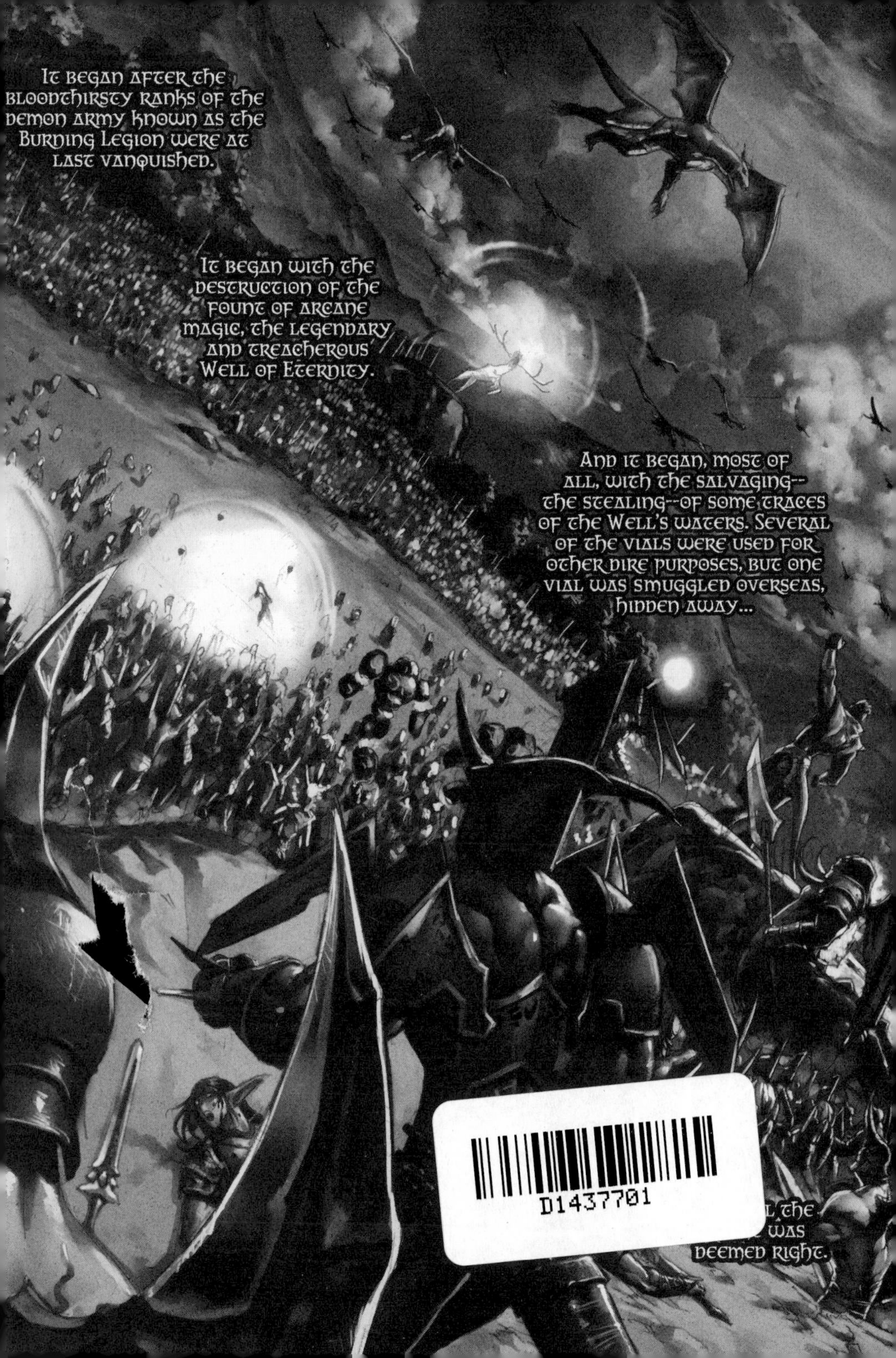
It began after the bloodthirsty ranks of the demon army known as the Burning Legion were at last vanquished.
It began with the destruction of the fount of arcane magic, the legendary and treacherous Well of Eternity.
And it began, most of all, with the salvaging--the stealing--of some traces of the Well's waters. Several of the vials were used for other dire purposes, but one vial was smuggled overseas, hidden away...
the
was
deemed right.

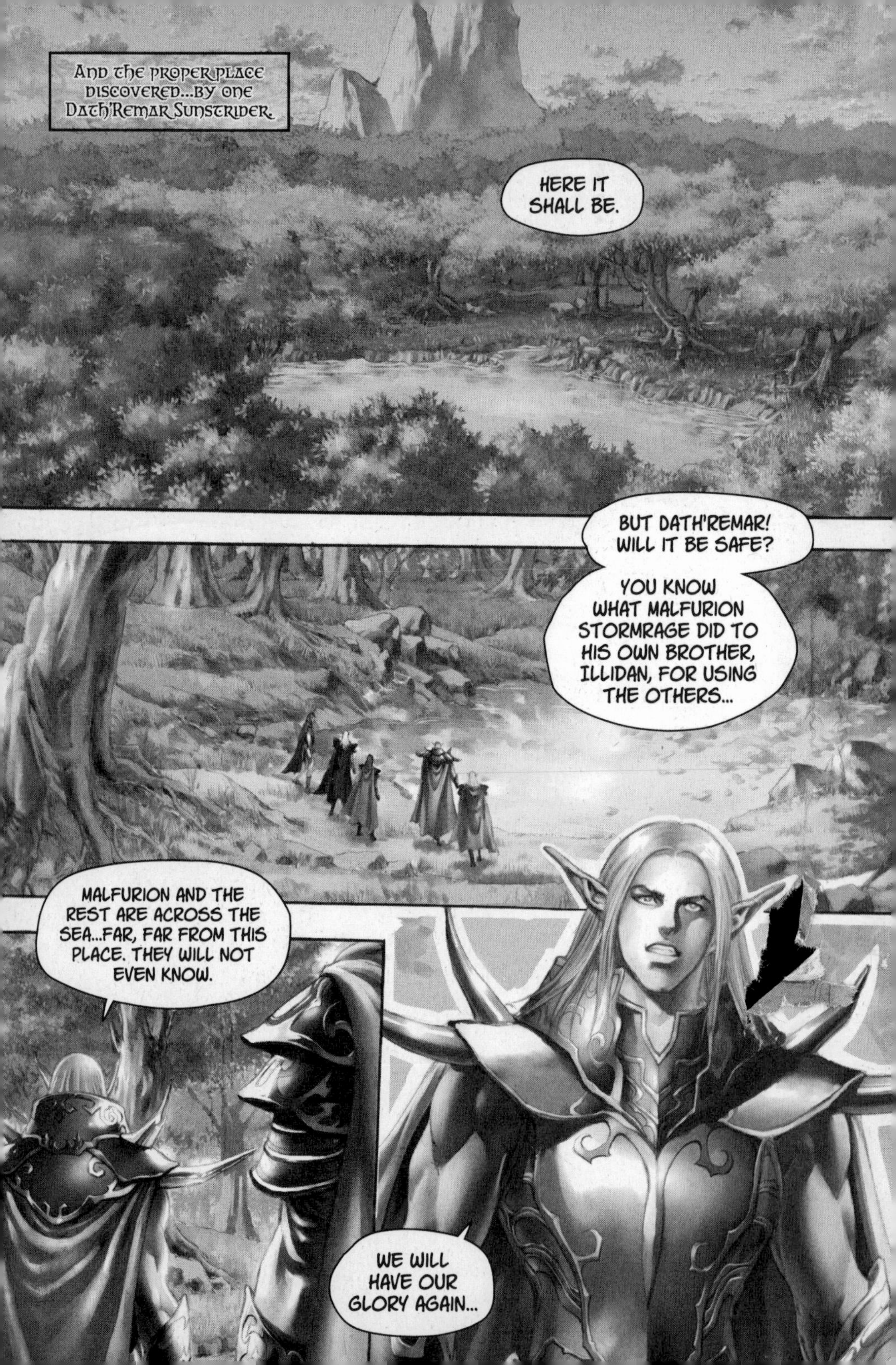
And the proper place discovered...by one Dath'Remar Sunstrider.
HERE IT SHALL BE.
BUT DATH'REMAR! WILL IT BE SAFE?
YOU KNOW WHAT MALFURION STORMRAGE DID TO HIS OWN BROTHER, ILLIDAN, FOR USING THE OTHERS...
MALFURION AND THE REST ARE ACROSS THE SEA...FAR, FAR FROM THIS PLACE. THEY WILL NOT EVEN KNOW.
WE WILL HAVE OUR GLORY AGAIN...

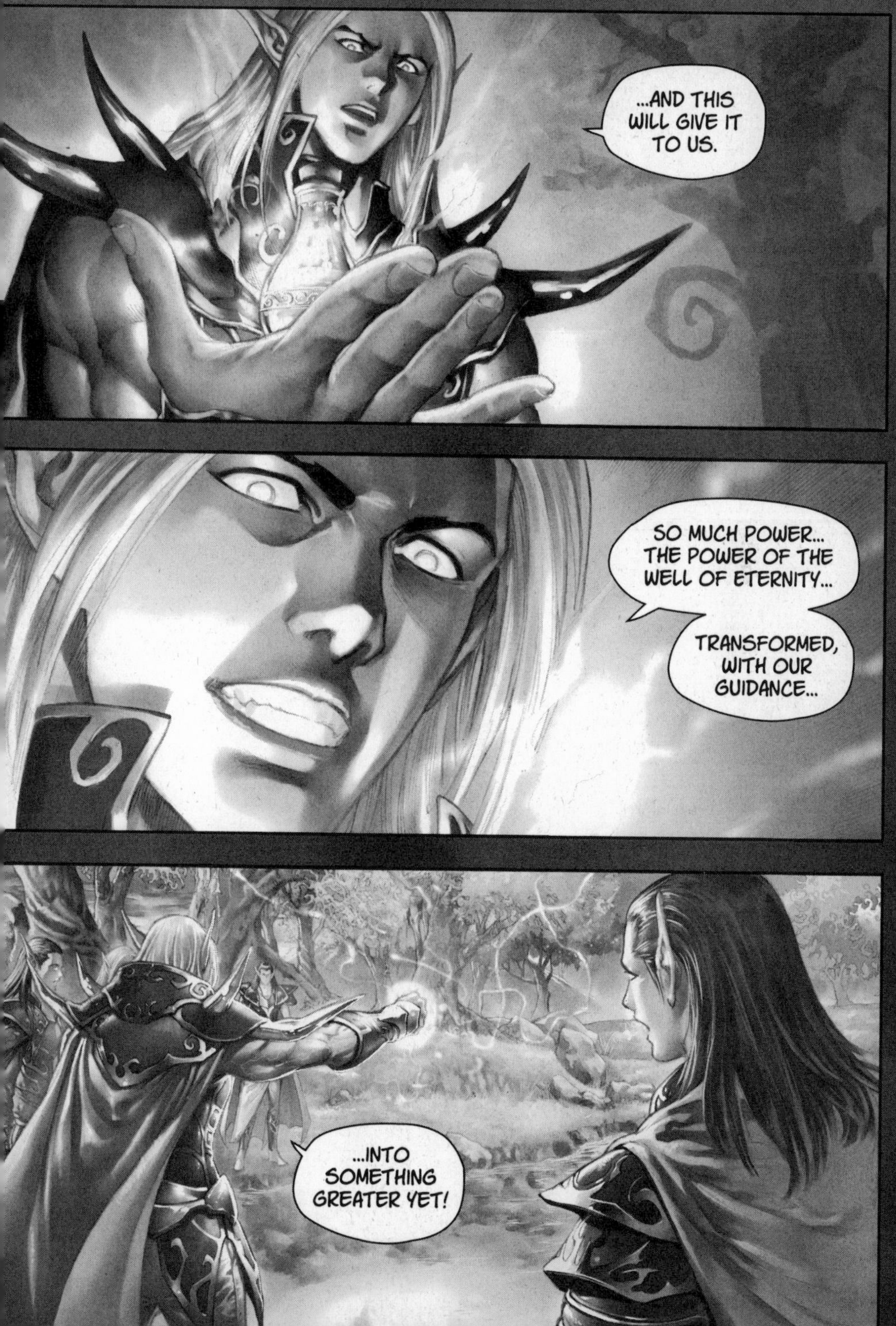
...AND THIS WILL GIVE IT TO US.
SO MUCH POWER... THE POWER OF THE WELL OF ETERNITY...
TRANSFORMED, WITH OUR GUIDANCE...
...INTO SOMETHING GREATER YET!

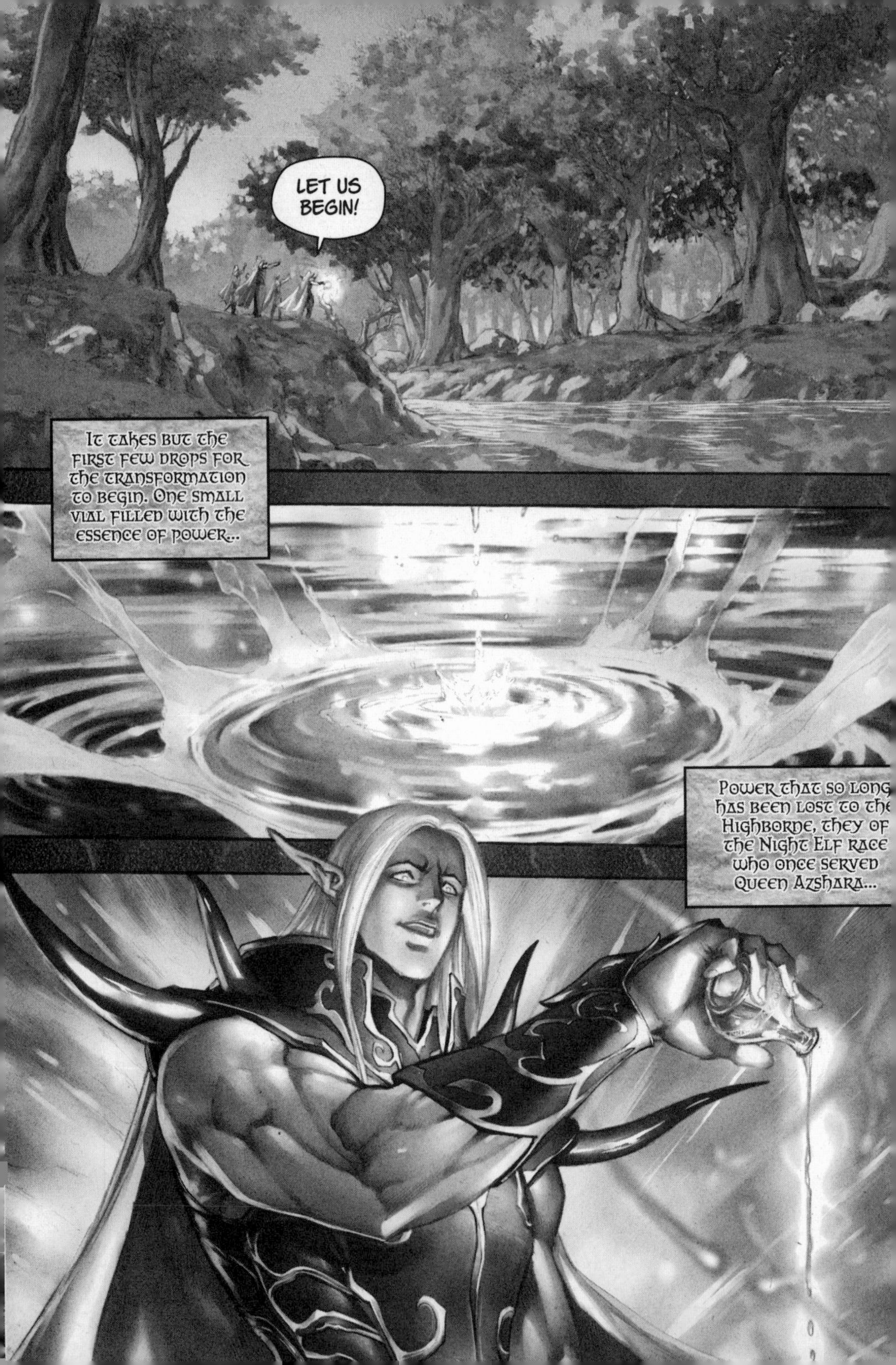
LET US BEGIN!
It takes but the first few drops for the transformation to begin. One small vial filled with the essence of power...
Power that so long has been lost to the Highborne, they of the Night Elf race who once served Queen Azshara...

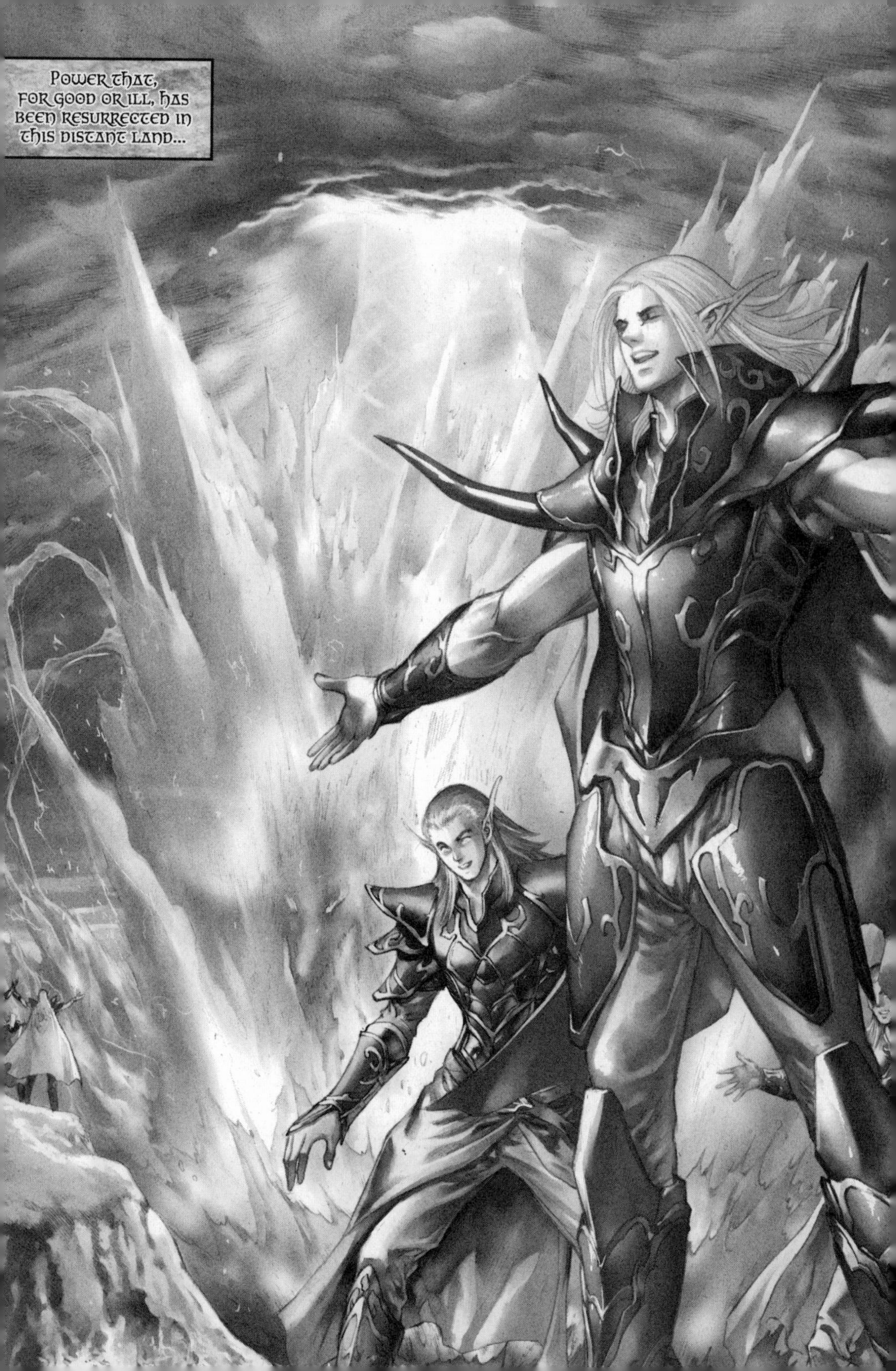
Power that, for good or ill, has been resurrected in this distant land...

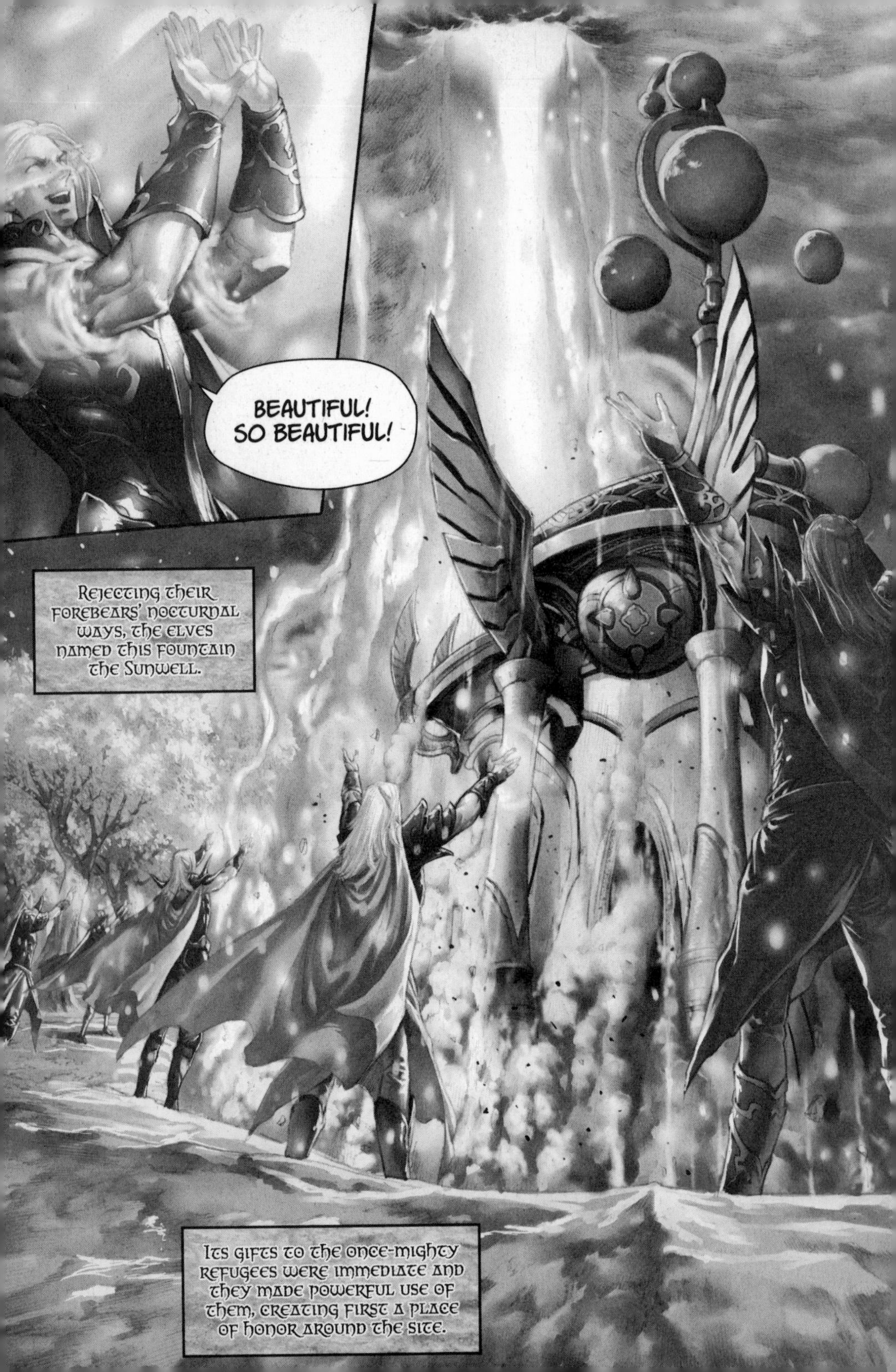
BEAUTIFUL! SO BEAUTIFUL!
Rejecting their forebears' nocturnal ways, the elves named this fountain the Sunwell.
Its gifts to the once-mighty refugees were immediate and they made powerful use of them, creating first a place of honor around the site.

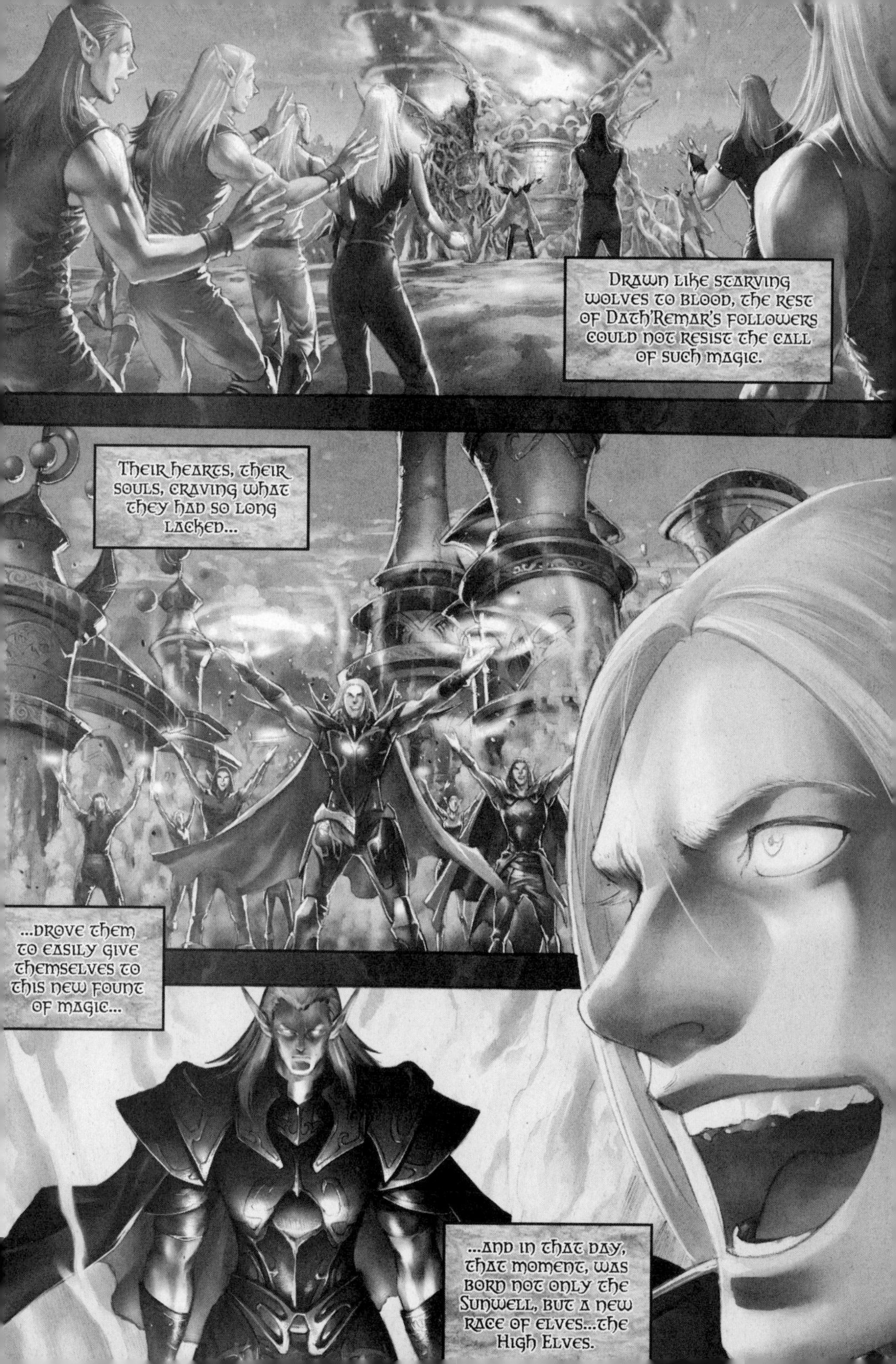
Drawn like starving wolves to blood, the rest of Dath'Remar's followers could not resist the call of such magic.
Their hearts, their souls, craving what they had so long lacked...
...drove them to easily give themselves to this new fount of magic...
...and in that day, that moment, was born not only the Sunwell, but a new race of elves...the High Elves.

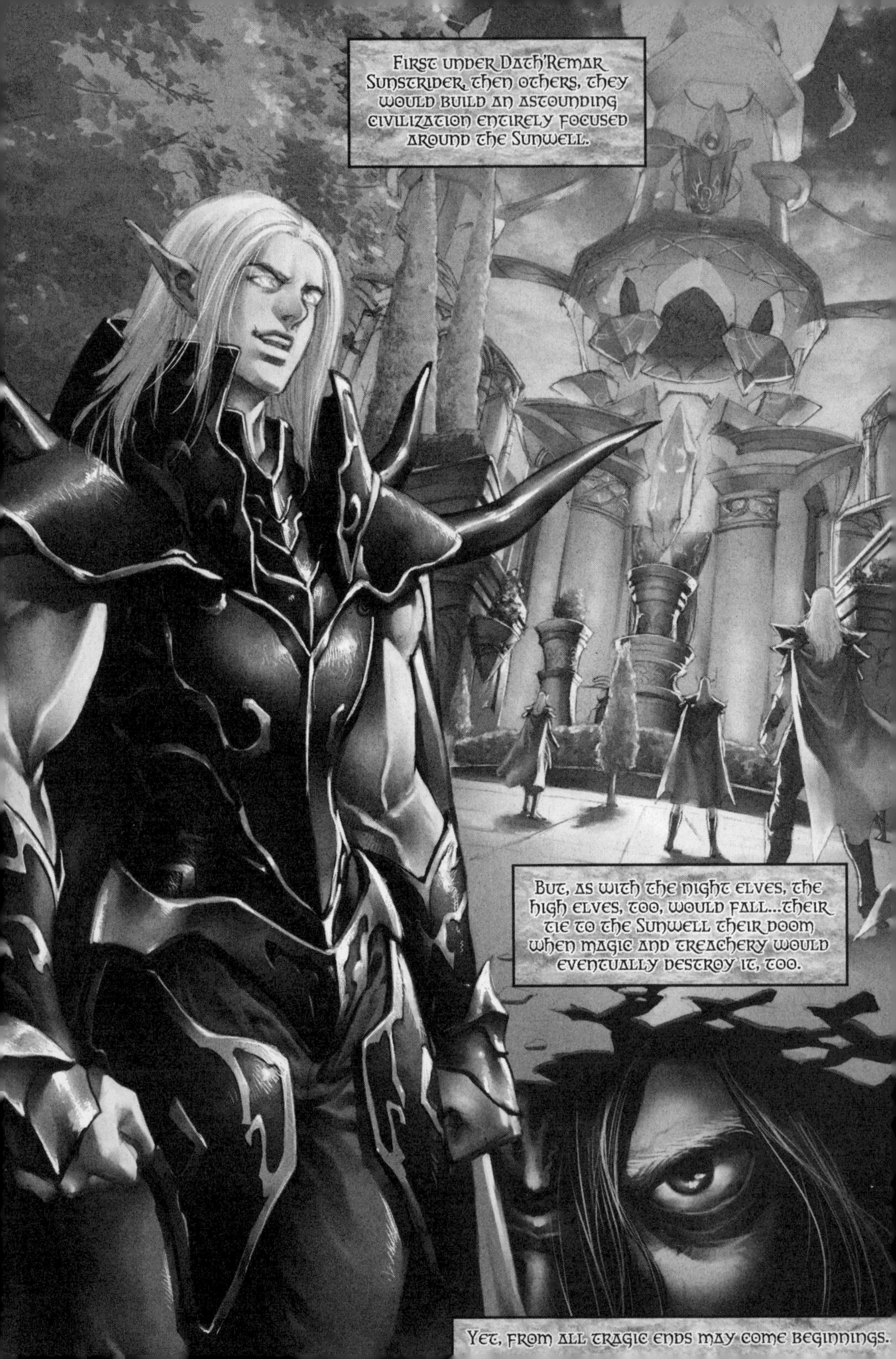
First under Dath'Remar Sunstrider, then others, they would build an astounding civilization entirely focused around the Sunwell.
But, as with the night elves, the high elves, too, would fall...their tie to the Sunwell their doom when magic and treachery would eventually destroy it, too.
Yet, from all tragic ends may come beginnings.

WORLD of WARCRAFT

The Essential Sunwell Collection

Written by
Richard A. Knaak

Illustrated by
Jae-Hwan Kim

HAMBURG // LONDON // LOS ANGELES // TOKYO

World of Warcraft: The Essential Sunwell Collection
Story by: Richard A. Knaak
Art by: Jae-Hwan Kim

Layout & Lettering - Rob Steen and Michael Paolilli
Creative Consultant - Michael Paolilli
Cover Designer - Louis Csontos
Cover Artist - Jae-Hwan Kim

Editors - Troy Lewter and Rob Tokar
Editorial Translator - Janice Kwon
Print Production Manager - Lucas Rivera
Managing Editor - Vy Nguyen
Senior Designer - Louis Csontos
Art Director - Al-Insan Lashley
Director of Sales and Manufacturing - Allyson De Simone
Associate Publisher - Marco F. Pavia
President and C.O.O. - John Parker
C.E.O. and Chief Creative Officer - Stu Levy

BLIZZARD ENTERTAINMENT
Senior Vice President, Creative Development - Chris Metzen
Director, Creative Development - Jeff Donais
Lead Developer, Licensed Products - Mike Hummel
Publishing Lead, Creative Development - Micky Neilson
Senior Story Developer - James Waugh
Art Director - Glenn Rane
Licensing Manager - Jason Bischoff
Historian - Evelyn Fredericksen
Additional Development - Samwise Didier, Cameron Dayton, Tommy Newcomer
and Max Thompson

A  Manga

TOKYOPOP Inc.
5900 Wilshire Blvd. Suite 2000
Los Angeles, CA 90036

E-mail: info@TOKYOPOP.com
Come visit us online at www.TOKYOPOP.com

ISBN: 978-1-4278-1897-3

First TOKYOPOP printing: November 2010
10 9 8 7 6 5 4 3 2 1
Printed in the USA

FOREWORD

Welcome to the saga of the Sunwell!

I'm pleased to be able to introduce this new collection, bringing together not only the original three-part Sunwell story, but much, much more! Not only did readers embrace the characters and their travails, but many elements of the trilogy have since become integral elements of the game world as well. Kalec the blue dragon, the innocent Anveena Teague, the overconfident Tyri, and the fallen paladin Jorad Mace are all a part of *World of Warcraft* now...as are even the villainous high elf, Dar'Khan, and the loyal tauren, Trag Highmountain.

When we created this trilogy, we knew that we were not only giving fans of the game a new way to experience Azeroth through the medium of the manga, but also introducing *World of Warcraft* to other manga readers as well. Greatly aiding in that effort was the choice for artist, Jae-Hwan Kim, another long-time WoW player himself. I couldn't have asked for a better partner in this effort, as Jae-Hwan presented one fantastic page after another, bringing each character to life with perfection.

The Sunwell Trilogy has been reprinted time and time again in fifty countries, translated into thirty languages (Icelandic included!), and has seen the return of some of its characters in the new **WORLD OF WARCRAFT: SHADOW WING** saga. So whether you are returning to this tale, or reading it for the first time, I hope you enjoy it!

And now, on to the adventure!

Sincerely

Richard A. Knaak

History of the World of Warcraft

No one knows exactly how the universe began, but it is clear that the titans--a race of powerful, metal-skinned beings from the far reaches of the cosmos--explored the newborn universe and made it their mission to bring stability to the various worlds and ensure a safe future for whoever would follow in their footsteps. As part of their unfathomable, far-sighted plan to create order out of chaos, the titans reshaped the worlds by raising mighty mountains, digging out vast seas, and breathing skies and raging atmospheres into being, and they empowered primitive races to maintain their worlds.

Ruled by an elite sect known as the Pantheon, the titans brought order to a hundred million worlds scattered throughout the Great Dark Beyond during the first ages of creation. The benevolent Pantheon assigned its greatest warrior, Sargeras, to be the first line of defense against the extra-dimensional demonic beings of the Twisting Nether who sought only to destroy life and devour the energies of the living universe. Sargeras was more than powerful enough to defeat any and all threats he faced… except one. Unfortunately for the Pantheon, the titans' inability to conceive of evil or wickedness in any form worked against Sargeras. After countless millennia of witnessing the atrocities of the demonic beings he fought, Sargeras eventually fell into a state of deep confusion, despair, and madness.

Sargeras ultimately lost all faith in his mission and the titans' vision of an ordered universe after he recognized the inherent flaws in creation. It wasn't long before he came to believe that the concept of order itself was folly and that chaos and depravity were the only absolutes within the dark, lonely universe. Viewing the titans themselves as responsible for creation's failure, Sargeras resolved to form an unstoppable army that would undo the benevolent creators' works throughout the universe and set reality aflame.

Even Sargeras's titanic form became distorted from the corruption that plagued his once-noble heart. His eyes, hair, and beard erupted in fire, and his metallic bronze skin split open to reveal an endless furnace of blistering hate.

In his fury, Sargeras freed the loathsome demons he'd previously imprisoned. These cunning creatures bowed before the Dark Titan's vast rage and offered to serve him in whatever malicious ways they could. Yet Sargeras remained unsatisfied. Thus he worked to corrupt other races, and from the ranks of one of the most intelligent of those--the eredar--he picked two champions to command his demonic army of destruction. Kil'jaeden the Deceiver was chosen to seek out the darkest races in the universe and recruit them into Sargeras's ranks. The second champion, Archimonde the Defiler, was chosen to lead Sargeras's vast armies into battle against any who might resist the twisted titan's will.

Once Sargeras saw that his armies were amassed and ready to follow his every command, he dubbed them the Burning Legion and launched them into the vastness of the Great Dark. To this date, it is still unclear how many worlds they ravaged on their unholy Burning Crusade across the universe.

Unaware of Sargeras's mission to undo their countless works, the titans continued to move across the universe, shaping and ordering each world as they saw fit. Along their journey, they happened upon a small world whose inhabitants would later name Azeroth.

For many ages, the titans guided races such as the earthen--who carved out the world's mountains--and the sea giants--responsible for dredging out vast seas--to move and shape Azeroth until at last there remained one perfect continent. At the continent's center the titans crafted a lake of scintillating energies. The lake, which they named the Well of Eternity, was to be the fount of life for the world. The Well's potent energies would nurture the bones of the world and empower life to take root in the land's rich soil. Over time, plants, trees, monsters, and creatures of every kind began to thrive on the primordial continent. As twilight fell on the final day of their labors, the titans named the continent Kalimdor: "land of eternal starlight."

Satisfied that the small world had been ordered and that their work was done, the titans prepared to leave Azeroth. However, before they departed, they charged the world's greatest species with the task of watching over Kalimdor lest any force should threaten its perfect tranquility. In that age there were many dragonflights, yet there were five that held dominion over their brethren. It was these five dragonflights that the titans chose to shepherd the budding world. The greatest members of the Pantheon bestowed a portion of their power upon each dragonflight's leader. These majestic dragons became known as the Great Aspects, or the Dragon Aspects.

Empowered by the Pantheon, the five Aspects were responsible for the world's defense in the titans' absence. With the dragons prepared to safeguard their creation, the titans left Azeroth behind forever. Unfortunately, it was only a matter of time before Sargeras learned of the newborn world's existence.

In time, a primitive tribe of nocturnal beings cautiously made its way to the edges of the mesmerizing enchanted lake. Drawn by the Well's strange energies, these feral, nomadic humanoids built crude homes upon the lake's tranquil shores. Over time, the Well's cosmic power affected the tribe, making its members strong, wise, and virtually immortal. The tribe adopted the name kaldorei, which meant "children of the stars" in its native tongue. To celebrate their budding society, the kaldorei constructed great structures and temples around the lake's periphery.

The kaldorei--or night elves, as they would later be known--worshipped the moon goddess, Elune, and believed that she slept within the Well's shimmering depths during the daylight hours. The early night elf priests and seers studied the Well with an insatiable curiosity, driven to discover its untold secrets and power. As the seemingly endless ages passed, night elven civilization expanded, and Azshara, the night elves' beautiful and gifted queen, built an immense, wondrous palace on the Well's shore that housed her favored servitors within its bejeweled halls. These servitors, who were from the highest caste of night elf nobility, grew even more influential during Azshara's rule. Now considering themselves greater than the rest of their brethren, they called themselves the quel'dorei, or "Highborne." Azshara declared the name official, which served only to increase the Highborne's desire for more power.

Sharing the priests' curiosity about the Well of Eternity, Azshara ordered the Highborne to learn its secrets and reveal its true purpose in the world. The Highborne buried themselves in their work and studied the Well ceaselessly. In time, they developed the ability to manipulate and control the Well's cosmic energies. As their experiments progressed, the Highborne found that they could use their growing powers either to create or destroy with tremendous ease. Despite the fact that they had previously declared magic to be dangerous if handled irresponsibly, Azshara and her Highborne dove into their new abilities with reckless abandon.

The Highborne's increasingly careless use of magic sent ripples of energy spiraling out from the Well of Eternity and into the Great Dark Beyond, where they were felt by Sargeras, the Great Enemy of all life. Spying Azeroth and sensing the limitless energies of the Well of Eternity, Sargeras resolved to destroy the fledgling world and claim its energies as his own.

Gathering his vast Burning Legion, Sargeras made his way toward the unsuspecting world of Azeroth. The Legion was composed of a million screaming demons, all ripped from the far corners of the universe and hungering for conquest.

To gain entrance into Azeroth, Sargeras enticed Queen Azshara and the Highborne with the promise of remaking their world into a paradise. Enthralled by the offer, the queen and her servitors opened a vast swirling portal within their palace for the Dark Titan to cross over. Initially, the way was too small for Sargeras himself to enter, but several of his demonic envoys stormed through the portal with ease. These agents of the Burning Legion quickly spread out from the capital of Zin-Azshari to the unsuspecting lands beyond, leaving only ash and sorrow in their wake. Though brave kaldorei rushed to defend their ancient homeland, they were forced to give ground, inch by inch, before the fury of the Legion's onslaught.

When the dragons, led by the red Dragon Aspect, Alexstrasza, sent their mighty forces to engage the demons and their infernal masters, all-out warfare erupted. As the battle raged across the burning fields of Kalimdor, a terrible turn of events unfolded. The other dragons didn't know it, but Neltharion, the Dragon Aspect of the earth, had gone mad. Guided by voices whispering in his head, he betrayed his brethren during a critical engagement against the Burning Legion and renamed himself Deathwing. The corrupted Dragon Aspect's sudden treachery was so destructive that the dragonflights never truly recovered. Wounded and shocked, Alexstrasza and the other noble dragons were forced to abandon their allies.

Hatching a desperate plot to destroy the Well of Eternity, a band of night elf defenders clashed with the Highborne at the Well's edge. There, a new portal was being formed within the Well itself, one large enough for Sargeras to pass through. The ensuing battle threw the Highborne's carefully crafted spellwork into chaos, destabilizing the vortex inside the Well and igniting a catastrophic chain of events that forever sundered the world. A massive explosion from the Well shattered the earth and blotted out the skies.

As the aftershocks from the Well's implosion rattled the bones of Azeroth, the seas rushed in to fill the gaping wound left in the earth. Nearly eighty percent of Kalimdor's landmass had been blasted apart, leaving only a handful of separate continents surrounding a raging sea. At the center of the new sea, where the Well of Eternity once stood, was a tumultuous storm of tidal fury and chaotic energies. This terrible scar, known as the Maelstrom, would never cease its furious spinning. It would remain a constant reminder of the terrible catastrophe... and the utopian era that had been lost forever.

The night elf survivors fled to safety on the slopes of Mount Hyjal. Surveying the wreckage of their world from the great mountain, they realized that their passions had brought about the destruction all around them. Though Sargeras and most of the Legion had been ripped from the world by the Well's destruction, the kaldorei were left to ponder the terrible cost of victory.

Unbeknownst to the other night elves, Illidan Stormrage, twin brother of the druid Malfurion, had reached Hyjal's summit before his kin. Using waters stolen from the Well of Eternity, Illidan created a second Well, believing that by doing so he was salvaging the lifeblood of his race. Ultimately he was punished for his transgression, but the deed had been done.

The Dragon Aspects Alexstrasza, Ysera, and Nozdormu learned of the second Well and feared that, as long as it existed, Azeroth would be threatened by the Legion. Thus, the night elves and the mighty dragons made a pact to keep the Well safe. Alexstrasza placed a single enchanted acorn within the heart of the new Well, and the colossal World Tree known as *Nordrassil* grew from the magical waters. She also blessed the tree so that it would give the night elves strength and health. Nozdormu in turn placed his own enchantment on the World Tree, granting immortality to the night elves. Both blessings would remain for as long as Nordrassil stood. Lastly, Ysera created a link between the World Tree and her own realm, the Emerald Dream, thus binding the night elf druids to the primal dimension.

As the centuries passed, the night elves' society flourished, but many of the original Highborne grew restless and began wielding magic again. Although Malfurion had forbidden the use of arcane magic on pain of death, the night elves were unable to impose such a harsh penalty on their wayward kin. Instead, they banished the Highborne from the night elven lands.

Glad to be rid of their conservative cousins, the exiles made their way to the eastern region that would later be called Lordaeron. The Highborne built their own magical kingdom, Quel'Thalas, and rejected the night elves' precepts of moon worship and nocturnal activity. Rather, they would embrace the sun and be known only as the high elves.

At some point during their long exile, the high elves discovered that they were no longer immortal or immune to the elements. They also shrank somewhat in height, and their skin lost its characteristic violet hue. Despite these hardships, the high elves encountered many wondrous creatures that had never been seen in Kalimdor... including humans.

Over the course of several thousand years, the high elves developed an insular society, creating alliances with their neighboring human nations only in times of crisis, such as the Troll Wars. Though these elves had constructed a series of monolithic Runestones at various points around Quel'Thalas to mask high elven magic from extra-dimensional threats, the humans who had learned magic from the elves were not so cautious. Sinister agents of the Burning Legion were lured back into the world by the heedless spellcasting of human magi of the city of Dalaran.

Under Sargeras's orders, the cunning demon lord Kil'jaeden plotted the Burning Legion's second invasion of Azeroth. Kil'jaeden surmised that he needed a new force to weaken Azeroth's defenses before the Legion even set foot upon the world. If the protectors of Azeroth, such as the night elves and dragons, were forced to contend with a new threat, they would be too weak to pose any real resistance when the Legion launched its true invasion.

Kil'jaeden found this new force while pursuing another old adversary. A group of eredar renegades, known as the draenei, had evaded the Legion's endless onslaughts for many years, eventually settling on a lush and peaceful world they called Draenor. Seeking a more efficient way of eliminating them, Kil'jaeden discovered the shamanic, clan-based orcs residing on the same world. Kil'jaeden knew that these noble clans had great potential to serve the Burning Legion if they could be cultivated properly and that, if the orcs succeeded against the draenei, Azeroth would be perfect as their next battlefield.

After enthralling the elder orc shaman Ner'zhul--in much the same way as Sargeras had brought Queen Azshara under his control in ages past--Sargeras spread bloodlust and savagery throughout the orc clans. To further fuel this corruption and better bind them to his desires, Sargeras sent the demon Mannoroth among the orc leaders and had them drink of his blood. The taint was thus quickly spread. Before long, the once-spiritual race had been transformed into a monstrous people now united into a single savage force known simply as the Horde.

Consumed with this new blood-curse, the orcs became the Burning Legion's greatest weapon. As they rampaged across Draenor, Sargeras moved forth with his plans for Azeroth. Subtly corrupting the mind of the great human mage Medivh, he used the mighty spellcaster to open the Dark Portal, which then linked the worlds of Azeroth and Draenor. The Horde poured through, and an all-out war ignited between orcs and humans. Though the humans of Azeroth fought valiantly, many of their cities were utterly devastated.

The orcs triumphed in what was known as the First War, but other enclaves of humanity remained untouched. Human refugees fled to the northern kingdom of Lordaeron, and the savage Horde relentlessly pursued. Convinced that the orcs would soon conquer all of Azeroth, Lordaeron and other disparate human kingdoms formed the Alliance and clashed with the marauding orcs in massive battles over land, sea, and air.

This Second War raged on, and with each passing day victory for the Horde seemed more imminent. Yet as the orcs prepared for their final assault on Lordaeron's Capital City, their dreams of conquest were shattered by betrayal from within. The orc warlock Gul'dan and his allies withdrew from the battle to seek out powerful relics for his own selfish desires, and the remaining, weakened Horde was forced to call off its attack. Seizing the opportunity, the humans retook their lands and even fought the orcs on Draenor, though many heroic humans lost their lives when Draenor tore itself apart. Victory in the Second War belonged to the Alliance, but the price was heavy for all.

Though Ner'zhul was one of many orcs who had escaped Draenor's destruction, as punishment, Kil'jaeden placed the shaman's spirit in stasis and slowly tore his body apart. The torture continued until the demon lord found another use for the orc as a means to soften Azeroth's defenders in preparation for the Legion's next invasion.

After Ner'zhul recklessly agreed to serve Kil'jaeden, the orc's spirit was placed within a specially crafted block of diamond-hard ice gathered from the far reaches of the Twisting Nether. Encased within the frozen cask, Ner'zhul felt his consciousness expand ten thousand-fold. Warped by the demon lord's chaotic powers, Ner'zhul became a spectral being of unfathomable power. At that moment, the orc known as Ner'zhul was transformed forever, and the Lich King was born.

The Lich King was to spread a plague of undeath and terror across Azeroth that would snuff out human civilization forever. All those who died from the dreaded plague would arise as the undead, and their spirits would be bound to the Lich King's iron will forever.

Though the Lich King fought for the total eradication of humankind, the wealthy and prestigious archmage Kel'Thuzad left the city of Dalaran to serve the evil creature. As the forces of the undead swept across Lordaeron, King Terenas's only son, Prince Arthas, took up the fight against the Scourge. Arthas succeeded in killing Kel'Thuzad, but even so, the undead ranks swelled with every soldier who fell defending the land. Frustrated and stymied by the seemingly unstoppable enemy, Arthas took increasingly extreme steps to conquer it. Finally Arthas's comrades warned him that he was losing his hold on his humanity.

Arthas's fearlessness and resolve proved to be his undoing. Believing that it would save his people, Arthas took up the cursed runeblade Frostmourne. The sword granted him unfathomable power, but it also stole his soul and transformed him into the greatest of the Lich King's death knights. With his soul cast aside and his sanity shattered, Arthas led the Scourge against his kingdom. Ultimately, Arthas murdered his own father, King Terenas, and crushed Lordaeron under the Lich King's iron heel.

Not long after Arthas and his army of undead swept across the land, he used the high elves' current fount of power, the Sunwell, to resurrect Kel'Thuzad. Under the leadership of the prince of Quel'Thalas, Kael'thas Sunstrider, the high elves destroyed the tainted Sunwell before it could further affect the remaining members of their race. The glorious homeland of the high elves, which had stood for some seven thousand years, was no more. Arthas subsequently led the Scourge south to Dalaran and then to Kalimdor.

In Kalimdor, the night elves braced themselves and fought the Burning Legion with grim determination. Allied with humans and orcs (now freed of their savage bloodlust), the night elves severed the Legion's anchor to the second Well of Eternity. Unable to draw power from the Well itself, the Burning Legion began to crumble under the combined might of the mortal armies.

By this time, the Scourge had essentially transformed Lordaeron and Quel'Thalas into the toxic Plaguelands. The high elves grieved for the loss of their homeland. Kael'thas convinced most of them to follow him on a new, more desperate path to find a source of power to replace the Sunwell. In honor of his fallen kin, Kael'thas renamed his loyal followers the *sin'dorei*, or "blood elves."

Meanwhile, some of the Scourge forces staged a coup to break free of the Lich King's control. Eventually, the Banshee Queen, Sylvanas Windrunner, and her rebel undead--known as the Forsaken--claimed the ruined Capital City of Lordaeron as their own and vowed to drive the Scourge and Kel'Thuzad from the land.

Although he was weakened, Arthas outmaneuvered the enemy forces that were closing in on the Lich King. Donning Ner'zhul's unimaginably powerful helm, Arthas's spirit fused with Ner'zhul's to form a single mighty being--the new Lich King--and Arthas became one of the most powerful entities the world had ever known.

Currently, Arthas, the new and immortal Lich King, resides in Northrend; he is rumored to be rebuilding the citadel of Icecrown. His trusted lieutenant Kel'Thuzad, commands the Scourge in the Plaguelands. Sylvanas and her rebel Forsaken hold only Tirisfal Glades, a small portion of the war-torn kingdom of Lordaeron, while the humans, orcs, and night elves are trying to rebuild their

After what seemed like ages of bloody conflict, the denizens of Azeroth thought they had at last found peace. The Second War against the brutish orcs had come to a definitive conclusion. The remnants of the Horde had been rounded up into enclaves and kept under guard. Eventually, the orcs would liberate themselves and carve out their own territories.

Only a short period of time after the world had started to rebuild, however, a monstrous new evil arose. The demonic army of the Burning Legion, united with the undead Scourge, swept over human and orcish realms alike, forcing old enemies to band together.

Yet not until the aid of the mysterious night elves, who would give up their very immortality for their world, and the sacrifice of countless brave lives was the Burning Legion crushed. Nearly all of the high elven kingdom of Quel'Thalas and the human kingdom of Lordaeron lay in ruins, transformed into the foul Plaguelands by the Scourge.

Now an unsteady stalemate exists between the living and the undead, and forces from both sides seek out that which will decisively tip the scales in their favor.

Thus it is when a young blue dragon wings his way toward what little remains of southern Lordaeron....

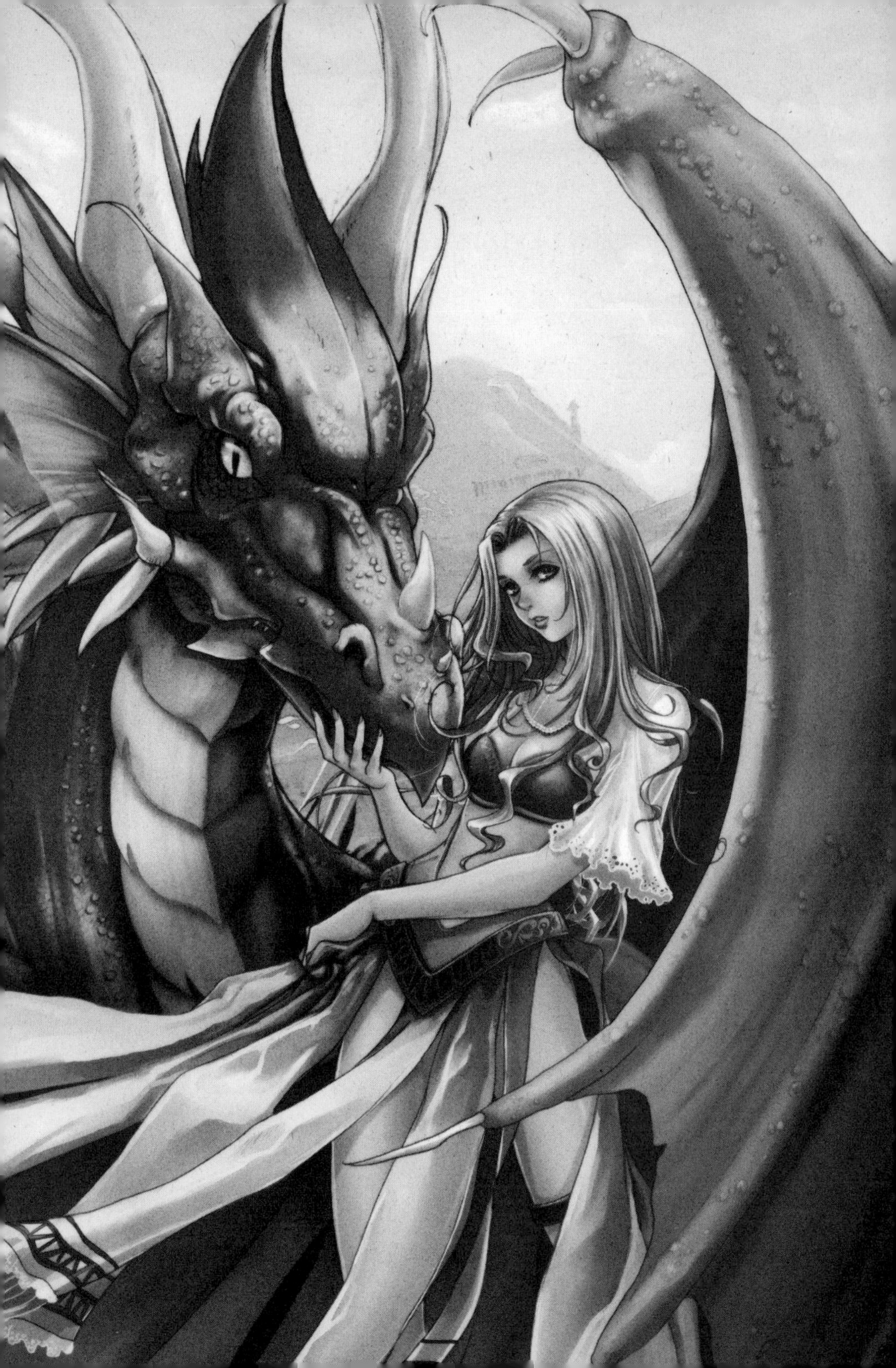

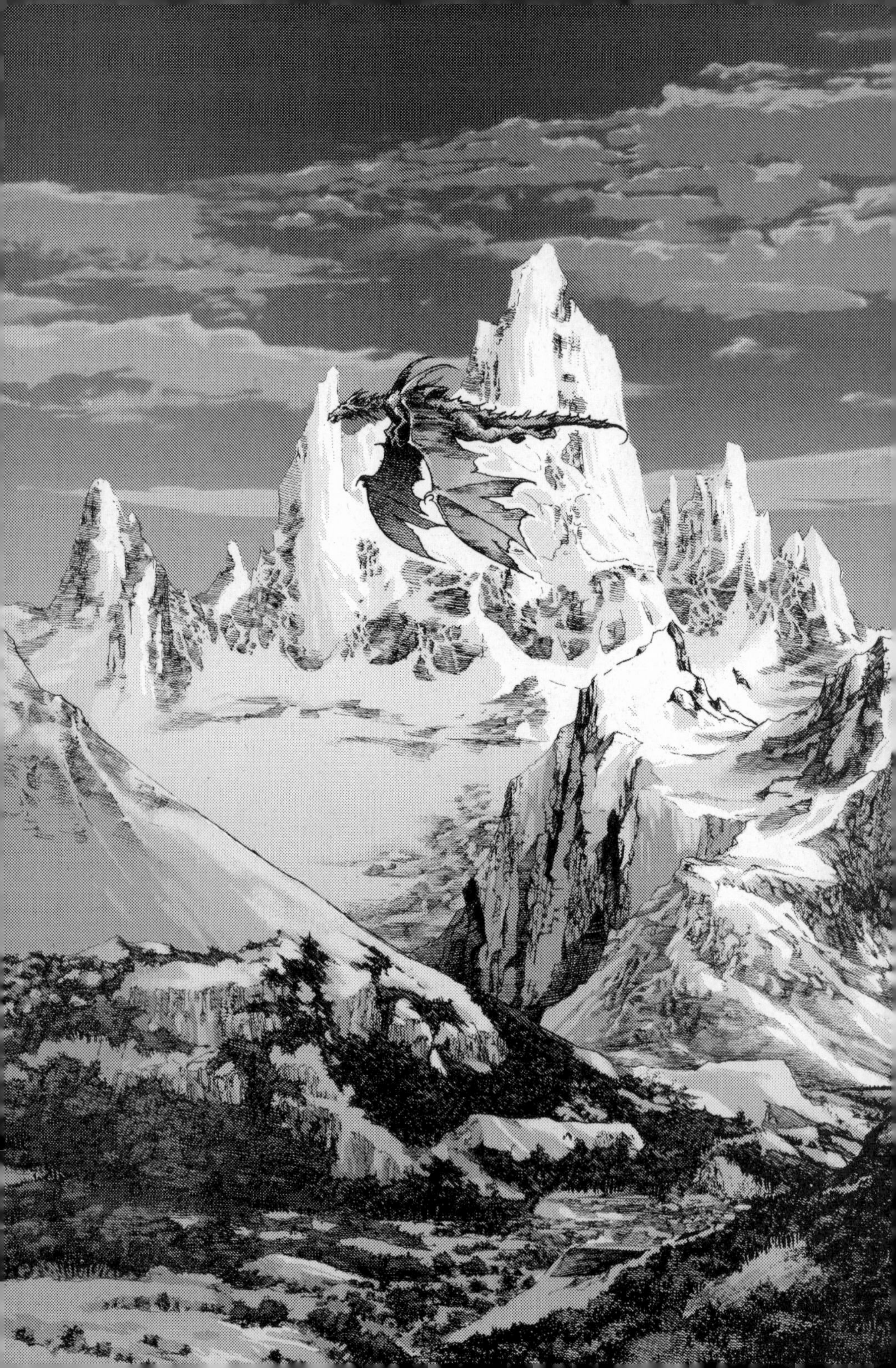

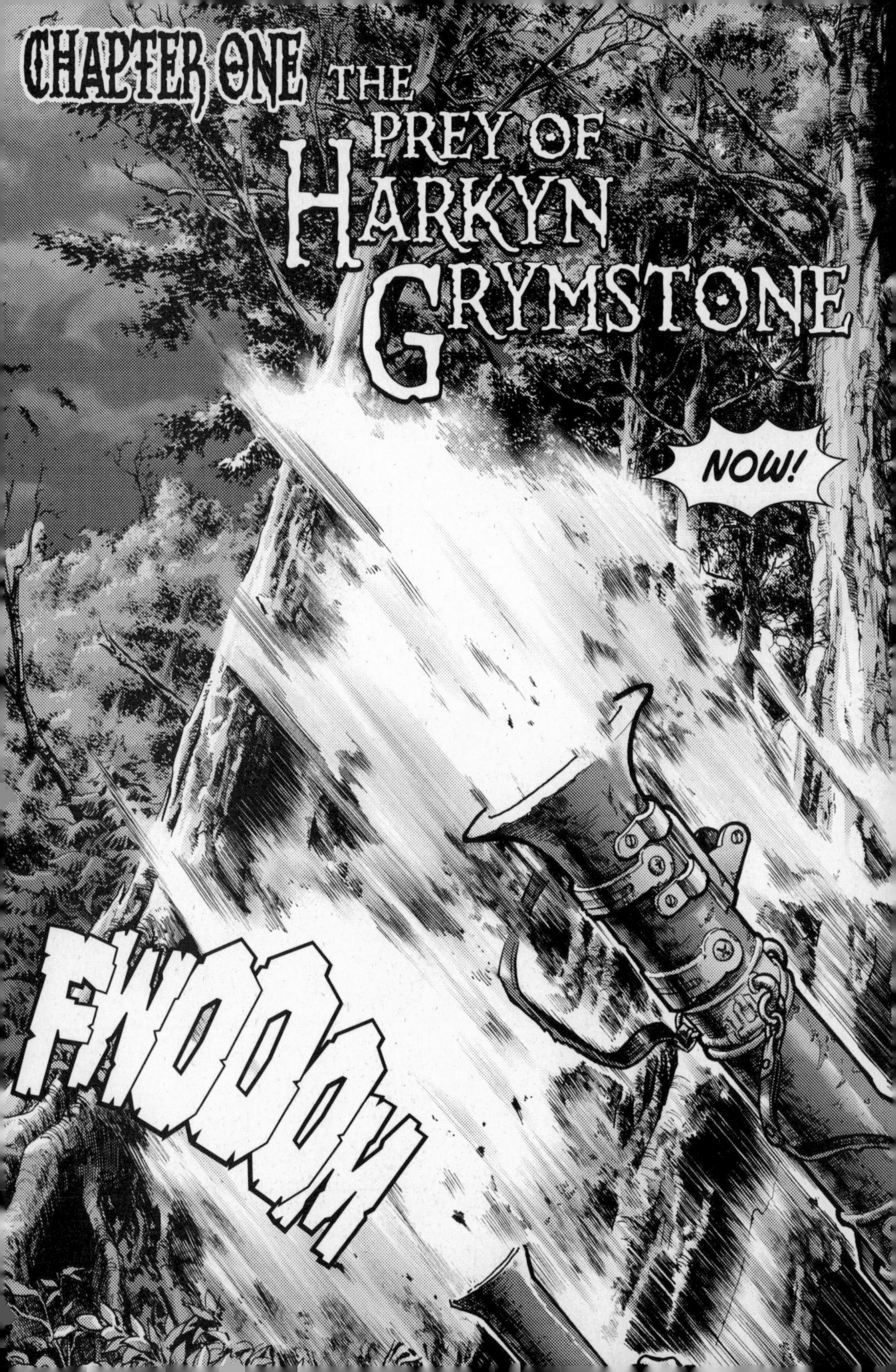
CHAPTER ONE THE PREY OF HARKYN GRYMSTONE
NOW!
FWOOM

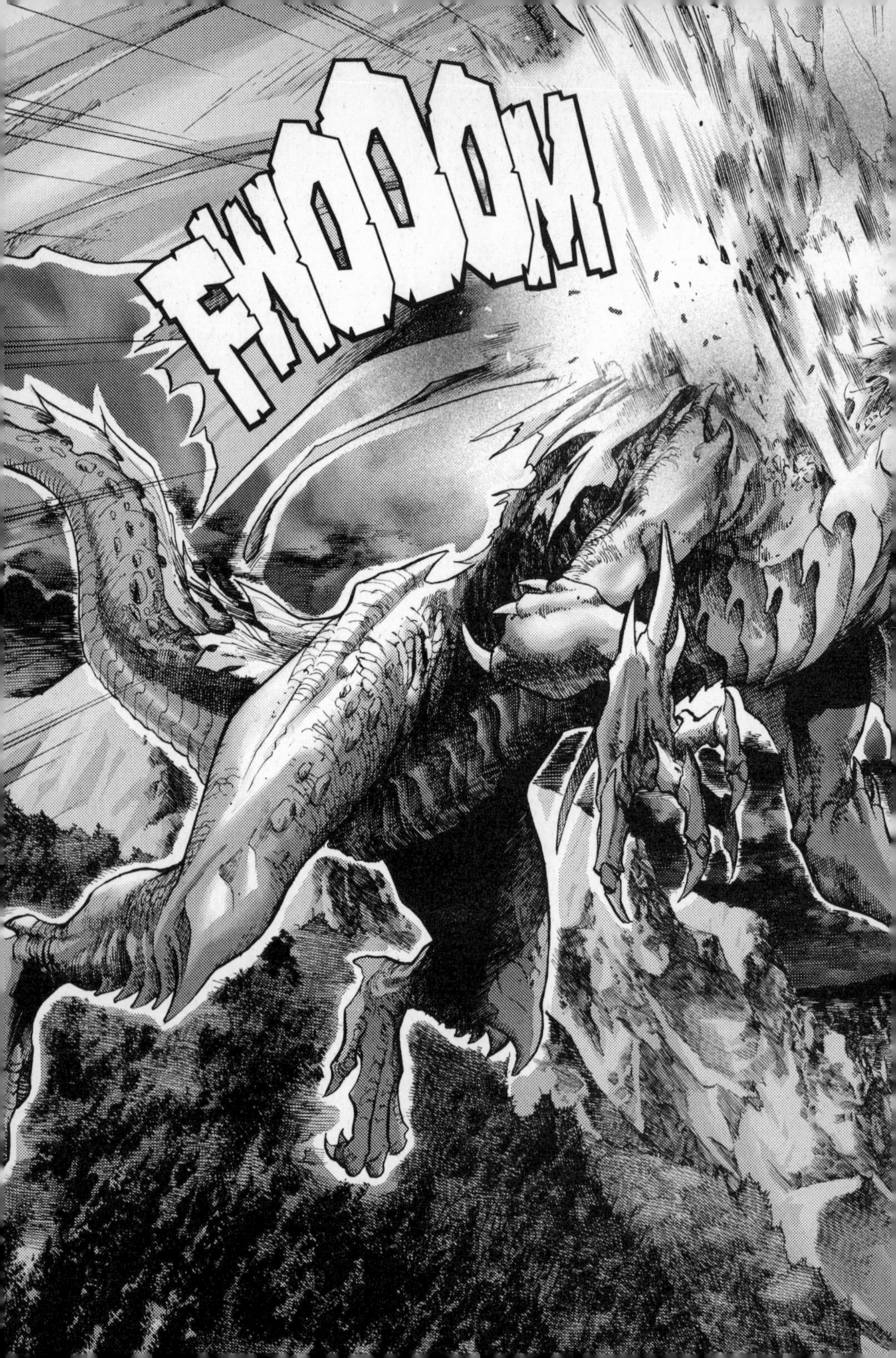
FWOOOM

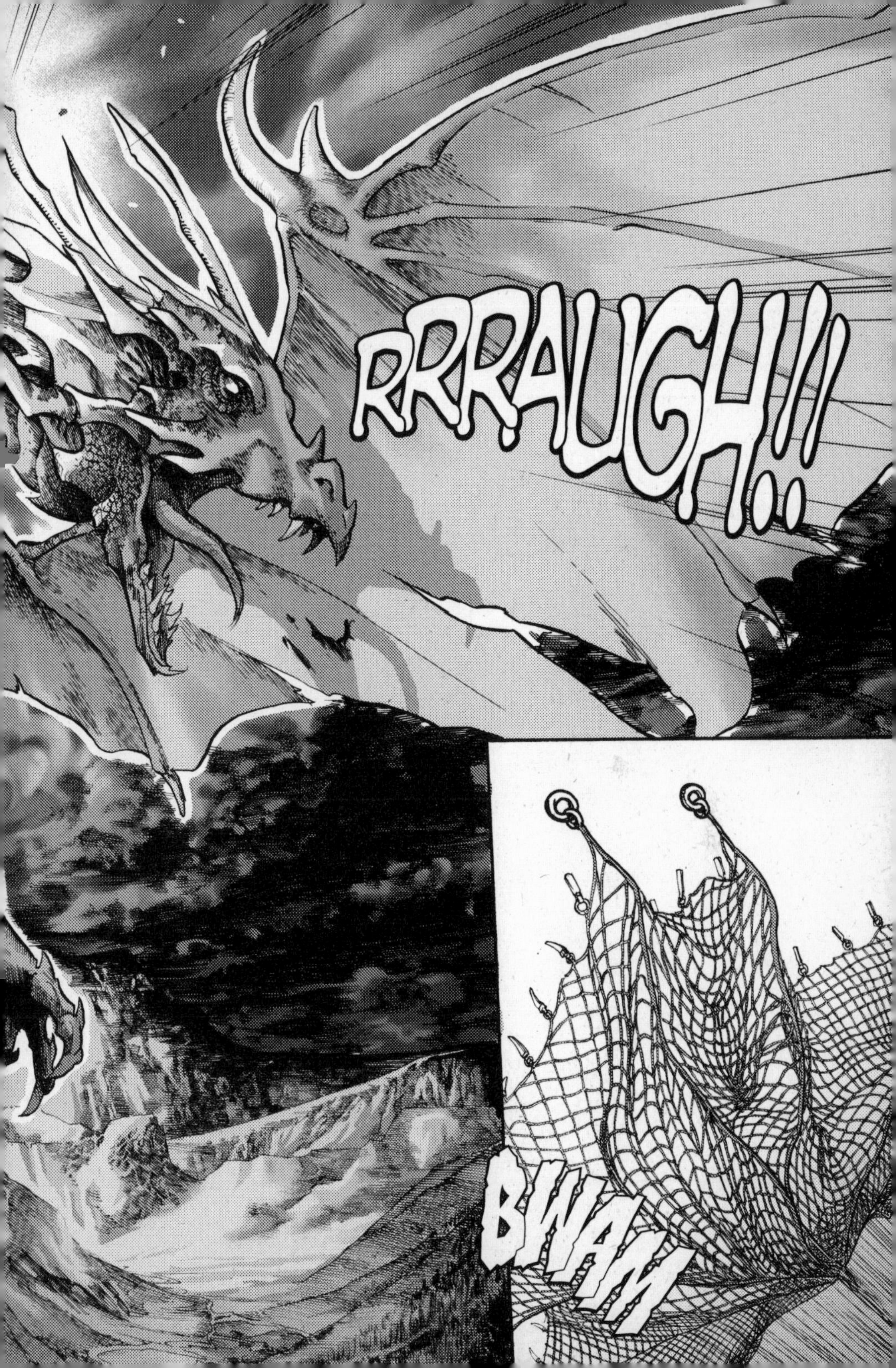
RRRAUGH!!
BWAM

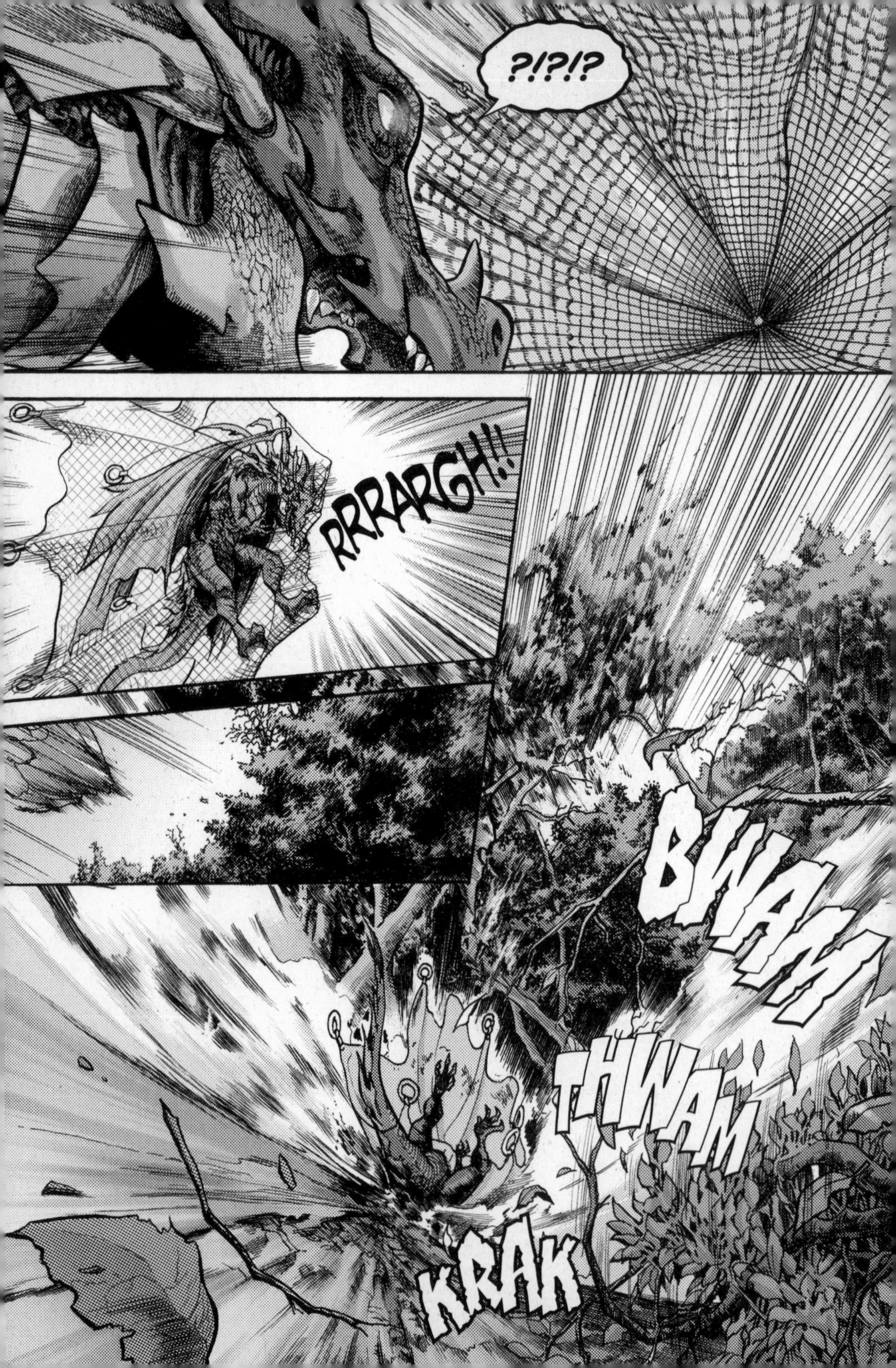
?!?!?
RRRARGH!!
BWAM
THWAM
KRAK

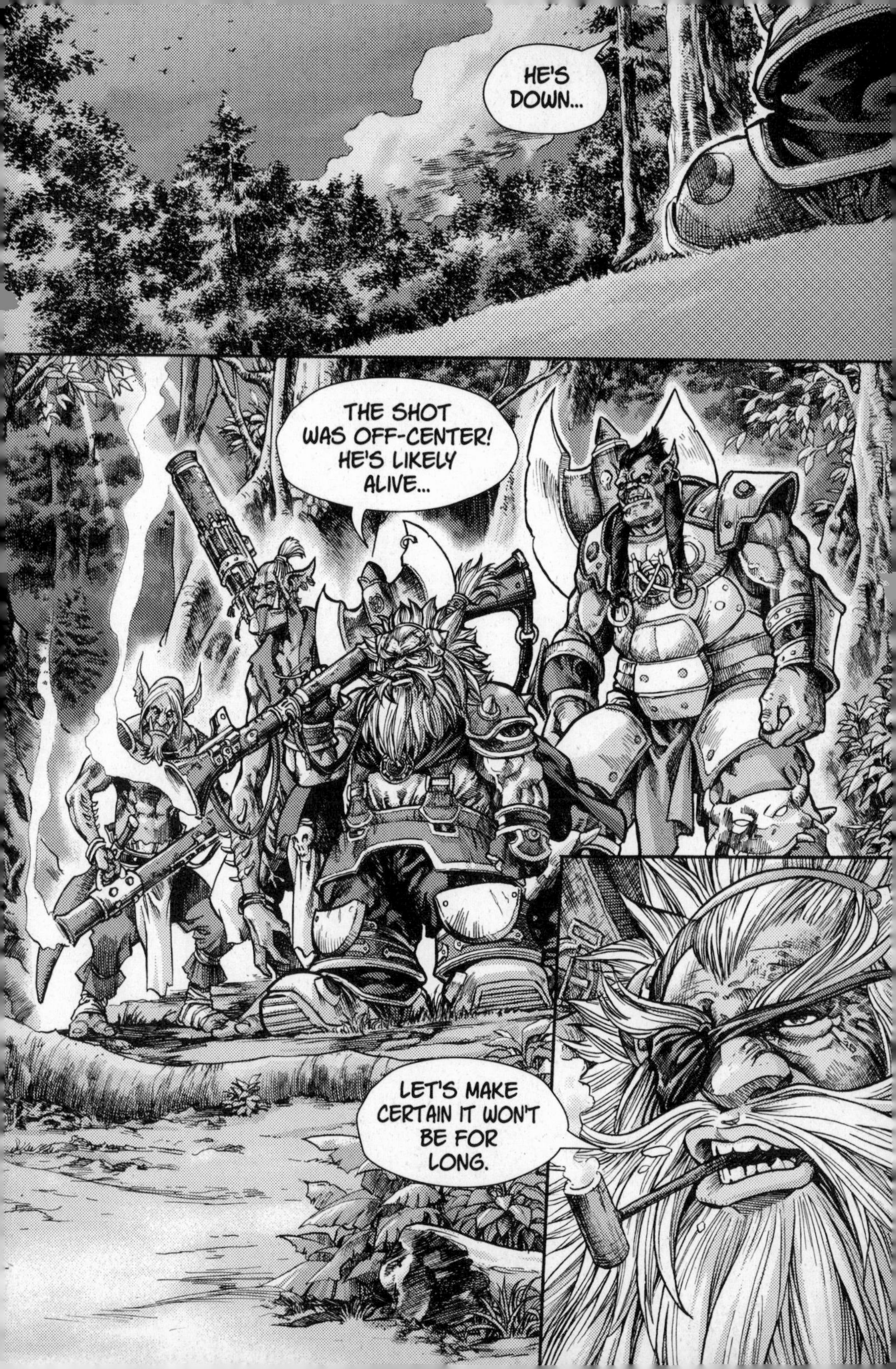
HE'S DOWN...
THE SHOT WAS OFF-CENTER! HE'S LIKELY ALIVE...
LET'S MAKE CERTAIN IT WON'T BE FOR LONG.

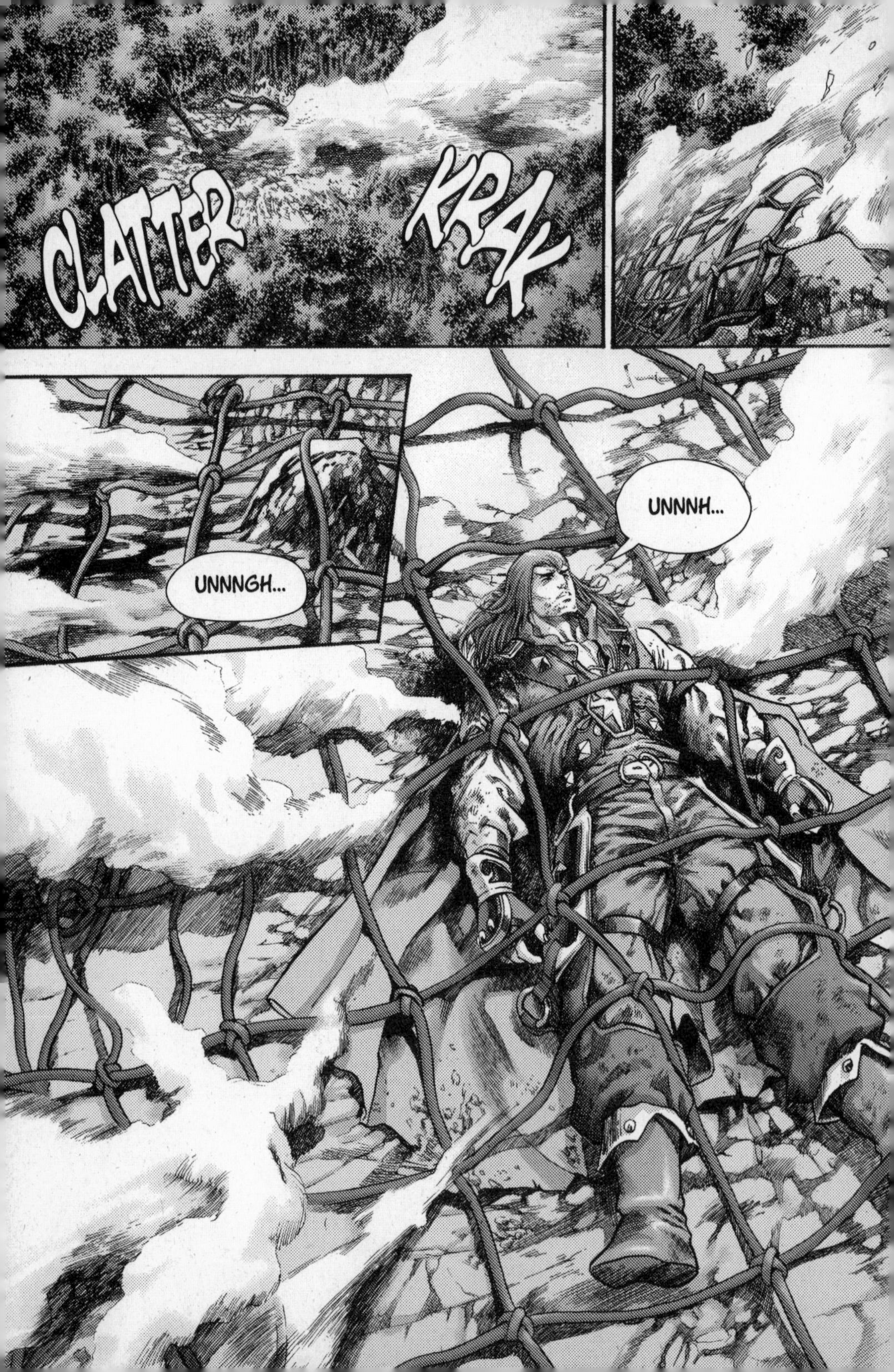
KRAK
CLATTER
UNNNH...
UNNNGH...

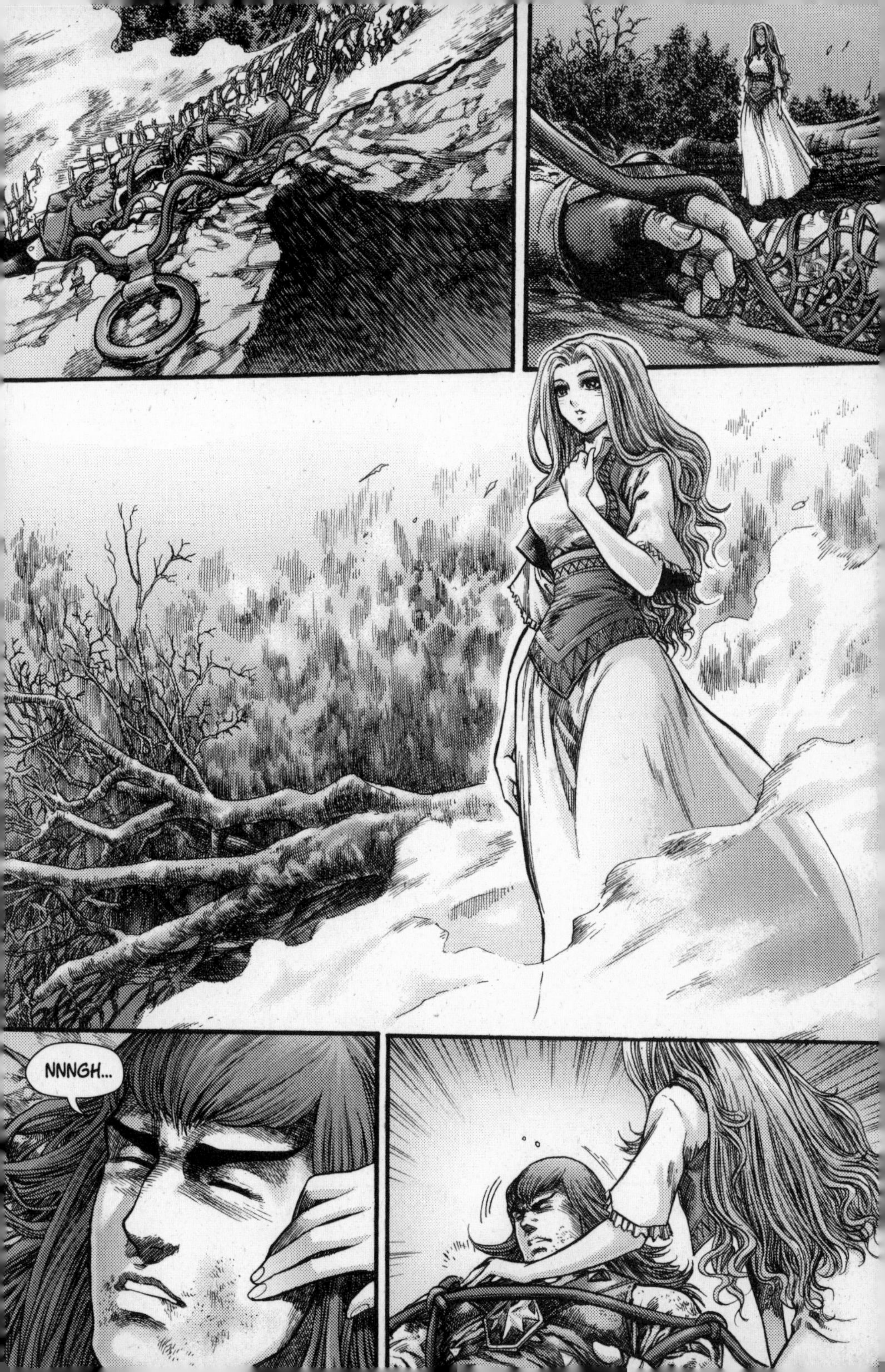
NNNGH...

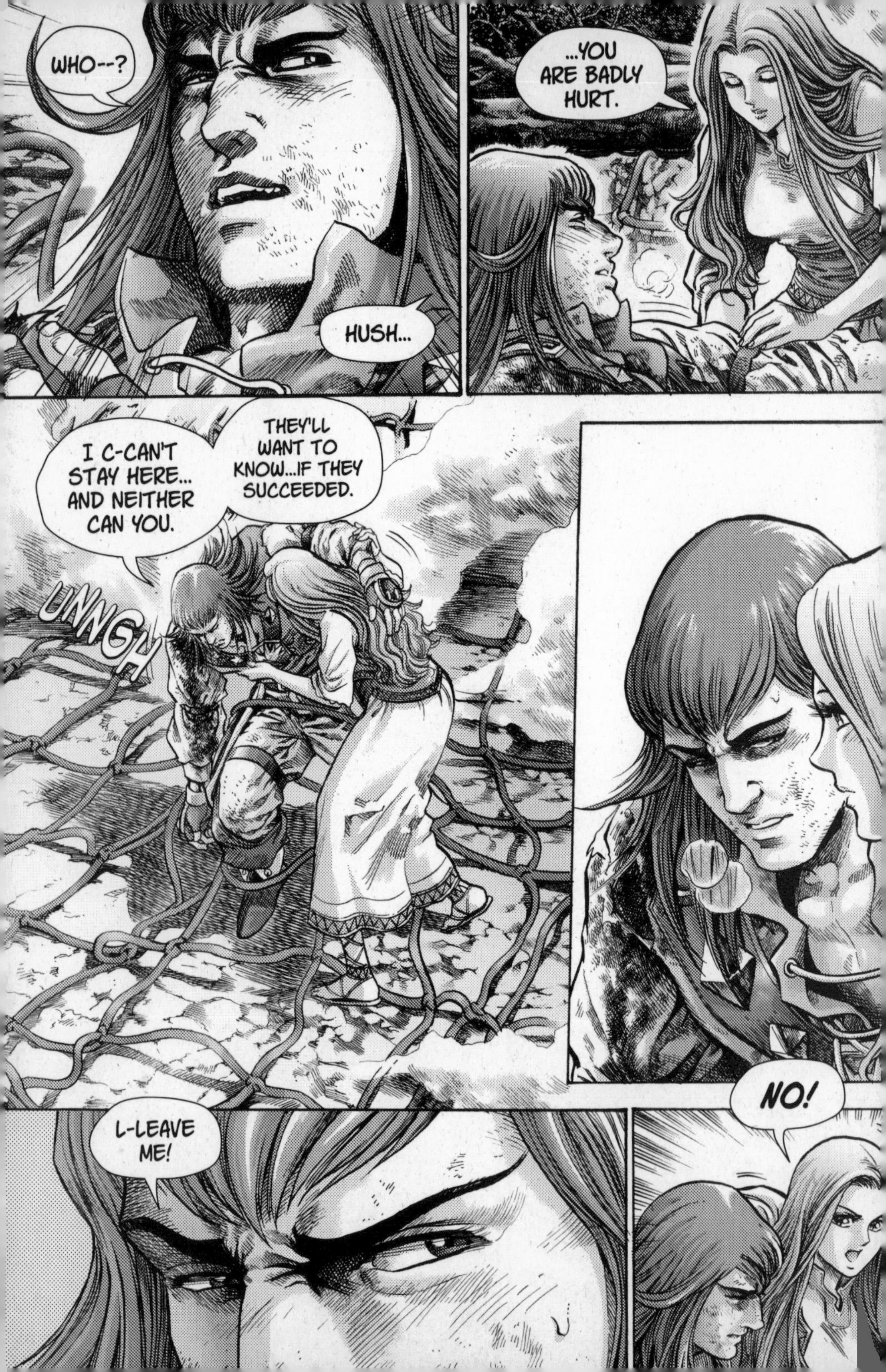
WHO--?
HUSH...
...YOU ARE BADLY HURT.
UNNGH
I C-CAN'T STAY HERE... AND NEITHER CAN YOU.
THEY'LL WANT TO KNOW...IF THEY SUCCEEDED.
L-LEAVE ME!
NO!

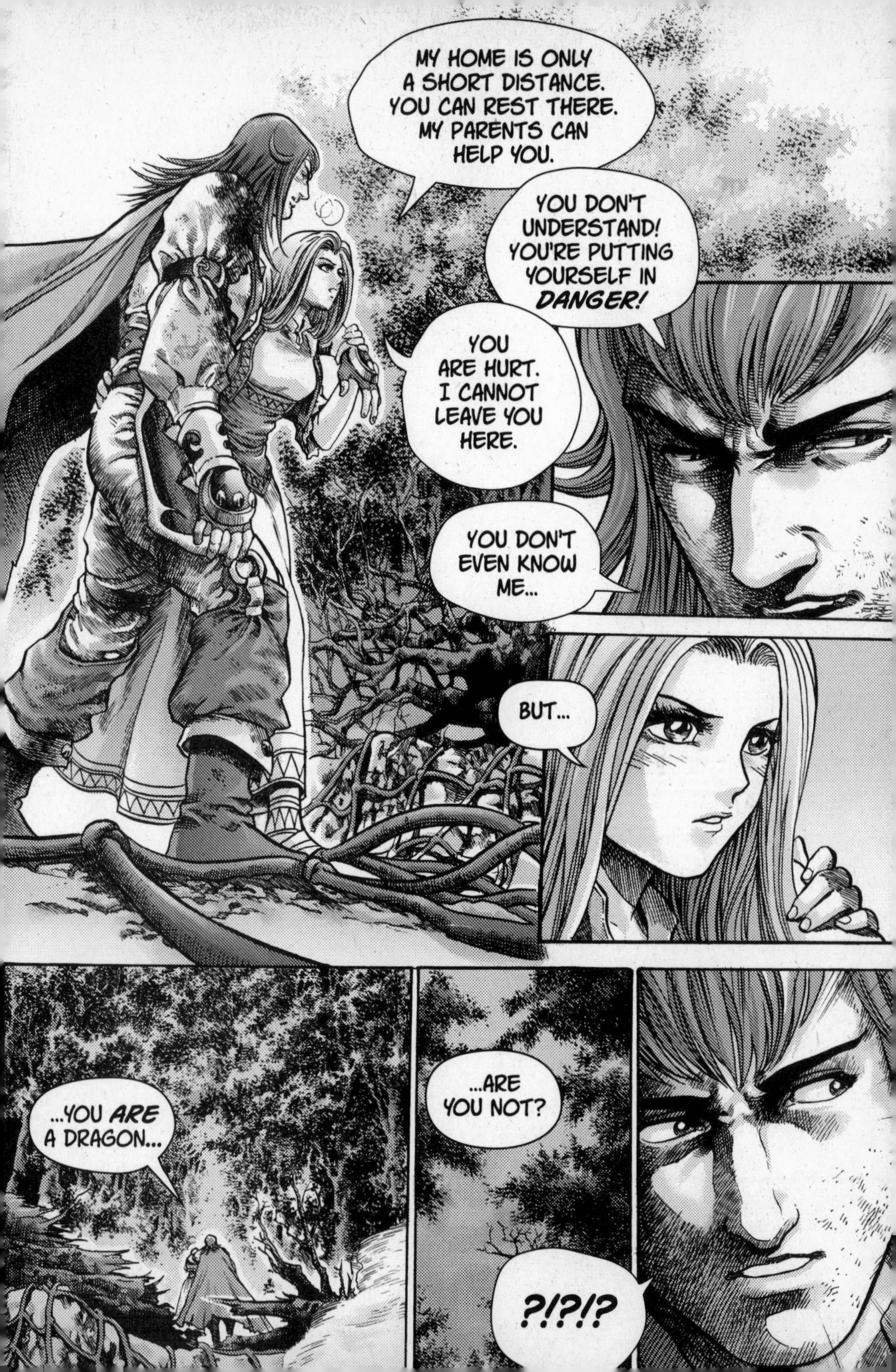
MY HOME IS ONLY A SHORT DISTANCE. YOU CAN REST THERE. MY PARENTS CAN HELP YOU.
YOU DON'T UNDERSTAND! YOU'RE PUTTING YOURSELF IN DANGER!
YOU ARE HURT. I CANNOT LEAVE YOU HERE.
YOU DON'T EVEN KNOW ME...
BUT...
...YOU ARE A DRAGON...
...ARE YOU NOT?
?!?!?

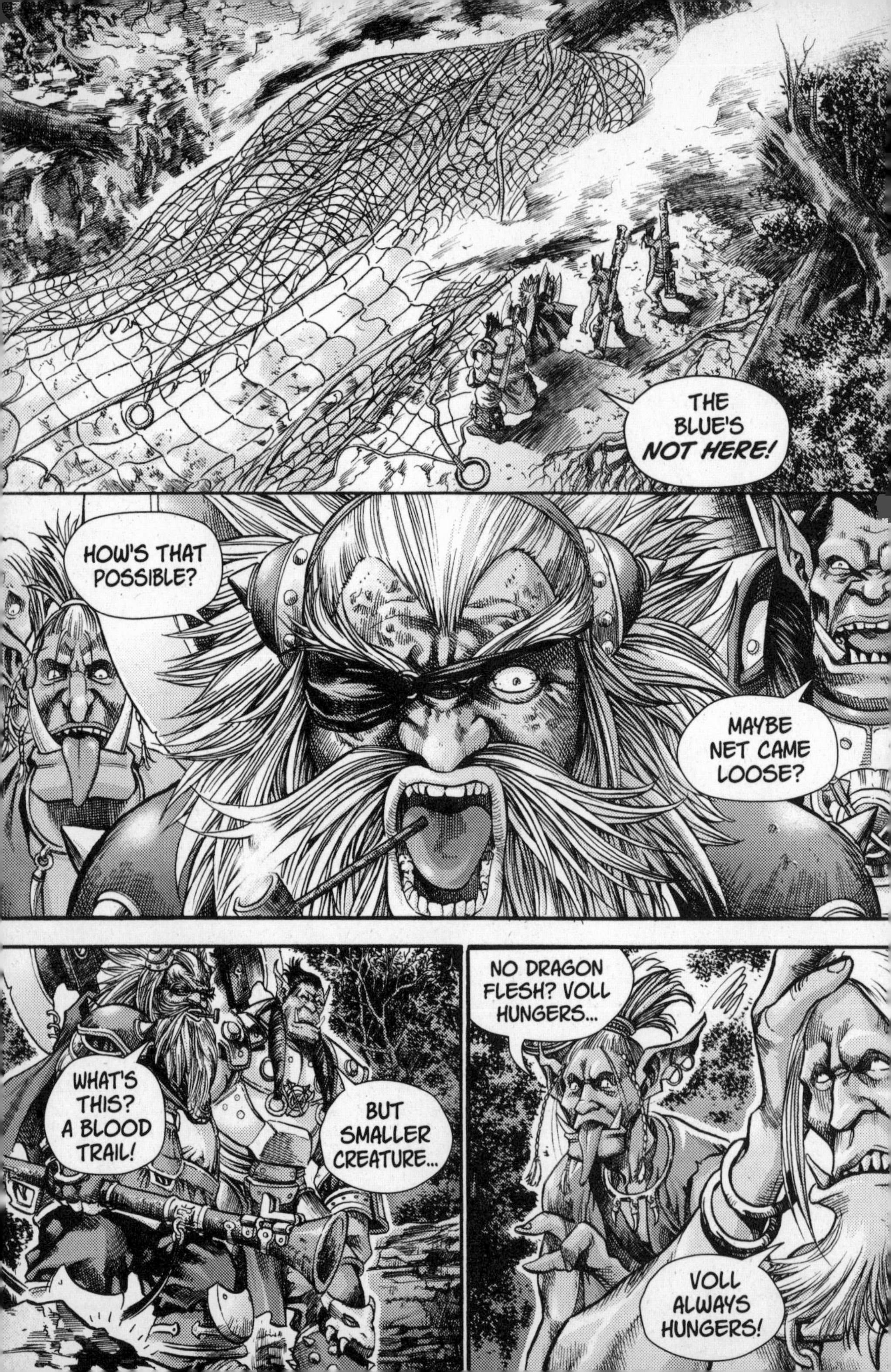
THE BLUE'S *NOT HERE!*
HOW'S THAT POSSIBLE?
MAYBE NET CAME LOOSE?
WHAT'S THIS? A BLOOD TRAIL!
BUT SMALLER CREATURE...
NO DRAGON FLESH? VOLL HUNGERS...
VOLL ALWAYS HUNGERS!

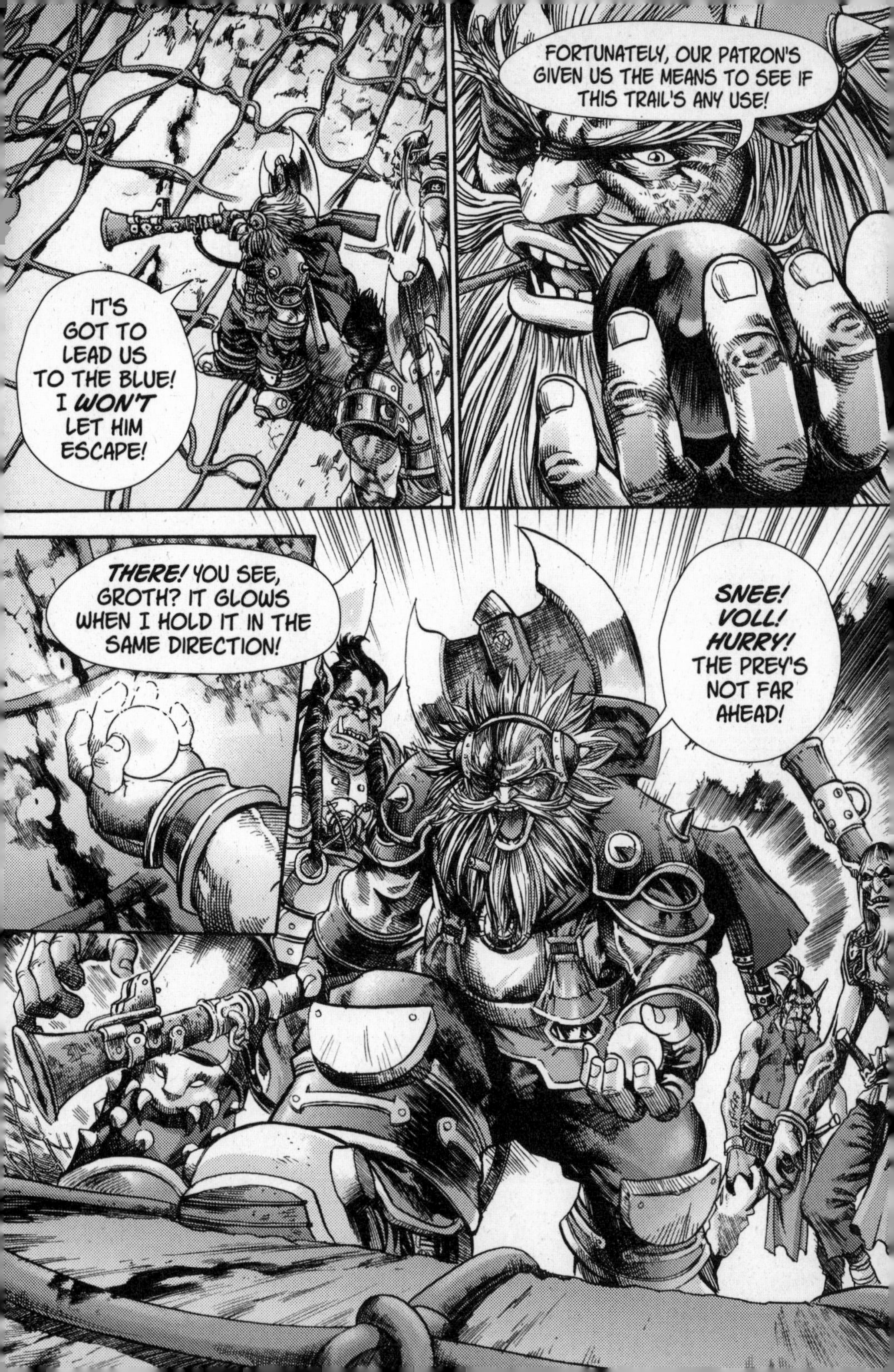
IT'S GOT TO LEAD US TO THE BLUE! I *WON'T* LET HIM ESCAPE!
FORTUNATELY, OUR PATRON'S GIVEN US THE MEANS TO SEE IF THIS TRAIL'S ANY USE!
THERE! YOU SEE, GROTH? IT GLOWS WHEN I HOLD IT IN THE SAME DIRECTION!
SNEE! VOLL! HURRY! THE PREY'S NOT FAR AHEAD!

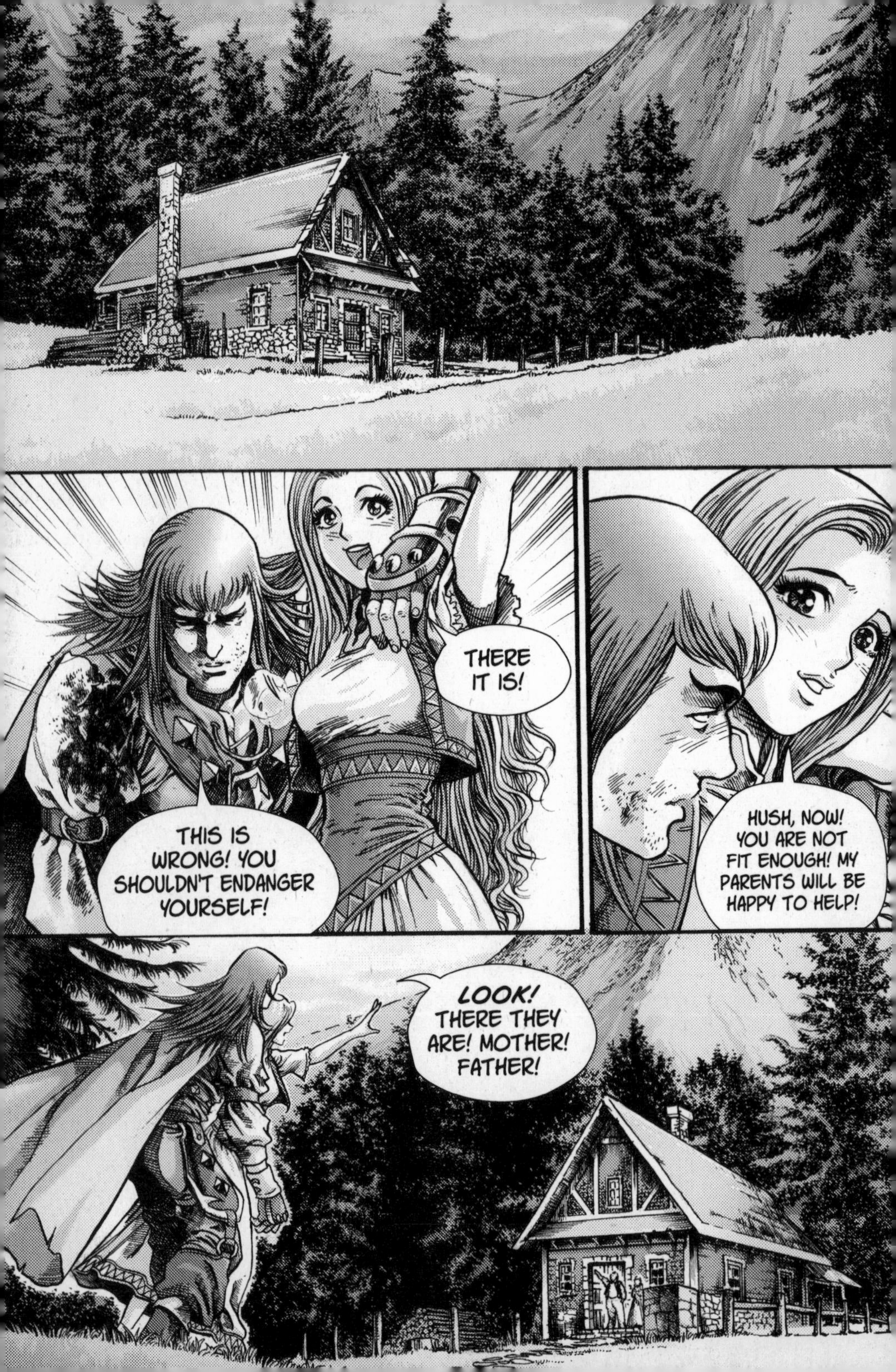
THERE IT IS!
THIS IS WRONG! YOU SHOULDN'T ENDANGER YOURSELF!
HUSH, NOW! YOU ARE NOT FIT ENOUGH! MY PARENTS WILL BE HAPPY TO HELP!
LOOK! THERE THEY ARE! MOTHER! FATHER!

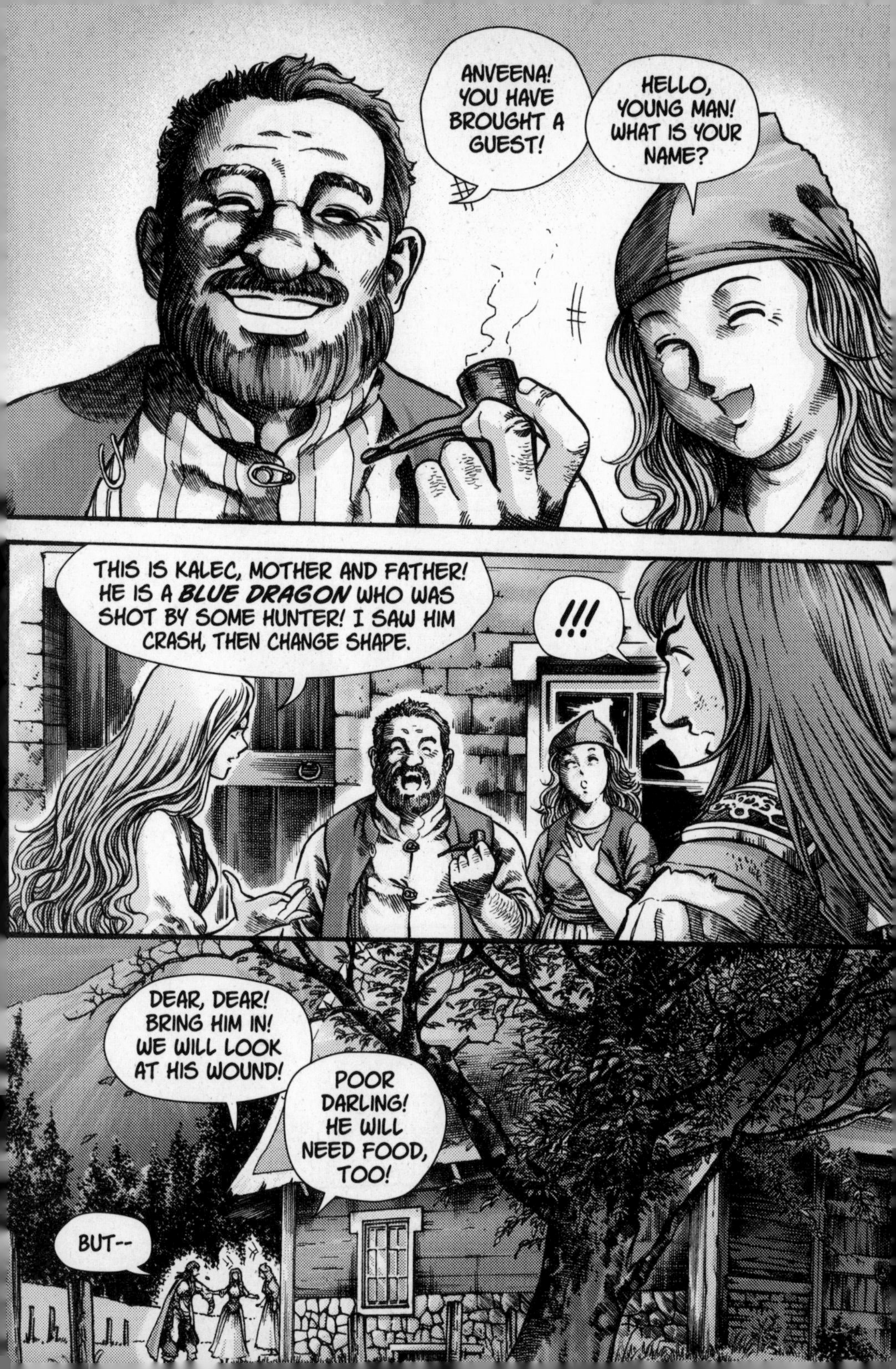
ANVEENA! YOU HAVE BROUGHT A GUEST!
HELLO, YOUNG MAN! WHAT IS YOUR NAME?
THIS IS KALEC, MOTHER AND FATHER! HE IS A *BLUE DRAGON* WHO WAS SHOT BY SOME HUNTER! I SAW HIM CRASH, THEN CHANGE SHAPE.
!!!
DEAR, DEAR! BRING HIM IN! WE WILL LOOK AT HIS WOUND!
POOR DARLING! HE WILL NEED FOOD, TOO!
BUT--

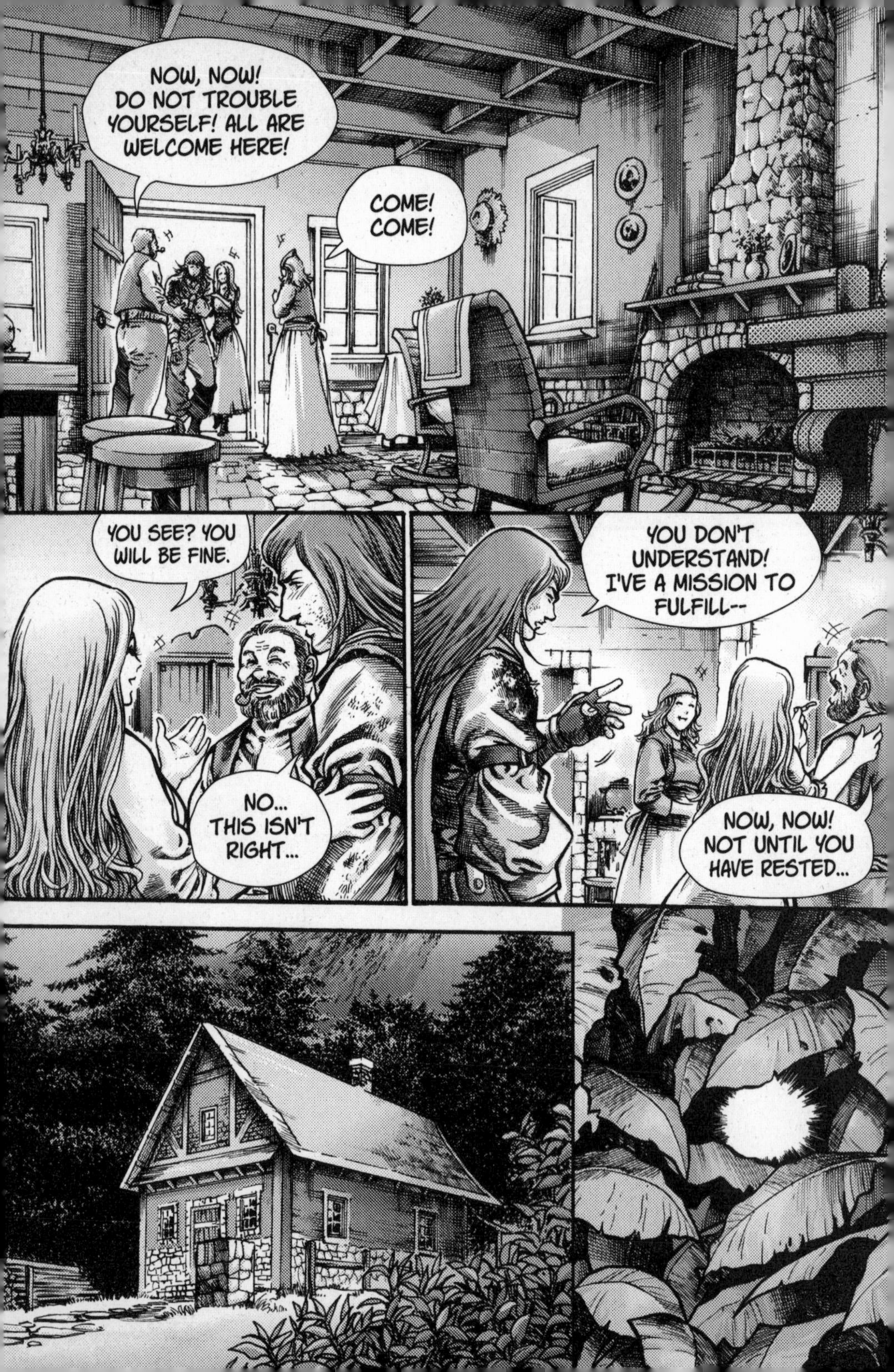
NOW, NOW! DO NOT TROUBLE YOURSELF! ALL ARE WELCOME HERE!
COME! COME!
YOU SEE? YOU WILL BE FINE.
NO... THIS ISN'T RIGHT...
YOU DON'T UNDERSTAND! I'VE A MISSION TO FULFILL--
NOW, NOW! NOT UNTIL YOU HAVE RESTED...

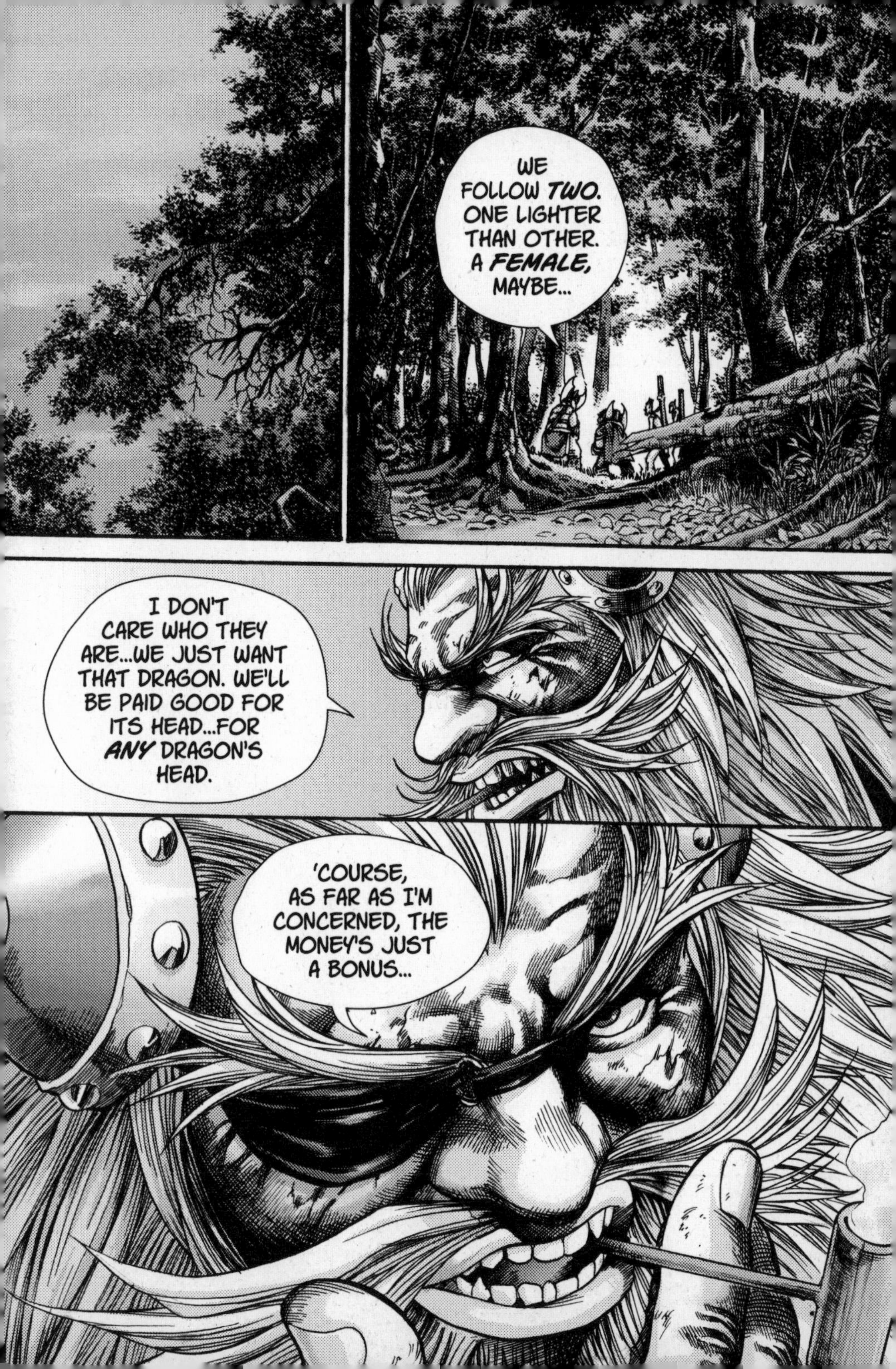
WE FOLLOW *TWO.* ONE LIGHTER THAN OTHER. A *FEMALE,* MAYBE...
I DON'T CARE WHO THEY ARE...WE JUST WANT THAT DRAGON. WE'LL BE PAID GOOD FOR ITS HEAD...FOR *ANY* DRAGON'S HEAD.
'COURSE, AS FAR AS I'M CONCERNED, THE MONEY'S JUST A BONUS...

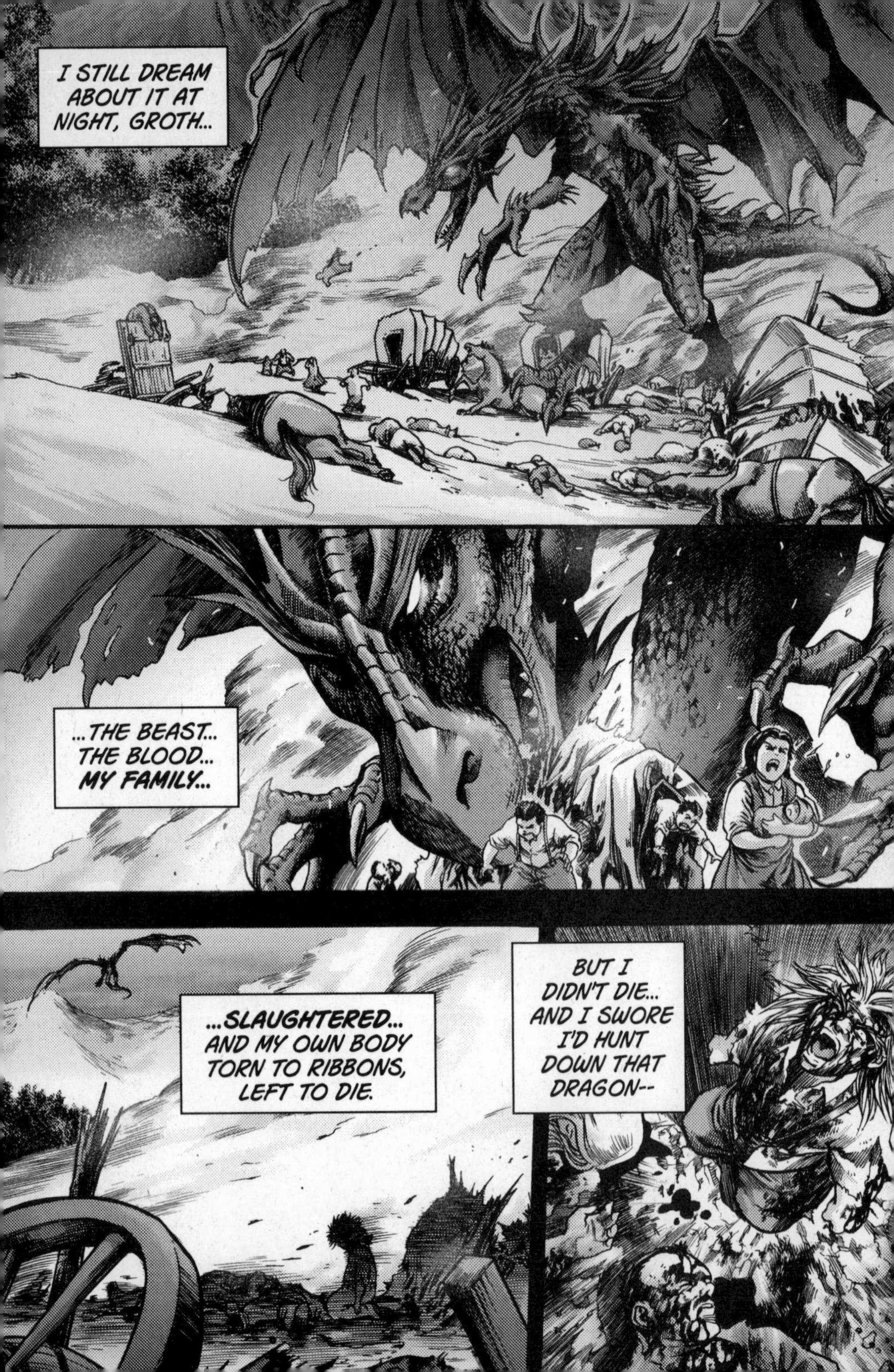
I STILL DREAM ABOUT IT AT NIGHT, GROTH...
...THE BEAST... THE BLOOD... MY FAMILY...
...SLAUGHTERED... AND MY OWN BODY TORN TO RIBBONS, LEFT TO DIE.
BUT I DIDN'T DIE... AND I SWORE I'D HUNT DOWN THAT DRAGON--

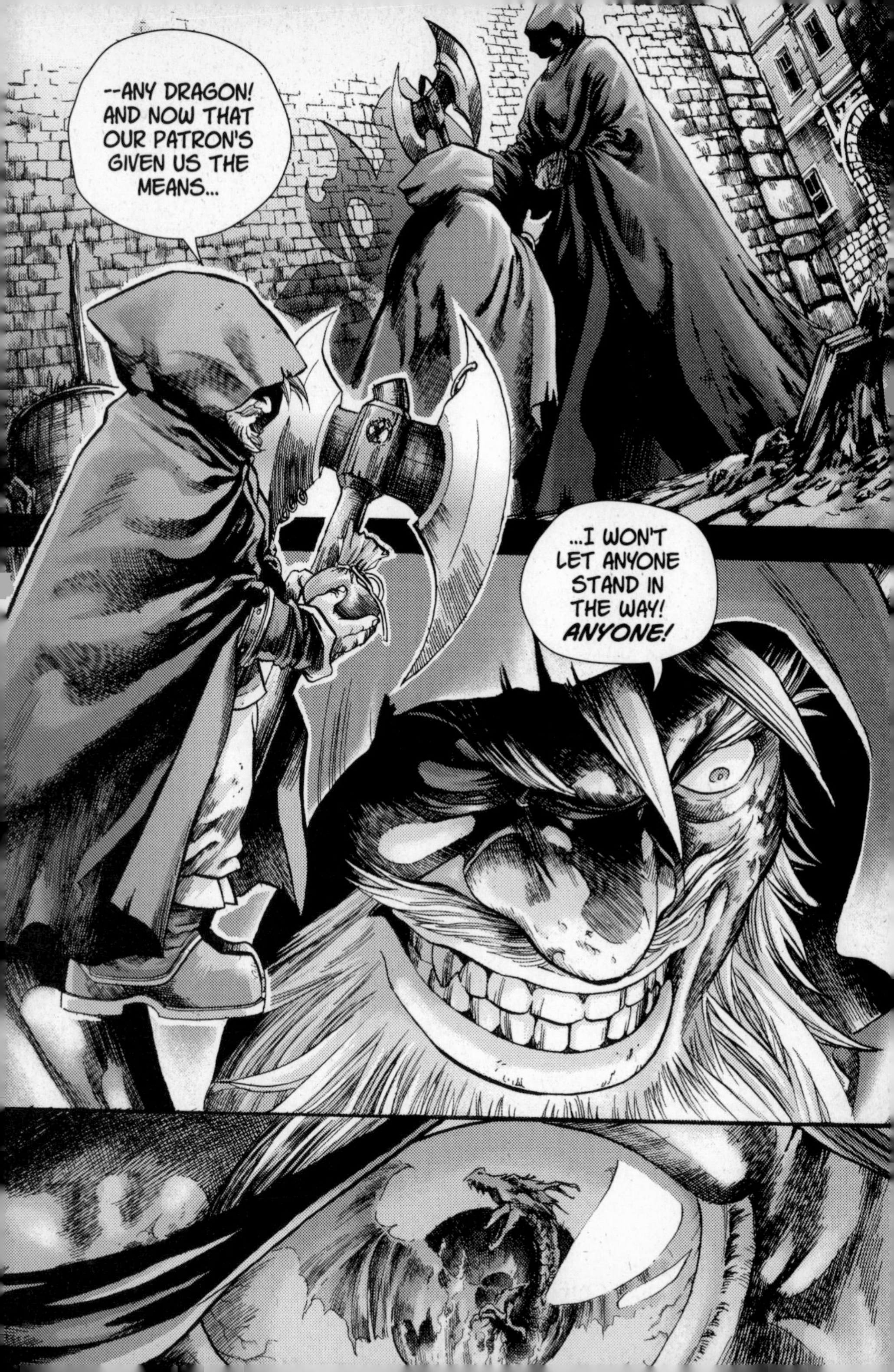
--ANY DRAGON! AND NOW THAT OUR PATRON'S GIVEN US THE MEANS...
...I WON'T LET ANYONE STAND IN THE WAY! *ANYONE!*

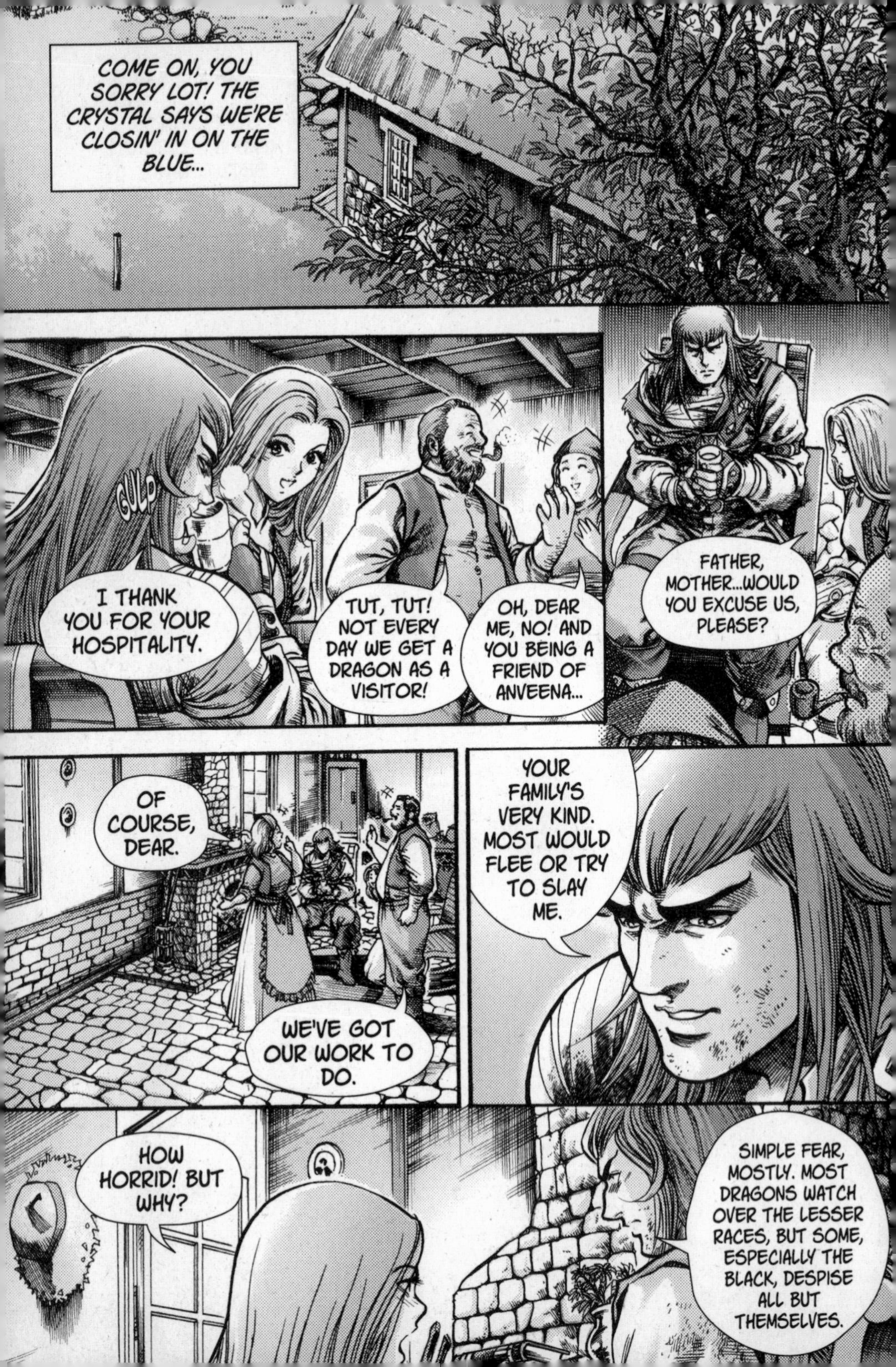
COME ON, YOU SORRY LOT! THE CRYSTAL SAYS WE'RE CLOSIN' IN ON THE BLUE...
GULP
I THANK YOU FOR YOUR HOSPITALITY.
TUT, TUT! NOT EVERY DAY WE GET A DRAGON AS A VISITOR!
OH, DEAR ME, NO! AND YOU BEING A FRIEND OF ANVEENA...
FATHER, MOTHER...WOULD YOU EXCUSE US, PLEASE?
OF COURSE, DEAR.
WE'VE GOT OUR WORK TO DO.
YOUR FAMILY'S VERY KIND. MOST WOULD FLEE OR TRY TO SLAY ME.
HOW HORRID! BUT WHY?
SIMPLE FEAR, MOSTLY. MOST DRAGONS WATCH OVER THE LESSER RACES, BUT SOME, ESPECIALLY THE BLACK, DESPISE ALL BUT THEMSELVES.

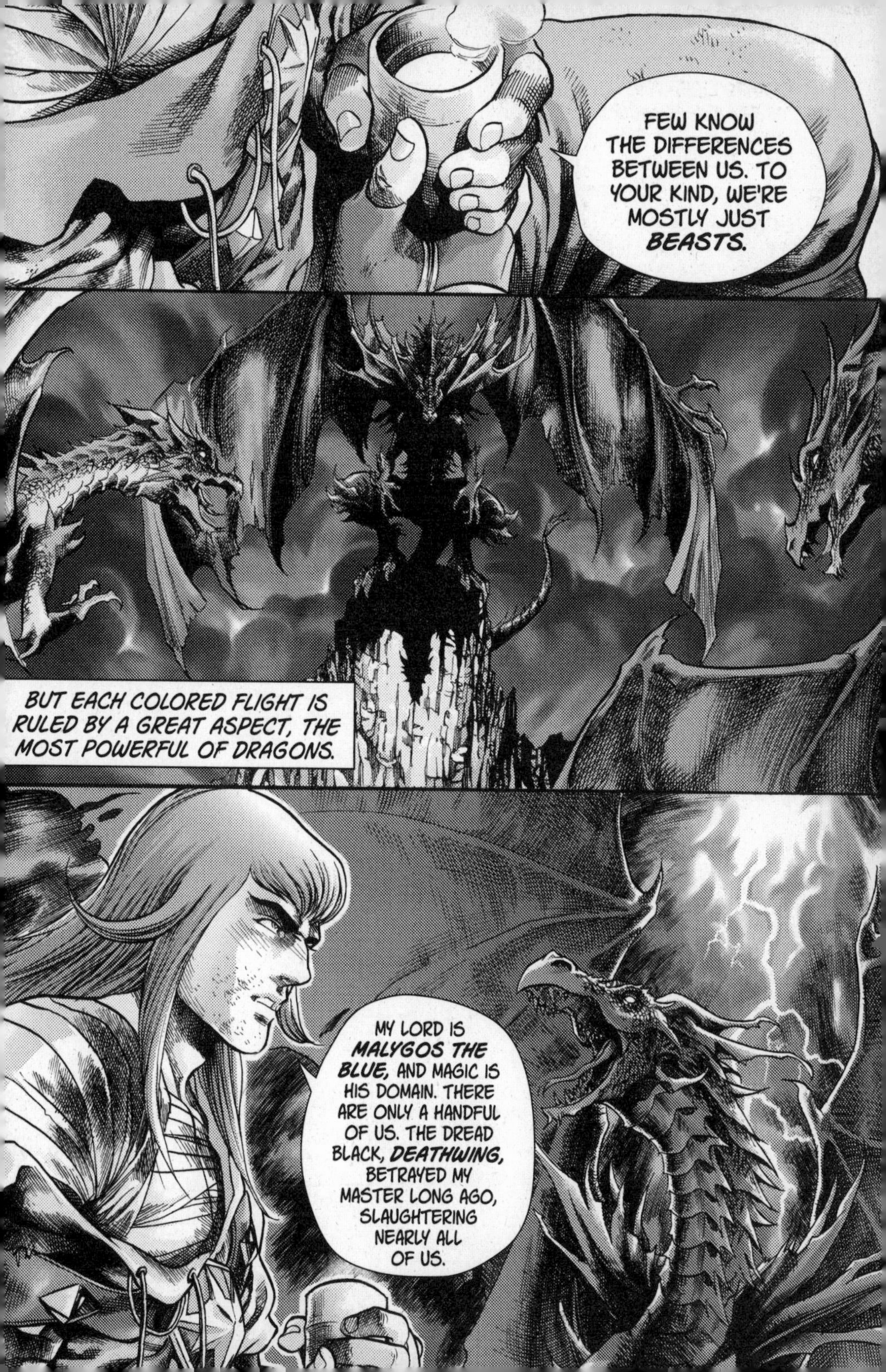
FEW KNOW THE DIFFERENCES BETWEEN US. TO YOUR KIND, WE'RE MOSTLY JUST *BEASTS.*
BUT EACH COLORED FLIGHT IS RULED BY A GREAT ASPECT, THE MOST POWERFUL OF DRAGONS.
MY LORD IS *MALYGOS THE BLUE,* AND MAGIC IS HIS DOMAIN. THERE ARE ONLY A HANDFUL OF US. THE DREAD BLACK, *DEATHWING,* BETRAYED MY MASTER LONG AGO, SLAUGHTERING NEARLY ALL OF US.

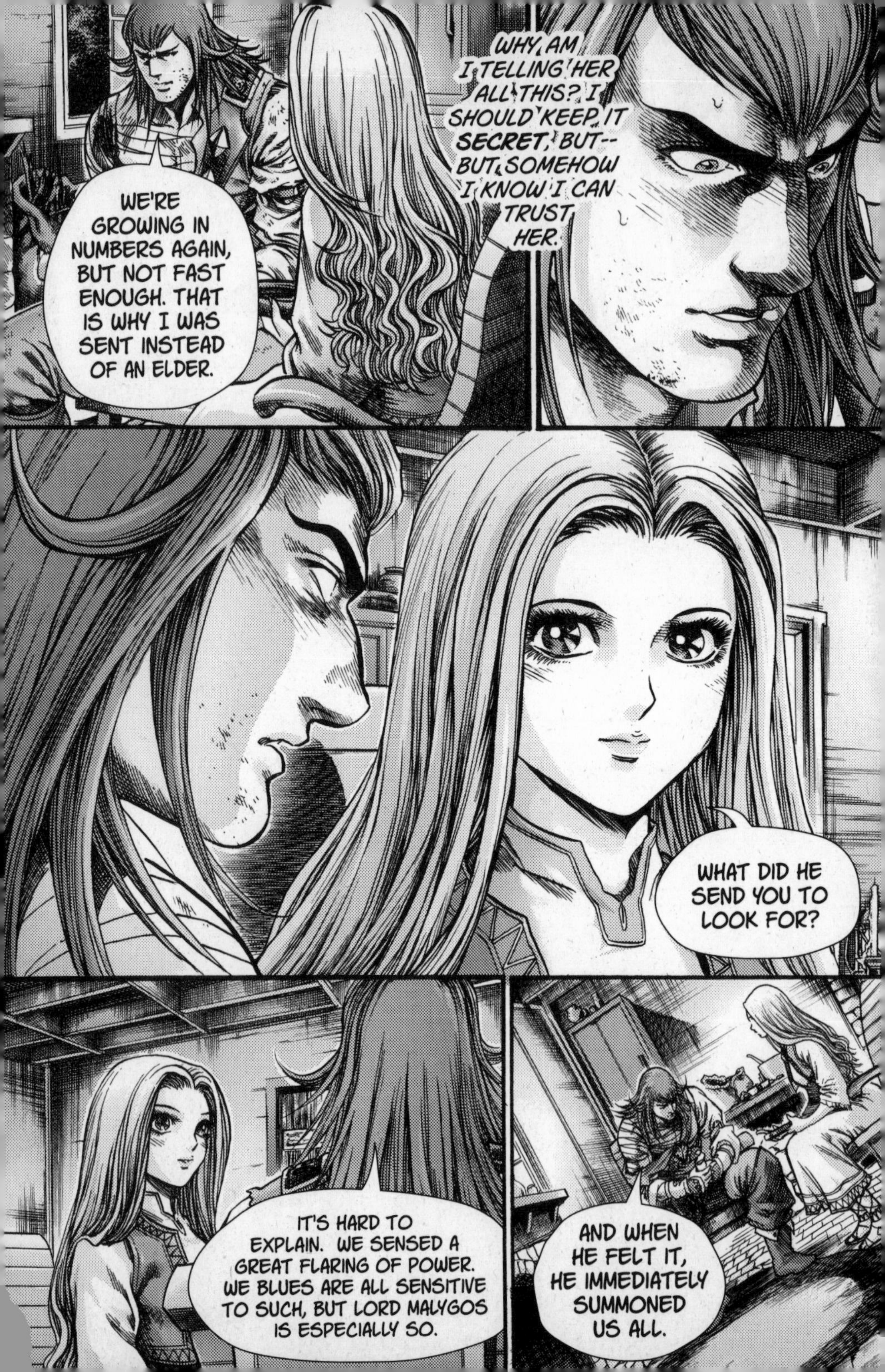
WE'RE GROWING IN NUMBERS AGAIN, BUT NOT FAST ENOUGH. THAT IS WHY I WAS SENT INSTEAD OF AN ELDER.
WHY AM I TELLING HER ALL THIS? I SHOULD KEEP IT **SECRET**, BUT-- BUT SOMEHOW I KNOW I CAN TRUST HER.
WHAT DID HE SEND YOU TO LOOK FOR?
IT'S HARD TO EXPLAIN. WE SENSED A GREAT FLARING OF POWER. WE BLUES ARE ALL SENSITIVE TO SUCH, BUT LORD MALYGOS IS ESPECIALLY SO.
AND WHEN HE FELT IT, HE IMMEDIATELY SUMMONED US ALL.

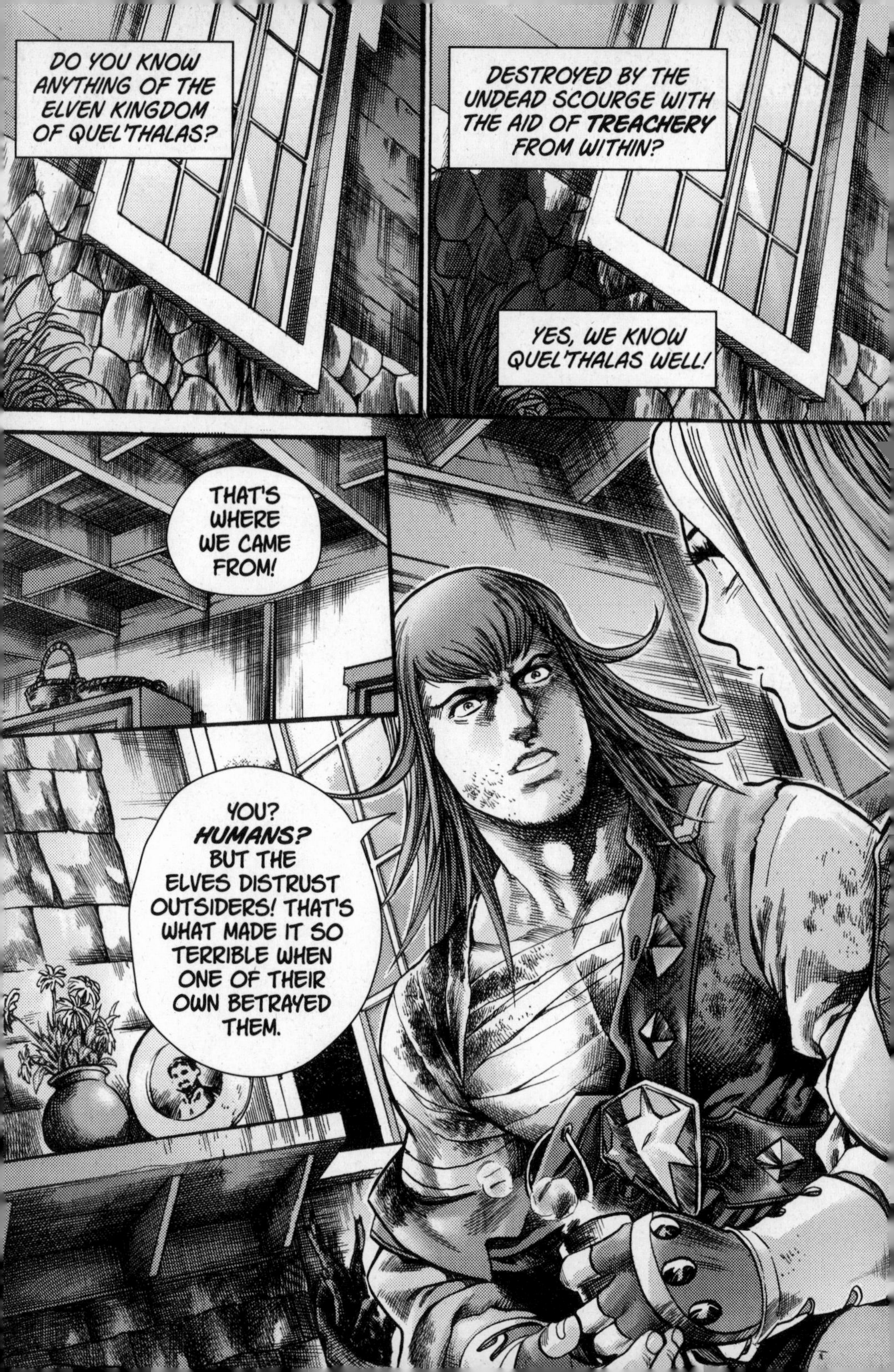
DO YOU KNOW ANYTHING OF THE ELVEN KINGDOM OF QUEL'THALAS?
DESTROYED BY THE UNDEAD SCOURGE WITH THE AID OF **TREACHERY** FROM WITHIN?
YES, WE KNOW QUEL'THALAS WELL!
THAT'S WHERE WE CAME FROM!
YOU? ***HUMANS?*** BUT THE ELVES DISTRUST OUTSIDERS! THAT'S WHAT MADE IT SO TERRIBLE WHEN ONE OF THEIR OWN BETRAYED THEM.

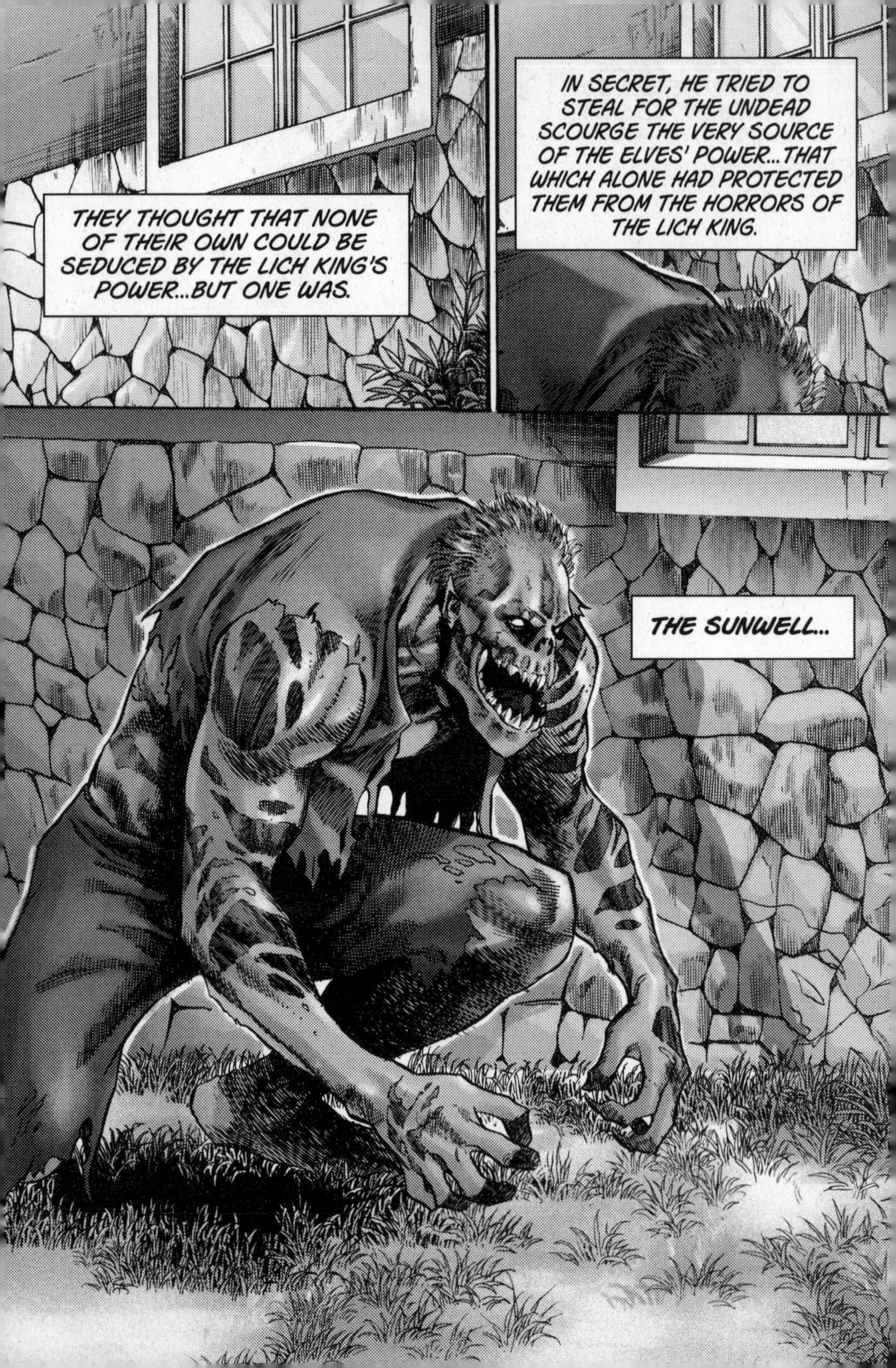
THEY THOUGHT THAT NONE OF THEIR OWN COULD BE SEDUCED BY THE LICH KING'S POWER...BUT ONE WAS.
IN SECRET, HE TRIED TO STEAL FOR THE UNDEAD SCOURGE THE VERY SOURCE OF THE ELVES' POWER...THAT WHICH ALONE HAD PROTECTED THEM FROM THE HORRORS OF THE LICH KING.
THE SUNWELL...

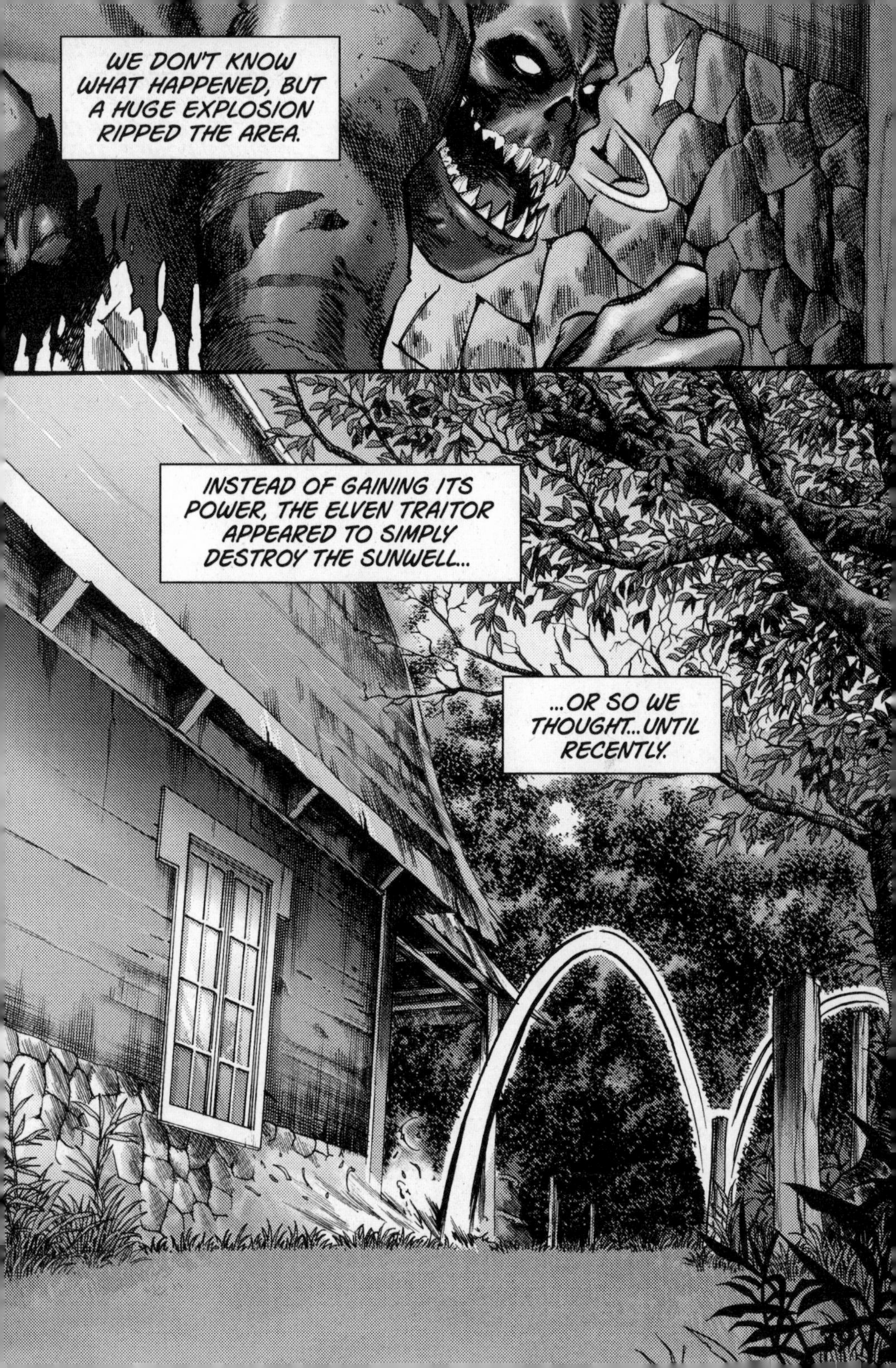
WE DON'T KNOW WHAT HAPPENED, BUT A HUGE EXPLOSION RIPPED THE AREA.
INSTEAD OF GAINING ITS POWER, THE ELVEN TRAITOR APPEARED TO SIMPLY DESTROY THE SUNWELL...
...OR SO WE THOUGHT...UNTIL RECENTLY.

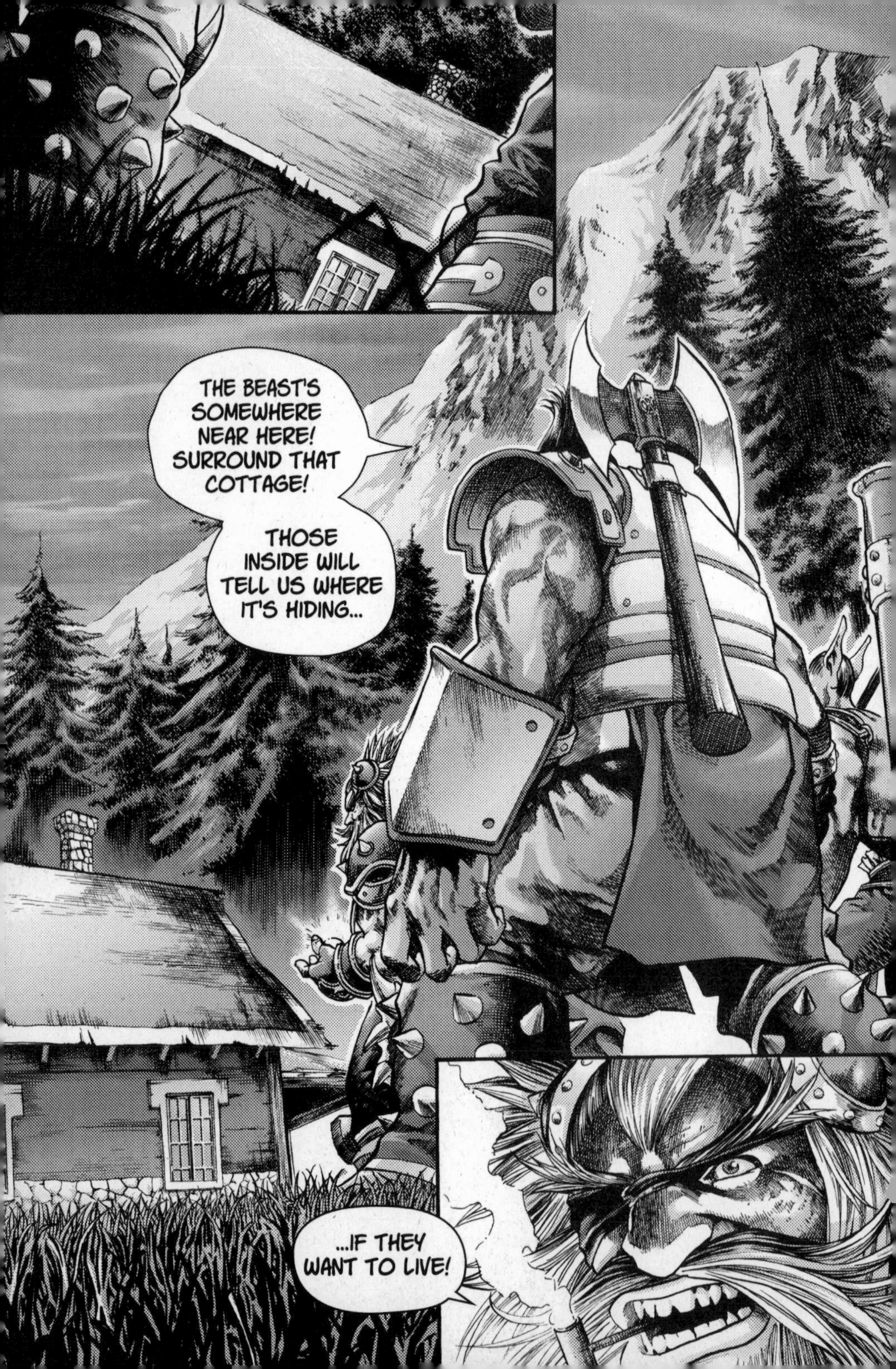
THE BEAST'S SOMEWHERE NEAR HERE! SURROUND THAT COTTAGE!
THOSE INSIDE WILL TELL US WHERE IT'S HIDING...
...IF THEY WANT TO LIVE!

CHAPTER TWO PURSUED

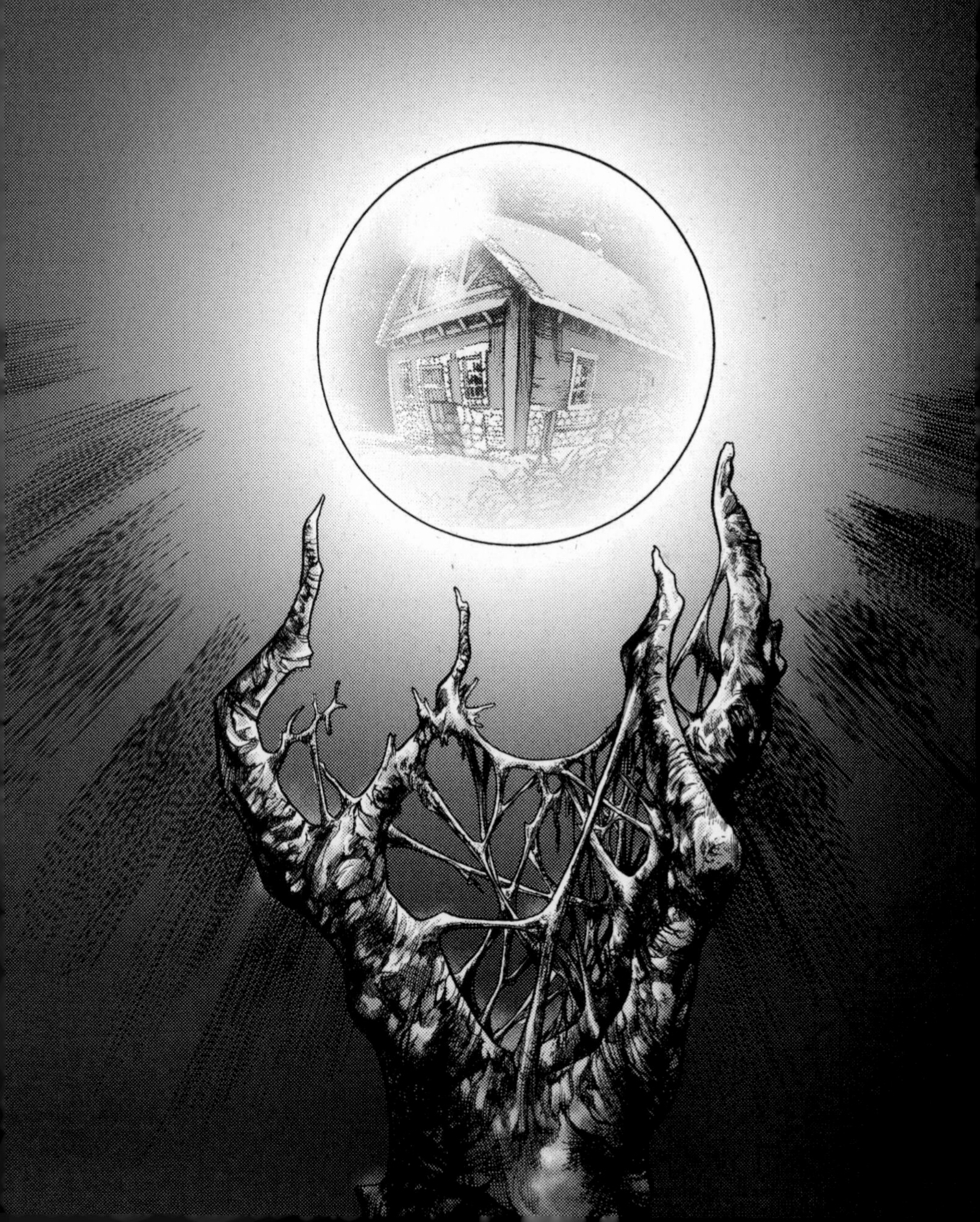

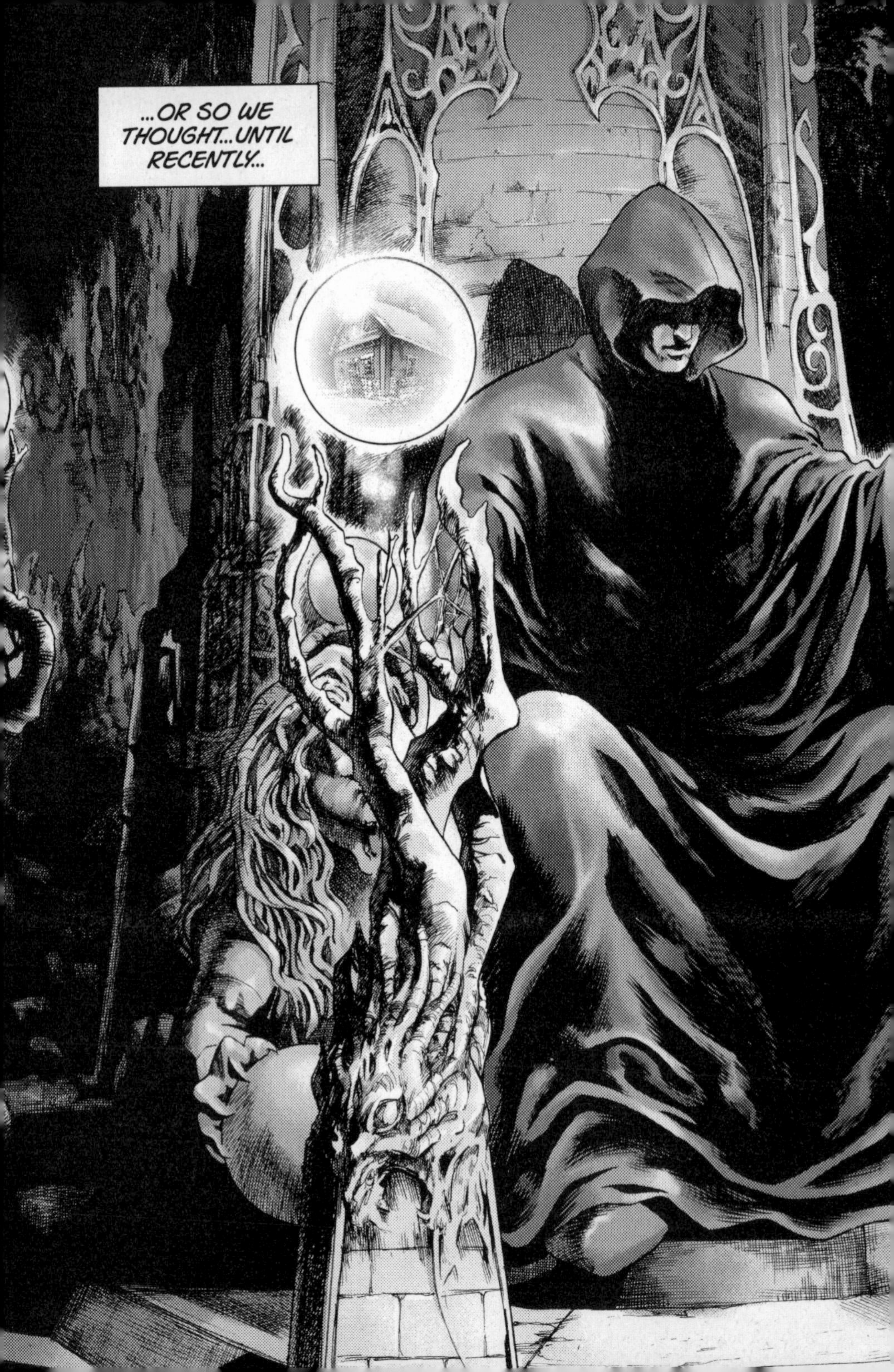
...OR SO WE THOUGHT...UNTIL RECENTLY...

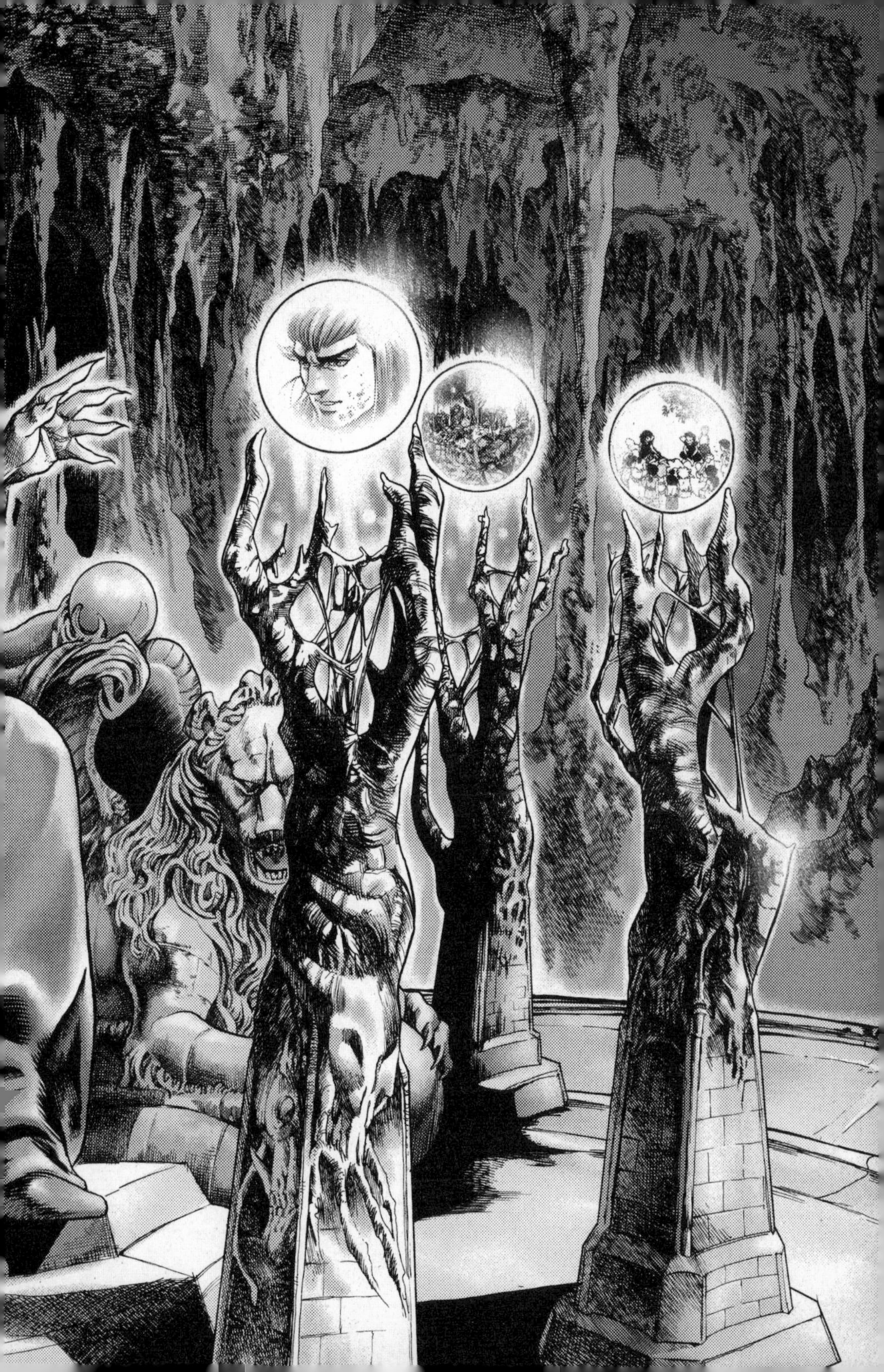

THE EMANATIONS CAME FROM VERY NEAR HERE. I WAS SEARCHING FOR THEIR SOURCE WHEN I WAS ATTACKED.

I'VE NO IDEA WHO ATTACKED ME, BUT THEY MUST BE AFTER THE SAME THING I AM.

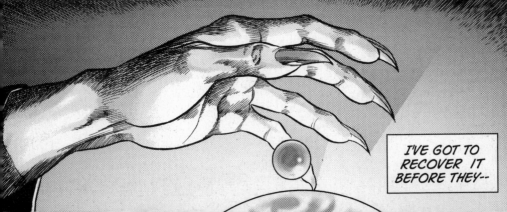

I'VE GOT TO RECOVER IT BEFORE THEY--

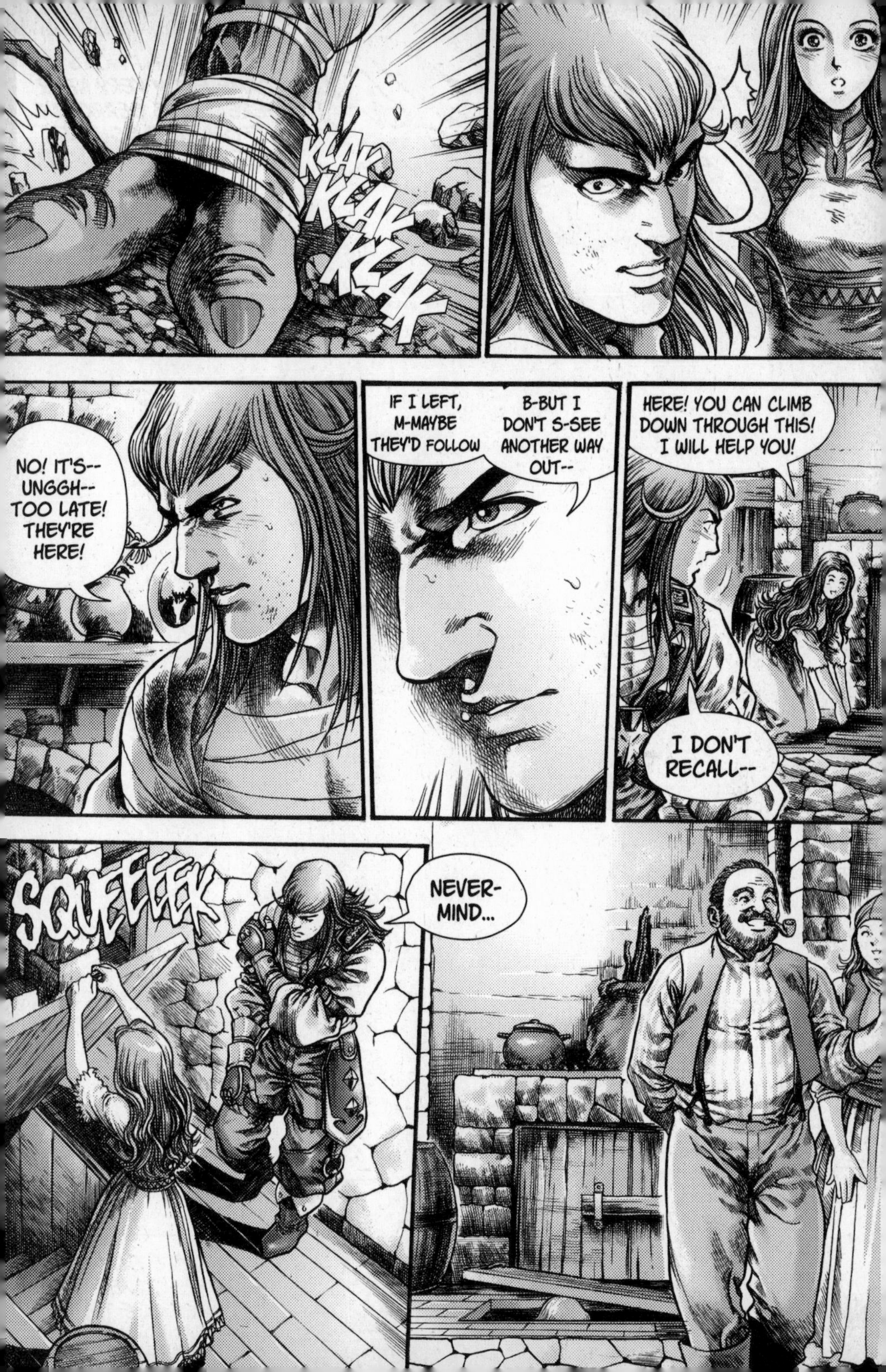
KLAK KLAK KLAK
NO! IT'S-- UNGGH-- TOO LATE! THEY'RE HERE!
IF I LEFT, M-MAYBE THEY'D FOLLOW
B-BUT I DON'T S-SEE ANOTHER WAY OUT--
HERE! YOU CAN CLIMB DOWN THROUGH THIS! I WILL HELP YOU!
I DON'T RECALL--
SQUEEEEK
NEVER-MIND...

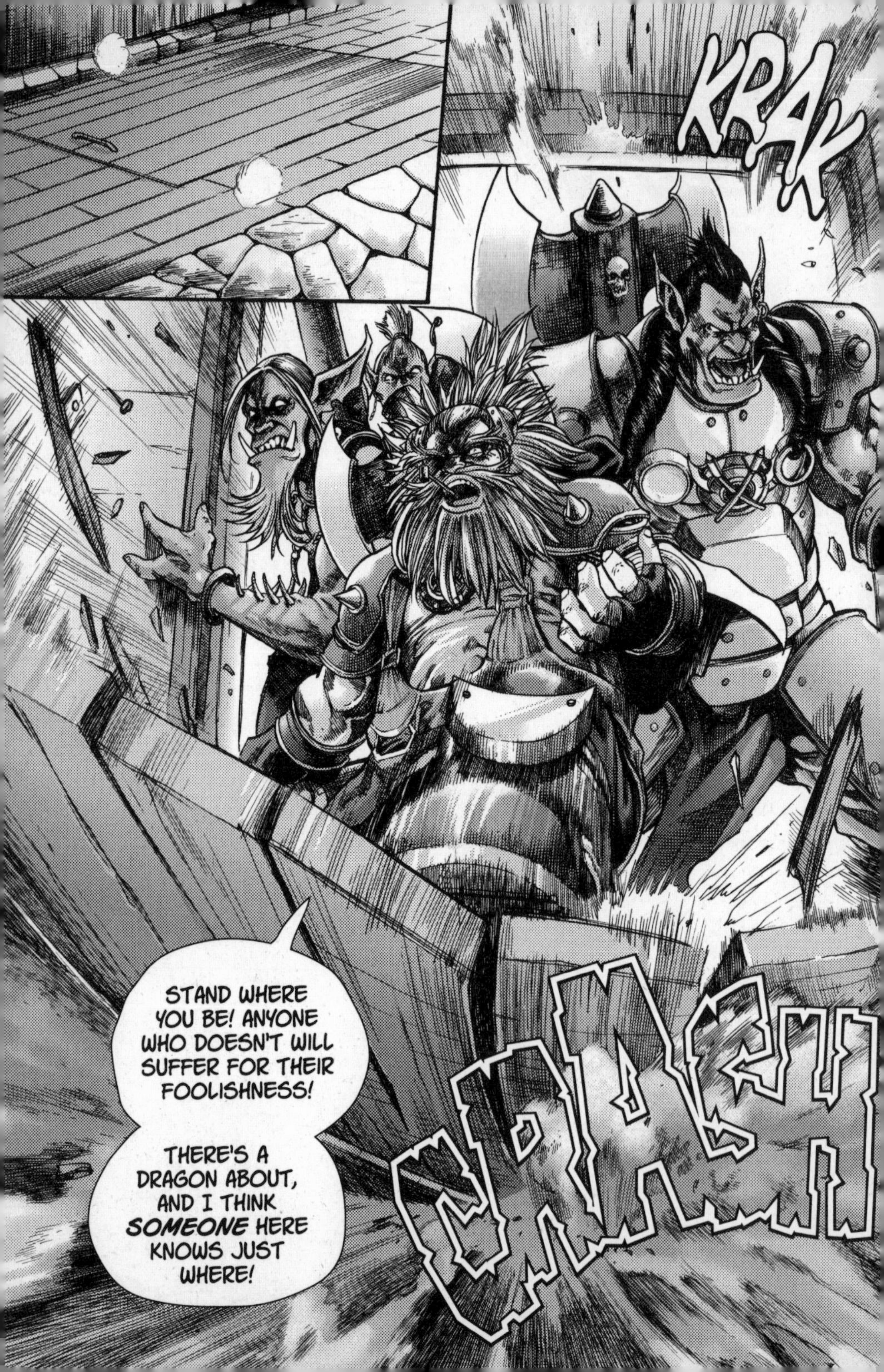
KRAK
STAND WHERE YOU BE! ANYONE WHO DOESN'T WILL SUFFER FOR THEIR FOOLISHNESS!
THERE'S A DRAGON ABOUT, AND I THINK *SOMEONE* HERE KNOWS JUST WHERE!
SMASH

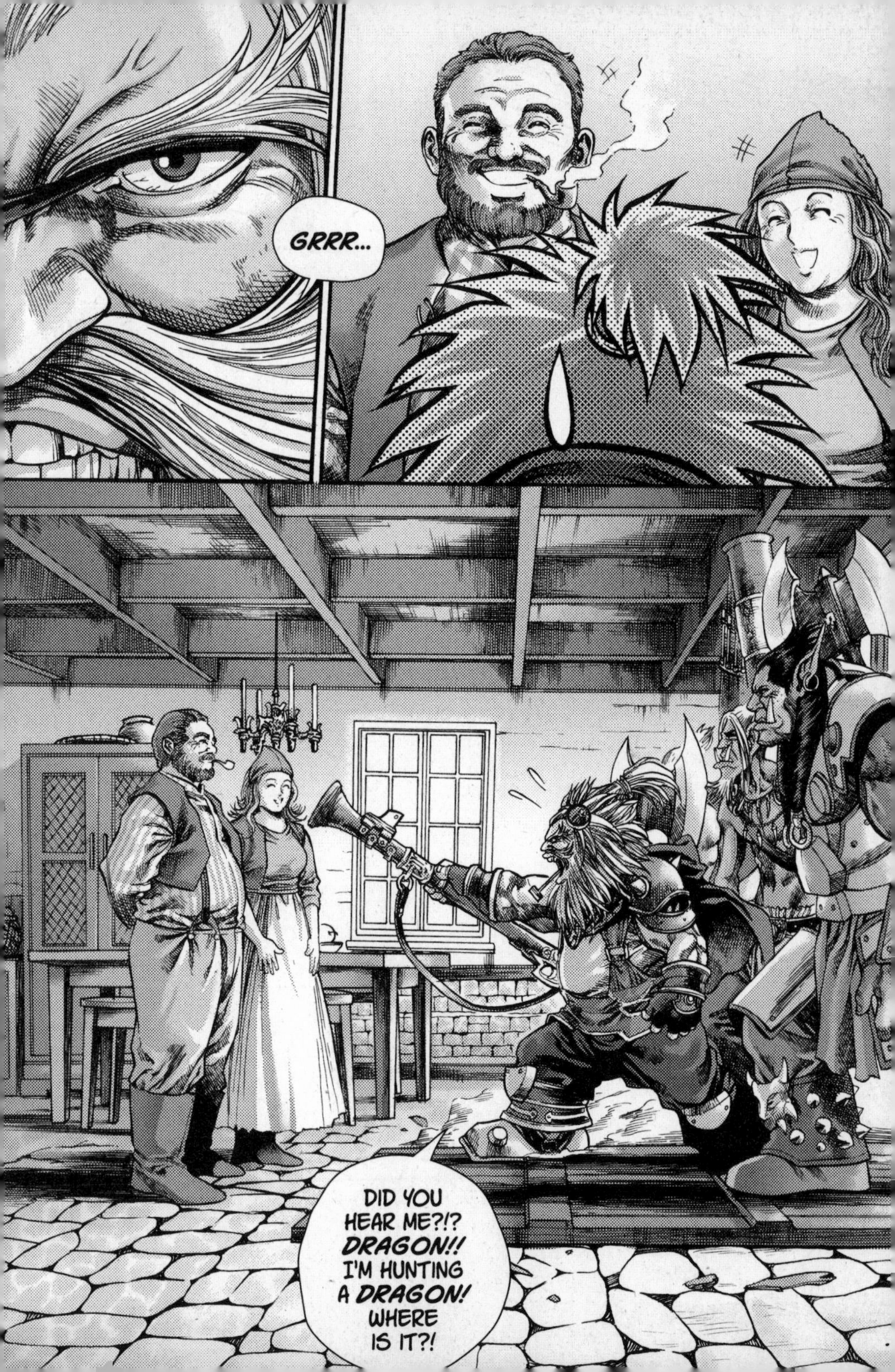
GRRR...
DID YOU HEAR ME?!? DRAGON!! I'M HUNTING A DRAGON! WHERE IS IT?!

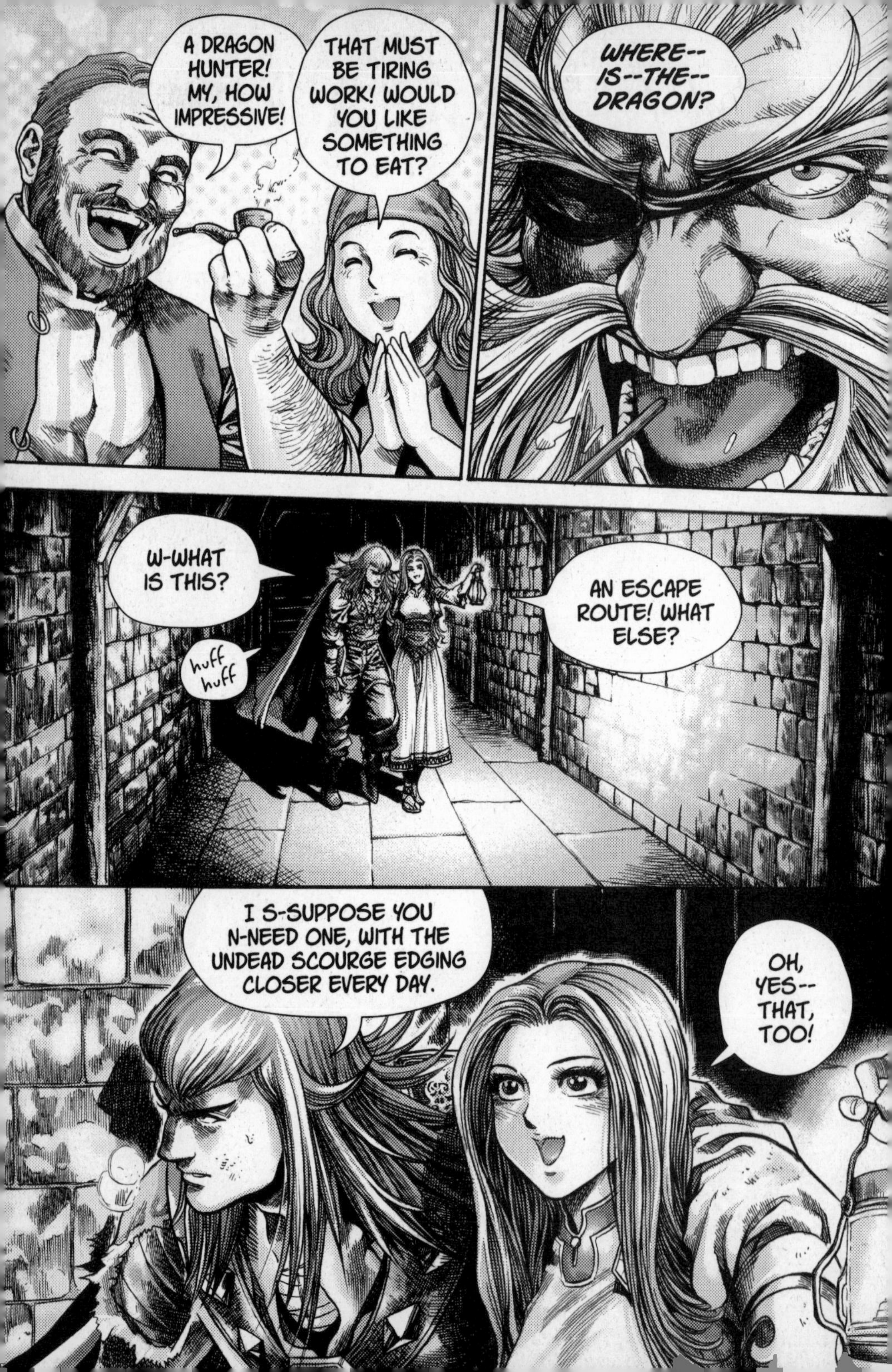
A DRAGON HUNTER! MY, HOW IMPRESSIVE!
THAT MUST BE TIRING WORK! WOULD YOU LIKE SOMETHING TO EAT?
WHERE--IS--THE--DRAGON?
W-WHAT IS THIS?
huff huff
AN ESCAPE ROUTE! WHAT ELSE?
I S-SUPPOSE YOU N-NEED ONE, WITH THE UNDEAD SCOURGE EDGING CLOSER EVERY DAY.
OH, YES--THAT, TOO!

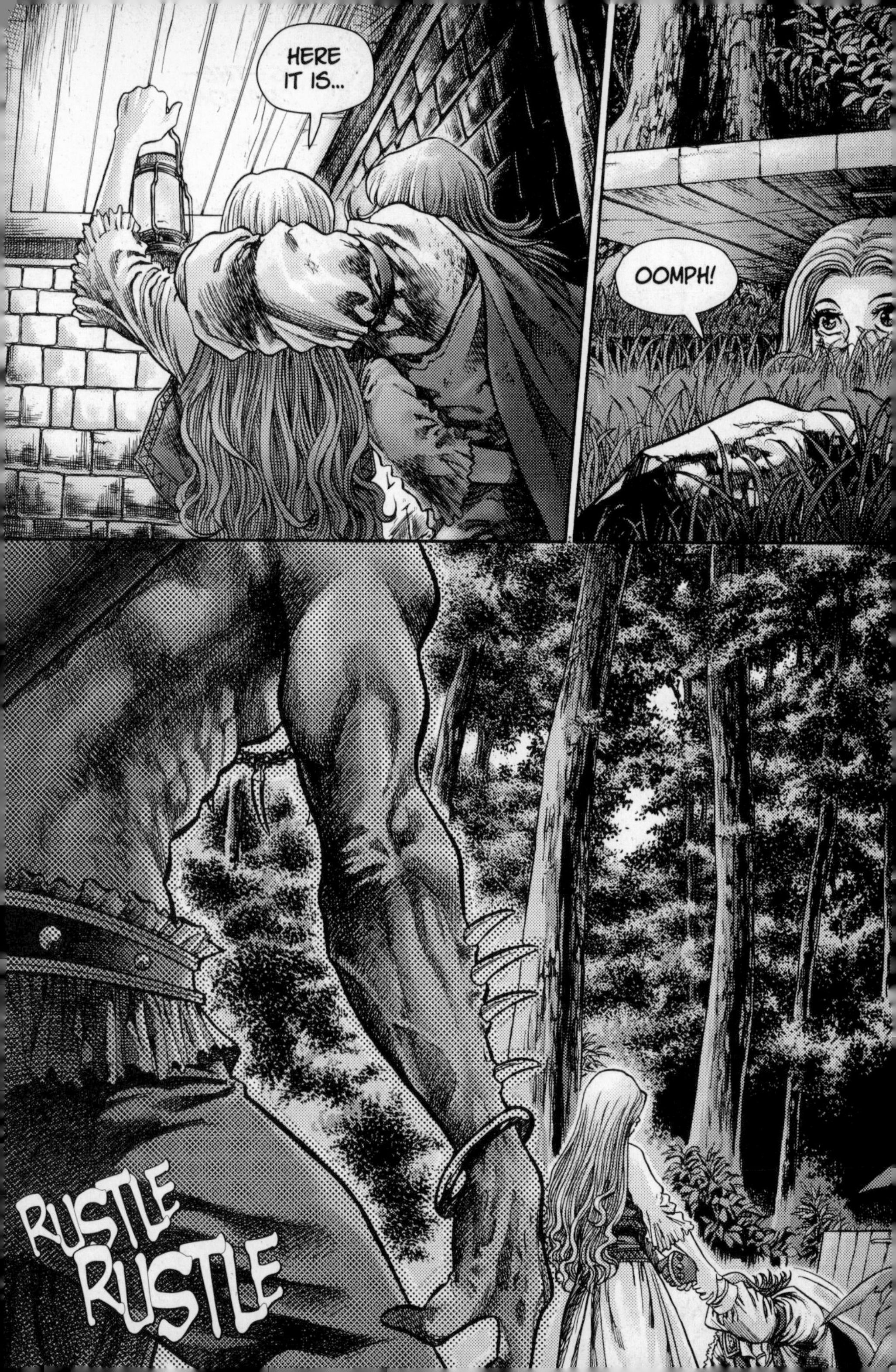
HERE IT IS...
OOMPH!
RUSTLE RUSTLE

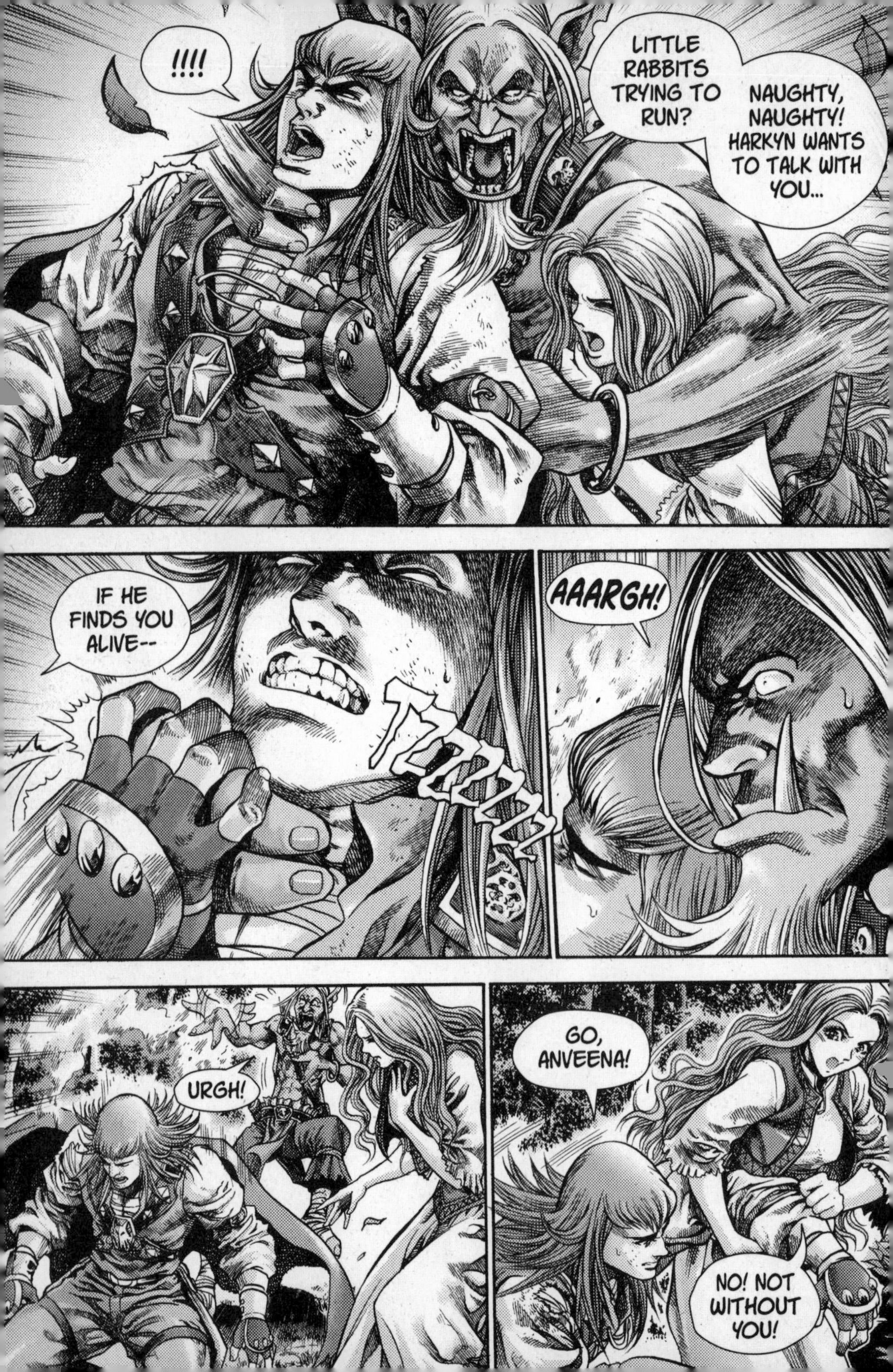
!!!!
LITTLE RABBITS TRYING TO RUN?
NAUGHTY, NAUGHTY! HARKYN WANTS TO TALK WITH YOU...
IF HE FINDS YOU ALIVE--
AAARGH!
URGH!
GO, ANVEENA!
NO! NOT WITHOUT YOU!

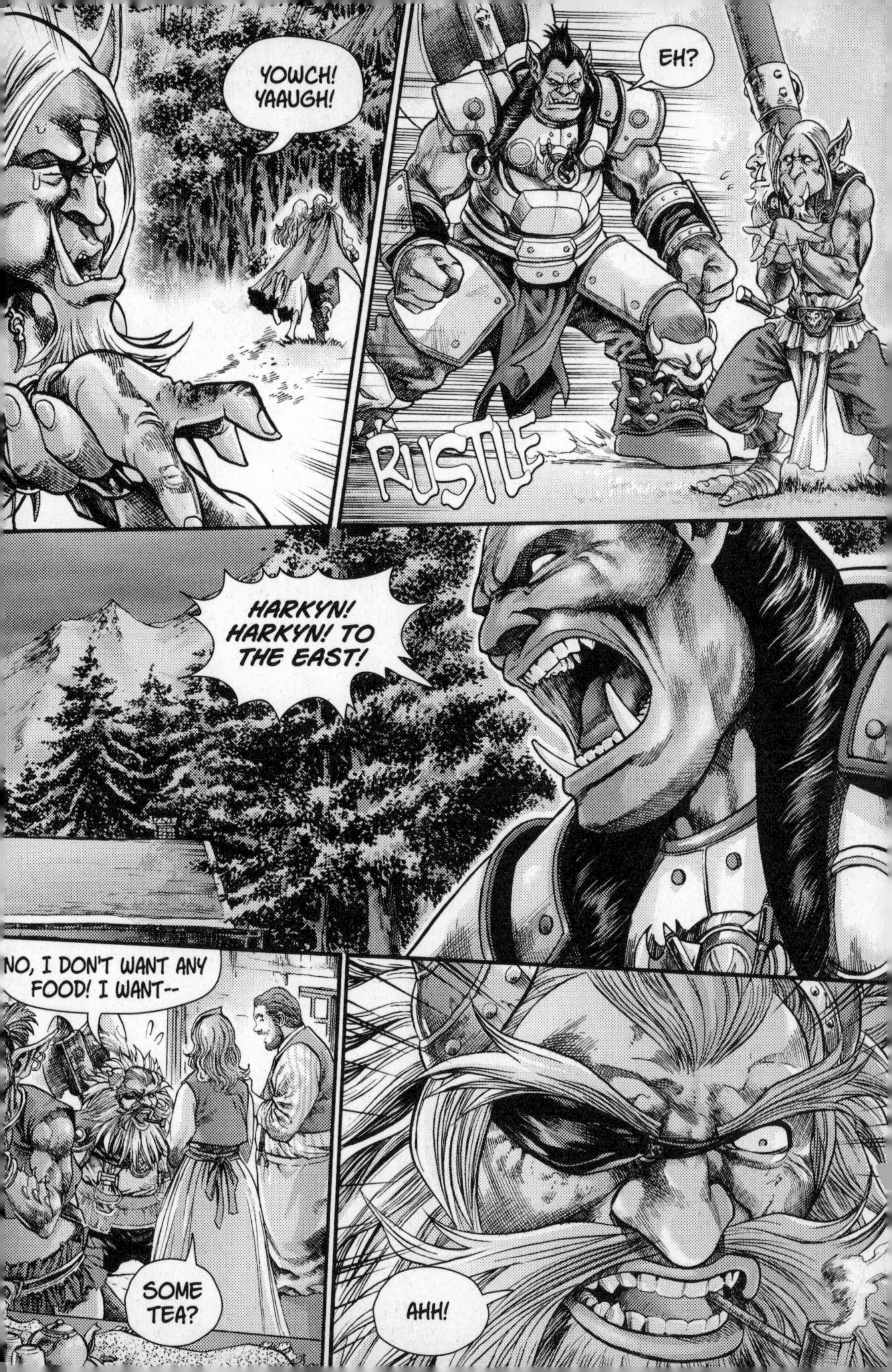
YOWCH! YAAUGH!
EH?
RUSTLE
HARKYN! HARKYN! TO THE EAST!
NO, I DON'T WANT ANY FOOD! I WANT--
SOME TEA?
AHH!

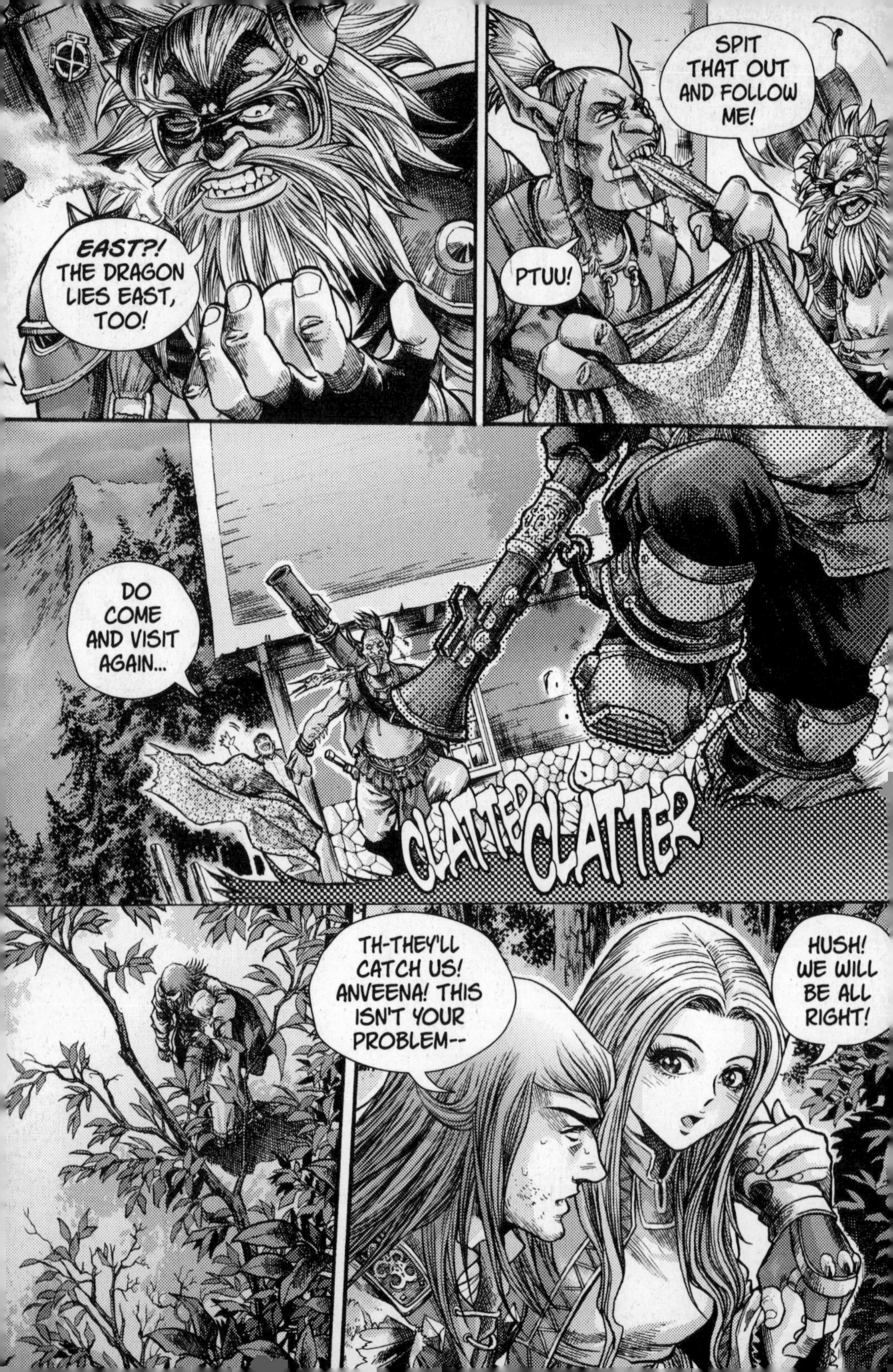
EAST?! THE DRAGON LIES EAST, TOO!
SPIT THAT OUT AND FOLLOW ME!
PTUU!
DO COME AND VISIT AGAIN...
CLATTER CLATTER
TH-THEY'LL CATCH US! ANVEENA! THIS ISN'T YOUR PROBLEM--
HUSH! WE WILL BE ALL RIGHT!

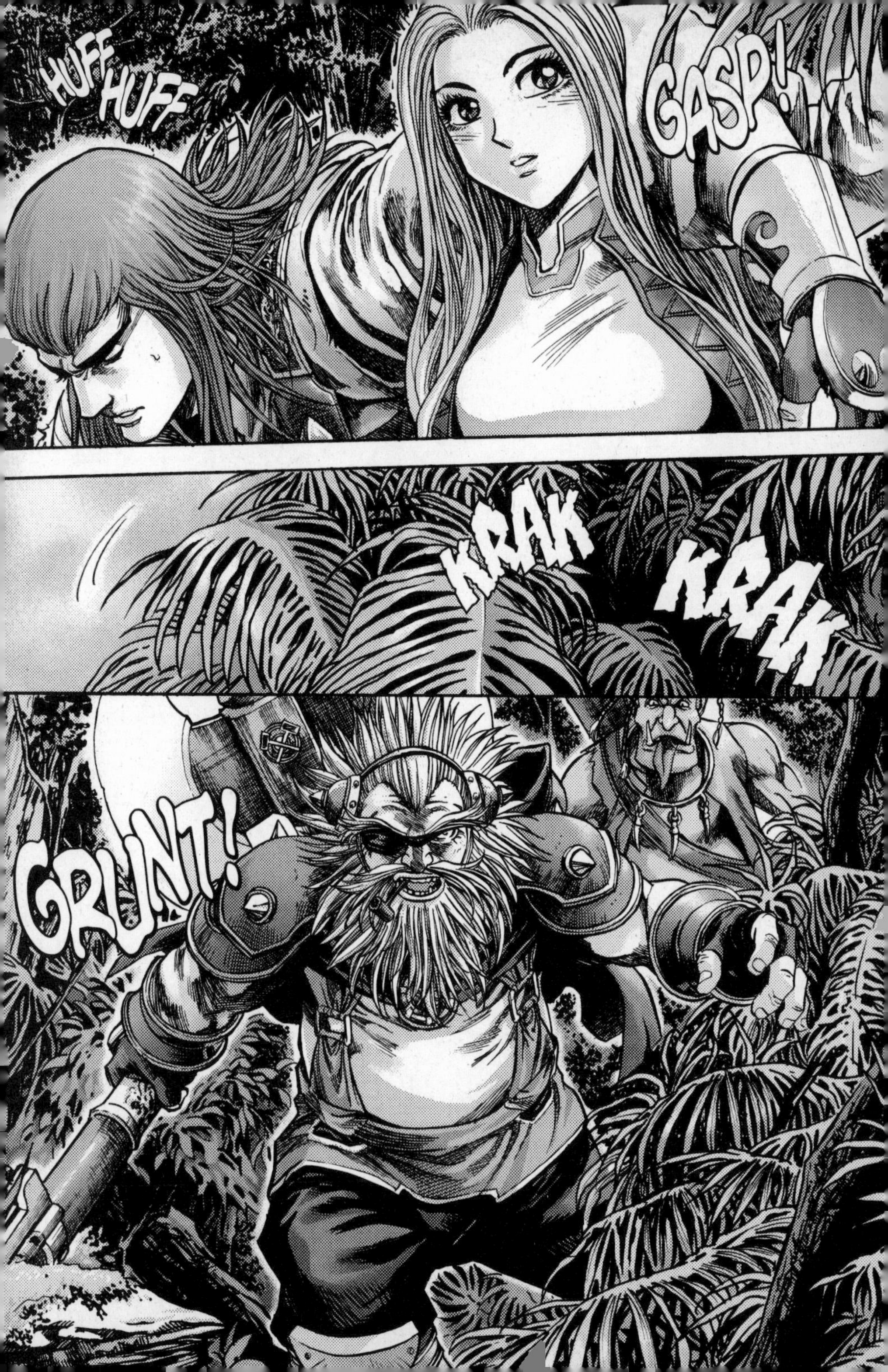
GASP!
HUFF HUFF
KRAK
KRAK
GRUNT!

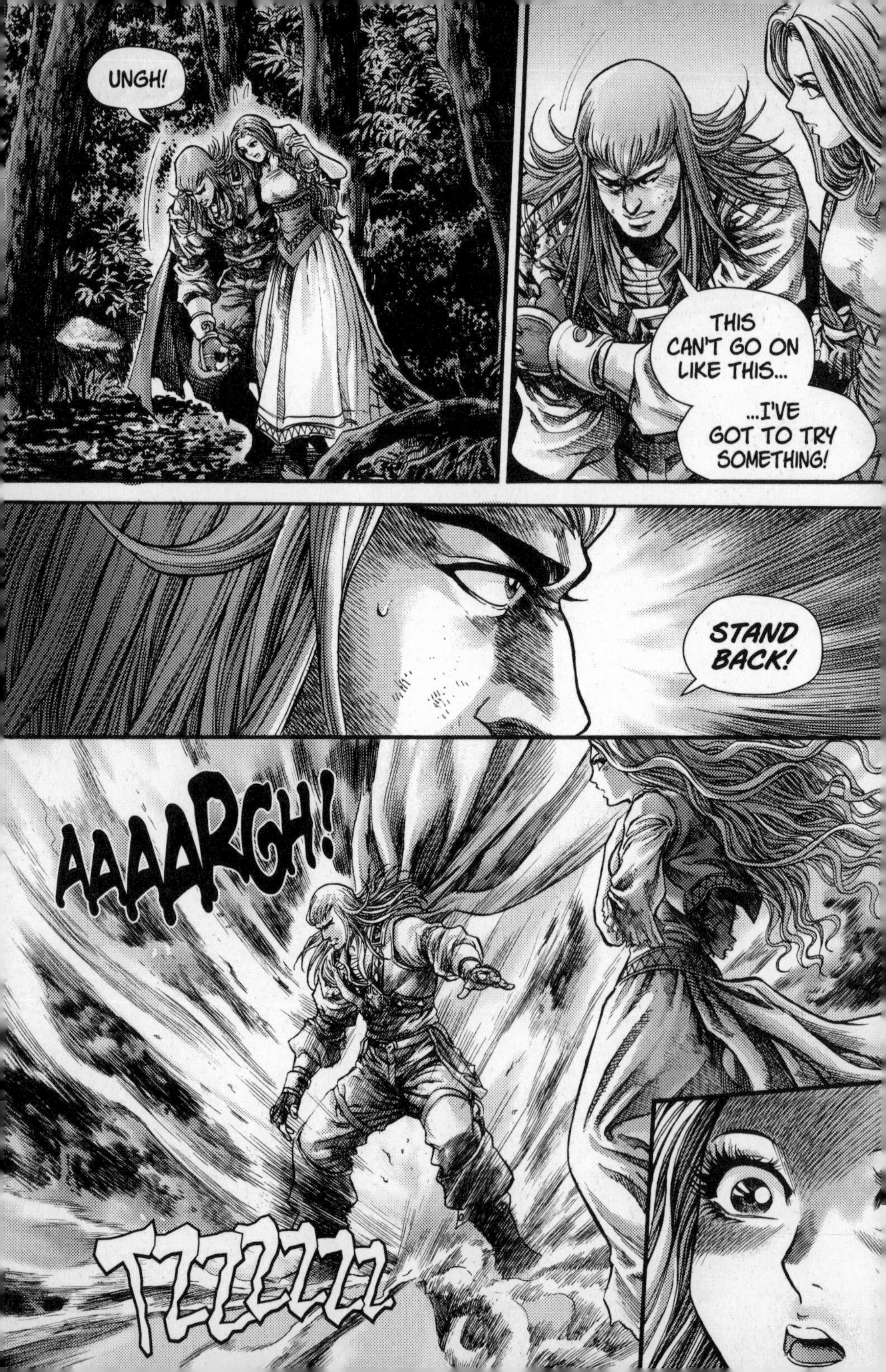
UNGH!
THIS CAN'T GO ON LIKE THIS...
...I'VE GOT TO TRY SOMETHING!
STAND BACK!
AAAARGH!
TZZZZZZZ

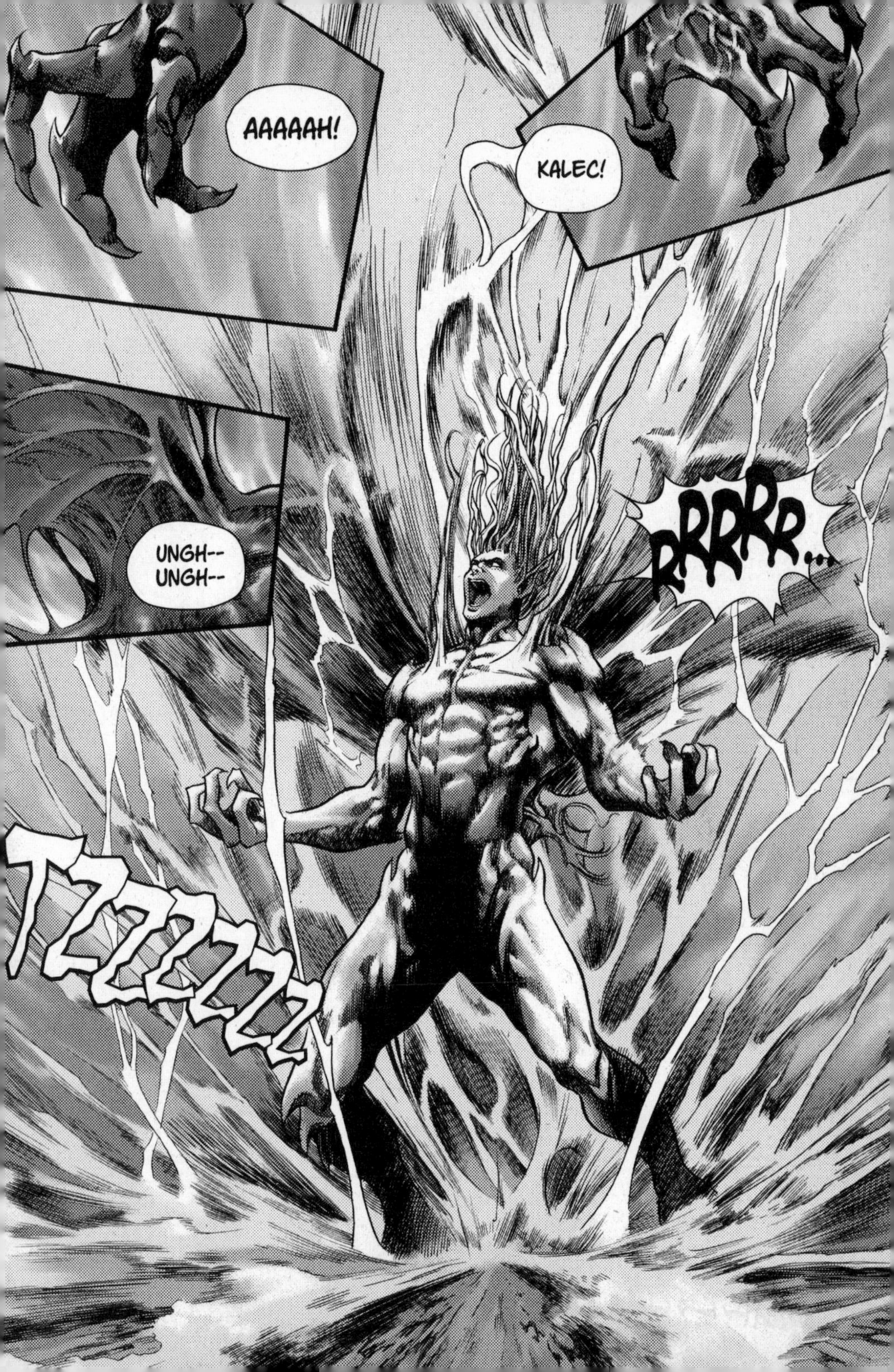
KALEC!
AAAAAH!
UNGH-- UNGH--
RRRRR...
TZZZZZZ

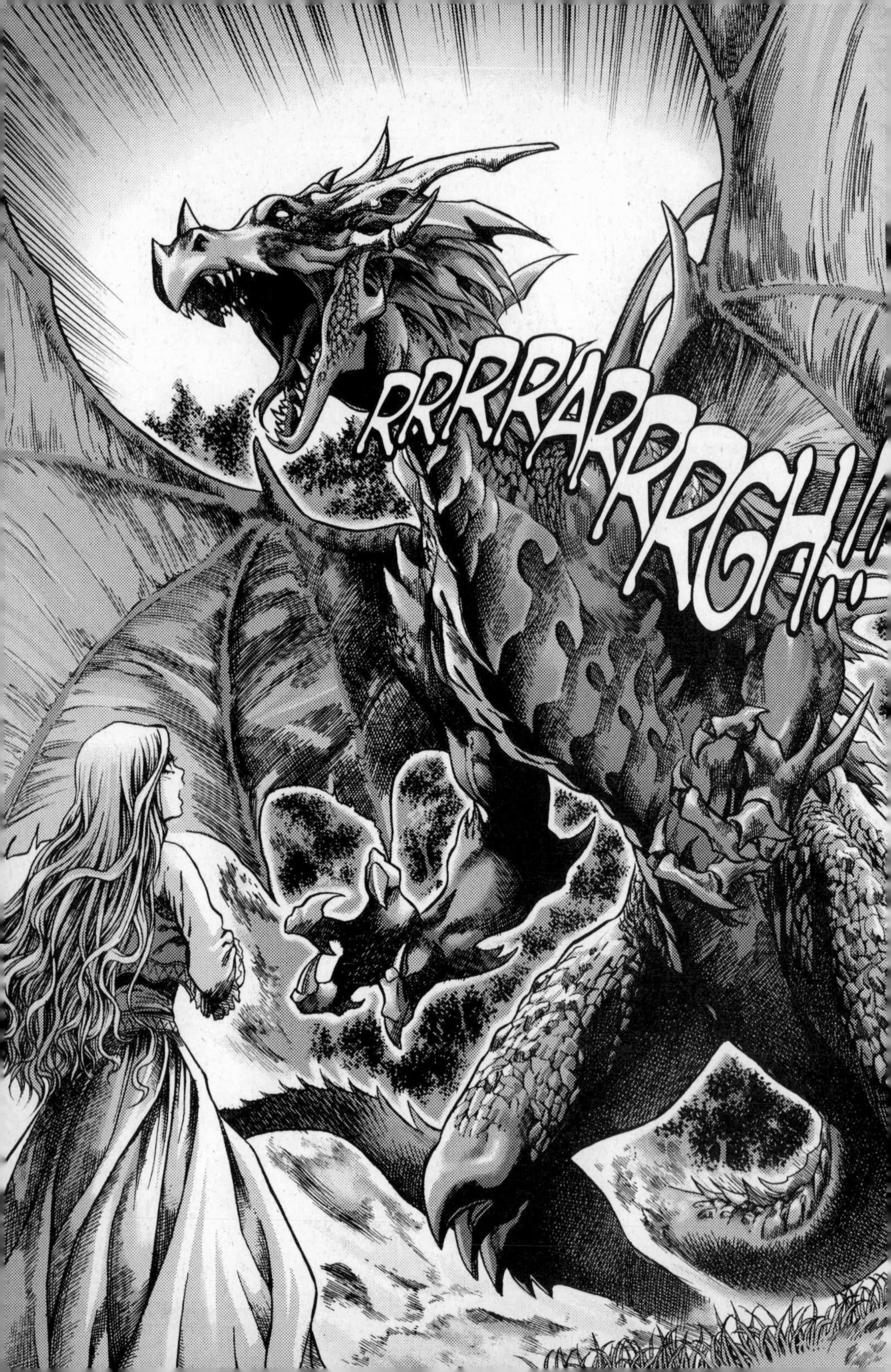
RRRRARRRGH!!

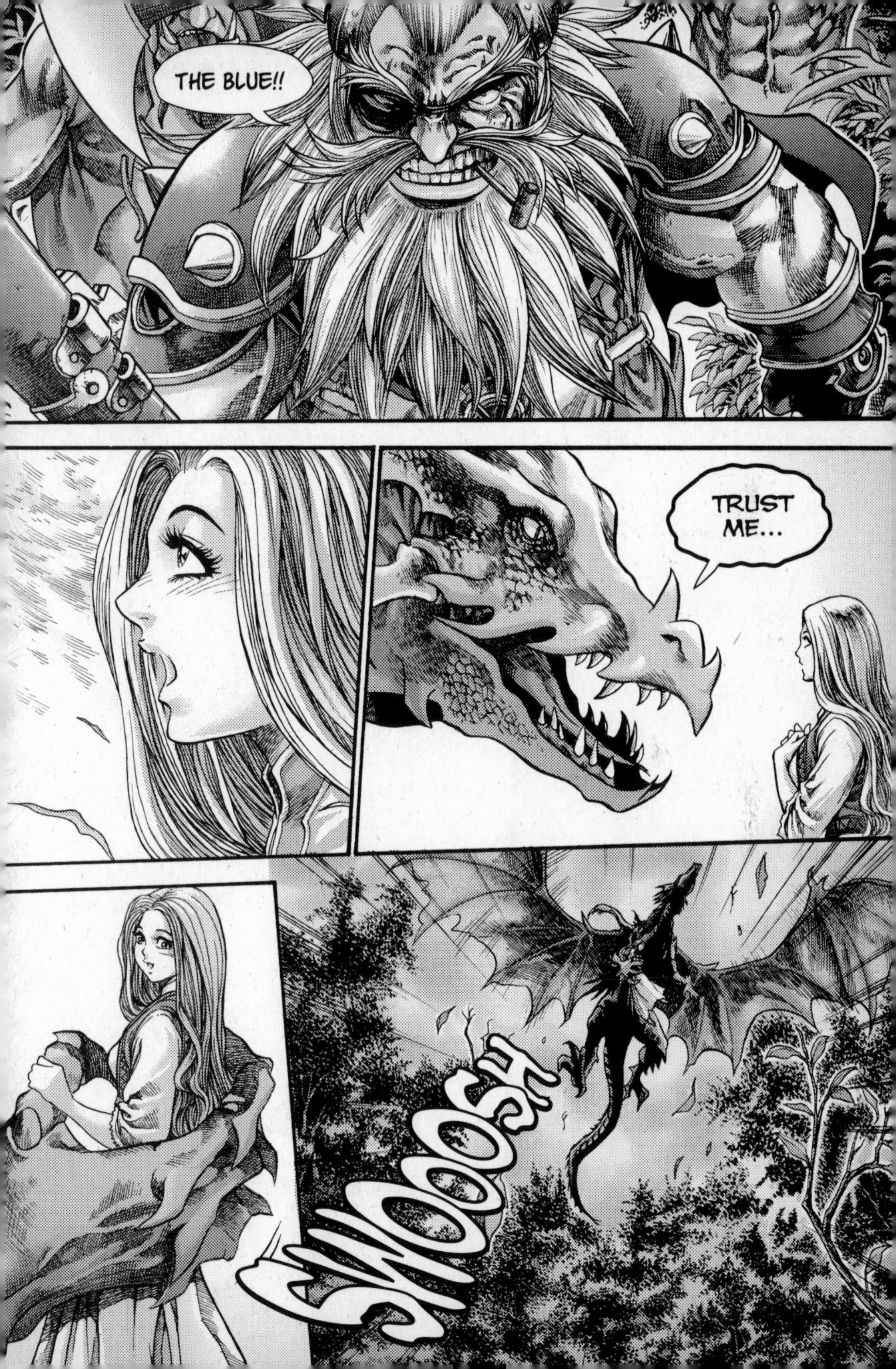
THE BLUE!!
TRUST ME...
SWOOOSH

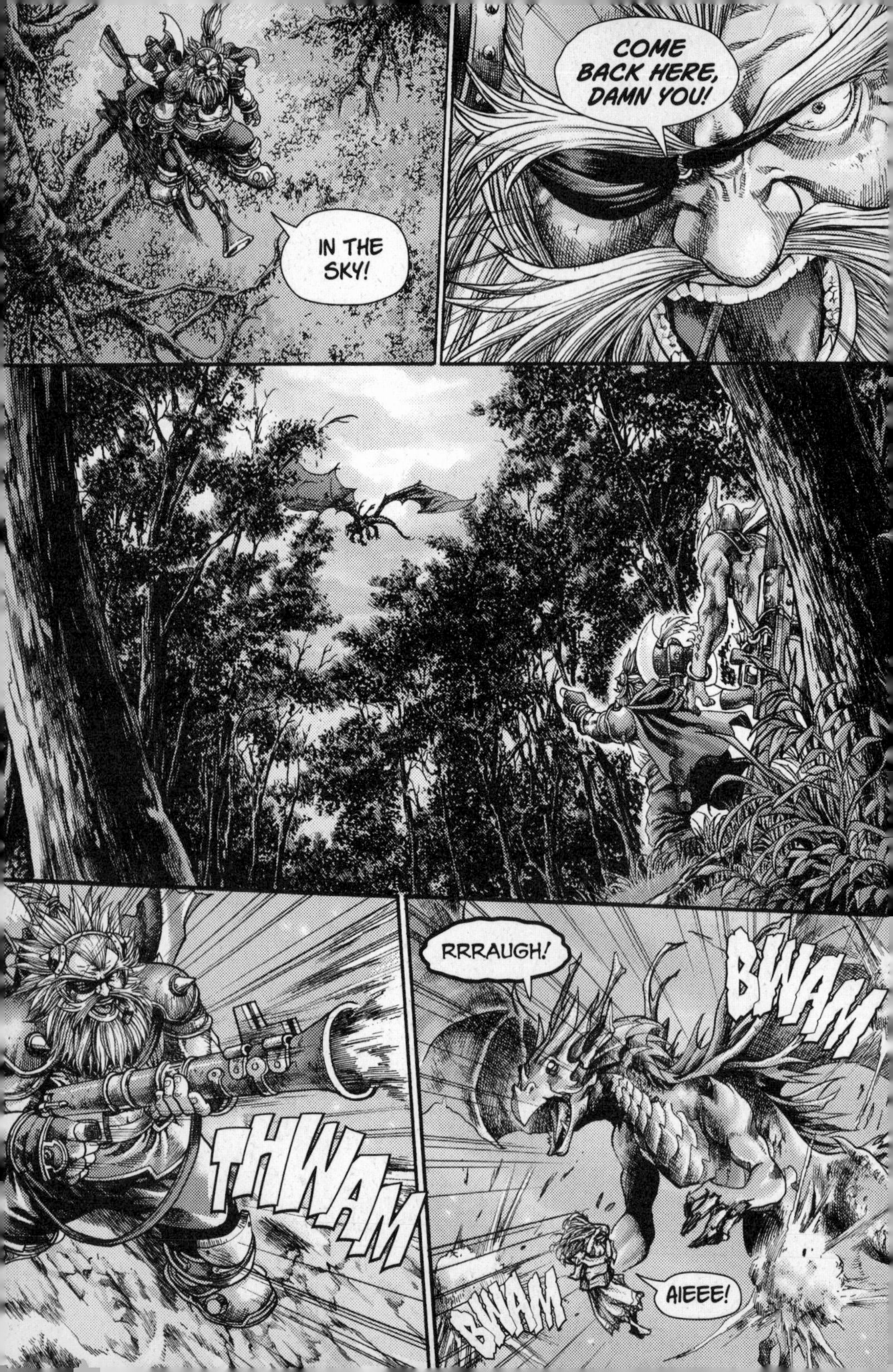
IN THE SKY!
COME BACK HERE, DAMN YOU!
THWAM
RRRAUGH!
BWAM
BWAM
AIEEE!

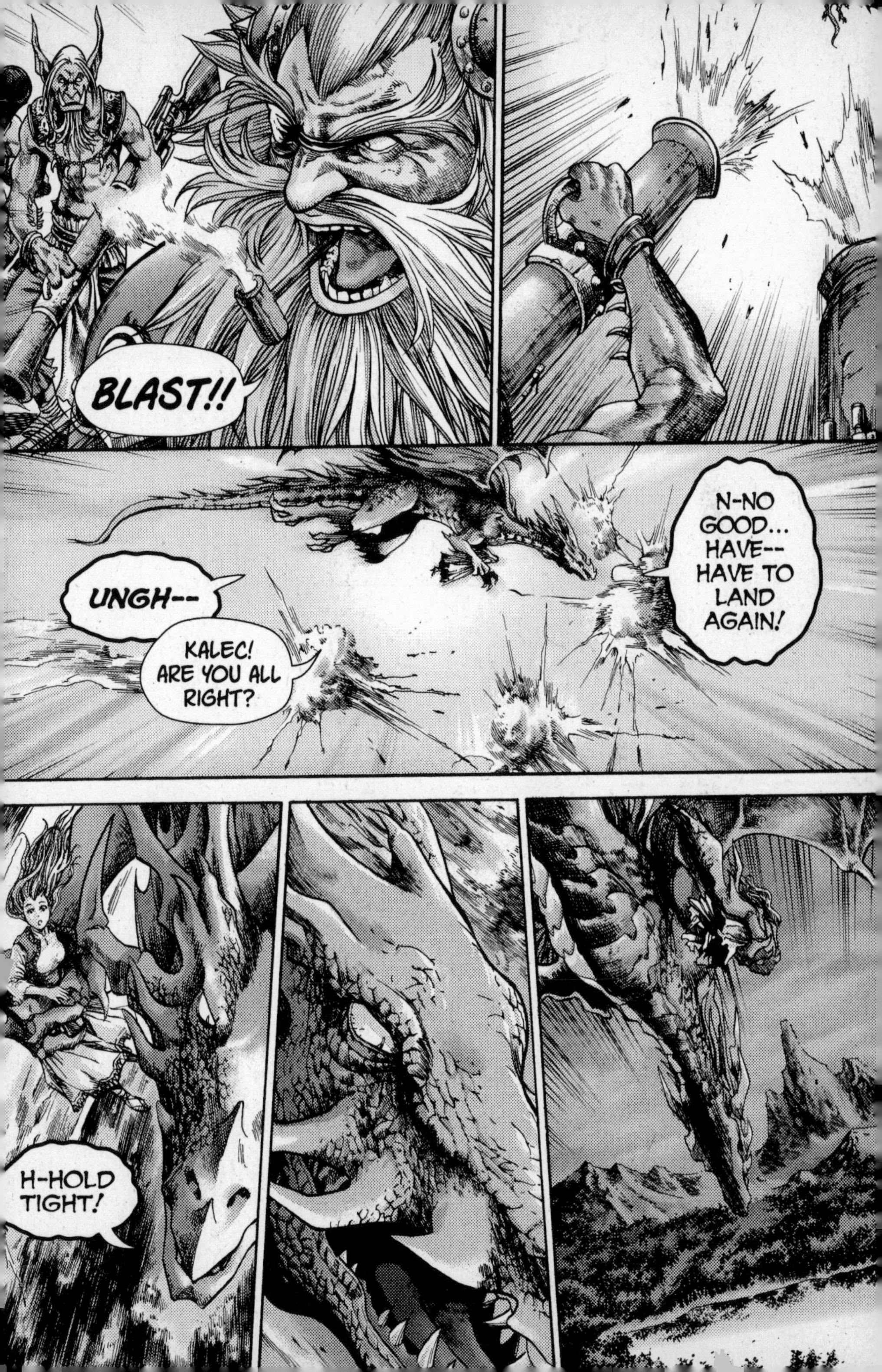
BLAST!!
UNGH--
KALEC! ARE YOU ALL RIGHT?
N-NO GOOD... HAVE-- HAVE TO LAND AGAIN!
H-HOLD TIGHT!

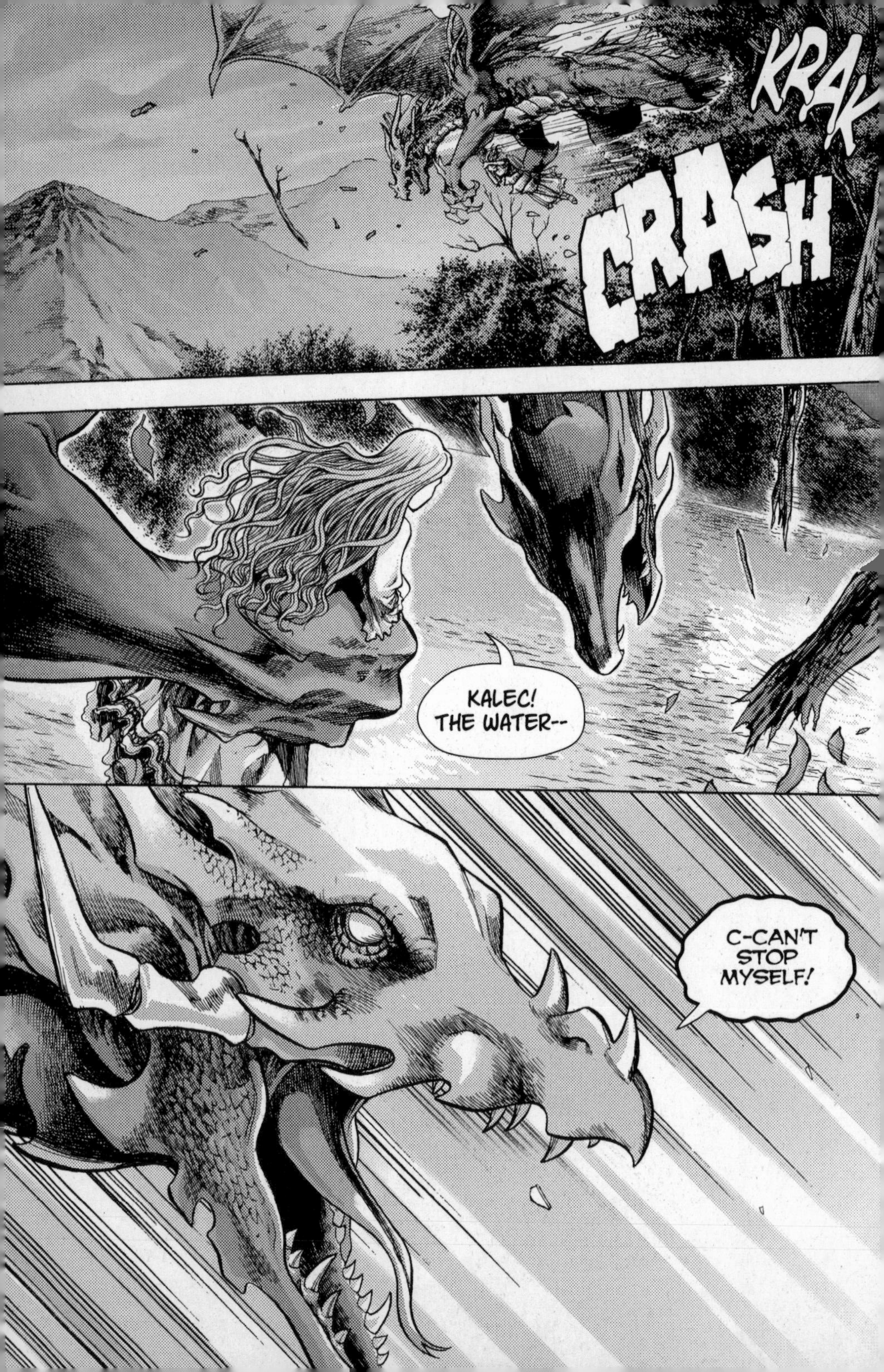
KRAK
CRASH
KALEC! THE WATER--
C-CAN'T STOP MYSELF!

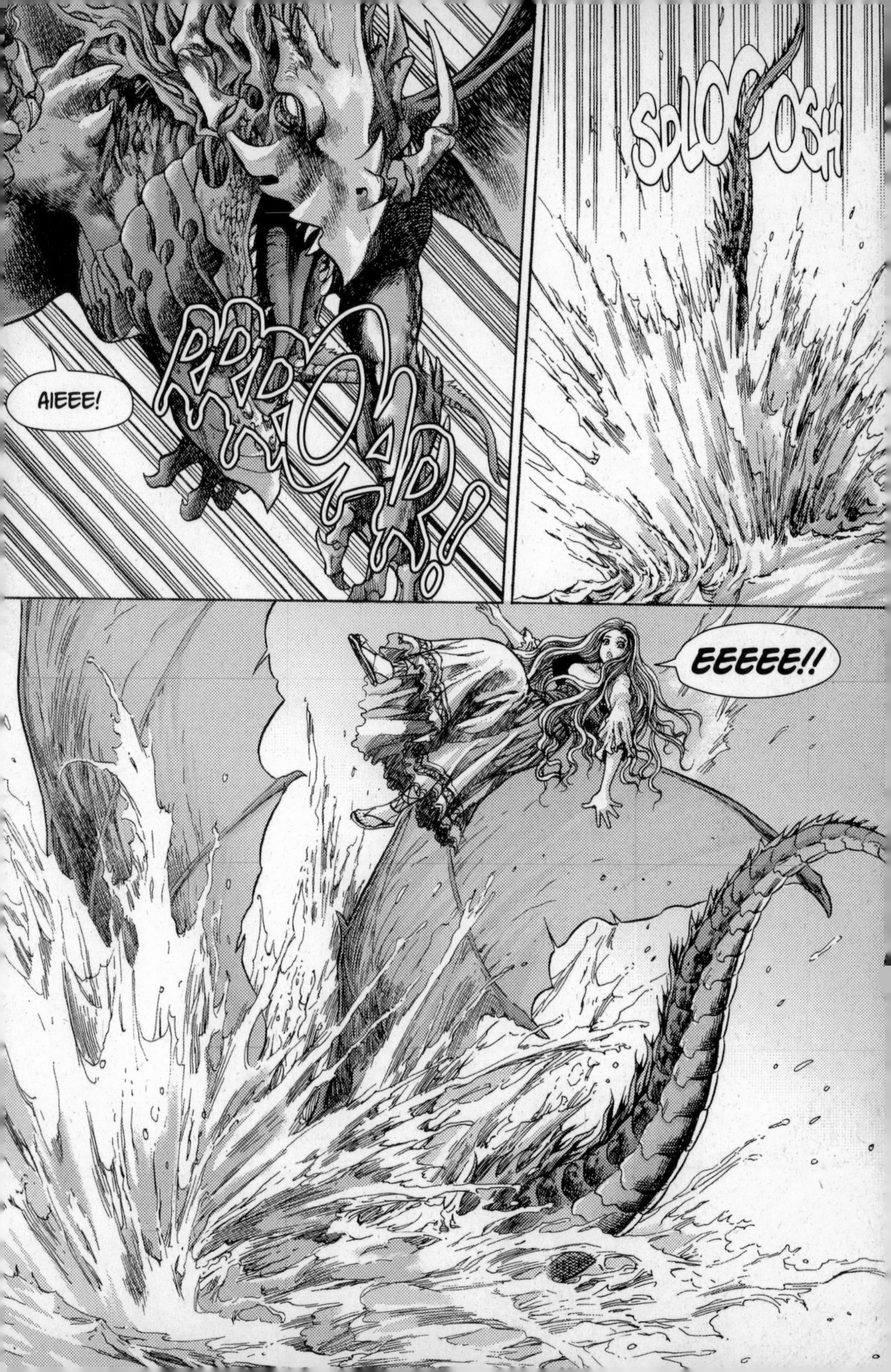
SPLOOOSH
AIEEE!
RRROAR!!
EEEEE!!

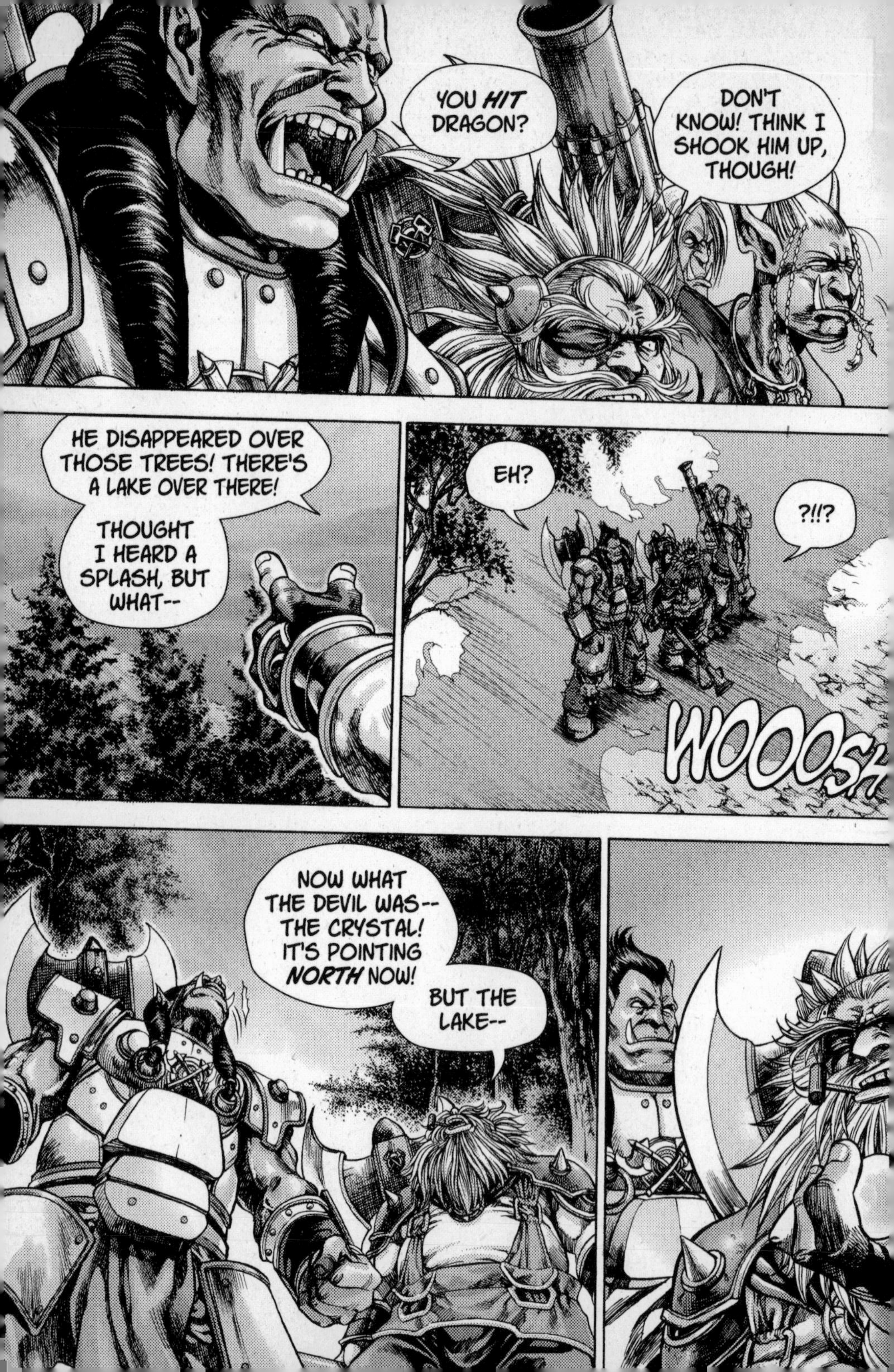
YOU *HIT* DRAGON?
DON'T KNOW! THINK I SHOOK HIM UP, THOUGH!
HE DISAPPEARED OVER THOSE TREES! THERE'S A LAKE OVER THERE!
THOUGHT I HEARD A SPLASH, BUT WHAT--
EH?
?!!?
WOOOSH
NOW WHAT THE DEVIL WAS-- THE CRYSTAL! IT'S POINTING *NORTH* NOW!
BUT THE LAKE--

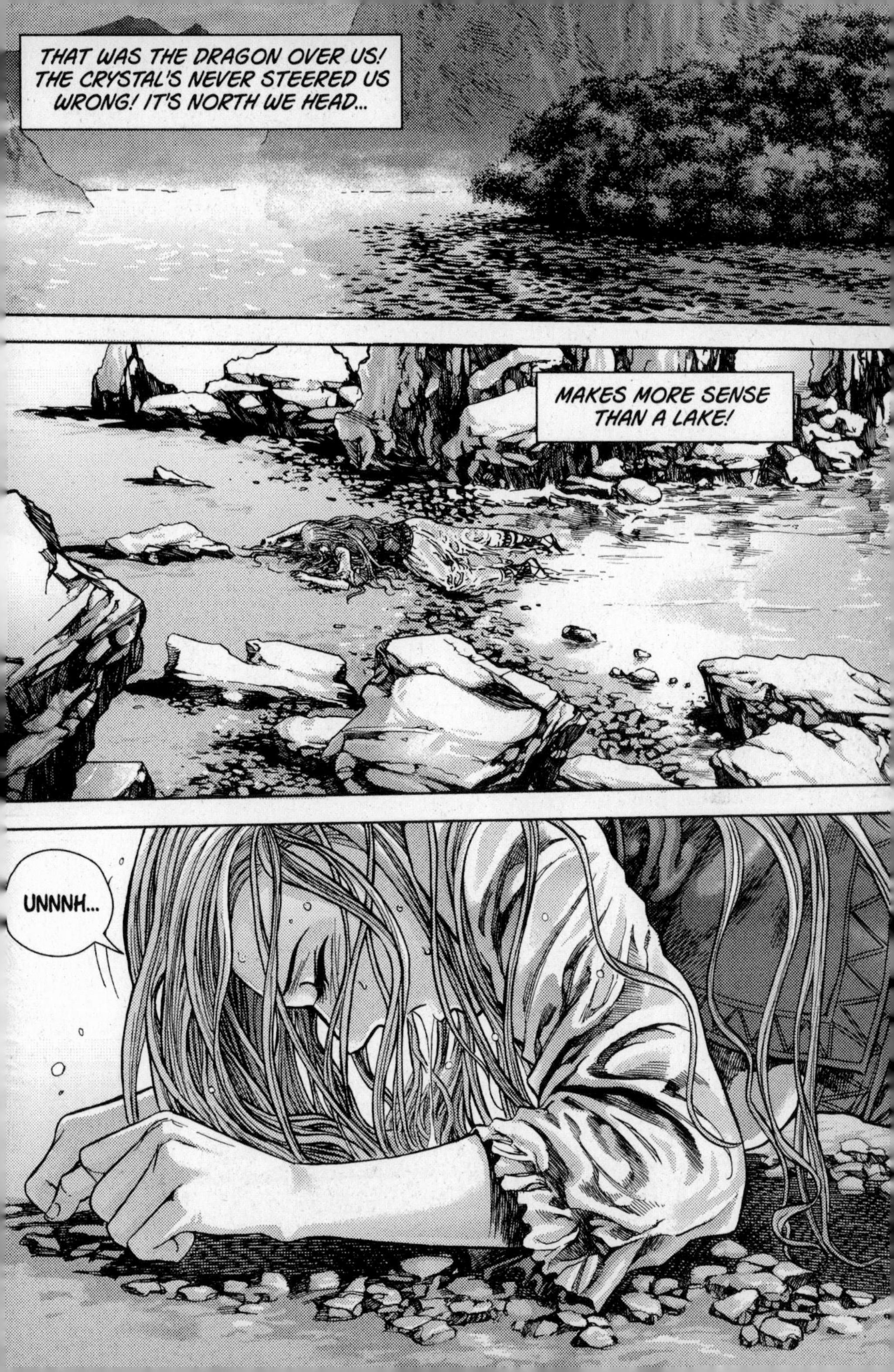
THAT WAS THE DRAGON OVER US! THE CRYSTAL'S NEVER STEERED US WRONG! IT'S NORTH WE HEAD...
MAKES MORE SENSE THAN A LAKE!
UNNNH...

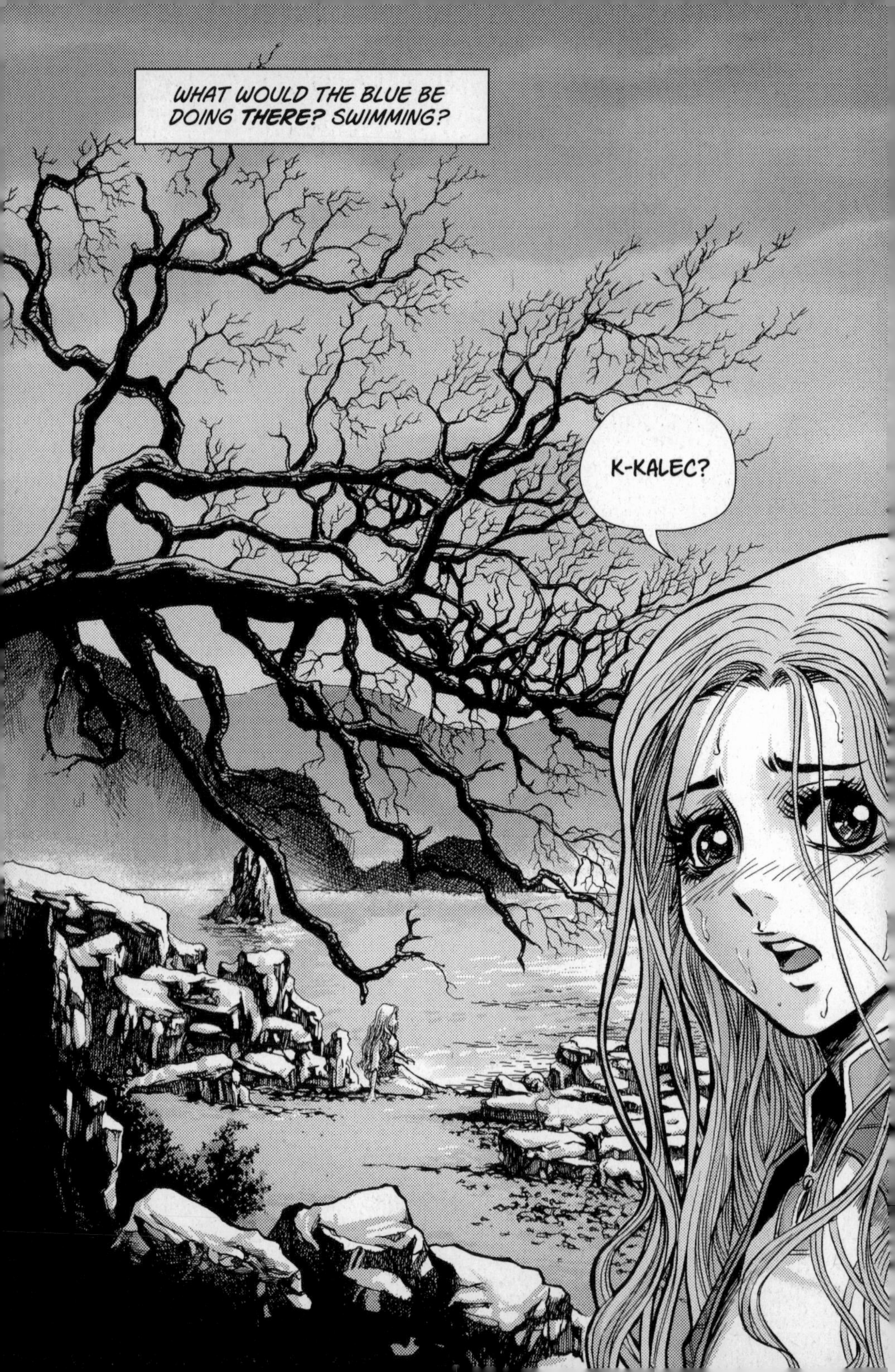
WHAT WOULD THE BLUE BE DOING **THERE?** SWIMMING?
K-KALEC?

CHAPTER THREE

DAR'KHAN

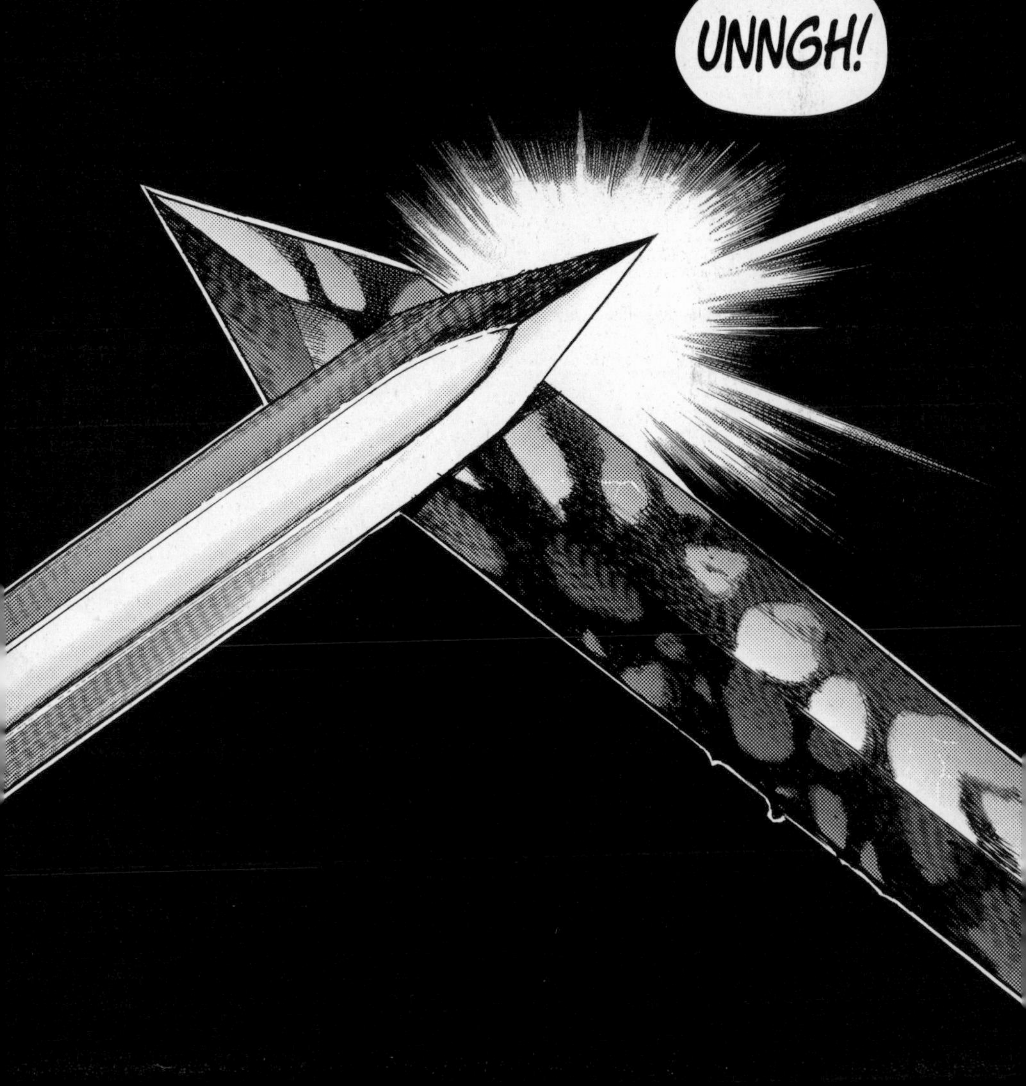
UNNGH!

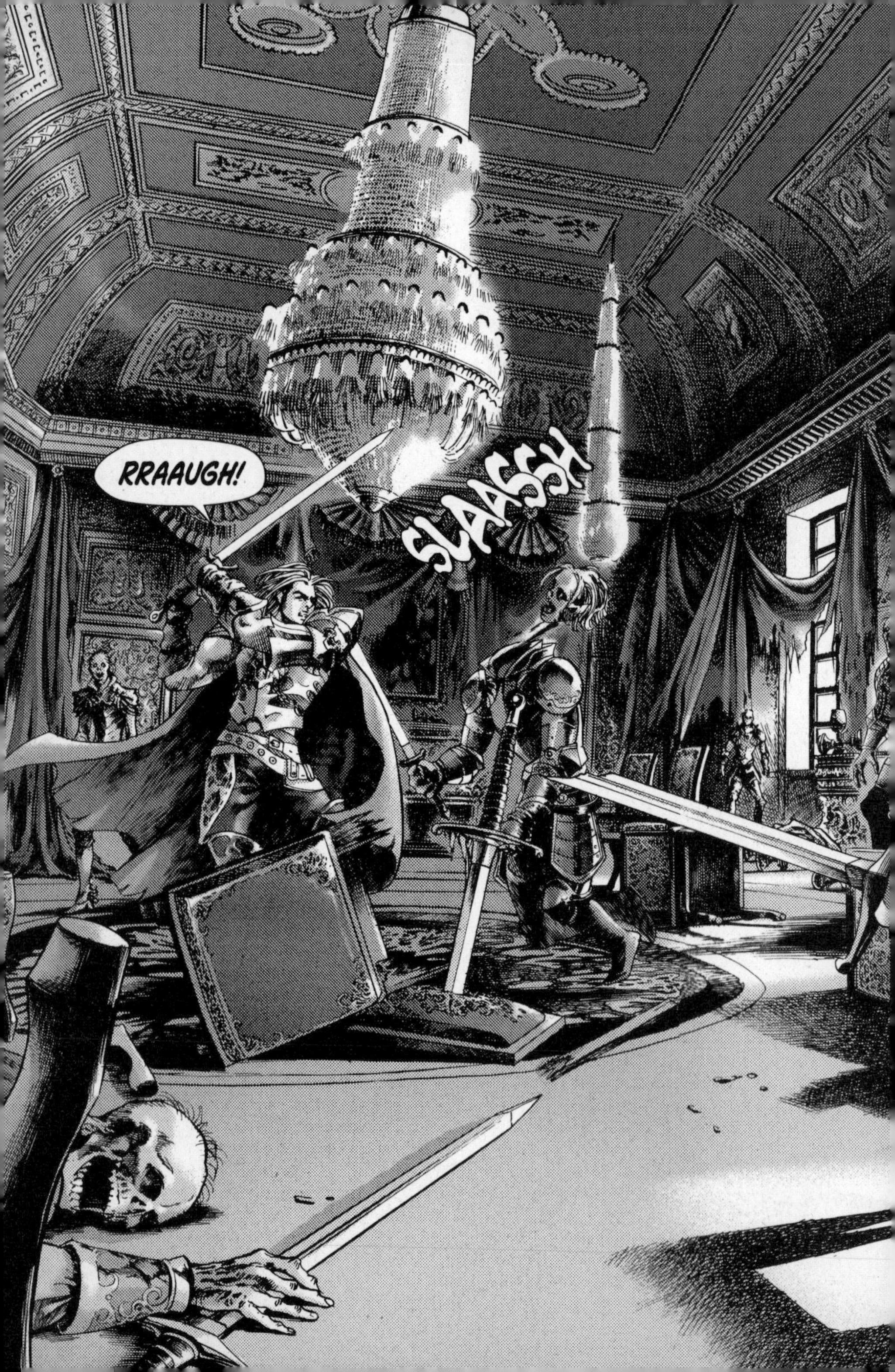
RRAAUGH!
SLASSH

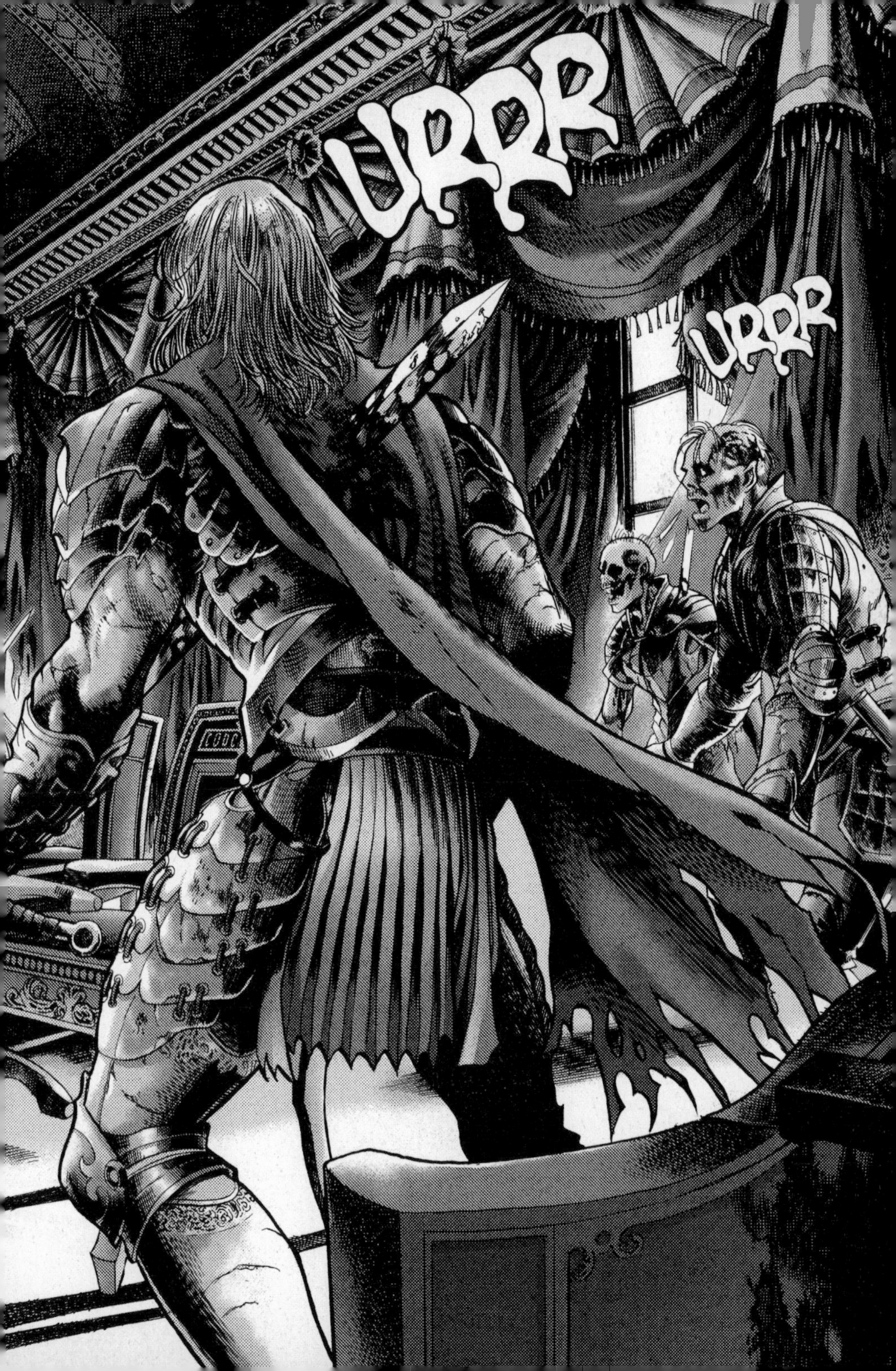
URRR
URRR

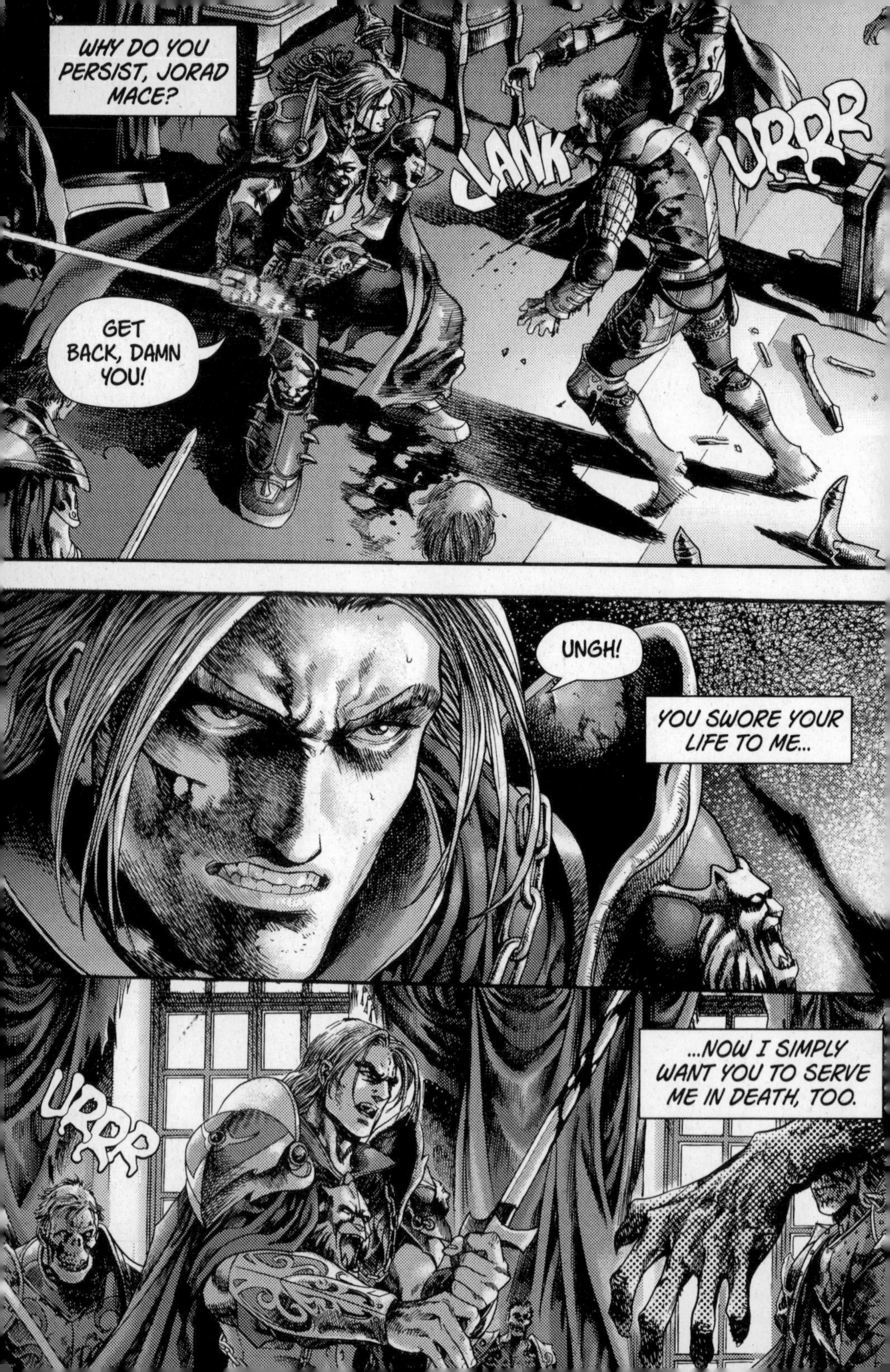
WHY DO YOU PERSIST, JORAD MACE?
CLANK
URRR
GET BACK, DAMN YOU!
UNGH!
YOU SWORE YOUR LIFE TO ME...
URRR
...NOW I SIMPLY WANT YOU TO SERVE ME IN DEATH, TOO.

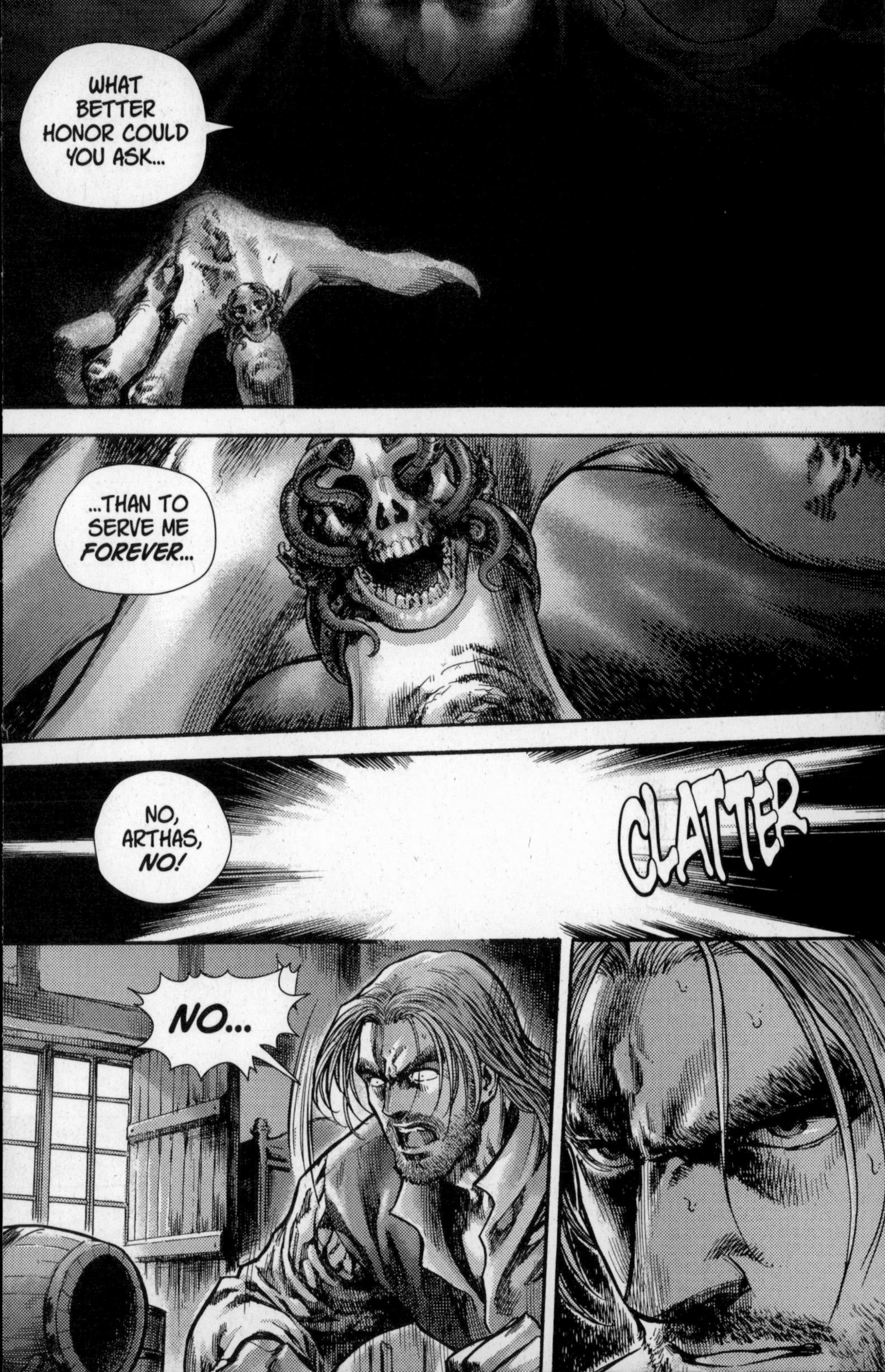
WHAT BETTER HONOR COULD YOU ASK...
...THAN TO SERVE ME *FOREVER*...
NO, ARTHAS, *NO!*
CLATTER
NO...

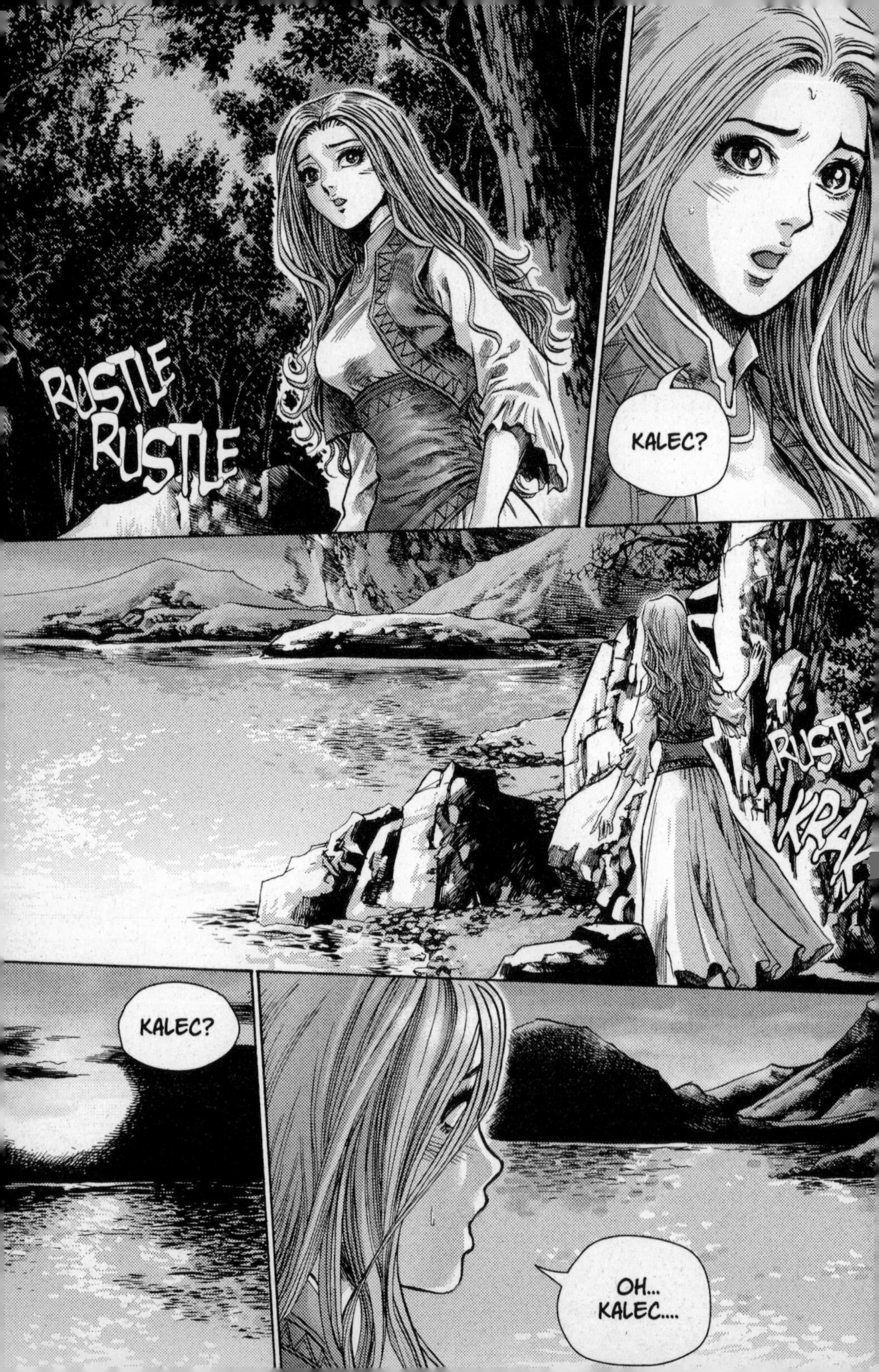
RUSTLE
RUSTLE
KALEC?
RUSTLE
KRAK
KALEC?
OH... KALEC....

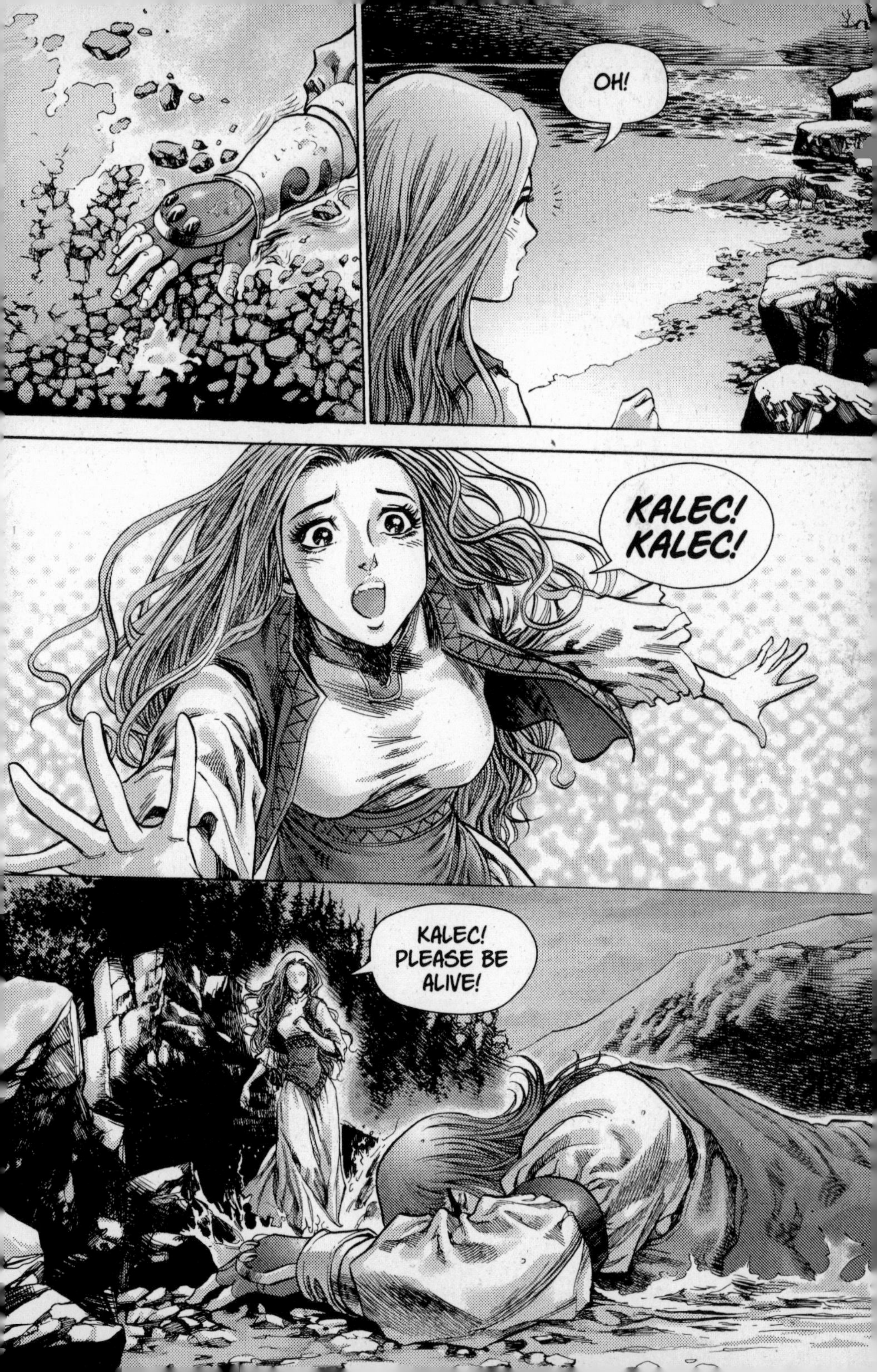
OH!
KALEC! KALEC!
KALEC! PLEASE BE ALIVE!

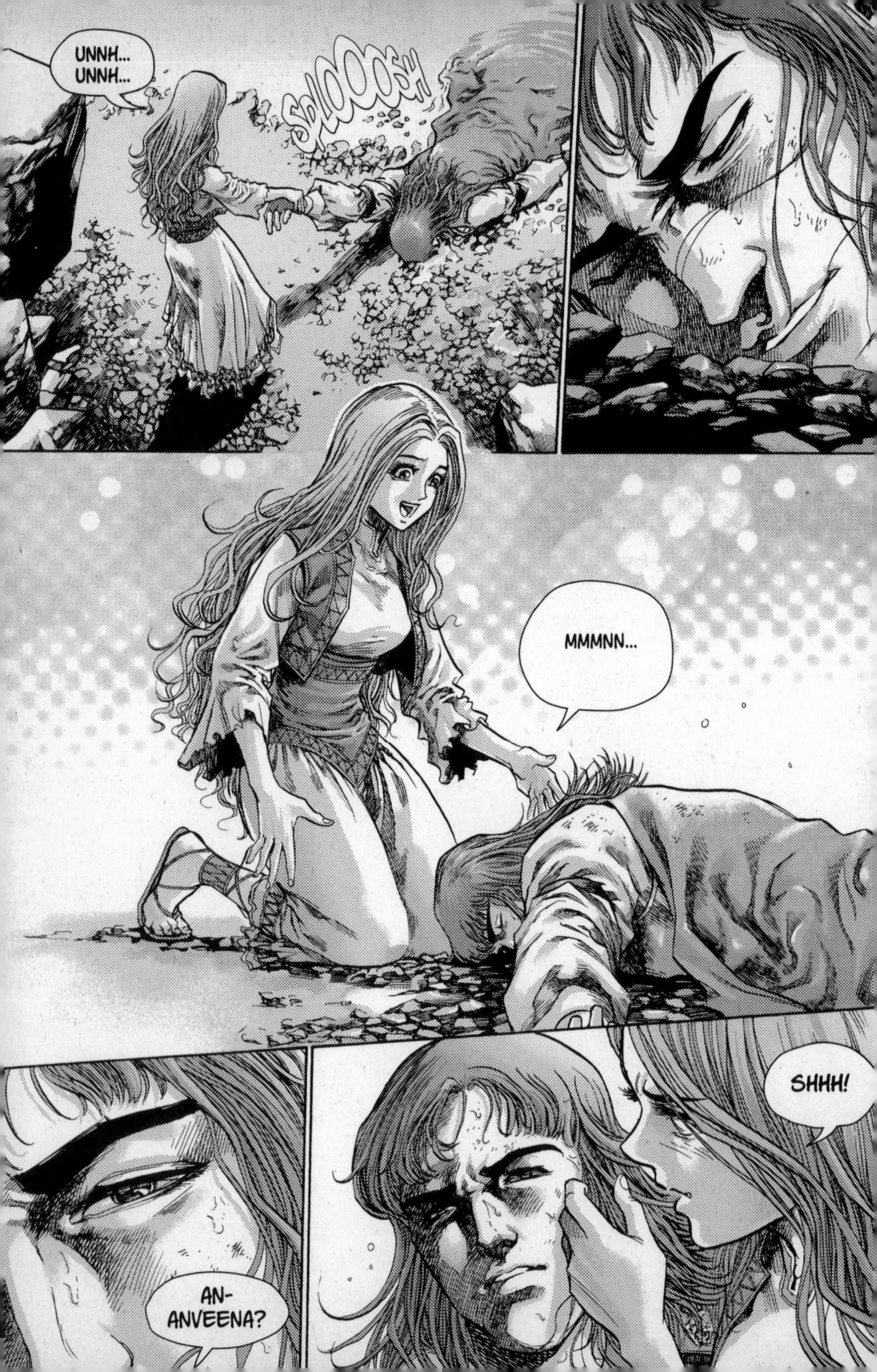
UNNH...
UNNH...
SPLOOOSH
MMMNN...
AN-
ANVEENA?
SHHH!

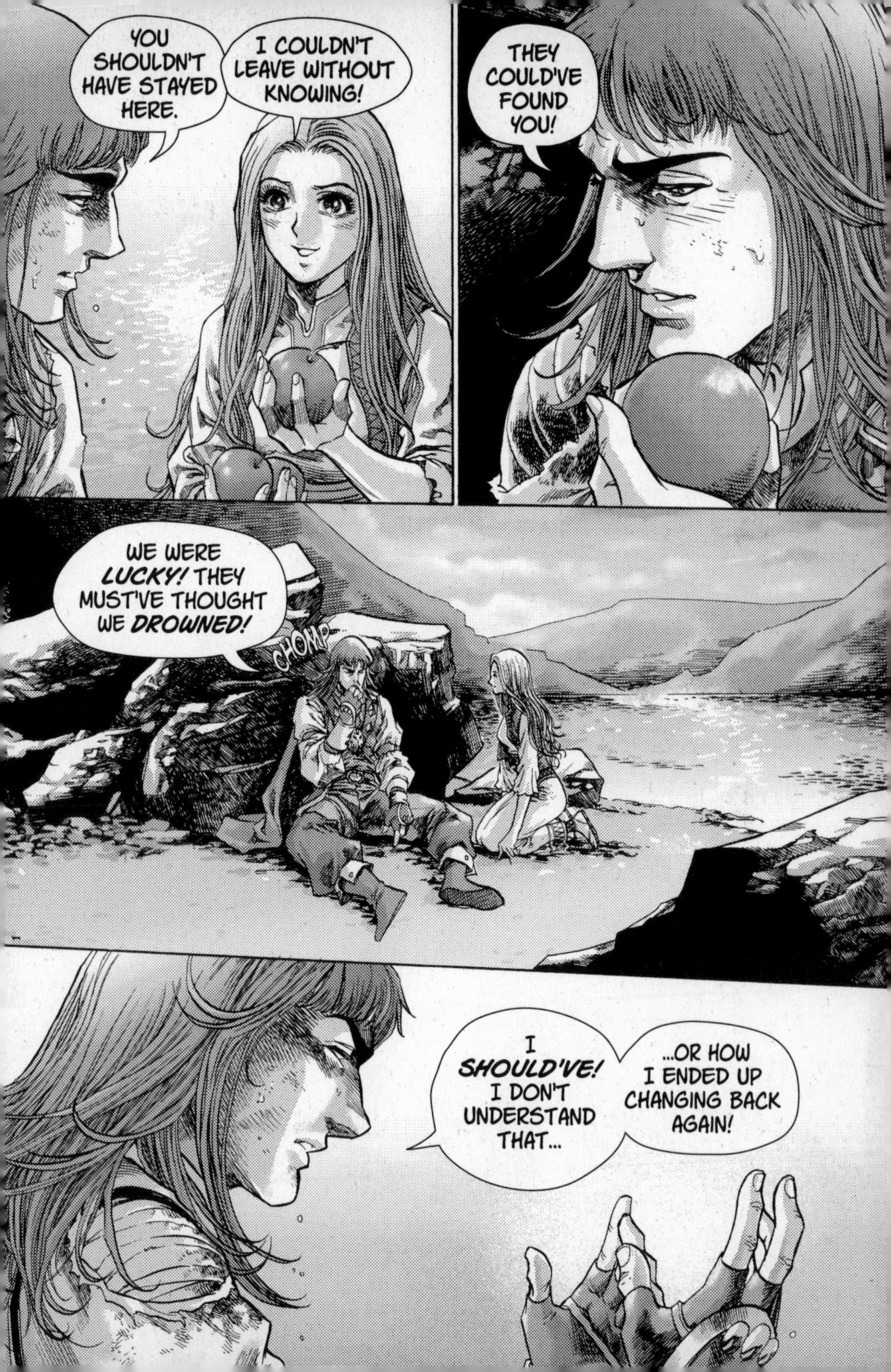
YOU SHOULDN'T HAVE STAYED HERE.
I COULDN'T LEAVE WITHOUT KNOWING!
THEY COULD'VE FOUND YOU!
WE WERE ***LUCKY!*** THEY MUST'VE THOUGHT WE ***DROWNED!***
CHOMP...
I ***SHOULD'VE!*** I DON'T UNDERSTAND THAT...
...OR HOW I ENDED UP CHANGING BACK AGAIN!

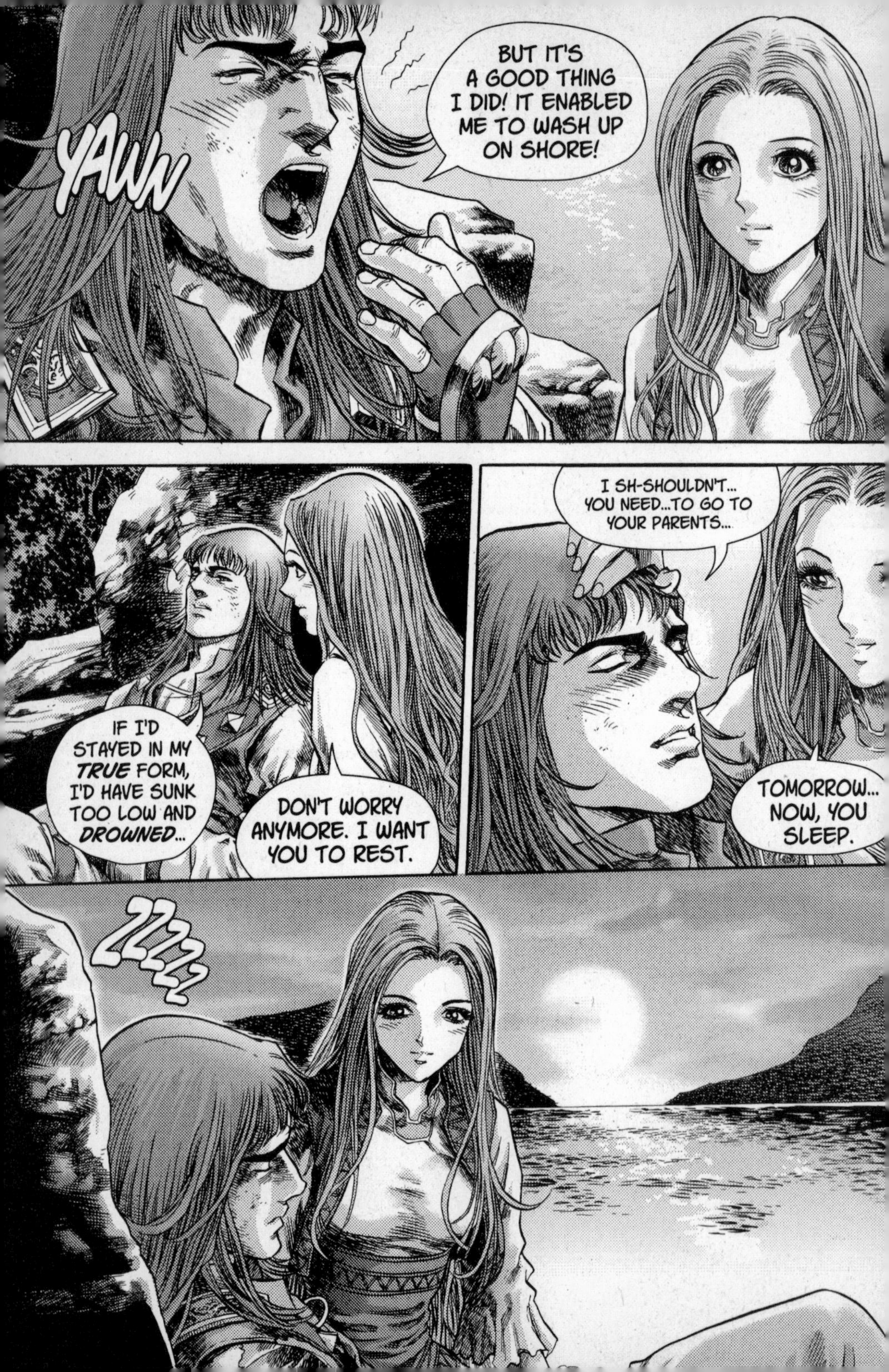
YAWN
BUT IT'S A GOOD THING I DID! IT ENABLED ME TO WASH UP ON SHORE!
IF I'D STAYED IN MY TRUE FORM, I'D HAVE SUNK TOO LOW AND DROWNED...
DON'T WORRY ANYMORE. I WANT YOU TO REST.
I SH-SHOULDN'T... YOU NEED...TO GO TO YOUR PARENTS...
TOMORROW... NOW, YOU SLEEP.
ZZZZZ

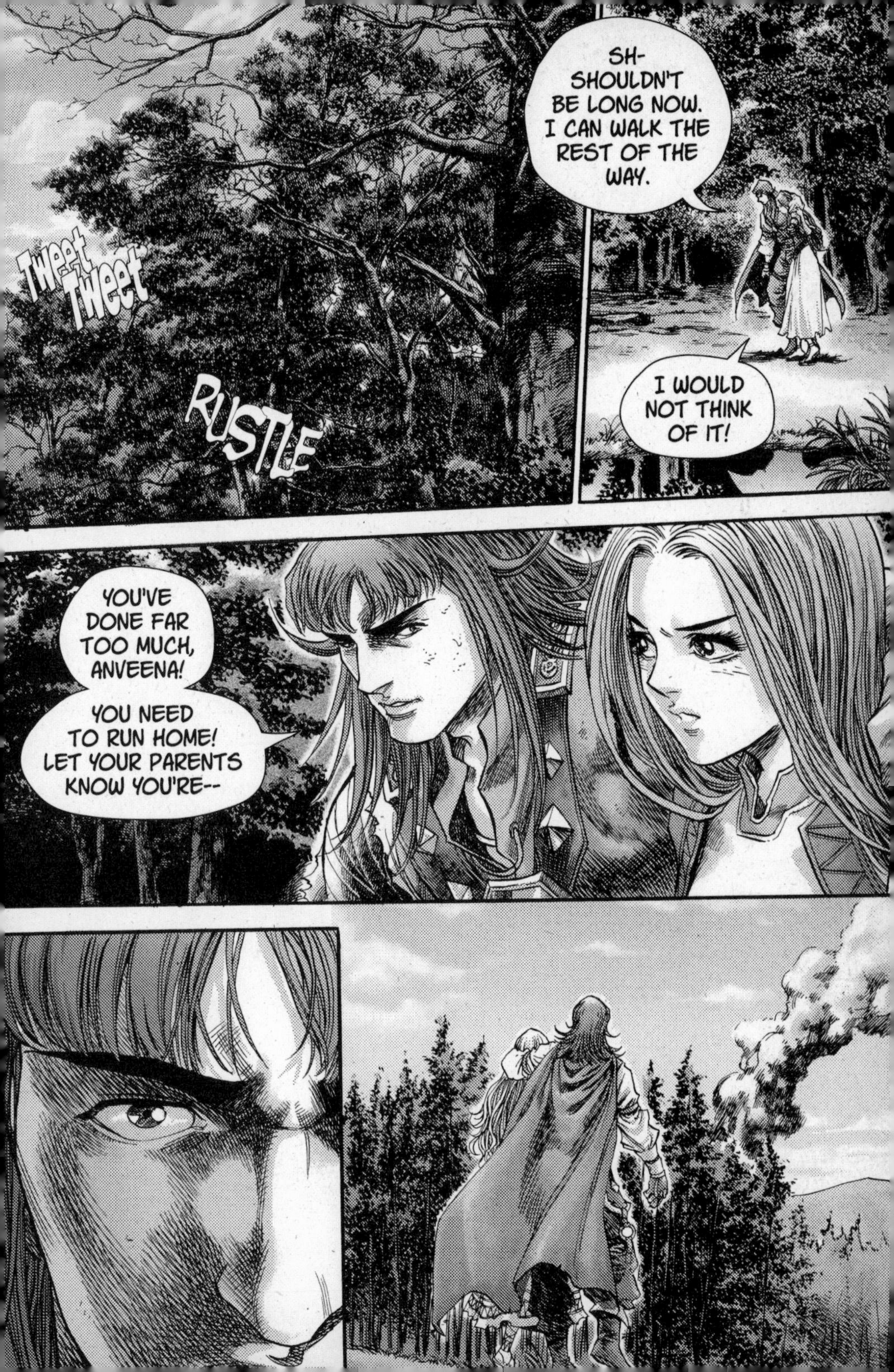
SH- SHOULDN'T BE LONG NOW. I CAN WALK THE REST OF THE WAY.
I WOULD NOT THINK OF IT!
Tweet Tweet
RUSTLE
YOU'VE DONE FAR TOO MUCH, ANVEENA!
YOU NEED TO RUN HOME! LET YOUR PARENTS KNOW YOU'RE--

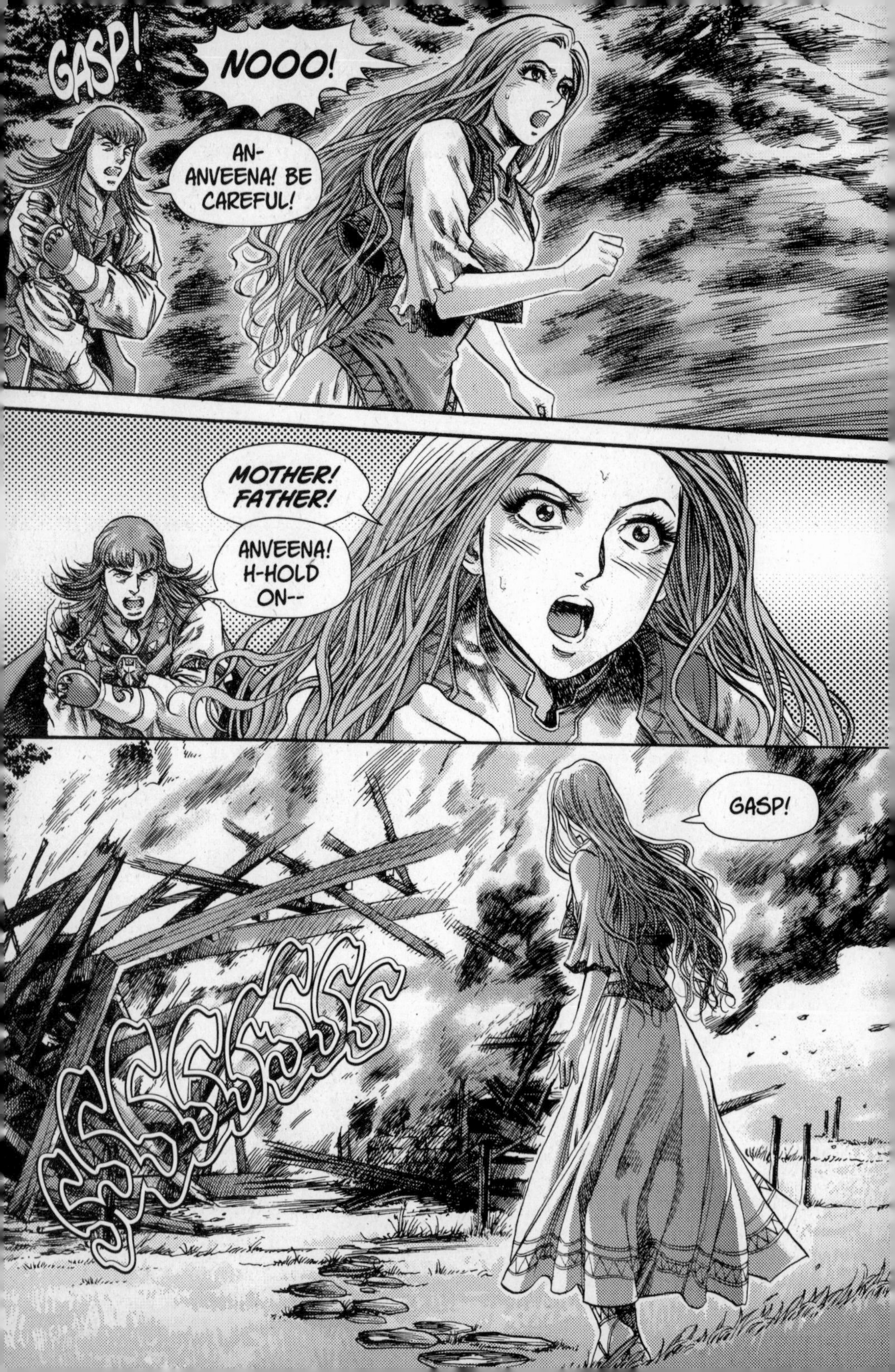
GASP!
NOOO!
AN- ANVEENA! BE CAREFUL!
MOTHER! FATHER!
ANVEENA! H-HOLD ON--
GASP!

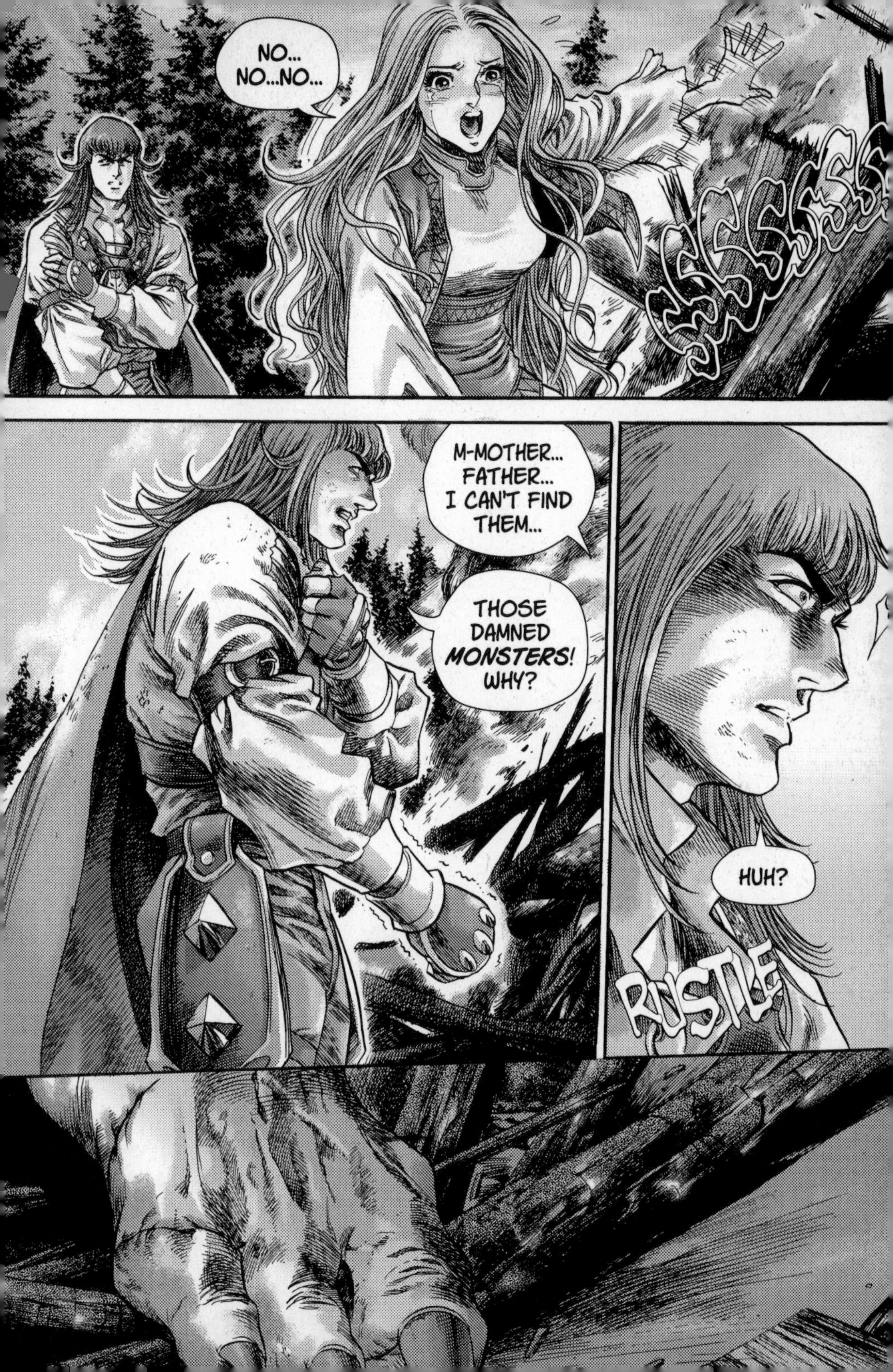
NO... NO...NO...
M-MOTHER... FATHER... I CAN'T FIND THEM...
THOSE DAMNED MONSTERS! WHY?
HUH?
RUSTLE

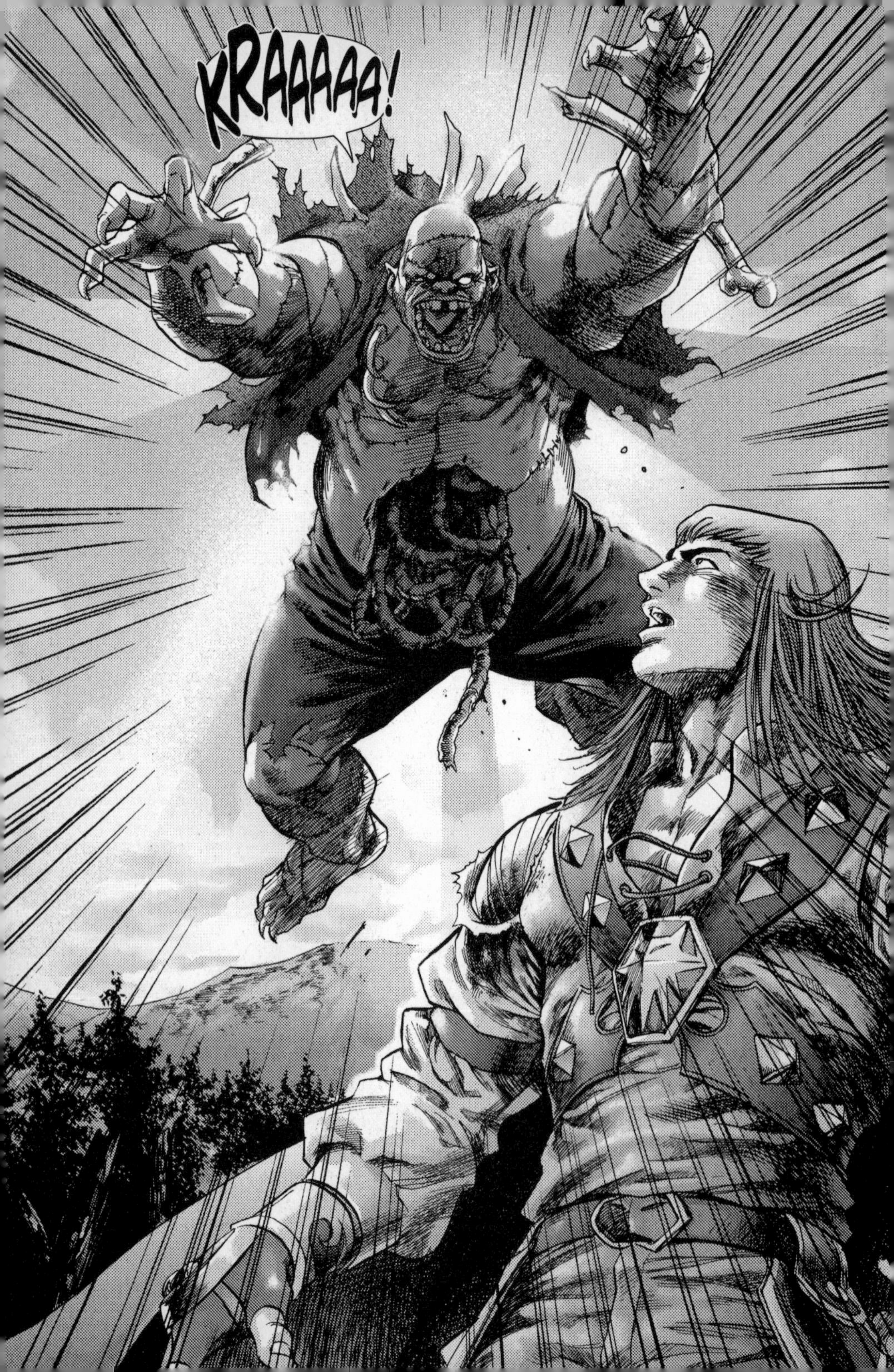
KRAAAAA!

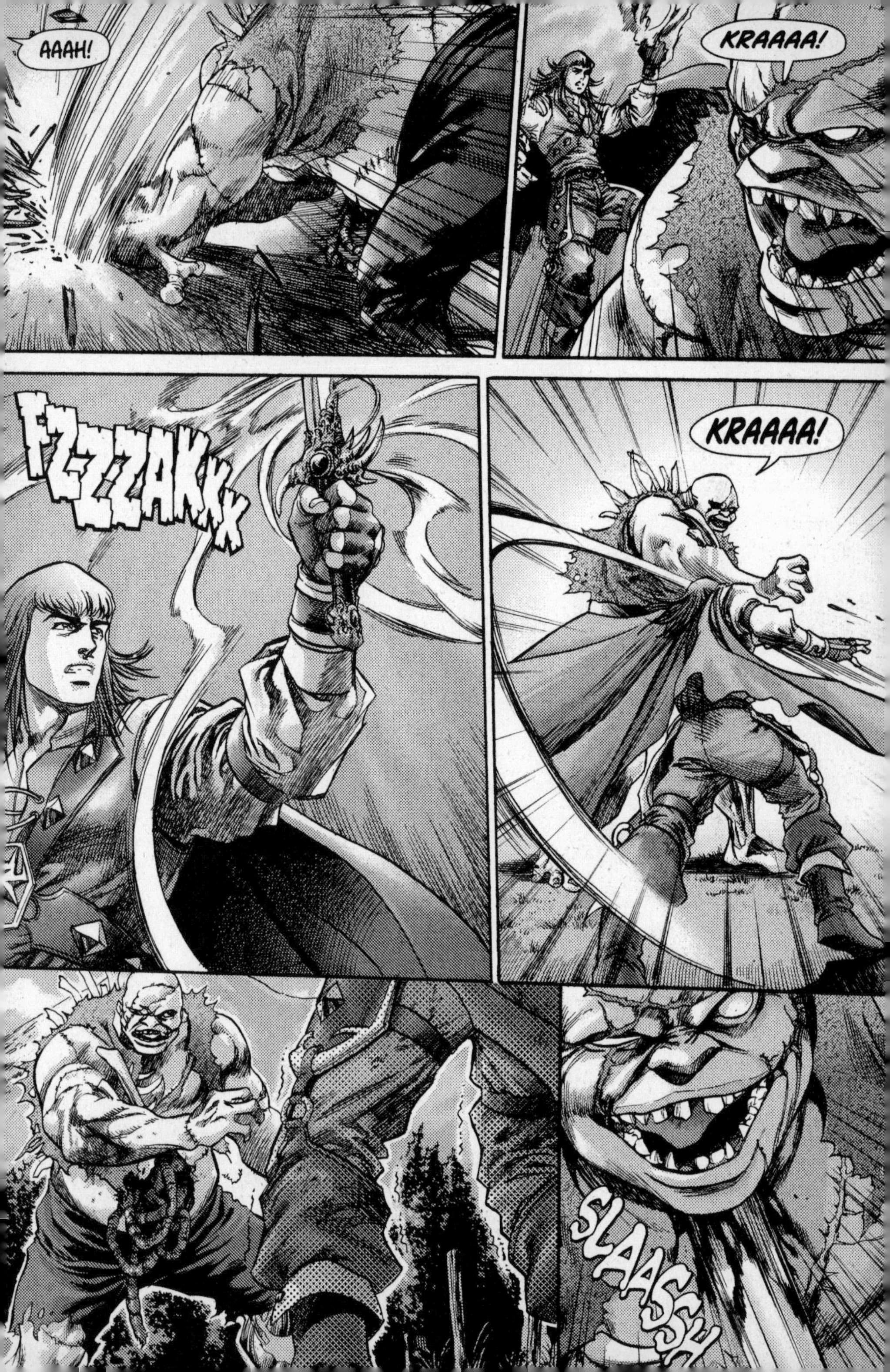
KRAAAA!
AAAH!
KRAAAA!
F-ZZZAKKKK
SLAASH

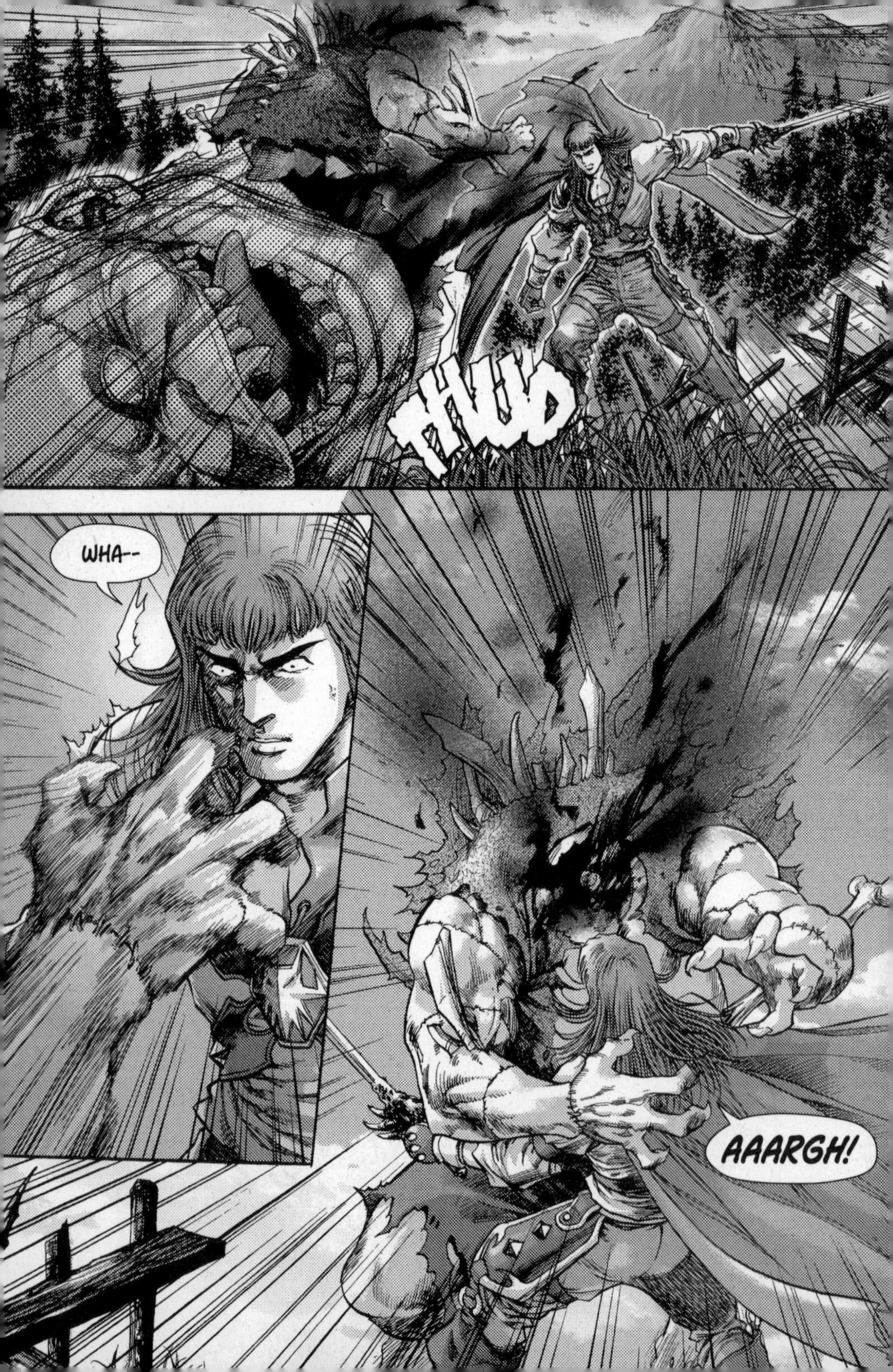
THUD
AAARGH!
WHA--

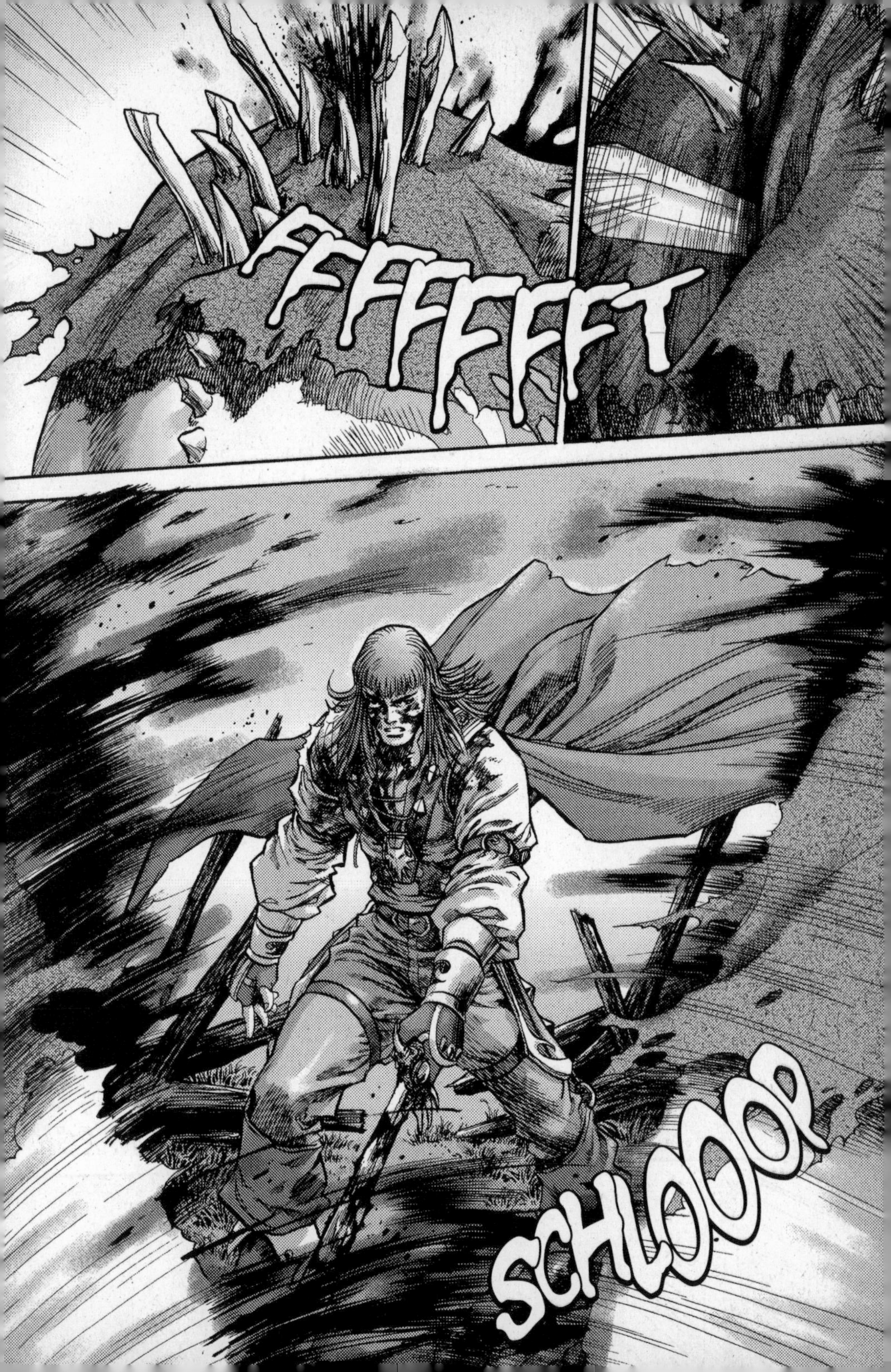
FFFFFFT
SCHLOOOOP

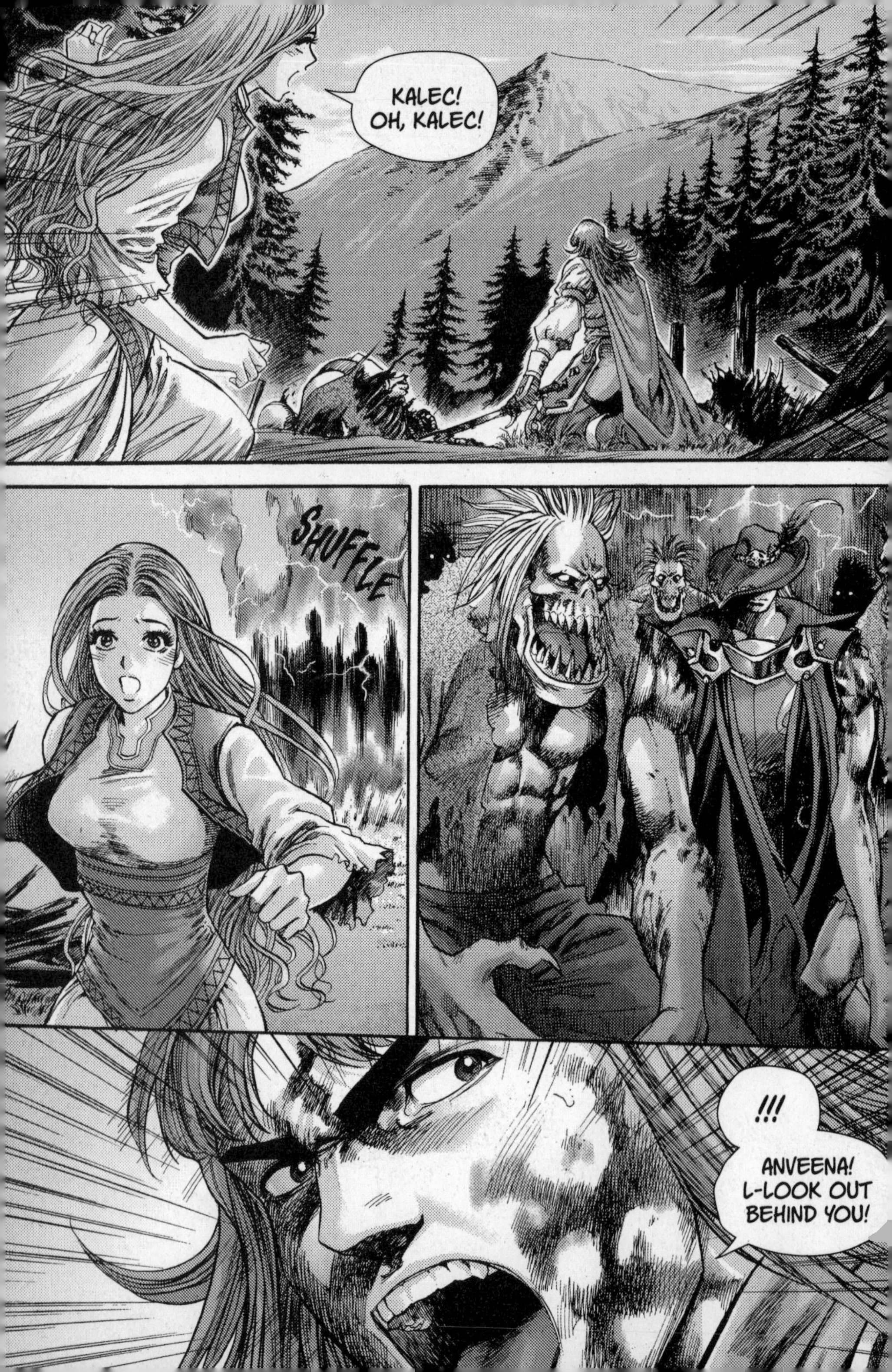
KALEC! OH, KALEC!
SHUFFLE
!!!
ANVEENA! L-LOOK OUT BEHIND YOU!

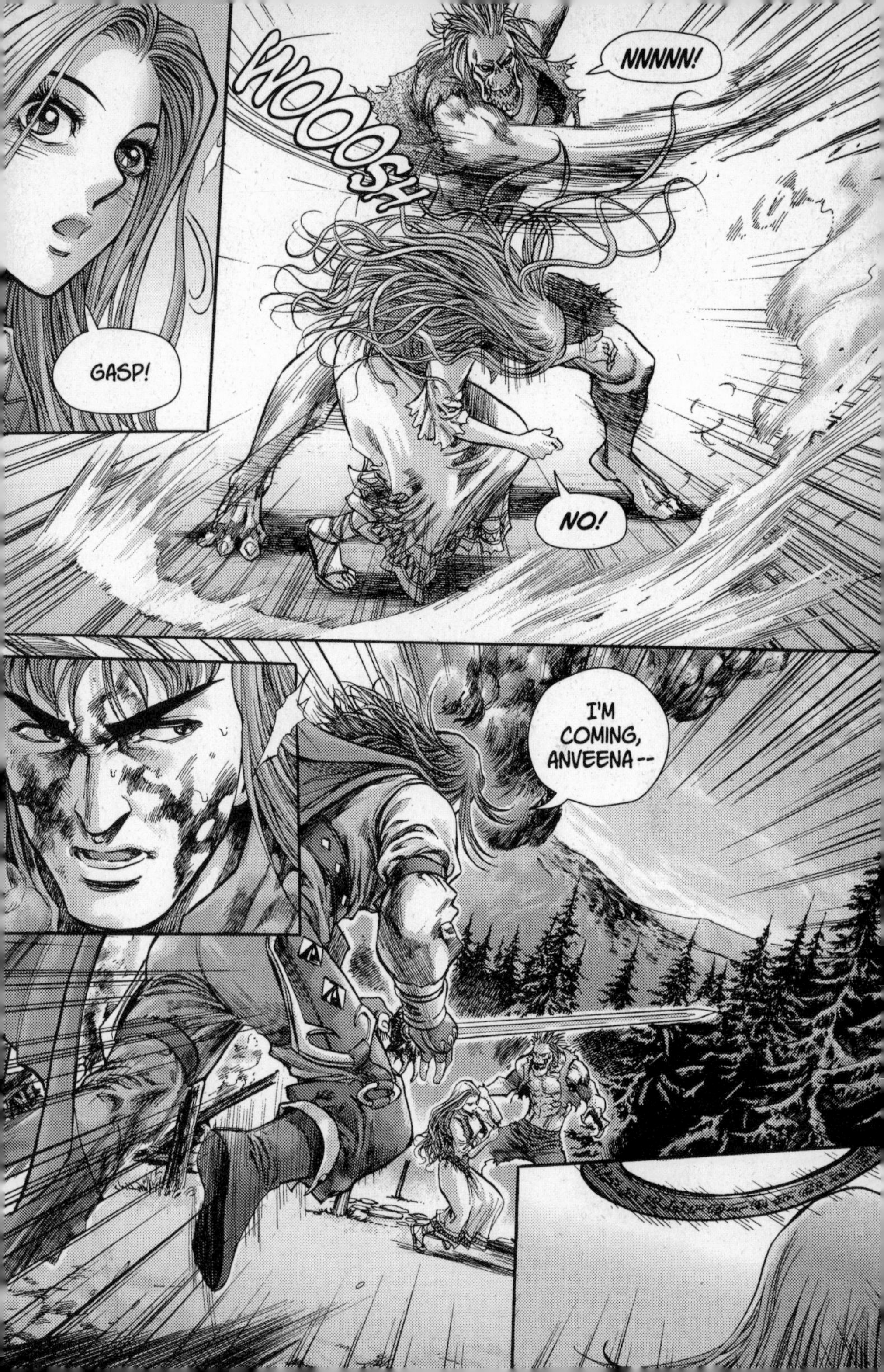
GASP!
WOOOSH
NNNNN!
NO!
I'M COMING, ANVEENA--

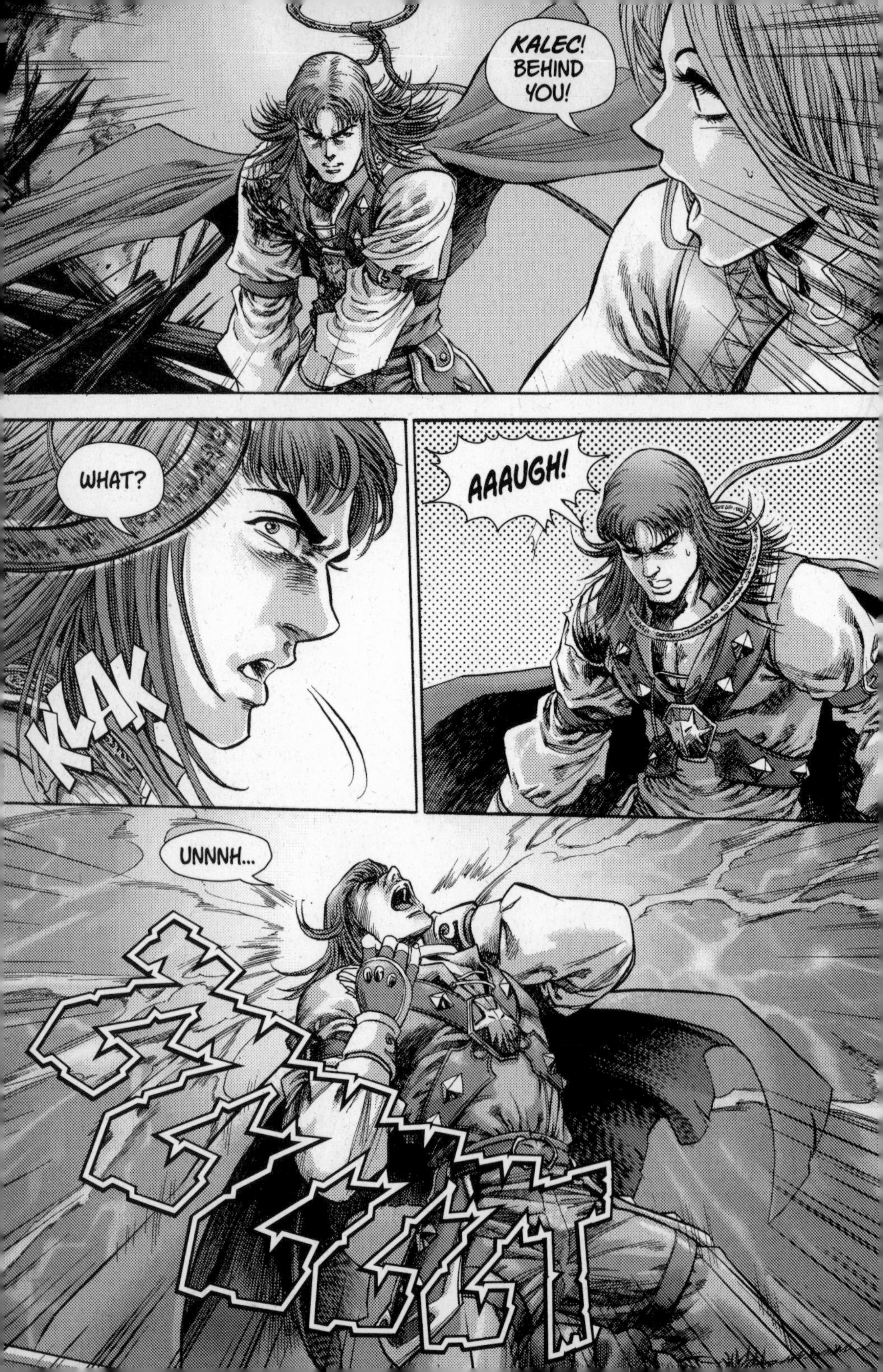
KALEC! BEHIND YOU!
WHAT?
KLAK
AAAUGH!
UNNNH...

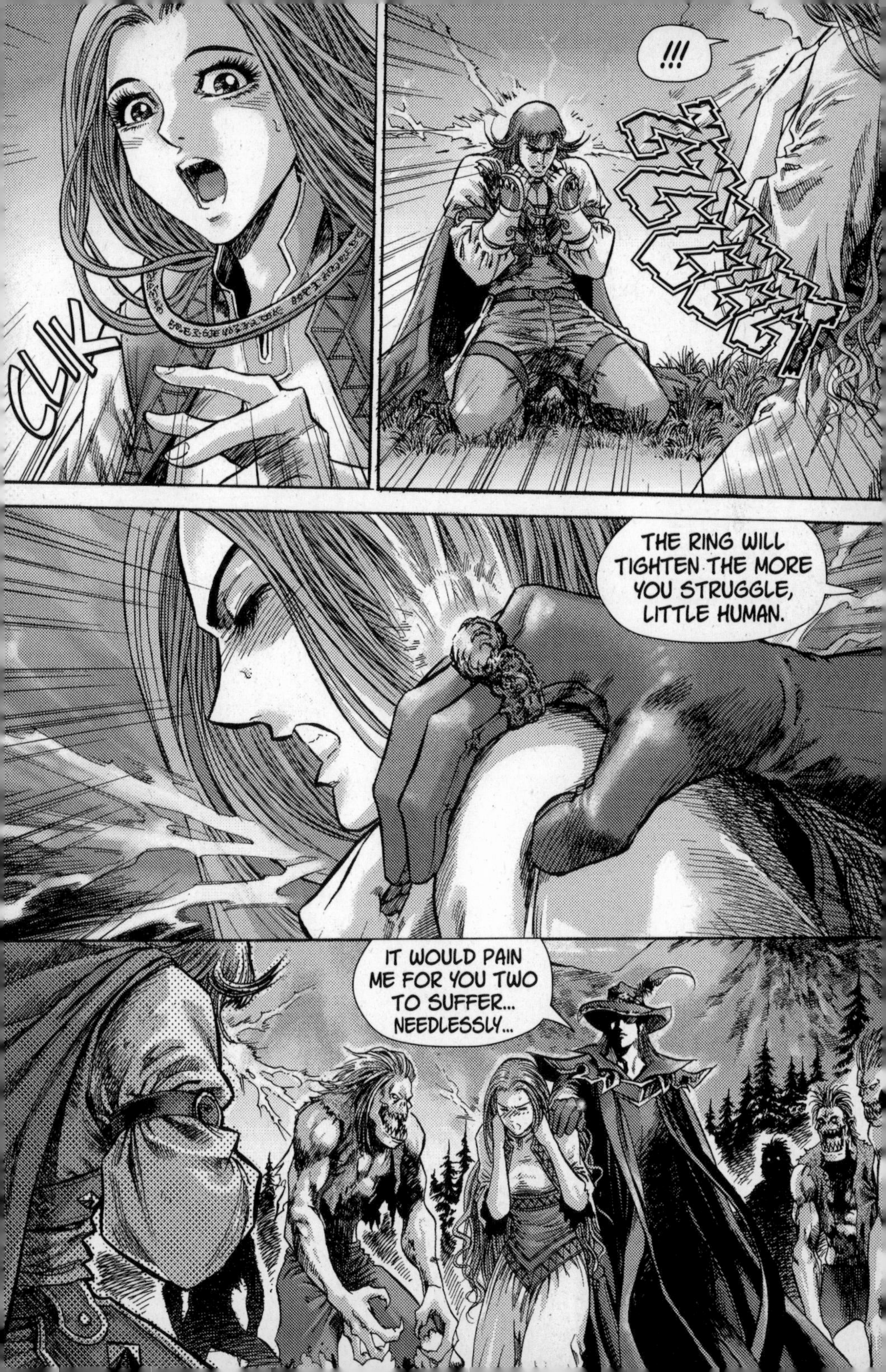
!!!
CLIK
THE RING WILL TIGHTEN THE MORE YOU STRUGGLE, LITTLE HUMAN.
IT WOULD PAIN ME FOR YOU TWO TO SUFFER... NEEDLESSLY...

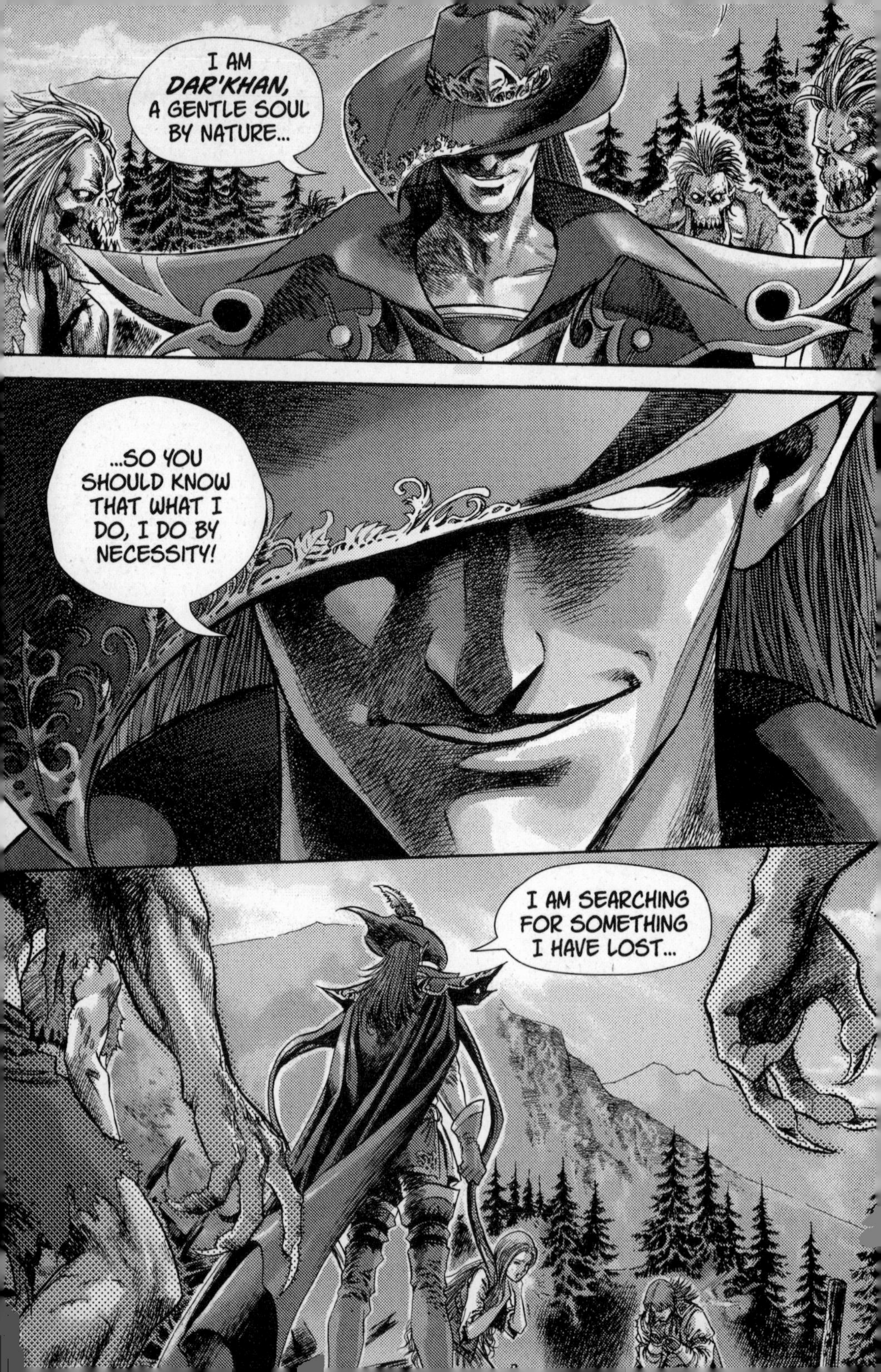
I AM *DAR'KHAN,* A GENTLE SOUL BY NATURE...
...SO YOU SHOULD KNOW THAT WHAT I DO, I DO BY NECESSITY!
I AM SEARCHING FOR SOMETHING I HAVE LOST...

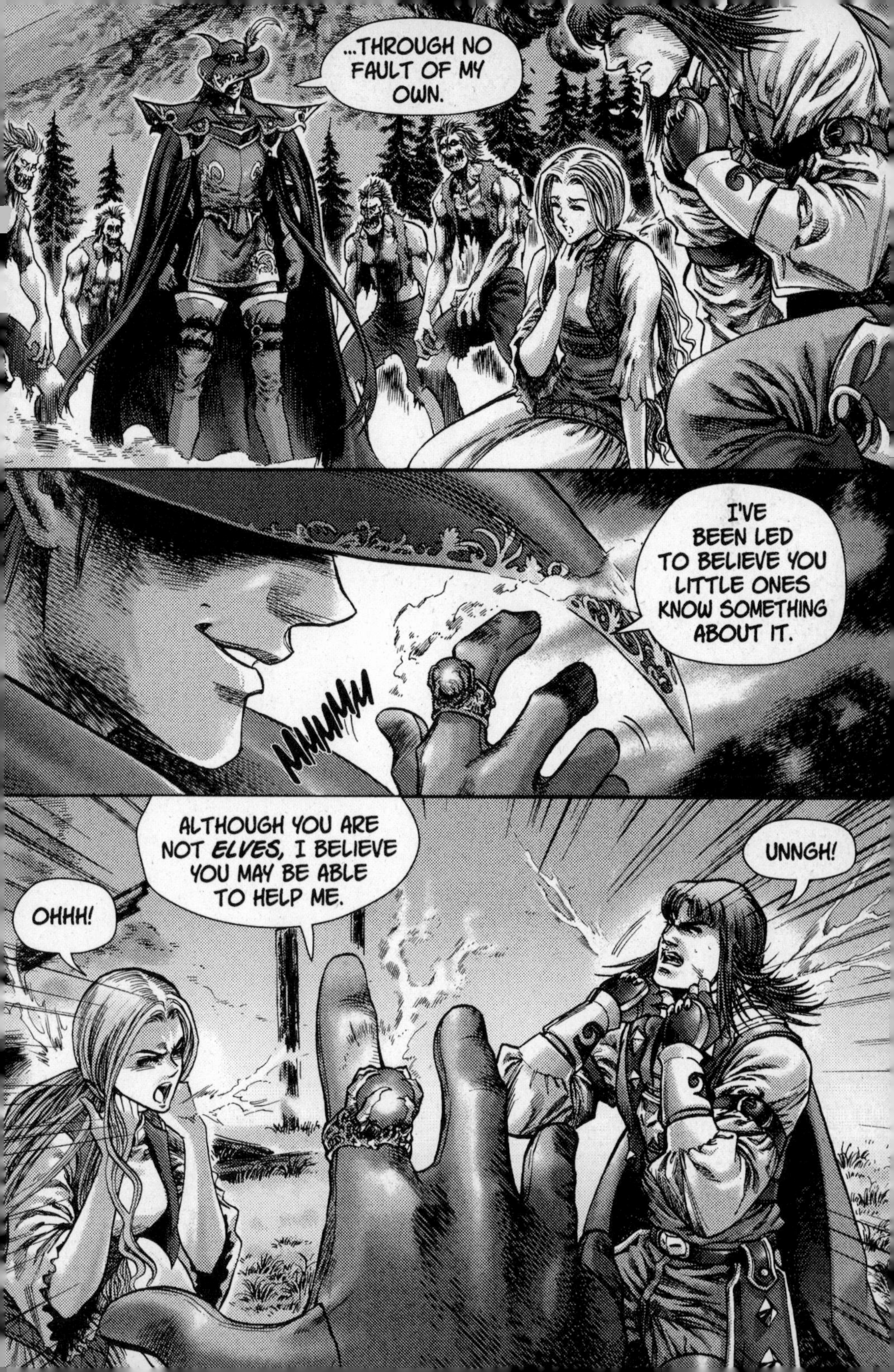
...THROUGH NO FAULT OF MY OWN.
I'VE BEEN LED TO BELIEVE YOU LITTLE ONES KNOW SOMETHING ABOUT IT.
MMMMM
UNNGH!
ALTHOUGH YOU ARE NOT *ELVES*, I BELIEVE YOU MAY BE ABLE TO HELP ME.
OHHH!

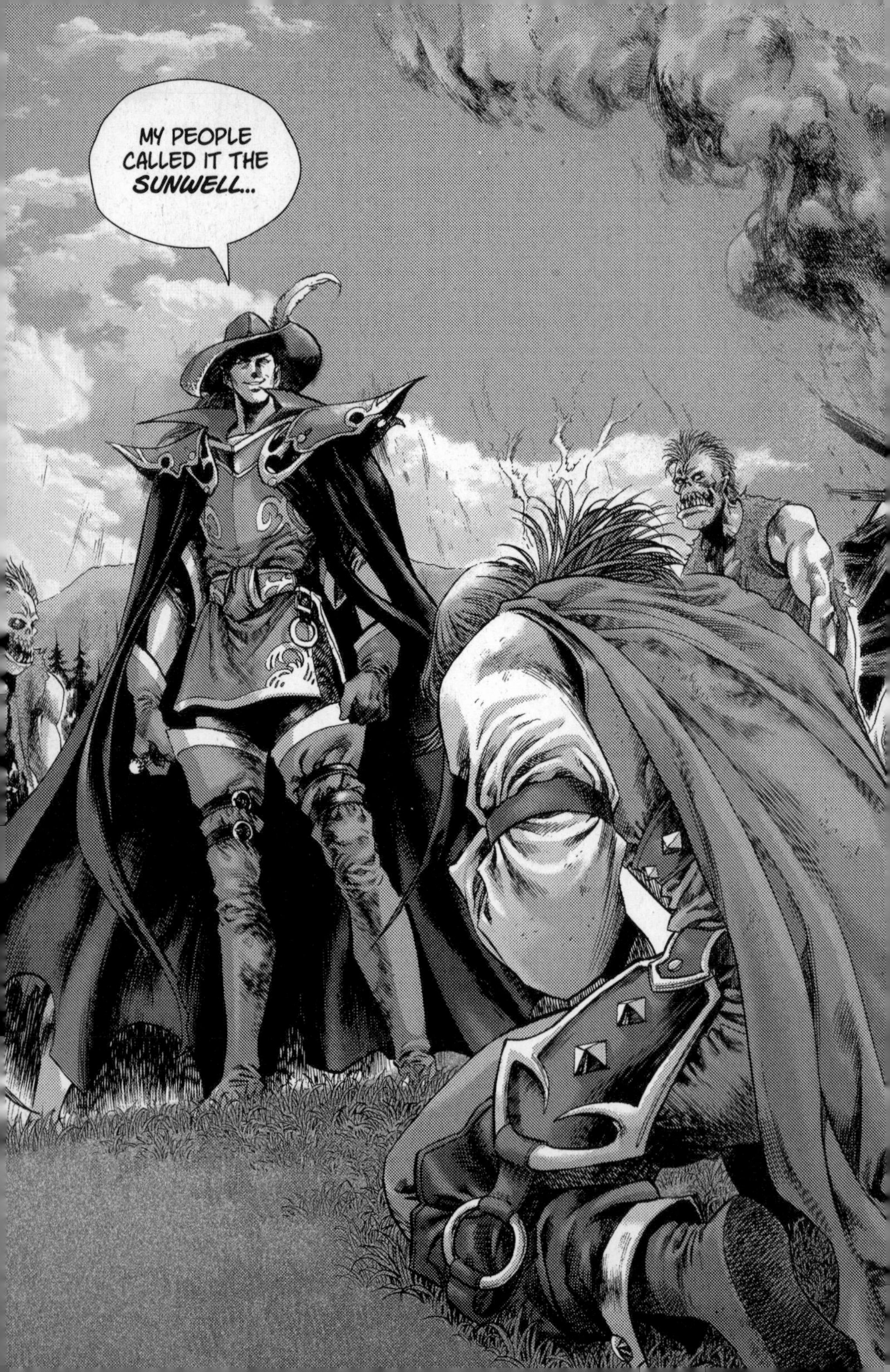
MY PEOPLE CALLED IT THE *SUNWELL*...

CHAPTER FOUR
LEGACY OF THE SUNWELL

IT WAS
THE ESSENCE OF
OUR LIVES...

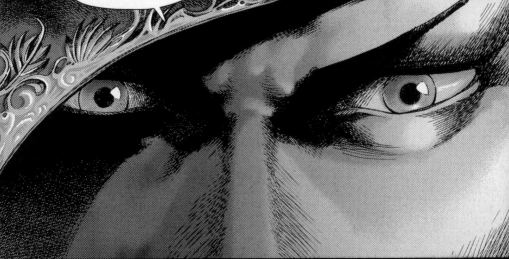

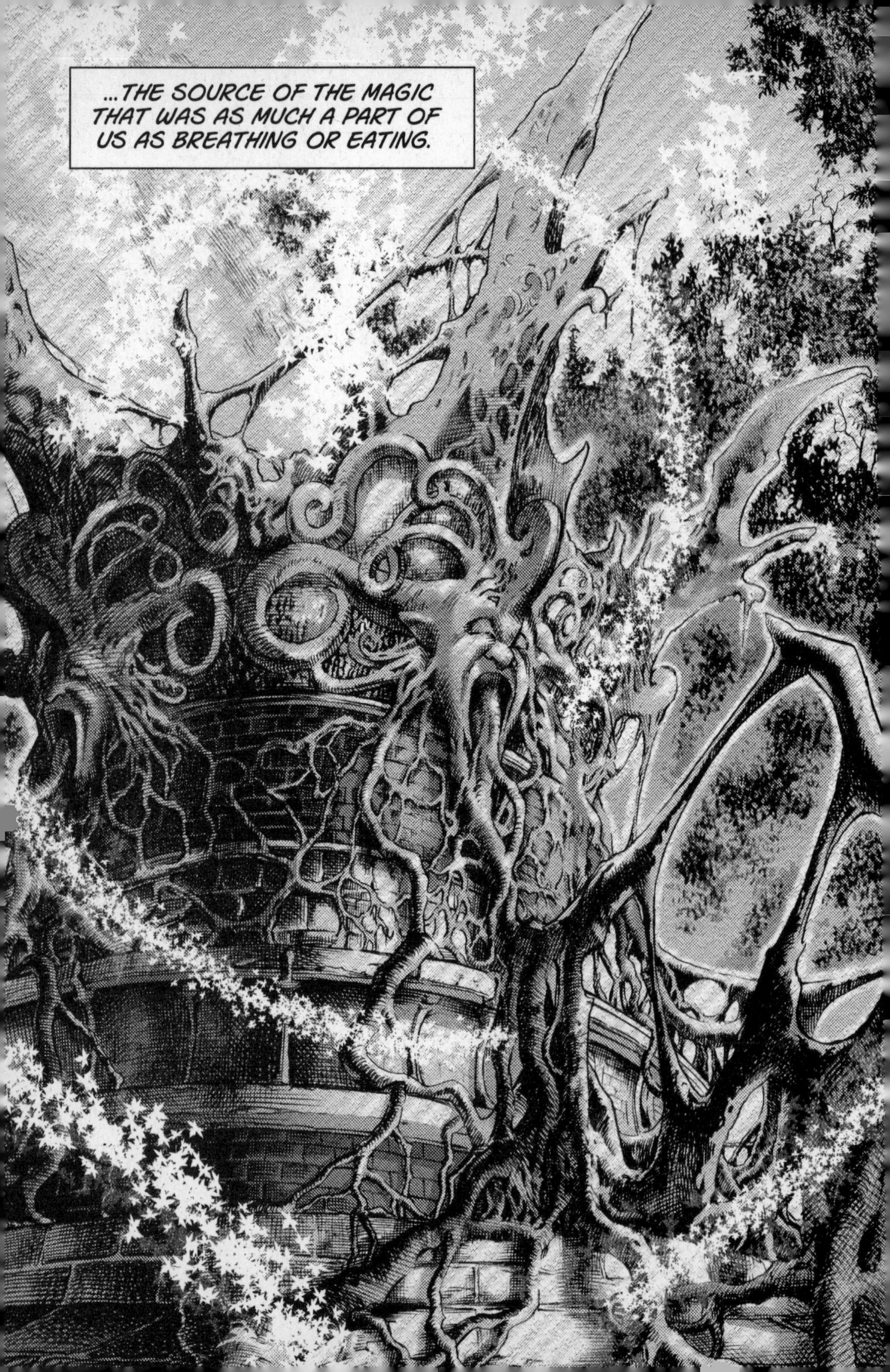
...THE SOURCE OF THE MAGIC THAT WAS AS MUCH A PART OF US AS BREATHING OR EATING.

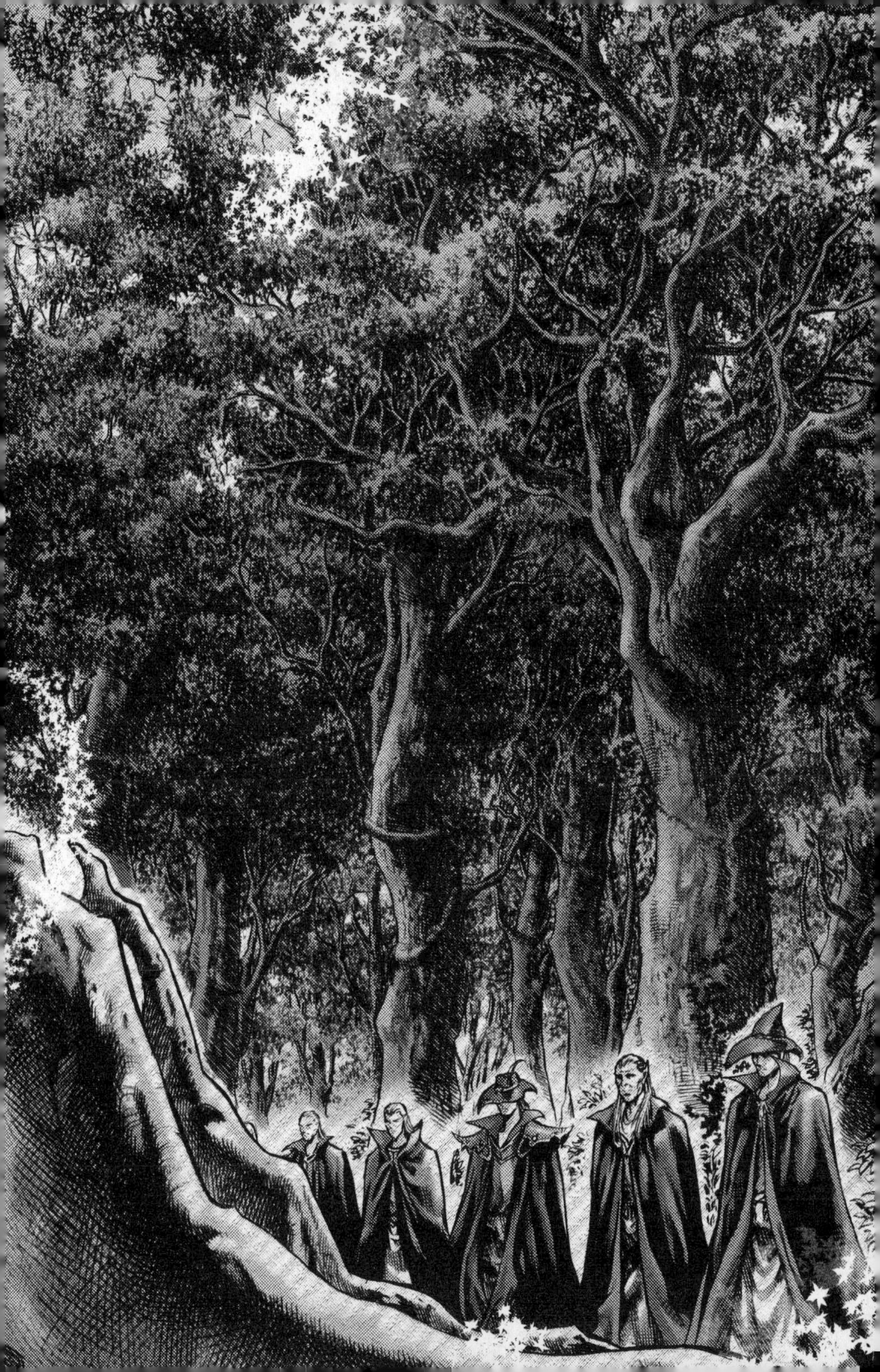

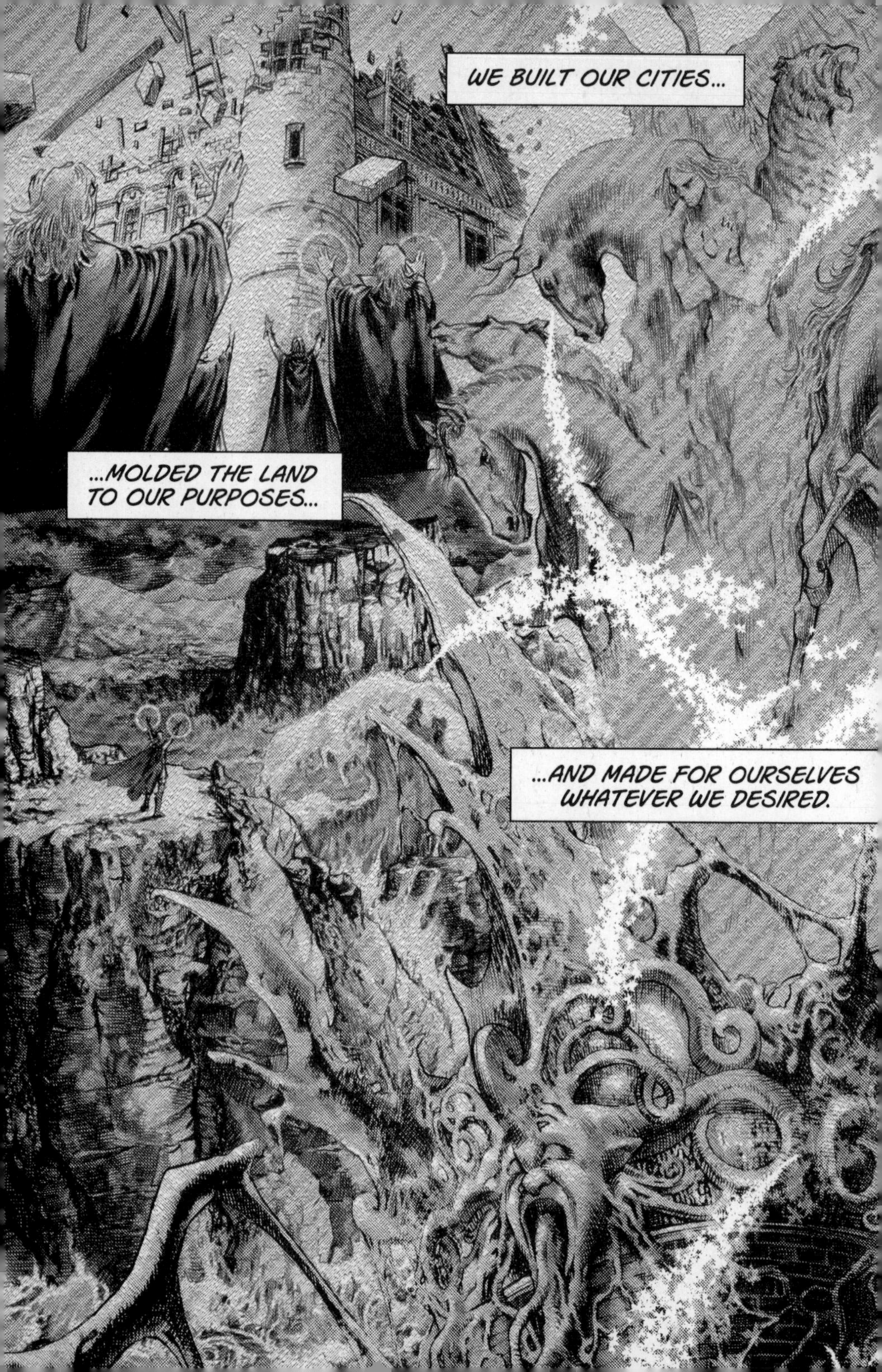
WE BUILT OUR CITIES...
...MOLDED THE LAND TO OUR PURPOSES...
...AND MADE FOR OURSELVES WHATEVER WE DESIRED.

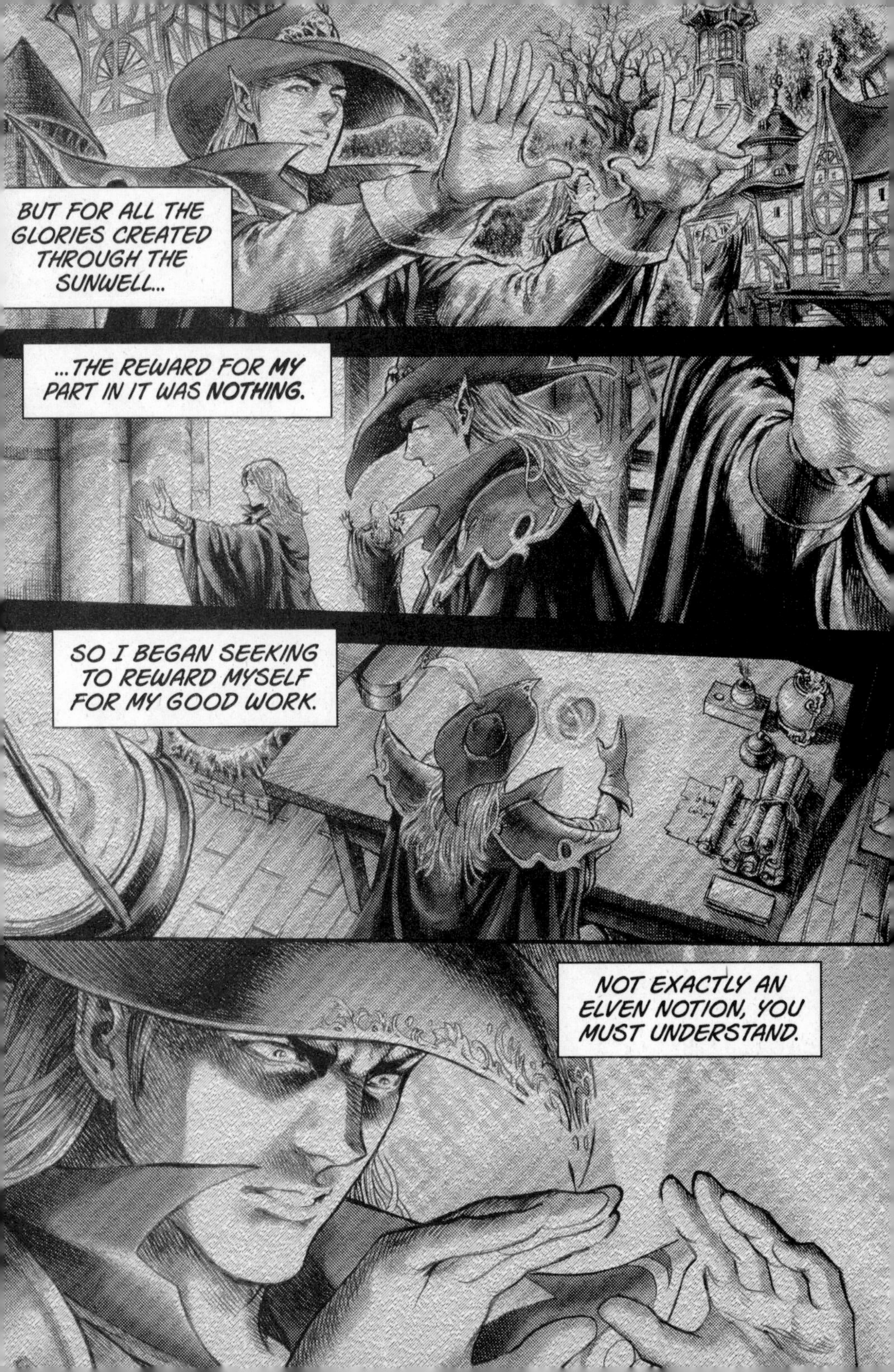
BUT FOR ALL THE GLORIES CREATED THROUGH THE SUNWELL...
...THE REWARD FOR MY PART IN IT WAS NOTHING.
SO I BEGAN SEEKING TO REWARD MYSELF FOR MY GOOD WORK.
NOT EXACTLY AN ELVEN NOTION, YOU MUST UNDERSTAND.

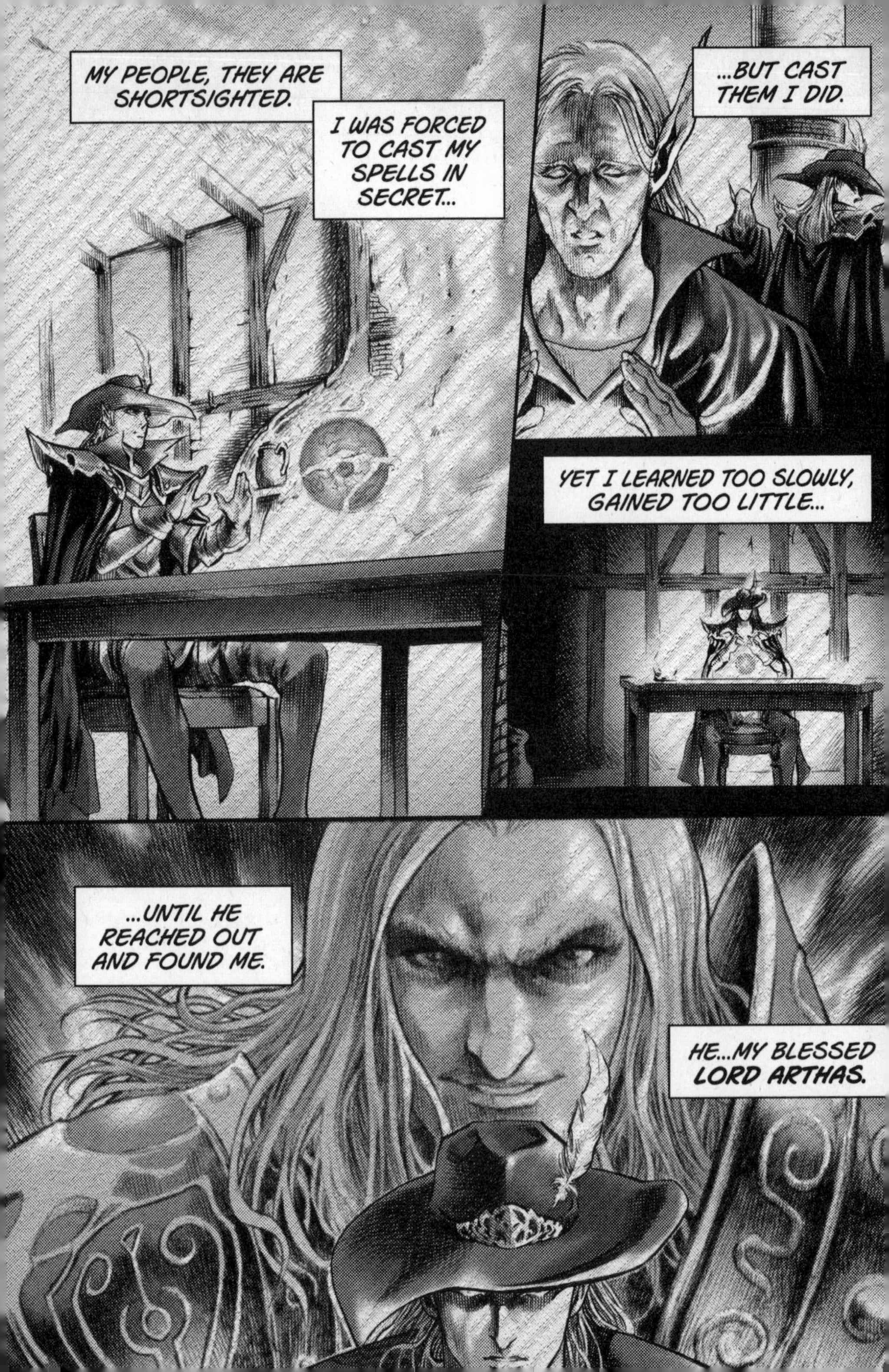
MY PEOPLE, THEY ARE SHORTSIGHTED.
I WAS FORCED TO CAST MY SPELLS IN SECRET...
...BUT CAST THEM I DID.
YET I LEARNED TOO SLOWLY, GAINED TOO LITTLE...
...UNTIL HE REACHED OUT AND FOUND ME.
HE...MY BLESSED LORD ARTHAS.

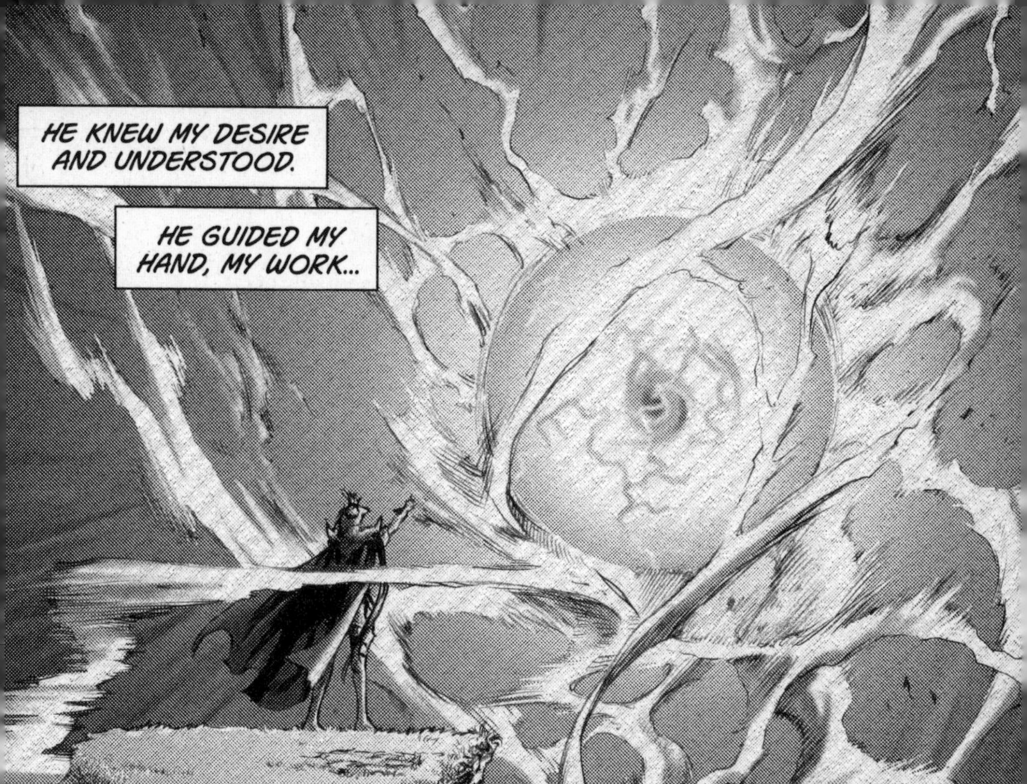
HE KNEW MY DESIRE AND UNDERSTOOD.
HE GUIDED MY HAND, MY WORK...
...AND SO I LEARNED...BUT STILL IT WAS NOT ENOUGH. I HAD REACHED THE LIMIT THAT MY CALLING ALLOWED FROM THE SUNWELL.
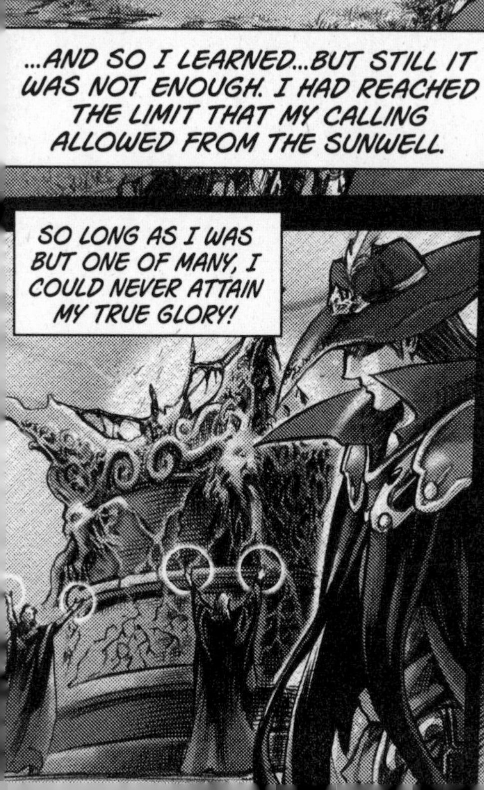
SO LONG AS I WAS BUT ONE OF MANY, I COULD NEVER ATTAIN MY TRUE GLORY!
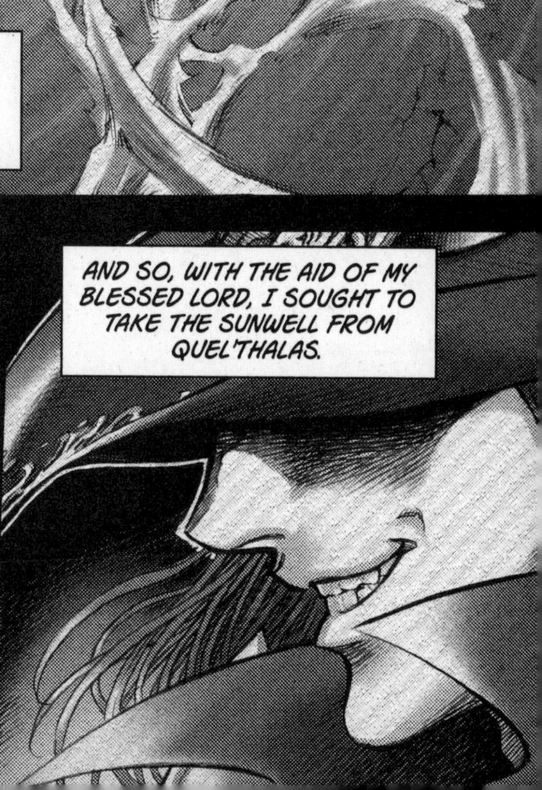
AND SO, WITH THE AID OF MY BLESSED LORD, I SOUGHT TO TAKE THE SUNWELL FROM QUEL'THALAS.

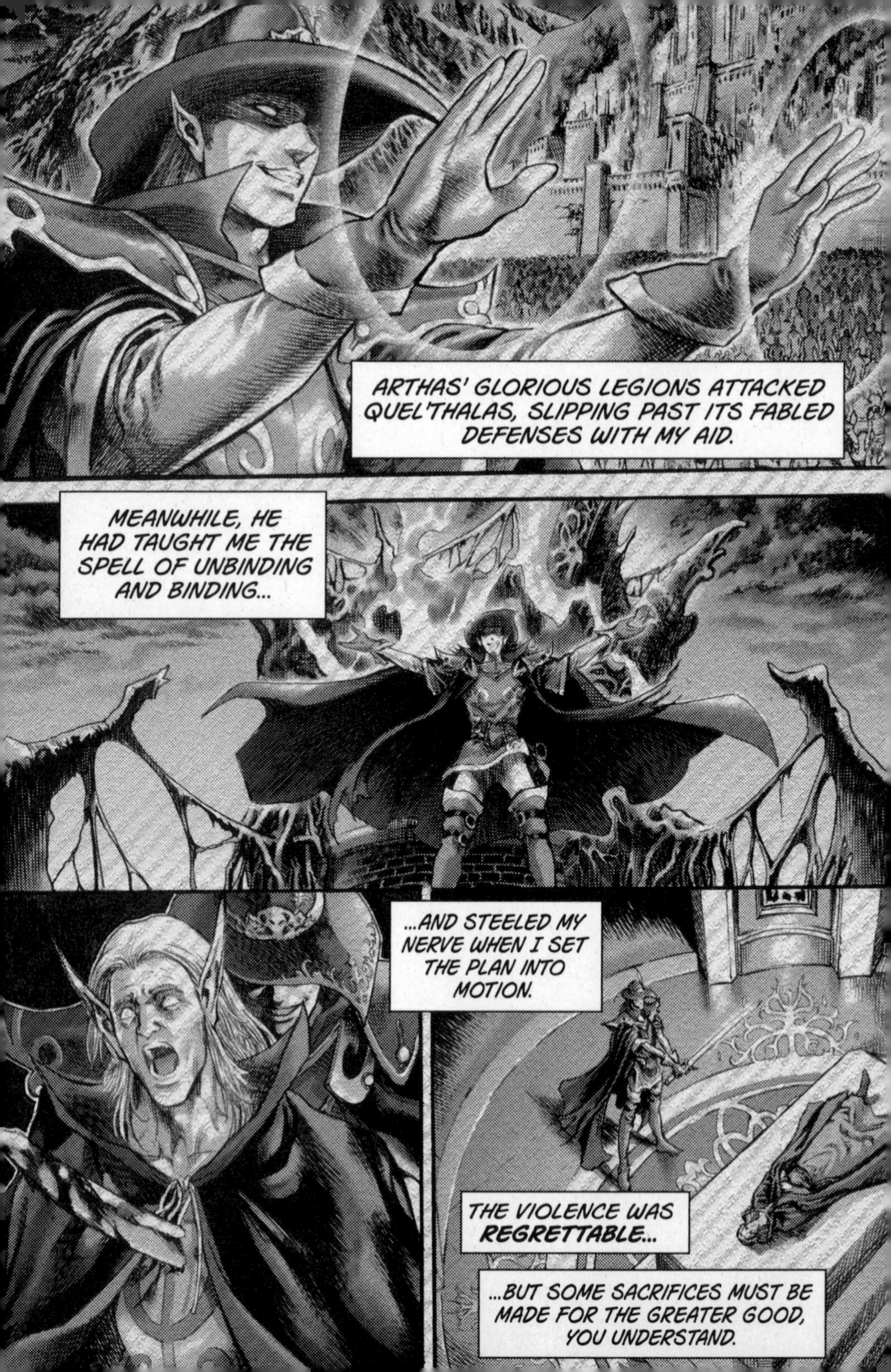
ARTHAS' GLORIOUS LEGIONS ATTACKED QUEL'THALAS, SLIPPING PAST ITS FABLED DEFENSES WITH MY AID.
MEANWHILE, HE HAD TAUGHT ME THE SPELL OF UNBINDING AND BINDING...
...AND STEELED MY NERVE WHEN I SET THE PLAN INTO MOTION.
THE VIOLENCE WAS REGRETTABLE...
...BUT SOME SACRIFICES MUST BE MADE FOR THE GREATER GOOD, YOU UNDERSTAND.

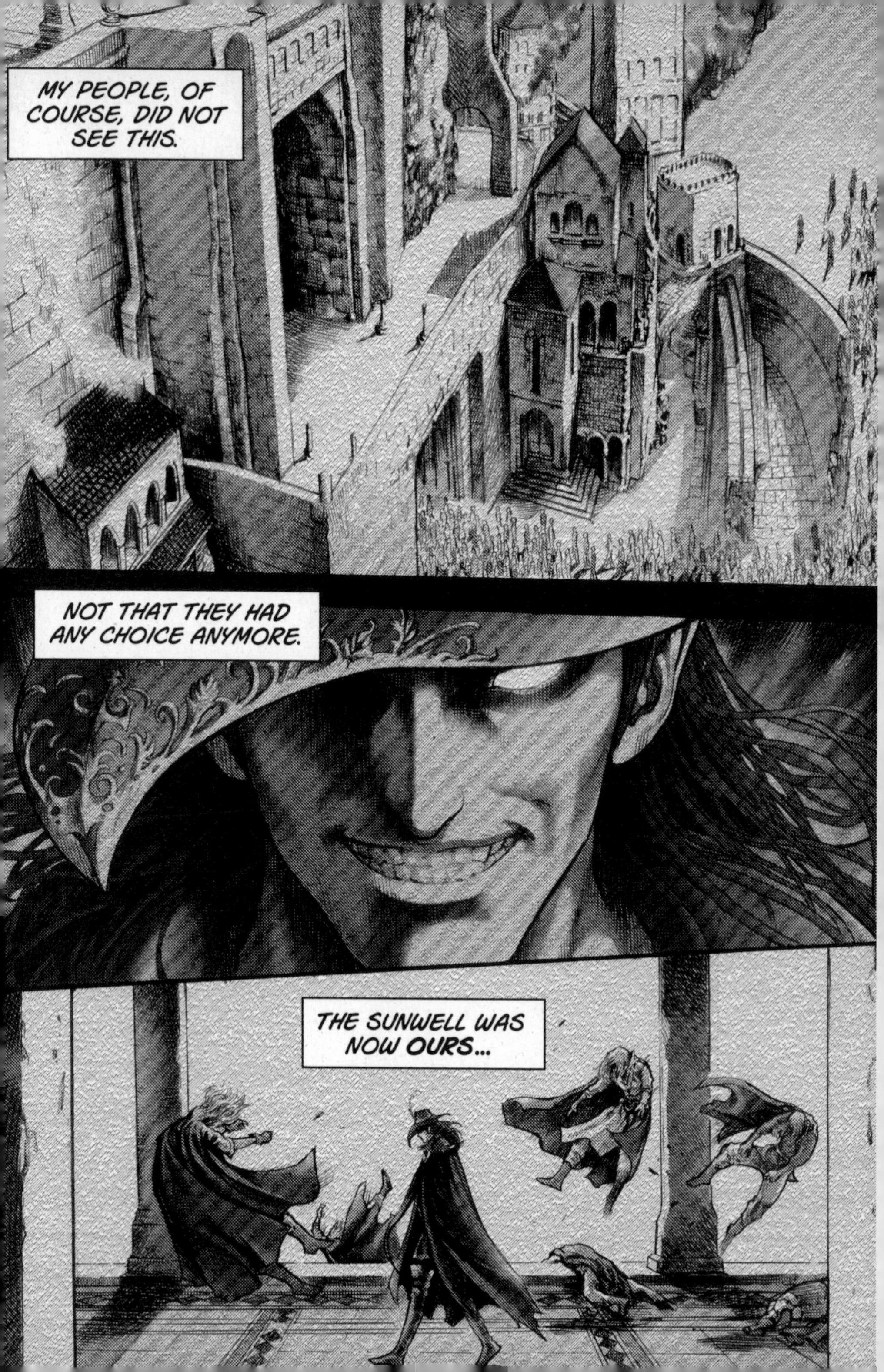
MY PEOPLE, OF COURSE, DID NOT SEE THIS.
NOT THAT THEY HAD ANY CHOICE ANYMORE.
THE SUNWELL WAS NOW OURS...

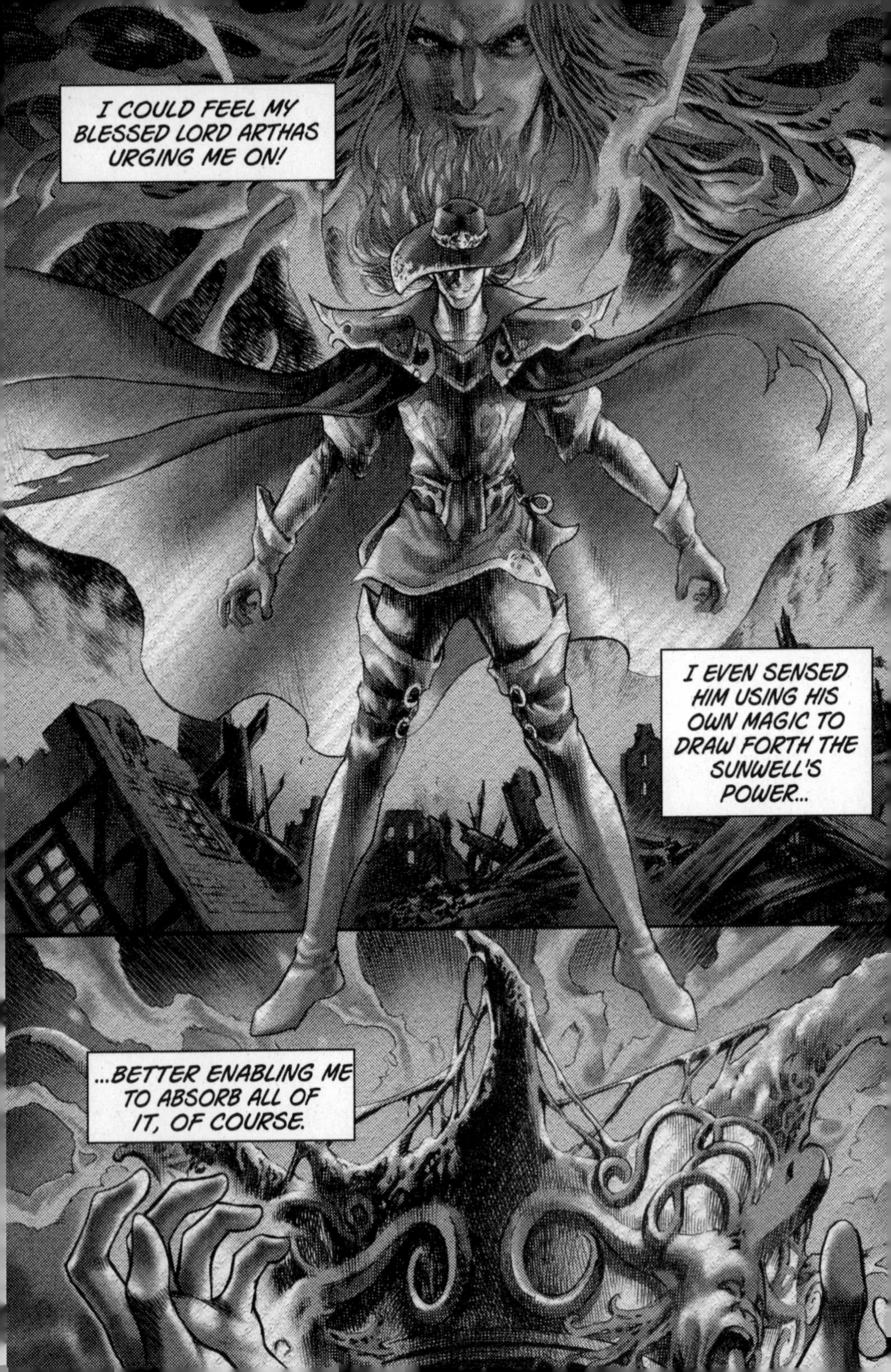
I COULD FEEL MY BLESSED LORD ARTHAS URGING ME ON!
I EVEN SENSED HIM USING HIS OWN MAGIC TO DRAW FORTH THE SUNWELL'S POWER...
...BETTER ENABLING ME TO ABSORB ALL OF IT, OF COURSE.

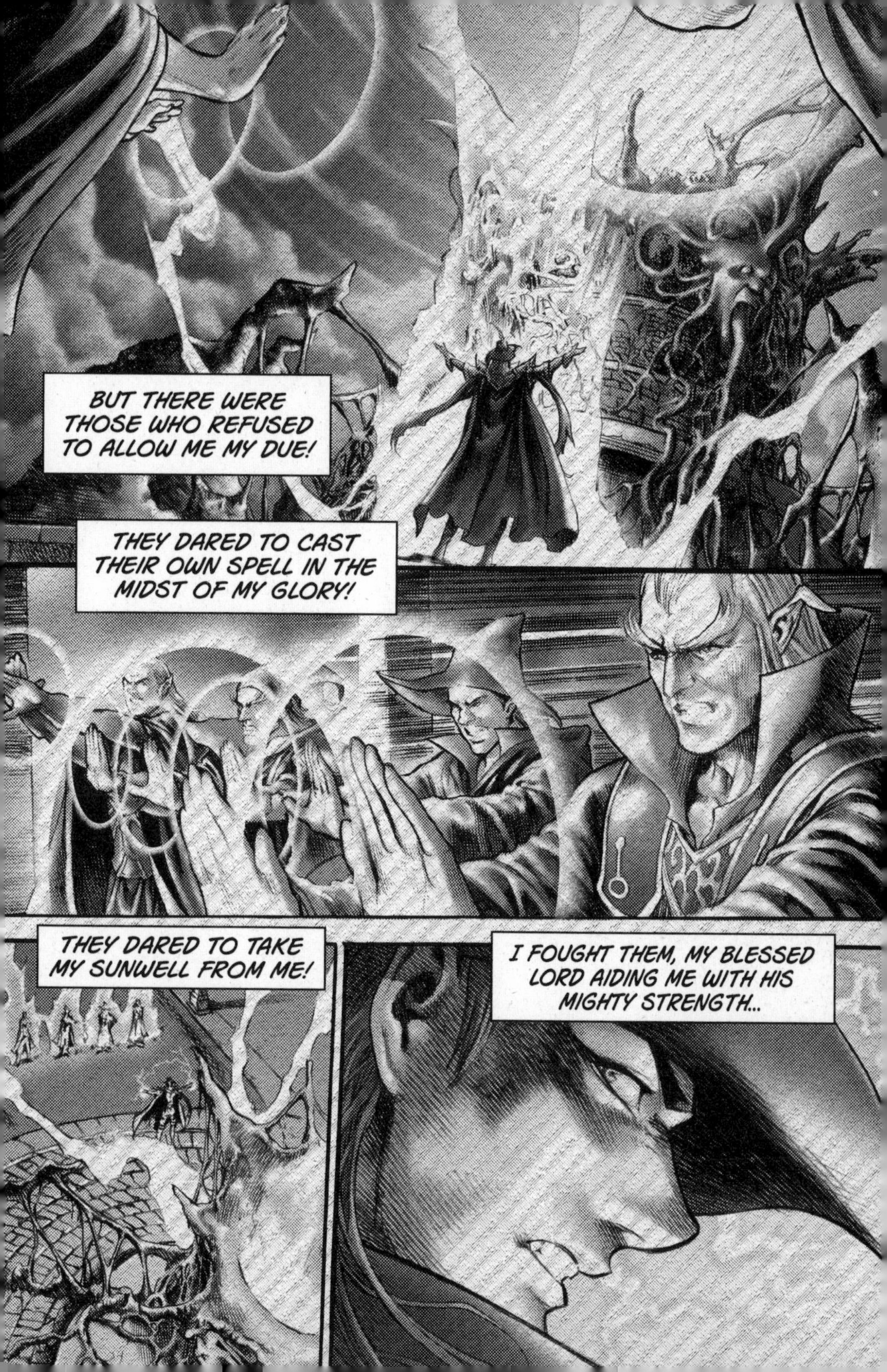
BUT THERE WERE THOSE WHO REFUSED TO ALLOW ME MY DUE!
THEY DARED TO CAST THEIR OWN SPELL IN THE MIDST OF MY GLORY!
THEY DARED TO TAKE MY SUNWELL FROM ME!
I FOUGHT THEM, MY BLESSED LORD AIDING ME WITH HIS MIGHTY STRENGTH...

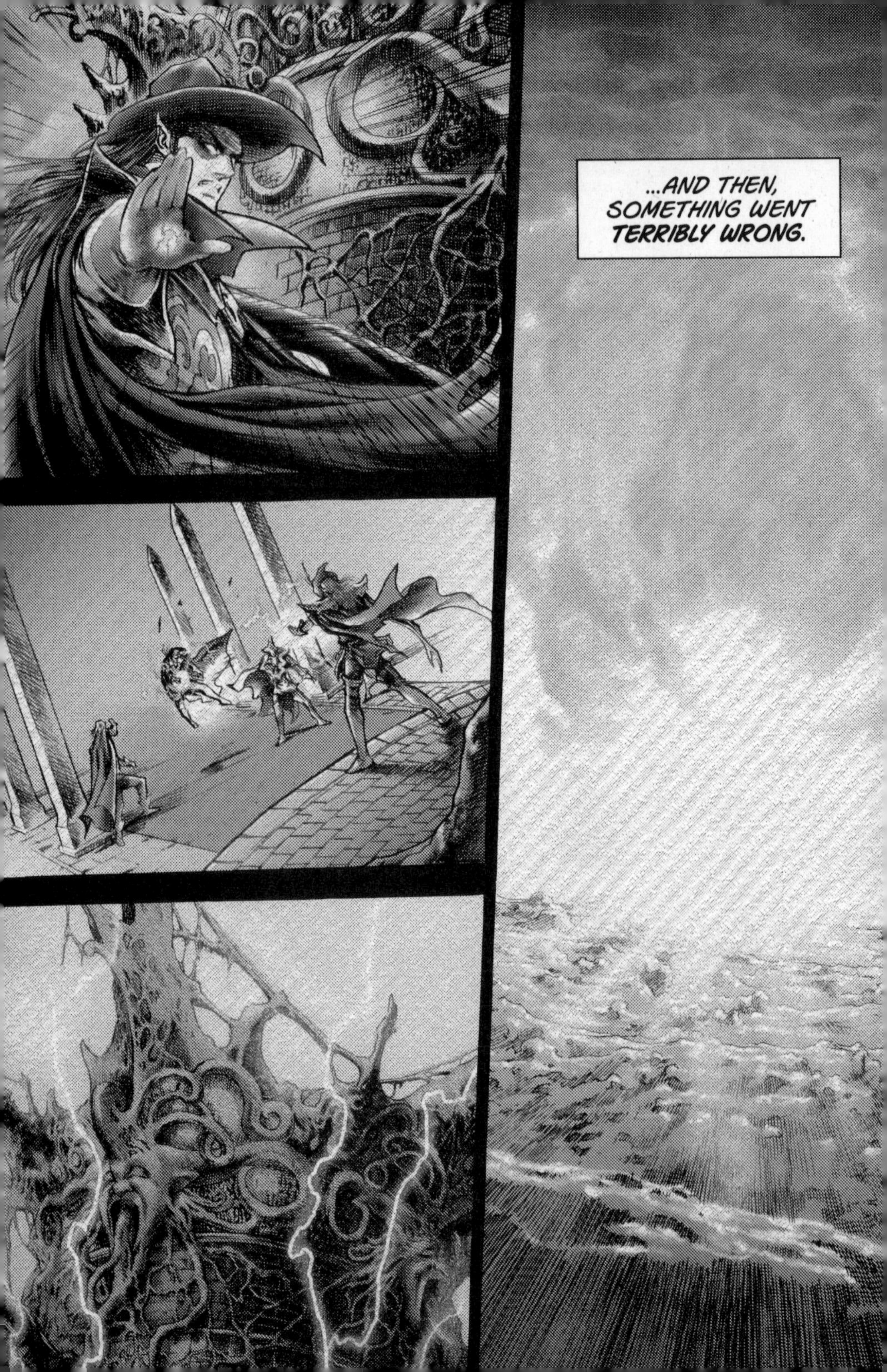
...AND THEN, SOMETHING WENT TERRIBLY WRONG.

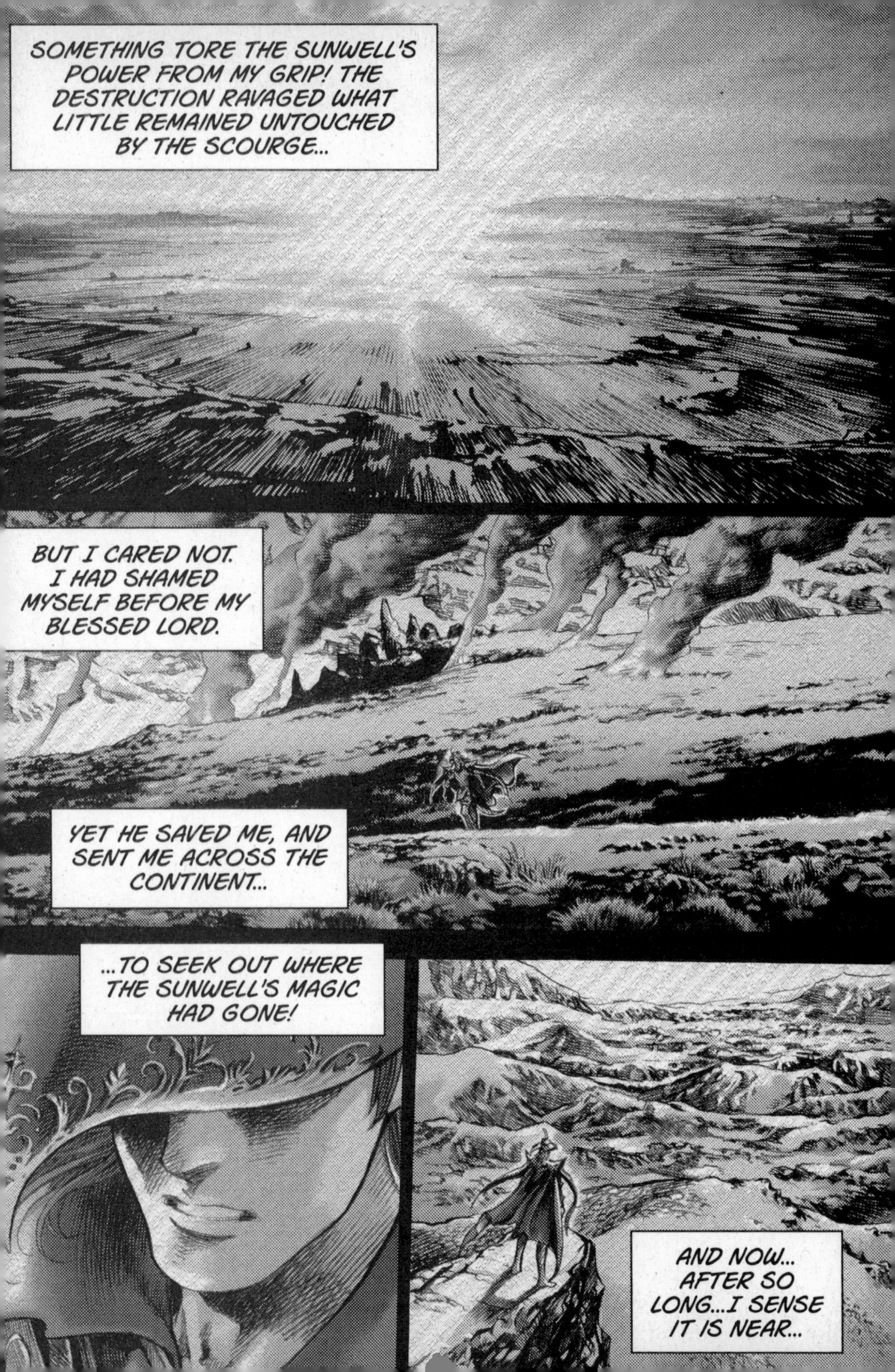
SOMETHING TORE THE SUNWELL'S POWER FROM MY GRIP! THE DESTRUCTION RAVAGED WHAT LITTLE REMAINED UNTOUCHED BY THE SCOURGE...
BUT I CARED NOT. I HAD SHAMED MYSELF BEFORE MY BLESSED LORD.
YET HE SAVED ME, AND SENT ME ACROSS THE CONTINENT...
...TO SEEK OUT WHERE THE SUNWELL'S MAGIC HAD GONE!
AND NOW... AFTER SO LONG...I SENSE IT IS NEAR...

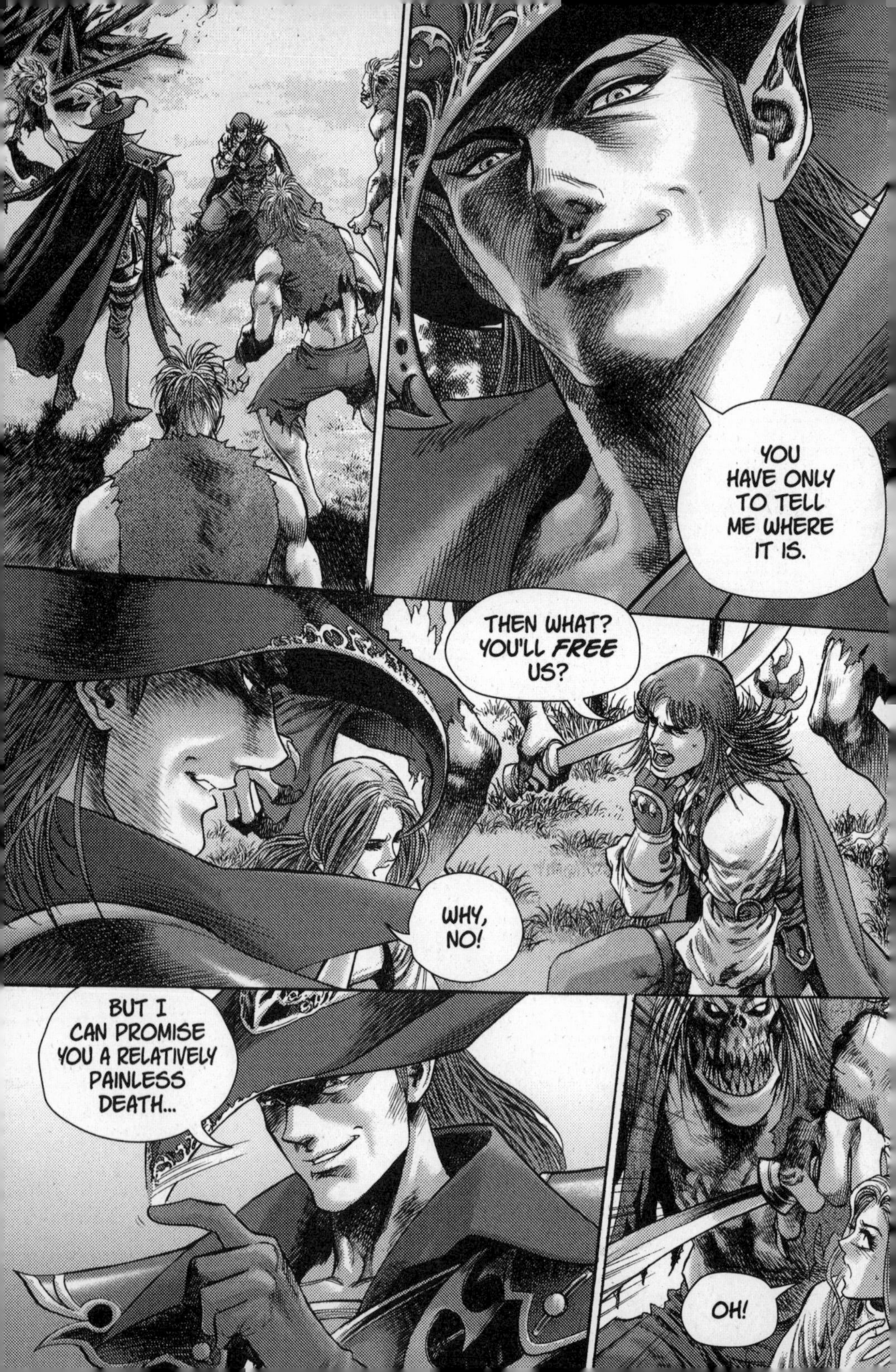
YOU HAVE ONLY TO TELL ME WHERE IT IS.
THEN WHAT? YOU'LL *FREE* US?
WHY, NO!
BUT I CAN PROMISE YOU A RELATIVELY PAINLESS DEATH...
OH!

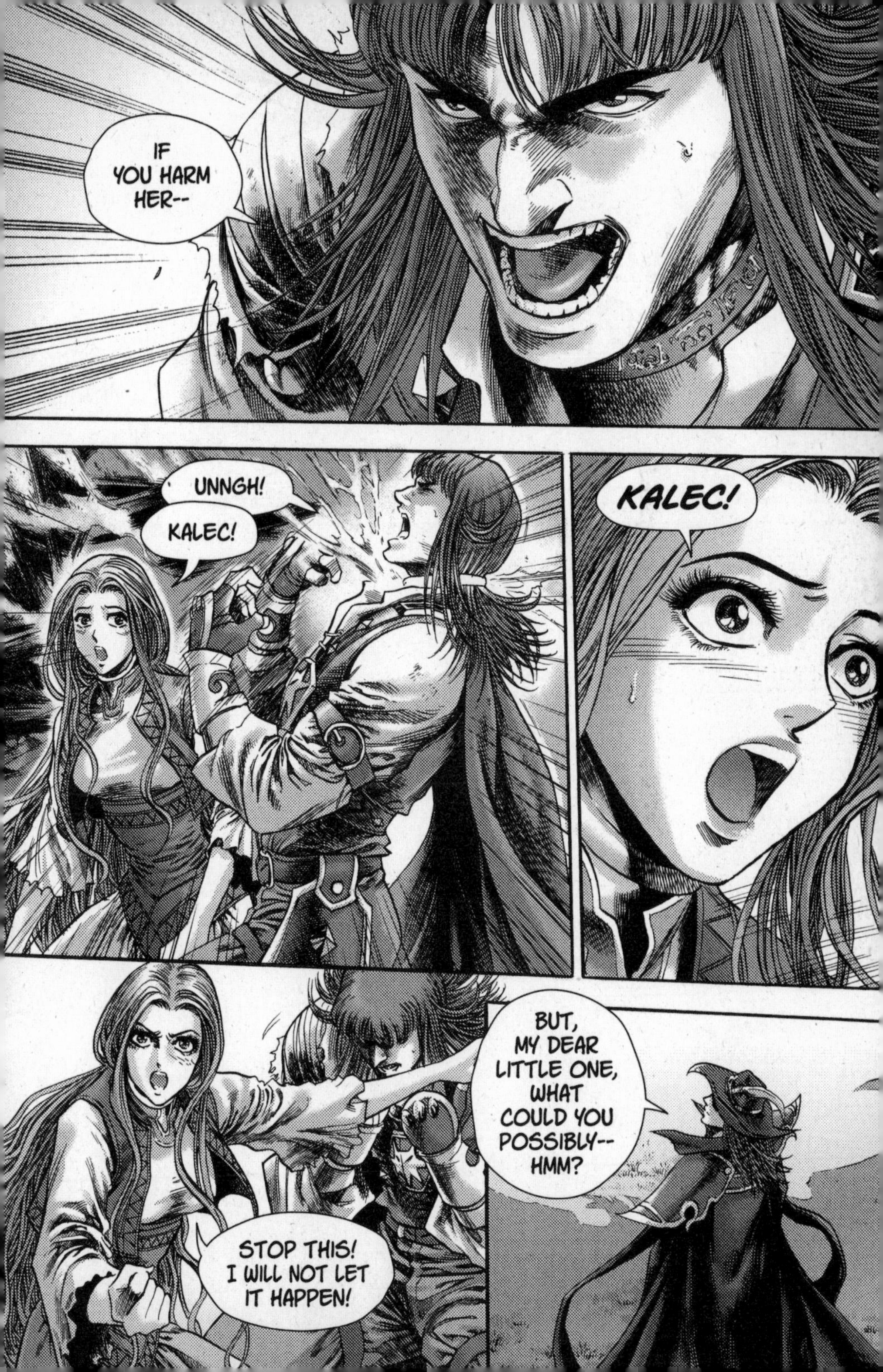
IF YOU HARM HER--
UNNGH!
KALEC!
KALEC!
STOP THIS! I WILL NOT LET IT HAPPEN!
BUT, MY DEAR LITTLE ONE, WHAT COULD YOU POSSIBLY-- HMM?

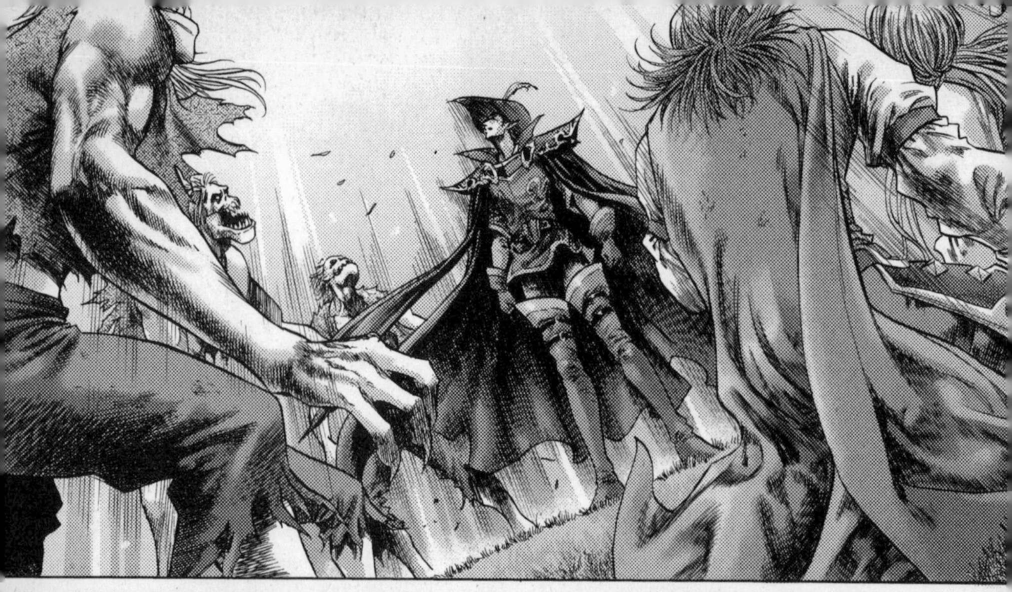

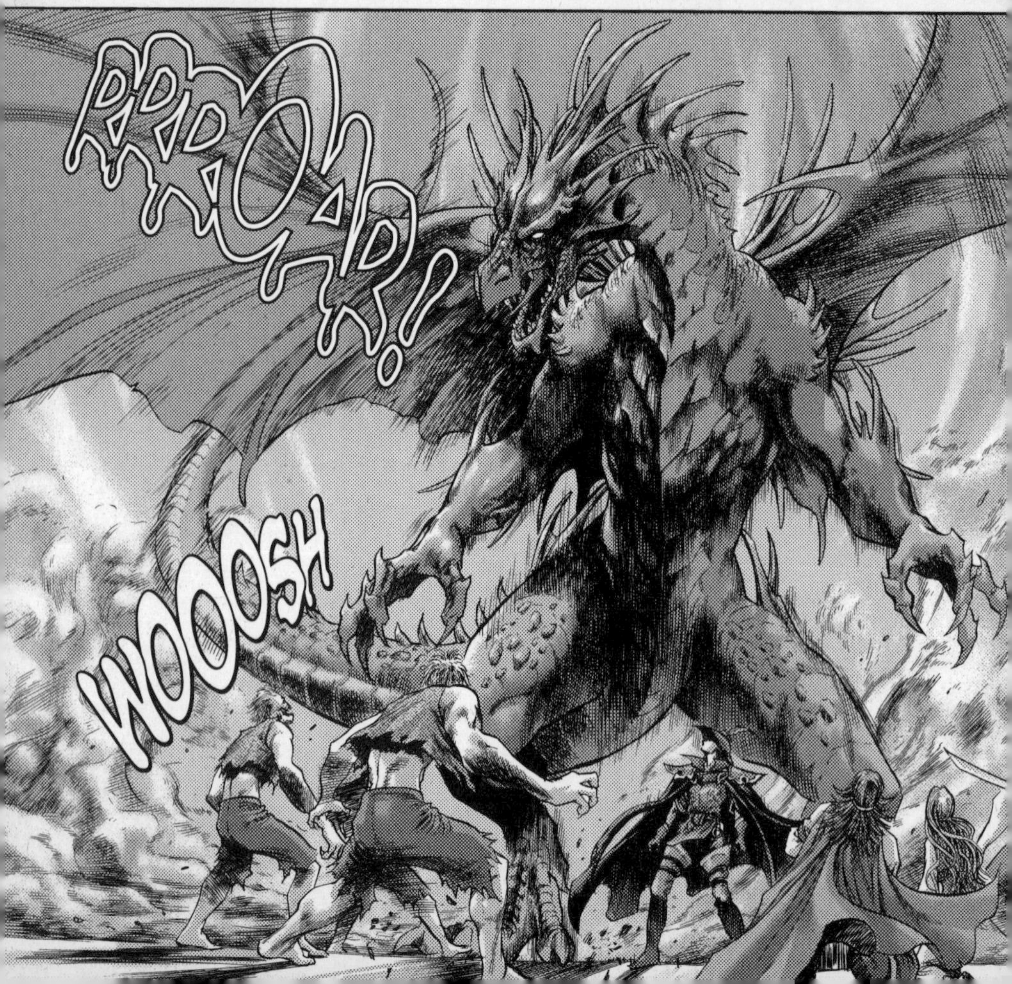
RRROAR!!
WOOOSH

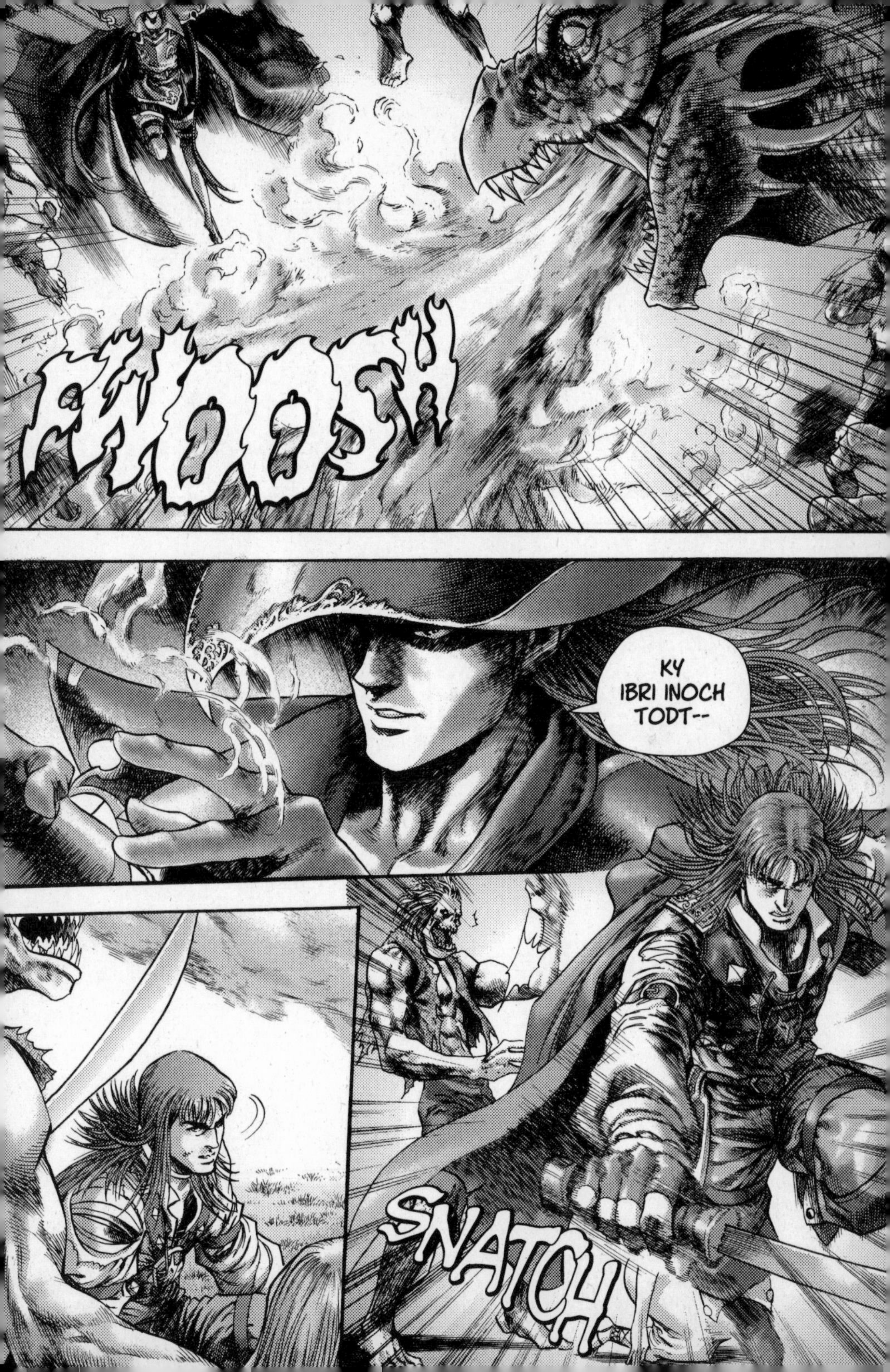
FWOOSH
KY IBRI INOCH TODT--
SNATCH

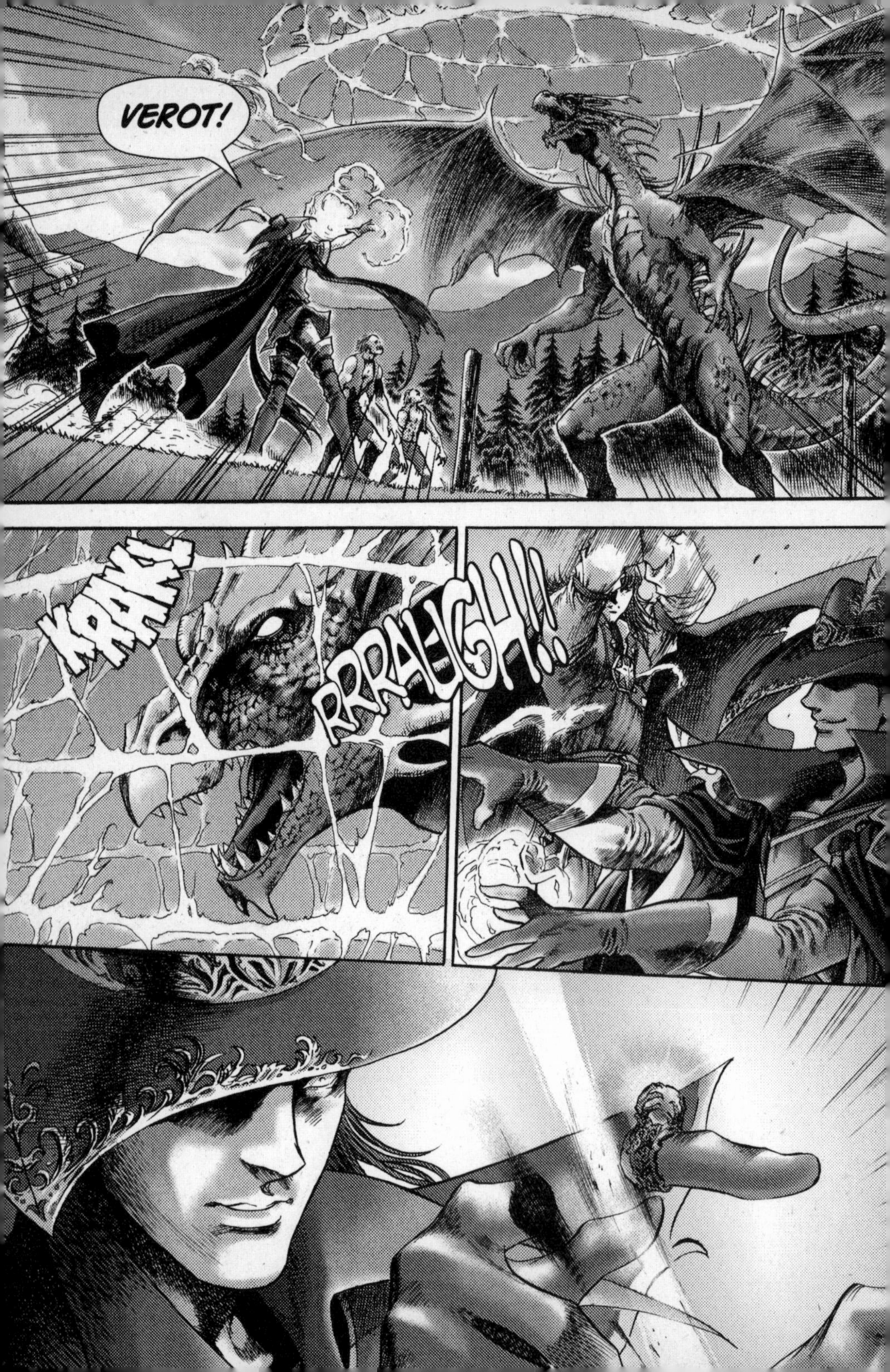
VEROT!
RRRAUGH!!!
KRAK!

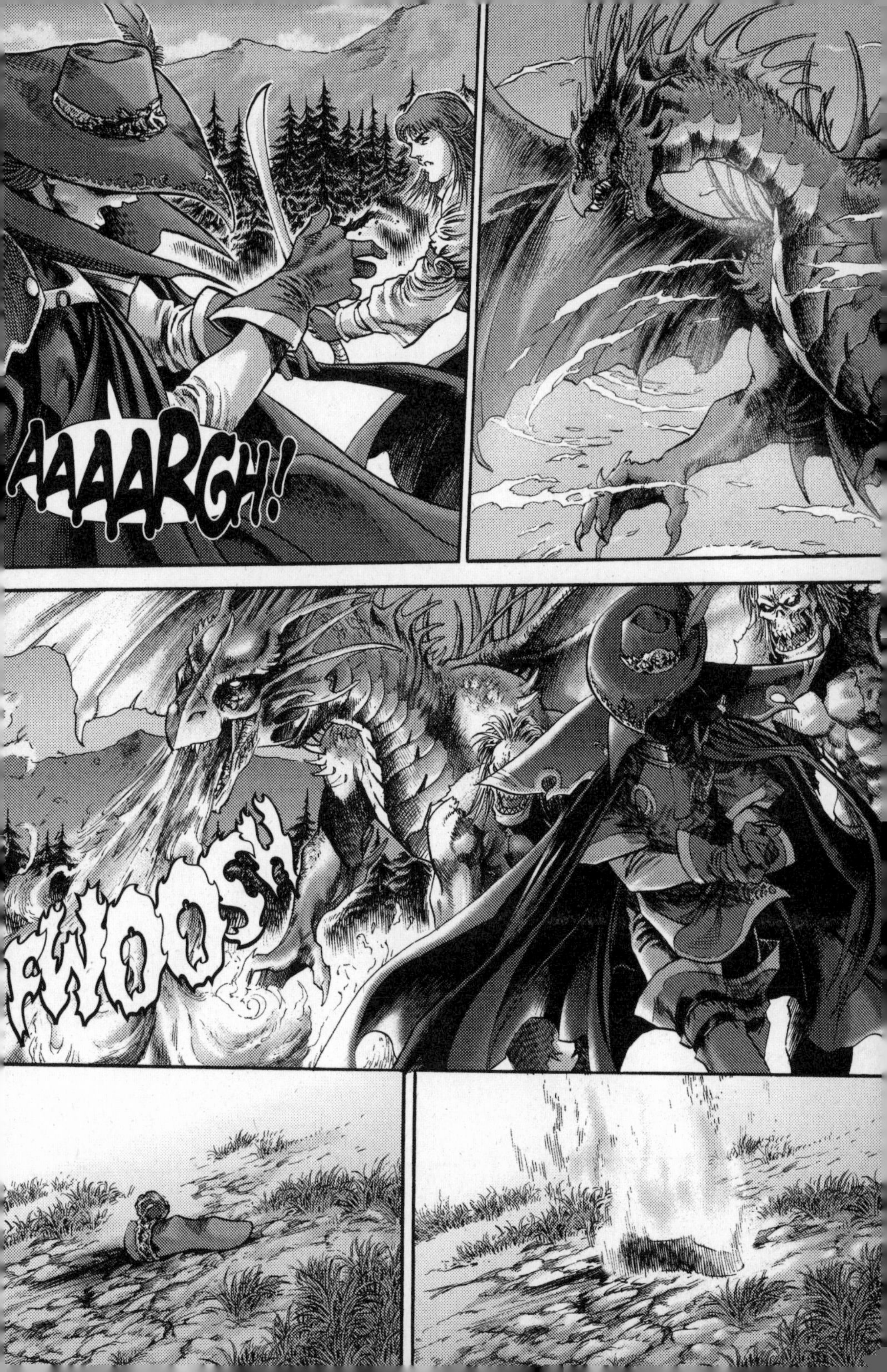
AAAARGH!
FWOOSH

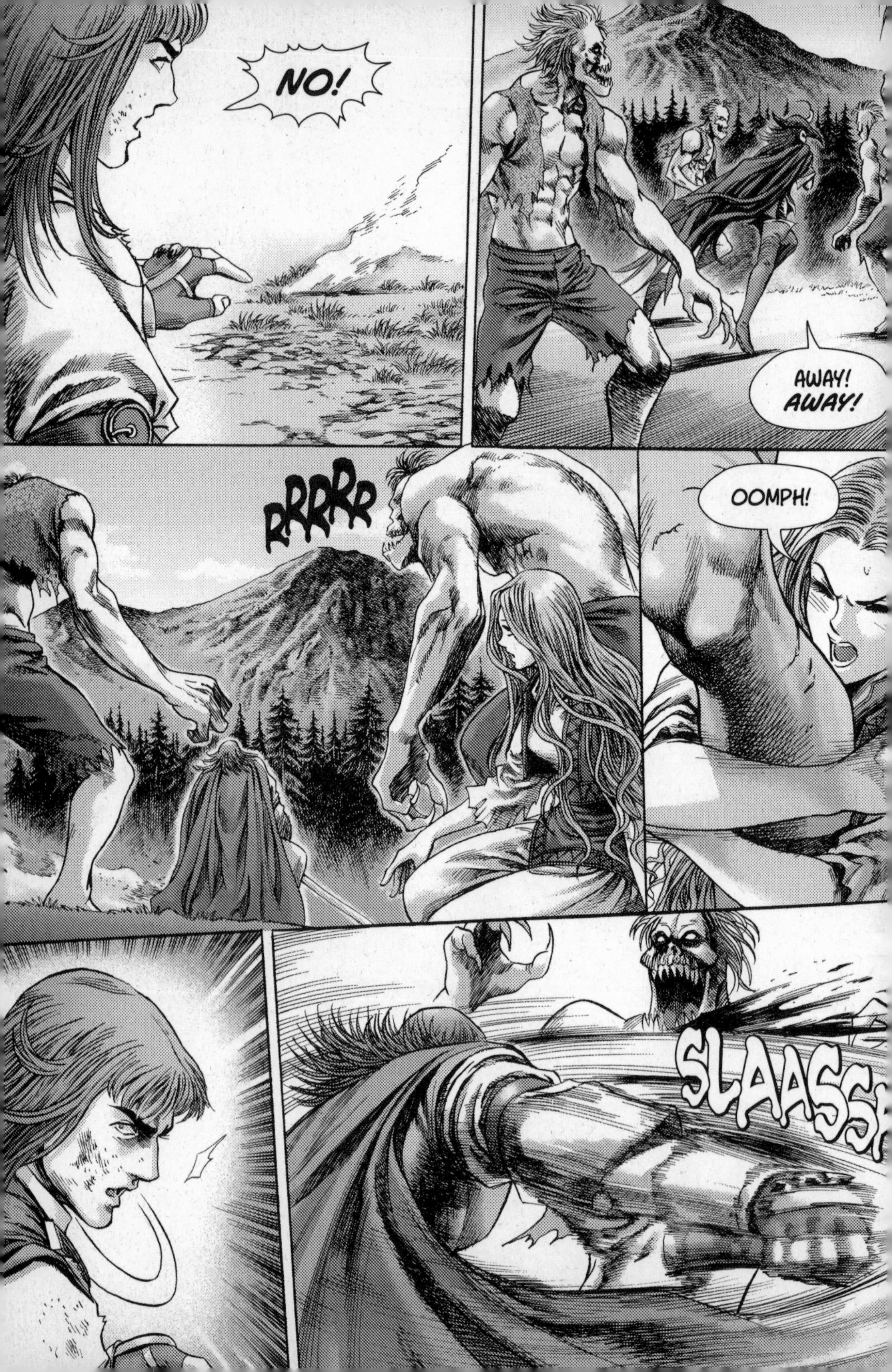
NO!
AWAY! AWAY!
RRRRR
OOMPH!
SLAASS

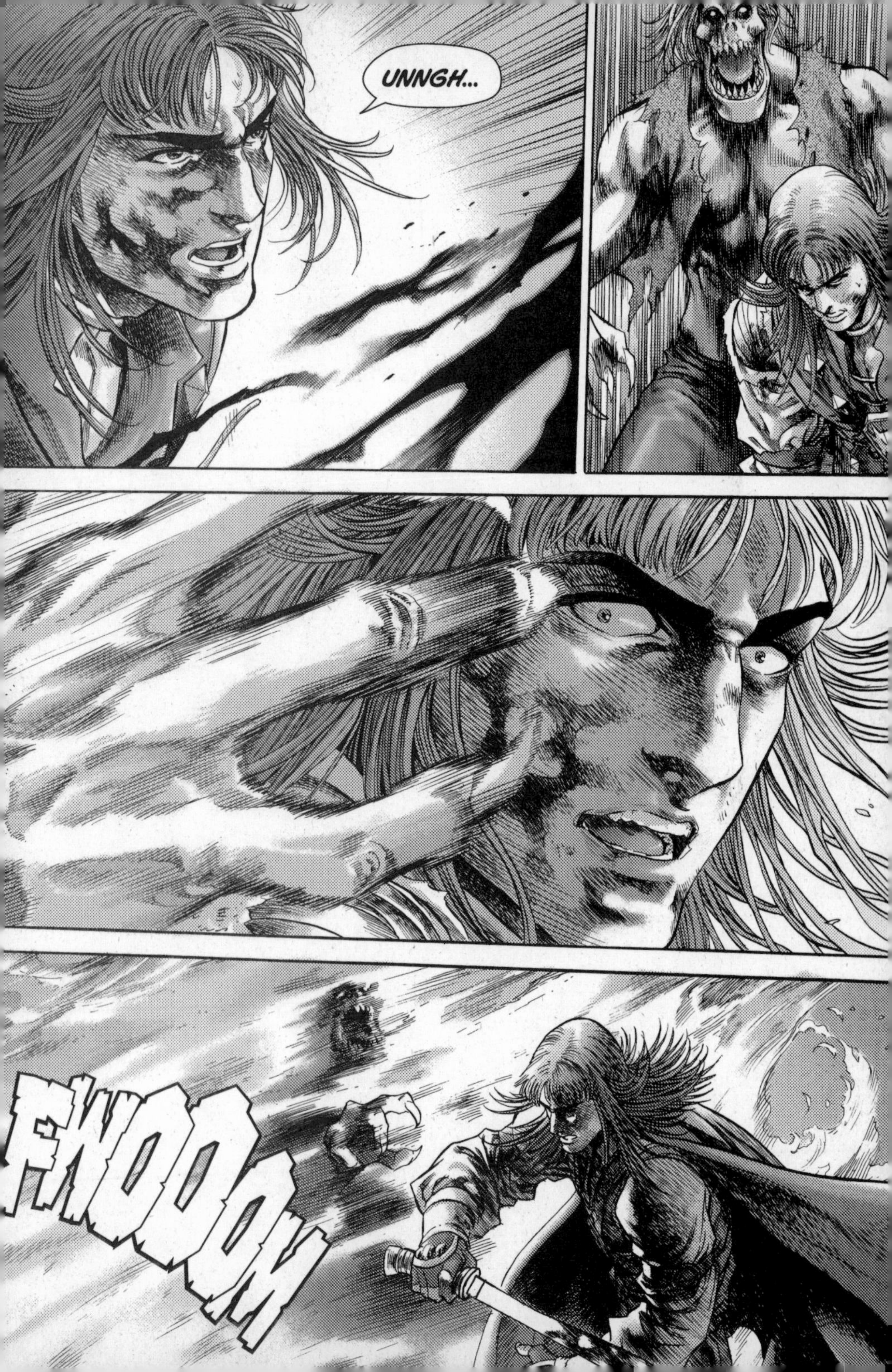
UNNGH...
FWOOOM

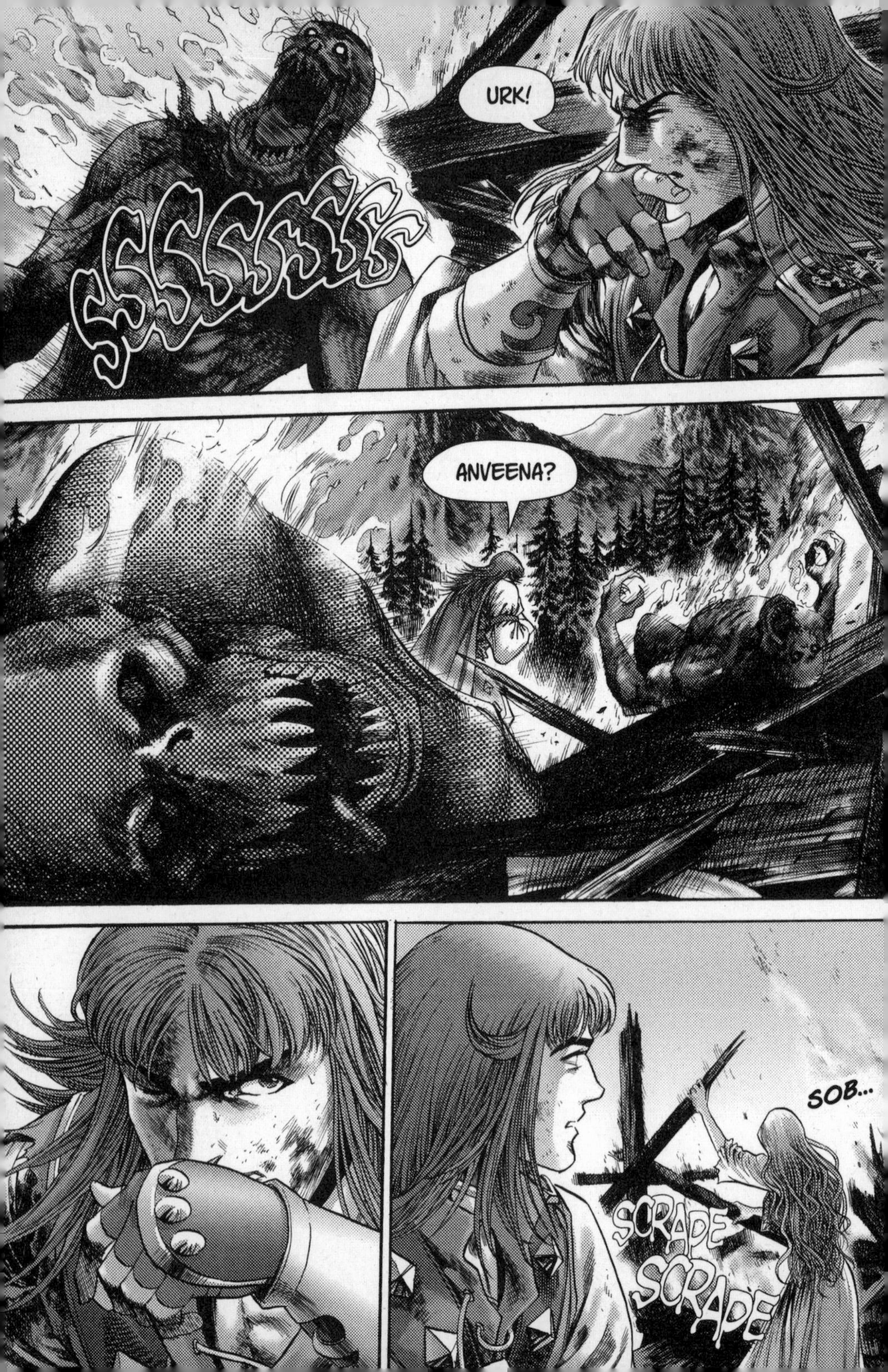
URK!
ANVEENA?
SOB...
SCRAPE
SCRAPE

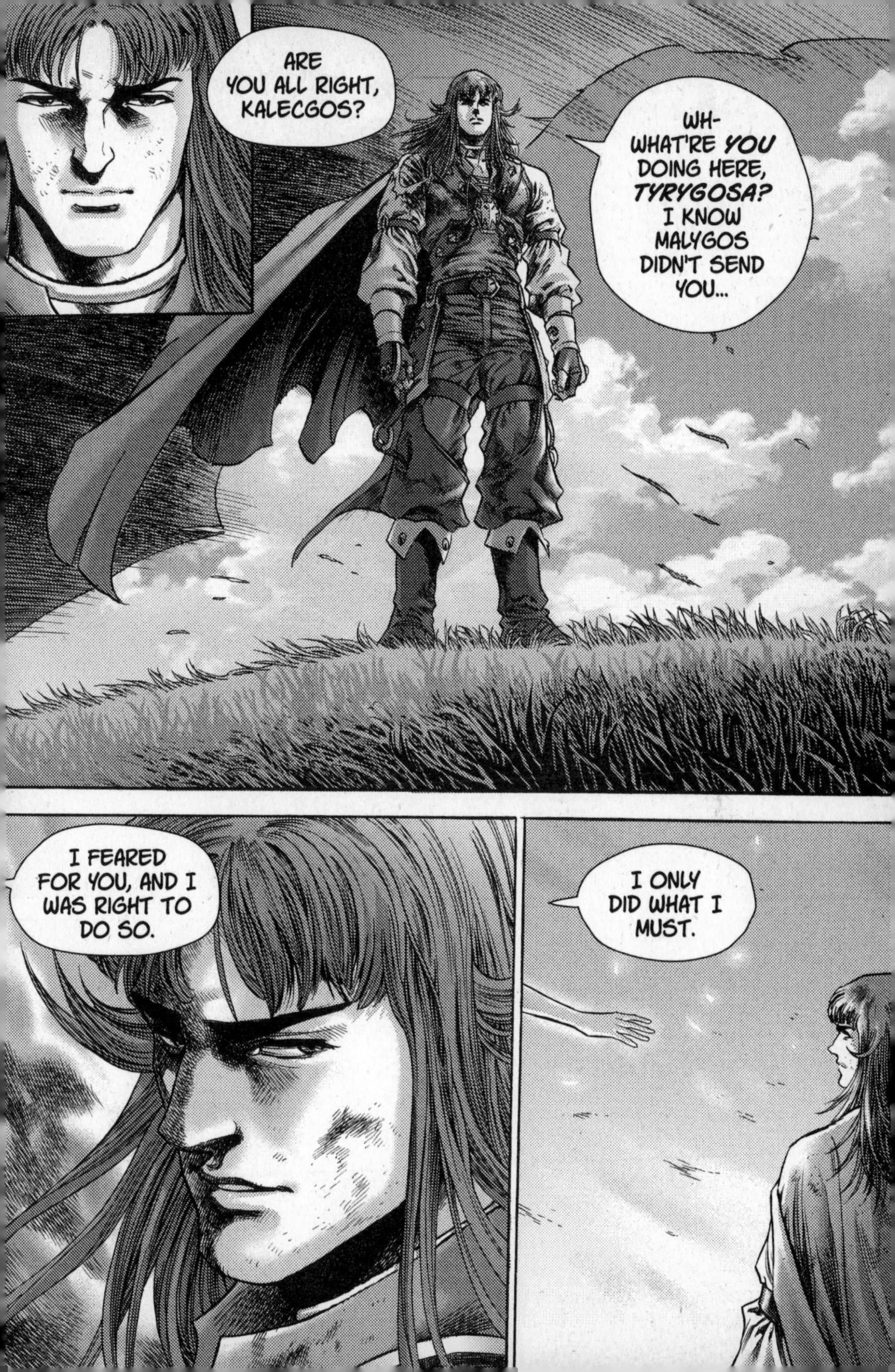
ARE YOU ALL RIGHT, KALECGOS?
WH- WHAT'RE *YOU* DOING HERE, *TYRYGOSA?* I KNOW MALYGOS DIDN'T SEND YOU...
I FEARED FOR YOU, AND I WAS RIGHT TO DO SO.
I ONLY DID WHAT I MUST.

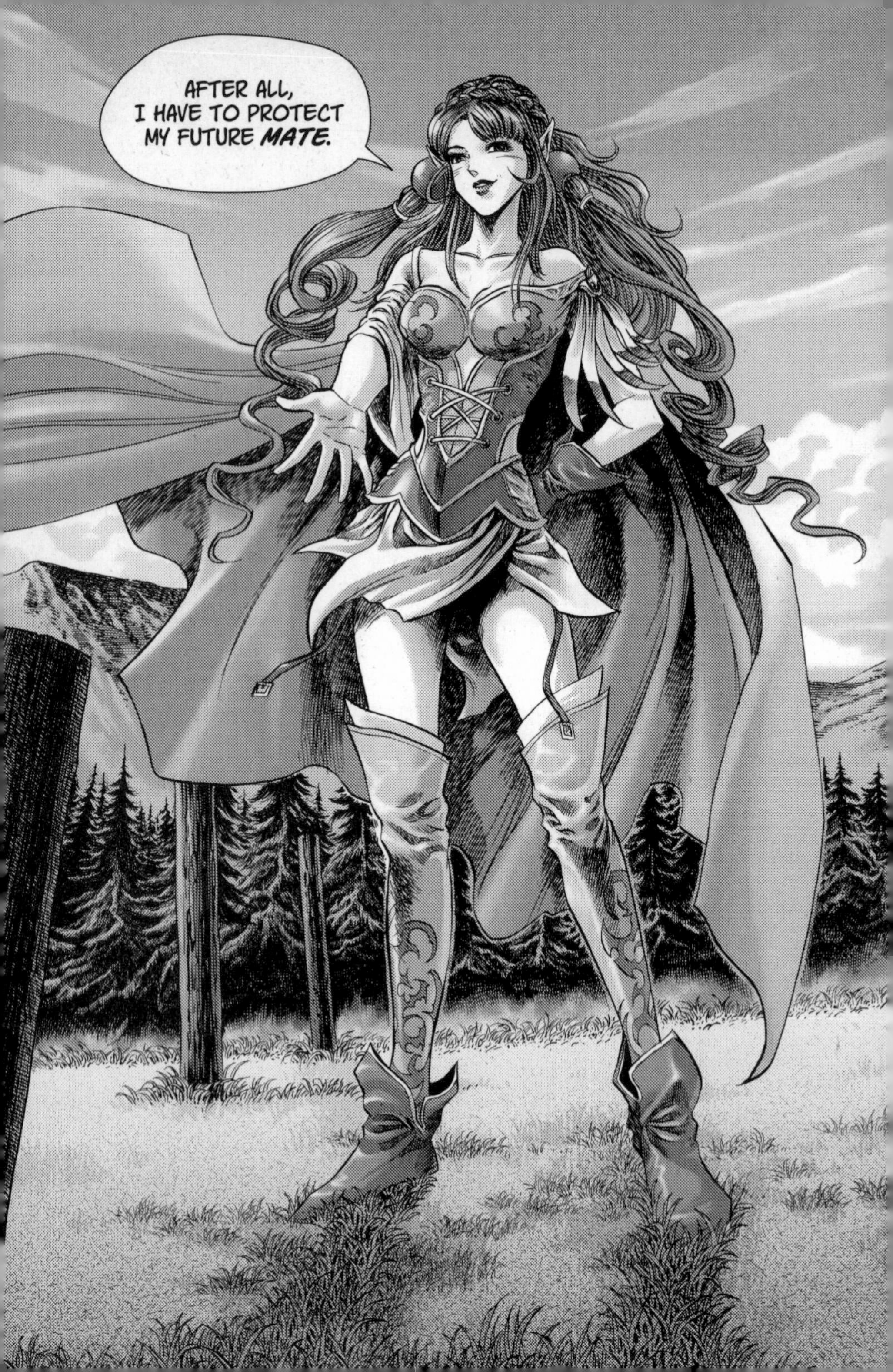
AFTER ALL, I HAVE TO PROTECT MY FUTURE *MATE*.

CHAPTER FIVE TARREN MILL

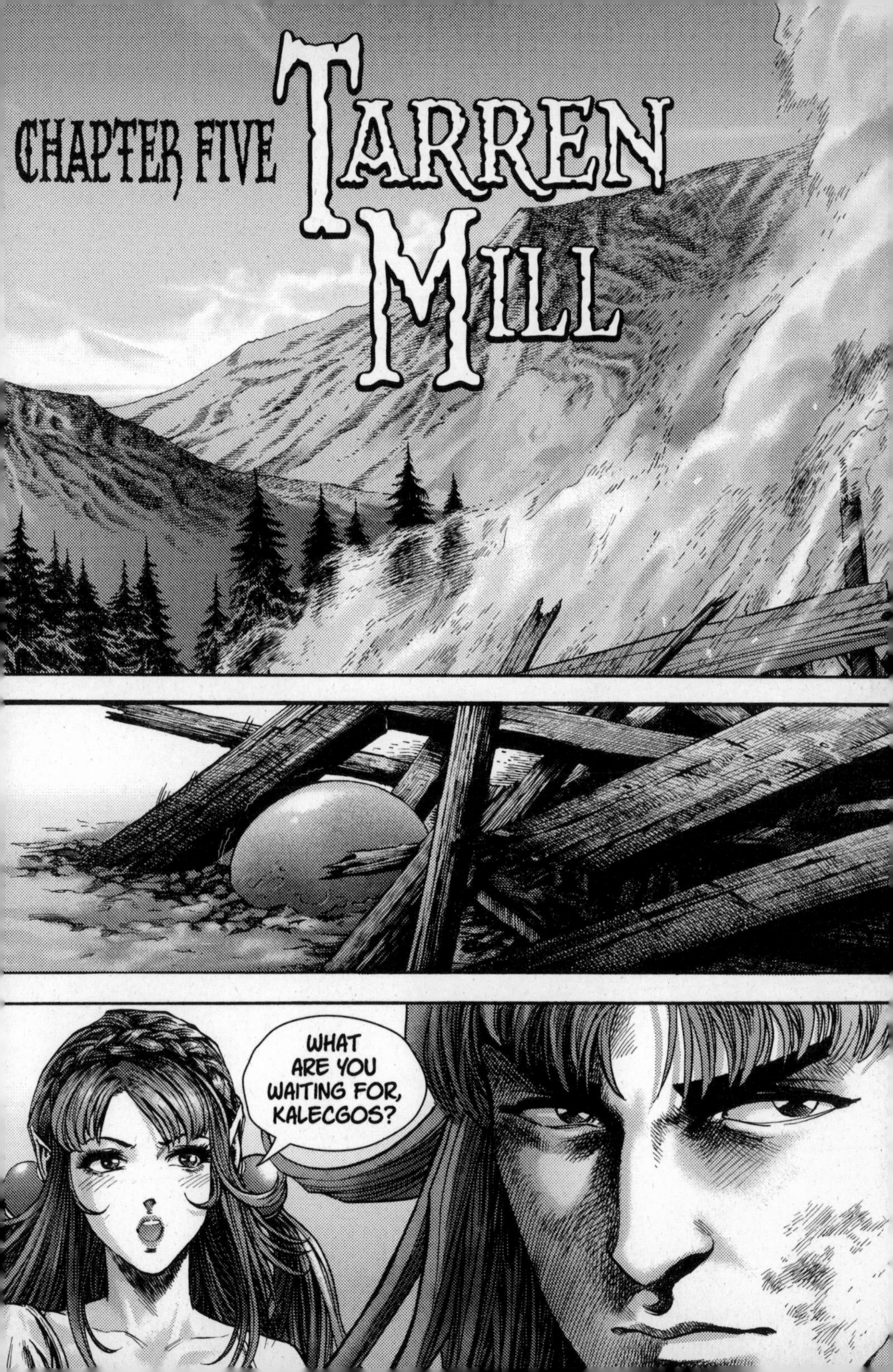
WHAT ARE YOU WAITING FOR, KALECGOS?

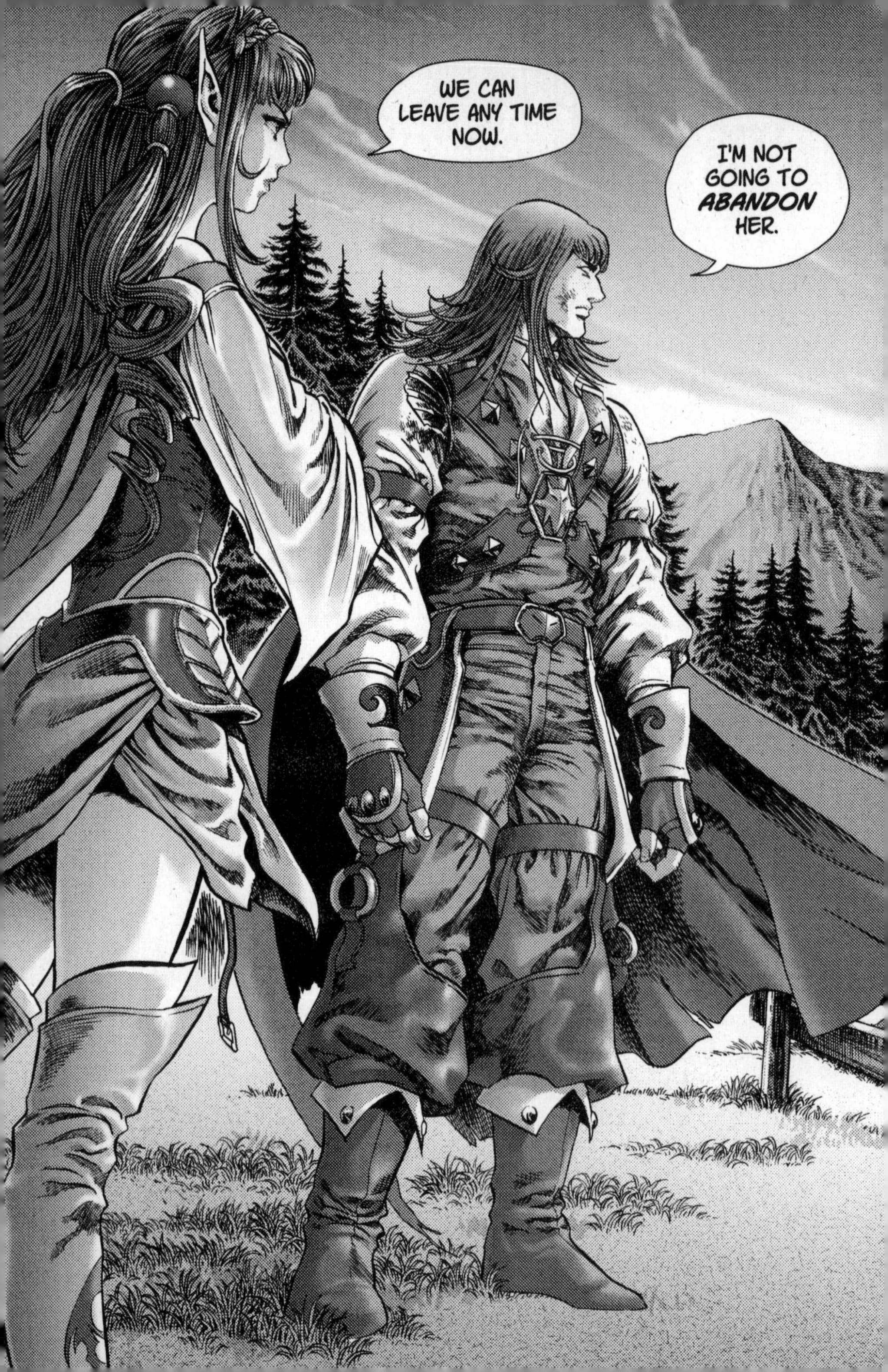
I'M NOT GOING TO ABANDON HER.
WE CAN LEAVE ANY TIME NOW.

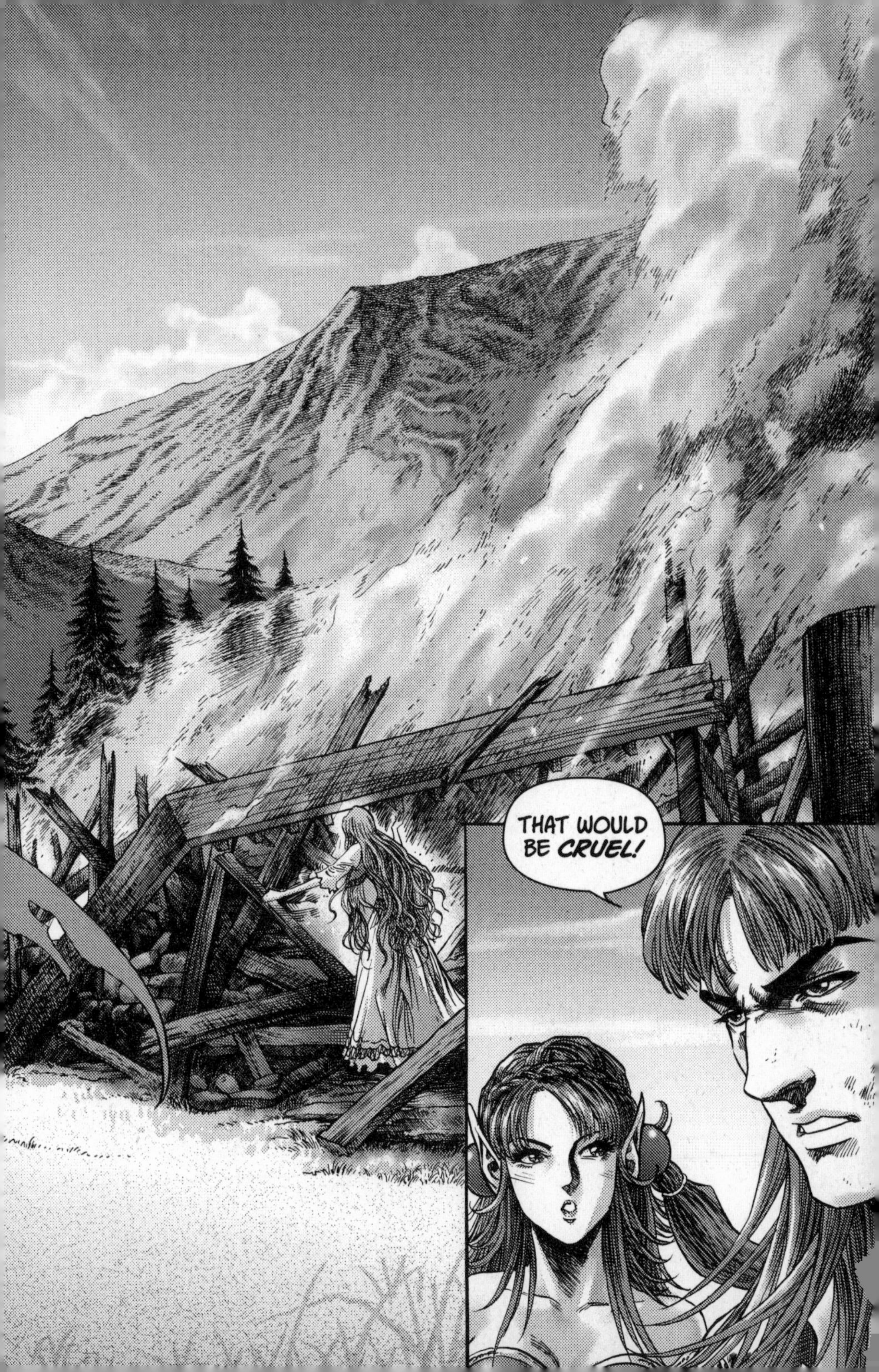
THAT WOULD BE *CRUEL!*

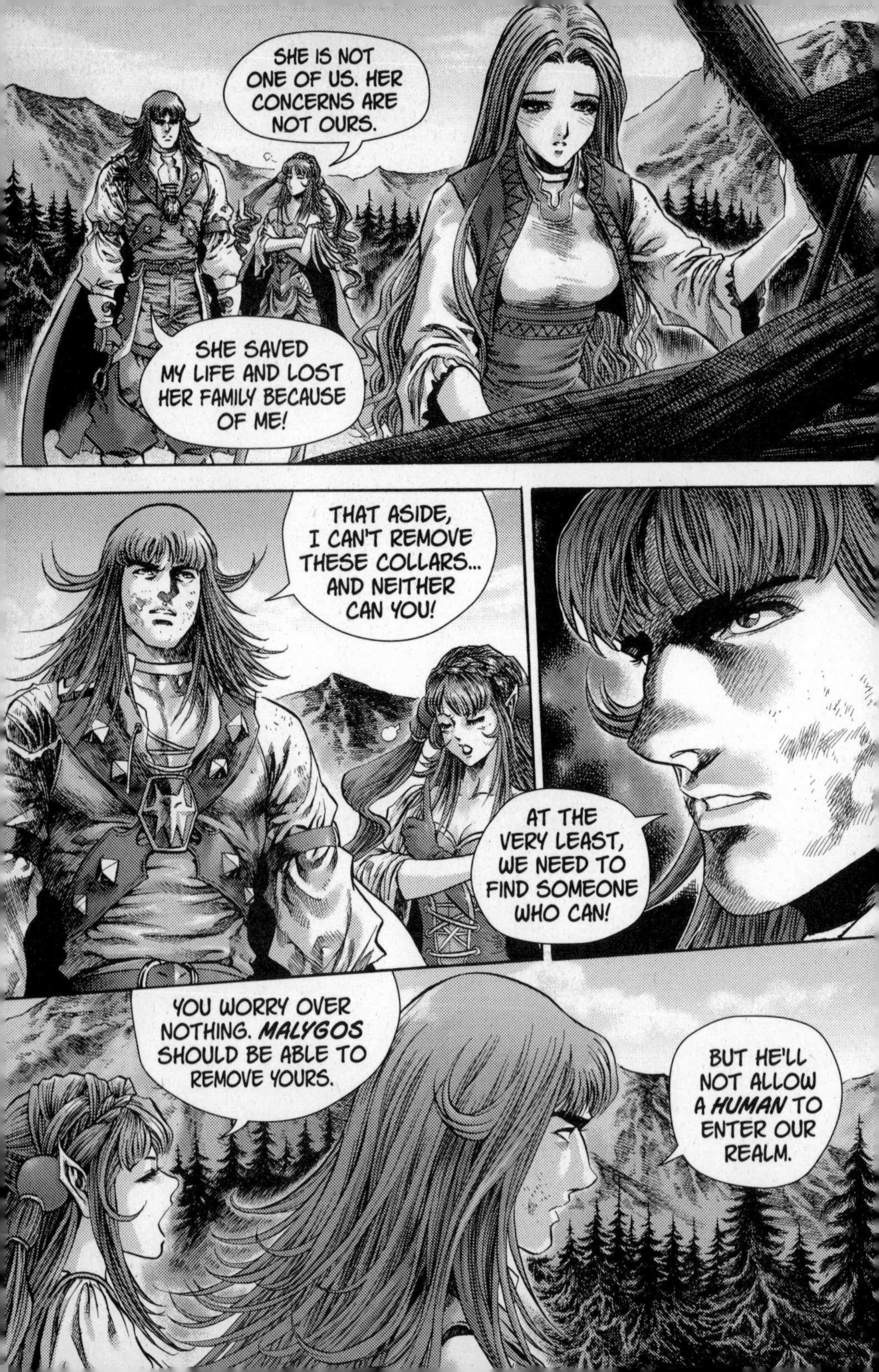
SHE IS NOT ONE OF US. HER CONCERNS ARE NOT OURS.
SHE SAVED MY LIFE AND LOST HER FAMILY BECAUSE OF ME!
THAT ASIDE, I CAN'T REMOVE THESE COLLARS... AND NEITHER CAN YOU!
AT THE VERY LEAST, WE NEED TO FIND SOMEONE WHO CAN!
YOU WORRY OVER NOTHING. *MALYGOS* SHOULD BE ABLE TO REMOVE YOURS.
BUT HE'LL NOT ALLOW A *HUMAN* TO ENTER OUR REALM.

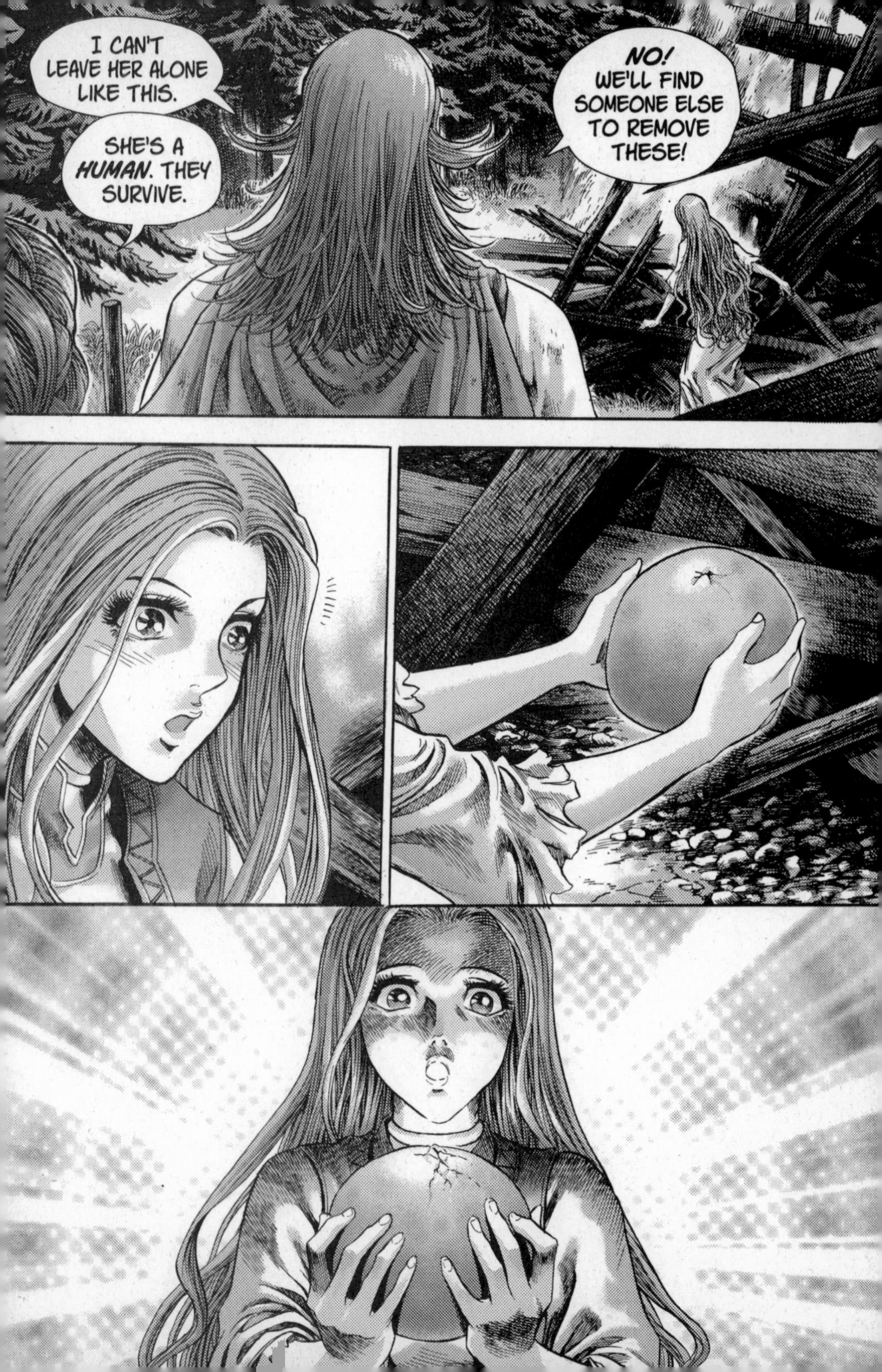
NO! WE'LL FIND SOMEONE ELSE TO REMOVE THESE!
I CAN'T LEAVE HER ALONE LIKE THIS.
SHE'S A *HUMAN*. THEY SURVIVE.

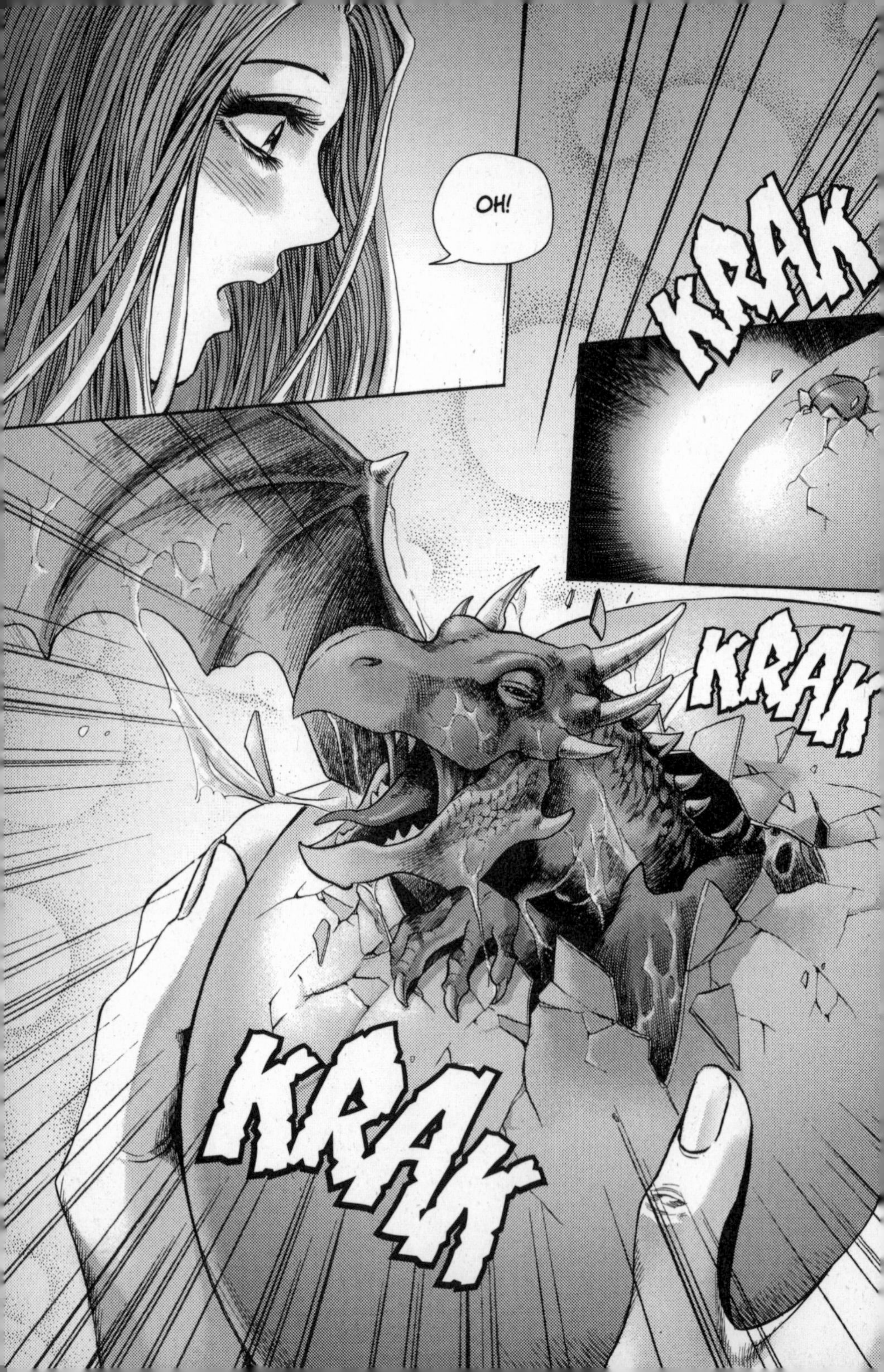
KRAK
OH!
KRAK
KRAK

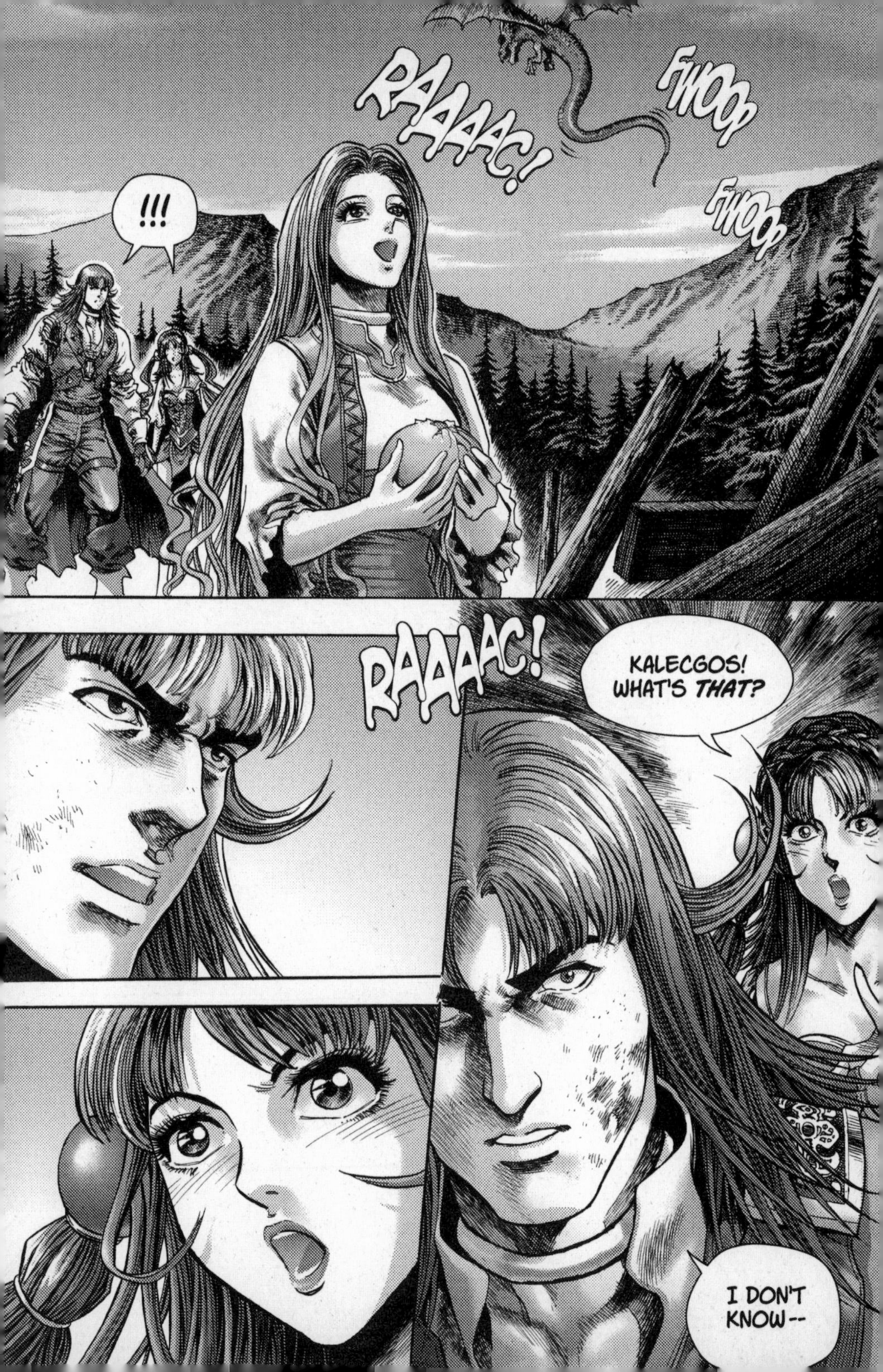
RAAAAC!
FWOOP
FWOOP
!!!
RAAAAC!
KALECGOS! WHAT'S *THAT?*
I DON'T KNOW--

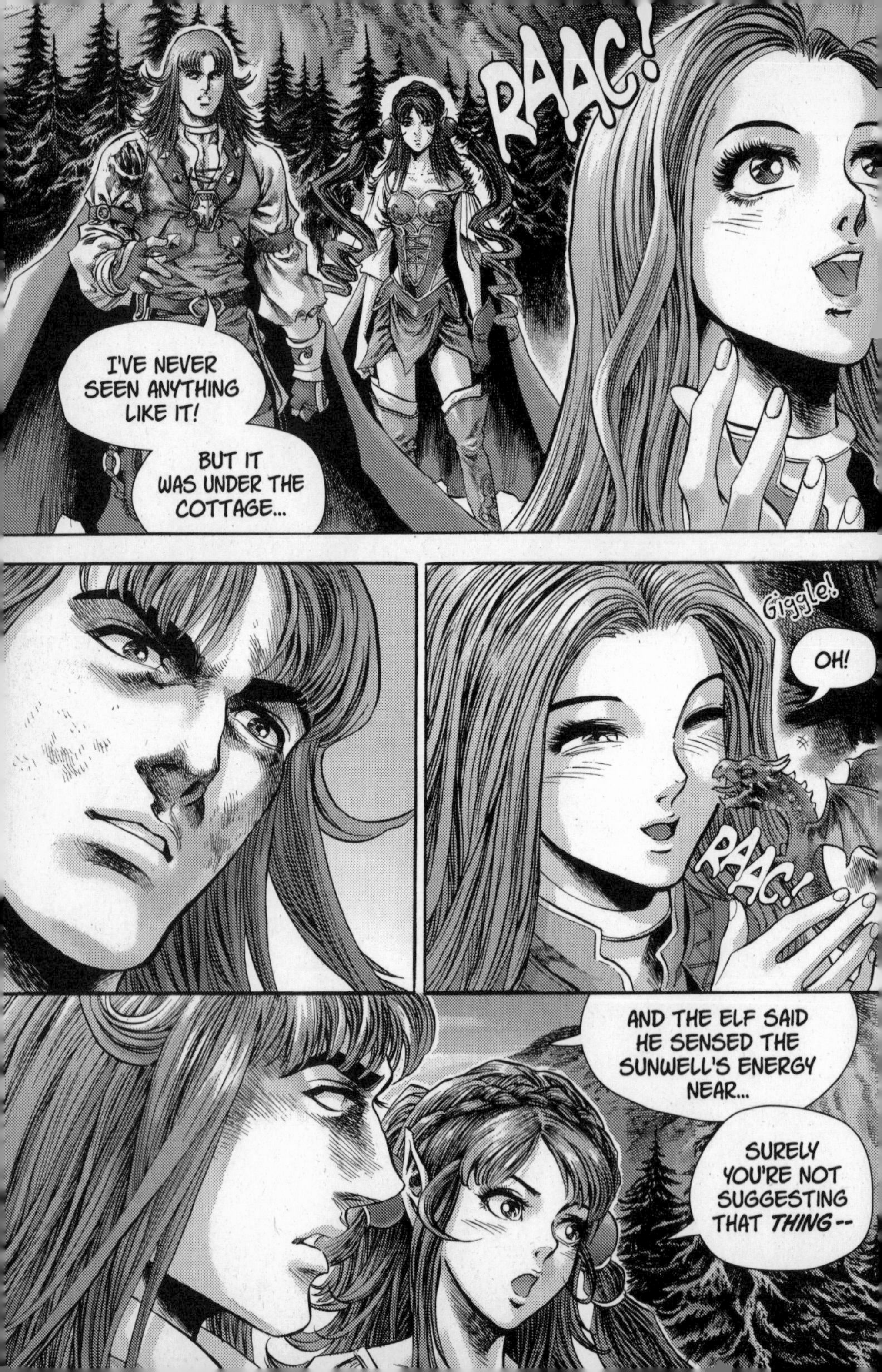
I'VE NEVER SEEN ANYTHING LIKE IT!
BUT IT WAS UNDER THE COTTAGE...
RAAC!
Giggle!
OH!
RAAC!
AND THE ELF SAID HE SENSED THE SUNWELL'S ENERGY NEAR...
SURELY YOU'RE NOT SUGGESTING THAT *THING*--

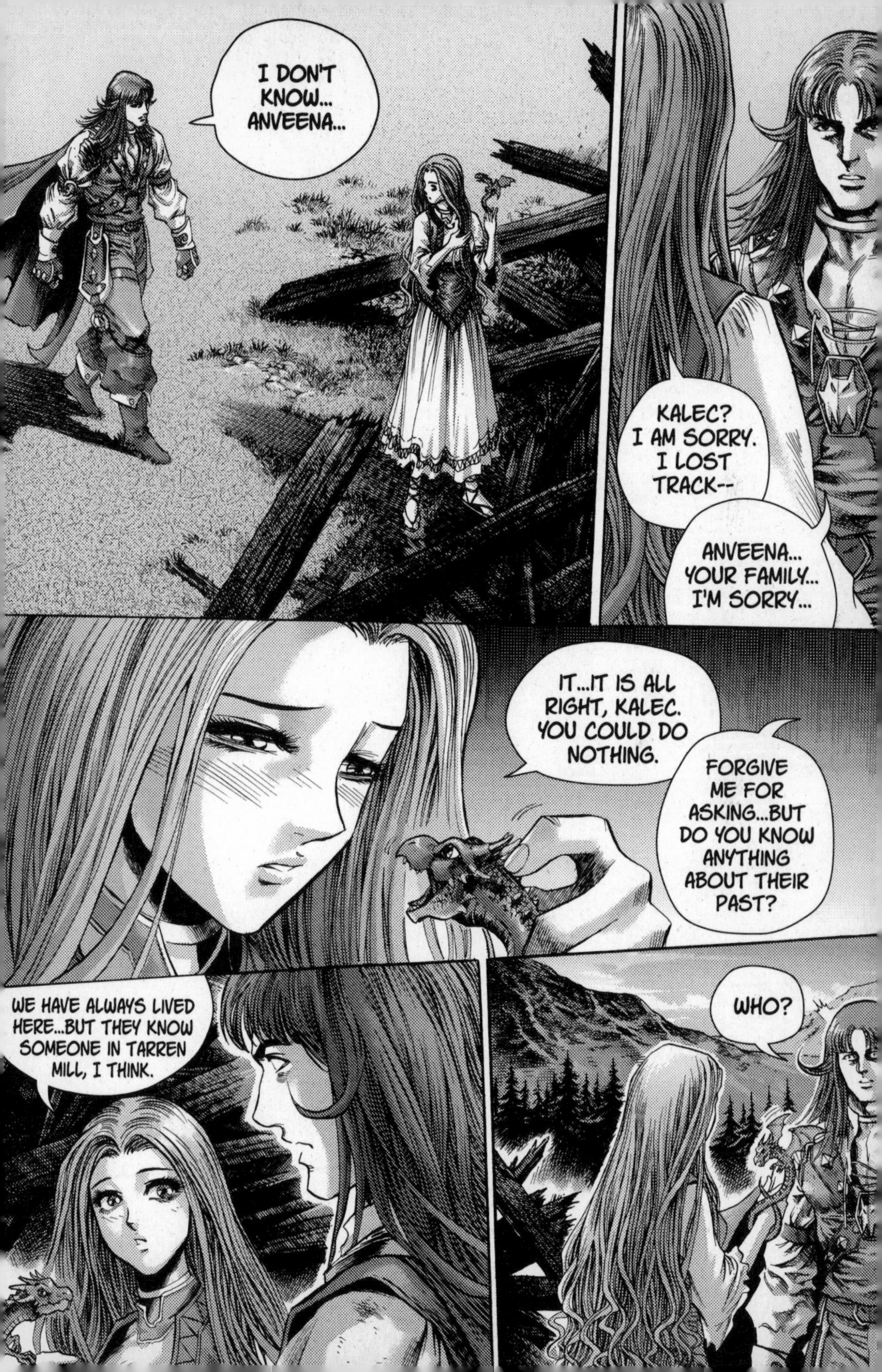
I DON'T KNOW... ANVEENA...
KALEC? I AM SORRY. I LOST TRACK--
ANVEENA... YOUR FAMILY... I'M SORRY...
IT...IT IS ALL RIGHT, KALEC. YOU COULD DO NOTHING.
FORGIVE ME FOR ASKING...BUT DO YOU KNOW ANYTHING ABOUT THEIR PAST?
WE HAVE ALWAYS LIVED HERE...BUT THEY KNOW SOMEONE IN TARREN MILL, I THINK.
WHO?

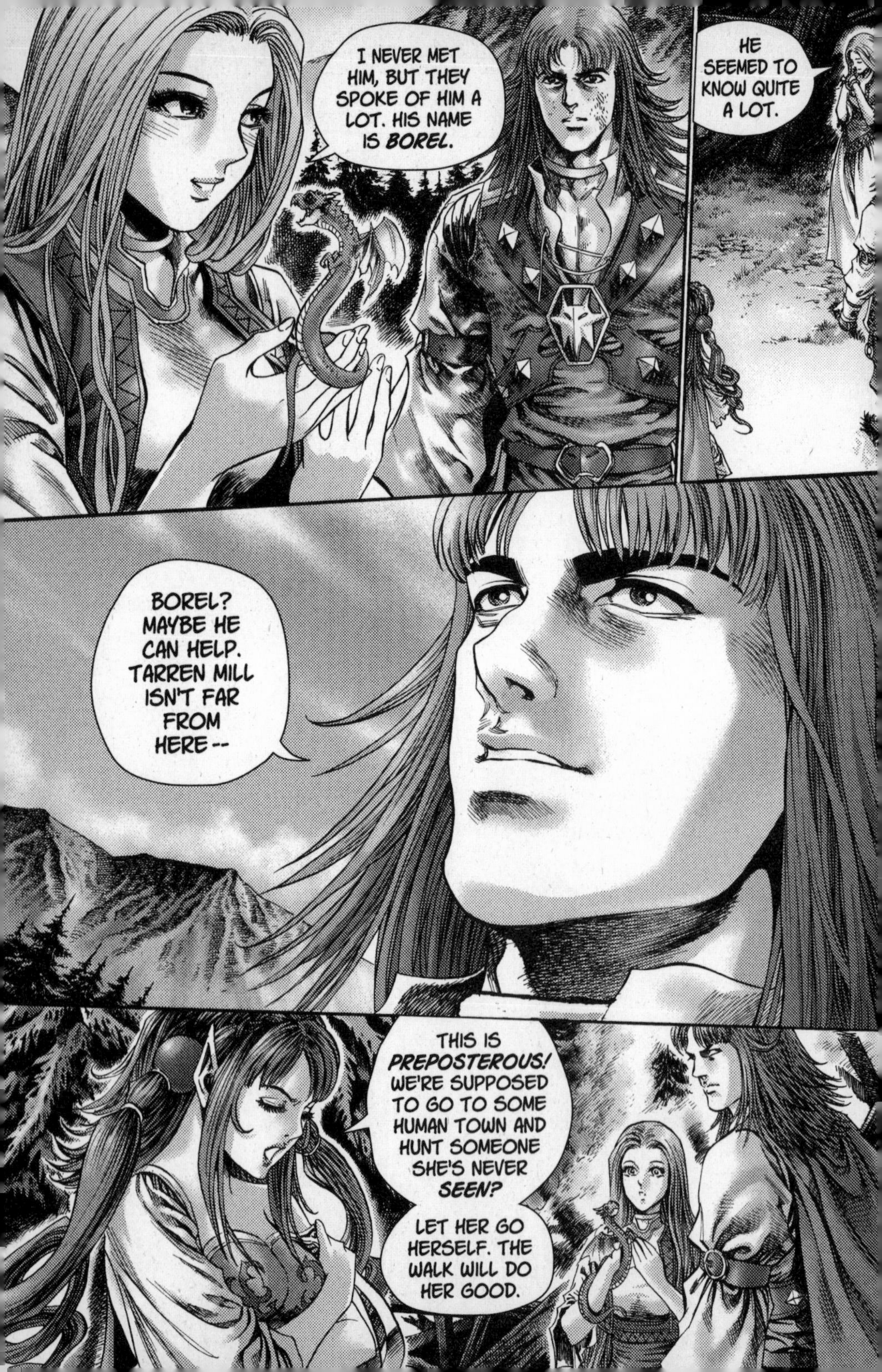
I NEVER MET HIM, BUT THEY SPOKE OF HIM A LOT. HIS NAME IS *BOREL.*
HE SEEMED TO KNOW QUITE A LOT.
BOREL? MAYBE HE CAN HELP. TARREN MILL ISN'T FAR FROM HERE--
THIS IS *PREPOSTEROUS!* WE'RE SUPPOSED TO GO TO SOME HUMAN TOWN AND HUNT SOMEONE SHE'S NEVER *SEEN?*
LET HER GO HERSELF. THE WALK WILL DO HER GOOD.

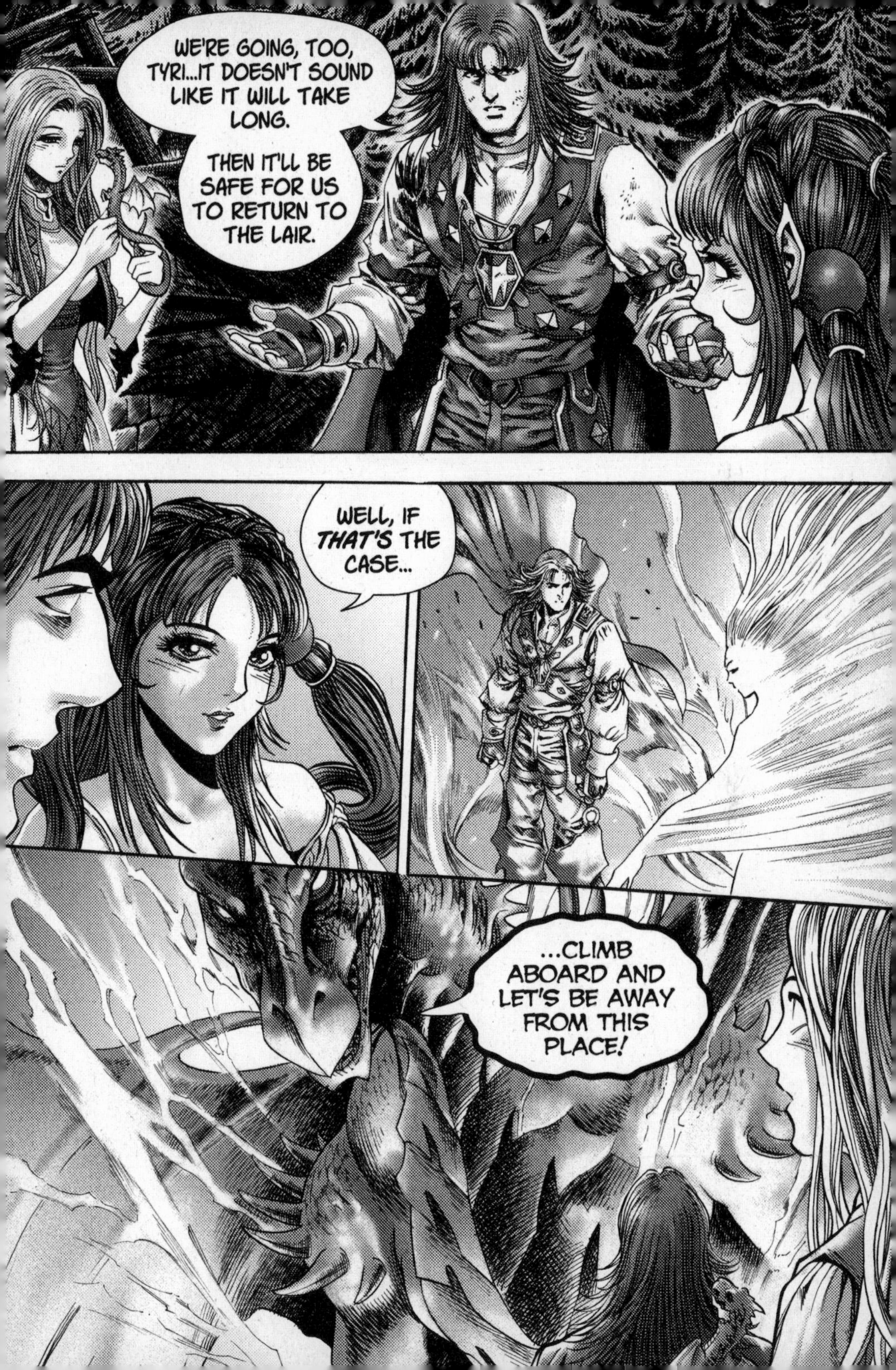
WE'RE GOING, TOO, TYRI...IT DOESN'T SOUND LIKE IT WILL TAKE LONG.
THEN IT'LL BE SAFE FOR US TO RETURN TO THE LAIR.
WELL, IF *THAT'S* THE CASE...
...CLIMB ABOARD AND LET'S BE AWAY FROM THIS PLACE!

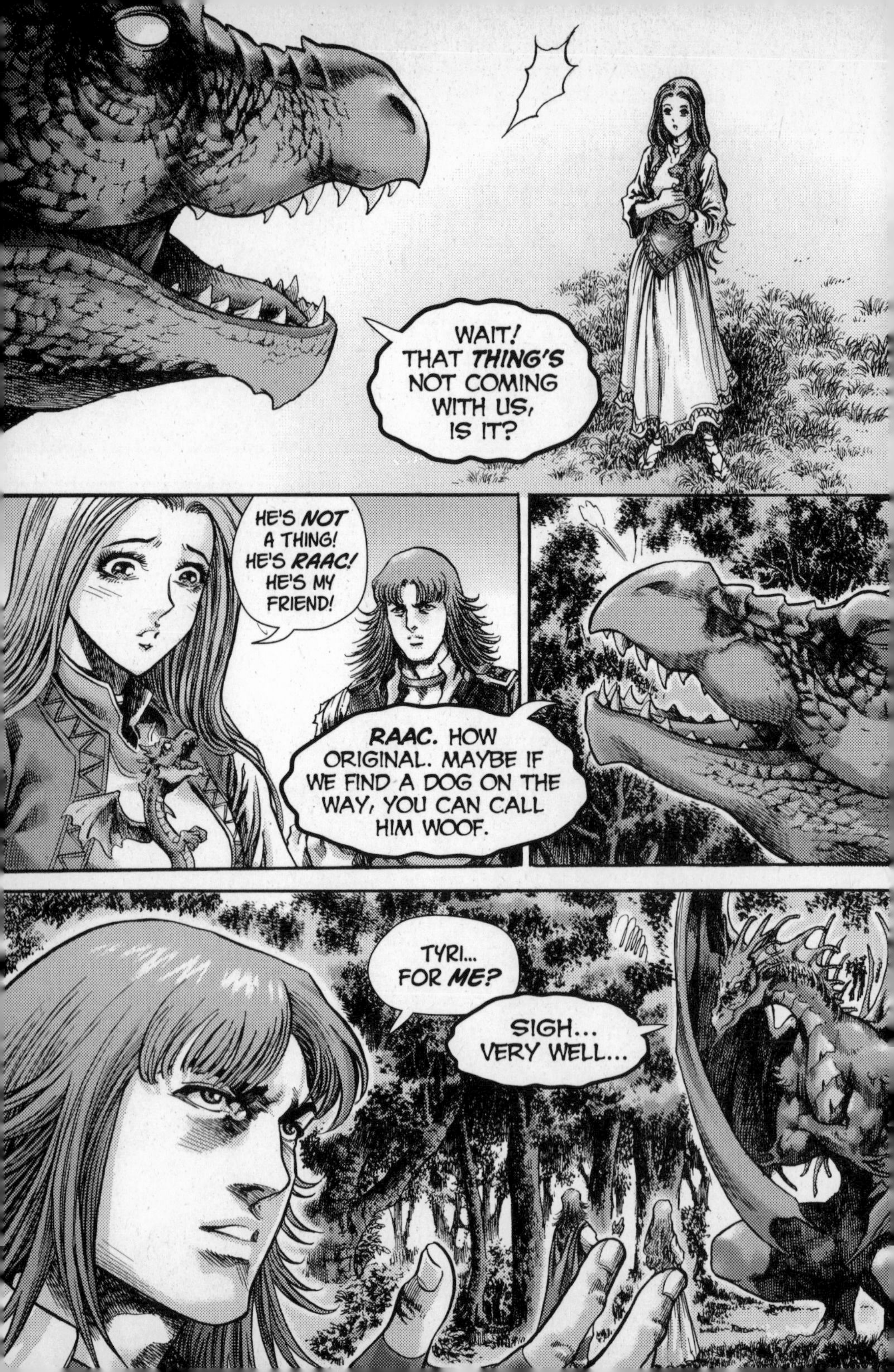
WAIT! THAT *THING'S* NOT COMING WITH US, IS IT?
HE'S *NOT* A THING! HE'S *RAAC!* HE'S MY FRIEND!
RAAC. HOW ORIGINAL. MAYBE IF WE FIND A DOG ON THE WAY, YOU CAN CALL HIM WOOF.
TYRI... FOR *ME?*
SIGH... VERY WELL...

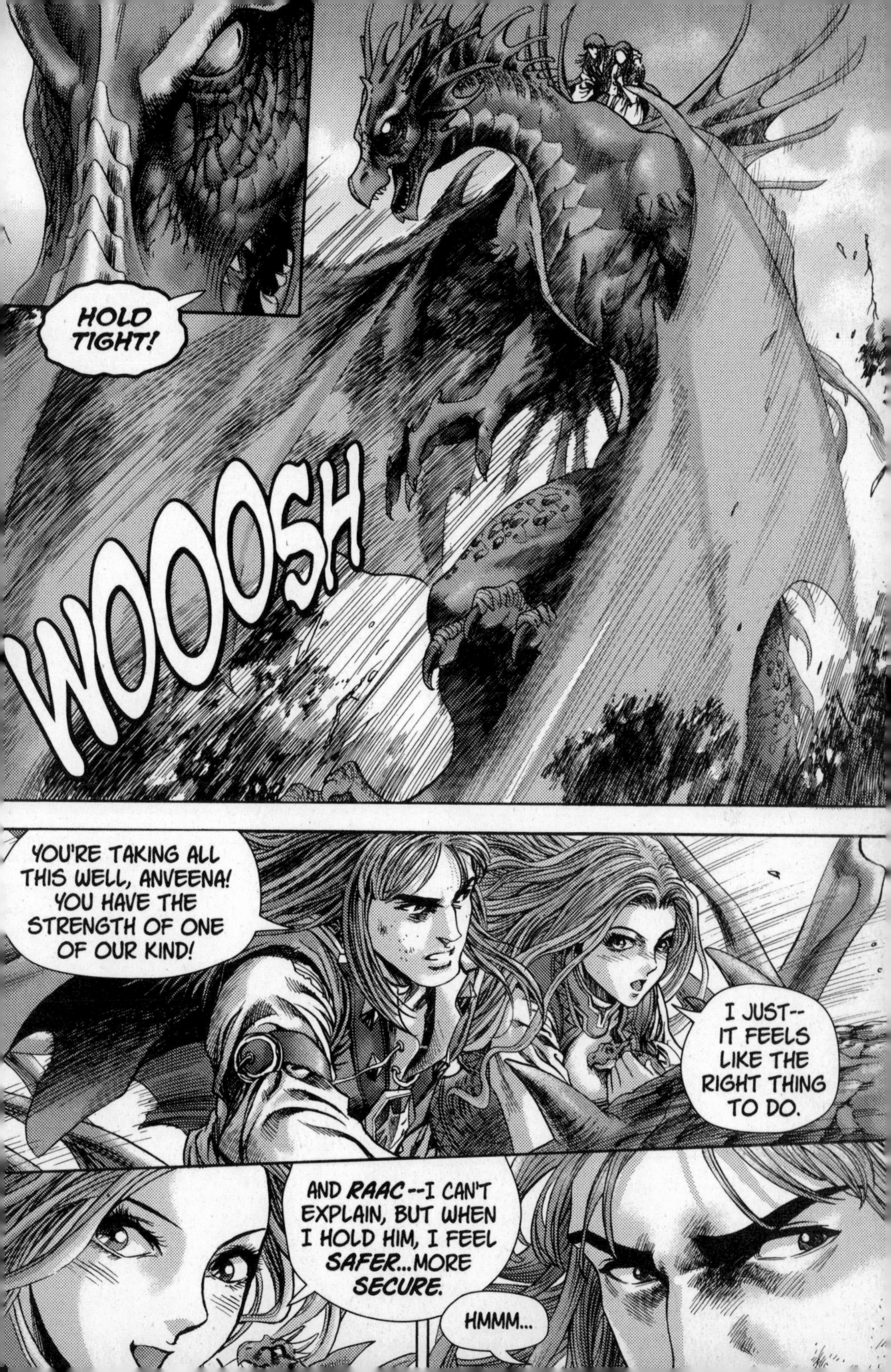
HOLD TIGHT!
WOOOSH
YOU'RE TAKING ALL THIS WELL, ANVEENA! YOU HAVE THE STRENGTH OF ONE OF OUR KIND!
I JUST-- IT FEELS LIKE THE RIGHT THING TO DO.
AND RAAC--I CAN'T EXPLAIN, BUT WHEN I HOLD HIM, I FEEL SAFER...MORE SECURE.
HMMM...

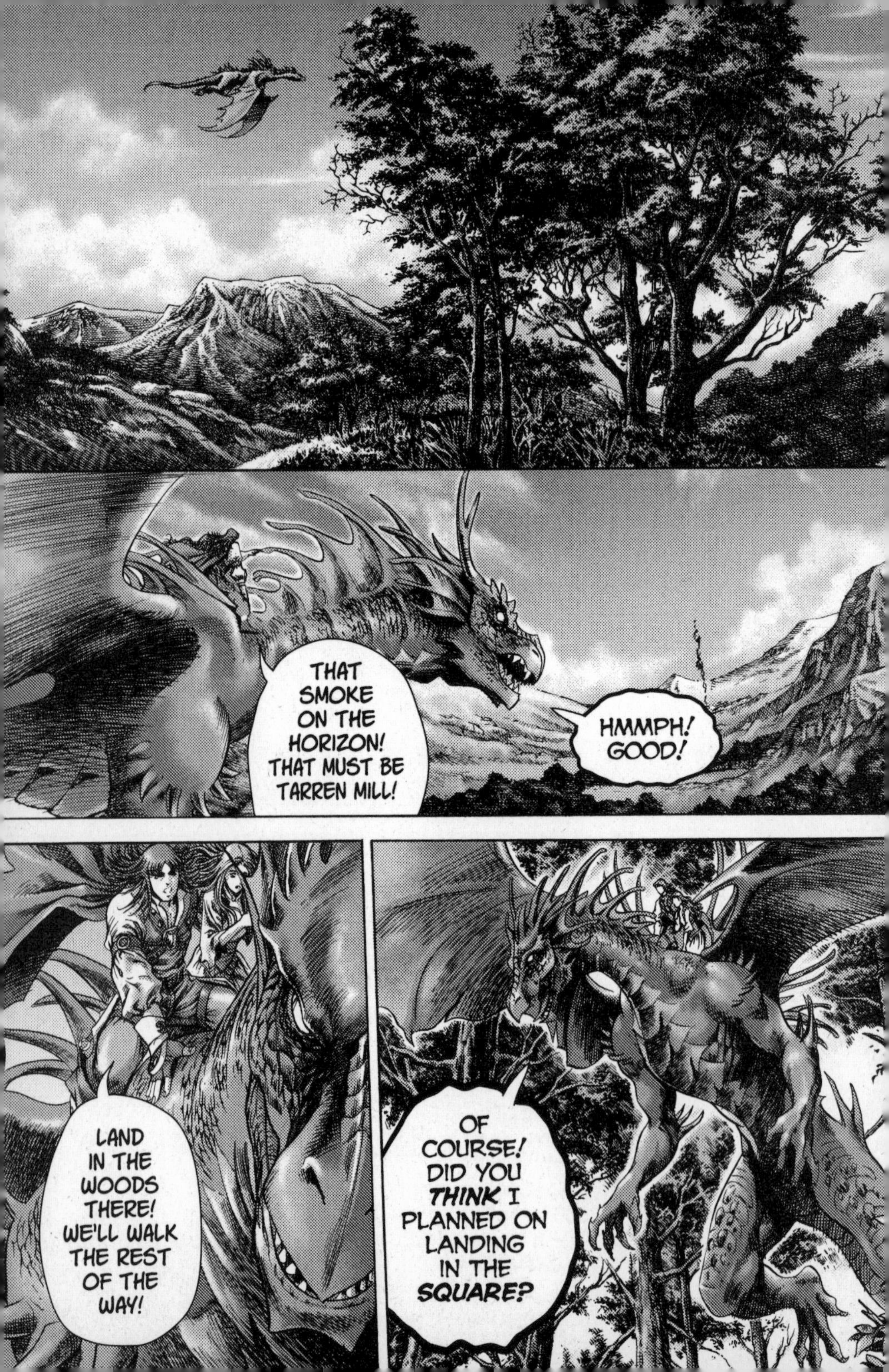
THAT SMOKE ON THE HORIZON! THAT MUST BE TARREN MILL!
HMMPH! GOOD!
LAND IN THE WOODS THERE! WE'LL WALK THE REST OF THE WAY!
OF COURSE! DID YOU *THINK* I PLANNED ON LANDING IN THE *SQUARE?*

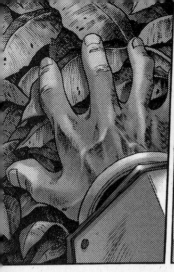

AH!

I HAVE NEVER SEEN SO MANY PEOPLE! IT IS *AMAZING!*

THIS BACKWATER SETTLEMENT? AMAZING?

CLATTER

CLANK

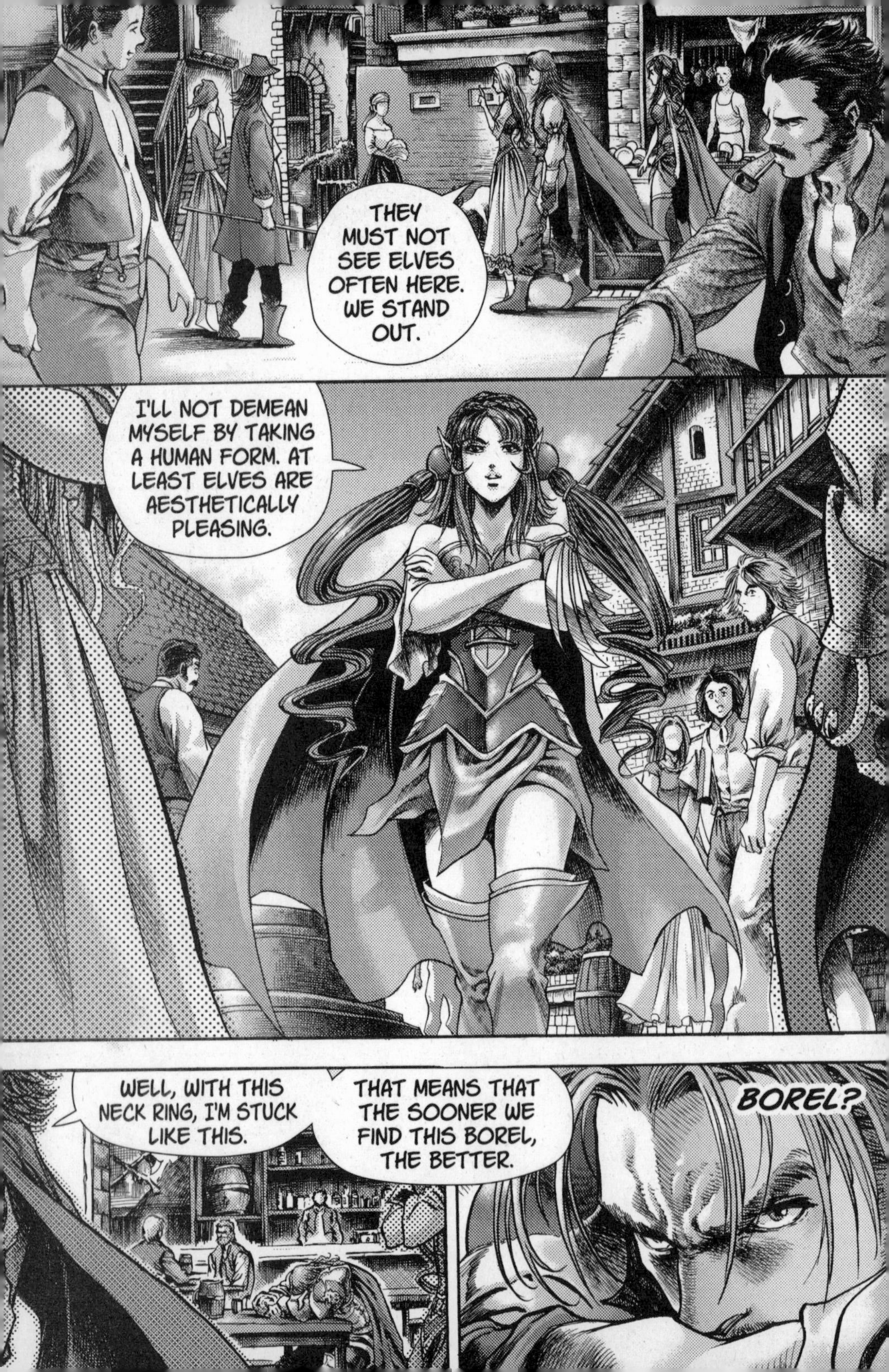
THEY MUST NOT SEE ELVES OFTEN HERE. WE STAND OUT.
I'LL NOT DEMEAN MYSELF BY TAKING A HUMAN FORM. AT LEAST ELVES ARE AESTHETICALLY PLEASING.
WELL, WITH THIS NECK RING, I'M STUCK LIKE THIS.
THAT MEANS THAT THE SOONER WE FIND THIS BOREL, THE BETTER.
BOREL?

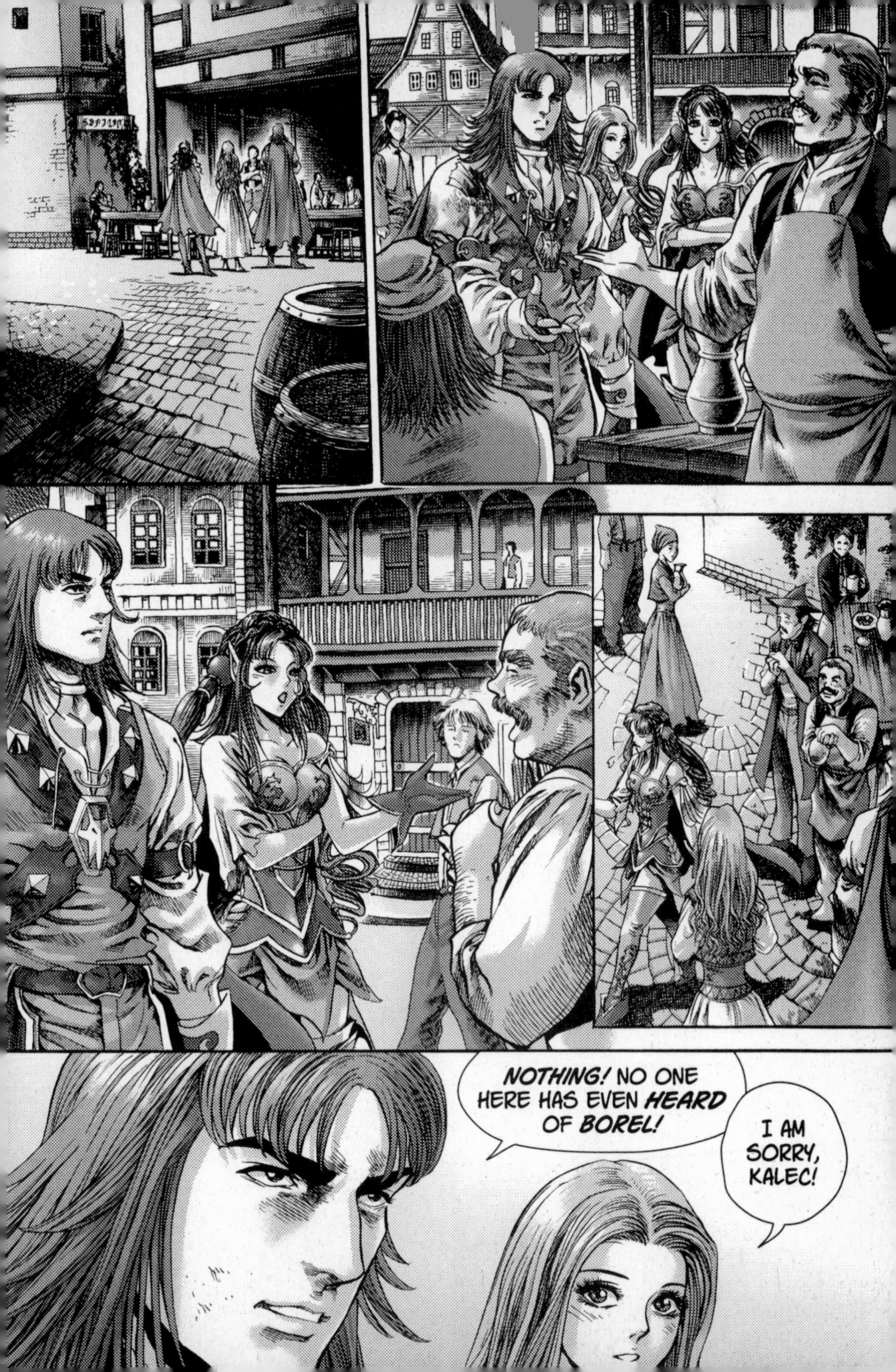
NOTHING! NO ONE HERE HAS EVEN HEARD OF BOREL!
I AM SORRY, KALEC!

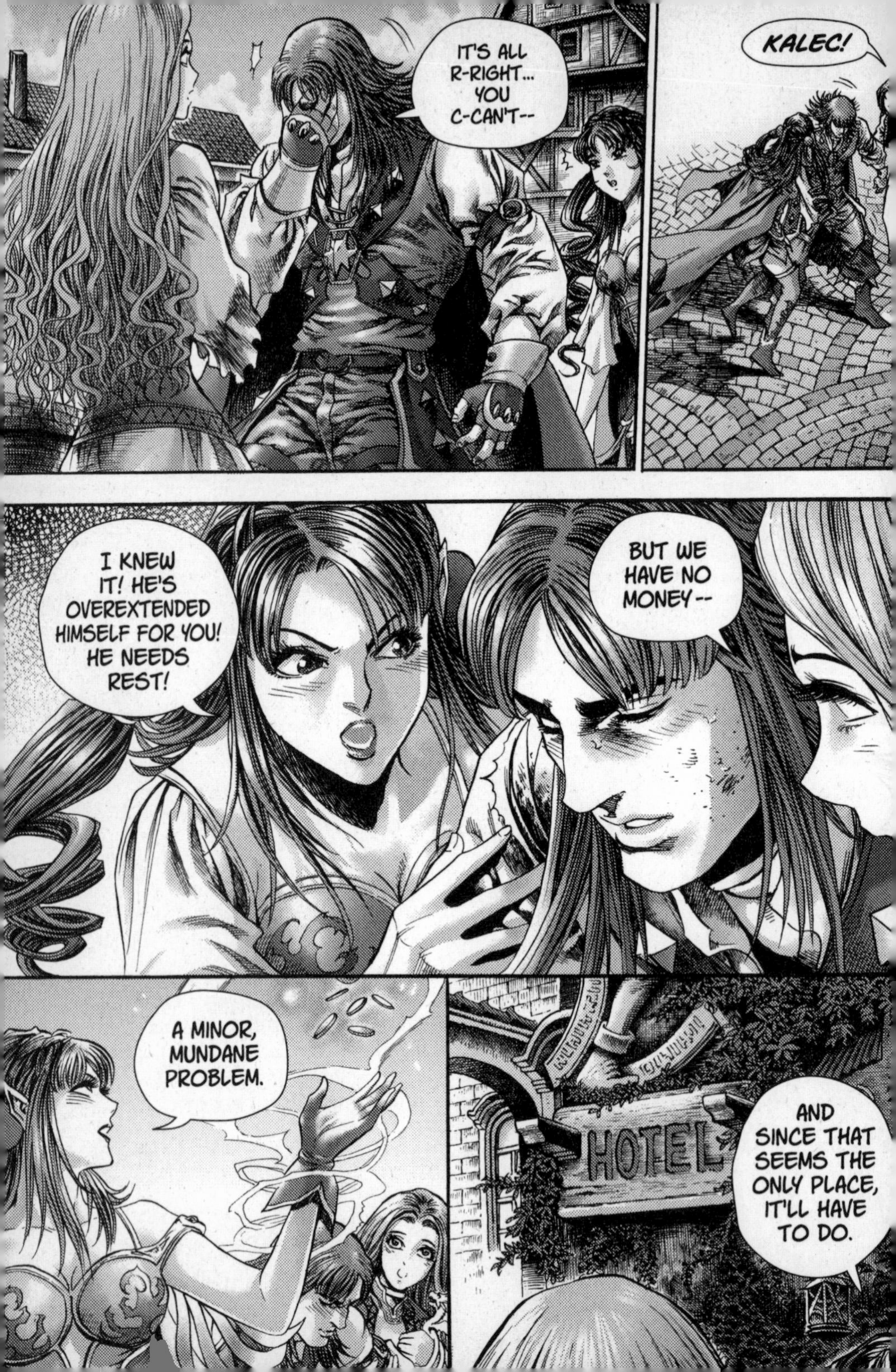
IT'S ALL R-RIGHT... YOU C-CAN'T--
KALEC!
I KNEW IT! HE'S OVEREXTENDED HIMSELF FOR YOU! HE NEEDS REST!
BUT WE HAVE NO MONEY--
A MINOR, MUNDANE PROBLEM.
HOTEL
AND SINCE THAT SEEMS THE ONLY PLACE, IT'LL HAVE TO DO.

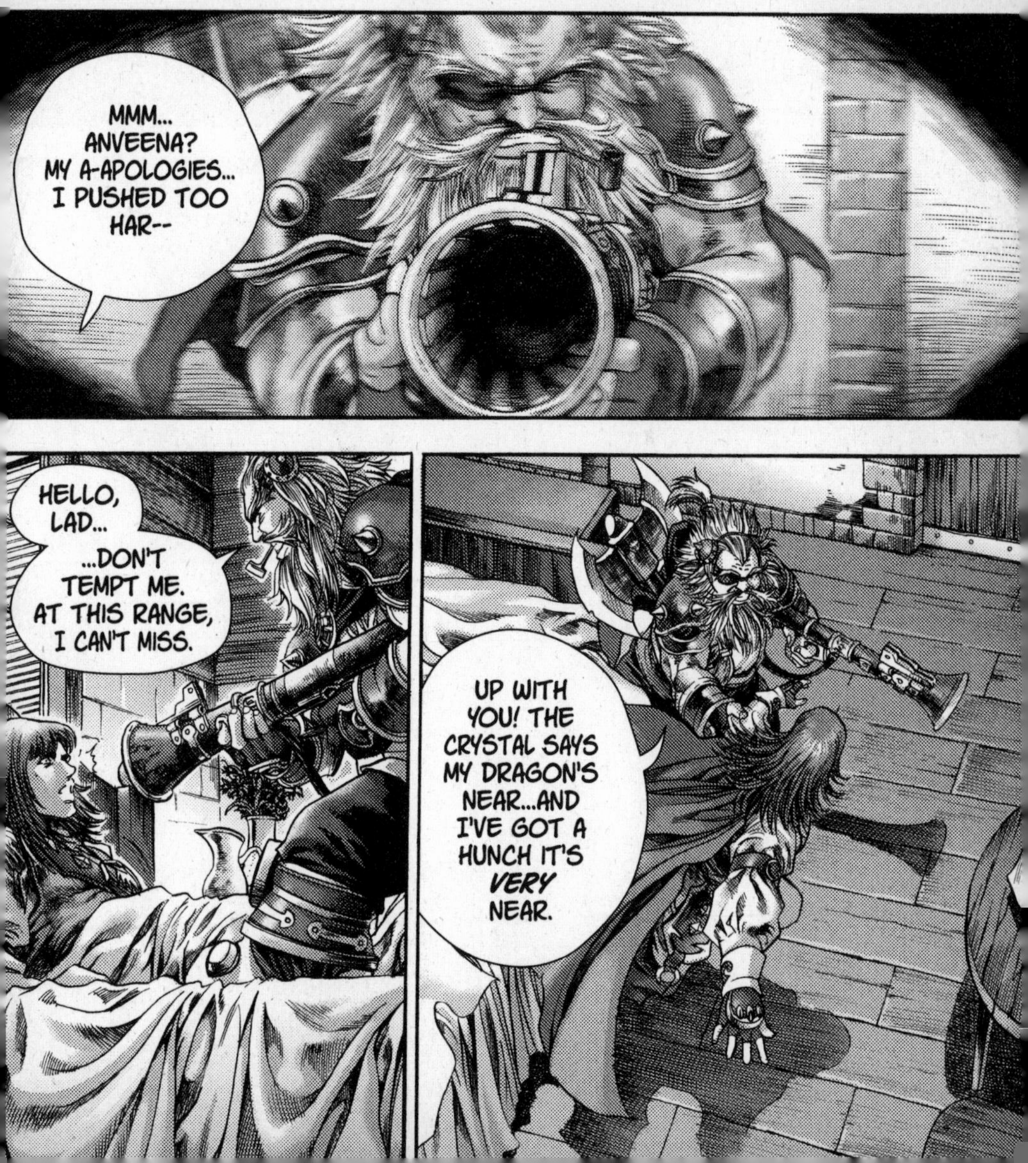
MMM... ANVEENA? MY A-APOLOGIES... I PUSHED TOO HAR--
UP WITH YOU! THE CRYSTAL SAYS MY DRAGON'S NEAR...AND I'VE GOT A HUNCH IT'S *VERY* NEAR.
HELLO, LAD...
...DON'T TEMPT ME. AT THIS RANGE, I CAN'T MISS.

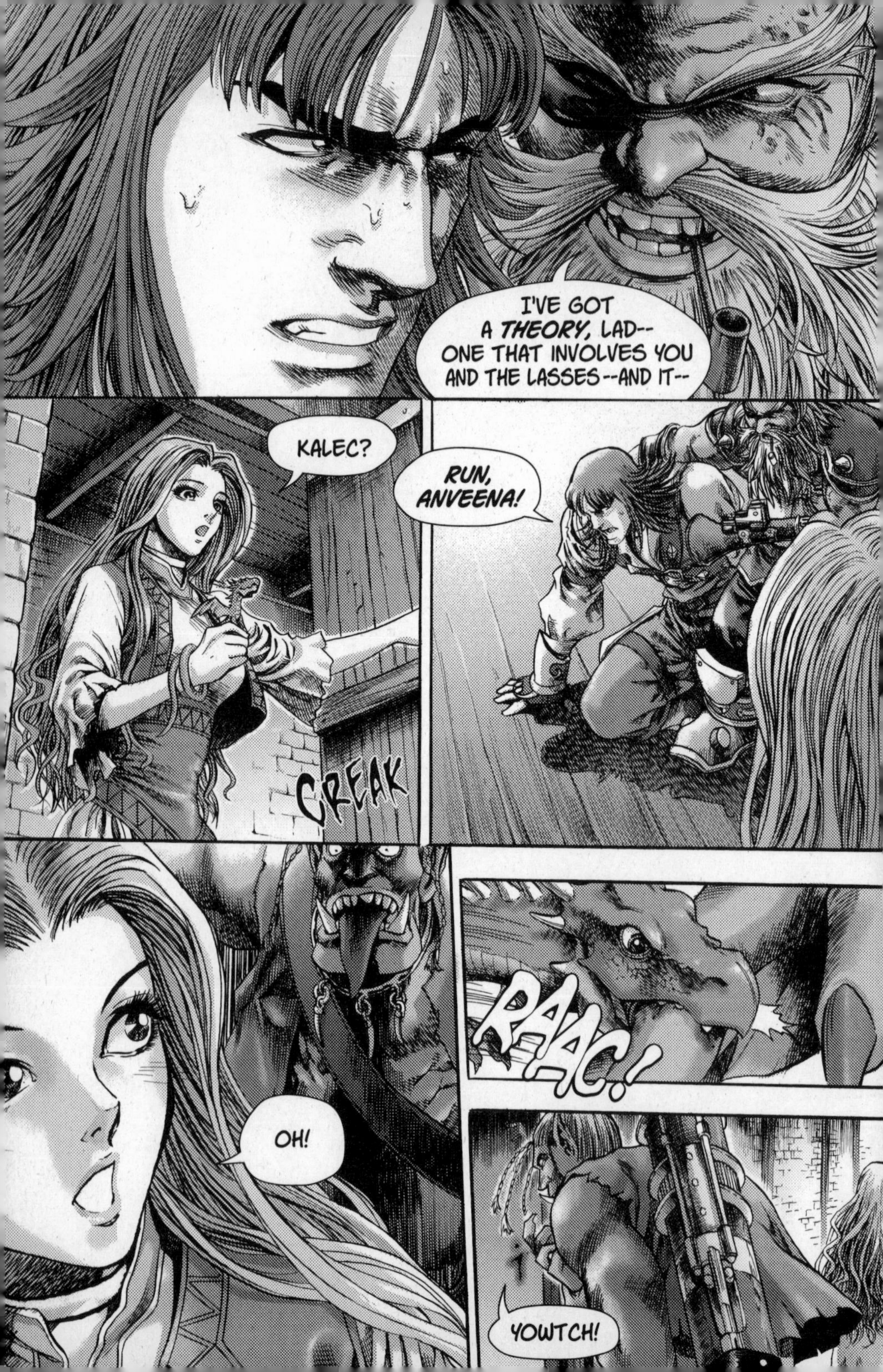
I'VE GOT A *THEORY,* LAD-- ONE THAT INVOLVES YOU AND THE LASSES --AND IT--
KALEC?
CREAK
RUN, ANVEENA!
OH!
RAAAC!
YOWTCH!

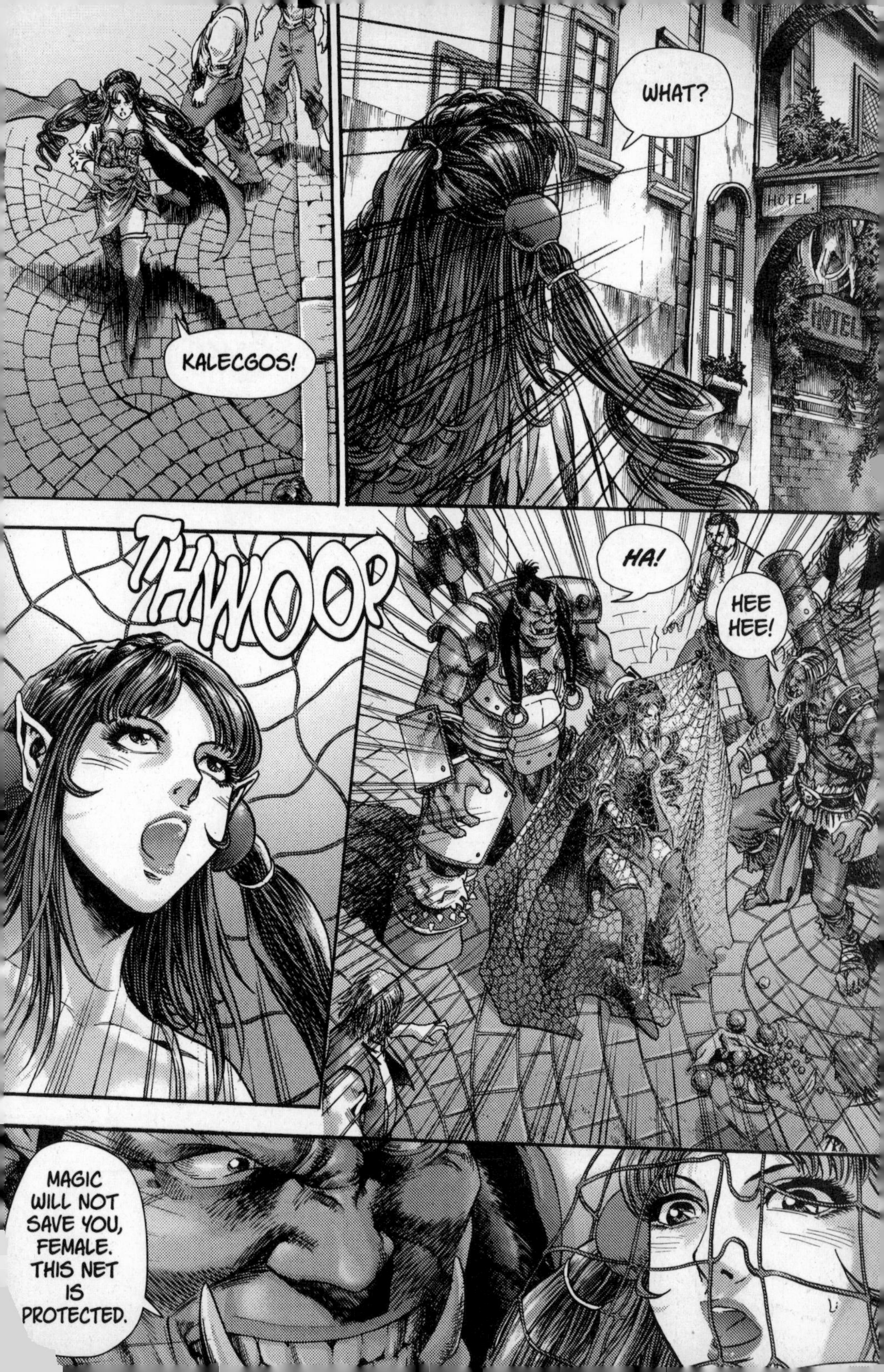
KALECGOS!
WHAT?
HOTEL
THWOOP
HA!
HEE HEE!
MAGIC WILL NOT SAVE YOU, FEMALE. THIS NET IS PROTECTED.

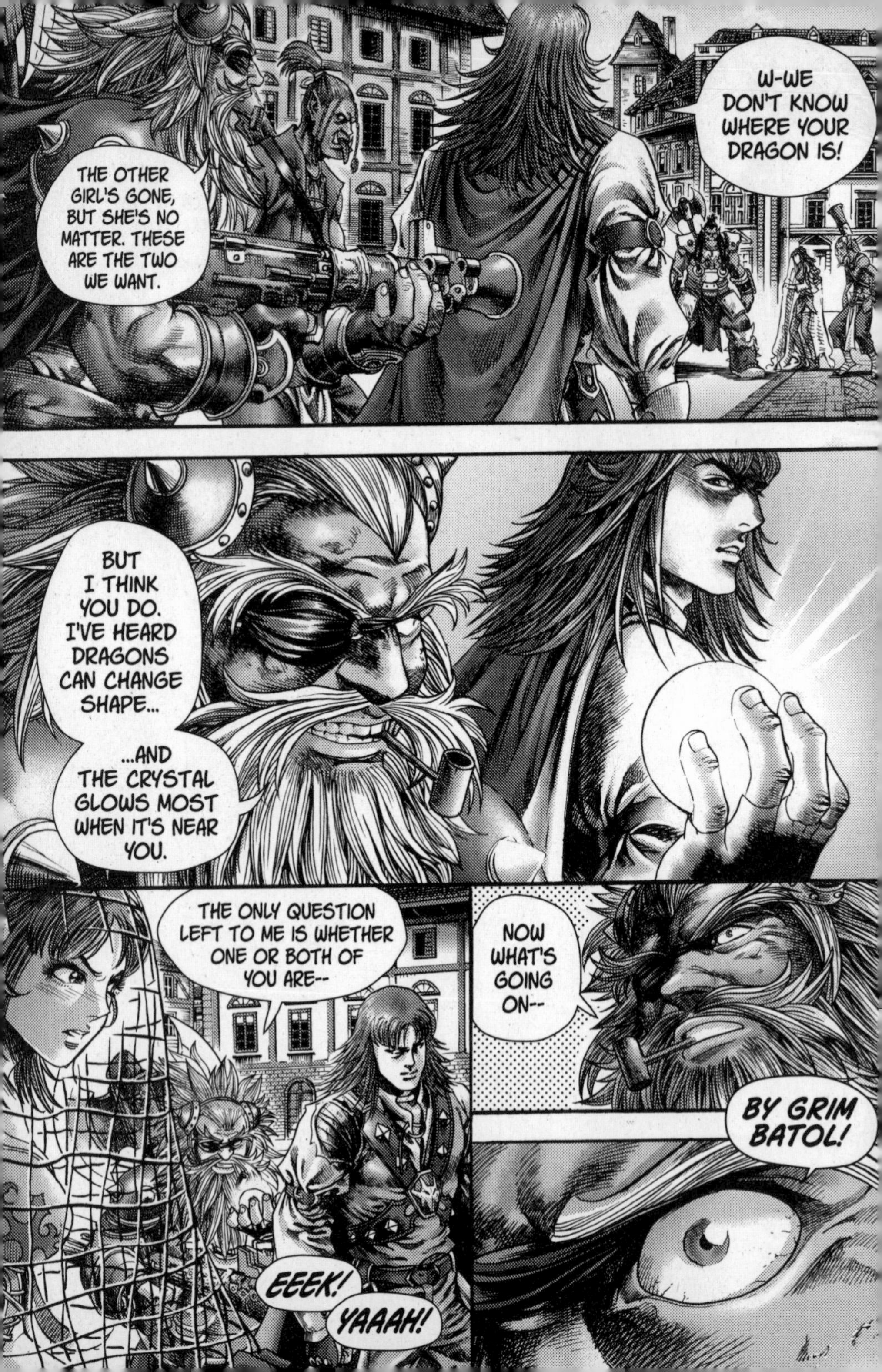
THE OTHER GIRL'S GONE, BUT SHE'S NO MATTER. THESE ARE THE TWO WE WANT.
W-WE DON'T KNOW WHERE YOUR DRAGON IS!
BUT I THINK YOU DO. I'VE HEARD DRAGONS CAN CHANGE SHAPE...
...AND THE CRYSTAL GLOWS MOST WHEN IT'S NEAR YOU.
THE ONLY QUESTION LEFT TO ME IS WHETHER ONE OR BOTH OF YOU ARE--
EEEK!
YAAAH!
NOW WHAT'S GOING ON--
BY GRIM BATOL!

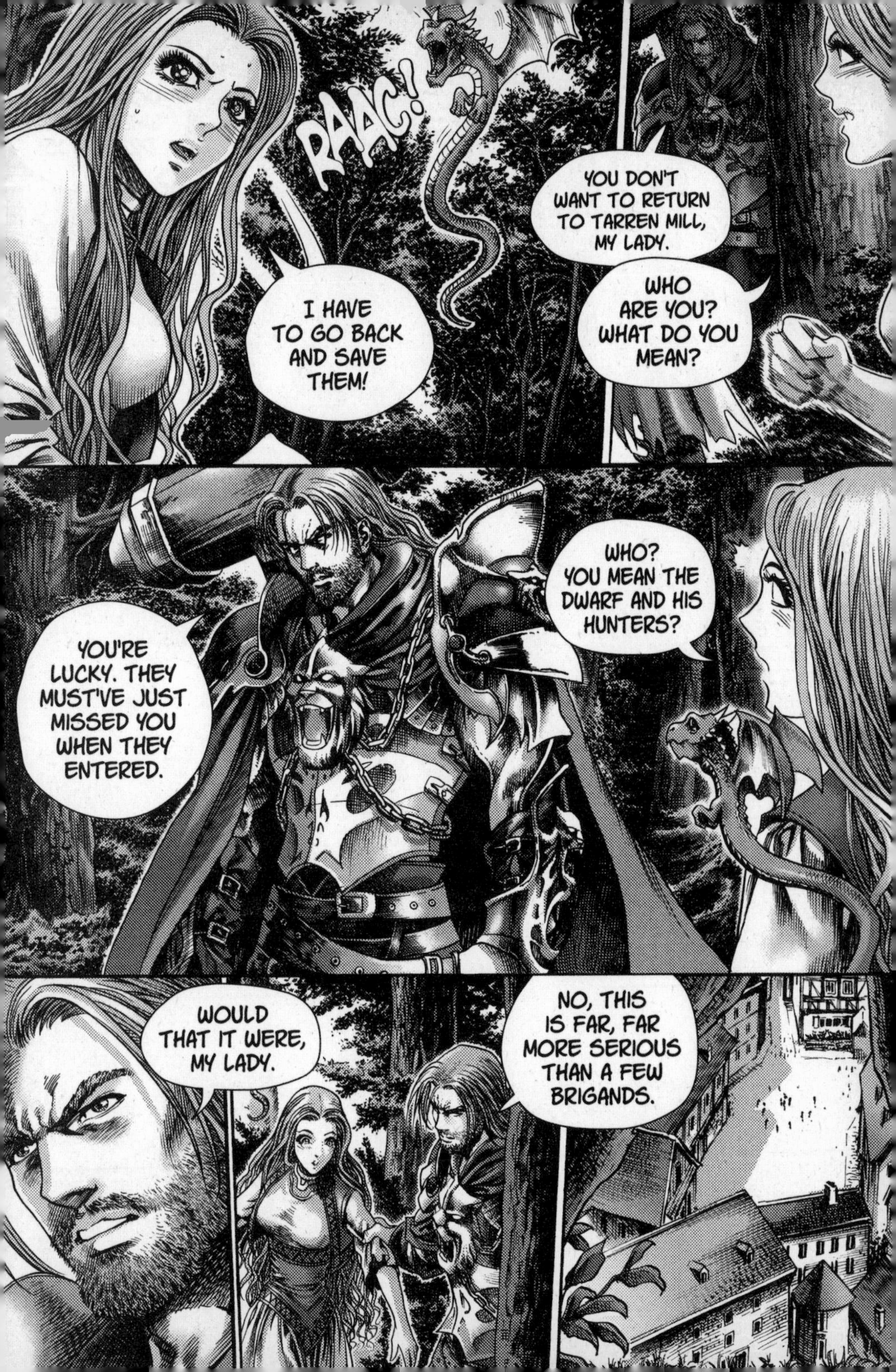
RAAC!
I HAVE TO GO BACK AND SAVE THEM!
YOU DON'T WANT TO RETURN TO TARREN MILL, MY LADY.
WHO ARE YOU? WHAT DO YOU MEAN?
YOU'RE LUCKY. THEY MUST'VE JUST MISSED YOU WHEN THEY ENTERED.
WHO? YOU MEAN THE DWARF AND HIS HUNTERS?
WOULD THAT IT WERE, MY LADY.
NO, THIS IS FAR, FAR MORE SERIOUS THAN A FEW BRIGANDS.

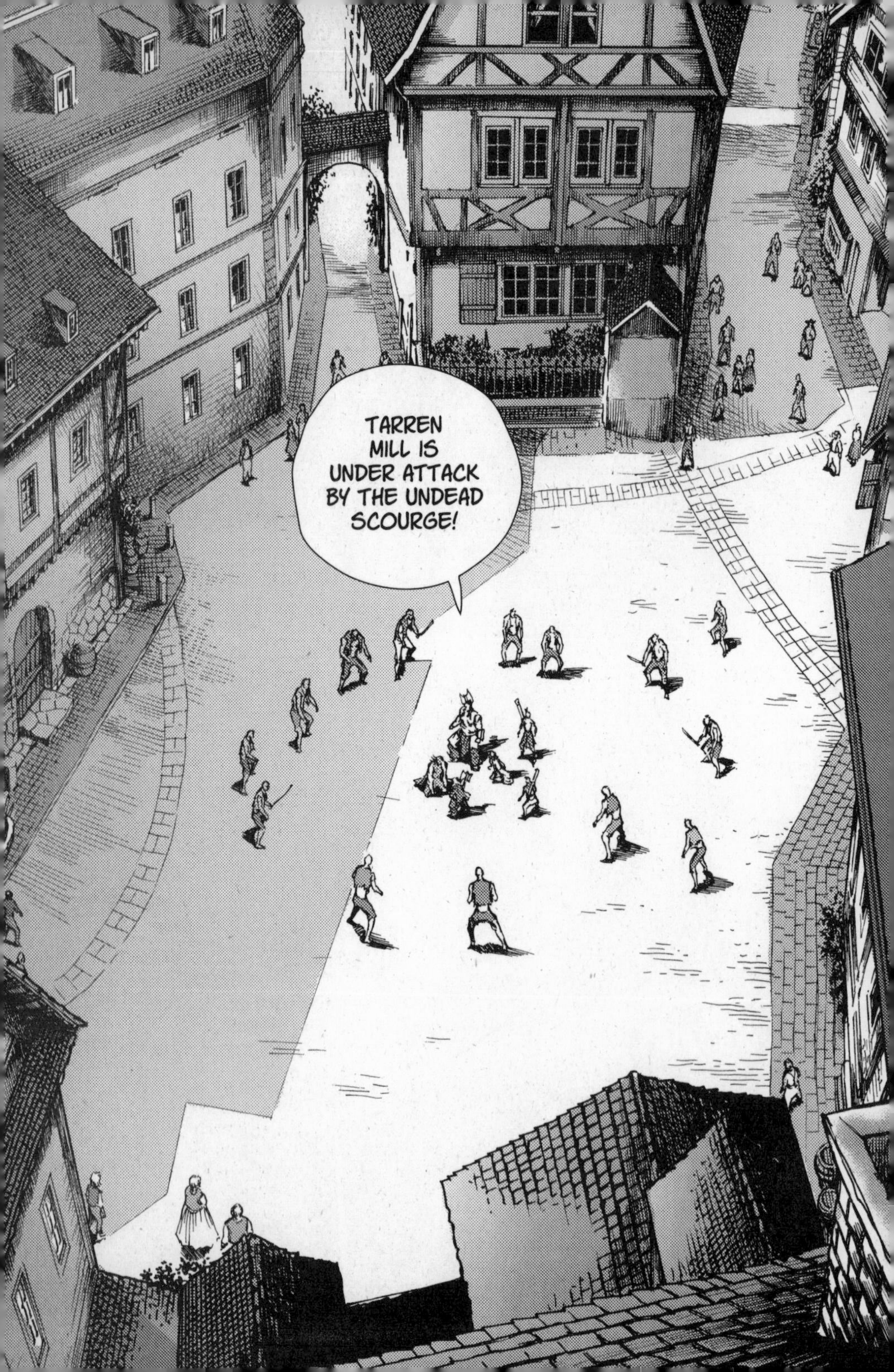
TARREN MILL IS UNDER ATTACK BY THE UNDEAD SCOURGE!

CHAPTER SIX
Against the Scourge

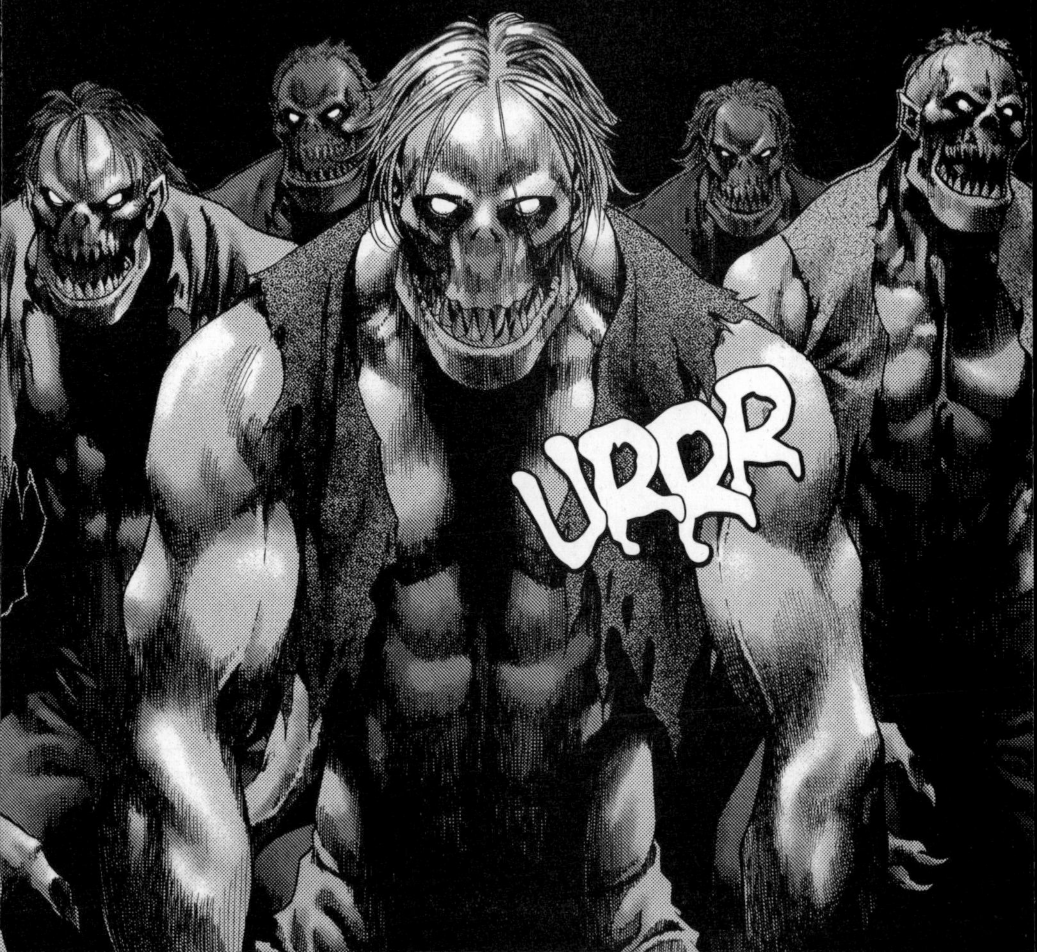
URRR

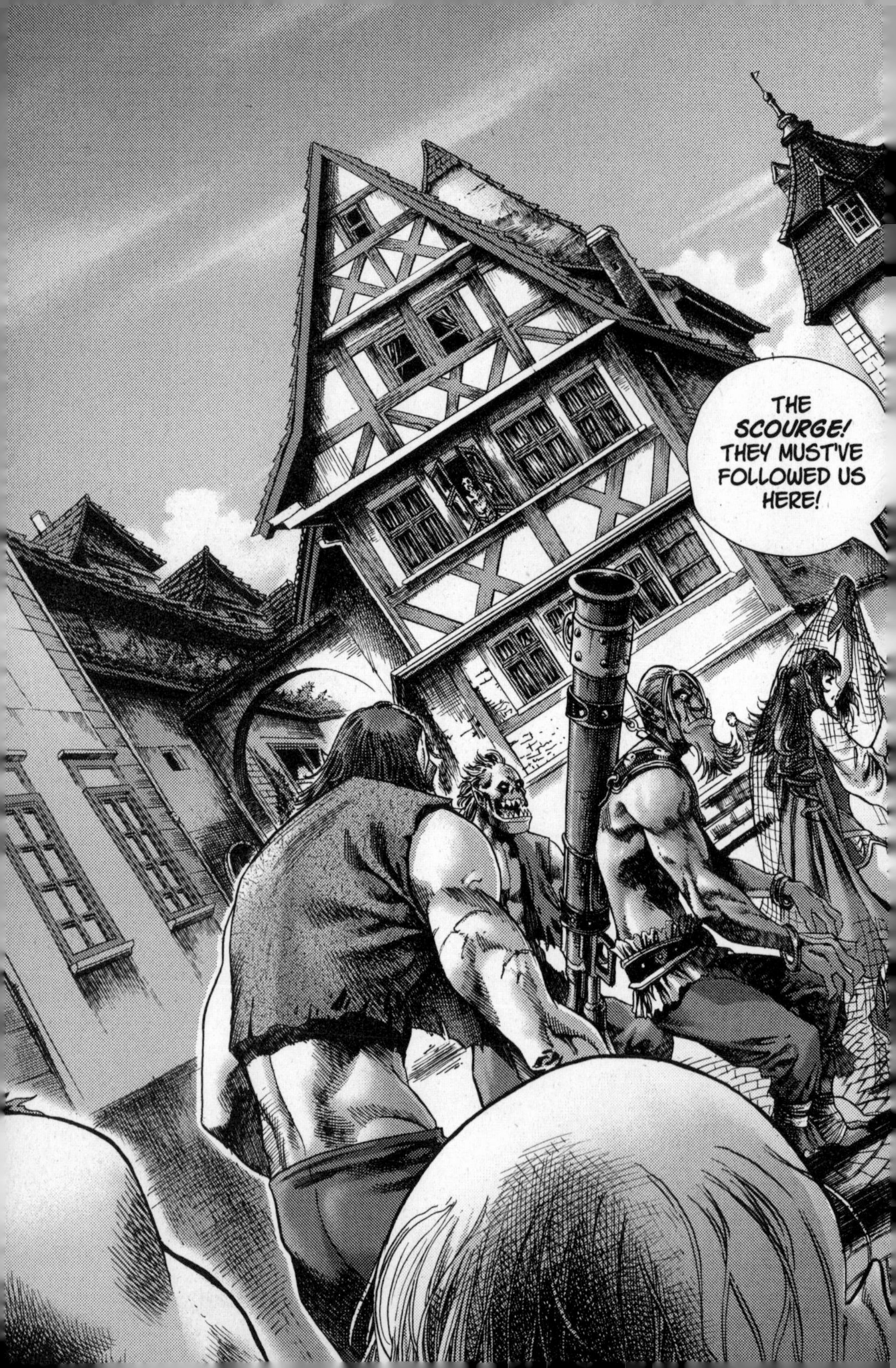
THE SCOURGE! THEY MUST'VE FOLLOWED US HERE!

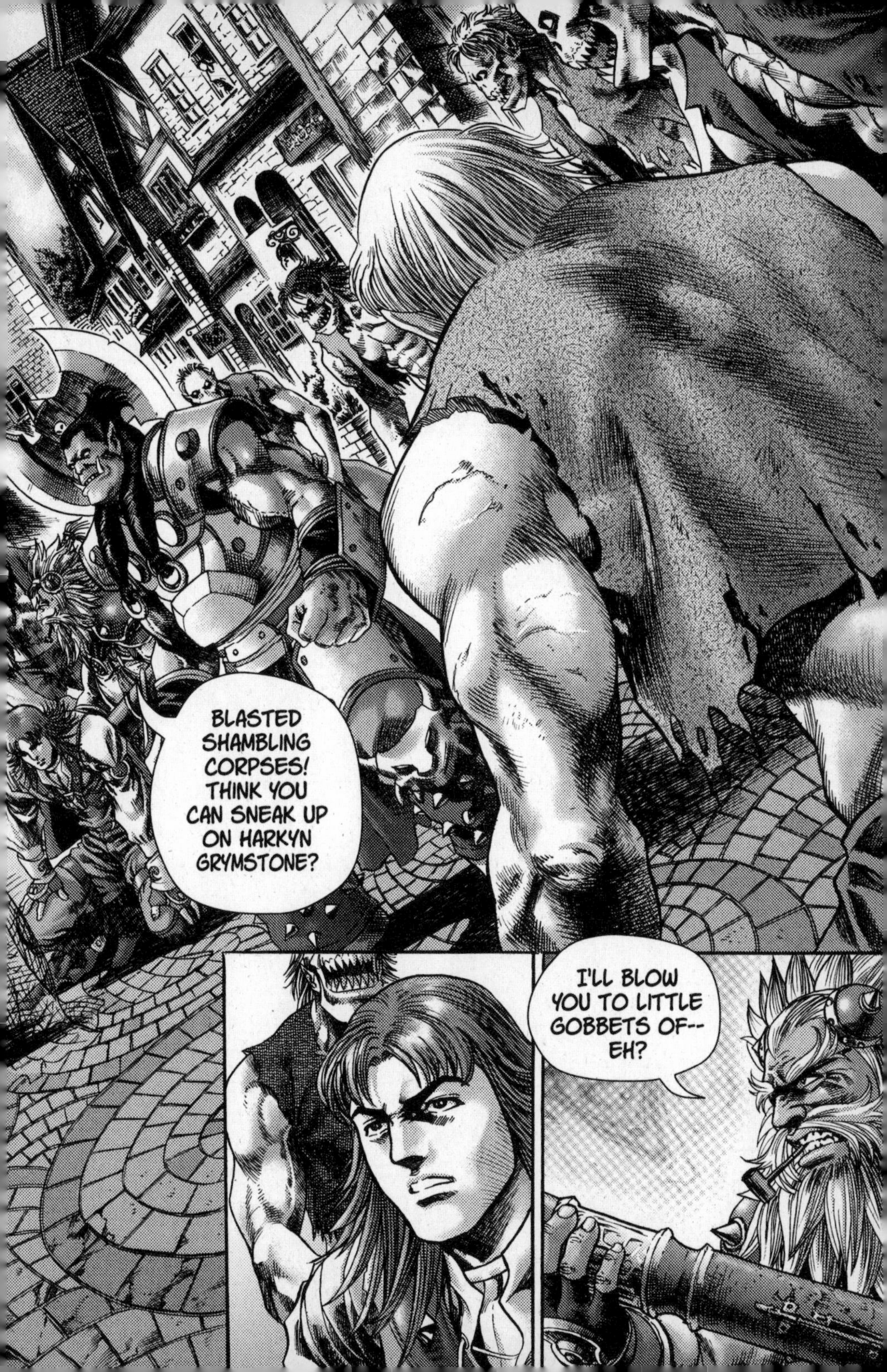
BLASTED SHAMBLING CORPSES! THINK YOU CAN SNEAK UP ON HARKYN GRYMSTONE?
I'LL BLOW YOU TO LITTLE GOBBETS OF-- EH?

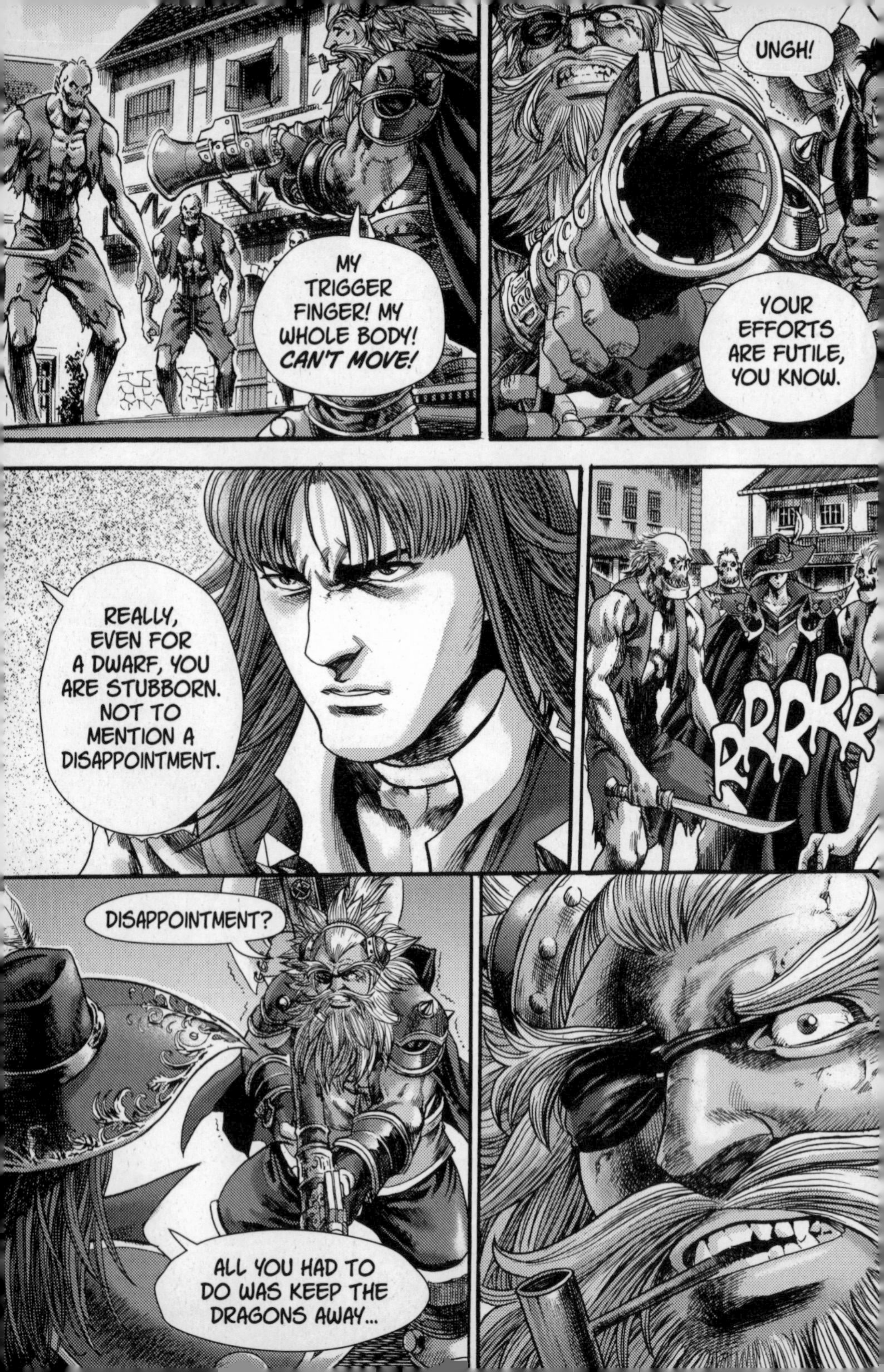

MY TRIGGER FINGER! MY WHOLE BODY! *CAN'T MOVE!*
UNGH!
YOUR EFFORTS ARE FUTILE, YOU KNOW.
REALLY, EVEN FOR A DWARF, YOU ARE STUBBORN. NOT TO MENTION A DISAPPOINTMENT.
RRRRR
DISAPPOINTMENT?
ALL YOU HAD TO DO WAS KEEP THE DRAGONS AWAY...

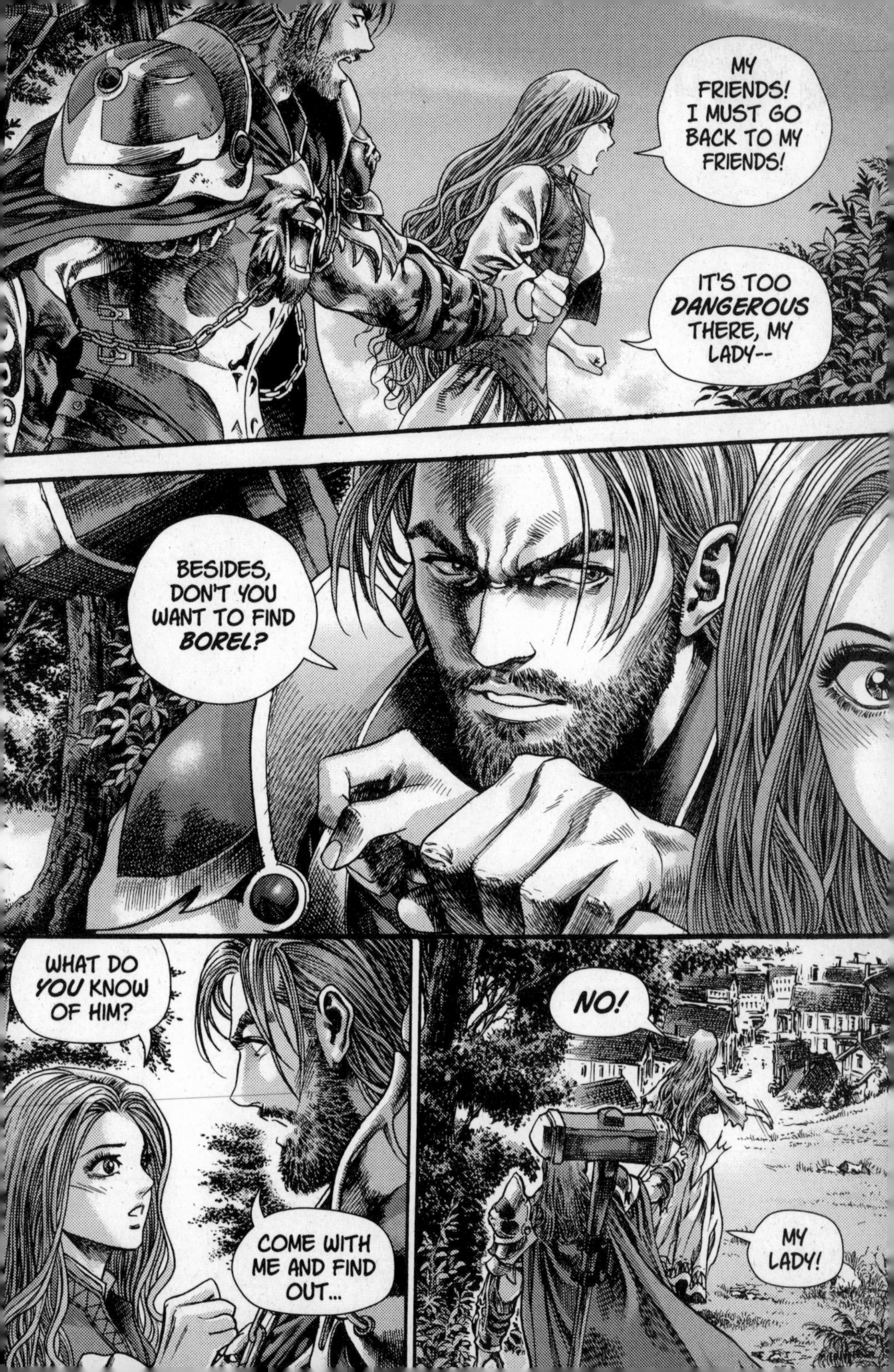
MY FRIENDS! I MUST GO BACK TO MY FRIENDS!
IT'S TOO DANGEROUS THERE, MY LADY--
BESIDES, DON'T YOU WANT TO FIND BOREL?
WHAT DO YOU KNOW OF HIM?
COME WITH ME AND FIND OUT...
NO!
MY LADY!

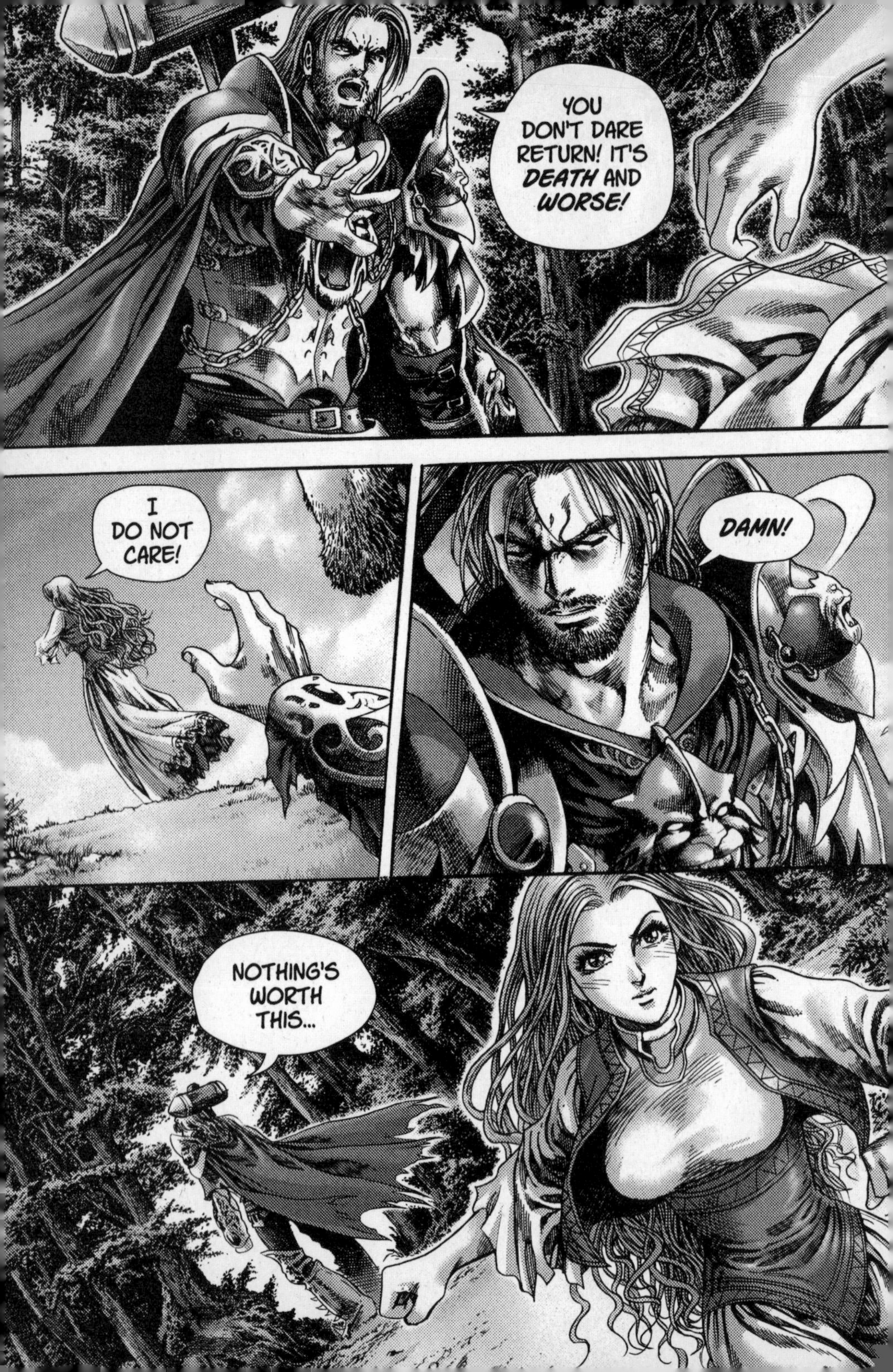
YOU DON'T DARE RETURN! IT'S *DEATH* AND *WORSE!*
I DO NOT CARE!
DAMN!
NOTHING'S WORTH THIS...

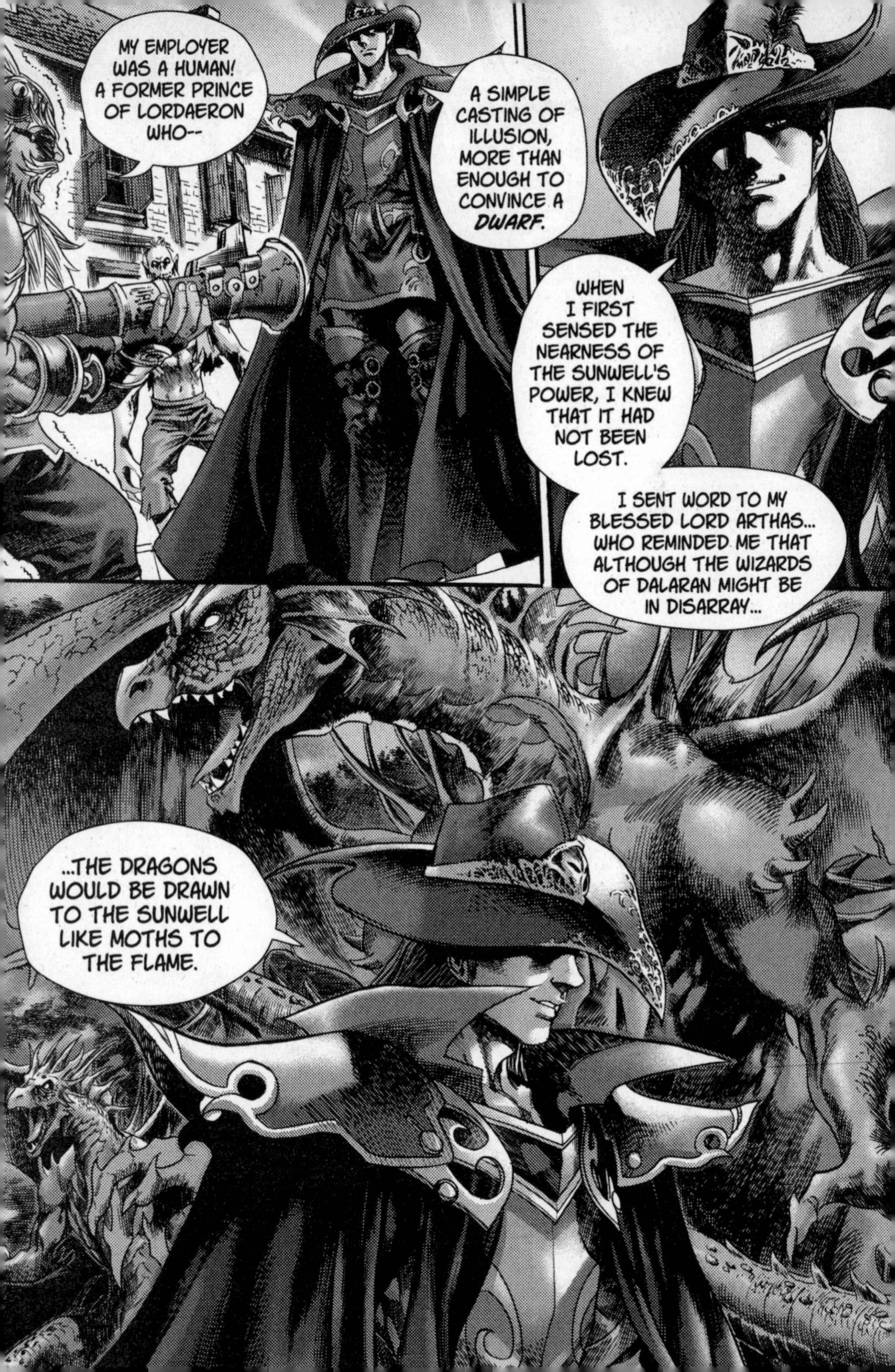
MY EMPLOYER WAS A HUMAN! A FORMER PRINCE OF LORDAERON WHO--
A SIMPLE CASTING OF ILLUSION, MORE THAN ENOUGH TO CONVINCE A *DWARF*.
WHEN I FIRST SENSED THE NEARNESS OF THE SUNWELL'S POWER, I KNEW THAT IT HAD NOT BEEN LOST.
I SENT WORD TO MY BLESSED LORD ARTHAS... WHO REMINDED ME THAT ALTHOUGH THE WIZARDS OF DALARAN MIGHT BE IN DISARRAY...
...THE DRAGONS WOULD BE DRAWN TO THE SUNWELL LIKE MOTHS TO THE FLAME.

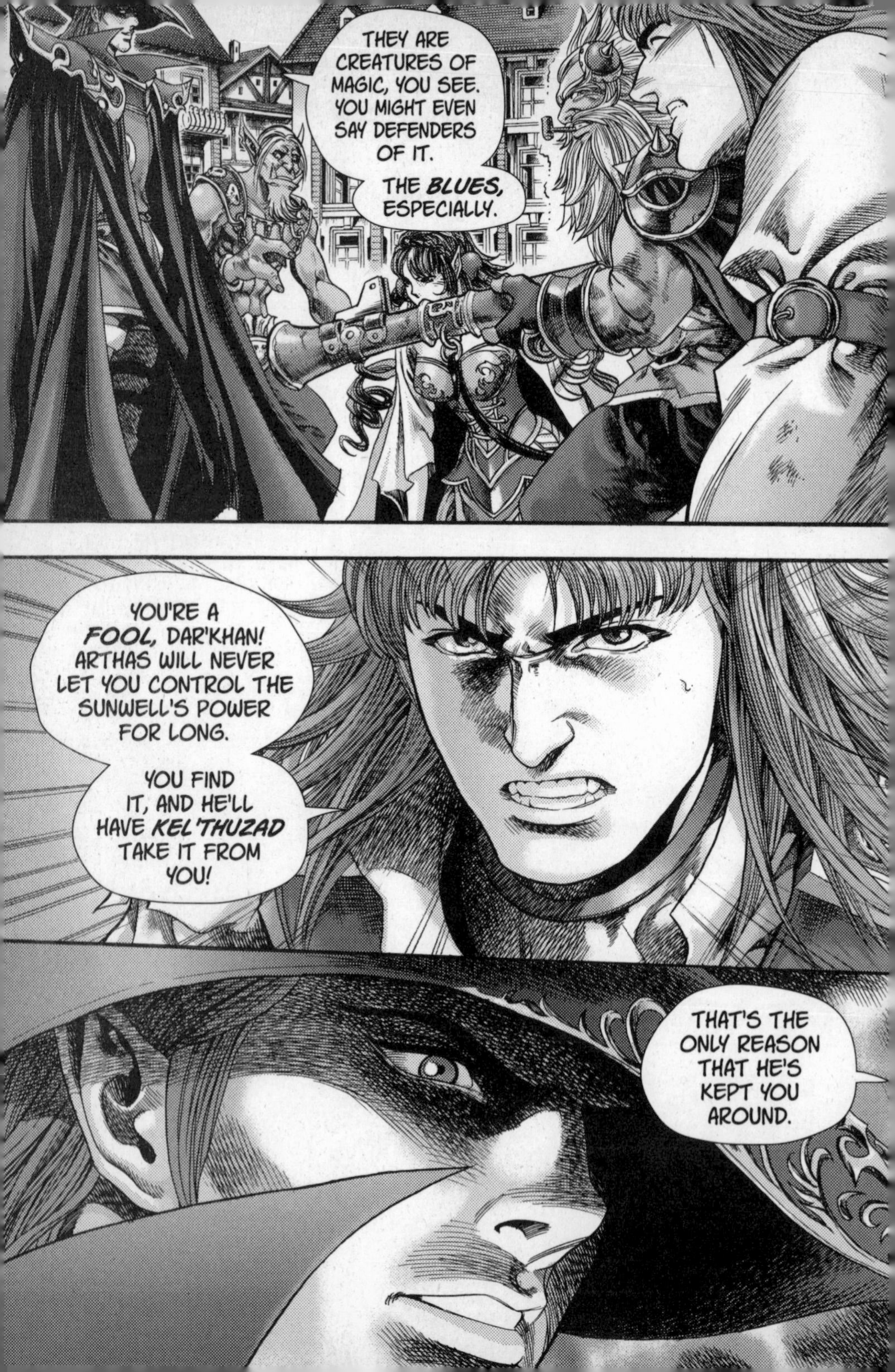
THEY ARE CREATURES OF MAGIC, YOU SEE. YOU MIGHT EVEN SAY DEFENDERS OF IT.
THE BLUES, ESPECIALLY.
YOU'RE A FOOL, DAR'KHAN! ARTHAS WILL NEVER LET YOU CONTROL THE SUNWELL'S POWER FOR LONG.
YOU FIND IT, AND HE'LL HAVE KEL'THUZAD TAKE IT FROM YOU!
THAT'S THE ONLY REASON THAT HE'S KEPT YOU AROUND.

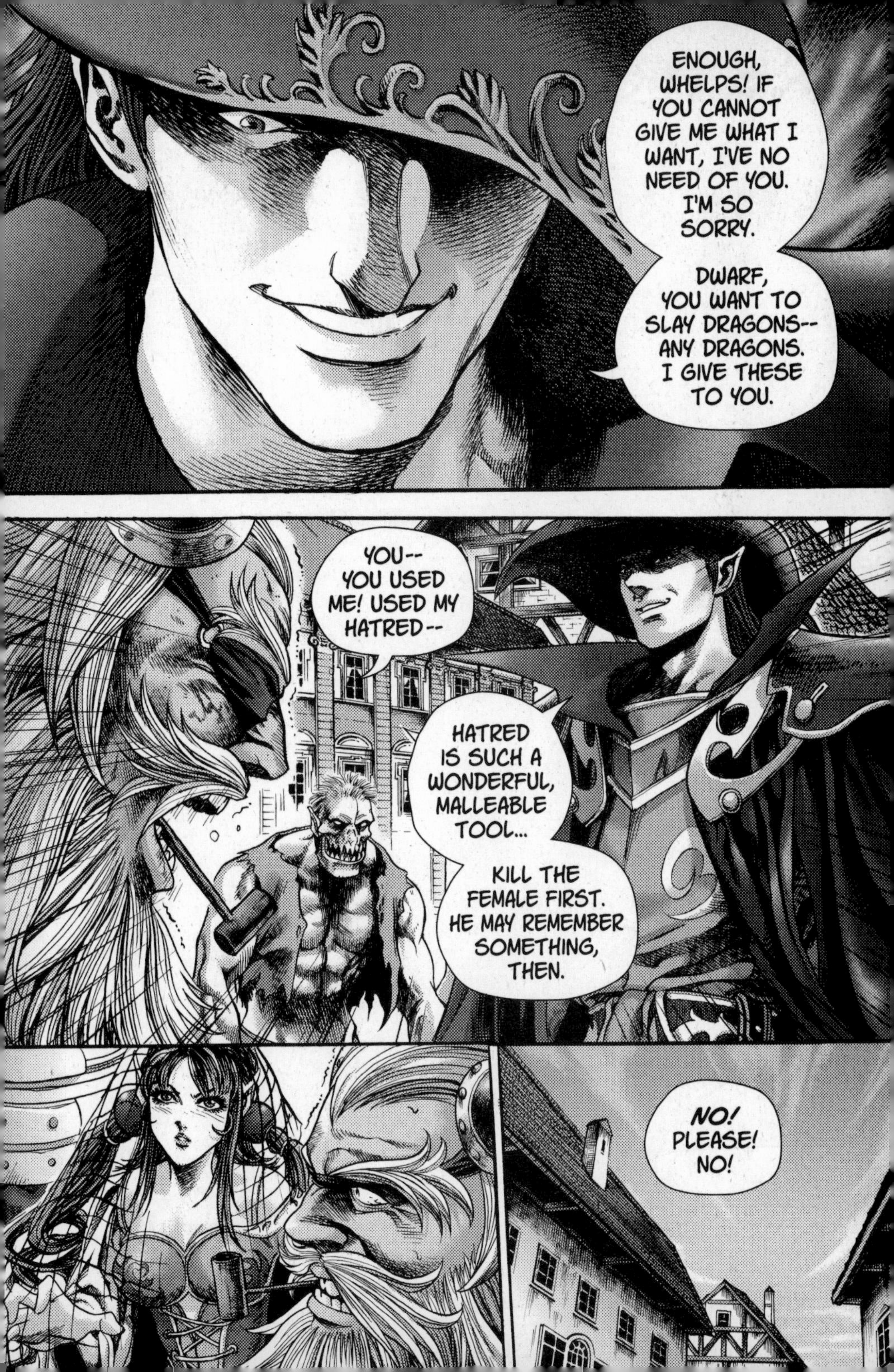
ENOUGH, WHELPS! IF YOU CANNOT GIVE ME WHAT I WANT, I'VE NO NEED OF YOU. I'M SO SORRY.
DWARF, YOU WANT TO SLAY DRAGONS-- ANY DRAGONS. I GIVE THESE TO YOU.
YOU-- YOU USED ME! USED MY HATRED--
HATRED IS SUCH A WONDERFUL, MALLEABLE TOOL...
KILL THE FEMALE FIRST. HE MAY REMEMBER SOMETHING, THEN.
NO! PLEASE! NO!

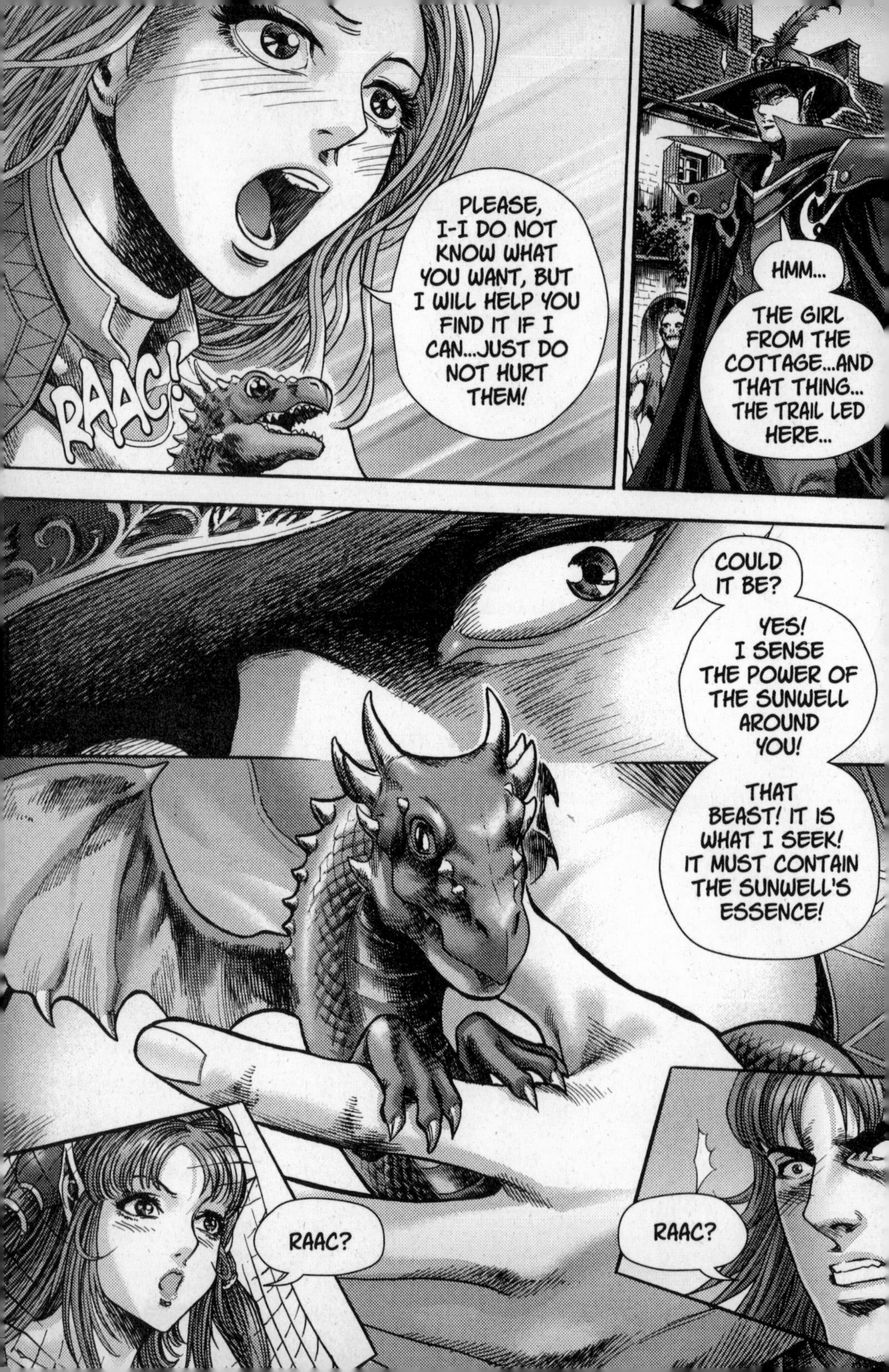
PLEASE, I-I DO NOT KNOW WHAT YOU WANT, BUT I WILL HELP YOU FIND IT IF I CAN...JUST DO NOT HURT THEM!
RAAC!
HMM...
THE GIRL FROM THE COTTAGE...AND THAT THING... THE TRAIL LED HERE...
COULD IT BE?
YES! I SENSE THE POWER OF THE SUNWELL AROUND YOU!
THAT BEAST! IT IS WHAT I SEEK! IT MUST CONTAIN THE SUNWELL'S ESSENCE!
RAAC?
RAAC?

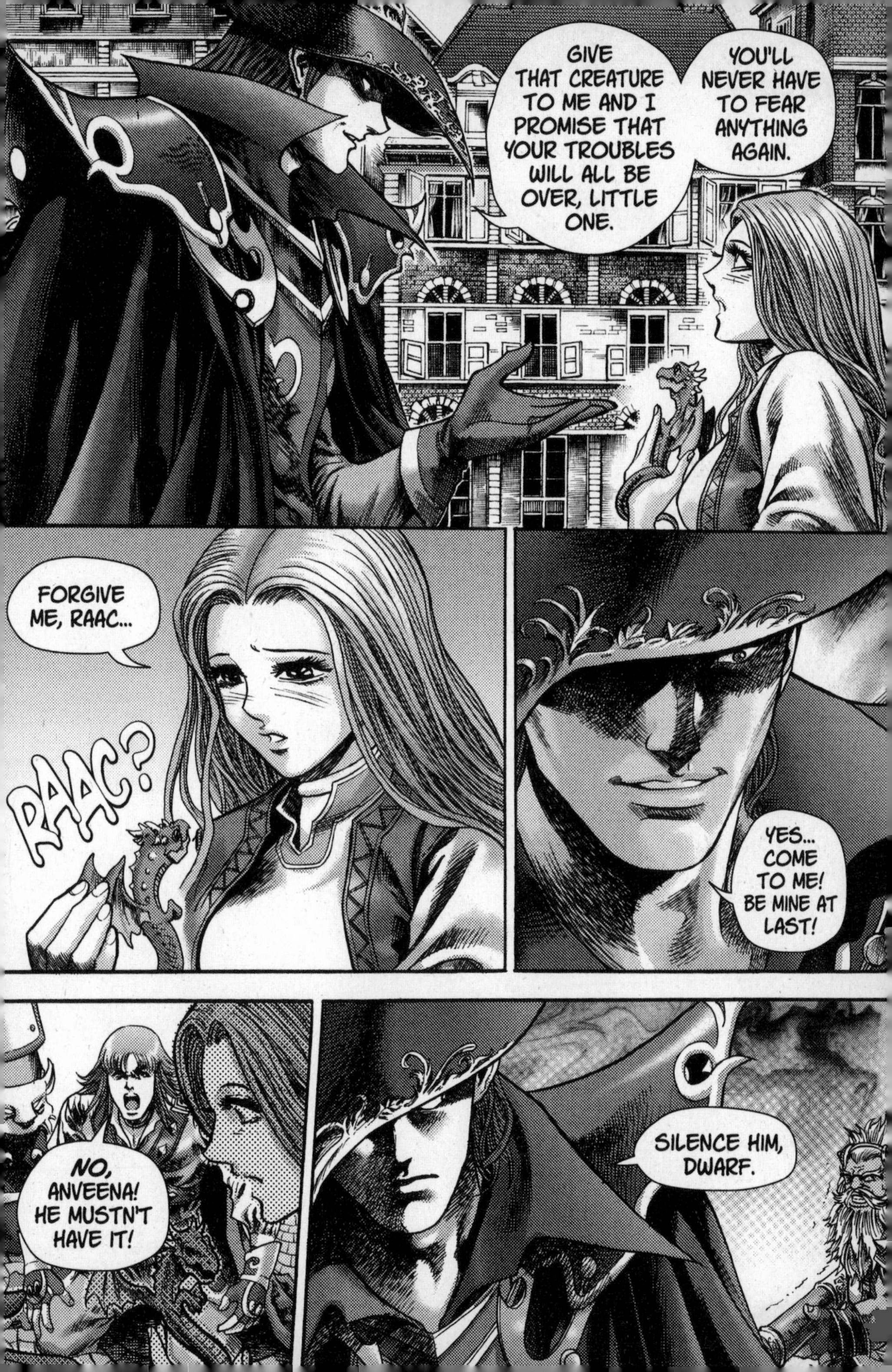
GIVE THAT CREATURE TO ME AND I PROMISE THAT YOUR TROUBLES WILL ALL BE OVER, LITTLE ONE.
YOU'LL NEVER HAVE TO FEAR ANYTHING AGAIN.
FORGIVE ME, RAAC...
RAAC?
YES... COME TO ME! BE MINE AT LAST!
NO, ANVEENA! HE MUSTN'T HAVE IT!
SILENCE HIM, DWARF.

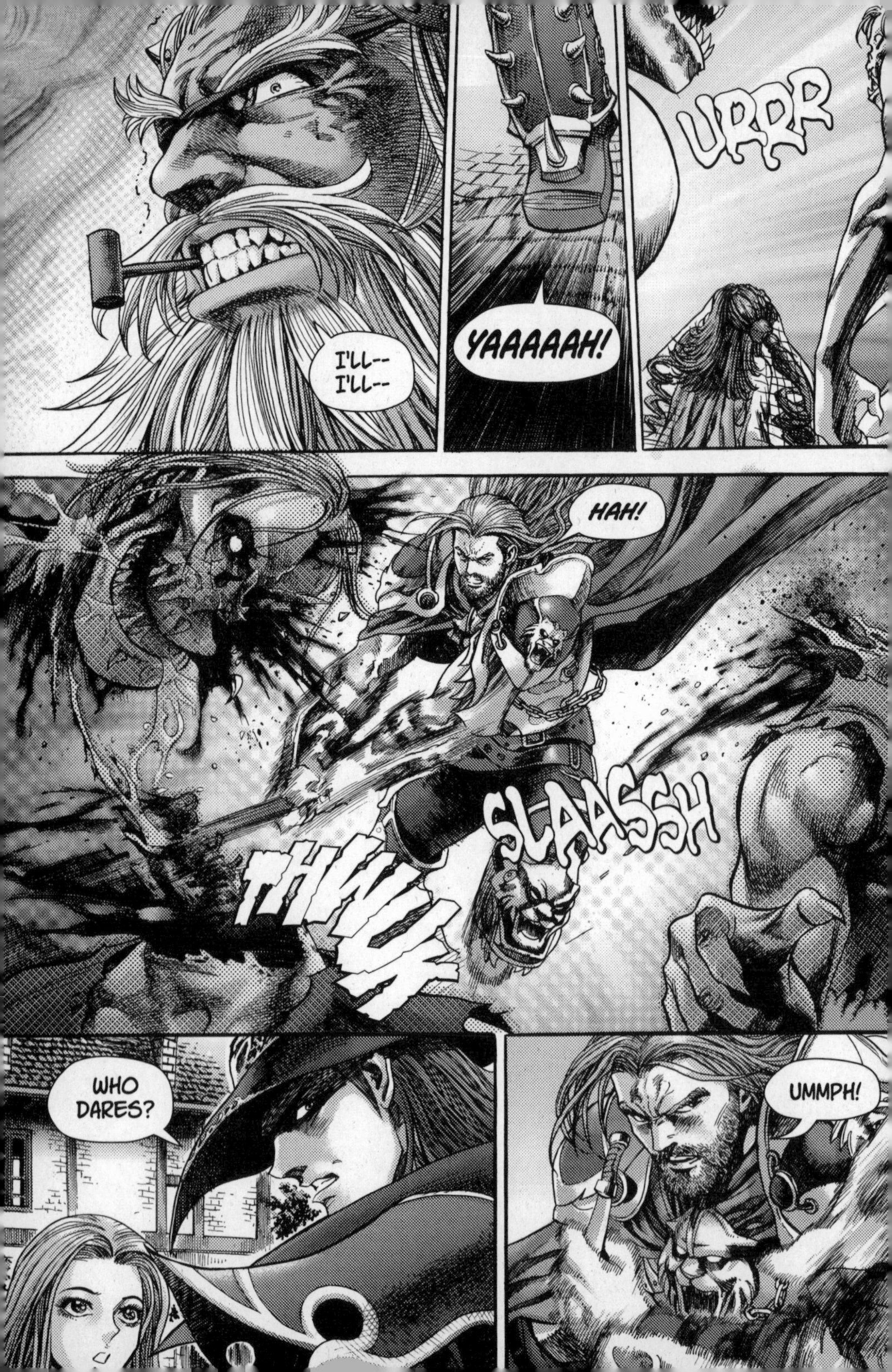
I'LL--
I'LL--
YAAAAAH!
URRR
HAH!
SLAASSH
THWOK
WHO DARES?
UMMPH!

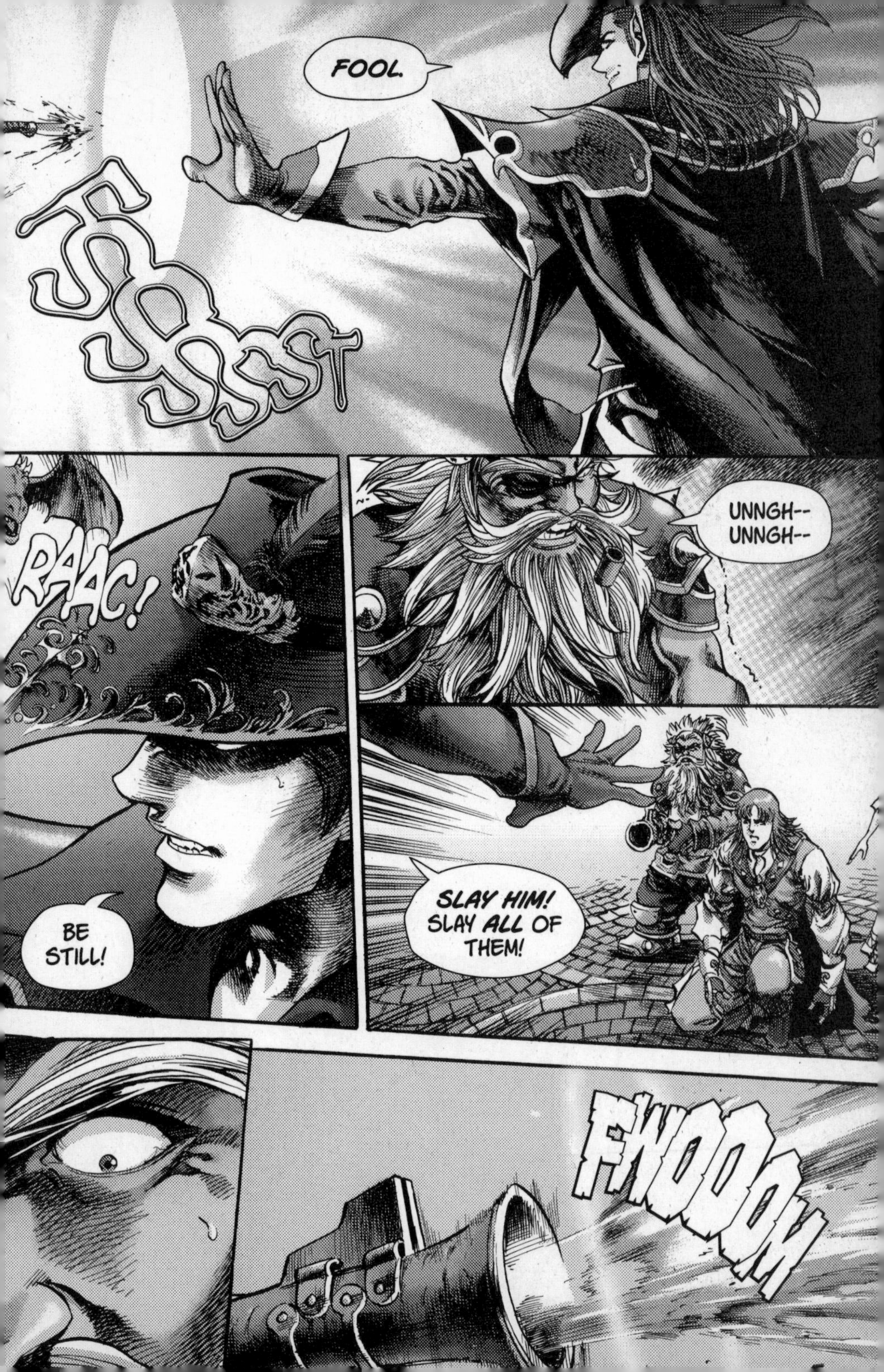
FOOL.
FSSSST
UNNGH--
UNNGH--
SLAY HIM! SLAY ALL OF THEM!
RAAC!
BE STILL!
FWOOOM

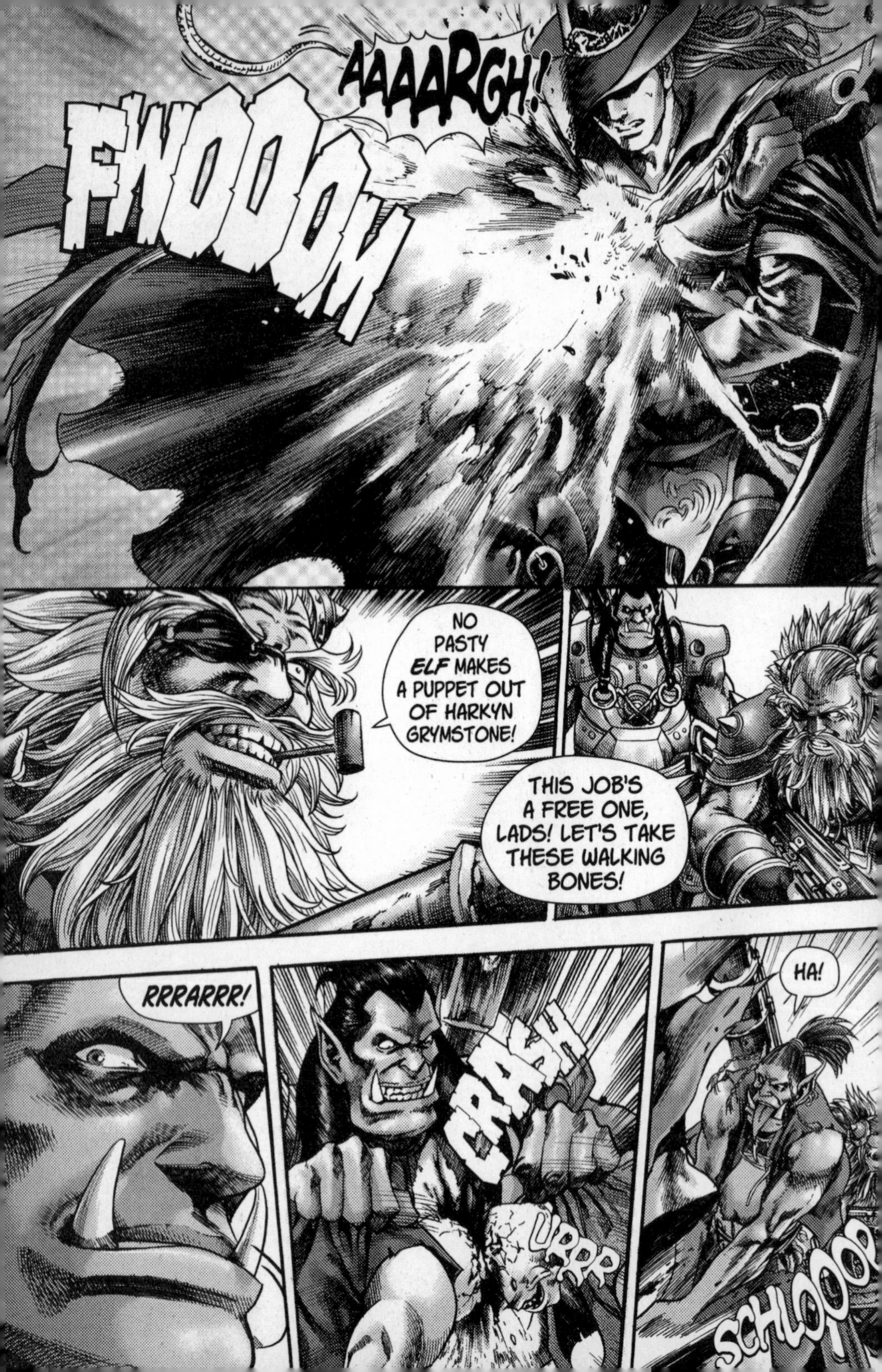
AAAARGH!
FWOOOM
NO PASTY *ELF* MAKES A PUPPET OUT OF HARKYN GRYMSTONE!
THIS JOB'S A FREE ONE, LADS! LET'S TAKE THESE WALKING BONES!
RRRARRR!
CRASH
URRR
HA!
SCHLOOOP

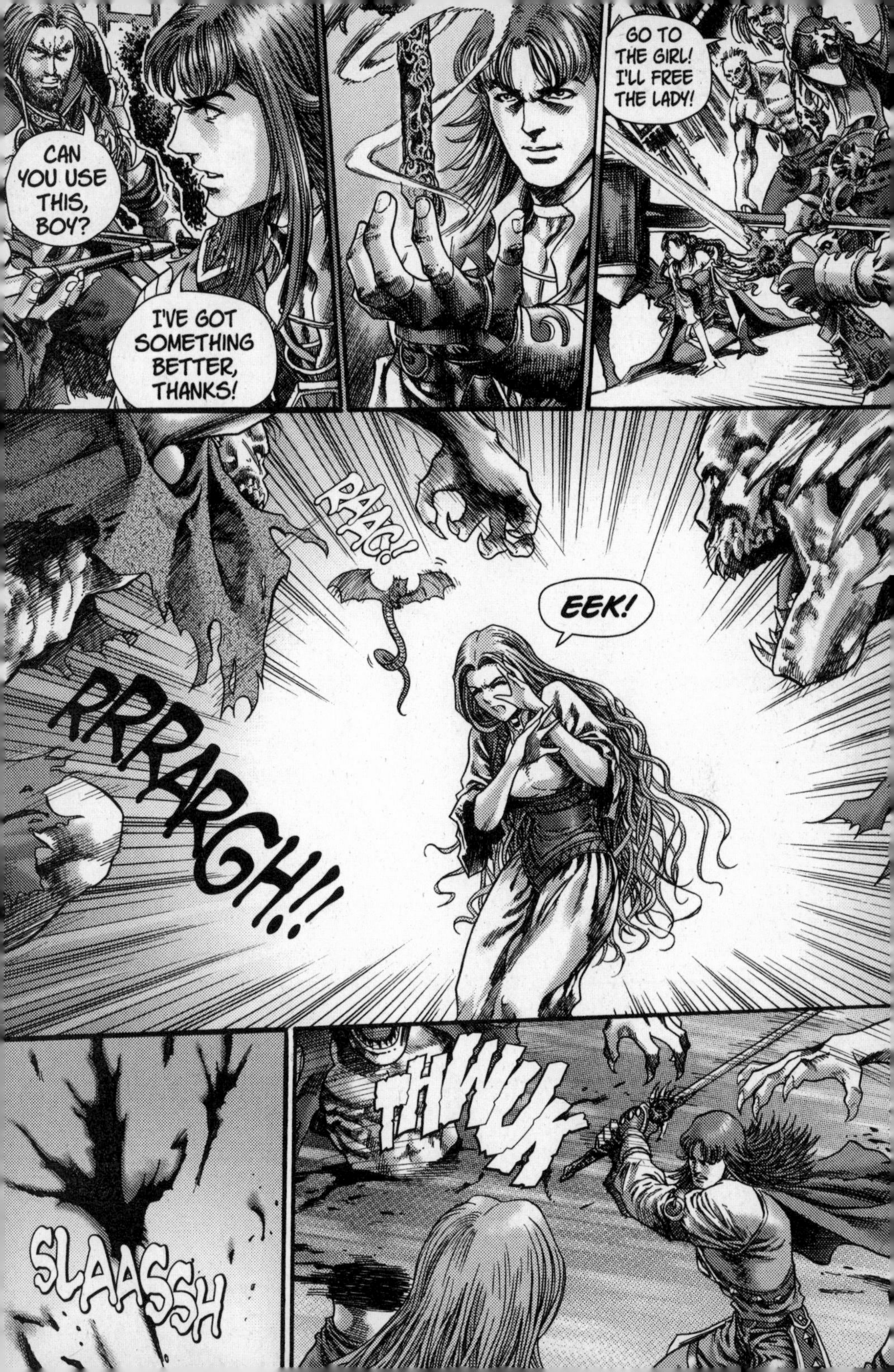
CAN YOU USE THIS, BOY?
I'VE GOT SOMETHING BETTER, THANKS!
GO TO THE GIRL! I'LL FREE THE LADY!
RAAG!
EEK!
RRRARGH!!!
SLAASSH
THWUK

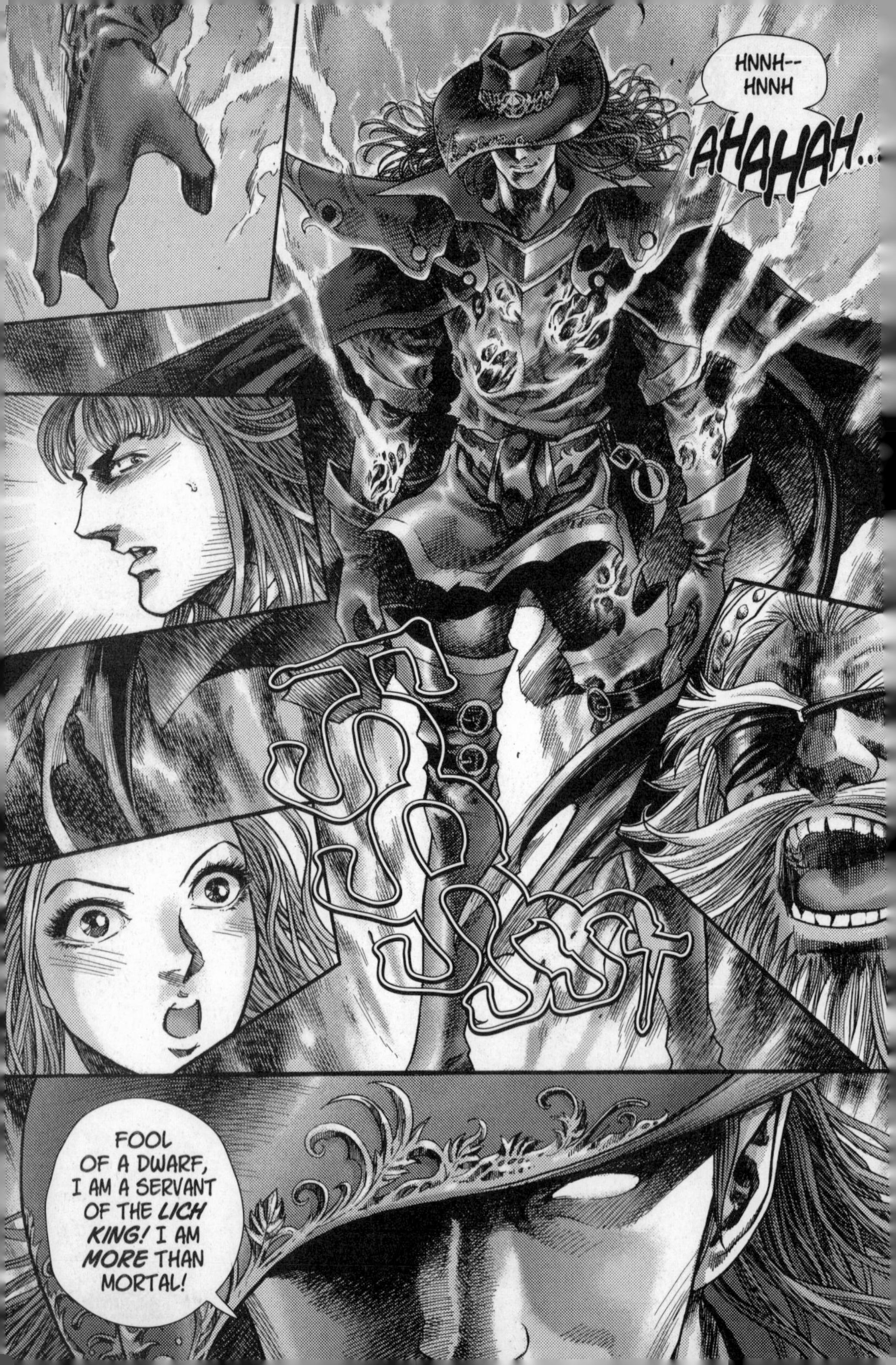
HNNH--
HNNH
AHAHAH...
FOOL OF A DWARF, I AM A SERVANT OF THE LICH KING! I AM MORE THAN MORTAL!

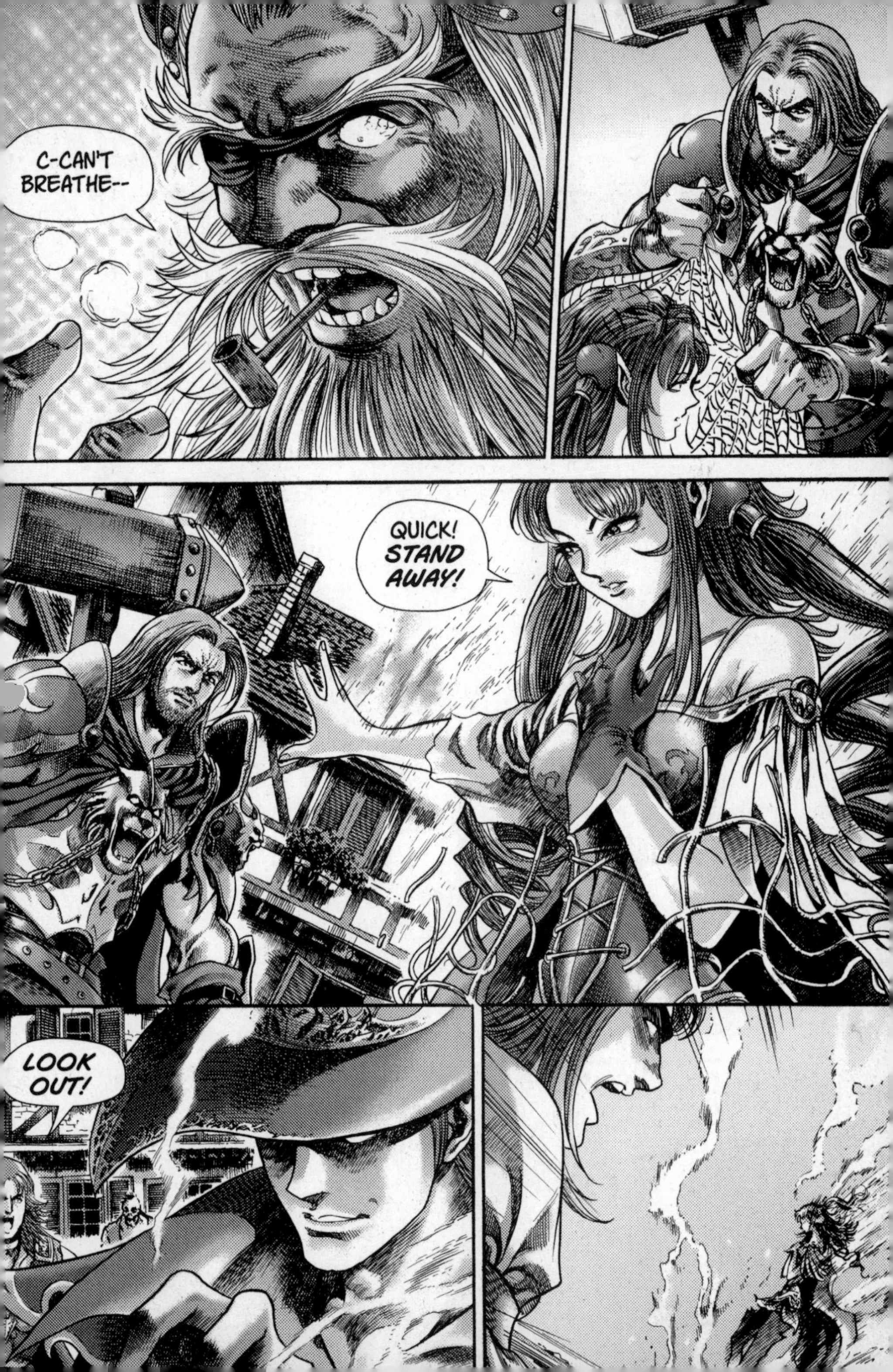
C-CAN'T BREATHE--
QUICK! STAND AWAY!
LOOK OUT!

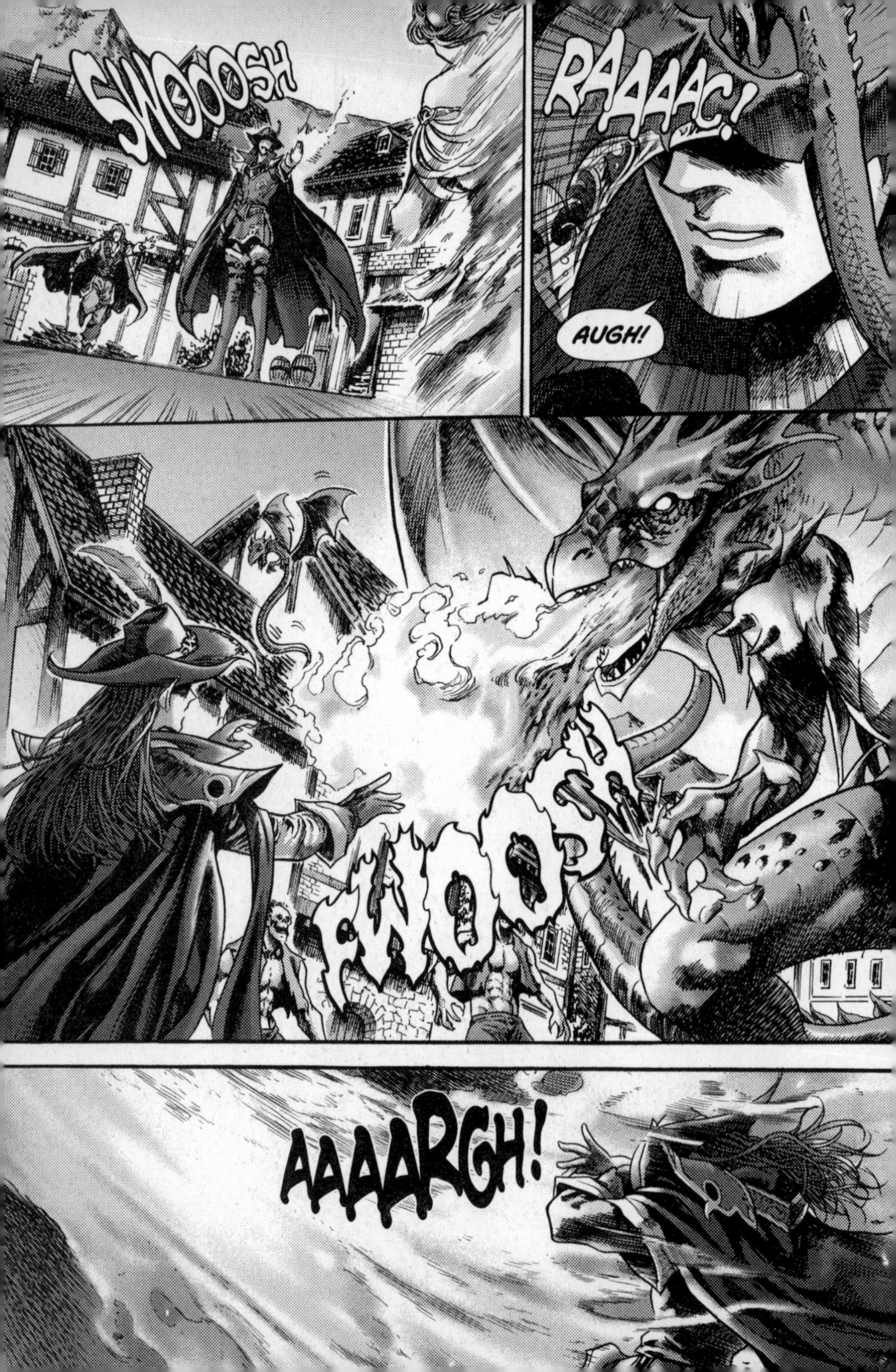
RAAAAC!
AUGH!
SHOOOSH
AAAARGH!

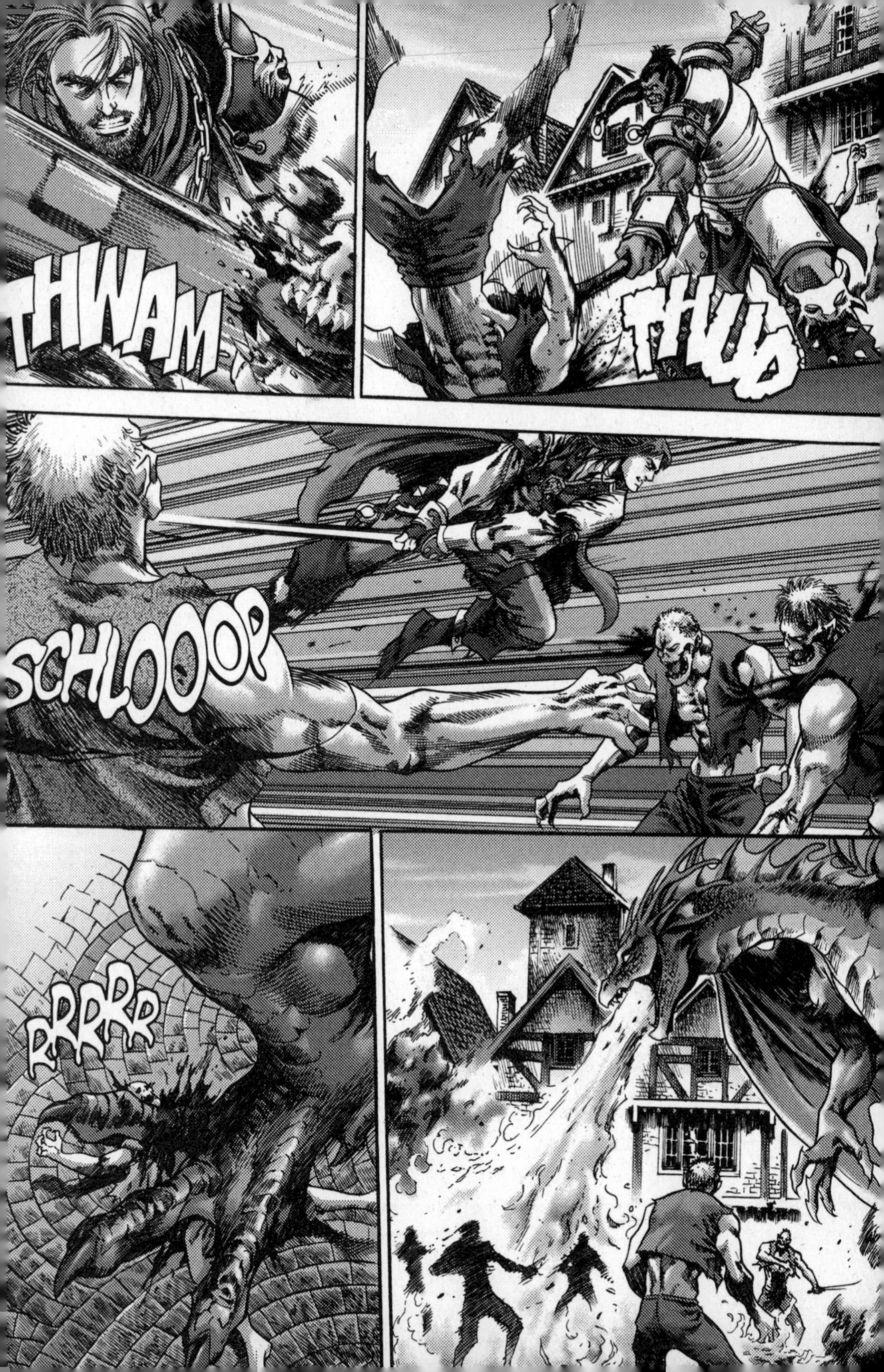
THWAM
THUD
SCHLOOOP
RRRRR

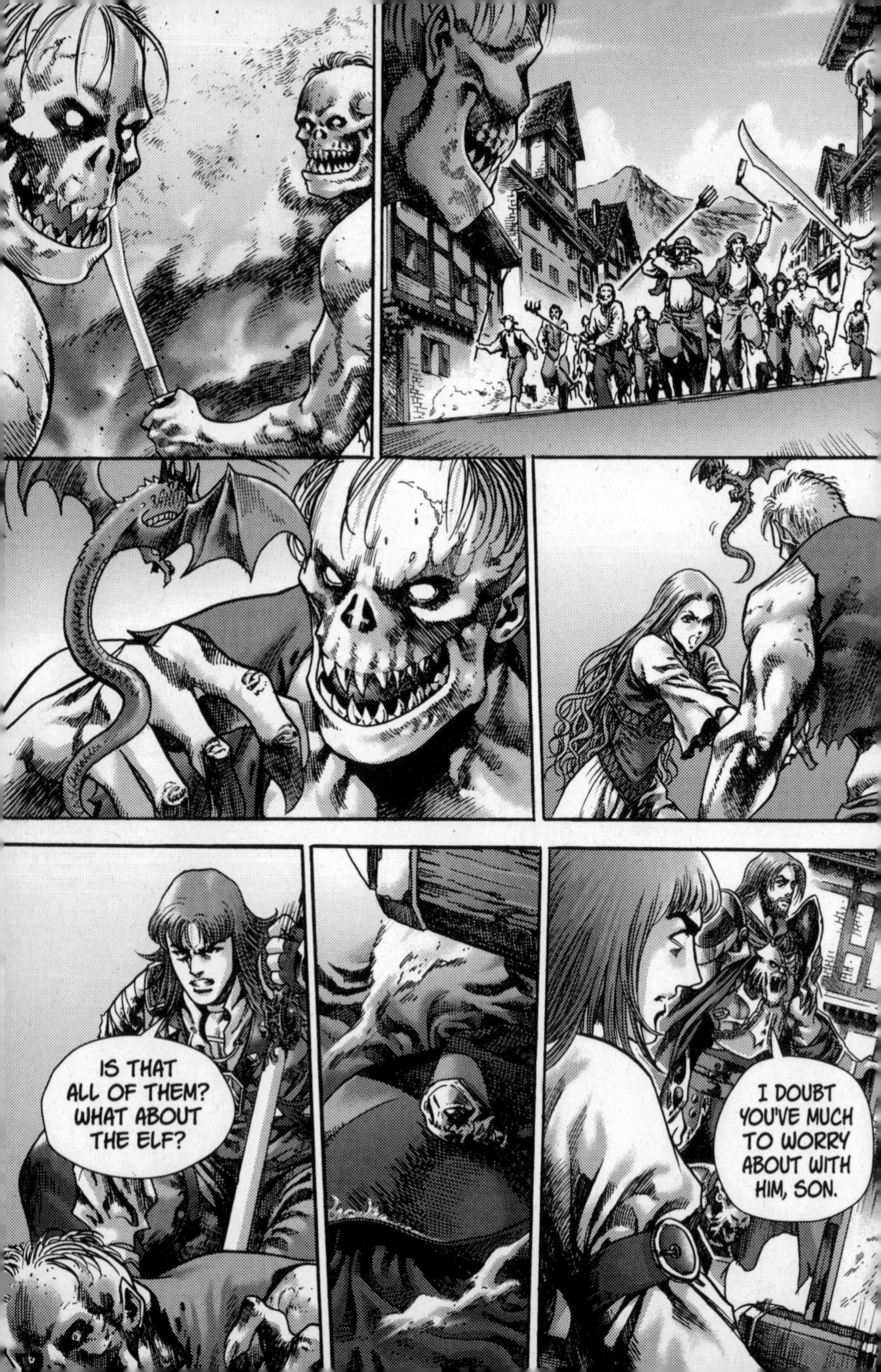
IS THAT ALL OF THEM? WHAT ABOUT THE ELF?
I DOUBT YOU'VE MUCH TO WORRY ABOUT WITH HIM, SON.

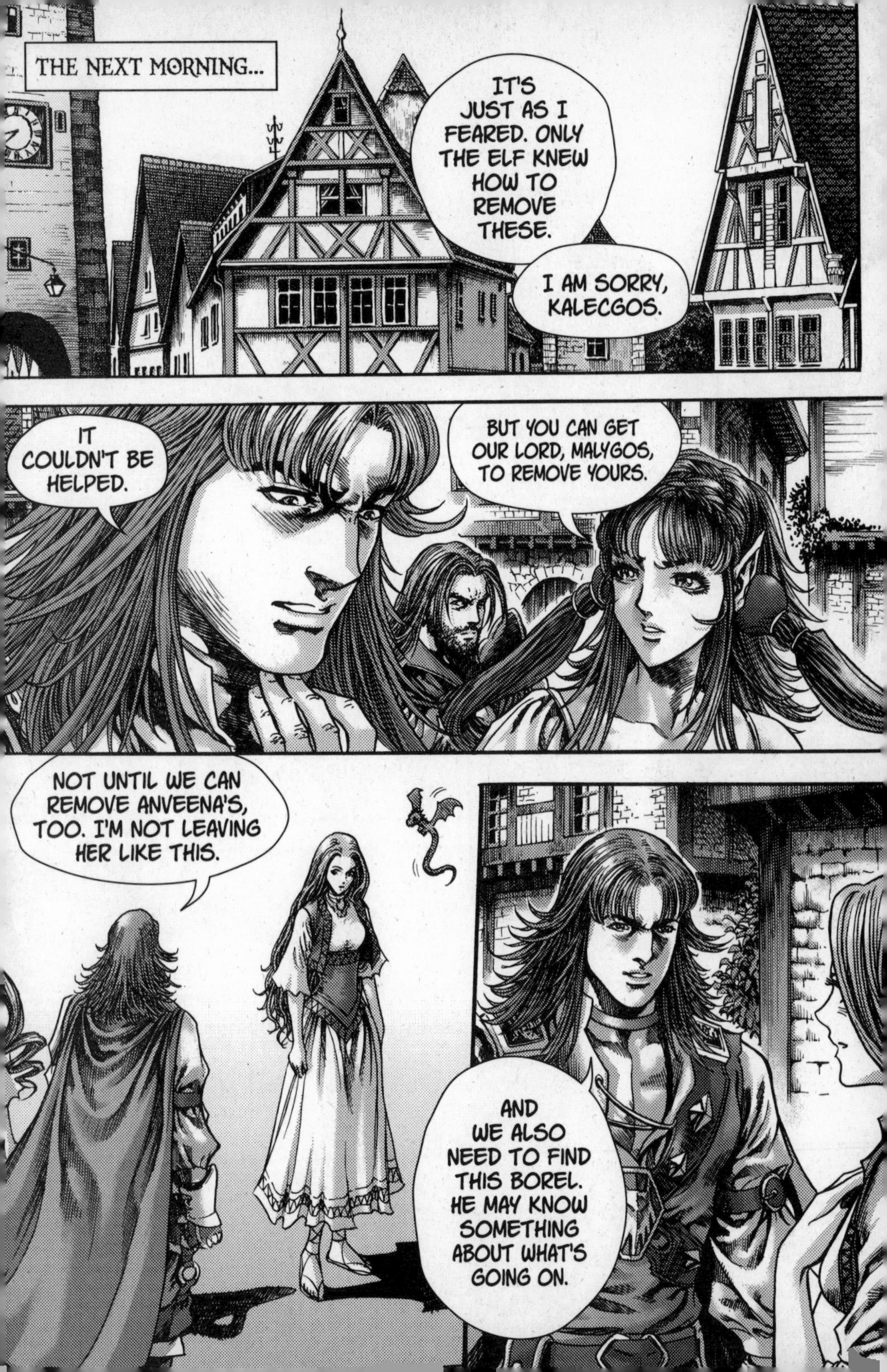
THE NEXT MORNING...
IT'S JUST AS I FEARED. ONLY THE ELF KNEW HOW TO REMOVE THESE.
I AM SORRY, KALECGOS.
IT COULDN'T BE HELPED.
BUT YOU CAN GET OUR LORD, MALYGOS, TO REMOVE YOURS.
NOT UNTIL WE CAN REMOVE ANVEENA'S, TOO. I'M NOT LEAVING HER LIKE THIS.
AND WE ALSO NEED TO FIND THIS BOREL. HE MAY KNOW SOMETHING ABOUT WHAT'S GOING ON.

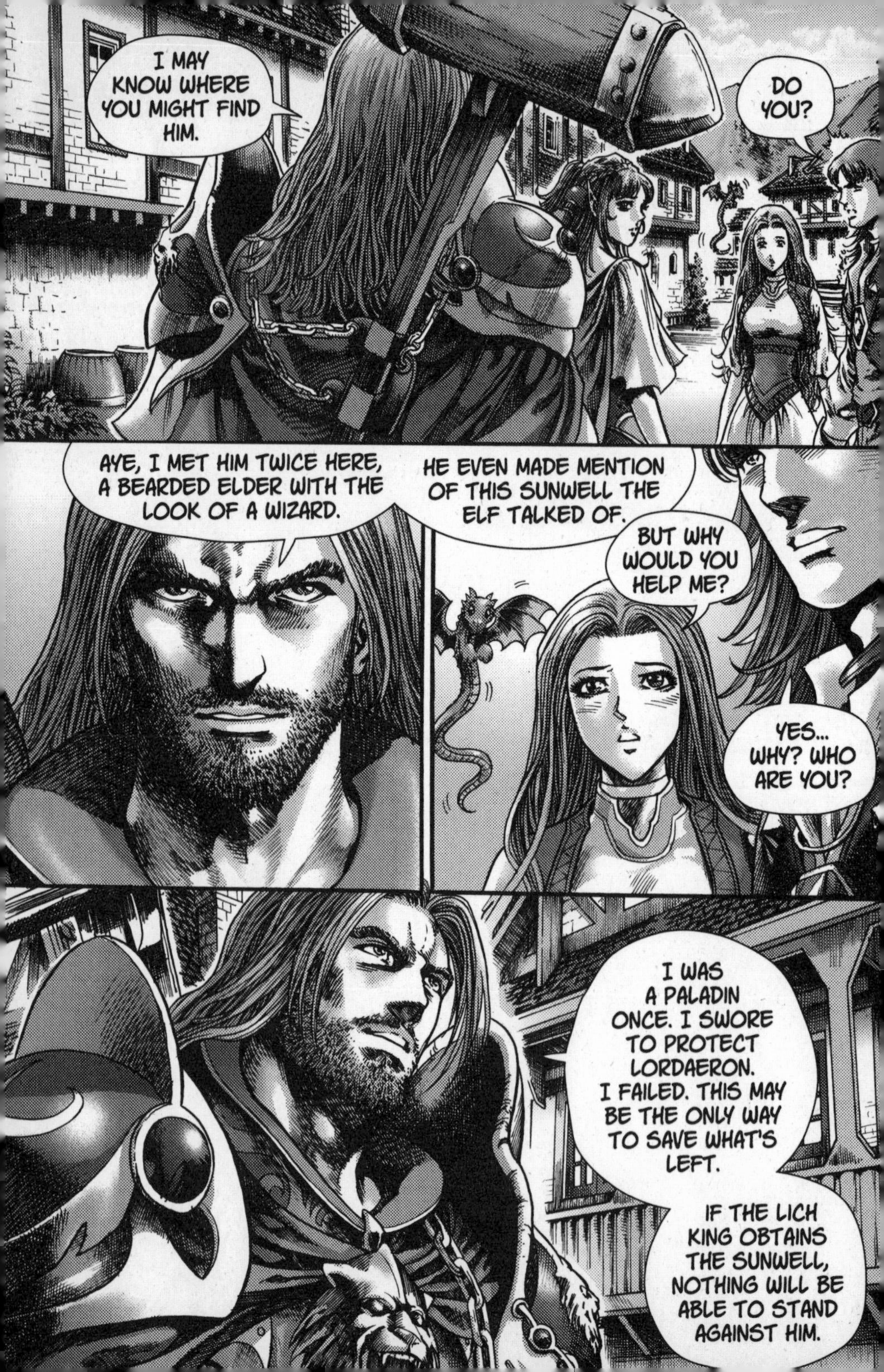
I MAY KNOW WHERE YOU MIGHT FIND HIM.
DO YOU?
AYE, I MET HIM TWICE HERE, A BEARDED ELDER WITH THE LOOK OF A WIZARD.
HE EVEN MADE MENTION OF THIS SUNWELL THE ELF TALKED OF.
BUT WHY WOULD YOU HELP ME?
YES... WHY? WHO ARE YOU?
I WAS A PALADIN ONCE. I SWORE TO PROTECT LORDAERON. I FAILED. THIS MAY BE THE ONLY WAY TO SAVE WHAT'S LEFT.
IF THE LICH KING OBTAINS THE SUNWELL, NOTHING WILL BE ABLE TO STAND AGAINST HIM.

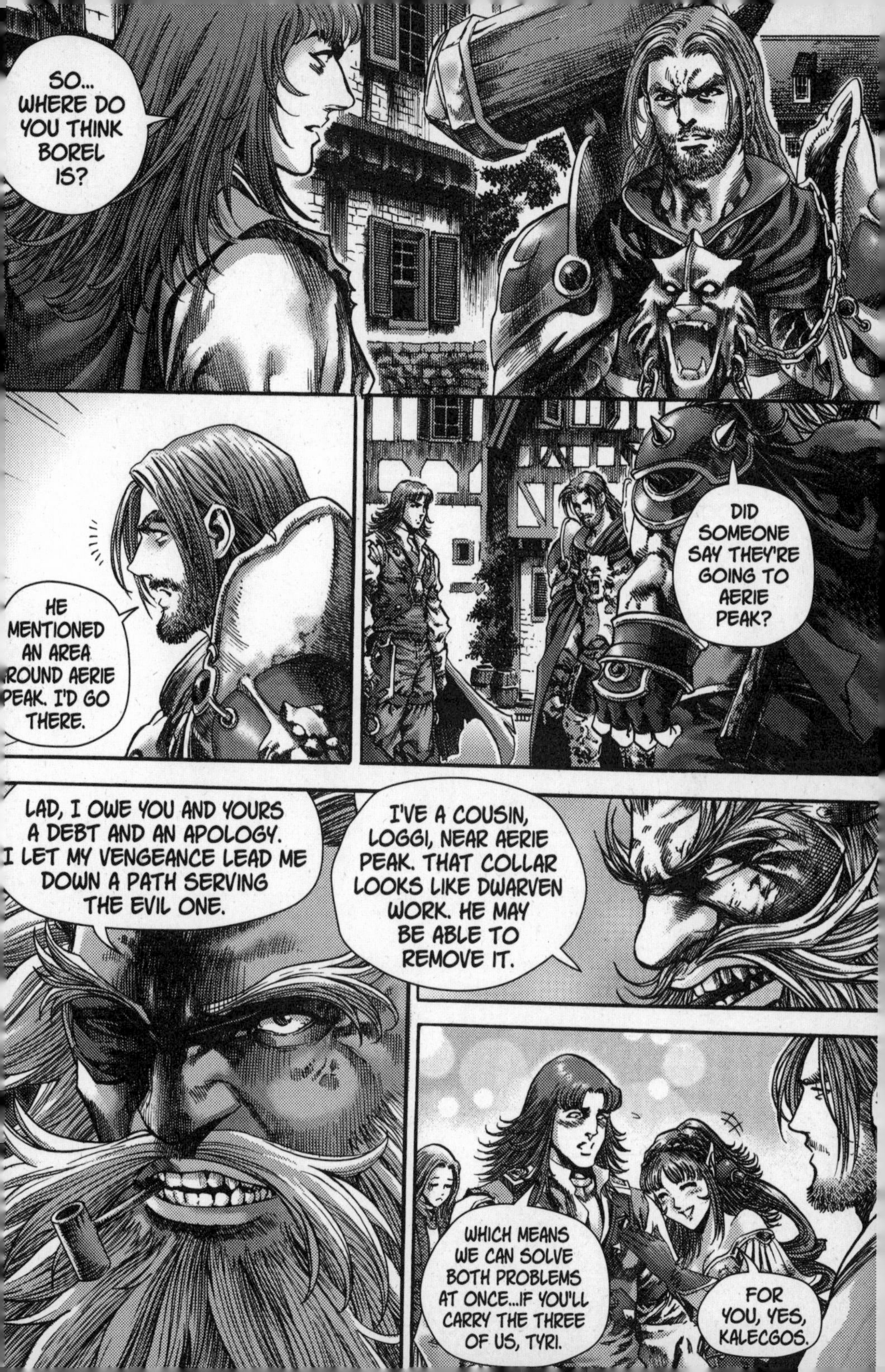
SO... WHERE DO YOU THINK BOREL IS?
HE MENTIONED AN AREA ROUND AERIE PEAK. I'D GO THERE.
DID SOMEONE SAY THEY'RE GOING TO AERIE PEAK?
LAD, I OWE YOU AND YOURS A DEBT AND AN APOLOGY. I LET MY VENGEANCE LEAD ME DOWN A PATH SERVING THE EVIL ONE.
I'VE A COUSIN, LOGGI, NEAR AERIE PEAK. THAT COLLAR LOOKS LIKE DWARVEN WORK. HE MAY BE ABLE TO REMOVE IT.
WHICH MEANS WE CAN SOLVE BOTH PROBLEMS AT ONCE...IF YOU'LL CARRY THE THREE OF US, TYRI.
FOR YOU, YES, KALECGOS.

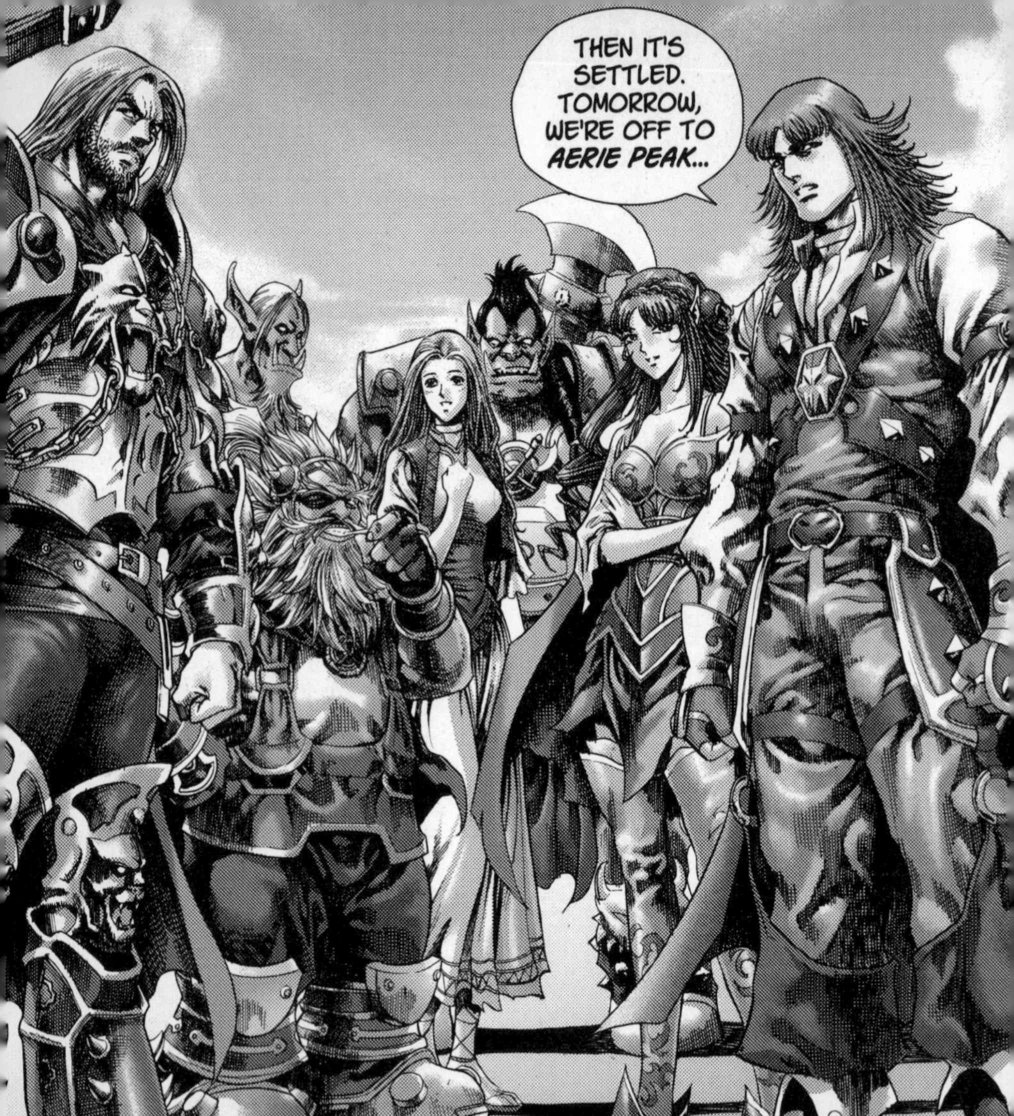
THEN IT'S SETTLED. TOMORROW, WE'RE OFF TO AERIE PEAK...
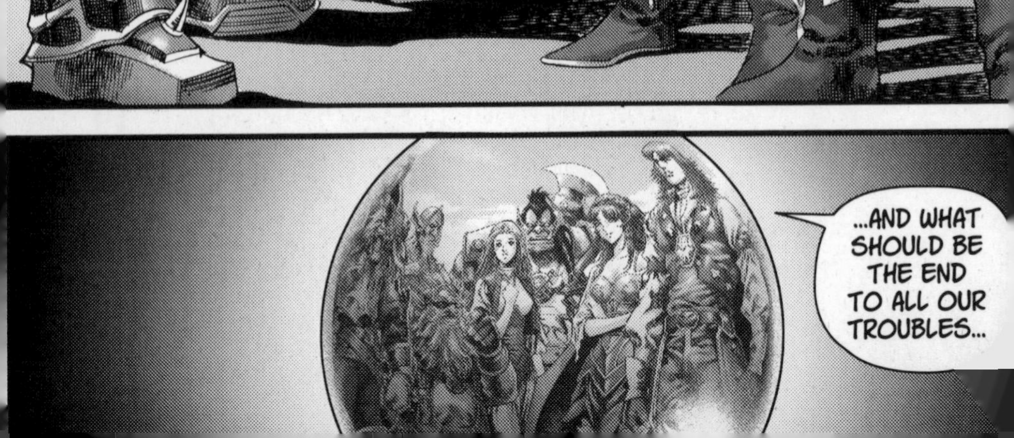
...AND WHAT SHOULD BE THE END TO ALL OUR TROUBLES...

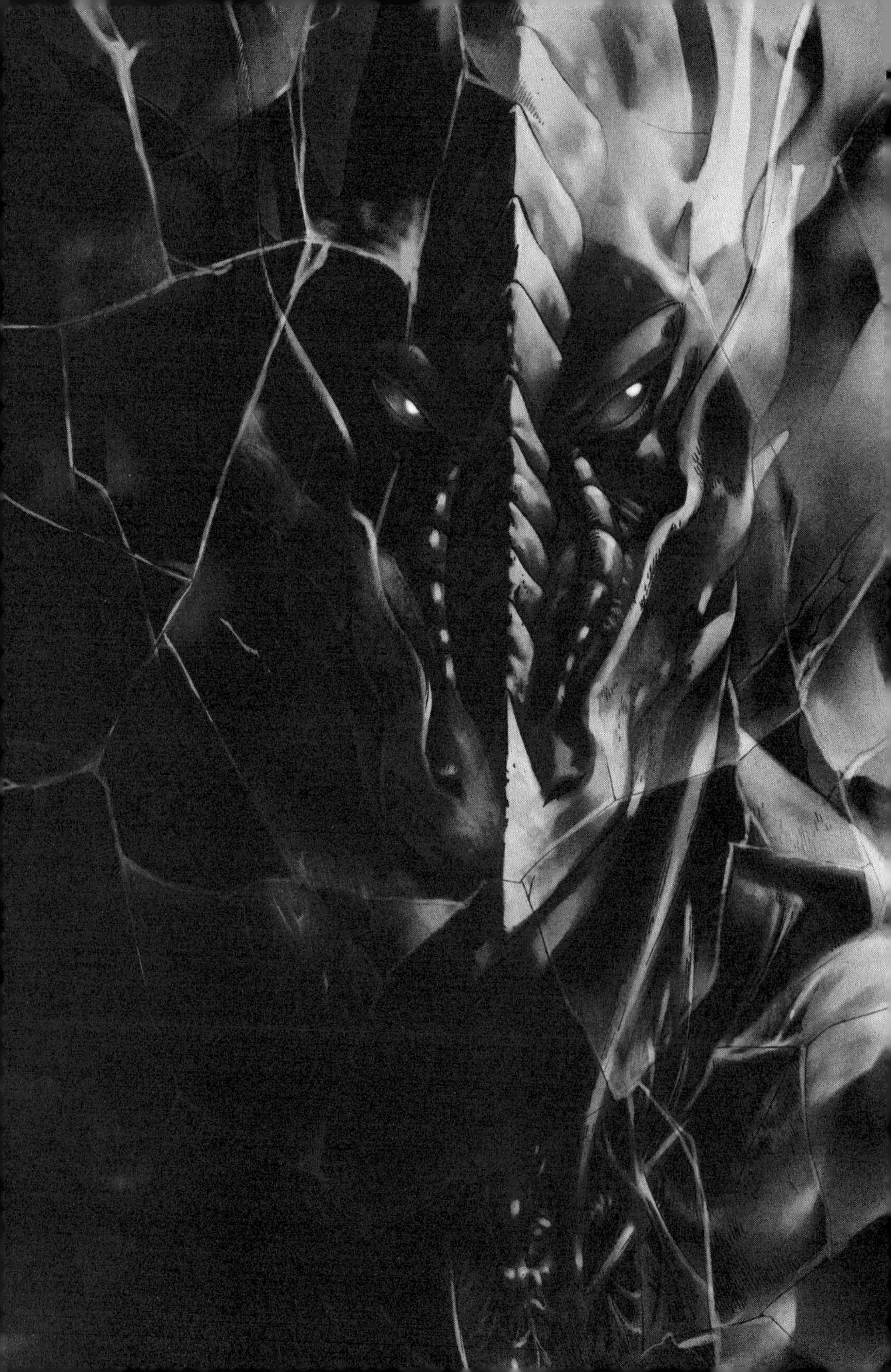

CHAPTER ONE
Terror on the Mountain

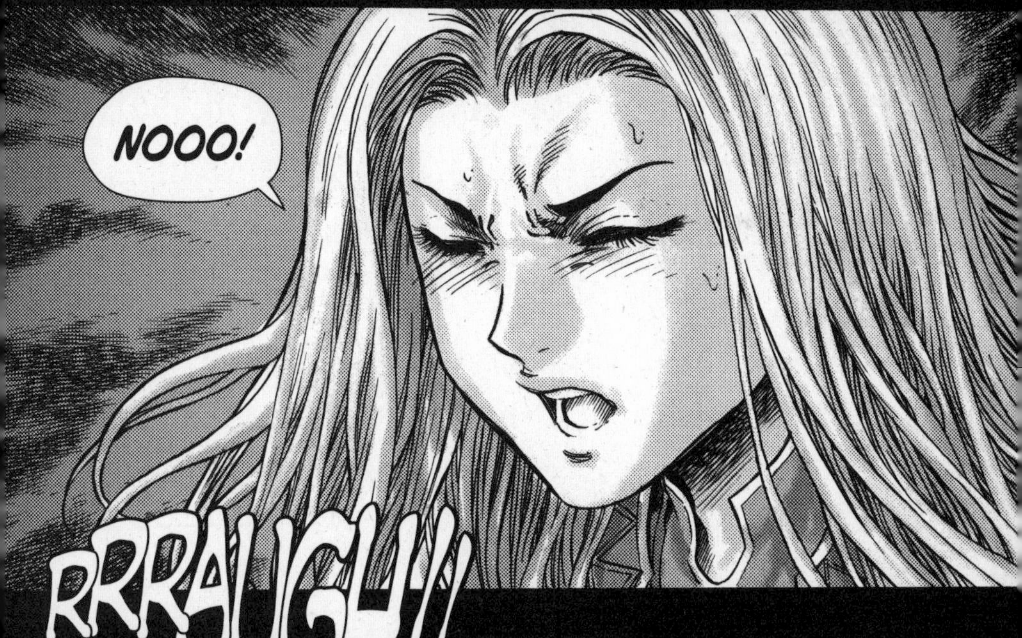
NOOO!
RRRAUGH!!

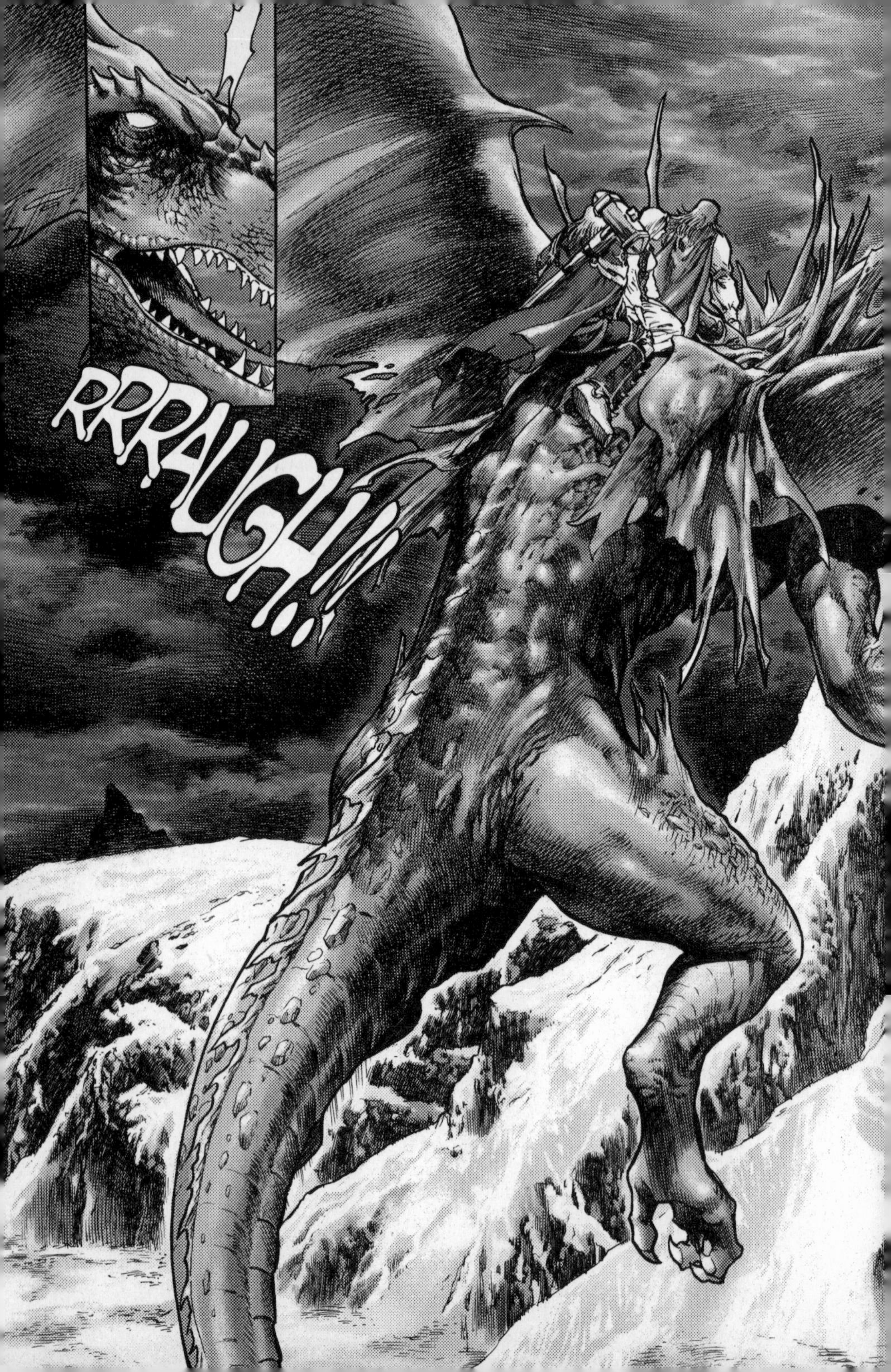
RRRRAUGH!!

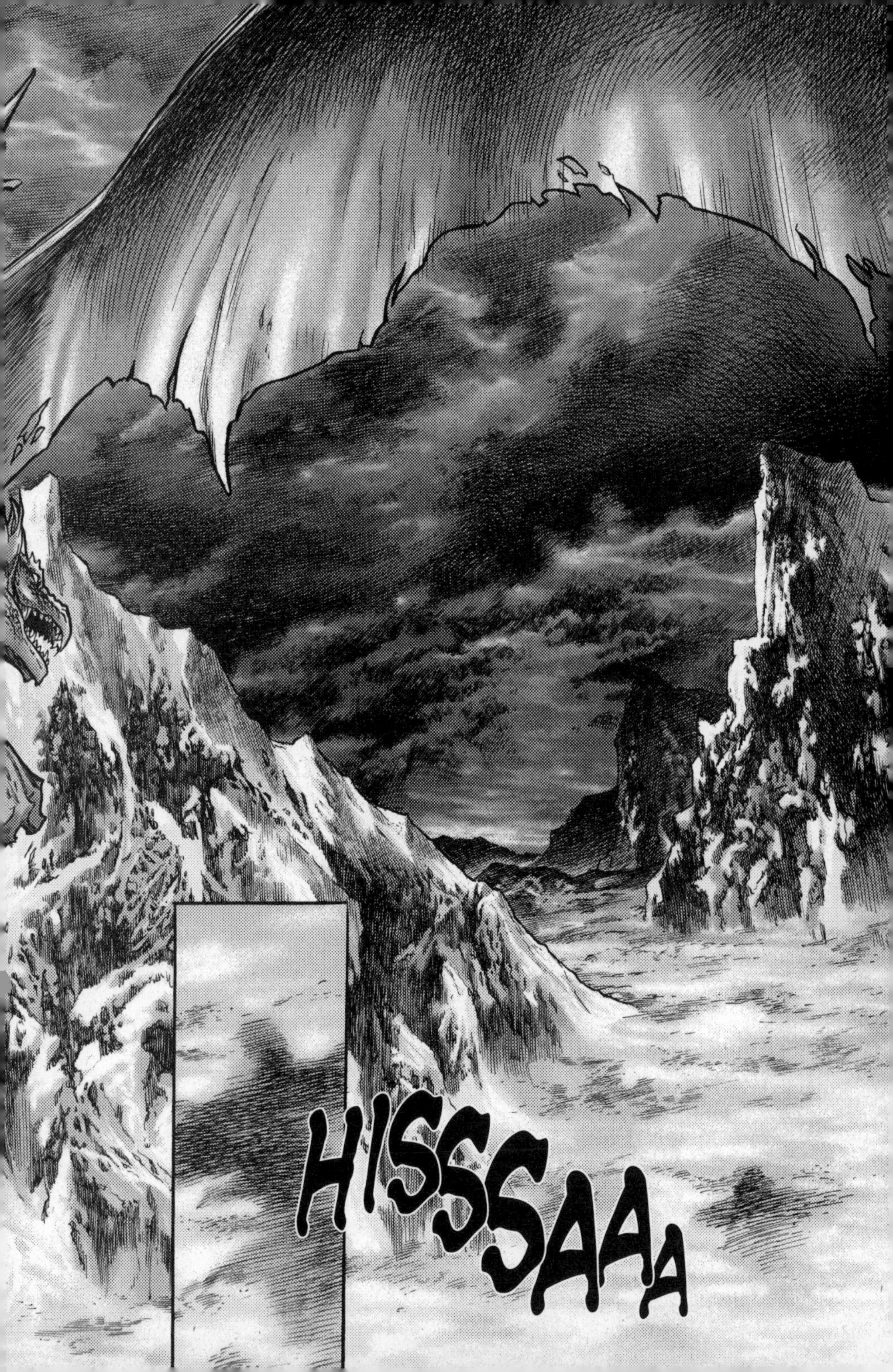
HISSSAAA

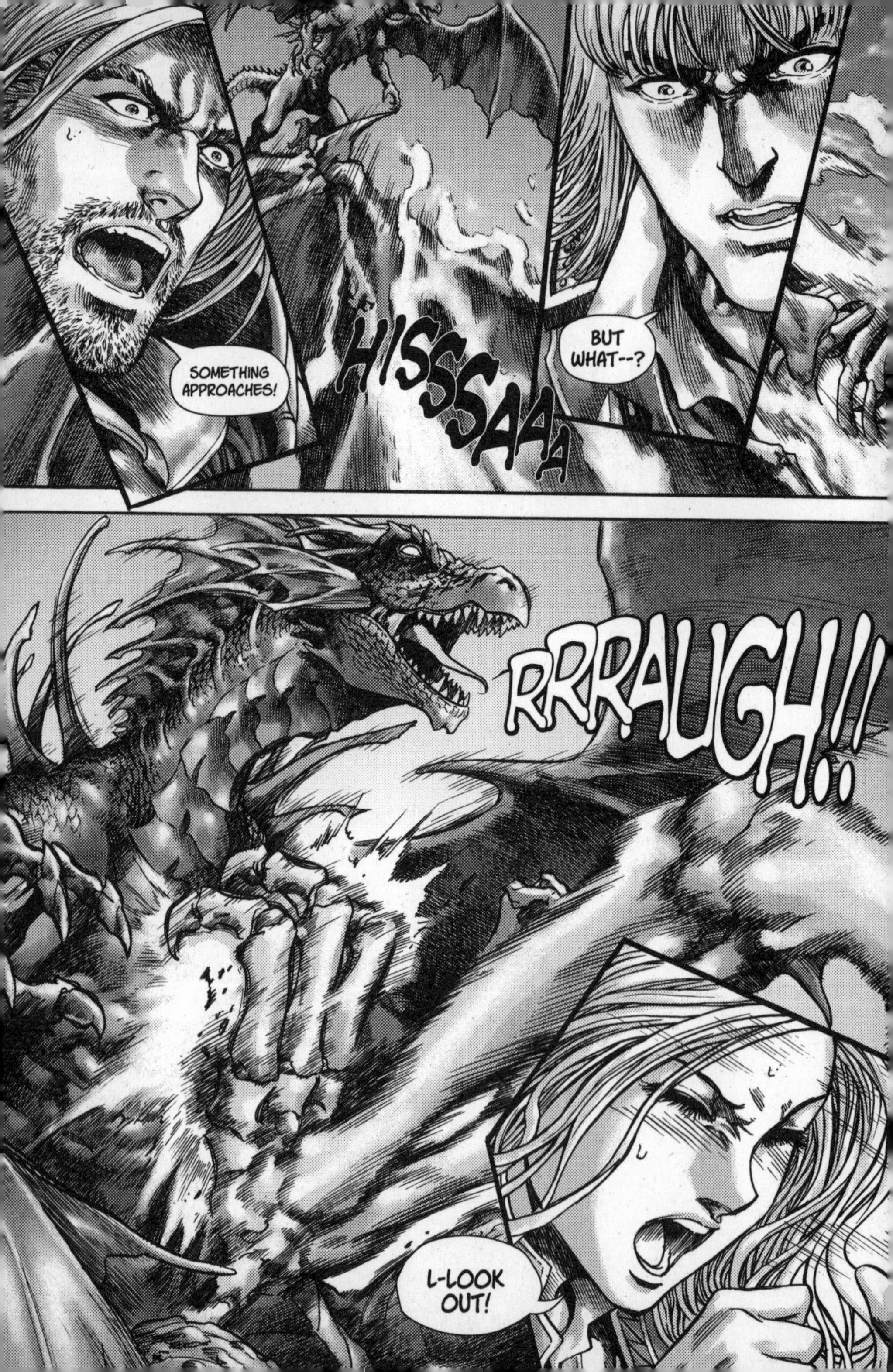
SOMETHING APPROACHES!
HISSSAAAA
BUT WHAT--?
RRRAUGH!!
L-LOOK OUT!

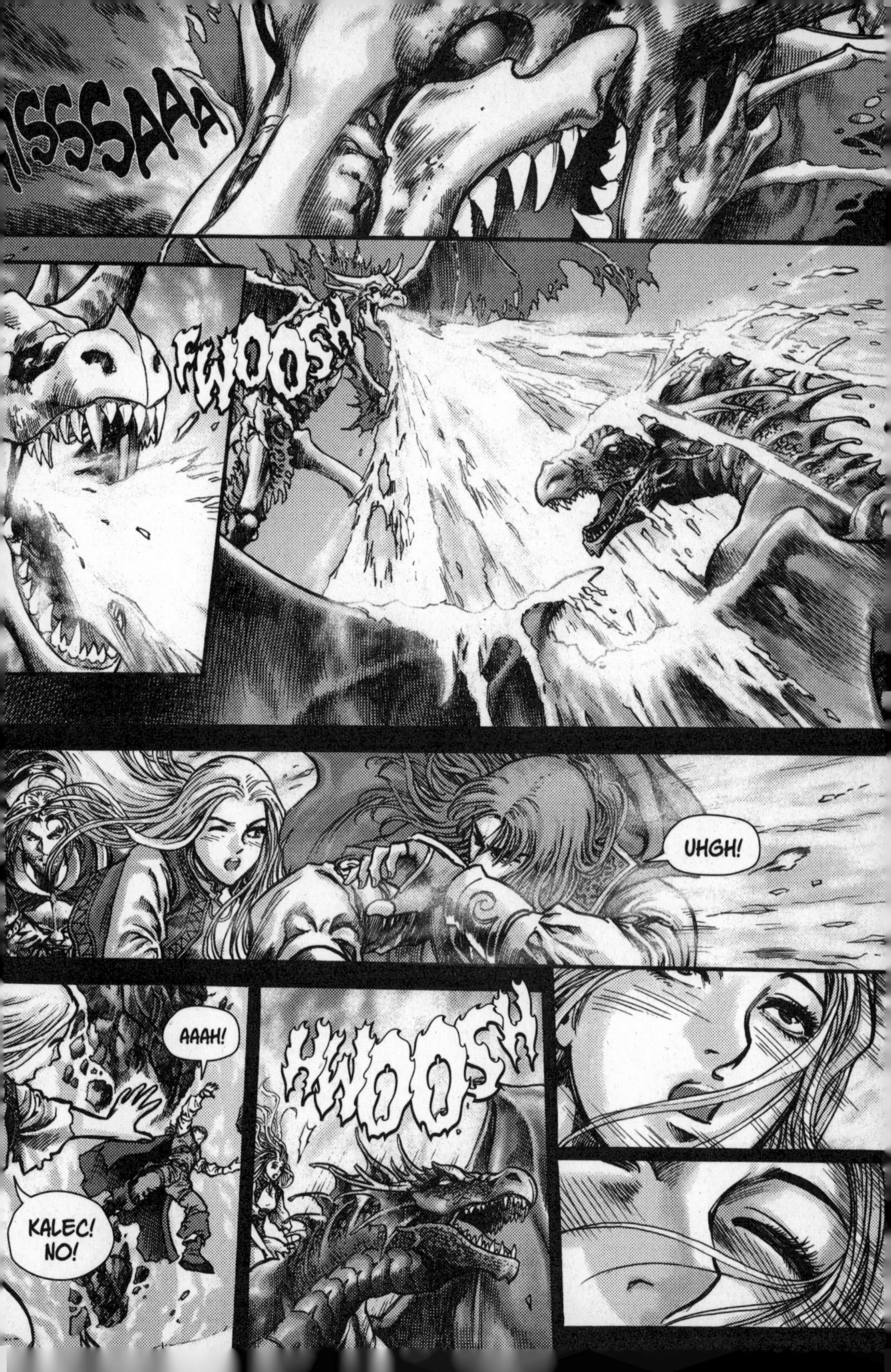
ISSSSAAA
FWOOSH
UHGH!
AAAH!
KALEC! NO!
FWOOSH

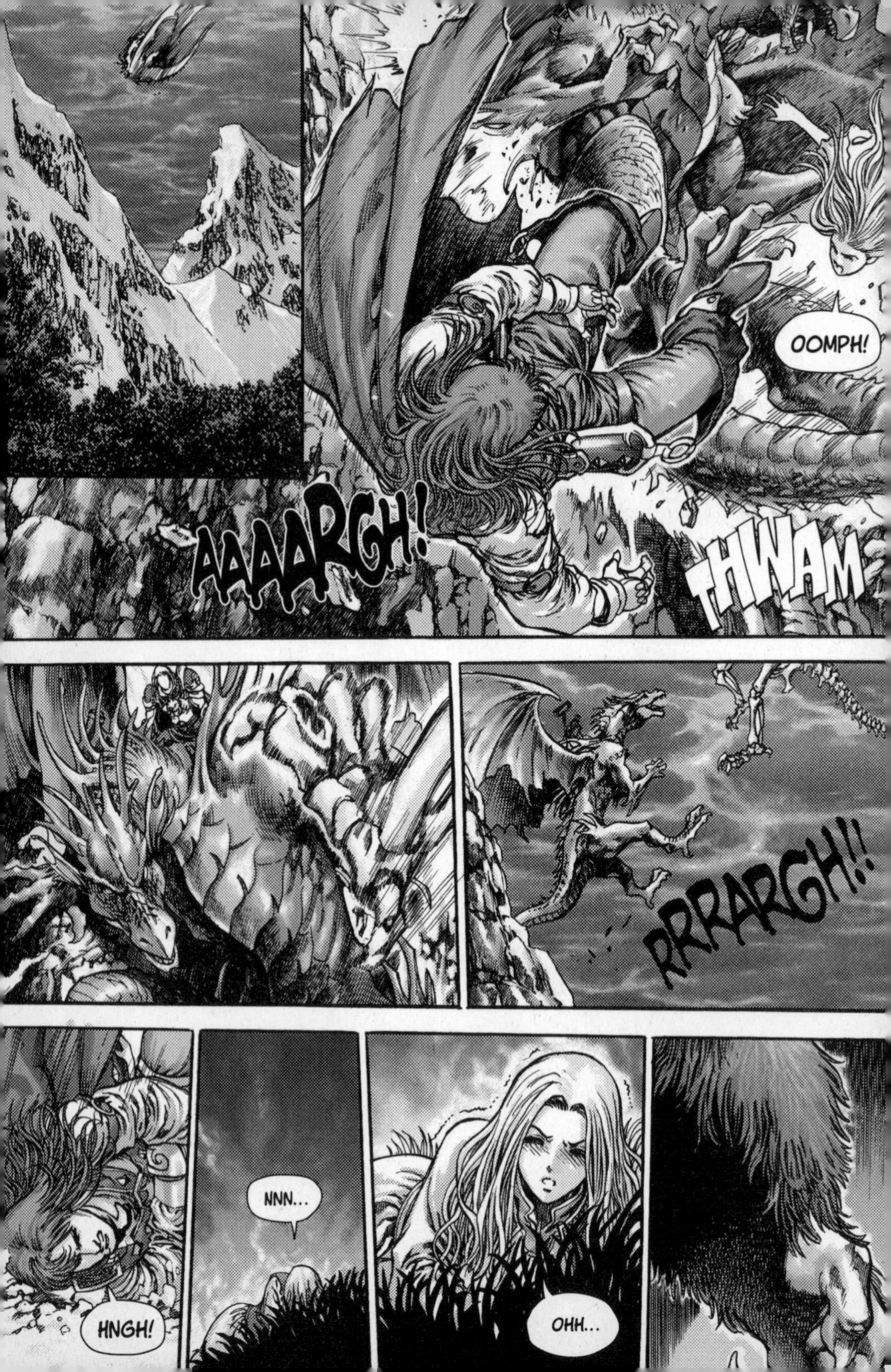
OOMPH!
THWAM
AAAARGH!
RRRARGH!!
OHH...
NNN...
HNGH!

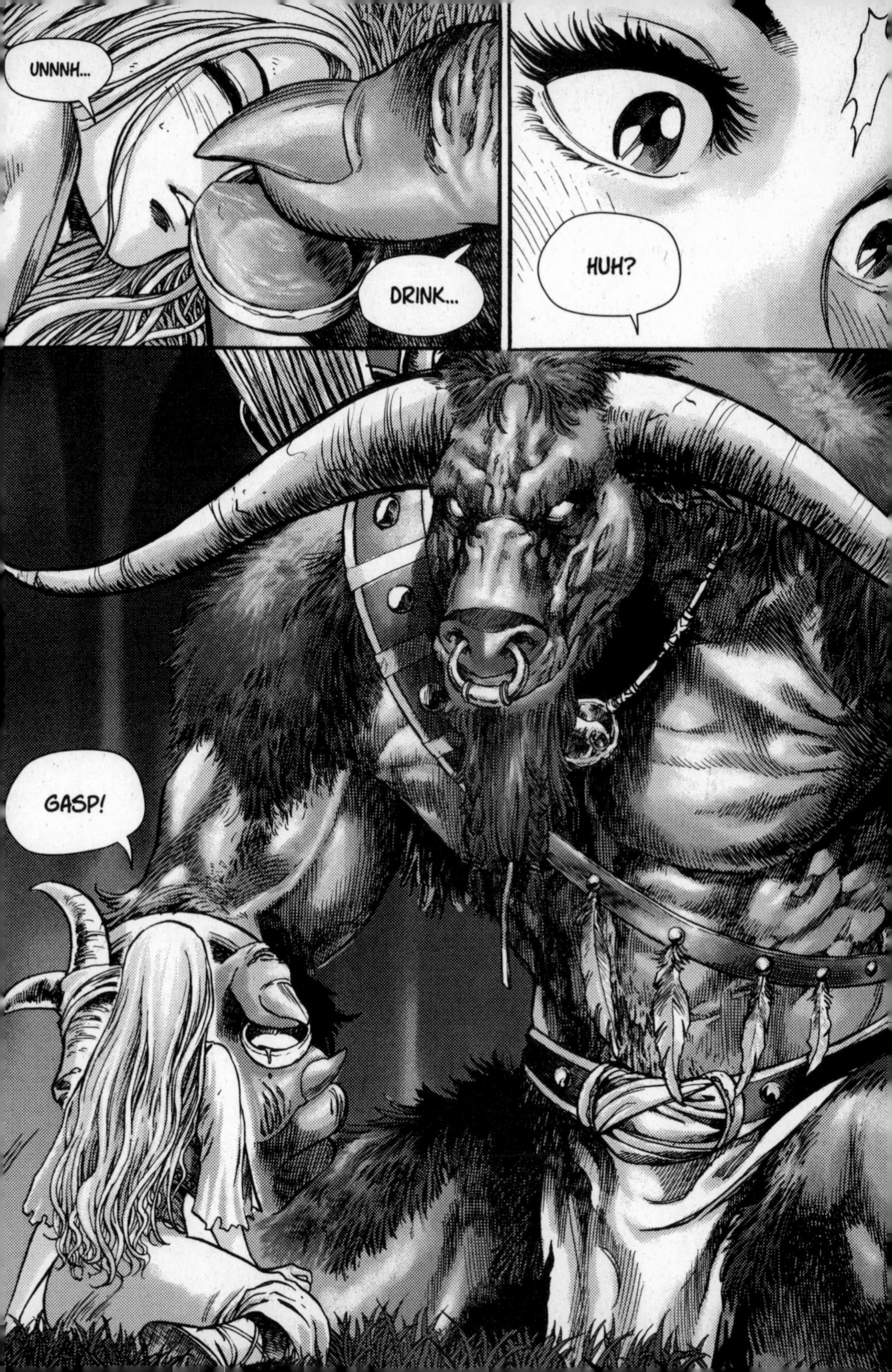
UNNNH...
DRINK...
HUH?
GASP!

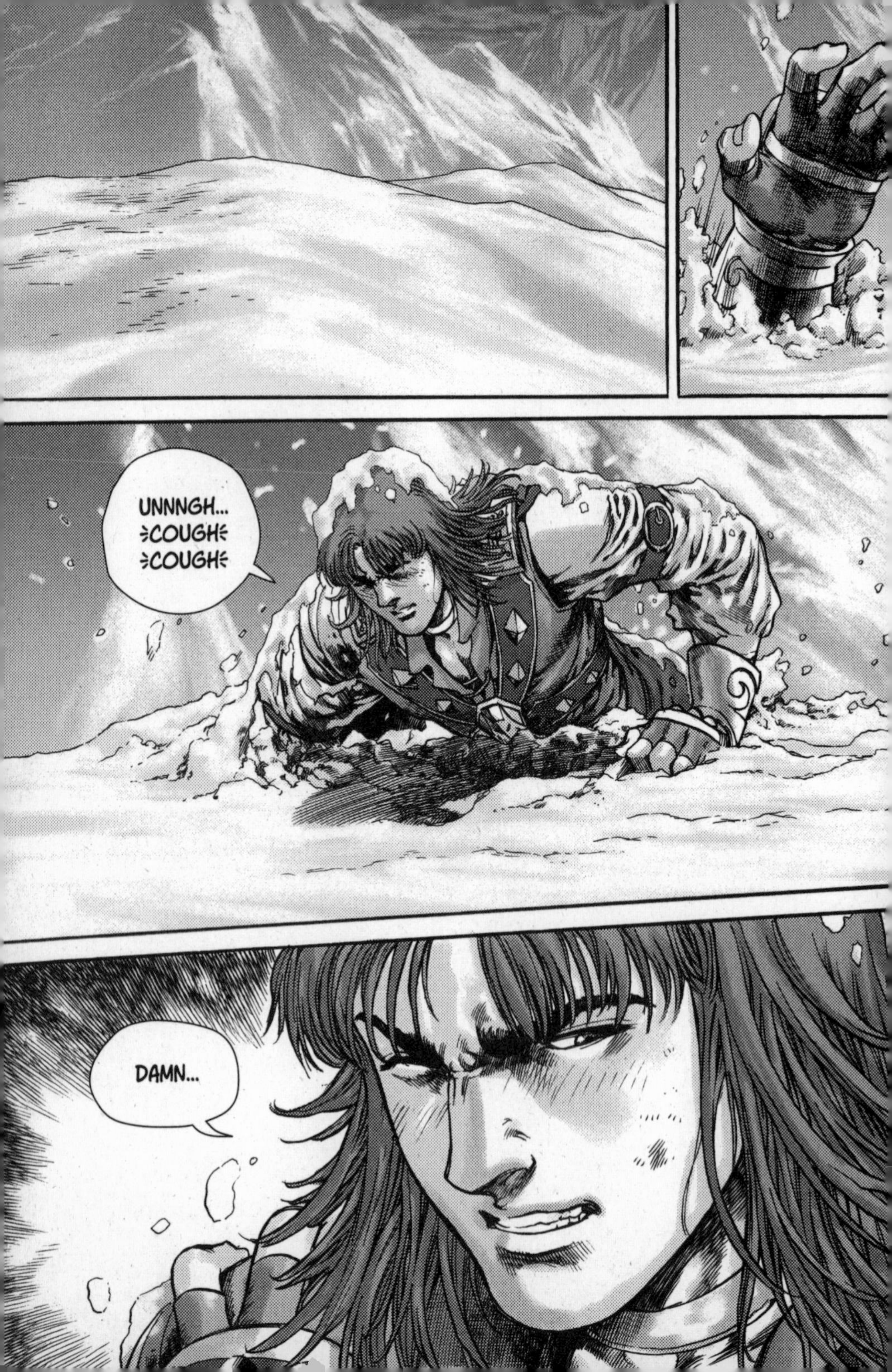
UNNNGH...
COUGH
COUGH
DAMN...

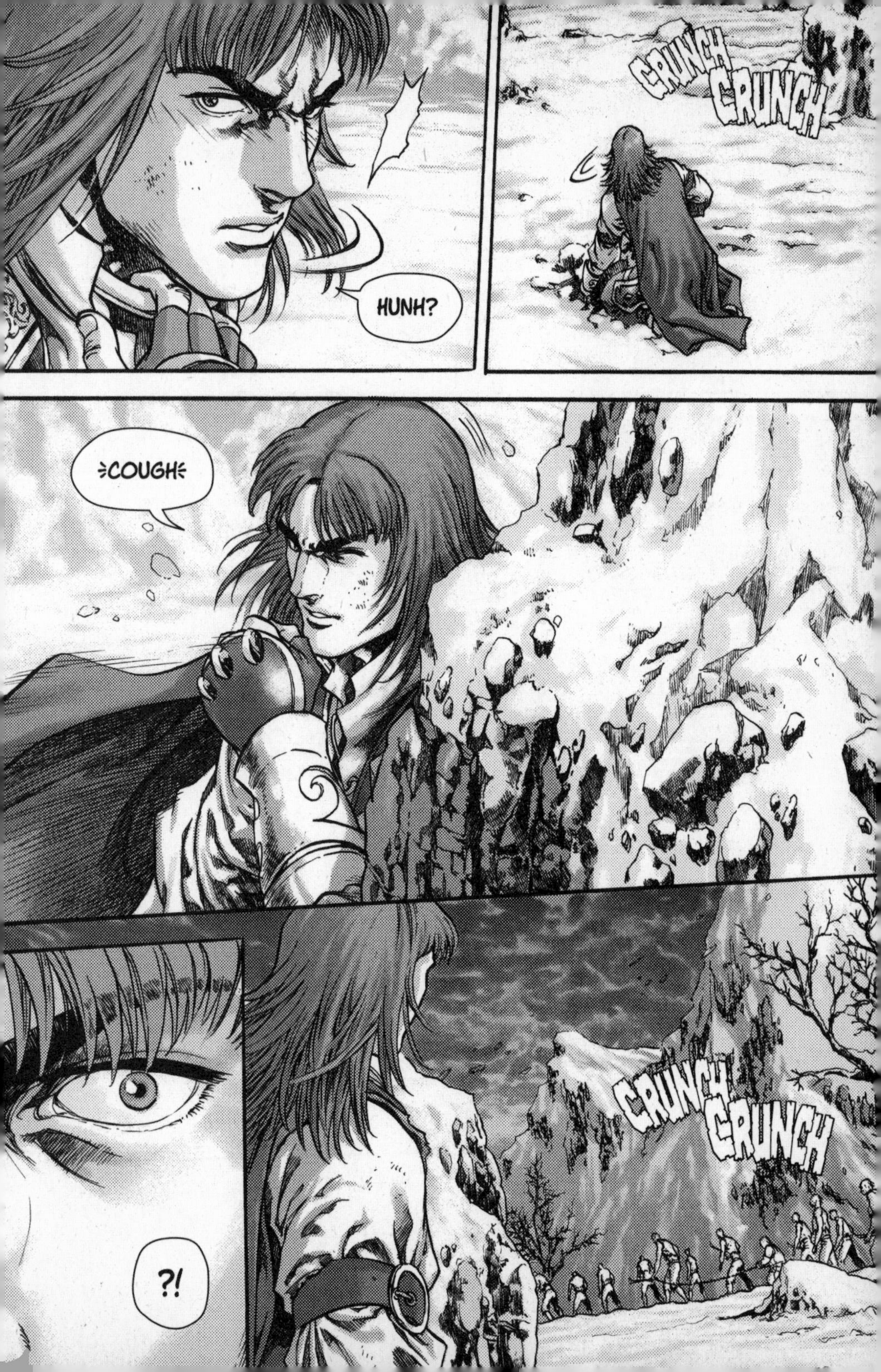
CRUNCH CRUNCH
HUNH?
COUGH
CRUNCH CRUNCH
?!

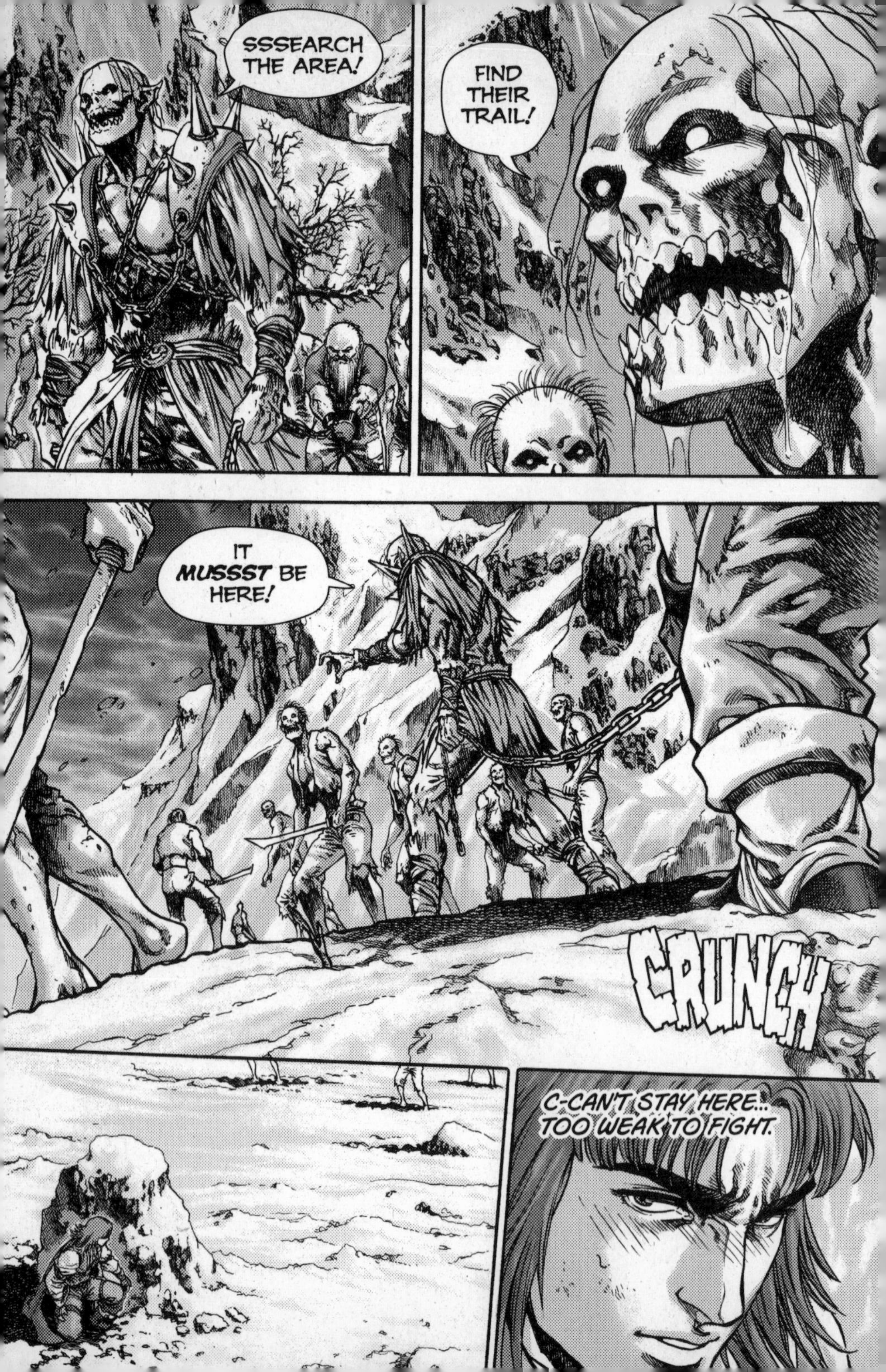
SSSEARCH THE AREA!
FIND THEIR TRAIL!
IT MUSSST BE HERE!
CRUNCH
C-CAN'T STAY HERE... TOO WEAK TO FIGHT.

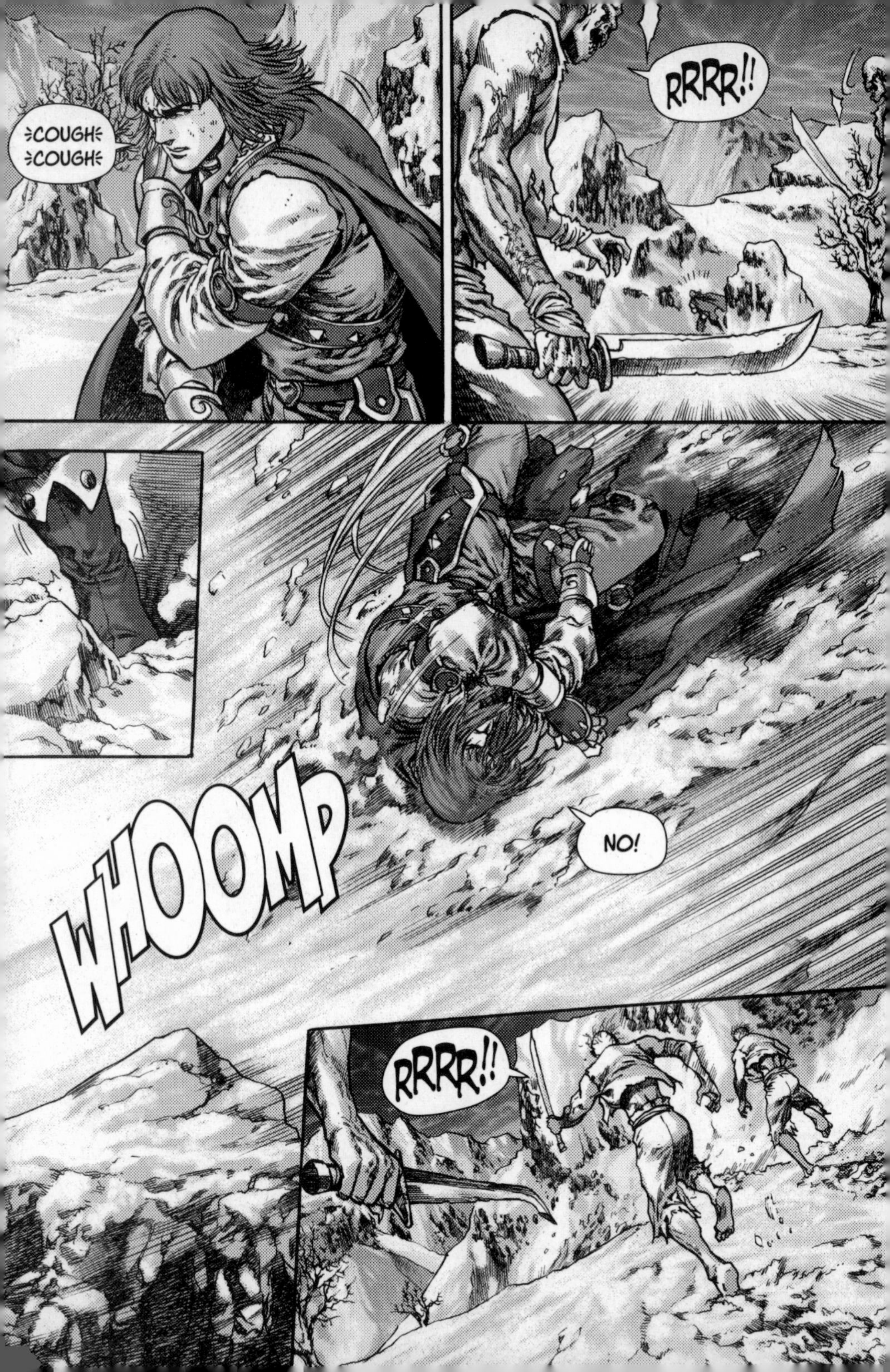
RRRR!!
COUGH COUGH
WHOOMP
NO!
RRRR!!

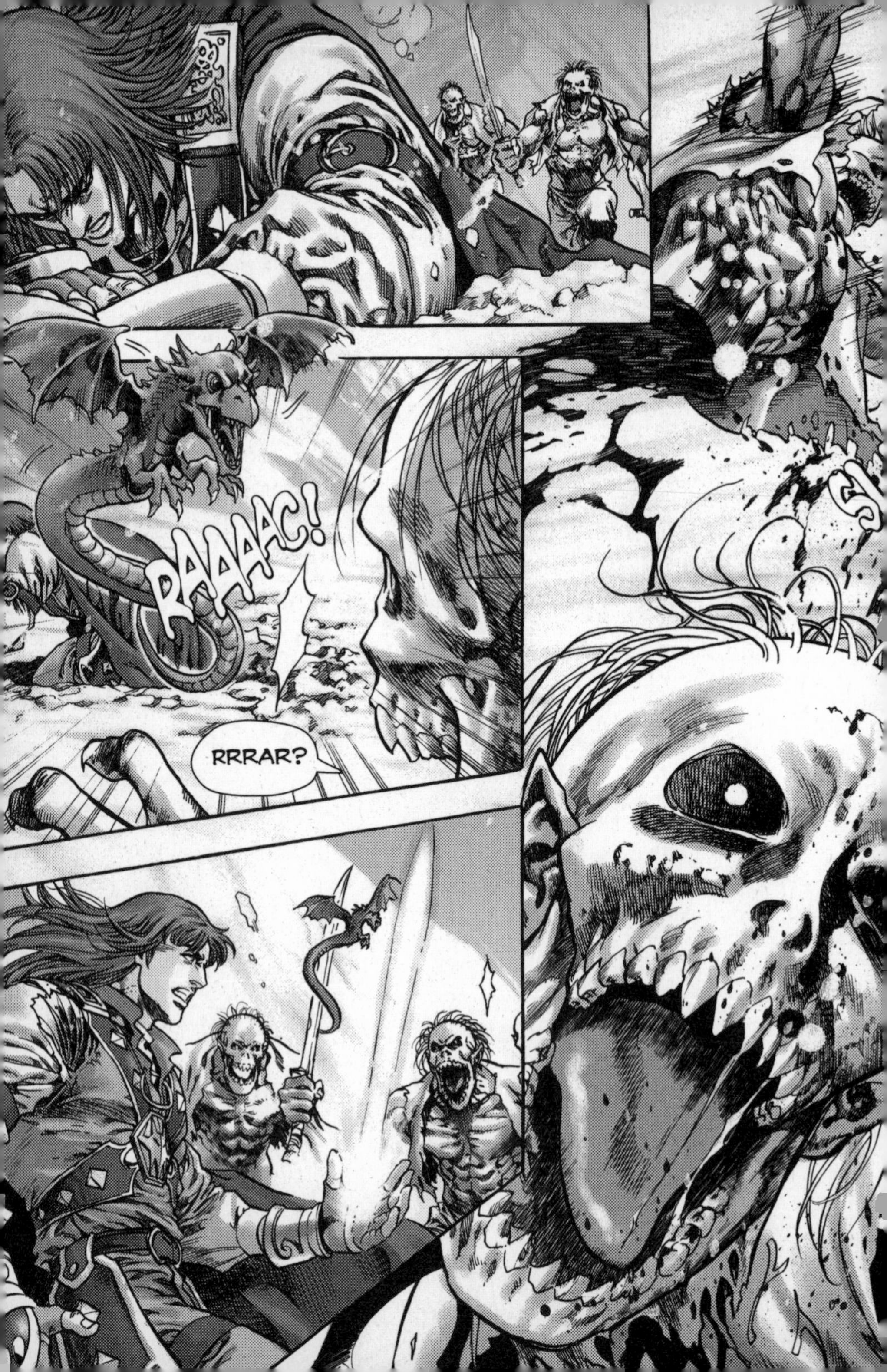
RAAAAC!
RRRAR?

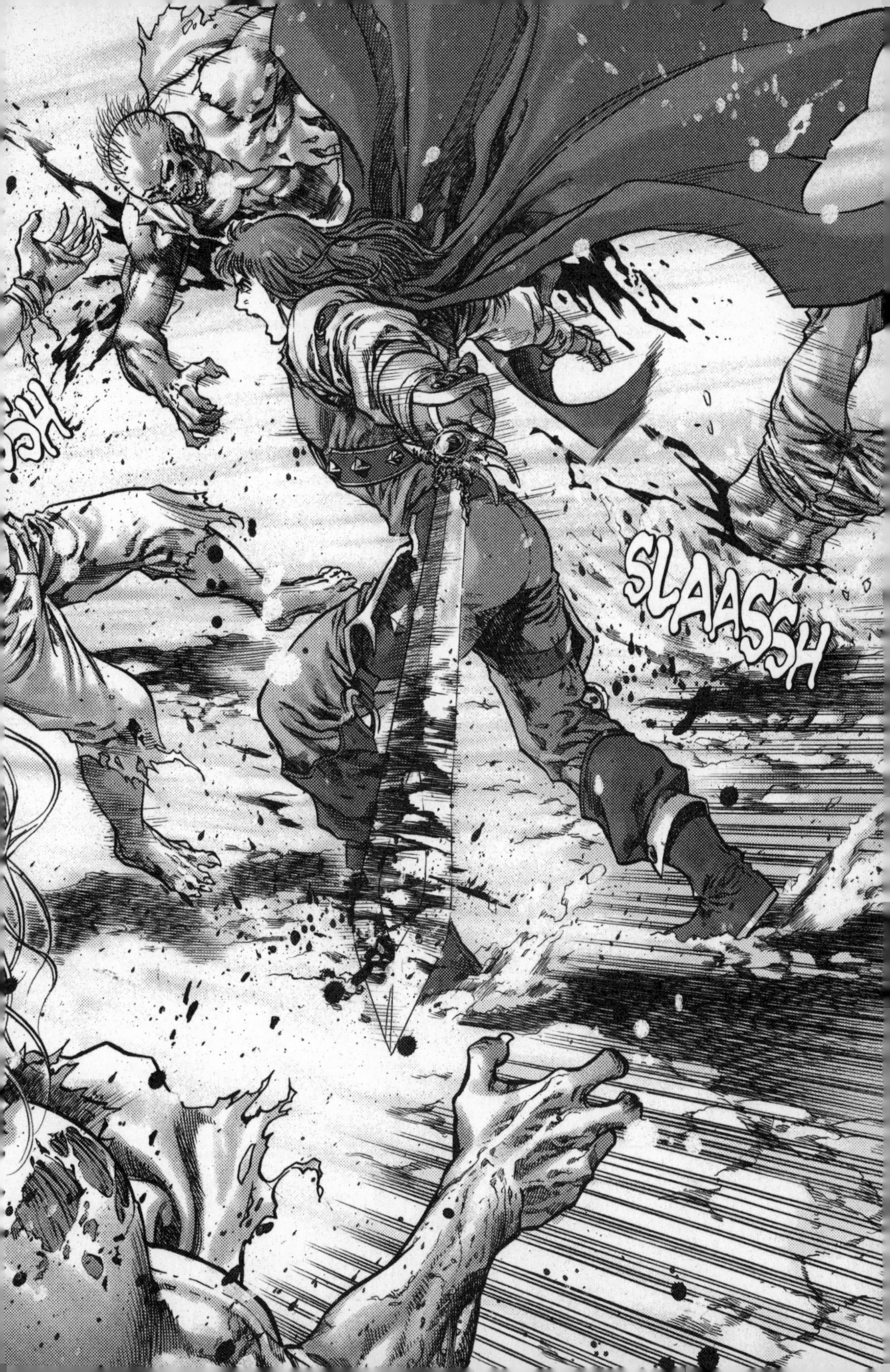
SLAASSH

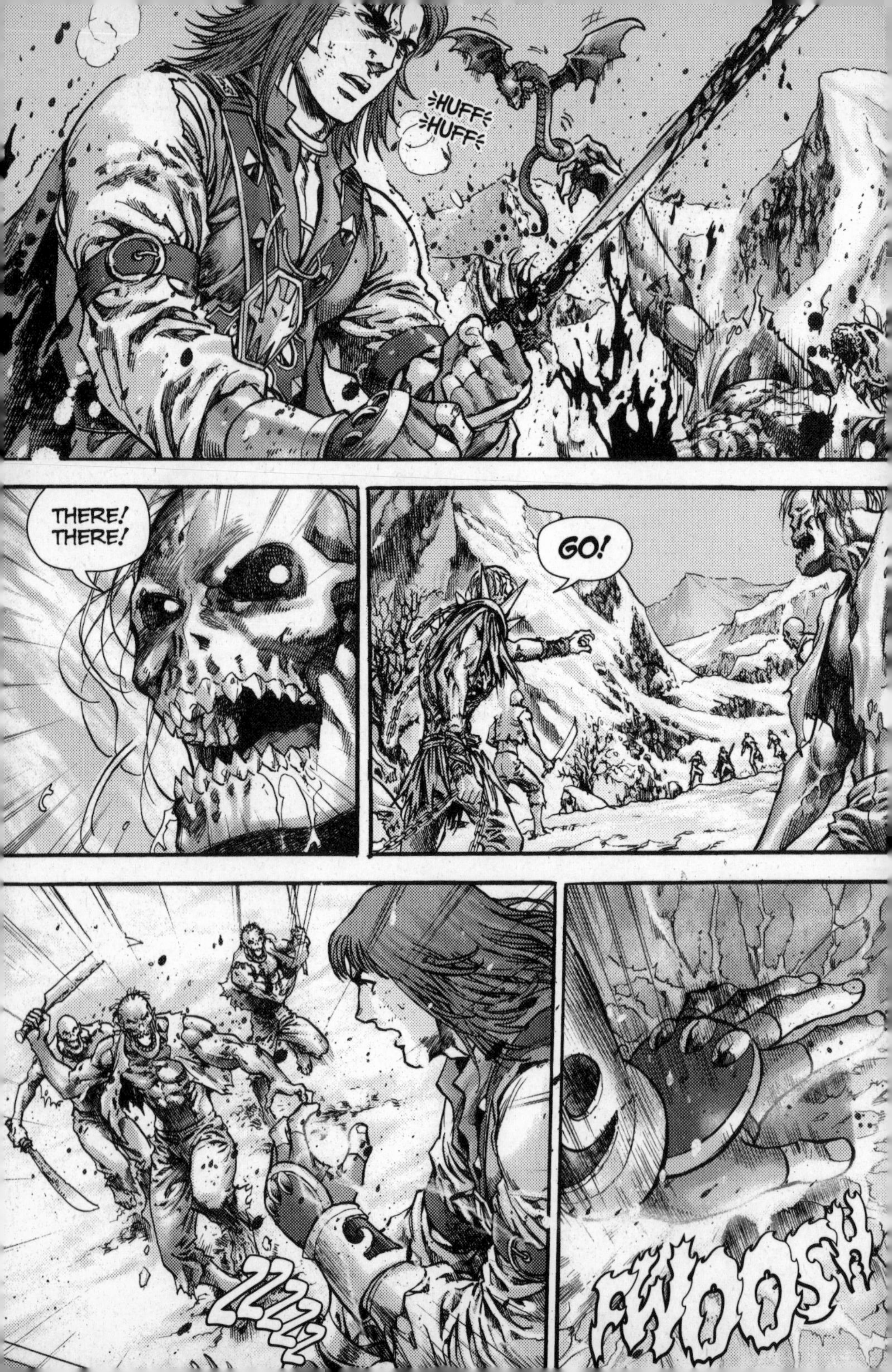

HUFF
HUFF
THERE! THERE!
GO!
ZZZZZ
FWOOSH

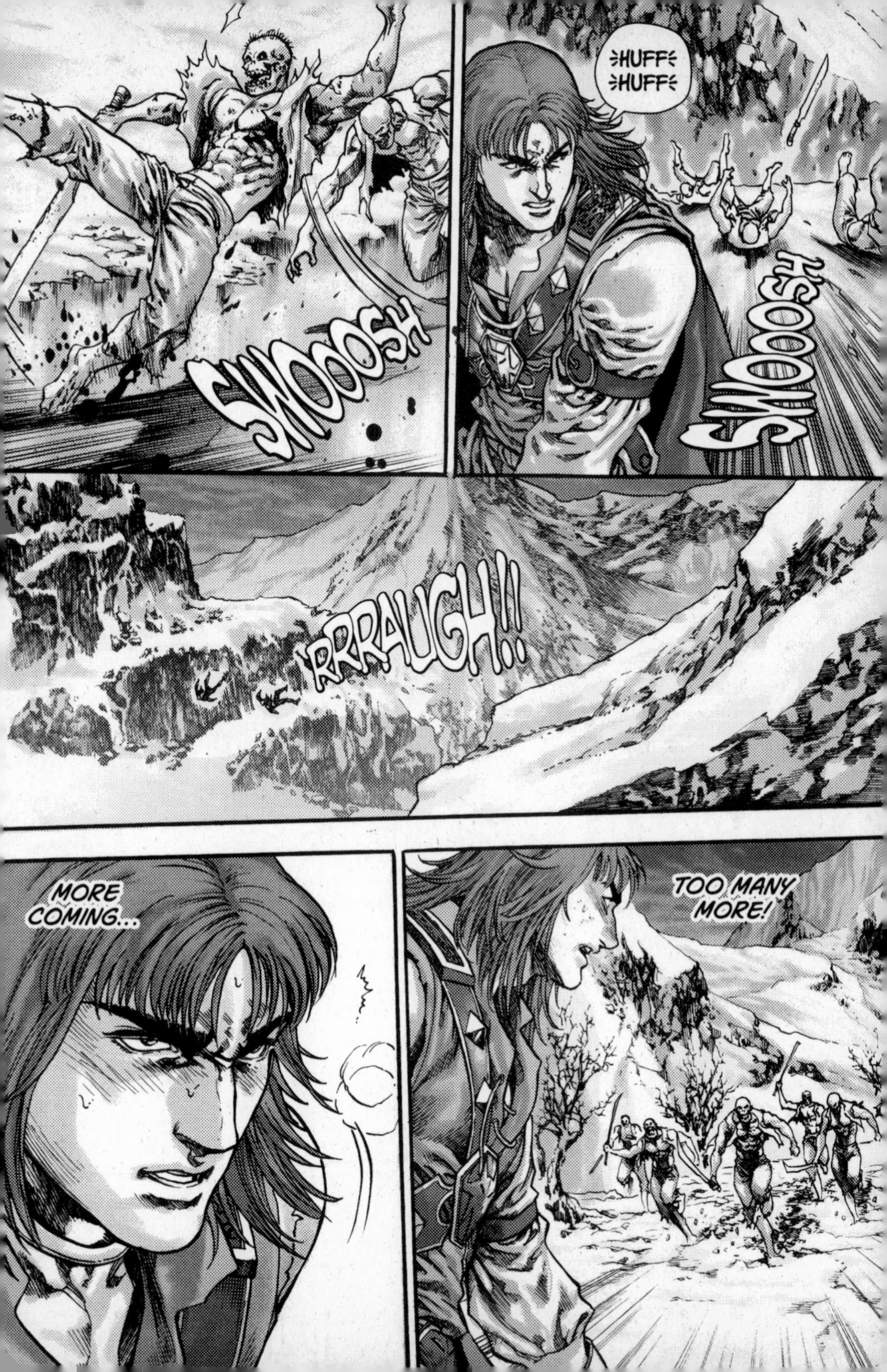
SWOOSH
HUFF HUFF
SWOOSH
RRRAUGH!!
MORE COMING...
TOO MANY MORE!

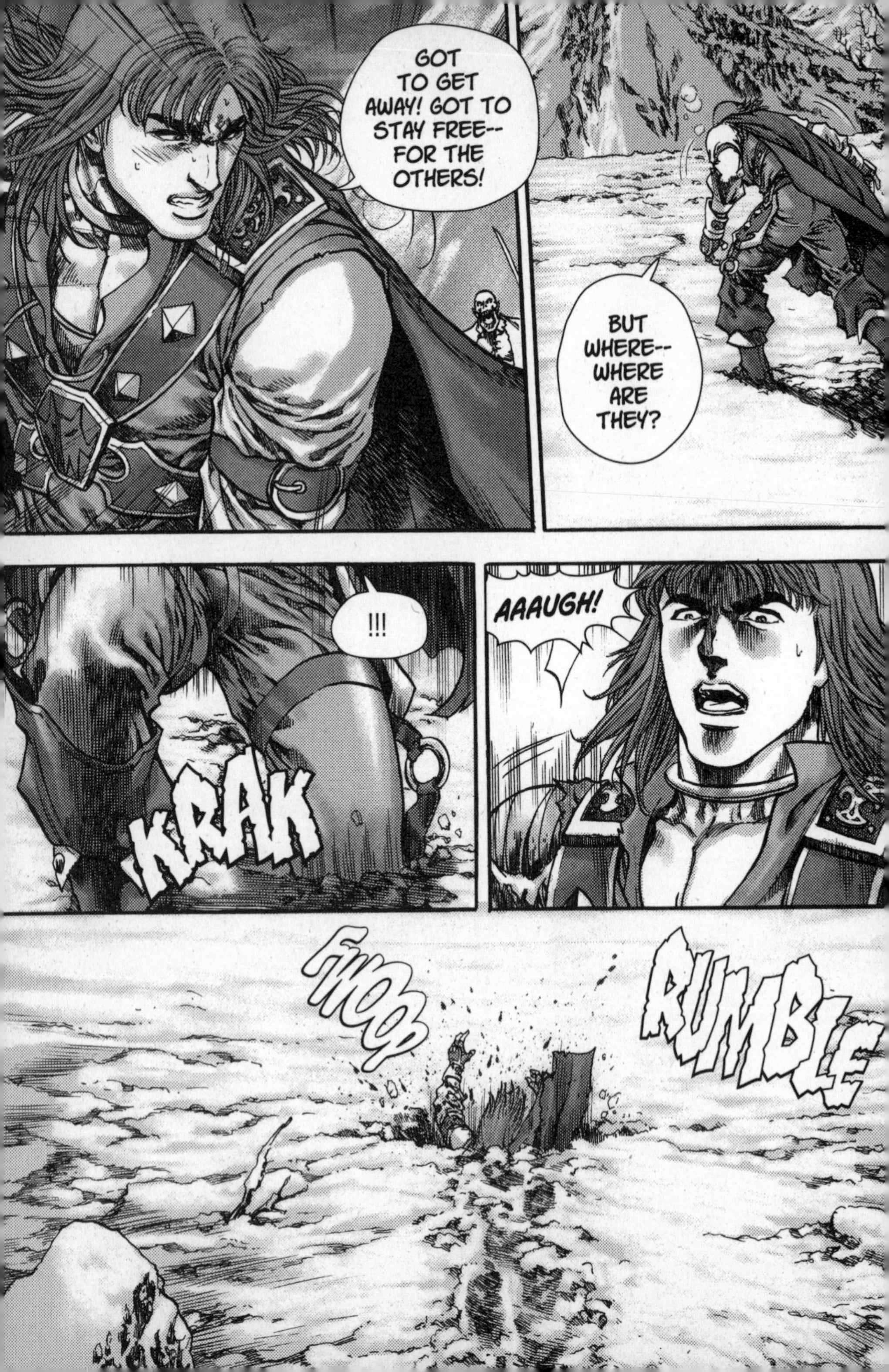
GOT TO GET AWAY! GOT TO STAY FREE-- FOR THE OTHERS!
BUT WHERE-- WHERE ARE THEY?
!!!
KRAK
AAAUGH!
FWOOSH
RUMBLE

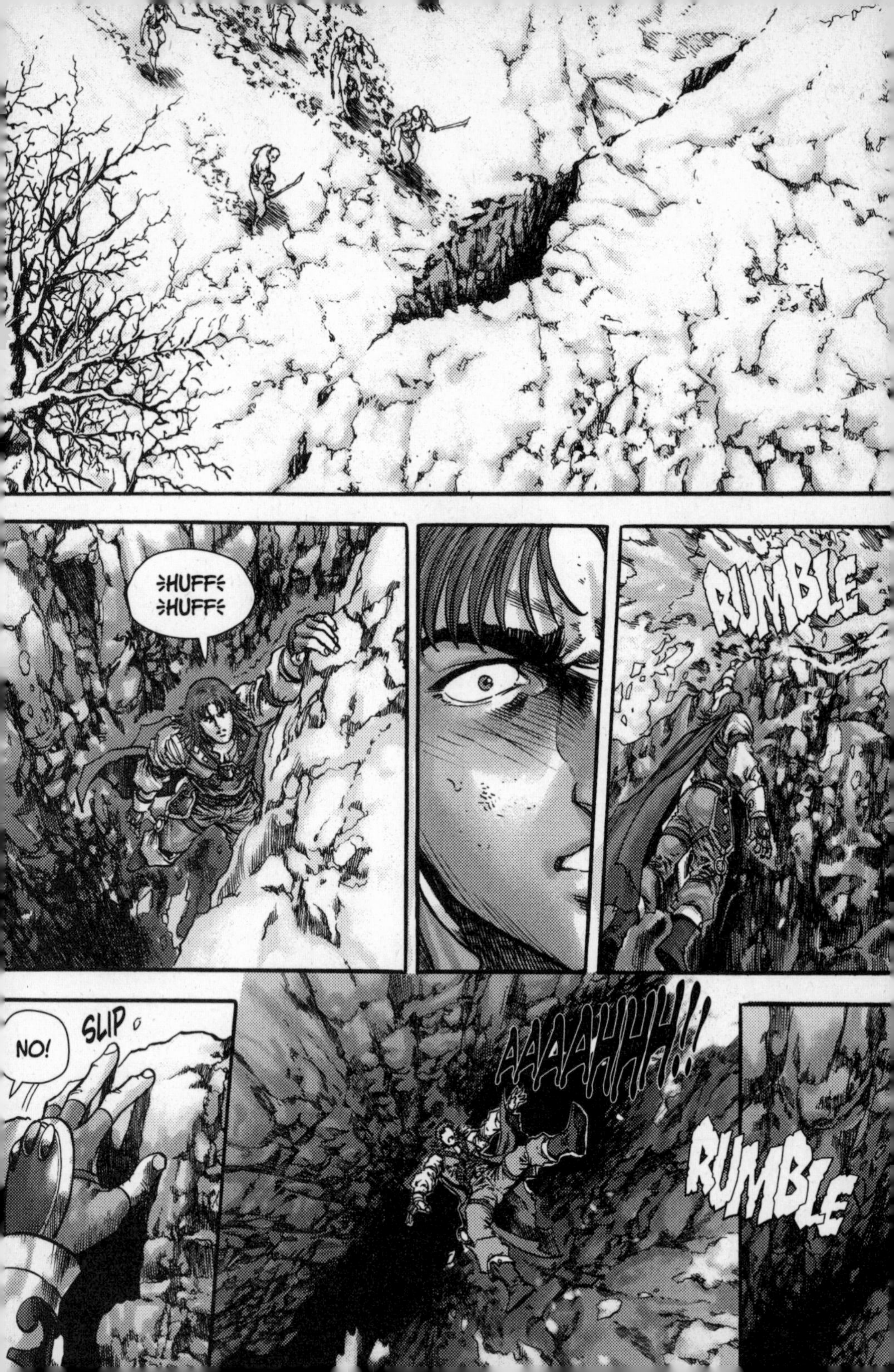
HUFF
HUFF
RUMBLE
NO!
SLIP
AAAAHHH!!
RUMBLE

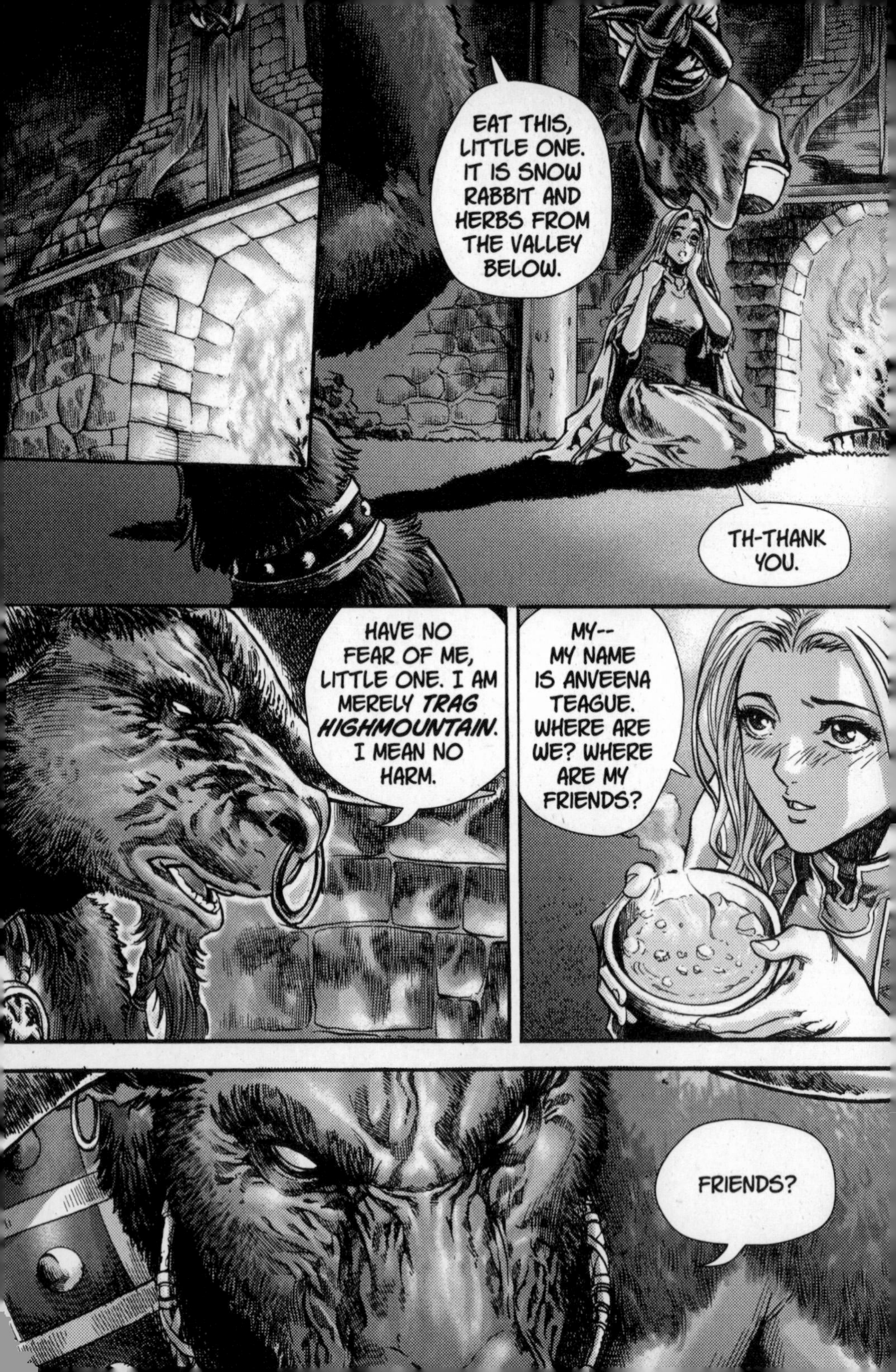
EAT THIS, LITTLE ONE. IT IS SNOW RABBIT AND HERBS FROM THE VALLEY BELOW.
TH-THANK YOU.
HAVE NO FEAR OF ME, LITTLE ONE. I AM MERELY *TRAG HIGHMOUNTAIN*. I MEAN NO HARM.
MY-- MY NAME IS ANVEENA TEAGUE. WHERE ARE WE? WHERE ARE MY FRIENDS?
FRIENDS?

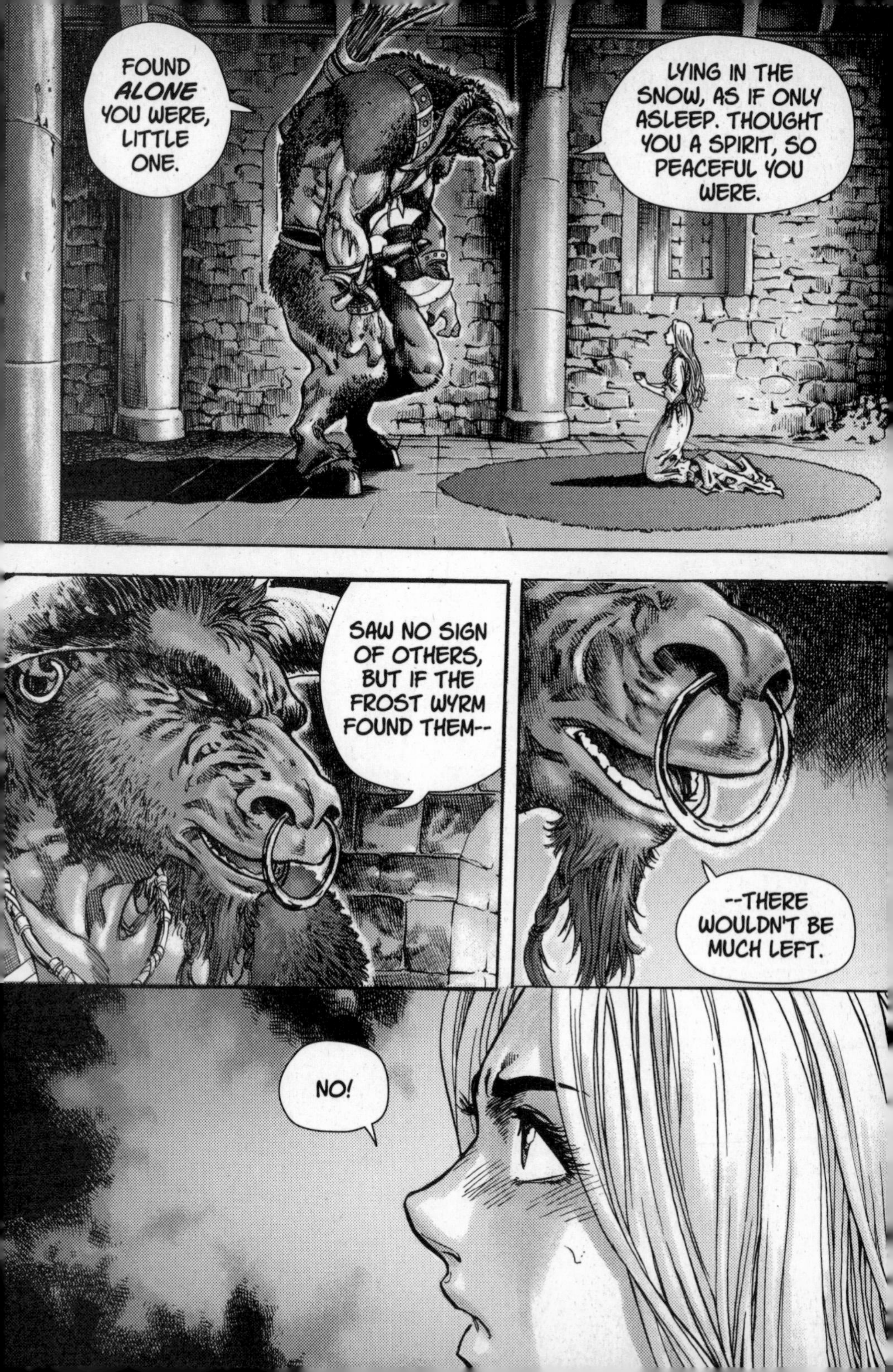
FOUND *ALONE* YOU WERE, LITTLE ONE.
LYING IN THE SNOW, AS IF ONLY ASLEEP. THOUGHT YOU A SPIRIT, SO PEACEFUL YOU WERE.
SAW NO SIGN OF OTHERS, BUT IF THE FROST WYRM FOUND THEM--
--THERE WOULDN'T BE MUCH LEFT.
NO!

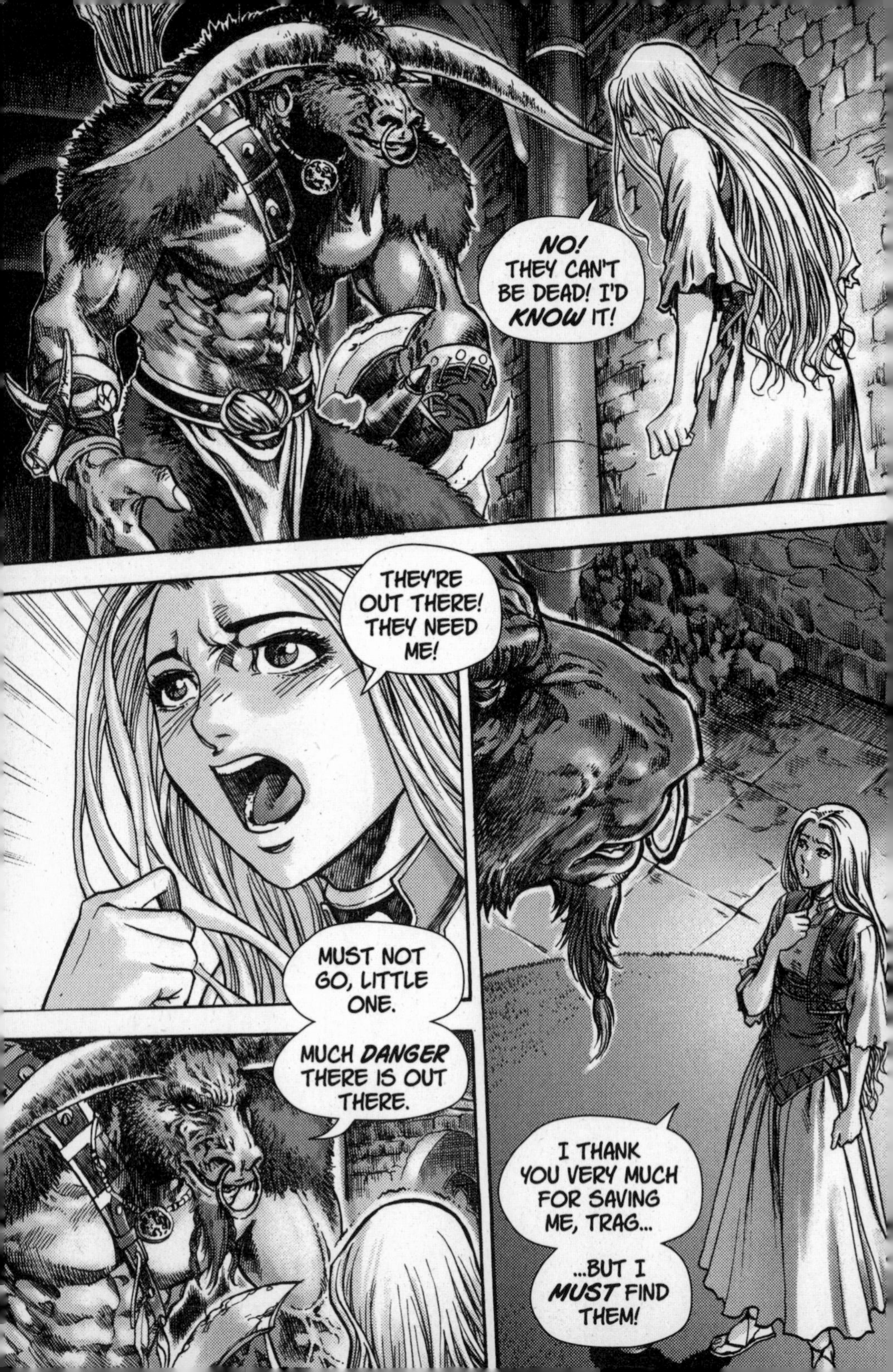
NO! THEY CAN'T BE DEAD! I'D KNOW IT!
THEY'RE OUT THERE! THEY NEED ME!
MUST NOT GO, LITTLE ONE.
MUCH DANGER THERE IS OUT THERE.
I THANK YOU VERY MUCH FOR SAVING ME, TRAG...
...BUT I MUST FIND THEM!

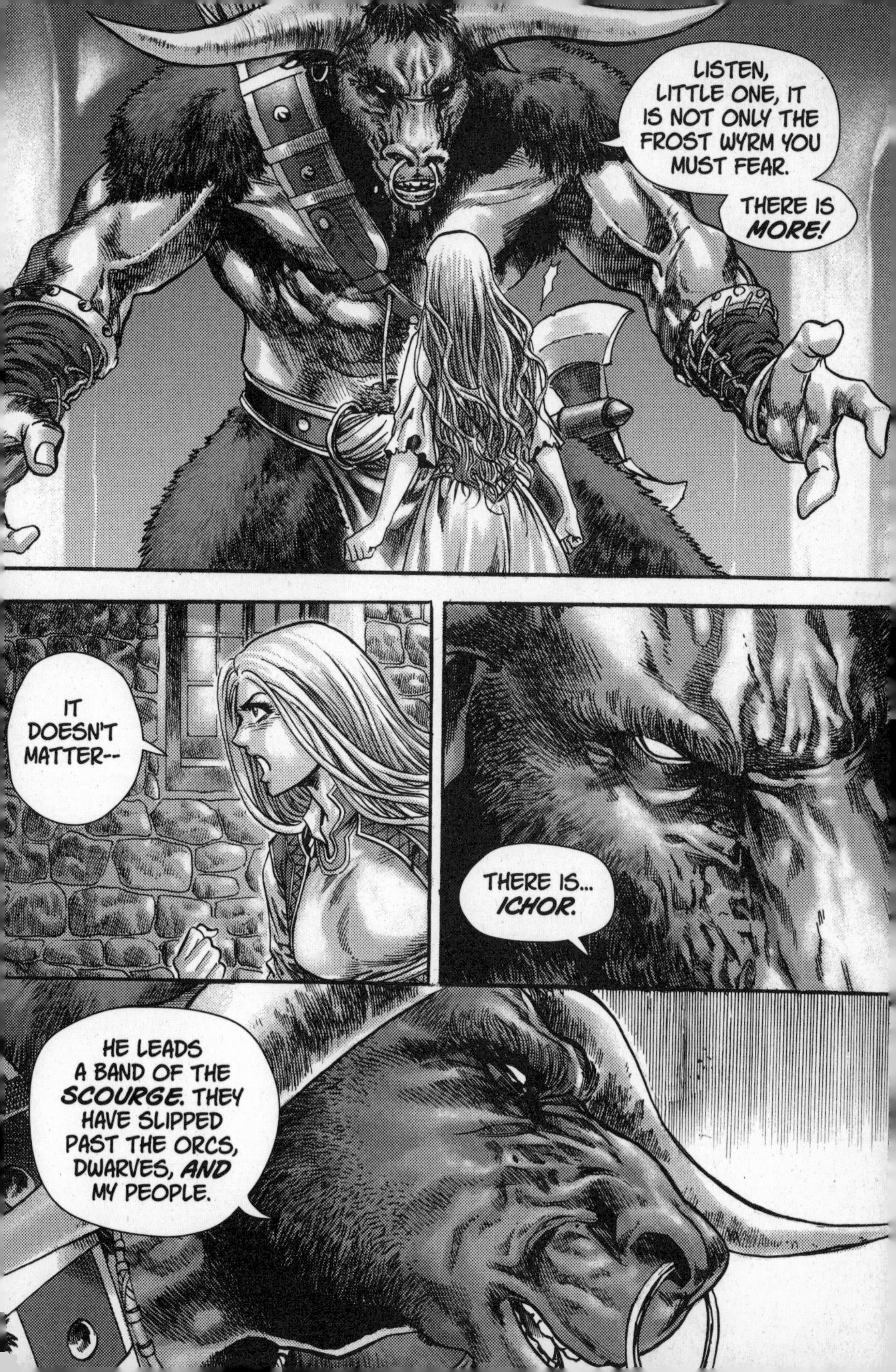
LISTEN, LITTLE ONE, IT IS NOT ONLY THE FROST WYRM YOU MUST FEAR.
THERE IS *MORE!*
IT DOESN'T MATTER--
THERE IS... *ICHOR.*
HE LEADS A BAND OF THE *SCOURGE.* THEY HAVE SLIPPED PAST THE ORCS, DWARVES, *AND* MY PEOPLE.

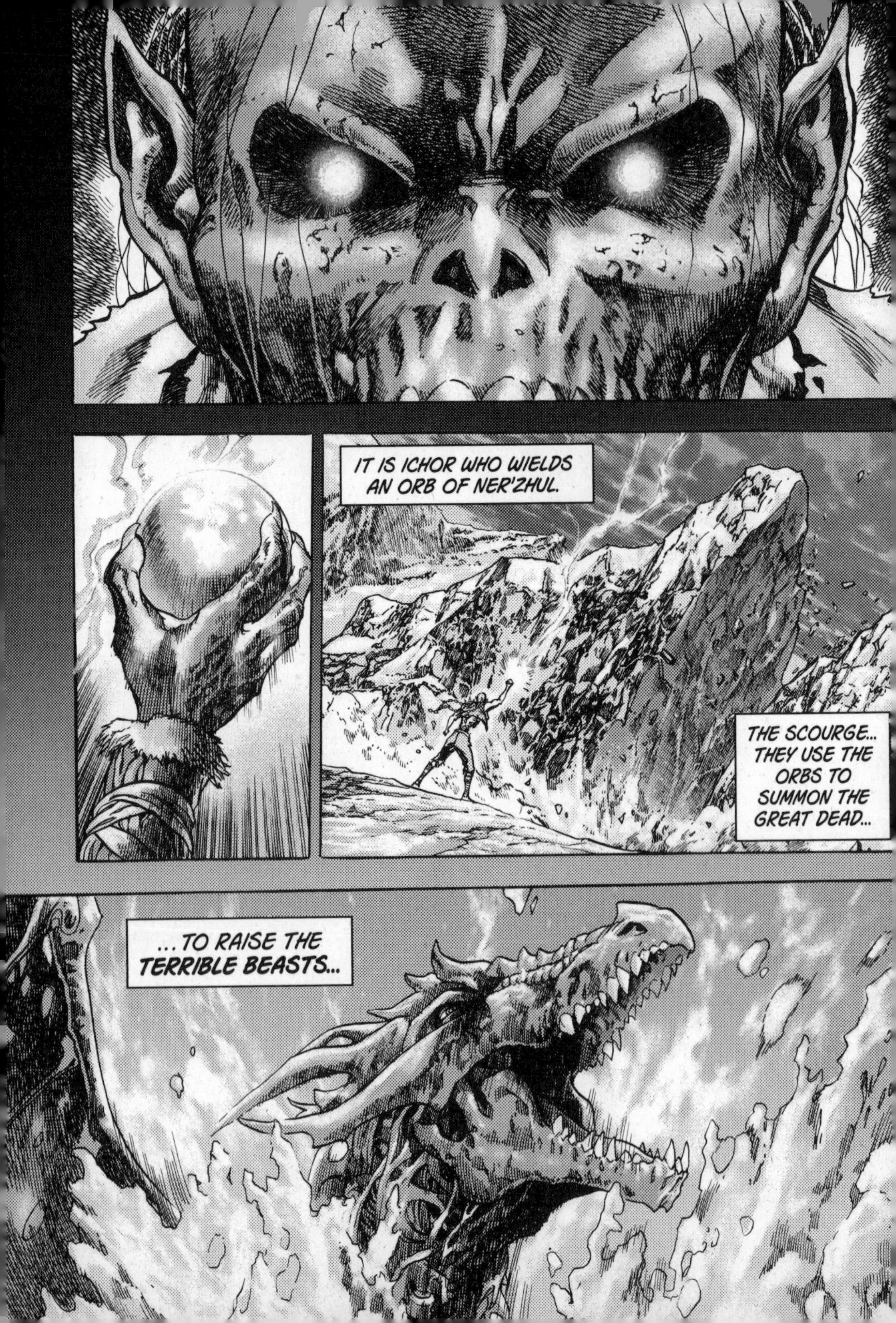
IT IS ICHOR WHO WIELDS AN ORB OF NER'ZHUL.
THE SCOURGE... THEY USE THE ORBS TO SUMMON THE GREAT DEAD...
...TO RAISE THE TERRIBLE BEASTS...

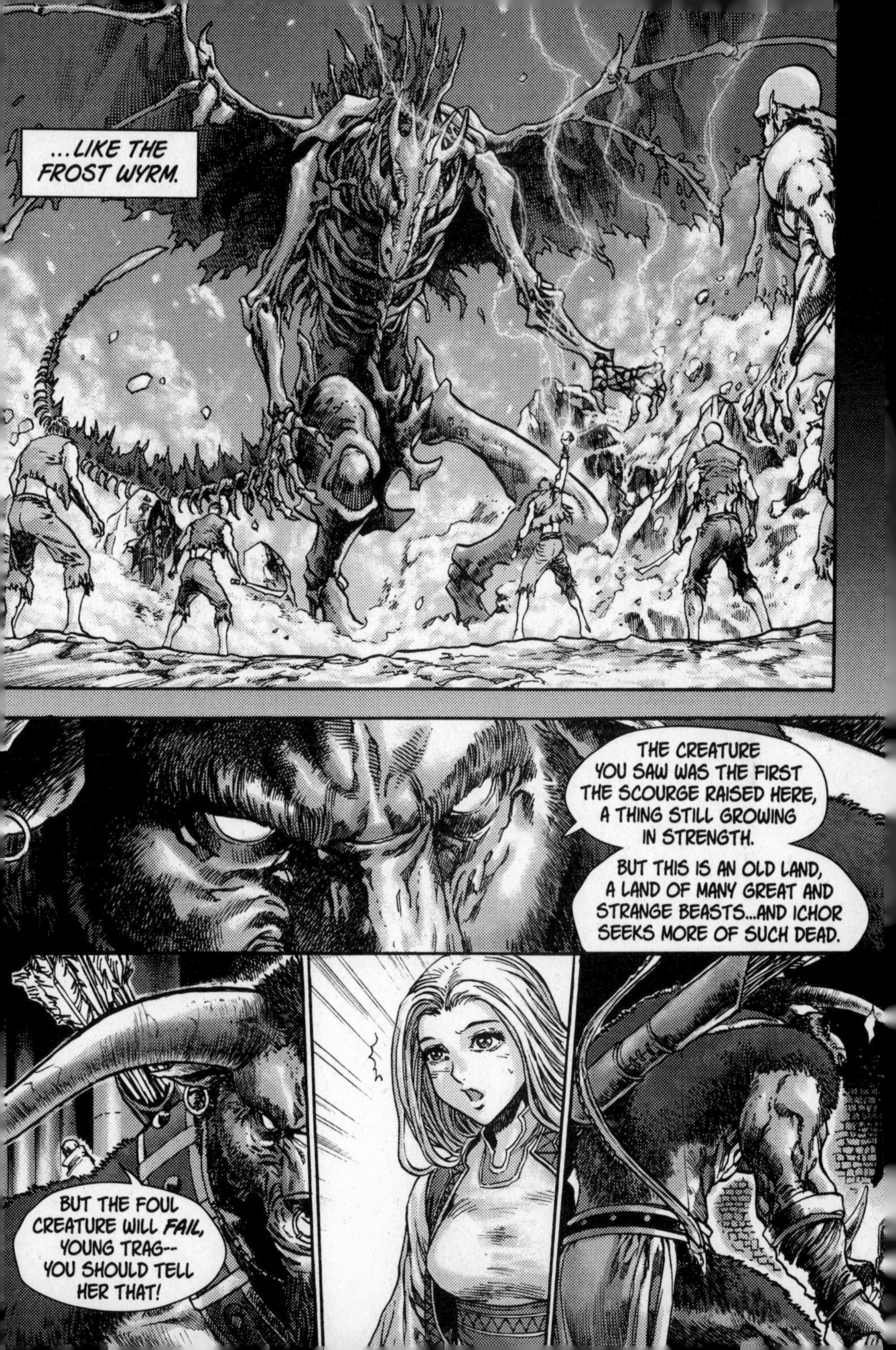
...LIKE THE FROST WYRM.
THE CREATURE YOU SAW WAS THE FIRST THE SCOURGE RAISED HERE, A THING STILL GROWING IN STRENGTH.
BUT THIS IS AN OLD LAND, A LAND OF MANY GREAT AND STRANGE BEASTS...AND ICHOR SEEKS MORE OF SUCH DEAD.
BUT THE FOUL CREATURE WILL *FAIL*, YOUNG TRAG-- YOU SHOULD TELL HER THAT!

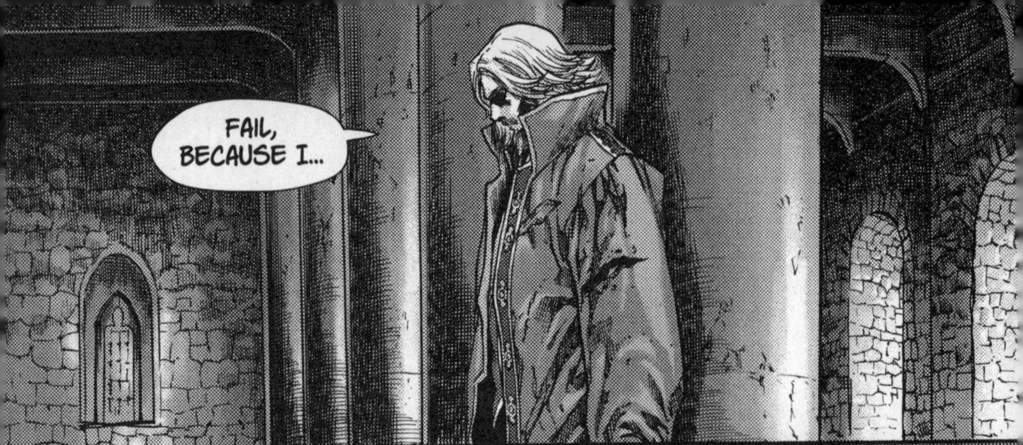
FAIL, BECAUSE I...
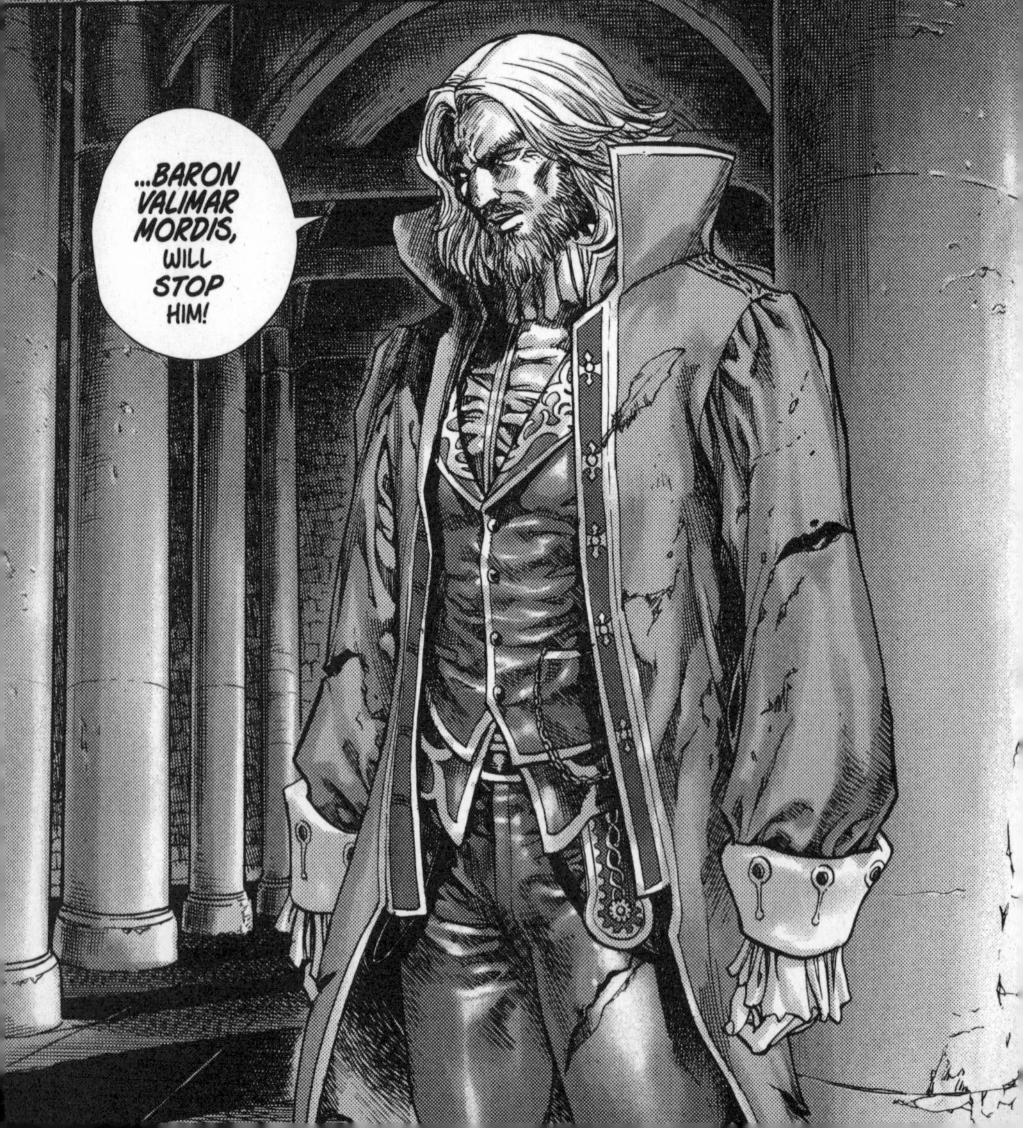
...BARON VALIMAR MORDIS, WILL STOP HIM!

CHAPTER TWO
BARON MORDIS

B-BOREL...

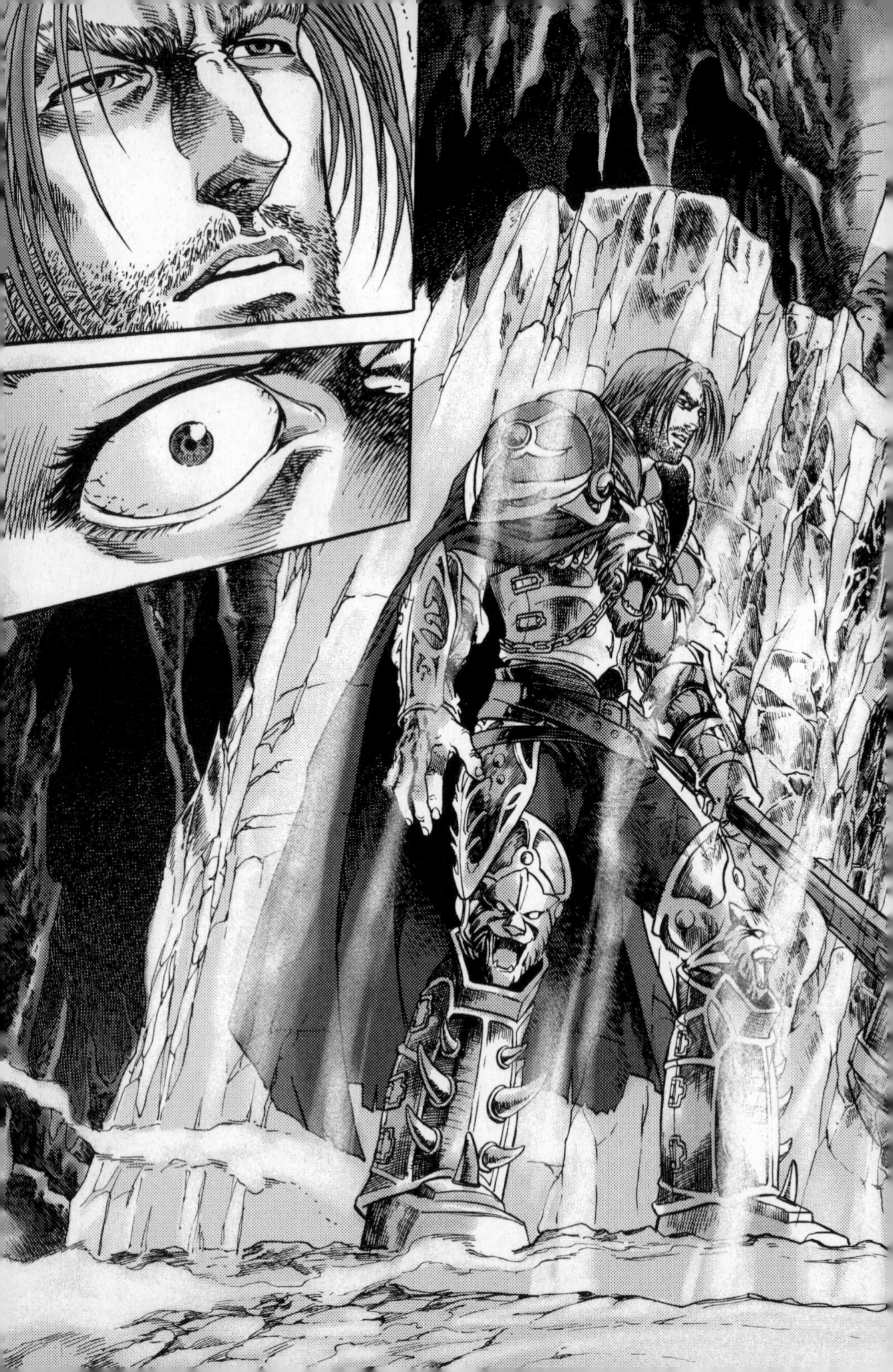

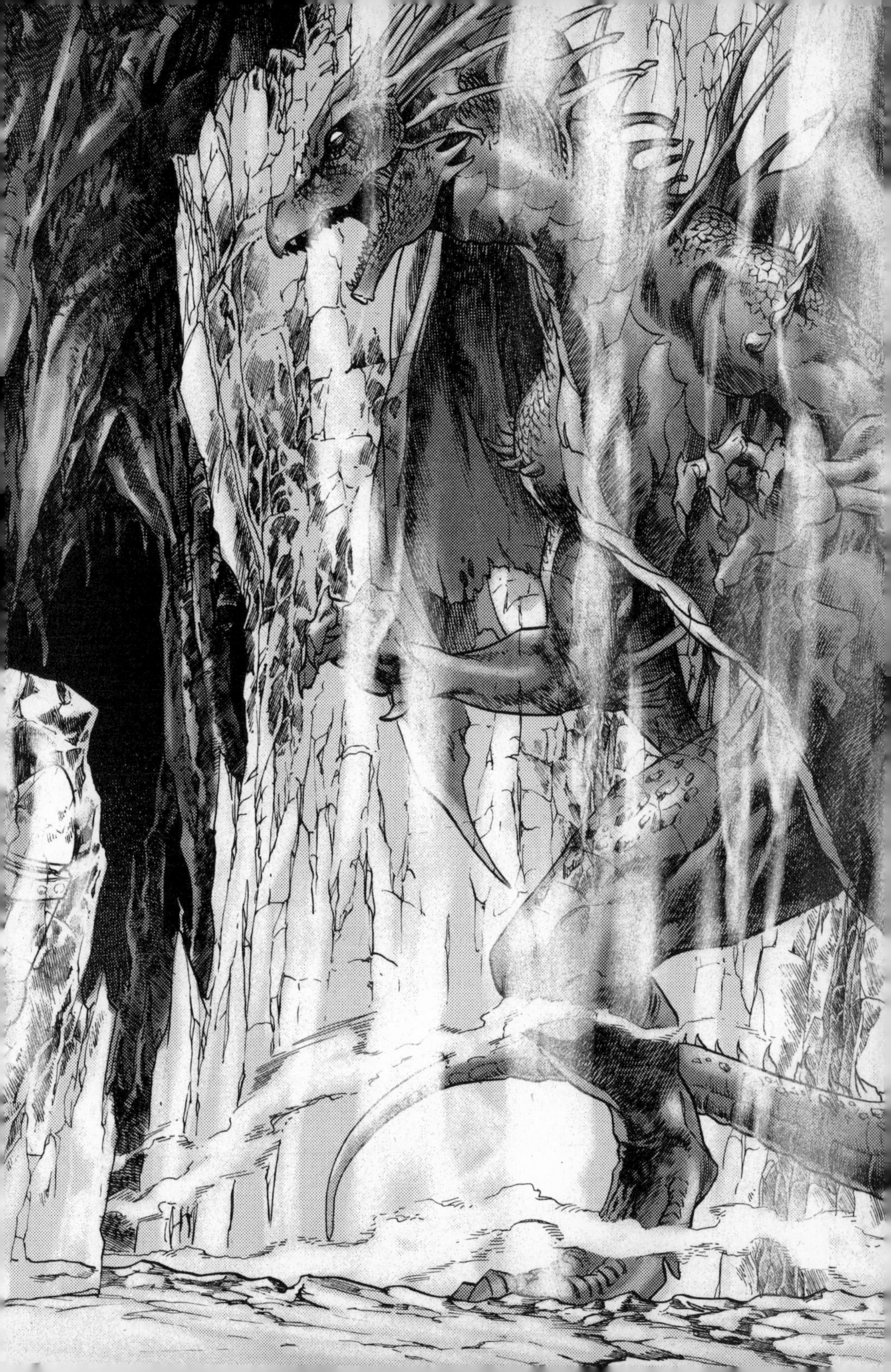

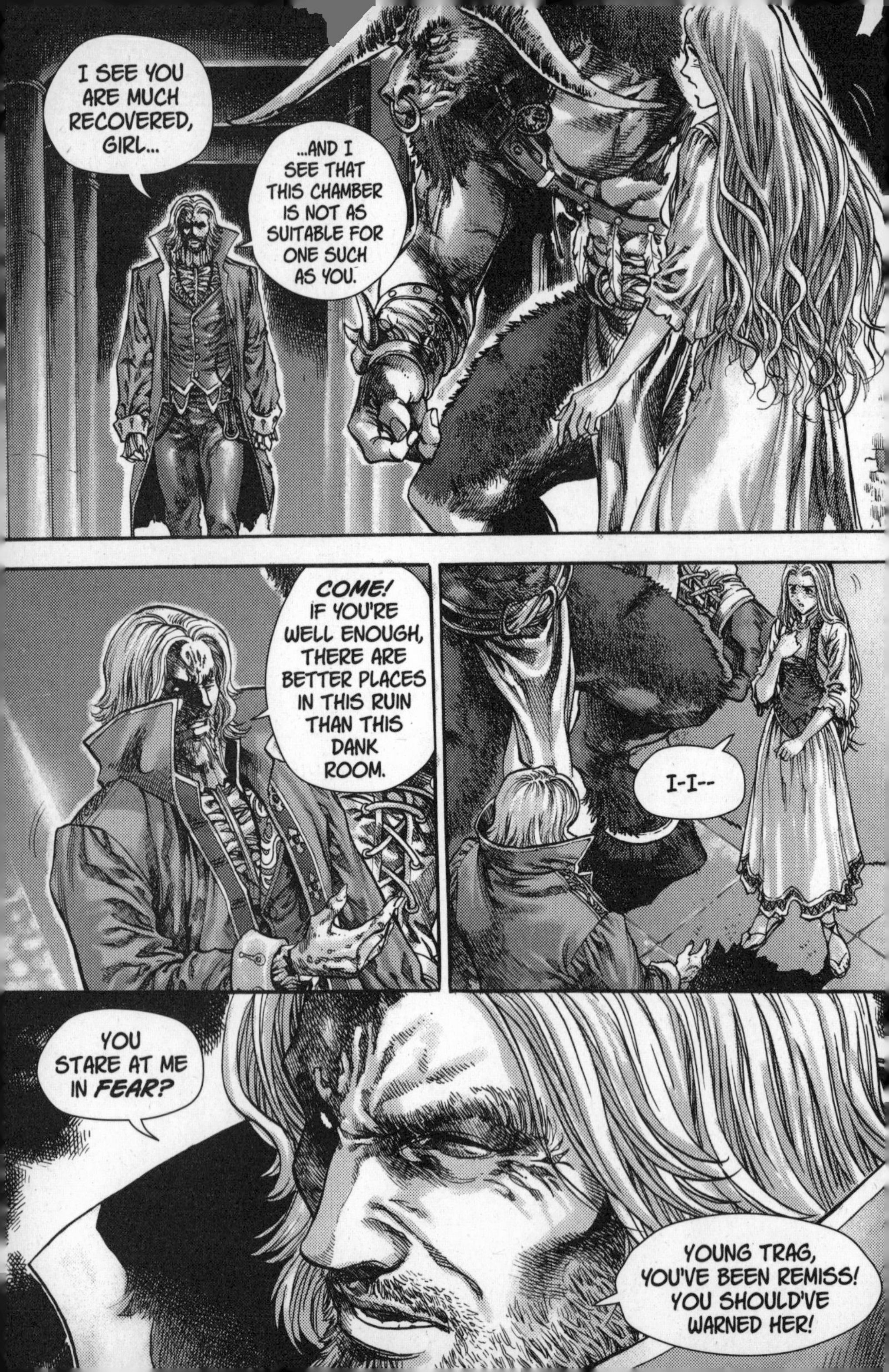
I SEE YOU ARE MUCH RECOVERED, GIRL...
...AND I SEE THAT THIS CHAMBER IS NOT AS SUITABLE FOR ONE SUCH AS YOU.
COME! IF YOU'RE WELL ENOUGH, THERE ARE BETTER PLACES IN THIS RUIN THAN THIS DANK ROOM.
I-I--
YOU STARE AT ME IN *FEAR?*
YOUNG TRAG, YOU'VE BEEN REMISS! YOU SHOULD'VE WARNED HER!

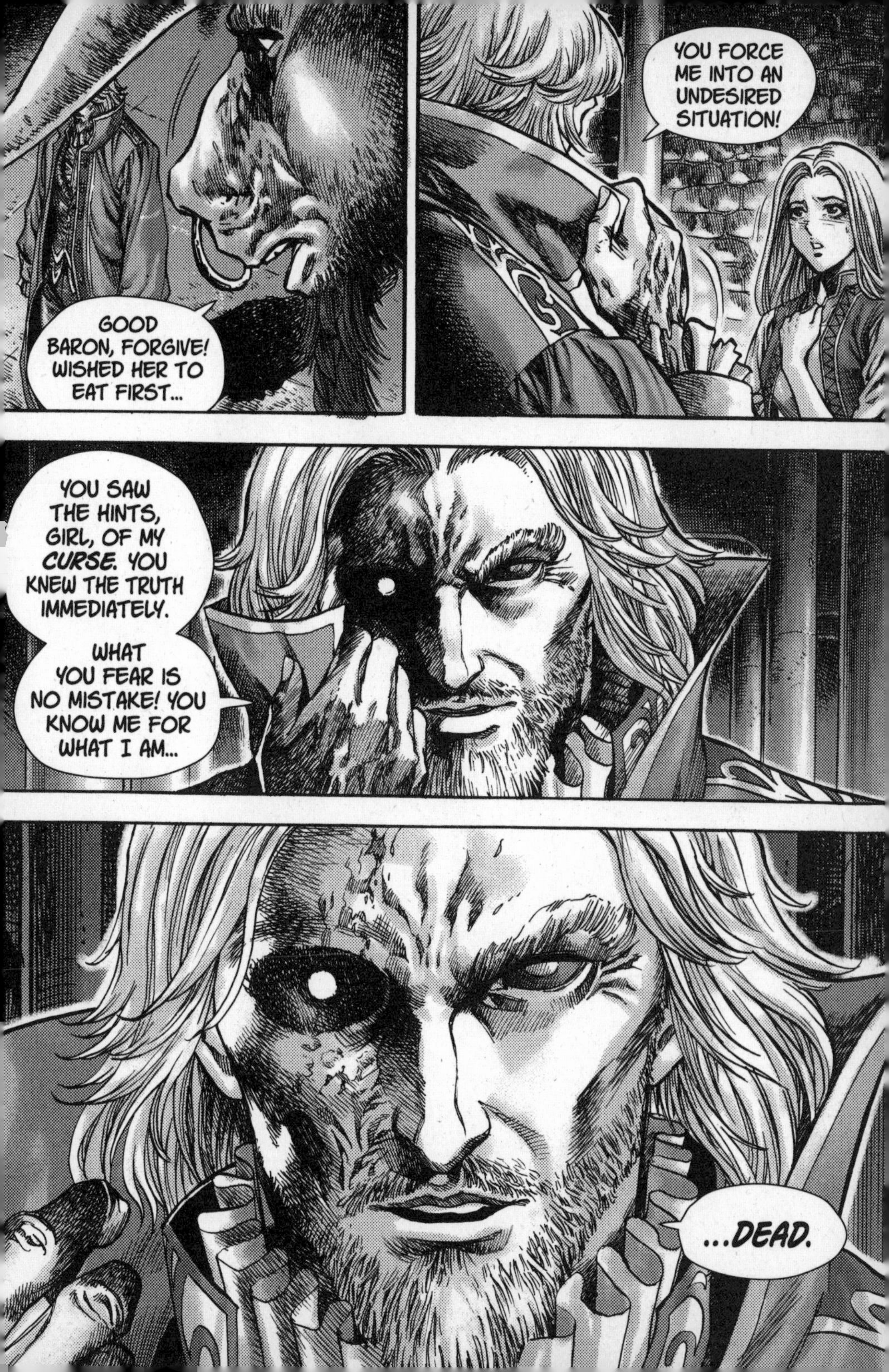
GOOD BARON, FORGIVE! WISHED HER TO EAT FIRST...
YOU FORCE ME INTO AN UNDESIRED SITUATION!
YOU SAW THE HINTS, GIRL, OF MY CURSE. YOU KNEW THE TRUTH IMMEDIATELY.
WHAT YOU FEAR IS NO MISTAKE! YOU KNOW ME FOR WHAT I AM...
...DEAD.

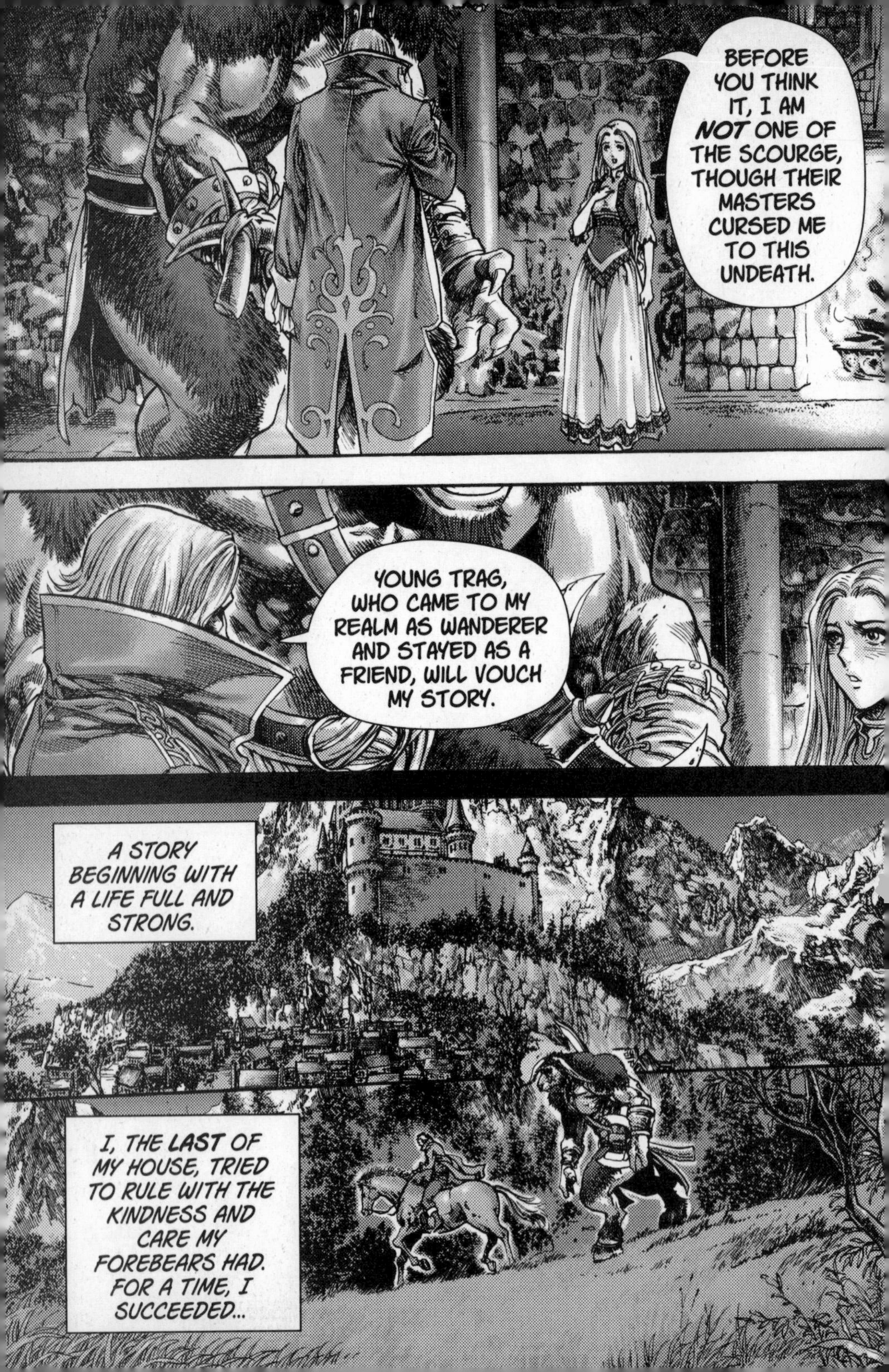
BEFORE YOU THINK IT, I AM NOT ONE OF THE SCOURGE, THOUGH THEIR MASTERS CURSED ME TO THIS UNDEATH.
YOUNG TRAG, WHO CAME TO MY REALM AS WANDERER AND STAYED AS A FRIEND, WILL VOUCH MY STORY.
A STORY BEGINNING WITH A LIFE FULL AND STRONG.
I, THE LAST OF MY HOUSE, TRIED TO RULE WITH THE KINDNESS AND CARE MY FOREBEARS HAD. FOR A TIME, I SUCCEEDED...

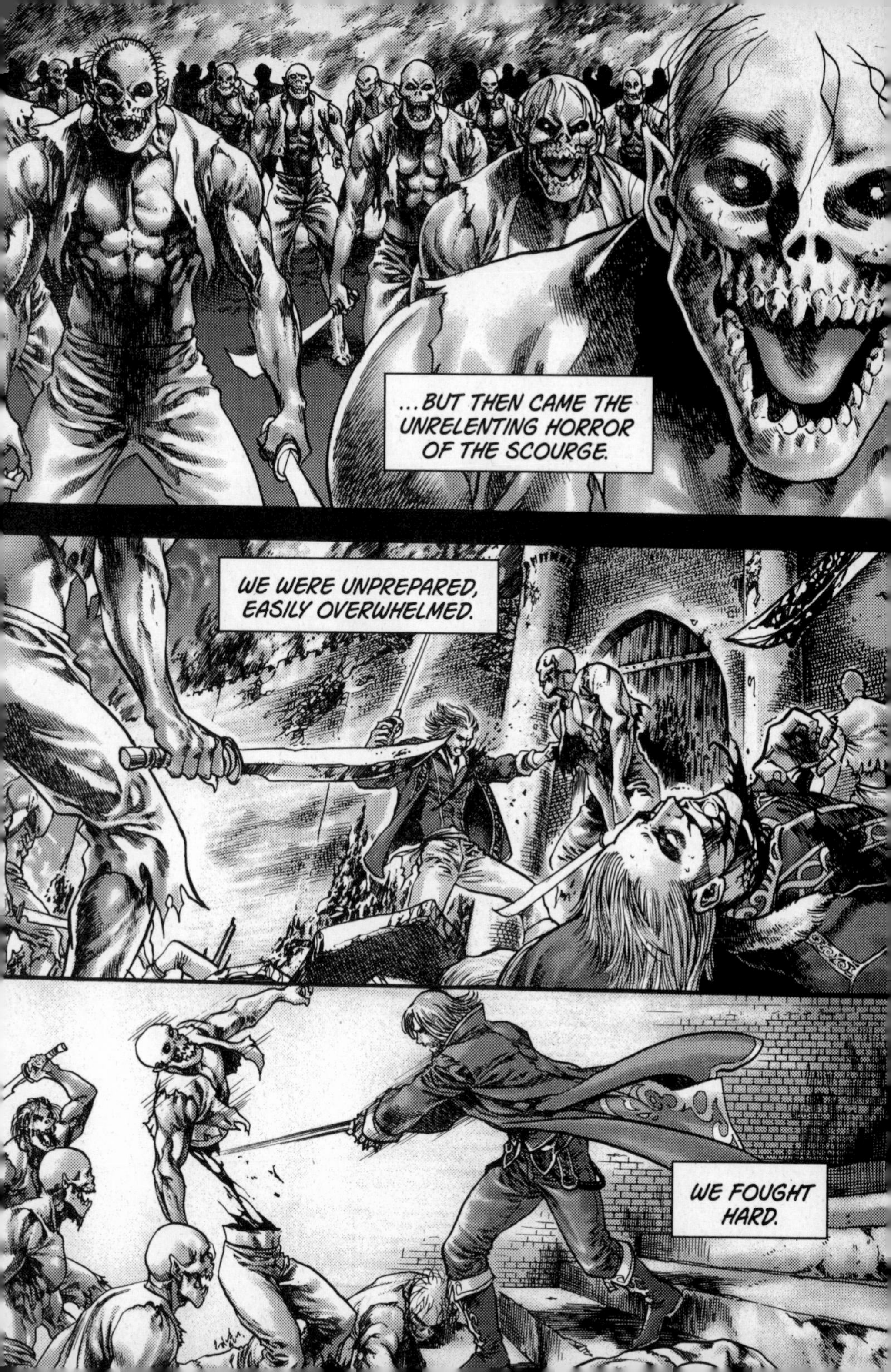
...BUT THEN CAME THE UNRELENTING HORROR OF THE SCOURGE.
WE WERE UNPREPARED, EASILY OVERWHELMED.
WE FOUGHT HARD.

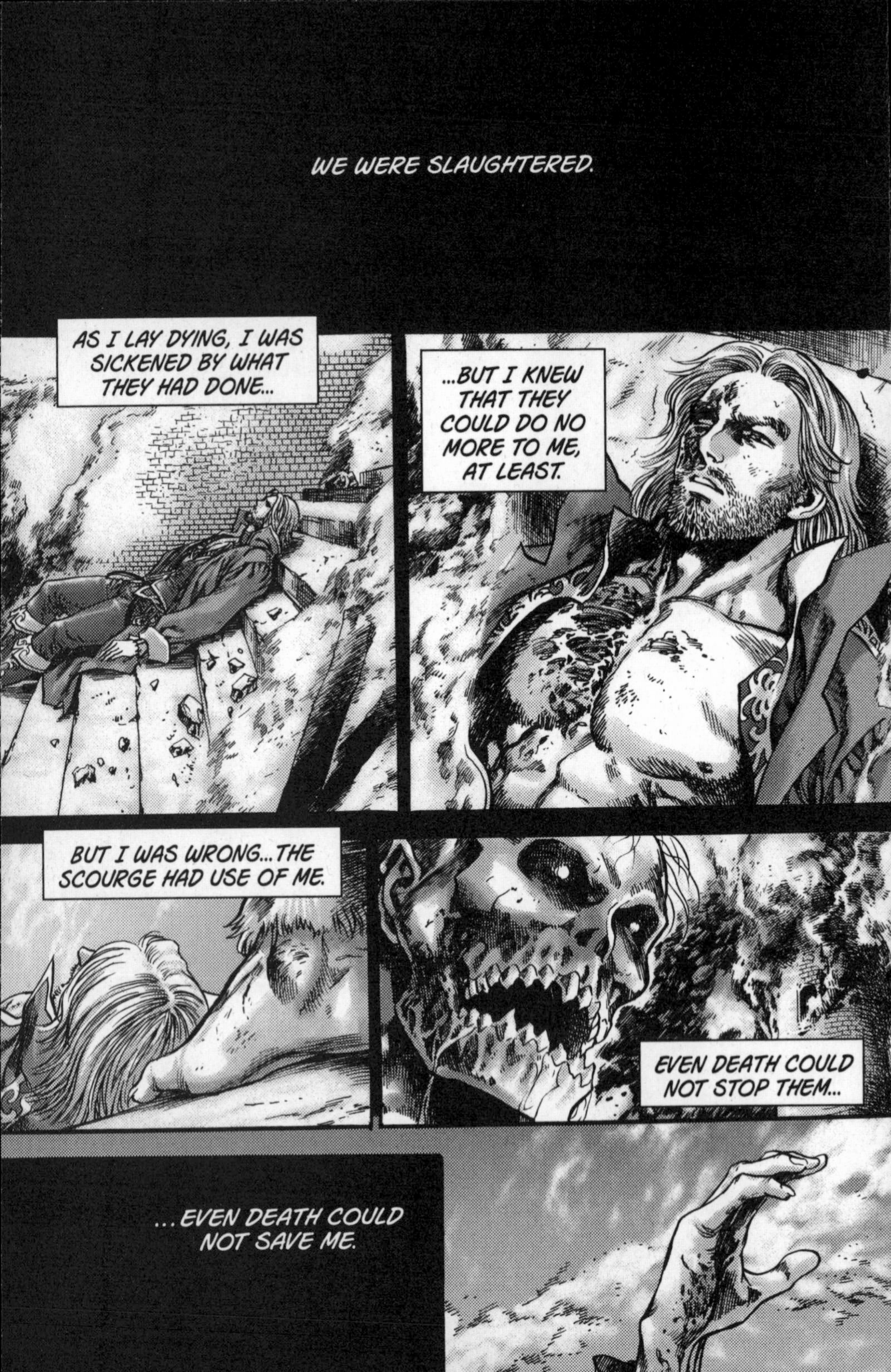
WE WERE SLAUGHTERED.
AS I LAY DYING, I WAS SICKENED BY WHAT THEY HAD DONE...
...BUT I KNEW THAT THEY COULD DO NO MORE TO ME, AT LEAST.
BUT I WAS WRONG...THE SCOURGE HAD USE OF ME.
EVEN DEATH COULD NOT STOP THEM...
...EVEN DEATH COULD NOT SAVE ME.

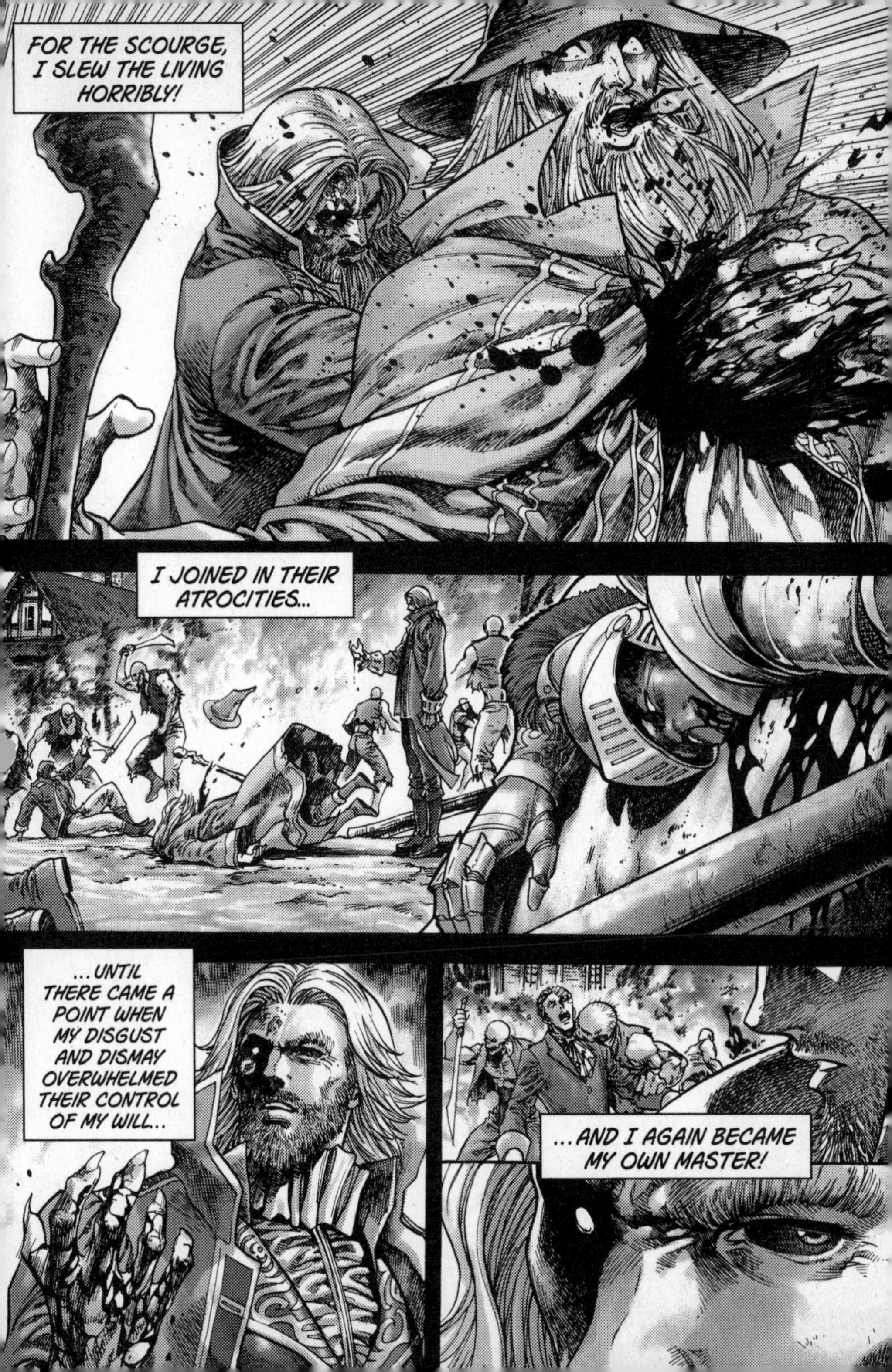
FOR THE SCOURGE, I SLEW THE LIVING HORRIBLY!
I JOINED IN THEIR ATROCITIES...
...UNTIL THERE CAME A POINT WHEN MY DISGUST AND DISMAY OVERWHELMED THEIR CONTROL OF MY WILL...
...AND I AGAIN BECAME MY OWN MASTER!

I KNEW THAT IF I STAYED AND FOUGHT, I WOULD QUICKLY BE DESTROYED--SO I FLED IN SECRET!

THE SCOURGE GAVE CHASE, BUT I ELUDED THEM!

I WAS CONFUSED, NEEDED TO THINK, AND SO I RETURNED TO MY HOME... OR WHAT LITTLE REMAINED...

THERE...THE FULL REALIZATION OF MY CURSE HIT ME...

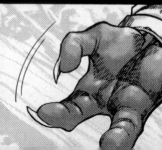

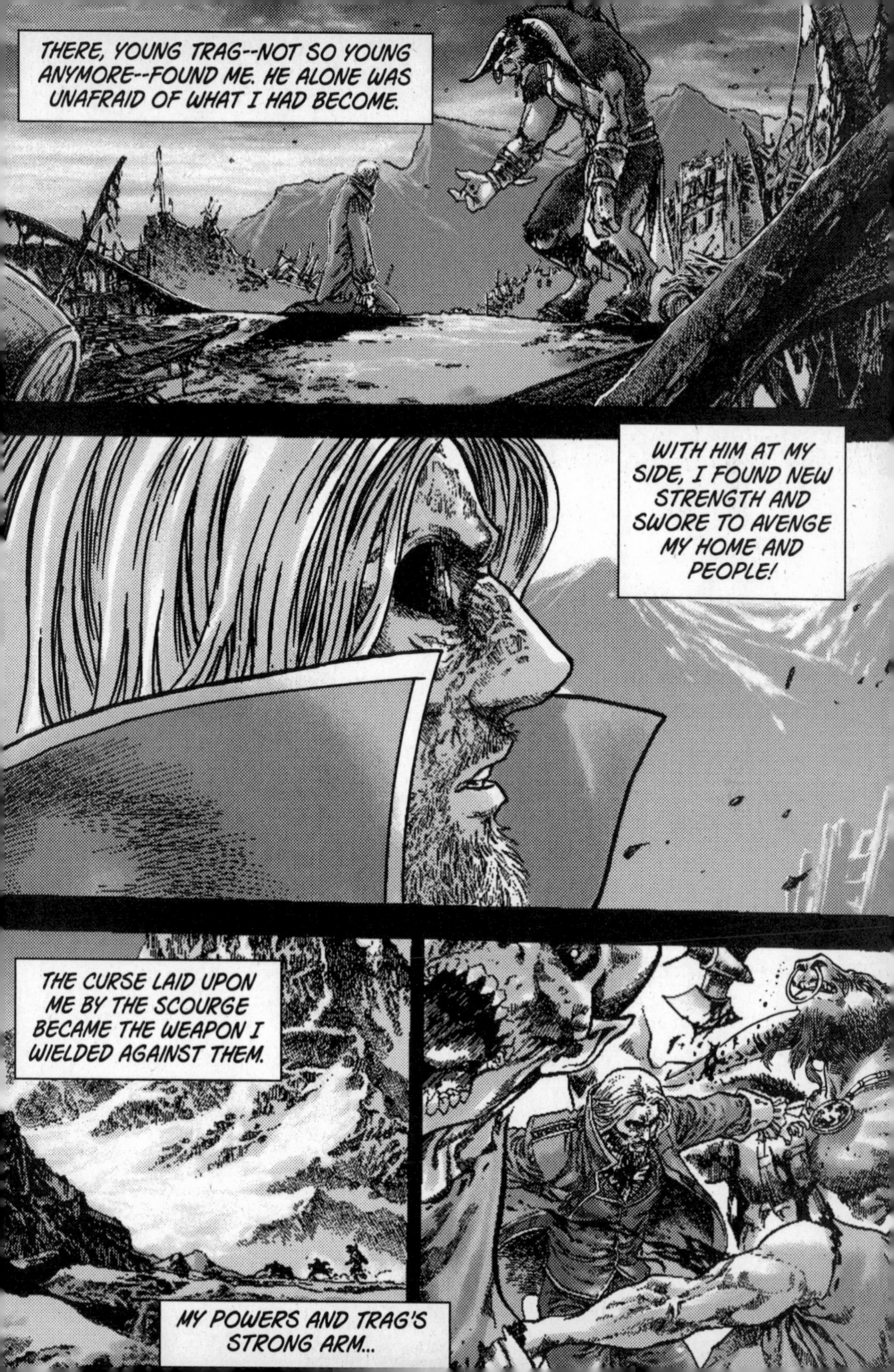
THERE, YOUNG TRAG--NOT SO YOUNG ANYMORE--FOUND ME. HE ALONE WAS UNAFRAID OF WHAT I HAD BECOME.
WITH HIM AT MY SIDE, I FOUND NEW STRENGTH AND SWORE TO AVENGE MY HOME AND PEOPLE!
THE CURSE LAID UPON ME BY THE SCOURGE BECAME THE WEAPON I WIELDED AGAINST THEM.
MY POWERS AND TRAG'S STRONG ARM...

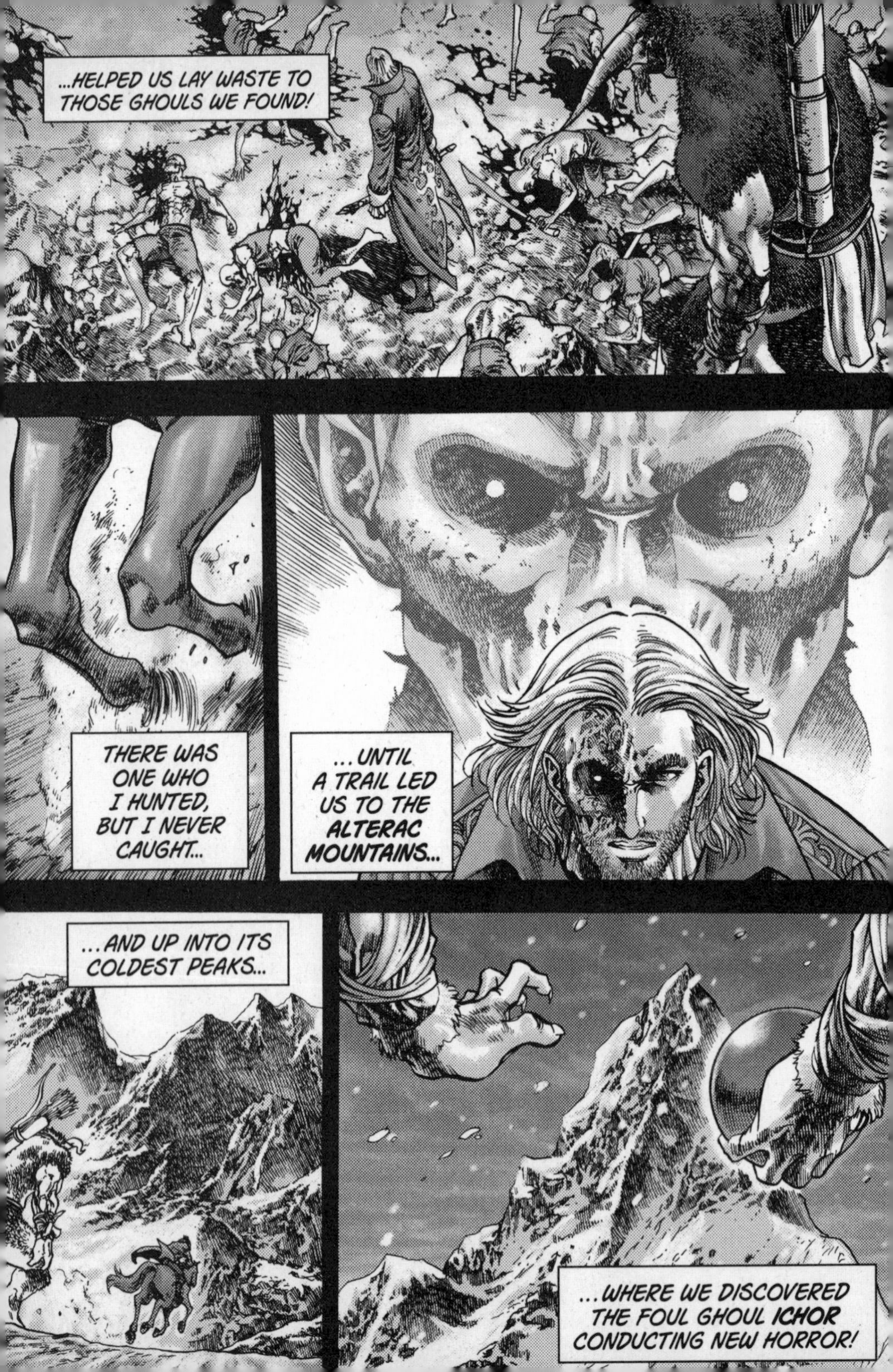
...HELPED US LAY WASTE TO THOSE GHOULS WE FOUND!
THERE WAS ONE WHO I HUNTED, BUT I NEVER CAUGHT...
...UNTIL A TRAIL LED US TO THE ALTERAC MOUNTAINS...
...AND UP INTO ITS COLDEST PEAKS...
...WHERE WE DISCOVERED THE FOUL GHOUL ICHOR CONDUCTING NEW HORROR!

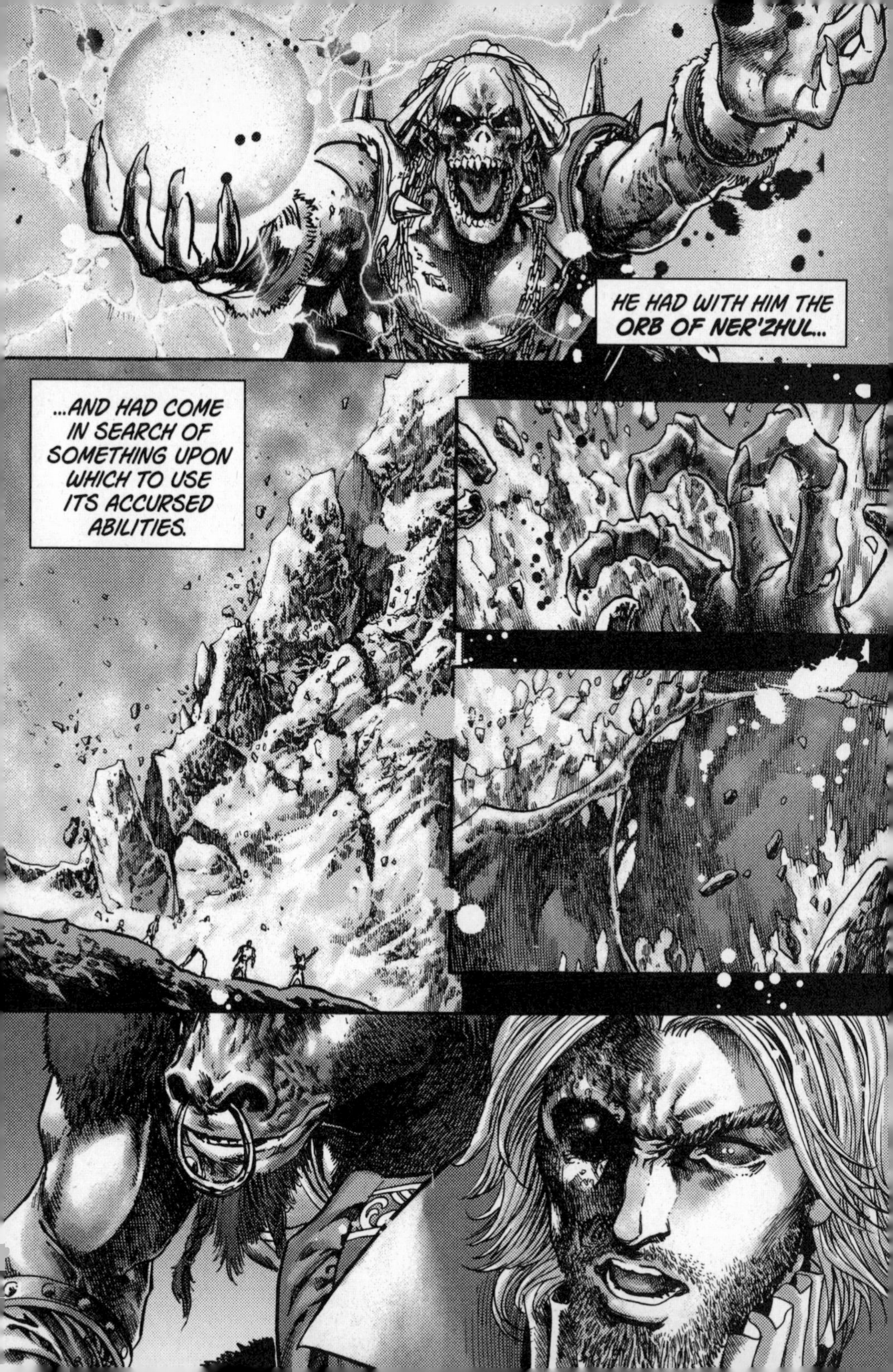
HE HAD WITH HIM THE ORB OF NER'ZHUL...
...AND HAD COME IN SEARCH OF SOMETHING UPON WHICH TO USE ITS ACCURSED ABILITIES.

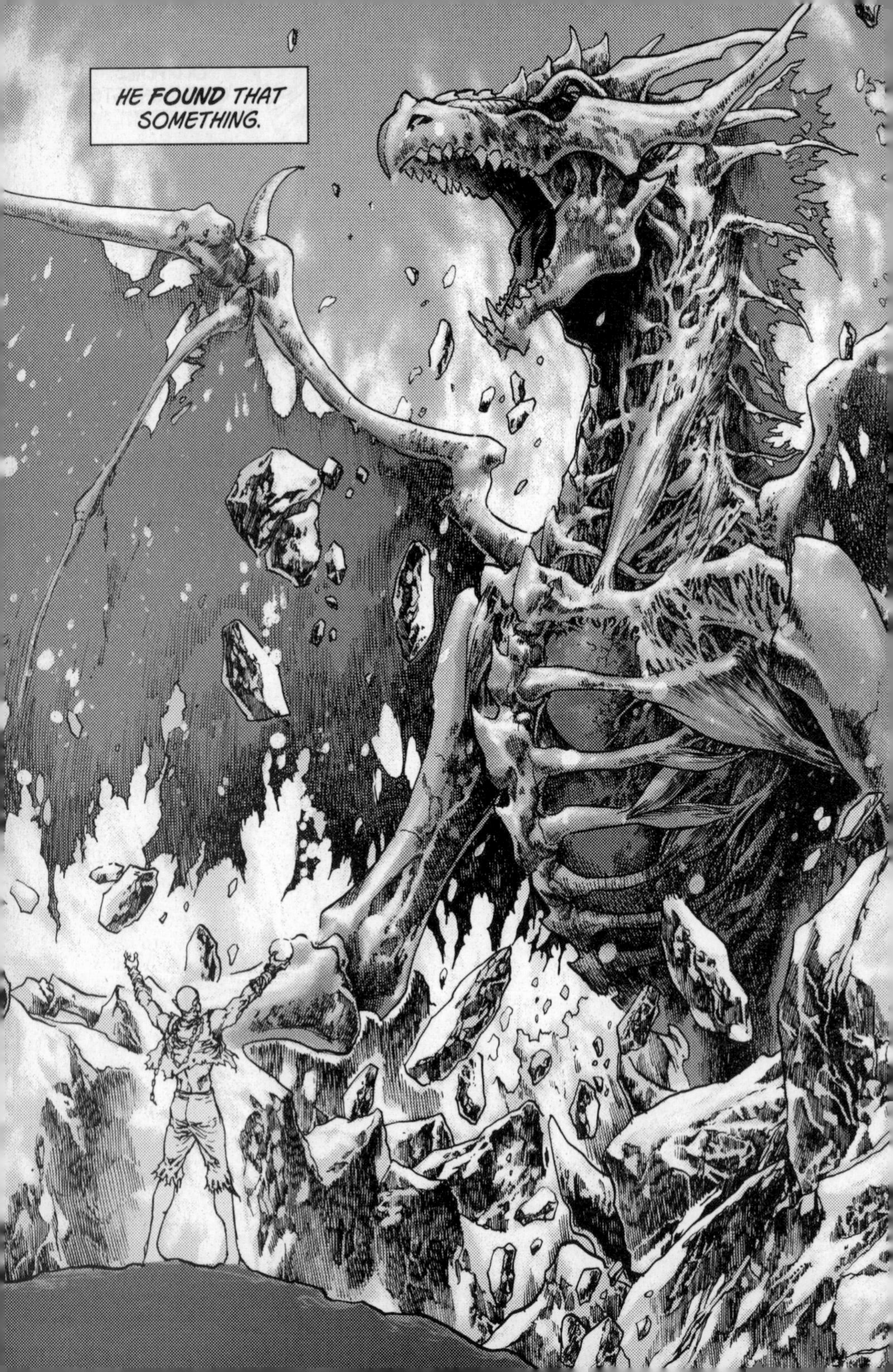
HE FOUND THAT SOMETHING.

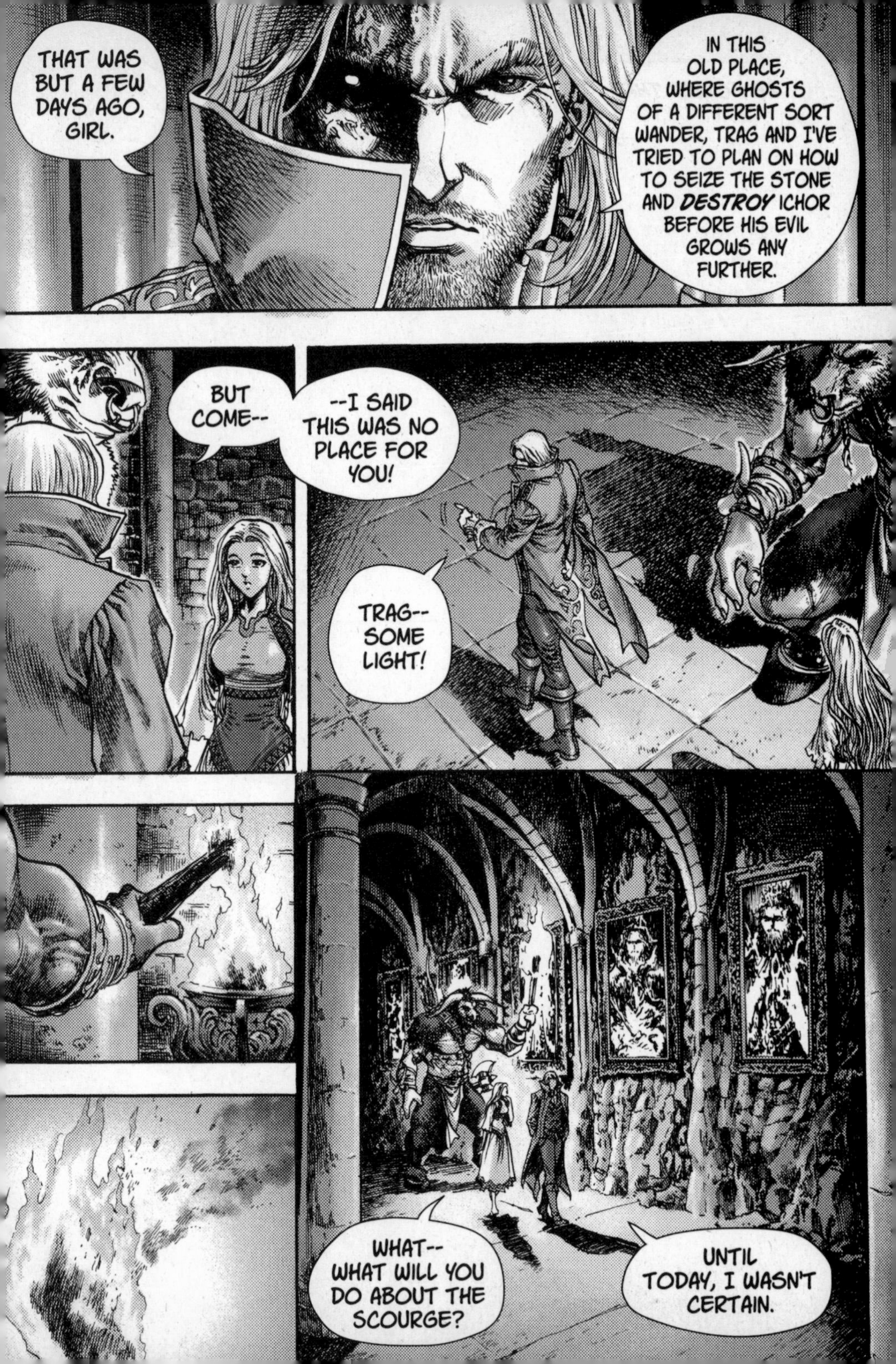
THAT WAS BUT A FEW DAYS AGO, GIRL.
IN THIS OLD PLACE, WHERE GHOSTS OF A DIFFERENT SORT WANDER, TRAG AND I'VE TRIED TO PLAN ON HOW TO SEIZE THE STONE AND DESTROY ICHOR BEFORE HIS EVIL GROWS ANY FURTHER.
BUT COME--
--I SAID THIS WAS NO PLACE FOR YOU!
TRAG-- SOME LIGHT!
WHAT-- WHAT WILL YOU DO ABOUT THE SCOURGE?
UNTIL TODAY, I WASN'T CERTAIN.

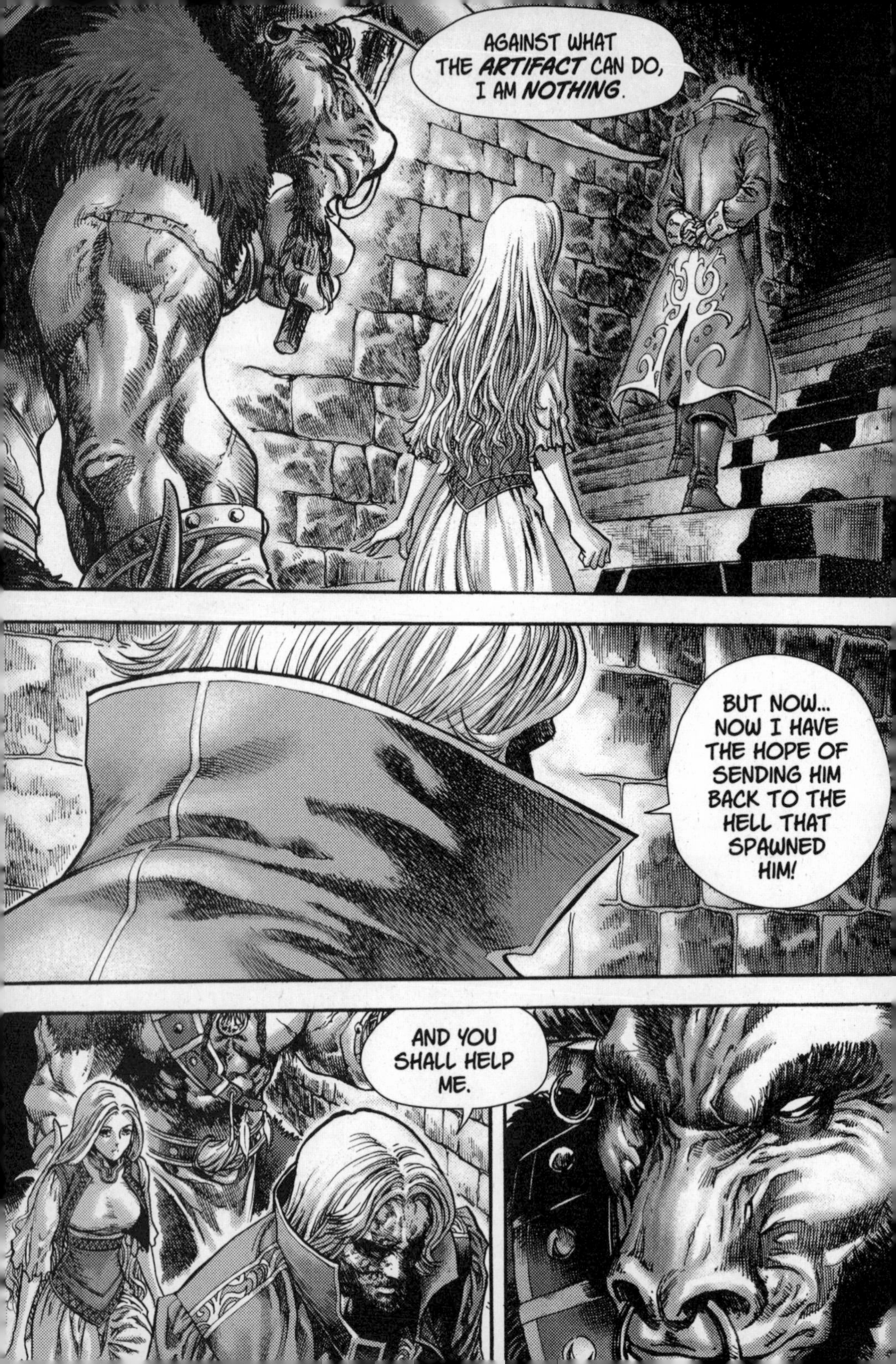
AGAINST WHAT THE ARTIFACT CAN DO, I AM NOTHING.
BUT NOW... NOW I HAVE THE HOPE OF SENDING HIM BACK TO THE HELL THAT SPAWNED HIM!
AND YOU SHALL HELP ME.

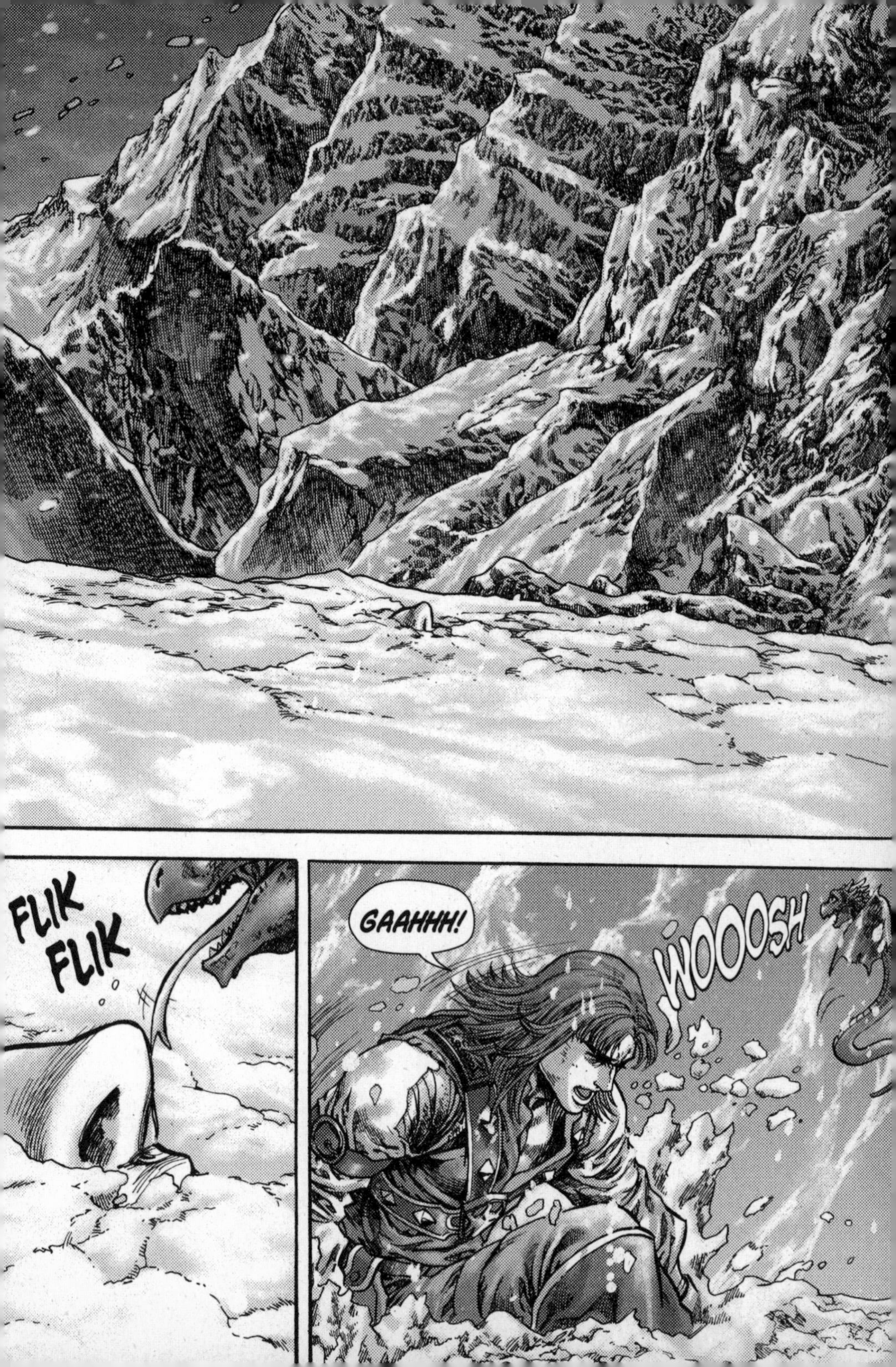
FLIK FLIK
GAAHHH!
WOOOSH

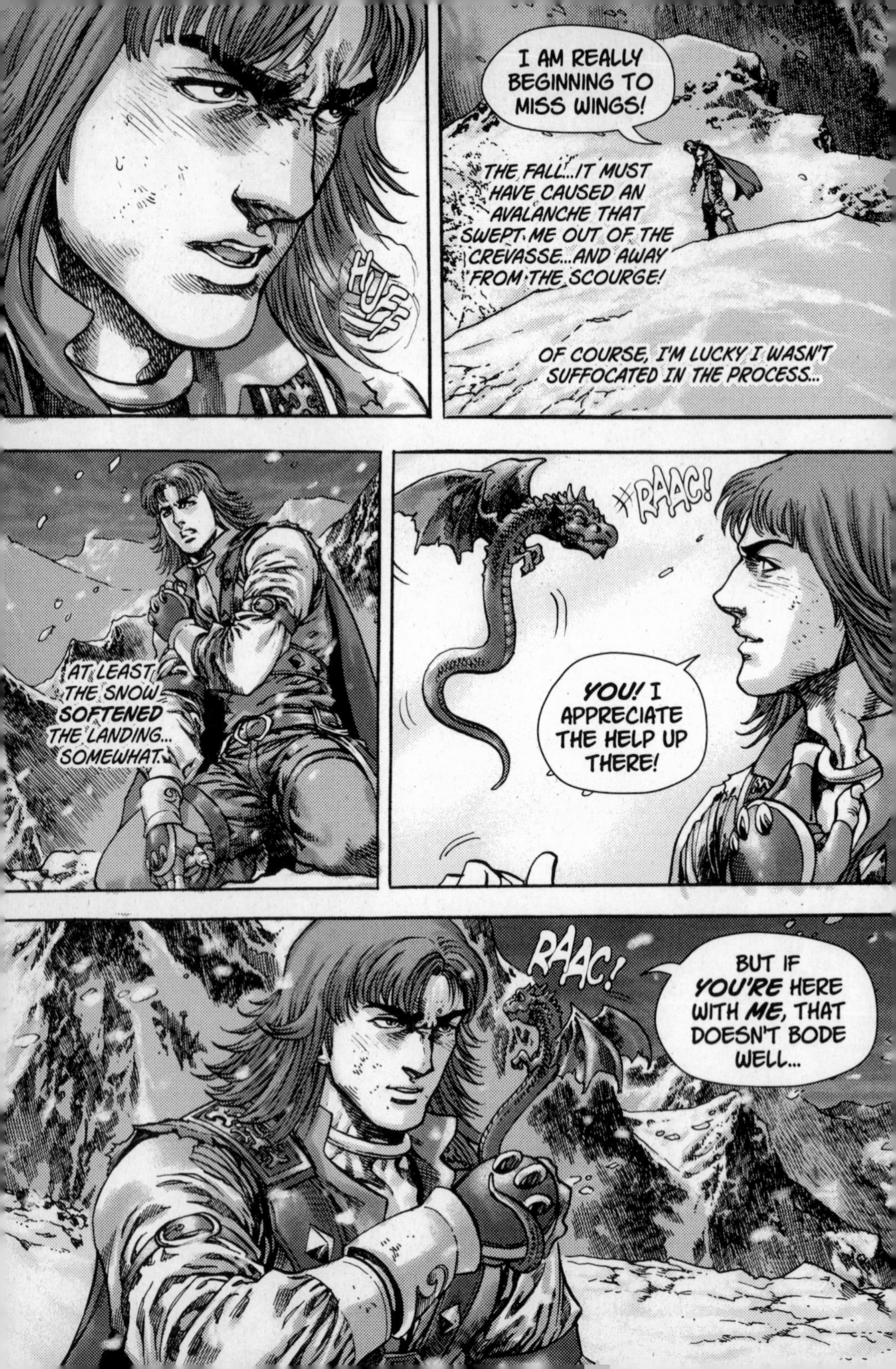
HUFF
I AM REALLY BEGINNING TO MISS WINGS!
THE FALL...IT MUST HAVE CAUSED AN AVALANCHE THAT SWEPT ME OUT OF THE CREVASSE...AND AWAY FROM THE SCOURGE!
OF COURSE, I'M LUCKY I WASN'T SUFFOCATED IN THE PROCESS...
AT LEAST THE SNOW SOFTENED THE LANDING... SOMEWHAT.
RAAC!
YOU! I APPRECIATE THE HELP UP THERE!
RAAC!
BUT IF YOU'RE HERE WITH ME, THAT DOESN'T BODE WELL...

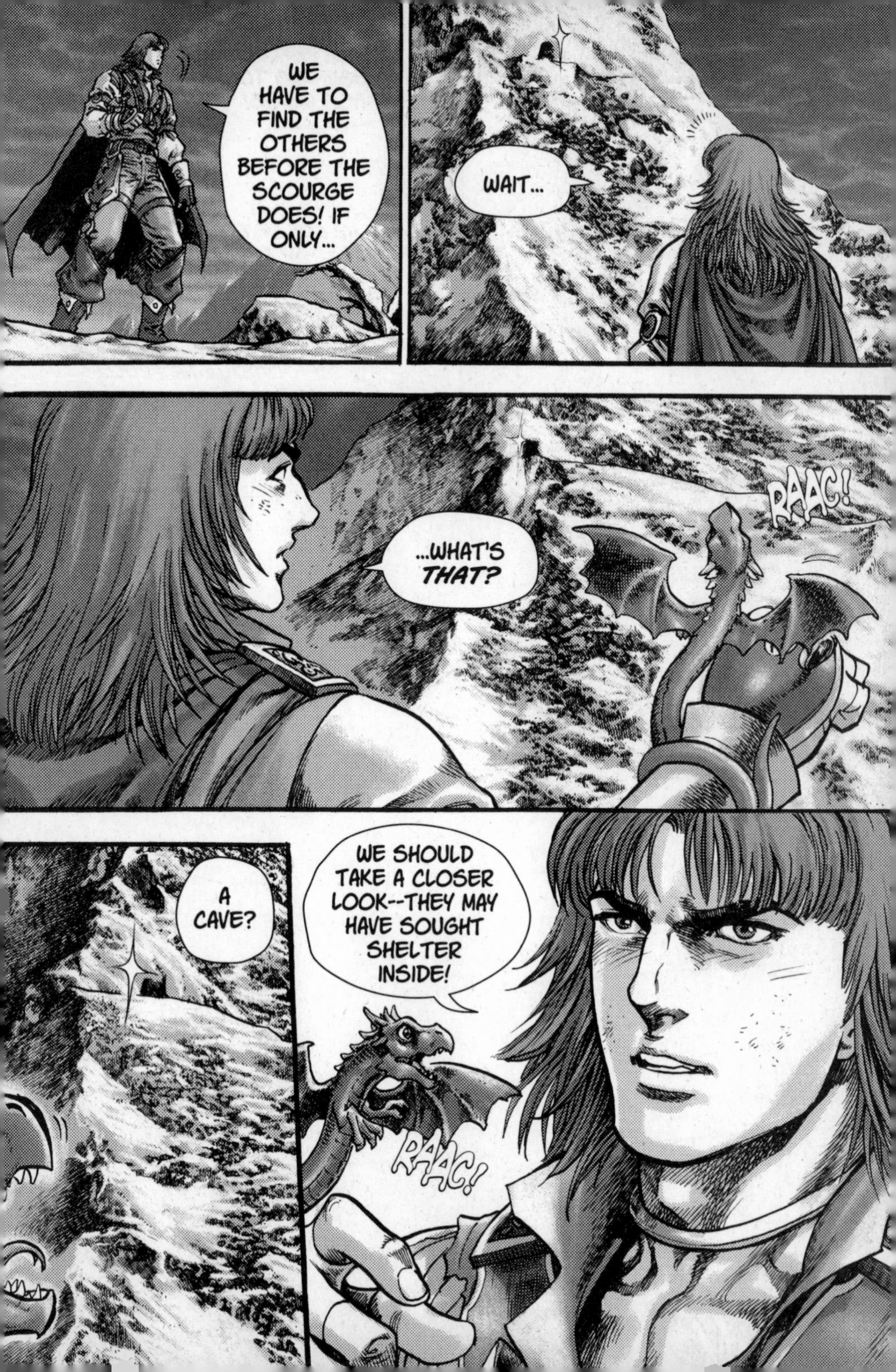

WE HAVE TO FIND THE OTHERS BEFORE THE SCOURGE DOES! IF ONLY...
WAIT...
RAAC!
...WHAT'S *THAT?*
A CAVE?
WE SHOULD TAKE A CLOSER LOOK--THEY MAY HAVE SOUGHT SHELTER INSIDE!
RAAC!

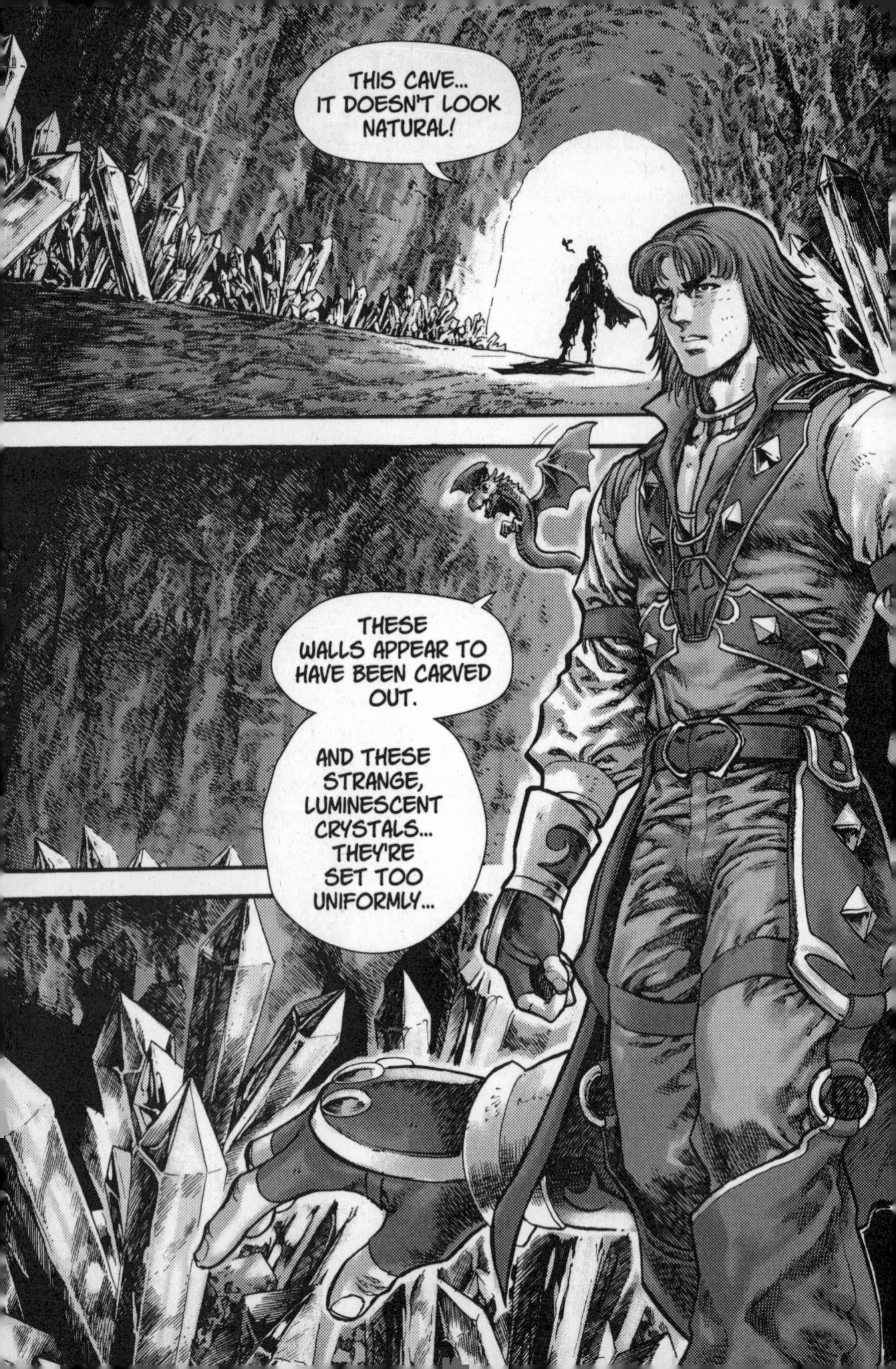
THIS CAVE... IT DOESN'T LOOK NATURAL!
THESE WALLS APPEAR TO HAVE BEEN CARVED OUT.
AND THESE STRANGE, LUMINESCENT CRYSTALS... THEY'RE SET TOO UNIFORMLY...

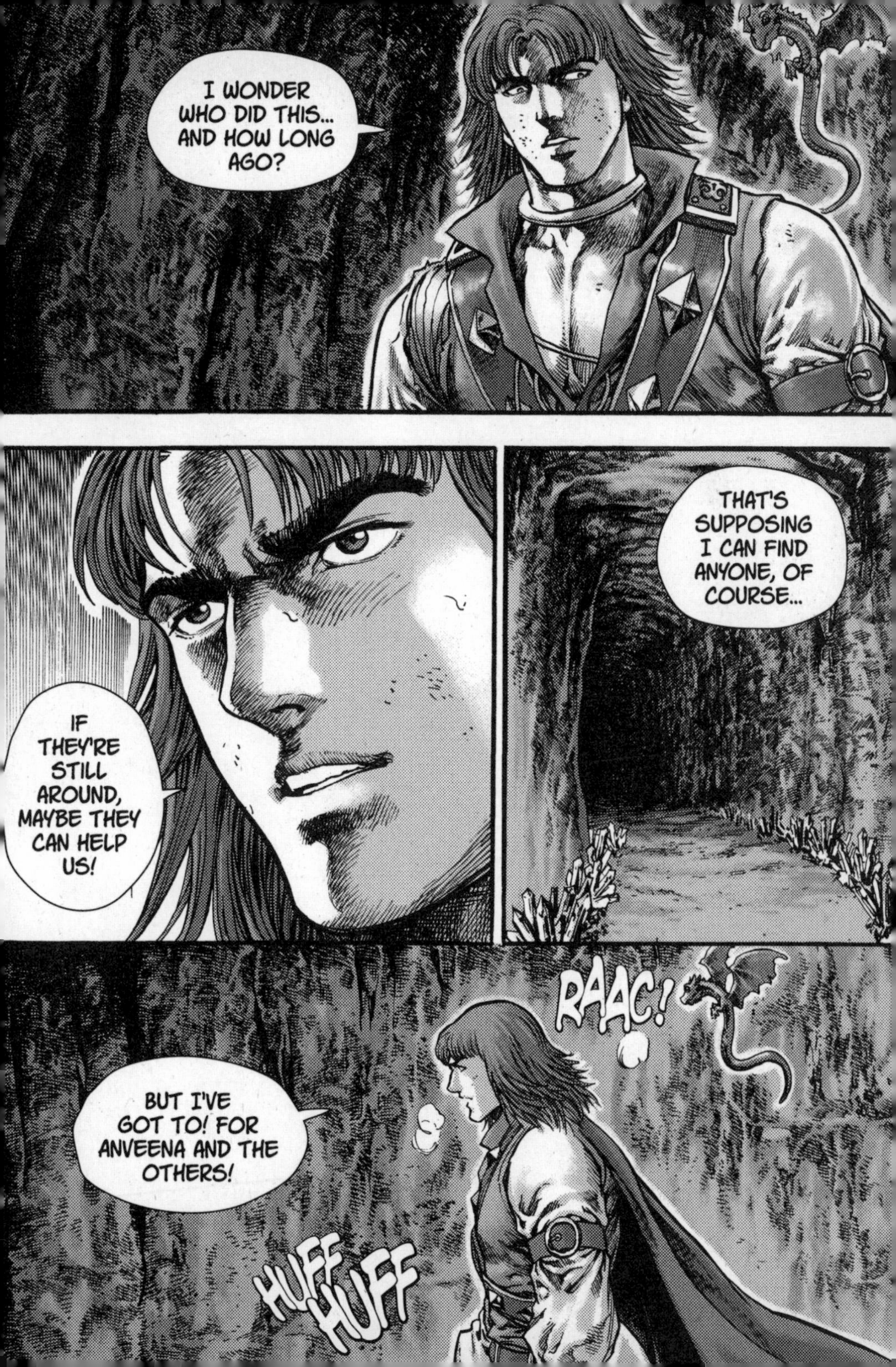
I WONDER WHO DID THIS... AND HOW LONG AGO?
IF THEY'RE STILL AROUND, MAYBE THEY CAN HELP US!
THAT'S SUPPOSING I CAN FIND ANYONE, OF COURSE...
RAAC!
BUT I'VE GOT TO! FOR ANVEENA AND THE OTHERS!
HUFF HUFF

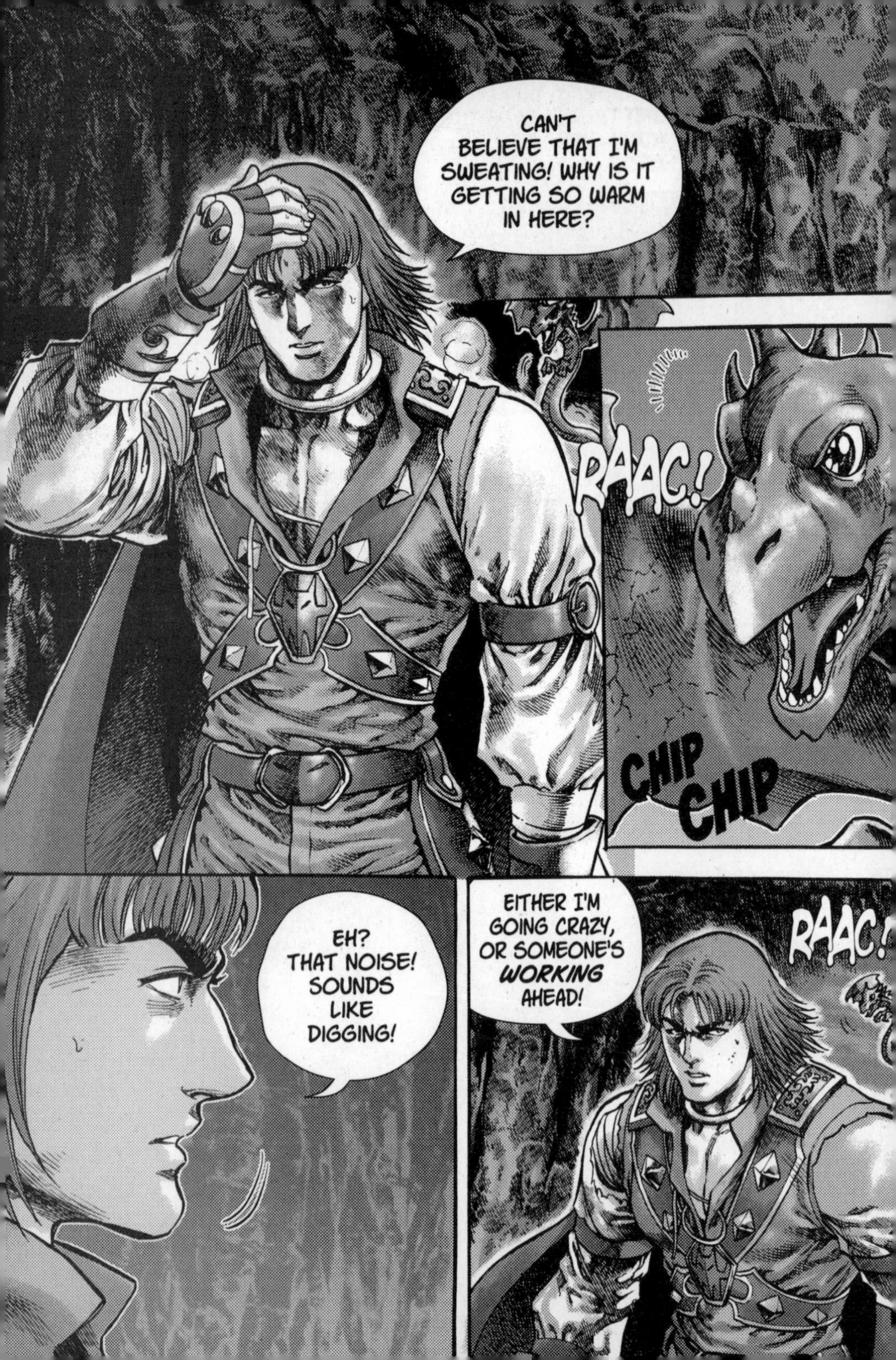
CAN'T BELIEVE THAT I'M SWEATING! WHY IS IT GETTING SO WARM IN HERE?
RAAC!
CHIP CHIP
EH? THAT NOISE! SOUNDS LIKE DIGGING!
EITHER I'M GOING CRAZY, OR SOMEONE'S *WORKING* AHEAD!
RAAC!

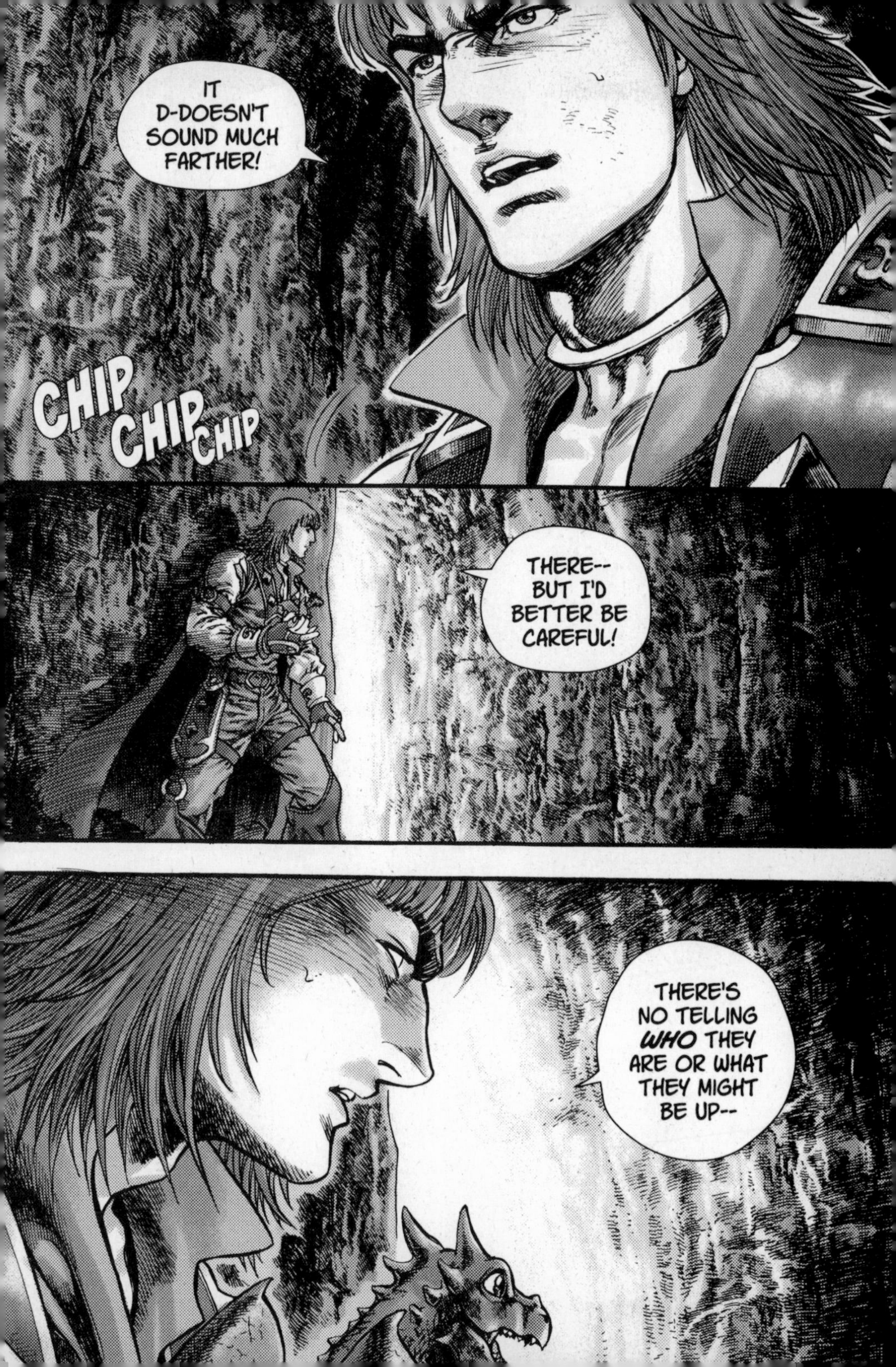
IT D-DOESN'T SOUND MUCH FARTHER!
CHIP CHIP CHIP
THERE-- BUT I'D BETTER BE CAREFUL!
THERE'S NO TELLING *WHO* THEY ARE OR WHAT THEY MIGHT BE UP--

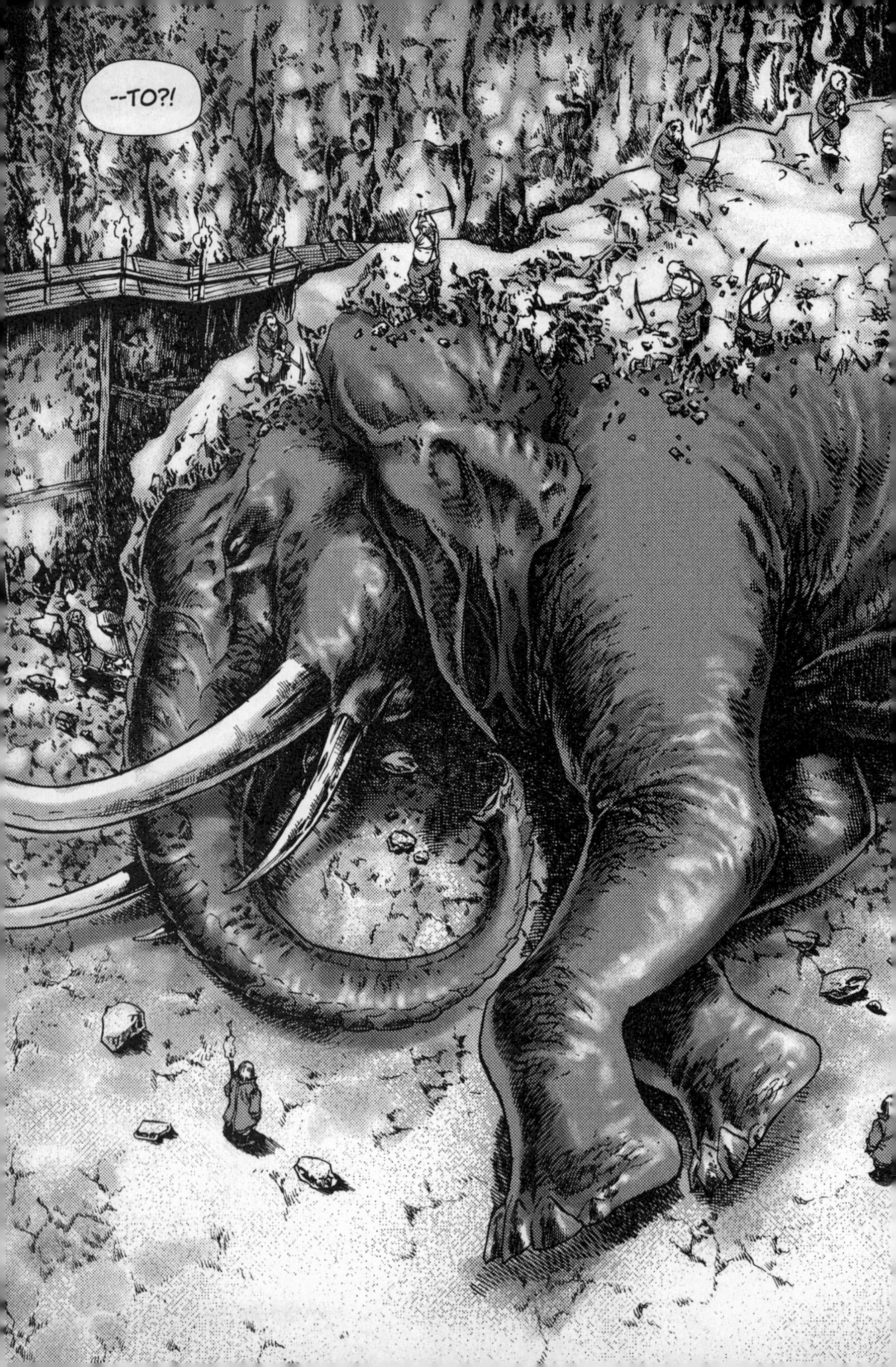
--TO?!

CHAPTER THREE
CAVERNS OF THE DEAD

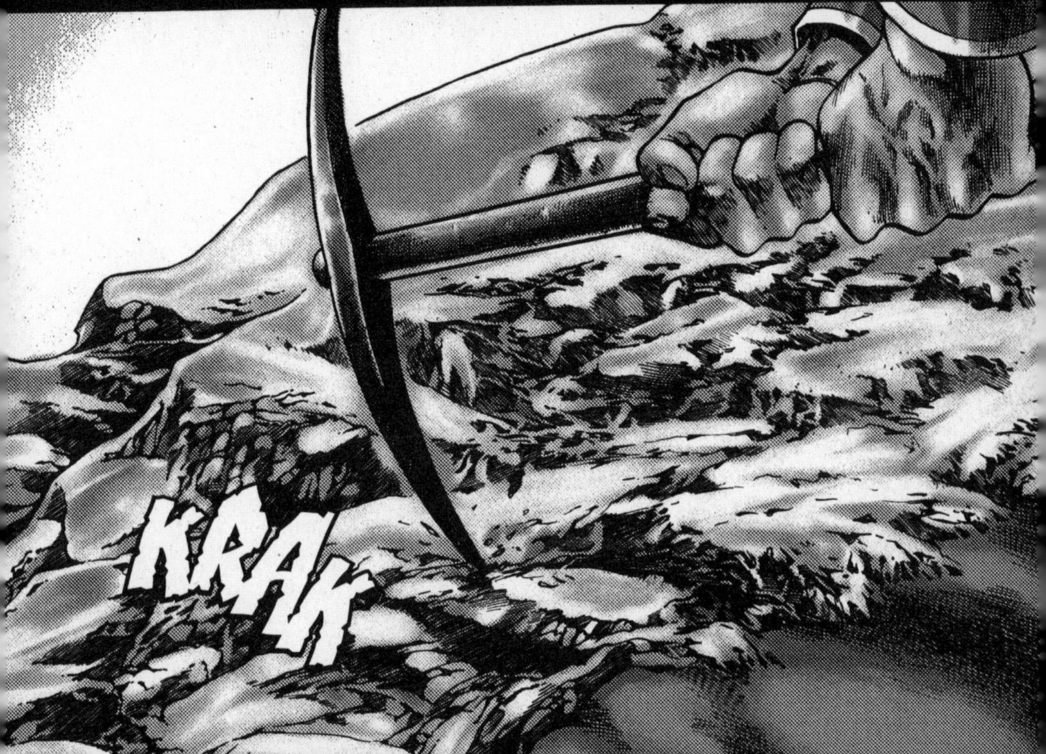
KRAK

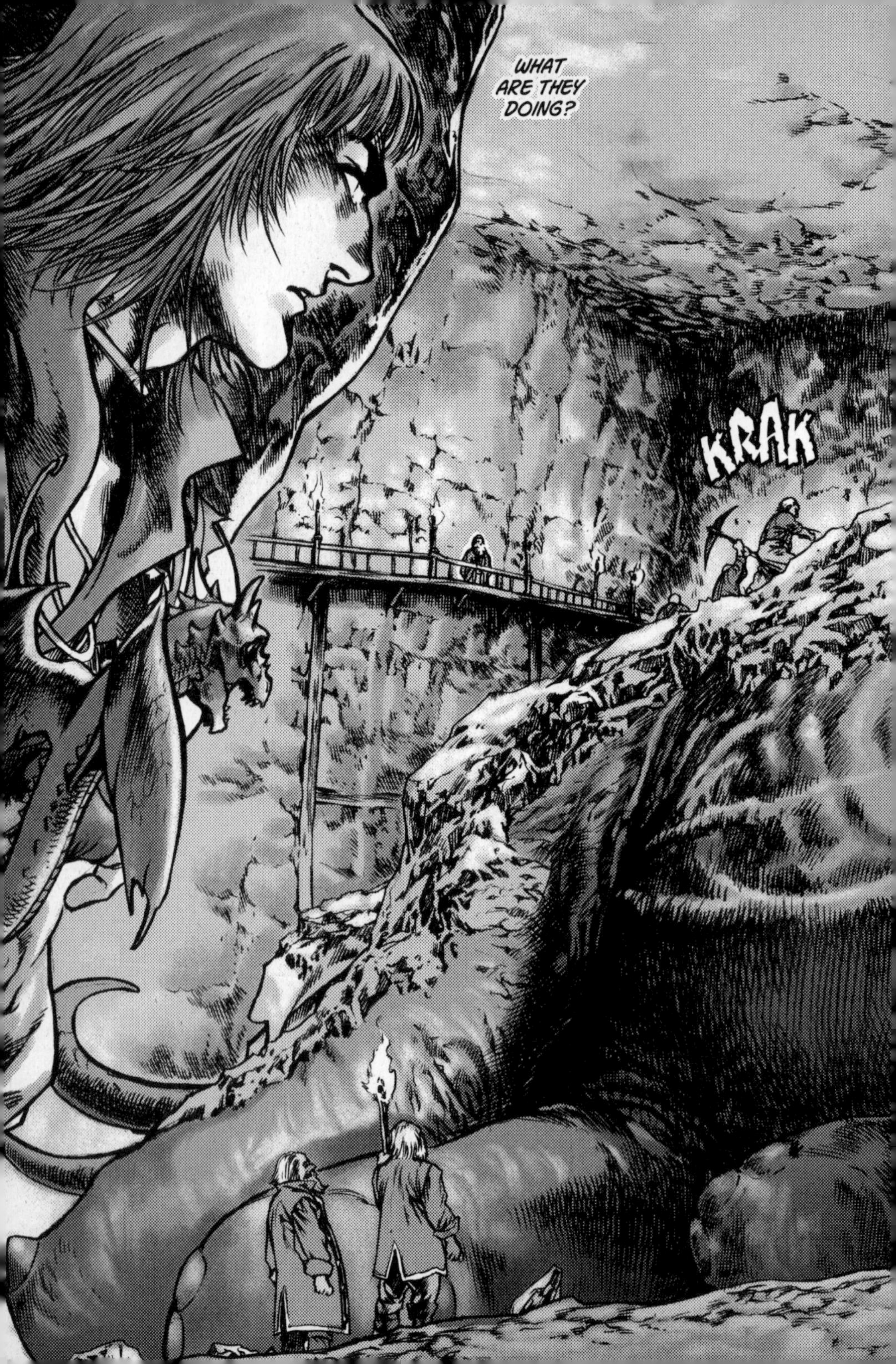
WHAT ARE THEY DOING?
KRAK

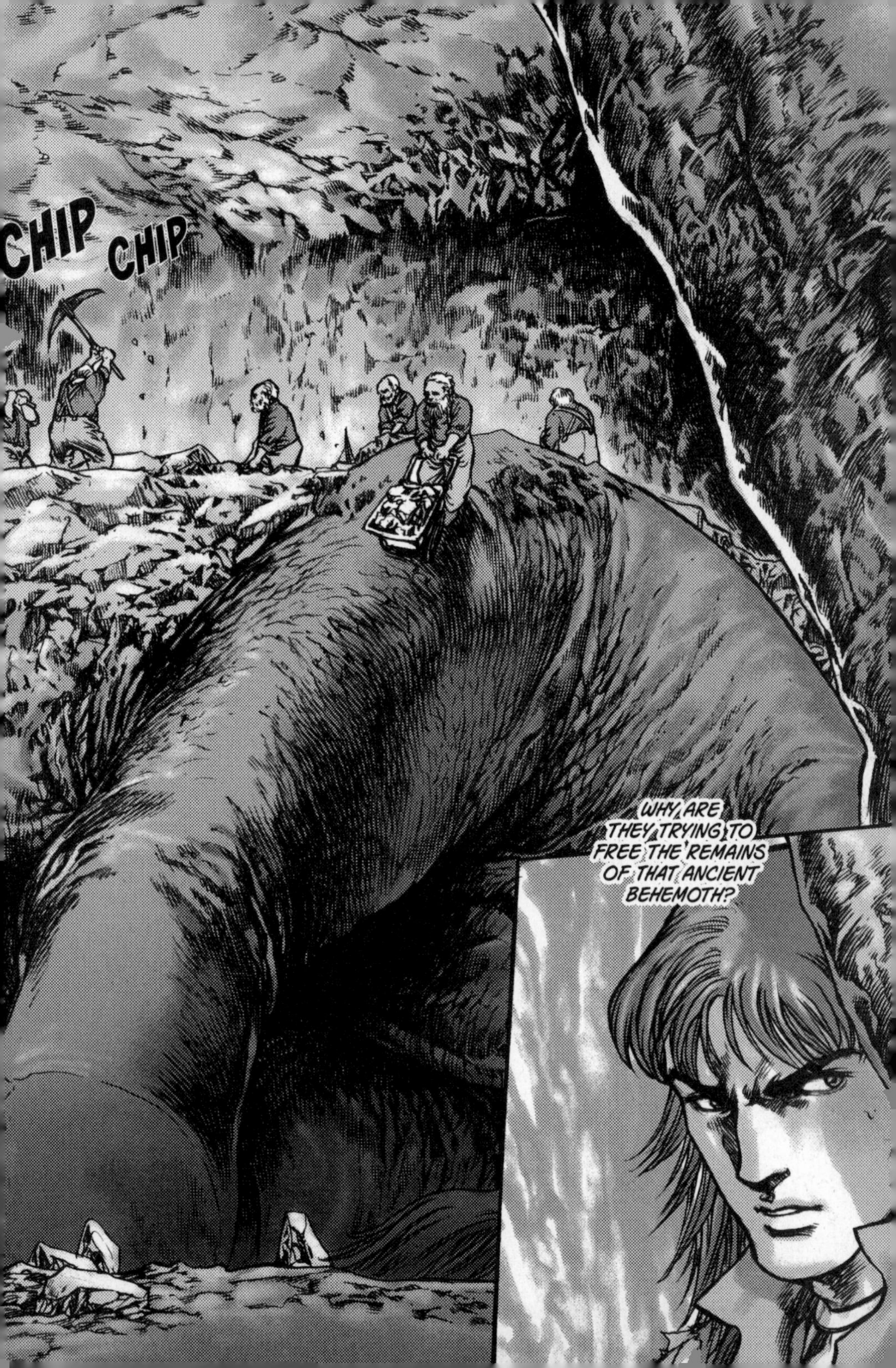
CHIP CHIP
WHY ARE THEY TRYING TO FREE THE REMAINS OF THAT ANCIENT BEHEMOTH?

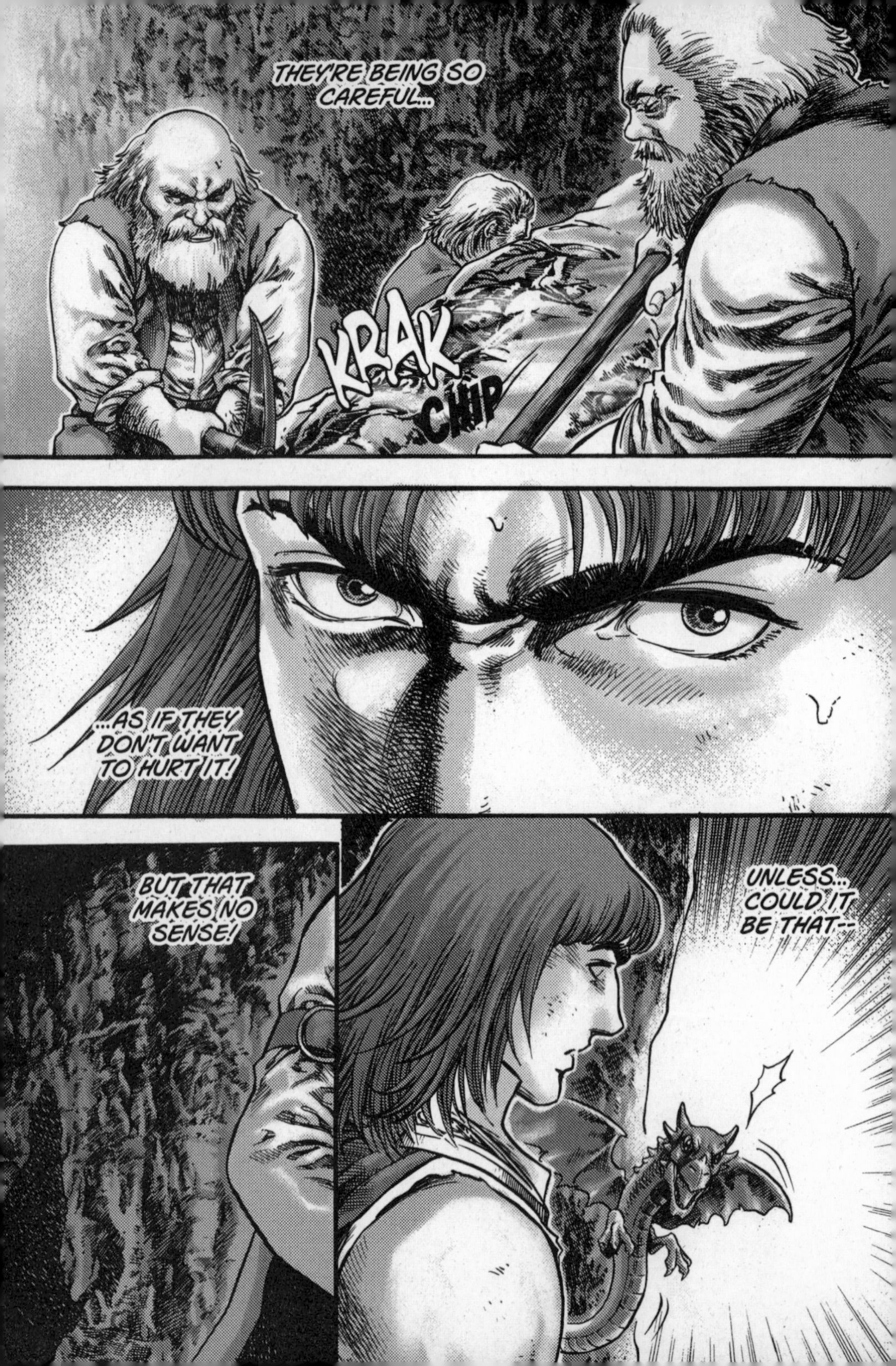
THEY'RE BEING SO CAREFUL...
KRAK
CHIP
...AS IF THEY DON'T WANT TO HURT IT!
BUT THAT MAKES NO SENSE!
UNLESS... COULD IT BE THAT--

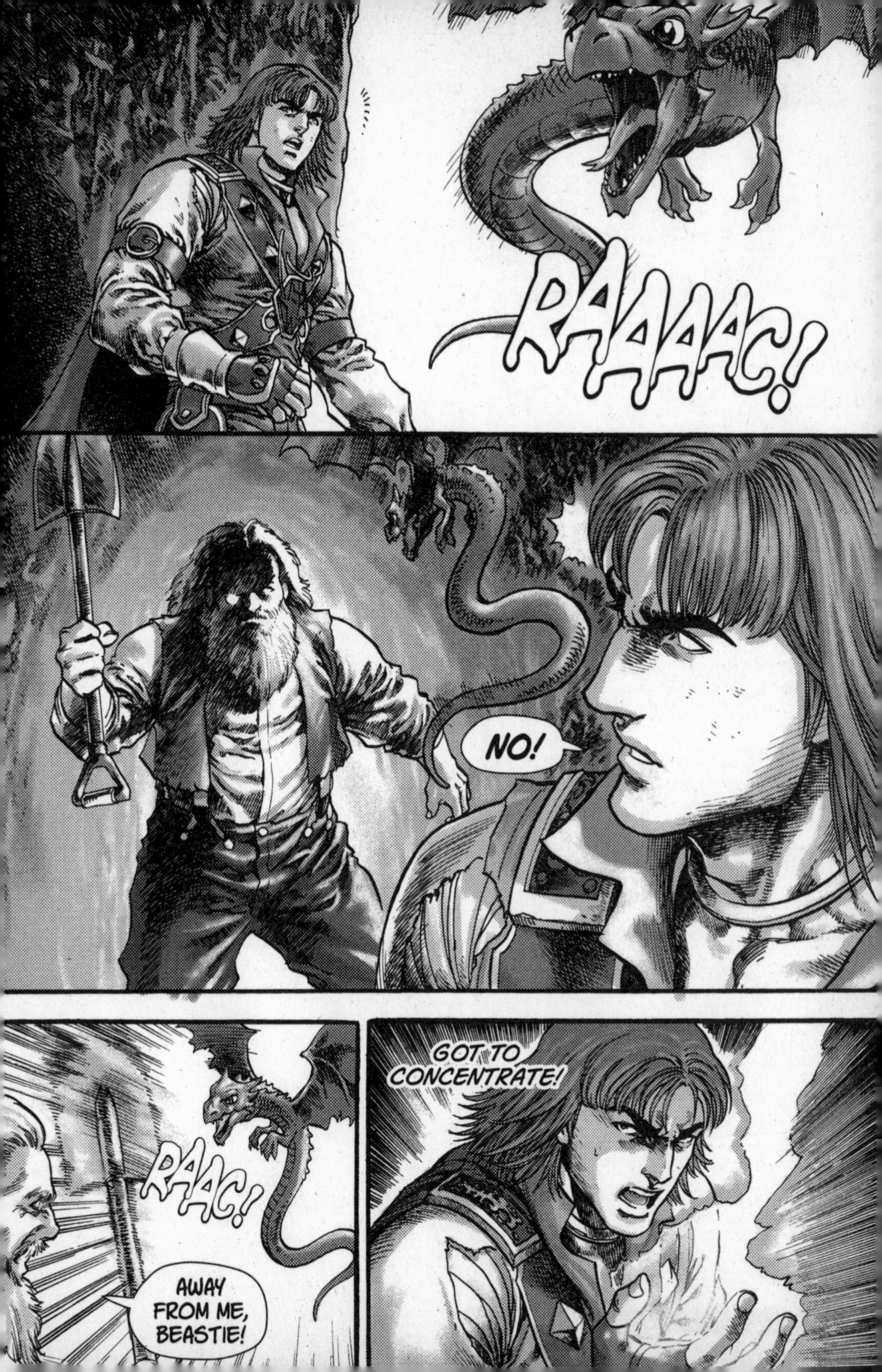
RAAAAC!
NO!
RAAC!
AWAY FROM ME, BEASTIE!
GOT TO CONCENTRATE!

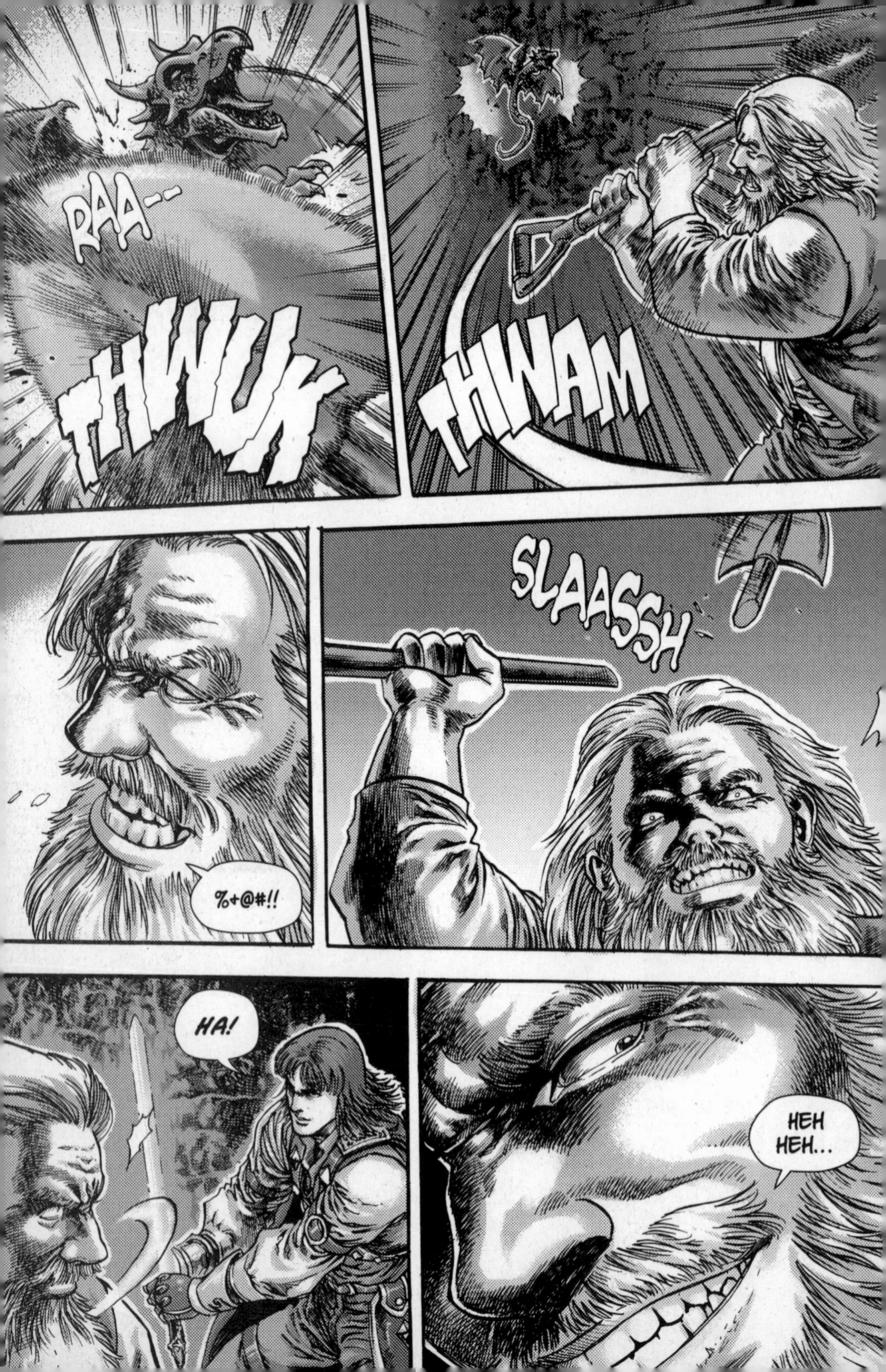
RAA--
THWUK
THWAM
%+@#!!
SLAASSH
HA!
HEH HEH...

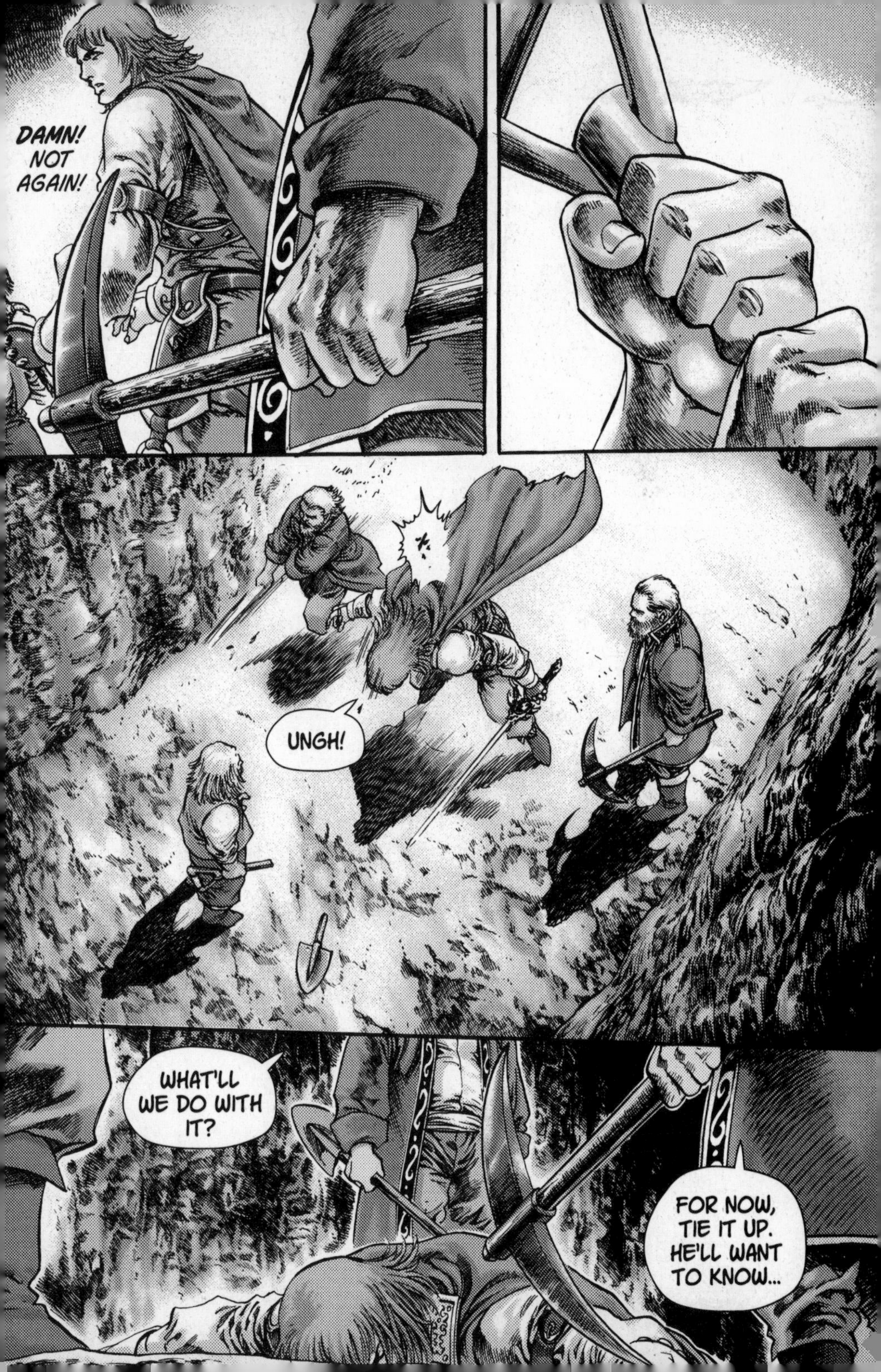
DAMN! NOT AGAIN!
UNGH!
WHAT'LL WE DO WITH IT?
FOR NOW, TIE IT UP. HE'LL WANT TO KNOW...

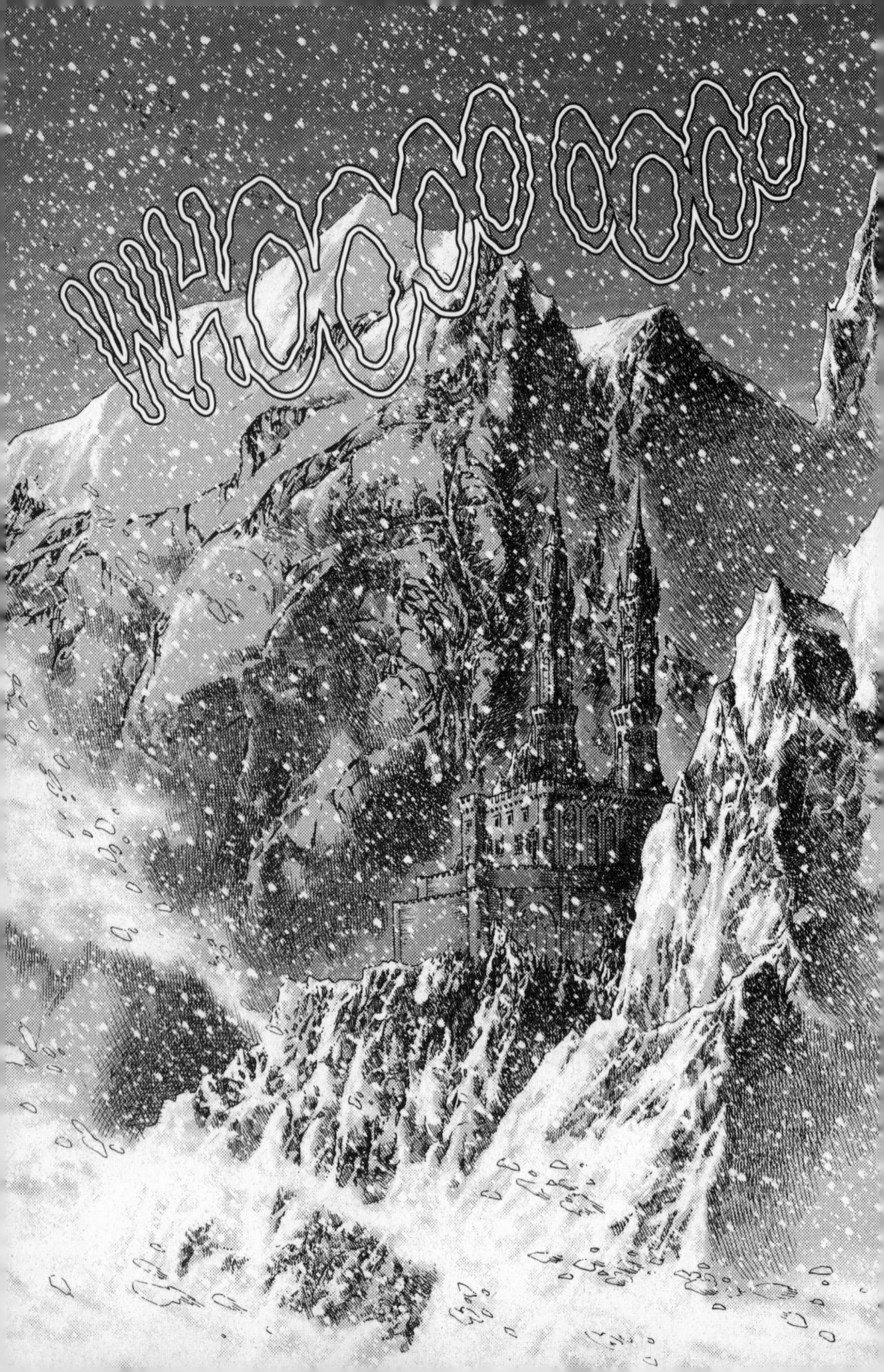
WHOOOOOOOO

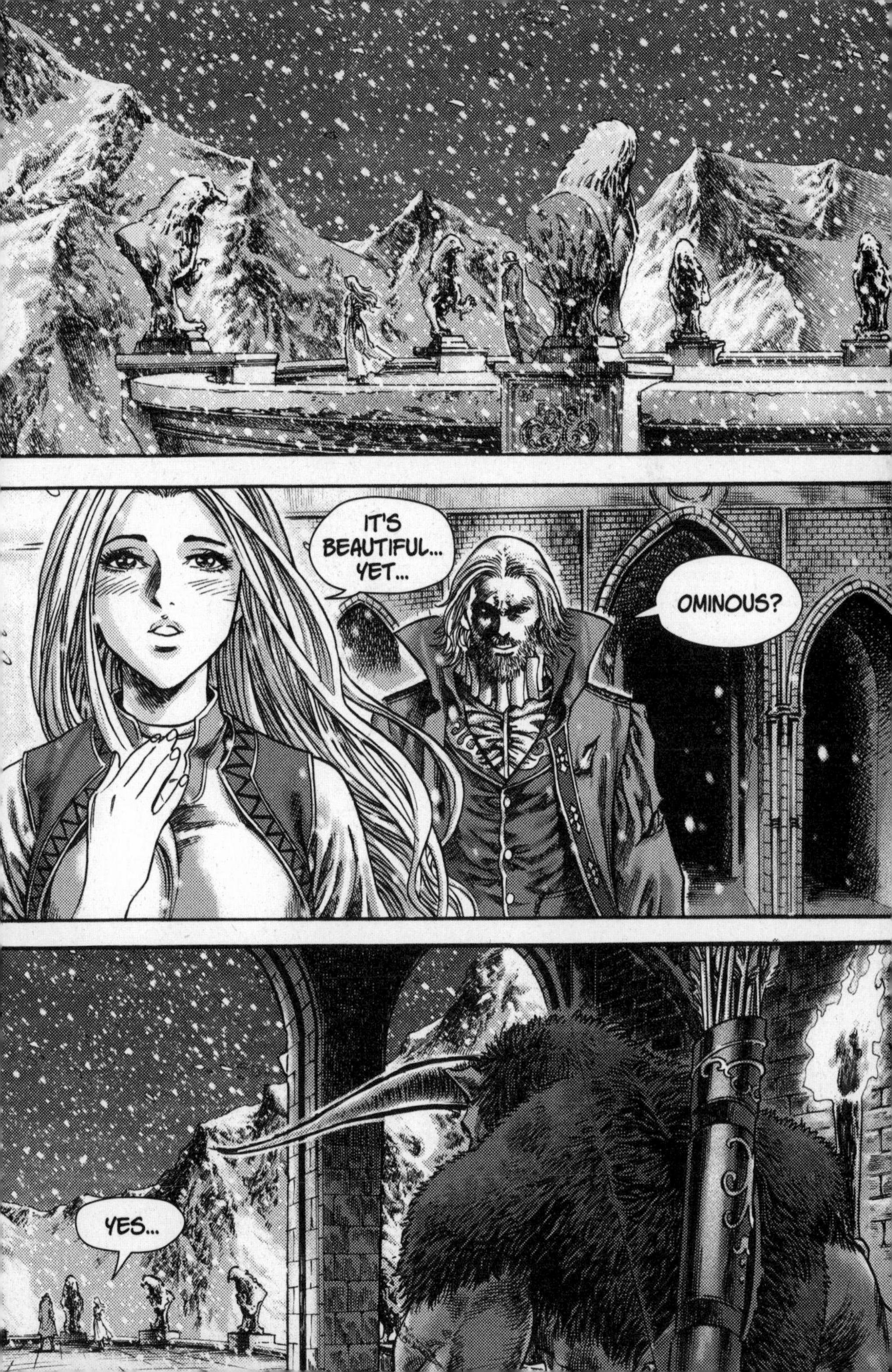
IT'S BEAUTIFUL... YET...
OMINOUS?
YES...

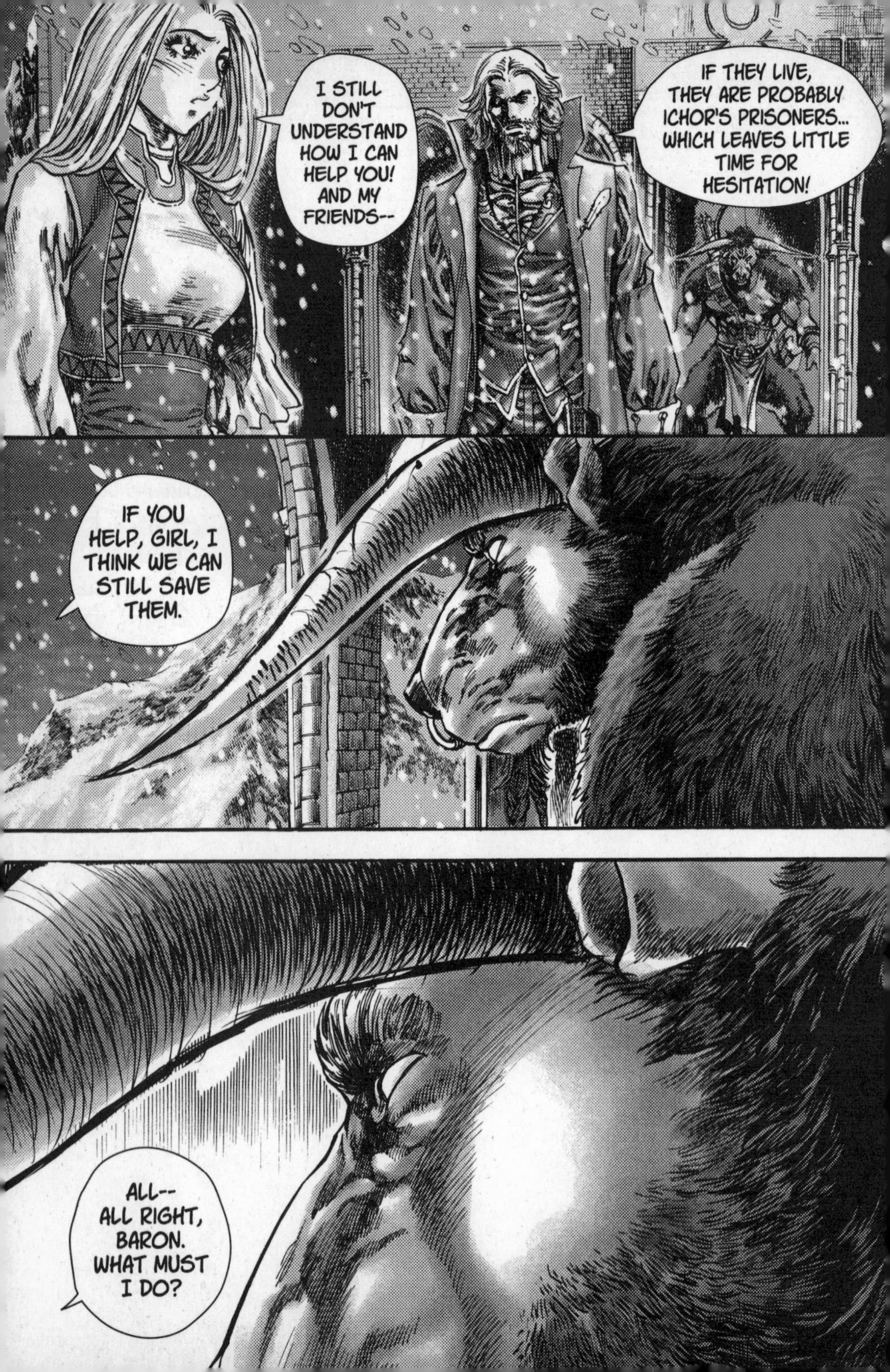
I STILL DON'T UNDERSTAND HOW I CAN HELP YOU! AND MY FRIENDS--
IF THEY LIVE, THEY ARE PROBABLY ICHOR'S PRISONERS... WHICH LEAVES LITTLE TIME FOR HESITATION!
IF YOU HELP, GIRL, I THINK WE CAN STILL SAVE THEM.
ALL-- ALL RIGHT, BARON. WHAT MUST I DO?

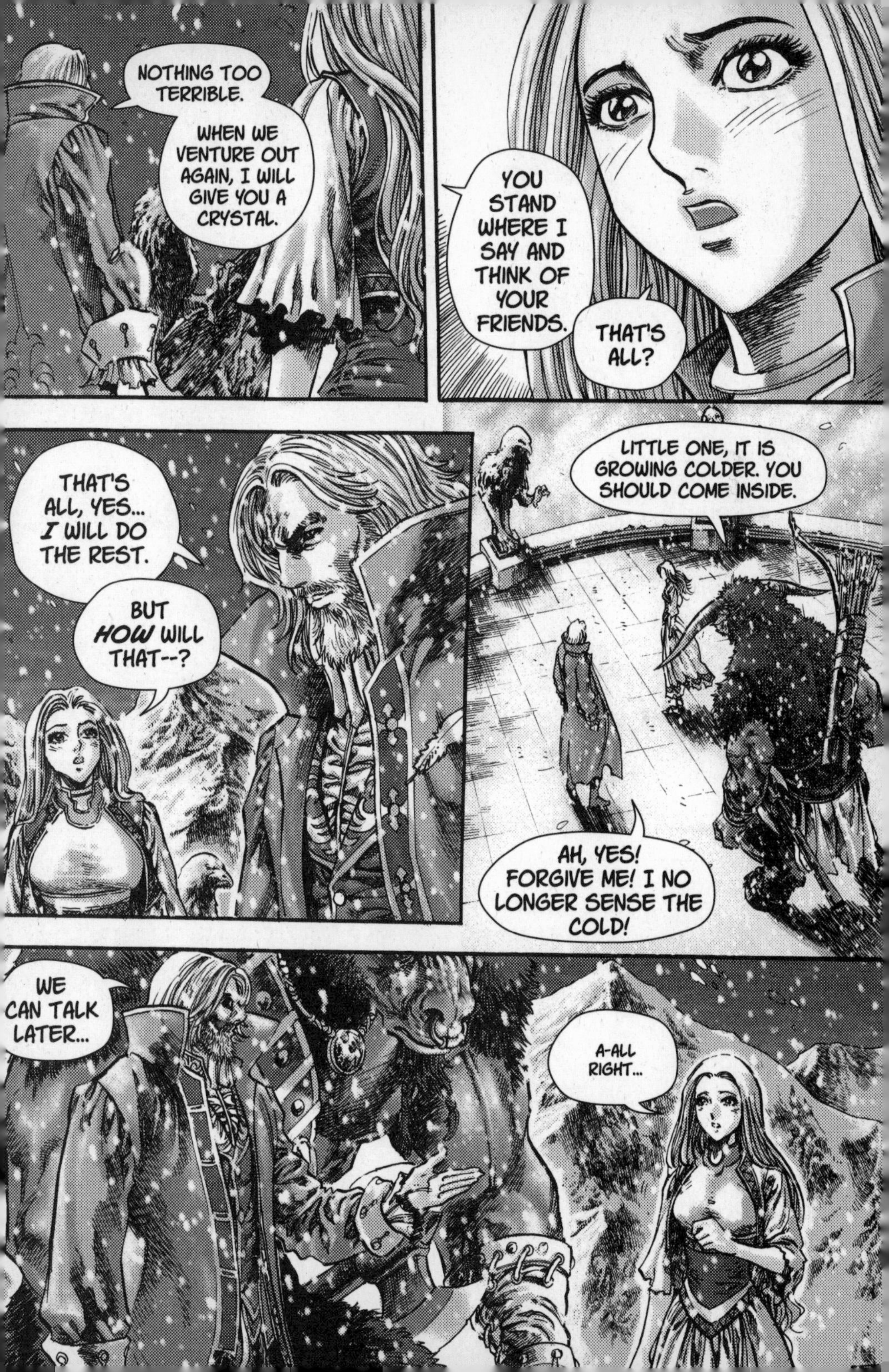
NOTHING TOO TERRIBLE.
WHEN WE VENTURE OUT AGAIN, I WILL GIVE YOU A CRYSTAL.
YOU STAND WHERE I SAY AND THINK OF YOUR FRIENDS.
THAT'S ALL?
THAT'S ALL, YES... *I* WILL DO THE REST.
BUT ***HOW*** WILL THAT--?
LITTLE ONE, IT IS GROWING COLDER. YOU SHOULD COME INSIDE.
AH, YES! FORGIVE ME! I NO LONGER SENSE THE COLD!
WE CAN TALK LATER...
A-ALL RIGHT...

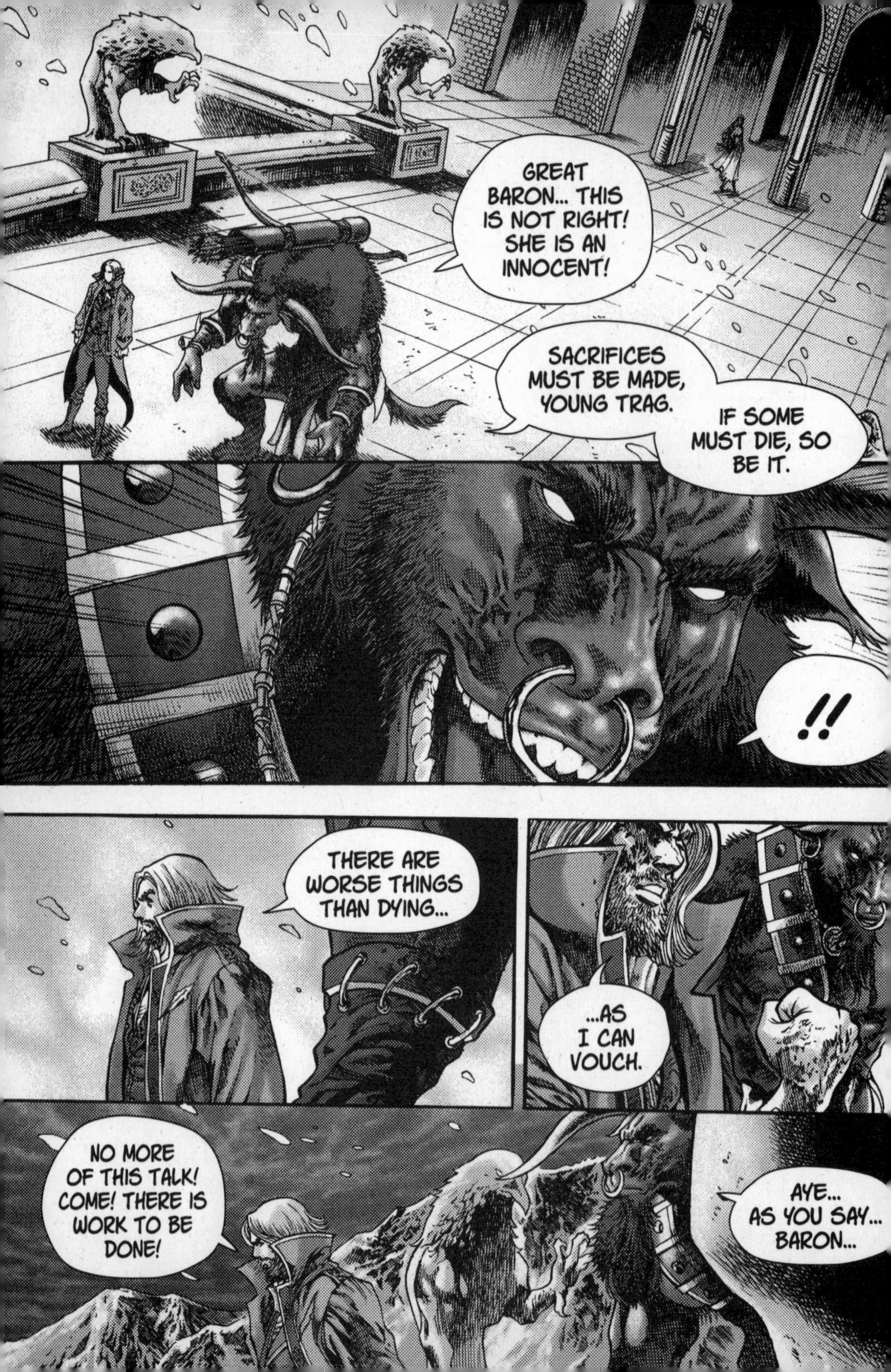
GREAT BARON... THIS IS NOT RIGHT! SHE IS AN INNOCENT!
SACRIFICES MUST BE MADE, YOUNG TRAG.
IF SOME MUST DIE, SO BE IT.
!!
THERE ARE WORSE THINGS THAN DYING...
...AS I CAN VOUCH.
NO MORE OF THIS TALK! COME! THERE IS WORK TO BE DONE!
AYE... AS YOU SAY... BARON...

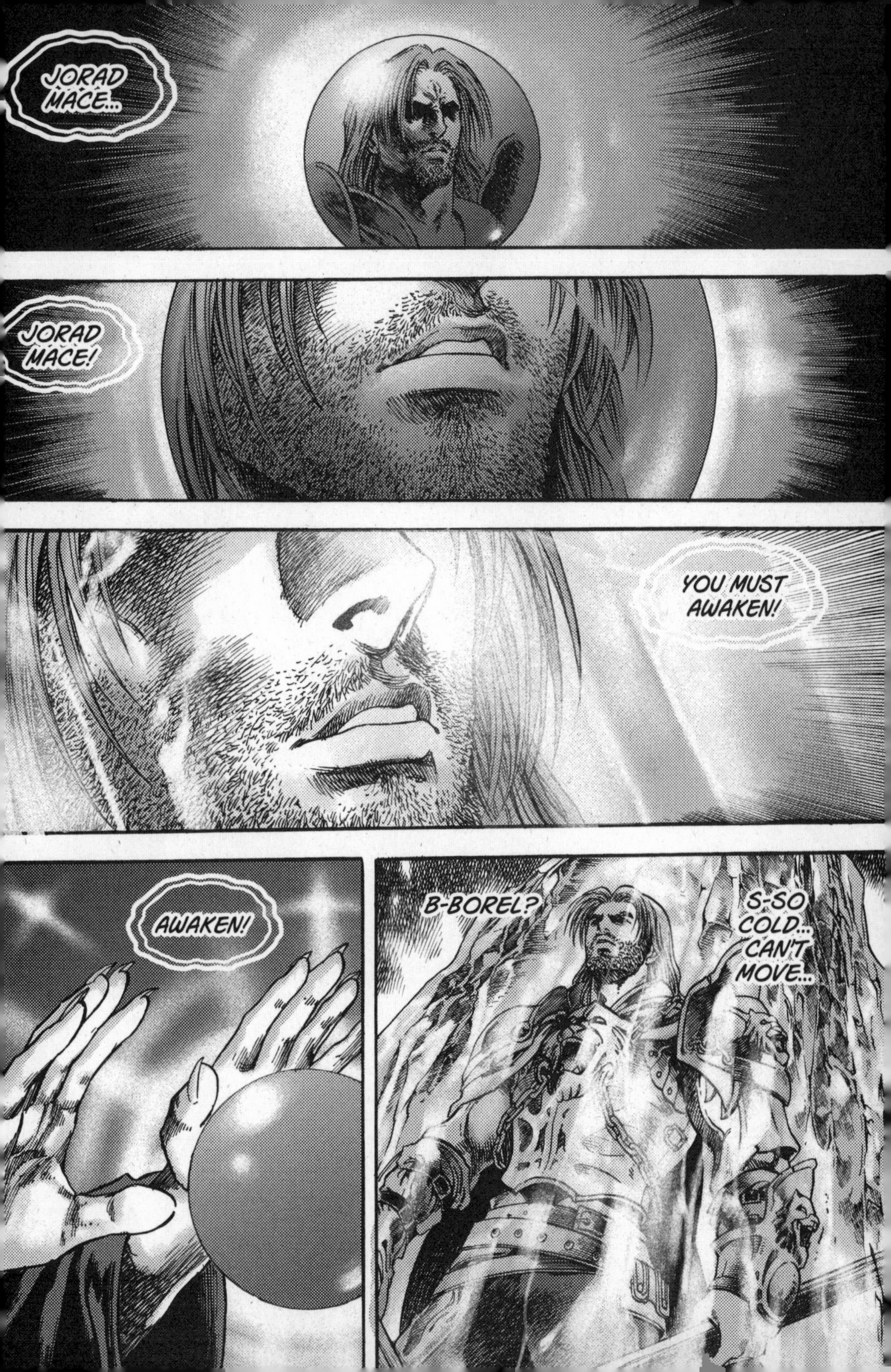
JORAD MACE...
JORAD MACE!
YOU MUST AWAKEN!
AWAKEN!
B-BOREL?
S-SO COLD... CAN'T MOVE...

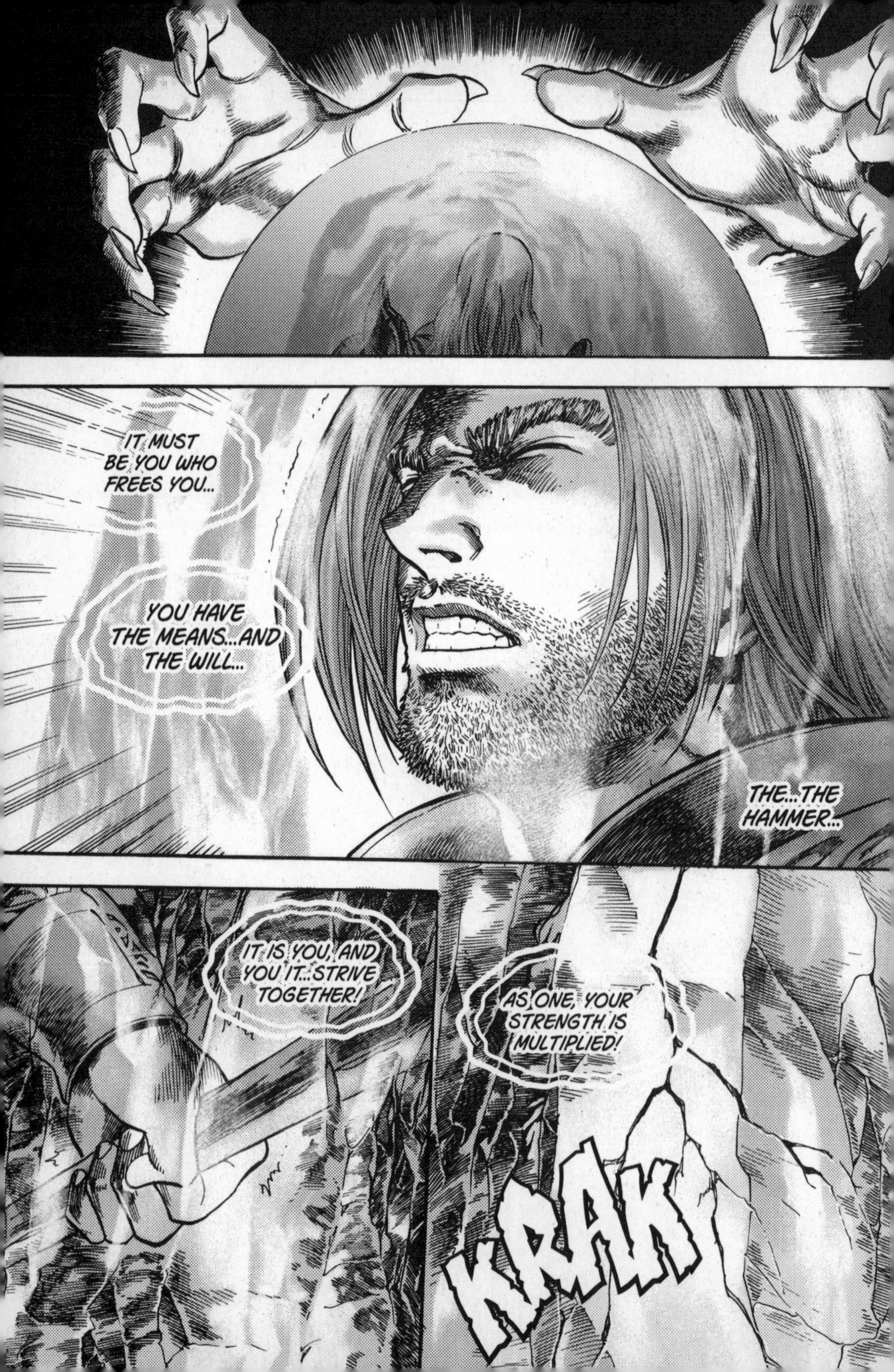
IT MUST BE YOU WHO FREES YOU...
YOU HAVE THE MEANS...AND THE WILL...
THE...THE HAMMER...
IT IS YOU, AND YOU IT...STRIVE TOGETHER!
AS ONE, YOUR STRENGTH IS MULTIPLIED!
KRAK

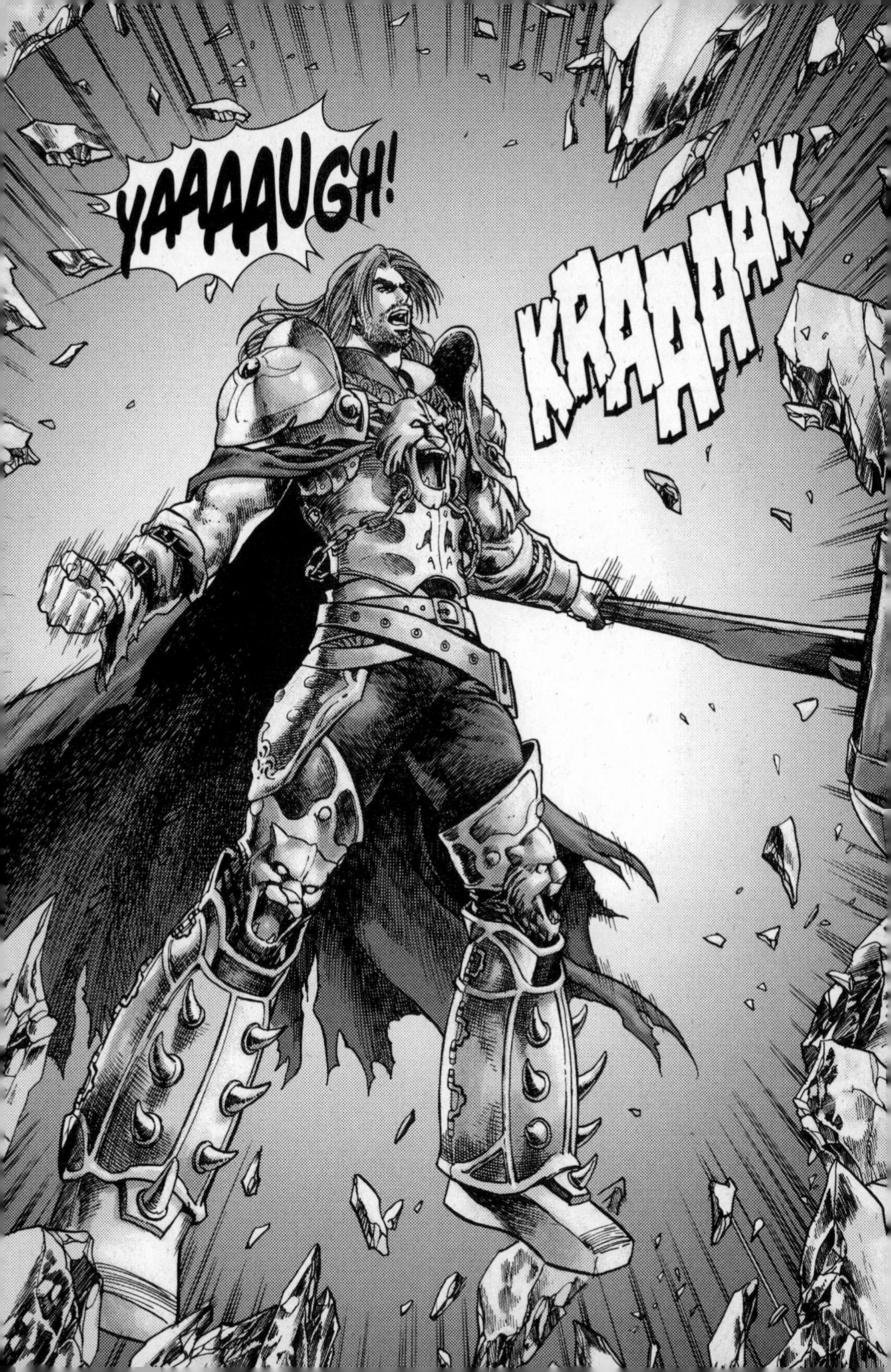
YAAAAUGH!
KRAAAAK

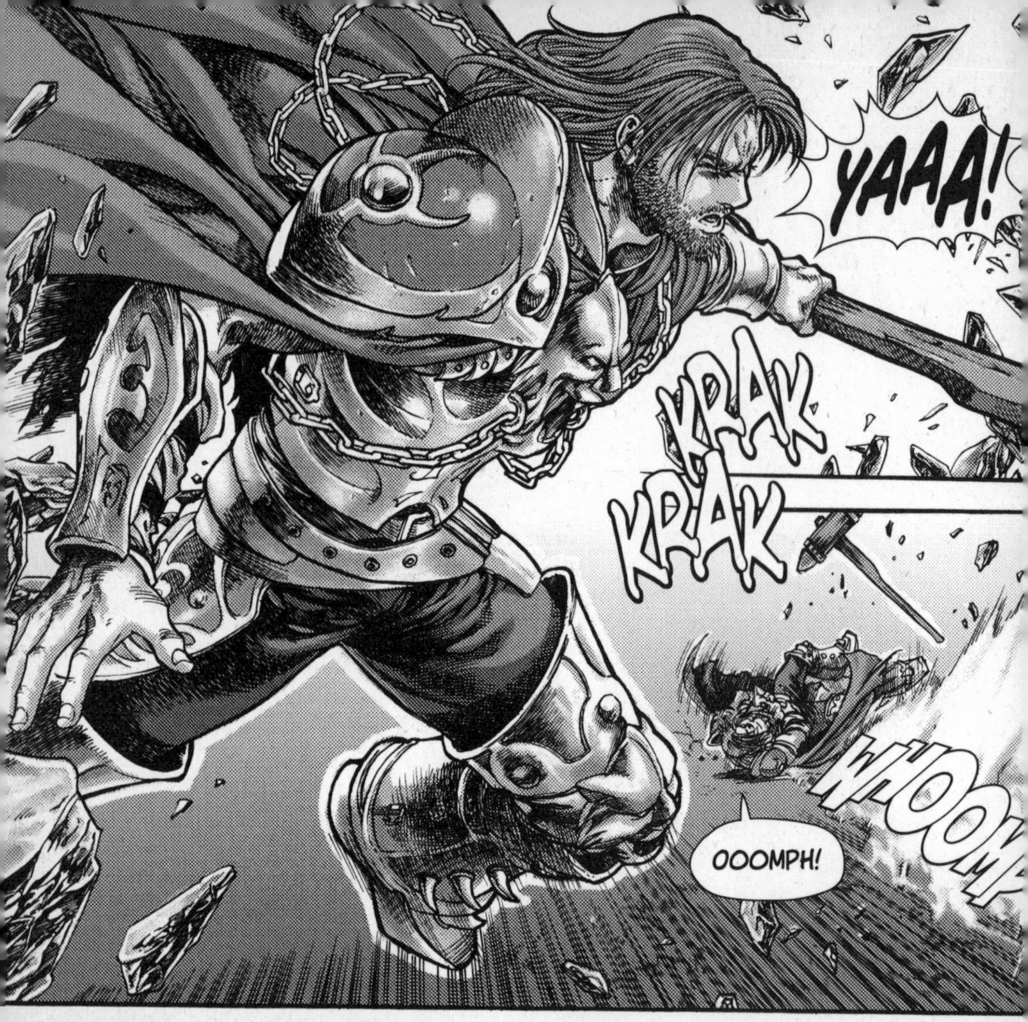
YAAAA!
KRAK
KRAK
WHOOM
OOOMPH!

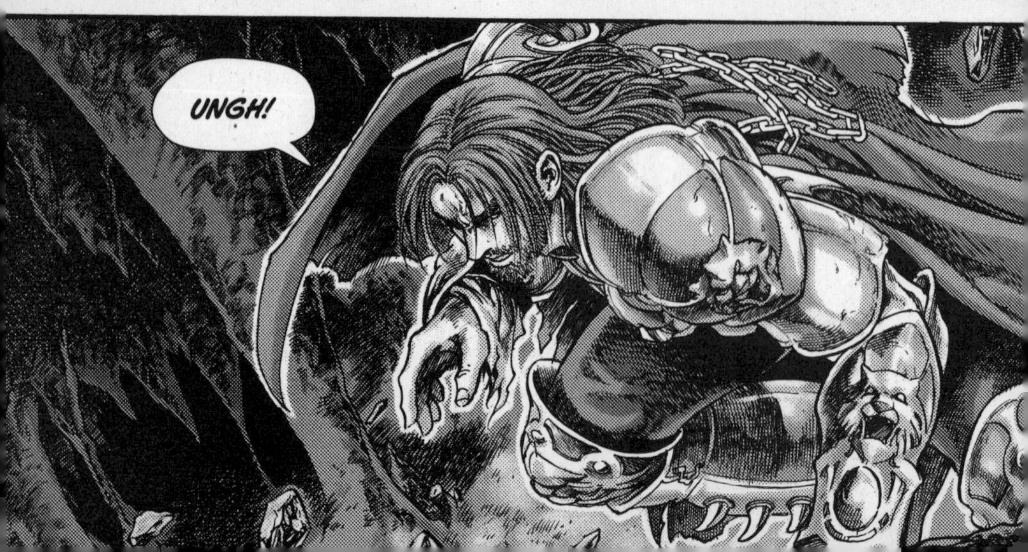
UNGH!

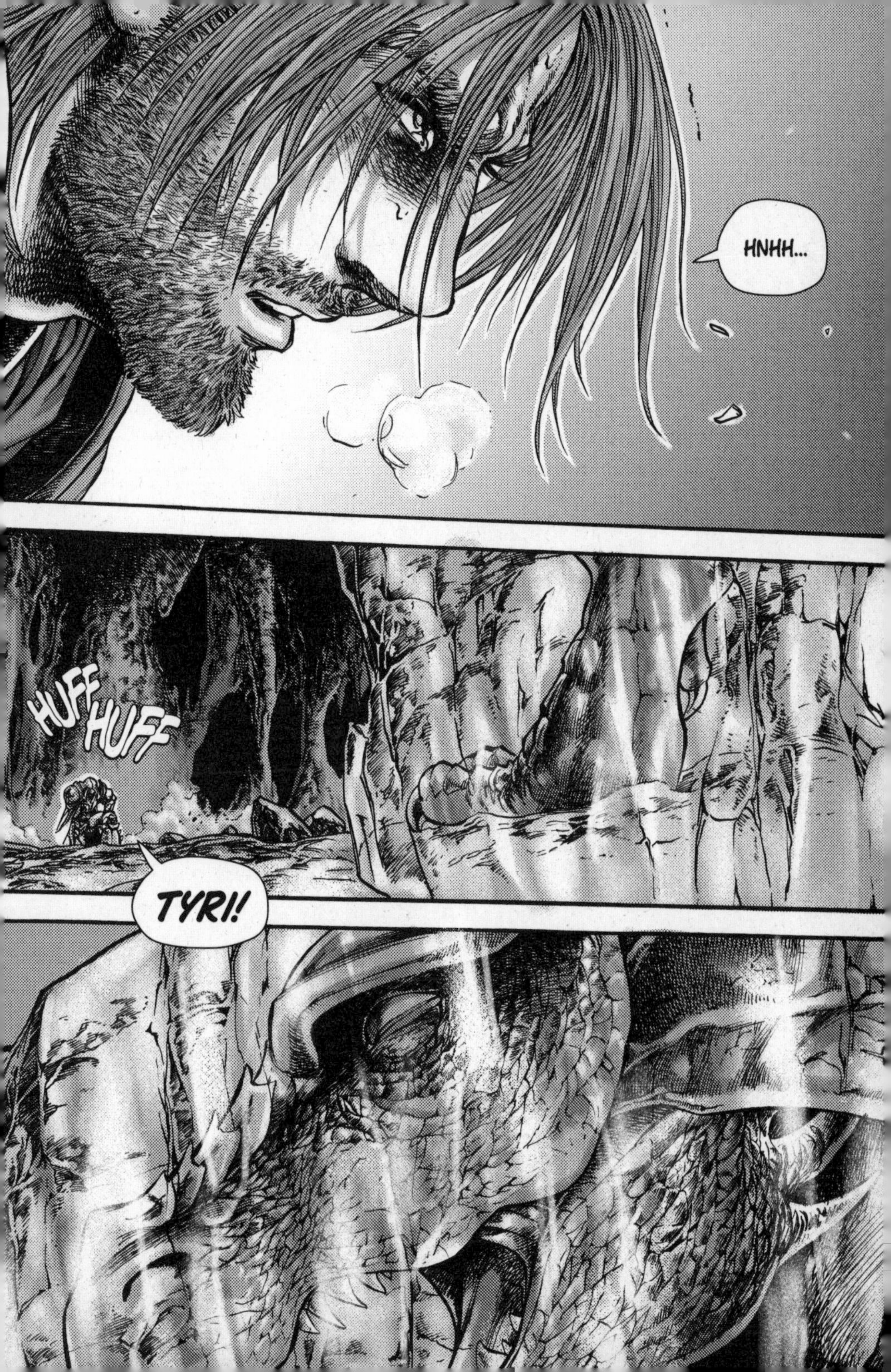
HNHH...
HUFF HUFF
TYRI!

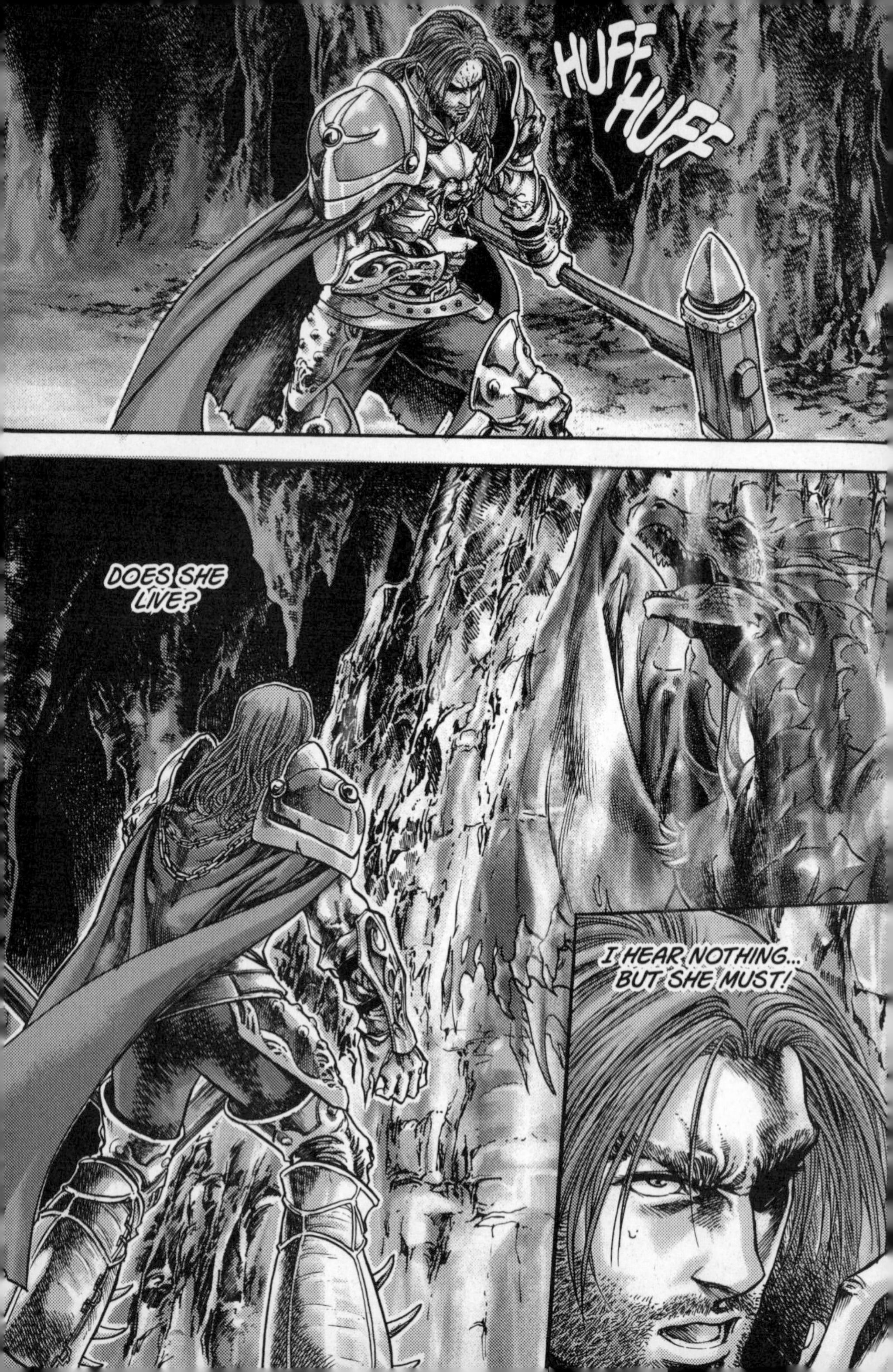
HUFF HUFF
DOES SHE LIVE?
I HEAR NOTHING... BUT SHE MUST!

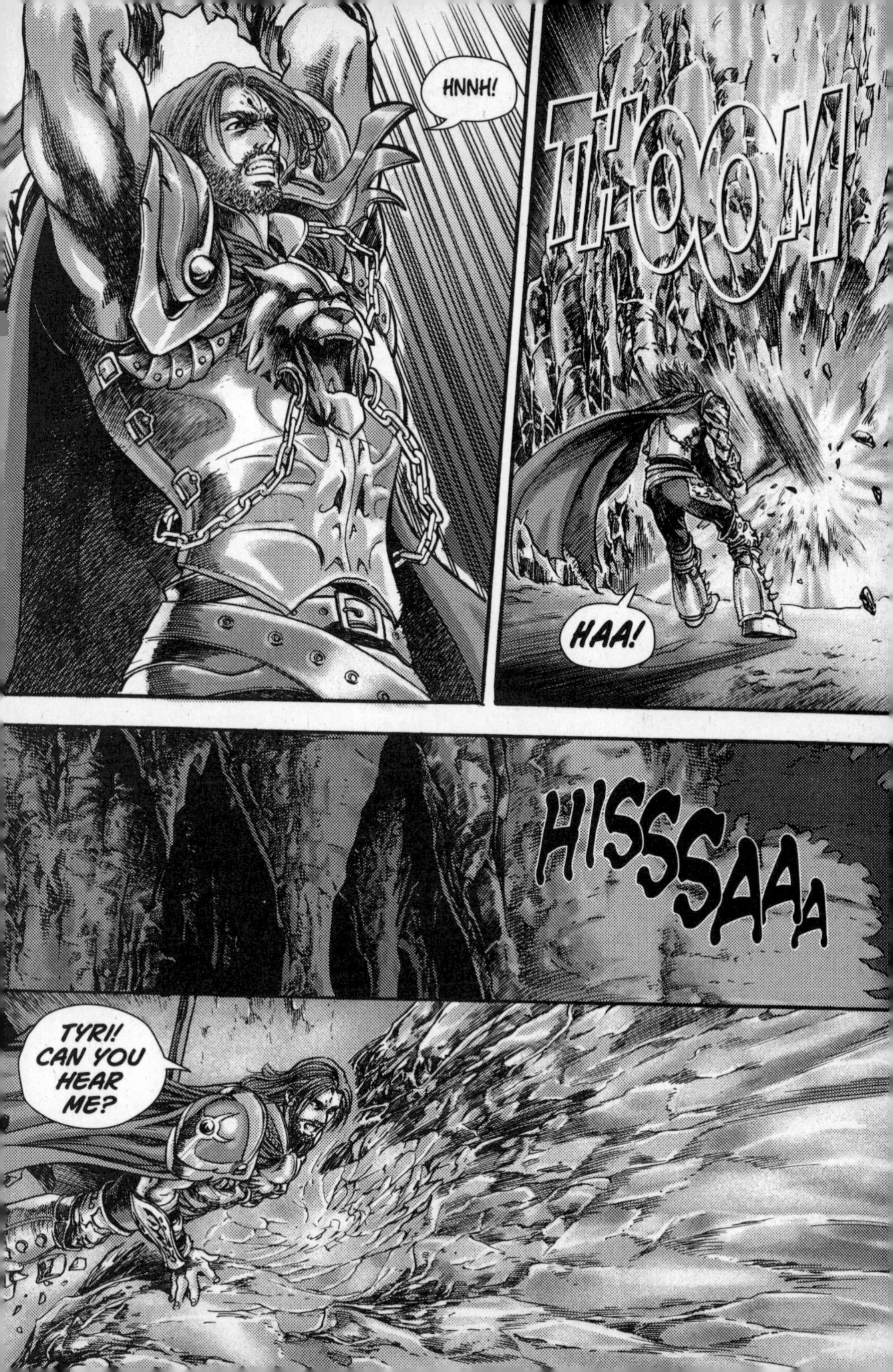
HNNH!
THOOM
HAA!
HISSSAAAA
TYRI! CAN YOU HEAR ME?

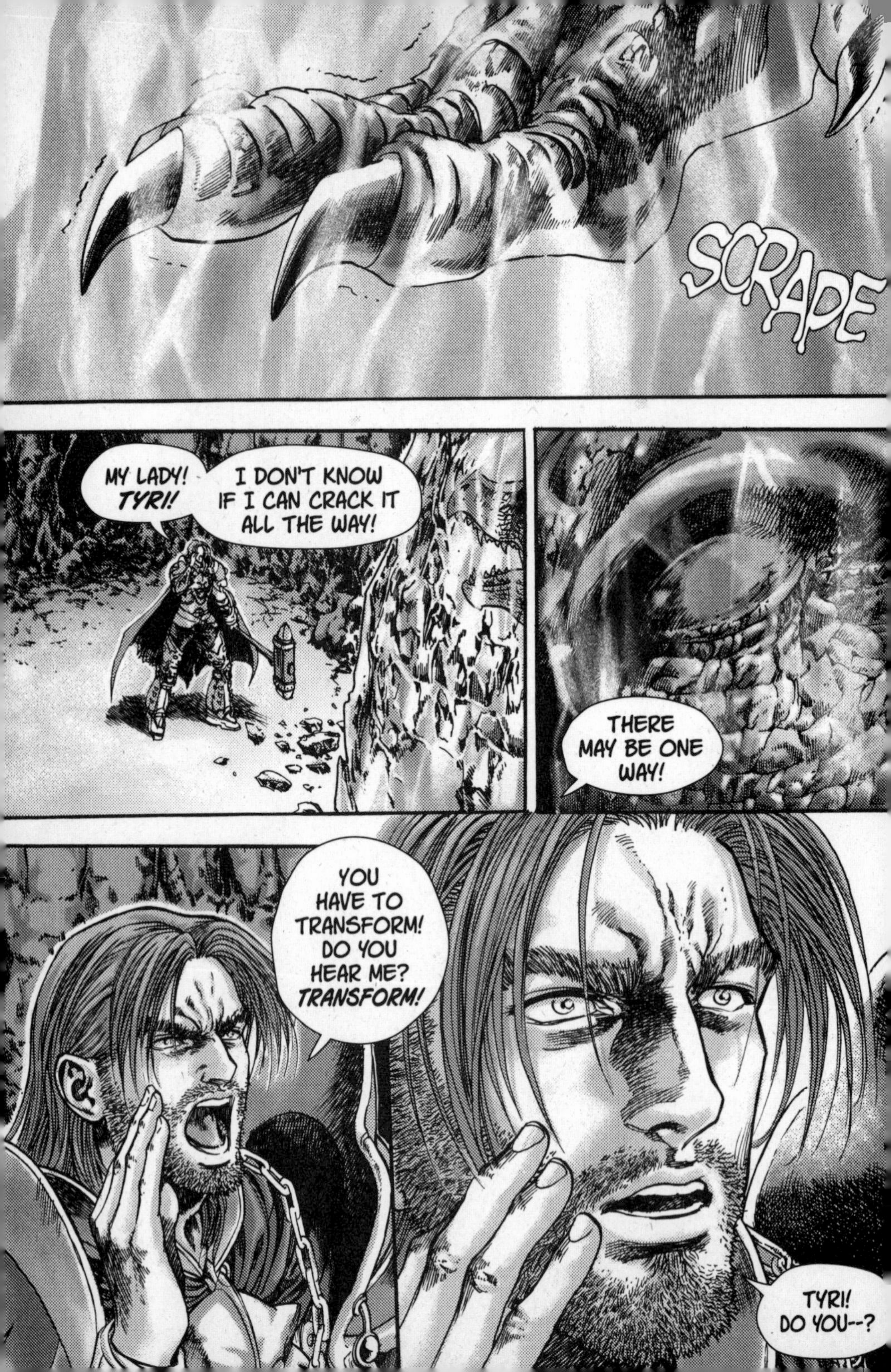
SCRAPE
MY LADY! TYRI!
I DON'T KNOW IF I CAN CRACK IT ALL THE WAY!
THERE MAY BE ONE WAY!
YOU HAVE TO TRANSFORM! DO YOU HEAR ME? TRANSFORM!
TYRI! DO YOU--?

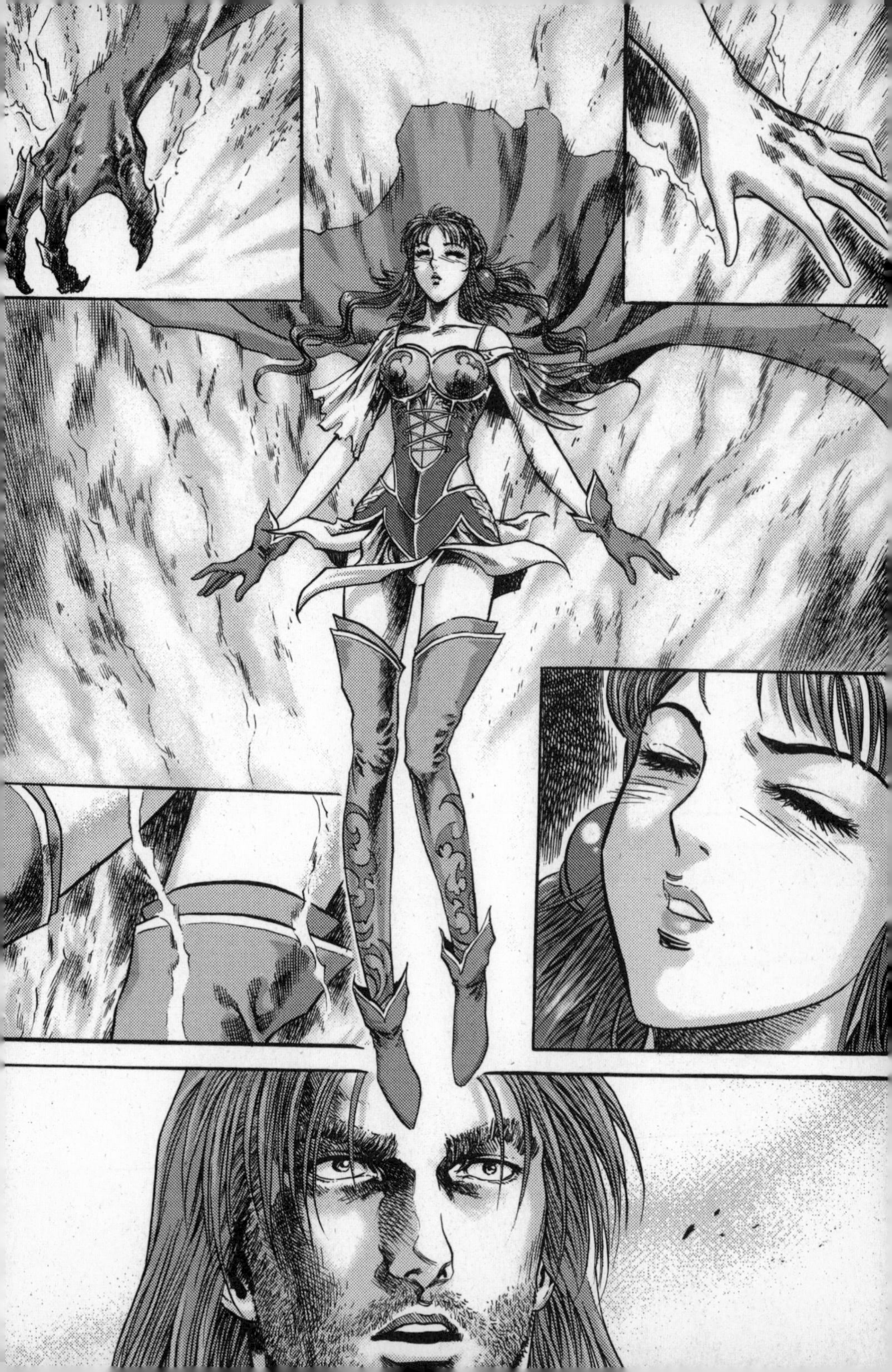

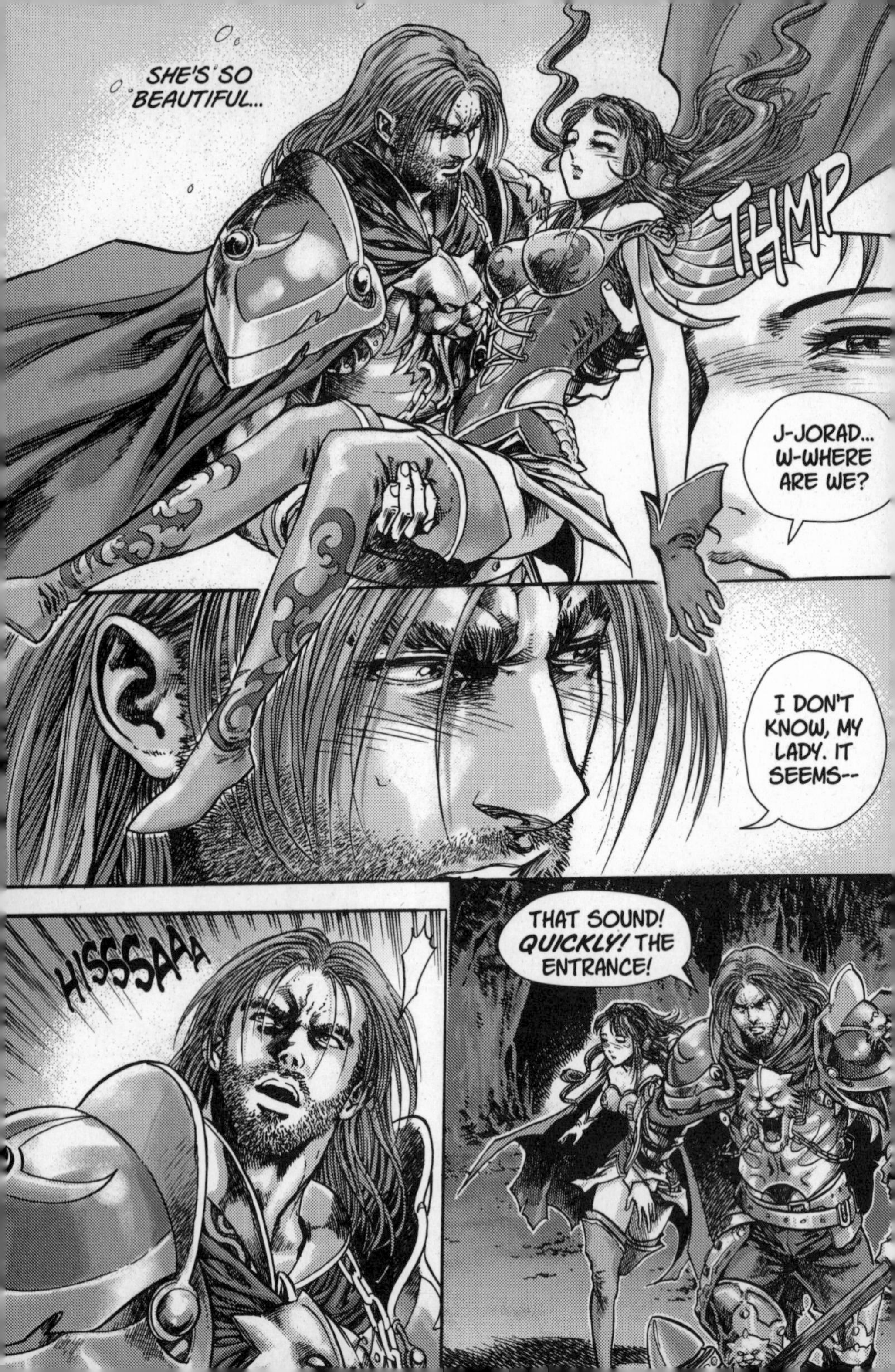
SHE'S SO BEAUTIFUL...
THMP
J-JORAD... W-WHERE ARE WE?
I DON'T KNOW, MY LADY. IT SEEMS--
HISSSAAA
THAT SOUND! *QUICKLY!* THE ENTRANCE!

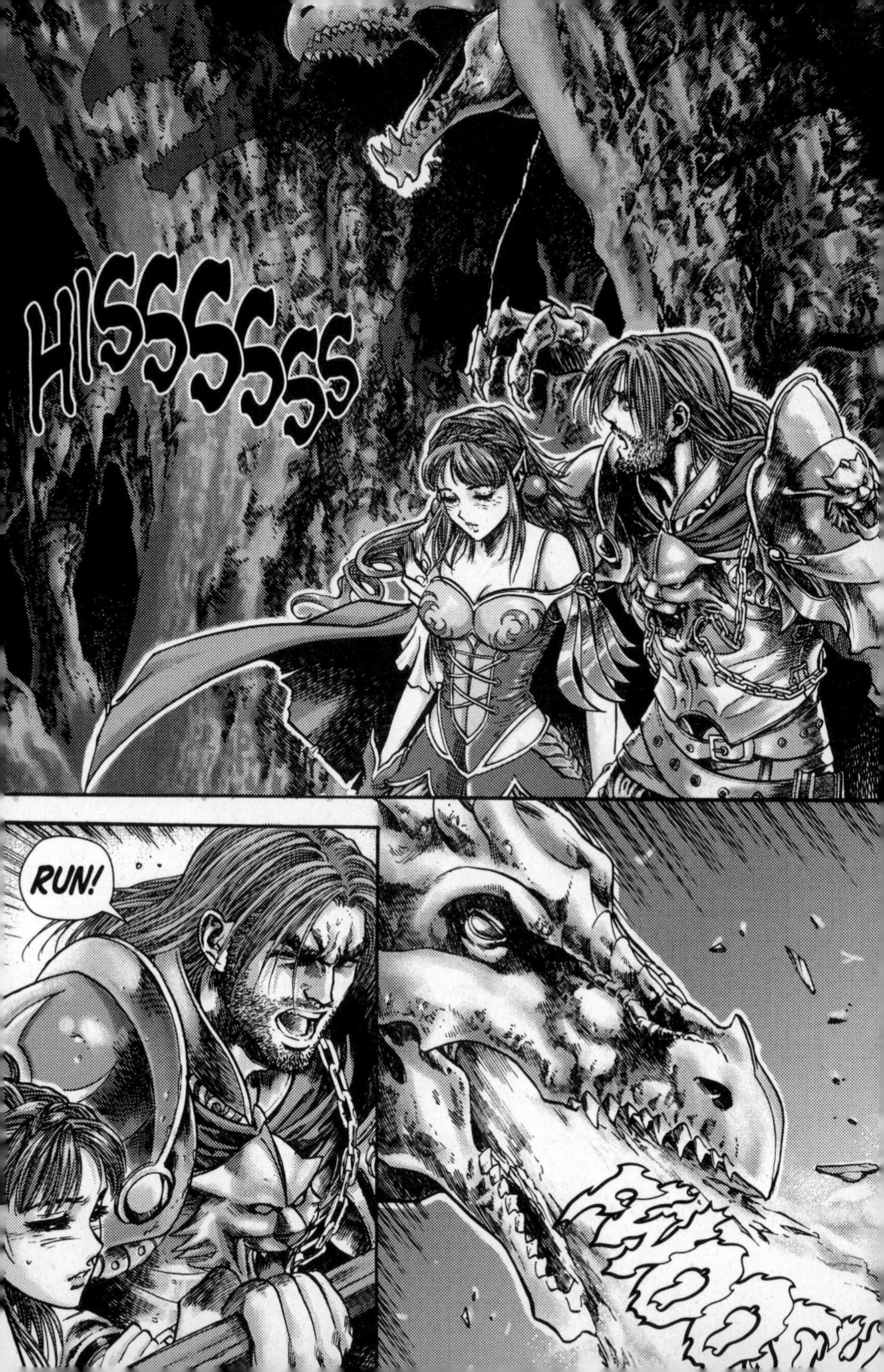
HISSSSSSS
RUN!

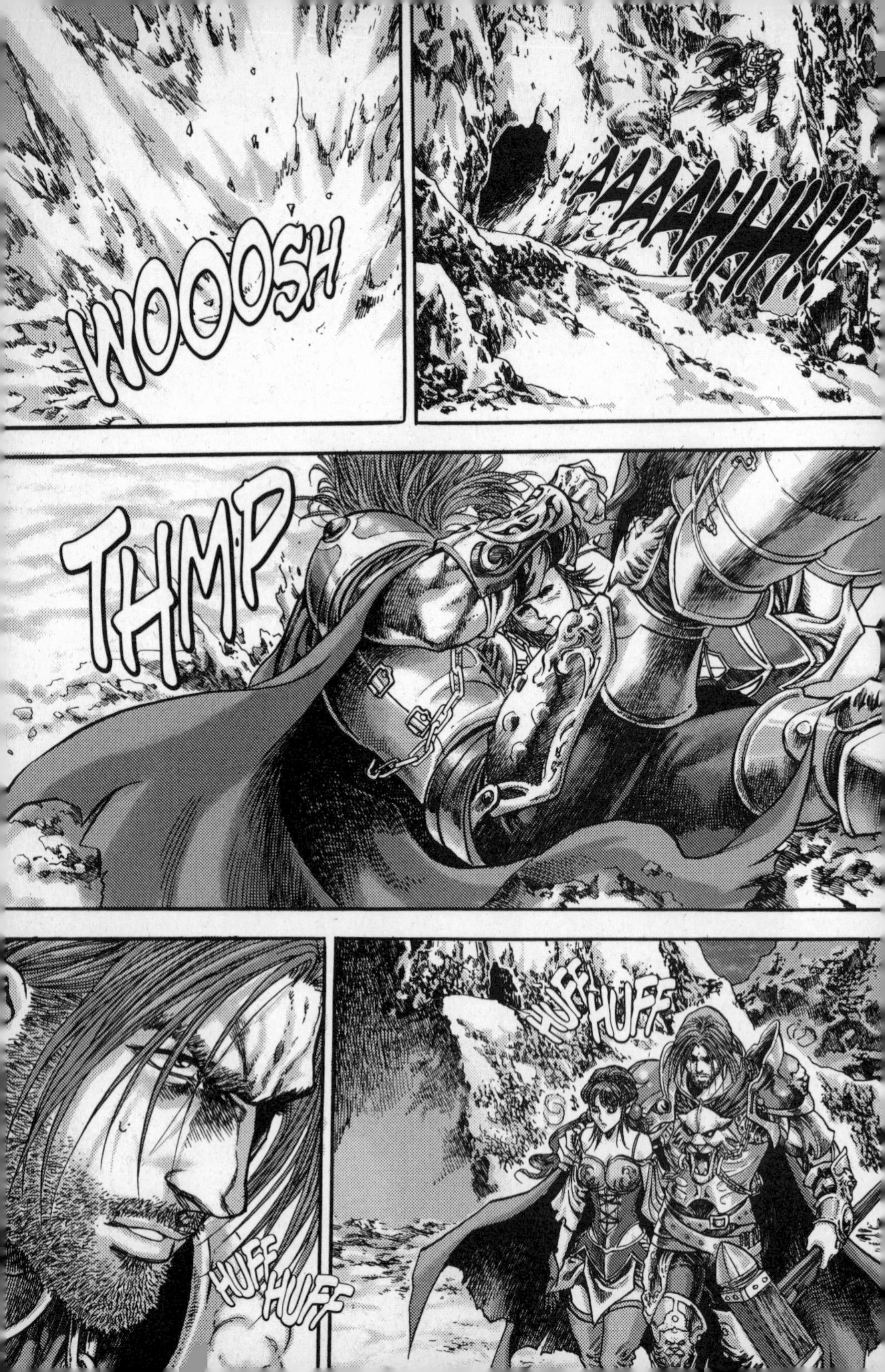
AAAAHHH!!!
WOOOSH
THMP
HUFF HUFF
HUFF HUFF

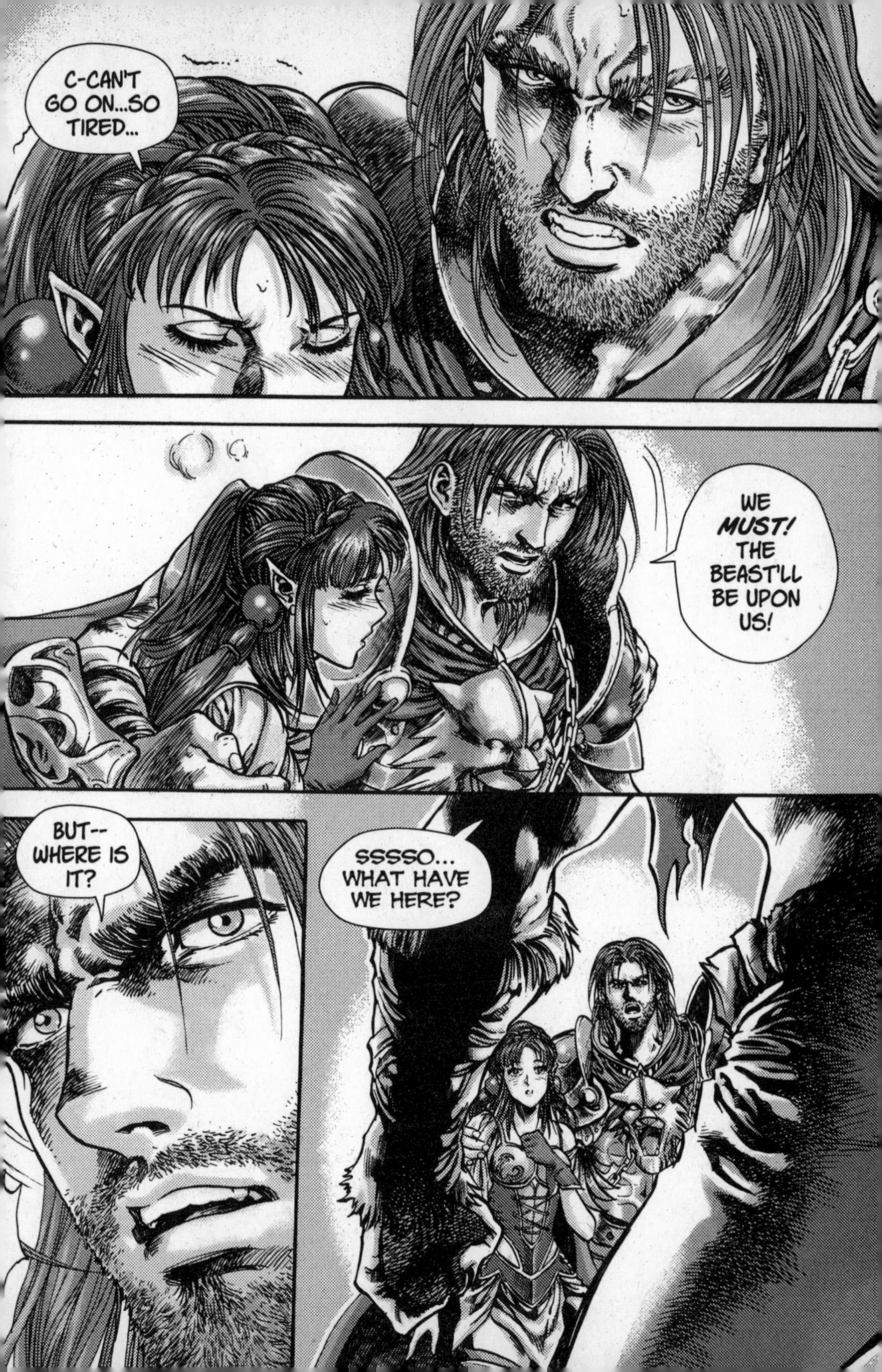
C-CAN'T GO ON...SO TIRED...
WE *MUST!* THE BEAST'LL BE UPON US!
BUT-- WHERE IS IT?
SSSSO... WHAT HAVE WE HERE?

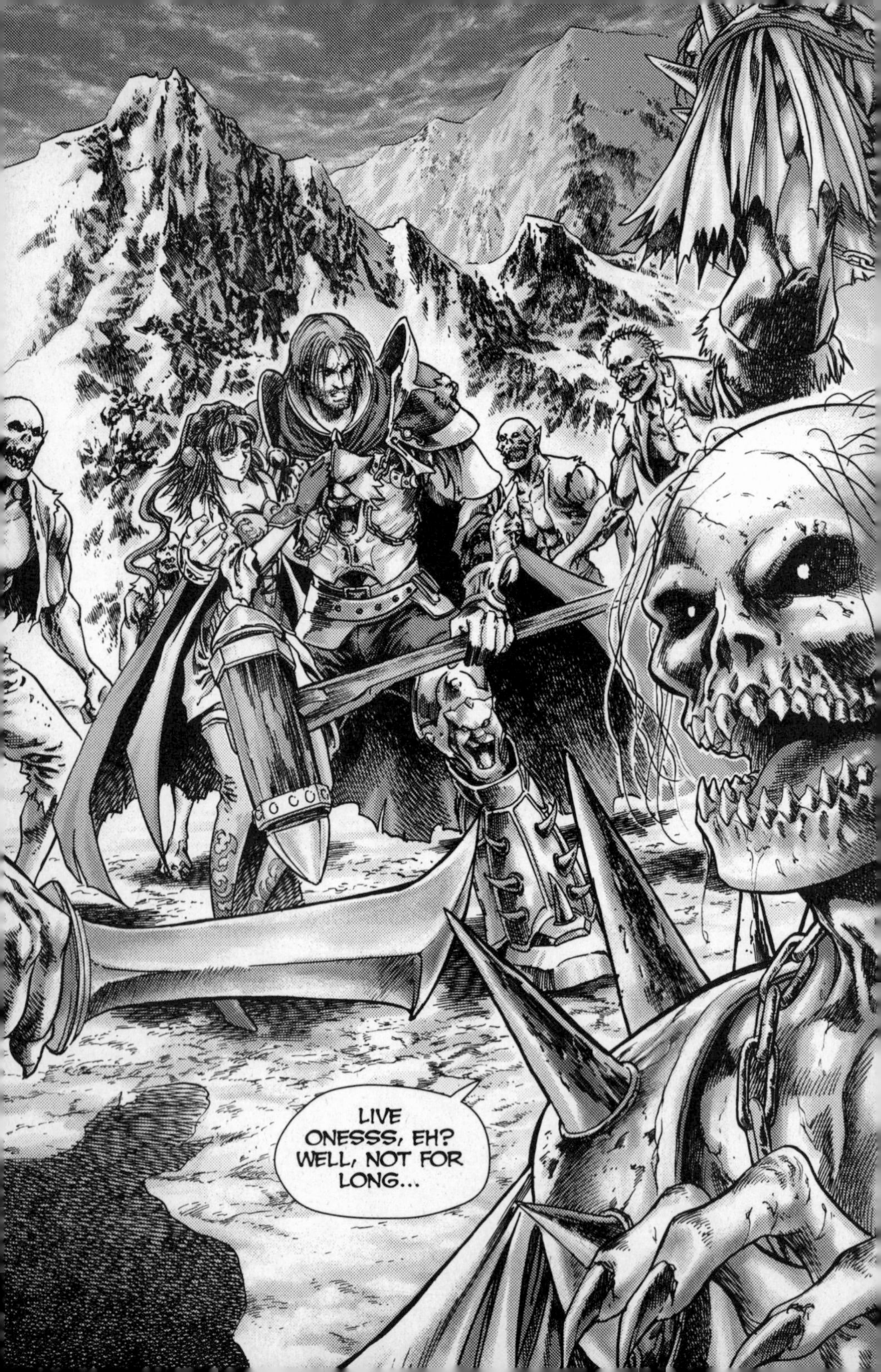
LIVE ONESSS, EH? WELL, NOT FOR LONG...

CHAPTER FOUR

The Dwellers Beneath

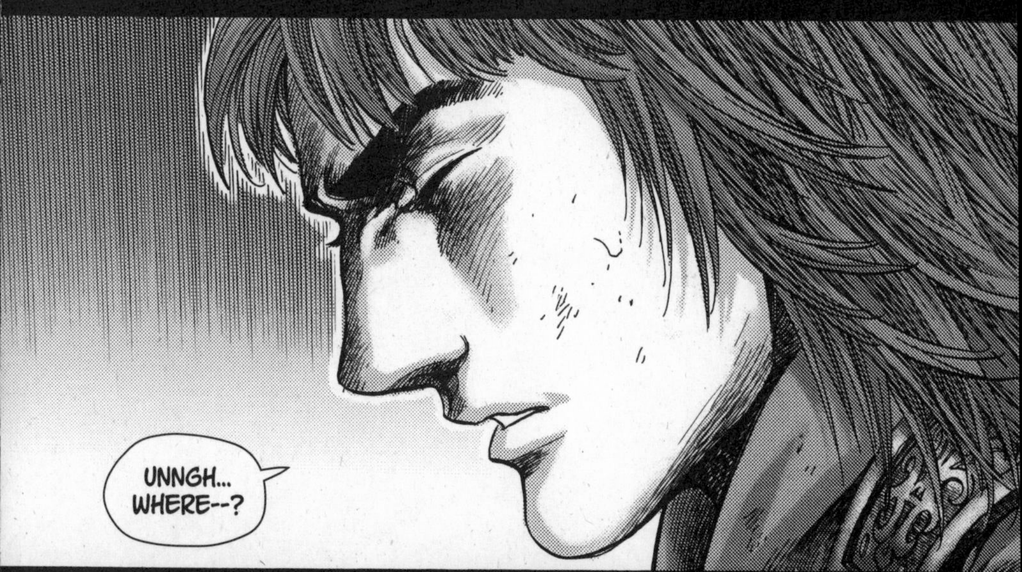
UNNGH... WHERE--?

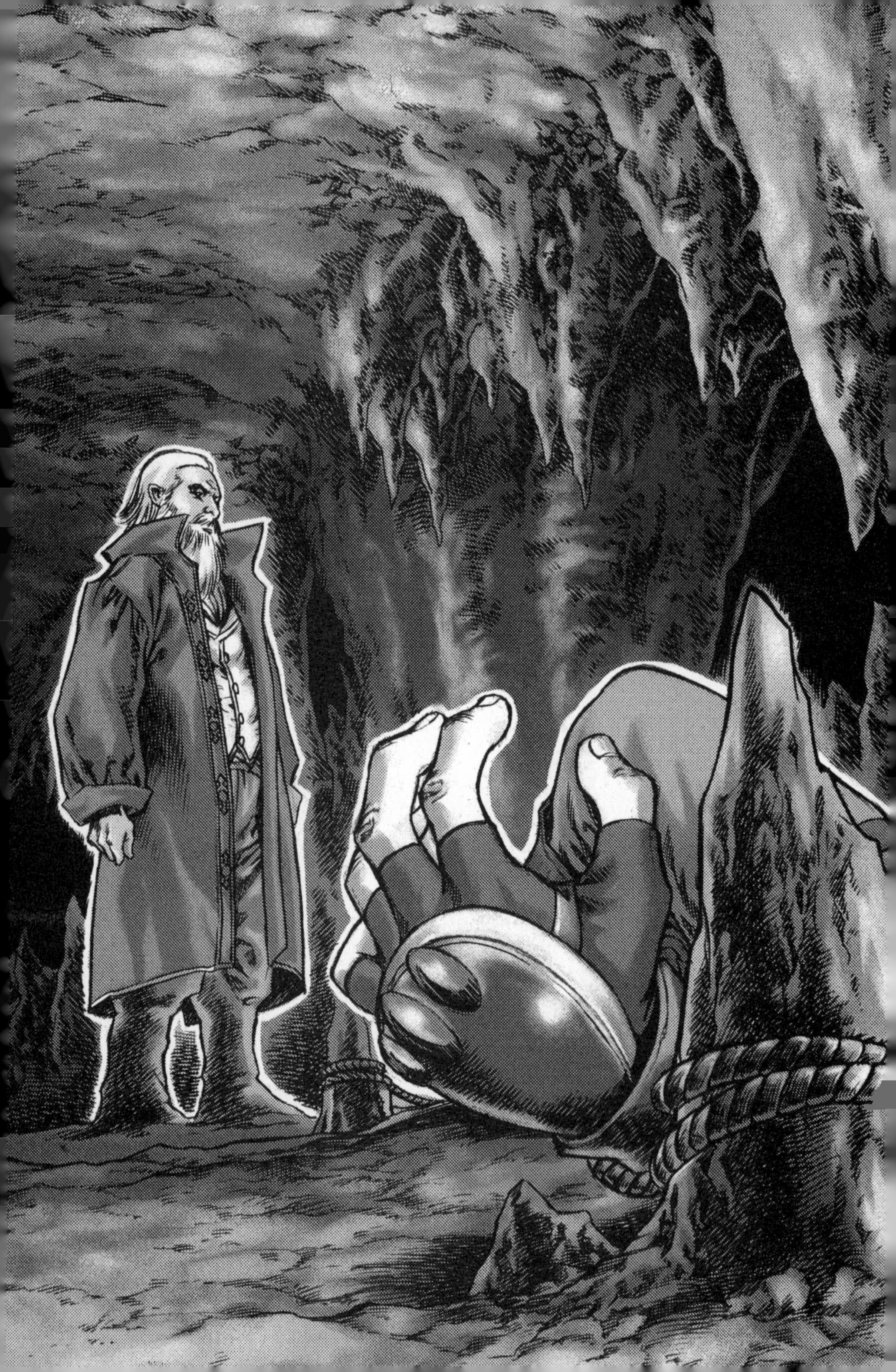

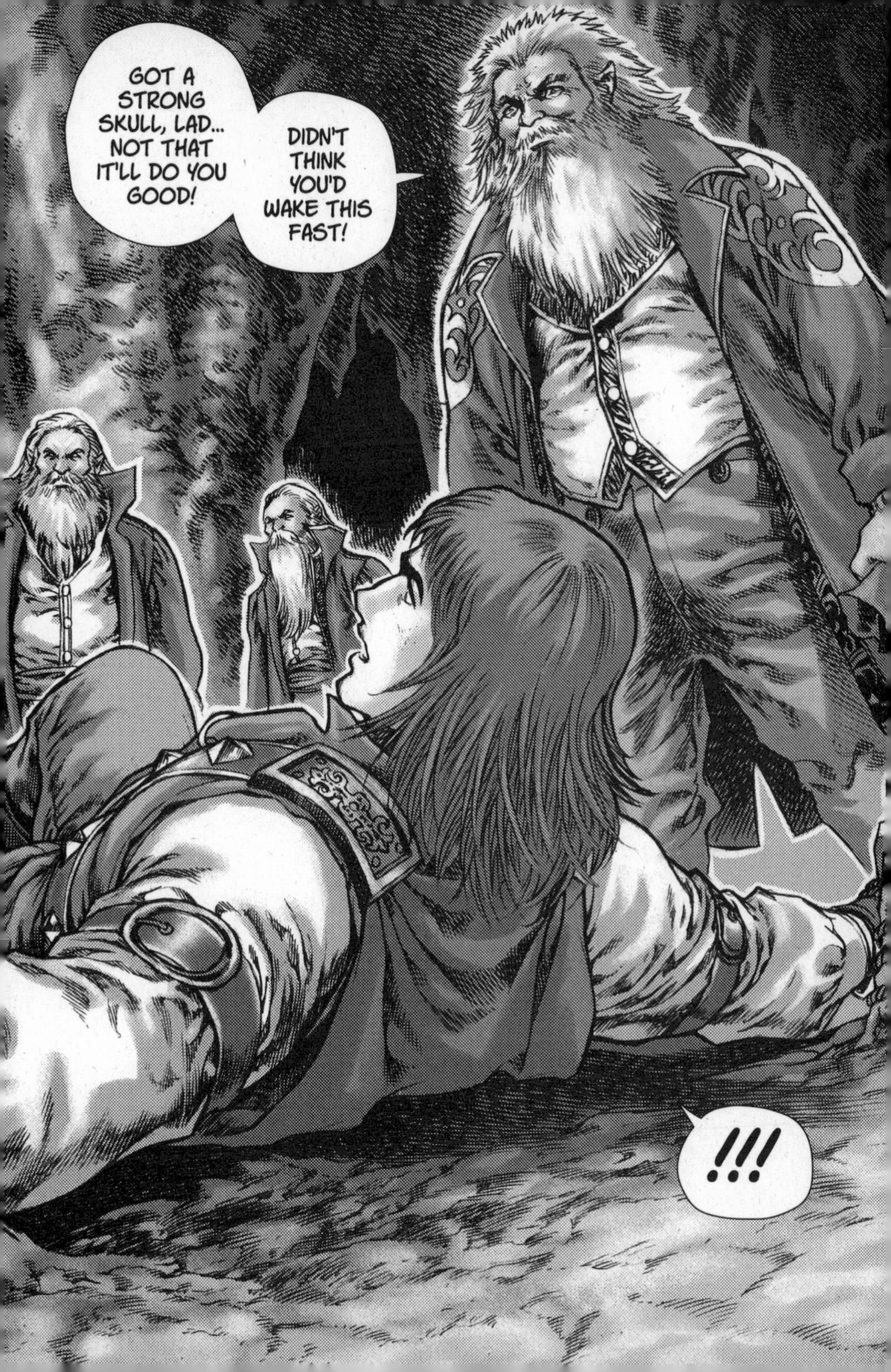
DIDN'T THINK YOU'D WAKE THIS FAST!
GOT A STRONG SKULL, LAD... NOT THAT IT'LL DO YOU GOOD!
!!!

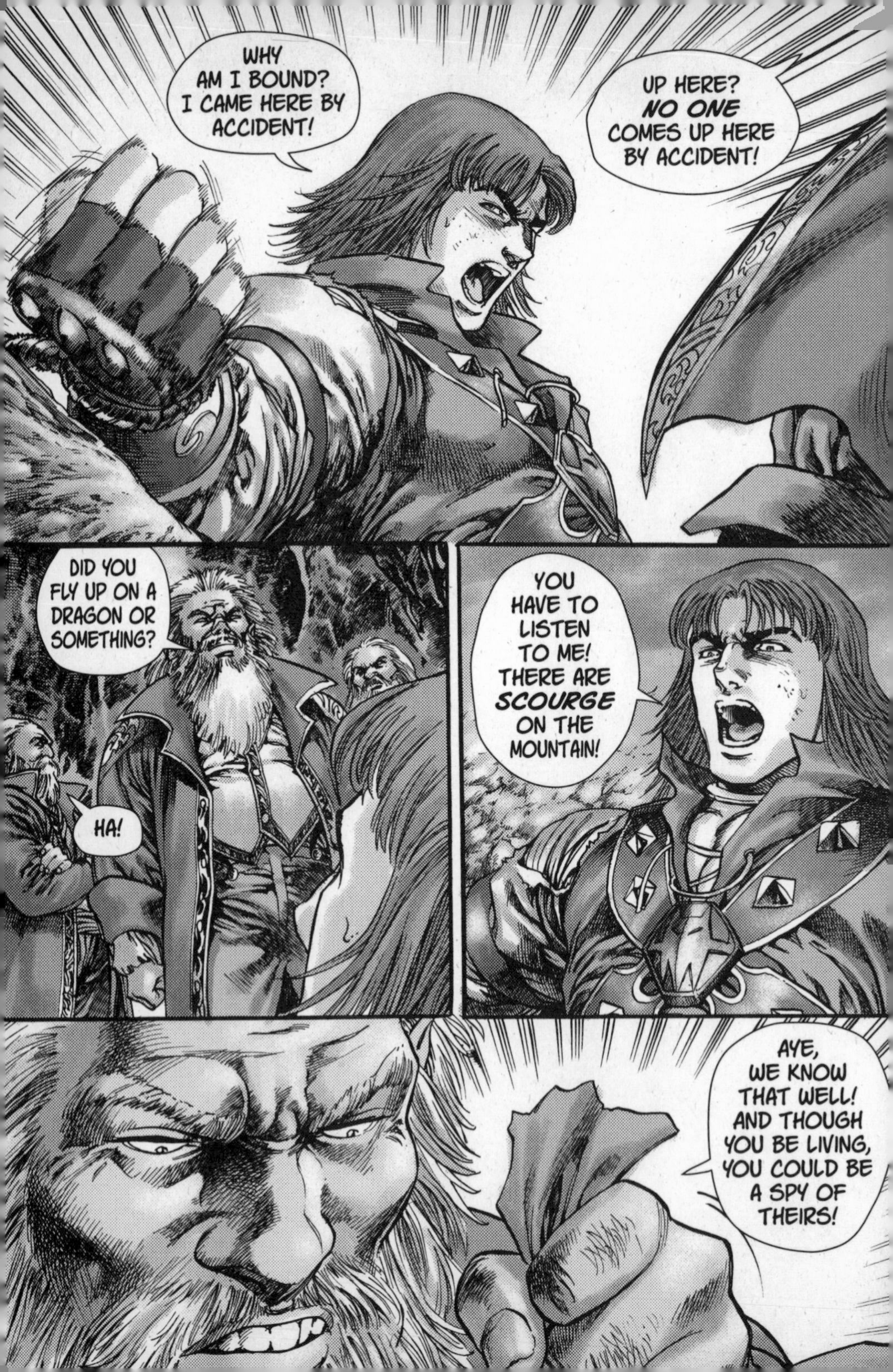
WHY AM I BOUND? I CAME HERE BY ACCIDENT!
UP HERE? *NO ONE* COMES UP HERE BY ACCIDENT!
DID YOU FLY UP ON A DRAGON OR SOMETHING?
HA!
YOU HAVE TO LISTEN TO ME! THERE ARE *SCOURGE* ON THE MOUNTAIN!
AYE, WE KNOW THAT WELL! AND THOUGH YOU BE LIVING, YOU COULD BE A SPY OF THEIRS!

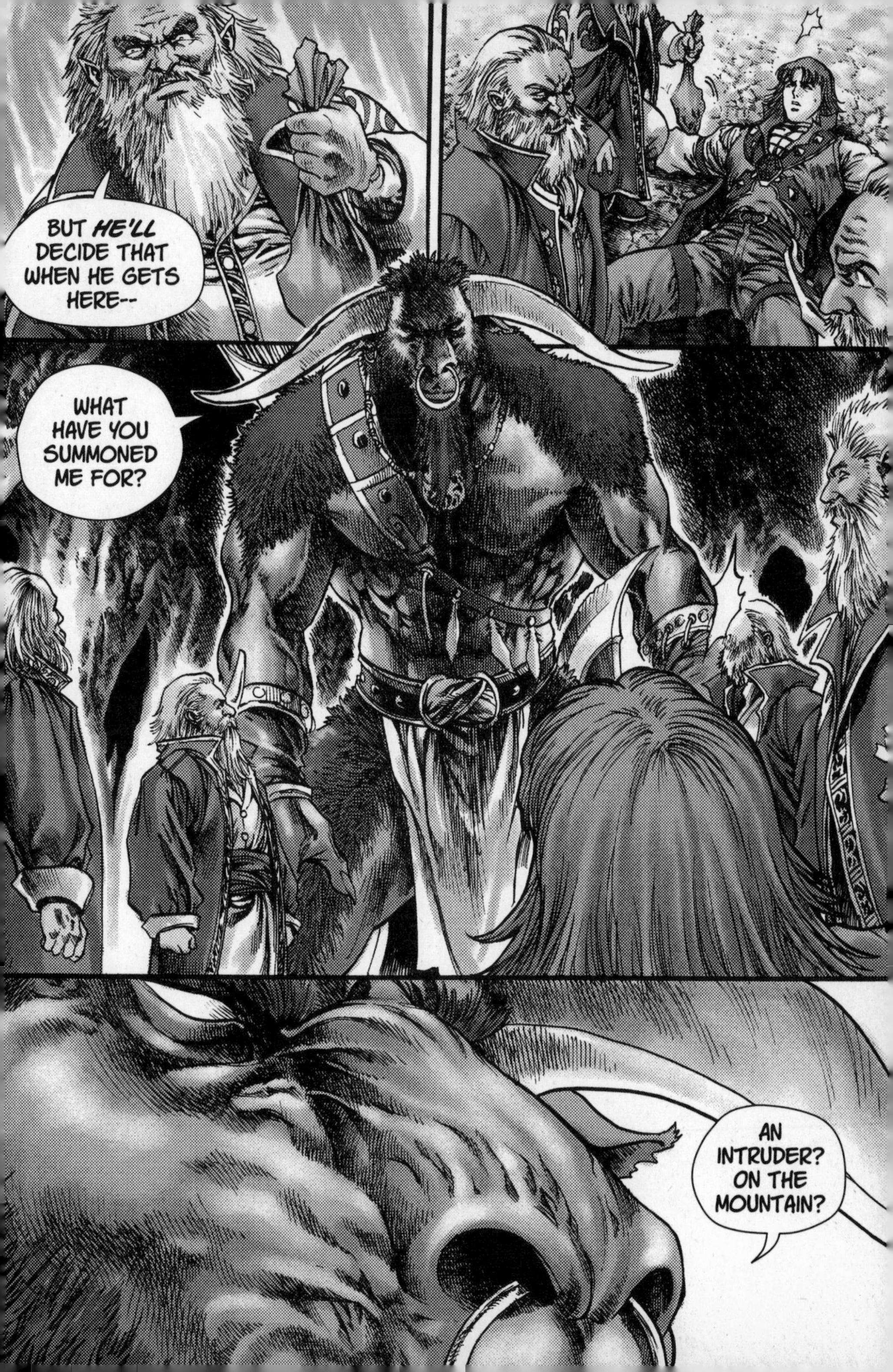

BUT HE'LL DECIDE THAT WHEN HE GETS HERE--
WHAT HAVE YOU SUMMONED ME FOR?
AN INTRUDER? ON THE MOUNTAIN?

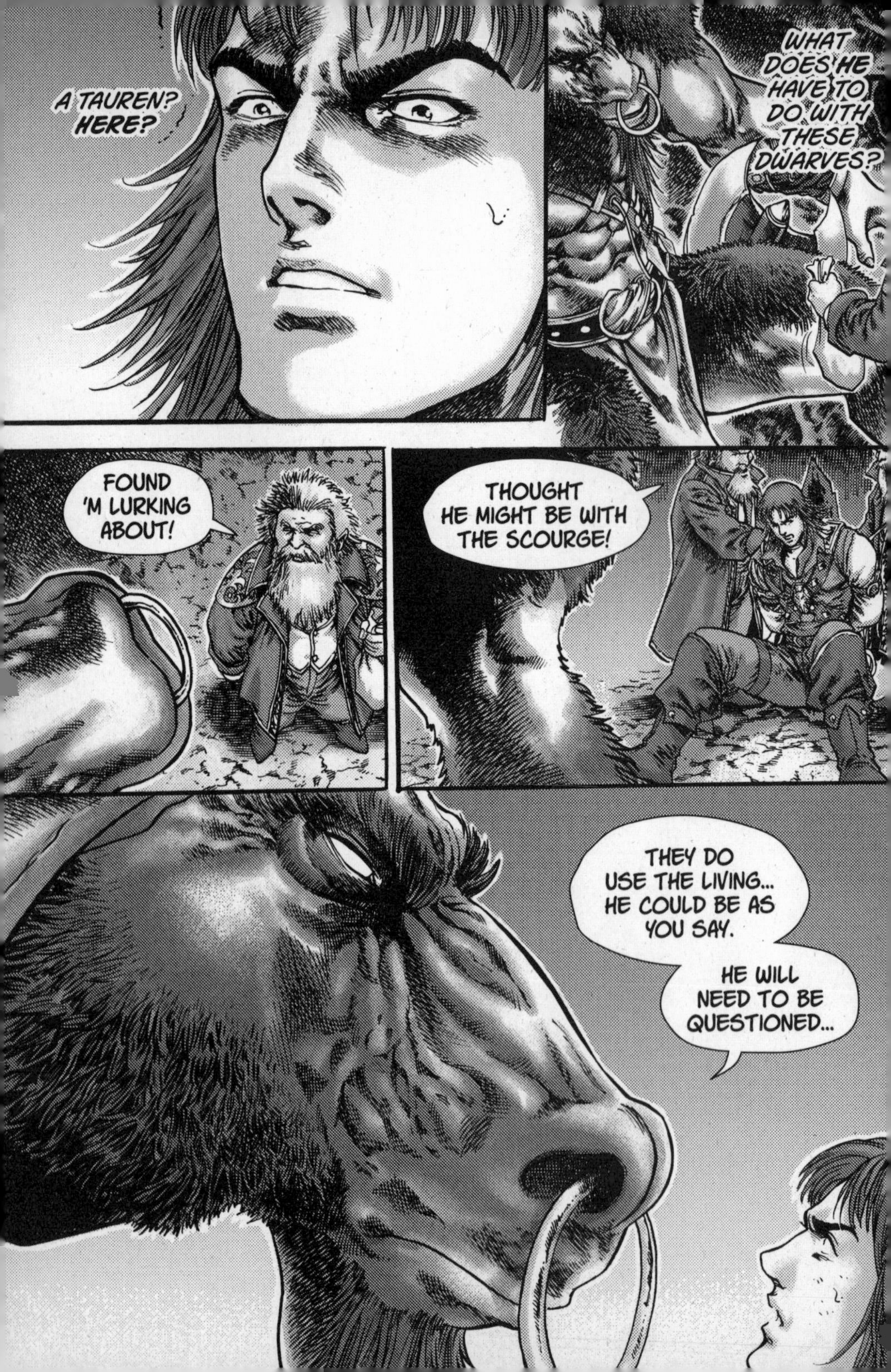
A TAUREN? HERE?
WHAT DOES HE HAVE TO DO WITH THESE DWARVES?
FOUND 'M LURKING ABOUT!
THOUGHT HE MIGHT BE WITH THE SCOURGE!
THEY DO USE THE LIVING... HE COULD BE AS YOU SAY.
HE WILL NEED TO BE QUESTIONED...

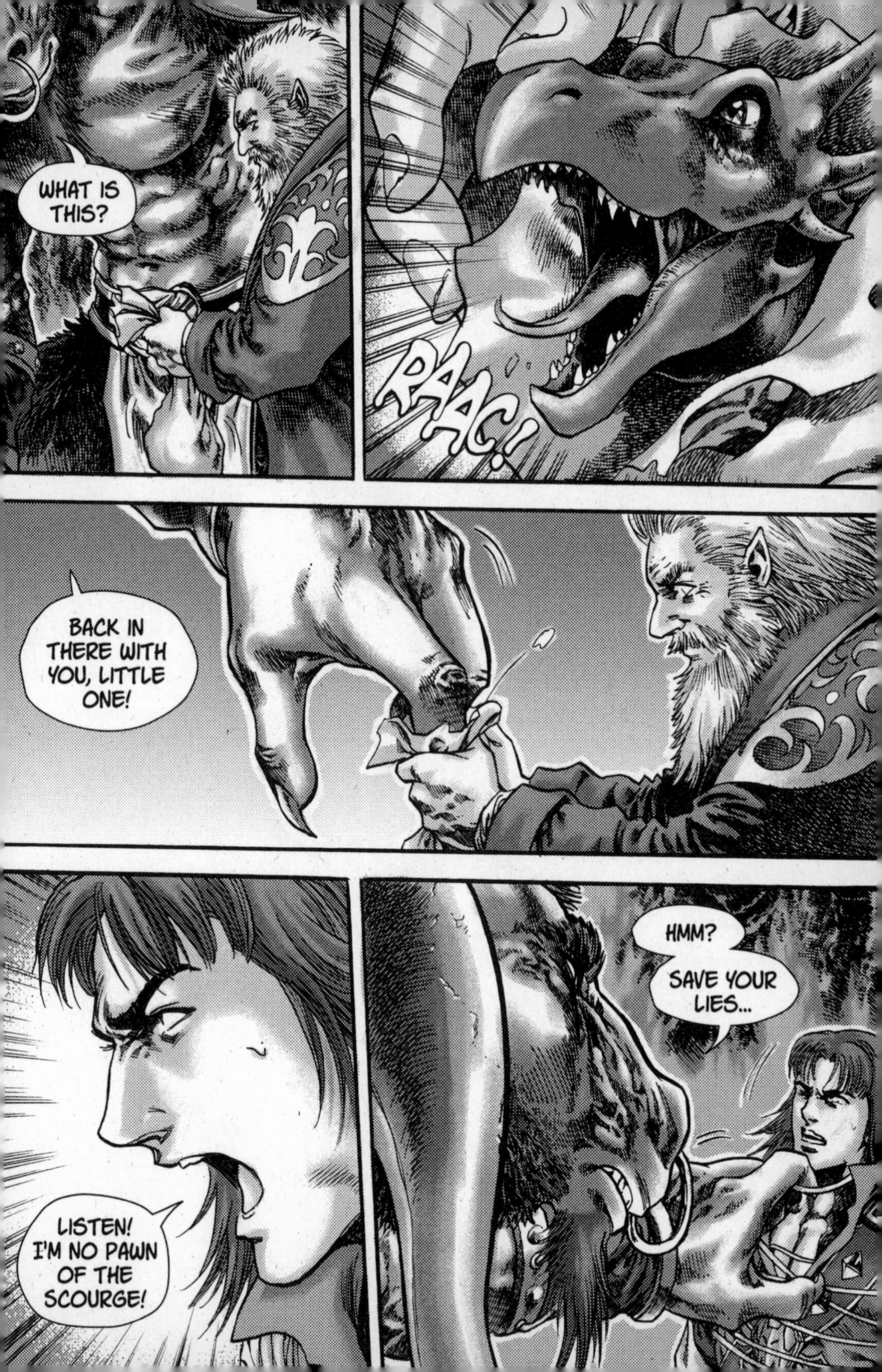
WHAT IS THIS?
RAAC!!
BACK IN THERE WITH YOU, LITTLE ONE!
LISTEN! I'M NO PAWN OF THE SCOURGE!
HMM?
SAVE YOUR LIES...

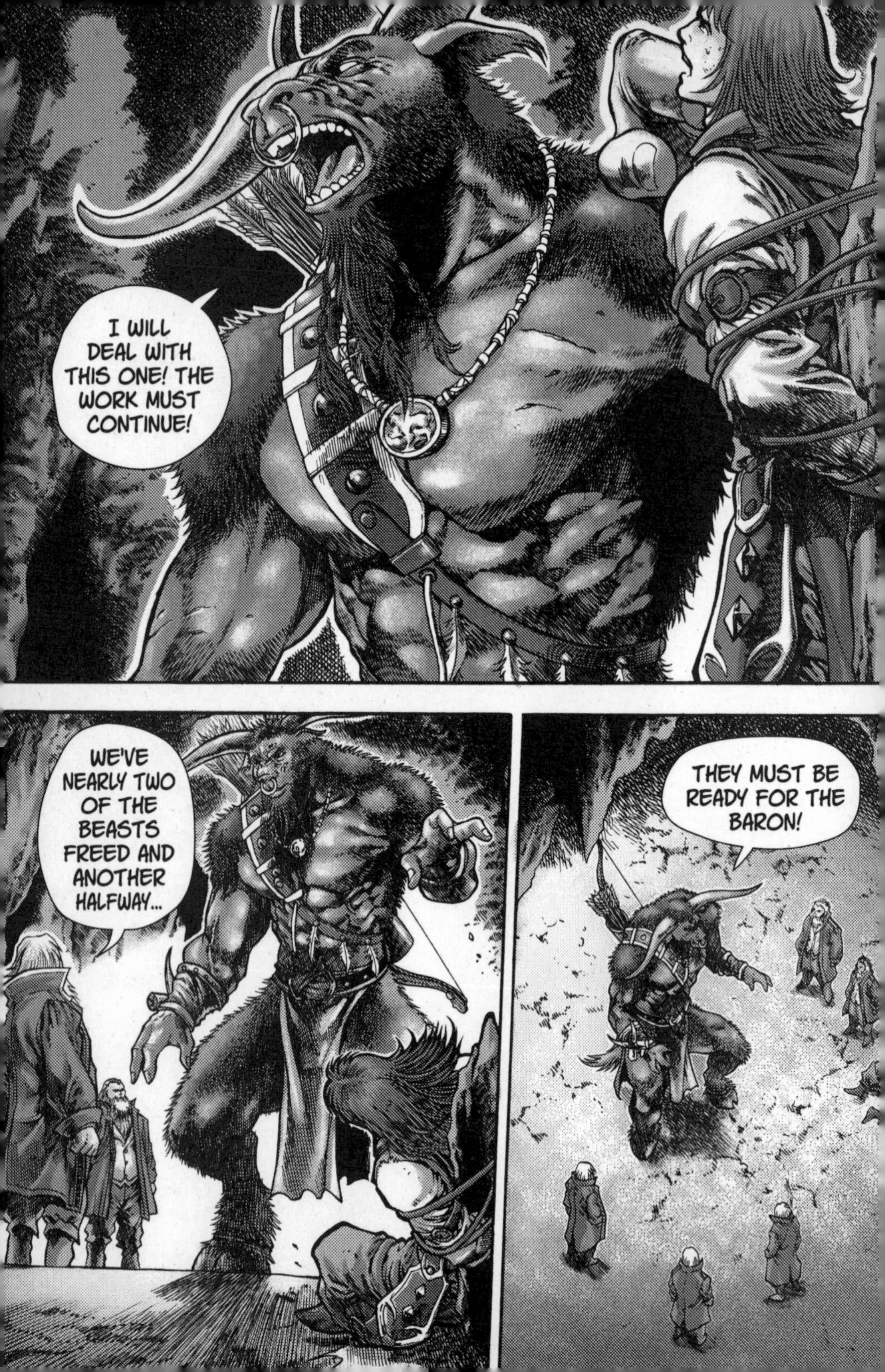
I WILL DEAL WITH THIS ONE! THE WORK MUST CONTINUE!
WE'VE NEARLY TWO OF THE BEASTS FREED AND ANOTHER HALFWAY...
THEY MUST BE READY FOR THE BARON!

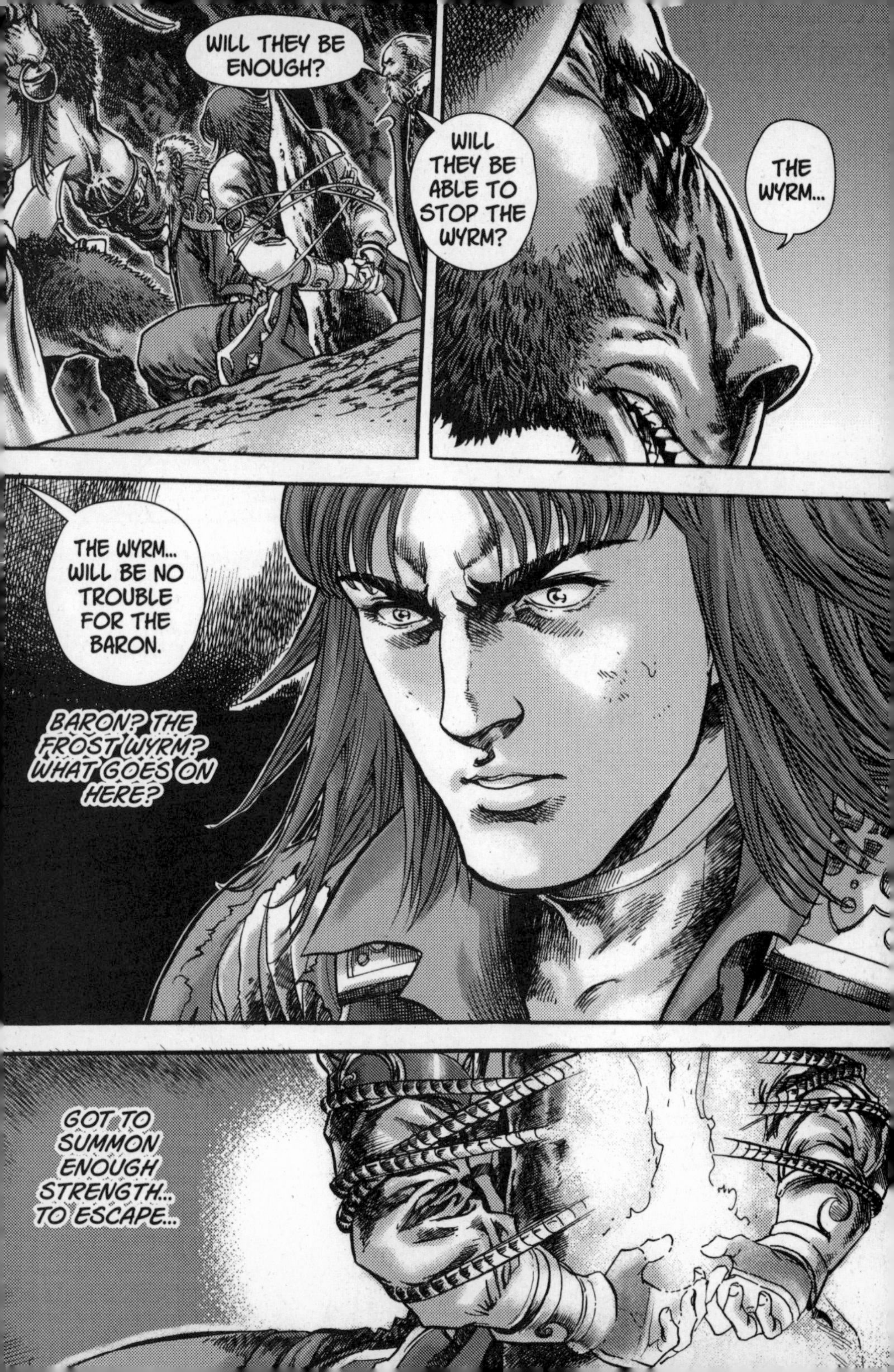
WILL THEY BE ENOUGH?
WILL THEY BE ABLE TO STOP THE WYRM?
THE WYRM...
THE WYRM... WILL BE NO TROUBLE FOR THE BARON.
BARON? THE FROST WYRM? WHAT GOES ON HERE?
GOT TO SUMMON ENOUGH STRENGTH... TO ESCAPE...

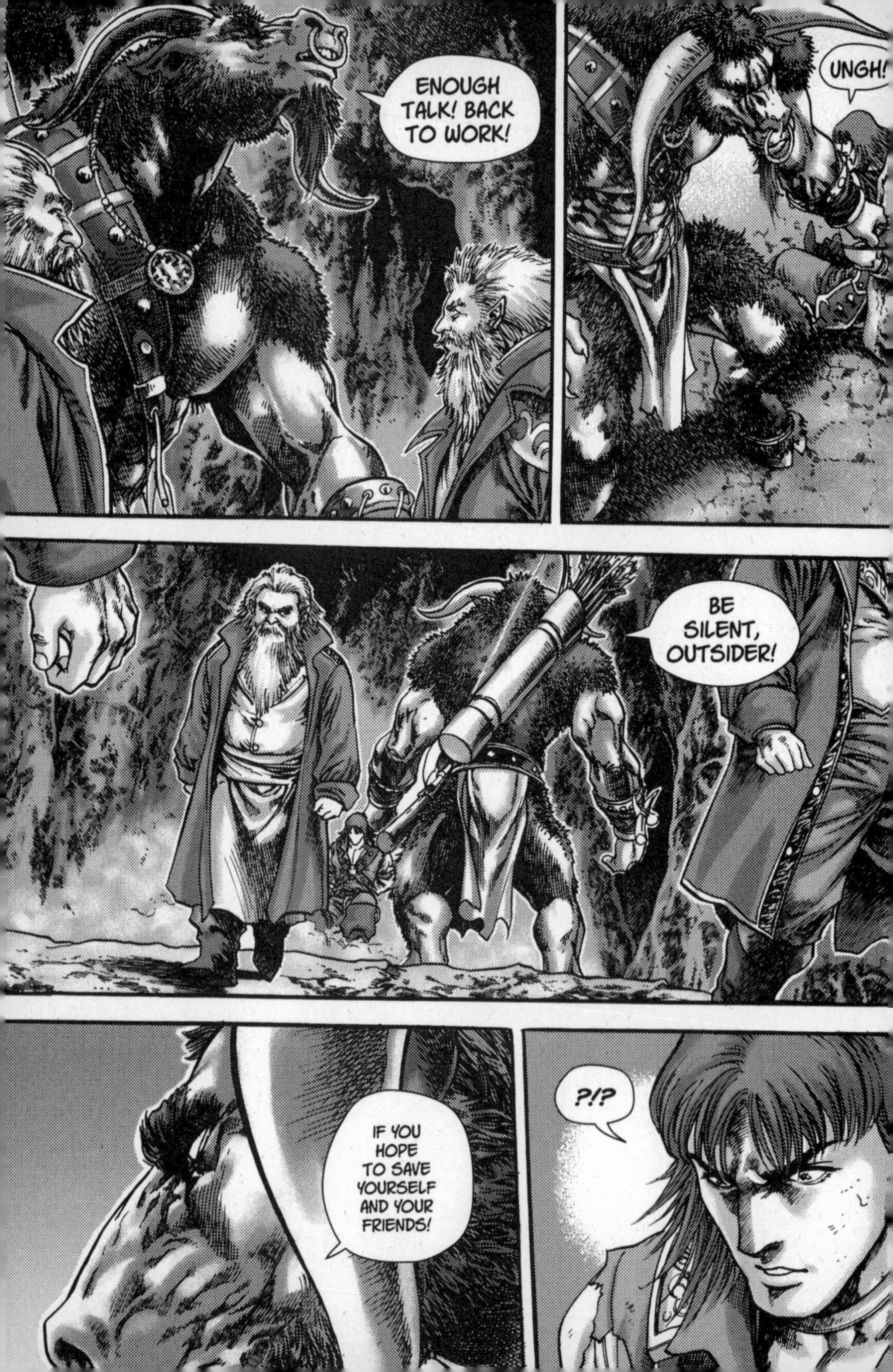
ENOUGH TALK! BACK TO WORK!
UNGH!
BE SILENT, OUTSIDER!
IF YOU HOPE TO SAVE YOURSELF AND YOUR FRIENDS!
?!?

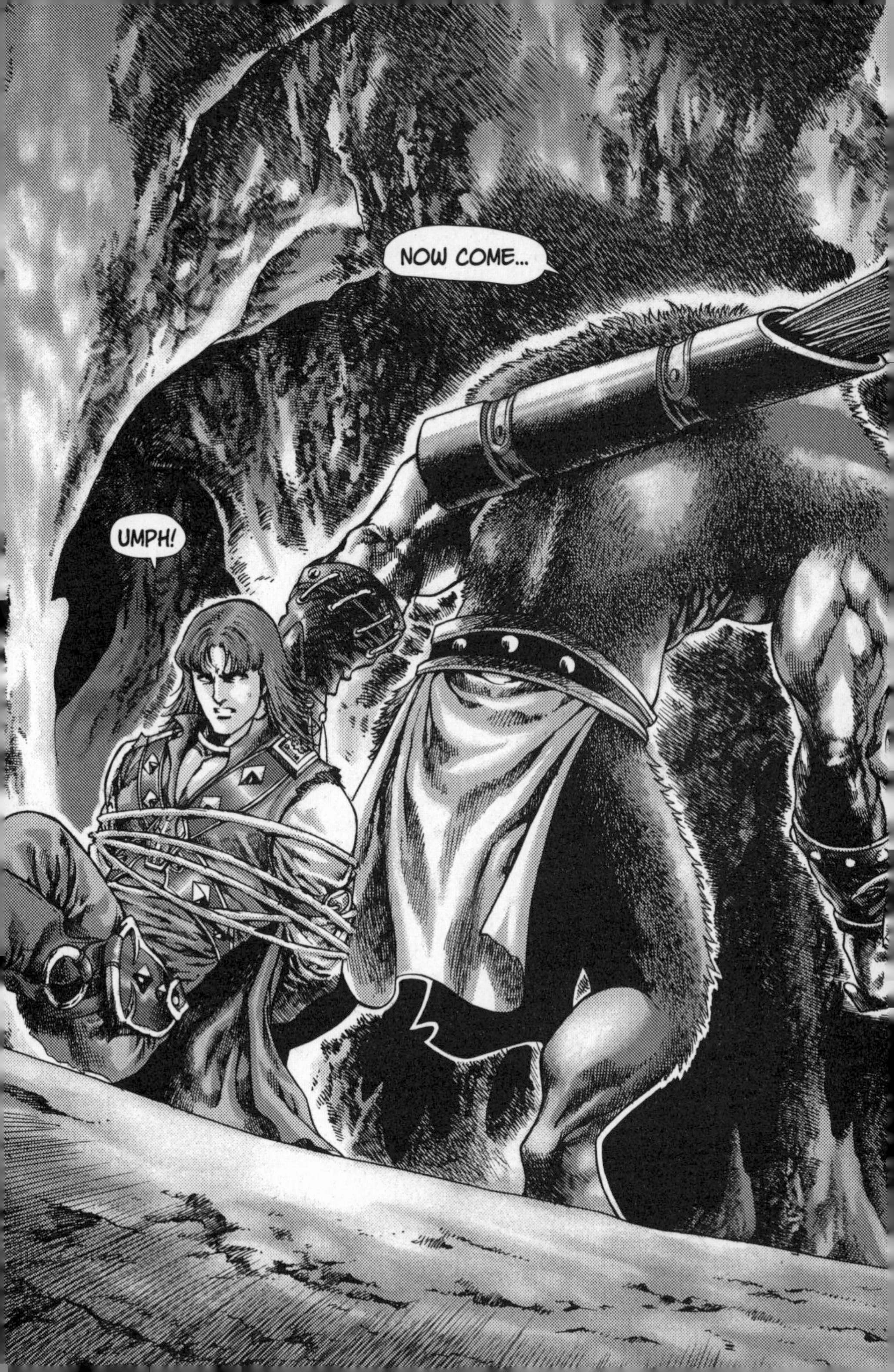
NOW COME...
UMPH!

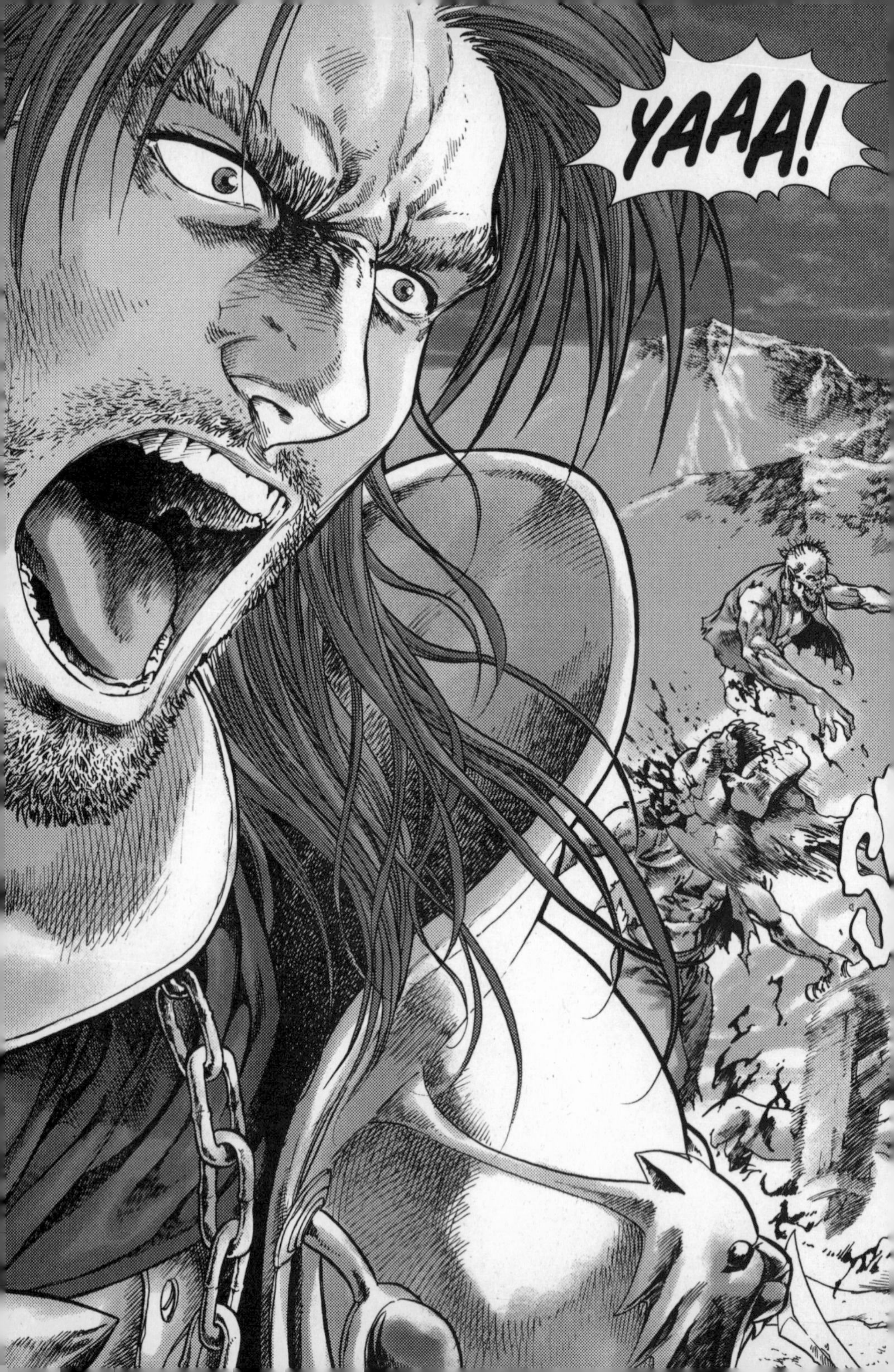
YAAA!

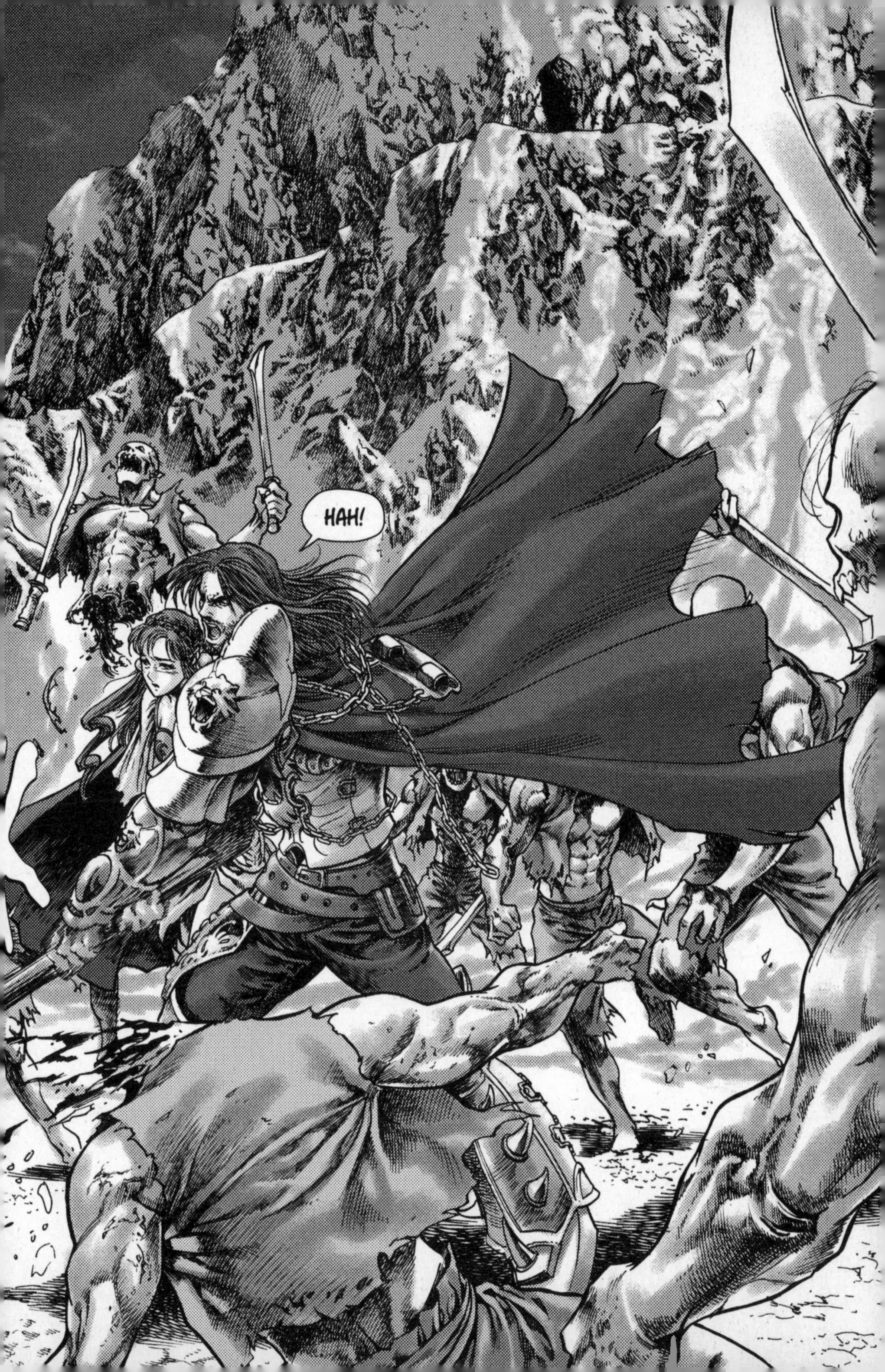
HAH!

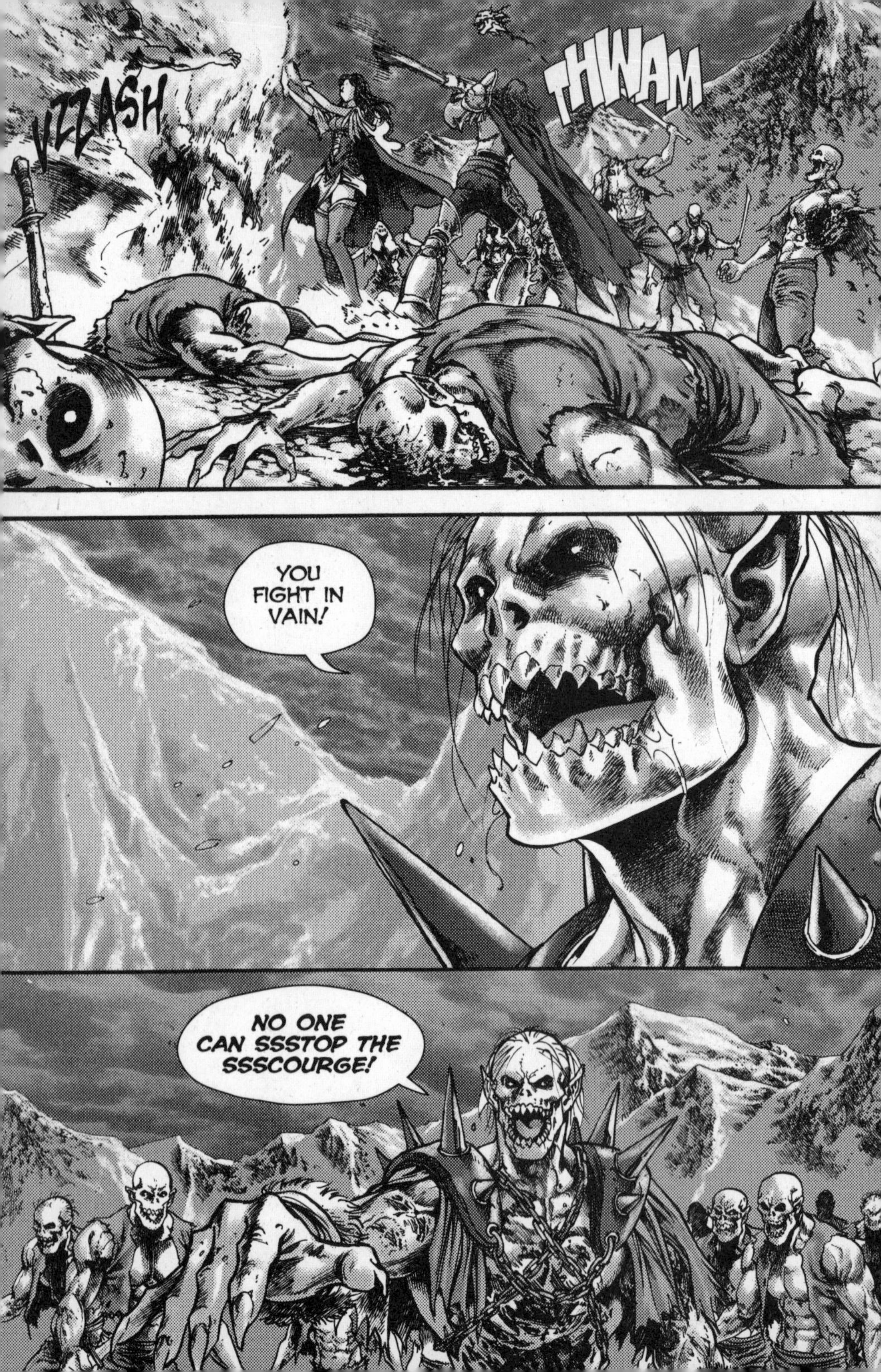
THWAM
VZZASH
YOU FIGHT IN VAIN!
NO ONE CAN SSSTOP THE SSSCOURGE!

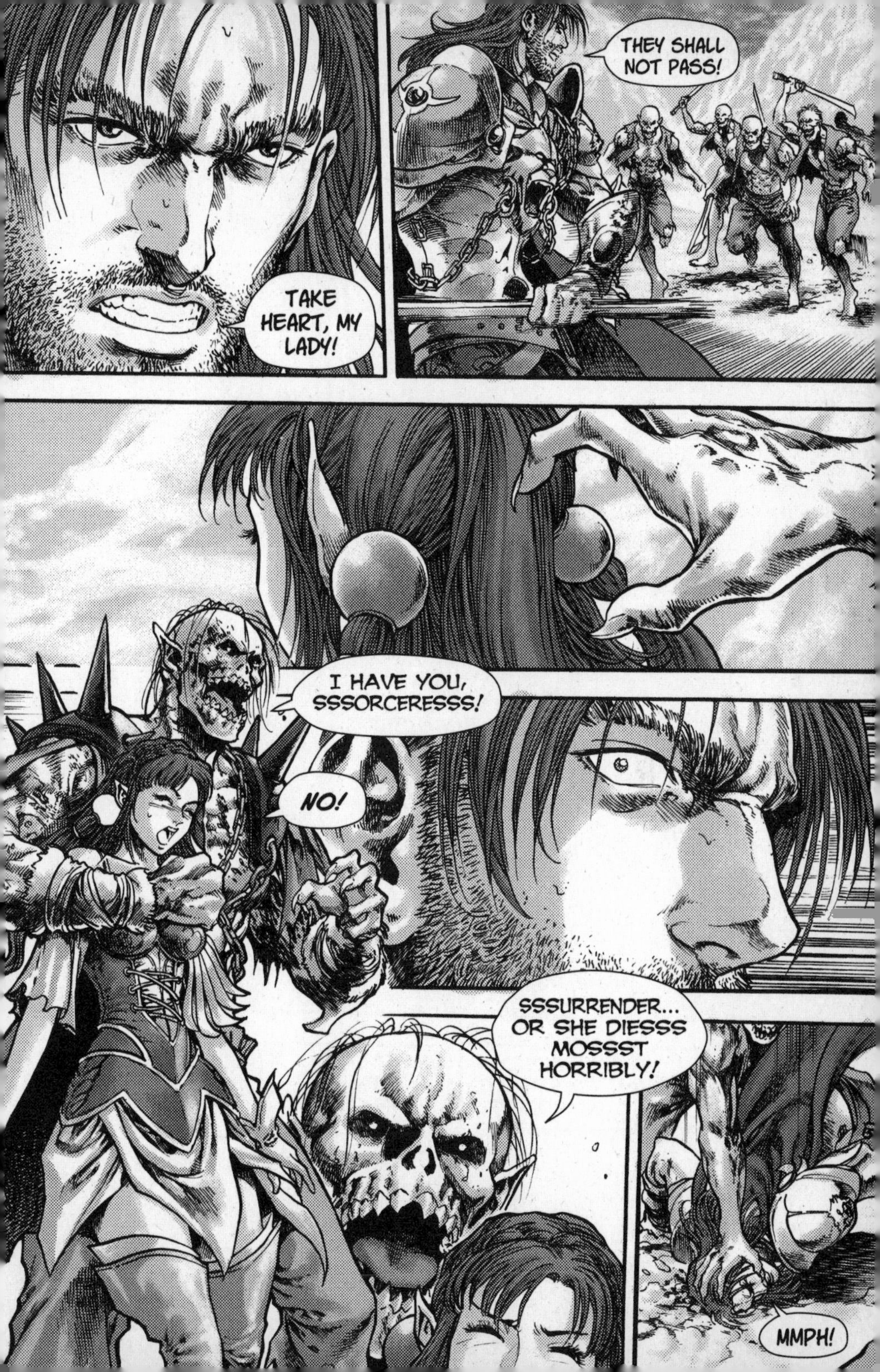
TAKE HEART, MY LADY!
THEY SHALL NOT PASS!
I HAVE YOU, SSSORCERESSS!
NO!
SSSURRENDER... OR SHE DIESSS MOSSST HORRIBLY!
MMPH!

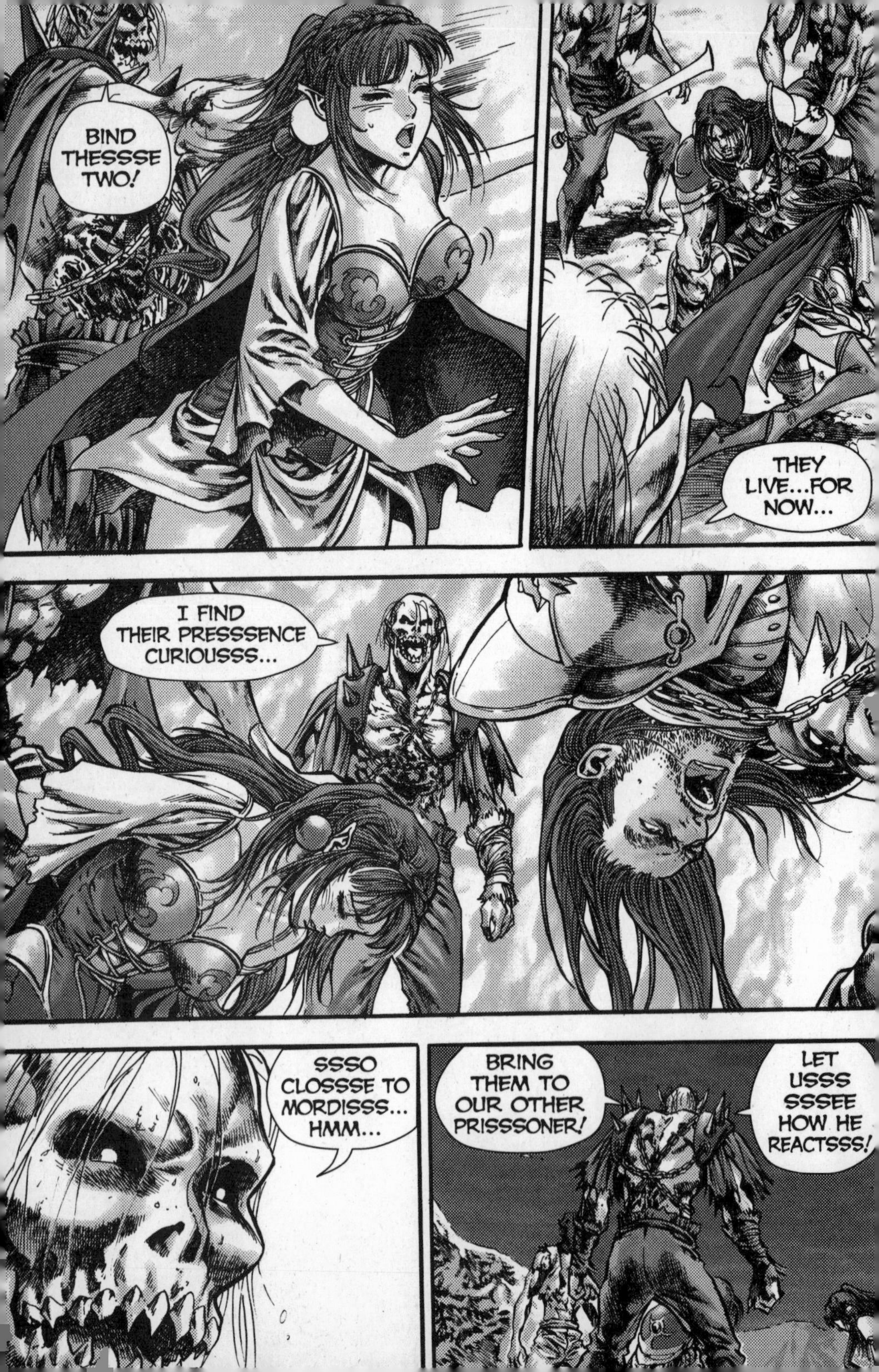
BIND THESSSE TWO!
THEY LIVE...FOR NOW...
I FIND THEIR PRESSSENCE CURIOUSSS...
SSSO CLOSSSE TO MORDISSS... HMM...
BRING THEM TO OUR OTHER PRISSSONER!
LET USSS SSSEE HOW HE REACTSSS!

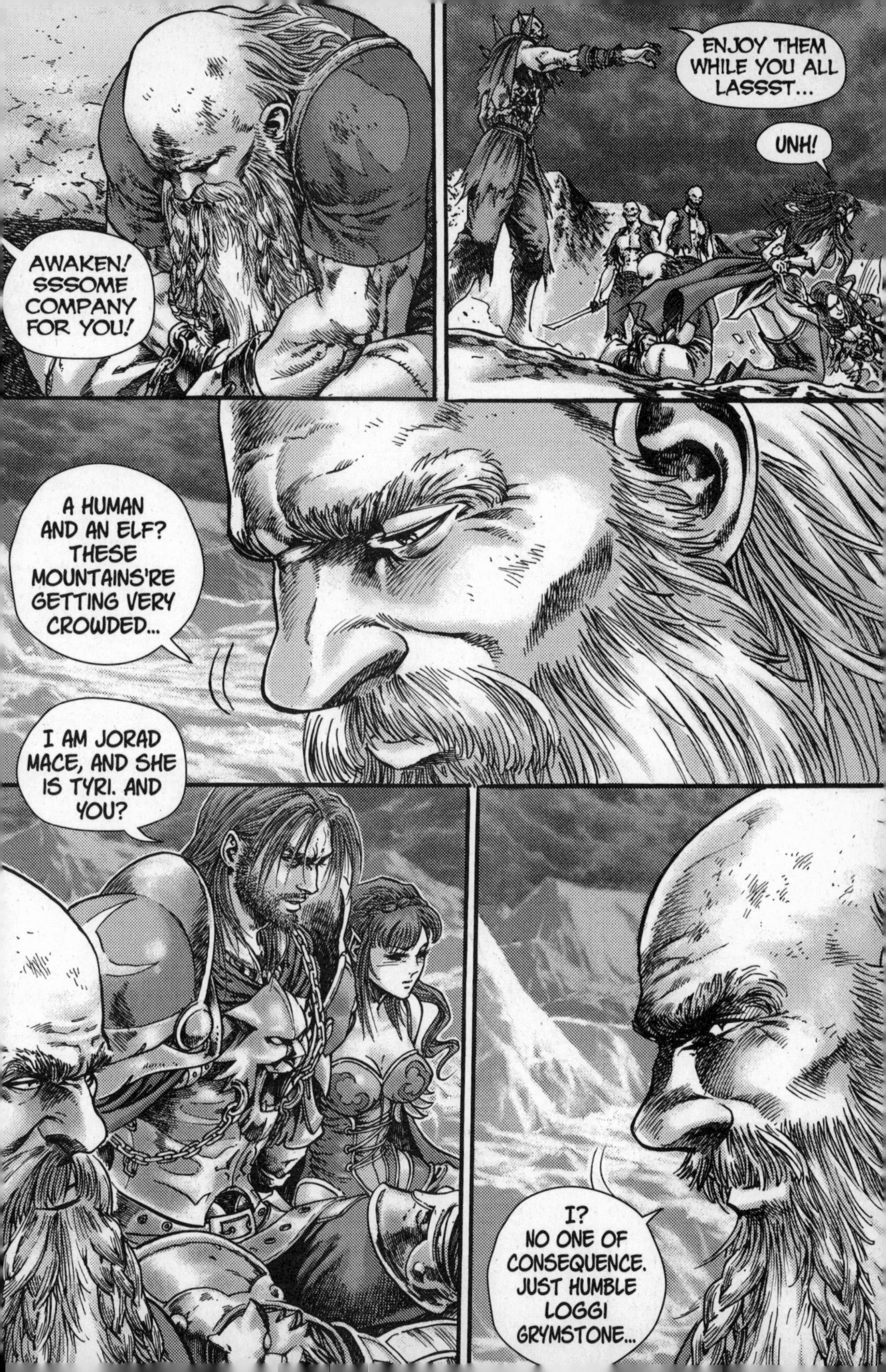
AWAKEN! SSSOME COMPANY FOR YOU!
ENJOY THEM WHILE YOU ALL LASSST...
UNH!
A HUMAN AND AN ELF? THESE MOUNTAINS'RE GETTING VERY CROWDED...
I AM JORAD MACE, AND SHE IS TYRI. AND YOU?
I? NO ONE OF CONSEQUENCE. JUST HUMBLE LOGGI GRYMSTONE...

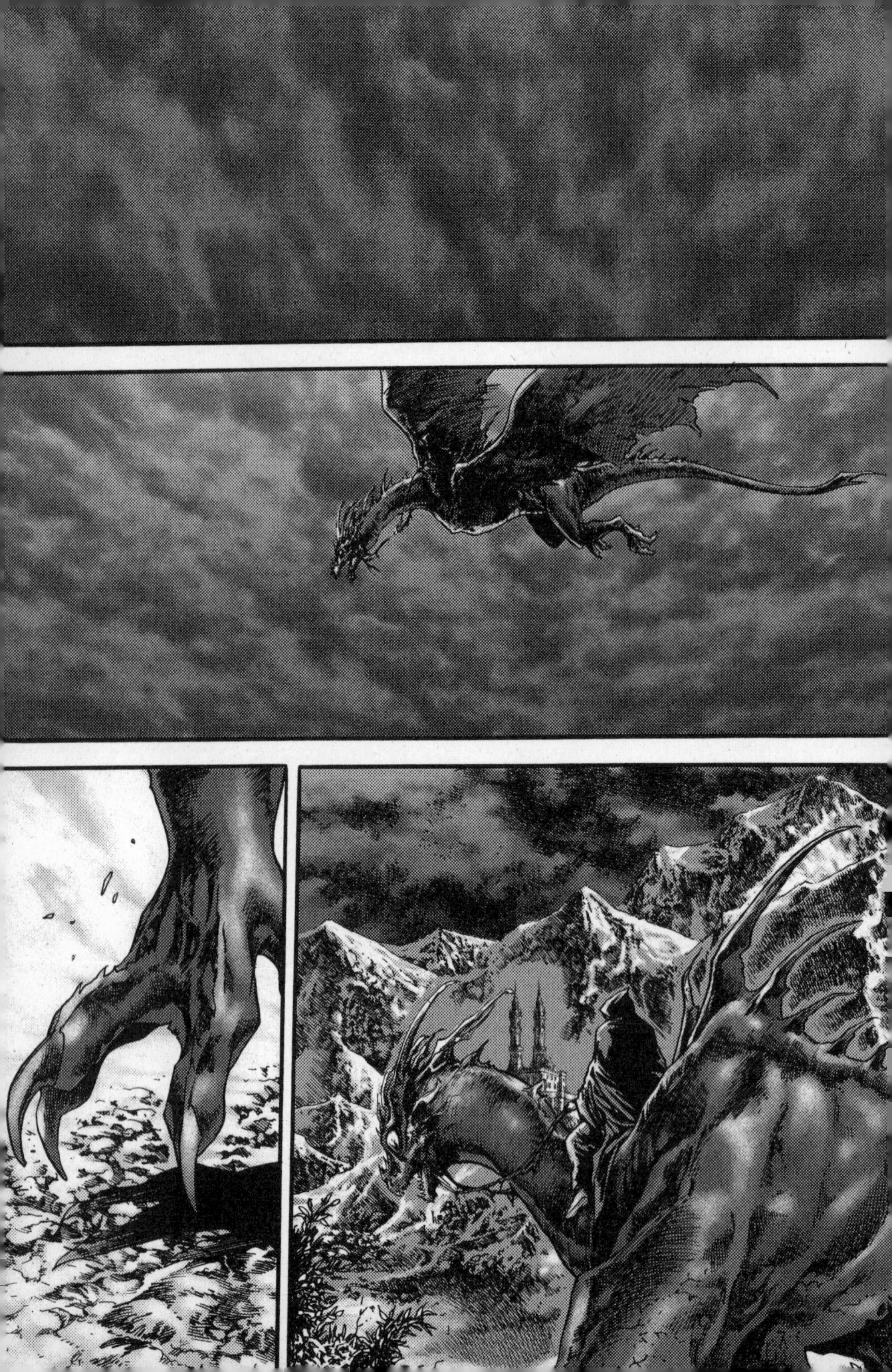

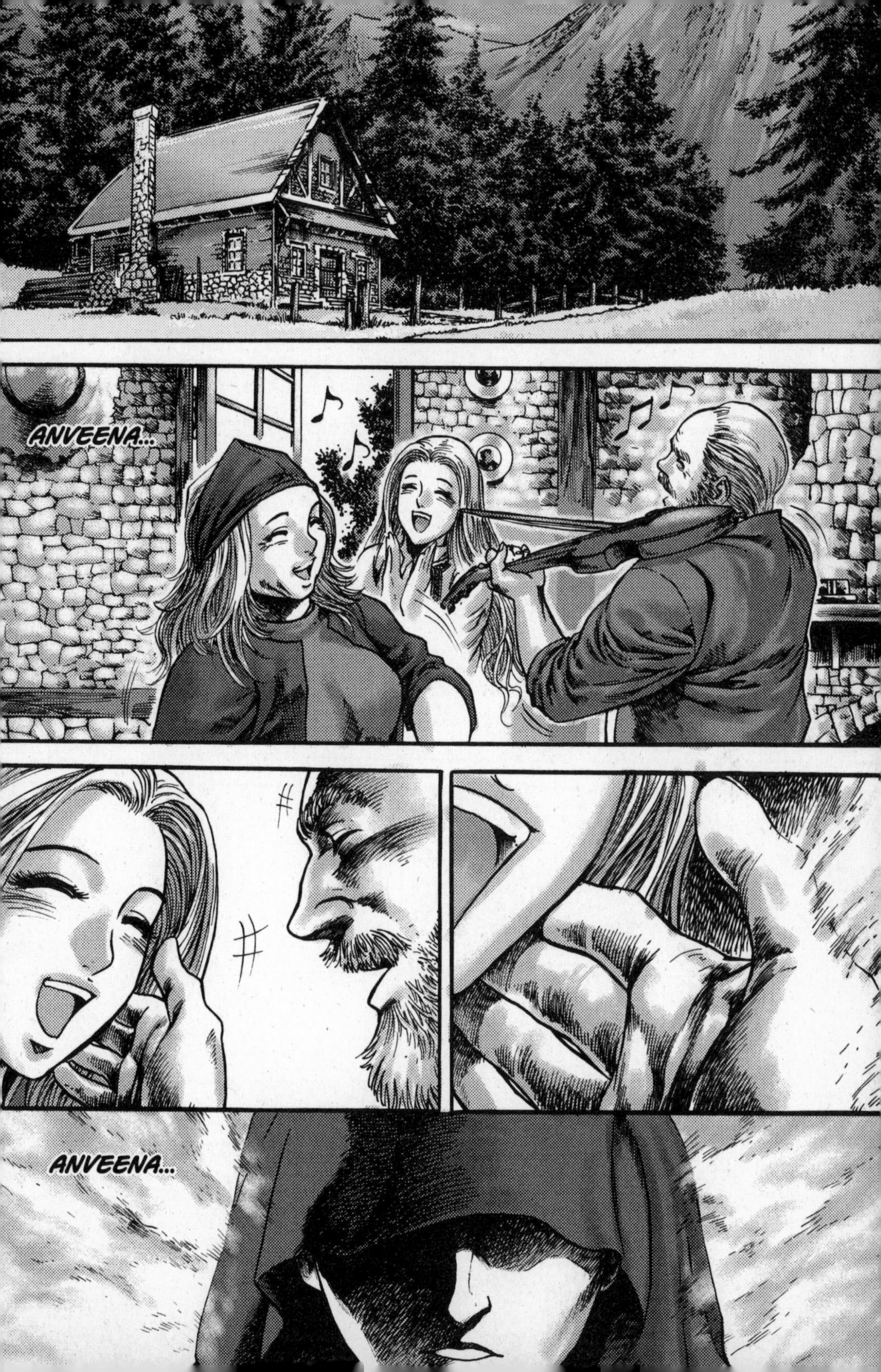
ANVEENA...
ANVEENA...

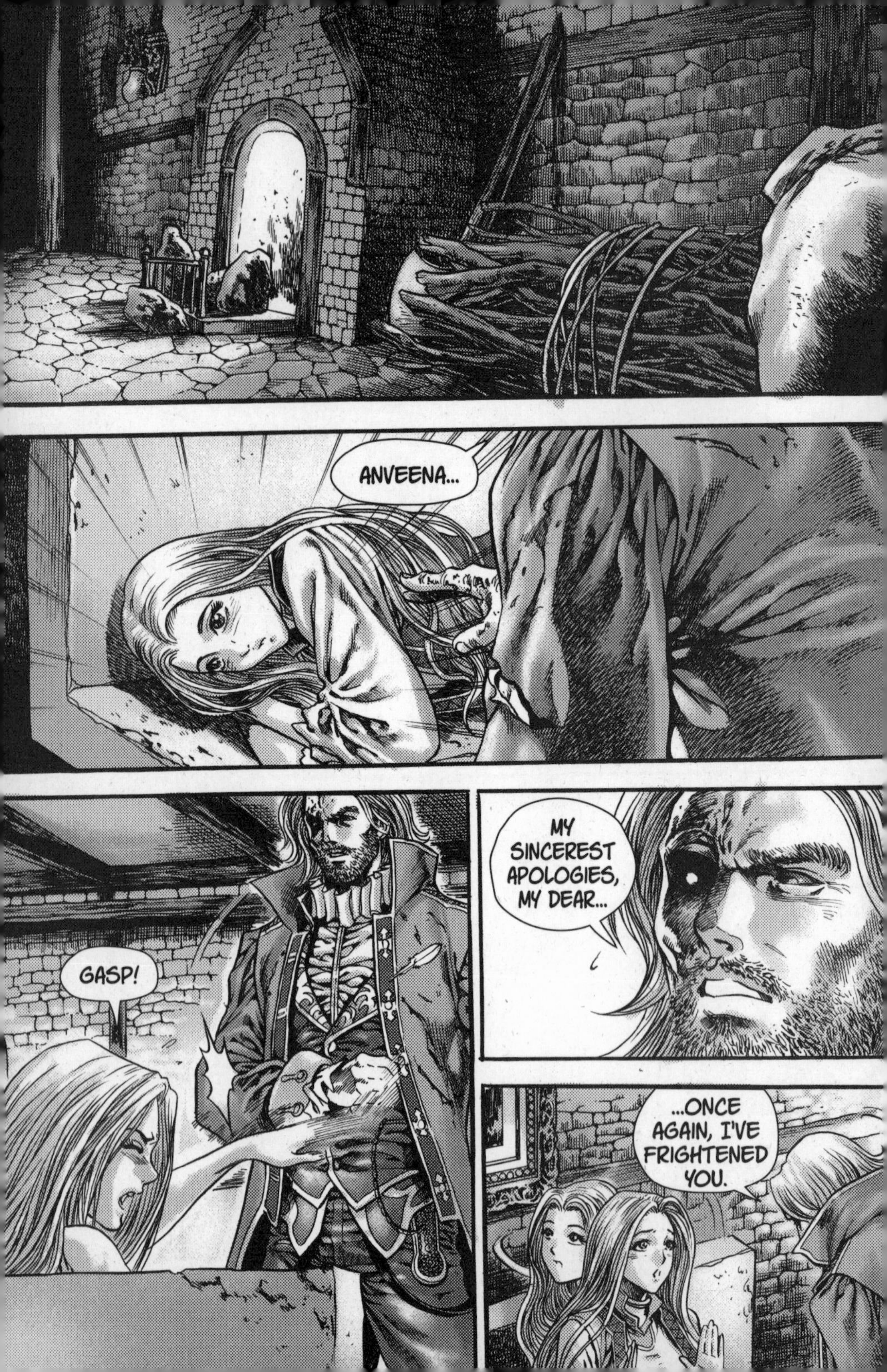
ANVEENA...
GASP!
MY SINCEREST APOLOGIES, MY DEAR...
...ONCE AGAIN, I'VE FRIGHTENED YOU.

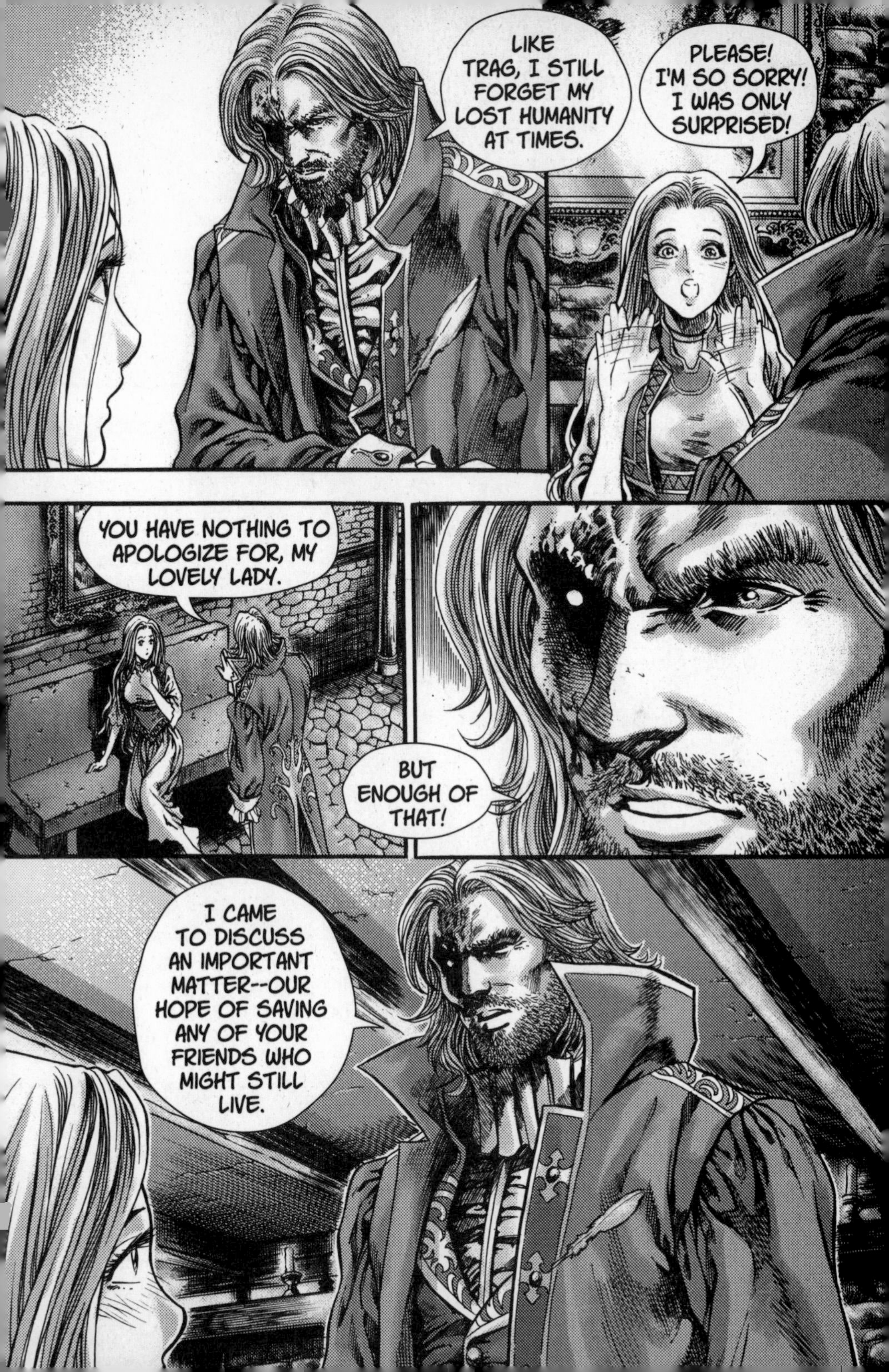
LIKE TRAG, I STILL FORGET MY LOST HUMANITY AT TIMES.
PLEASE! I'M SO SORRY! I WAS ONLY SURPRISED!
YOU HAVE NOTHING TO APOLOGIZE FOR, MY LOVELY LADY.
BUT ENOUGH OF THAT!
I CAME TO DISCUSS AN IMPORTANT MATTER--OUR HOPE OF SAVING ANY OF YOUR FRIENDS WHO MIGHT STILL LIVE.

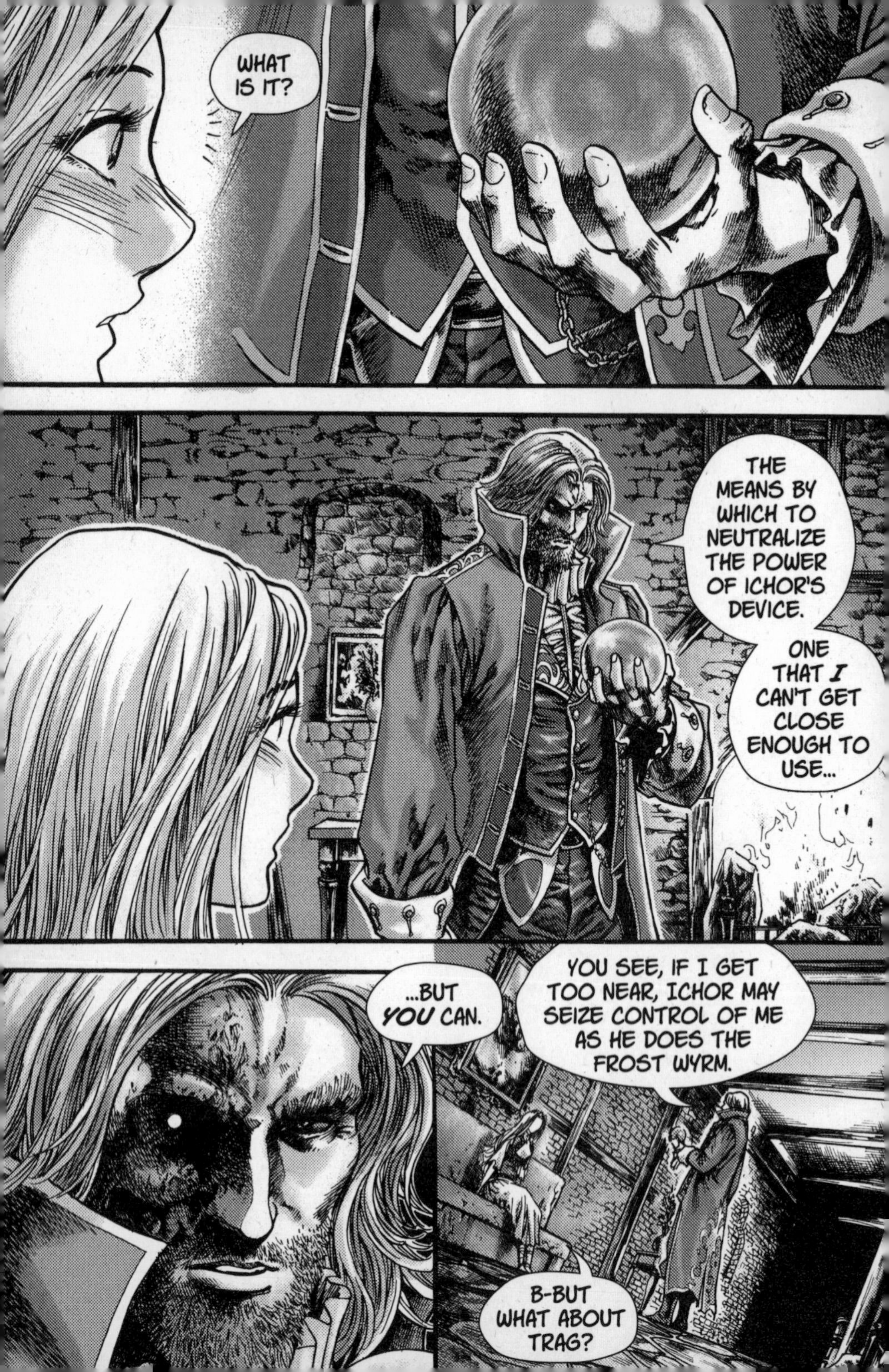
WHAT IS IT?
THE MEANS BY WHICH TO NEUTRALIZE THE POWER OF ICHOR'S DEVICE.
ONE THAT *I* CAN'T GET CLOSE ENOUGH TO USE...
...BUT *YOU* CAN.
YOU SEE, IF I GET TOO NEAR, ICHOR MAY SEIZE CONTROL OF ME AS HE DOES THE FROST WYRM.
B-BUT WHAT ABOUT TRAG?

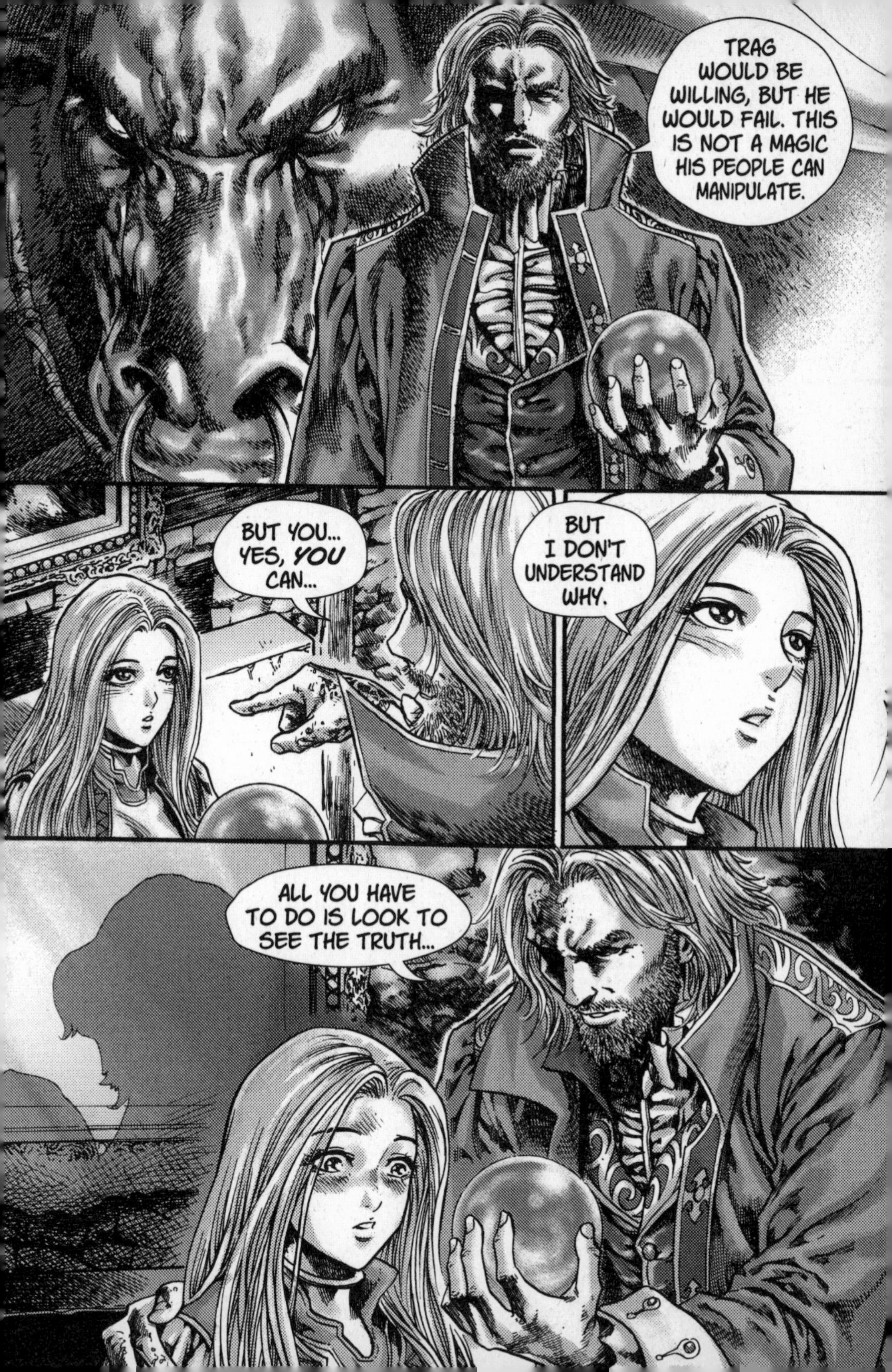
TRAG WOULD BE WILLING, BUT HE WOULD FAIL. THIS IS NOT A MAGIC HIS PEOPLE CAN MANIPULATE.
BUT YOU... YES, *YOU* CAN...
BUT I DON'T UNDERSTAND WHY.
ALL YOU HAVE TO DO IS LOOK TO SEE THE TRUTH...

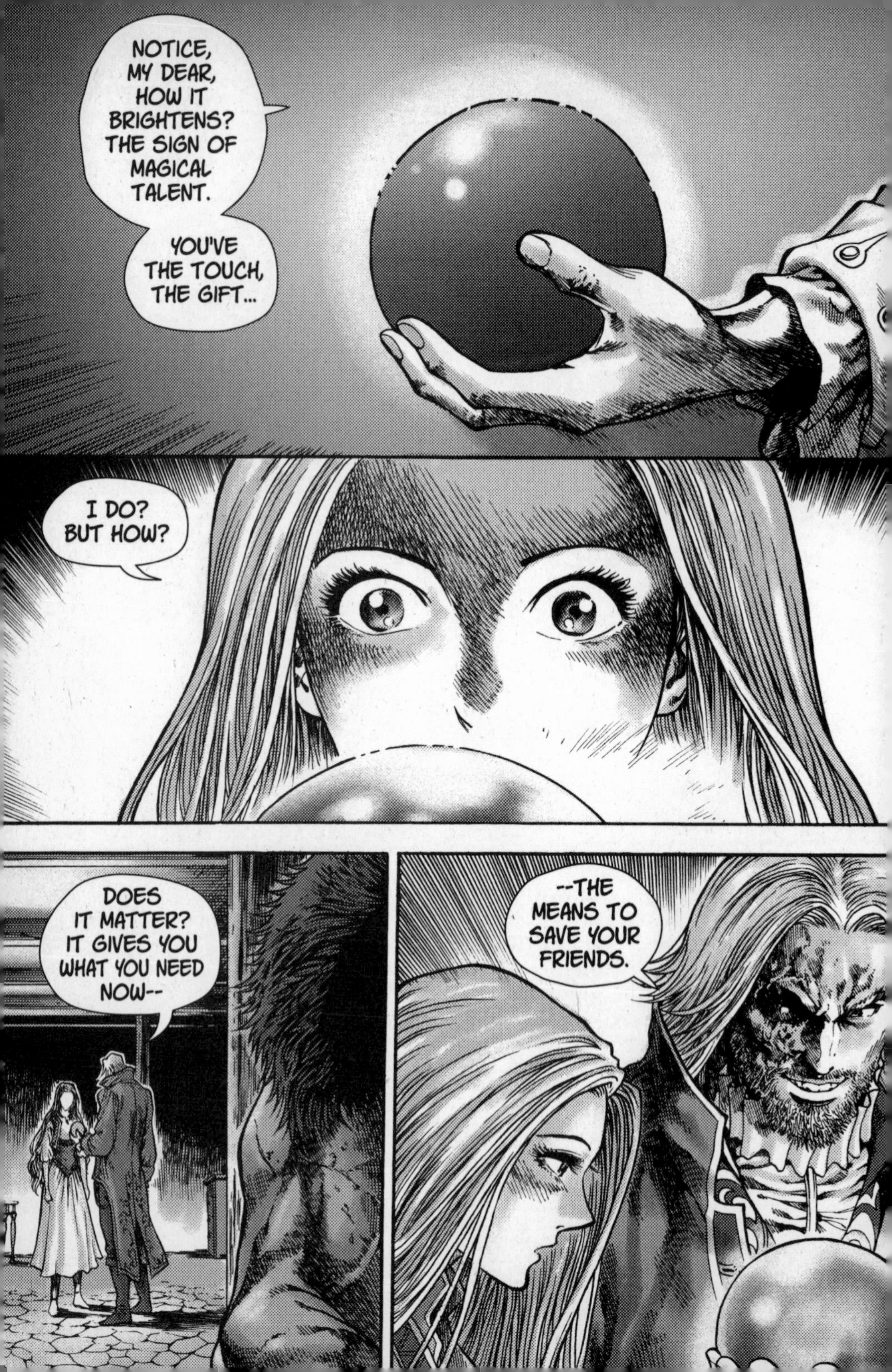
NOTICE, MY DEAR, HOW IT BRIGHTENS? THE SIGN OF MAGICAL TALENT.
YOU'VE THE TOUCH, THE GIFT...
I DO? BUT HOW?
DOES IT MATTER? IT GIVES YOU WHAT YOU NEED NOW--
--THE MEANS TO SAVE YOUR FRIENDS.

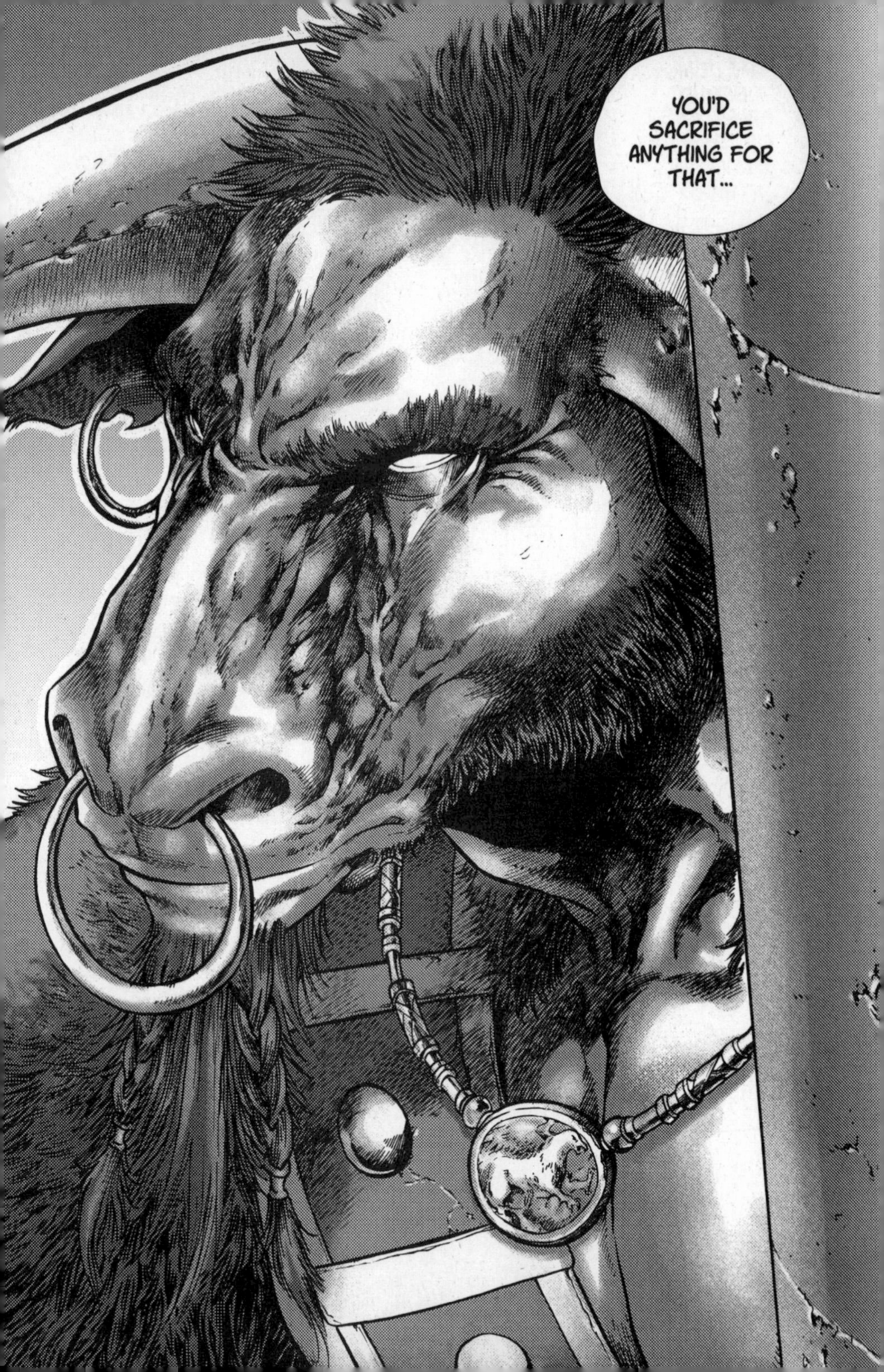
YOU'D SACRIFICE ANYTHING FOR THAT...

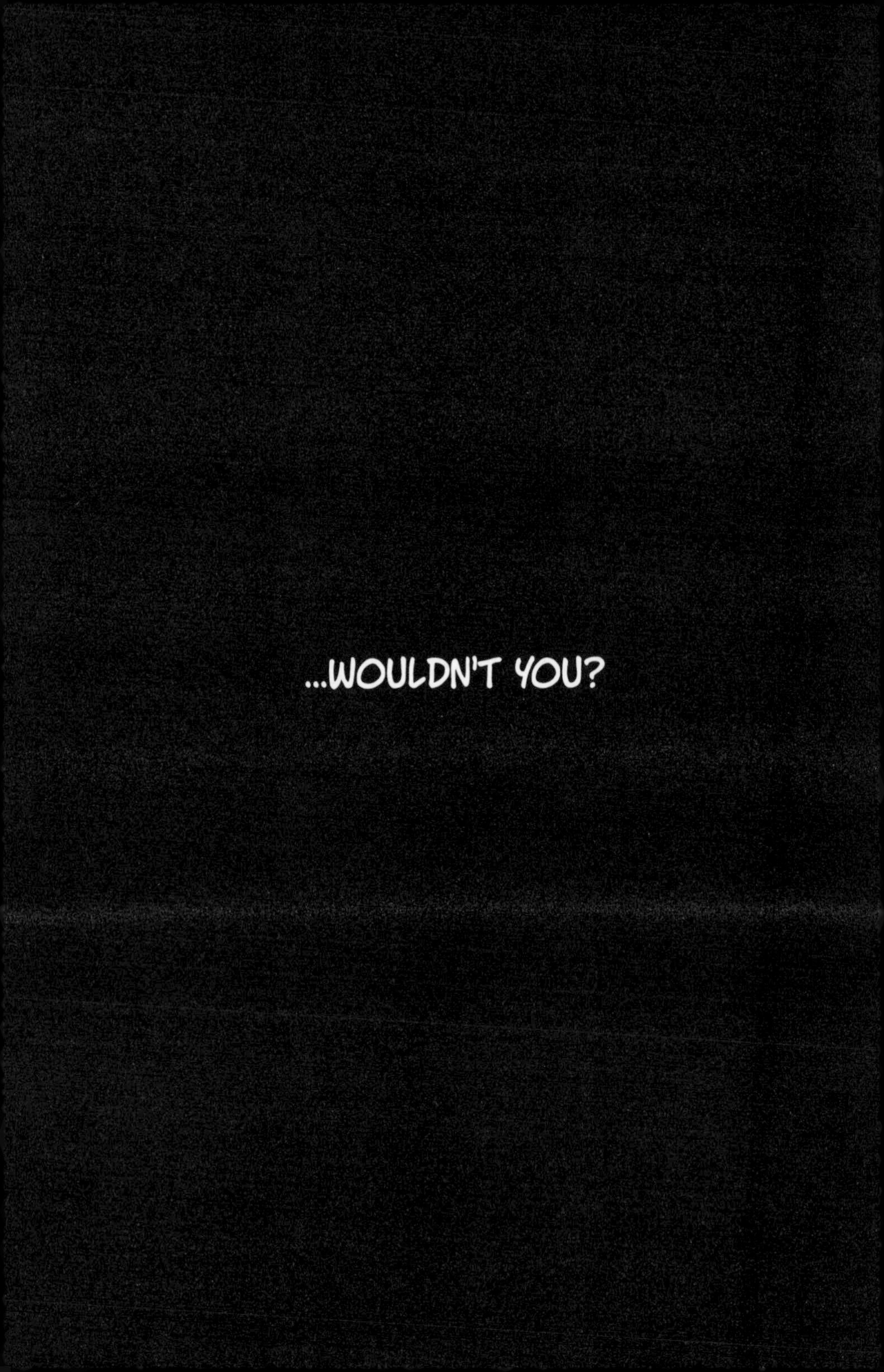
...WOULDN'T YOU?

CHAPTER FIVE
The Orb of Ner'zhul

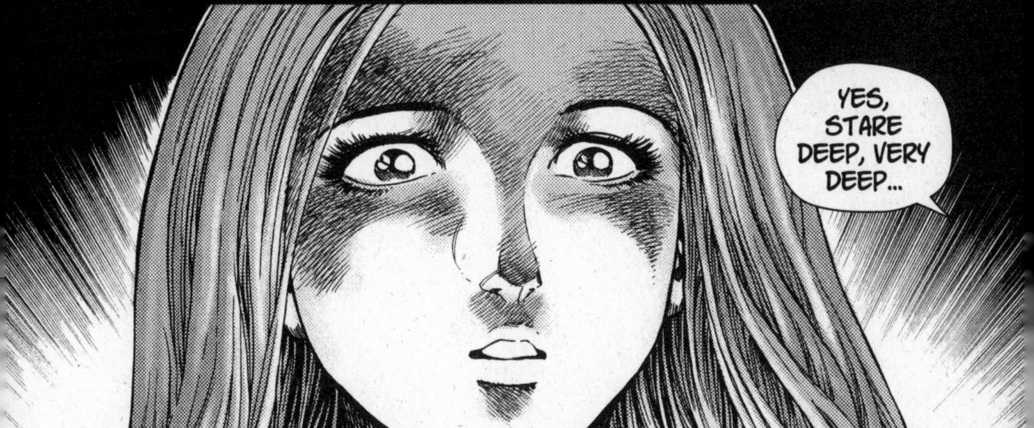
YES, STARE DEEP, VERY DEEP...

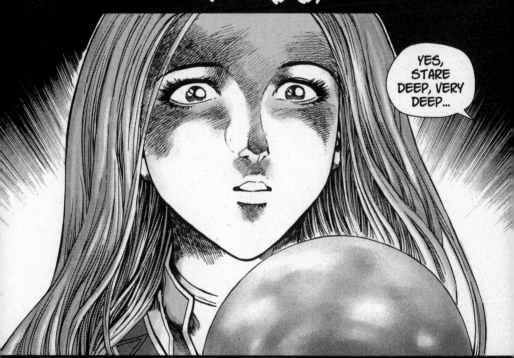

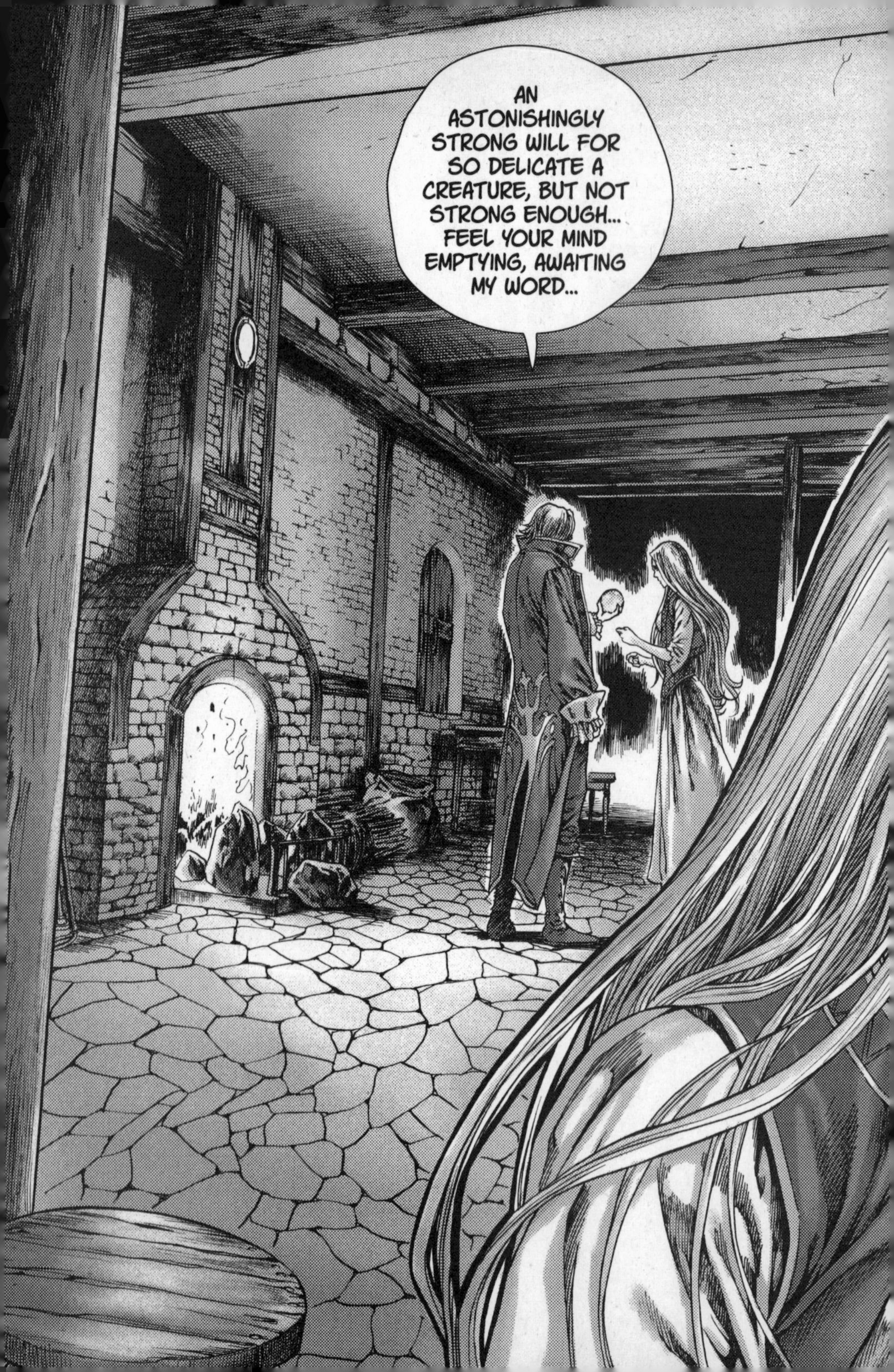
AN ASTONISHINGLY STRONG WILL FOR SO DELICATE A CREATURE, BUT NOT STRONG ENOUGH... FEEL YOUR MIND EMPTYING, AWAITING MY WORD...

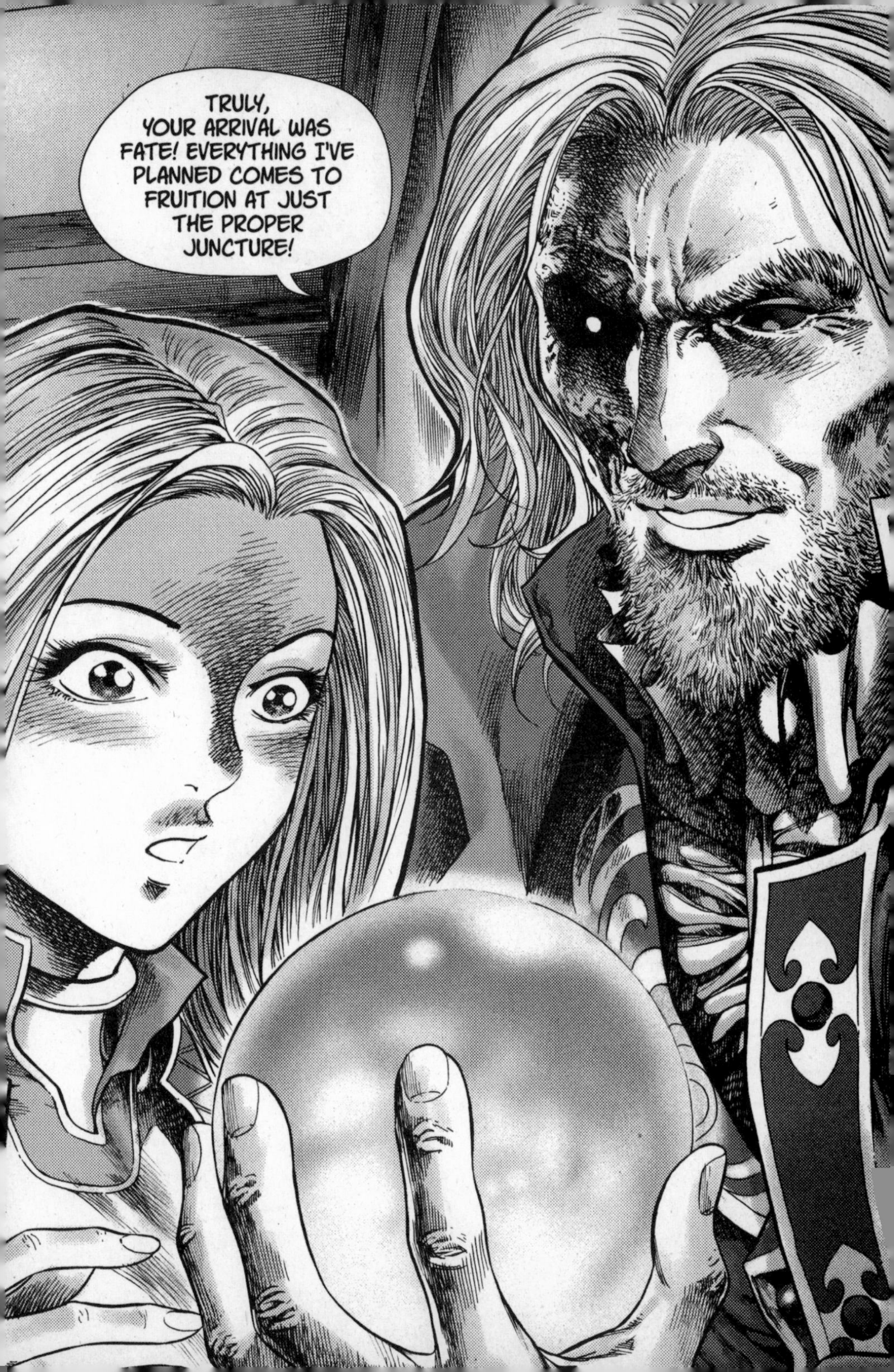
TRULY, YOUR ARRIVAL WAS FATE! EVERYTHING I'VE PLANNED COMES TO FRUITION AT JUST THE PROPER JUNCTURE!

WHEN I STOLE ONE OF THE ORBS OF NER'ZHUL FROM ICHOR, I SOUGHT IT SO THAT I MIGHT RAISE AN ARMY OF MY OWN!

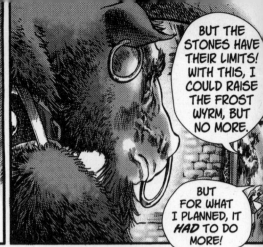

BUT THE STONES HAVE THEIR LIMITS! WITH THIS, I COULD RAISE THE FROST WYRM, BUT NO MORE.

BUT FOR WHAT I PLANNED, IT *HAD* TO DO MORE!

AND THEN YOU APPEARED...AND EVEN FROM WITHIN THIS PLACE, THE ORB SENSED YOUR POWER...POWER DEEPLY HIDDEN...

...POWER WITH WHICH I CAN CONTROL NOT ONLY THE WYRM...BUT MUCH, MUCH MORE.

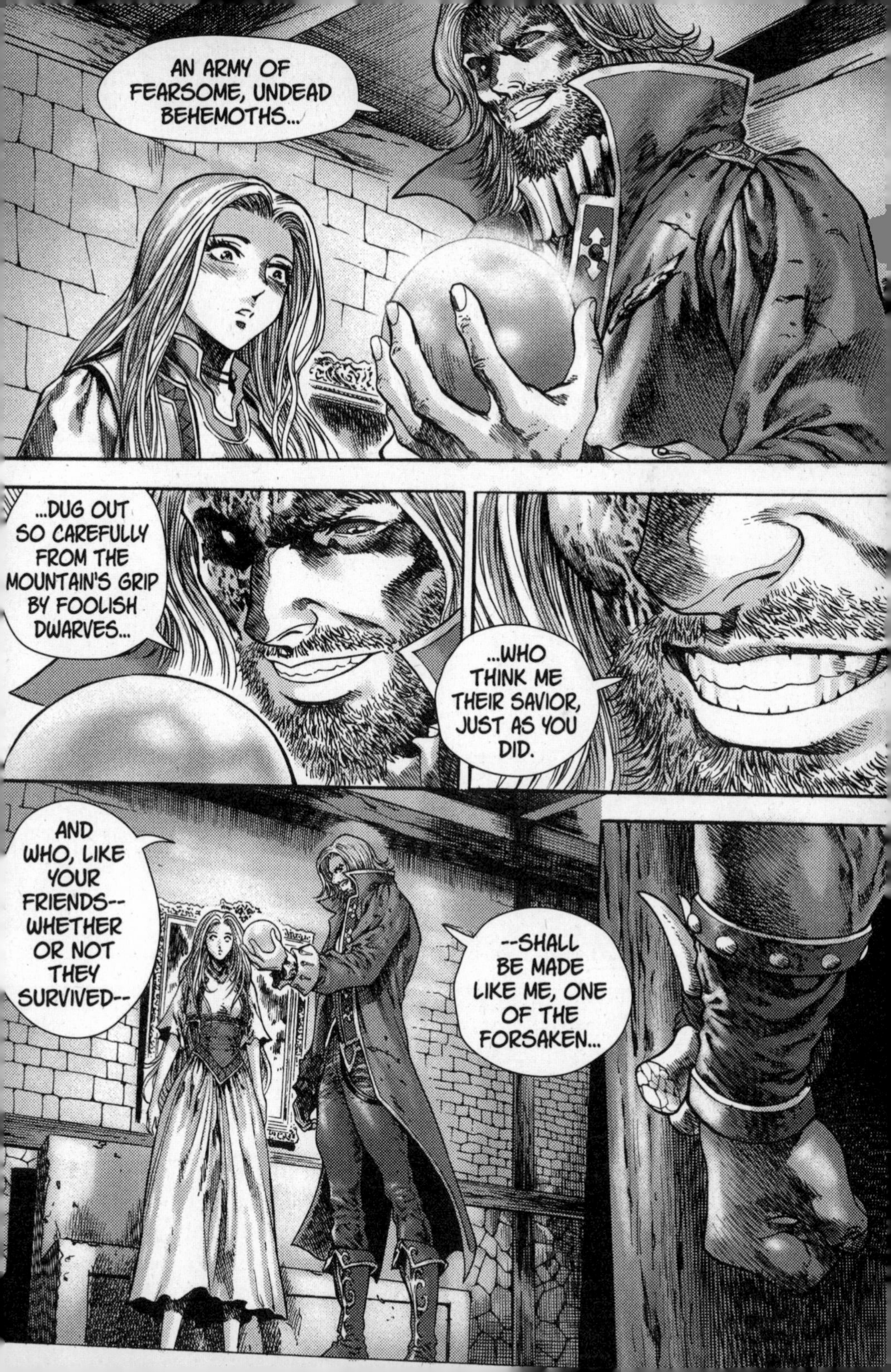
AN ARMY OF FEARSOME, UNDEAD BEHEMOTHS...
...DUG OUT SO CAREFULLY FROM THE MOUNTAIN'S GRIP BY FOOLISH DWARVES...
...WHO THINK ME THEIR SAVIOR, JUST AS YOU DID.
AND WHO, LIKE YOUR FRIENDS-- WHETHER OR NOT THEY SURVIVED--
--SHALL BE MADE LIKE ME, ONE OF THE FORSAKEN...

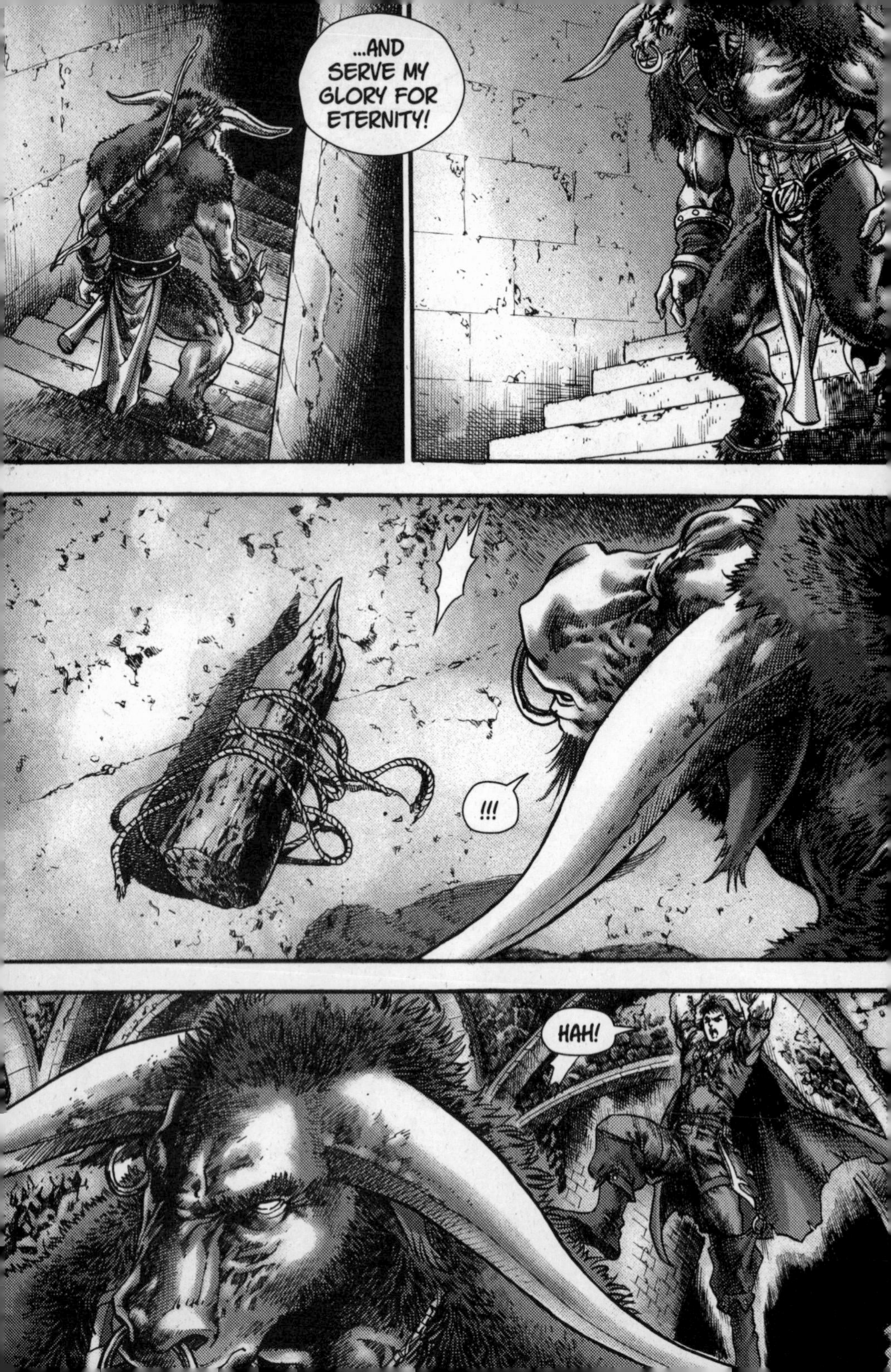
...AND SERVE MY GLORY FOR ETERNITY!
!!!
HAH!

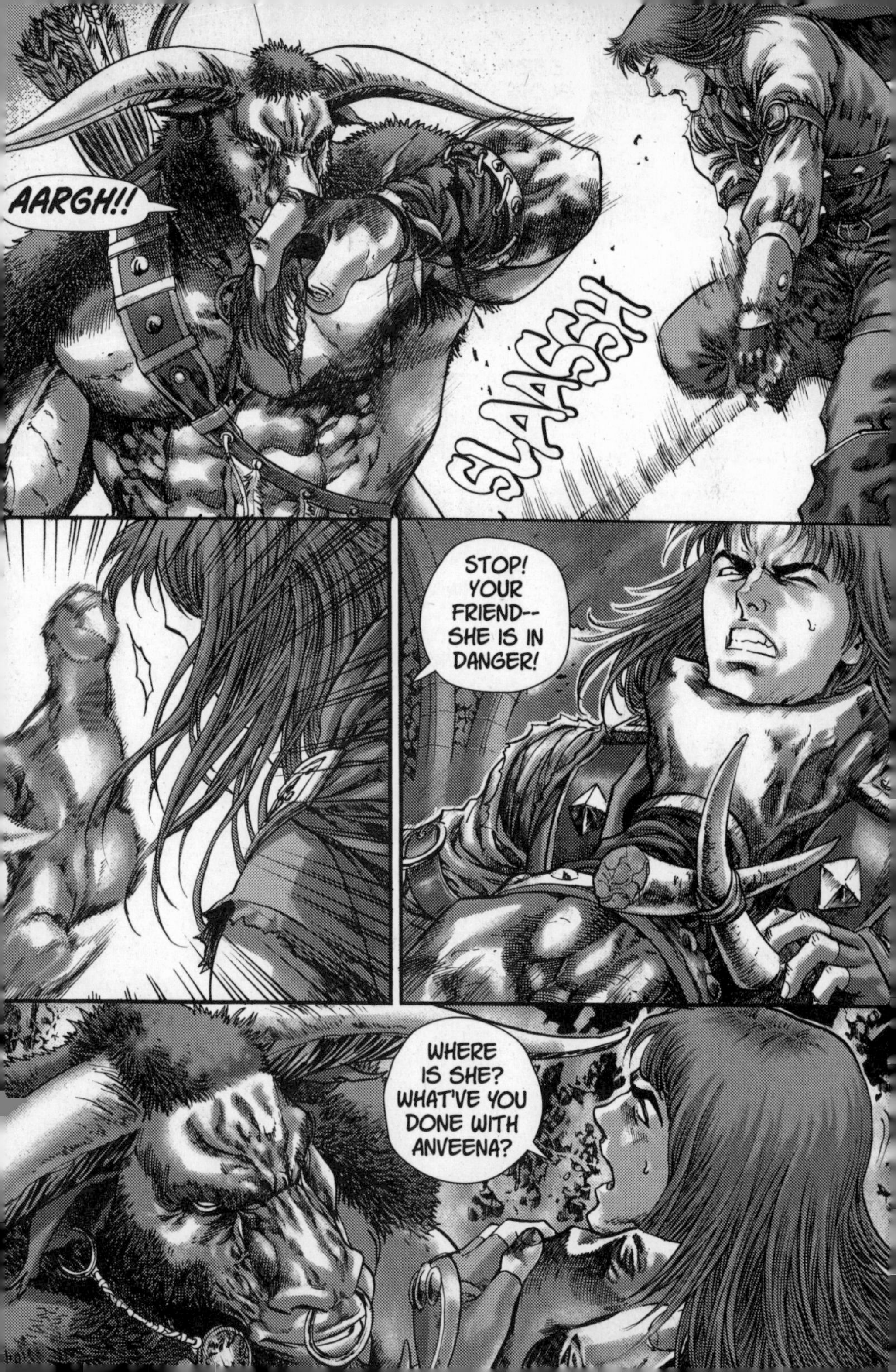
AARGH!!
SLASSH
STOP! YOUR FRIEND-- SHE IS IN DANGER!
WHERE IS SHE? WHAT'VE YOU DONE WITH ANVEENA?

I TRIED TO BRING HER HERE, BUT THE BARON IS WITH HER!

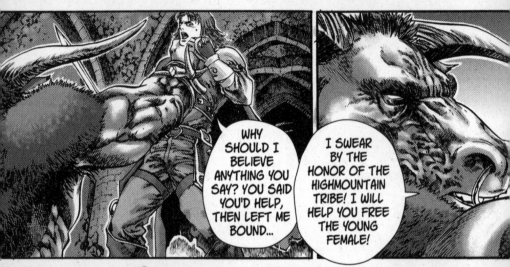

WHY SHOULD I BELIEVE ANYTHING YOU SAY? YOU SAID YOU'D HELP, THEN LEFT ME BOUND...

I SWEAR BY THE HONOR OF THE HIGHMOUNTAIN TRIBE! I WILL HELP YOU FREE THE YOUNG FEMALE!

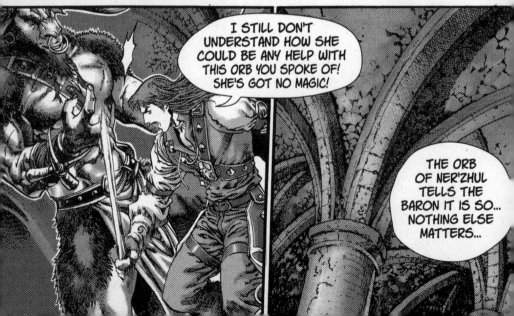

I STILL DON'T UNDERSTAND HOW SHE COULD BE ANY HELP WITH THIS ORB YOU SPOKE OF! SHE'S GOT NO MAGIC!

THE ORB OF NER'ZHUL TELLS THE BARON IT IS SO... NOTHING ELSE MATTERS...

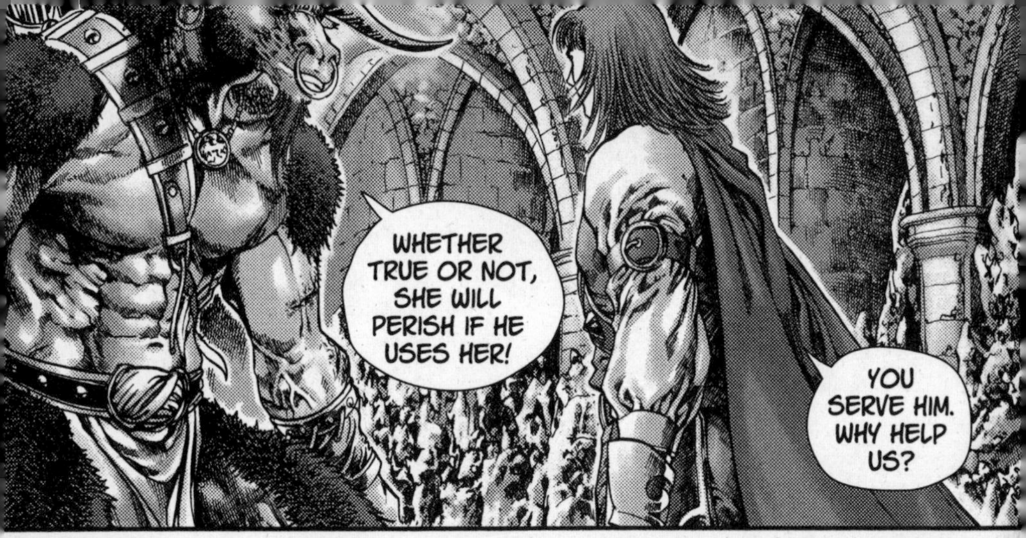
WHETHER TRUE OR NOT, SHE WILL PERISH IF HE USES HER!
YOU SERVE HIM. WHY HELP US?

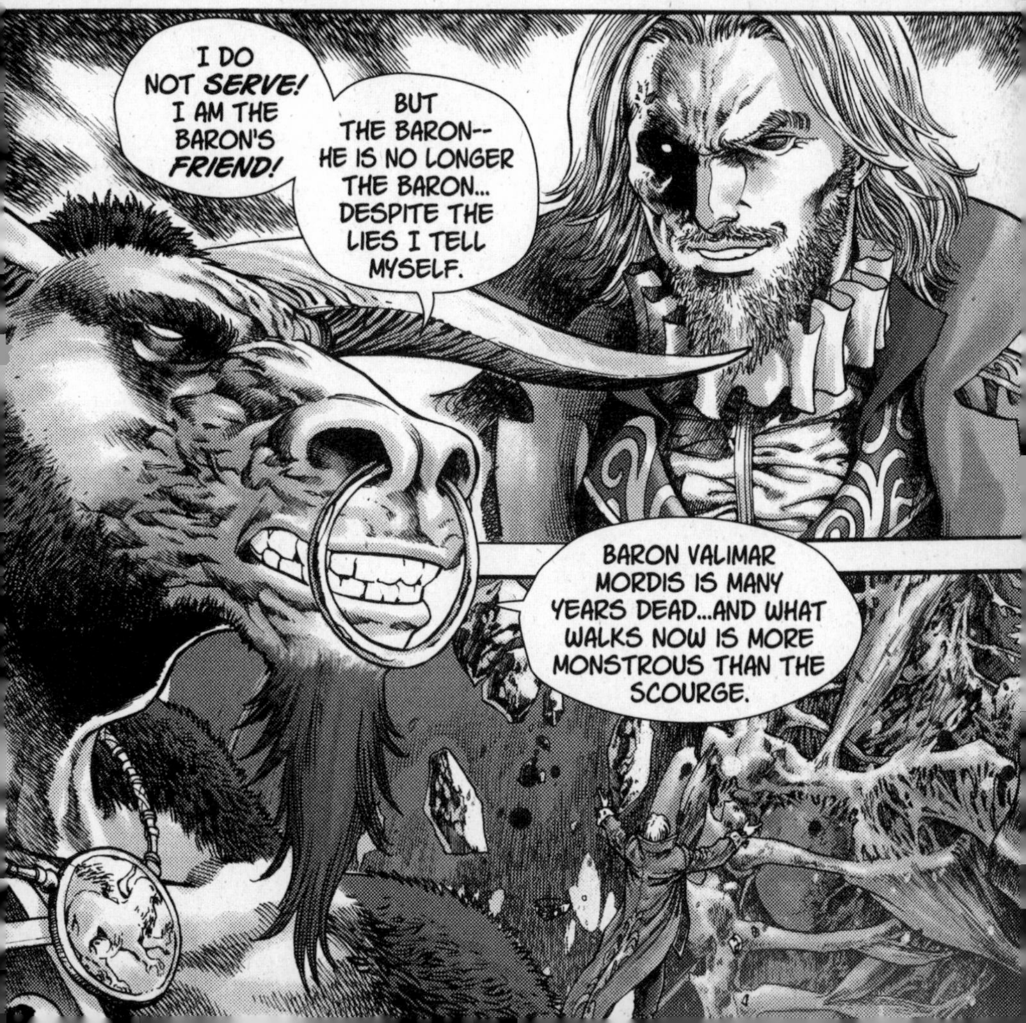
I DO NOT *SERVE!* I AM THE BARON'S *FRIEND!*
BUT THE BARON-- HE IS NO LONGER THE BARON... DESPITE THE LIES I TELL MYSELF.
BARON VALIMAR MORDIS IS MANY YEARS DEAD...AND WHAT WALKS NOW IS MORE MONSTROUS THAN THE SCOURGE.

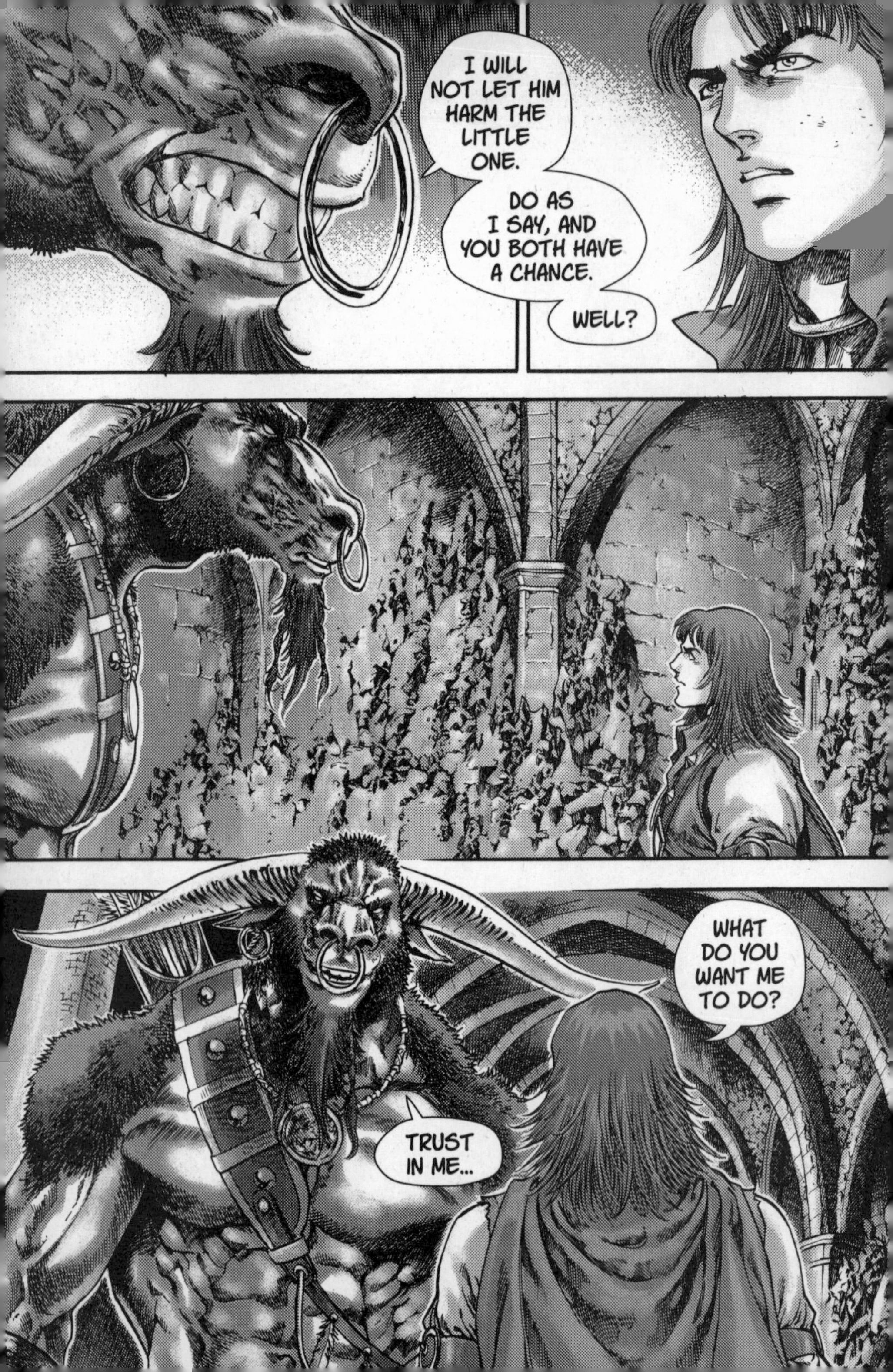
I WILL NOT LET HIM HARM THE LITTLE ONE.
DO AS I SAY, AND YOU BOTH HAVE A CHANCE.
WELL?
WHAT DO YOU WANT ME TO DO?
TRUST IN ME...

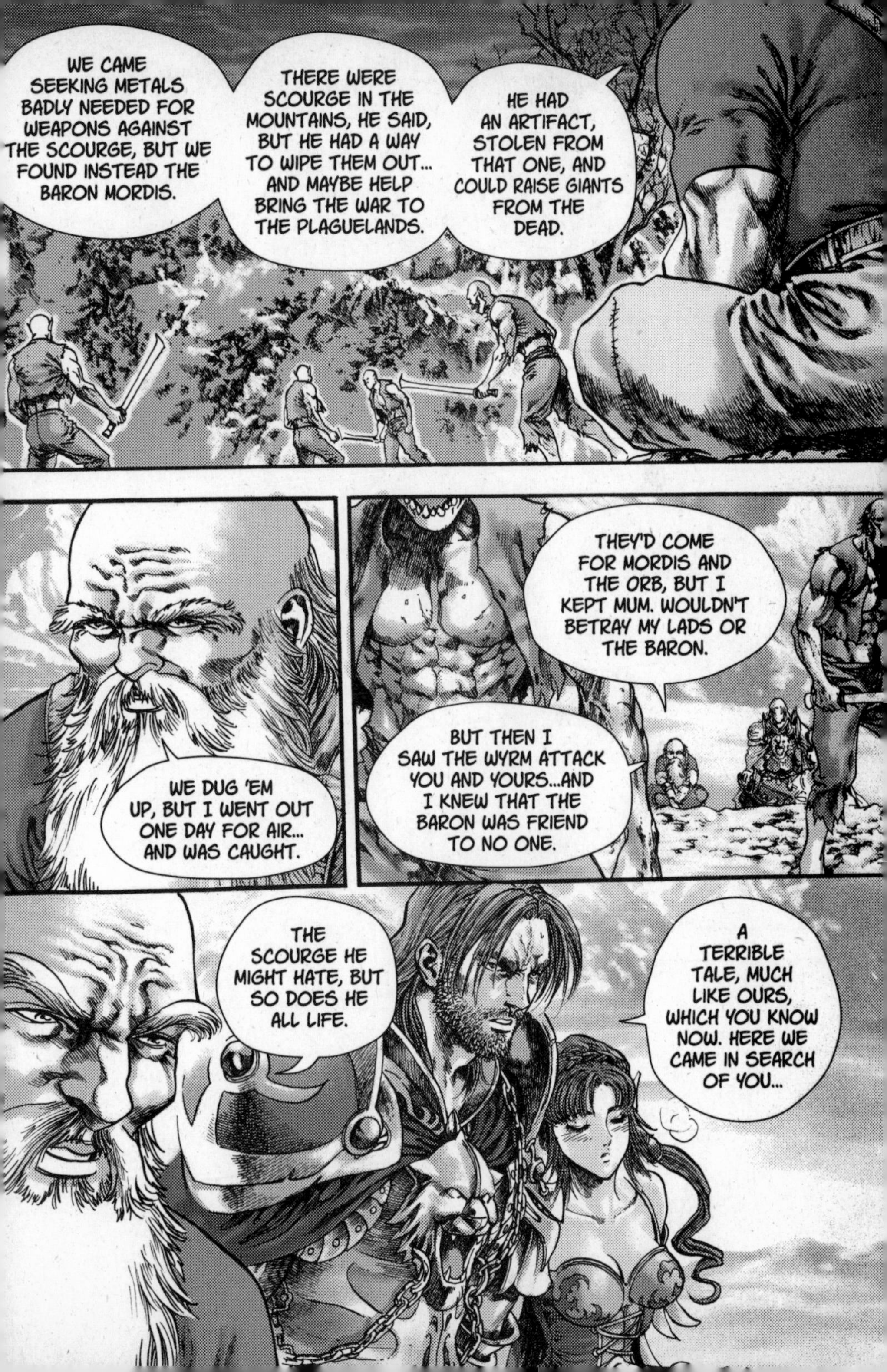
WE CAME SEEKING METALS BADLY NEEDED FOR WEAPONS AGAINST THE SCOURGE, BUT WE FOUND INSTEAD THE BARON MORDIS.
THERE WERE SCOURGE IN THE MOUNTAINS, HE SAID, BUT HE HAD A WAY TO WIPE THEM OUT... AND MAYBE HELP BRING THE WAR TO THE PLAGUELANDS.
HE HAD AN ARTIFACT, STOLEN FROM THAT ONE, AND COULD RAISE GIANTS FROM THE DEAD.
WE DUG 'EM UP, BUT I WENT OUT ONE DAY FOR AIR... AND WAS CAUGHT.
THEY'D COME FOR MORDIS AND THE ORB, BUT I KEPT MUM. WOULDN'T BETRAY MY LADS OR THE BARON.
BUT THEN I SAW THE WYRM ATTACK YOU AND YOURS...AND I KNEW THAT THE BARON WAS FRIEND TO NO ONE.
THE SCOURGE HE MIGHT HATE, BUT SO DOES HE ALL LIFE.
A TERRIBLE TALE, MUCH LIKE OURS, WHICH YOU KNOW NOW. HERE WE CAME IN SEARCH OF YOU...

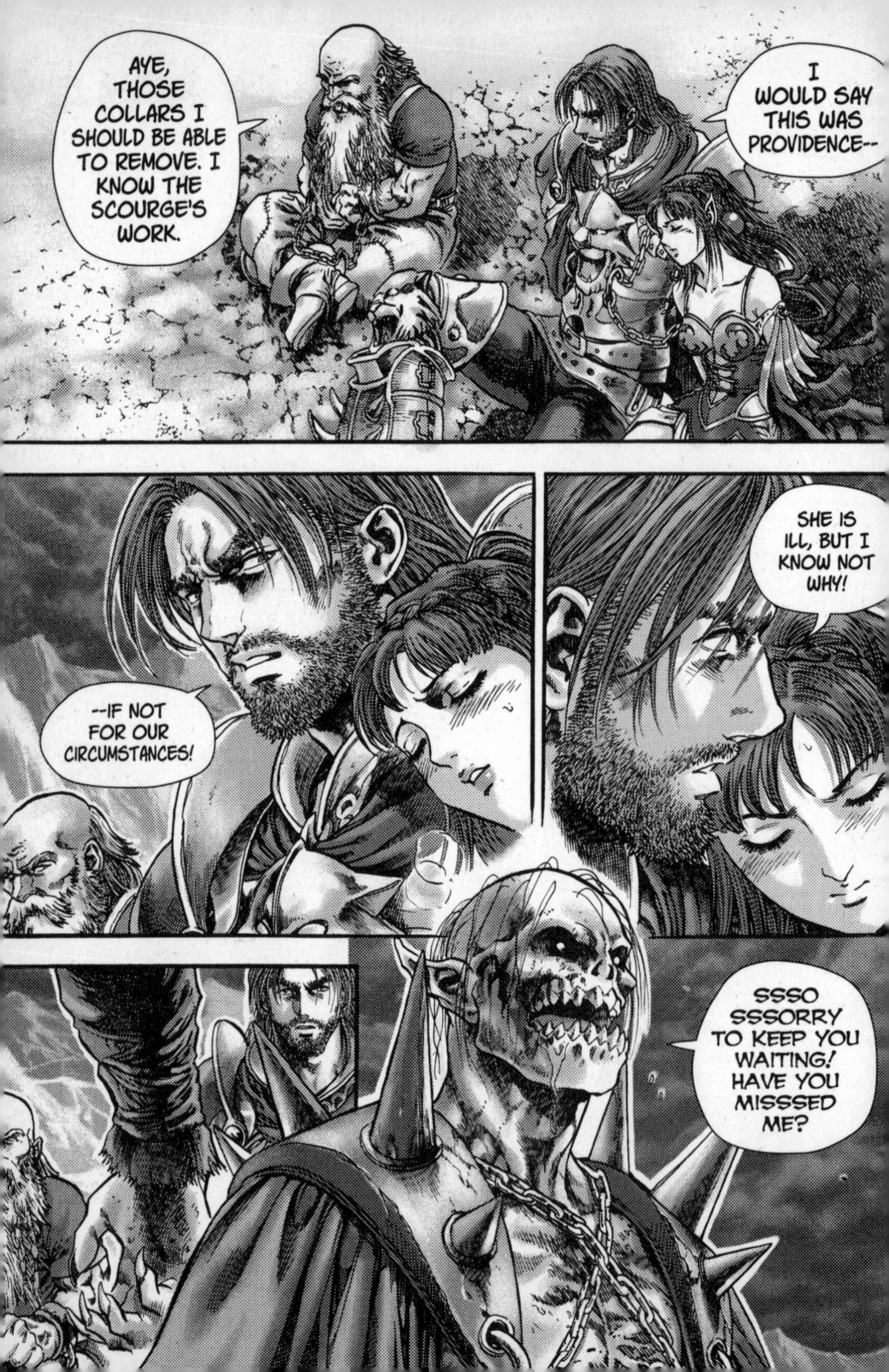
AYE, THOSE COLLARS I SHOULD BE ABLE TO REMOVE. I KNOW THE SCOURGE'S WORK.
I WOULD SAY THIS WAS PROVIDENCE--
--IF NOT FOR OUR CIRCUMSTANCES!
SHE IS ILL, BUT I KNOW NOT WHY!
SSSO SSSORRY TO KEEP YOU WAITING! HAVE YOU MISSSED ME?

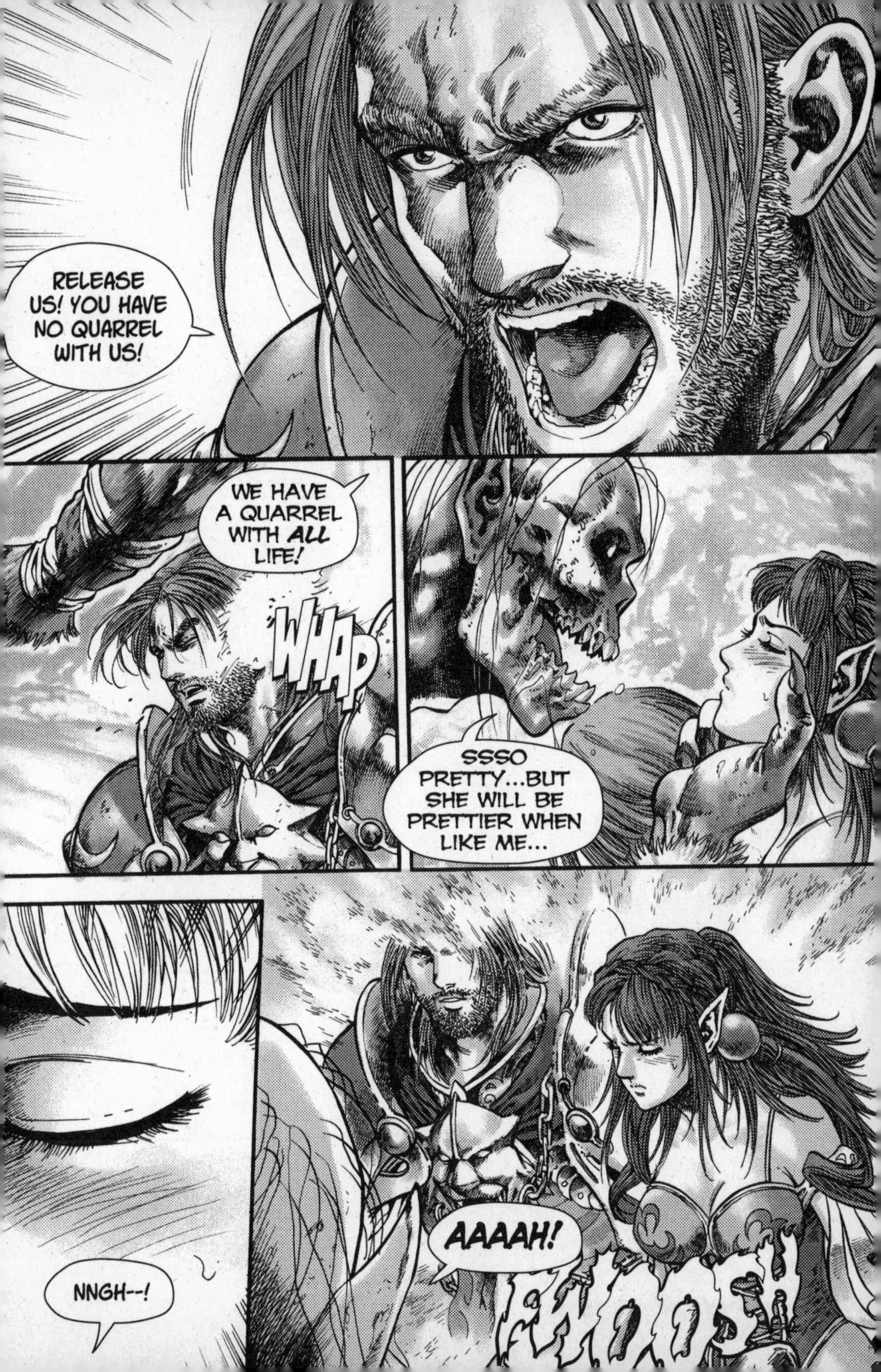
RELEASE US! YOU HAVE NO QUARREL WITH US!
WE HAVE A QUARREL WITH **ALL** LIFE!
WHAP
SSSO PRETTY...BUT SHE WILL BE PRETTIER WHEN LIKE ME...
NNGH--!
AAAAH!
FWOOSH

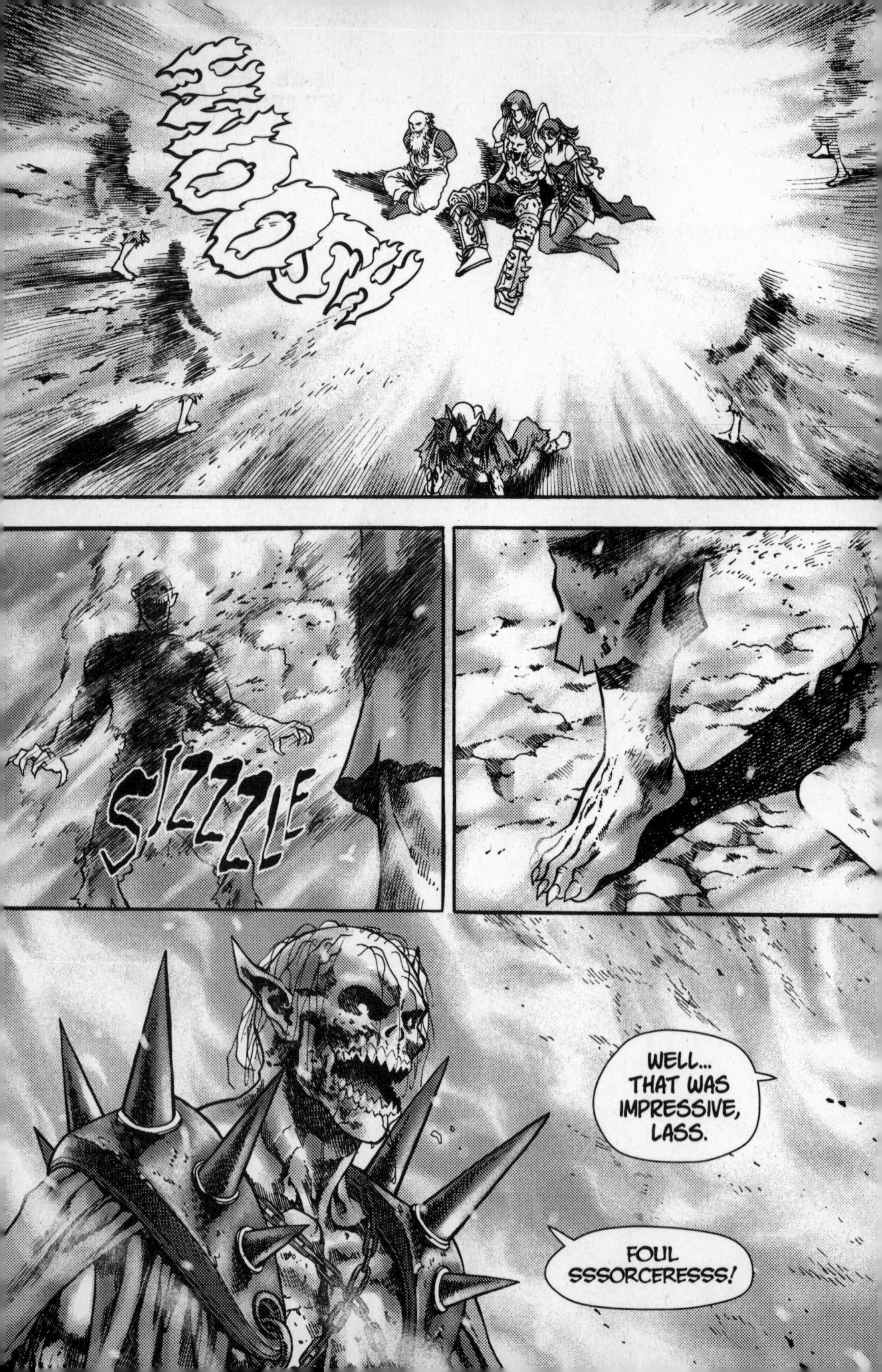
SIZZZLE
WELL... THAT WAS IMPRESSIVE, LASS.
FOUL SSSORCERESSS!

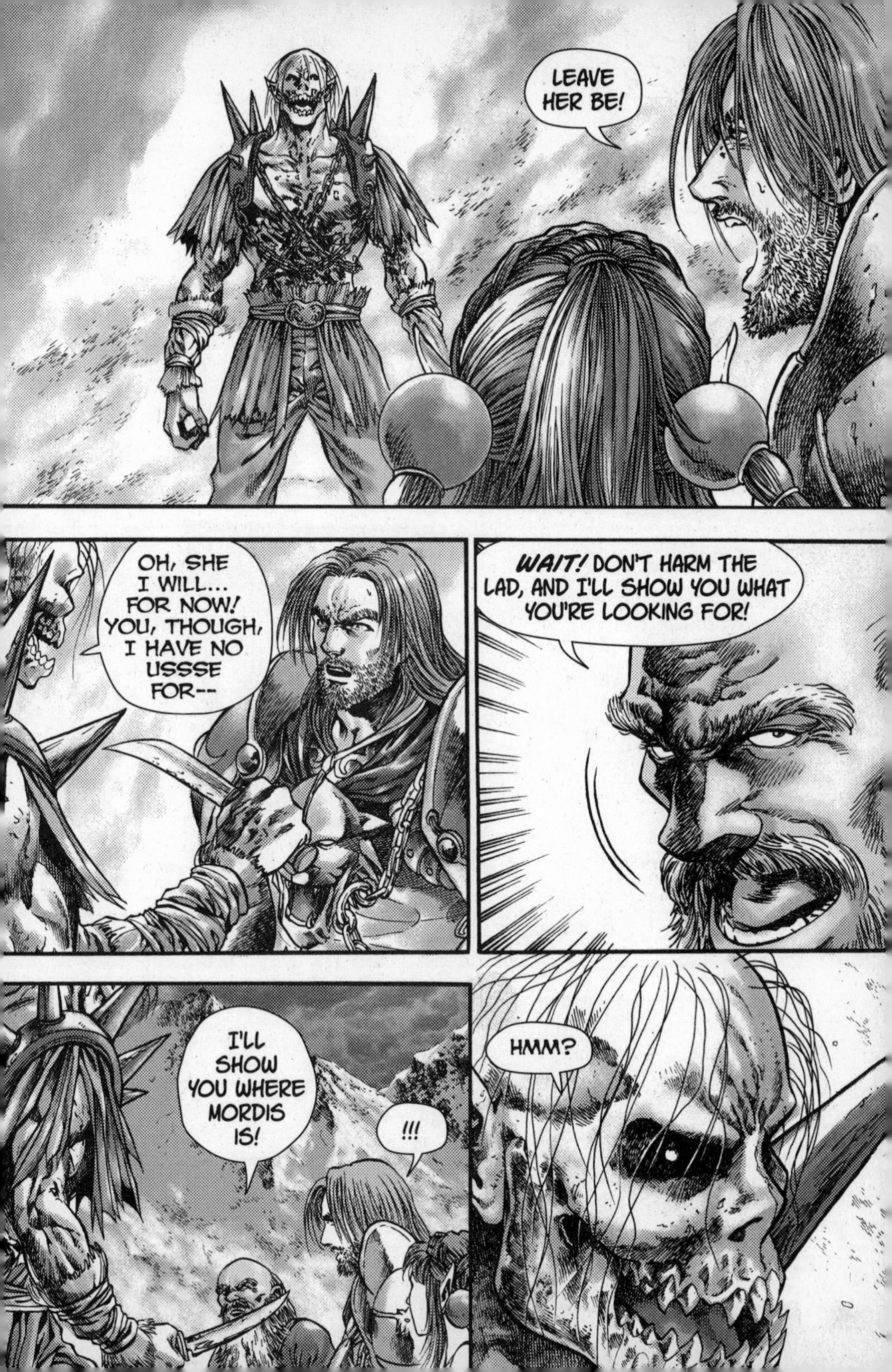
LEAVE HER BE!
OH, SHE I WILL... FOR NOW! YOU, THOUGH, I HAVE NO USSSE FOR--
WAIT! DON'T HARM THE LAD, AND I'LL SHOW YOU WHAT YOU'RE LOOKING FOR!
I'LL SHOW YOU WHERE MORDIS IS!
!!!
HMM?

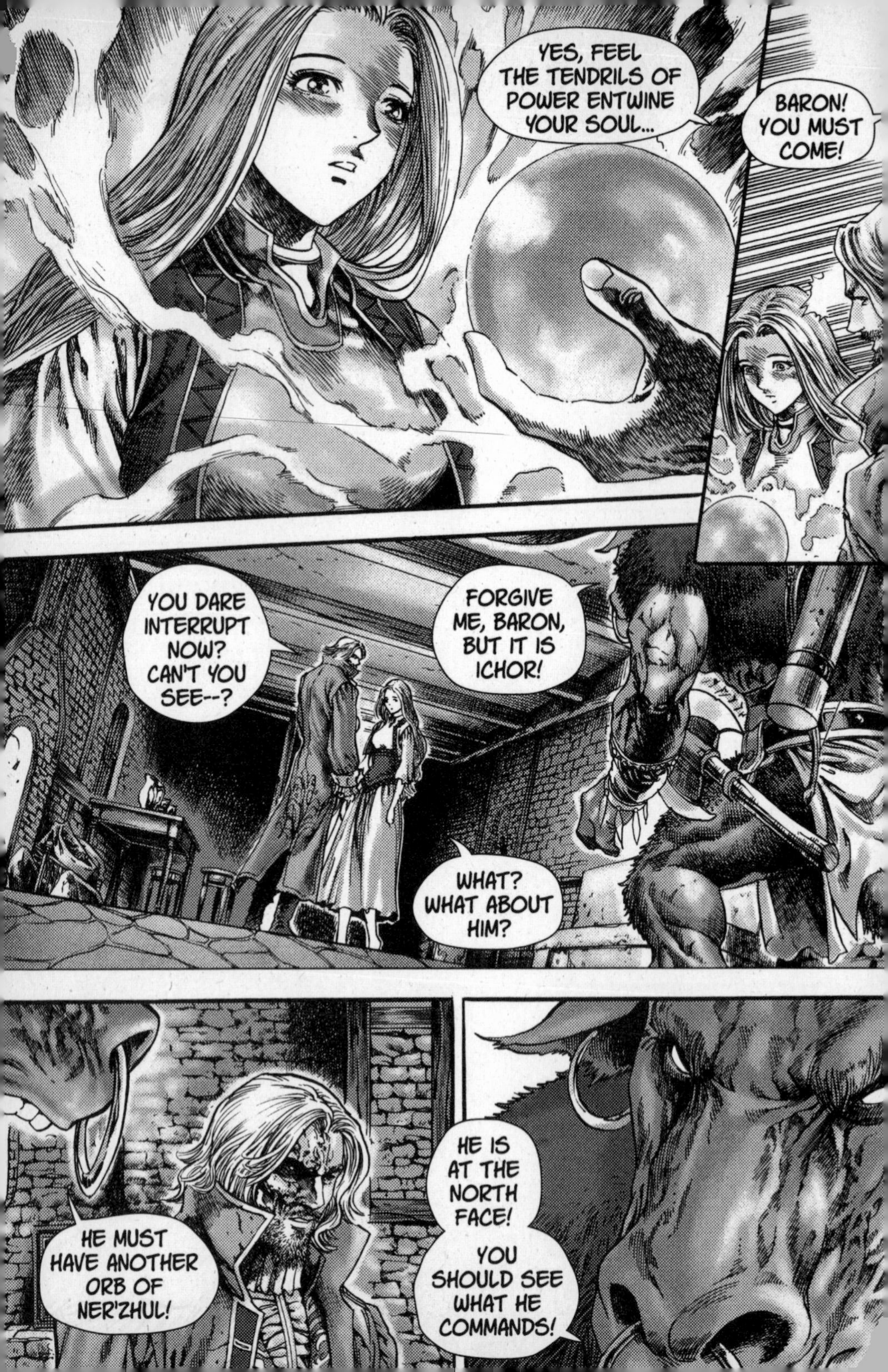
YES, FEEL THE TENDRILS OF POWER ENTWINE YOUR SOUL...
BARON! YOU MUST COME!
YOU DARE INTERRUPT NOW? CAN'T YOU SEE--?
FORGIVE ME, BARON, BUT IT IS ICHOR!
WHAT? WHAT ABOUT HIM?
HE MUST HAVE ANOTHER ORB OF NER'ZHUL!
HE IS AT THE NORTH FACE!
YOU SHOULD SEE WHAT HE COMMANDS!

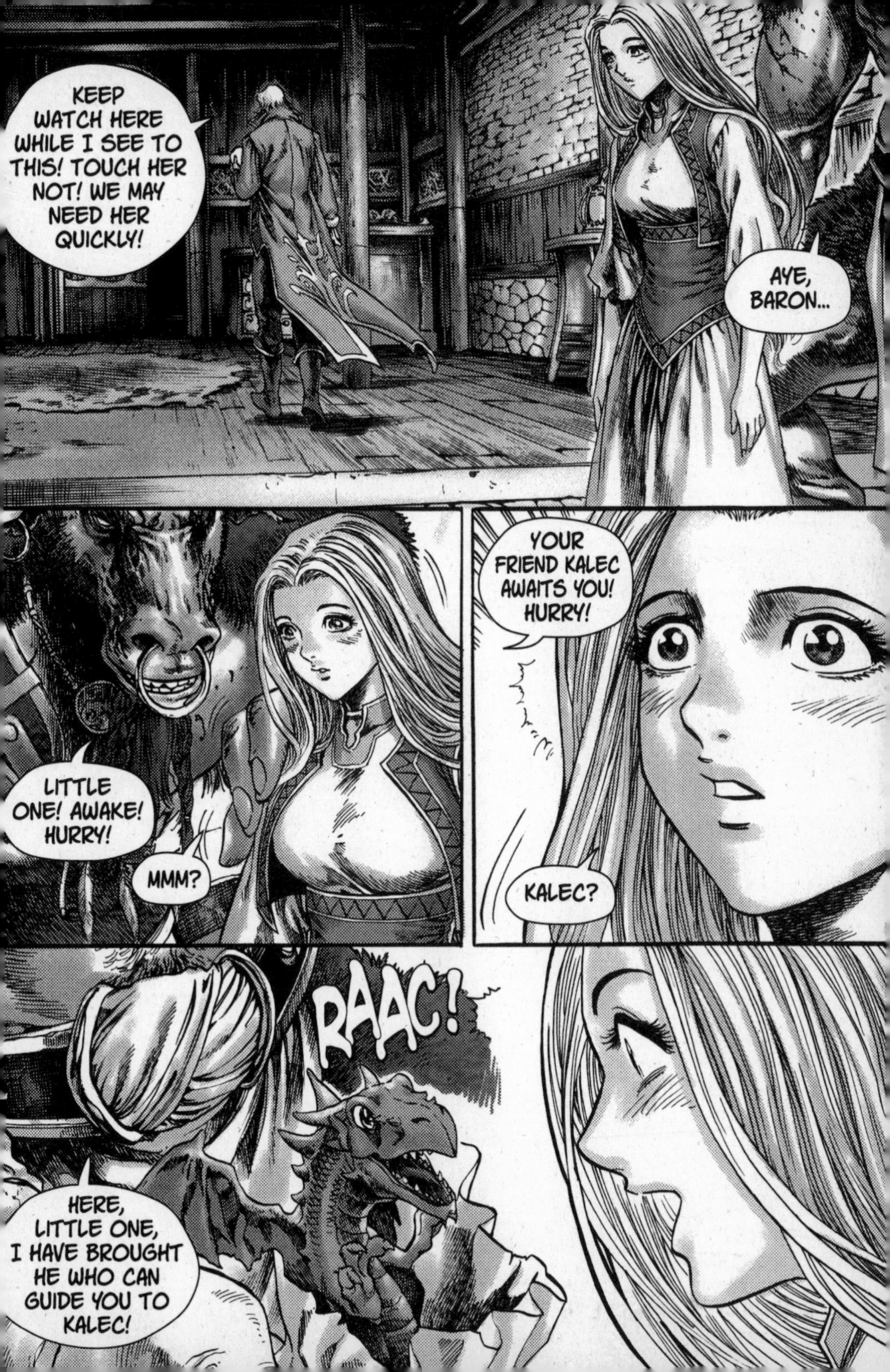
KEEP WATCH HERE WHILE I SEE TO THIS! TOUCH HER NOT! WE MAY NEED HER QUICKLY!
AYE, BARON...
LITTLE ONE! AWAKE! HURRY!
MMM?
YOUR FRIEND KALEC AWAITS YOU! HURRY!
KALEC?
RAAC!
HERE, LITTLE ONE, I HAVE BROUGHT HE WHO CAN GUIDE YOU TO KALEC!

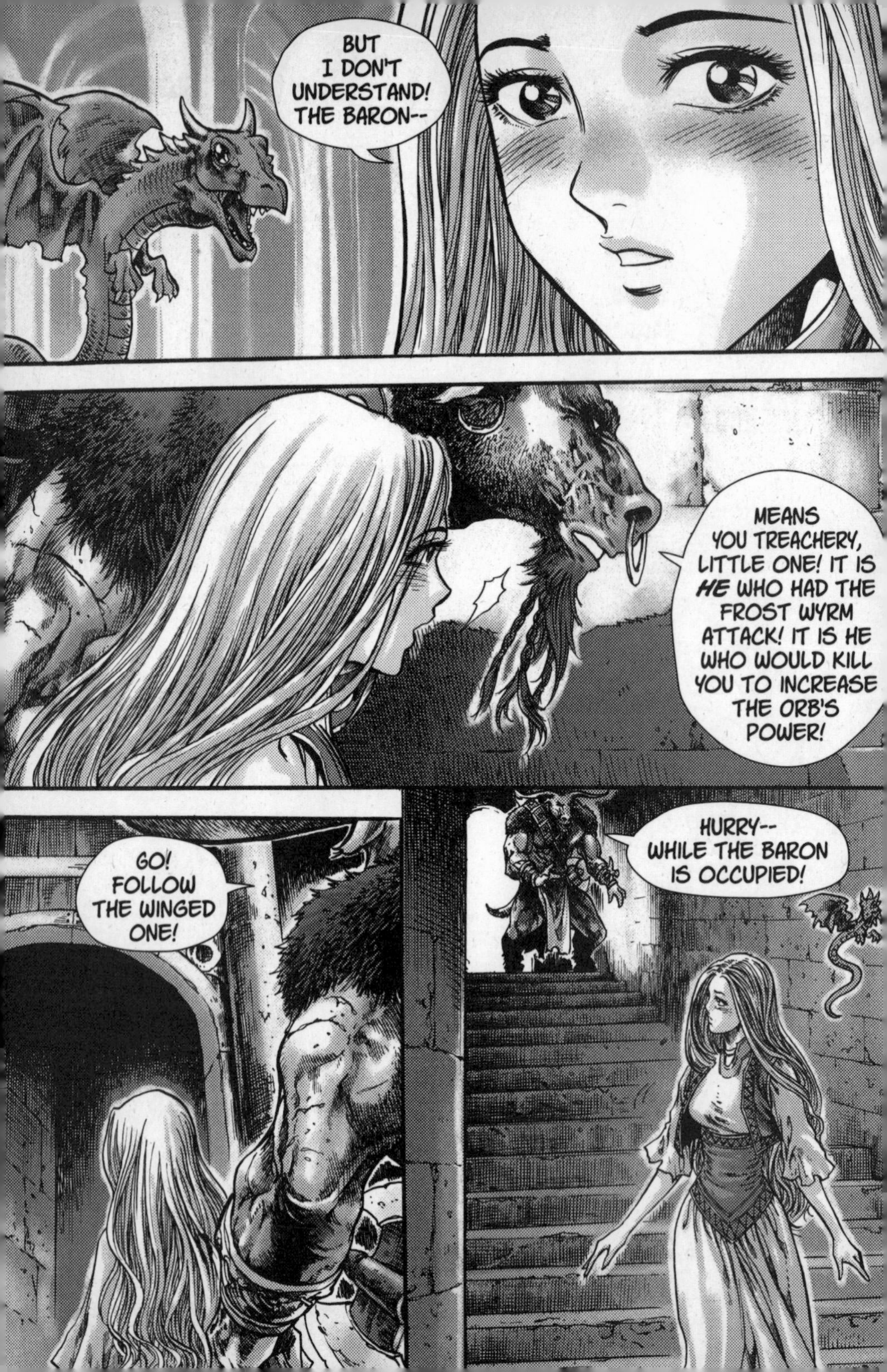
BUT I DON'T UNDERSTAND! THE BARON--
MEANS YOU TREACHERY, LITTLE ONE! IT IS *HE* WHO HAD THE FROST WYRM ATTACK! IT IS HE WHO WOULD KILL YOU TO INCREASE THE ORB'S POWER!
GO! FOLLOW THE WINGED ONE!
HURRY-- WHILE THE BARON IS OCCUPIED!

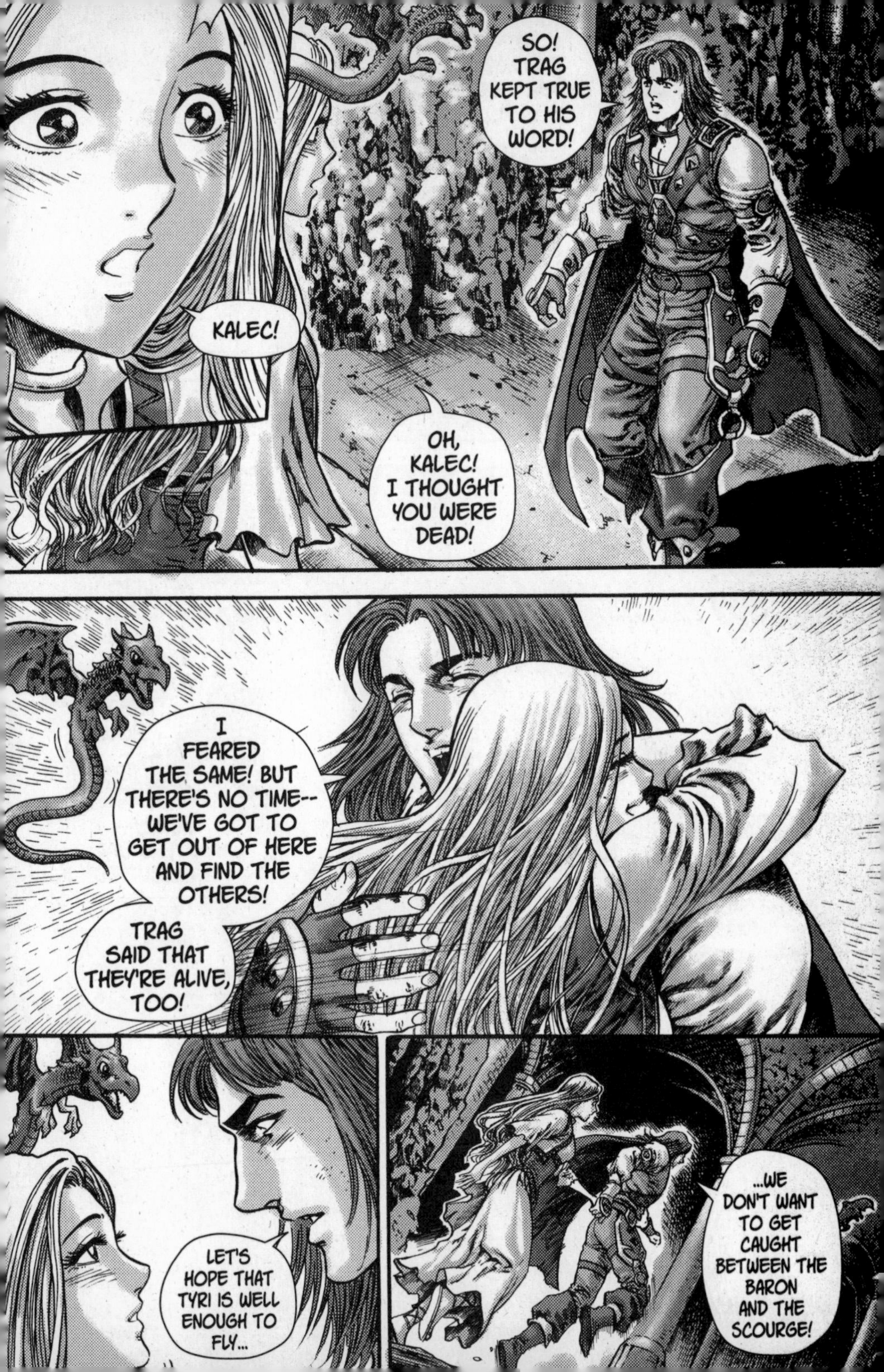
KALEC!
SO! TRAG KEPT TRUE TO HIS WORD!
OH, KALEC! I THOUGHT YOU WERE DEAD!
I FEARED THE SAME! BUT THERE'S NO TIME-- WE'VE GOT TO GET OUT OF HERE AND FIND THE OTHERS!
TRAG SAID THAT THEY'RE ALIVE, TOO!
LET'S HOPE THAT TYRI IS WELL ENOUGH TO FLY...
...WE DON'T WANT TO GET CAUGHT BETWEEN THE BARON AND THE SCOURGE!

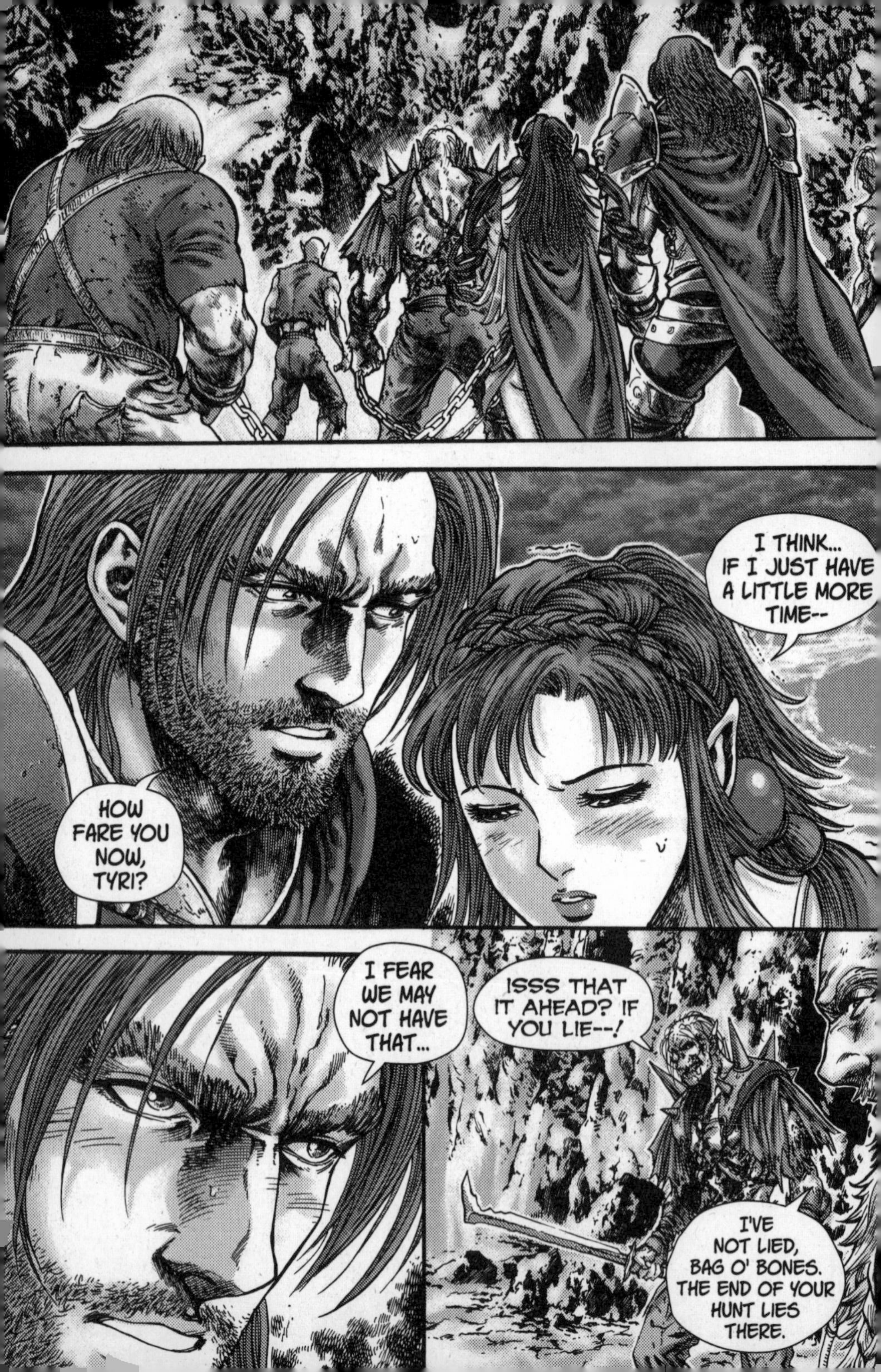
HOW FARE YOU NOW, TYRI?
I THINK... IF I JUST HAVE A LITTLE MORE TIME--
I FEAR WE MAY NOT HAVE THAT...
ISSS THAT IT AHEAD? IF YOU LIE--!
I'VE NOT LIED, BAG O' BONES. THE END OF YOUR HUNT LIES THERE.

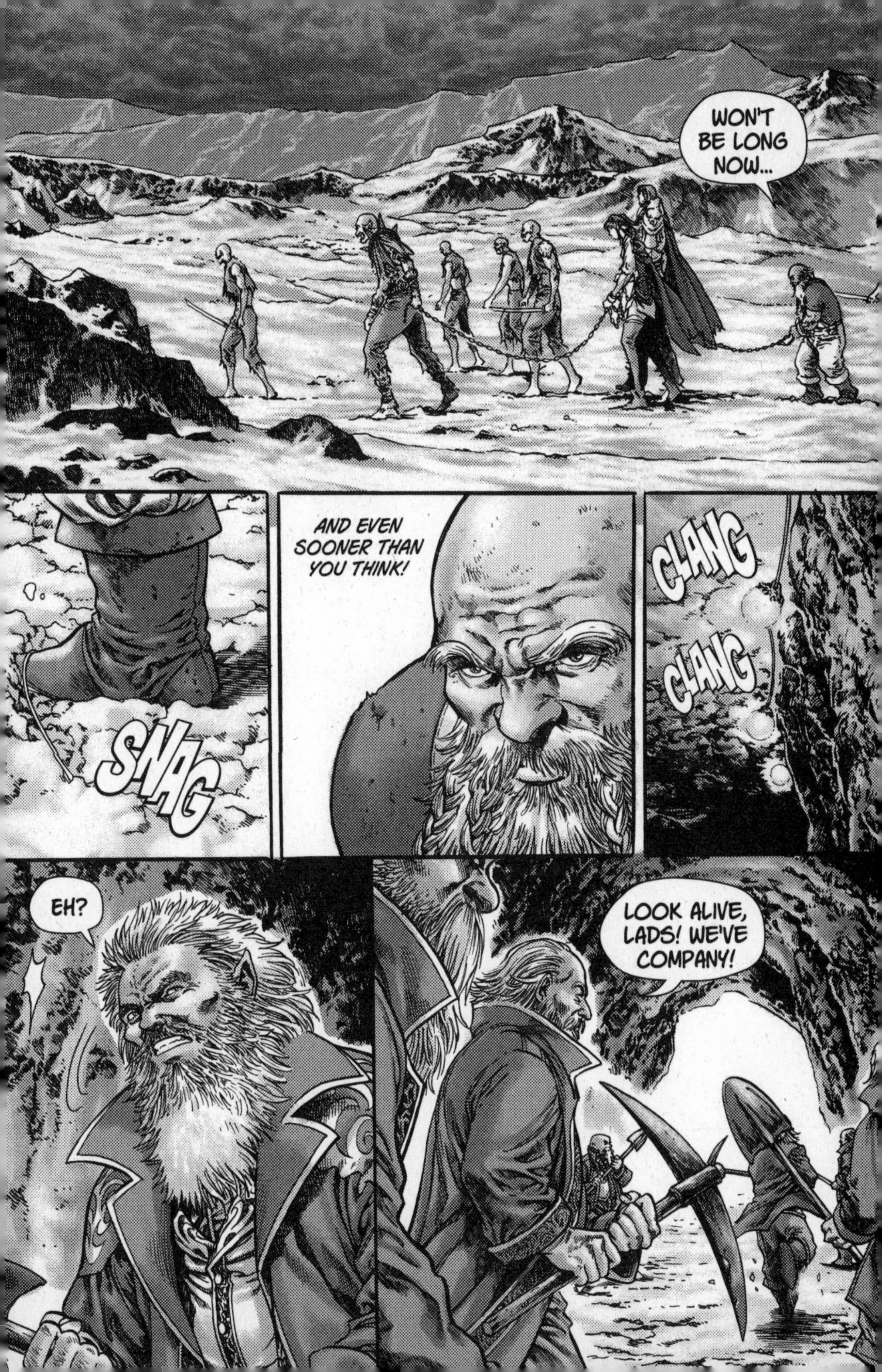
WON'T BE LONG NOW...
SNAG
AND EVEN SOONER THAN YOU THINK!
CLANG
CLANG
EH?
LOOK ALIVE, LADS! WE'VE COMPANY!

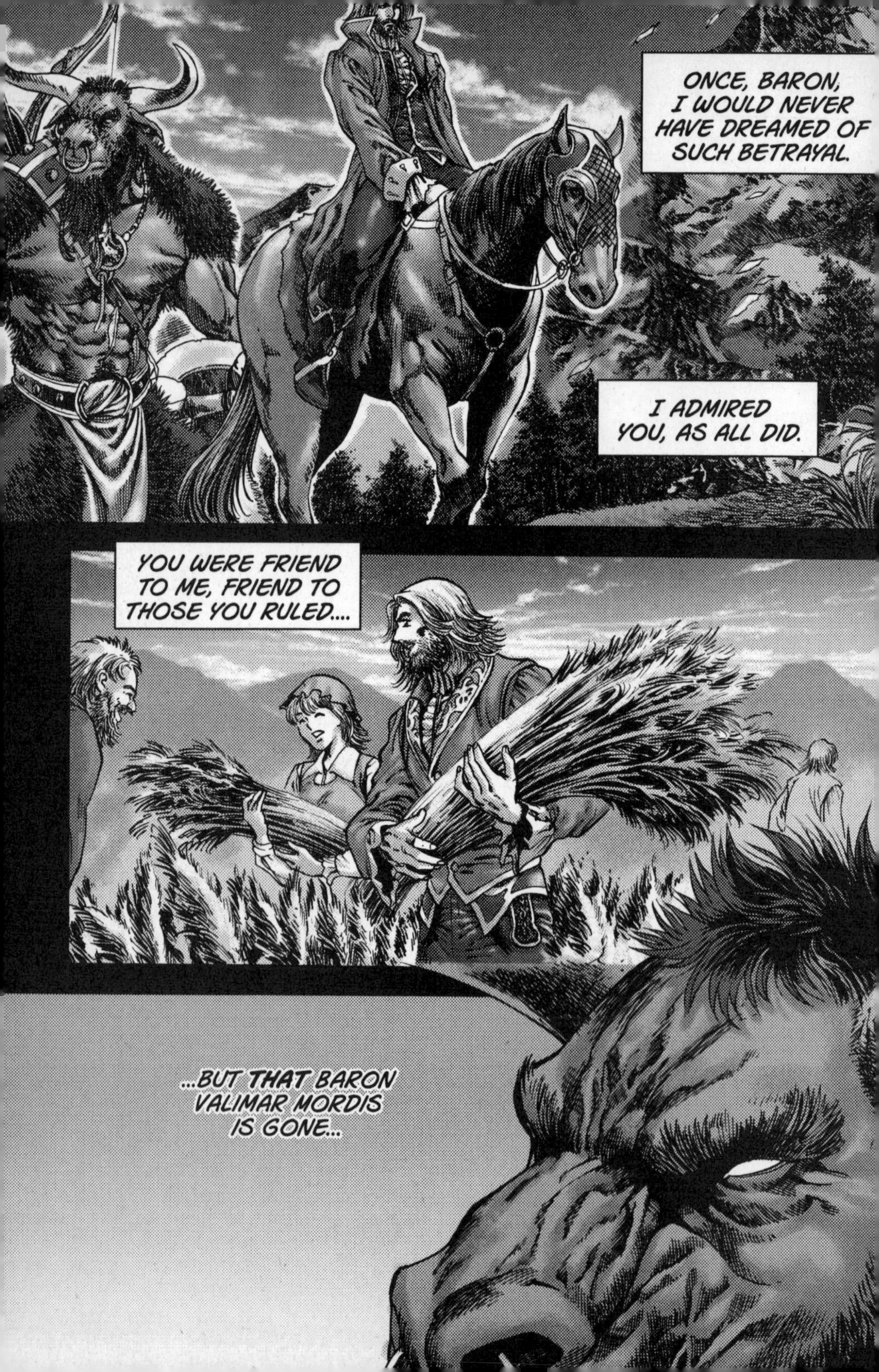
ONCE, BARON, I WOULD NEVER HAVE DREAMED OF SUCH BETRAYAL.
I ADMIRED YOU, AS ALL DID.
YOU WERE FRIEND TO ME, FRIEND TO THOSE YOU RULED....
...BUT THAT BARON VALIMAR MORDIS IS GONE...

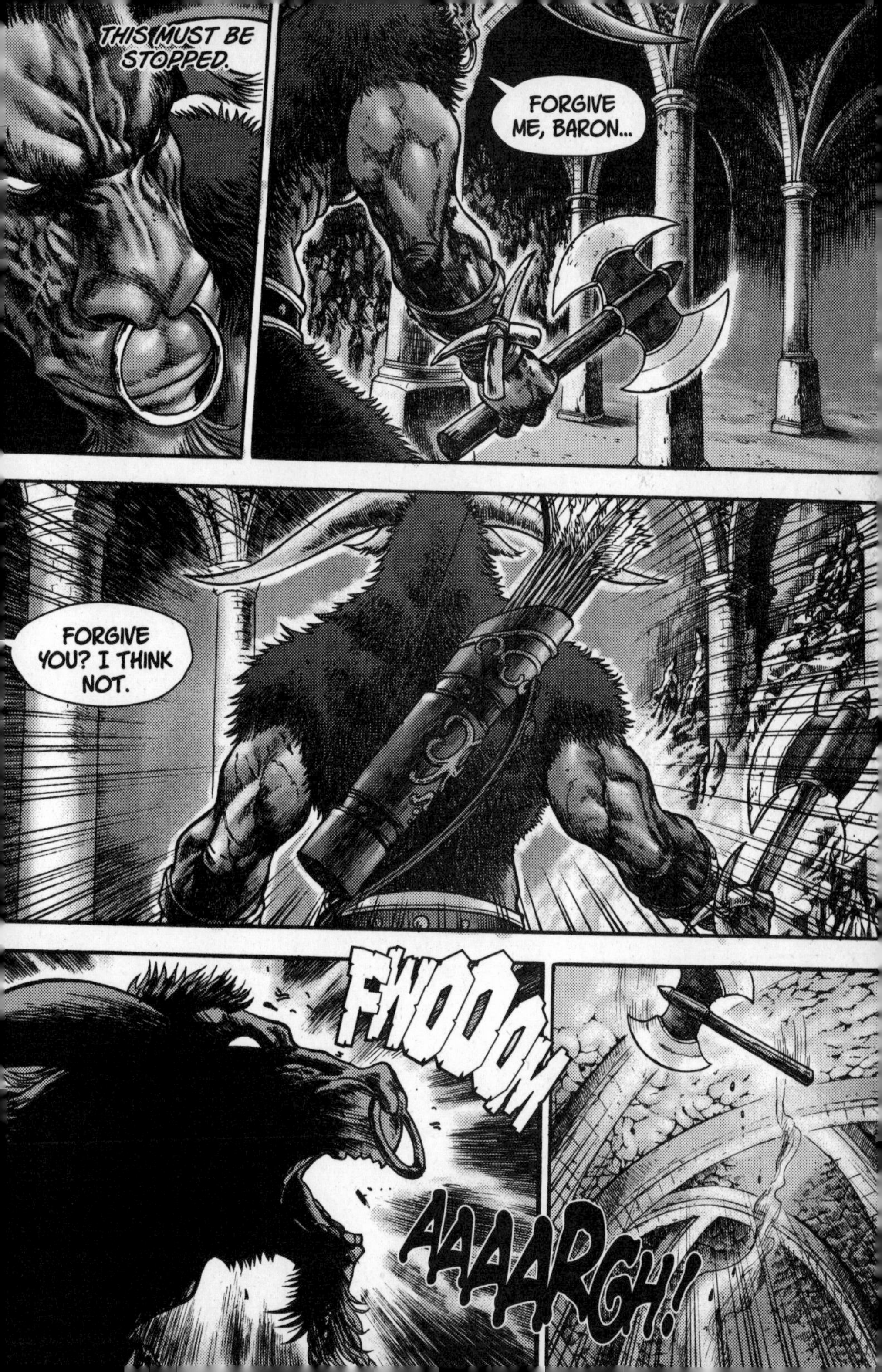
THIS MUST BE STOPPED.
FORGIVE ME, BARON...
FORGIVE YOU? I THINK NOT.
FWOOOM
AAAARGH!

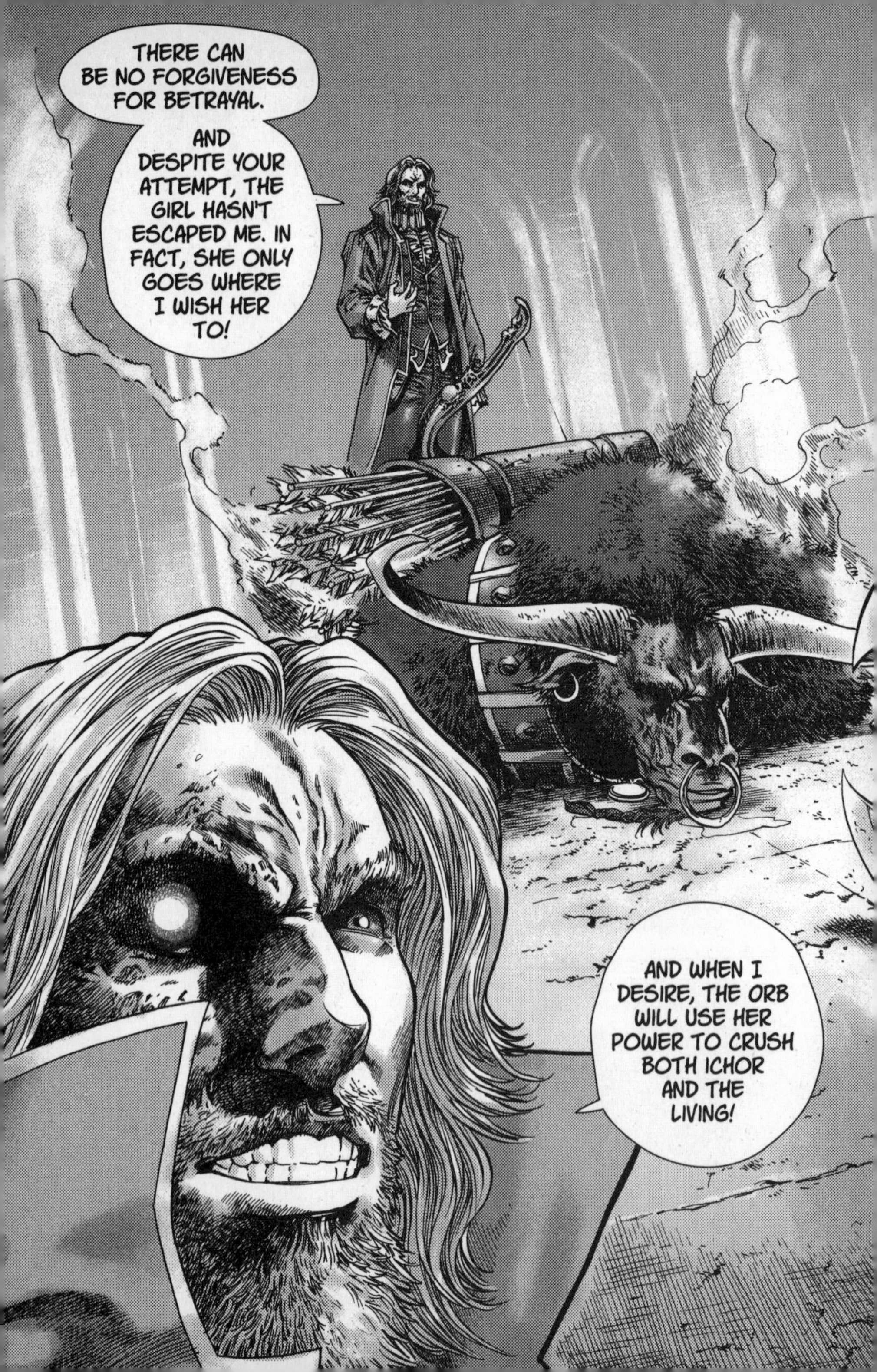
THERE CAN BE NO FORGIVENESS FOR BETRAYAL.
AND DESPITE YOUR ATTEMPT, THE GIRL HASN'T ESCAPED ME. IN FACT, SHE ONLY GOES WHERE I WISH HER TO!
AND WHEN I DESIRE, THE ORB WILL USE HER POWER TO CRUSH BOTH ICHOR AND THE LIVING!

CHAPTER SIX

Death on the Mountain

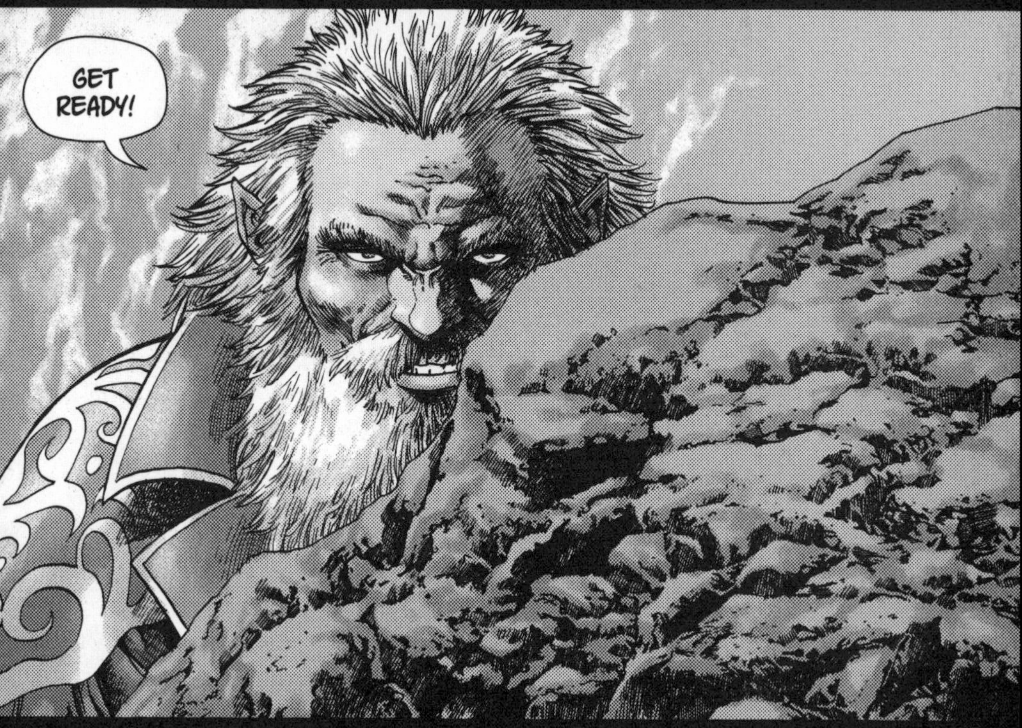
GET READY!

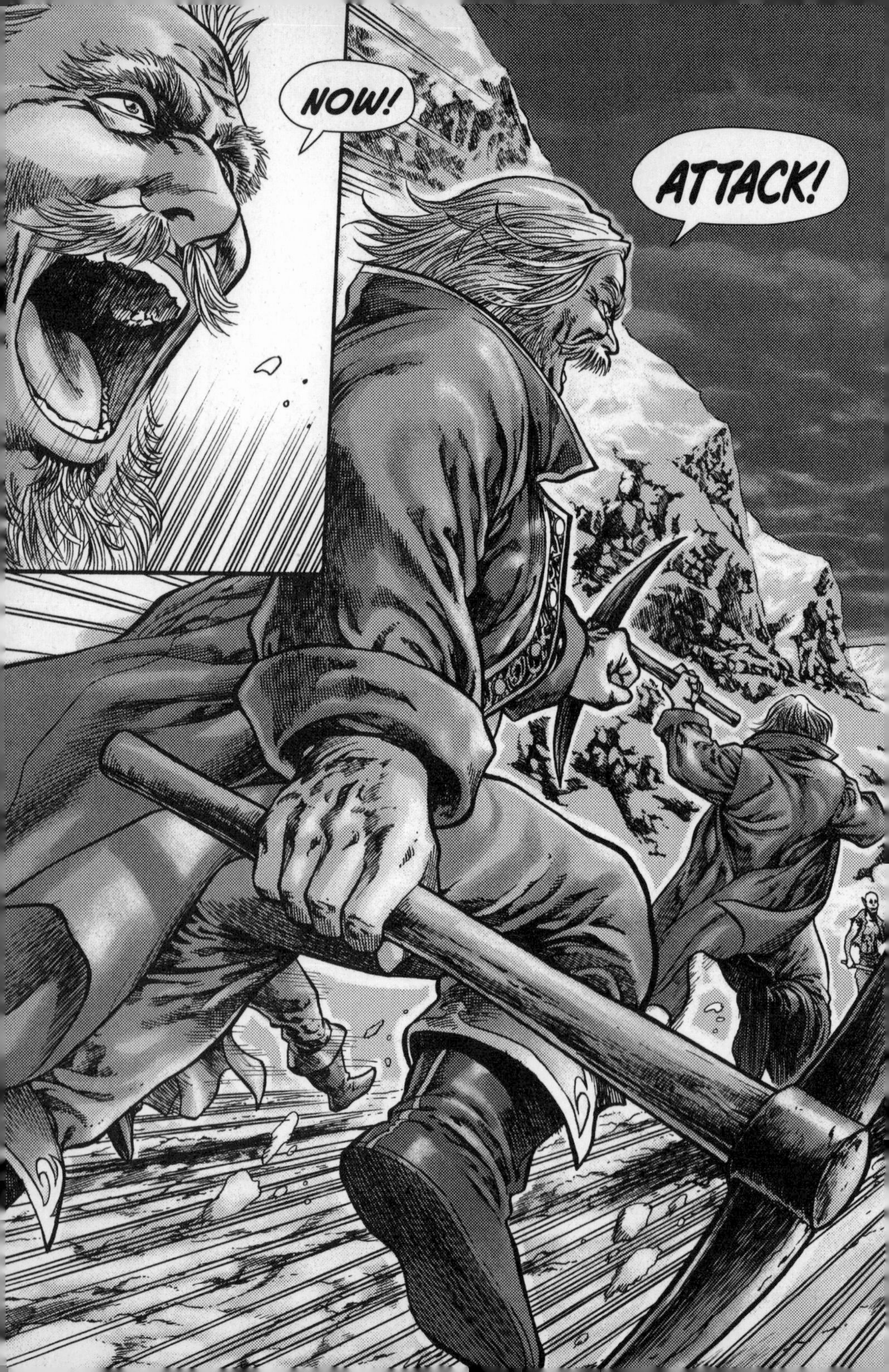
NOW!
ATTACK!

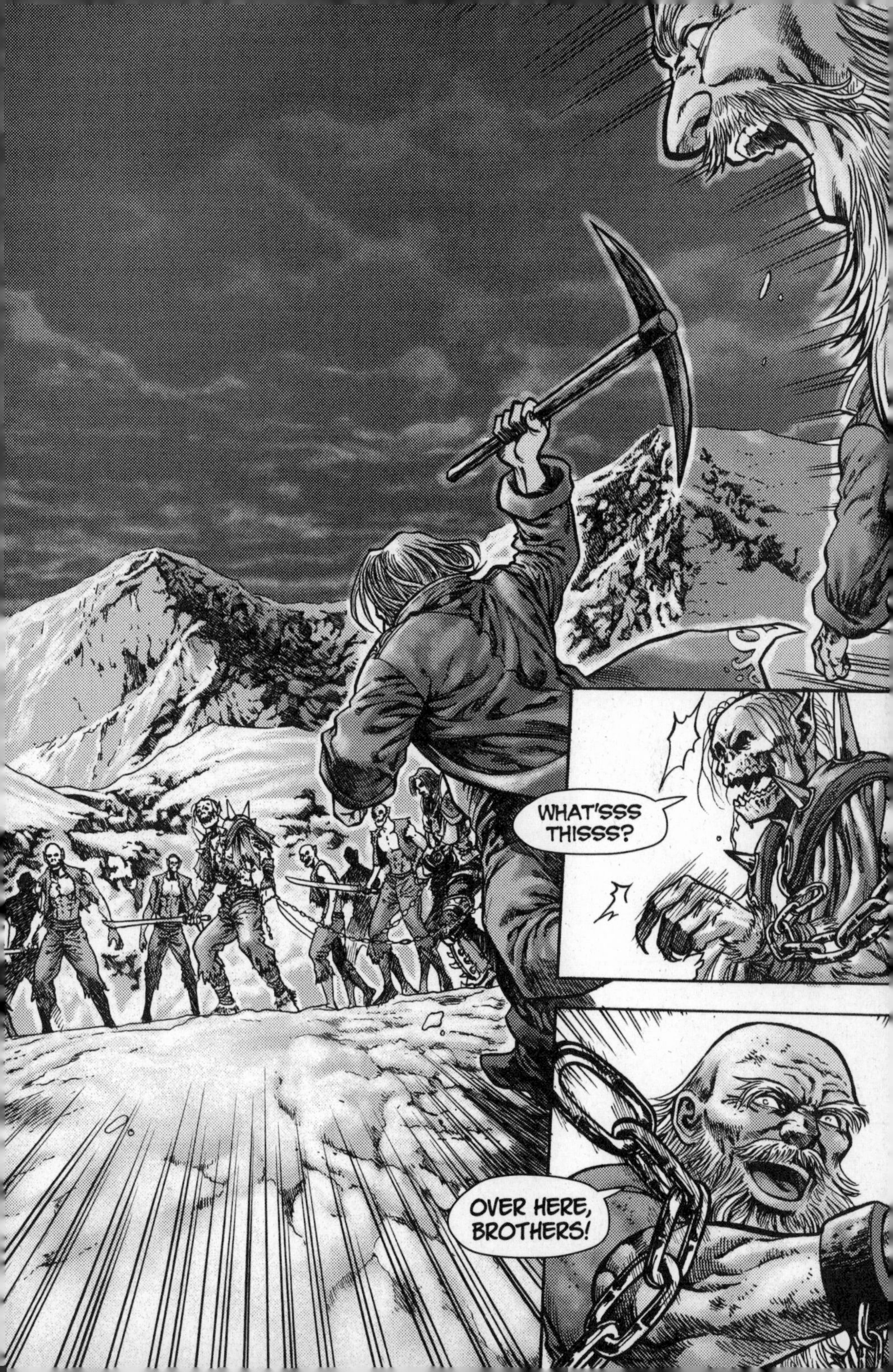
WHAT'SSS THISSS?
OVER HERE, BROTHERS!

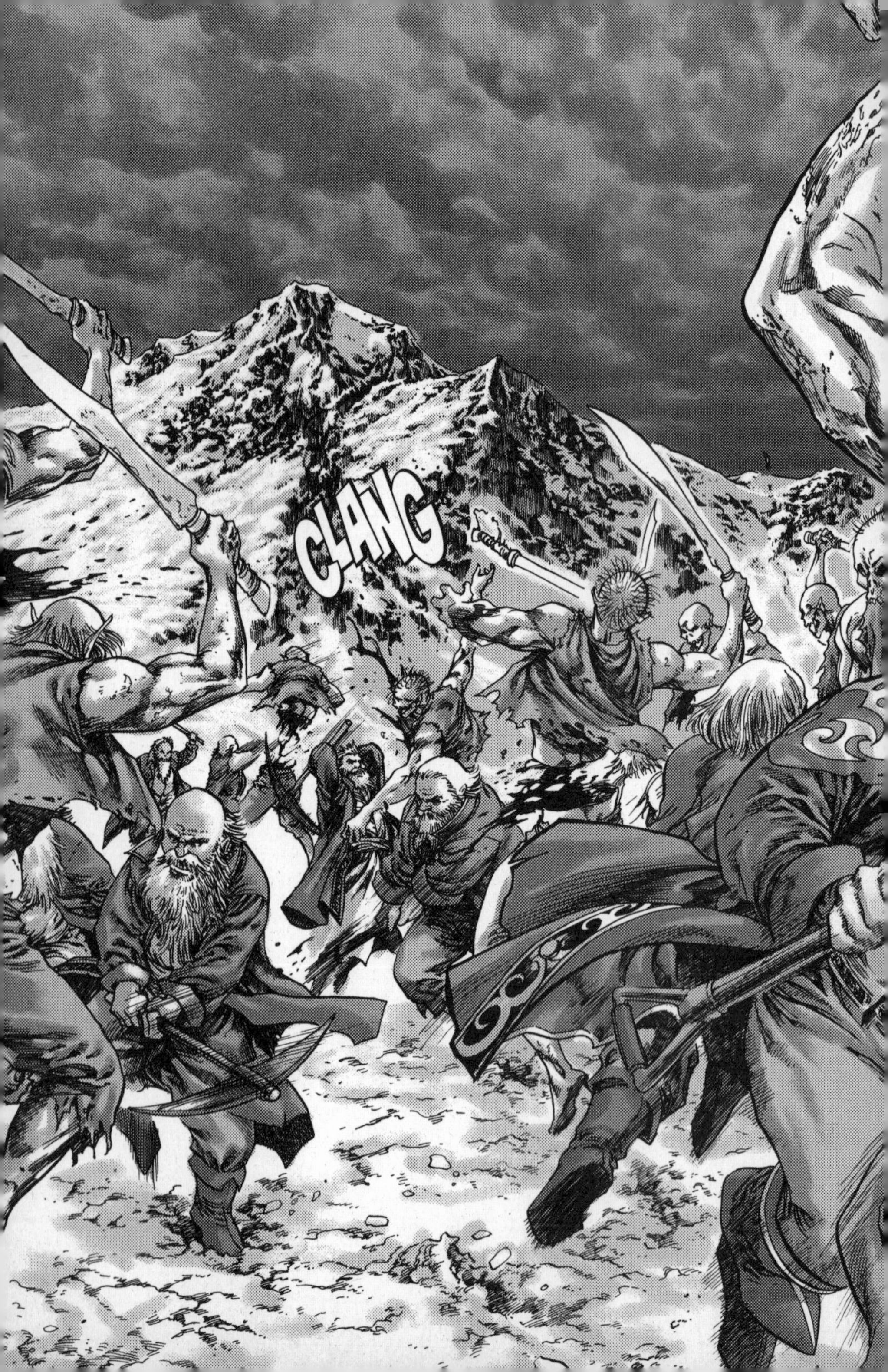
CLANG

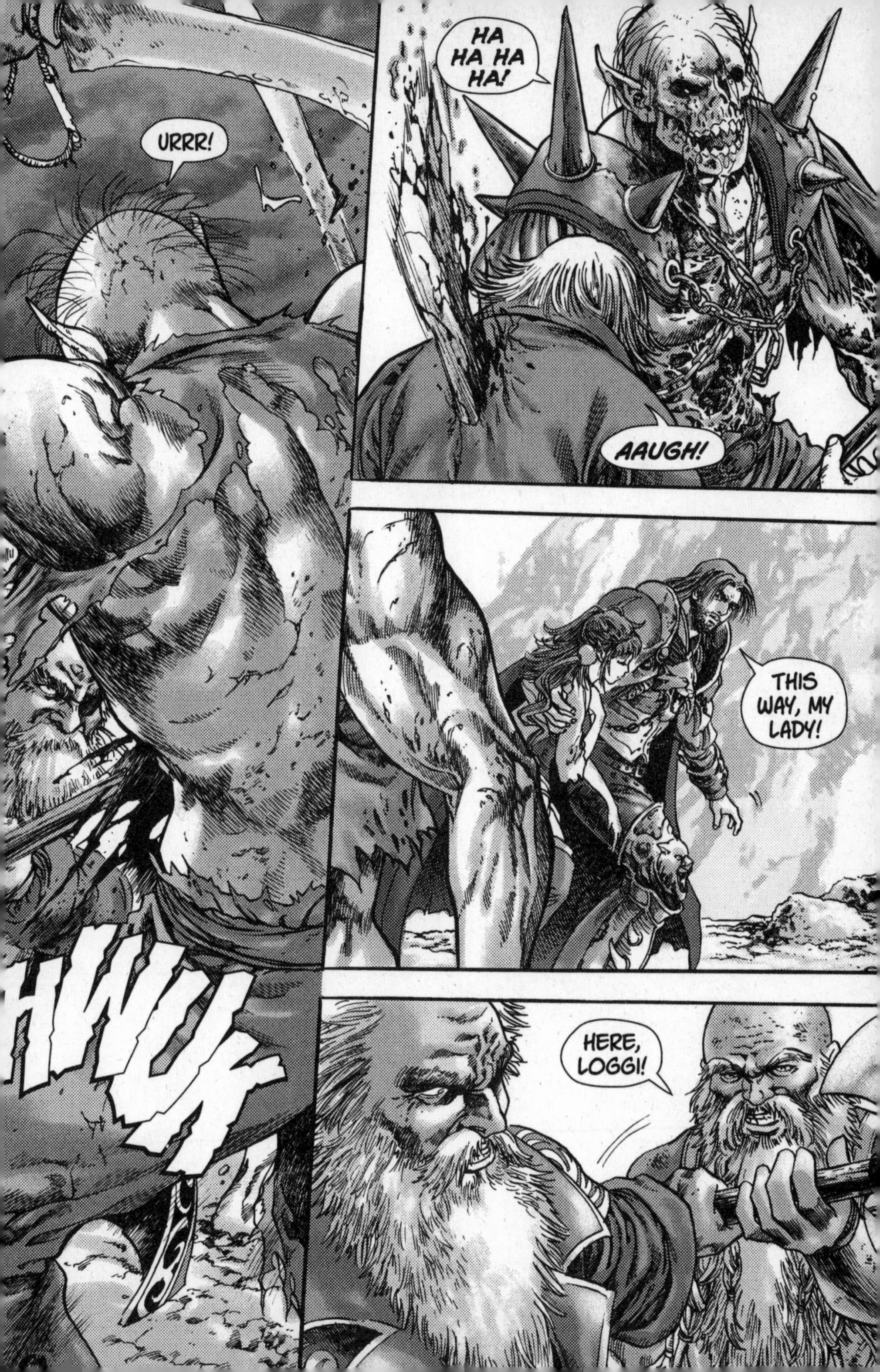
URRR!
HWUK
HA HA HA HA!
AAUGH!
THIS WAY, MY LADY!
HERE, LOGGI!

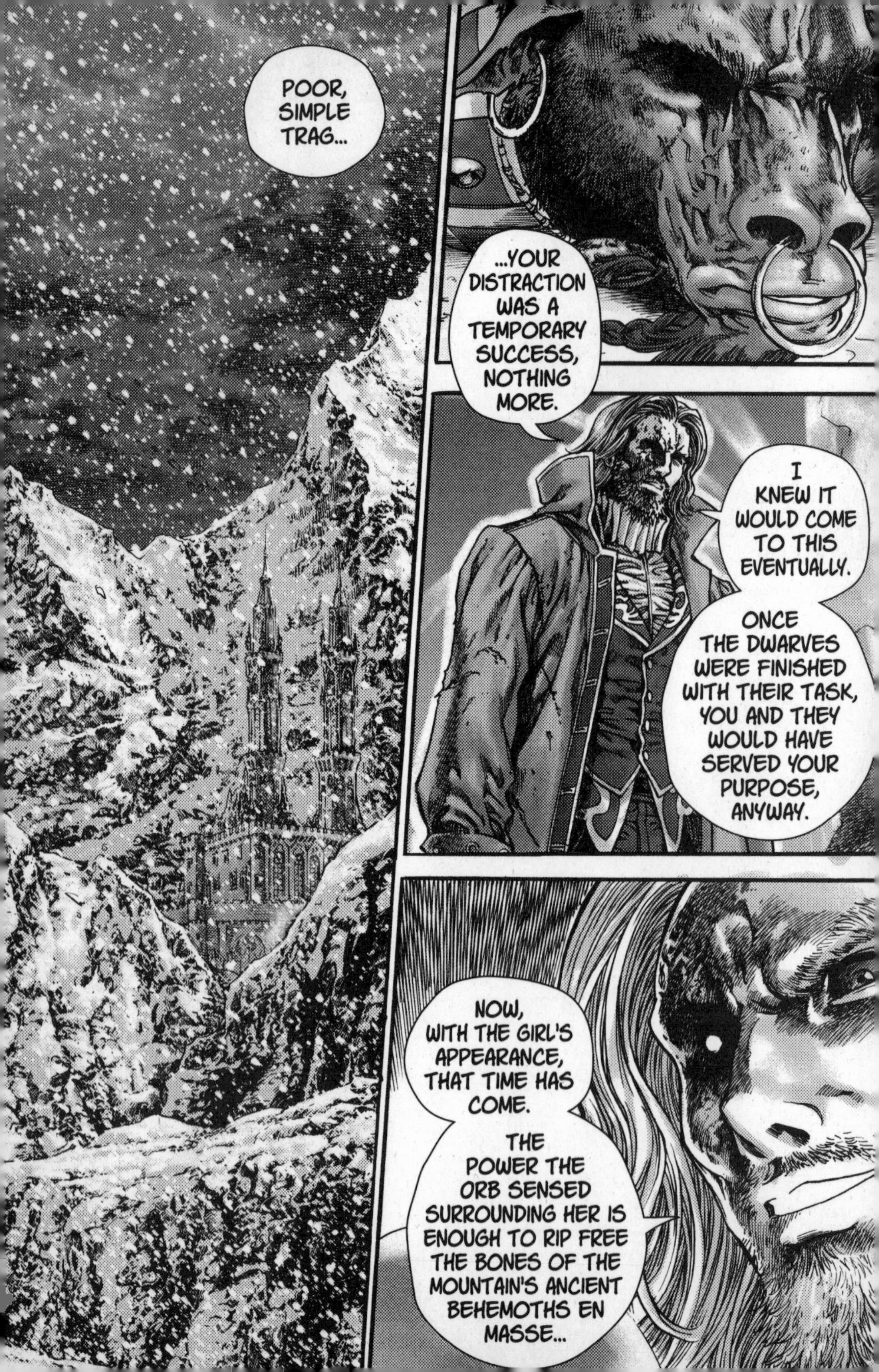
POOR, SIMPLE TRAG...
...YOUR DISTRACTION WAS A TEMPORARY SUCCESS, NOTHING MORE.
I KNEW IT WOULD COME TO THIS EVENTUALLY.
ONCE THE DWARVES WERE FINISHED WITH THEIR TASK, YOU AND THEY WOULD HAVE SERVED YOUR PURPOSE, ANYWAY.
NOW, WITH THE GIRL'S APPEARANCE, THAT TIME HAS COME.
THE POWER THE ORB SENSED SURROUNDING HER IS ENOUGH TO RIP FREE THE BONES OF THE MOUNTAIN'S ANCIENT BEHEMOTHS EN MASSE...

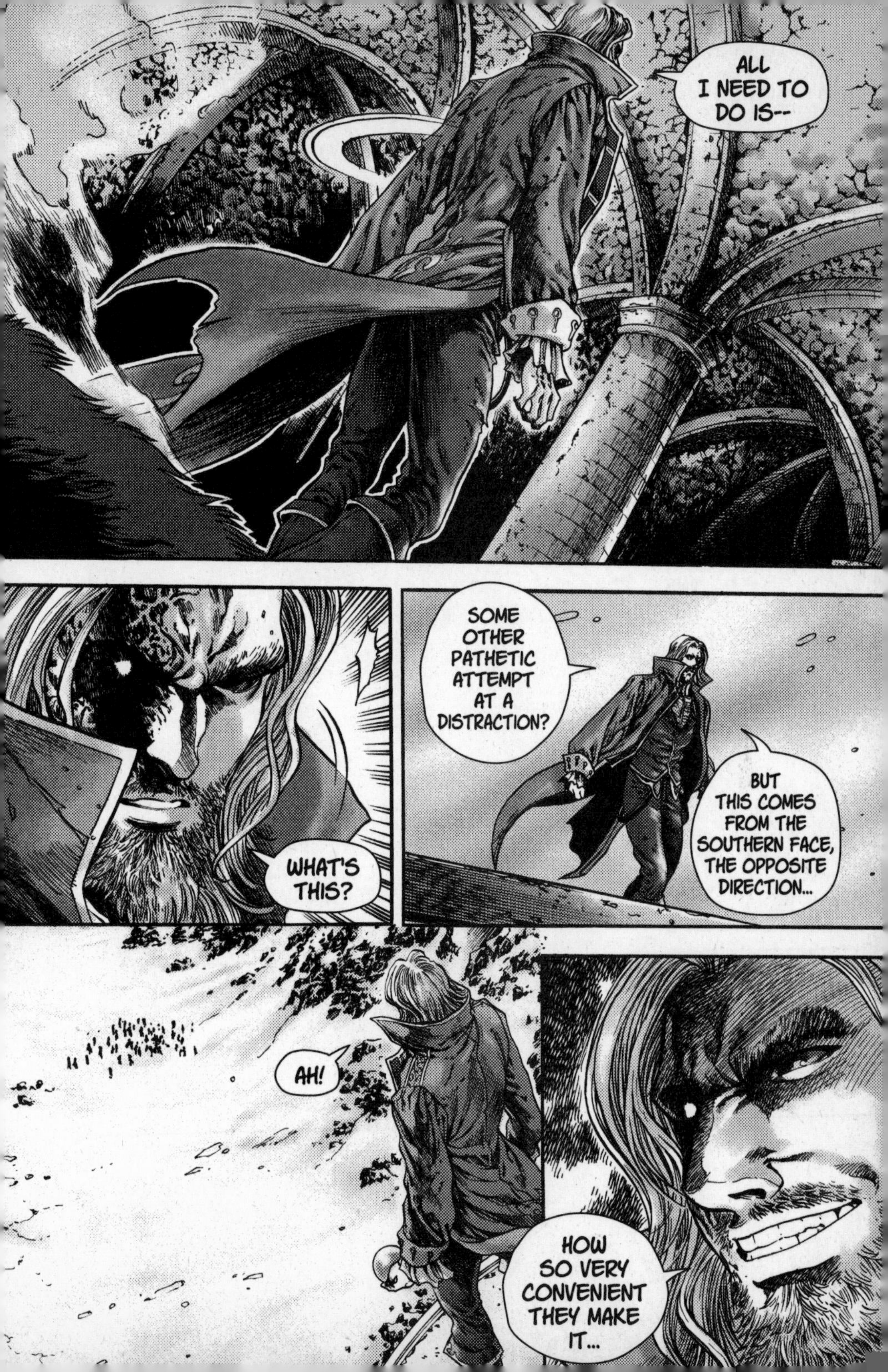
ALL I NEED TO DO IS--
WHAT'S THIS?
SOME OTHER PATHETIC ATTEMPT AT A DISTRACTION?
BUT THIS COMES FROM THE SOUTHERN FACE, THE OPPOSITE DIRECTION...
AH!
HOW SO VERY CONVENIENT THEY MAKE IT...

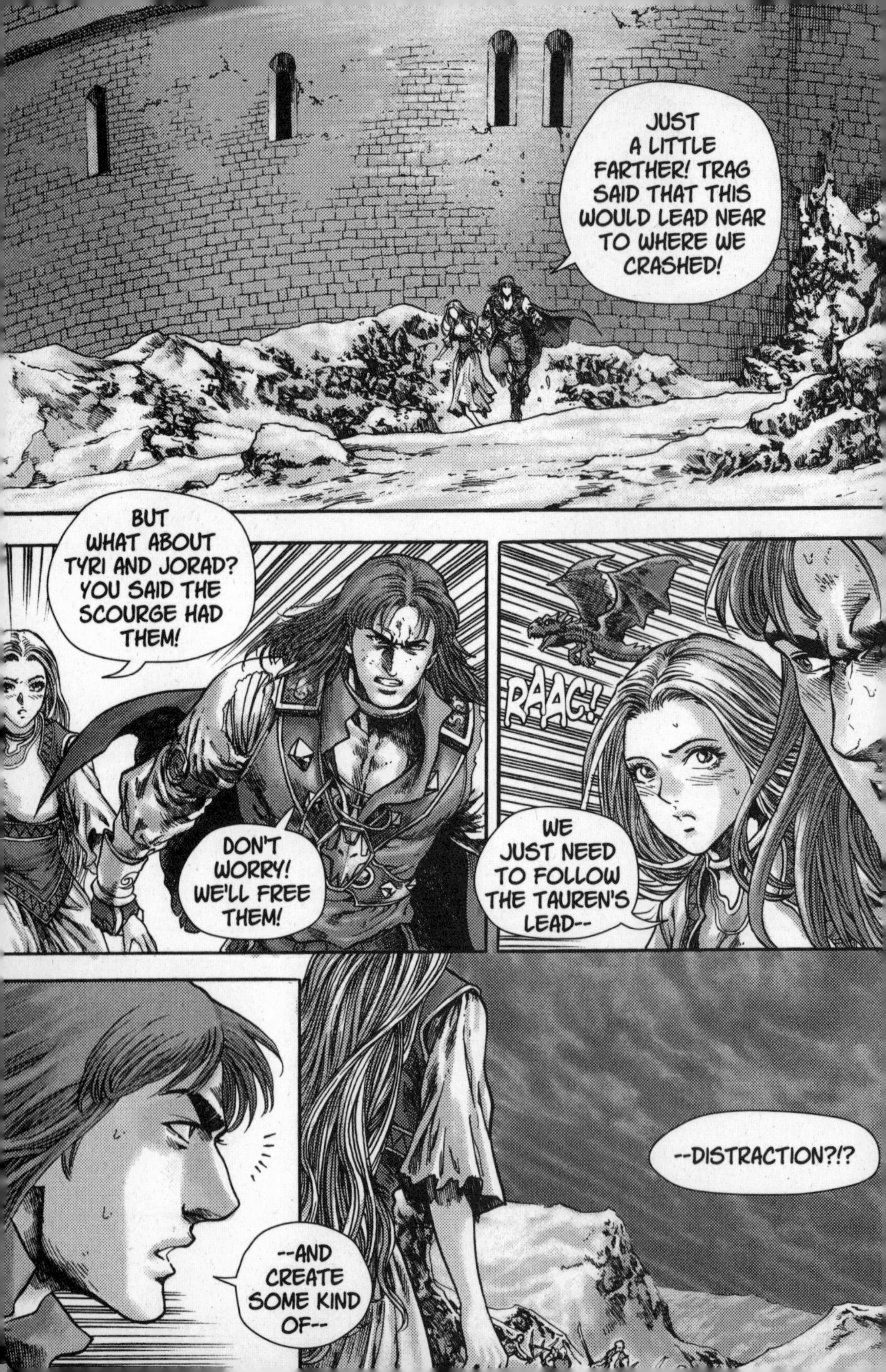
JUST A LITTLE FARTHER! TRAG SAID THAT THIS WOULD LEAD NEAR TO WHERE WE CRASHED!
BUT WHAT ABOUT TYRI AND JORAD? YOU SAID THE SCOURGE HAD THEM!
DON'T WORRY! WE'LL FREE THEM!
RAAC!
WE JUST NEED TO FOLLOW THE TAUREN'S LEAD--
--AND CREATE SOME KIND OF--
--DISTRACTION?!?

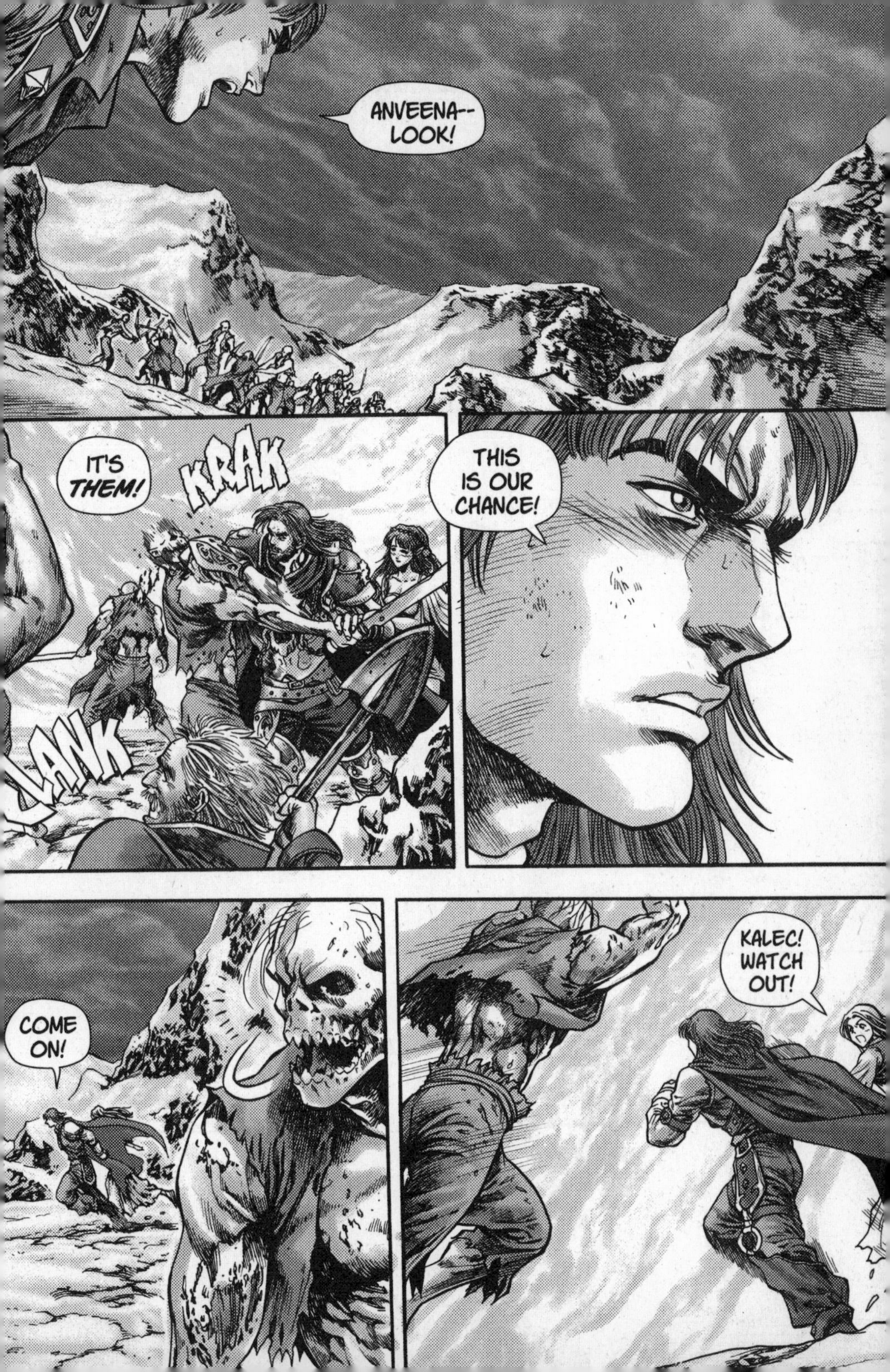

ANVEENA-- LOOK!
IT'S THEM!
KRAK
LANK
THIS IS OUR CHANCE!
COME ON!
KALEC! WATCH OUT!

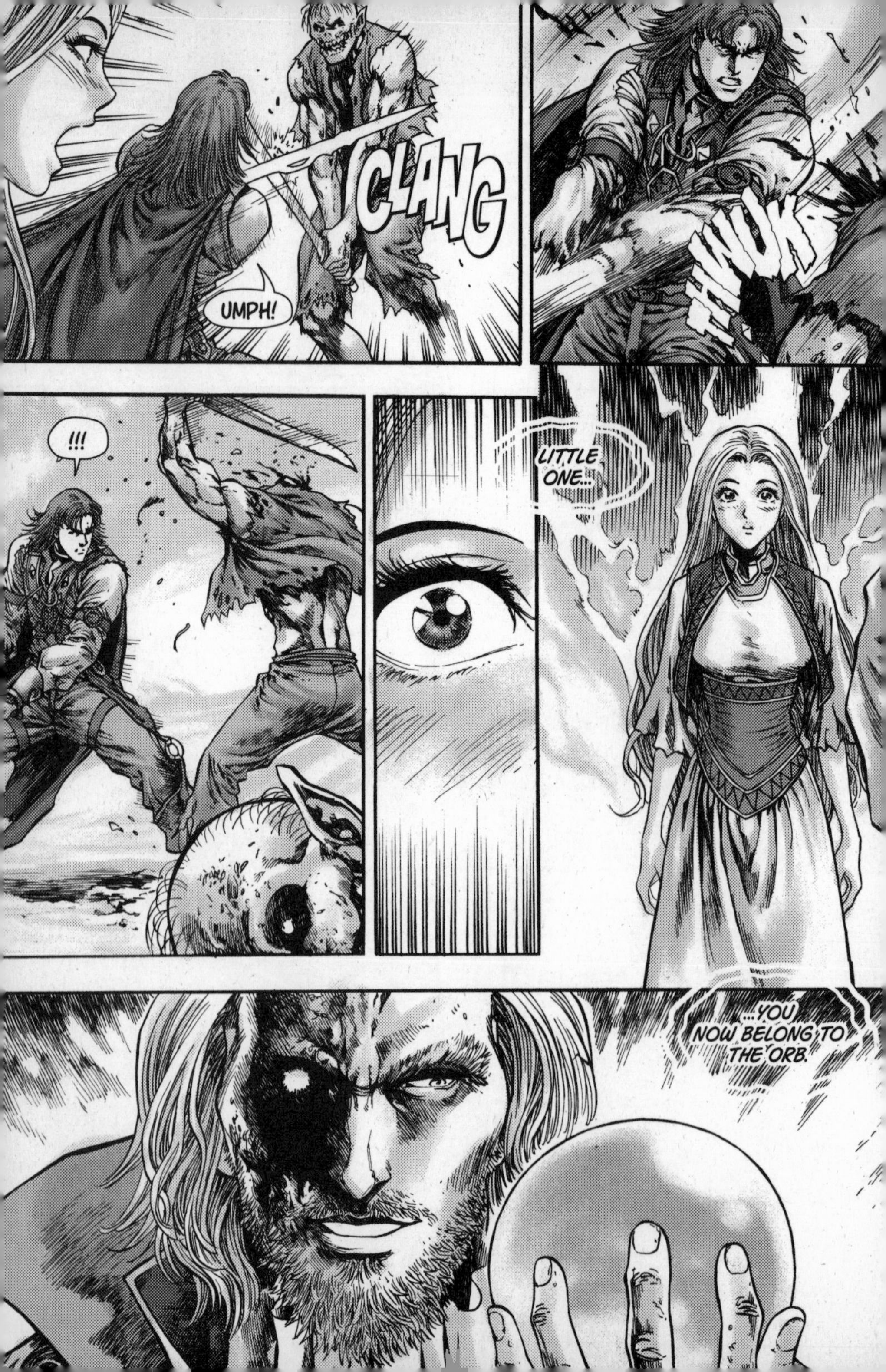
CLANG
UMPH!
THUNK
!!!
LITTLE ONE...
...YOU NOW BELONG TO THE ORB.

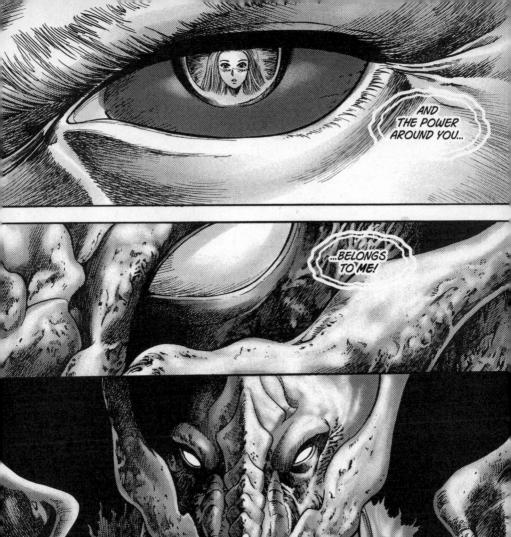

AND THE POWER AROUND YOU...

...BELONGS TO ME!

HISSSSSSAAA

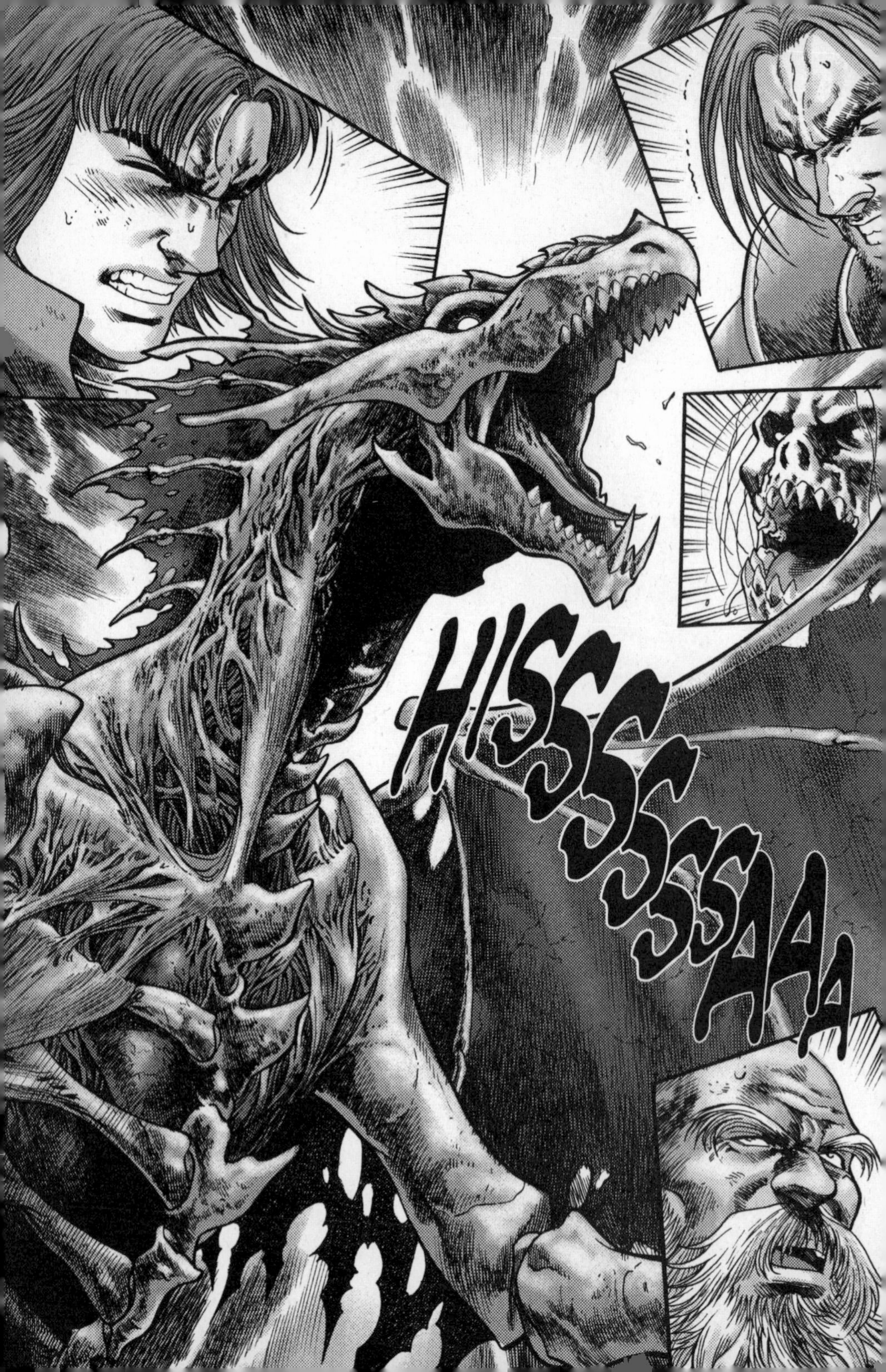
HISSSSSSAAAA

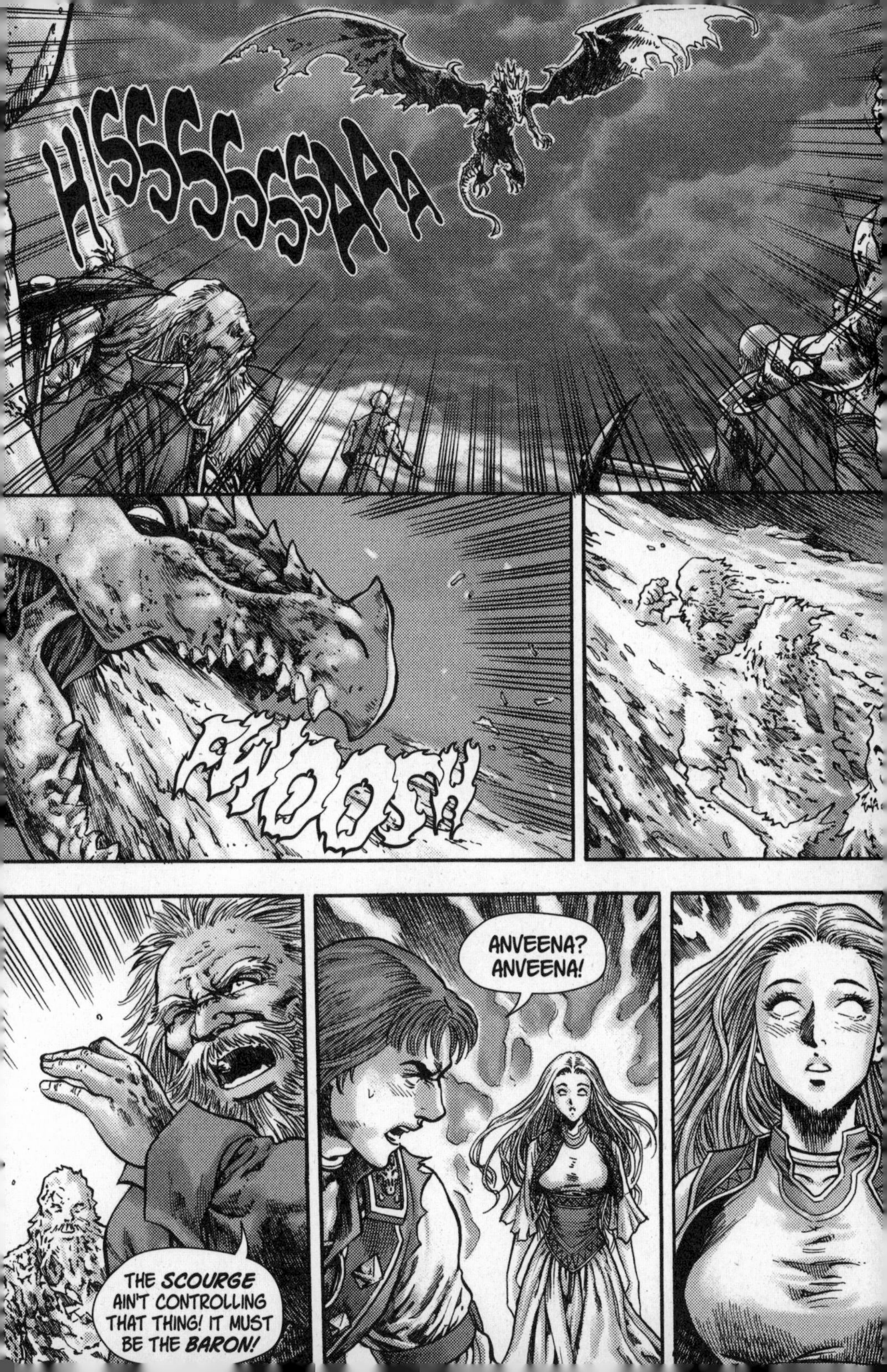
HISSSSSSAAA
FWOOSH
THE SCOURGE AIN'T CONTROLLING THAT THING! IT MUST BE THE BARON!
ANVEENA? ANVEENA!

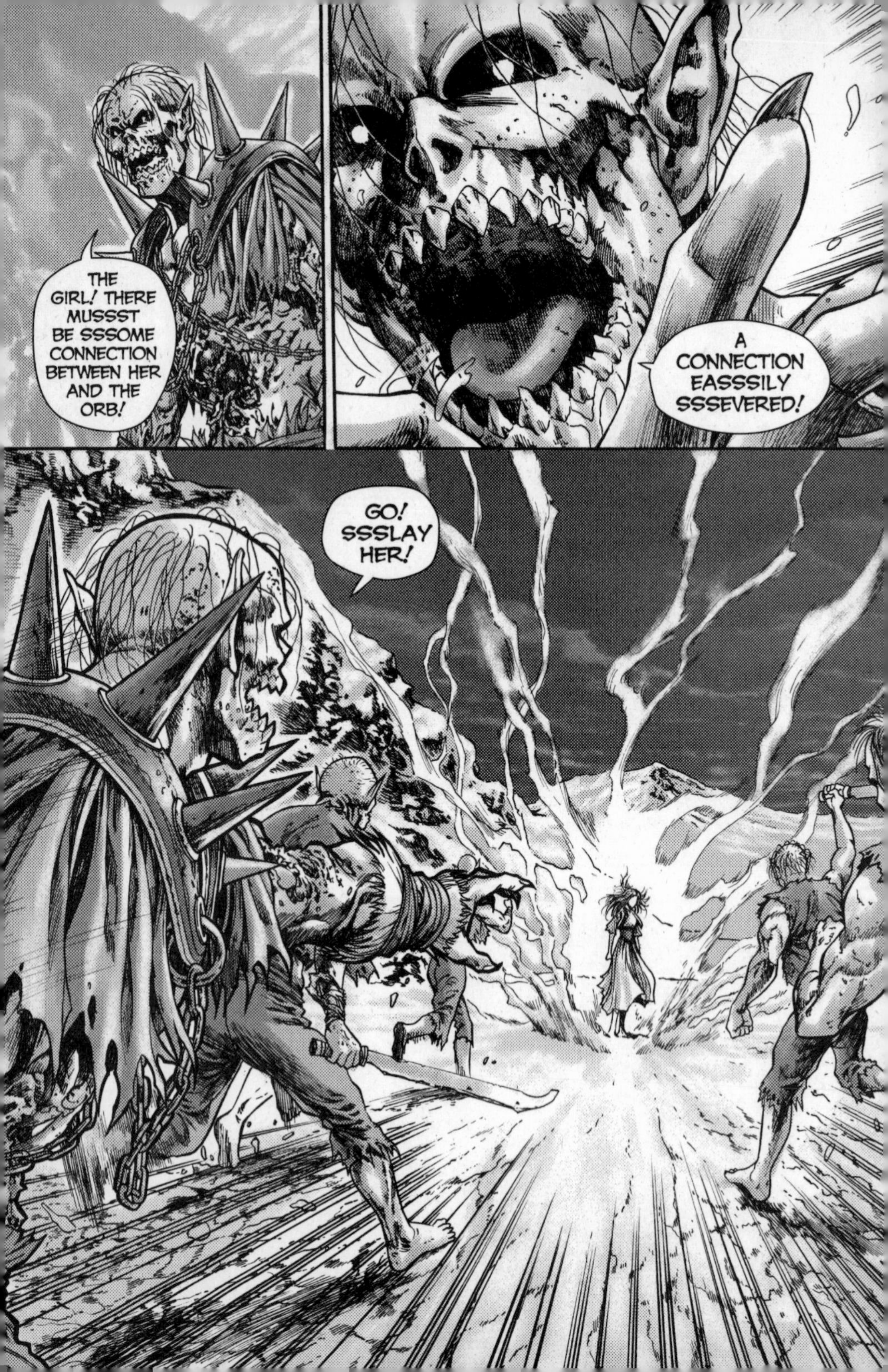
THE GIRL! THERE MUSSST BE SSSOME CONNECTION BETWEEN HER AND THE ORB!
A CONNECTION EASSSILY SSSEVERED!
GO! SSSLAY HER!

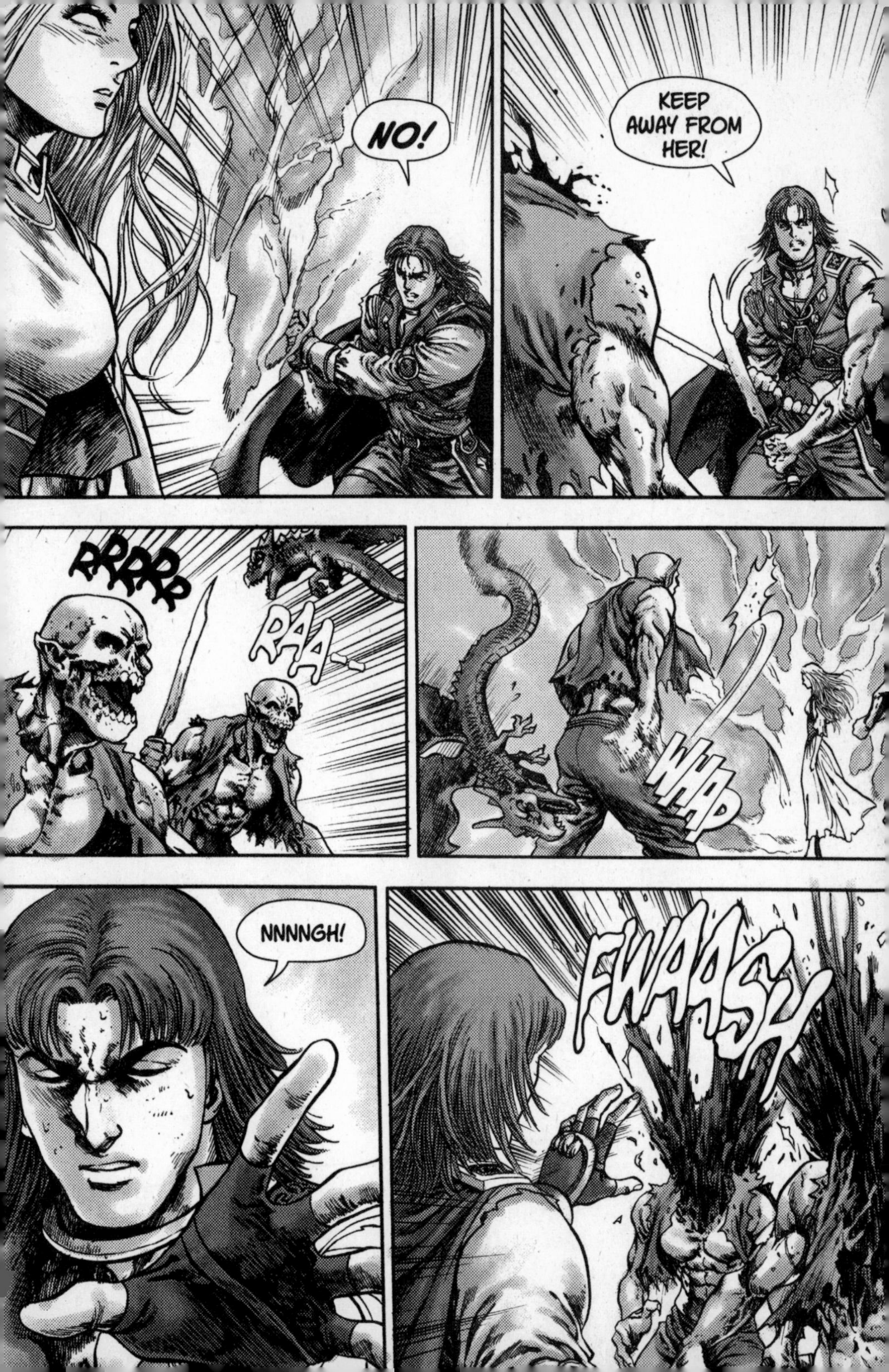
NO!
KEEP AWAY FROM HER!
RRRRR
RAA--
WHAP
NNNNGH!
FWAASH

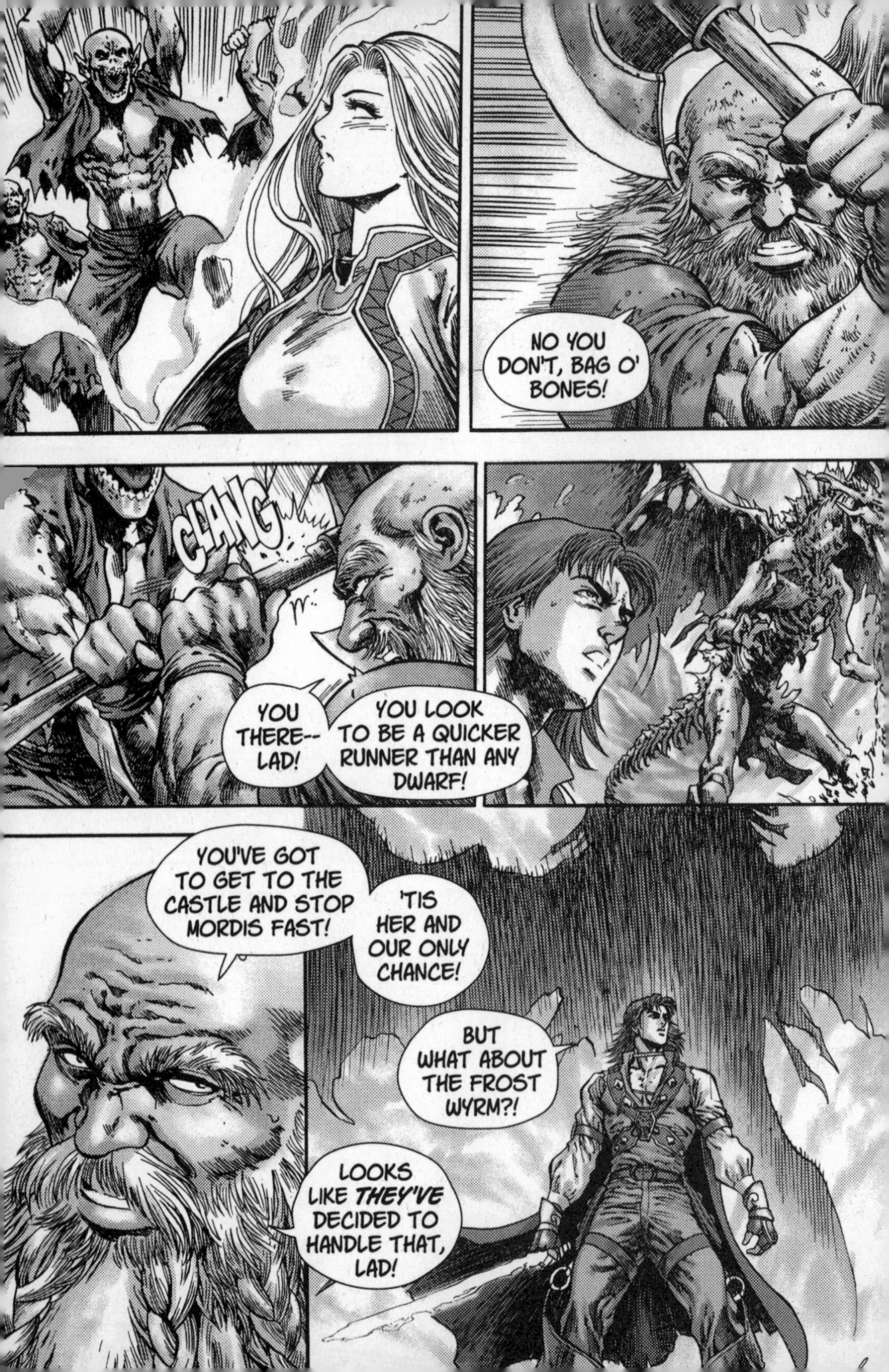
NO YOU DON'T, BAG O' BONES!
CLANG
YOU THERE-- LAD!
YOU LOOK TO BE A QUICKER RUNNER THAN ANY DWARF!
YOU'VE GOT TO GET TO THE CASTLE AND STOP MORDIS FAST!
'TIS HER AND OUR ONLY CHANCE!
BUT WHAT ABOUT THE FROST WYRM?!
LOOKS LIKE *THEY'VE* DECIDED TO HANDLE THAT, LAD!

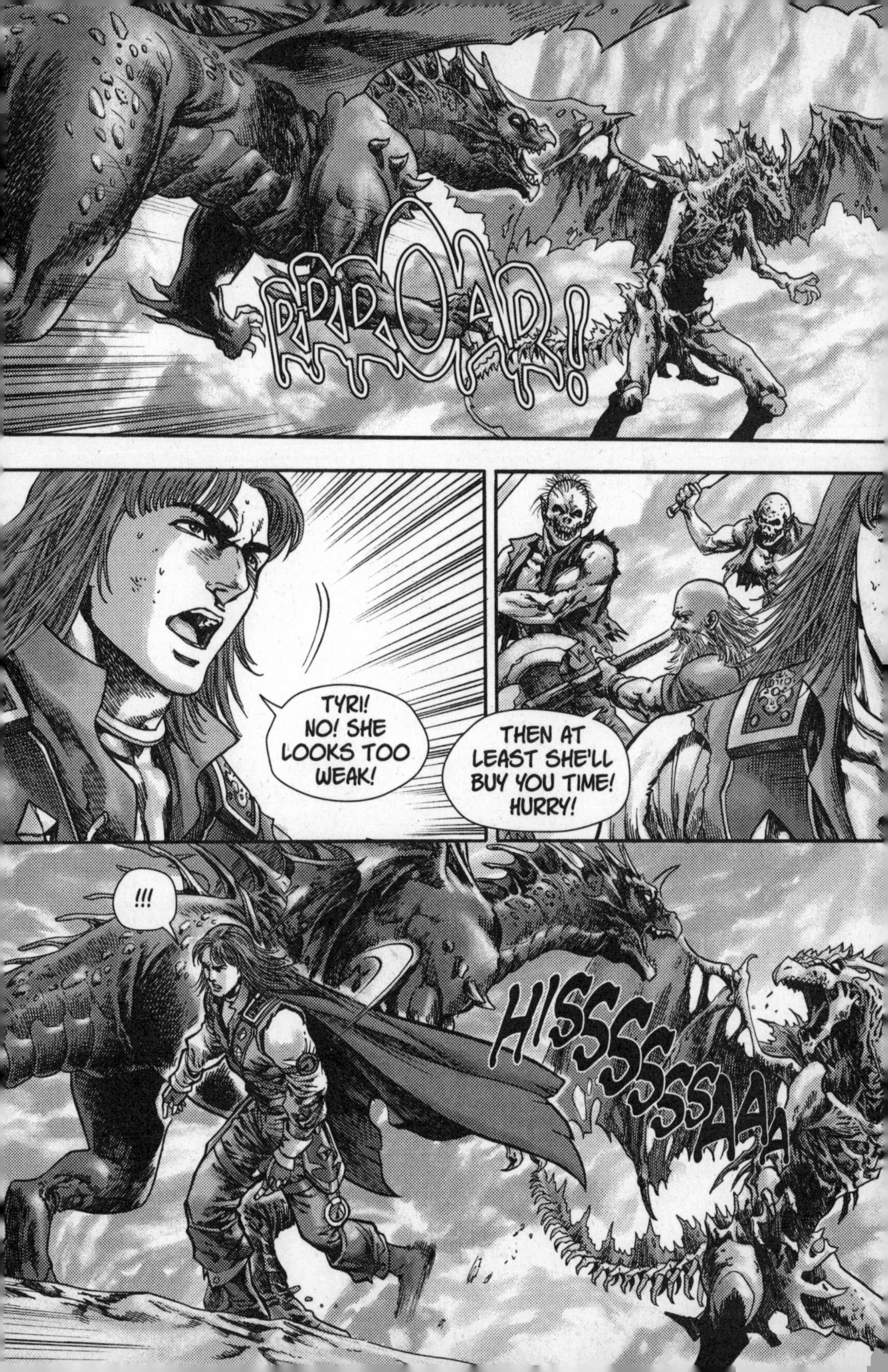
RRRROAR!
TYRI! NO! SHE LOOKS TOO WEAK!
THEN AT LEAST SHE'LL BUY YOU TIME! HURRY!
!!!
HISSSSSSAAA

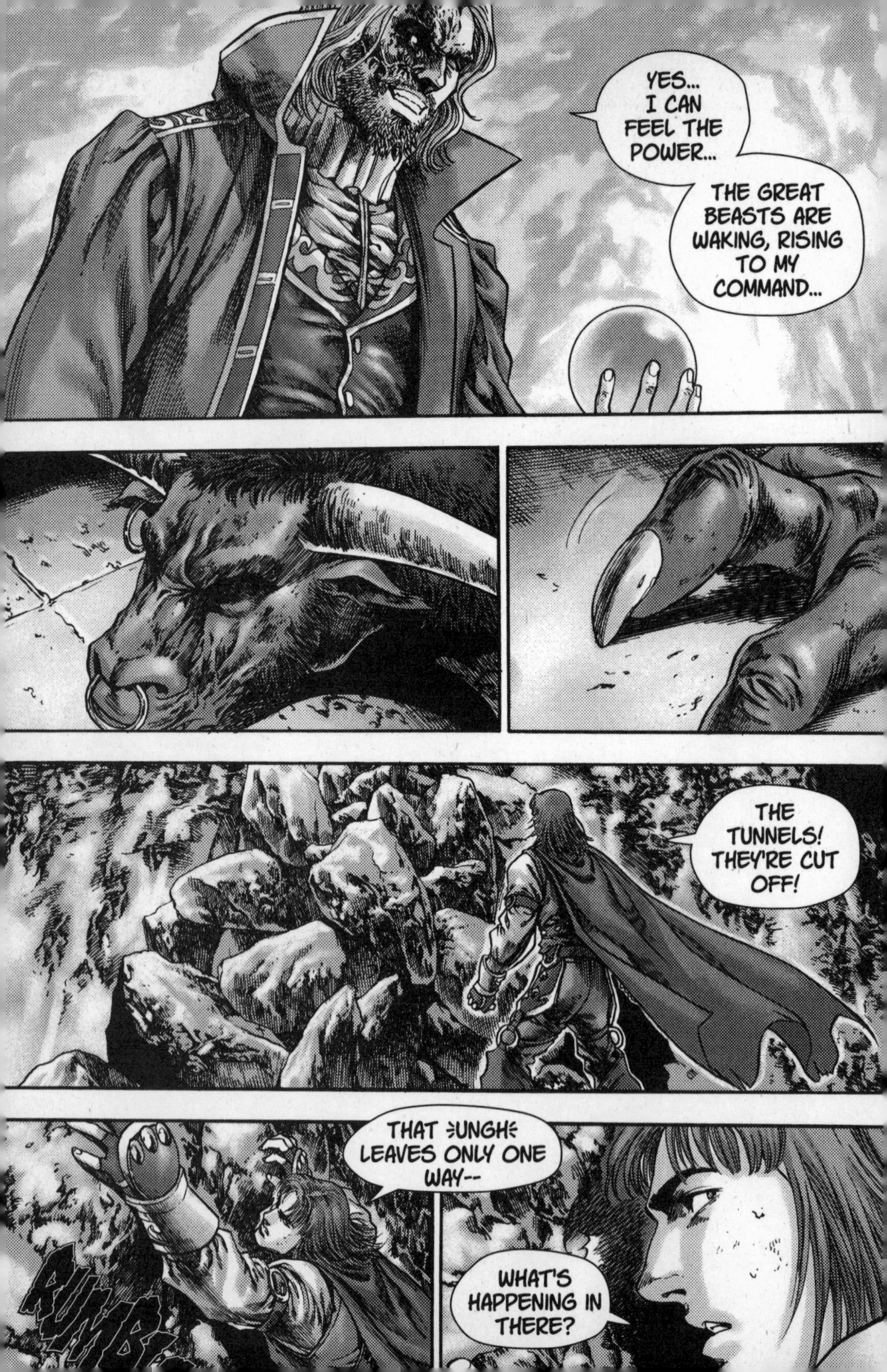
YES... I CAN FEEL THE POWER...
THE GREAT BEASTS ARE WAKING, RISING TO MY COMMAND...
THE TUNNELS! THEY'RE CUT OFF!
WHAT'S HAPPENING IN THERE?
THAT ≈UNGH≈ LEAVES ONLY ONE WAY--
RUMB

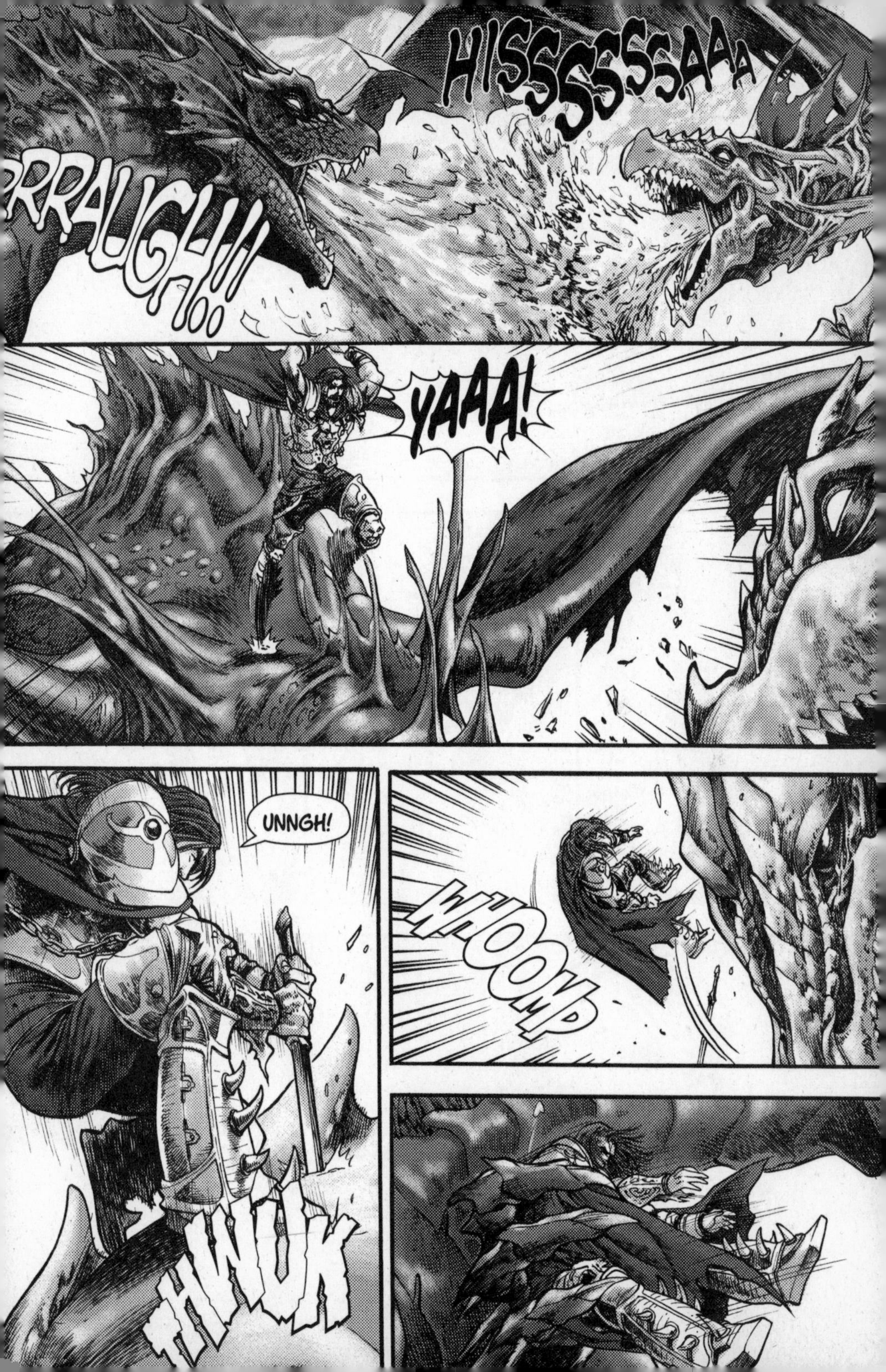

RRRAUGH!!!
HISSSSSSAAA
YAAA!
UNNGH!
THWUK
WHOOMP

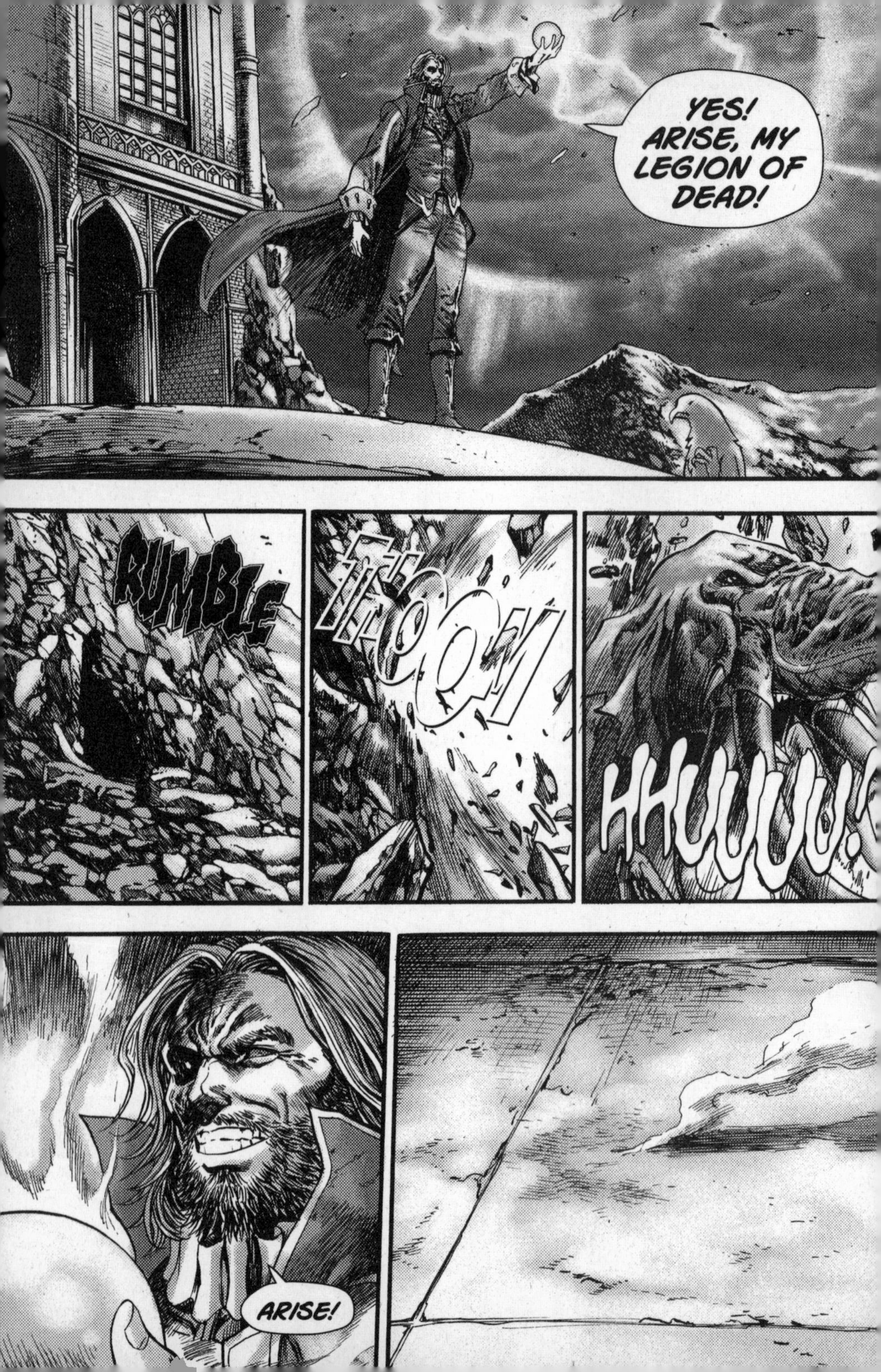
YES! ARISE, MY LEGION OF DEAD!
RUMBLE
HHUUUU!
ARISE!

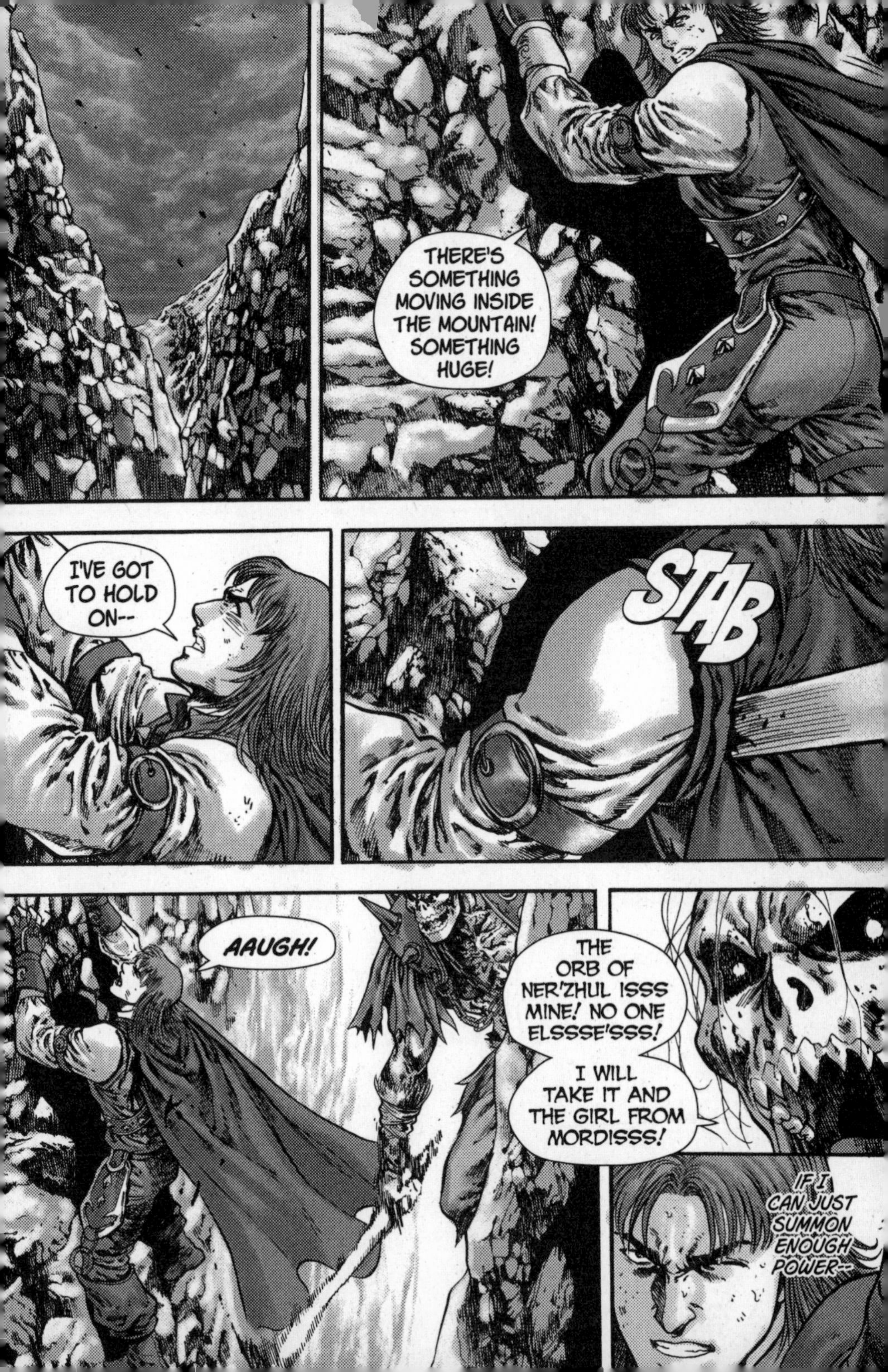
THERE'S SOMETHING MOVING INSIDE THE MOUNTAIN! SOMETHING HUGE!
I'VE GOT TO HOLD ON--
STAB
AAUGH!
THE ORB OF NER'ZHUL ISSS MINE! NO ONE ELSSSE'SSS!
I WILL TAKE IT AND THE GIRL FROM MORDISSS!
IF I CAN JUST SUMMON ENOUGH POWER--

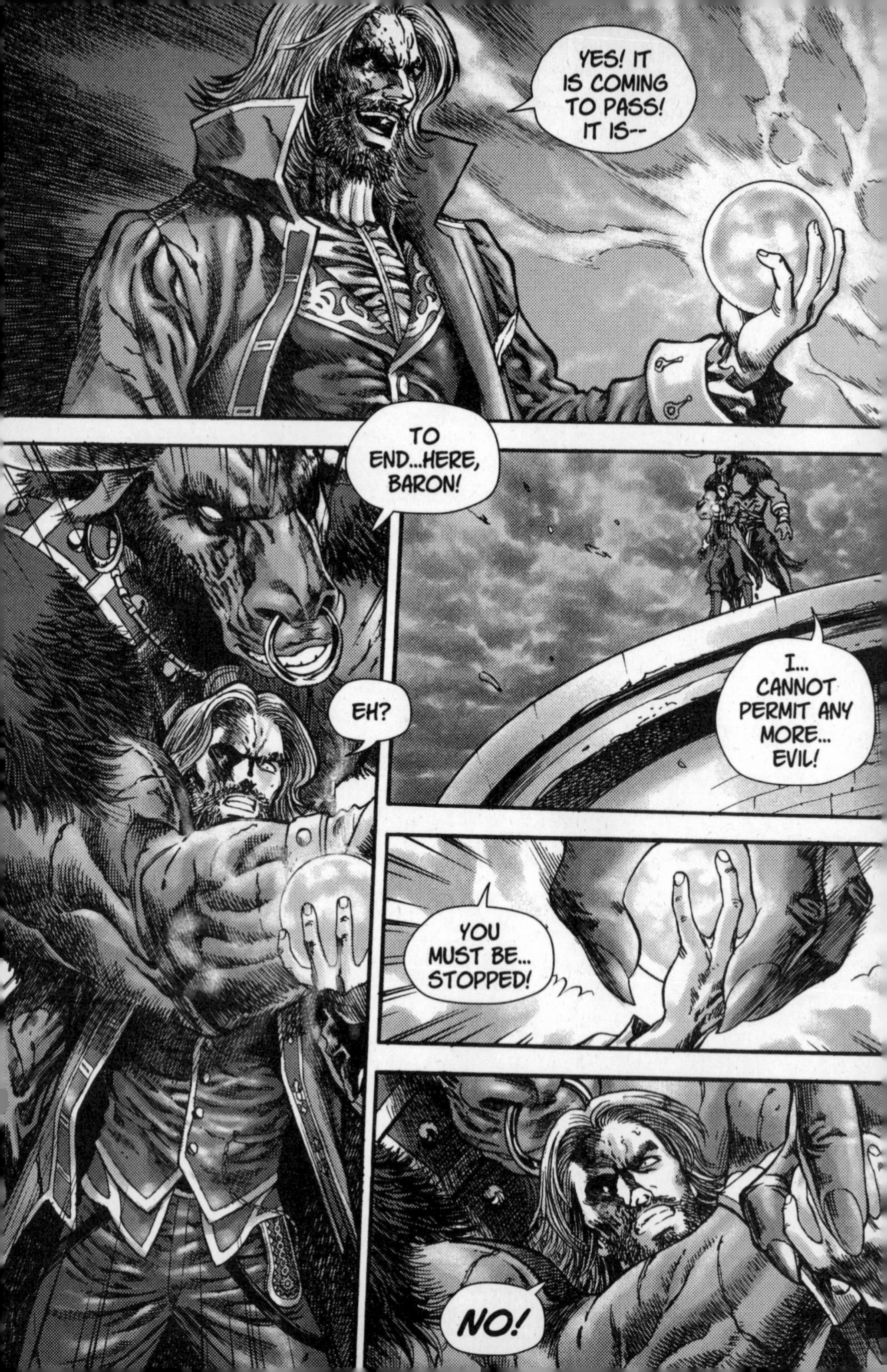
YES! IT IS COMING TO PASS! IT IS--
TO END...HERE, BARON!
EH?
I... CANNOT PERMIT ANY MORE... EVIL!
YOU MUST BE... STOPPED!
NO!

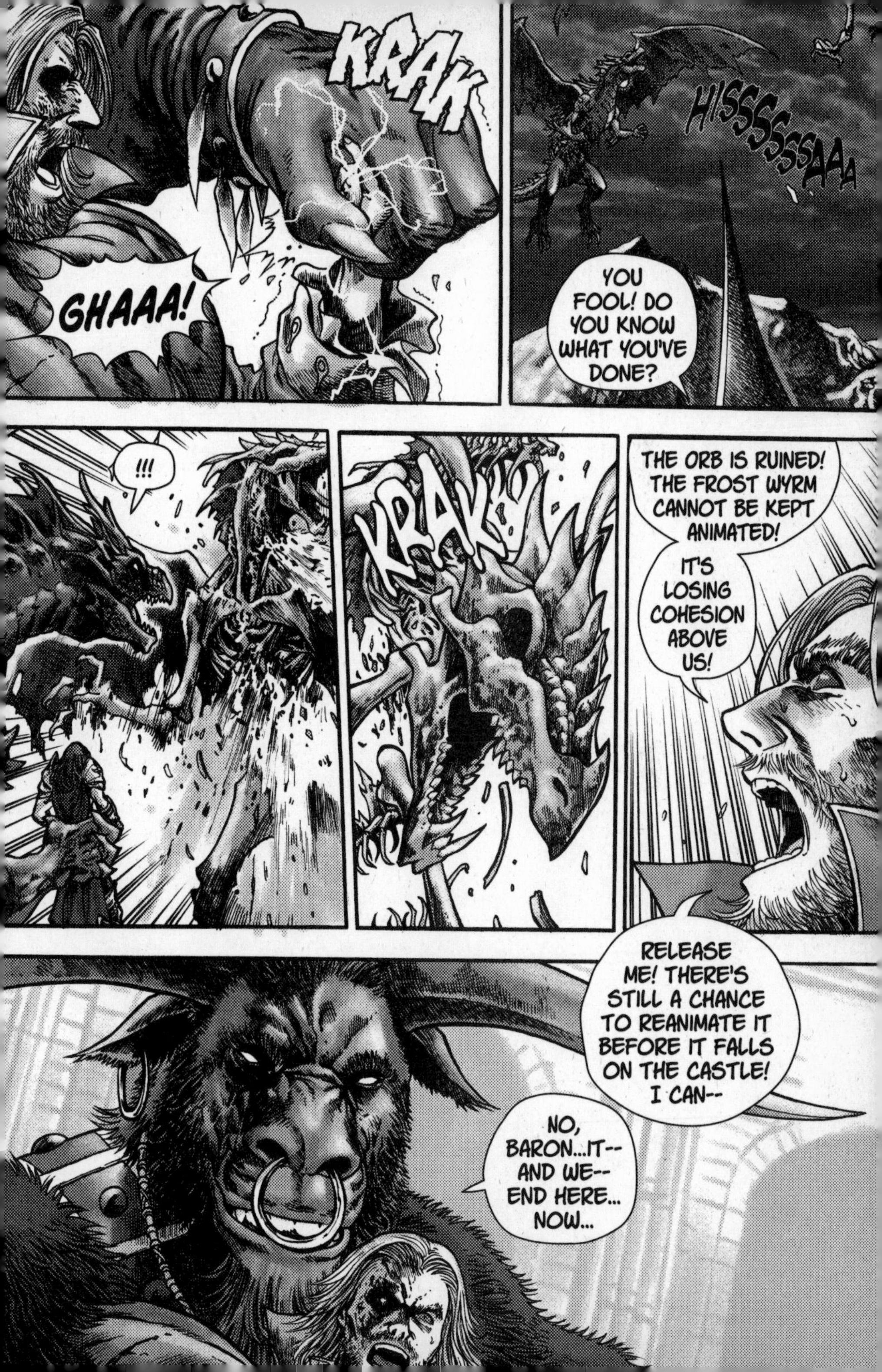
KRAK
GHAAA!
HISSSSSSSAAAA
YOU FOOL! DO YOU KNOW WHAT YOU'VE DONE?
!!!
KRAK
THE ORB IS RUINED! THE FROST WYRM CANNOT BE KEPT ANIMATED!
IT'S LOSING COHESION ABOVE US!
RELEASE ME! THERE'S STILL A CHANCE TO REANIMATE IT BEFORE IT FALLS ON THE CASTLE! I CAN--
NO, BARON...IT--AND WE--END HERE... NOW...

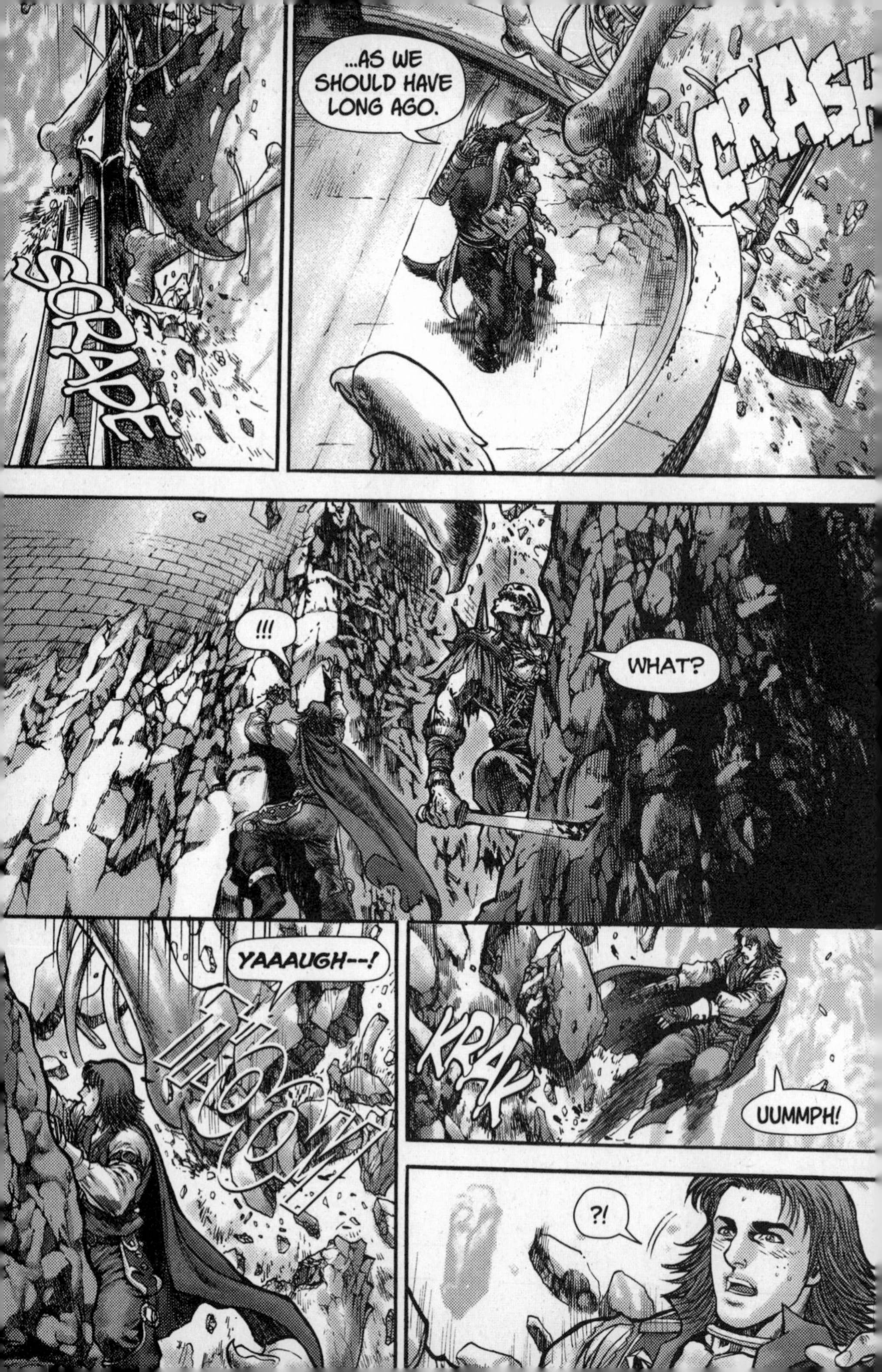
SCRAPE
...AS WE SHOULD HAVE LONG AGO.
CRASH
!!!
WHAT?
YAAAUGH--!
THOOM
KRAK
UUMMPH!
?!

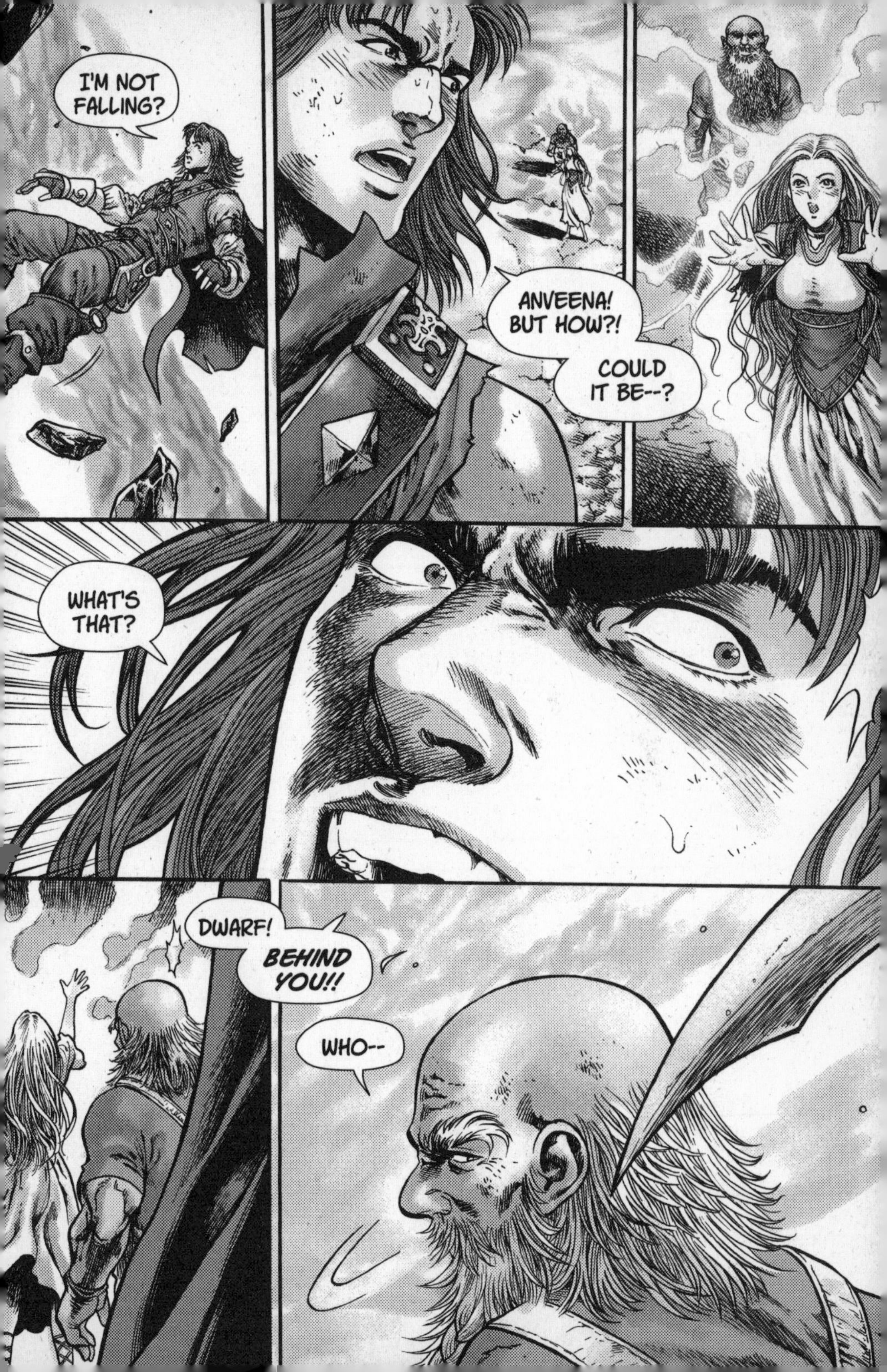
I'M NOT FALLING?
ANVEENA! BUT HOW?!
COULD IT BE--?
WHAT'S THAT?
DWARF! *BEHIND YOU!!*
WHO--

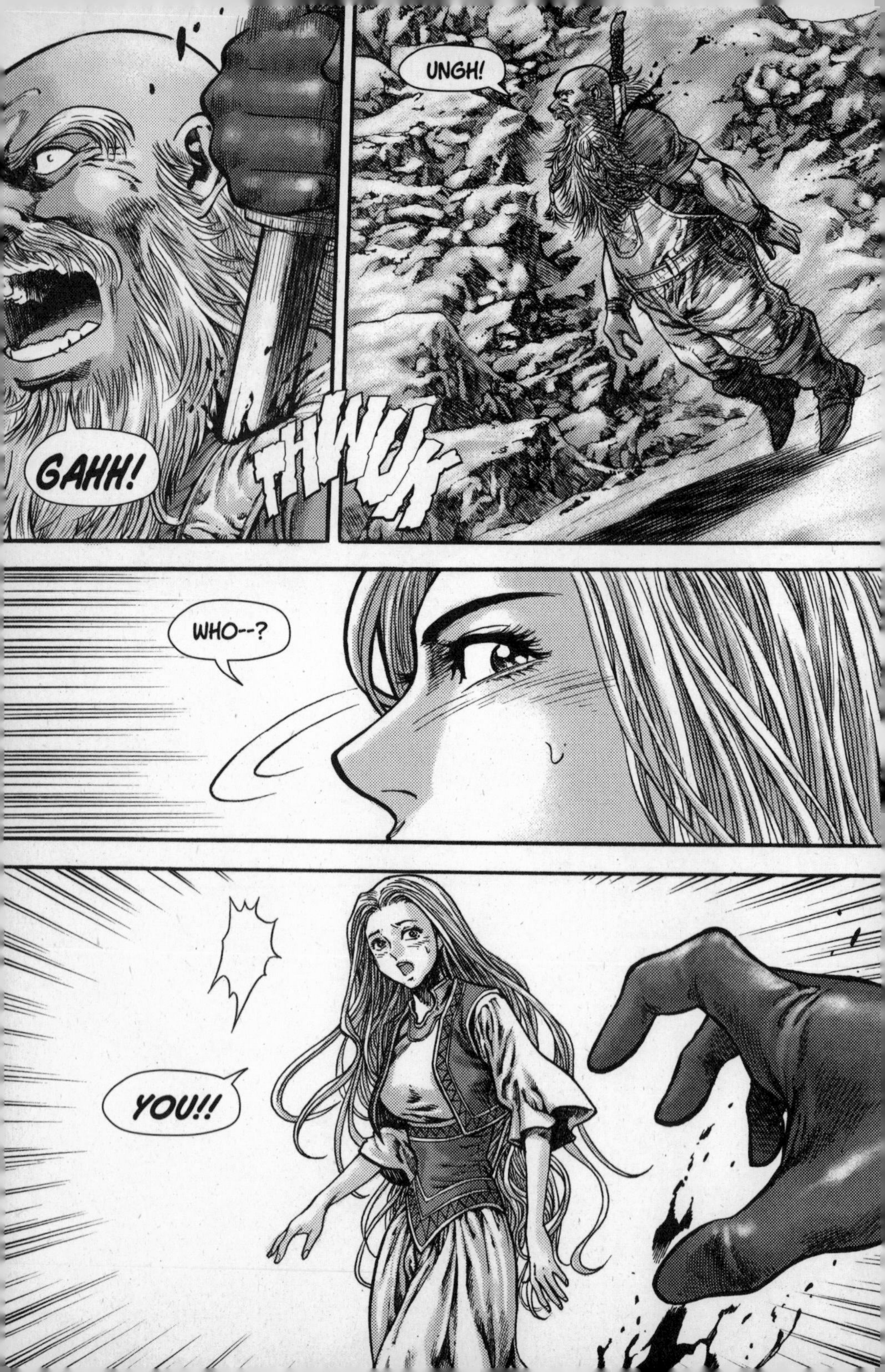
GAHH!
THWUK
UNGH!
WHO--?
YOU!!

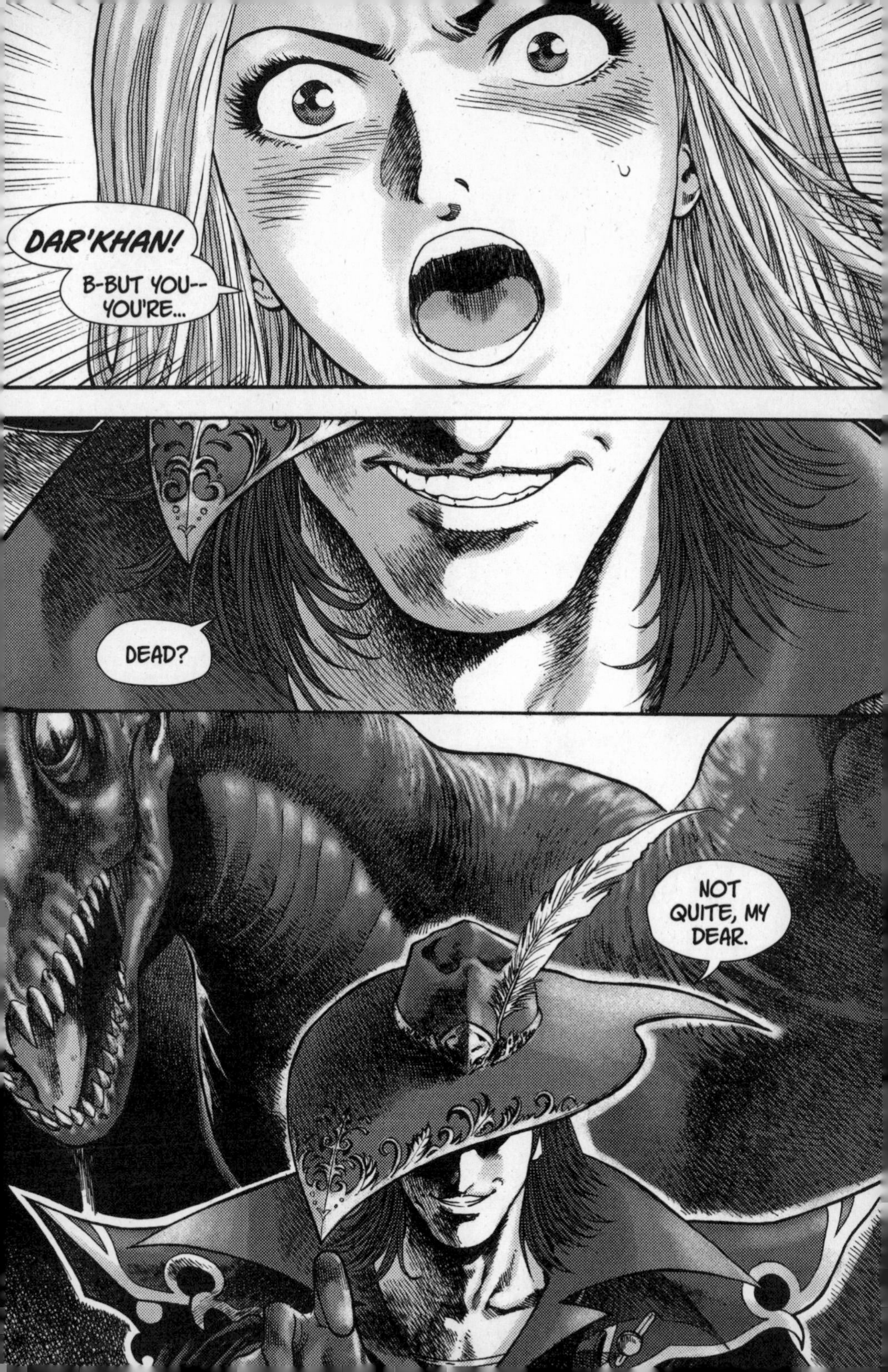
DAR'KHAN!
B-BUT YOU-- YOU'RE...
DEAD?
NOT QUITE, MY DEAR.

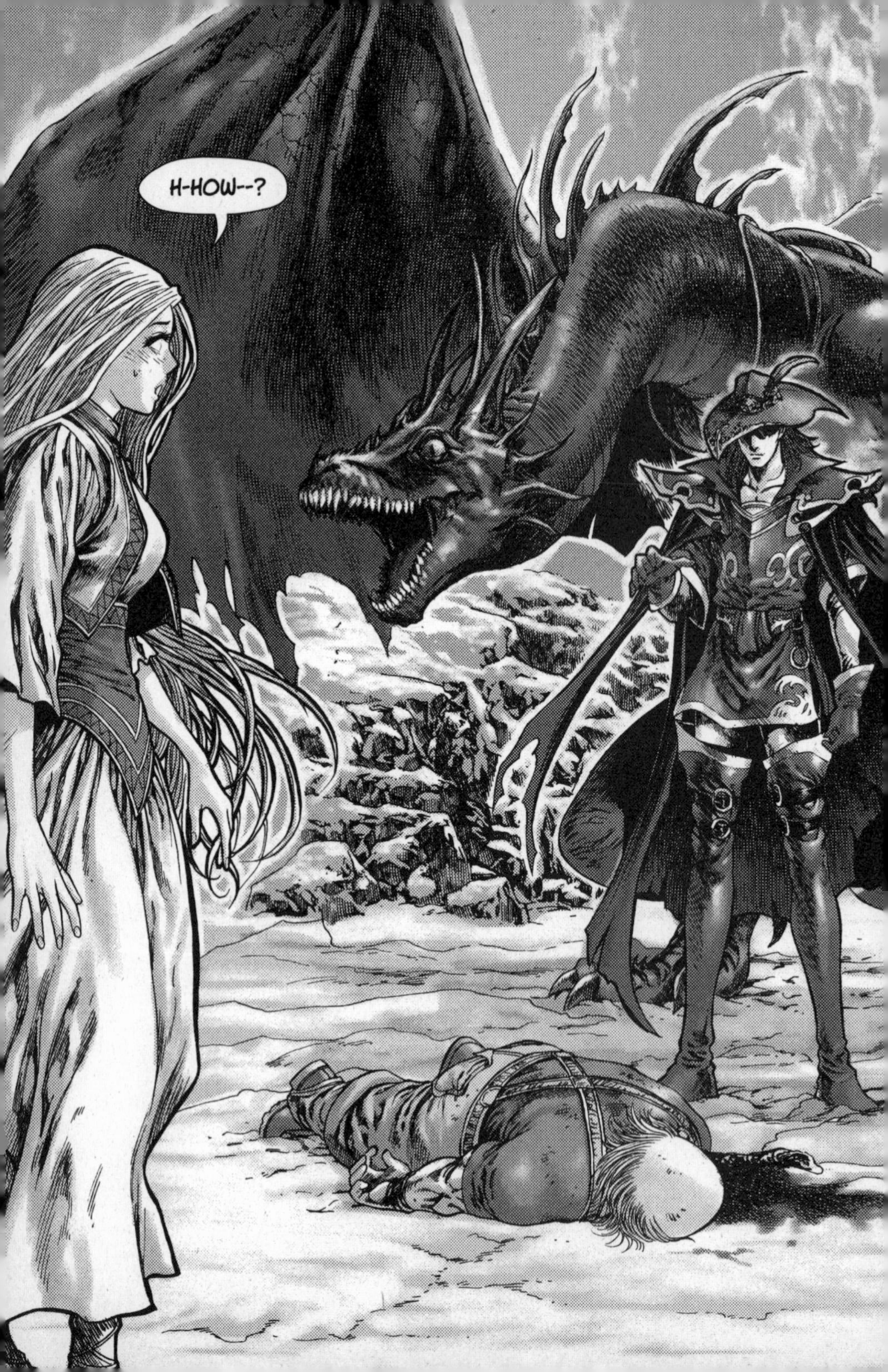
H-HOW--?

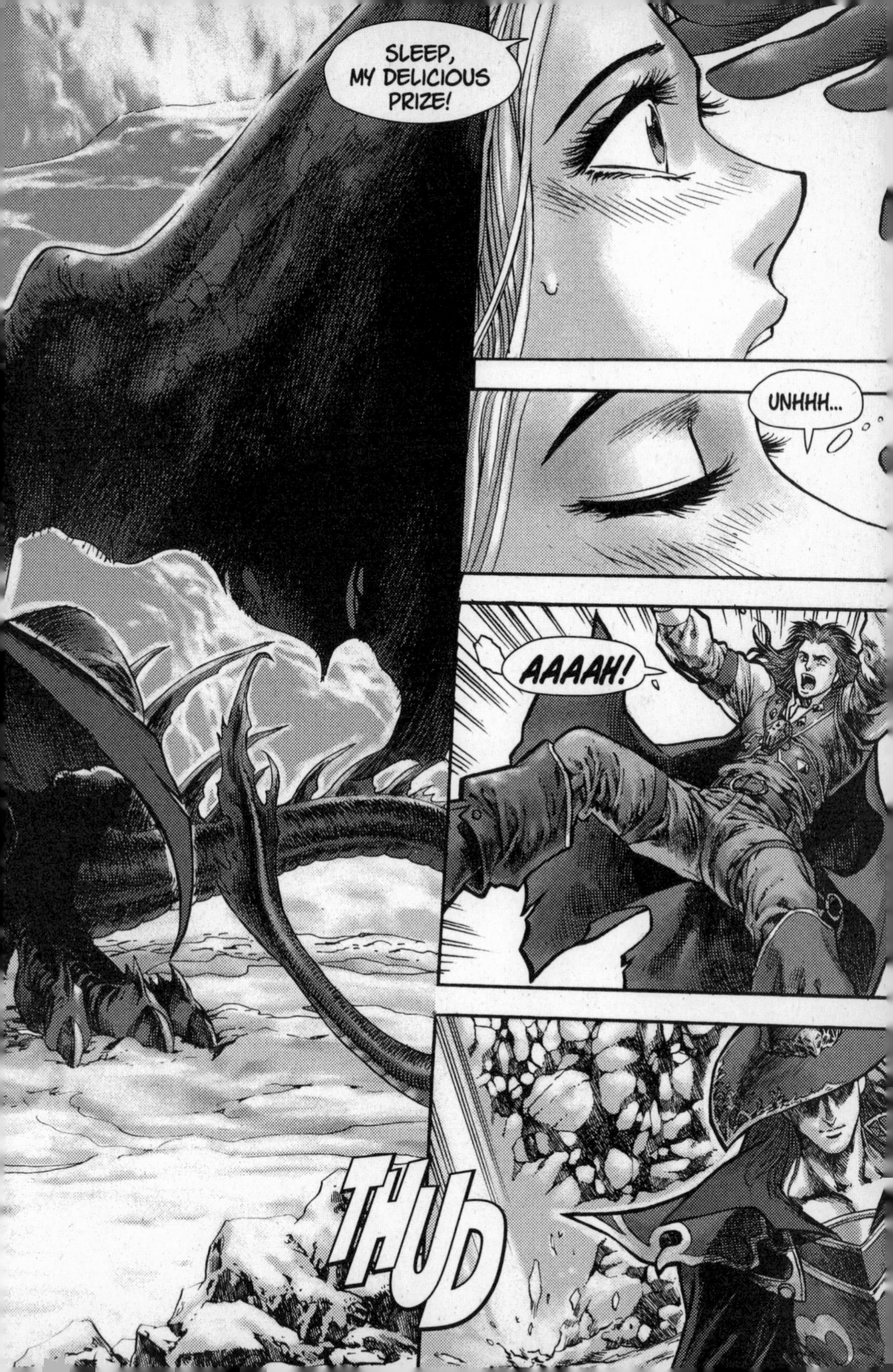
SLEEP, MY DELICIOUS PRIZE!
UNHHH...
AAAAH!
THUD

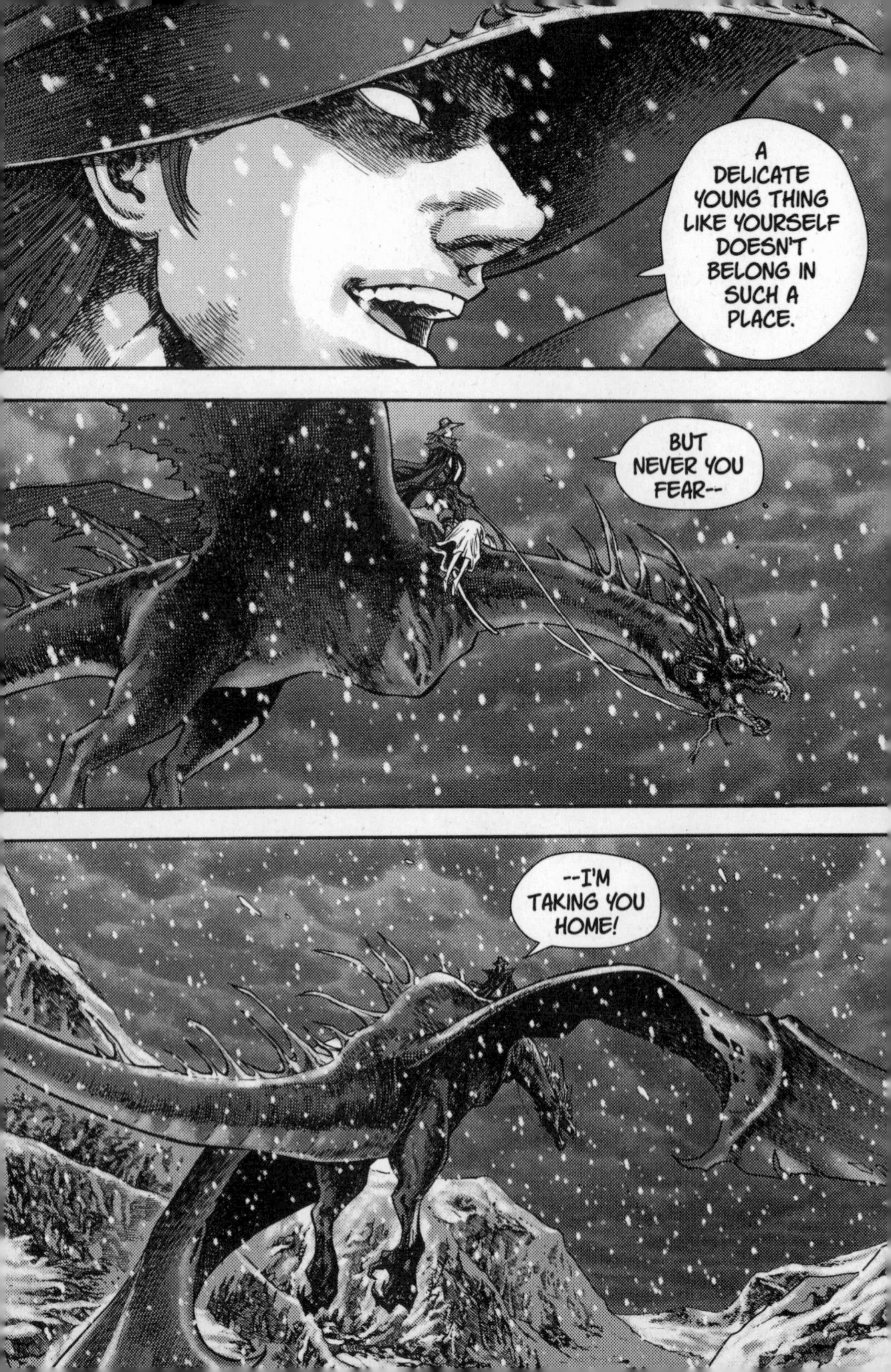
A DELICATE YOUNG THING LIKE YOURSELF DOESN'T BELONG IN SUCH A PLACE.
BUT NEVER YOU FEAR--
--I'M TAKING YOU HOME!

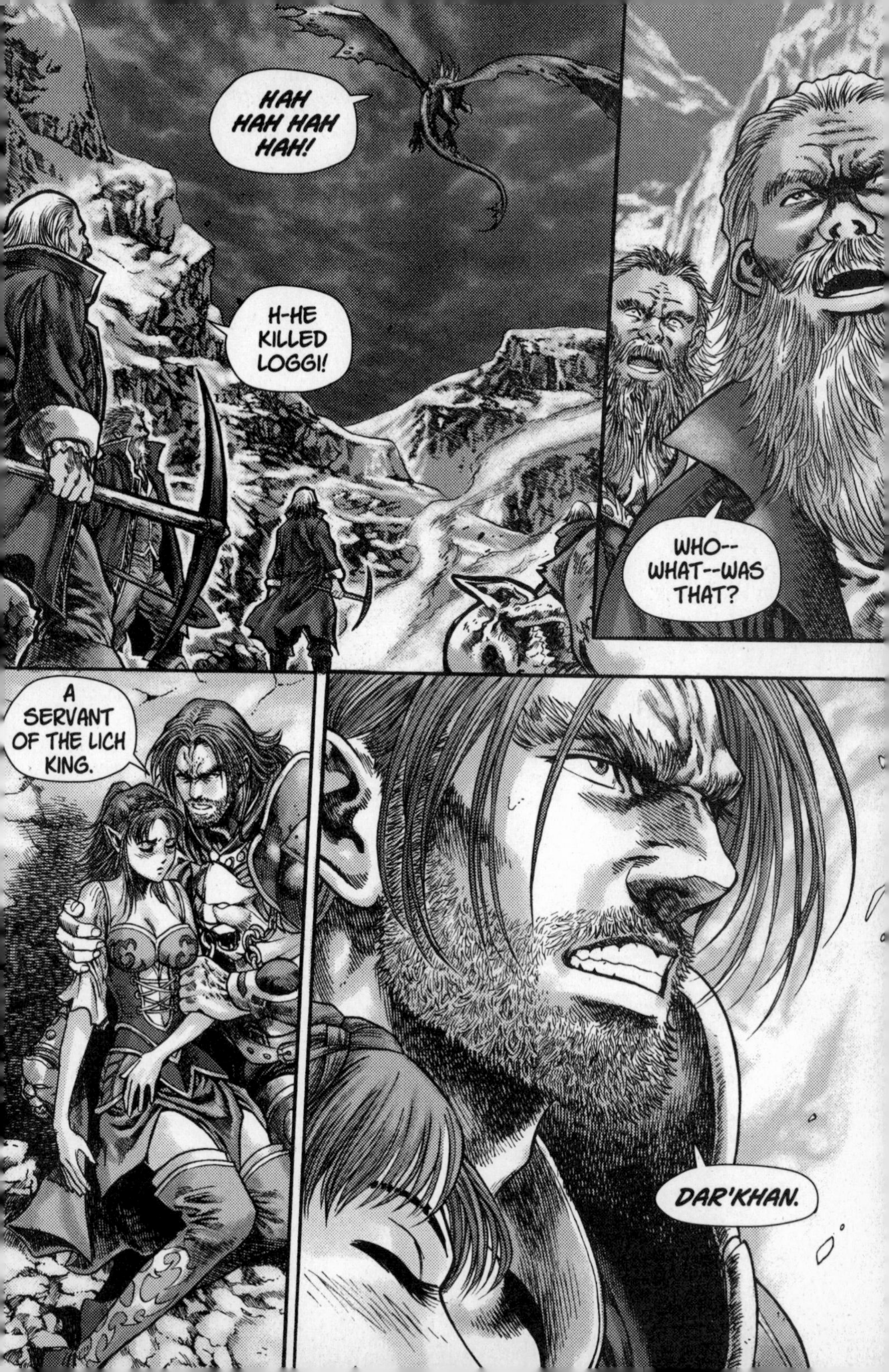
HAH HAH HAH HAH!
H-HE KILLED LOGGI!
WHO-- WHAT--WAS THAT?
A SERVANT OF THE LICH KING.
DAR'KHAN.

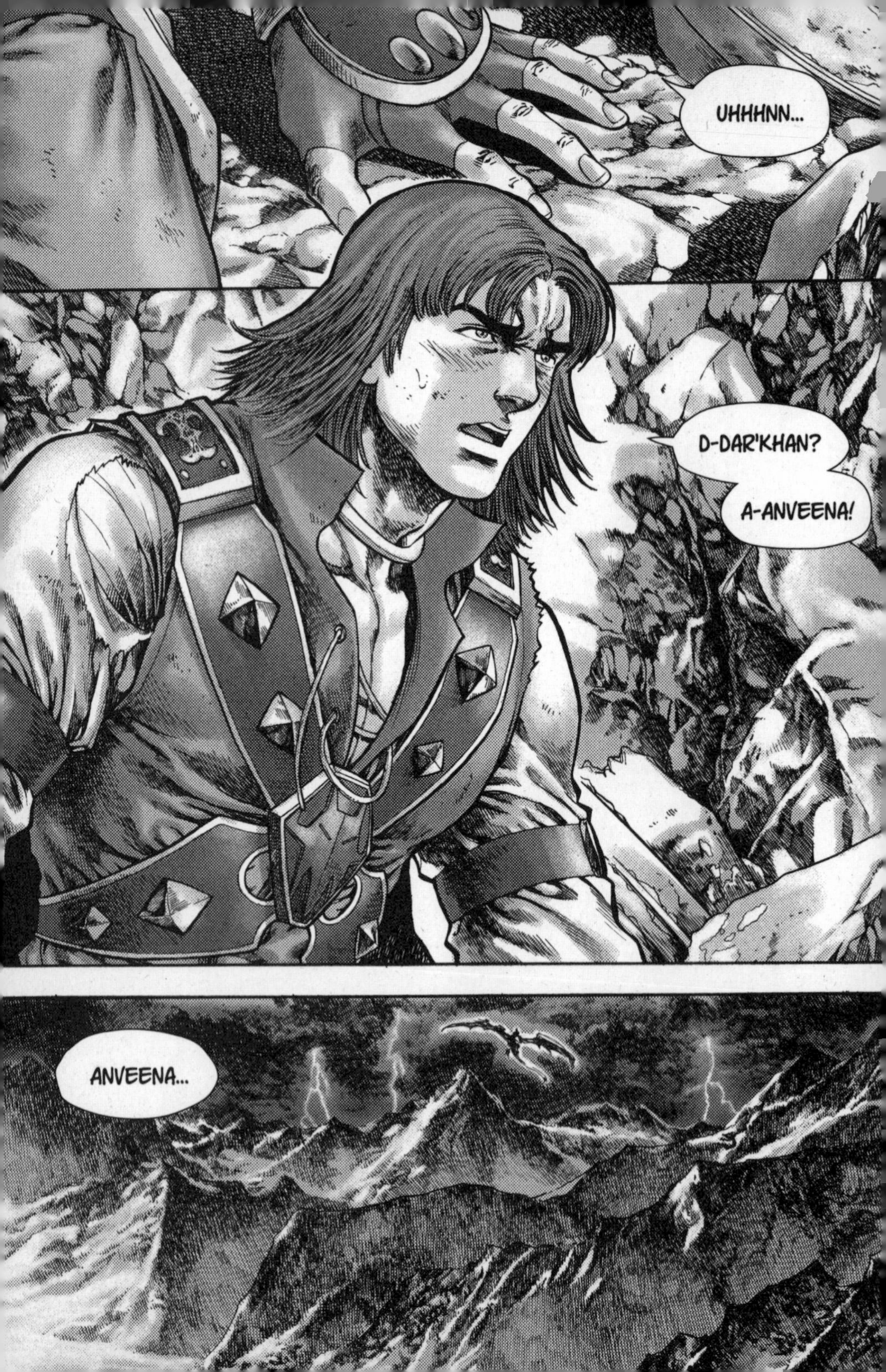
UHHHNN...
D-DAR'KHAN?
A-ANVEENA!
ANVEENA...

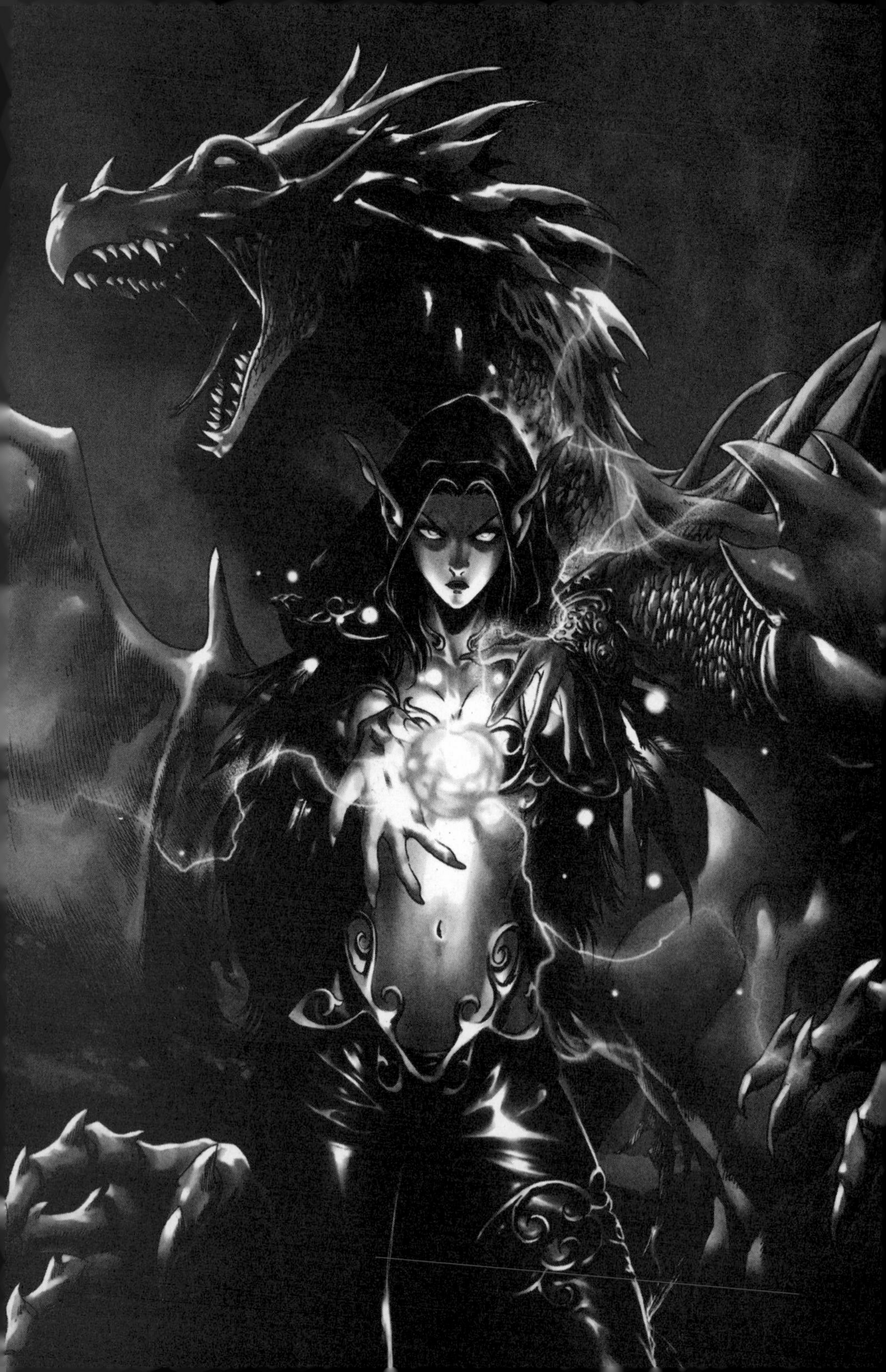

CHAPTER ONE

THE NIGHTMARE PLAINS

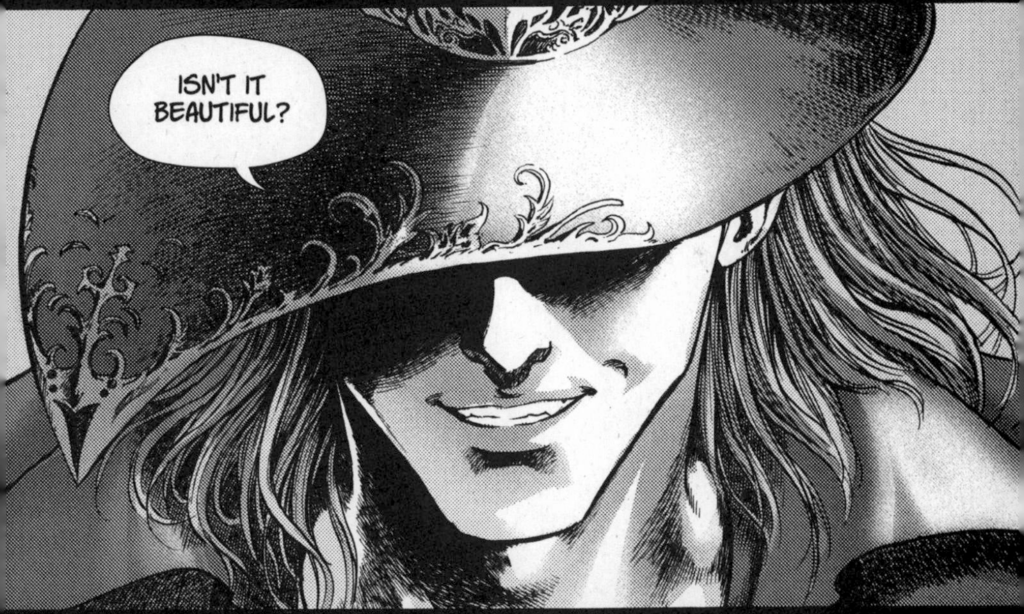
ISN'T IT BEAUTIFUL?

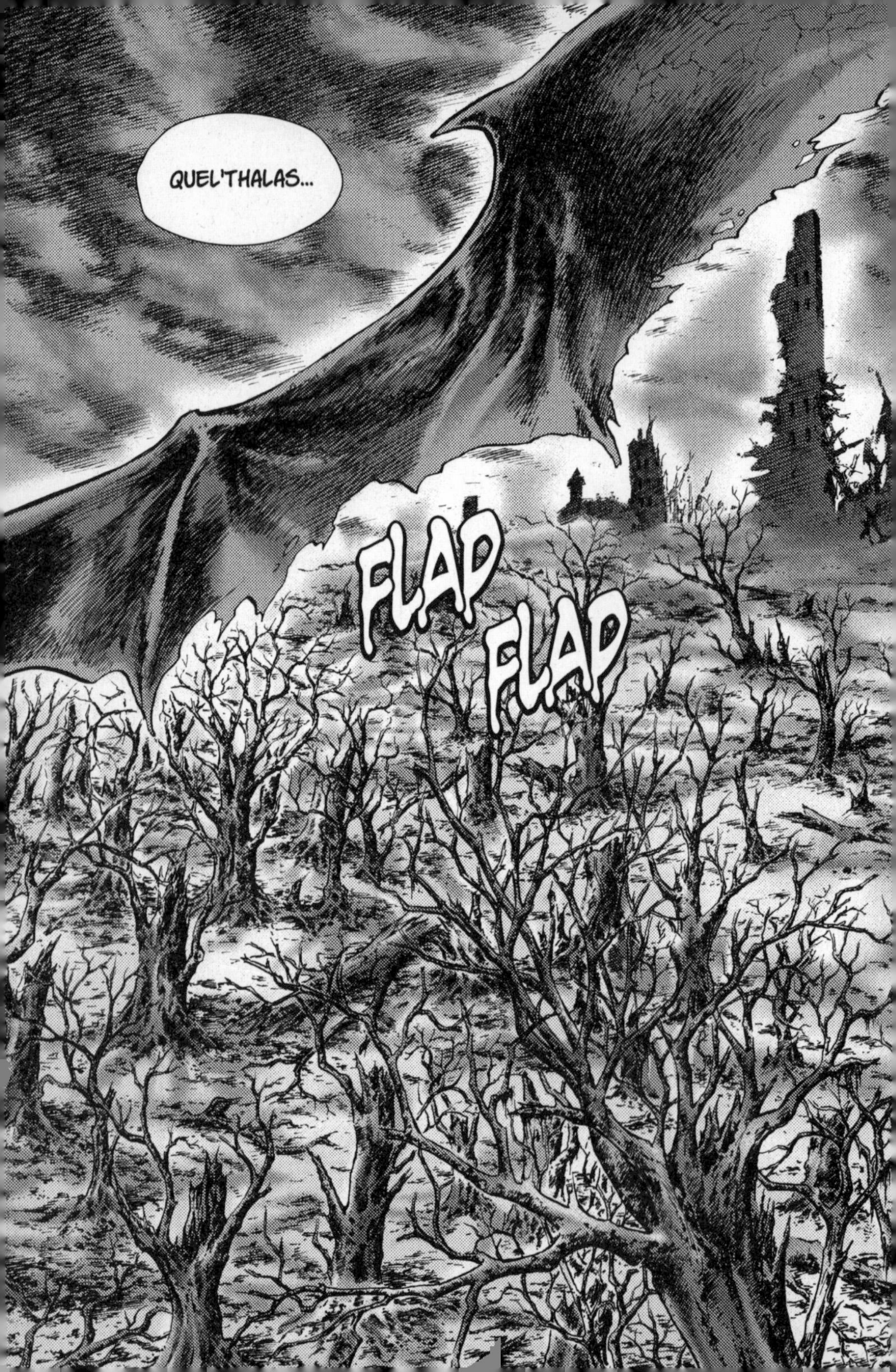
QUEL'THALAS...
FLAP
FLAP

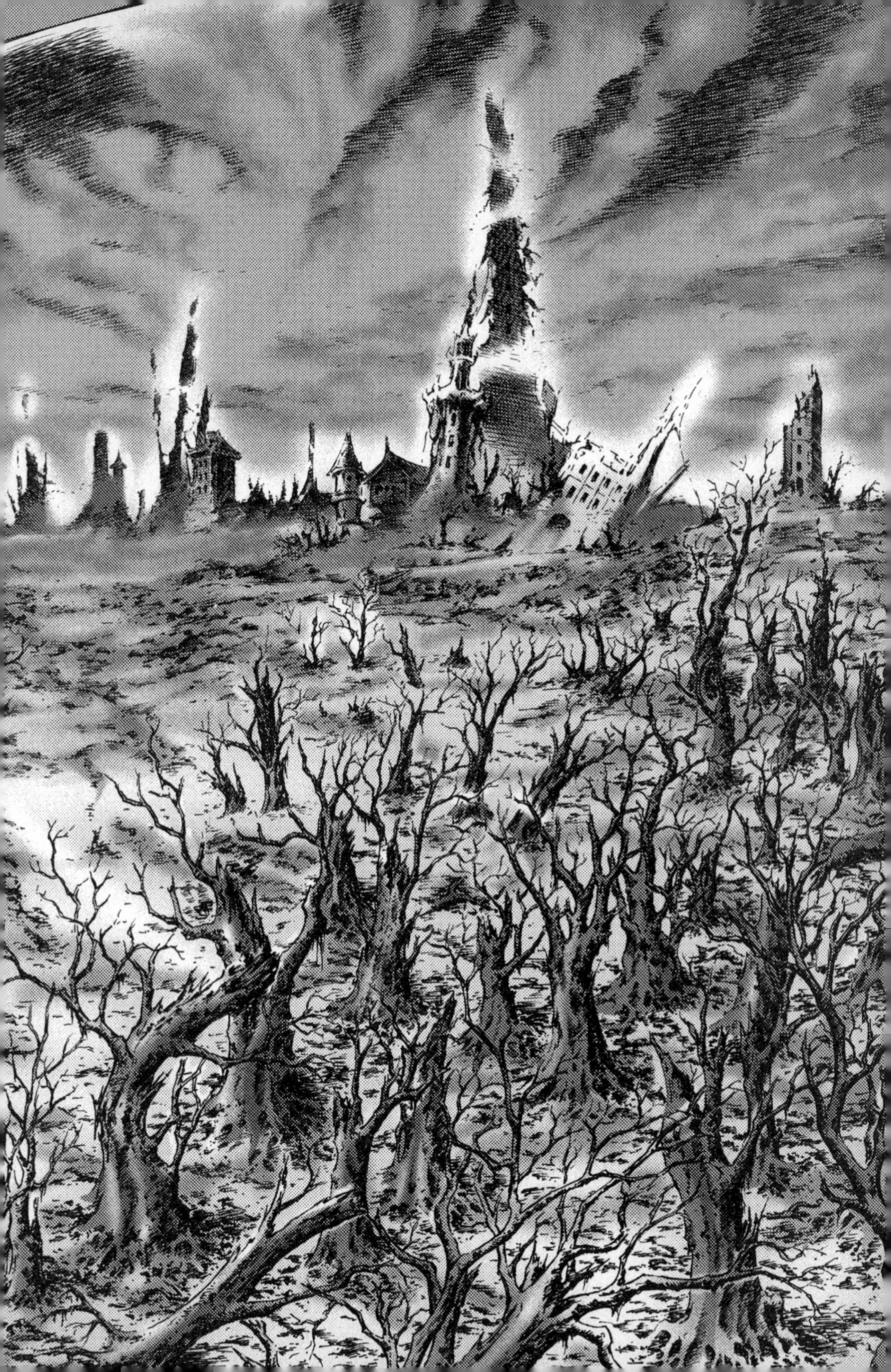

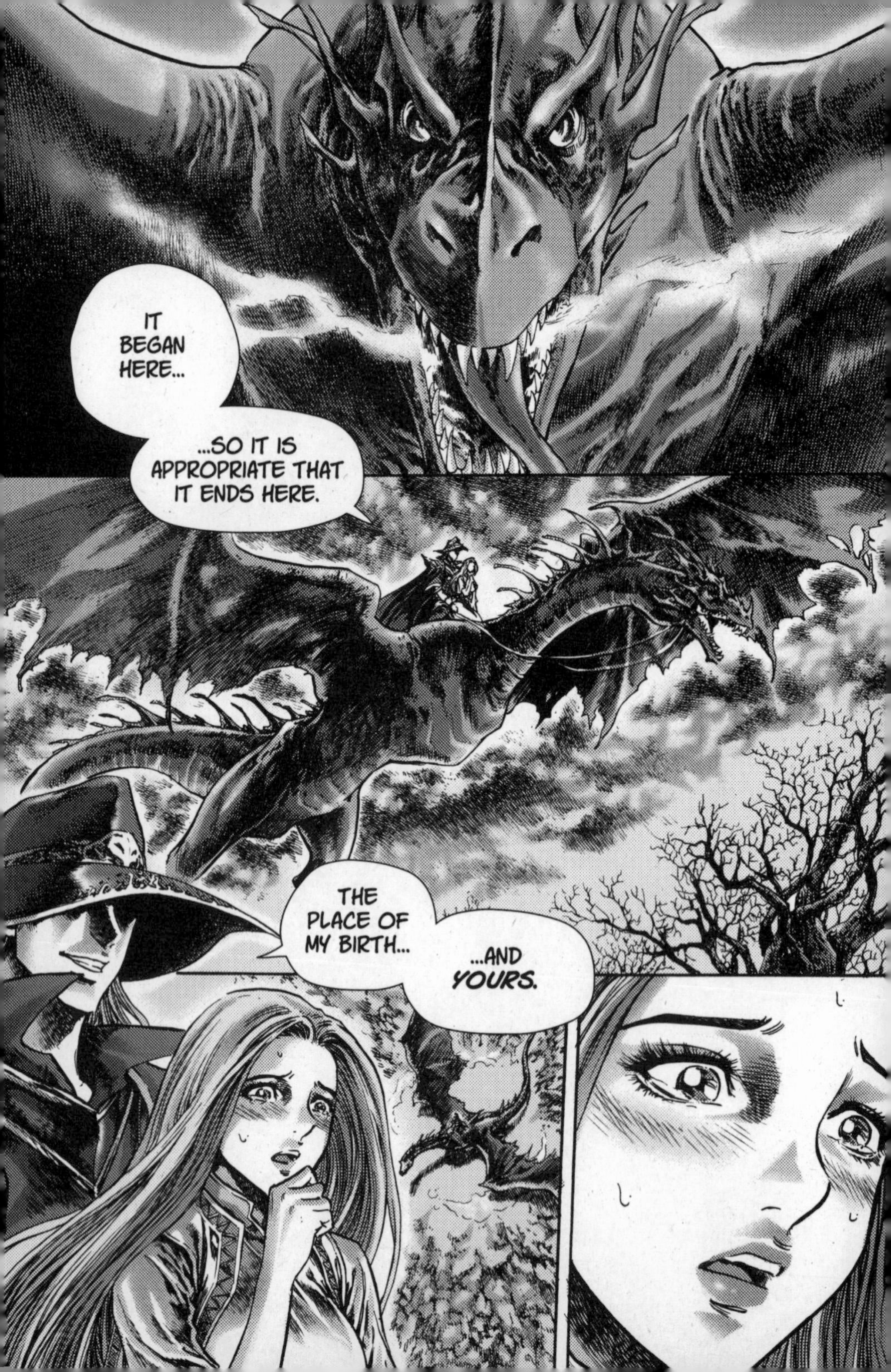
IT BEGAN HERE...
...SO IT IS APPROPRIATE THAT IT ENDS HERE.
THE PLACE OF MY BIRTH...
...AND *YOURS.*

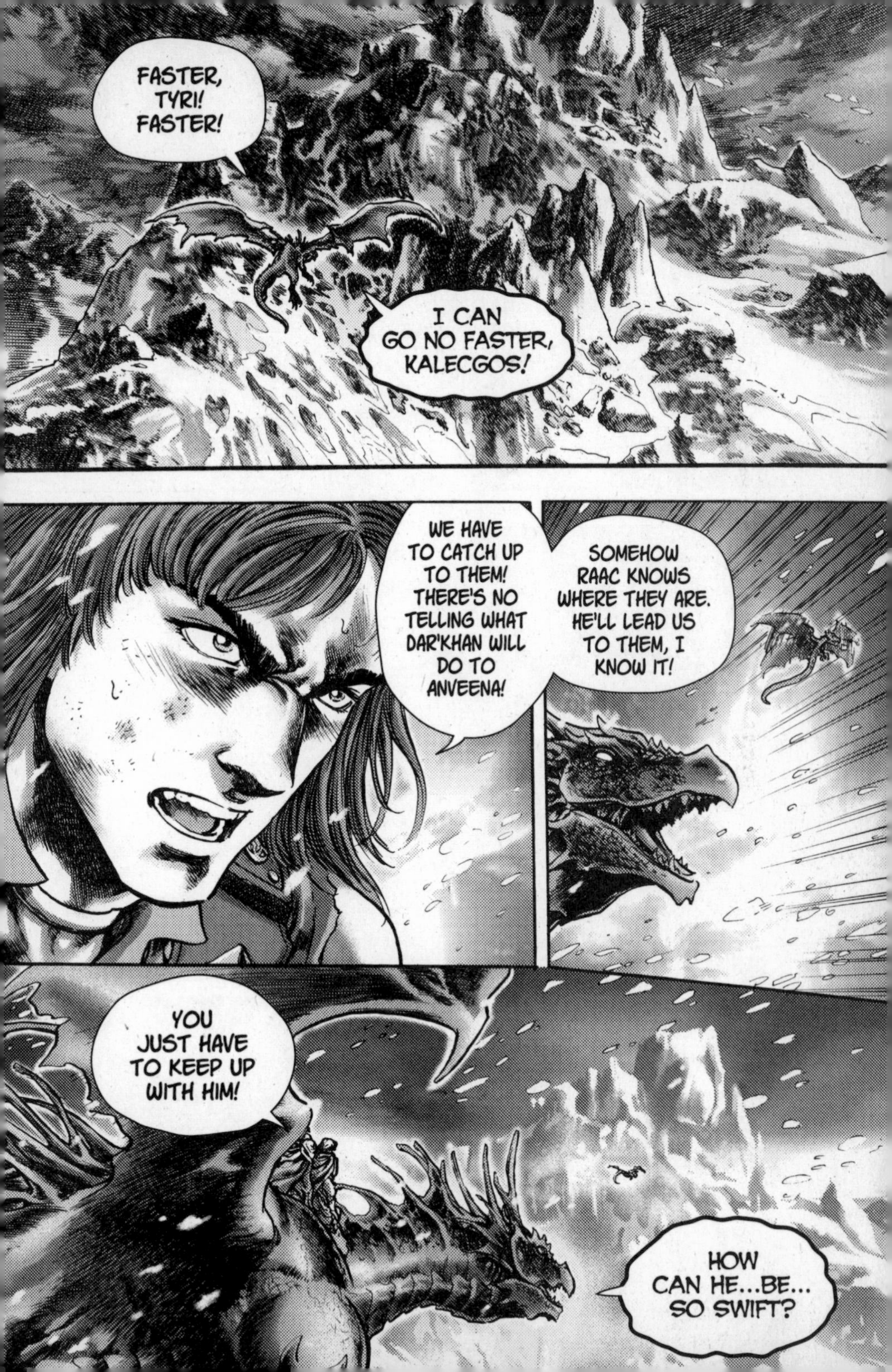
FASTER, TYRI! FASTER!
I CAN GO NO FASTER, KALECGOS!
WE HAVE TO CATCH UP TO THEM! THERE'S NO TELLING WHAT DAR'KHAN WILL DO TO ANVEENA!
SOMEHOW RAAC KNOWS WHERE THEY ARE. HE'LL LEAD US TO THEM, I KNOW IT!
YOU JUST HAVE TO KEEP UP WITH HIM!
HOW CAN HE...BE... SO SWIFT?

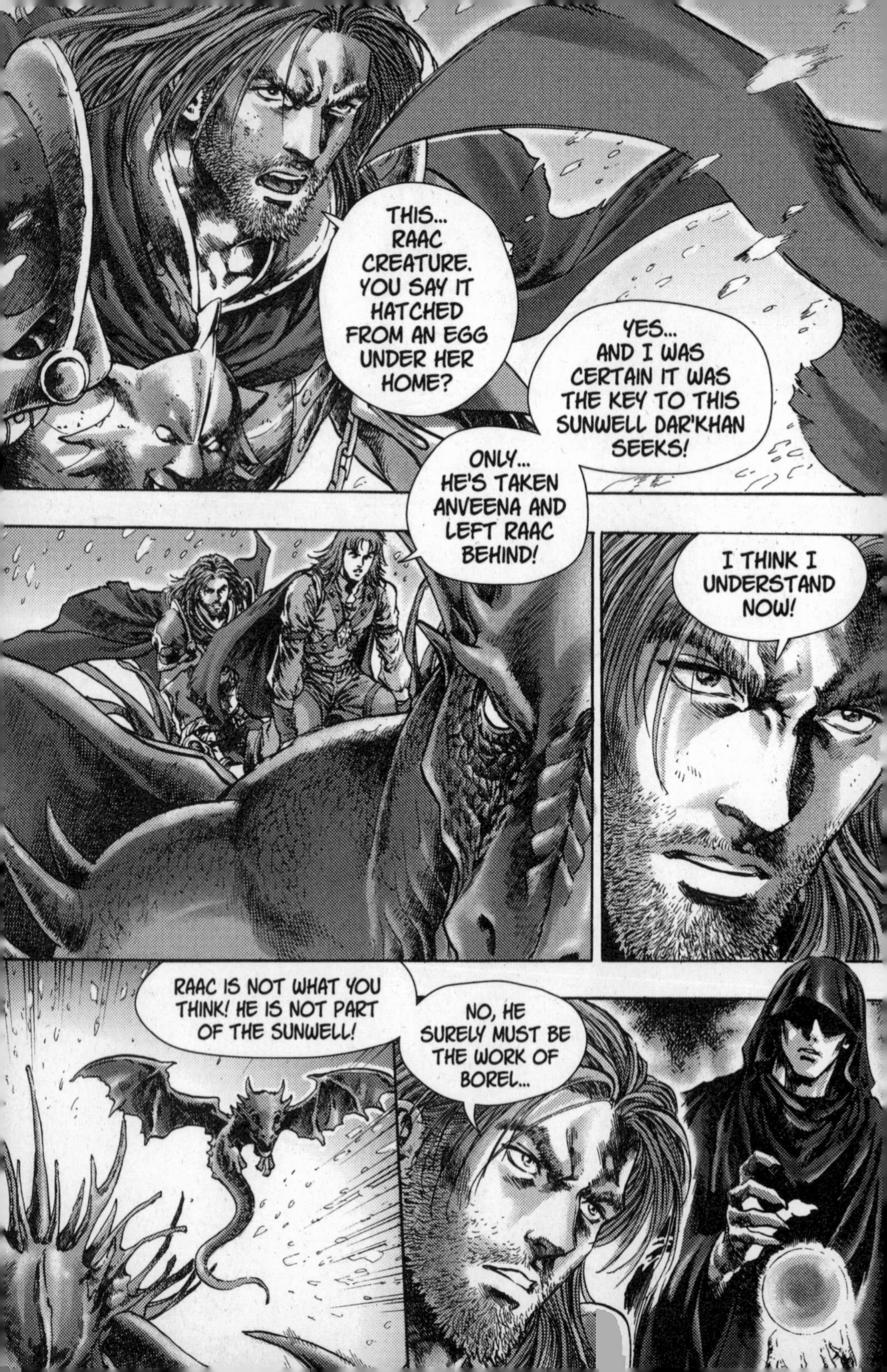
THIS... RAAC CREATURE. YOU SAY IT HATCHED FROM AN EGG UNDER HER HOME?
YES... AND I WAS CERTAIN IT WAS THE KEY TO THIS SUNWELL DAR'KHAN SEEKS!
ONLY... HE'S TAKEN ANVEENA AND LEFT RAAC BEHIND!
I THINK I UNDERSTAND NOW!
RAAC IS NOT WHAT YOU THINK! HE IS NOT PART OF THE SUNWELL!
NO, HE SURELY MUST BE THE WORK OF BOREL...

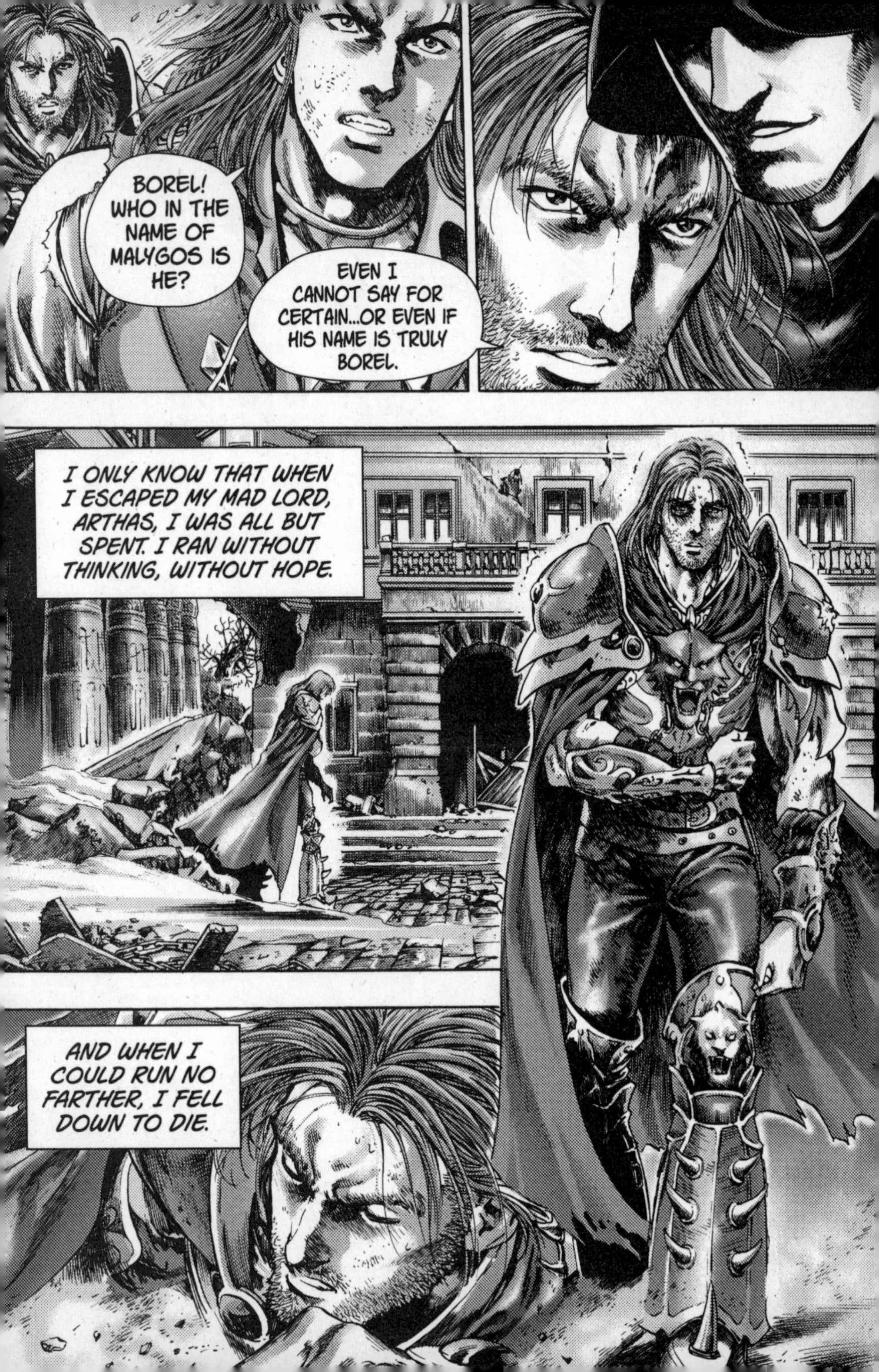
BOREL! WHO IN THE NAME OF MALYGOS IS HE?
EVEN I CANNOT SAY FOR CERTAIN...OR EVEN IF HIS NAME IS TRULY BOREL.
I ONLY KNOW THAT WHEN I ESCAPED MY MAD LORD, ARTHAS, I WAS ALL BUT SPENT. I RAN WITHOUT THINKING, WITHOUT HOPE.
AND WHEN I COULD RUN NO FARTHER, I FELL DOWN TO DIE.

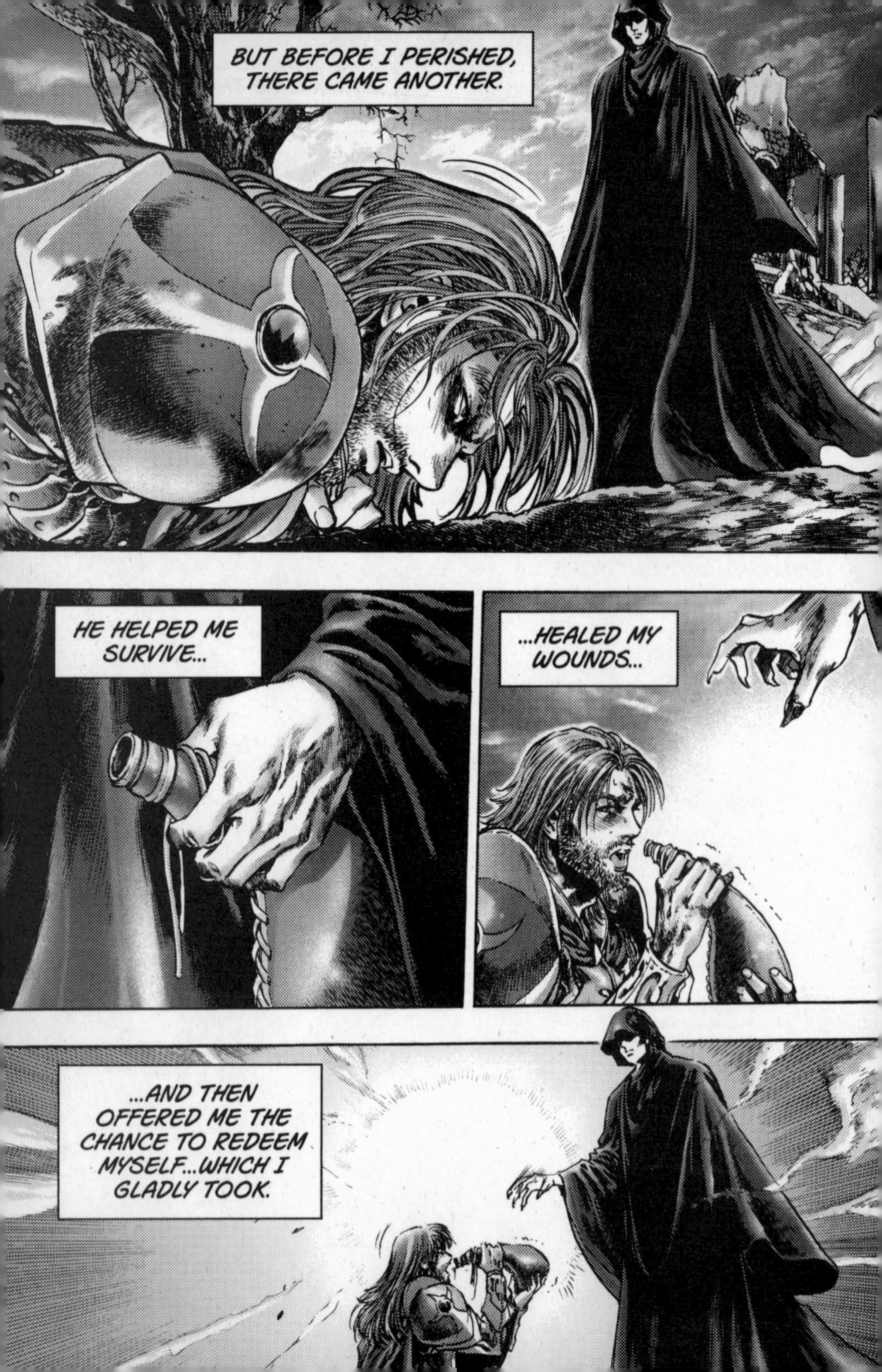
BUT BEFORE I PERISHED, THERE CAME ANOTHER.
HE HELPED ME SURVIVE...
...HEALED MY WOUNDS...
...AND THEN OFFERED ME THE CHANCE TO REDEEM MYSELF...WHICH I GLADLY TOOK.

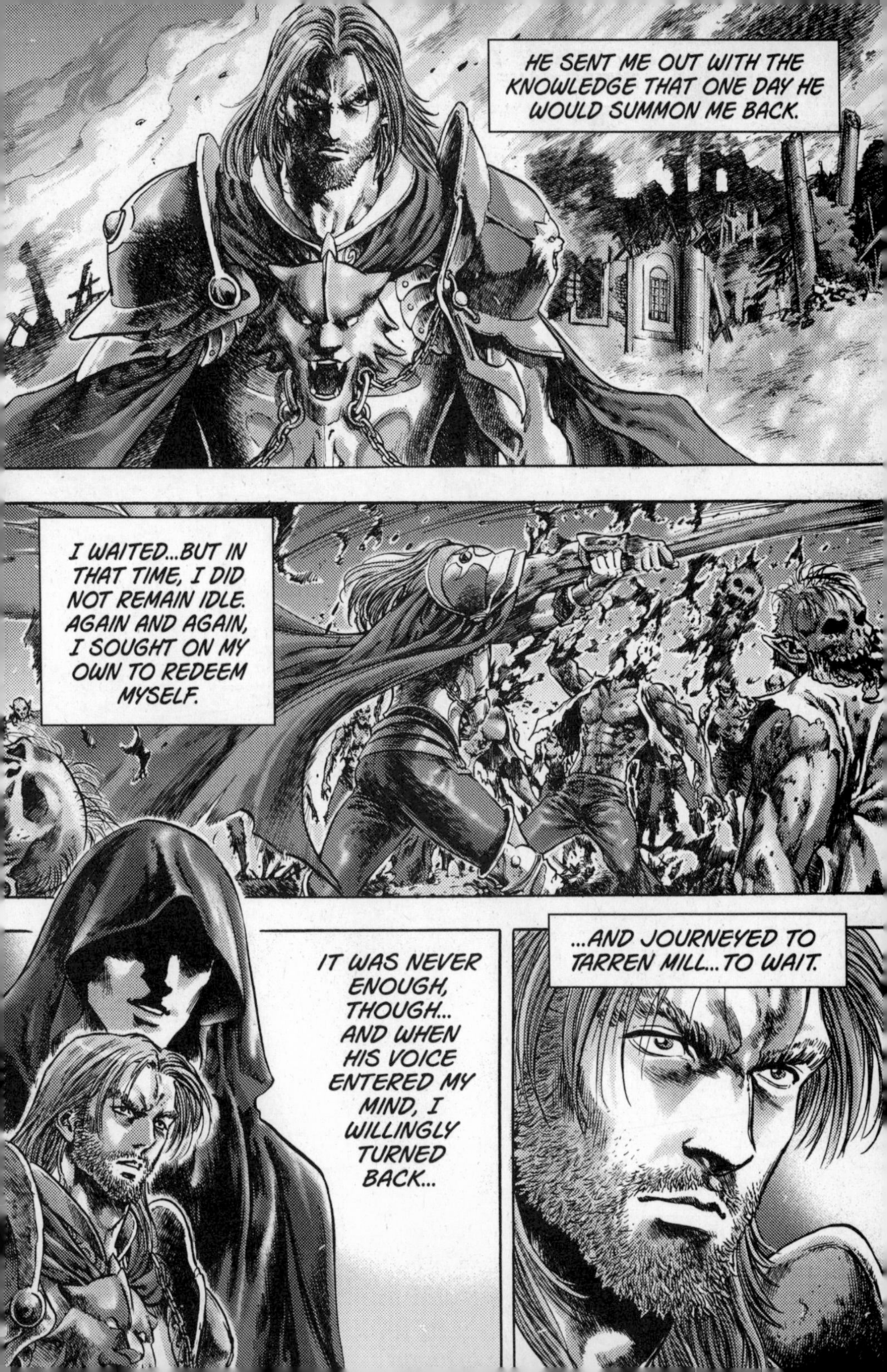
HE SENT ME OUT WITH THE KNOWLEDGE THAT ONE DAY HE WOULD SUMMON ME BACK.
I WAITED...BUT IN THAT TIME, I DID NOT REMAIN IDLE. AGAIN AND AGAIN, I SOUGHT ON MY OWN TO REDEEM MYSELF.
IT WAS NEVER ENOUGH, THOUGH... AND WHEN HIS VOICE ENTERED MY MIND, I WILLINGLY TURNED BACK...
...AND JOURNEYED TO TARREN MILL...TO WAIT.

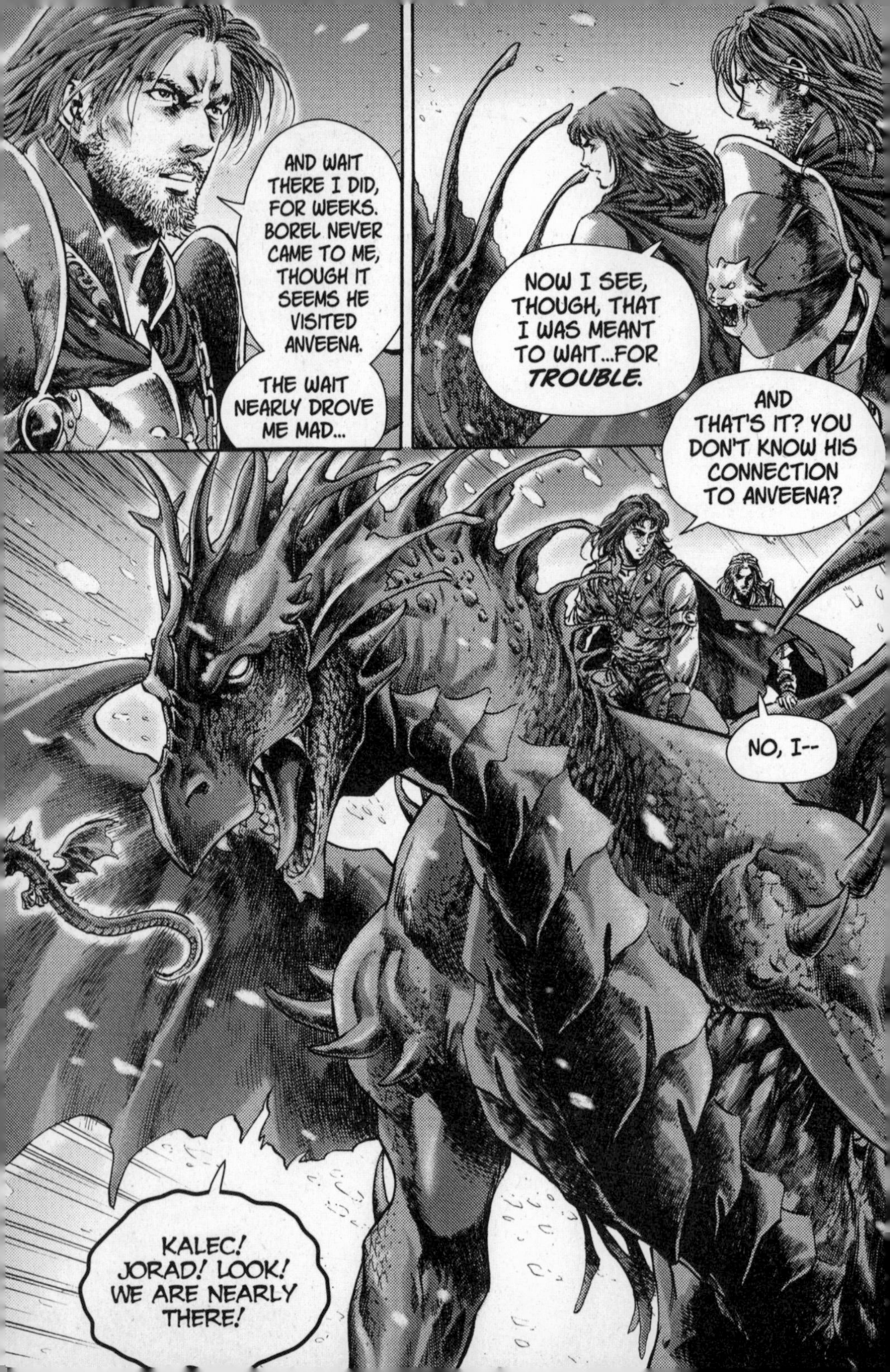
AND WAIT THERE I DID, FOR WEEKS. BOREL NEVER CAME TO ME, THOUGH IT SEEMS HE VISITED ANVEENA.
THE WAIT NEARLY DROVE ME MAD...
NOW I SEE, THOUGH, THAT I WAS MEANT TO WAIT...FOR *TROUBLE.*
AND THAT'S IT? YOU DON'T KNOW HIS CONNECTION TO ANVEENA?
NO, I--
KALEC! JORAD! LOOK! WE ARE NEARLY THERE!

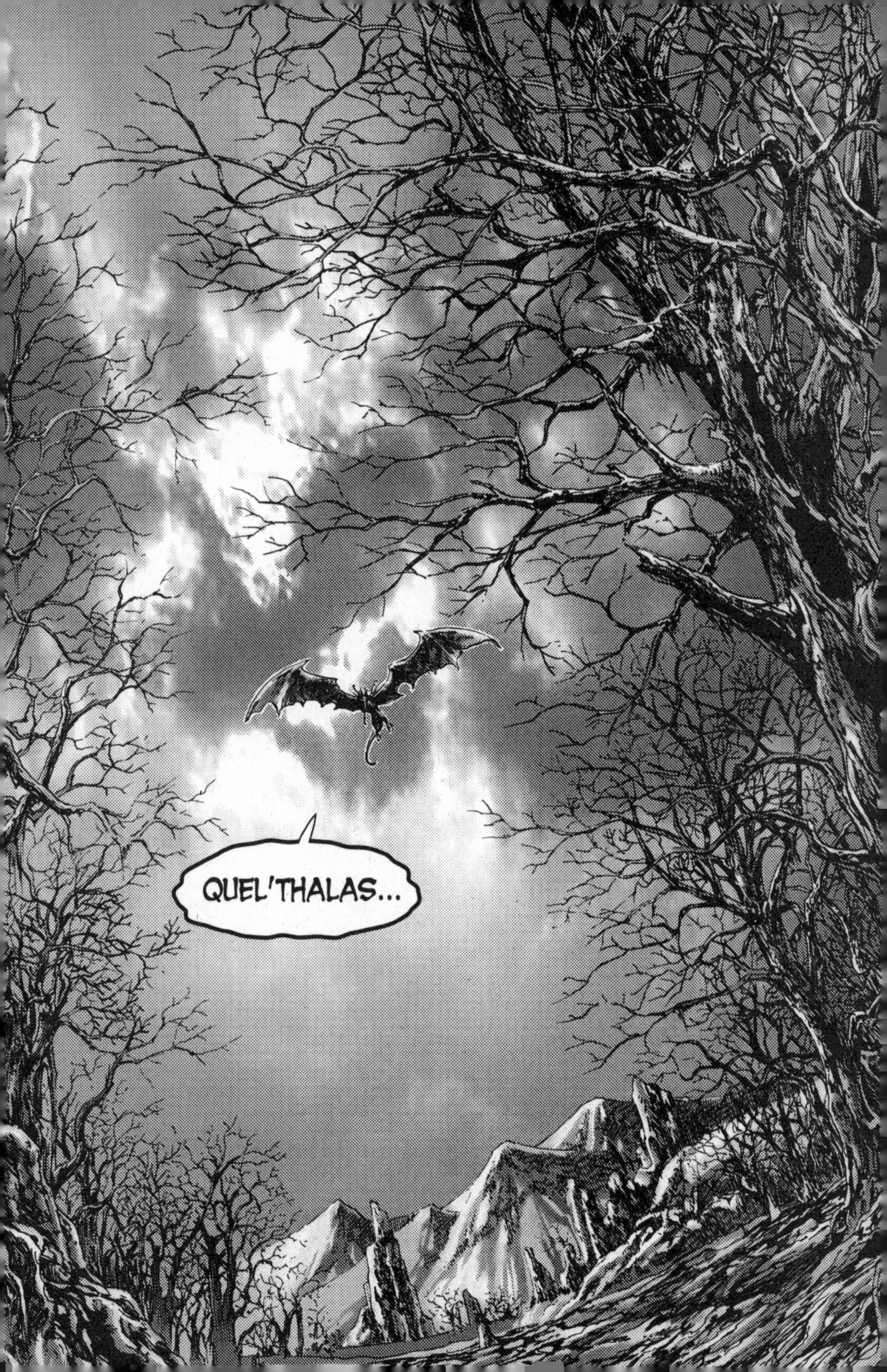
QUEL'THALAS...

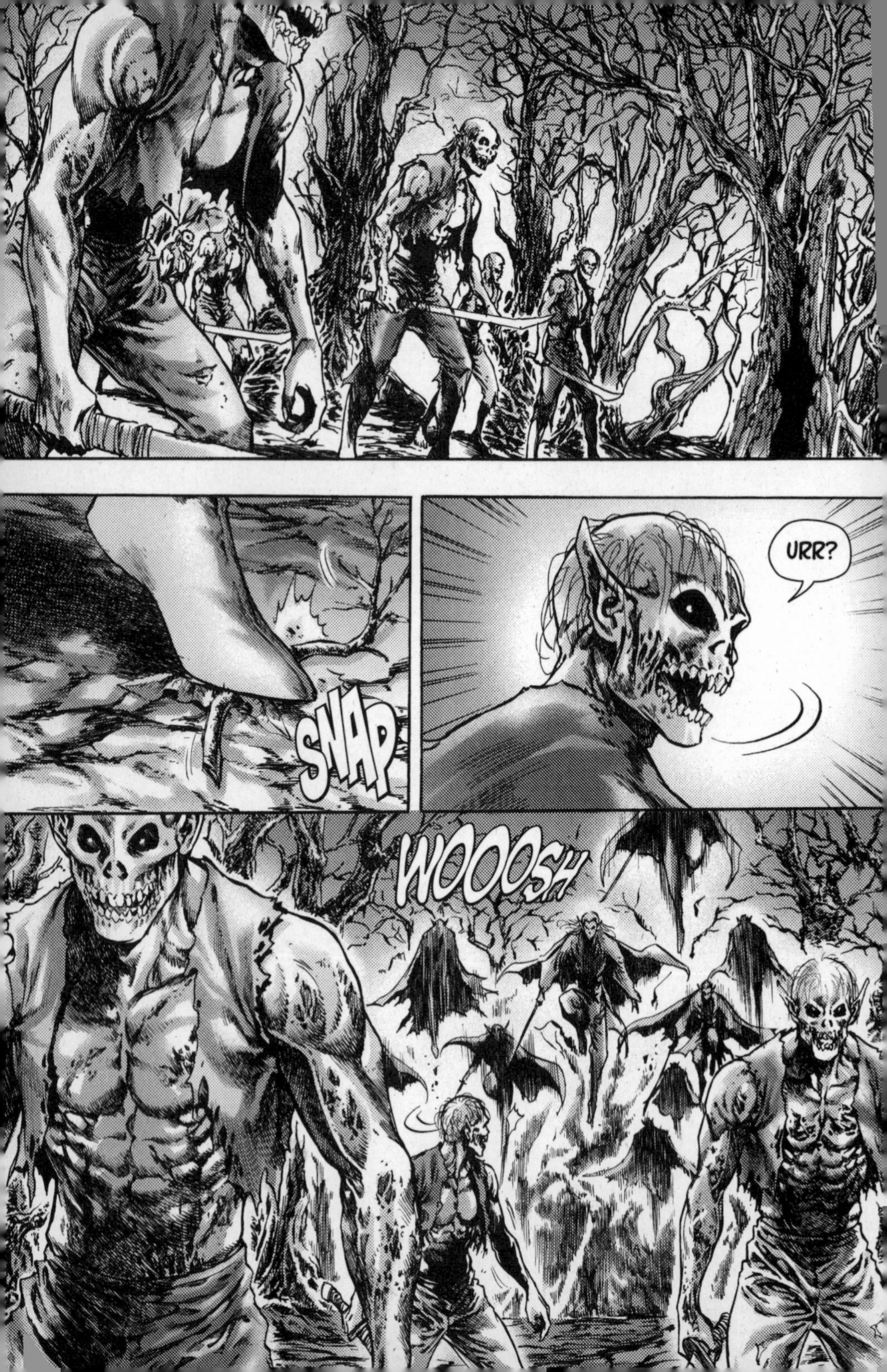
SNAP
URR?
WOOOSH

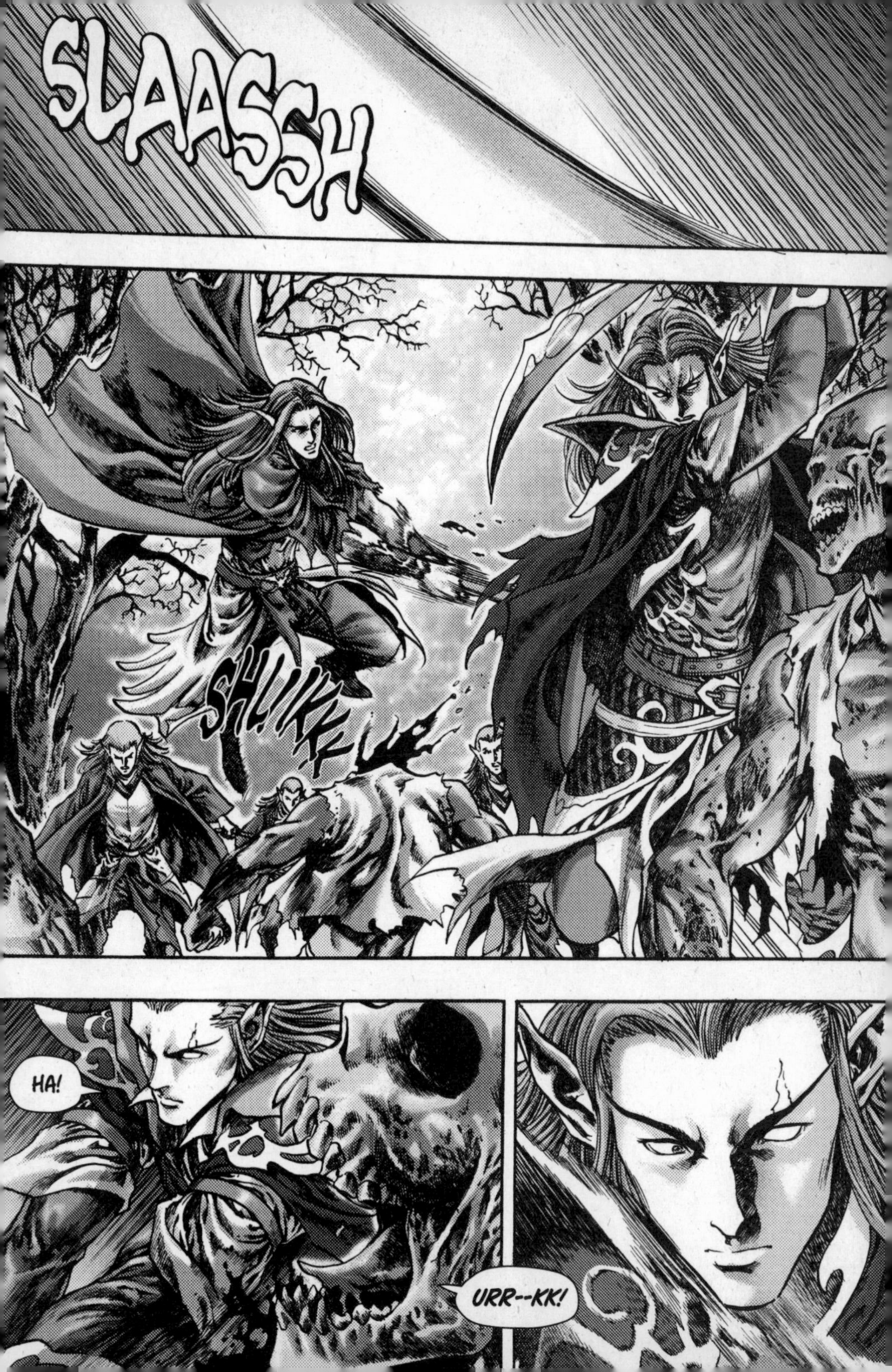
SLAASSH
SHIKKK
URR--KK!
HA!

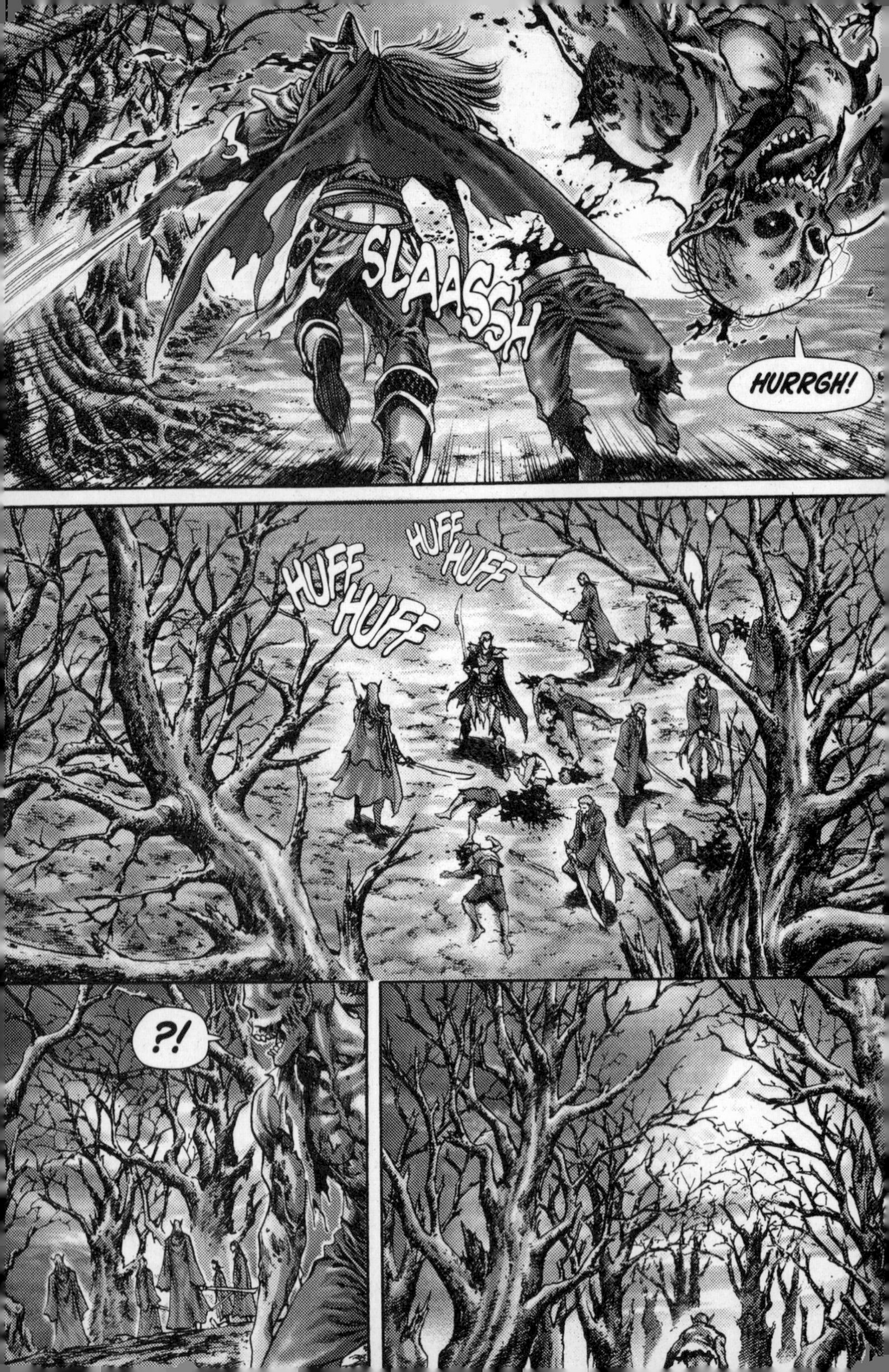
SLAASSH
HURRGH!
HUFF HUFF
HUFF HUFF
?!

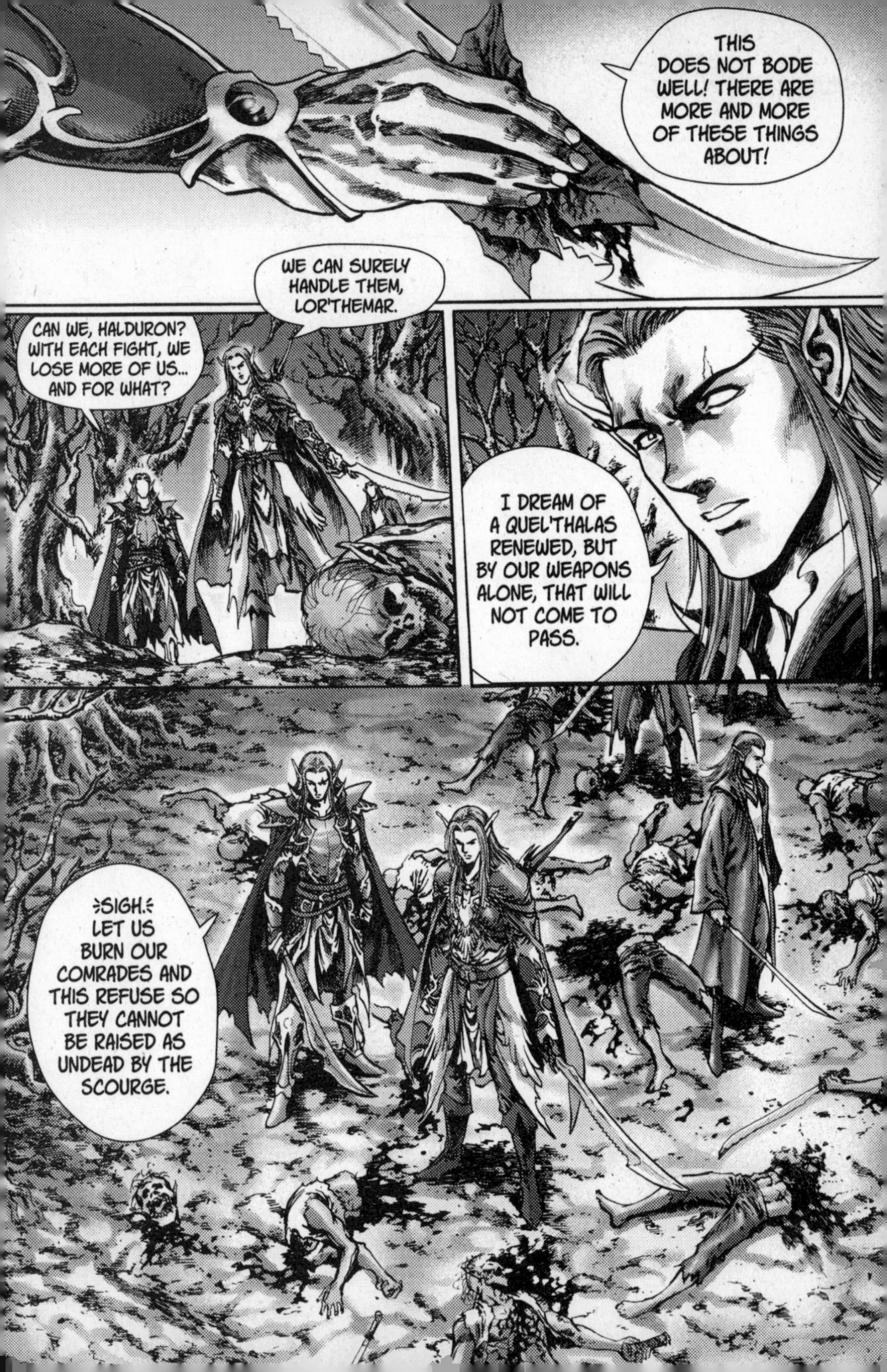
THIS DOES NOT BODE WELL! THERE ARE MORE AND MORE OF THESE THINGS ABOUT!
WE CAN SURELY HANDLE THEM, LOR'THEMAR.
CAN WE, HALDURON? WITH EACH FIGHT, WE LOSE MORE OF US... AND FOR WHAT?
I DREAM OF A QUEL'THALAS RENEWED, BUT BY OUR WEAPONS ALONE, THAT WILL NOT COME TO PASS.
SIGH. LET US BURN OUR COMRADES AND THIS REFUSE SO THEY CANNOT BE RAISED AS UNDEAD BY THE SCOURGE.

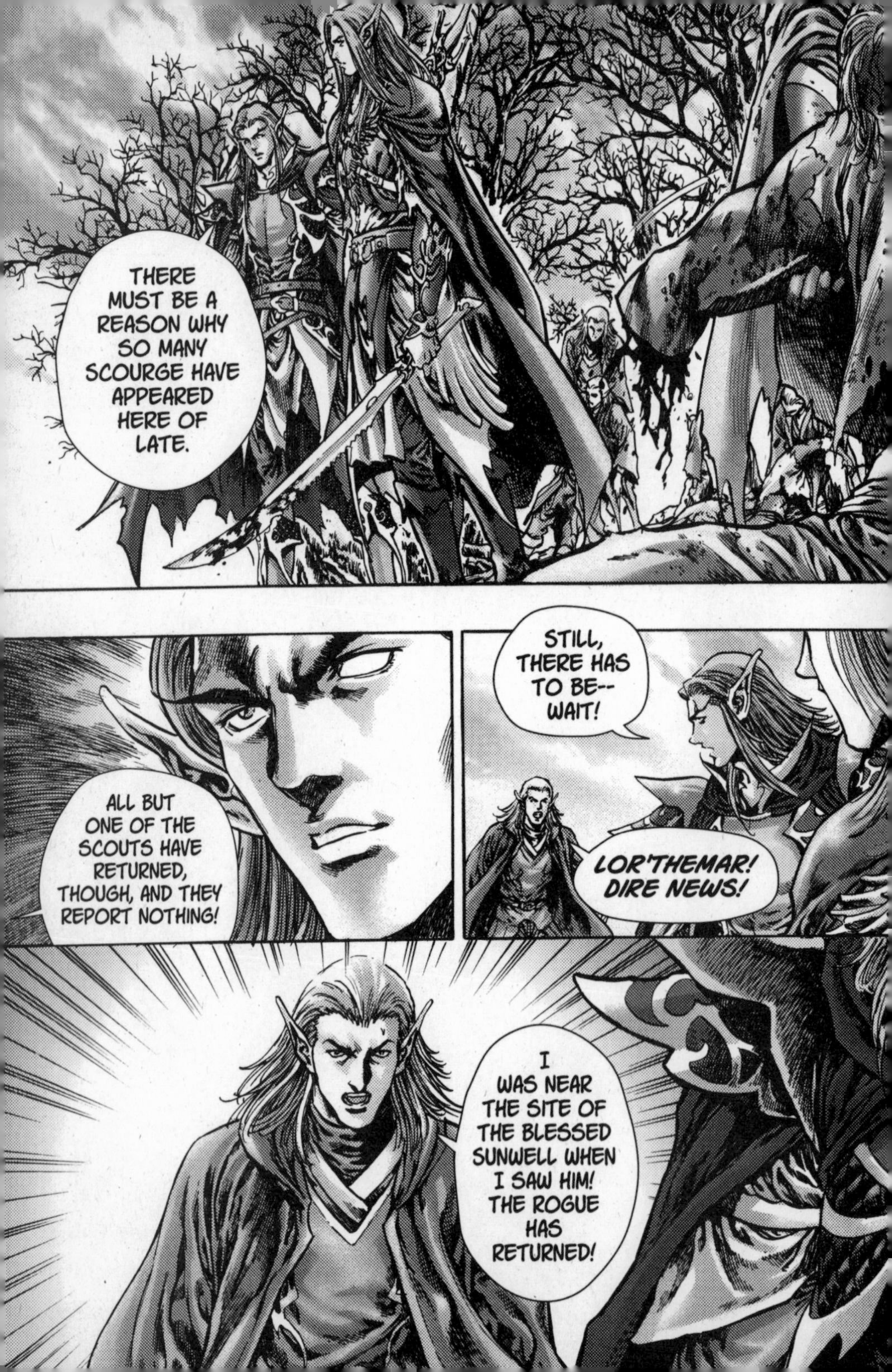
THERE MUST BE A REASON WHY SO MANY SCOURGE HAVE APPEARED HERE OF LATE.
ALL BUT ONE OF THE SCOUTS HAVE RETURNED, THOUGH, AND THEY REPORT NOTHING!
STILL, THERE HAS TO BE-- WAIT!
LOR'THEMAR! DIRE NEWS!
I WAS NEAR THE SITE OF THE BLESSED SUNWELL WHEN I SAW HIM! THE ROGUE HAS RETURNED!

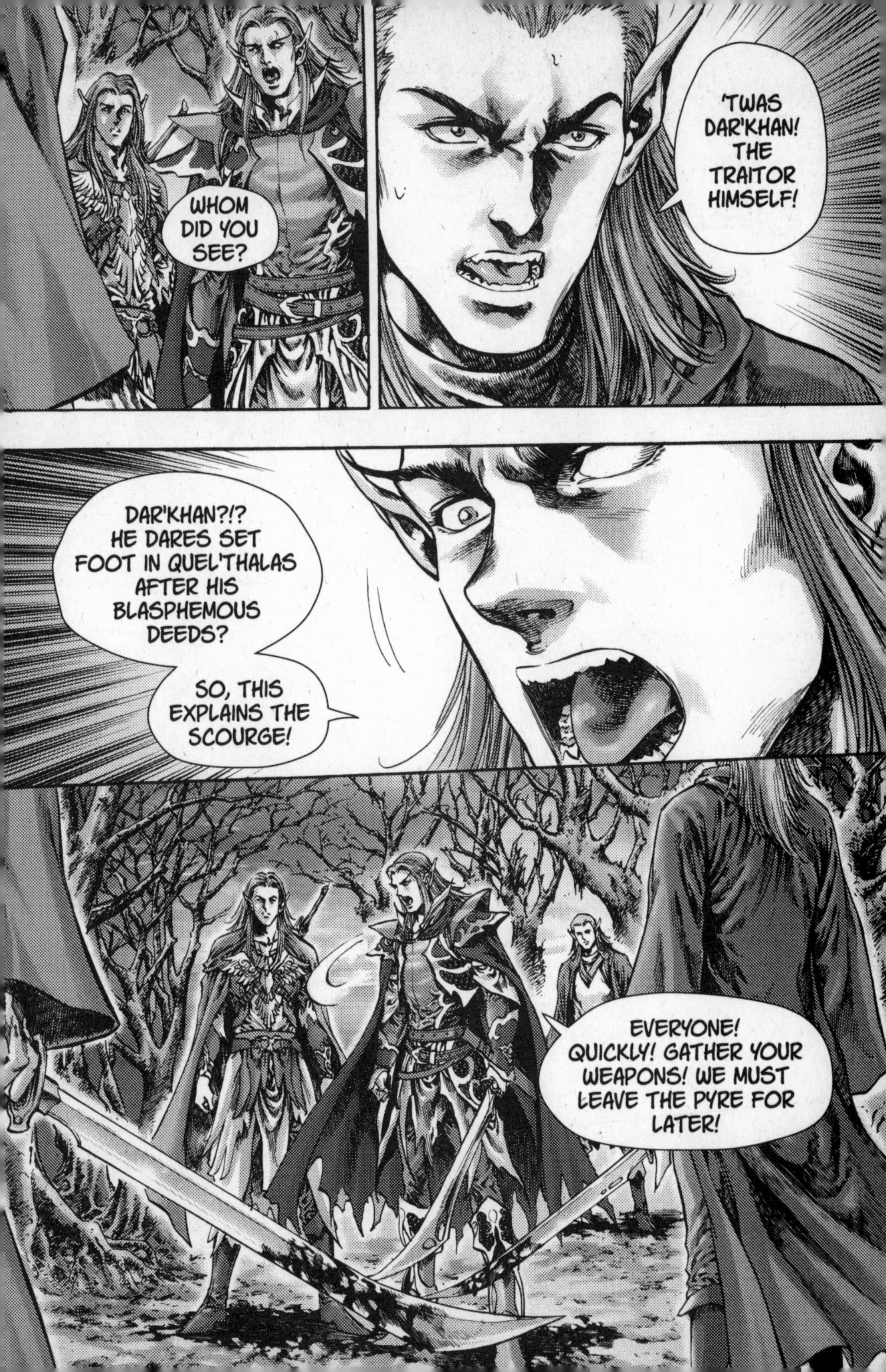
WHOM DID YOU SEE?
'TWAS DAR'KHAN! THE TRAITOR HIMSELF!
DAR'KHAN?!? HE DARES SET FOOT IN QUEL'THALAS AFTER HIS BLASPHEMOUS DEEDS?
SO, THIS EXPLAINS THE SCOURGE!
EVERYONE! QUICKLY! GATHER YOUR WEAPONS! WE MUST LEAVE THE PYRE FOR LATER!

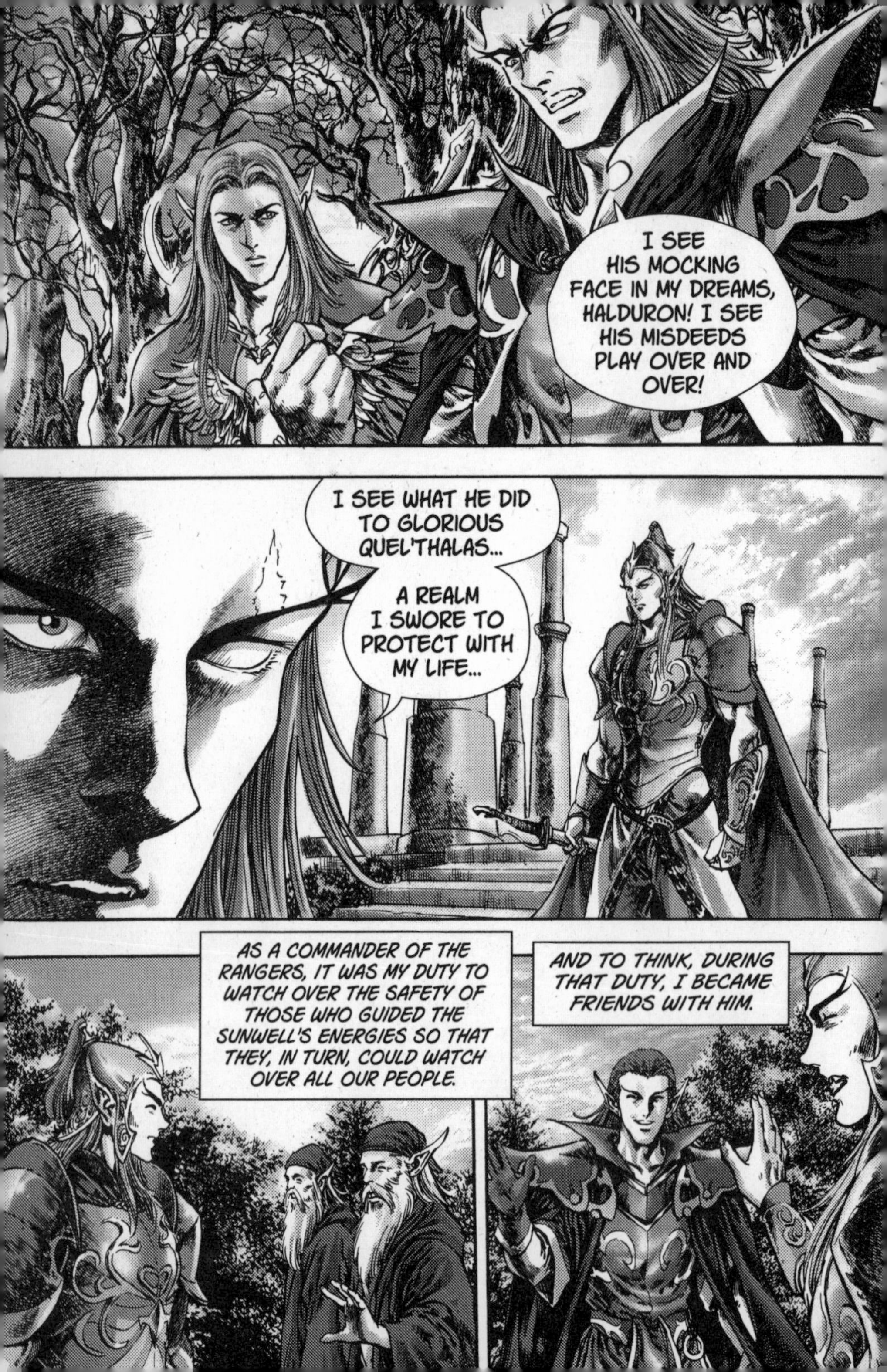
I SEE HIS MOCKING FACE IN MY DREAMS, HALDURON! I SEE HIS MISDEEDS PLAY OVER AND OVER!
I SEE WHAT HE DID TO GLORIOUS QUEL'THALAS...
A REALM I SWORE TO PROTECT WITH MY LIFE...
AS A COMMANDER OF THE RANGERS, IT WAS MY DUTY TO WATCH OVER THE SAFETY OF THOSE WHO GUIDED THE SUNWELL'S ENERGIES SO THAT THEY, IN TURN, COULD WATCH OVER ALL OUR PEOPLE.
AND TO THINK, DURING THAT DUTY, I BECAME FRIENDS WITH HIM.

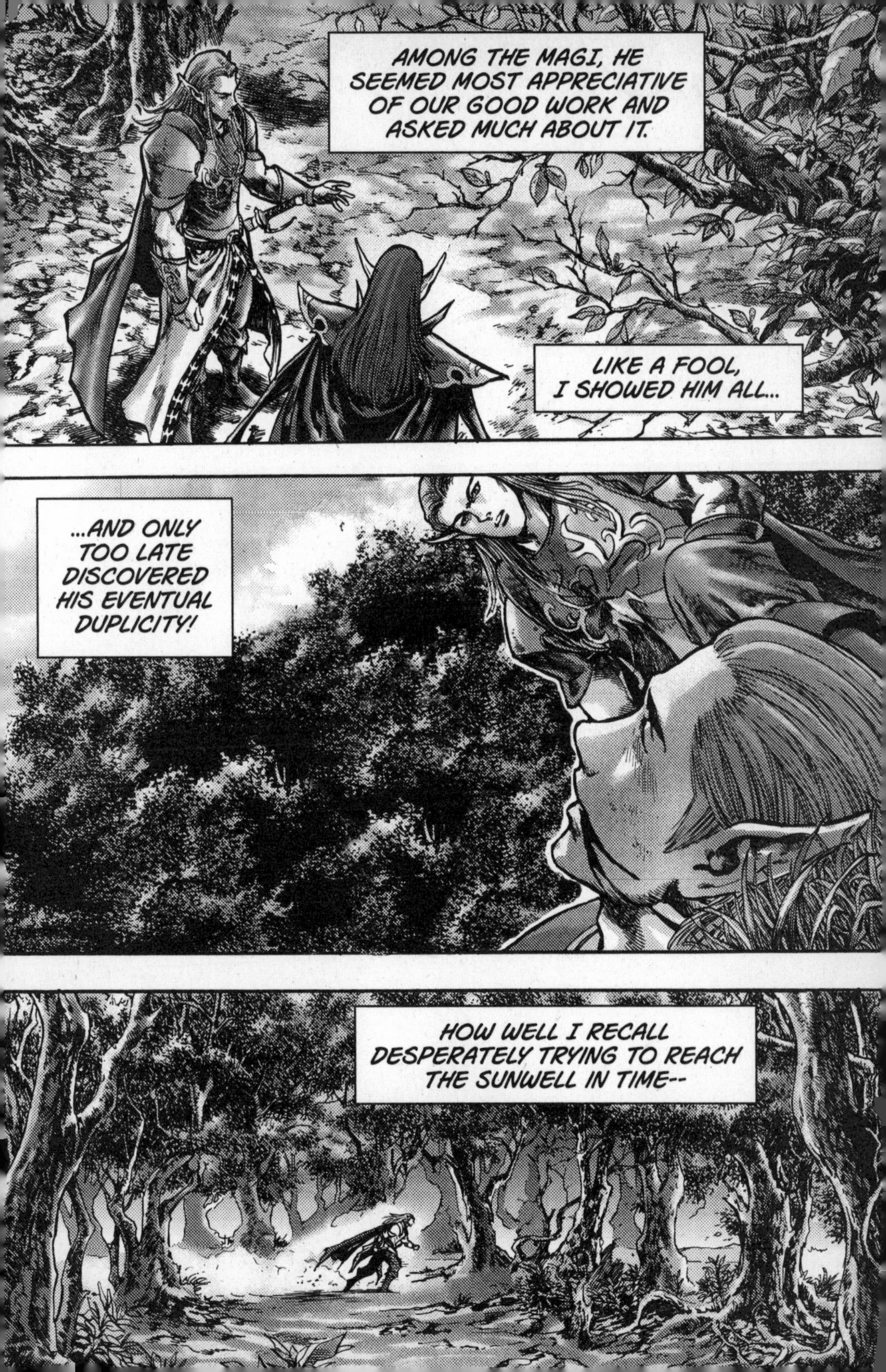
AMONG THE MAGI, HE SEEMED MOST APPRECIATIVE OF OUR GOOD WORK AND ASKED MUCH ABOUT IT.
LIKE A FOOL, I SHOWED HIM ALL...
...AND ONLY TOO LATE DISCOVERED HIS EVENTUAL DUPLICITY!
HOW WELL I RECALL DESPERATELY TRYING TO REACH THE SUNWELL IN TIME--

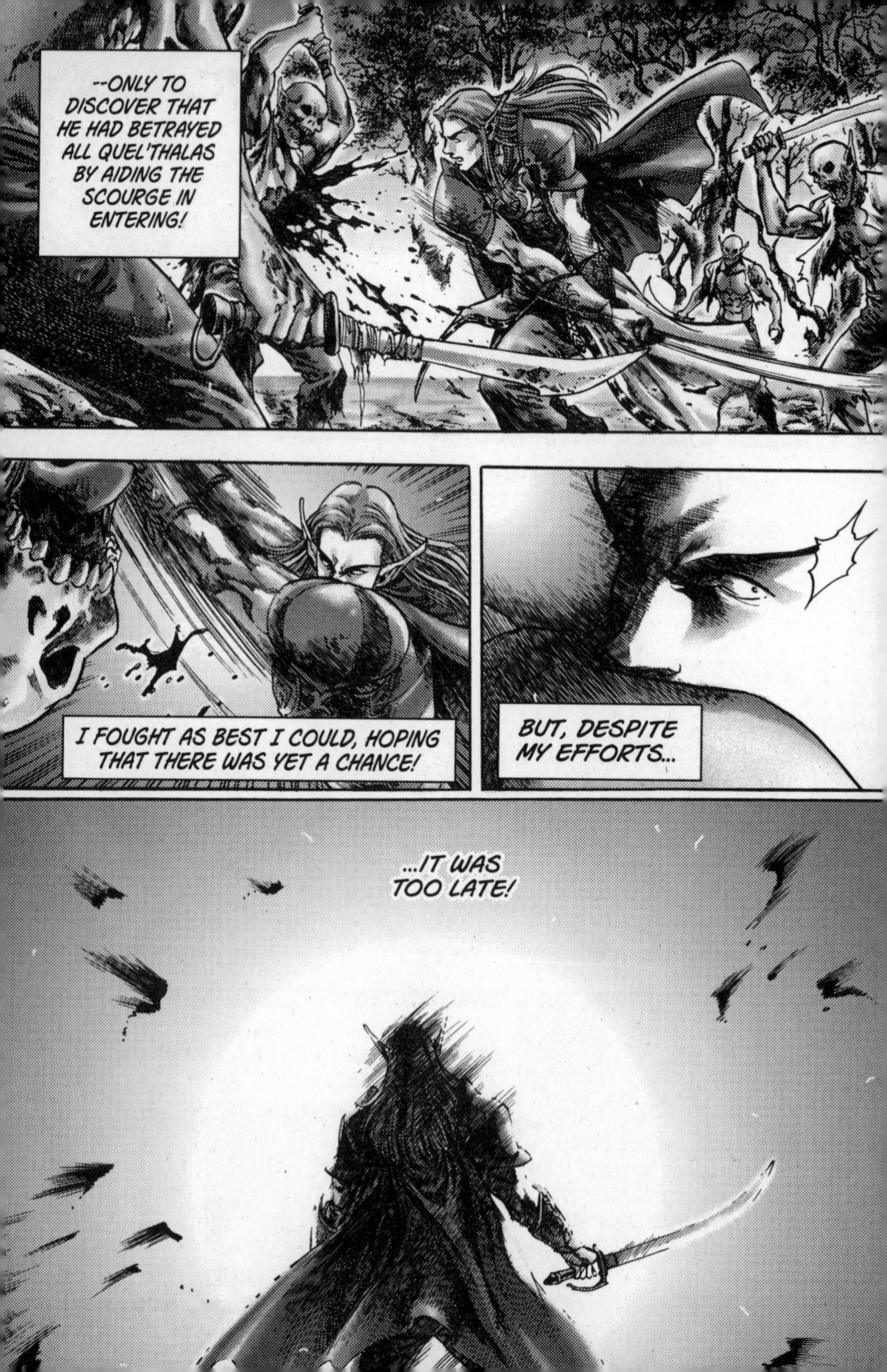
--ONLY TO DISCOVER THAT HE HAD BETRAYED ALL QUEL'THALAS BY AIDING THE SCOURGE IN ENTERING!
I FOUGHT AS BEST I COULD, HOPING THAT THERE WAS YET A CHANCE!
BUT, DESPITE MY EFFORTS...
...IT WAS TOO LATE!

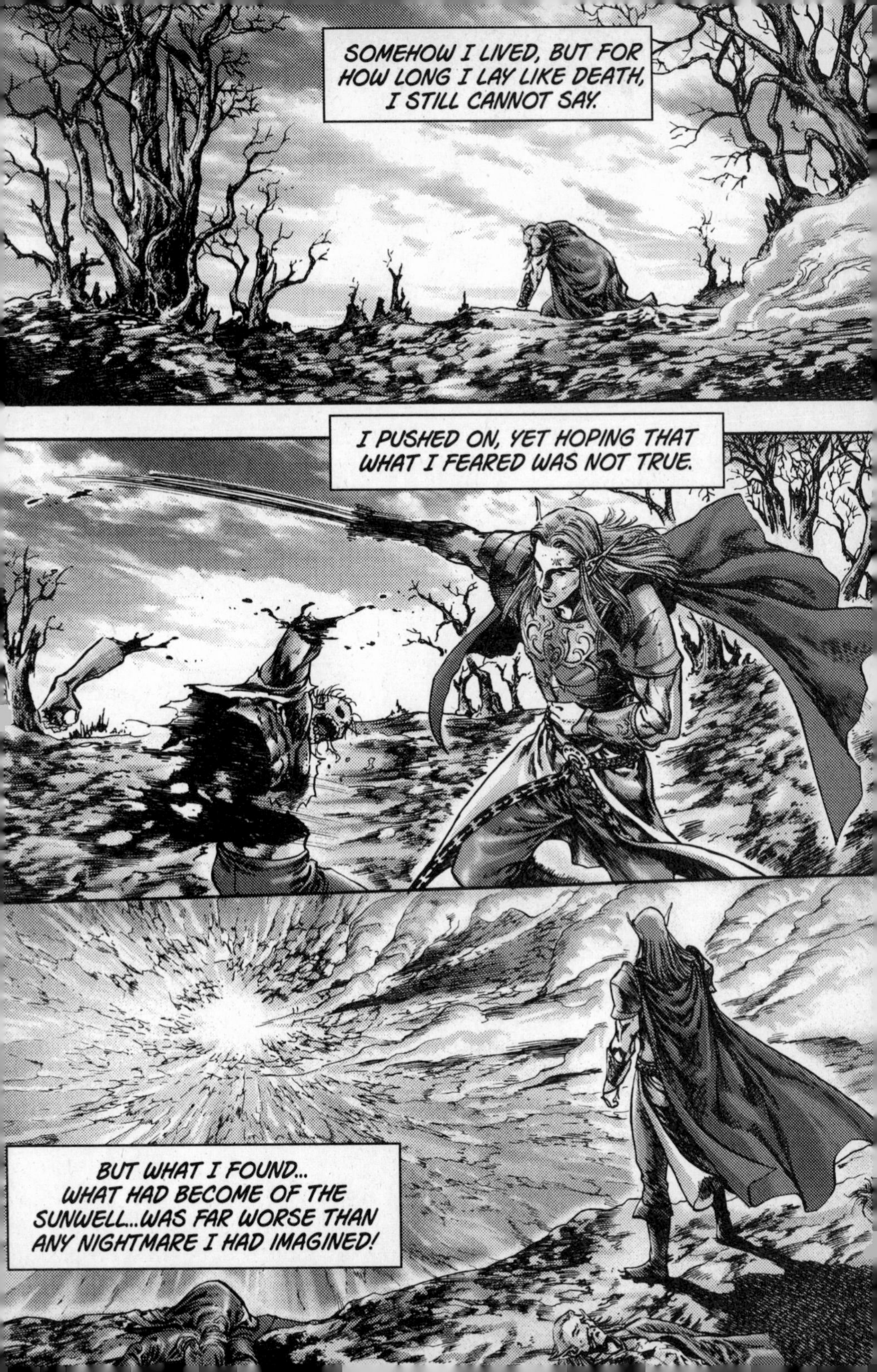
SOMEHOW I LIVED, BUT FOR HOW LONG I LAY LIKE DEATH, I STILL CANNOT SAY.
I PUSHED ON, YET HOPING THAT WHAT I FEARED WAS NOT TRUE.
BUT WHAT I FOUND... WHAT HAD BECOME OF THE SUNWELL...WAS FAR WORSE THAN ANY NIGHTMARE I HAD IMAGINED!

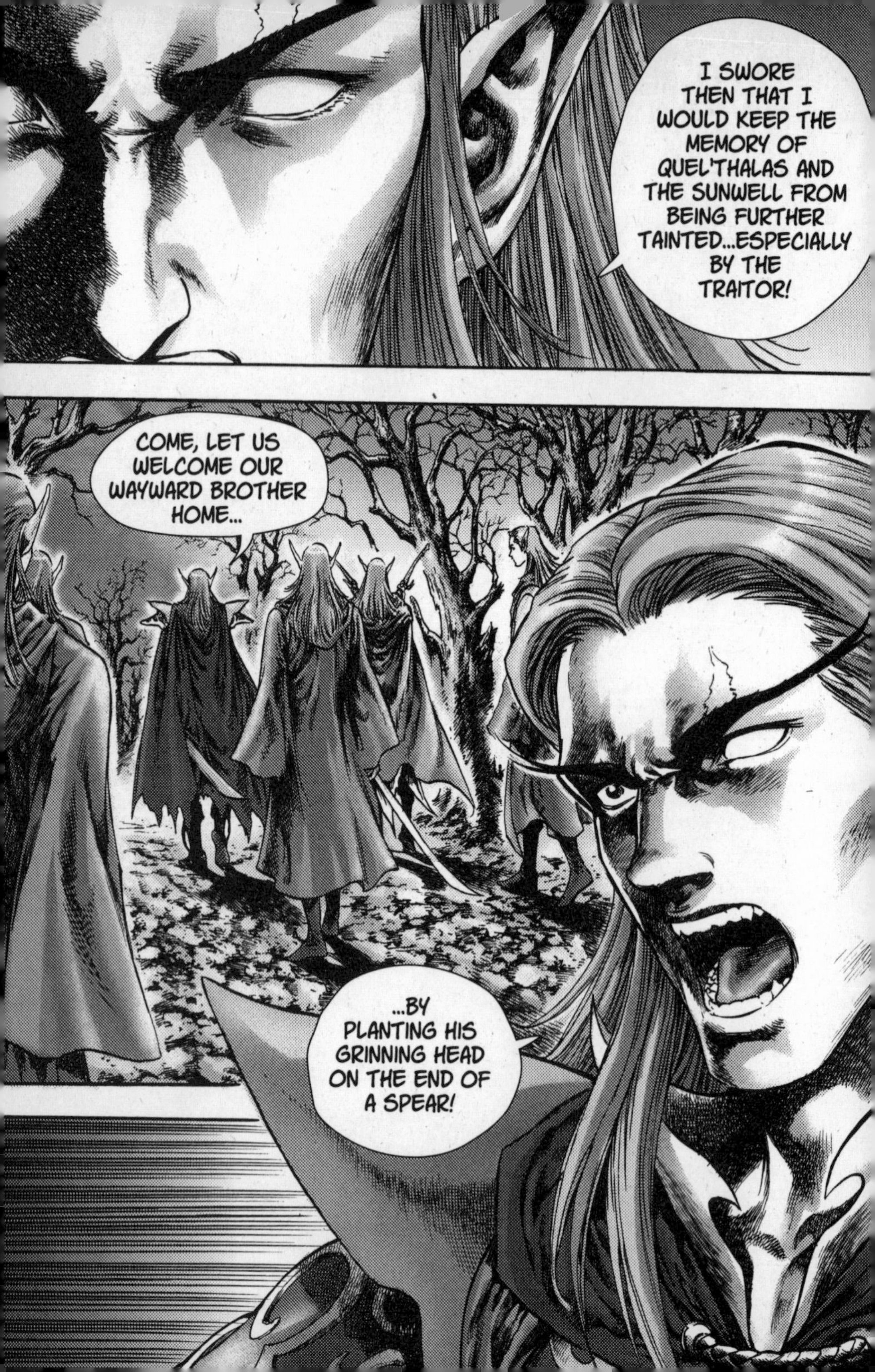
I SWORE THEN THAT I WOULD KEEP THE MEMORY OF QUEL'THALAS AND THE SUNWELL FROM BEING FURTHER TAINTED...ESPECIALLY BY THE TRAITOR!
COME, LET US WELCOME OUR WAYWARD BROTHER HOME...
...BY PLANTING HIS GRINNING HEAD ON THE END OF A SPEAR!

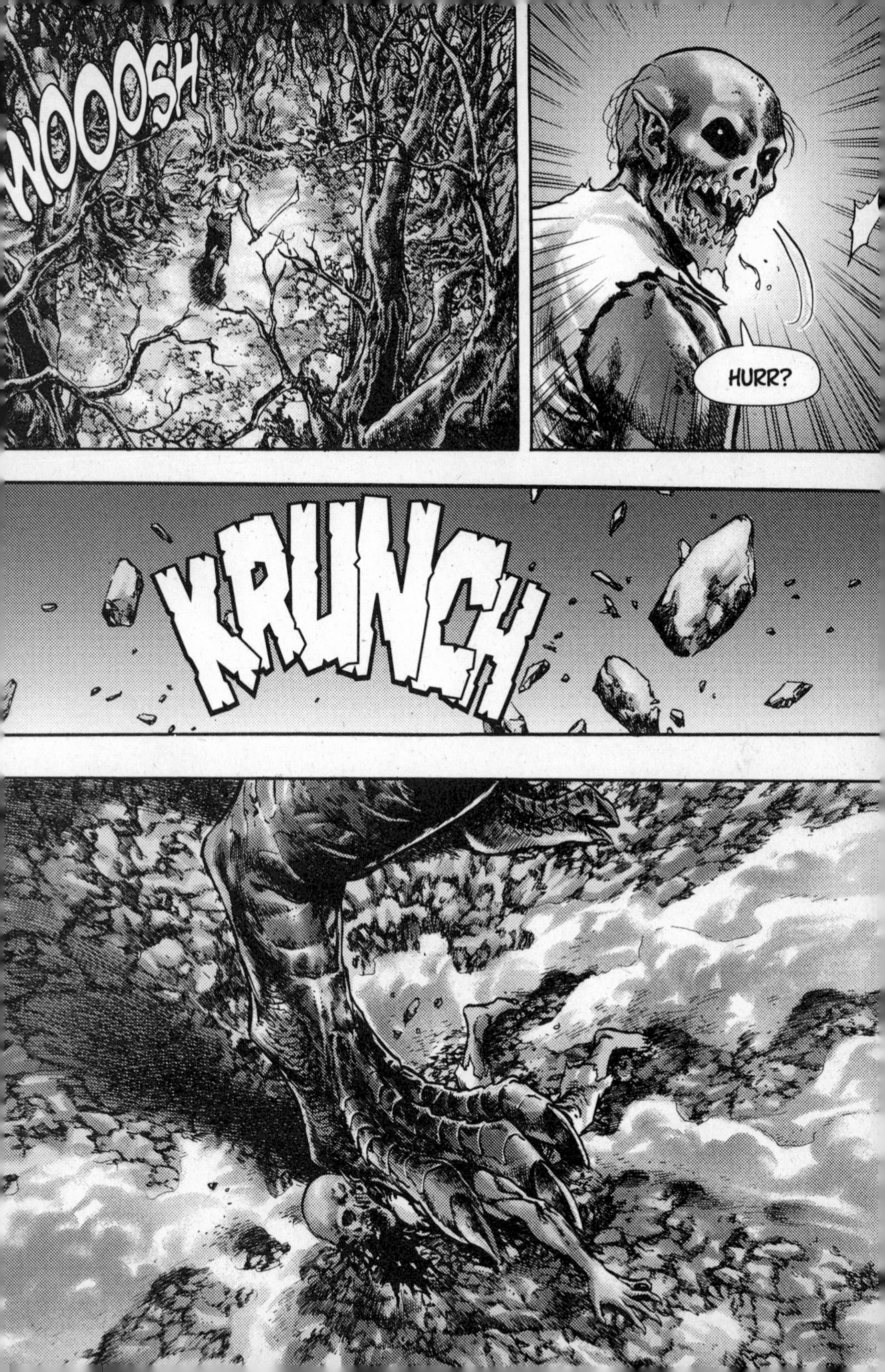
WOOOSH
HURR?
KRUNCH

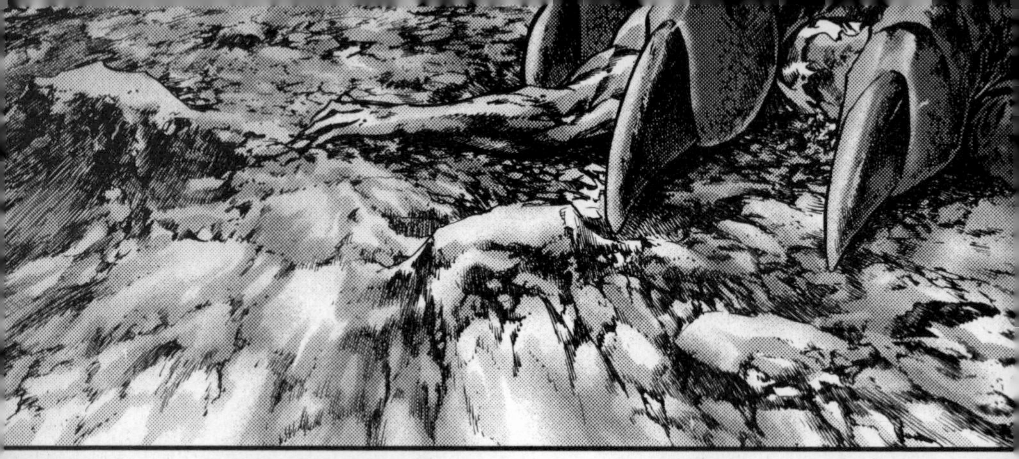
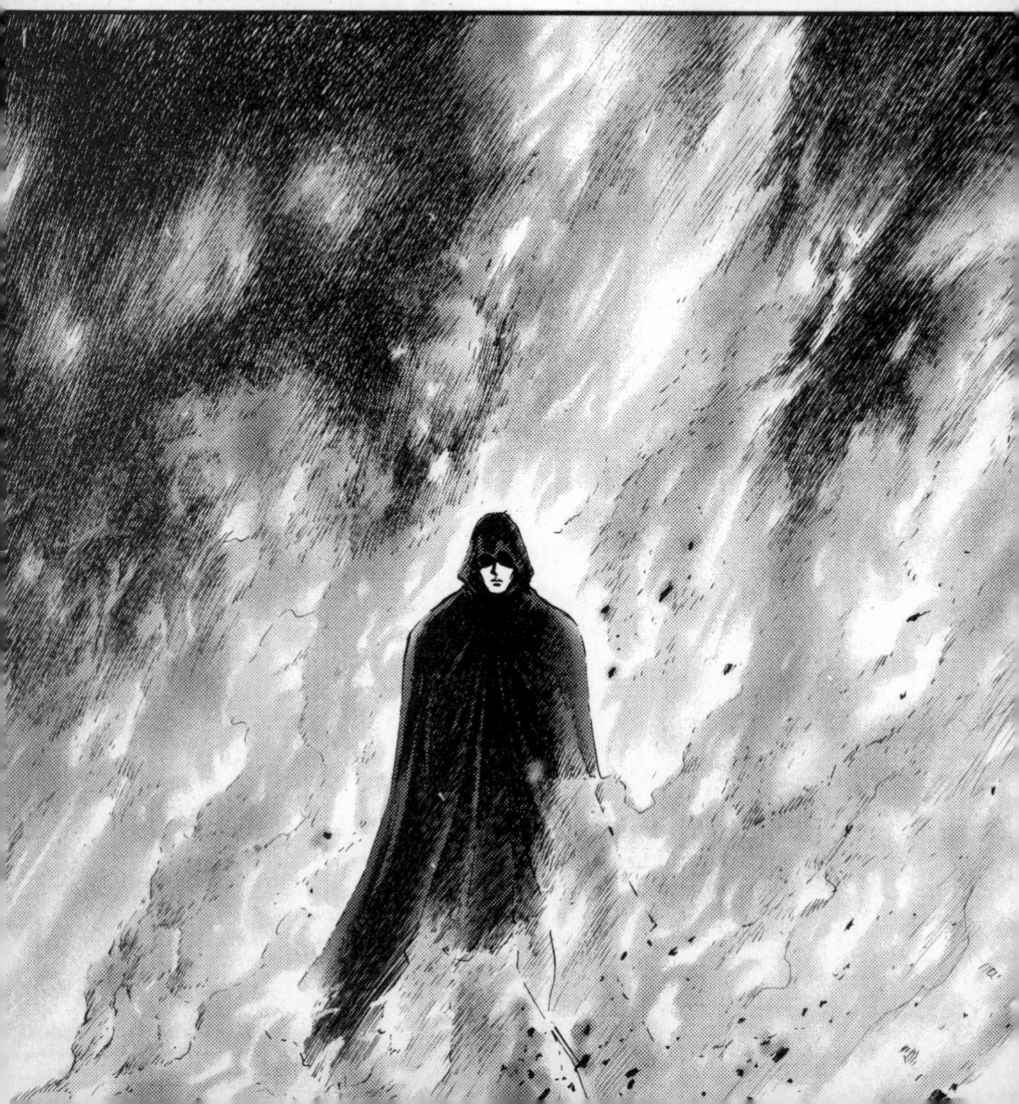

CHAPTER TWO

MASTER OF THE DEAD

HORRIBLE...

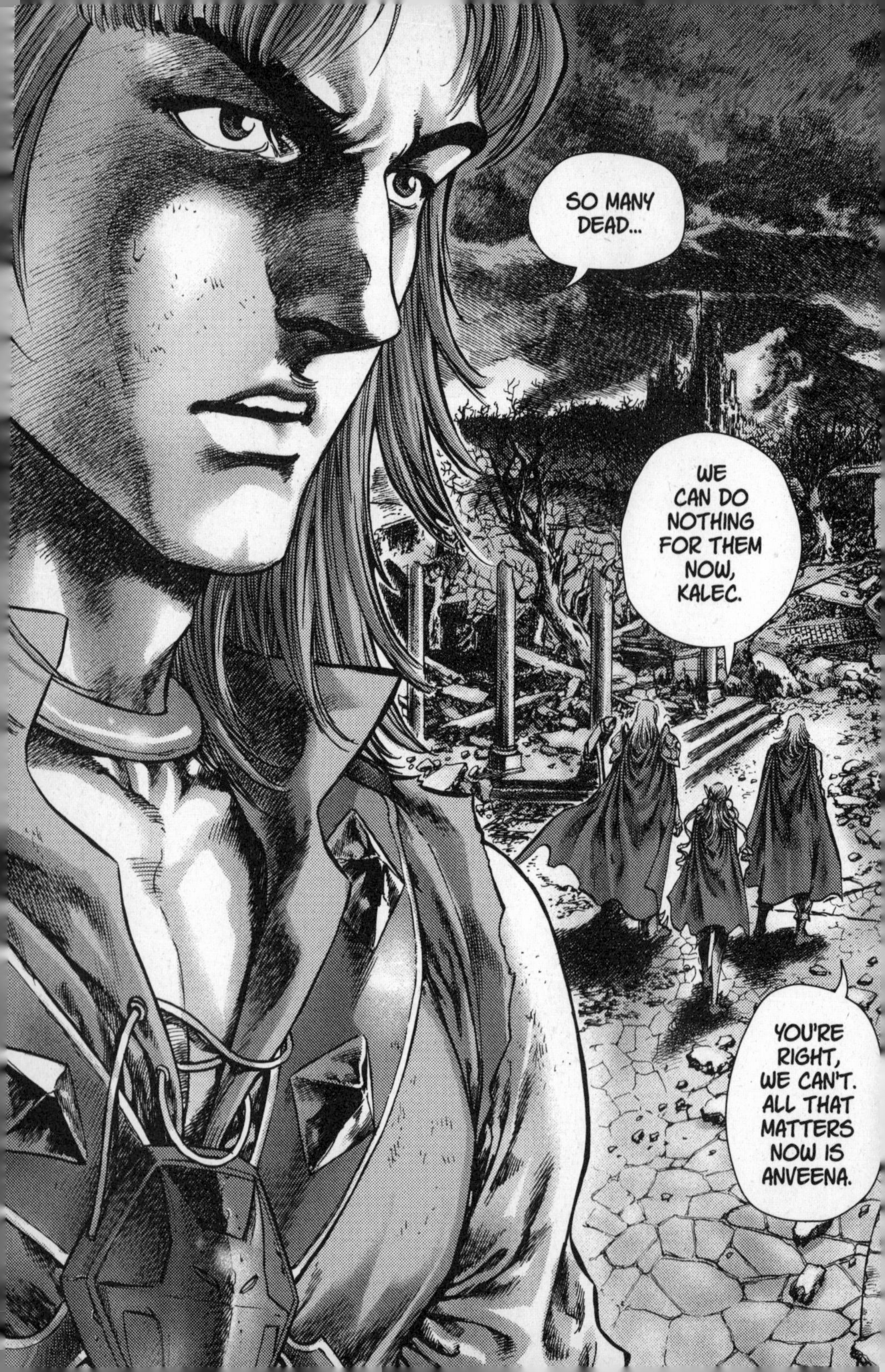
SO MANY DEAD...
WE CAN DO NOTHING FOR THEM NOW, KALEC.
YOU'RE RIGHT, WE CAN'T. ALL THAT MATTERS NOW IS ANVEENA.

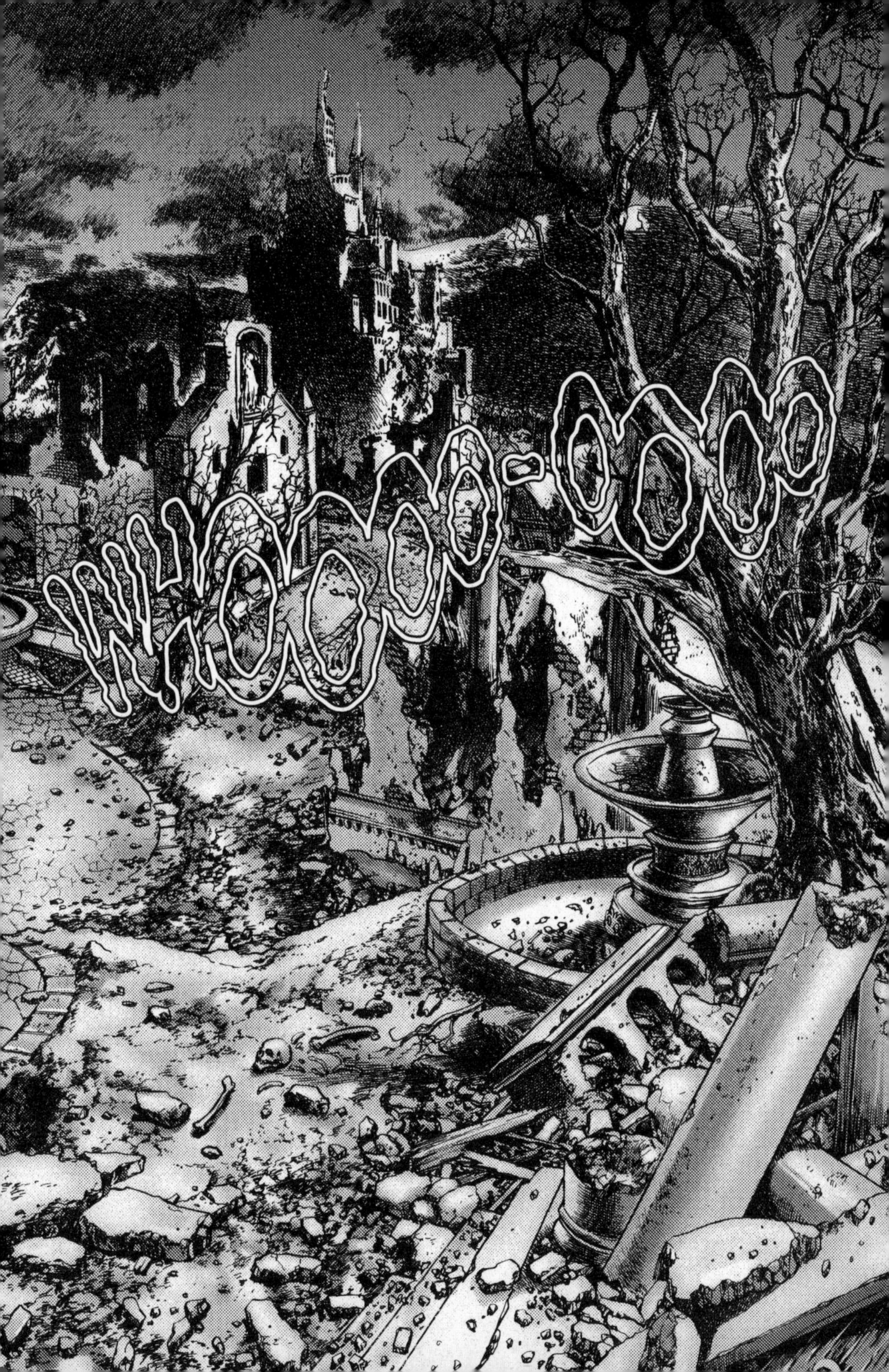
WHOOOO-OOOO

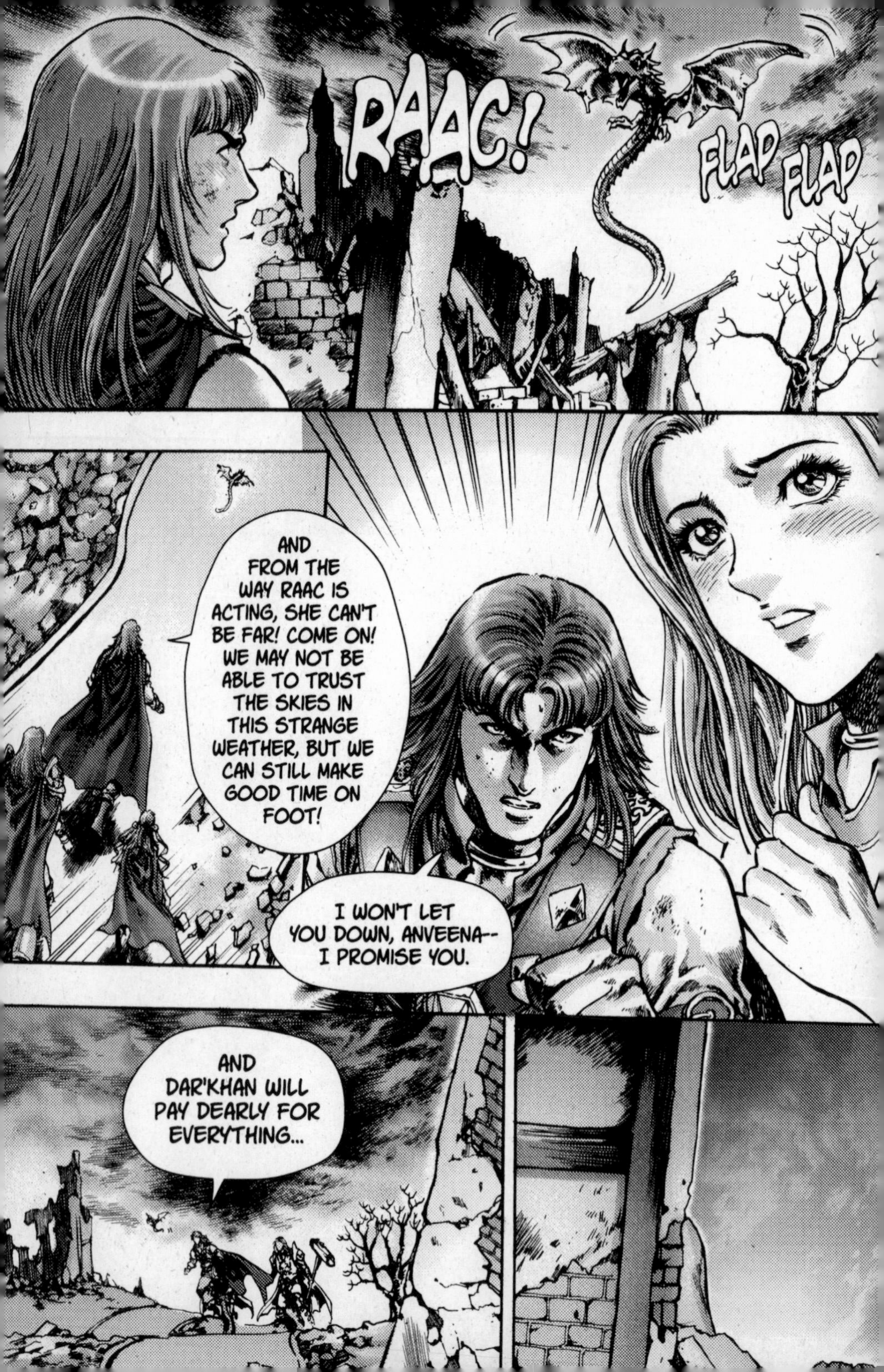
RAAC!
FLAP FLAP
AND FROM THE WAY RAAC IS ACTING, SHE CAN'T BE FAR! COME ON! WE MAY NOT BE ABLE TO TRUST THE SKIES IN THIS STRANGE WEATHER, BUT WE CAN STILL MAKE GOOD TIME ON FOOT!
I WON'T LET YOU DOWN, ANVEENA-- I PROMISE YOU.
AND DAR'KHAN WILL PAY DEARLY FOR EVERYTHING...

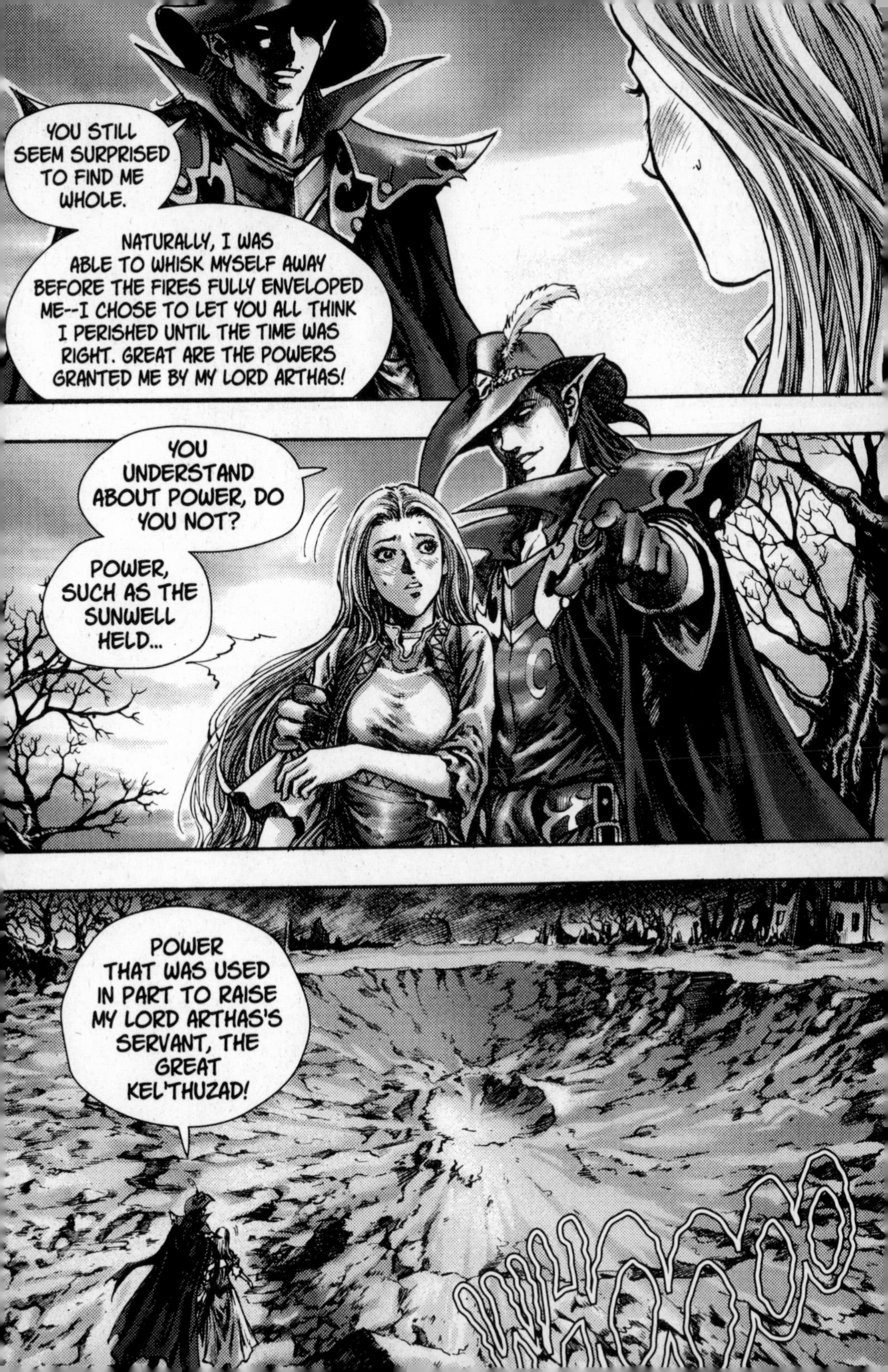
YOU STILL SEEM SURPRISED TO FIND ME WHOLE.
NATURALLY, I WAS ABLE TO WHISK MYSELF AWAY BEFORE THE FIRES FULLY ENVELOPED ME--I CHOSE TO LET YOU ALL THINK I PERISHED UNTIL THE TIME WAS RIGHT. GREAT ARE THE POWERS GRANTED ME BY MY LORD ARTHAS!
YOU UNDERSTAND ABOUT POWER, DO YOU NOT?
POWER, SUCH AS THE SUNWELL HELD...
POWER THAT WAS USED IN PART TO RAISE MY LORD ARTHAS'S SERVANT, THE GREAT KEL'THUZAD!

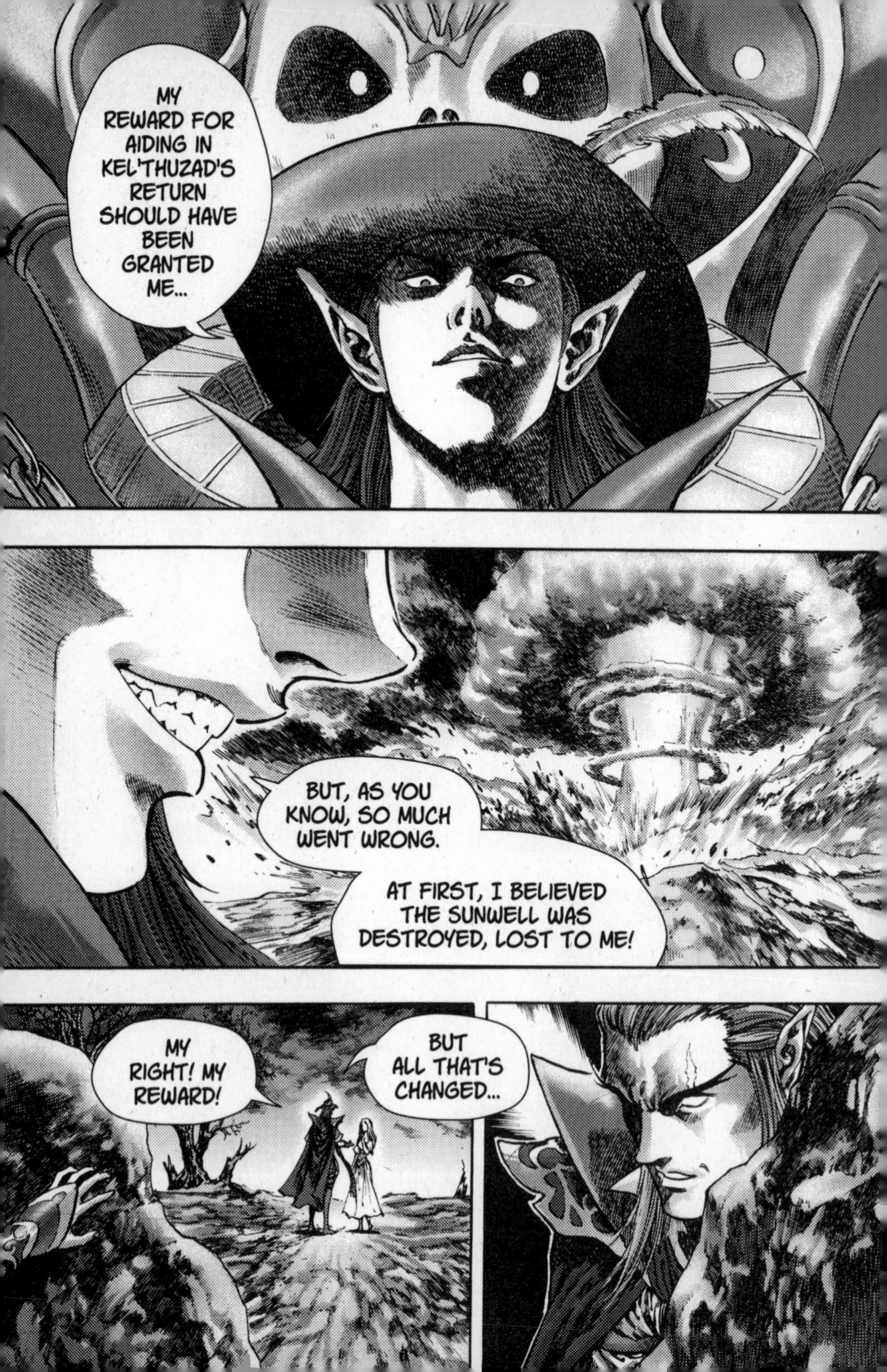
MY REWARD FOR AIDING IN KEL'THUZAD'S RETURN SHOULD HAVE BEEN GRANTED ME...
BUT, AS YOU KNOW, SO MUCH WENT WRONG.
AT FIRST, I BELIEVED THE SUNWELL WAS DESTROYED, LOST TO ME!
MY RIGHT! MY REWARD!
BUT ALL THAT'S CHANGED...

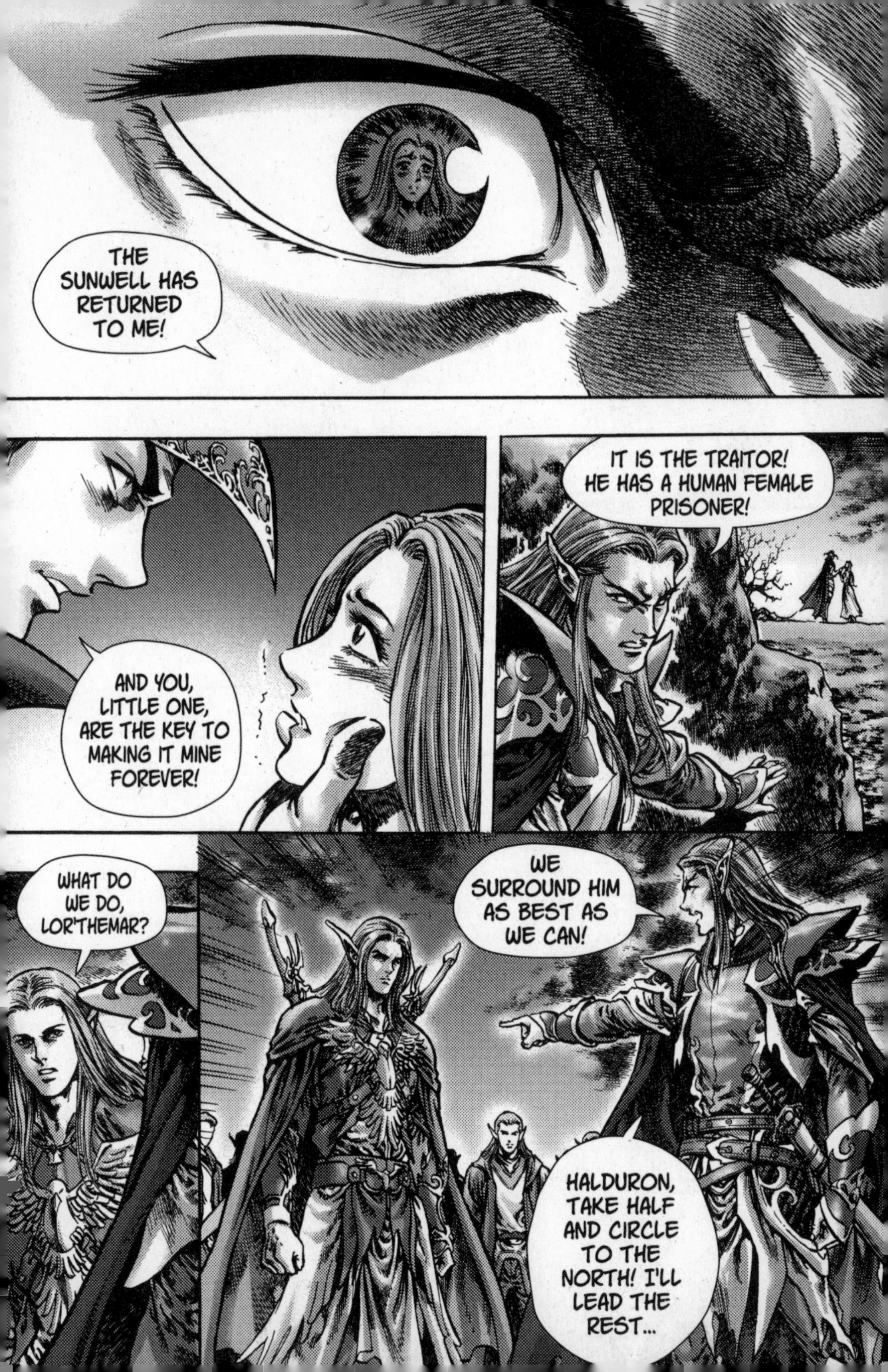
THE SUNWELL HAS RETURNED TO ME!
AND YOU, LITTLE ONE, ARE THE KEY TO MAKING IT MINE FOREVER!
IT IS THE TRAITOR! HE HAS A HUMAN FEMALE PRISONER!
WHAT DO WE DO, LOR'THEMAR?
WE SURROUND HIM AS BEST AS WE CAN!
HALDURON, TAKE HALF AND CIRCLE TO THE NORTH! I'LL LEAD THE REST...

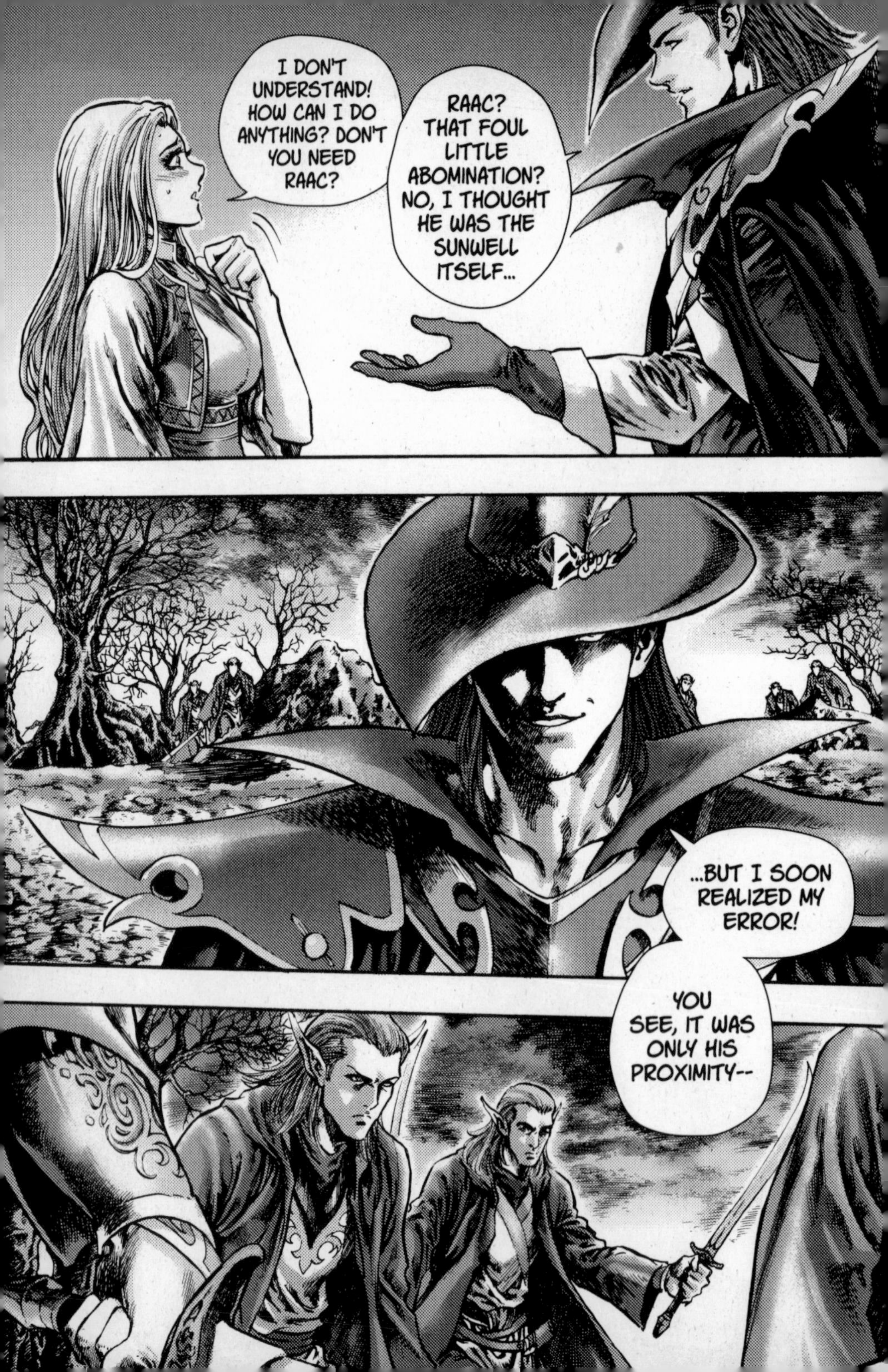
I DON'T UNDERSTAND! HOW CAN I DO ANYTHING? DON'T YOU NEED RAAC?
RAAC? THAT FOUL LITTLE ABOMINATION? NO, I THOUGHT HE WAS THE SUNWELL ITSELF...
...BUT I SOON REALIZED MY ERROR!
YOU SEE, IT WAS ONLY HIS PROXIMITY--

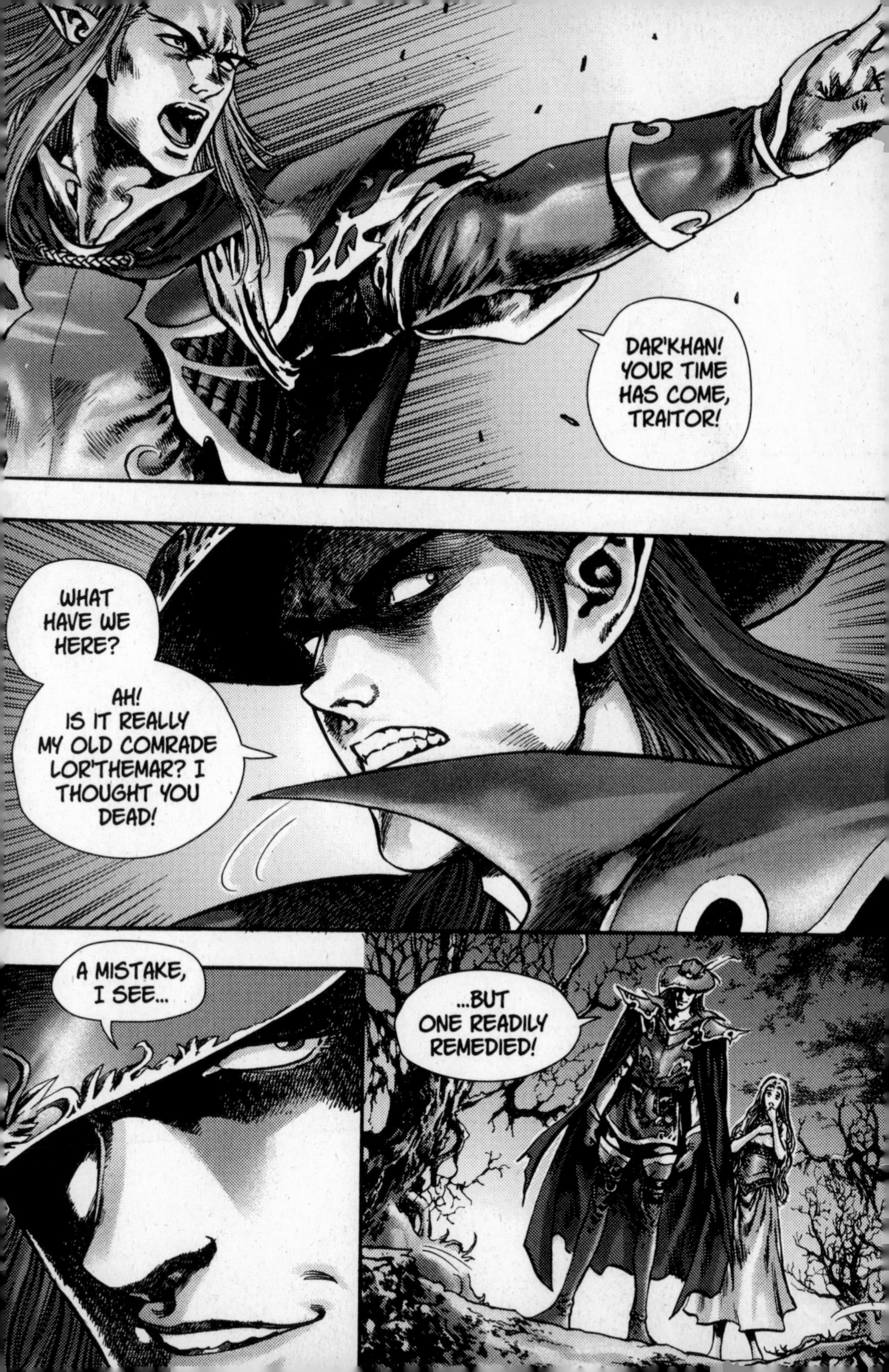
DAR'KHAN! YOUR TIME HAS COME, TRAITOR!
WHAT HAVE WE HERE?
AH! IS IT REALLY MY OLD COMRADE LOR'THEMAR? I THOUGHT YOU DEAD!
A MISTAKE, I SEE...
...BUT ONE READILY REMEDIED!

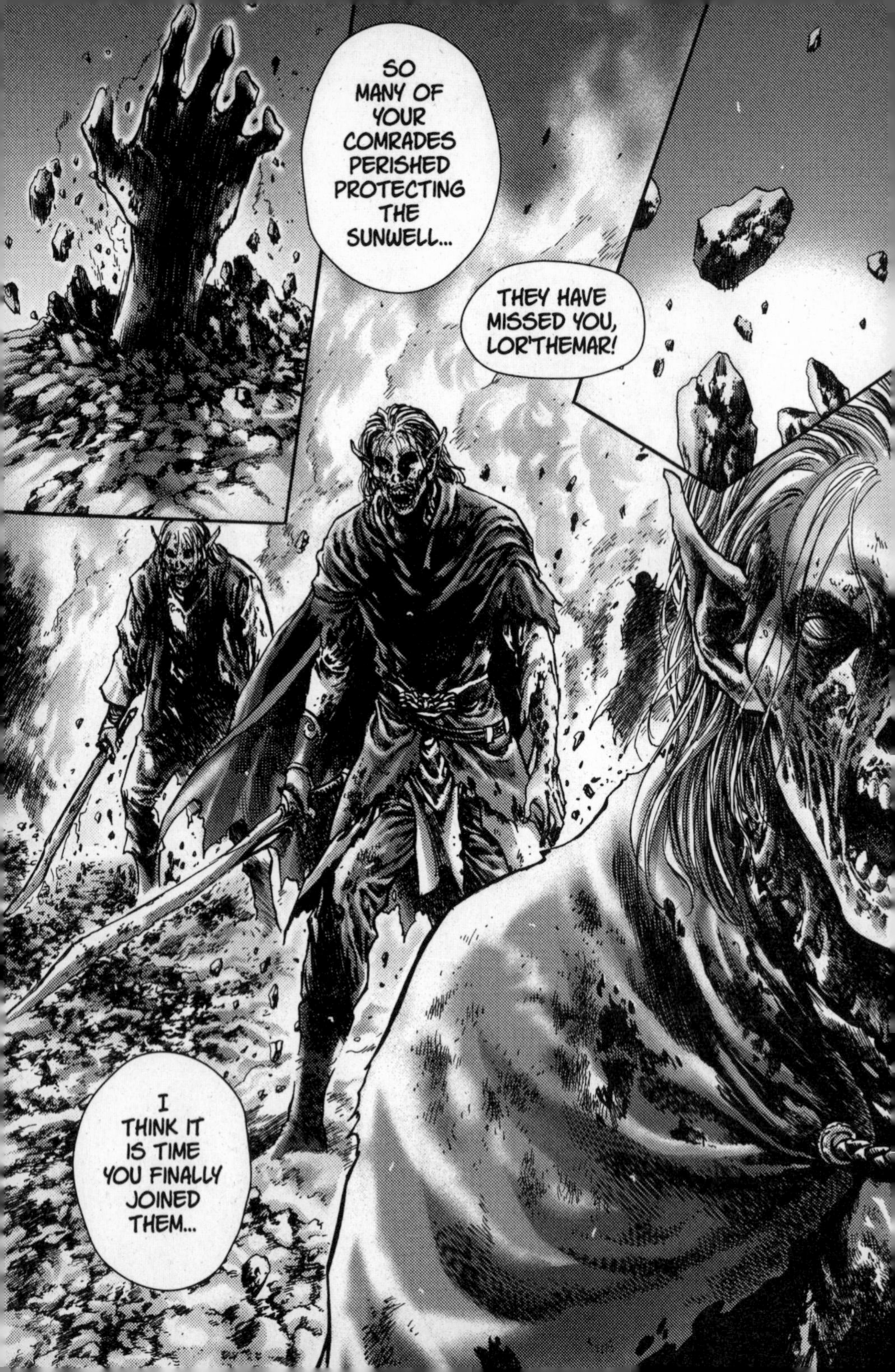
SO MANY OF YOUR COMRADES PERISHED PROTECTING THE SUNWELL...
THEY HAVE MISSED YOU, LOR'THEMAR!
I THINK IT IS TIME YOU FINALLY JOINED THEM...

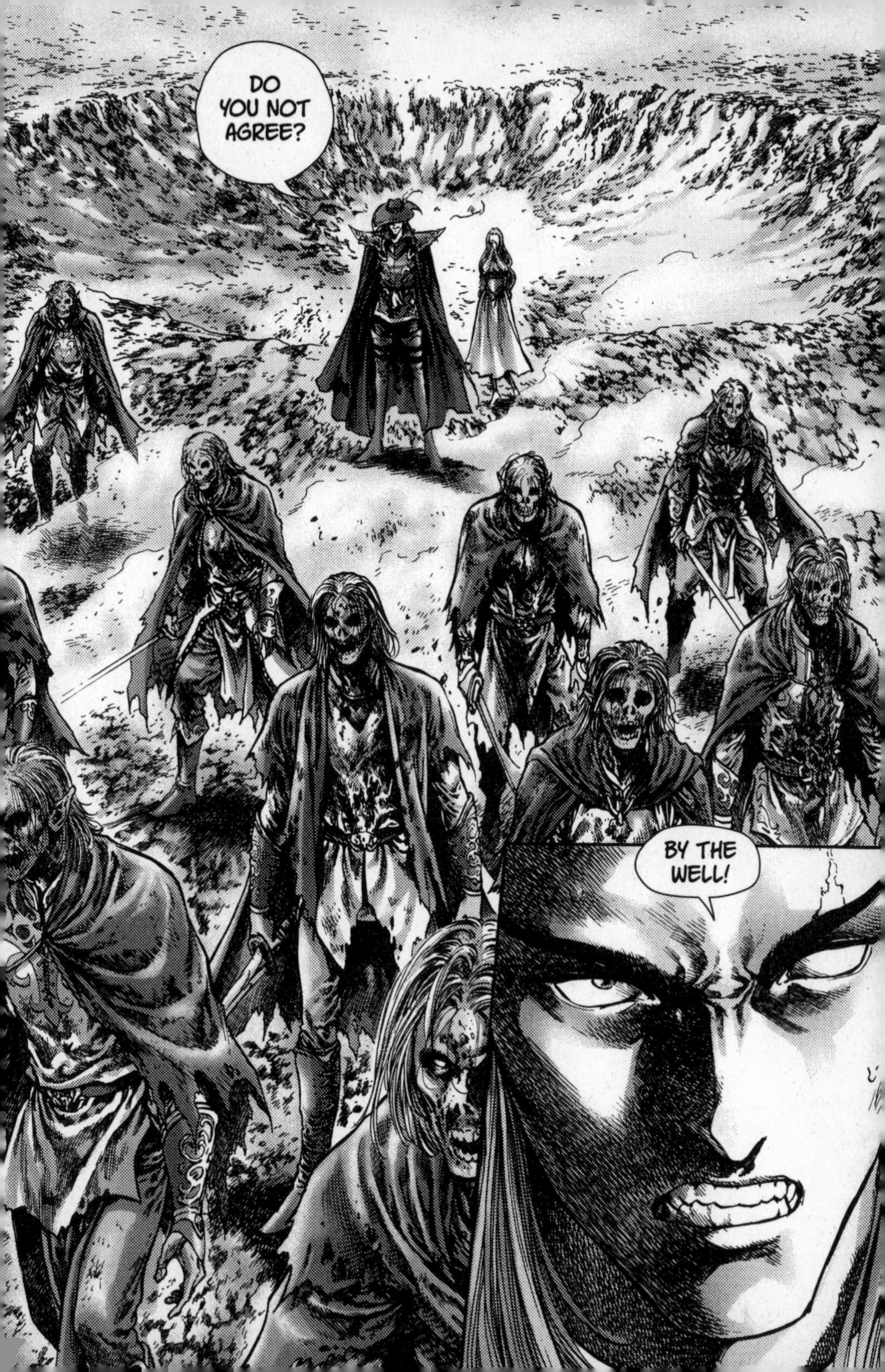
DO YOU NOT AGREE?
BY THE WELL!

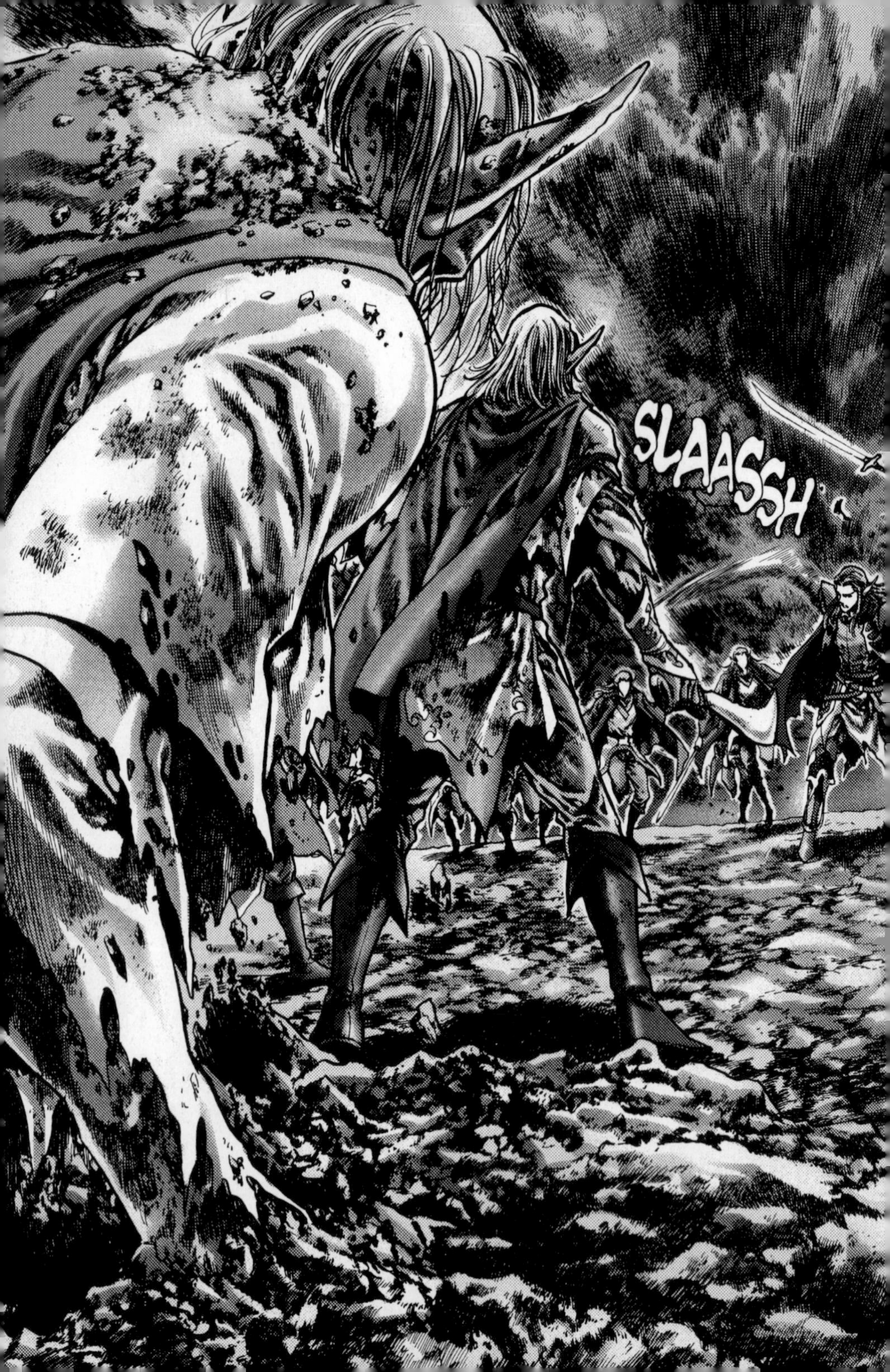
SLAASSH

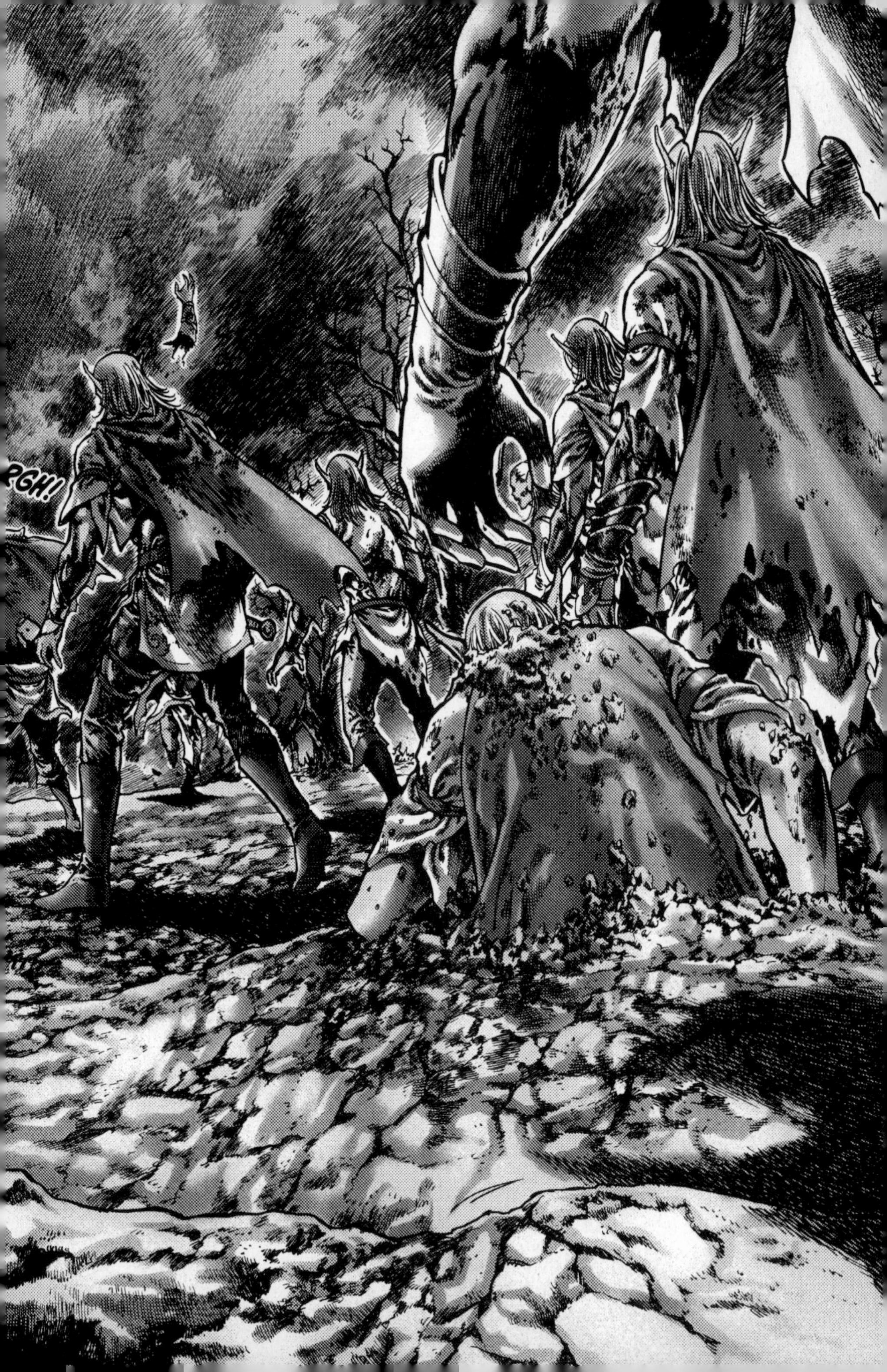
RGH!

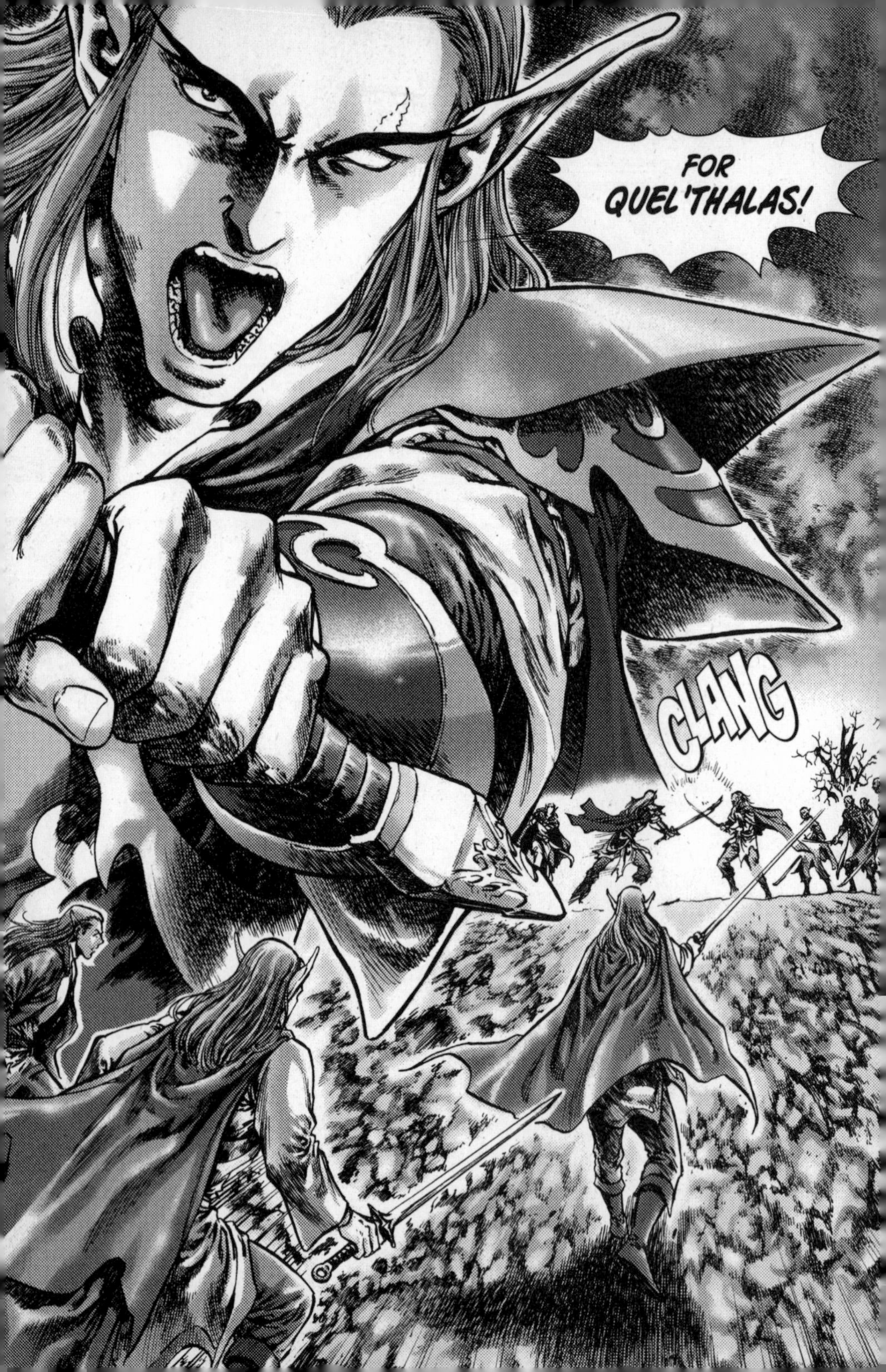
FOR QUEL'THALAS!
CLANG

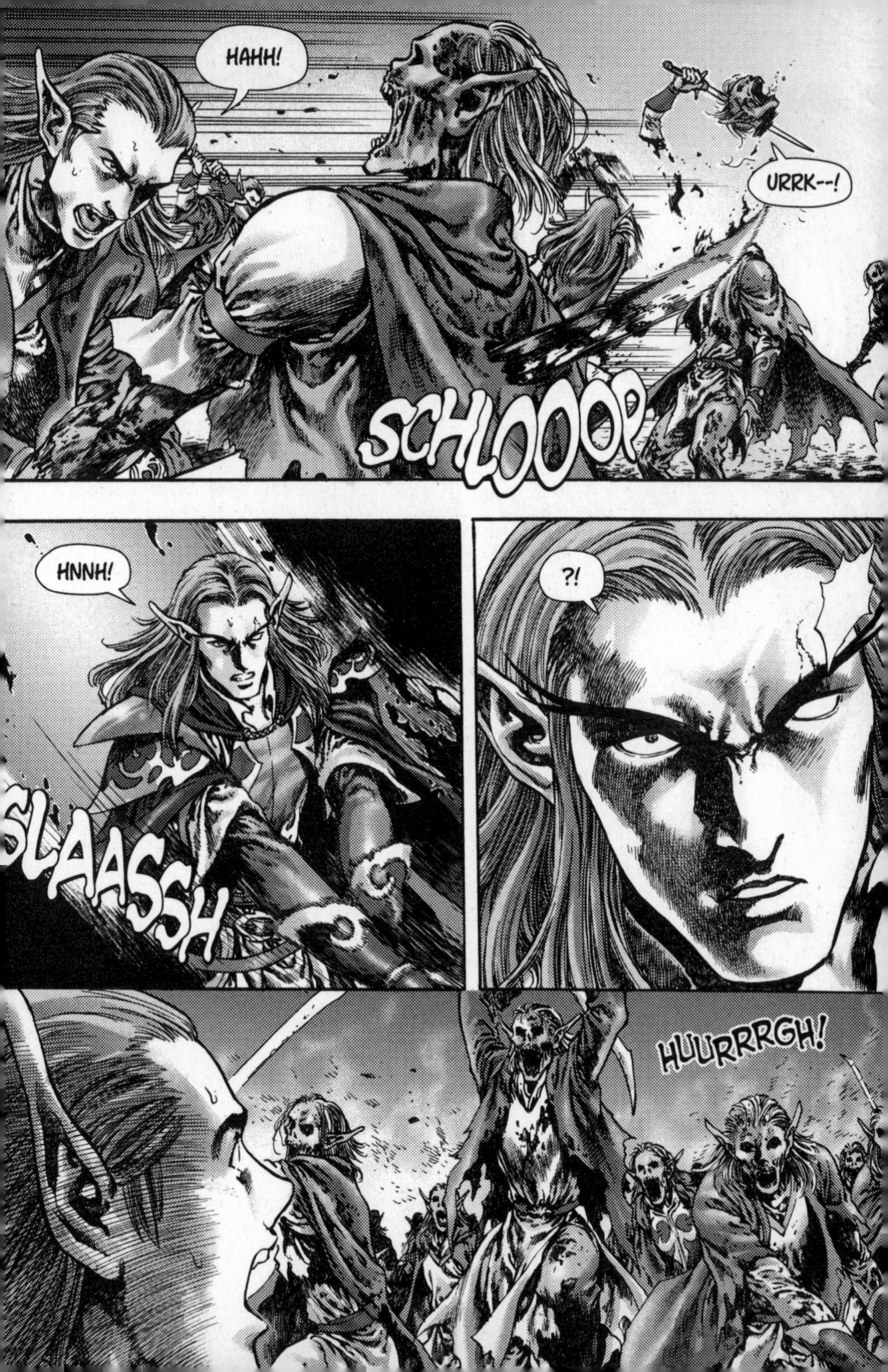
HAHH!
URRK--!
SCHLOOOP
HNNH!
SLAASSH
?!
HUURRRGH!

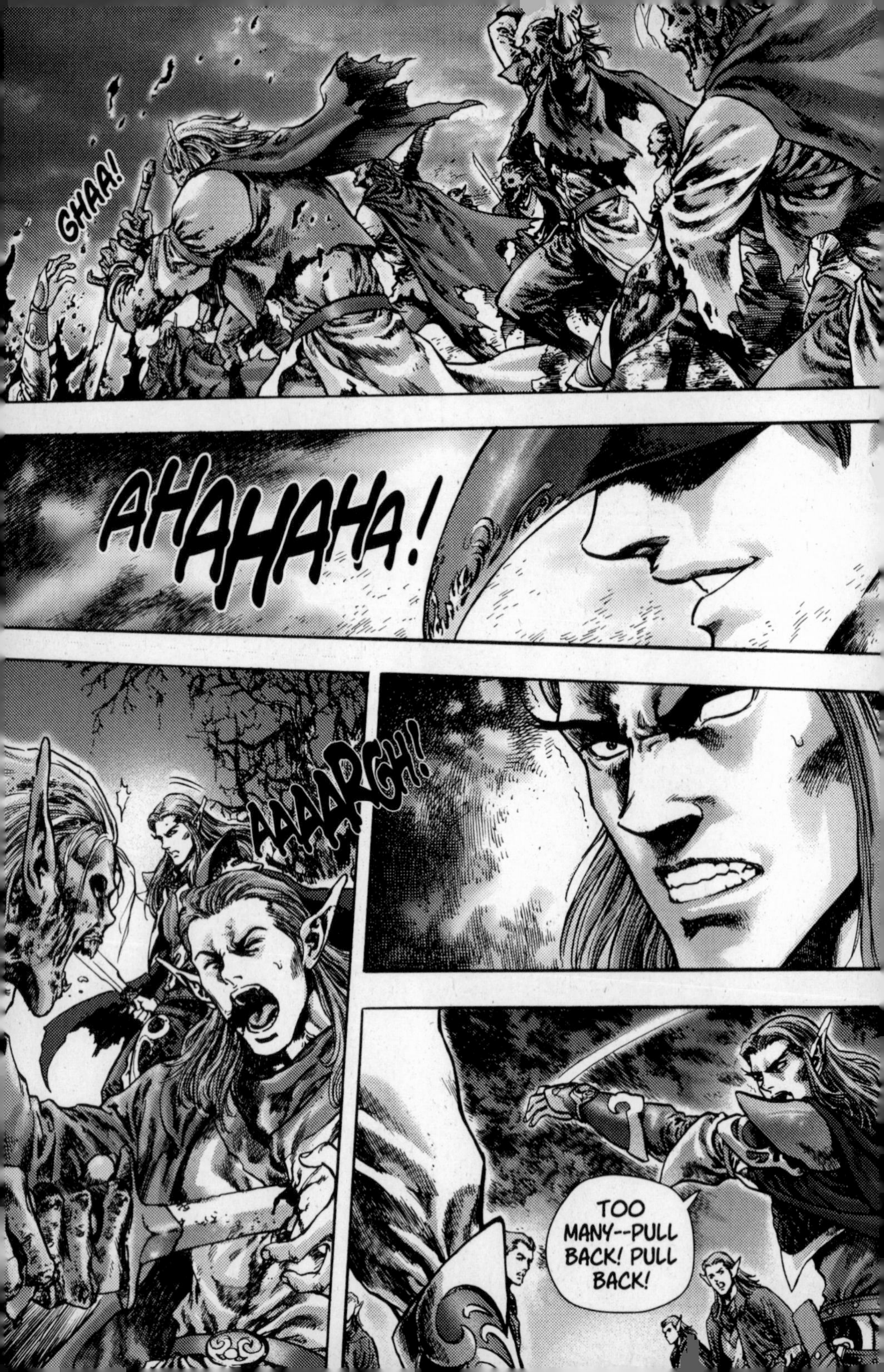
GHAA!
AHAHAHAHA!
AAAARGH!
TOO MANY--PULL BACK! PULL BACK!

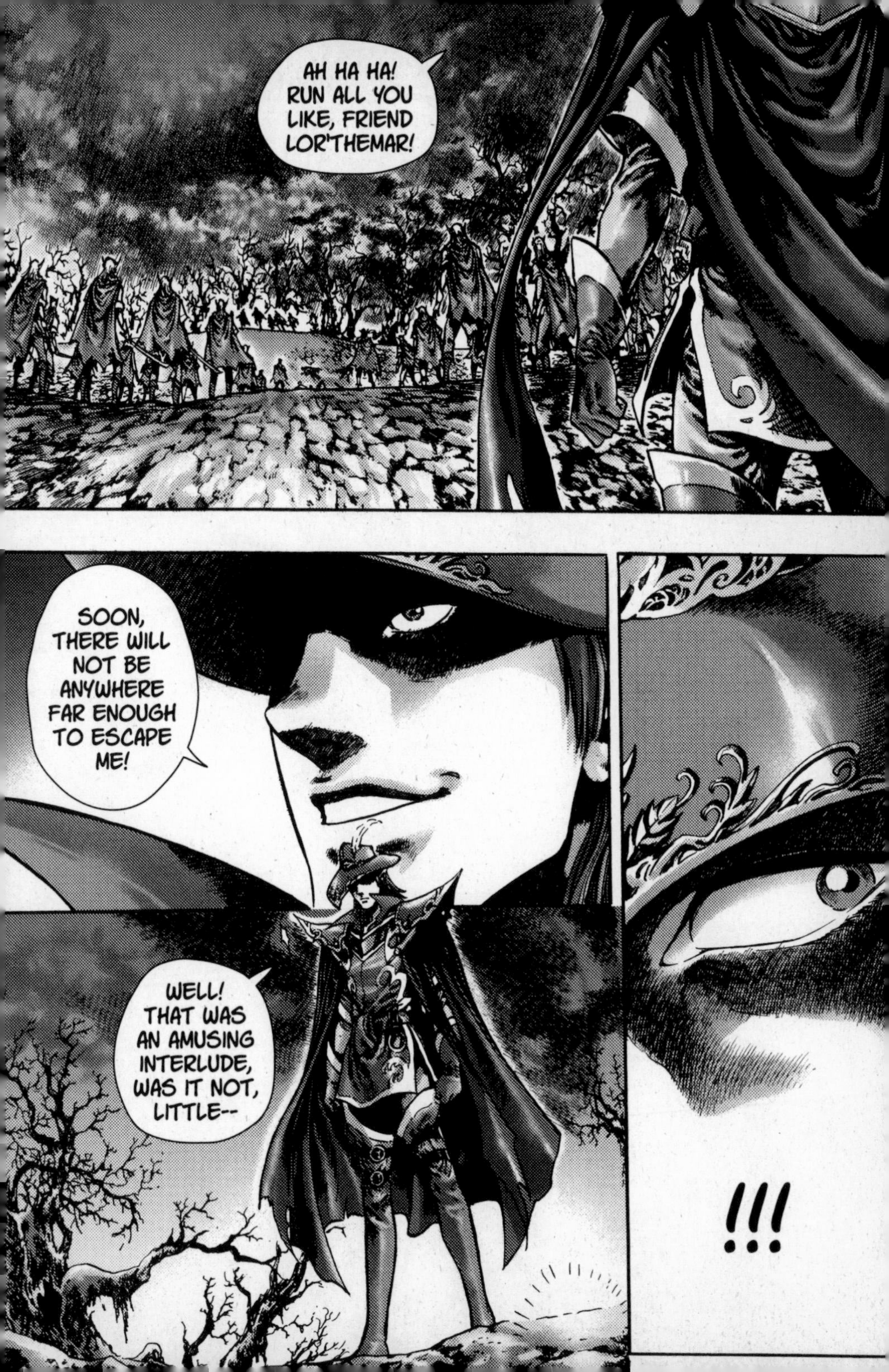
AH HA HA! RUN ALL YOU LIKE, FRIEND LOR'THEMAR!
SOON, THERE WILL NOT BE ANYWHERE FAR ENOUGH TO ESCAPE ME!
WELL! THAT WAS AN AMUSING INTERLUDE, WAS IT NOT, LITTLE--
!!!

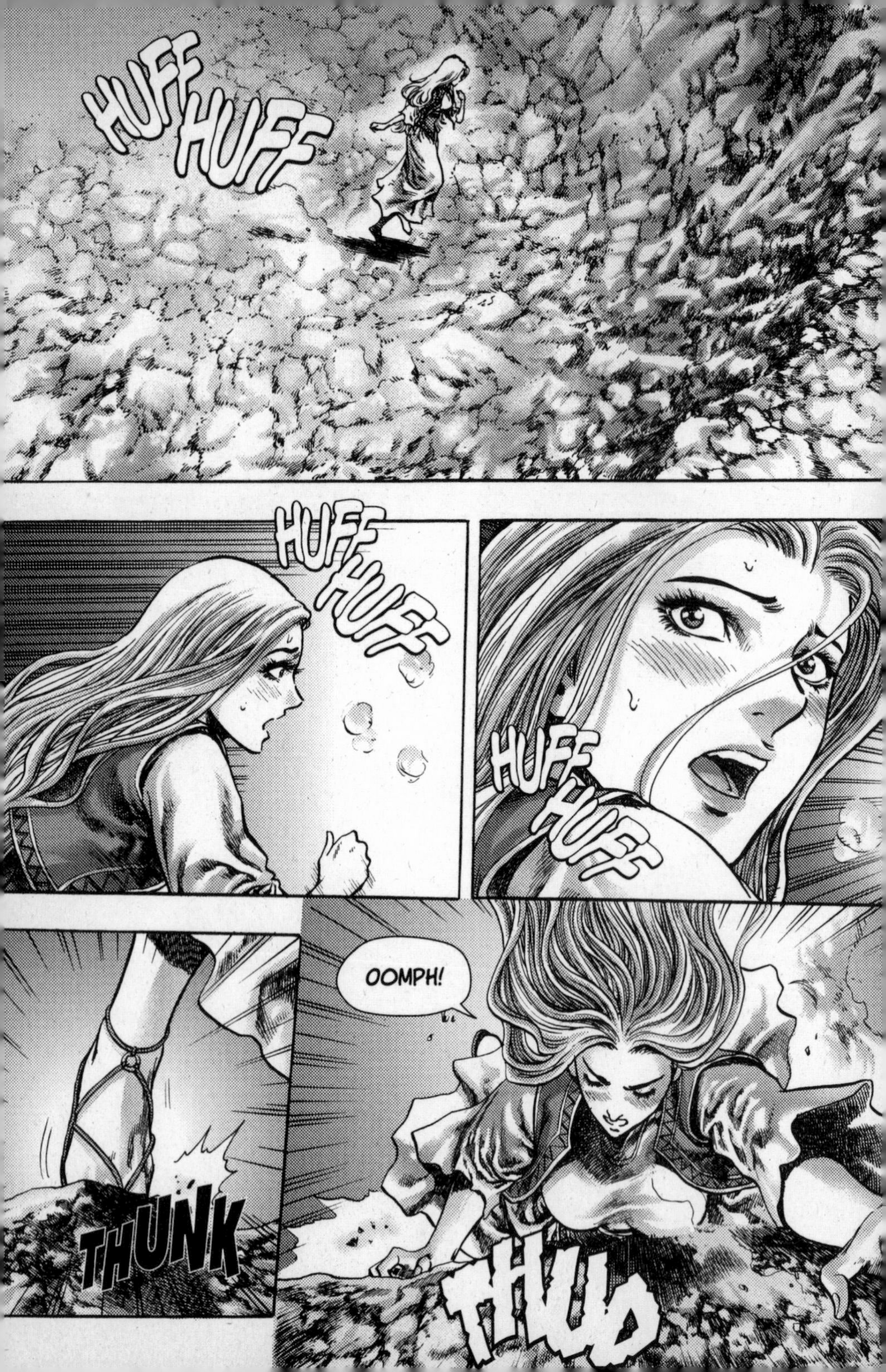
HUFF HUFF
HUFF HUFF
HUFF HUFF
OOMPH!
THUD
THUNK

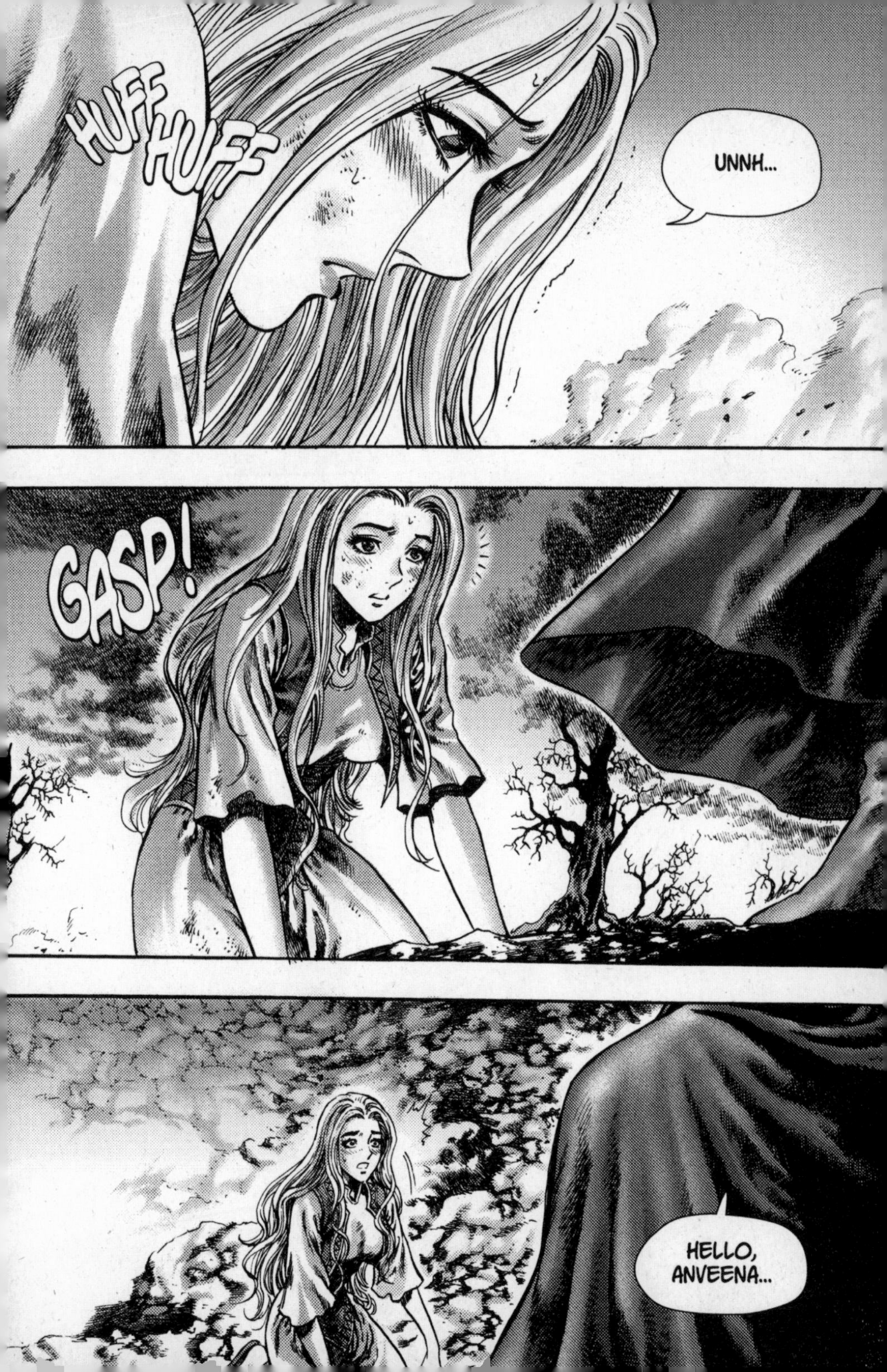
UNNH...
HUFF HUFF
GASP!
HELLO, ANVEENA...

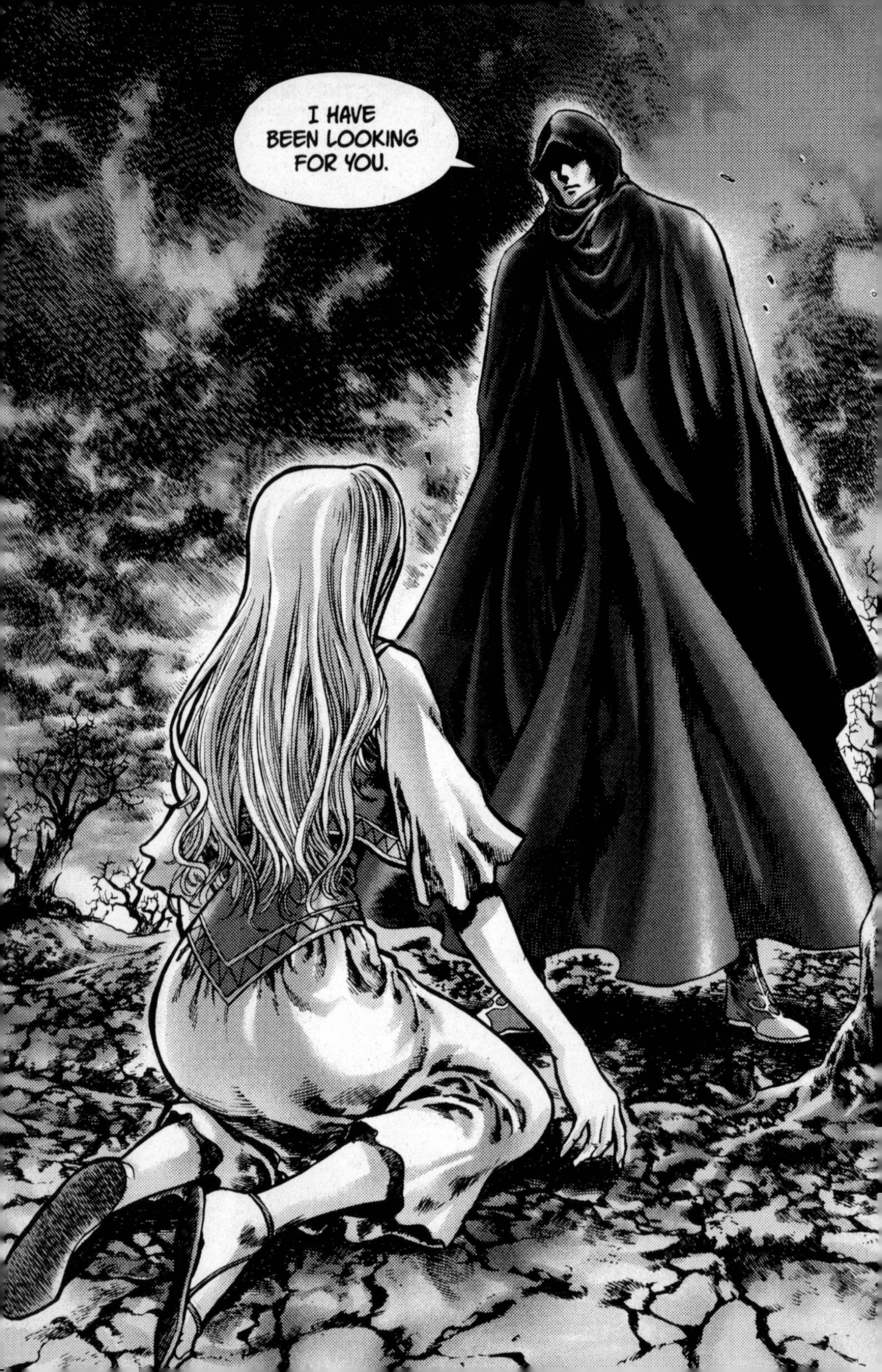
I HAVE BEEN LOOKING FOR YOU.

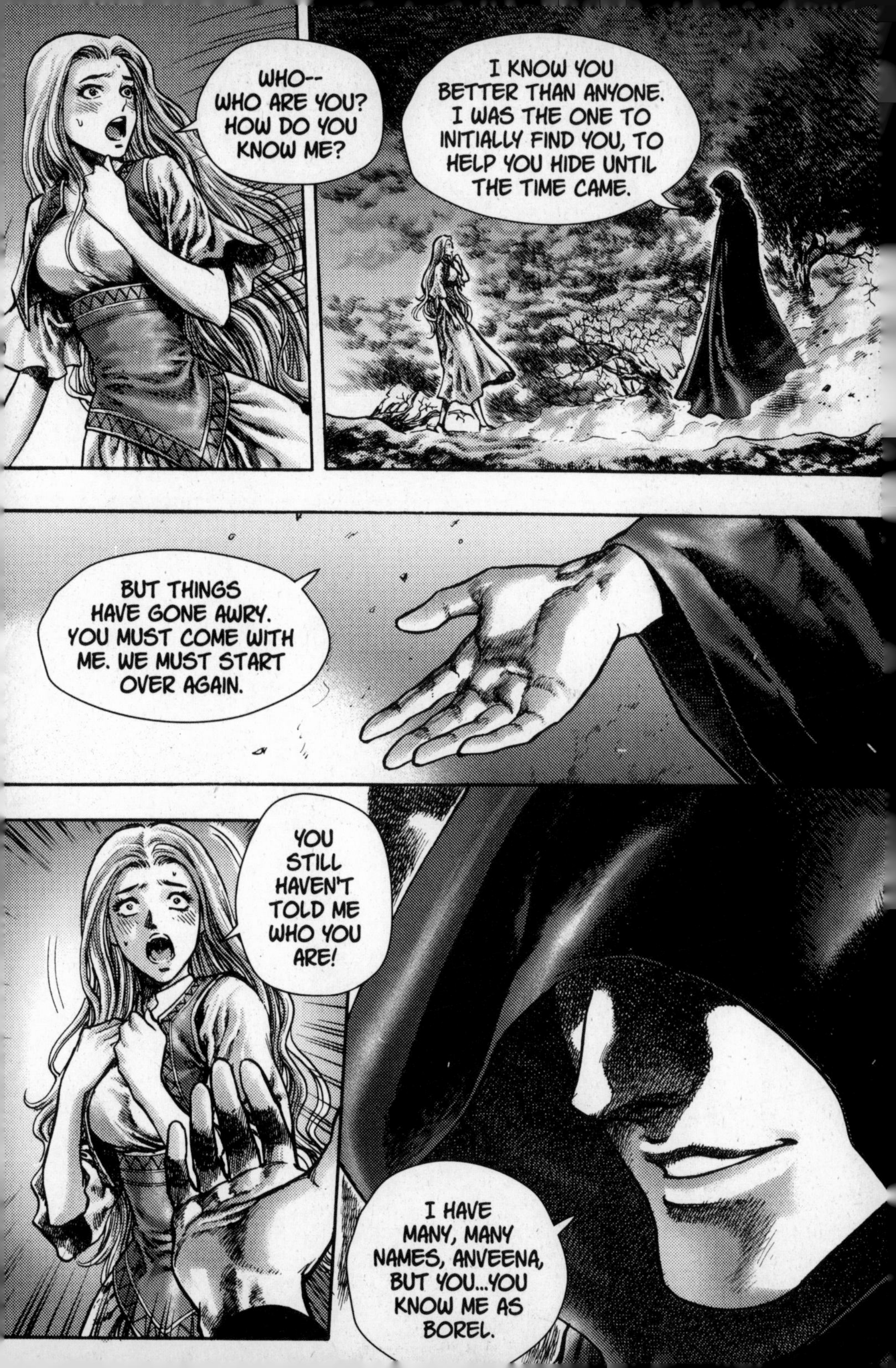
WHO-- WHO ARE YOU? HOW DO YOU KNOW ME?
I KNOW YOU BETTER THAN ANYONE. I WAS THE ONE TO INITIALLY FIND YOU, TO HELP YOU HIDE UNTIL THE TIME CAME.
BUT THINGS HAVE GONE AWRY. YOU MUST COME WITH ME. WE MUST START OVER AGAIN.
YOU STILL HAVEN'T TOLD ME WHO YOU ARE!
I HAVE MANY, MANY NAMES, ANVEENA, BUT YOU...YOU KNOW ME AS BOREL.

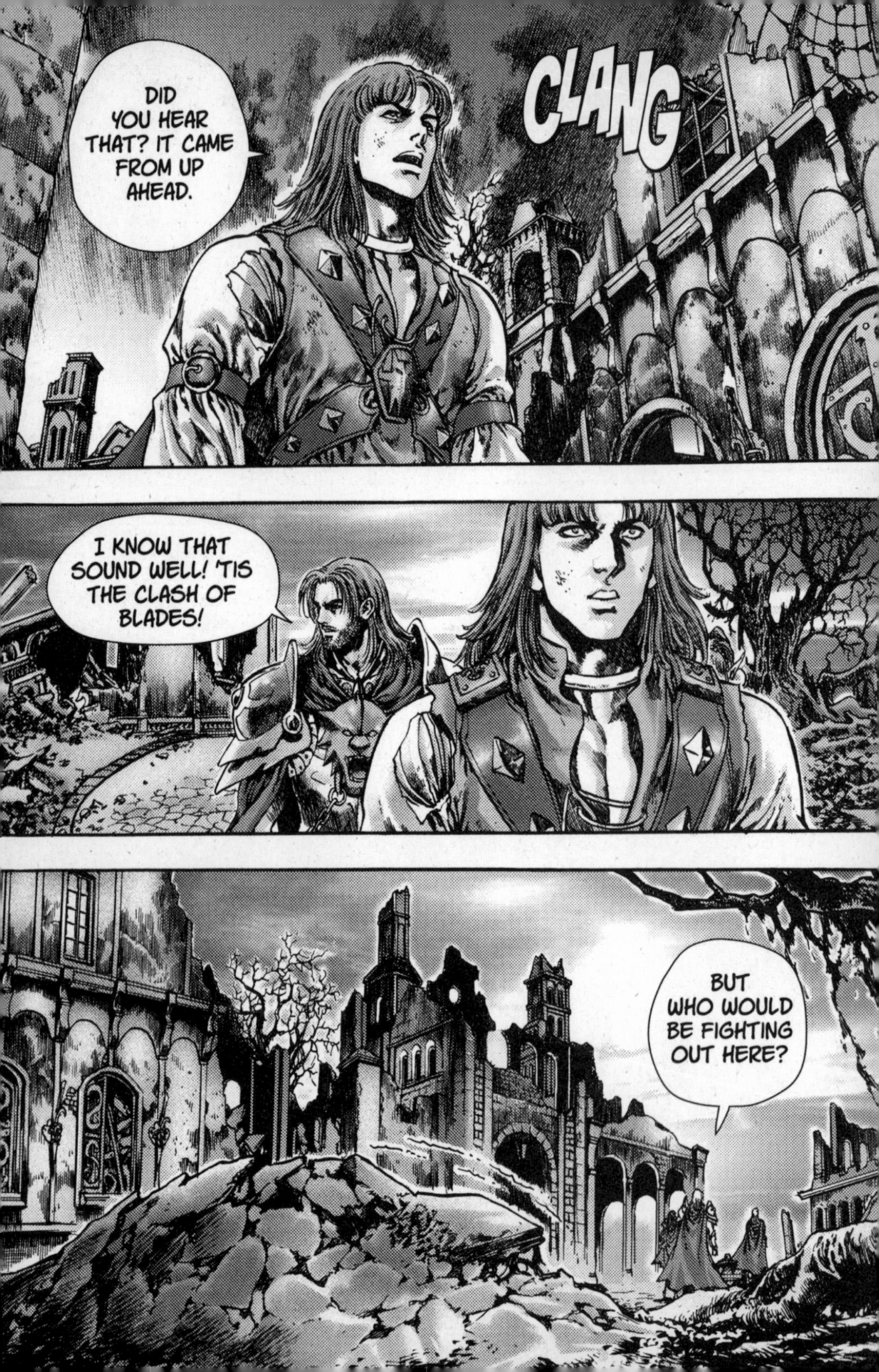
CLANG
DID YOU HEAR THAT? IT CAME FROM UP AHEAD.
I KNOW THAT SOUND WELL! 'TIS THE CLASH OF BLADES!
BUT WHO WOULD BE FIGHTING OUT HERE?

IT MUST HAVE SOMETHING TO DO WITH ANVEENA! SHE HAS TO BE NEAR!

IF SO, THEN I SHOULD TAKE THE LEAD! YOUR MAGIC IS HINDERED BY THE COLLAR, WHILE MINE REMAINS STRONG!

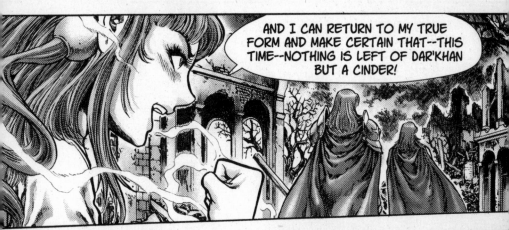

AND I CAN RETURN TO MY TRUE FORM AND MAKE CERTAIN THAT--THIS TIME--NOTHING IS LEFT OF DAR'KHAN BUT A CINDER!

THOUGH I AM LOATH TO ADMIT IT, SHE IS THE MOST POWERFUL OF US, KALEC.

MAYBE, BUT SHE'S ALSO THE MOST HEADSTRONG!

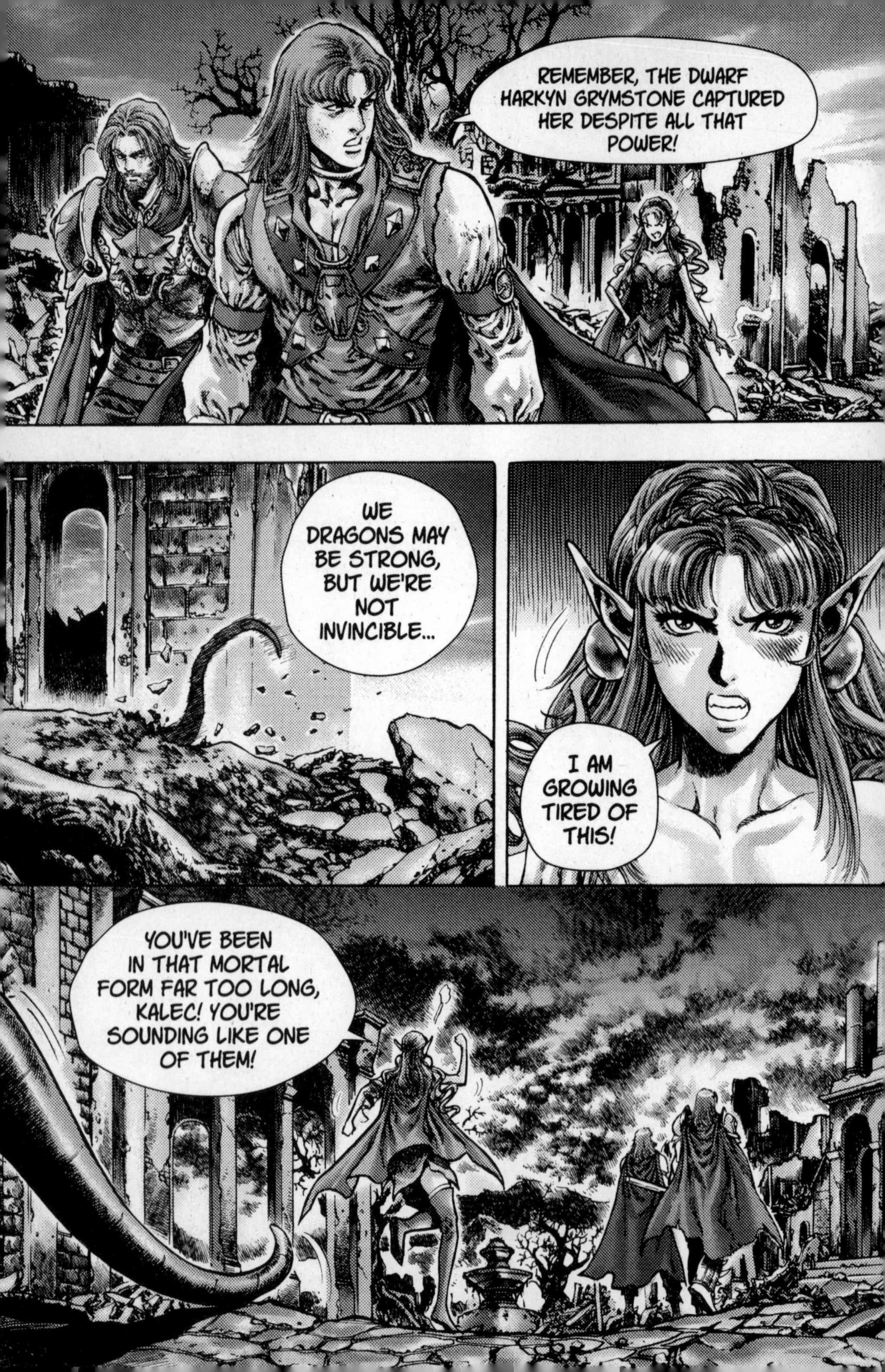
REMEMBER, THE DWARF HARKYN GRYMSTONE CAPTURED HER DESPITE ALL THAT POWER!
WE DRAGONS MAY BE STRONG, BUT WE'RE NOT INVINCIBLE...
I AM GROWING TIRED OF THIS!
YOU'VE BEEN IN THAT MORTAL FORM FAR TOO LONG, KALEC! YOU'RE SOUNDING LIKE ONE OF THEM!

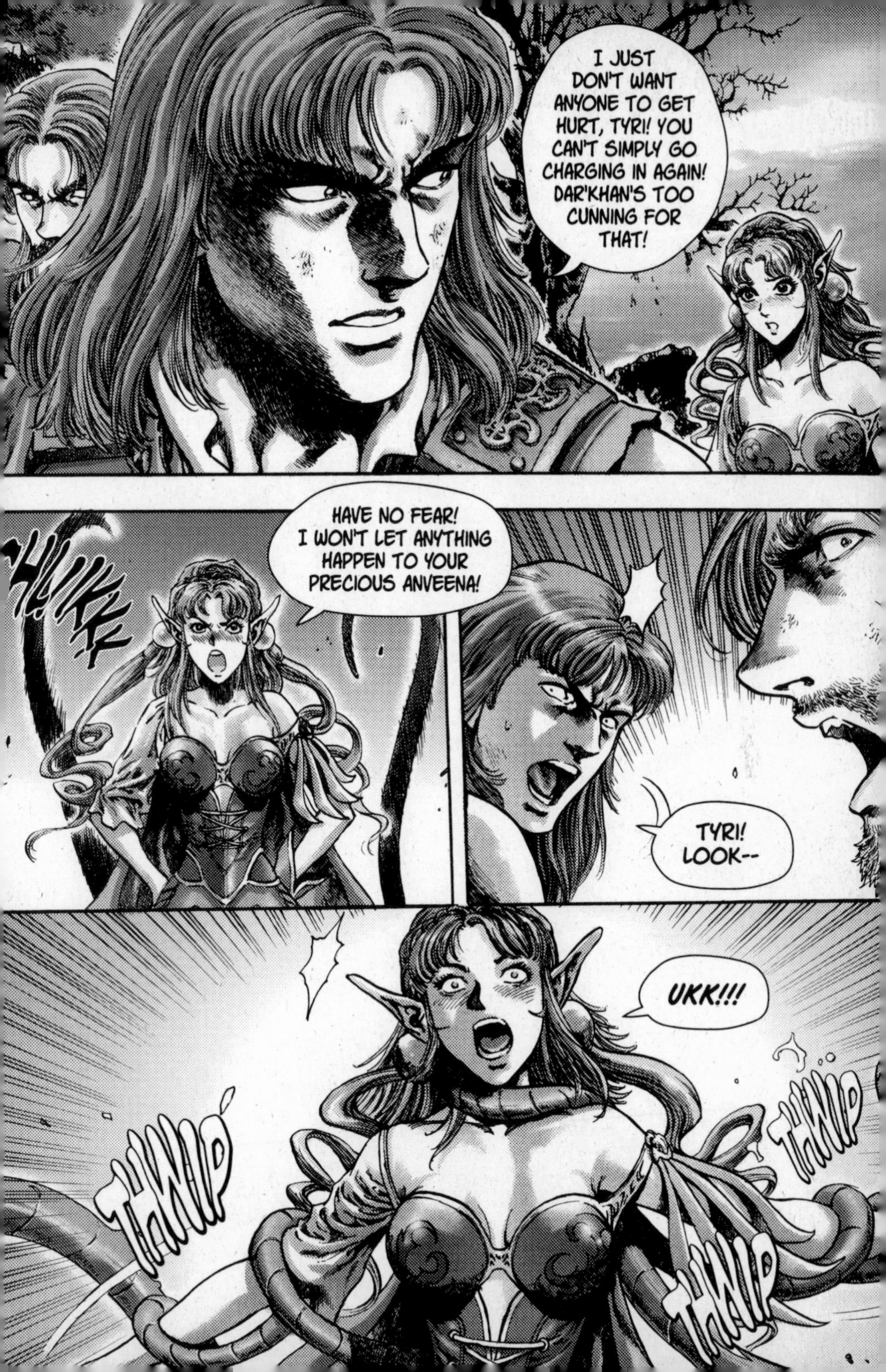
I JUST DON'T WANT ANYONE TO GET HURT, TYRI! YOU CAN'T SIMPLY GO CHARGING IN AGAIN! DAR'KHAN'S TOO CUNNING FOR THAT!
THUKKK
HAVE NO FEAR! I WON'T LET ANYTHING HAPPEN TO YOUR PRECIOUS ANVEENA!
TYRI! LOOK--
UKK!!!
THWIP
THWIP
THWIP

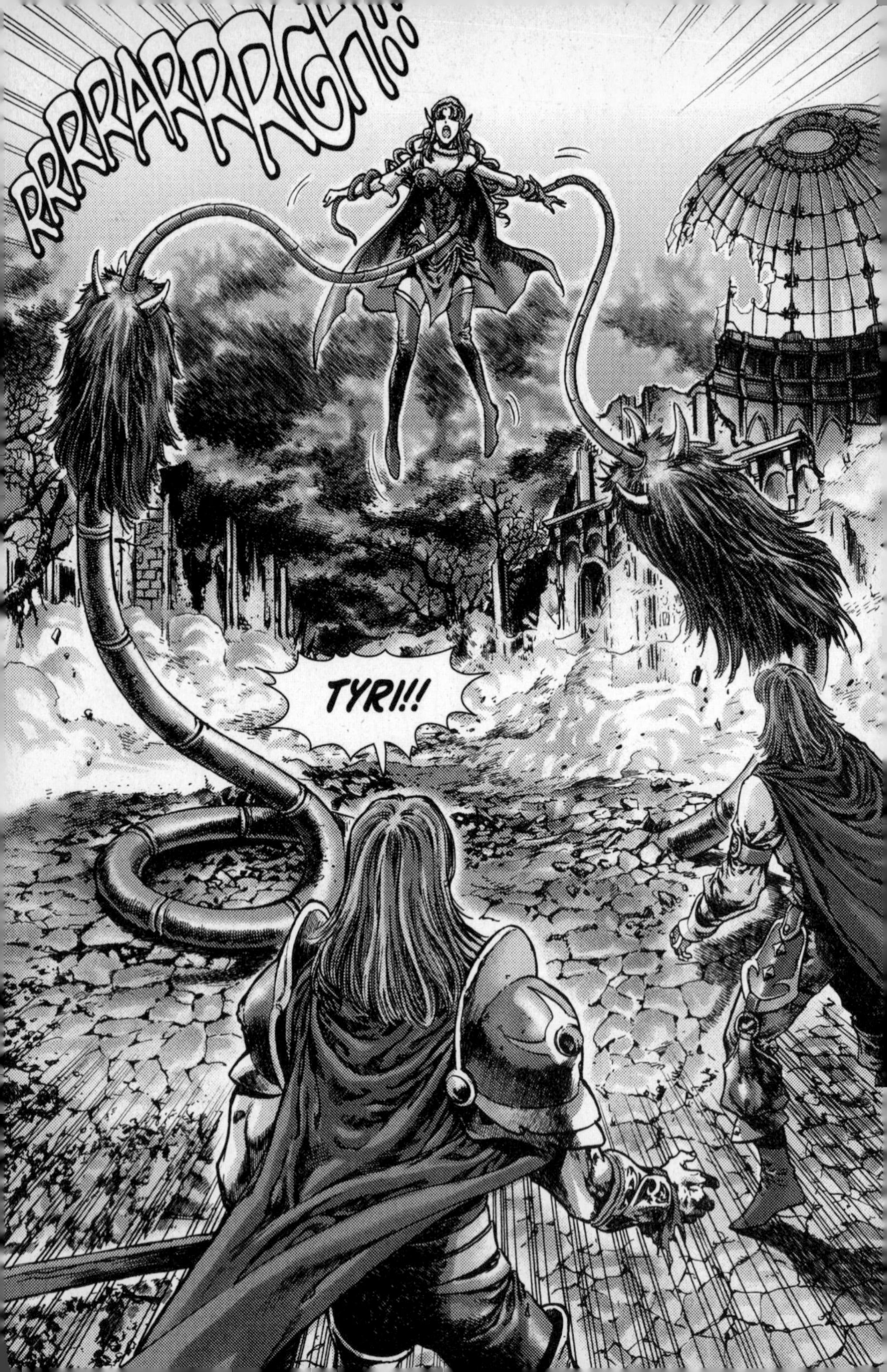
RRRRARRRGH!!
TYRI!!

CHAPTER THREE

CRY OF THE BANSHEE

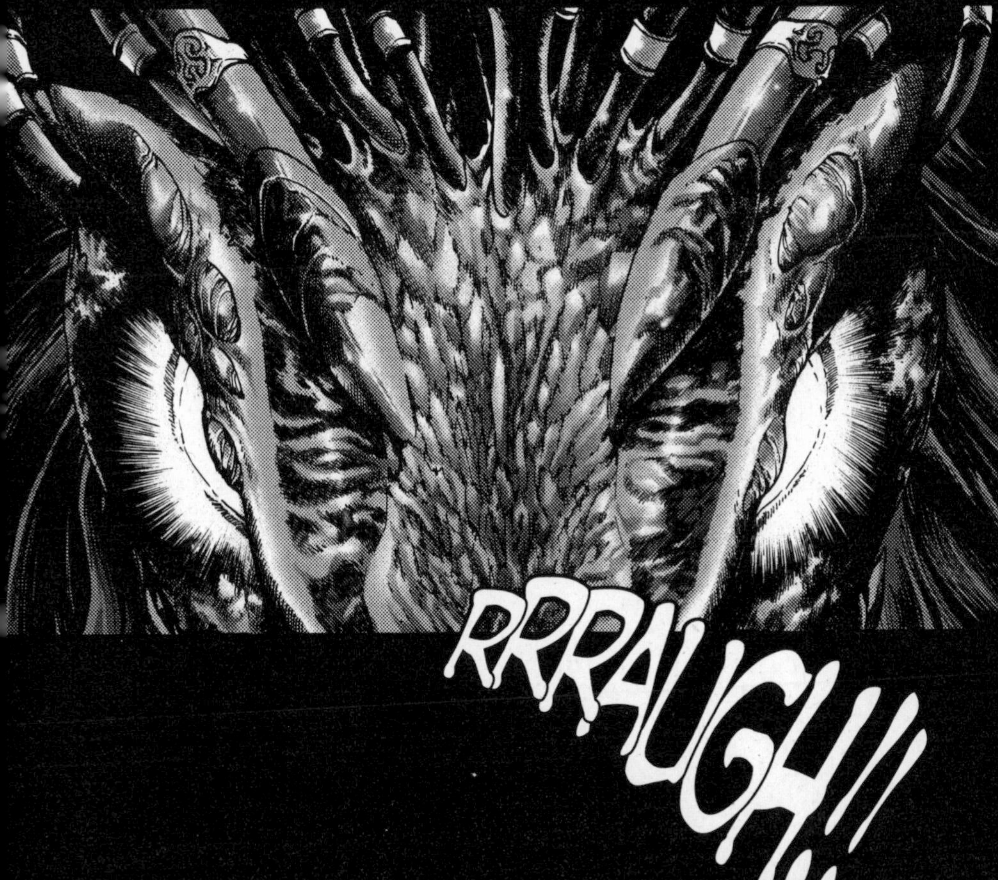
RRRAUGH!!

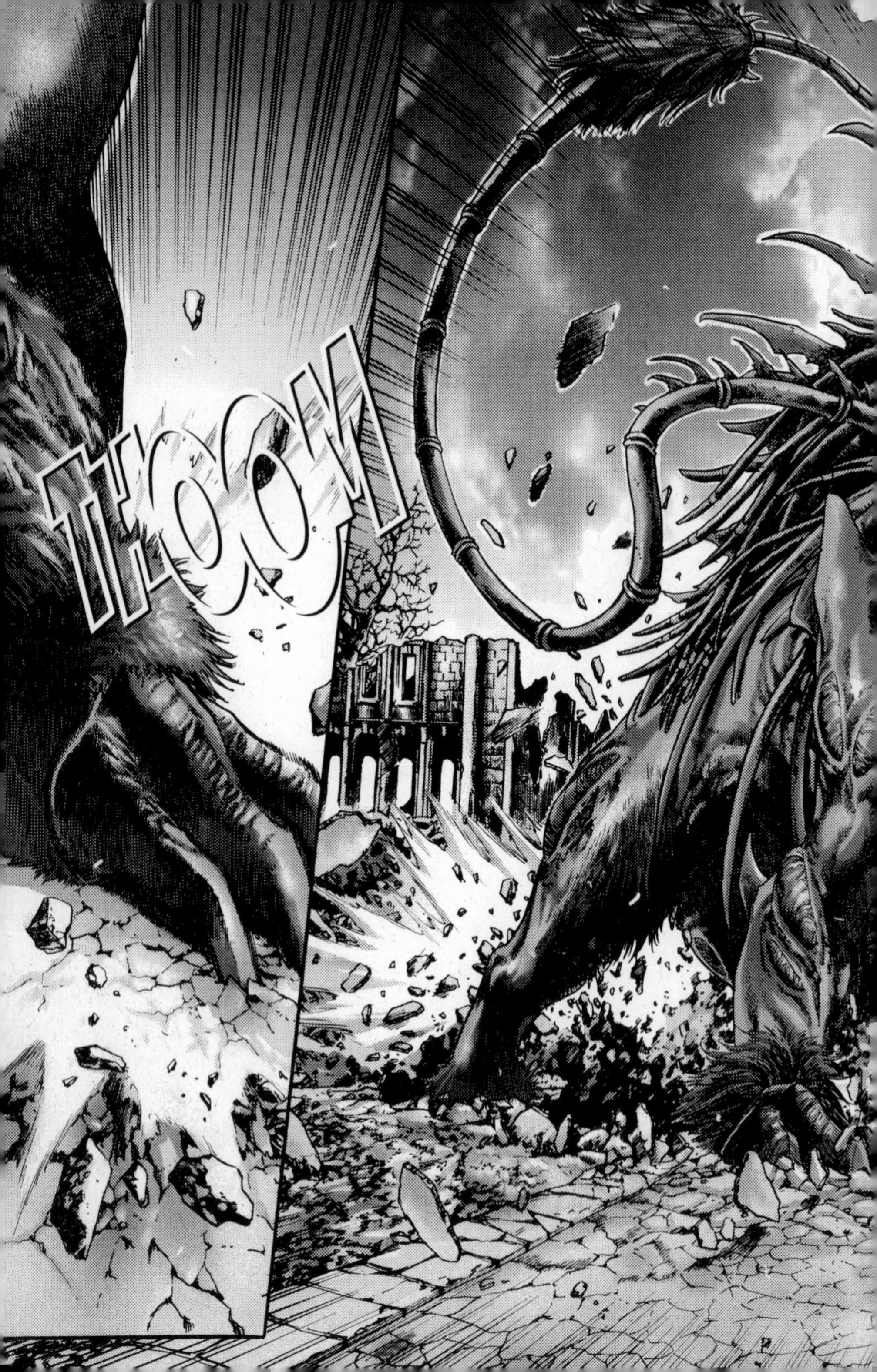
THOOM

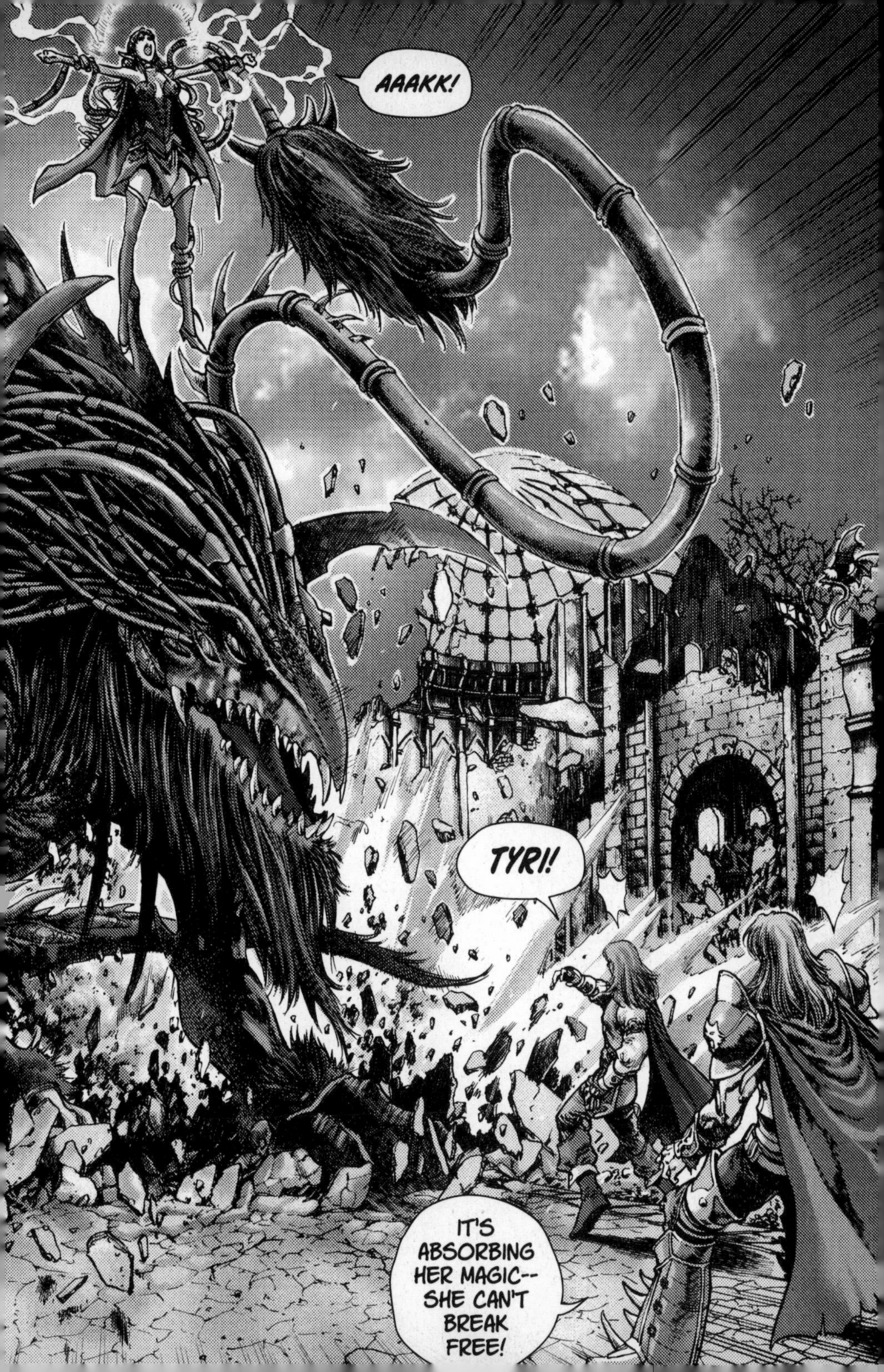
AAAKK!
TYRI!
IT'S ABSORBING HER MAGIC-- SHE CAN'T BREAK FREE!

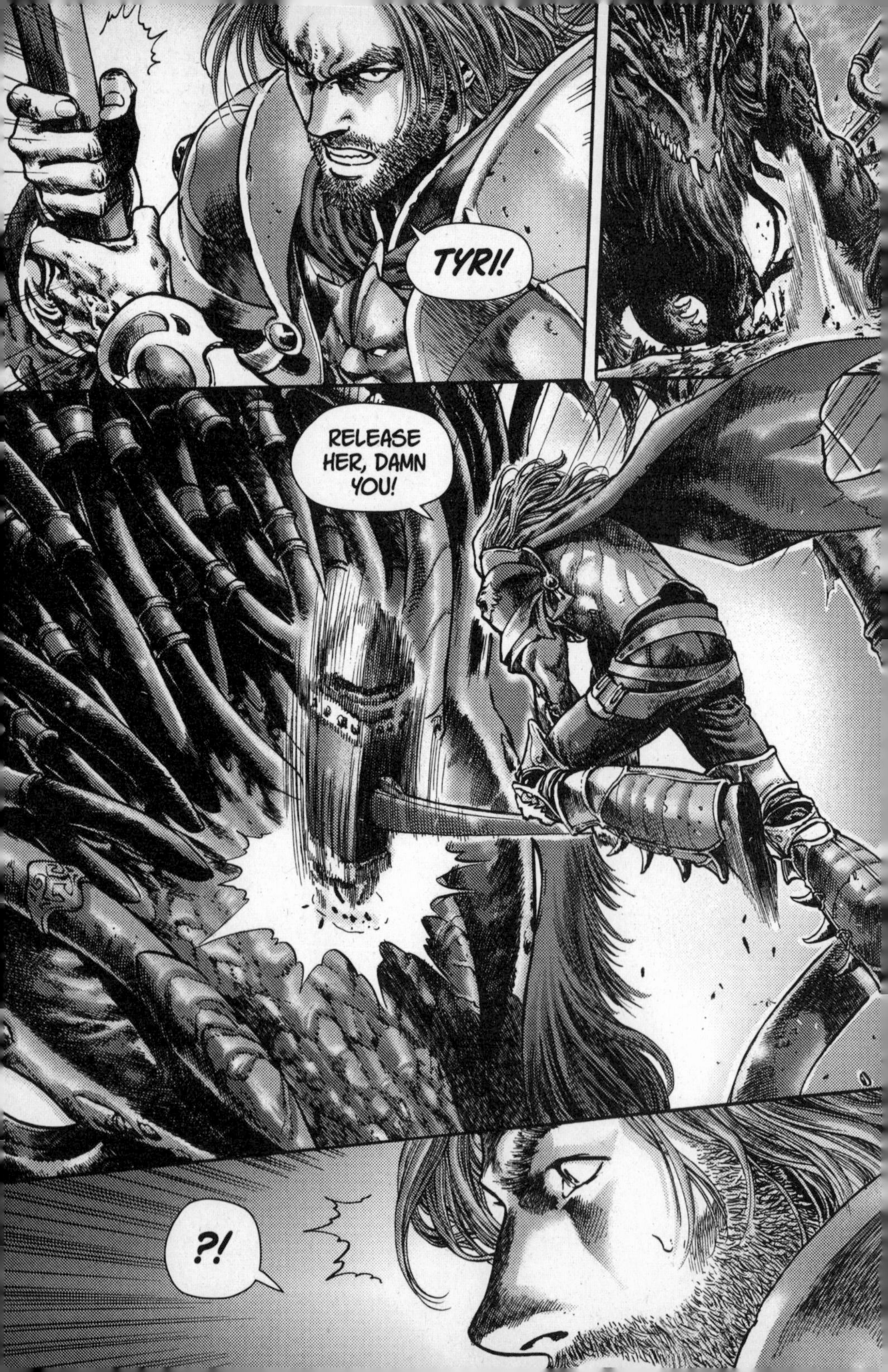
TYRI!
RELEASE HER, DAMN YOU!
?!

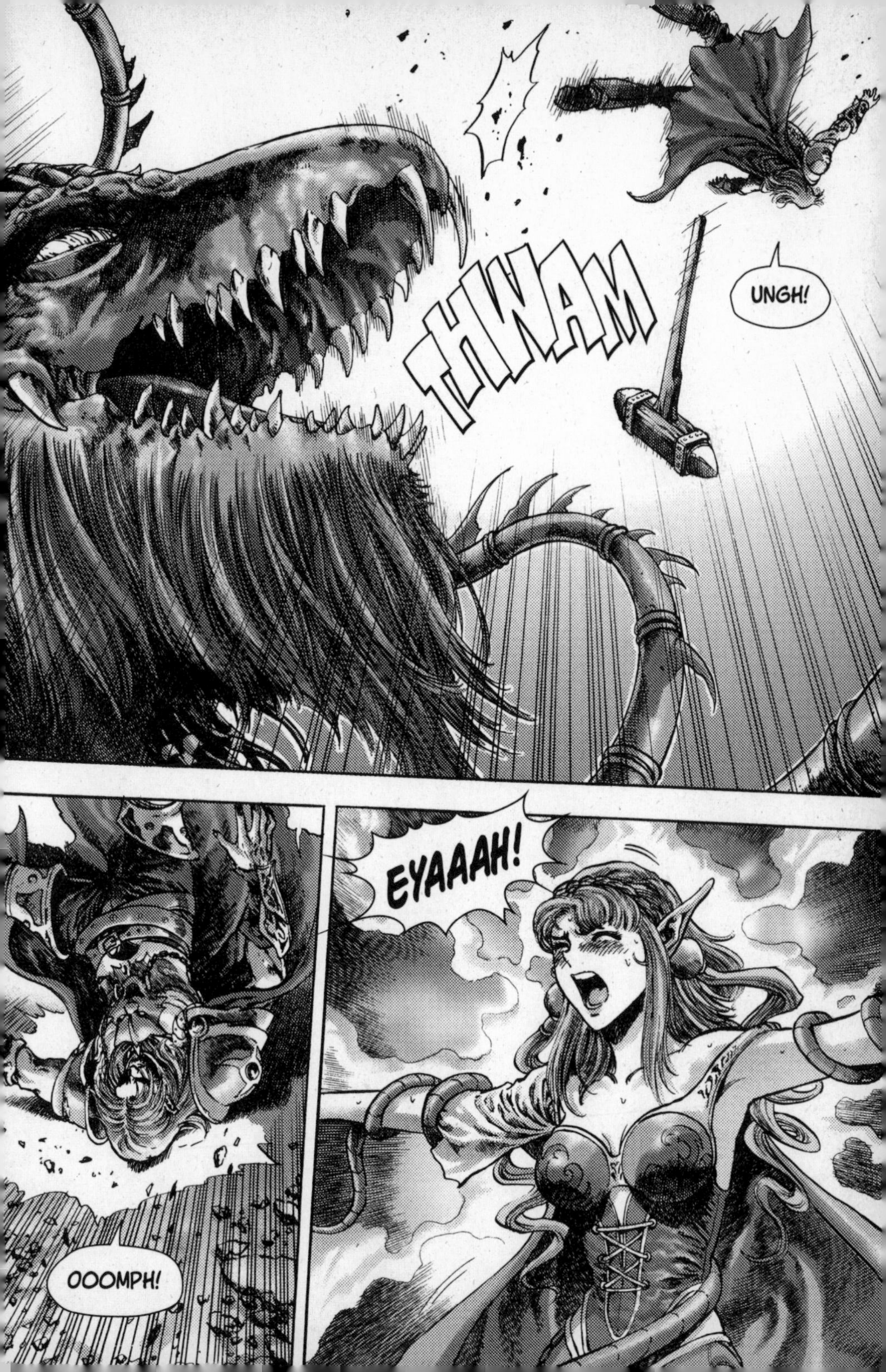
UNGH!
THWAM
EYAAAH!
OOOMPH!

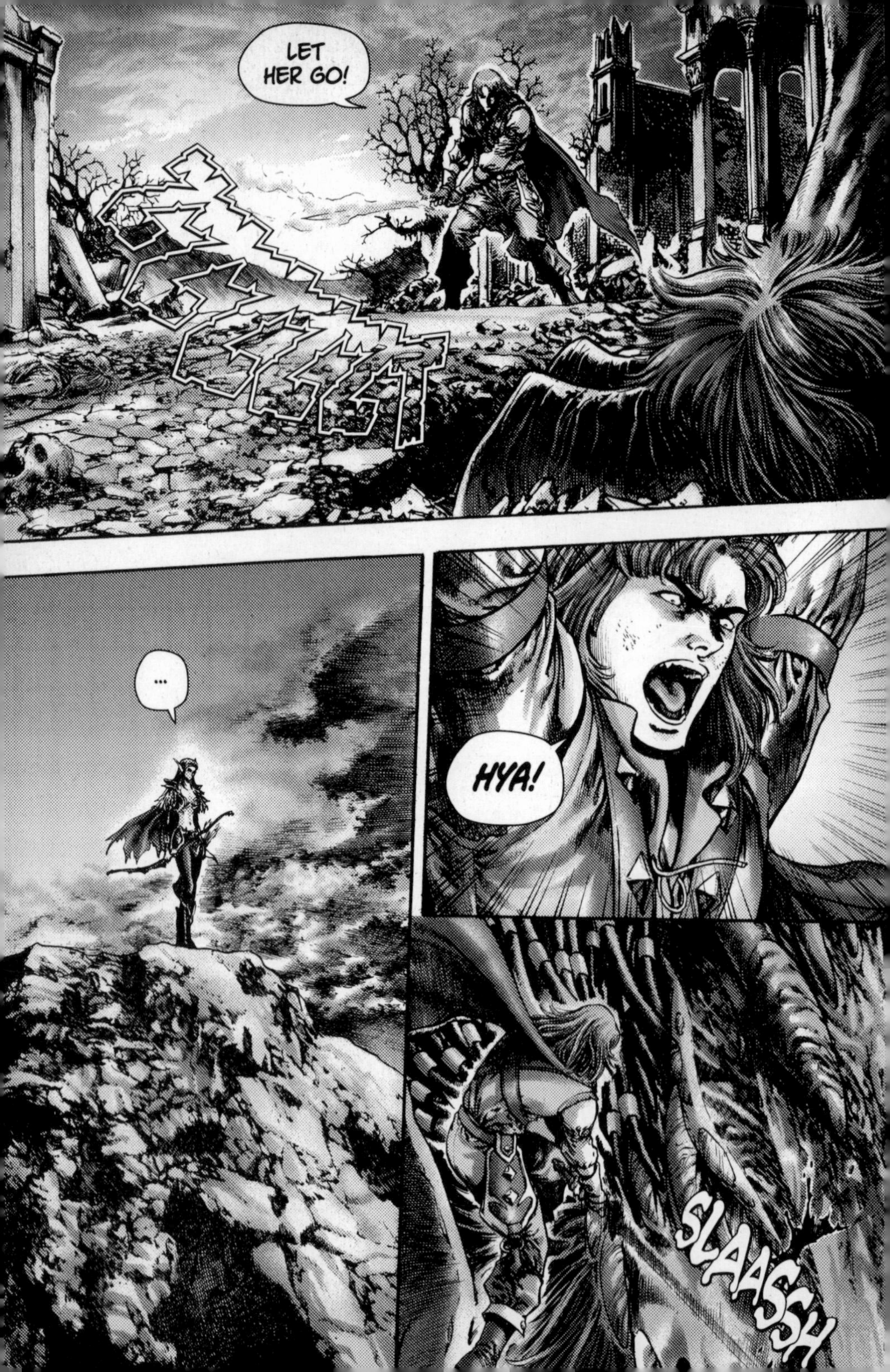
LET HER GO!
HYA!
SLAASSH
...

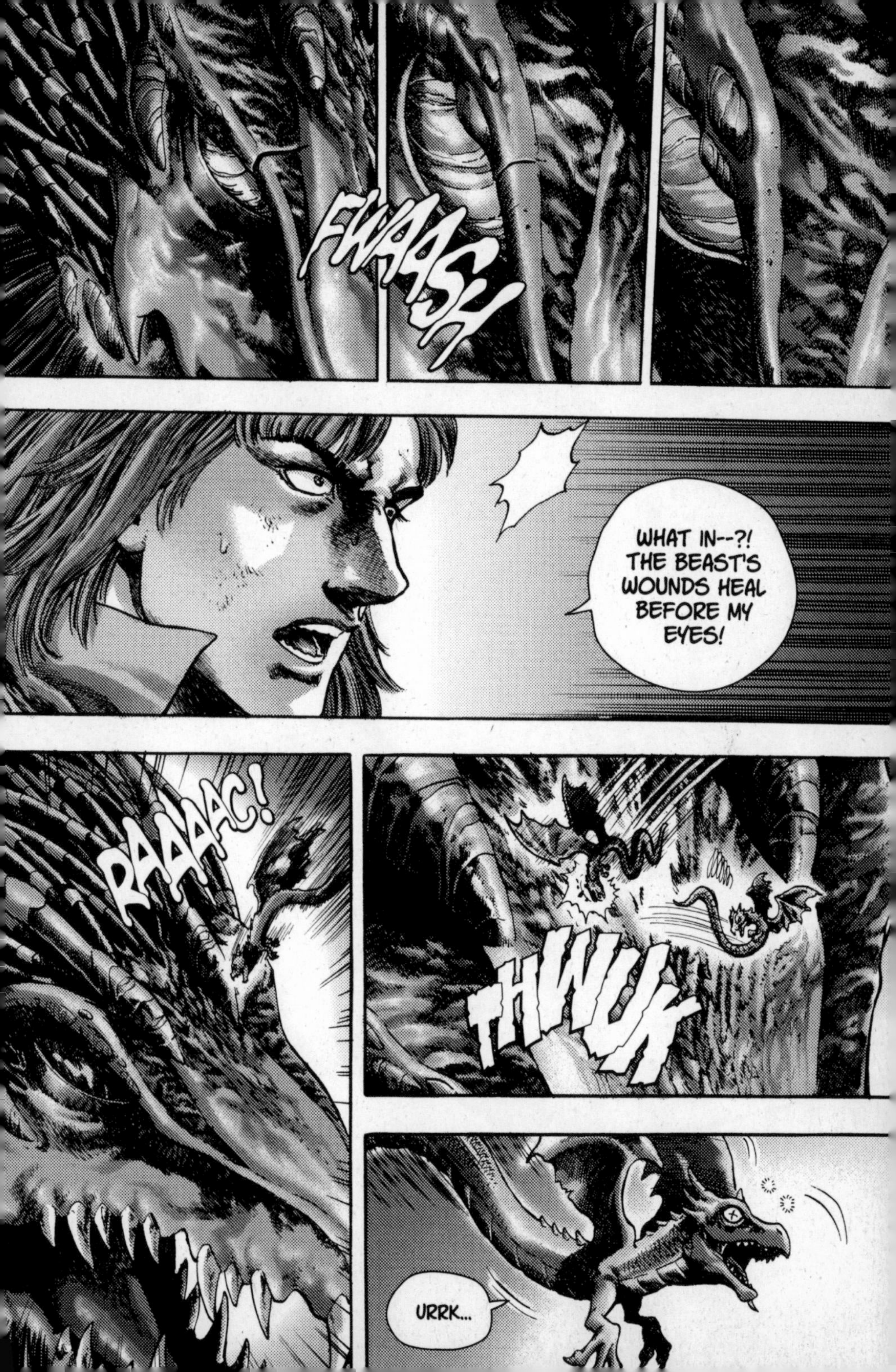
FWAASH
WHAT IN--?! THE BEAST'S WOUNDS HEAL BEFORE MY EYES!
THWUK
URRK...
RAAAAC!

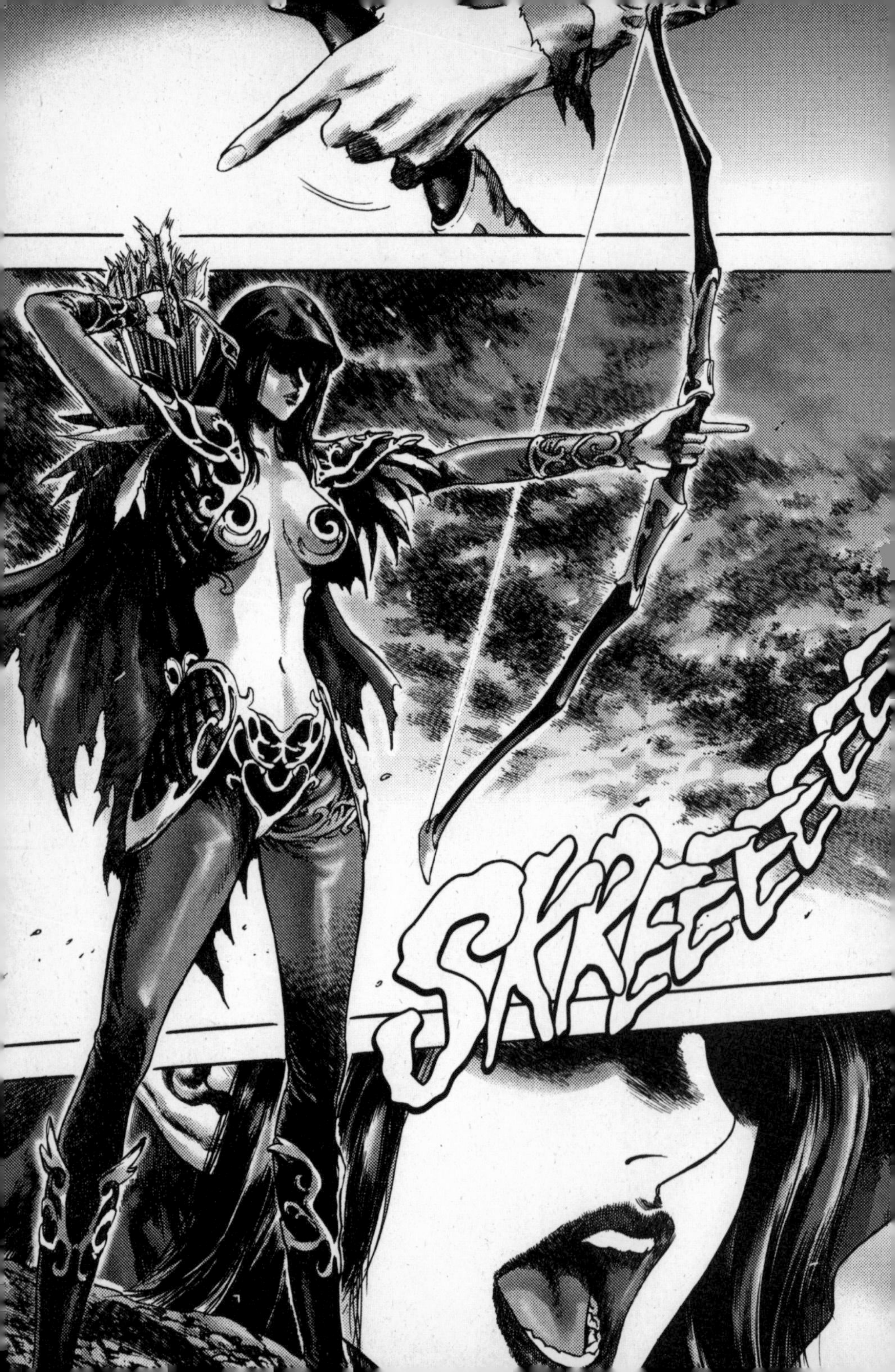
SKREEEEEEE

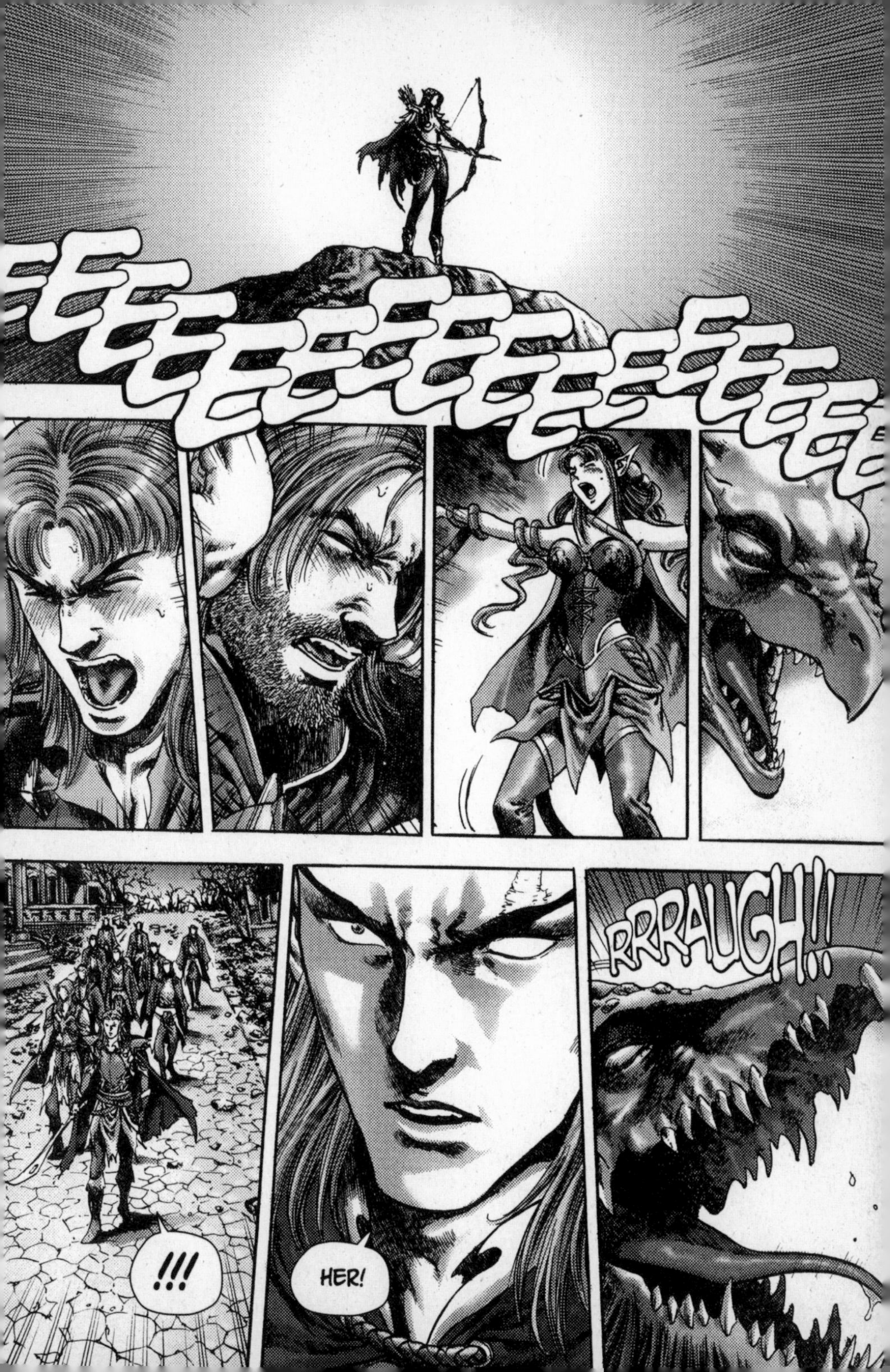
EEEEEEEEEEEEEEEEEEEEEEEEEEE
RRRAUGH!!
HER!
!!!

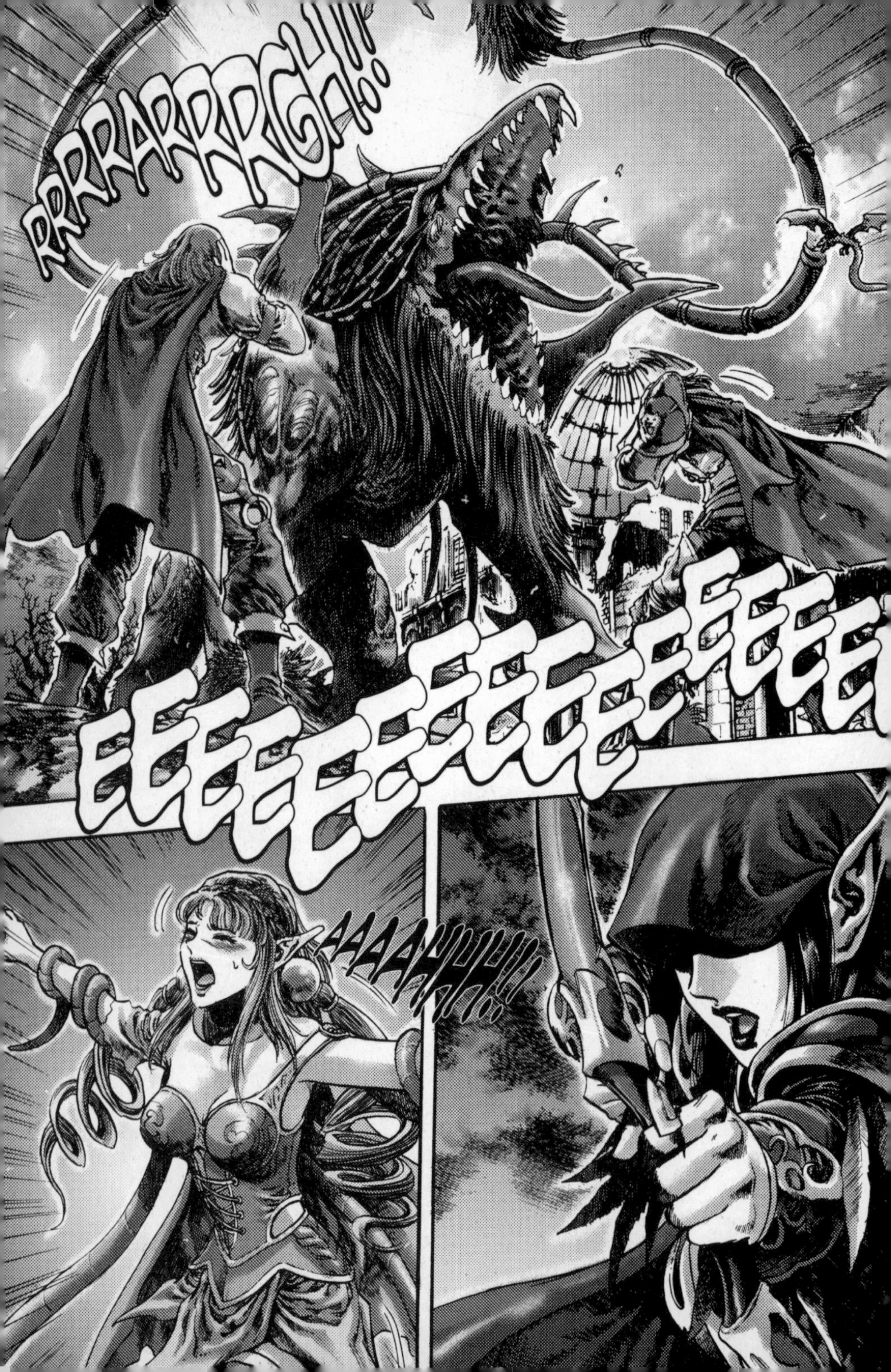
RRRRARRRGH!!!
EEEEEEEEEEEEEEEEEEE
AAAAAHHH!!!

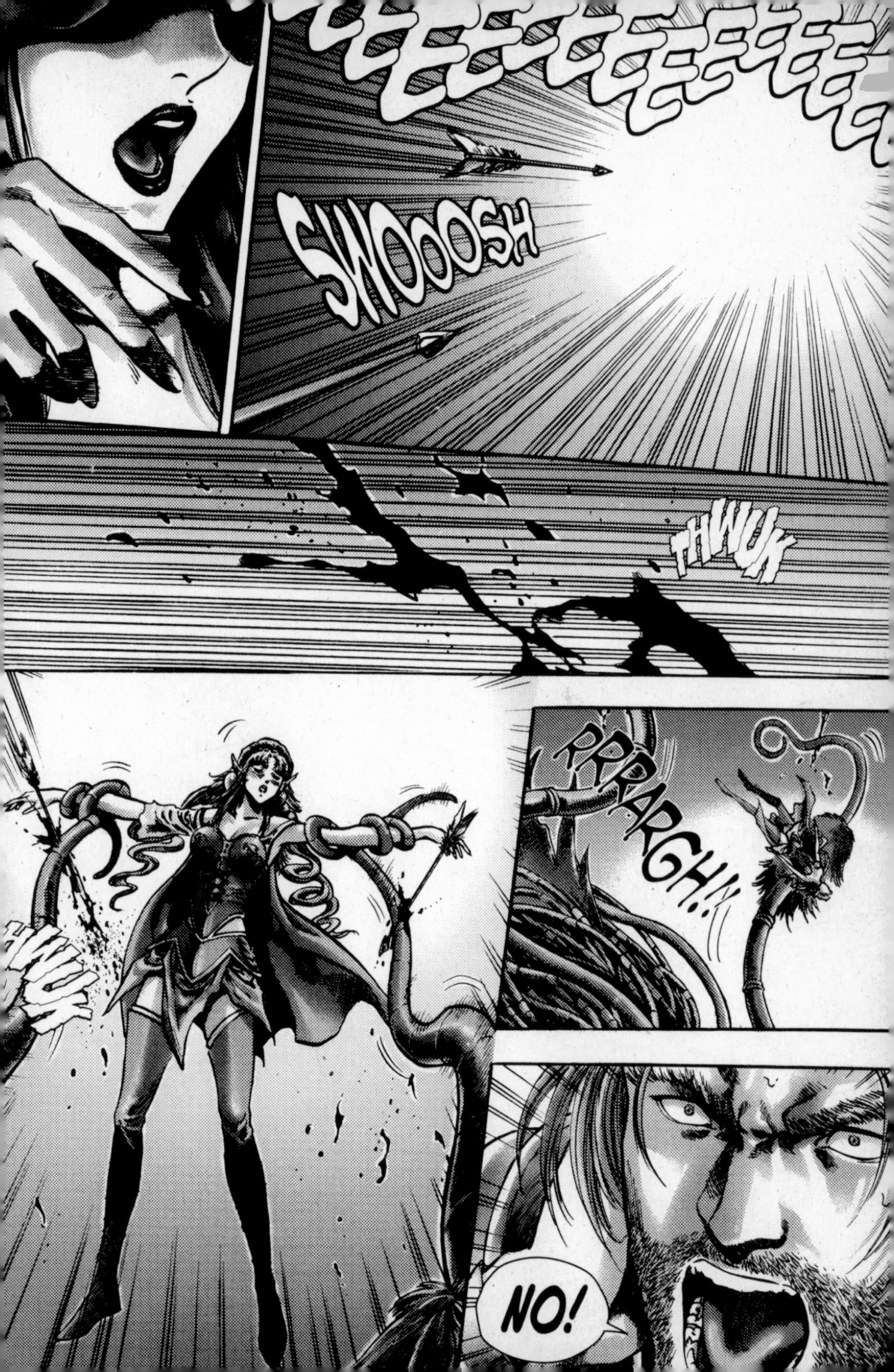
EEEEEEEEEEEEEEEEEEEE
SWOOOSH
THWUK
PRRARGH!!
THWUK
NO!

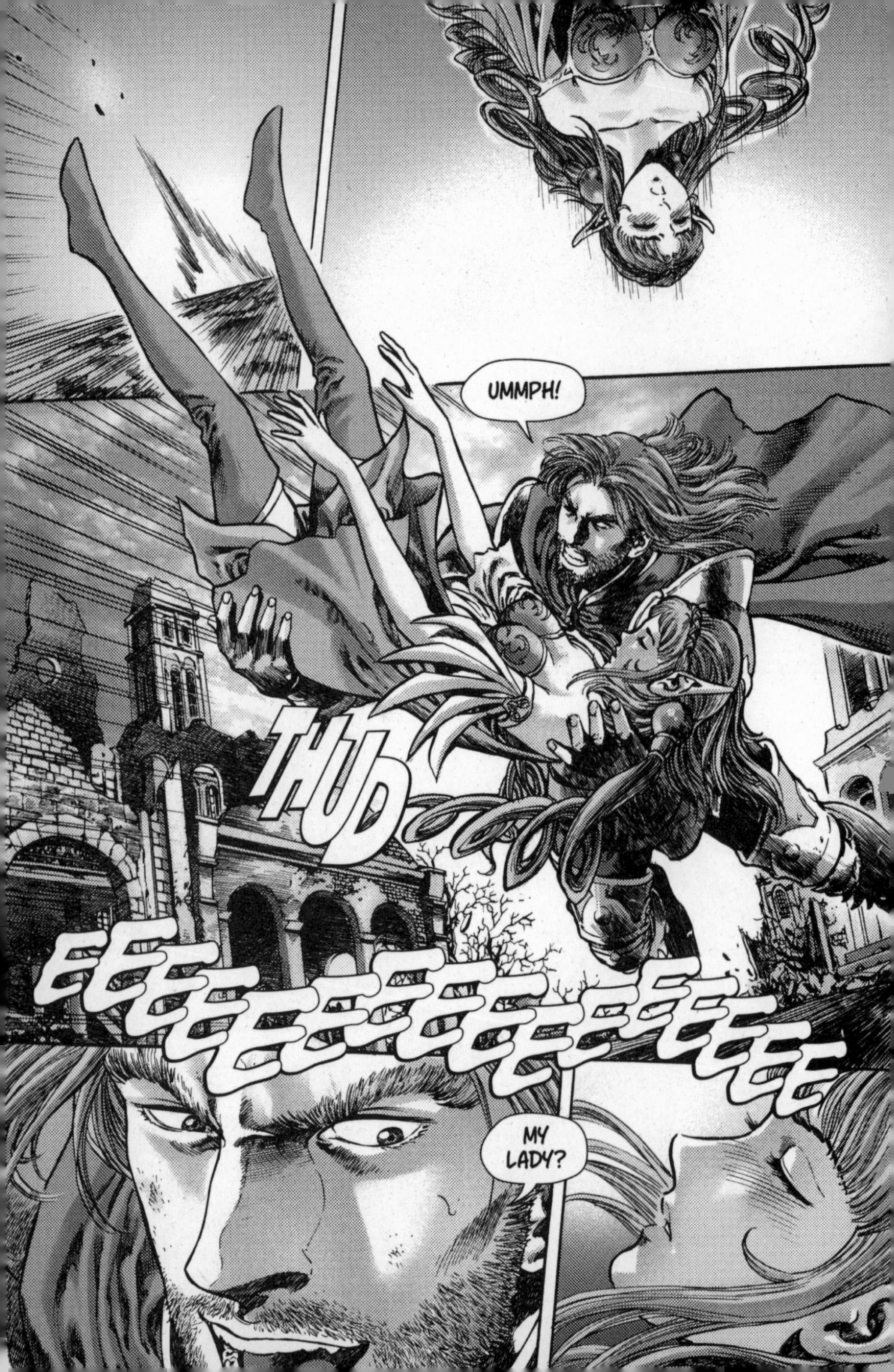
UMMPH!
THUD
EEEEEEEEEEEEEEEEEEEEEEEEEE
MY LADY?

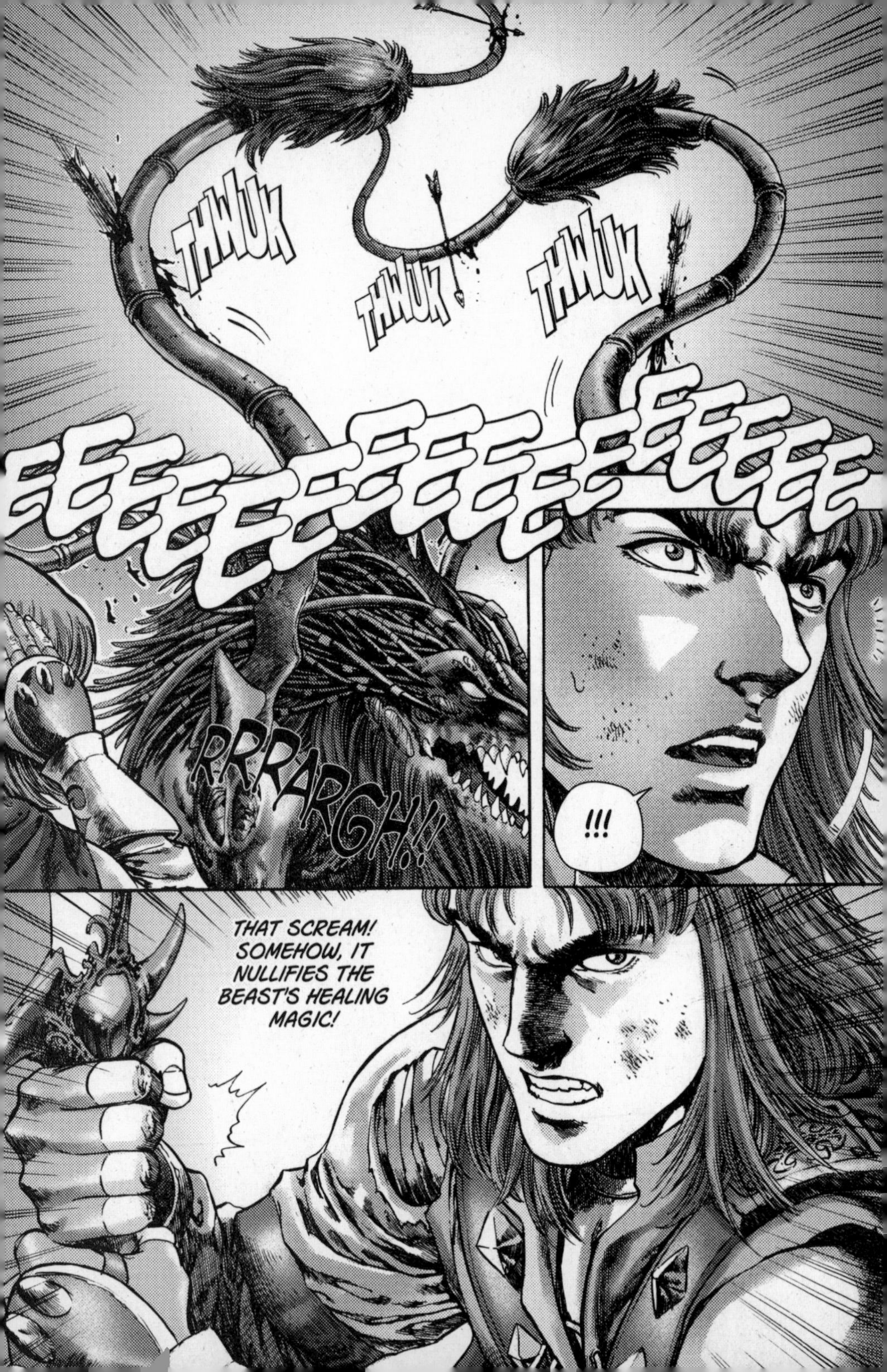
THWUK
THWUK
THWUK
EEEEEEEEEEEEEEEEEEEEEEEEE
!!!
RRRARGH!!
THAT SCREAM! SOMEHOW, IT NULLIFIES THE BEAST'S HEALING MAGIC!

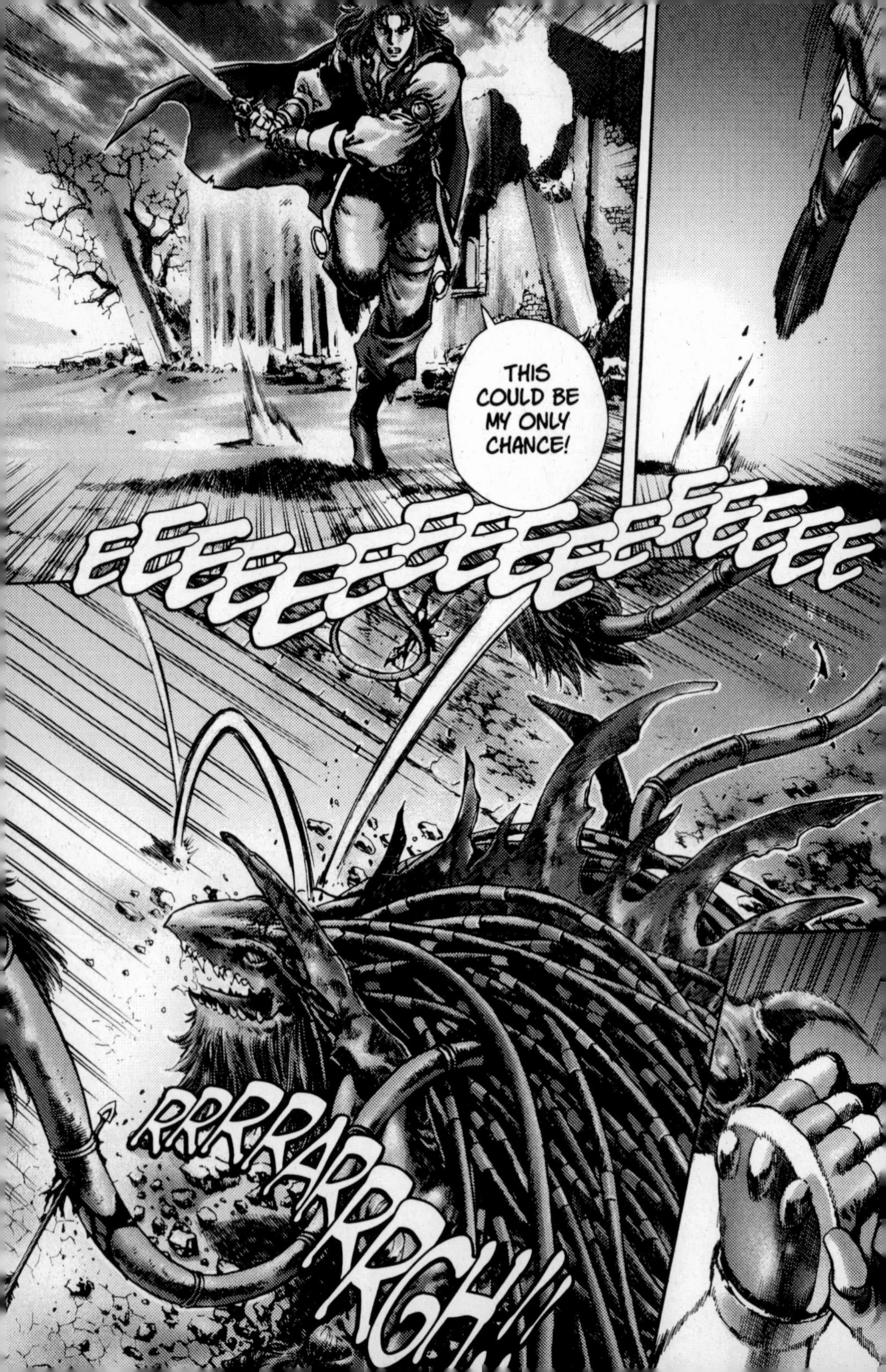
THIS COULD BE MY ONLY CHANCE!
EEEEEEEEEEEEEEEEEEEEEE
RRRRARRRGH!!

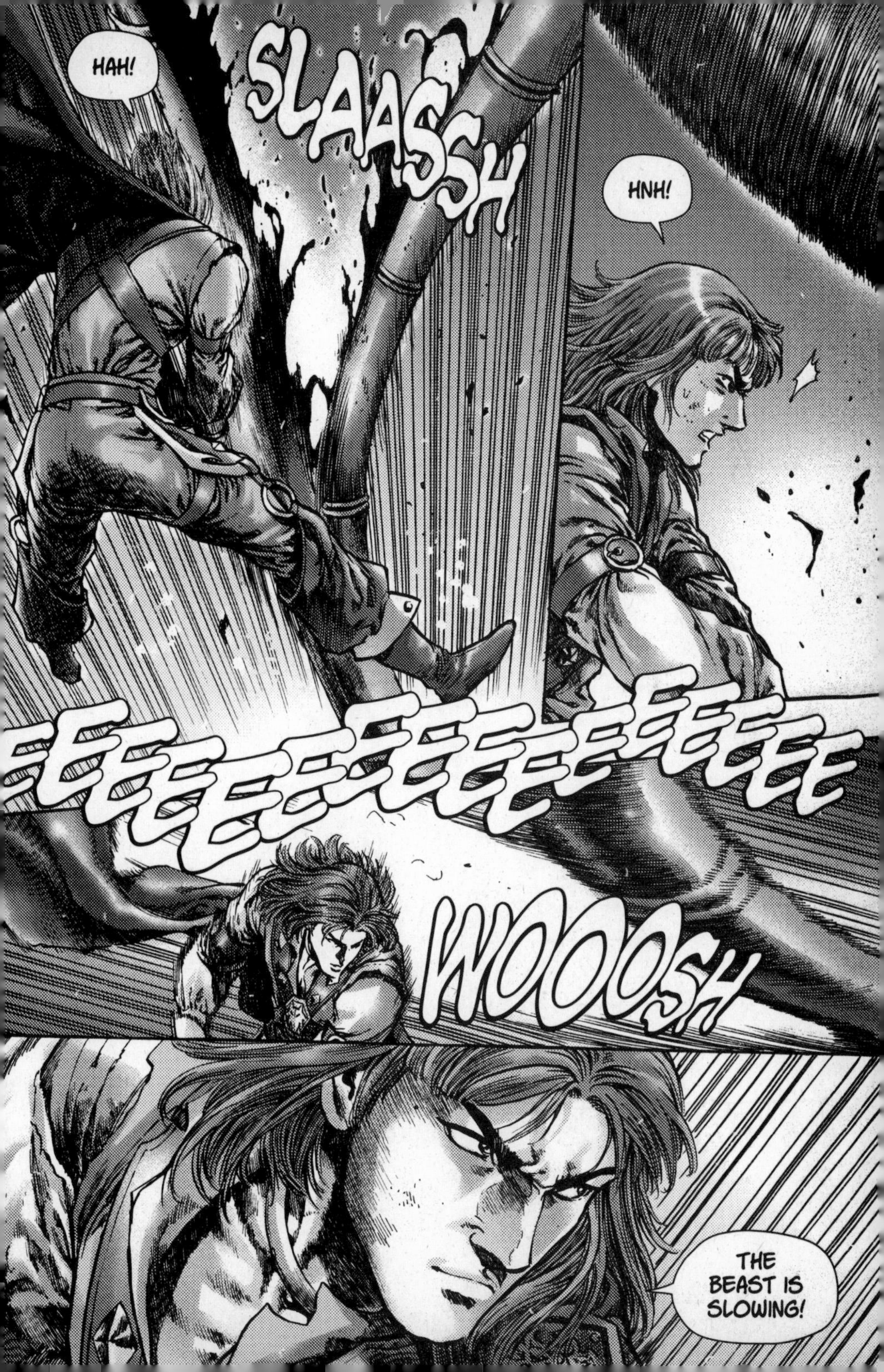
HNH!
HAH!
SLAASSH
EEEEEEEEEEEEEEEEEEEE
WOOOSH
THE BEAST IS SLOWING!

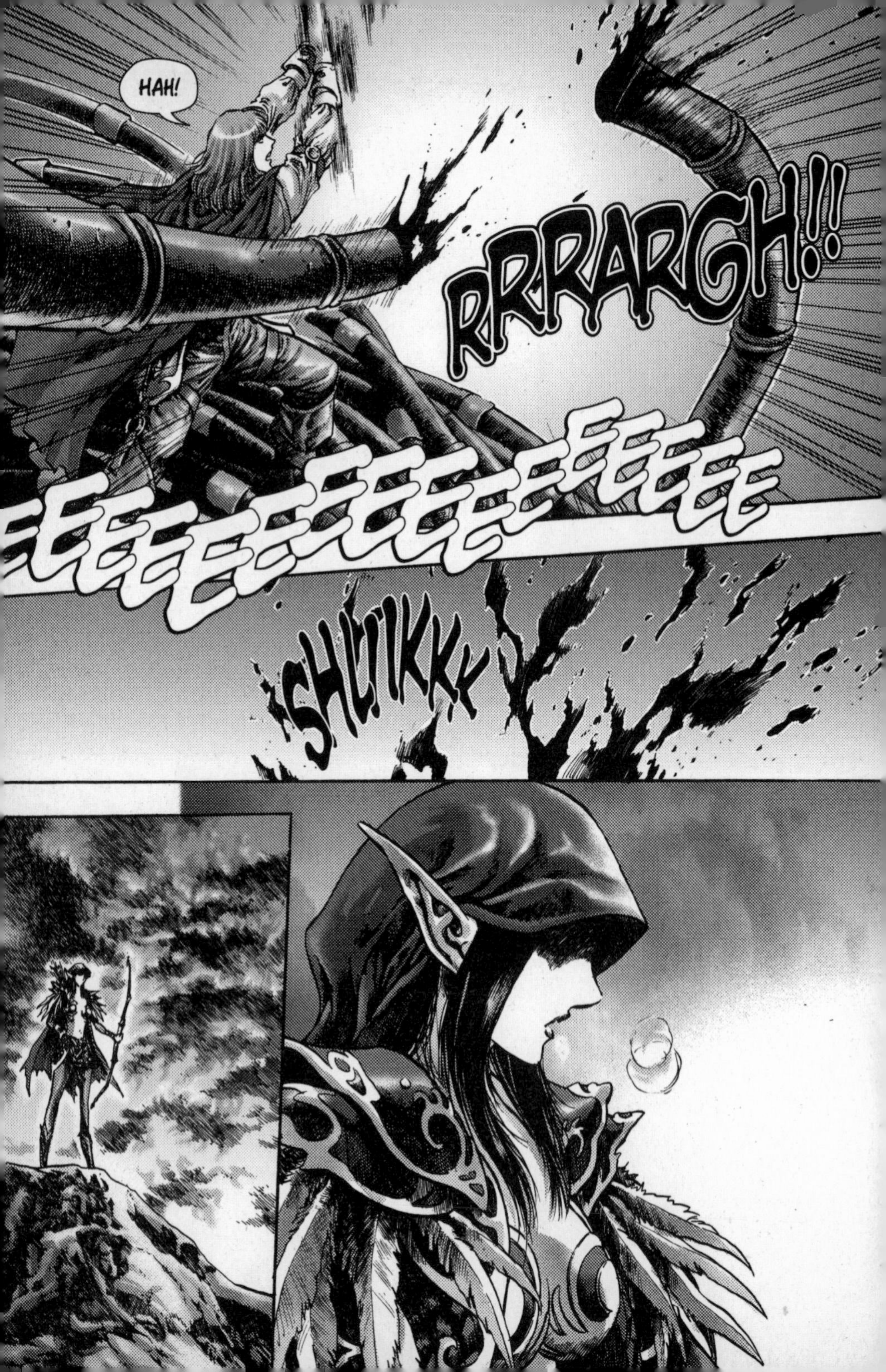
HAH!
RRRARGH!!

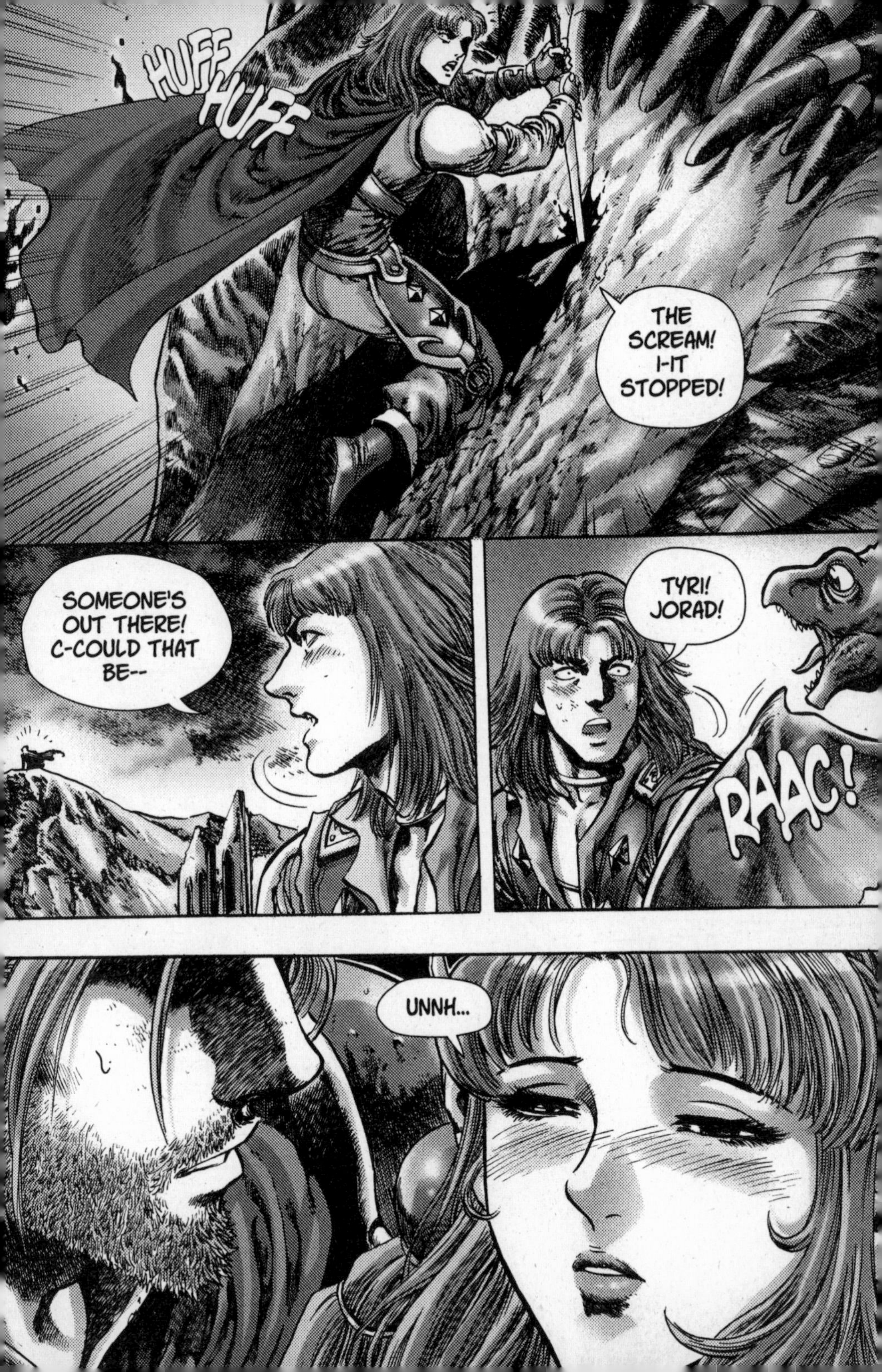
HUFF HUFF
THE SCREAM! I-IT STOPPED!
SOMEONE'S OUT THERE! C-COULD THAT BE--
TYRI! JORAD!
RAAC!
UNNH...

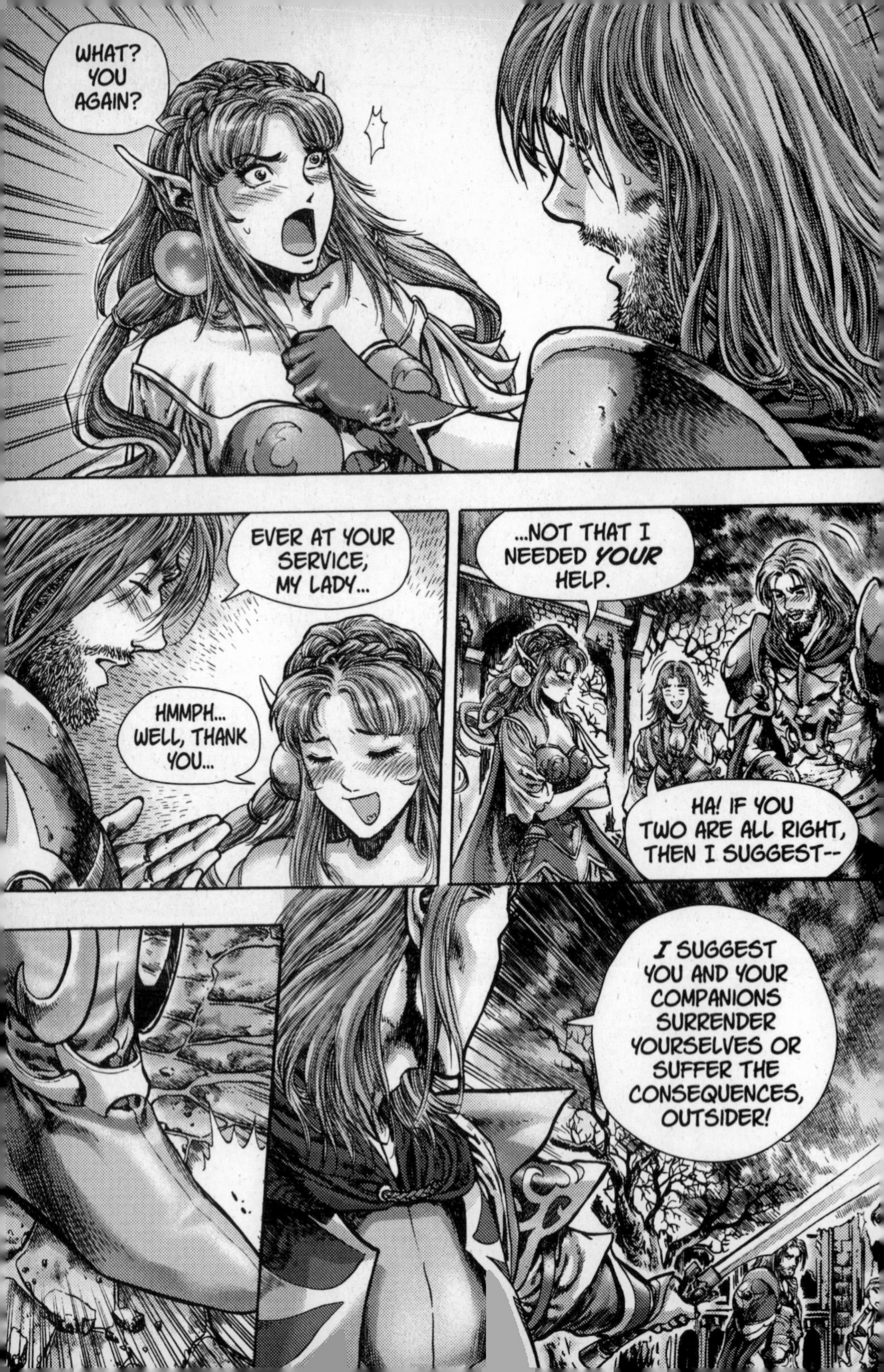
WHAT? YOU AGAIN?
EVER AT YOUR SERVICE, MY LADY...
HMMPH... WELL, THANK YOU...
...NOT THAT I NEEDED *YOUR* HELP.
HA! IF YOU TWO ARE ALL RIGHT, THEN I SUGGEST--
I SUGGEST YOU AND YOUR COMPANIONS SURRENDER YOURSELVES OR SUFFER THE CONSEQUENCES, OUTSIDER!

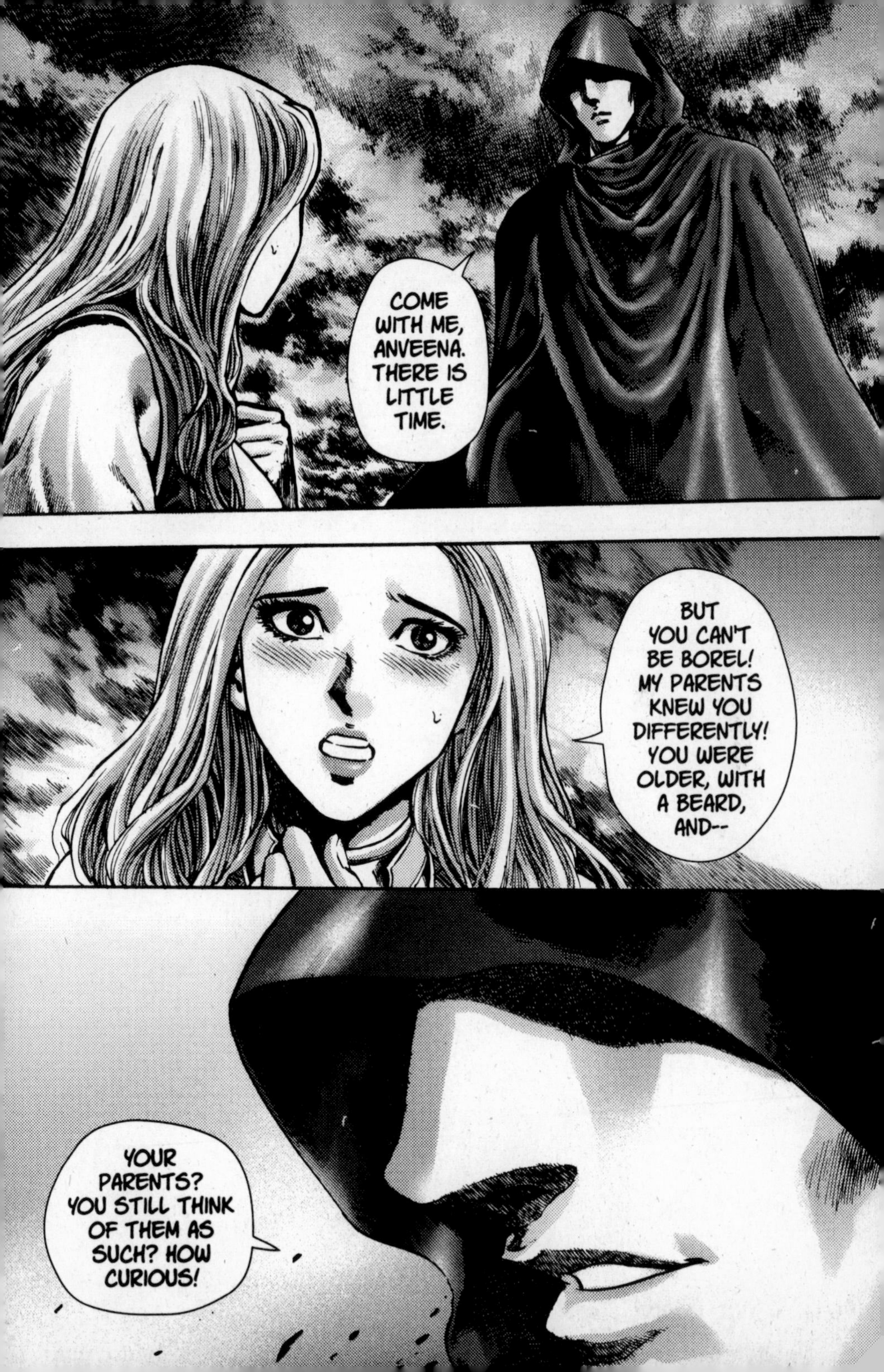
COME WITH ME, ANVEENA. THERE IS LITTLE TIME.
BUT YOU CAN'T BE BOREL! MY PARENTS KNEW YOU DIFFERENTLY! YOU WERE OLDER, WITH A BEARD, AND--
YOUR PARENTS? YOU STILL THINK OF THEM AS SUCH? HOW CURIOUS!

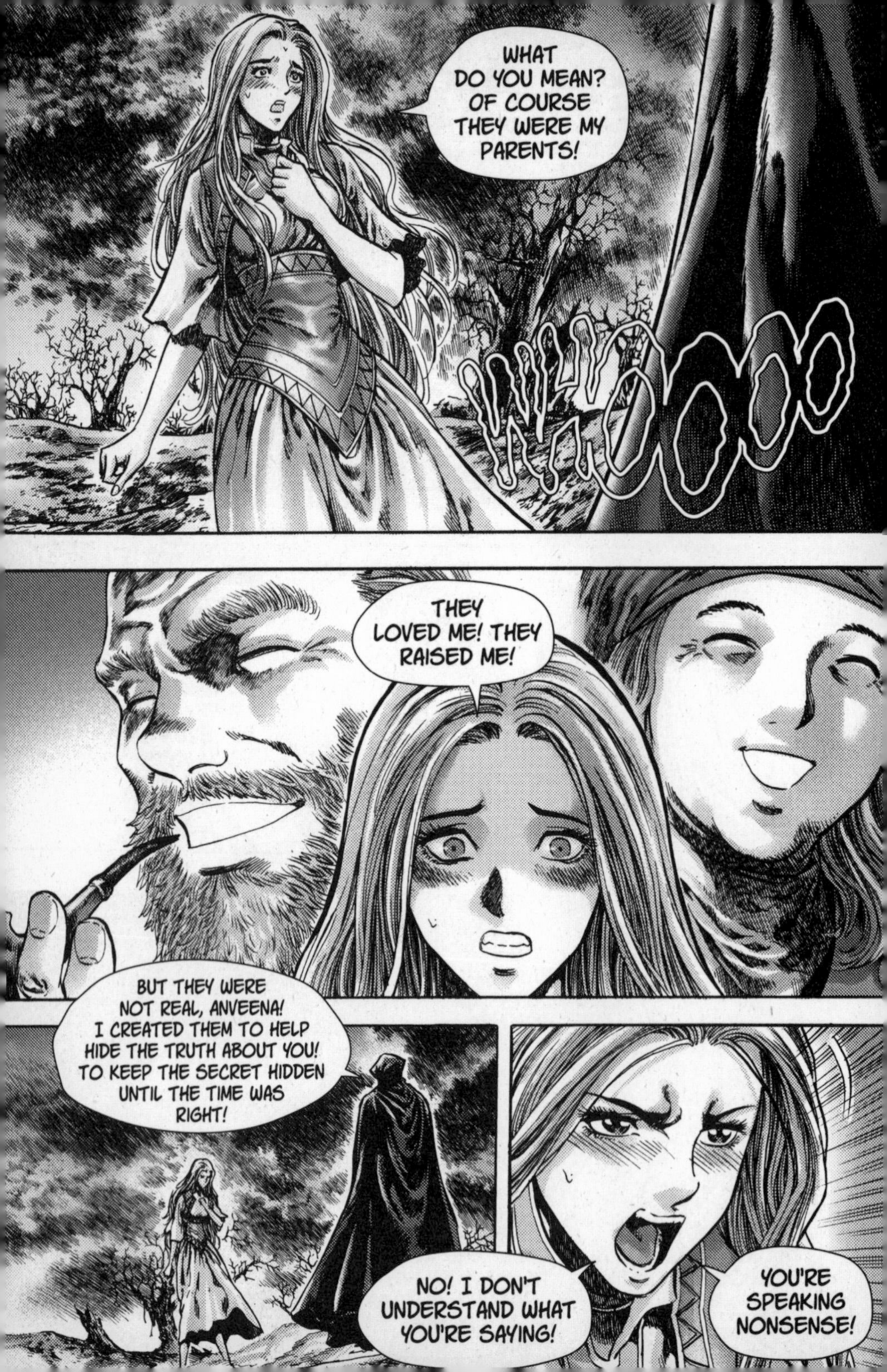
WHAT DO YOU MEAN? OF COURSE THEY WERE MY PARENTS!
WHOOOOO
THEY LOVED ME! THEY RAISED ME!
BUT THEY WERE NOT REAL, ANVEENA! I CREATED THEM TO HELP HIDE THE TRUTH ABOUT YOU! TO KEEP THE SECRET HIDDEN UNTIL THE TIME WAS RIGHT!
NO! I DON'T UNDERSTAND WHAT YOU'RE SAYING!
YOU'RE SPEAKING NONSENSE!

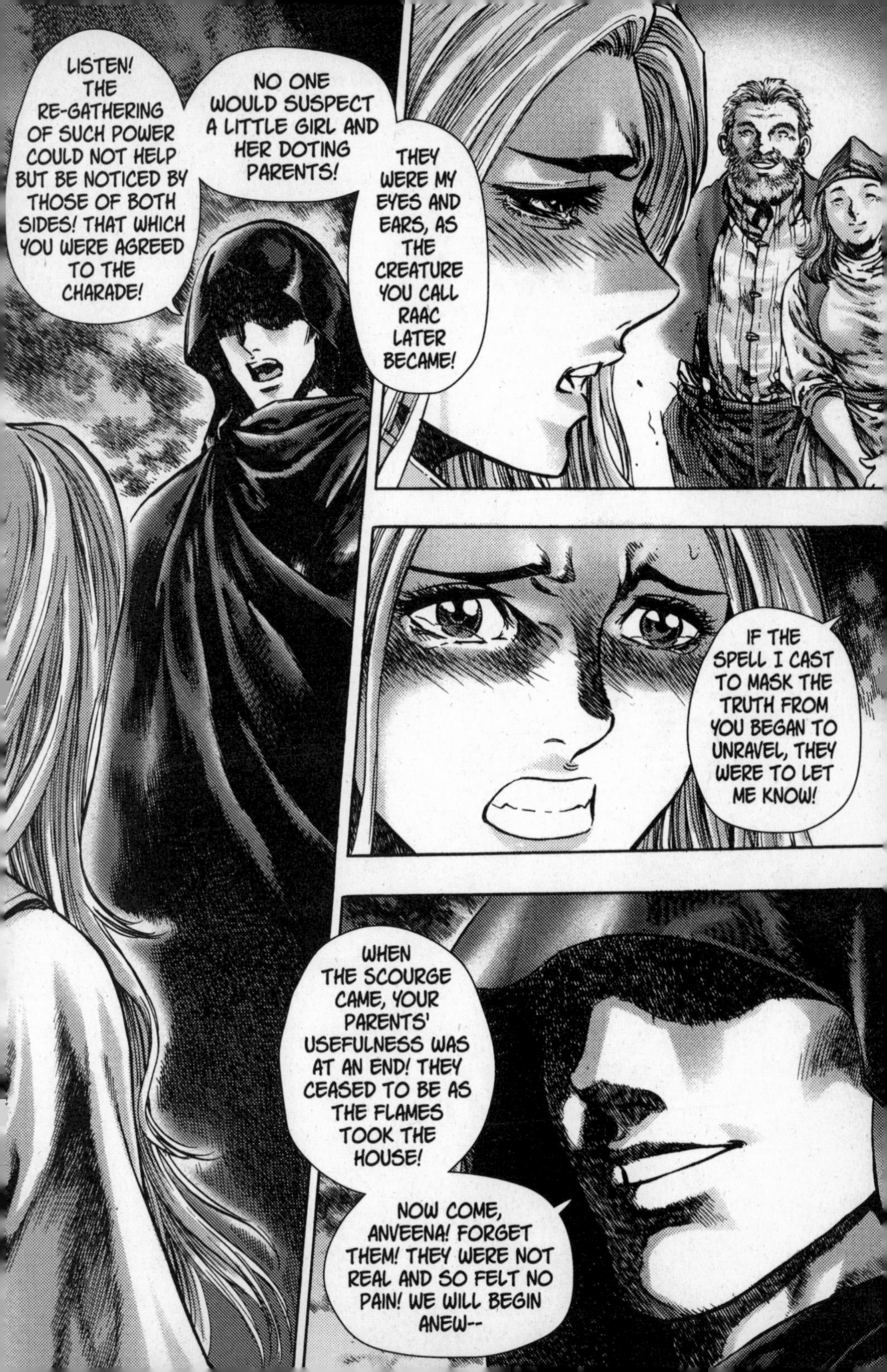
LISTEN! THE RE-GATHERING OF SUCH POWER COULD NOT HELP BUT BE NOTICED BY THOSE OF BOTH SIDES! THAT WHICH YOU WERE AGREED TO THE CHARADE!
NO ONE WOULD SUSPECT A LITTLE GIRL AND HER DOTING PARENTS!
THEY WERE MY EYES AND EARS, AS THE CREATURE YOU CALL RAAC LATER BECAME!
IF THE SPELL I CAST TO MASK THE TRUTH FROM YOU BEGAN TO UNRAVEL, THEY WERE TO LET ME KNOW!
WHEN THE SCOURGE CAME, YOUR PARENTS' USEFULNESS WAS AT AN END! THEY CEASED TO BE AS THE FLAMES TOOK THE HOUSE!
NOW COME, ANVEENA! FORGET THEM! THEY WERE NOT REAL AND SO FELT NO PAIN! WE WILL BEGIN ANEW--

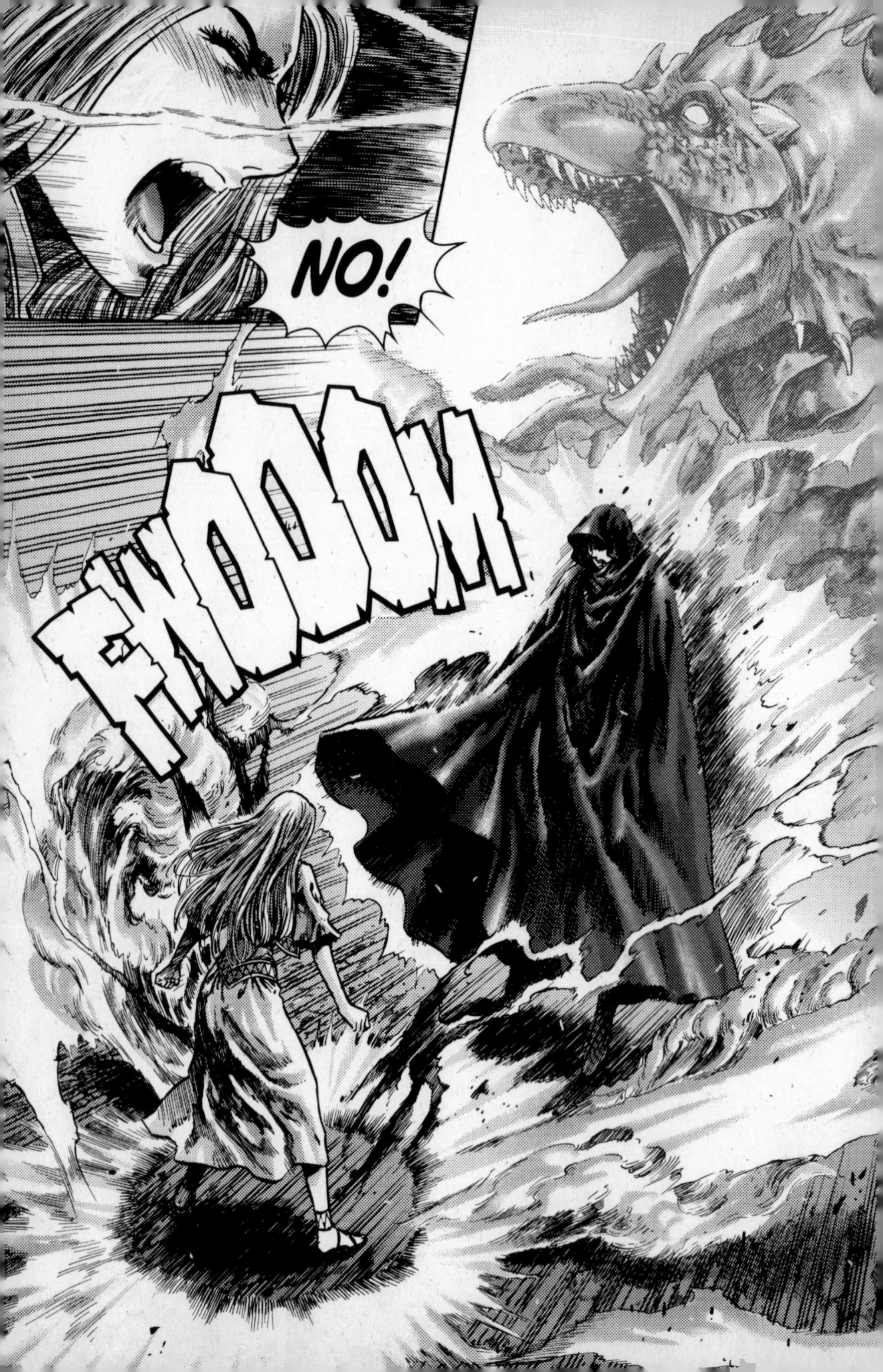
NO!
FWOOOM

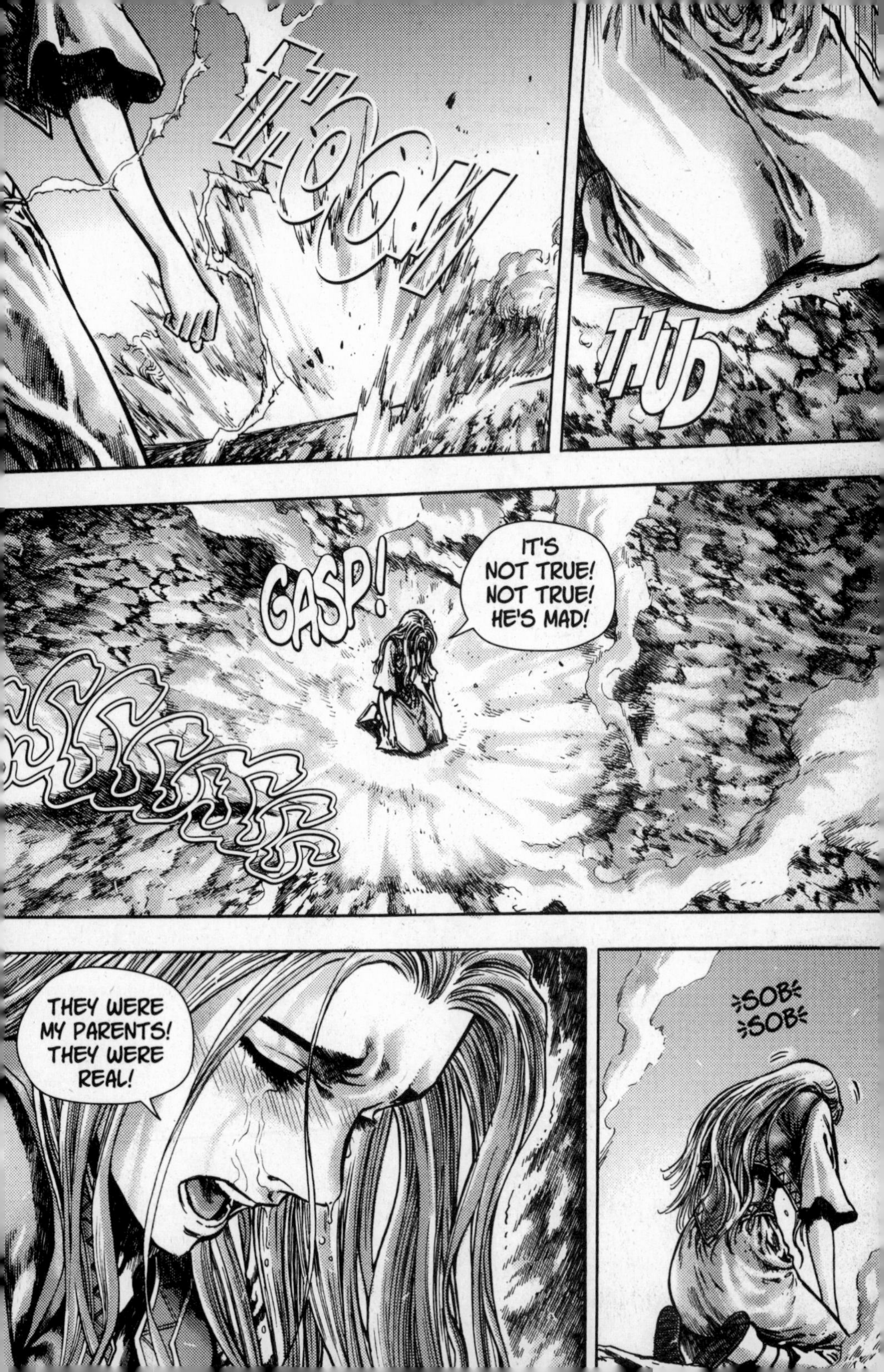
THUD
IT'S NOT TRUE! NOT TRUE! HE'S MAD!
GASP!
SOB SOB
THEY WERE MY PARENTS! THEY WERE REAL!

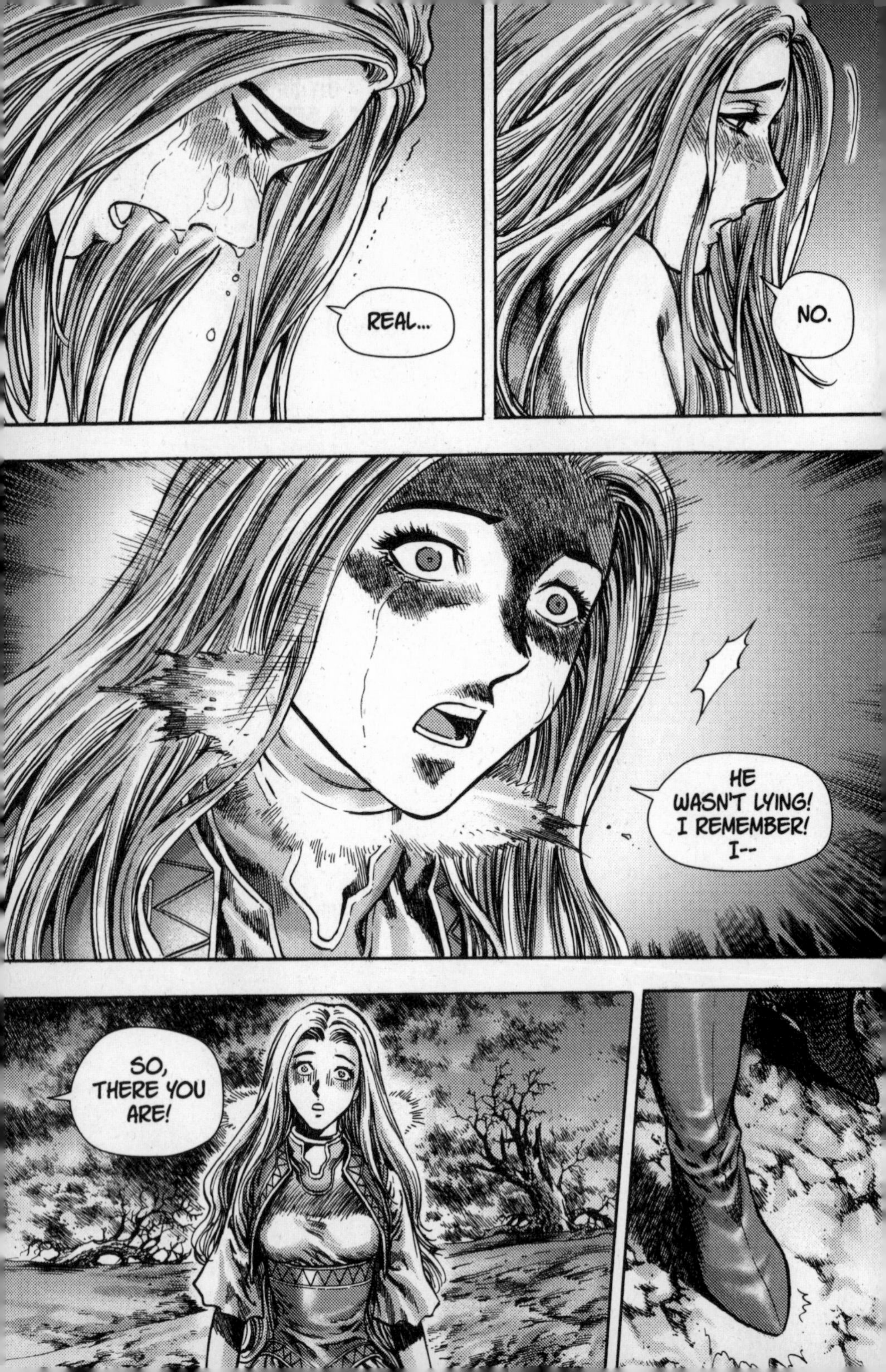
NO.
REAL...
HE WASN'T LYING! I REMEMBER! I--
SO, THERE YOU ARE!

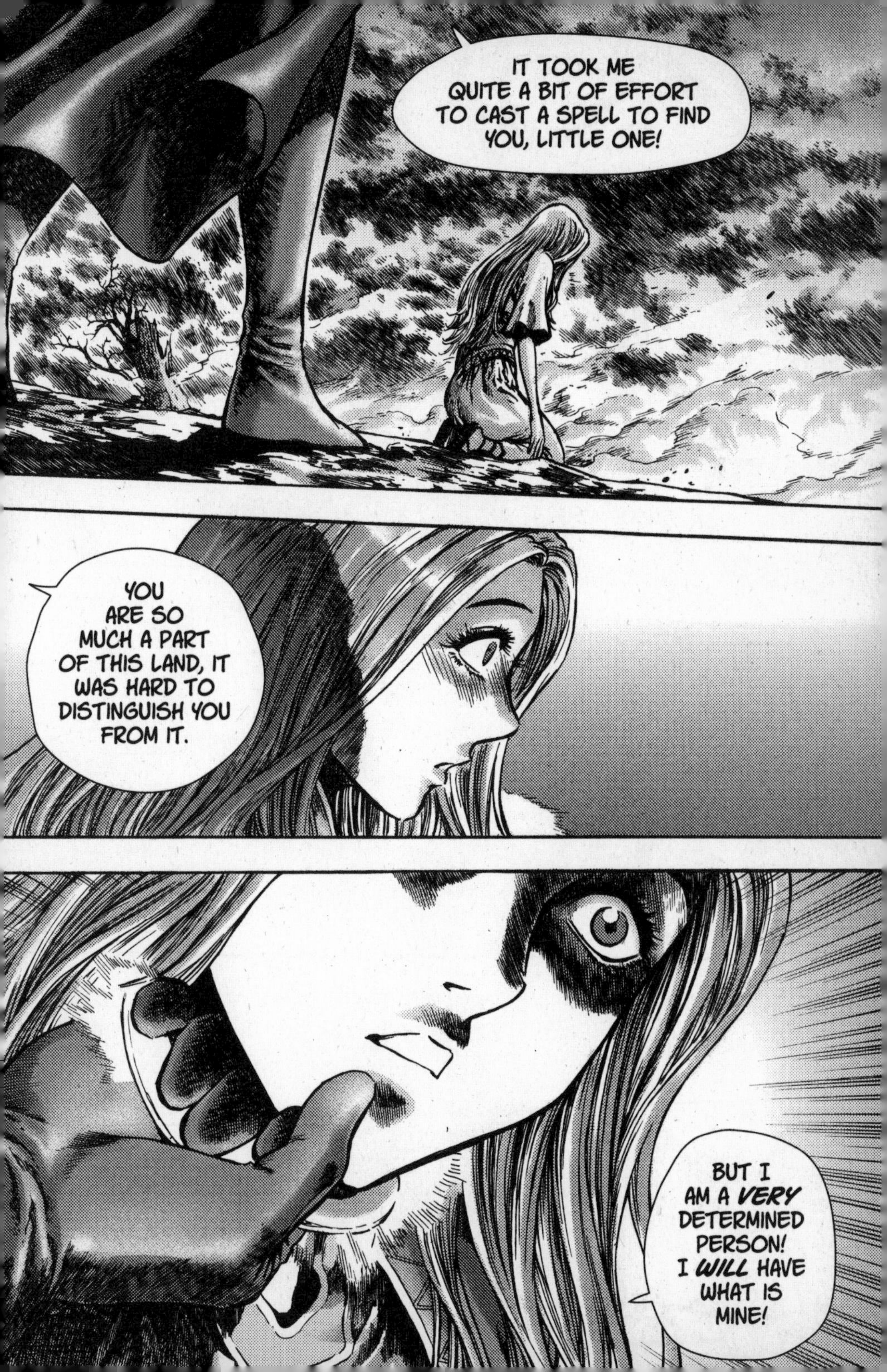
IT TOOK ME QUITE A BIT OF EFFORT TO CAST A SPELL TO FIND YOU, LITTLE ONE!
YOU ARE SO MUCH A PART OF THIS LAND, IT WAS HARD TO DISTINGUISH YOU FROM IT.
BUT I AM A ***VERY*** DETERMINED PERSON! I ***WILL*** HAVE WHAT IS MINE!

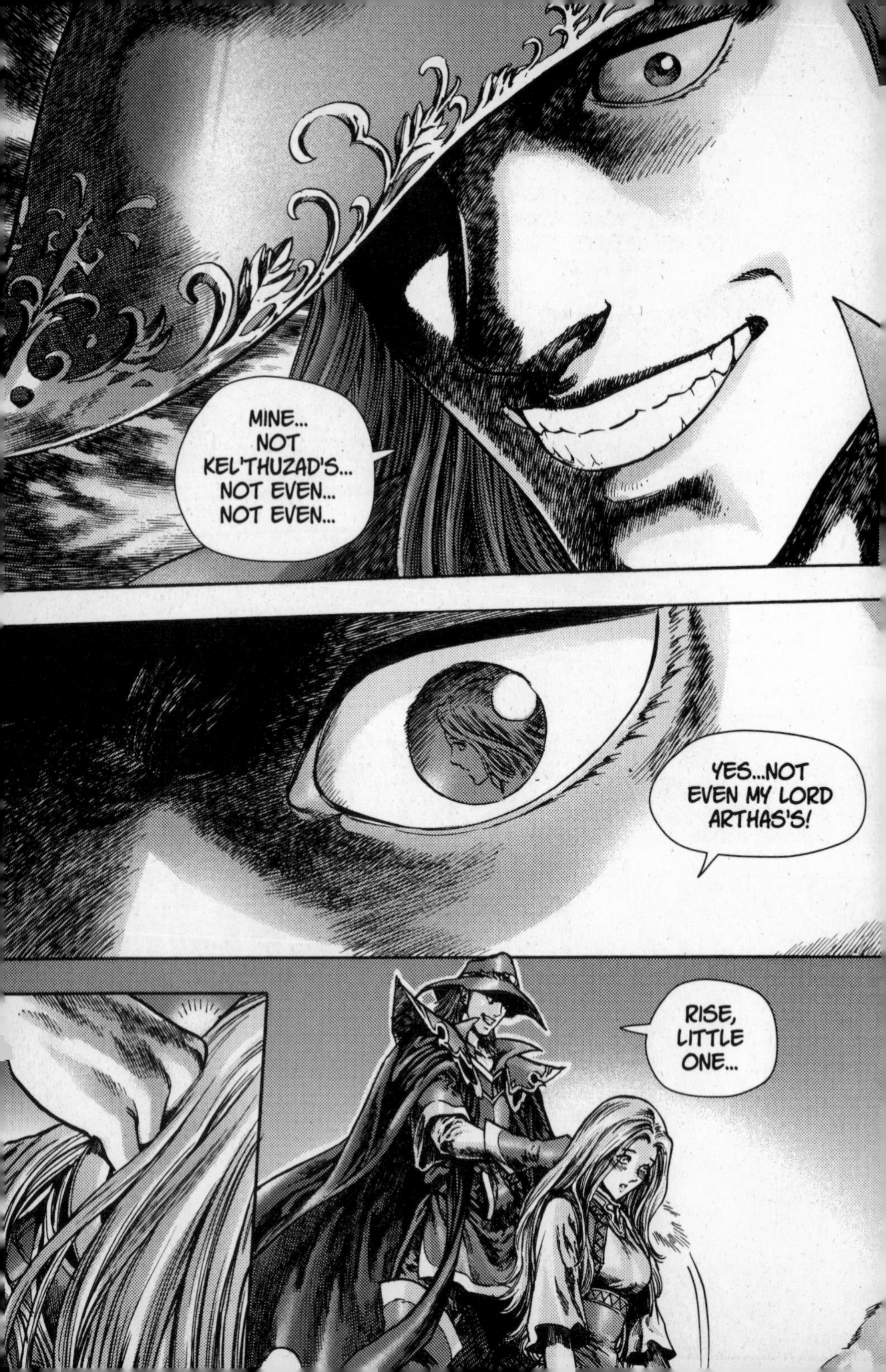
MINE... NOT KEL'THUZAD'S... NOT EVEN... NOT EVEN...
YES...NOT EVEN MY LORD ARTHAS'S!
RISE, LITTLE ONE...

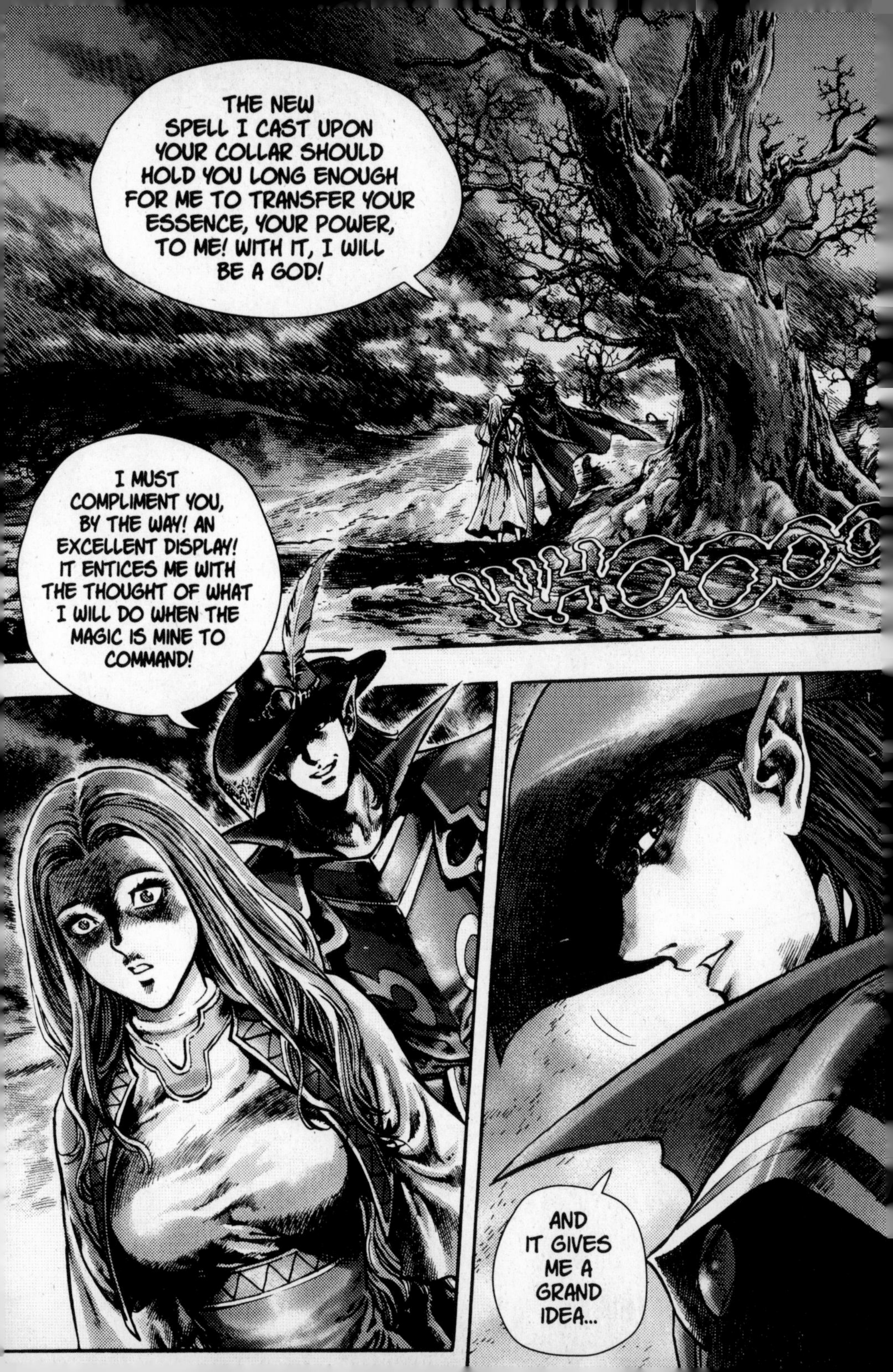
THE NEW SPELL I CAST UPON YOUR COLLAR SHOULD HOLD YOU LONG ENOUGH FOR ME TO TRANSFER YOUR ESSENCE, YOUR POWER, TO ME! WITH IT, I WILL BE A GOD!
WHOOOOO
I MUST COMPLIMENT YOU, BY THE WAY! AN EXCELLENT DISPLAY! IT ENTICES ME WITH THE THOUGHT OF WHAT I WILL DO WHEN THE MAGIC IS MINE TO COMMAND!
AND IT GIVES ME A GRAND IDEA...

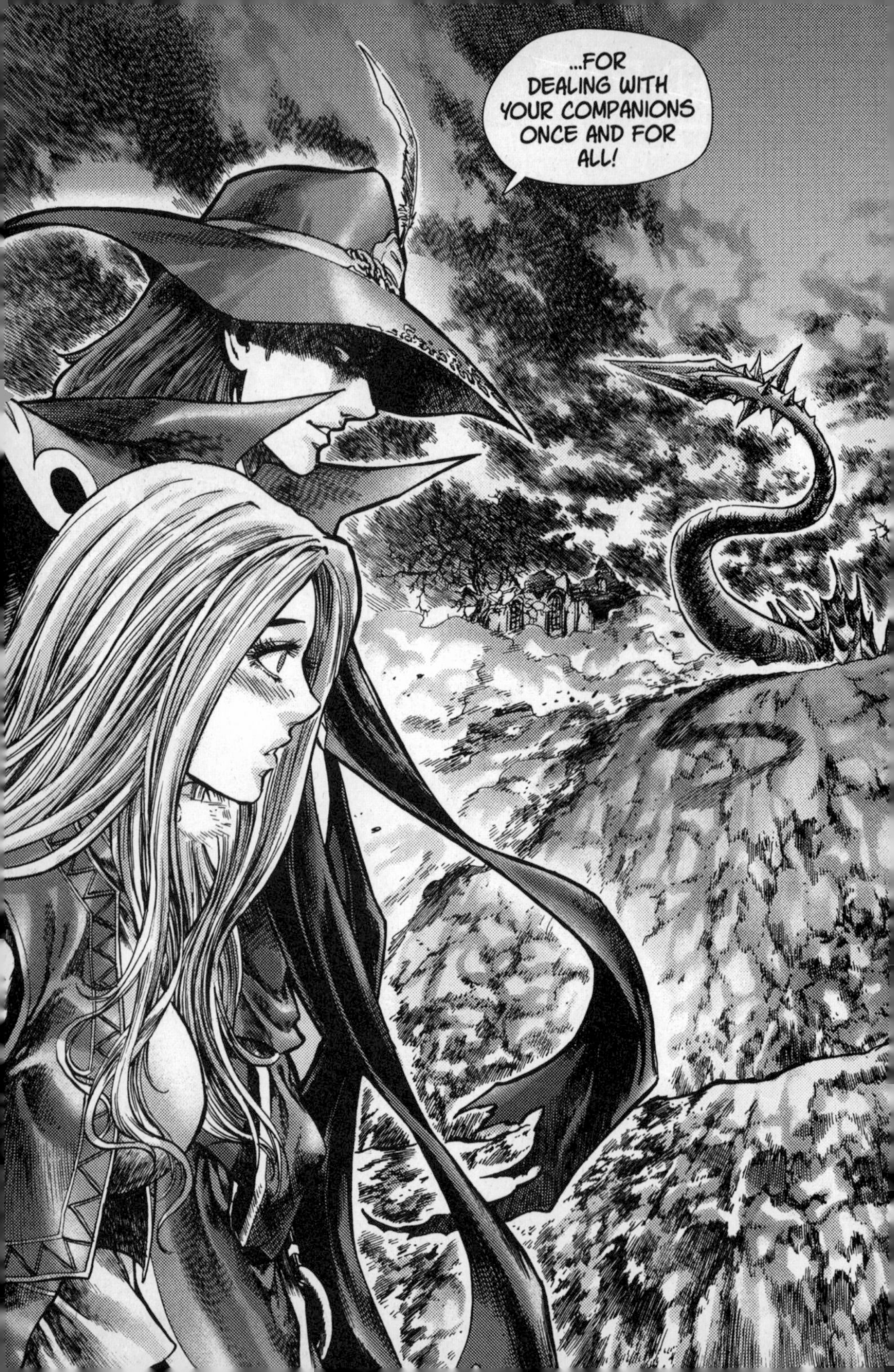
...FOR DEALING WITH YOUR COMPANIONS ONCE AND FOR ALL!

CHAPTER FOUR
DARK REUNION

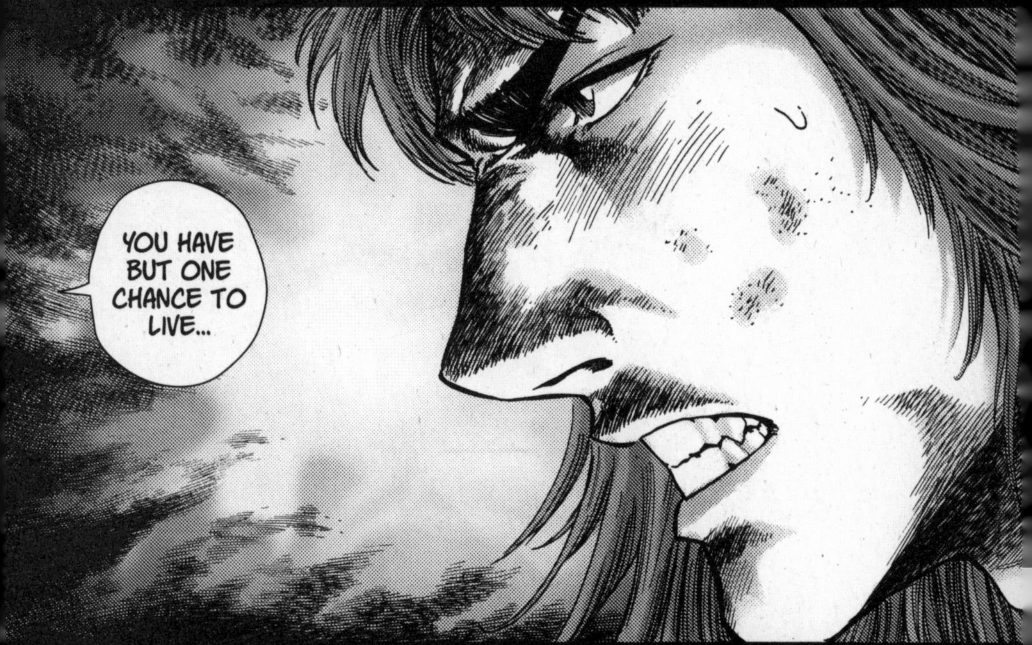
YOU HAVE BUT ONE CHANCE TO LIVE...

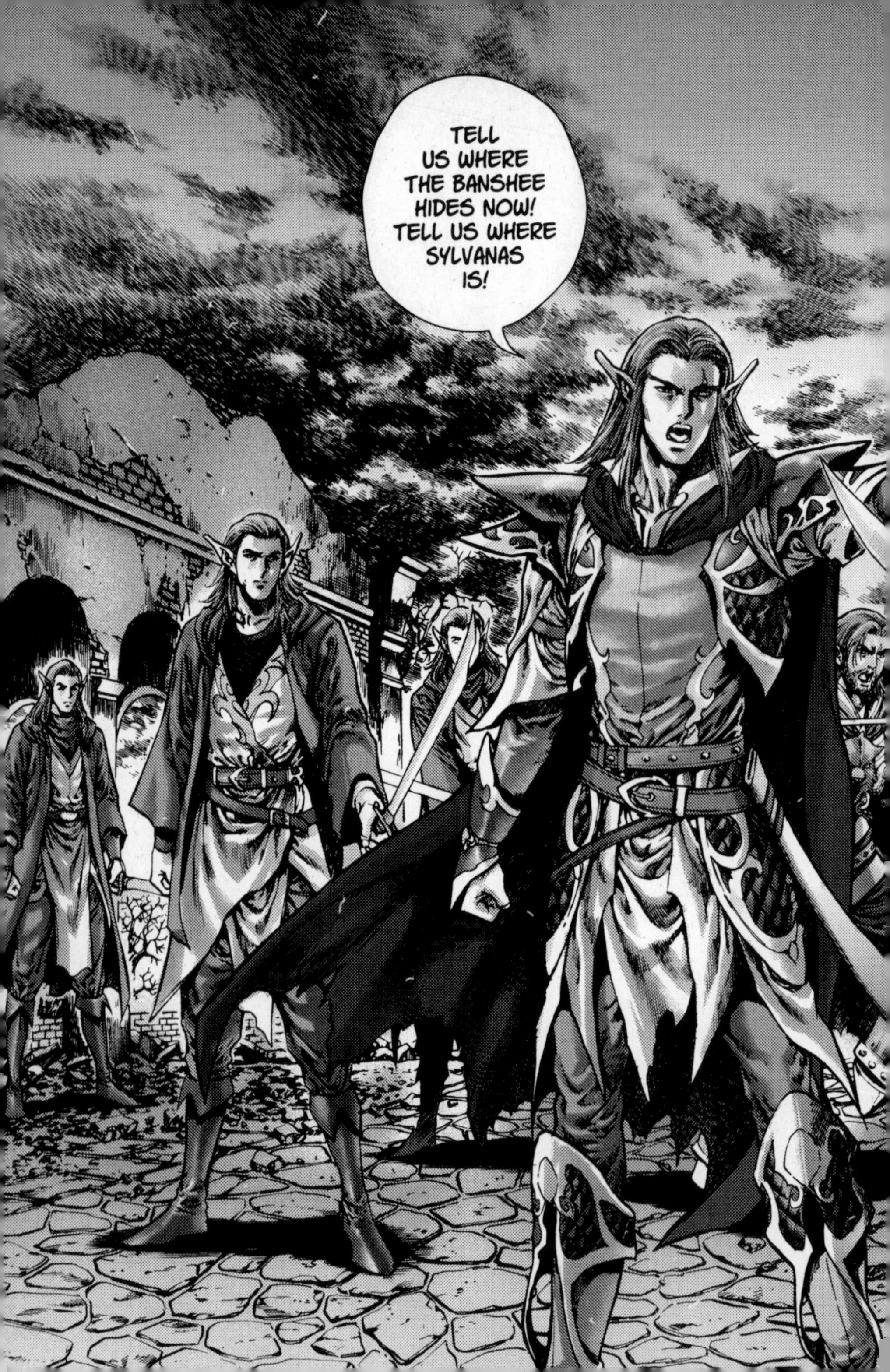
TELL US WHERE THE BANSHEE HIDES NOW! TELL US WHERE SYLVANAS IS!

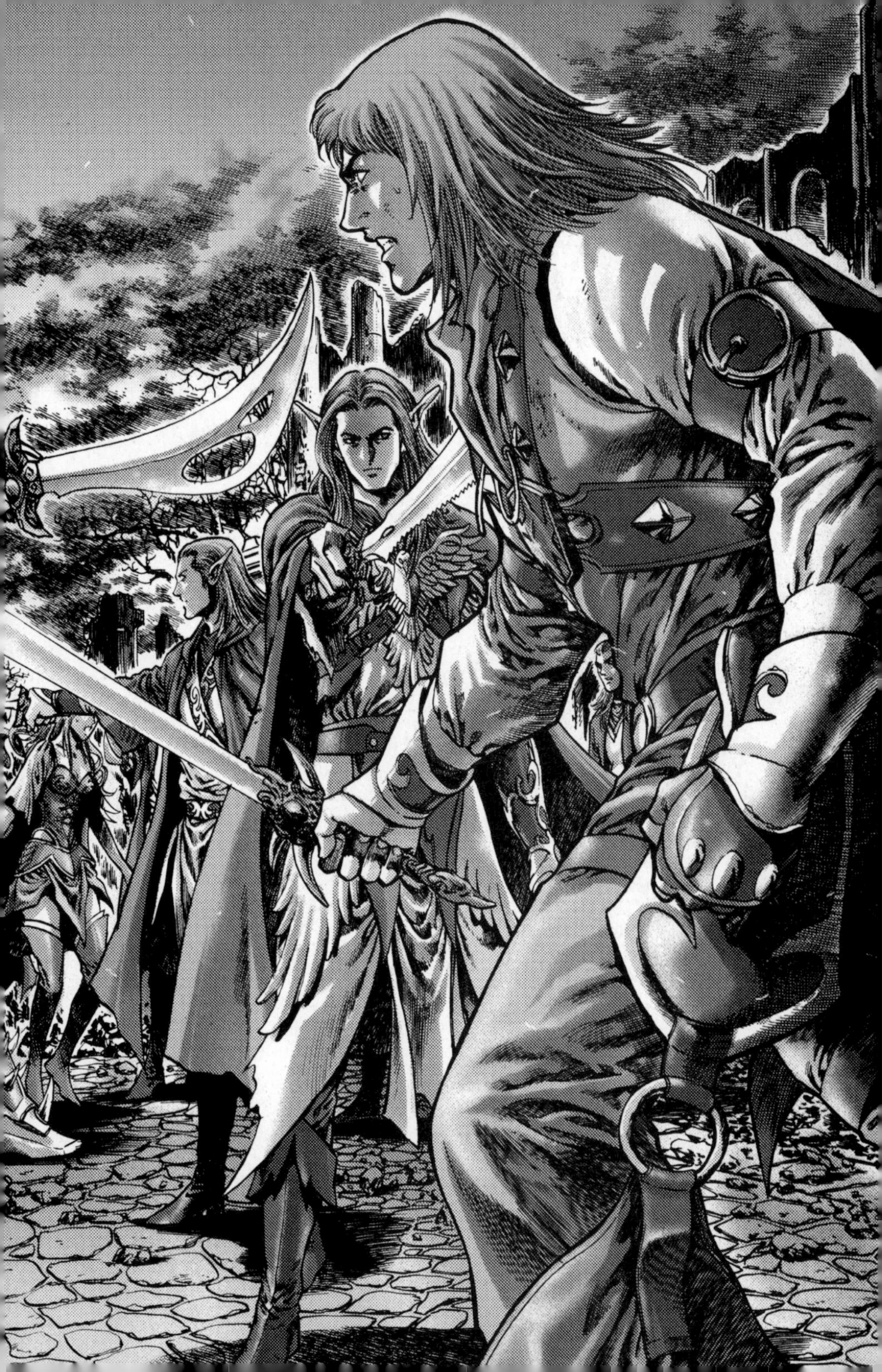

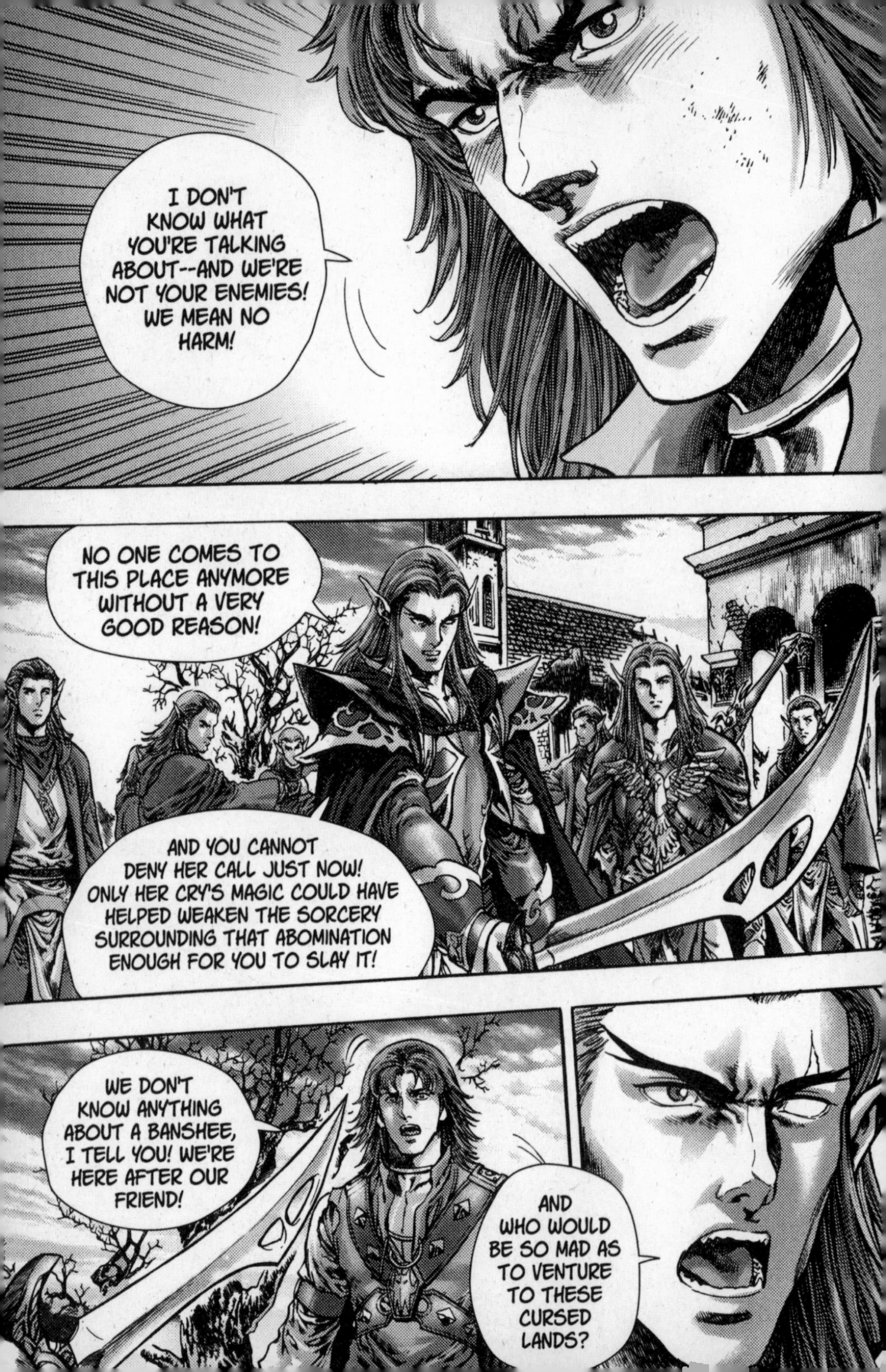
I DON'T KNOW WHAT YOU'RE TALKING ABOUT--AND WE'RE NOT YOUR ENEMIES! WE MEAN NO HARM!
NO ONE COMES TO THIS PLACE ANYMORE WITHOUT A VERY GOOD REASON!
AND YOU CANNOT DENY HER CALL JUST NOW! ONLY HER CRY'S MAGIC COULD HAVE HELPED WEAKEN THE SORCERY SURROUNDING THAT ABOMINATION ENOUGH FOR YOU TO SLAY IT!
WE DON'T KNOW ANYTHING ABOUT A BANSHEE, I TELL YOU! WE'RE HERE AFTER OUR FRIEND!
AND WHO WOULD BE SO MAD AS TO VENTURE TO THESE CURSED LANDS?

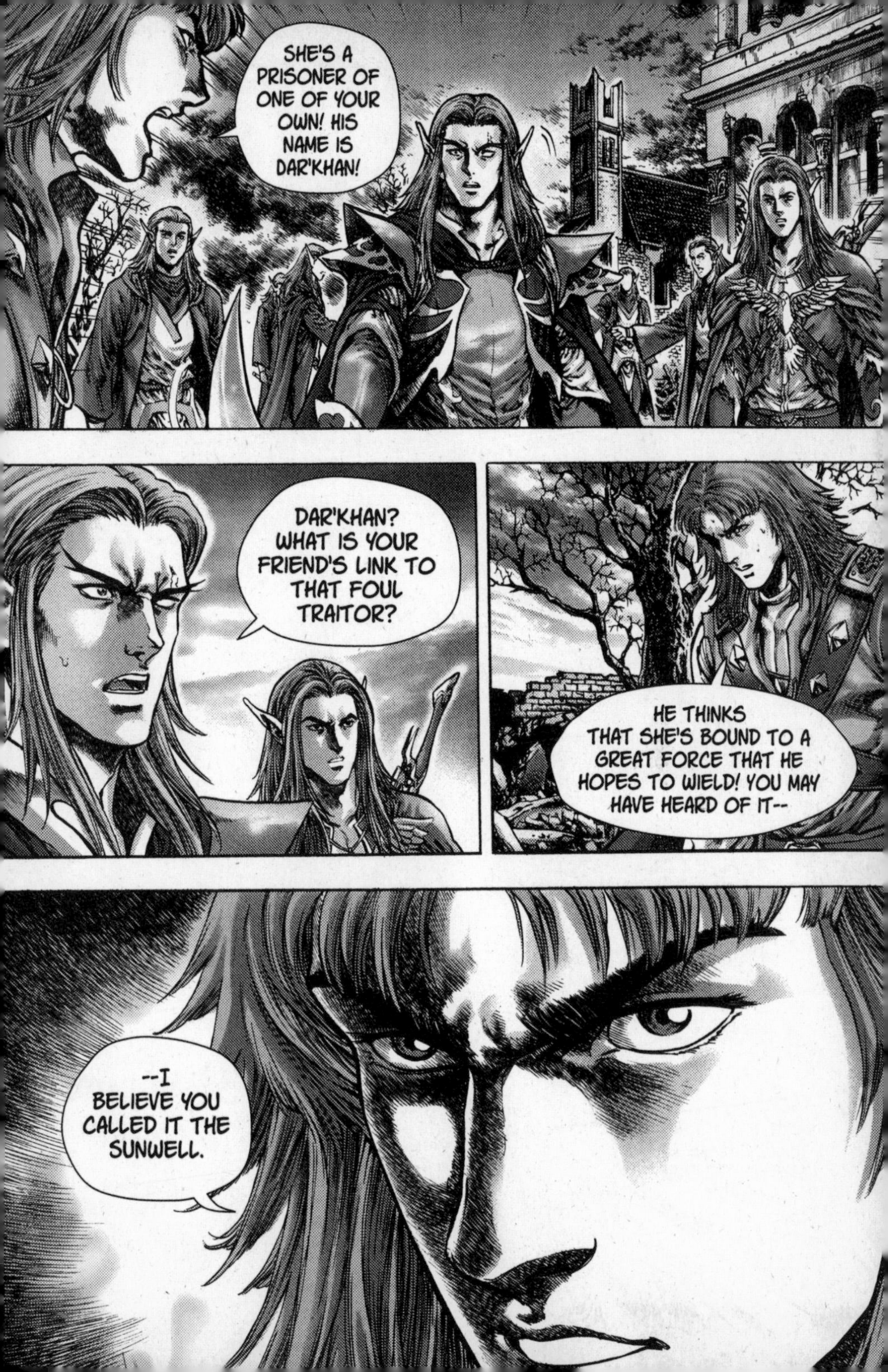
SHE'S A PRISONER OF ONE OF YOUR OWN! HIS NAME IS DAR'KHAN!
DAR'KHAN? WHAT IS YOUR FRIEND'S LINK TO THAT FOUL TRAITOR?
HE THINKS THAT SHE'S BOUND TO A GREAT FORCE THAT HE HOPES TO WIELD! YOU MAY HAVE HEARD OF IT--
--I BELIEVE YOU CALLED IT THE SUNWELL.

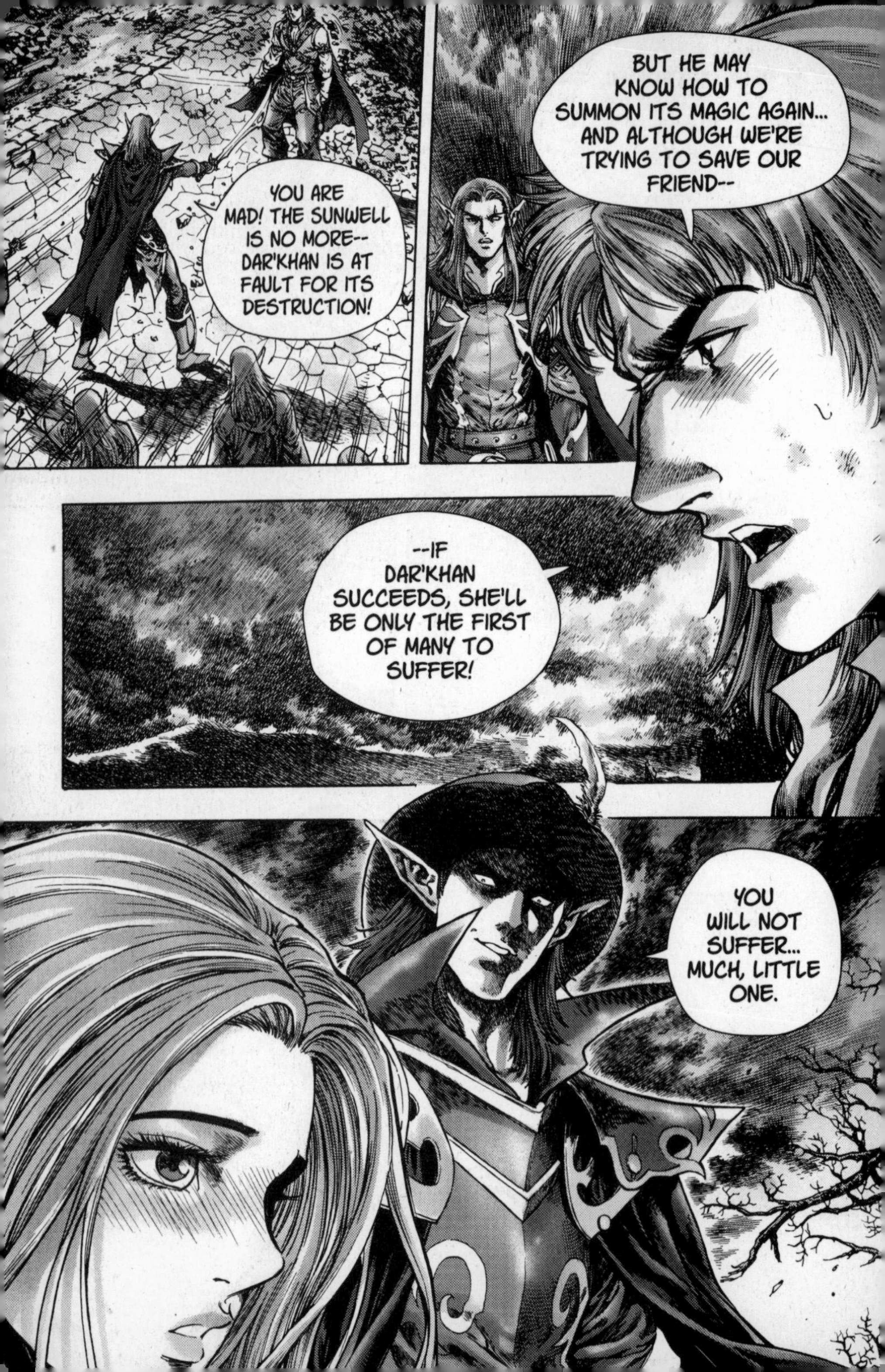
YOU ARE MAD! THE SUNWELL IS NO MORE-- DAR'KHAN IS AT FAULT FOR ITS DESTRUCTION!
BUT HE MAY KNOW HOW TO SUMMON ITS MAGIC AGAIN... AND ALTHOUGH WE'RE TRYING TO SAVE OUR FRIEND--
--IF DAR'KHAN SUCCEEDS, SHE'LL BE ONLY THE FIRST OF MANY TO SUFFER!
YOU WILL NOT SUFFER... MUCH, LITTLE ONE.

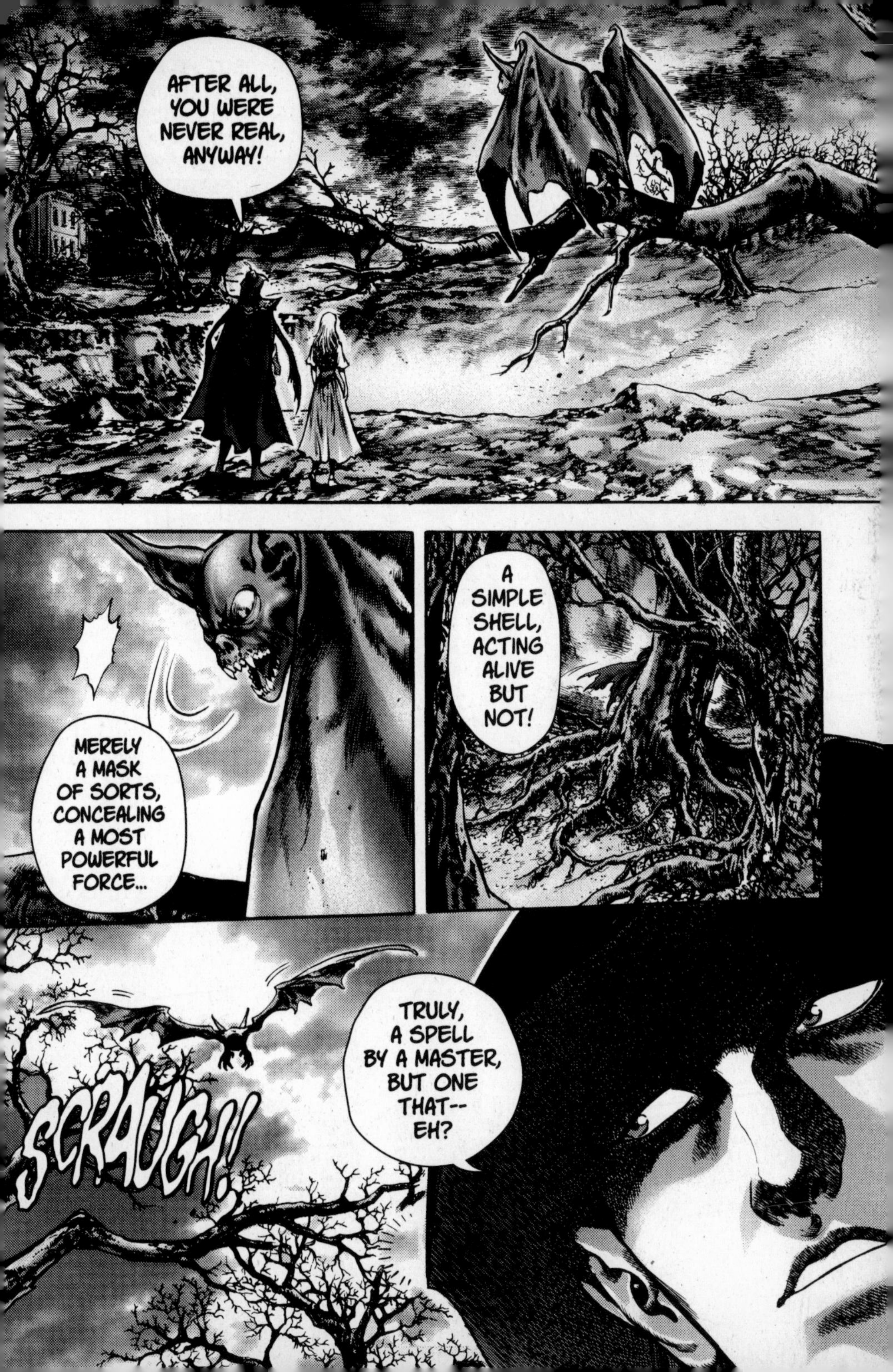
AFTER ALL, YOU WERE NEVER REAL, ANYWAY!
A SIMPLE SHELL, ACTING ALIVE BUT NOT!
MERELY A MASK OF SORTS, CONCEALING A MOST POWERFUL FORCE...
TRULY, A SPELL BY A MASTER, BUT ONE THAT-- EH?
SCRAUGH!!

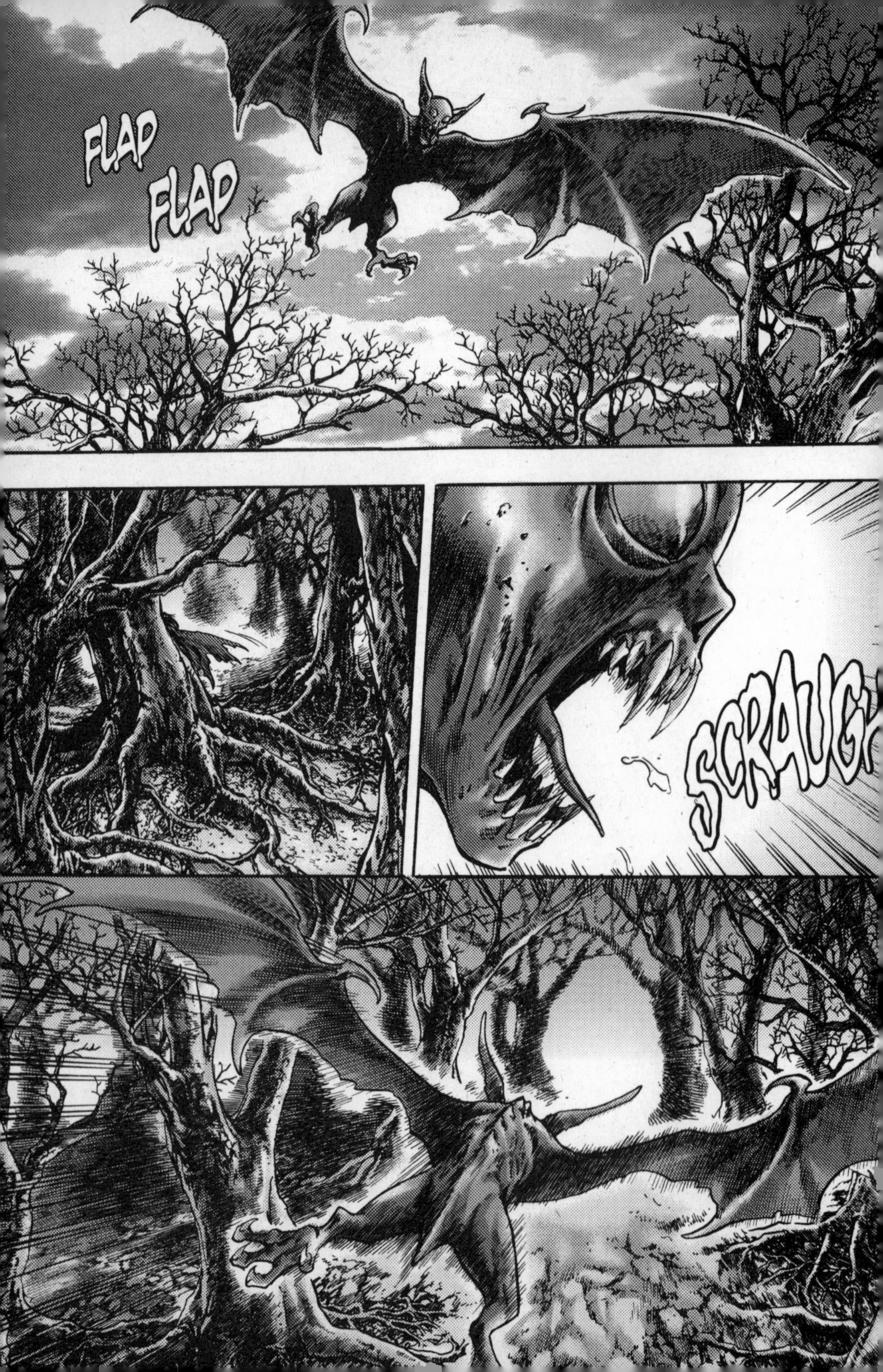
FLAP
FLAP
SCRAUGH

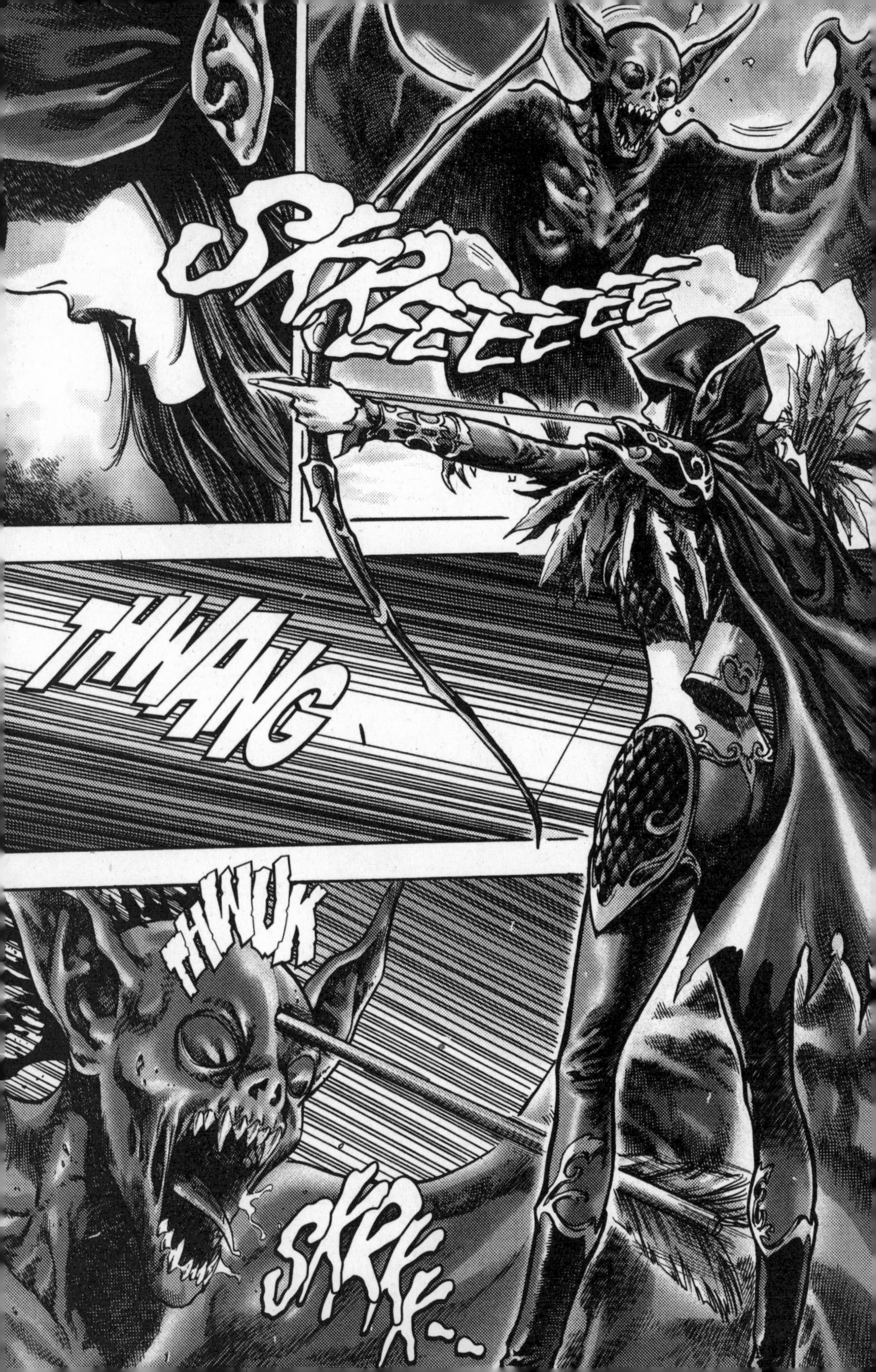
SKREEEEEEE
THWANG
THWUK
SKRKK..

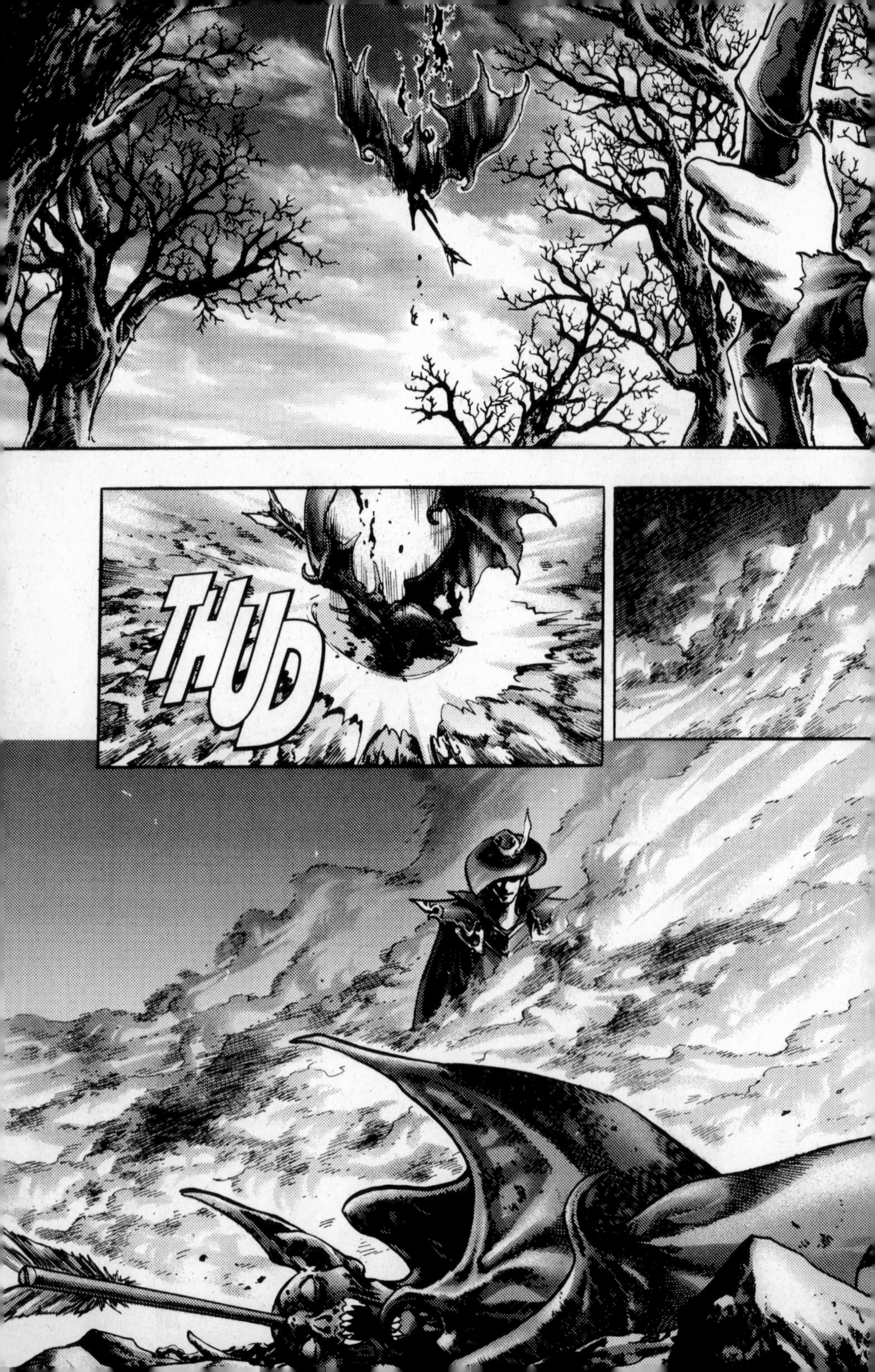
THUD

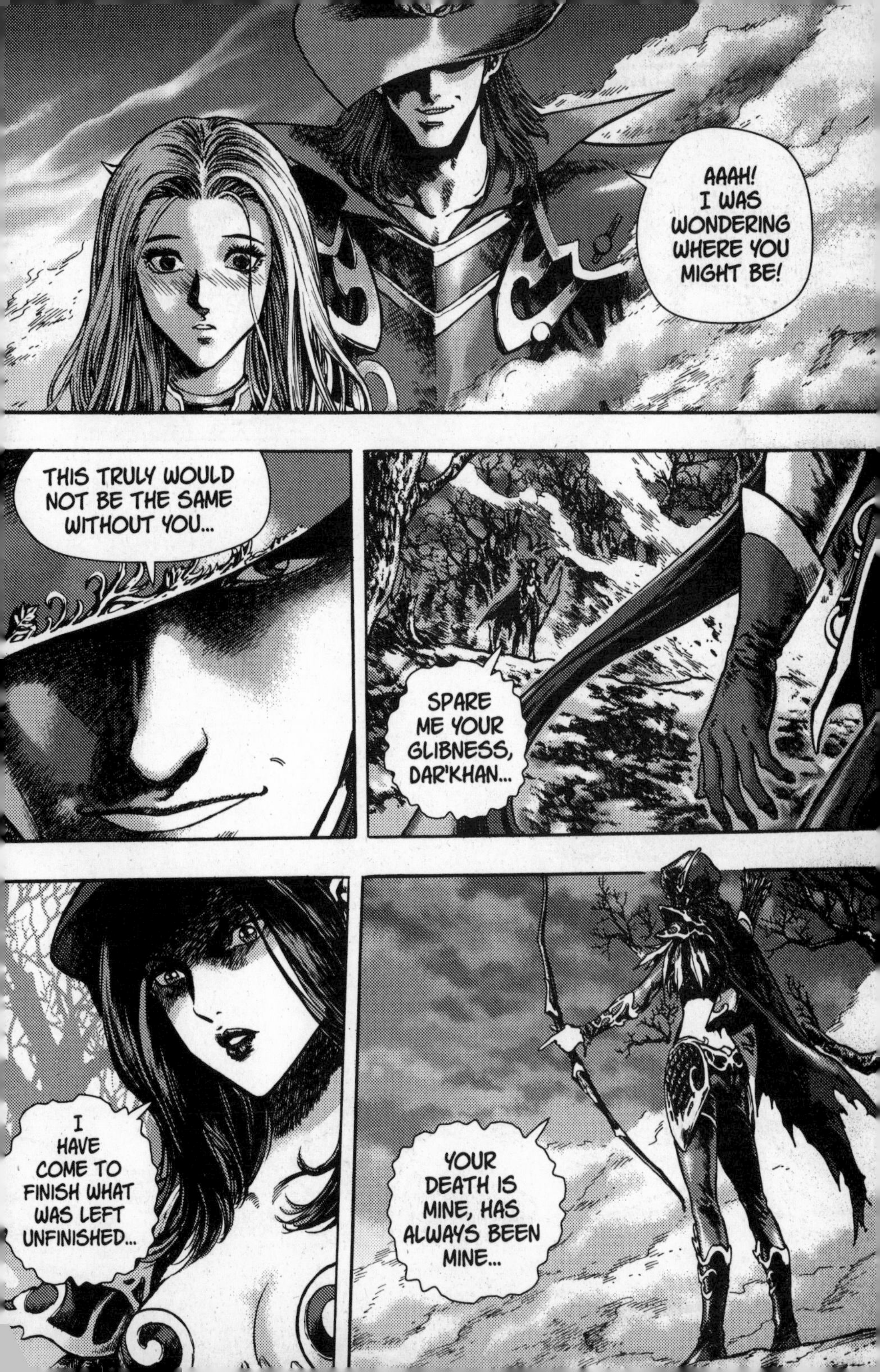
AAAH! I WAS WONDERING WHERE YOU MIGHT BE!
THIS TRULY WOULD NOT BE THE SAME WITHOUT YOU...
SPARE ME YOUR GLIBNESS, DAR'KHAN...
I HAVE COME TO FINISH WHAT WAS LEFT UNFINISHED...
YOUR DEATH IS MINE, HAS ALWAYS BEEN MINE...

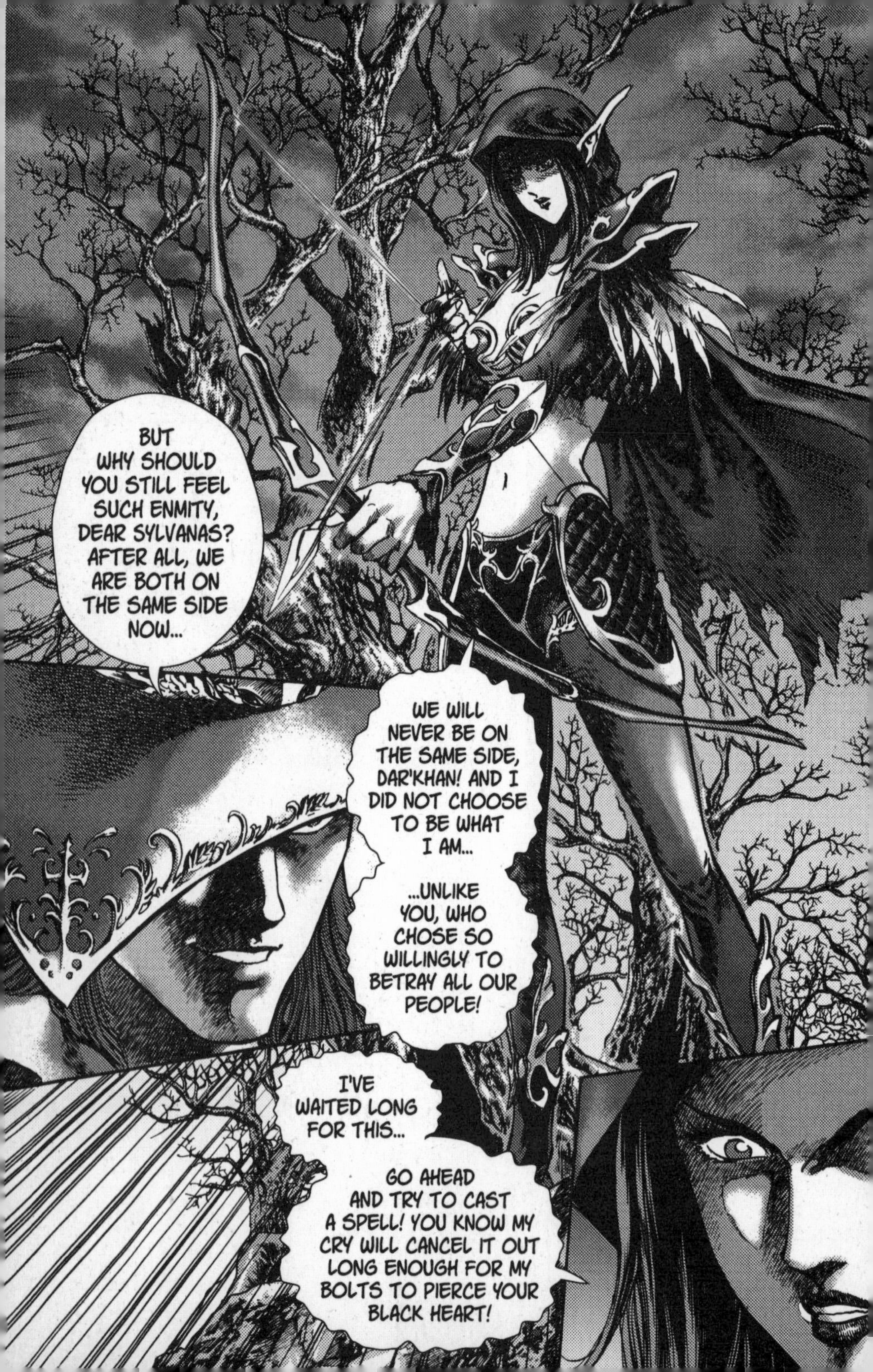
BUT WHY SHOULD YOU STILL FEEL SUCH ENMITY, DEAR SYLVANAS? AFTER ALL, WE ARE BOTH ON THE SAME SIDE NOW...
WE WILL NEVER BE ON THE SAME SIDE, DAR'KHAN! AND I DID NOT CHOOSE TO BE WHAT I AM...
...UNLIKE YOU, WHO CHOSE SO WILLINGLY TO BETRAY ALL OUR PEOPLE!
I'VE WAITED LONG FOR THIS...
GO AHEAD AND TRY TO CAST A SPELL! YOU KNOW MY CRY WILL CANCEL IT OUT LONG ENOUGH FOR MY BOLTS TO PIERCE YOUR BLACK HEART!

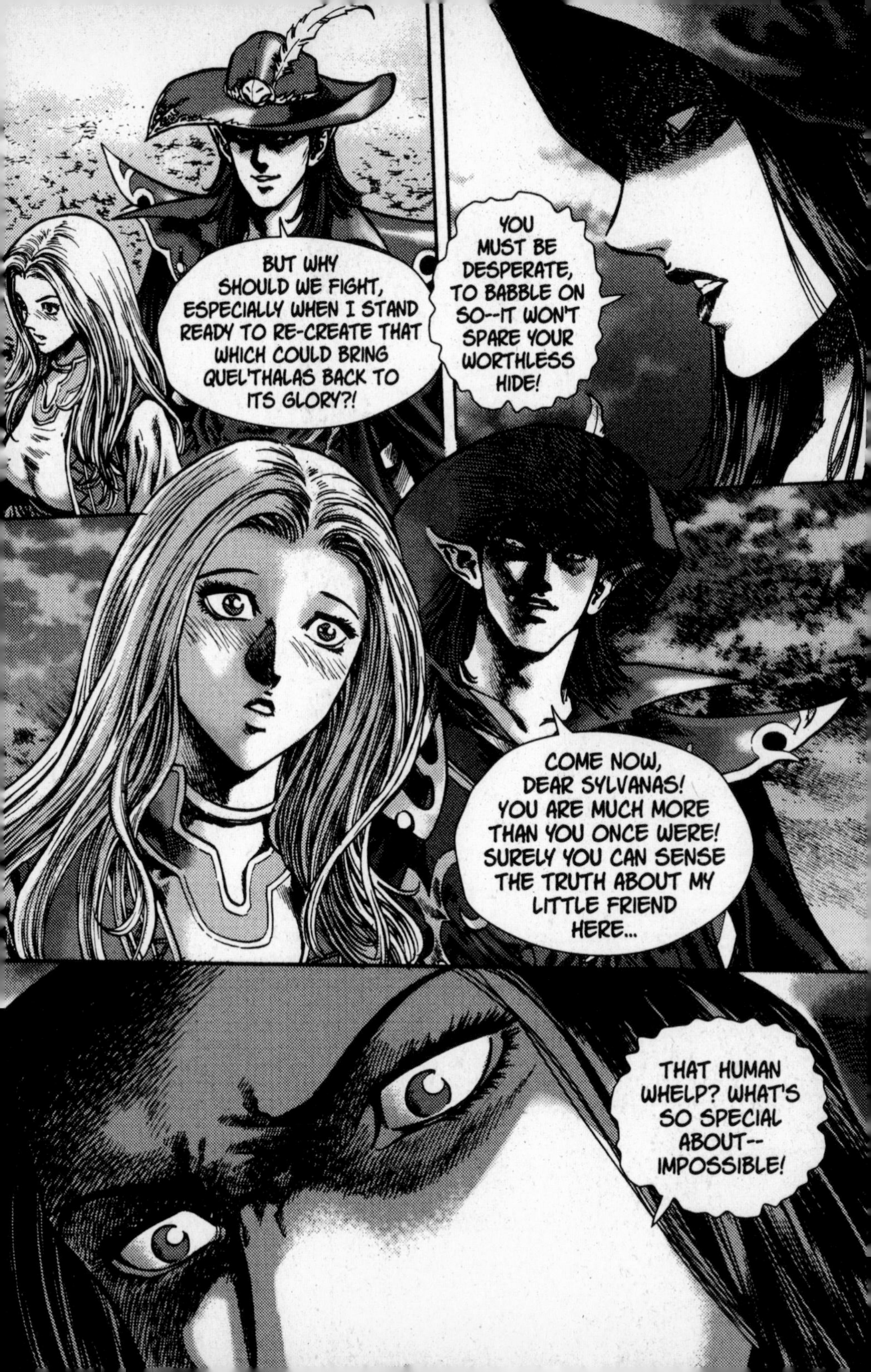
BUT WHY SHOULD WE FIGHT, ESPECIALLY WHEN I STAND READY TO RE-CREATE THAT WHICH COULD BRING QUEL'THALAS BACK TO ITS GLORY?!
YOU MUST BE DESPERATE, TO BABBLE ON SO--IT WON'T SPARE YOUR WORTHLESS HIDE!
COME NOW, DEAR SYLVANAS! YOU ARE MUCH MORE THAN YOU ONCE WERE! SURELY YOU CAN SENSE THE TRUTH ABOUT MY LITTLE FRIEND HERE...
THAT HUMAN WHELP? WHAT'S SO SPECIAL ABOUT-- IMPOSSIBLE!

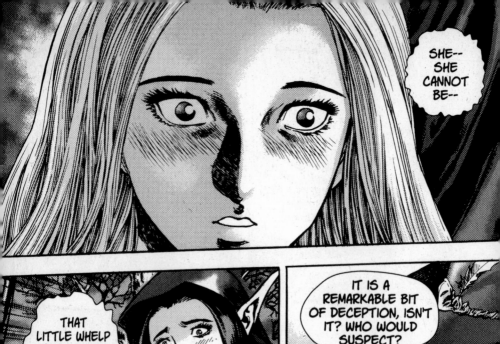

SHE-- SHE CANNOT BE--

THAT LITTLE WHELP CANNOT HOLD IN HER THE ESSENCE OF THE BLESSED SUNWELL!

IT IS A REMARKABLE BIT OF DECEPTION, ISN'T IT? WHO WOULD SUSPECT?

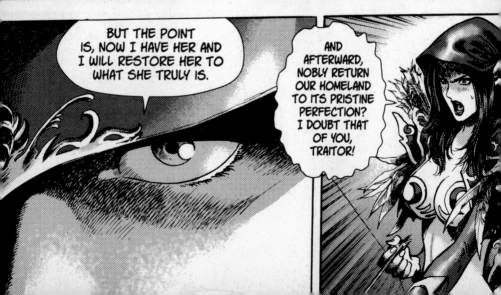

BUT THE POINT IS, NOW I HAVE HER AND I WILL RESTORE HER TO WHAT SHE TRULY IS.

AND AFTERWARD, NOBLY RETURN OUR HOMELAND TO ITS PRISTINE PERFECTION? I DOUBT THAT OF YOU, TRAITOR!

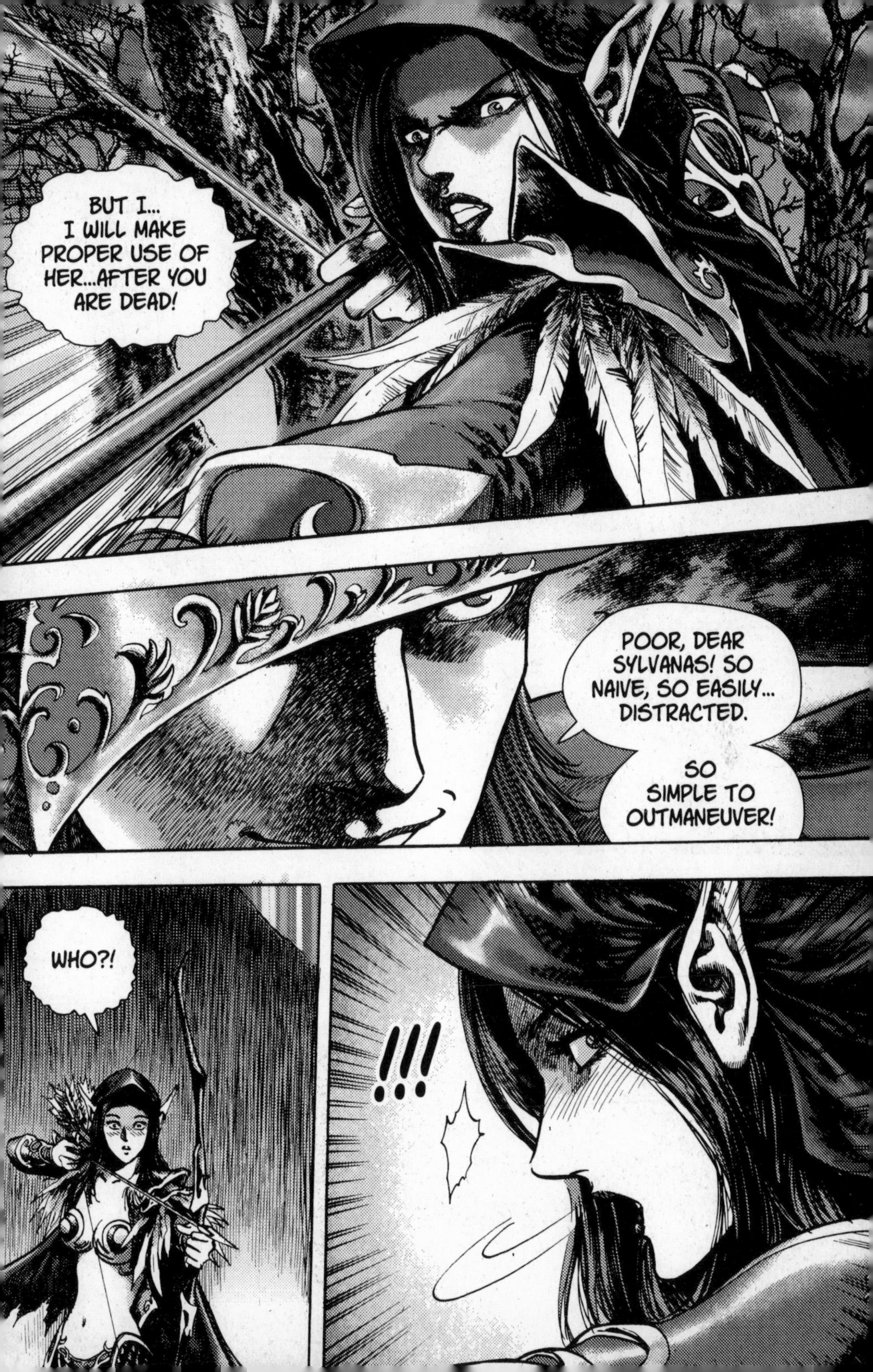
BUT I... I WILL MAKE PROPER USE OF HER...AFTER YOU ARE DEAD!
POOR, DEAR SYLVANAS! SO NAIVE, SO EASILY... DISTRACTED.
SO SIMPLE TO OUTMANEUVER!
WHO?!
!!!

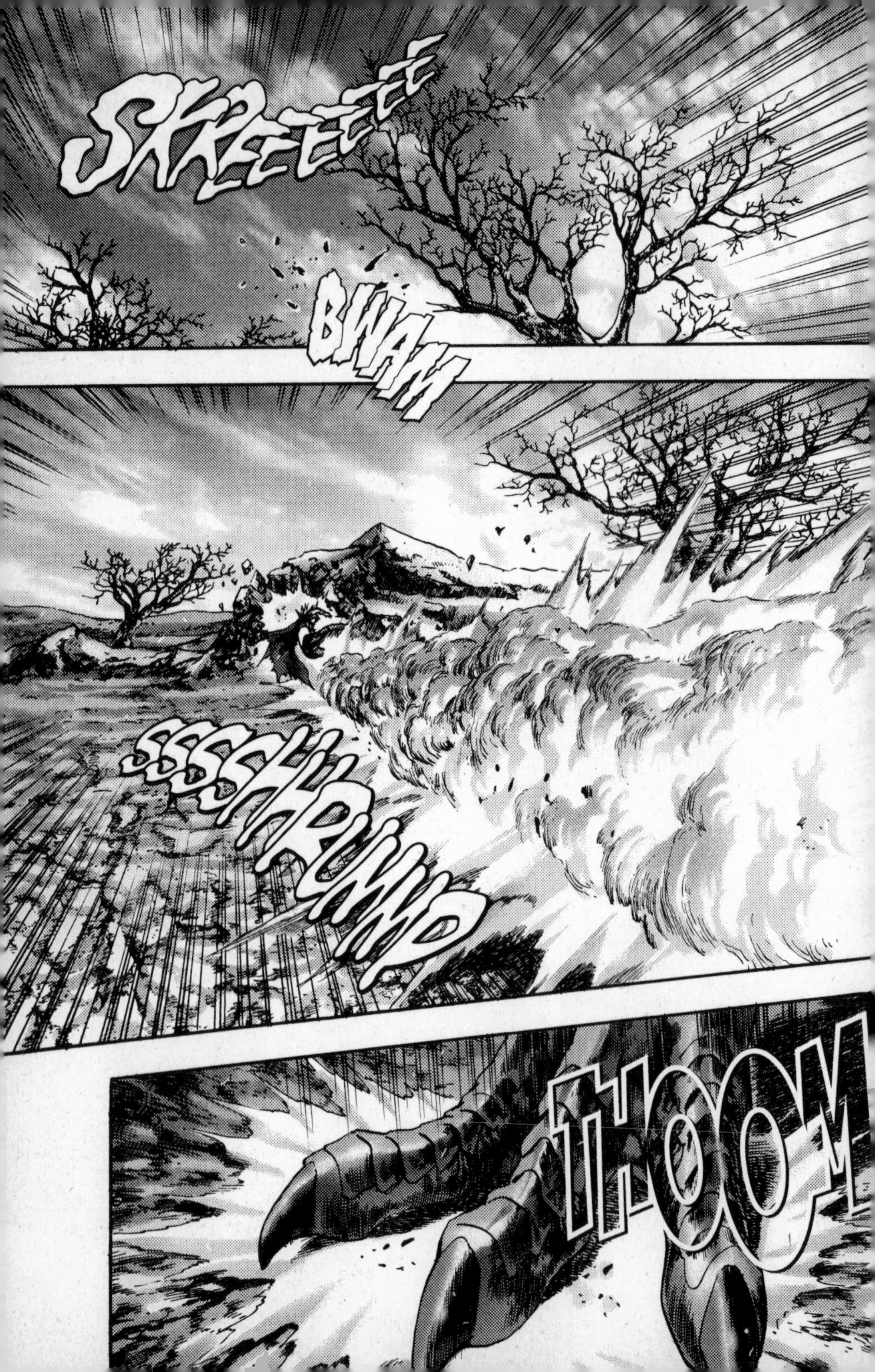
SKREEEEEE
BWAM
SSSSCHRUMMP
THOOM

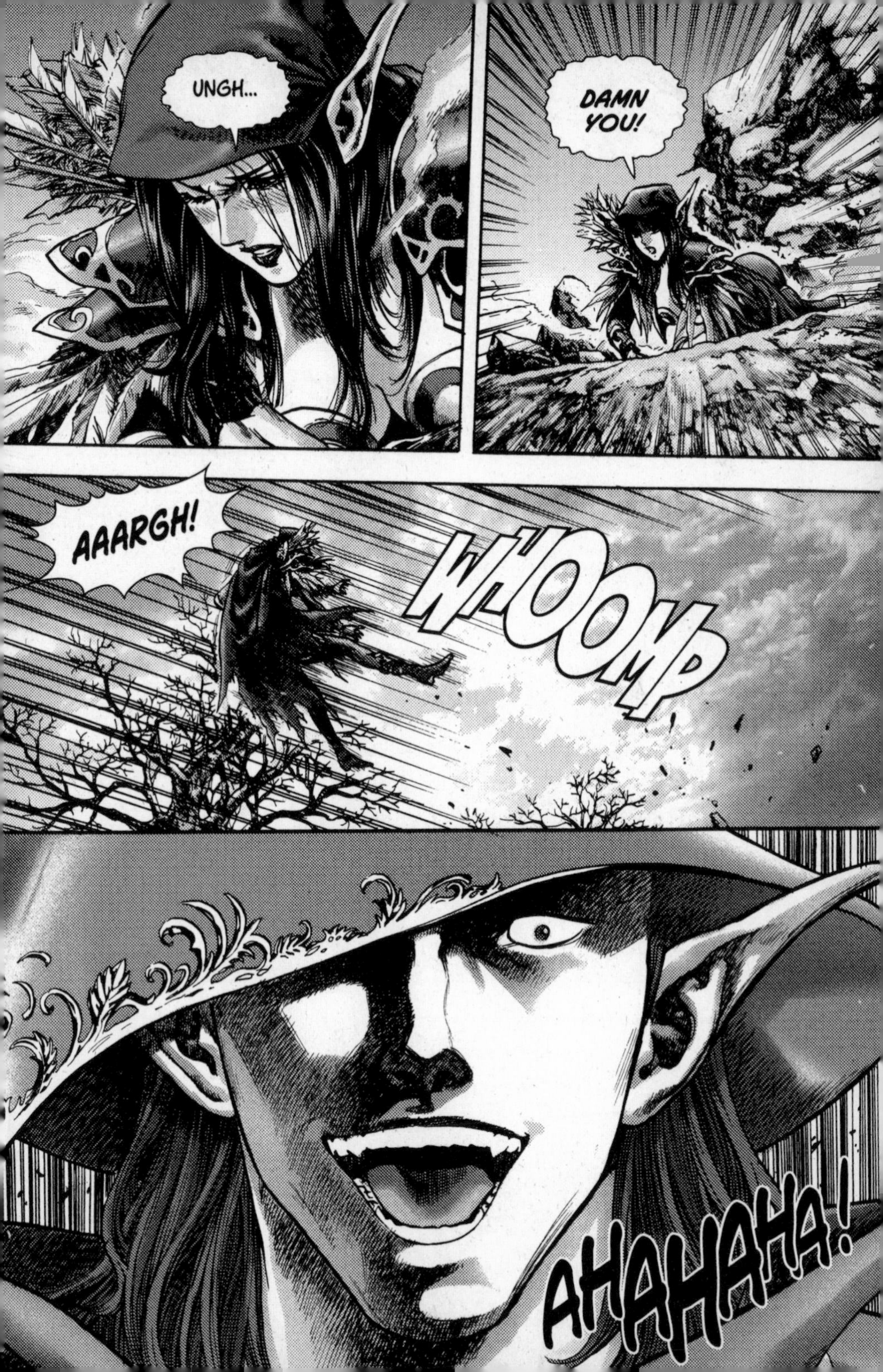
UNGH...
DAMN YOU!
AAARGH!
WHOOMP
AHAHAHA!

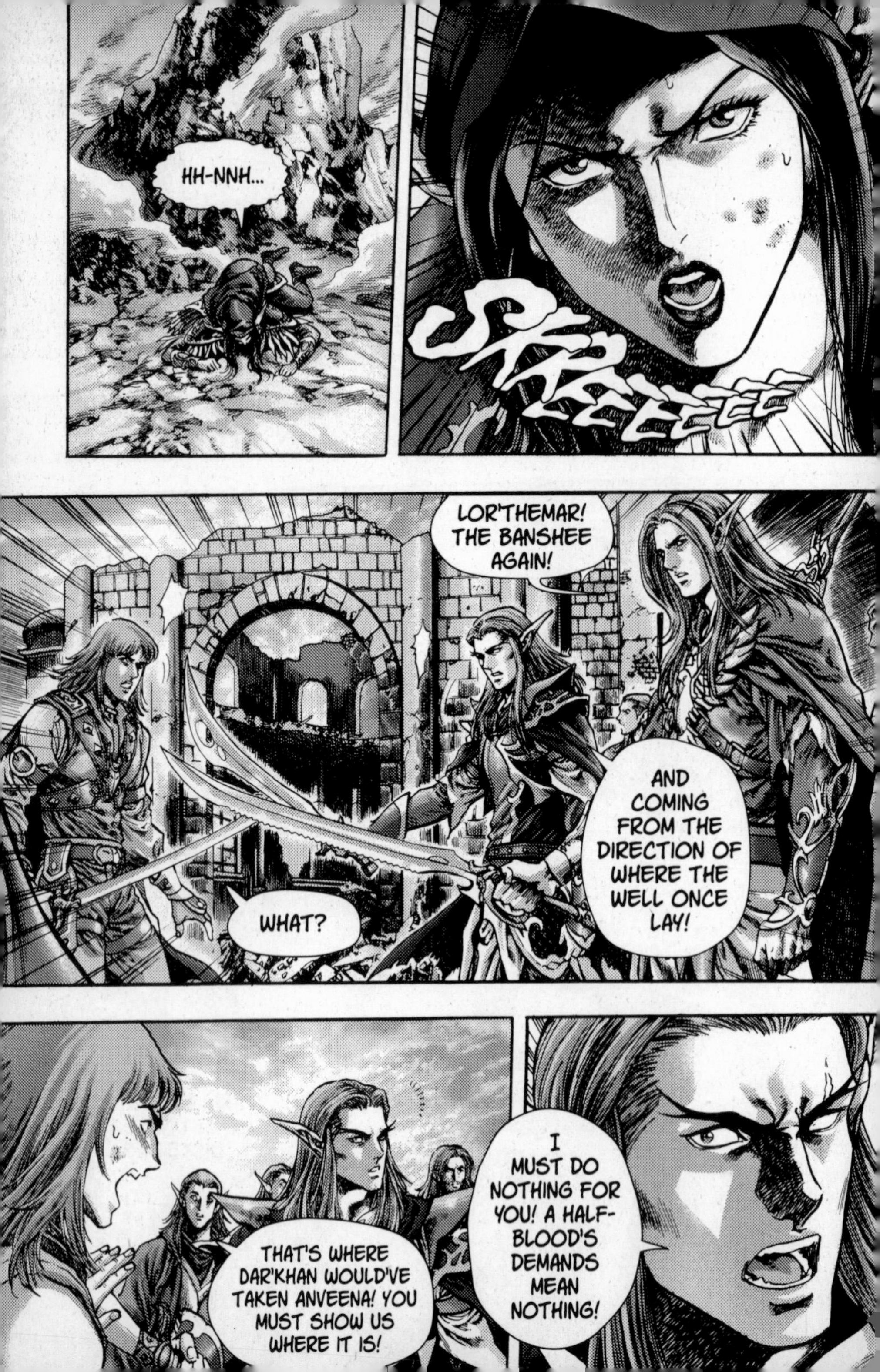
HH-NNH...
SKREEEEEE
LOR'THEMAR! THE BANSHEE AGAIN!
WHAT?
AND COMING FROM THE DIRECTION OF WHERE THE WELL ONCE LAY!
THAT'S WHERE DAR'KHAN WOULD'VE TAKEN ANVEENA! YOU MUST SHOW US WHERE IT IS!
I MUST DO NOTHING FOR YOU! A HALF-BLOOD'S DEMANDS MEAN NOTHING!

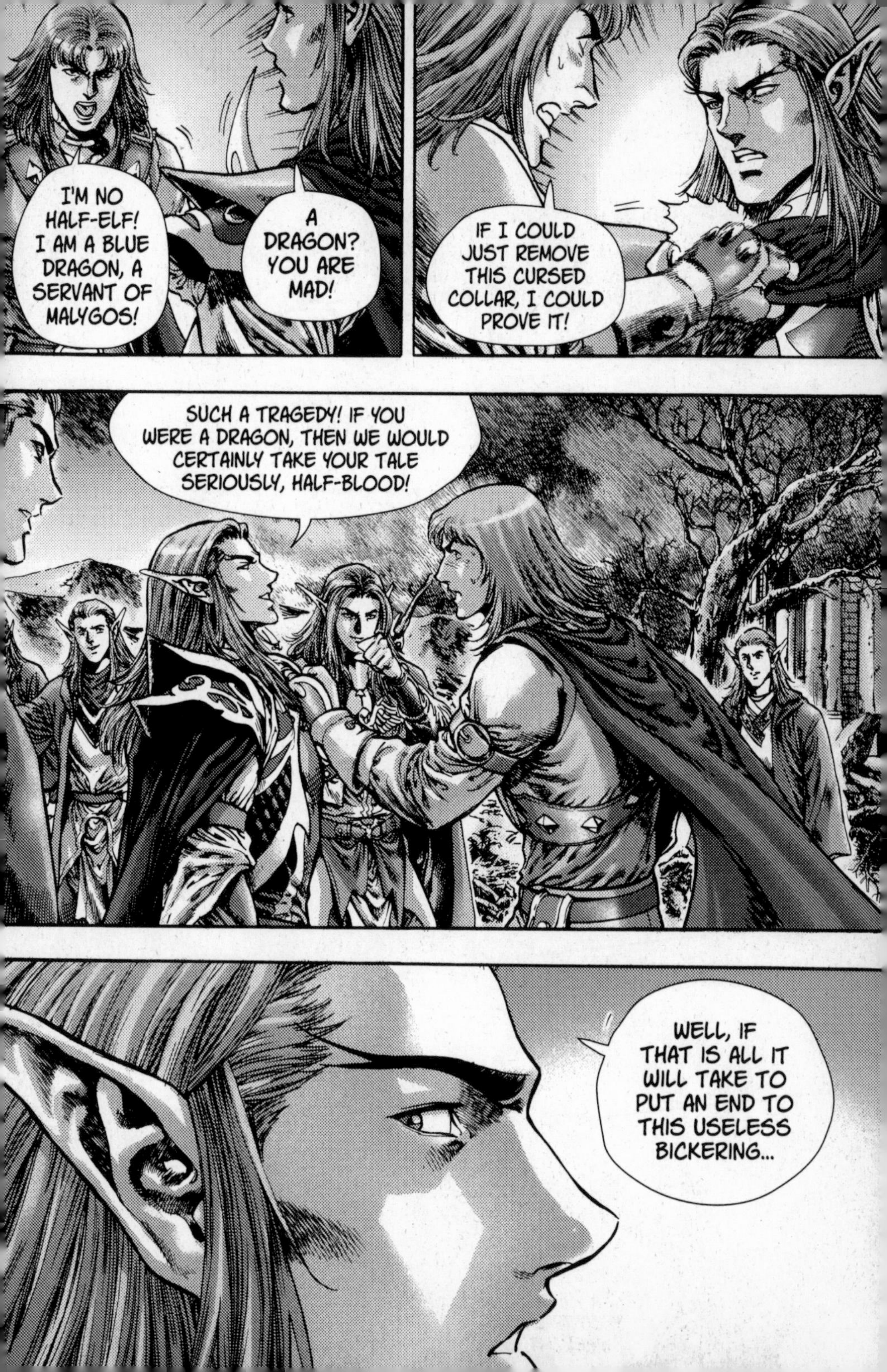
I'M NO HALF-ELF! I AM A BLUE DRAGON, A SERVANT OF MALYGOS!
A DRAGON? YOU ARE MAD!
IF I COULD JUST REMOVE THIS CURSED COLLAR, I COULD PROVE IT!
SUCH A TRAGEDY! IF YOU WERE A DRAGON, THEN WE WOULD CERTAINLY TAKE YOUR TALE SERIOUSLY, HALF-BLOOD!
WELL, IF THAT IS ALL IT WILL TAKE TO PUT AN END TO THIS USELESS BICKERING...

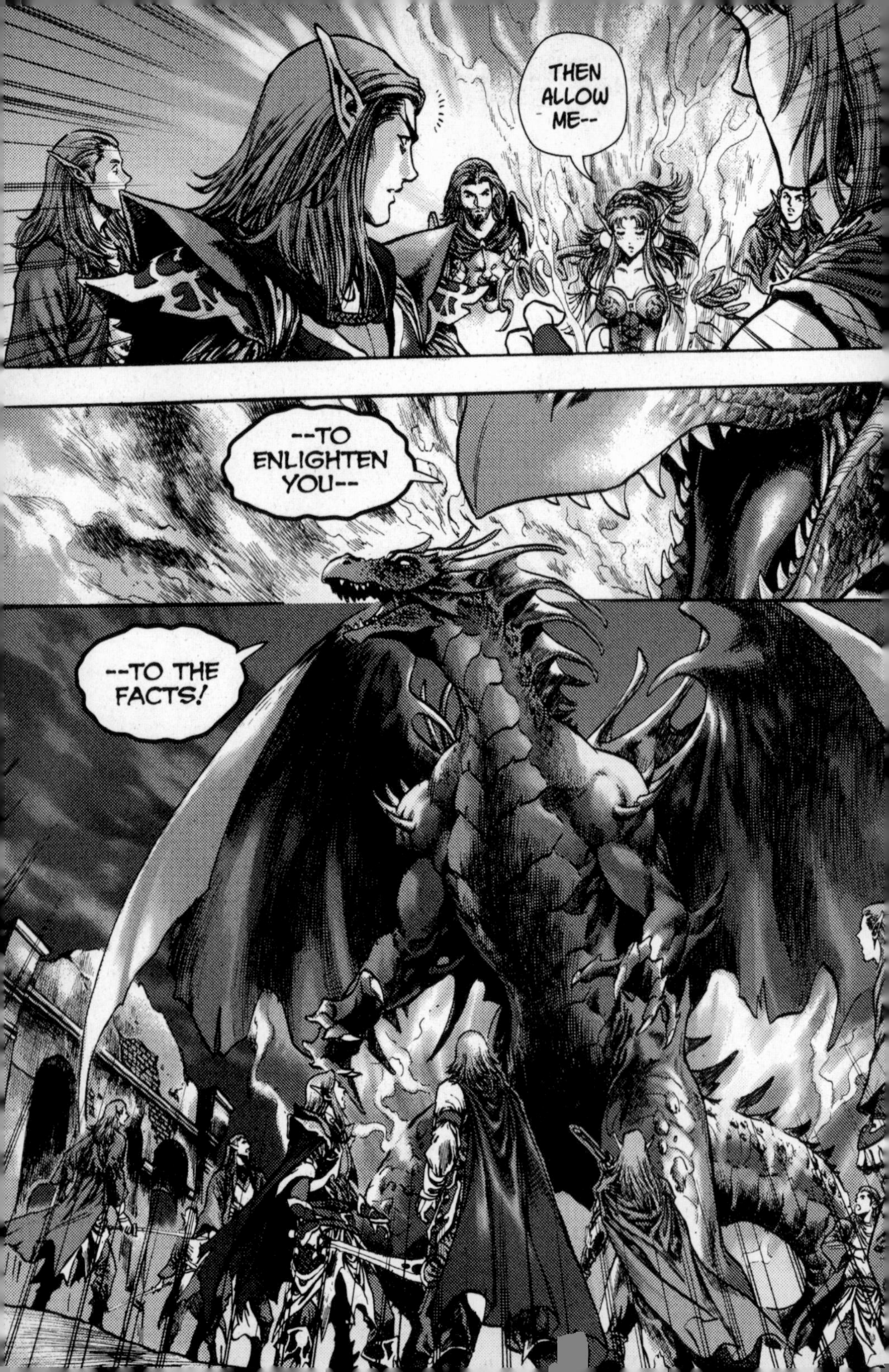
THEN ALLOW ME--
--TO ENLIGHTEN YOU--
--TO THE FACTS!

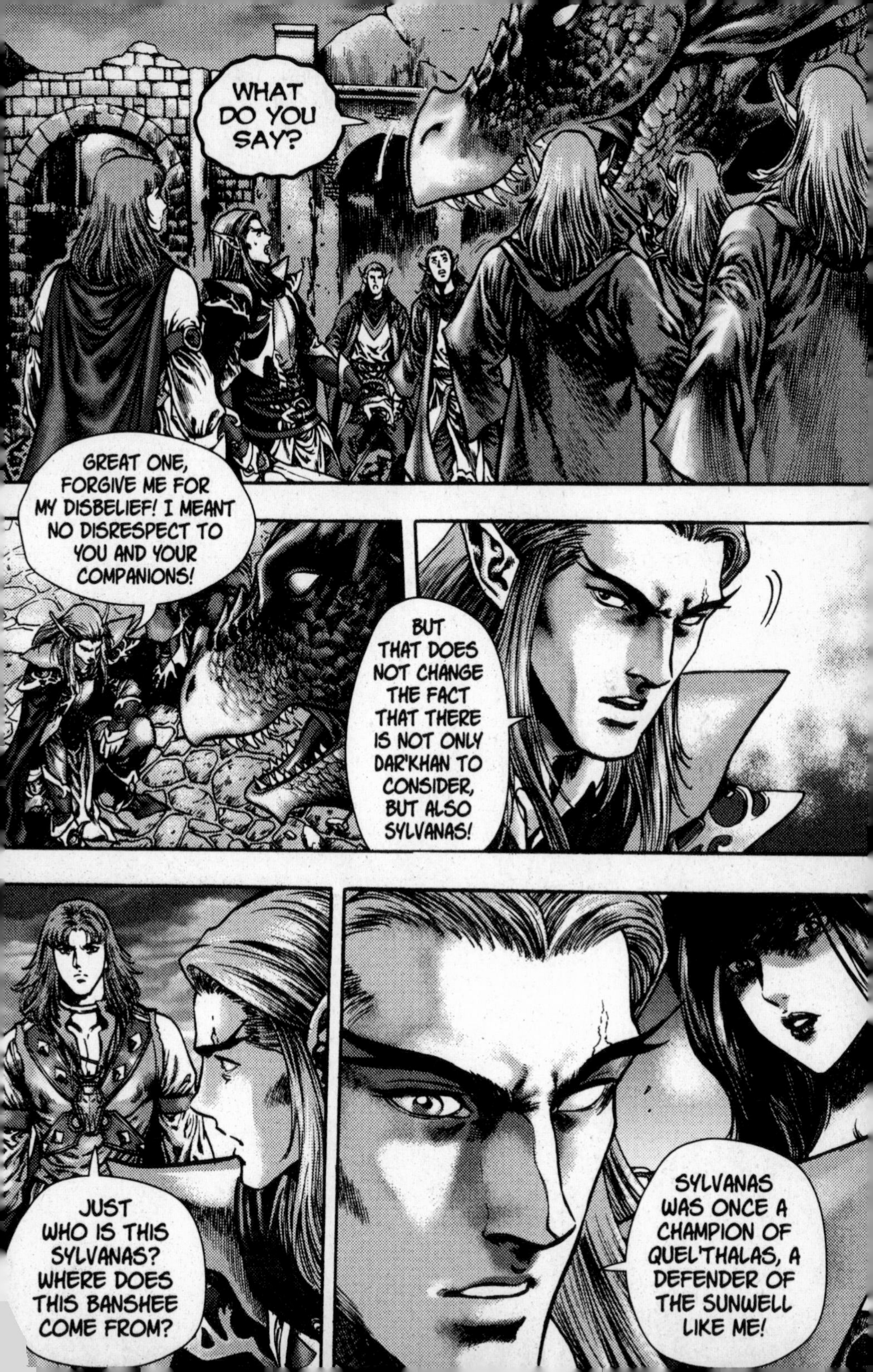
WHAT DO YOU SAY?
GREAT ONE, FORGIVE ME FOR MY DISBELIEF! I MEANT NO DISRESPECT TO YOU AND YOUR COMPANIONS!
BUT THAT DOES NOT CHANGE THE FACT THAT THERE IS NOT ONLY DAR'KHAN TO CONSIDER, BUT ALSO SYLVANAS!
JUST WHO IS THIS SYLVANAS? WHERE DOES THIS BANSHEE COME FROM?
SYLVANAS WAS ONCE A CHAMPION OF QUEL'THALAS, A DEFENDER OF THE SUNWELL LIKE ME!

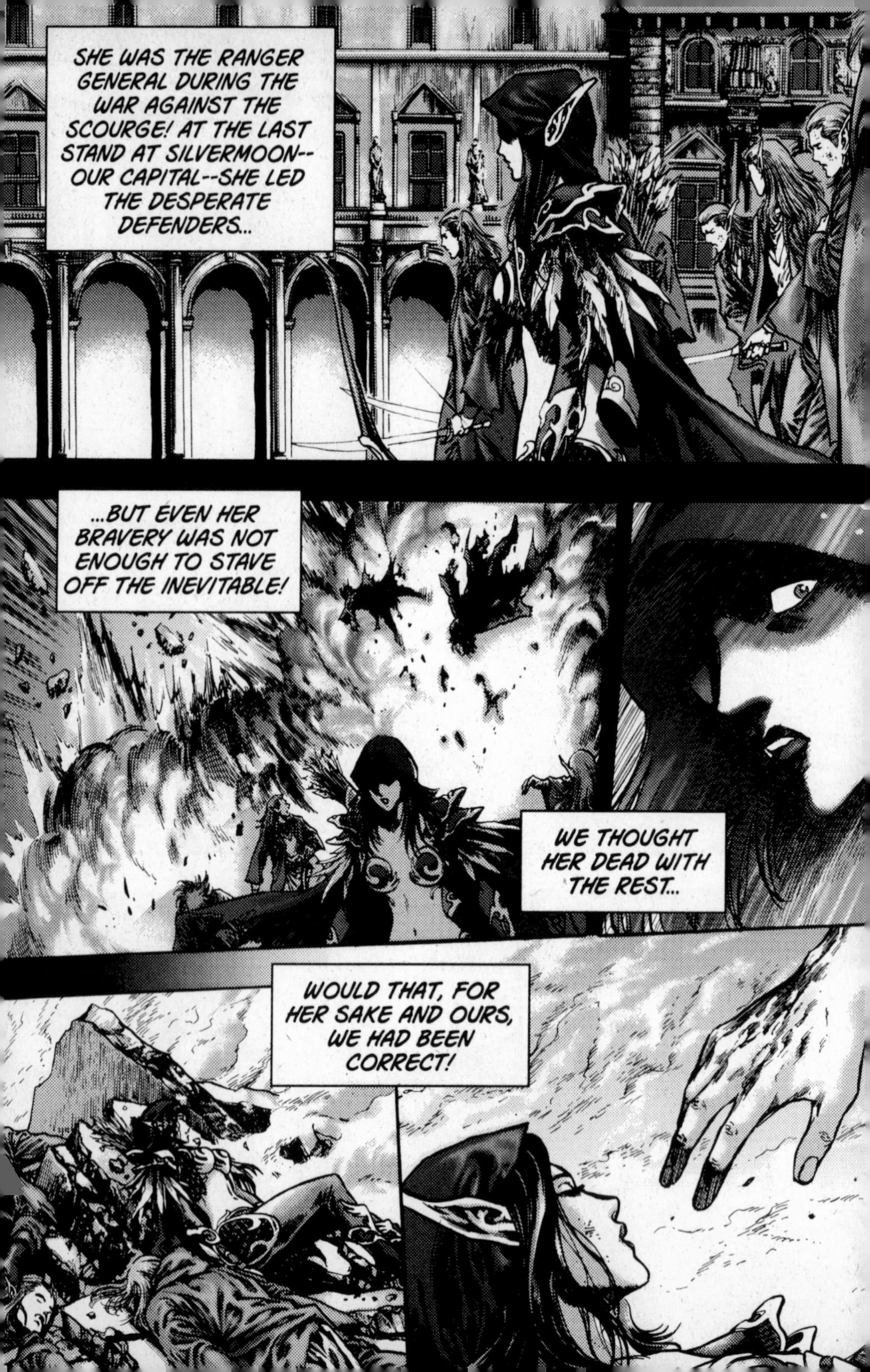
SHE WAS THE RANGER GENERAL DURING THE WAR AGAINST THE SCOURGE! AT THE LAST STAND AT SILVERMOON--OUR CAPITAL--SHE LED THE DESPERATE DEFENDERS...
...BUT EVEN HER BRAVERY WAS NOT ENOUGH TO STAVE OFF THE INEVITABLE!
WE THOUGHT HER DEAD WITH THE REST...
WOULD THAT, FOR HER SAKE AND OURS, WE HAD BEEN CORRECT!

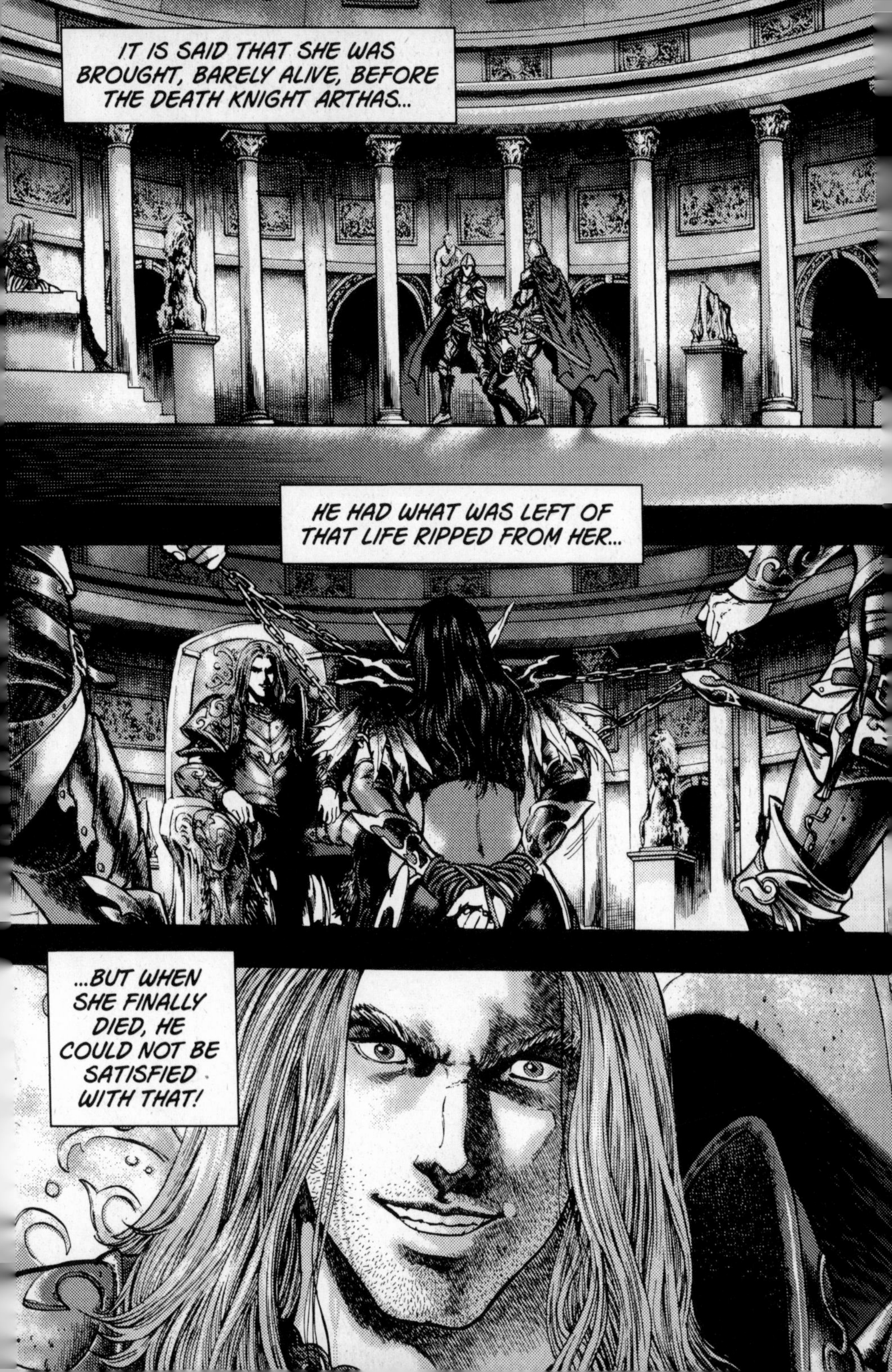
IT IS SAID THAT SHE WAS BROUGHT, BARELY ALIVE, BEFORE THE DEATH KNIGHT ARTHAS...
HE HAD WHAT WAS LEFT OF THAT LIFE RIPPED FROM HER...
...BUT WHEN SHE FINALLY DIED, HE COULD NOT BE SATISFIED WITH THAT!

HE TOOK HER RAVAGED BODY AND CAST UNHOLY SPELLS UPON IT!

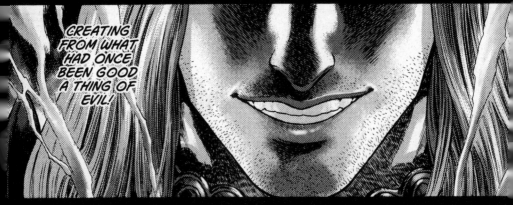

CREATING FROM WHAT HAD ONCE BEEN GOOD A THING OF EVIL!

HE TWISTED THE SOUL OF SYLVANAS WINDRUNNER--

--AND TURNED HER INTO THE BANSHEE SHE IS NOW!

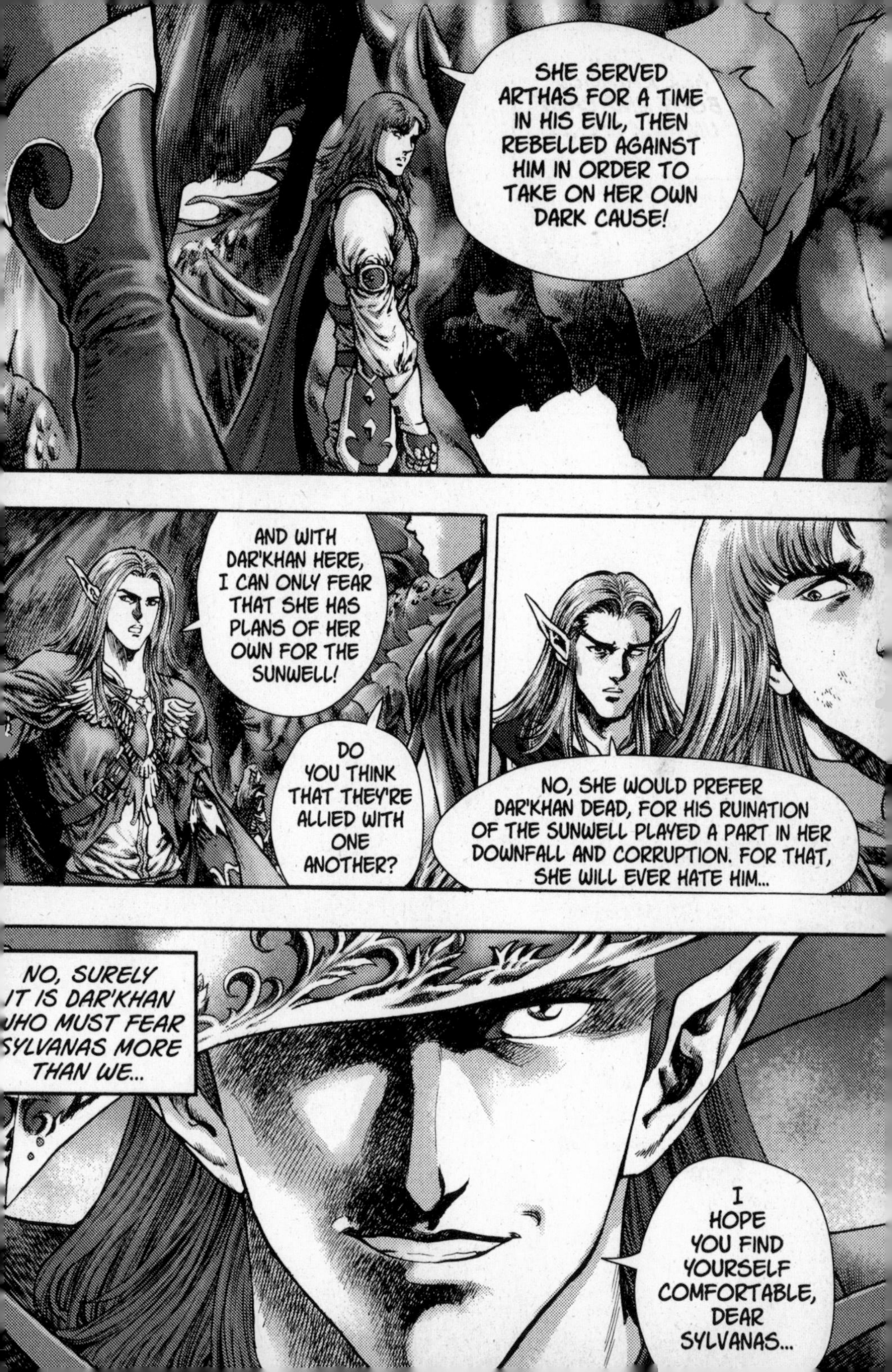
SHE SERVED ARTHAS FOR A TIME IN HIS EVIL, THEN REBELLED AGAINST HIM IN ORDER TO TAKE ON HER OWN DARK CAUSE!
AND WITH DAR'KHAN HERE, I CAN ONLY FEAR THAT SHE HAS PLANS OF HER OWN FOR THE SUNWELL!
DO YOU THINK THAT THEY'RE ALLIED WITH ONE ANOTHER?
NO, SHE WOULD PREFER DAR'KHAN DEAD, FOR HIS RUINATION OF THE SUNWELL PLAYED A PART IN HER DOWNFALL AND CORRUPTION. FOR THAT, SHE WILL EVER HATE HIM...
NO, SURELY IT IS DAR'KHAN WHO MUST FEAR SYLVANAS MORE THAN WE...
I HOPE YOU FIND YOURSELF COMFORTABLE, DEAR SYLVANAS...

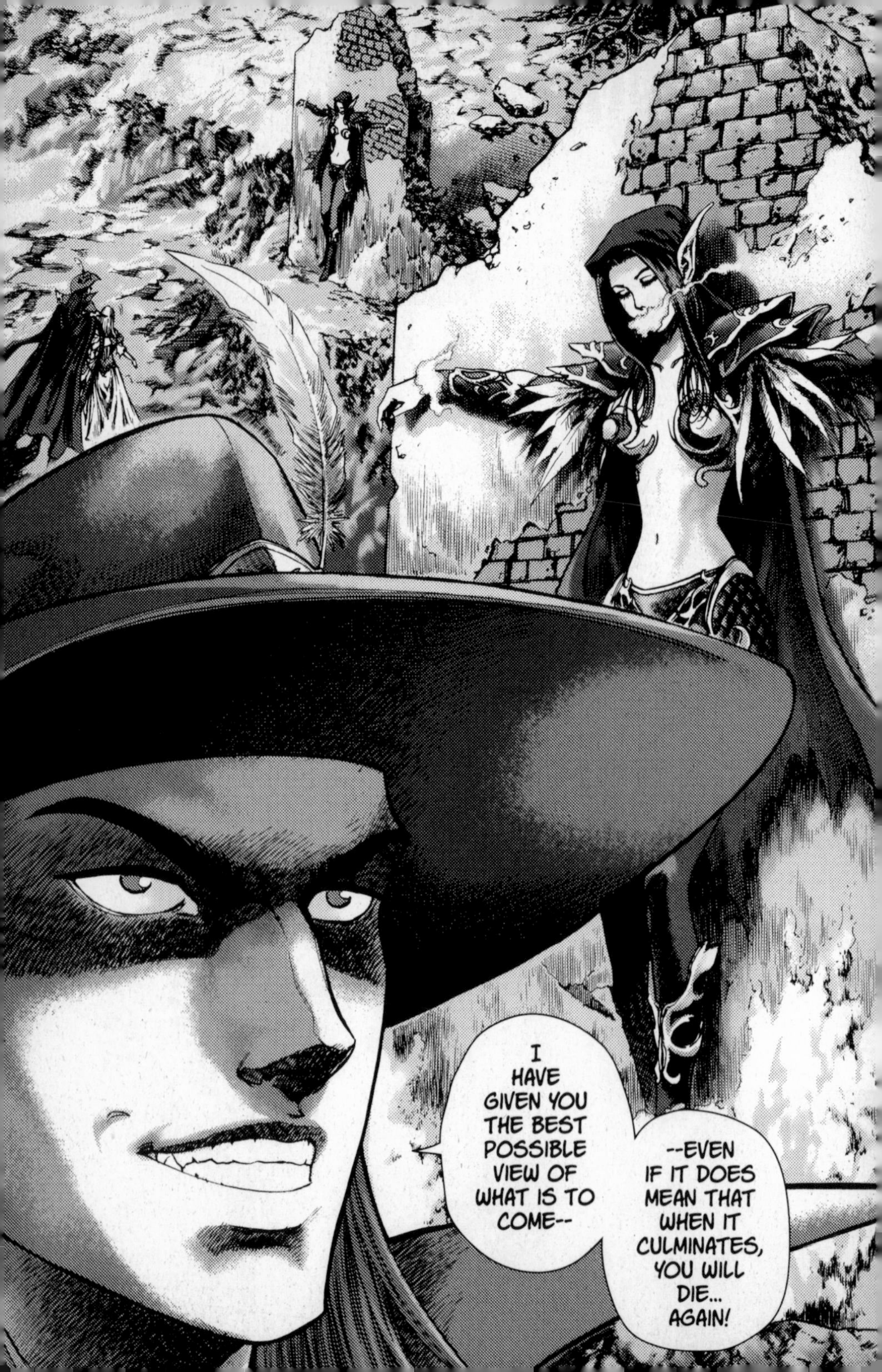
I HAVE GIVEN YOU THE BEST POSSIBLE VIEW OF WHAT IS TO COME--
--EVEN IF IT DOES MEAN THAT WHEN IT CULMINATES, YOU WILL DIE... AGAIN!

CHAPTER FIVE
EDGE OF THE ABYSS

THERE!
WE MUST
LAND
THERE!

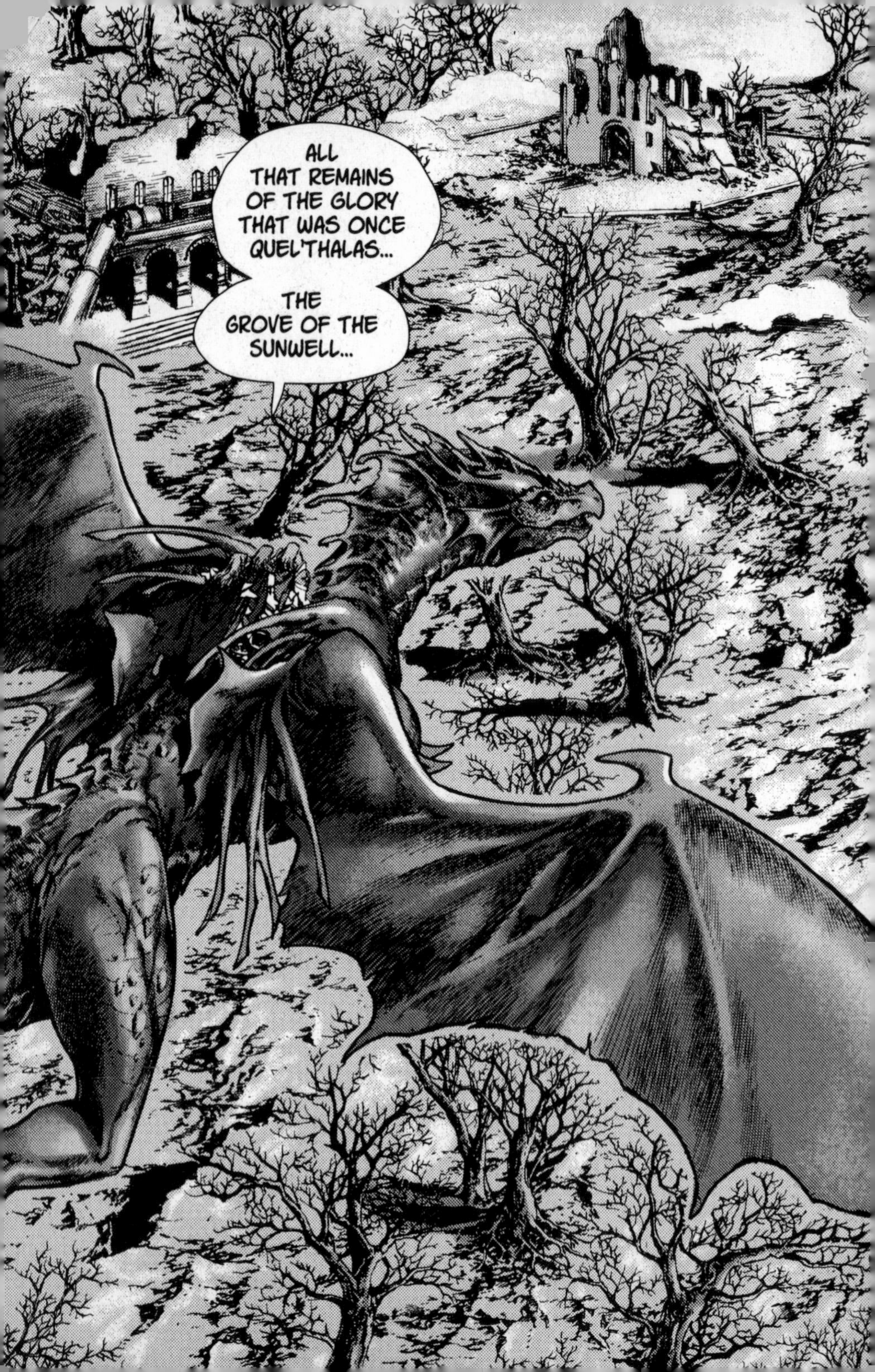
ALL THAT REMAINS OF THE GLORY THAT WAS ONCE QUEL'THALAS...
THE GROVE OF THE SUNWELL...

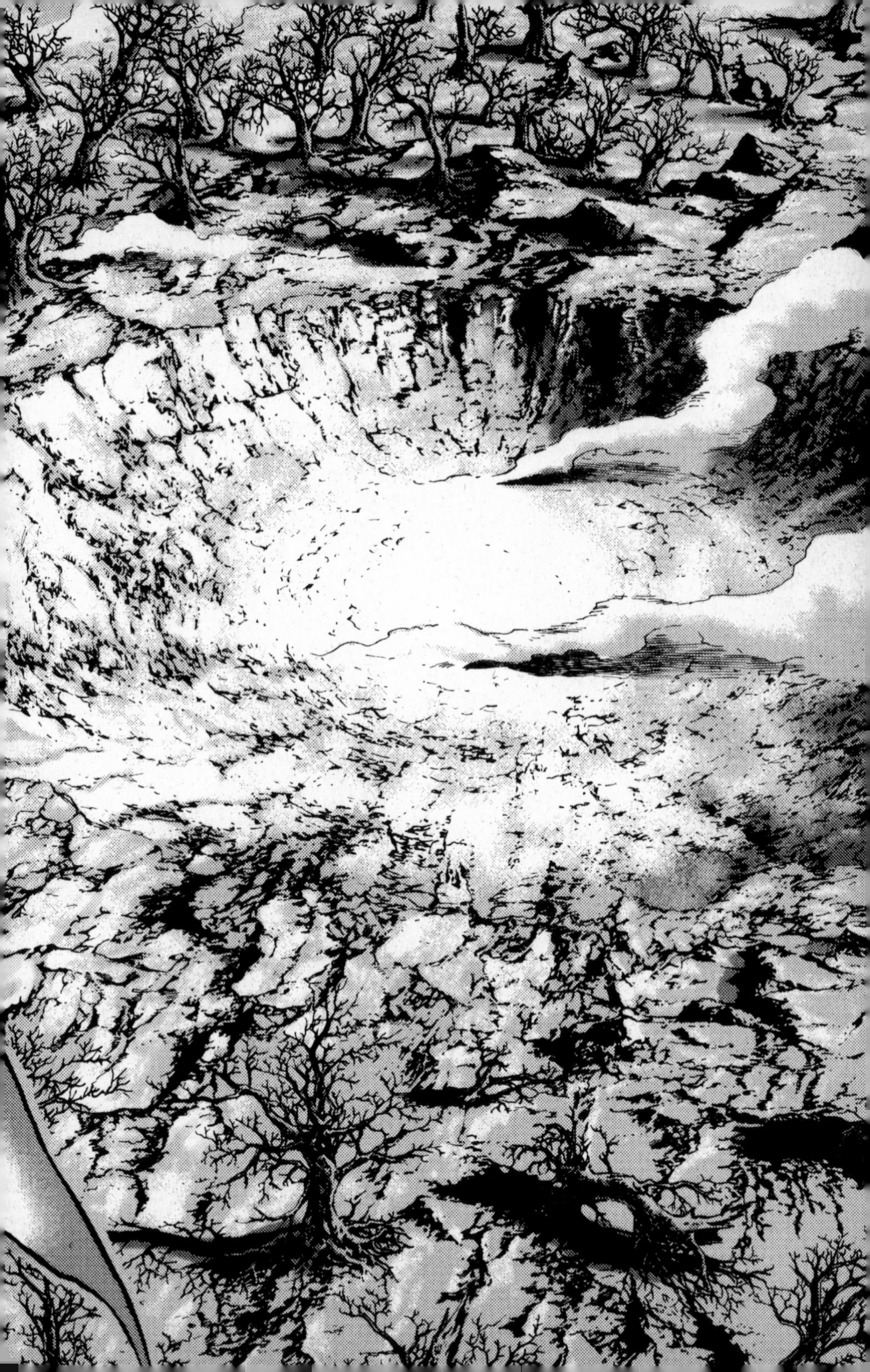

BUT THIS AREA IS HUGE! IF WE LAND WHERE YOU SAY, WE'LL STILL BE FAR FROM ANVEENA!

WE DARE NOT LAND NEARER! DAR'KHAN MUST NOT KNOW OF OUR PRESENCE!

I GUIDE US AS NEAR AS POSSIBLE!

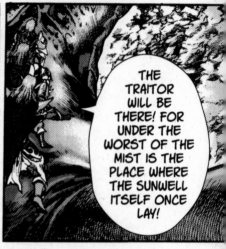

THE TRAITOR WILL BE THERE! FOR UNDER THE WORST OF THE MIST IS THE PLACE WHERE THE SUNWELL ITSELF ONCE LAY!

I DON'T CARE ANYTHING ABOUT THE SUNWELL! ALL THAT MATTERS IS ANVEENA...

BUT DO YOU NOT UNDERSTAND YET? I NOW DO!

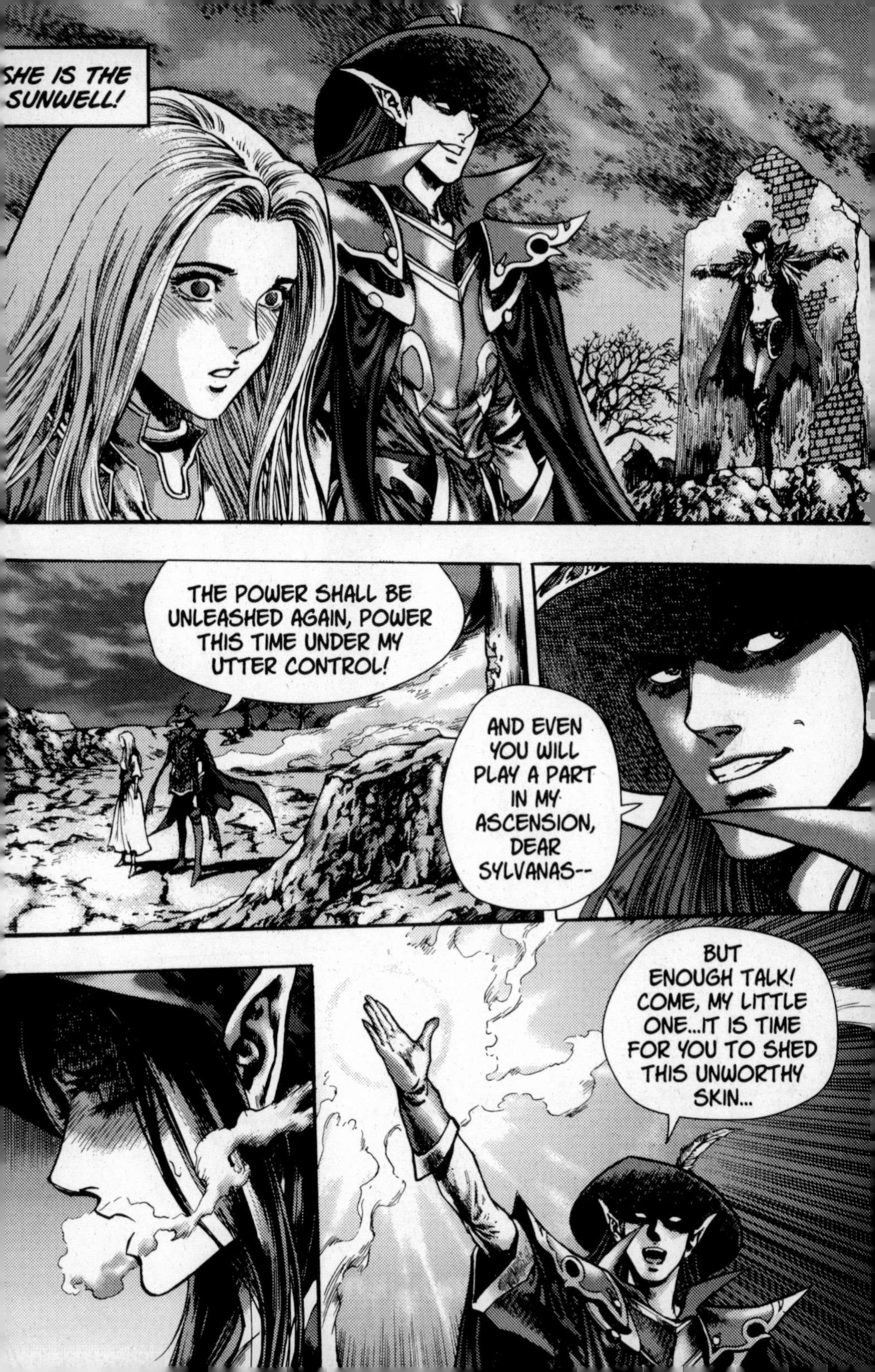
SHE IS THE SUNWELL!
THE POWER SHALL BE UNLEASHED AGAIN, POWER THIS TIME UNDER MY UTTER CONTROL!
AND EVEN YOU WILL PLAY A PART IN MY ASCENSION, DEAR SYLVANAS--
BUT ENOUGH TALK! COME, MY LITTLE ONE...IT IS TIME FOR YOU TO SHED THIS UNWORTHY SKIN...

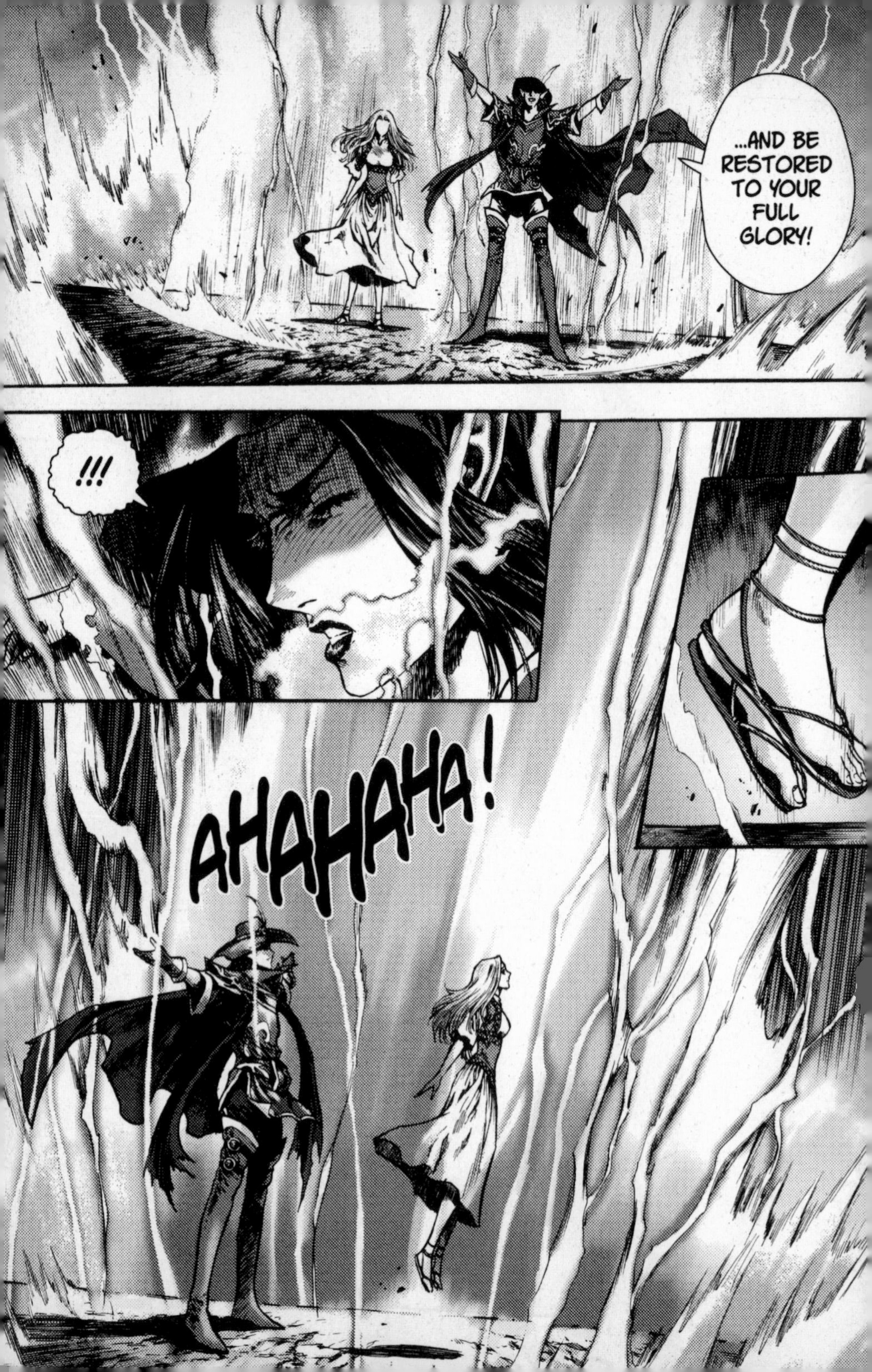
...AND BE RESTORED TO YOUR FULL GLORY!
!!!
AHAHAHA!

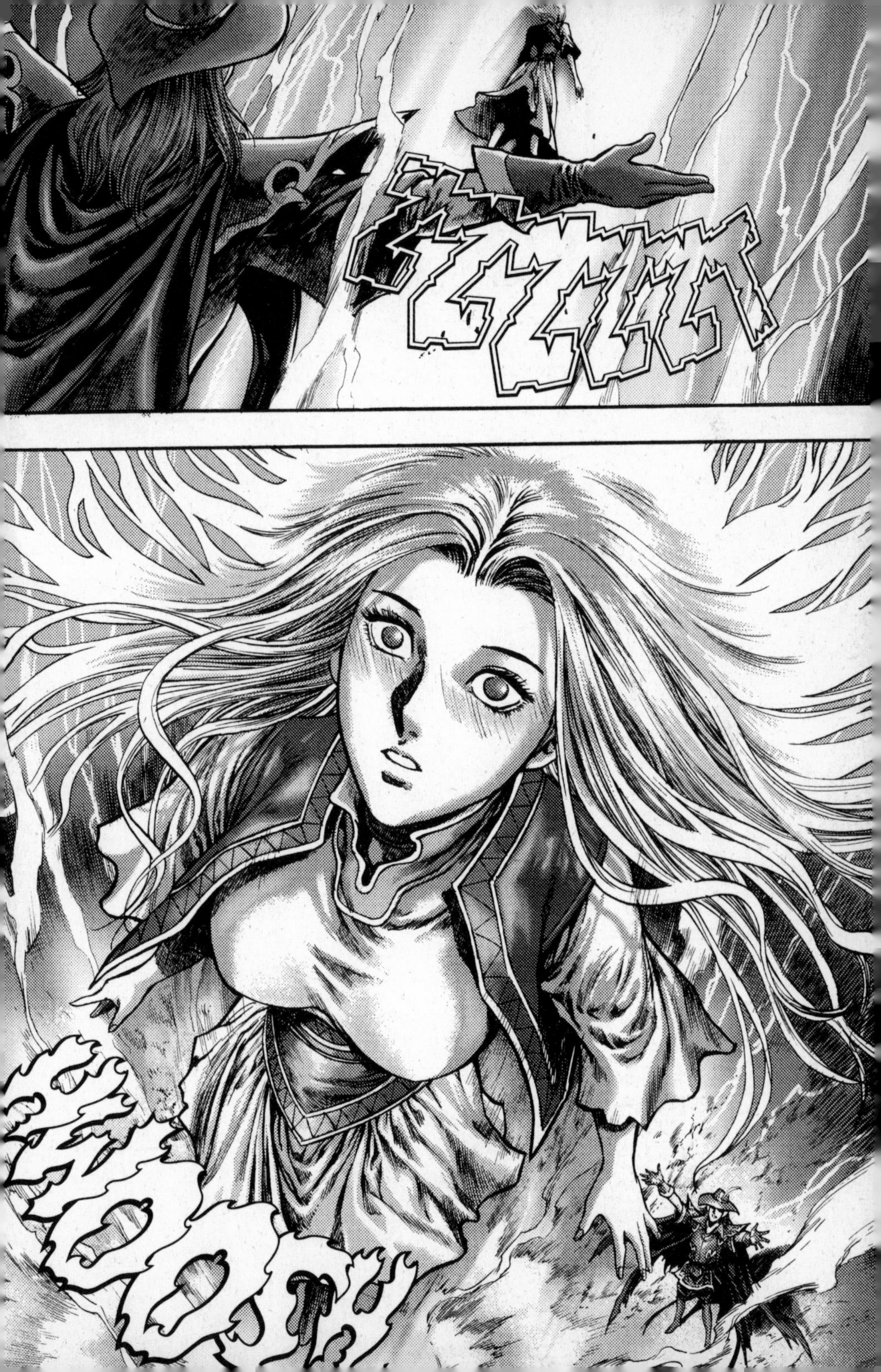

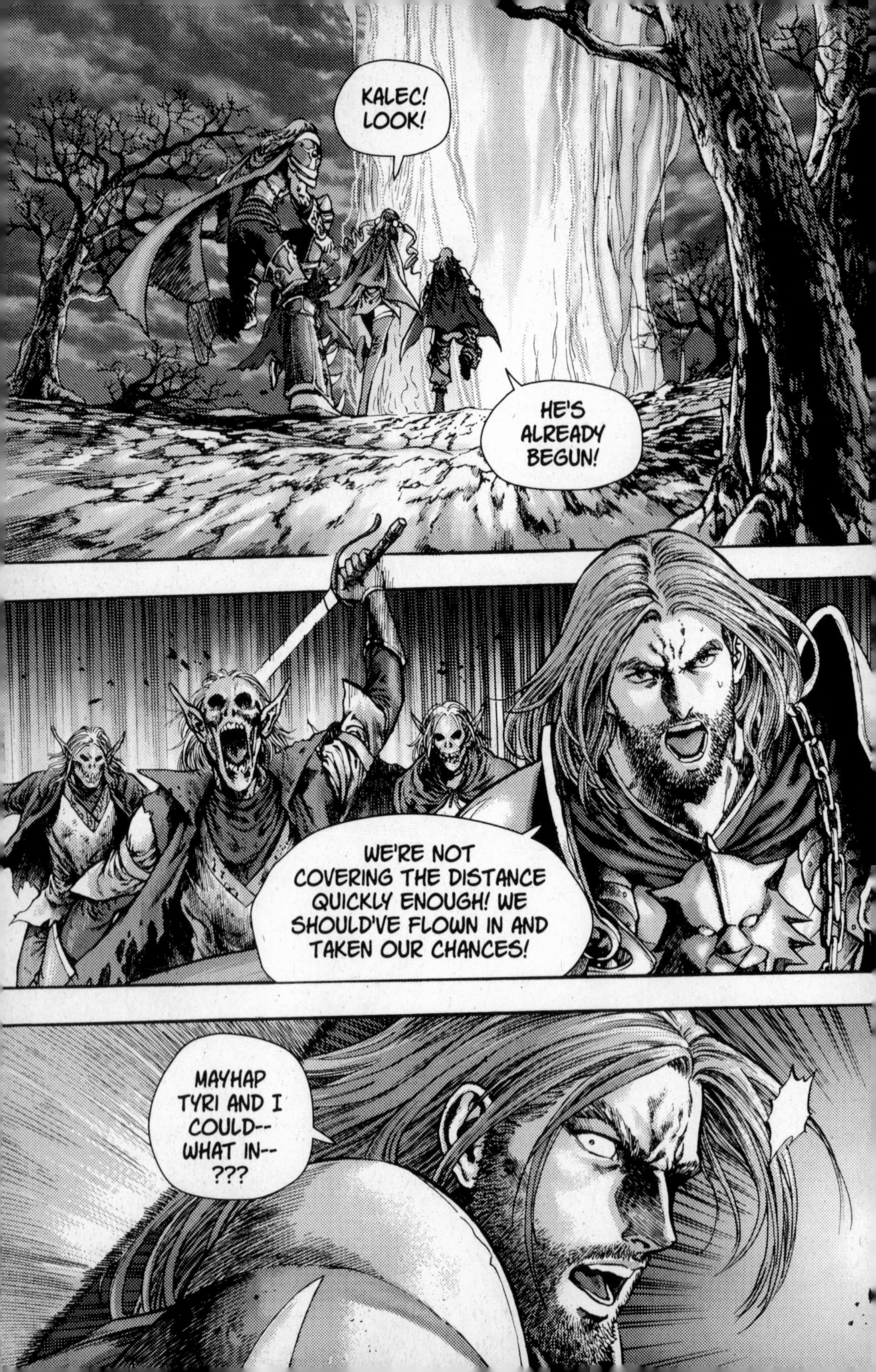
KALEC! LOOK!
HE'S ALREADY BEGUN!
WE'RE NOT COVERING THE DISTANCE QUICKLY ENOUGH! WE SHOULD'VE FLOWN IN AND TAKEN OUR CHANCES!
MAYHAP TYRI AND I COULD-- WHAT IN-- ???

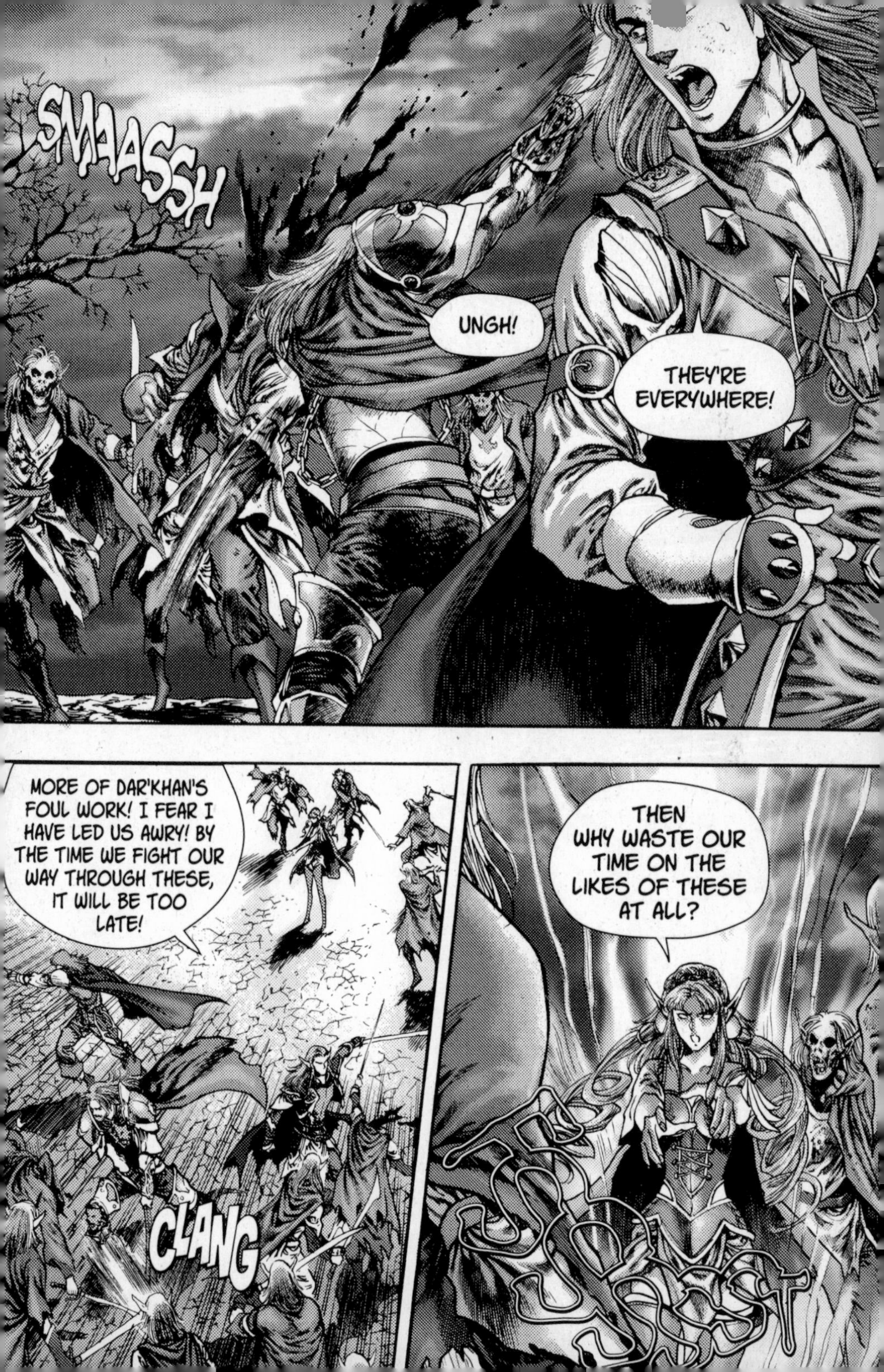
SMAASSH
UNGH!
THEY'RE EVERYWHERE!
MORE OF DAR'KHAN'S FOUL WORK! I FEAR I HAVE LED US AWRY! BY THE TIME WE FIGHT OUR WAY THROUGH THESE, IT WILL BE TOO LATE!
CLANG
THEN WHY WASTE OUR TIME ON THE LIKES OF THESE AT ALL?

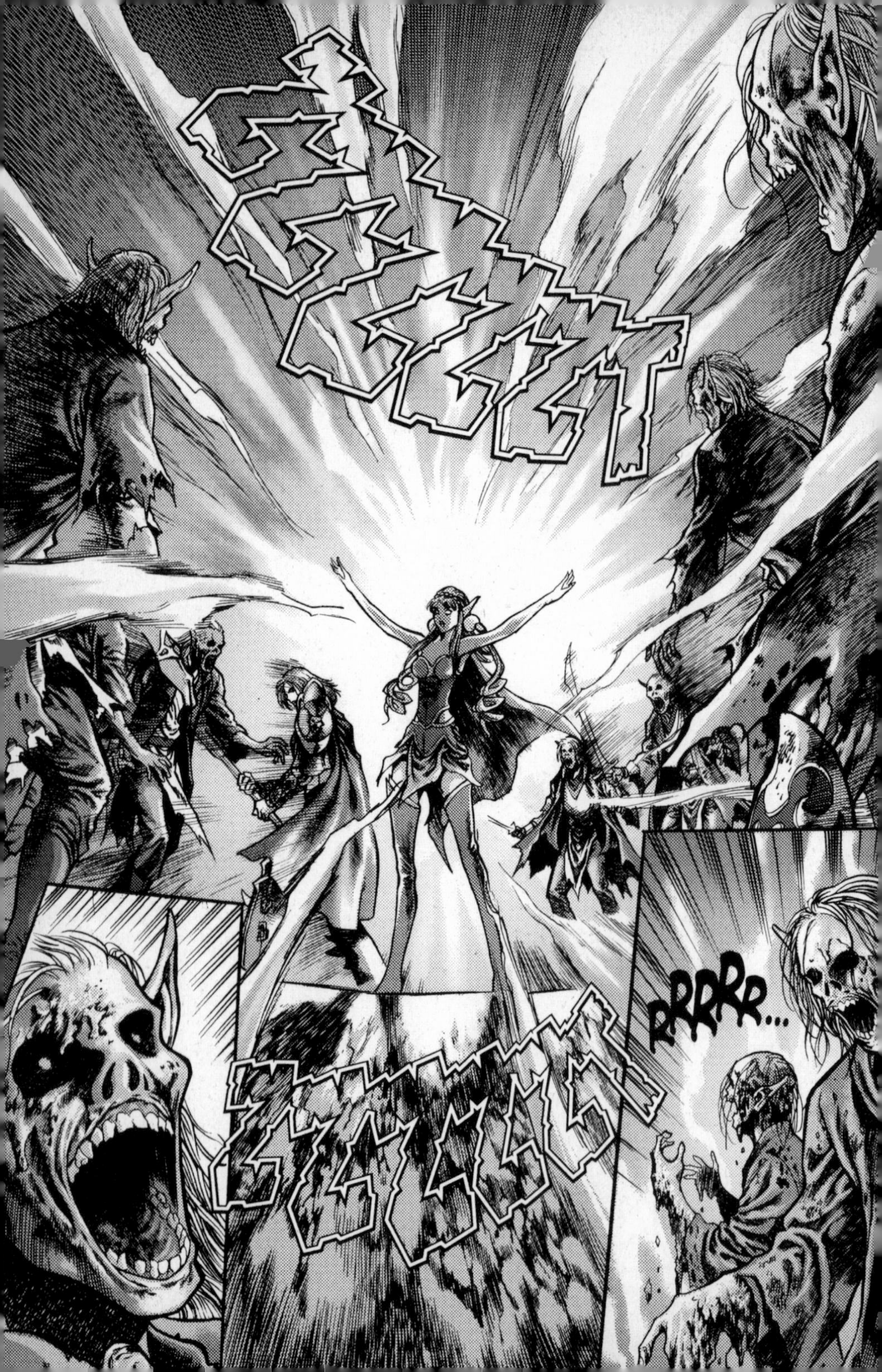
RRRRR...

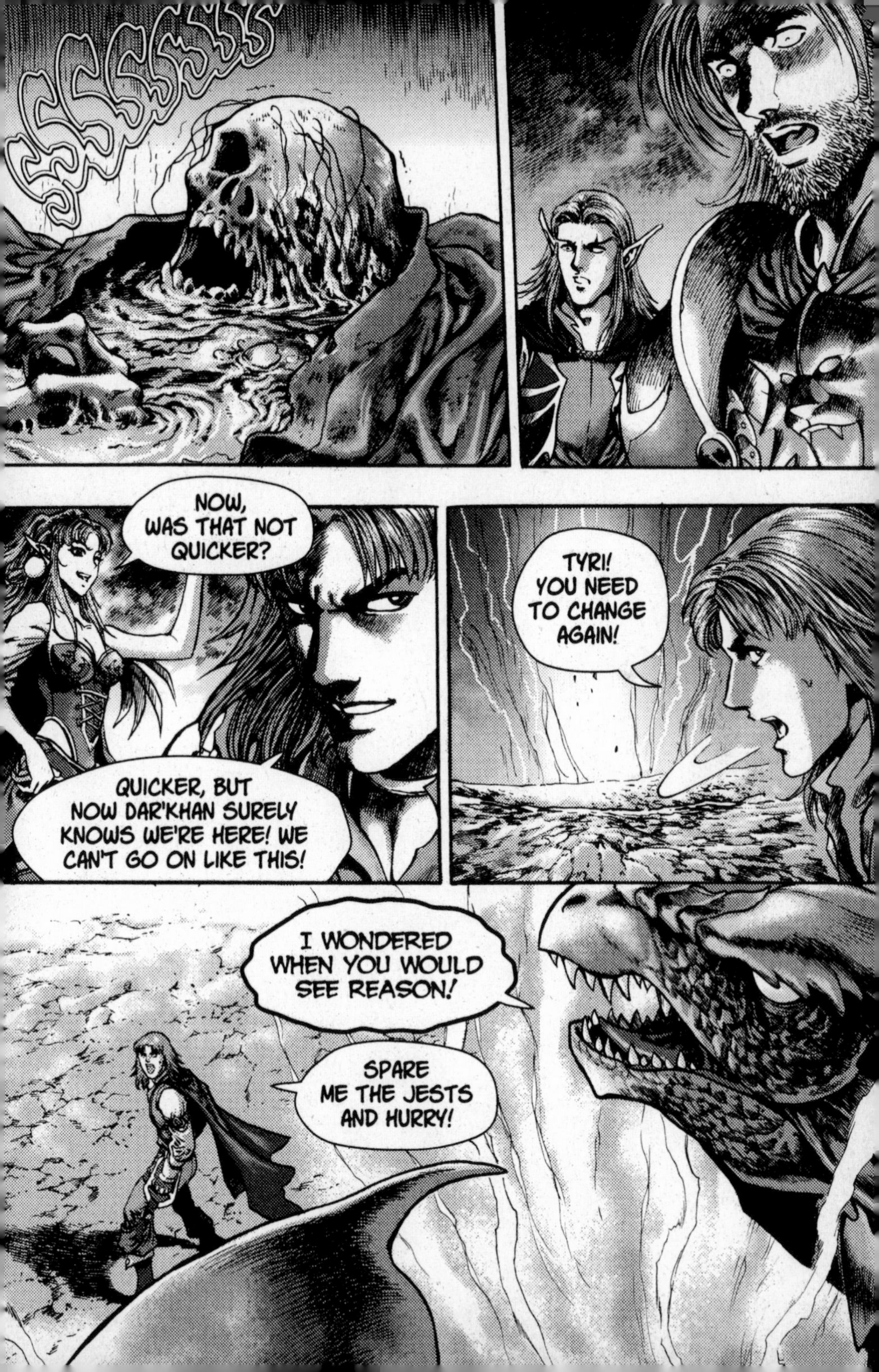

NOW, WAS THAT NOT QUICKER?
QUICKER, BUT NOW DAR'KHAN SURELY KNOWS WE'RE HERE! WE CAN'T GO ON LIKE THIS!
TYRI! YOU NEED TO CHANGE AGAIN!
I WONDERED WHEN YOU WOULD SEE REASON!
SPARE ME THE JESTS AND HURRY!

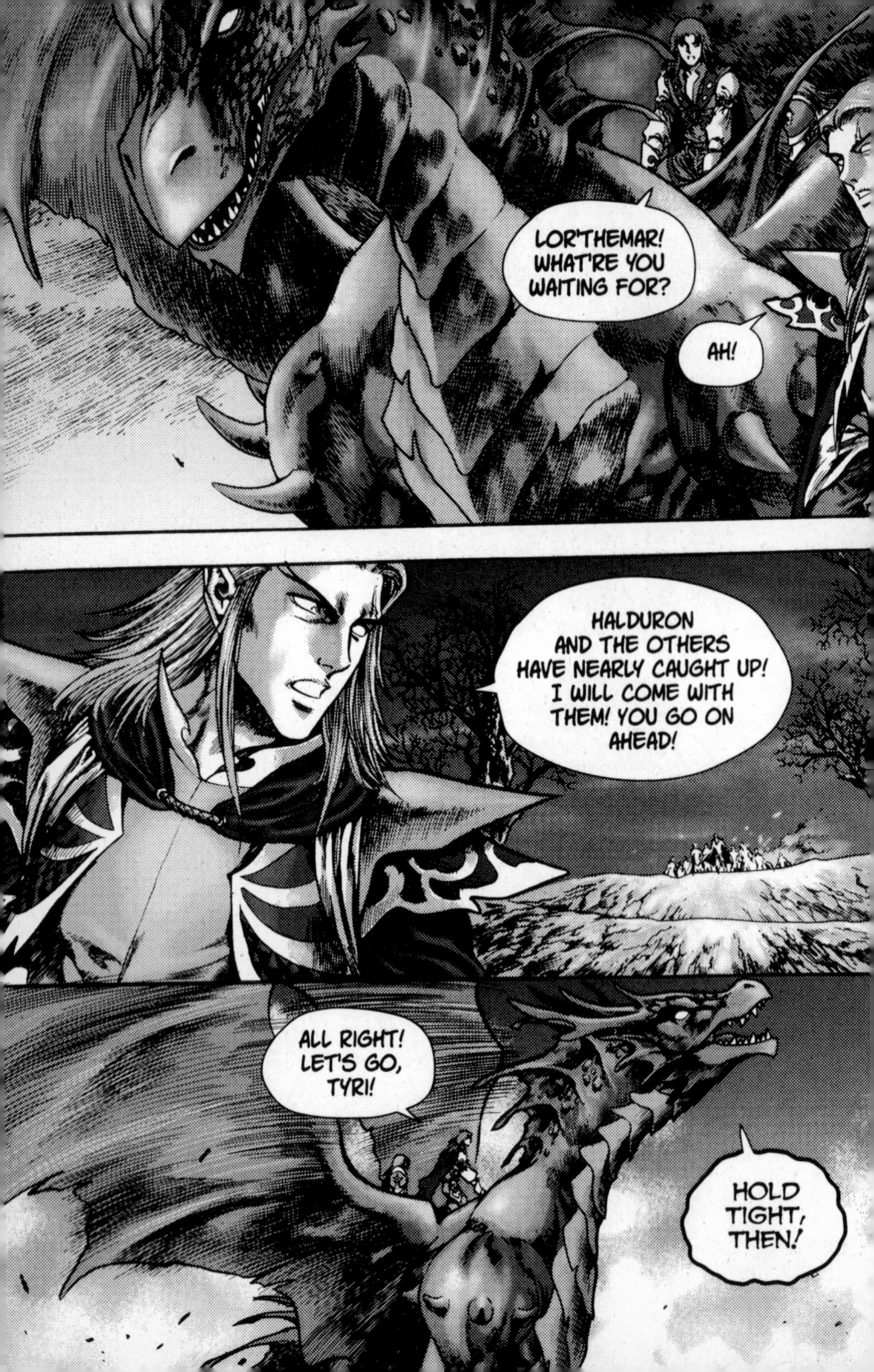
LOR'THEMAR! WHAT'RE YOU WAITING FOR?
AH!
HALDURON AND THE OTHERS HAVE NEARLY CAUGHT UP! I WILL COME WITH THEM! YOU GO ON AHEAD!
ALL RIGHT! LET'S GO, TYRI!
HOLD TIGHT, THEN!

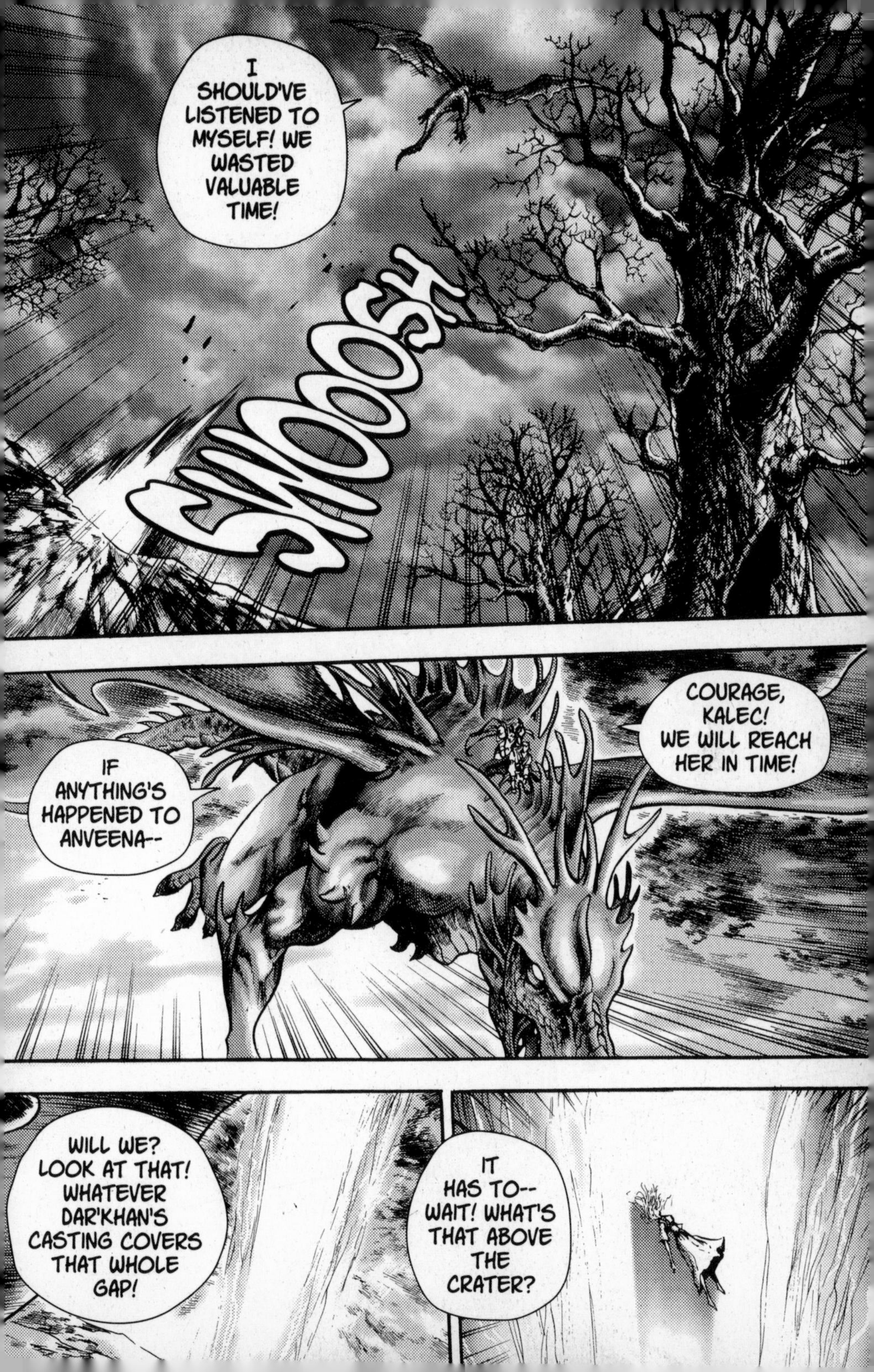
I SHOULD'VE LISTENED TO MYSELF! WE WASTED VALUABLE TIME!
SWOOOSH
IF ANYTHING'S HAPPENED TO ANVEENA--
COURAGE, KALEC! WE WILL REACH HER IN TIME!
WILL WE? LOOK AT THAT! WHATEVER DAR'KHAN'S CASTING COVERS THAT WHOLE GAP!
IT HAS TO-- WAIT! WHAT'S THAT ABOVE THE CRATER?

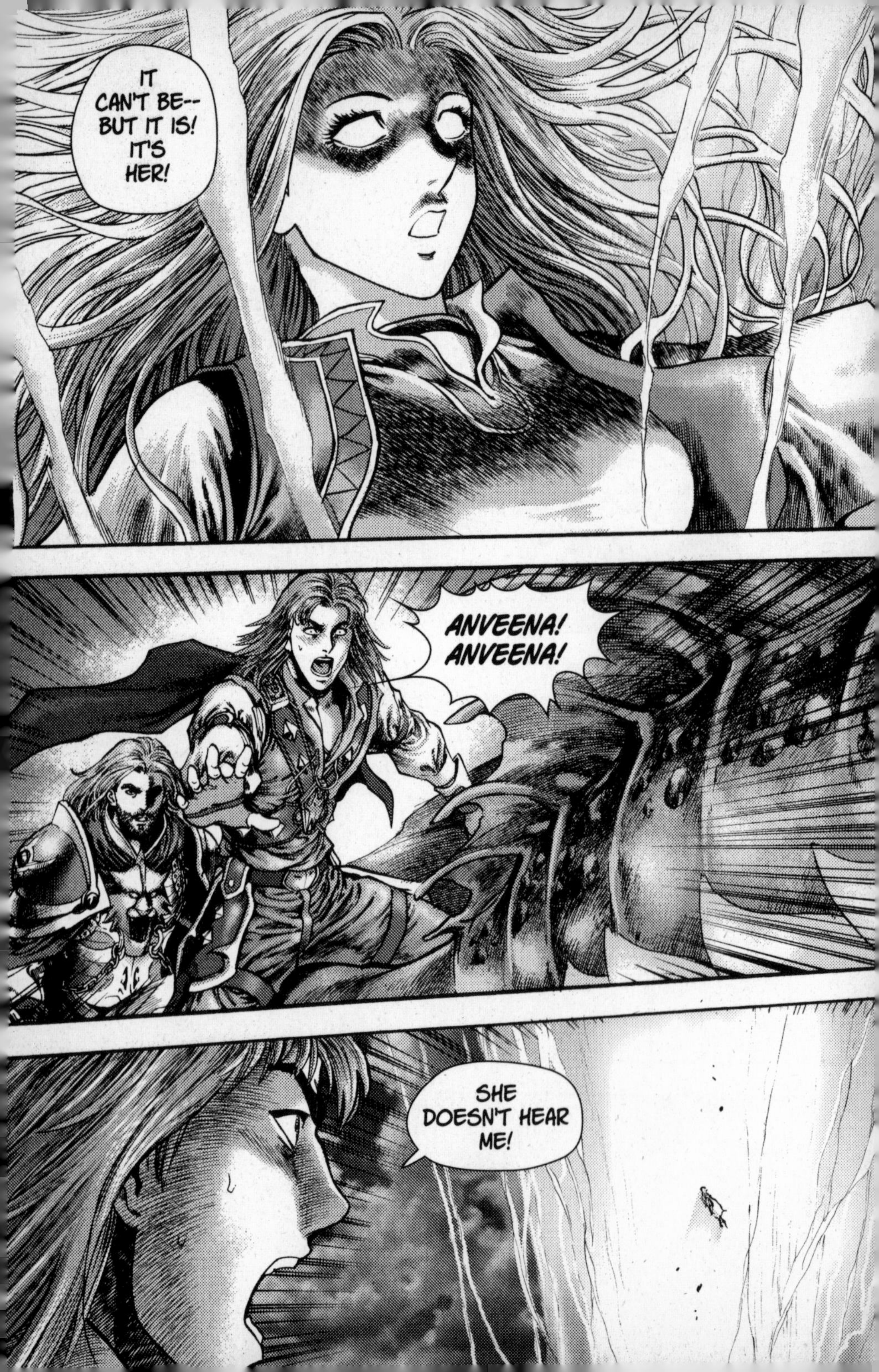
IT CAN'T BE-- BUT IT IS! IT'S HER!
ANVEENA! ANVEENA!
SHE DOESN'T HEAR ME!

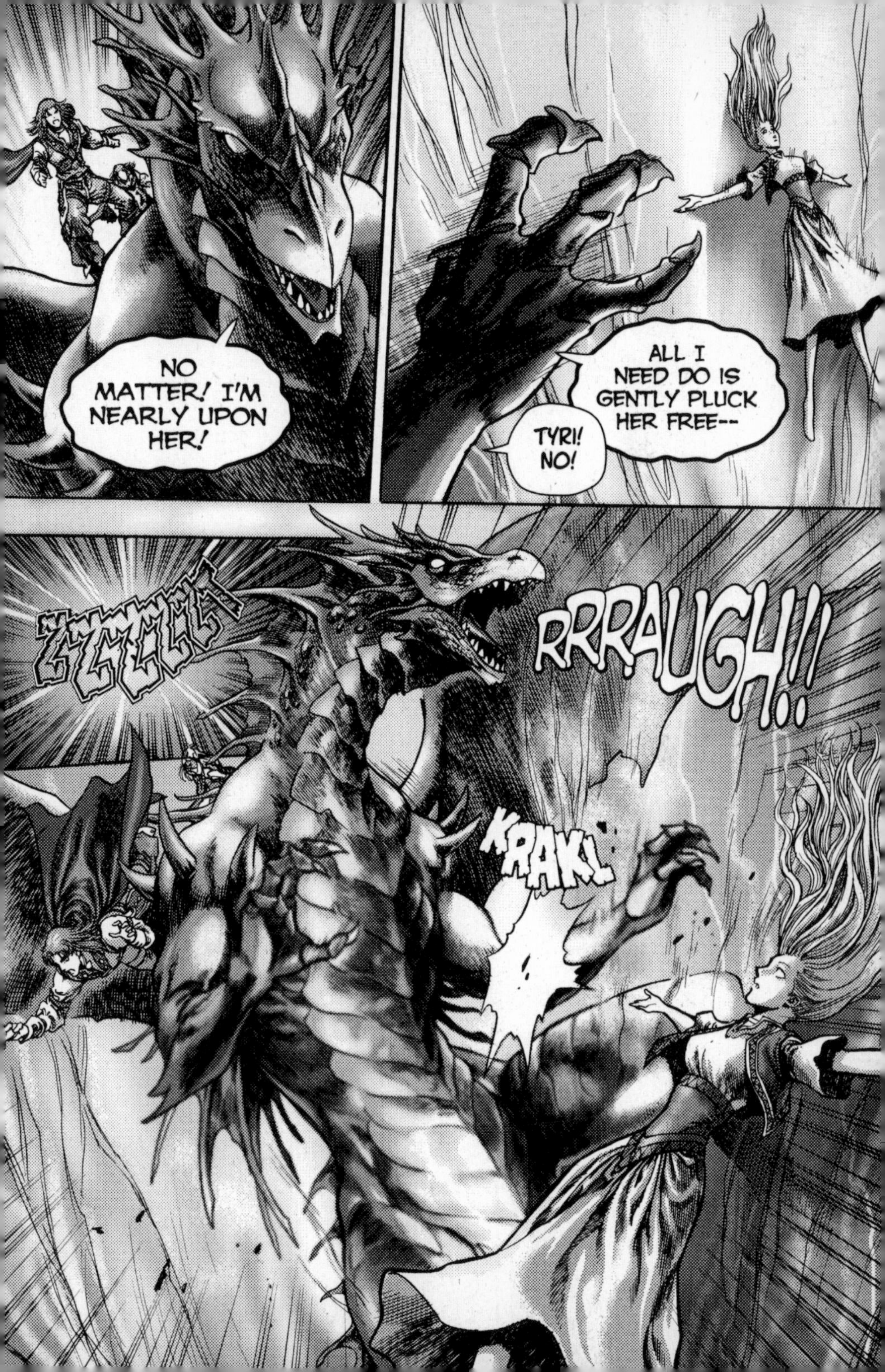
NO MATTER! I'M NEARLY UPON HER!
ALL I NEED DO IS GENTLY PLUCK HER FREE--
TYRI! NO!
RRRAUGH!!
KRAK!

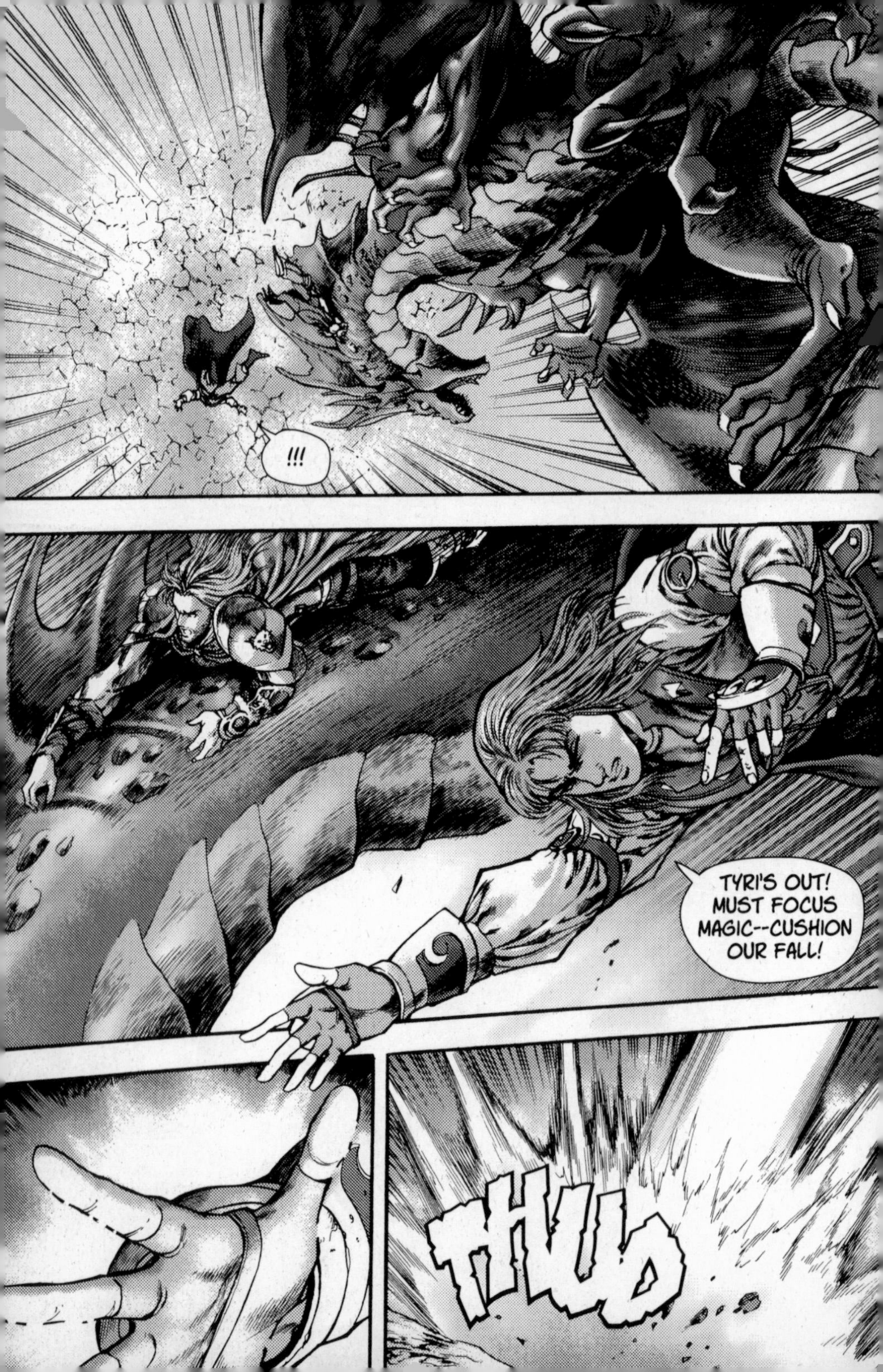
!!!
TYRI'S OUT! MUST FOCUS MAGIC--CUSHION OUR FALL!
THUD

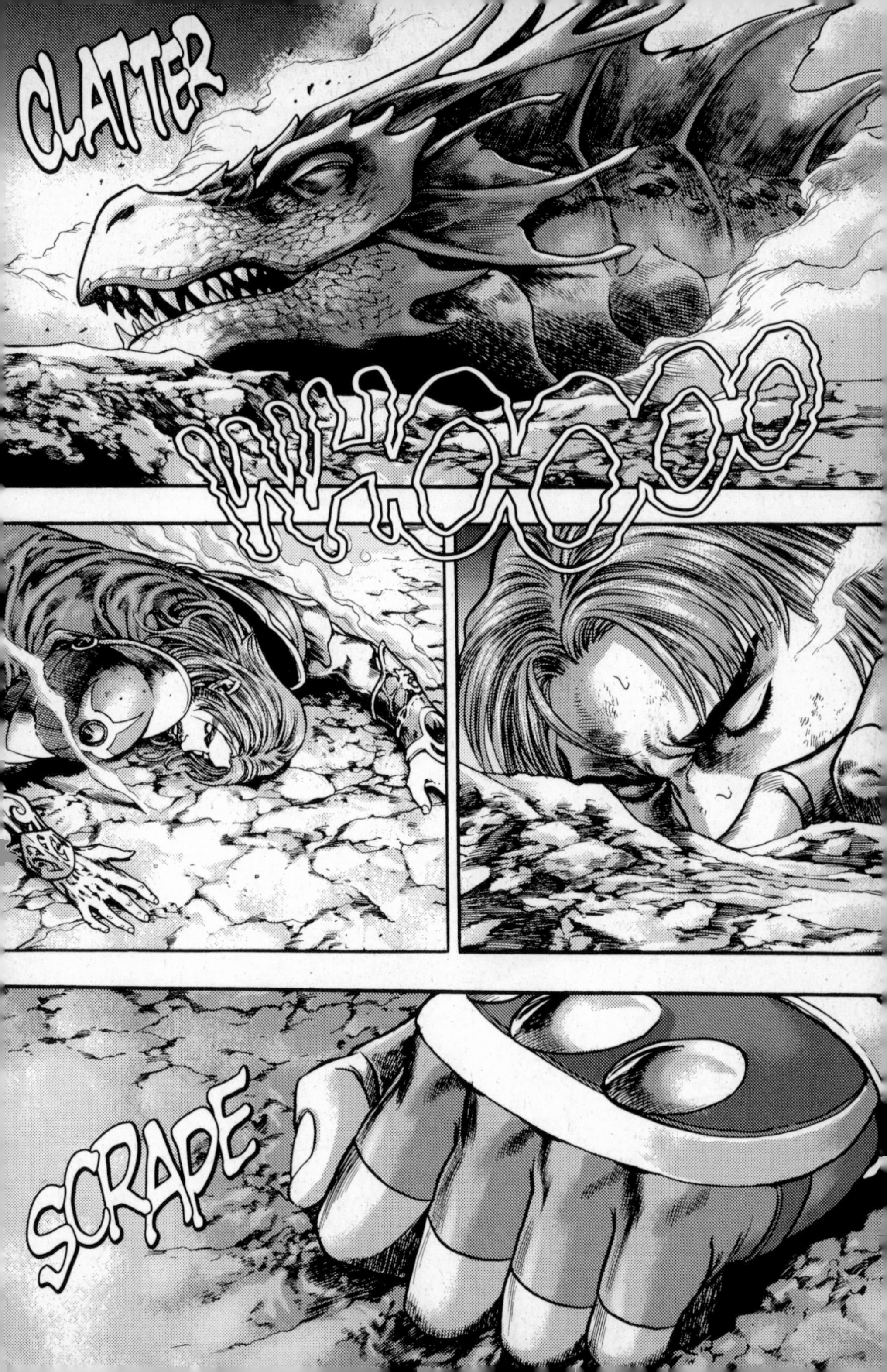
CLATTER
WHOOOOOO
SCRAPE

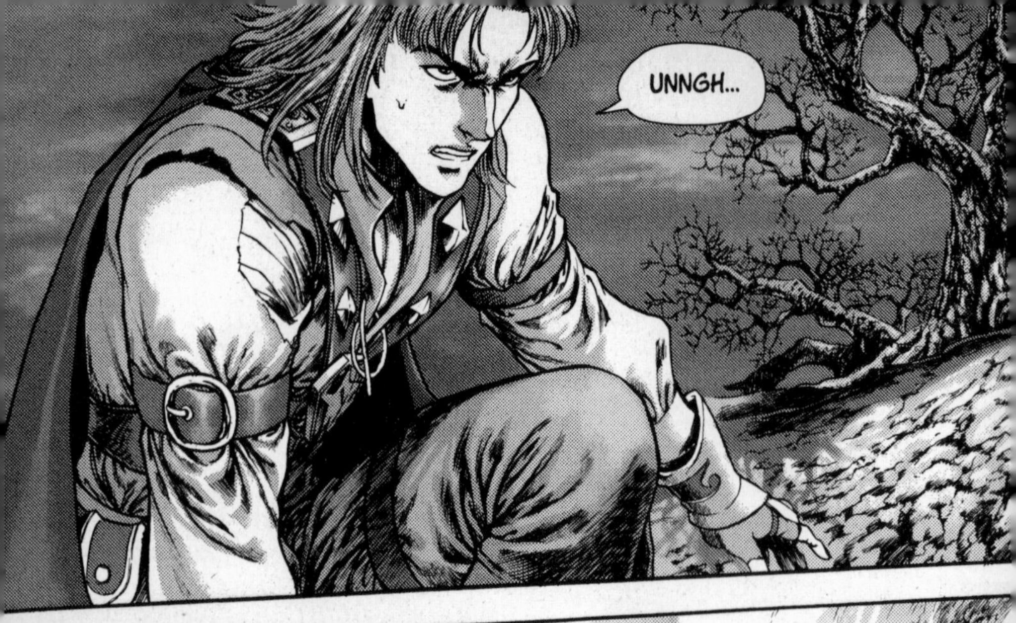
UNNGH...
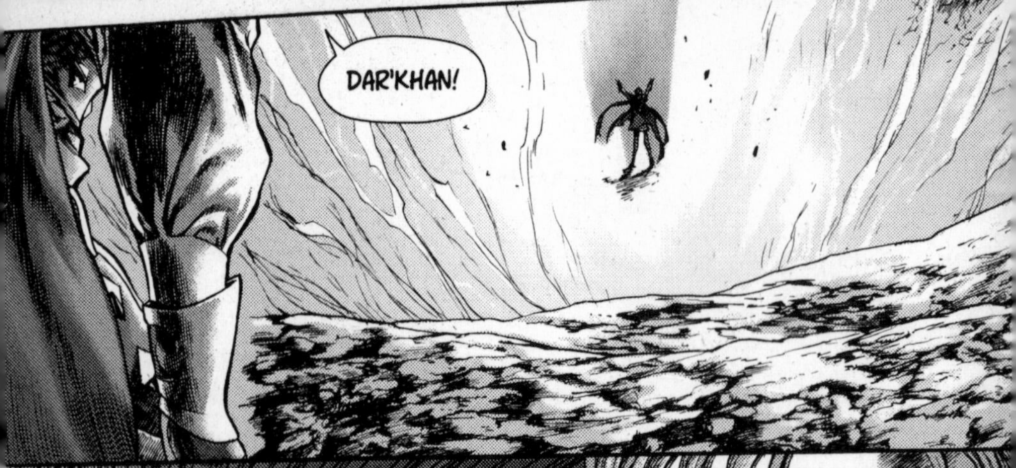
DAR'KHAN!
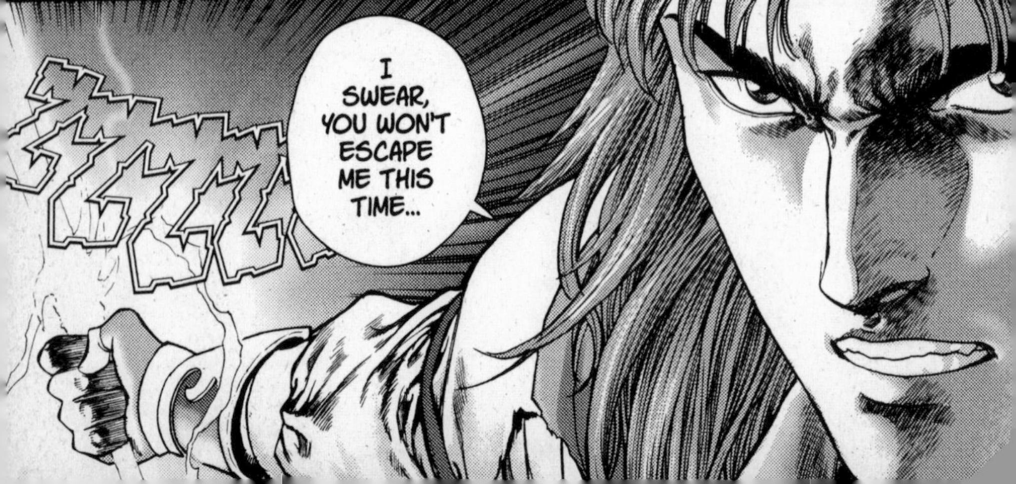
I SWEAR, YOU WON'T ESCAPE ME THIS TIME...

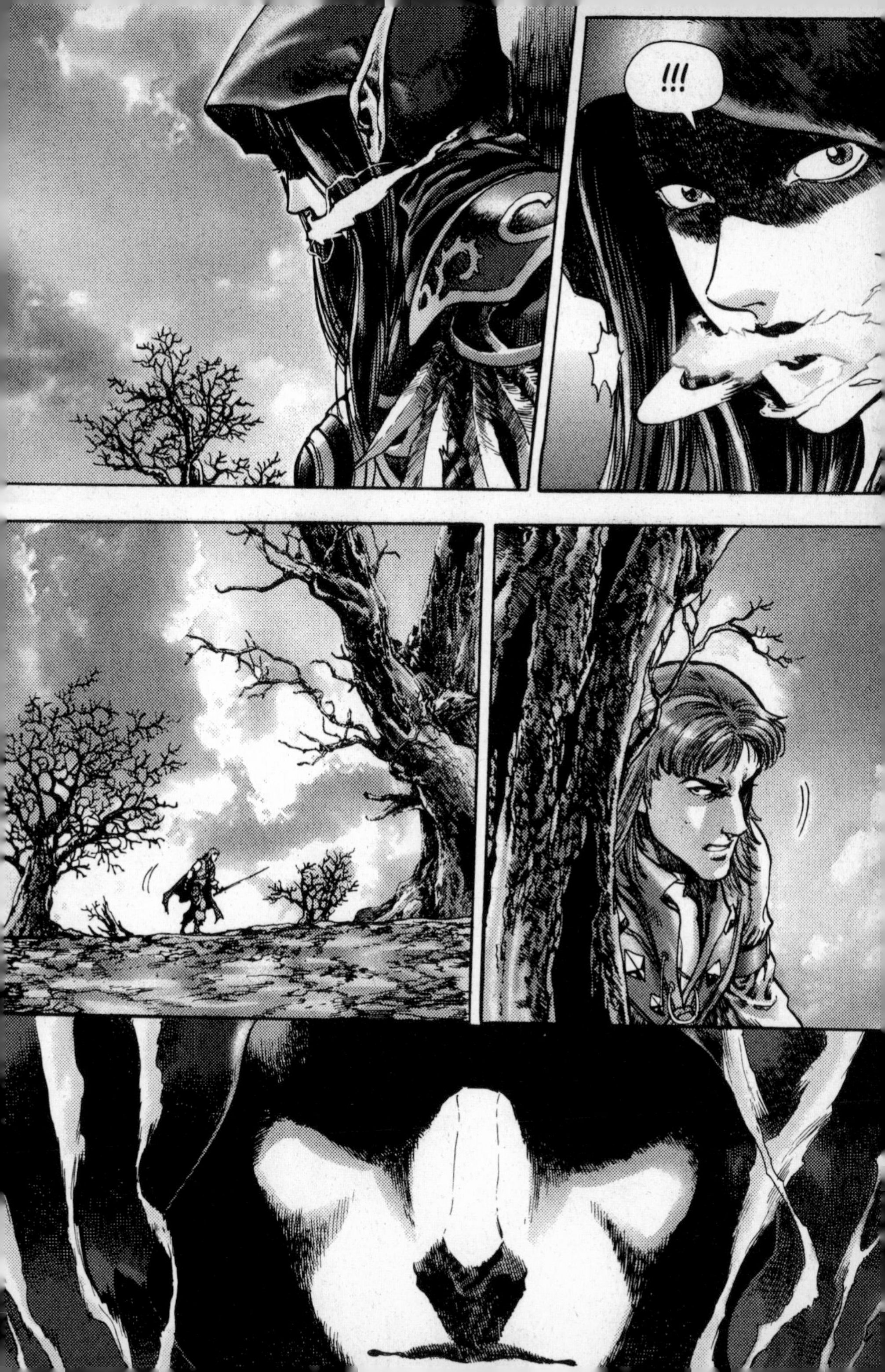
!!!

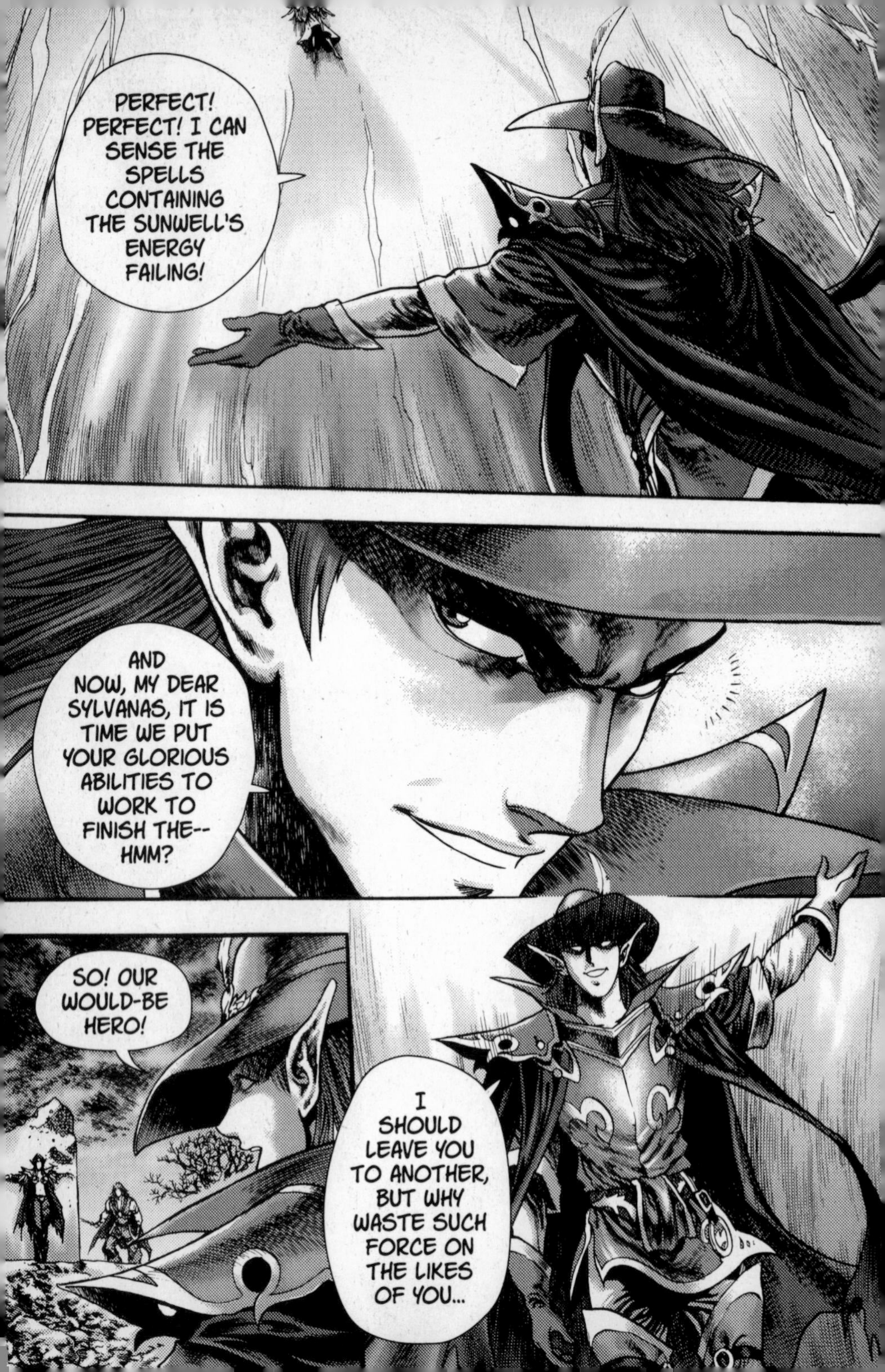
PERFECT! PERFECT! I CAN SENSE THE SPELLS CONTAINING THE SUNWELL'S ENERGY FAILING!
AND NOW, MY DEAR SYLVANAS, IT IS TIME WE PUT YOUR GLORIOUS ABILITIES TO WORK TO FINISH THE-- HMM?
SO! OUR WOULD-BE HERO!
I SHOULD LEAVE YOU TO ANOTHER, BUT WHY WASTE SUCH FORCE ON THE LIKES OF YOU...

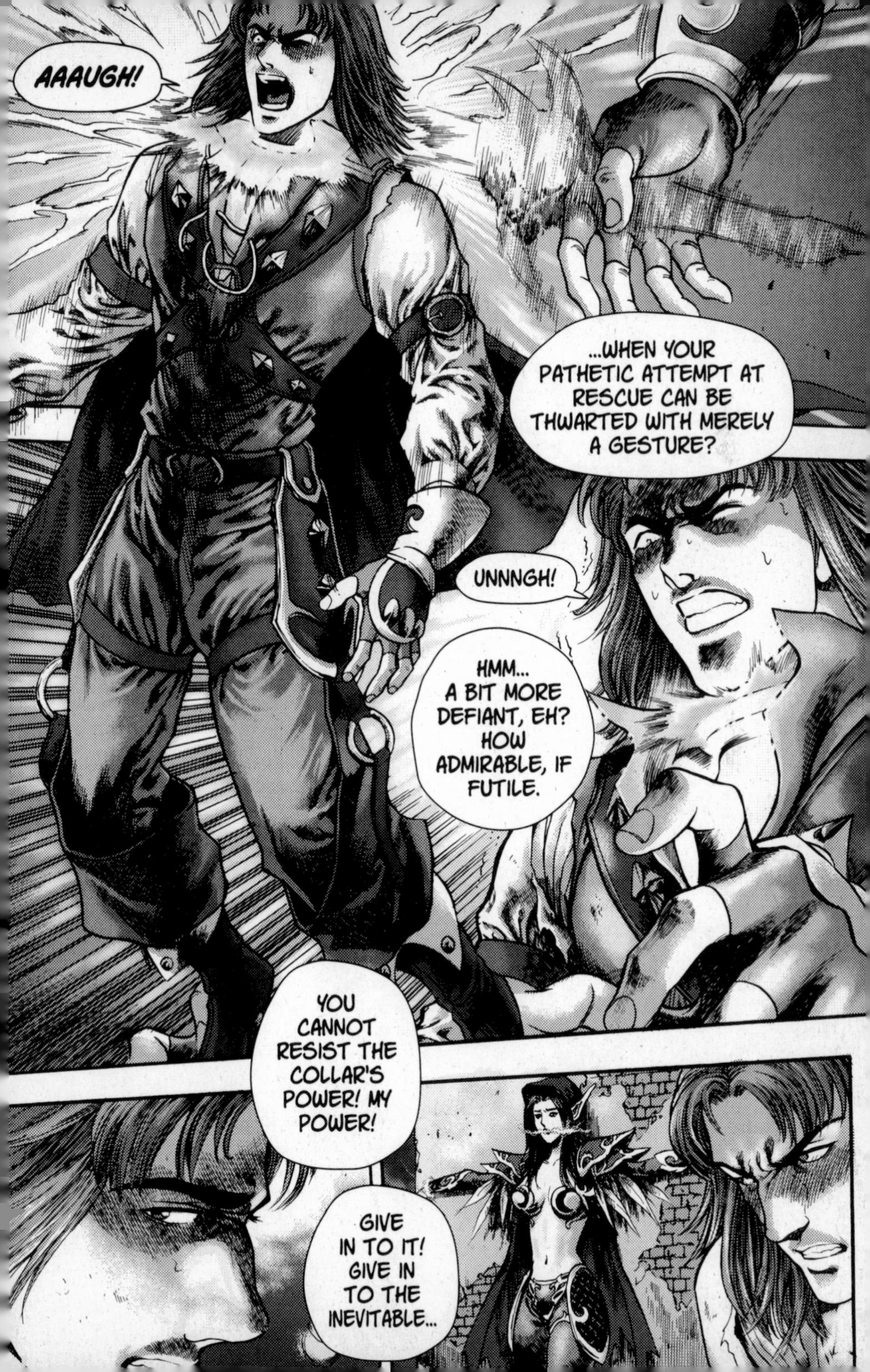
AAAUGH!
...WHEN YOUR PATHETIC ATTEMPT AT RESCUE CAN BE THWARTED WITH MERELY A GESTURE?
UNNNGH!
HMM... A BIT MORE DEFIANT, EH? HOW ADMIRABLE, IF FUTILE.
YOU CANNOT RESIST THE COLLAR'S POWER! MY POWER!
GIVE IN TO IT! GIVE IN TO THE INEVITABLE...

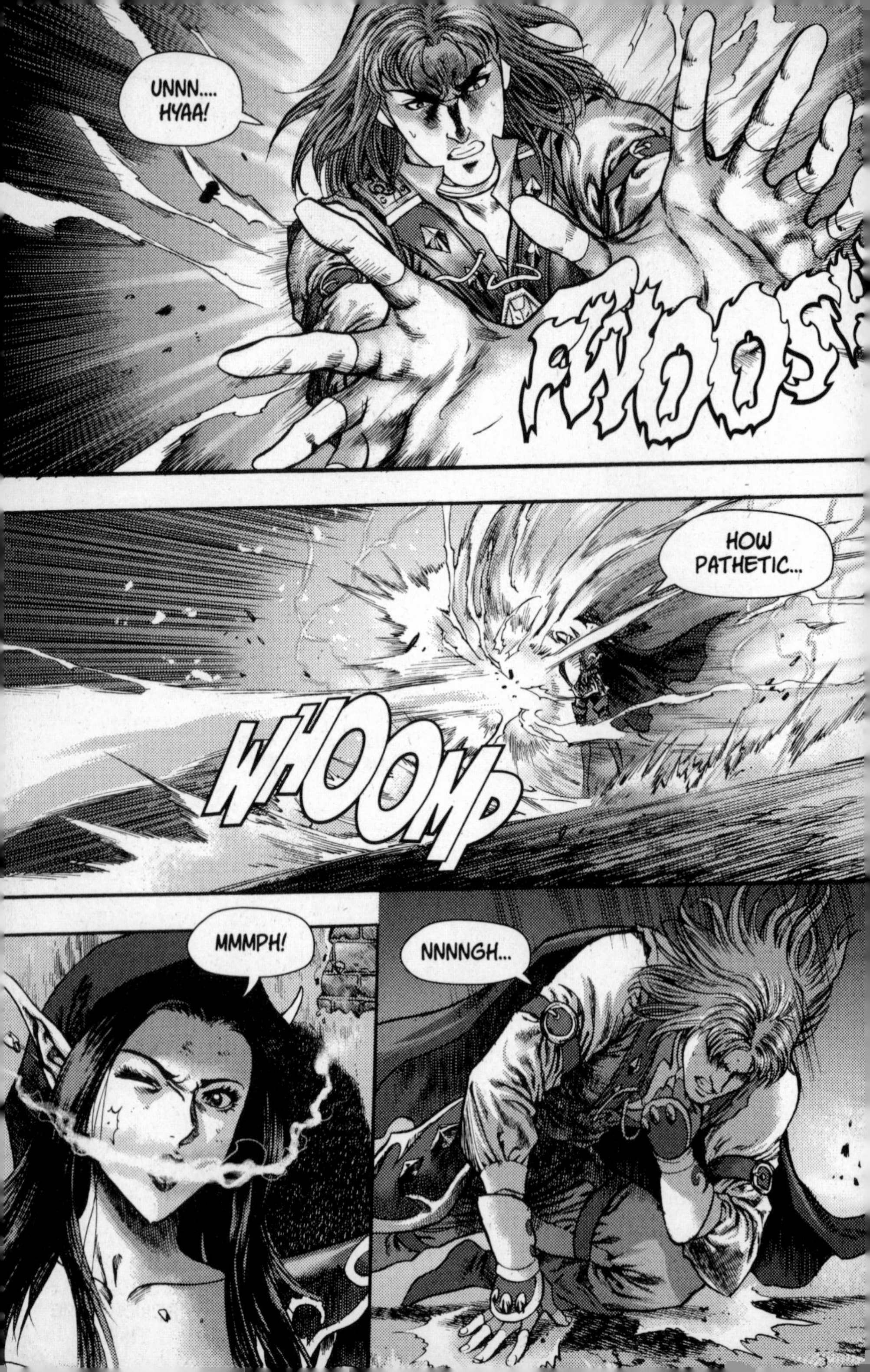
UNNN.... HYAA!
FWOOS
HOW PATHETIC...
WHOOMP
NNNNGH...
MMMPH!

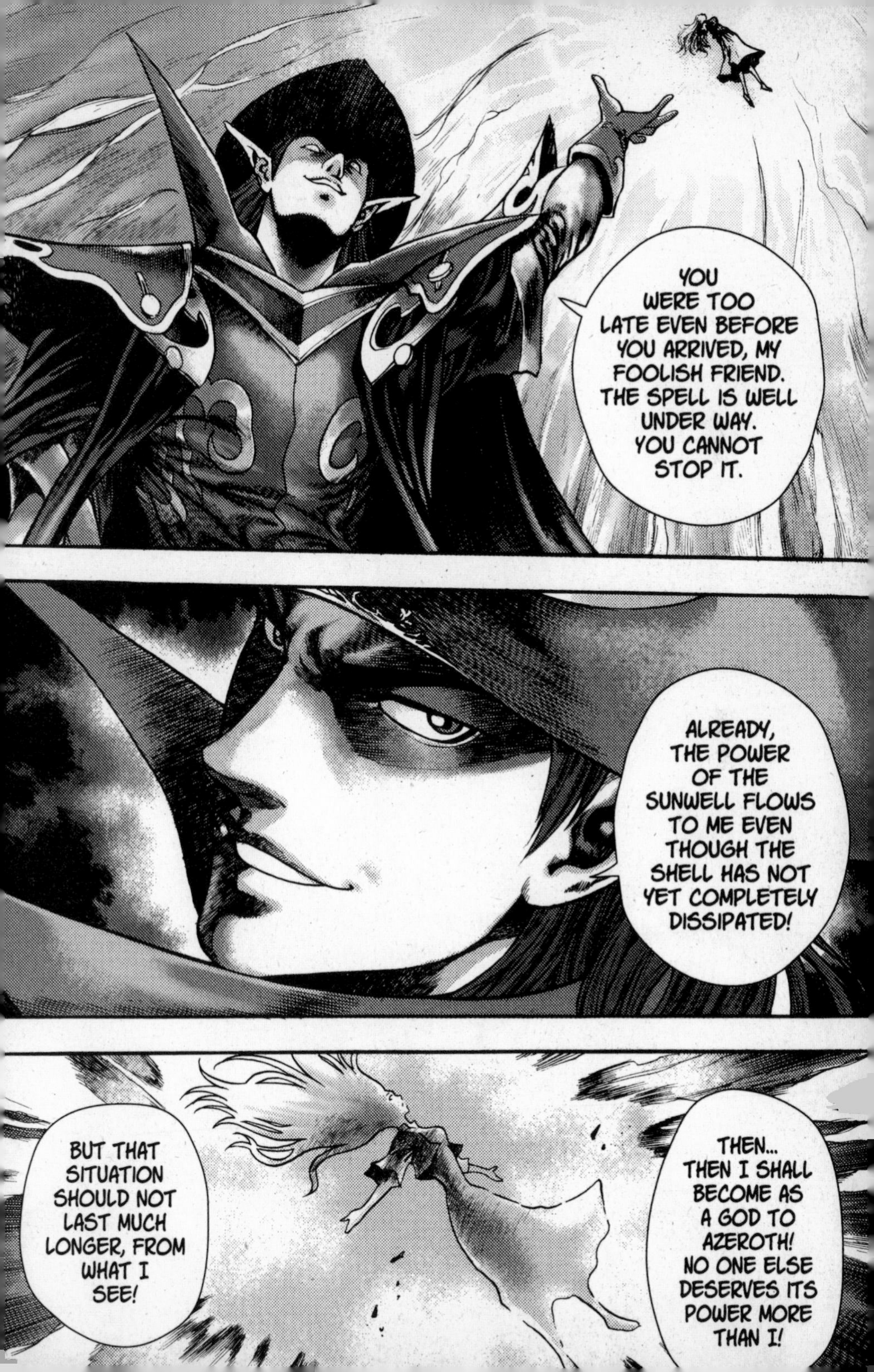
YOU WERE TOO LATE EVEN BEFORE YOU ARRIVED, MY FOOLISH FRIEND. THE SPELL IS WELL UNDER WAY. YOU CANNOT STOP IT.
ALREADY, THE POWER OF THE SUNWELL FLOWS TO ME EVEN THOUGH THE SHELL HAS NOT YET COMPLETELY DISSIPATED!
BUT THAT SITUATION SHOULD NOT LAST MUCH LONGER, FROM WHAT I SEE!
THEN... THEN I SHALL BECOME AS A GOD TO AZEROTH! NO ONE ELSE DESERVES ITS POWER MORE THAN I!

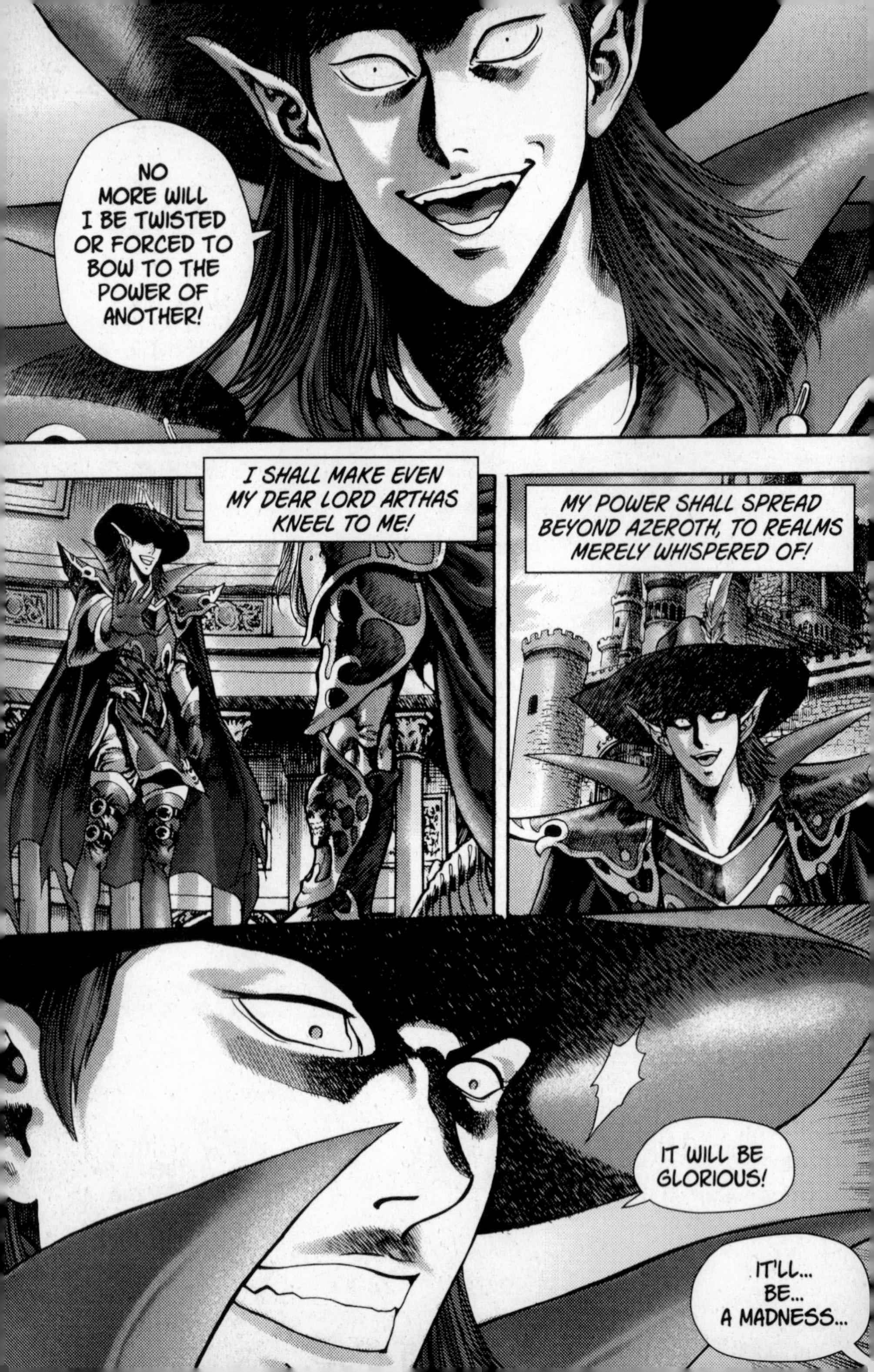
NO MORE WILL I BE TWISTED OR FORCED TO BOW TO THE POWER OF ANOTHER!
I SHALL MAKE EVEN MY DEAR LORD ARTHAS KNEEL TO ME!
MY POWER SHALL SPREAD BEYOND AZEROTH, TO REALMS MERELY WHISPERED OF!
IT WILL BE GLORIOUS!
IT'LL... BE... A MADNESS...

A MADNESS... YOU'LL NEVER SEE... COME TRUE!

SKREEEEE

UNNGH... HA!

MMMPH!

FWOOOM

EEEEEEEEEEE

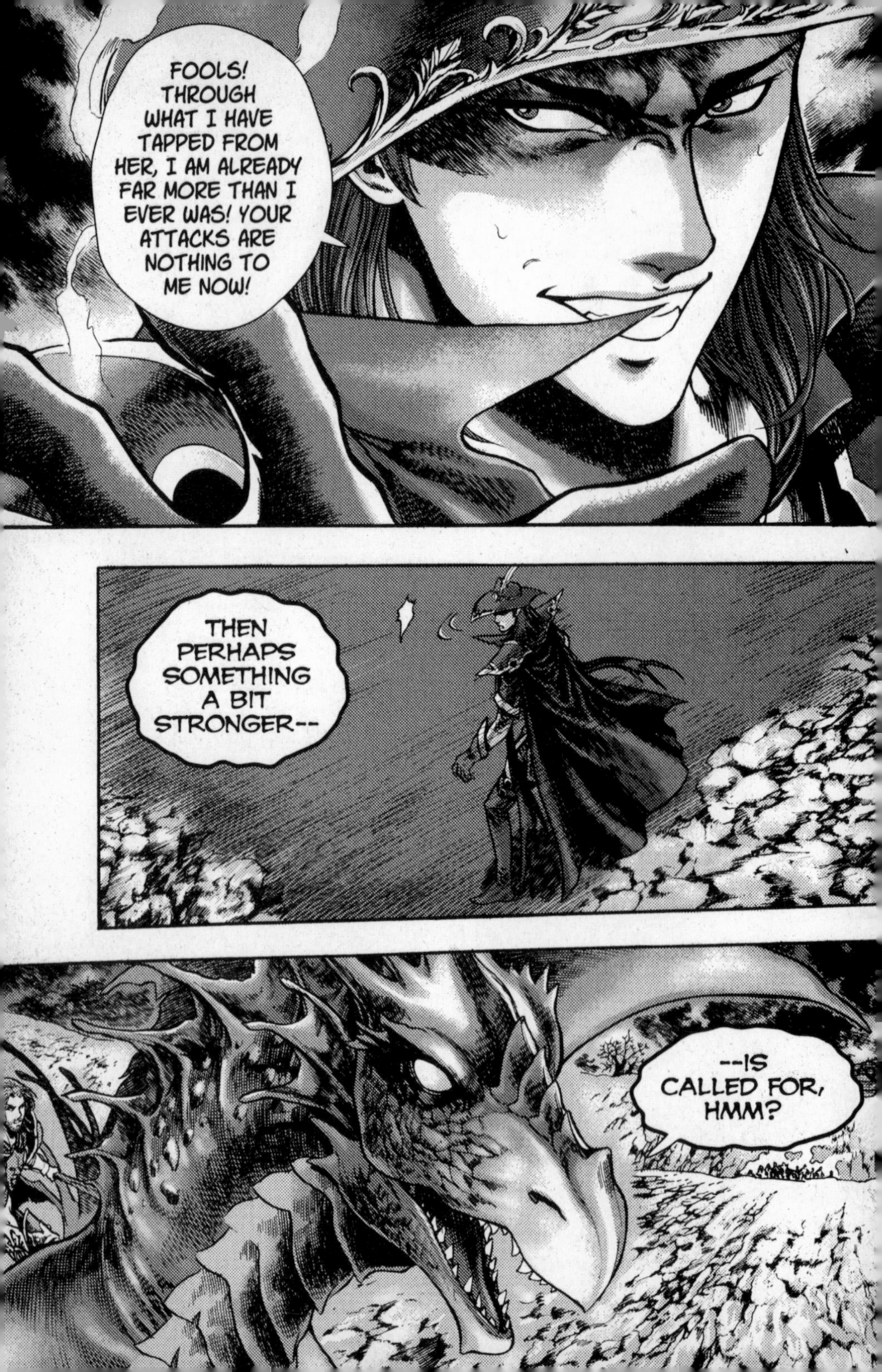
FOOLS! THROUGH WHAT I HAVE TAPPED FROM HER, I AM ALREADY FAR MORE THAN I EVER WAS! YOUR ATTACKS ARE NOTHING TO ME NOW!
THEN PERHAPS SOMETHING A BIT STRONGER--
--IS CALLED FOR, HMM?

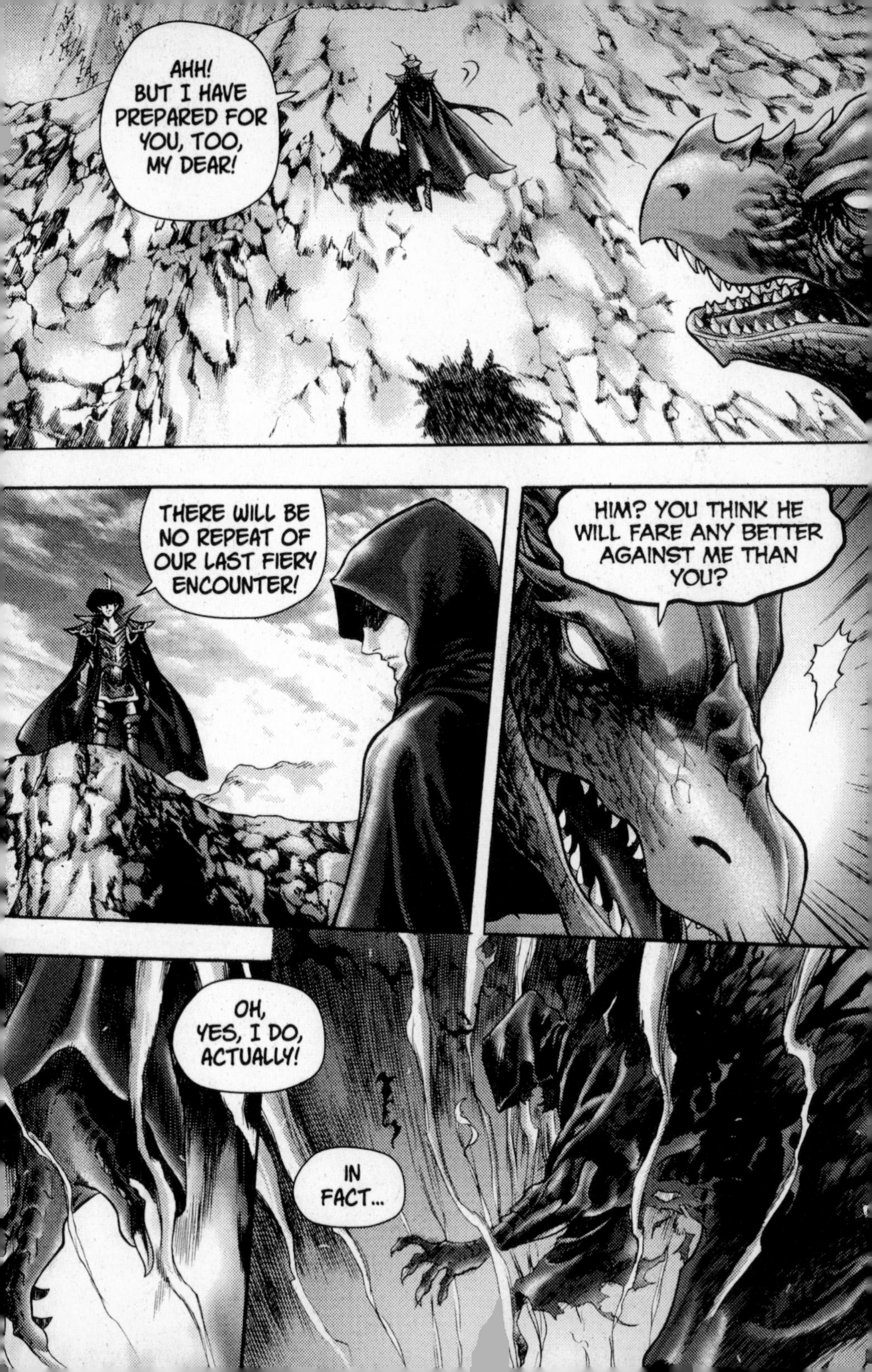
AHH! BUT I HAVE PREPARED FOR YOU, TOO, MY DEAR!
THERE WILL BE NO REPEAT OF OUR LAST FIERY ENCOUNTER!
HIM? YOU THINK HE WILL FARE ANY BETTER AGAINST ME THAN YOU?
OH, YES, I DO, ACTUALLY!
IN FACT...

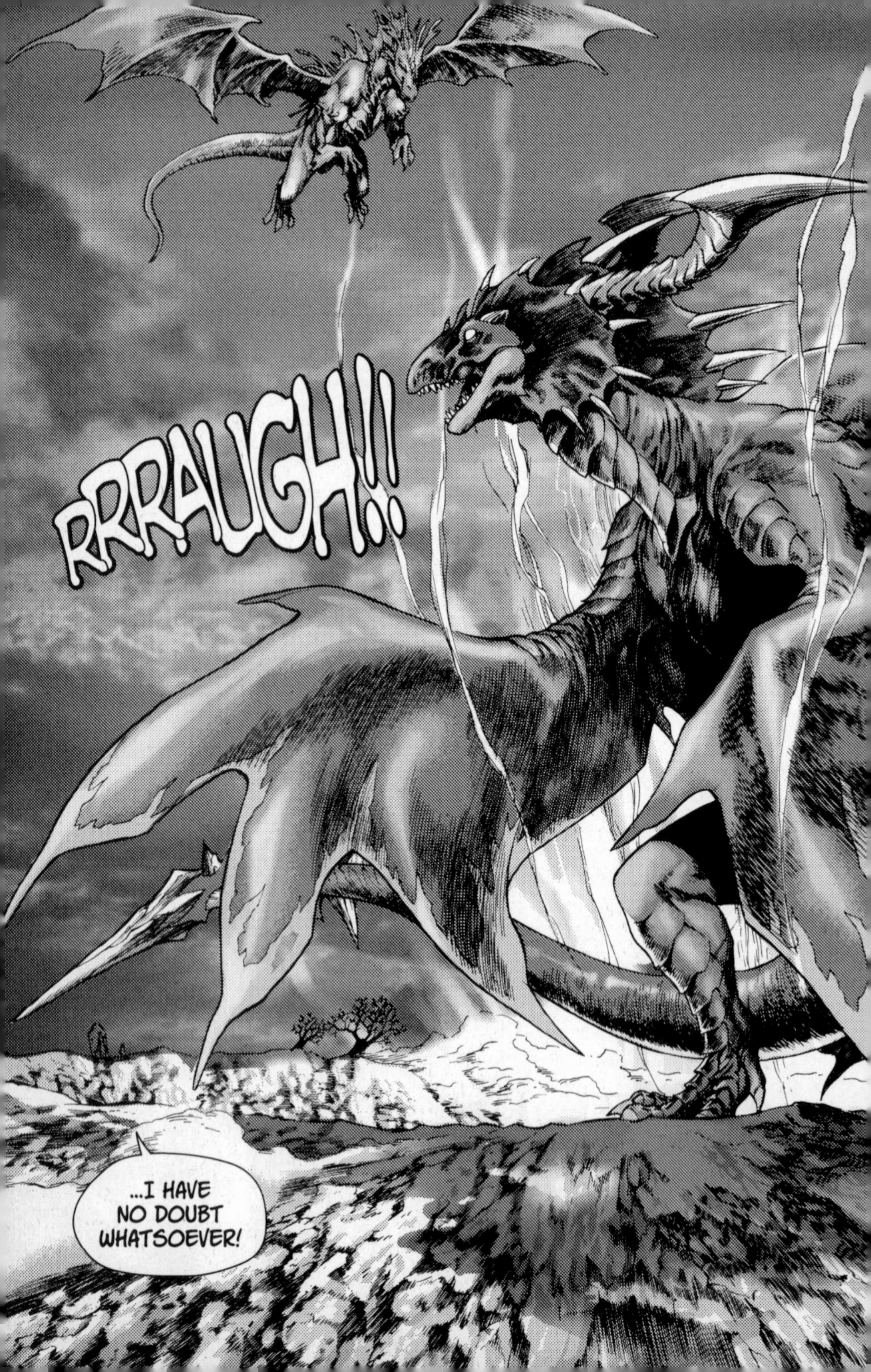
RRRAUGH!!!
...I HAVE NO DOUBT WHATSOEVER!

CHAPTER SIX
FIRE AND FURY

RRRARGH!!!

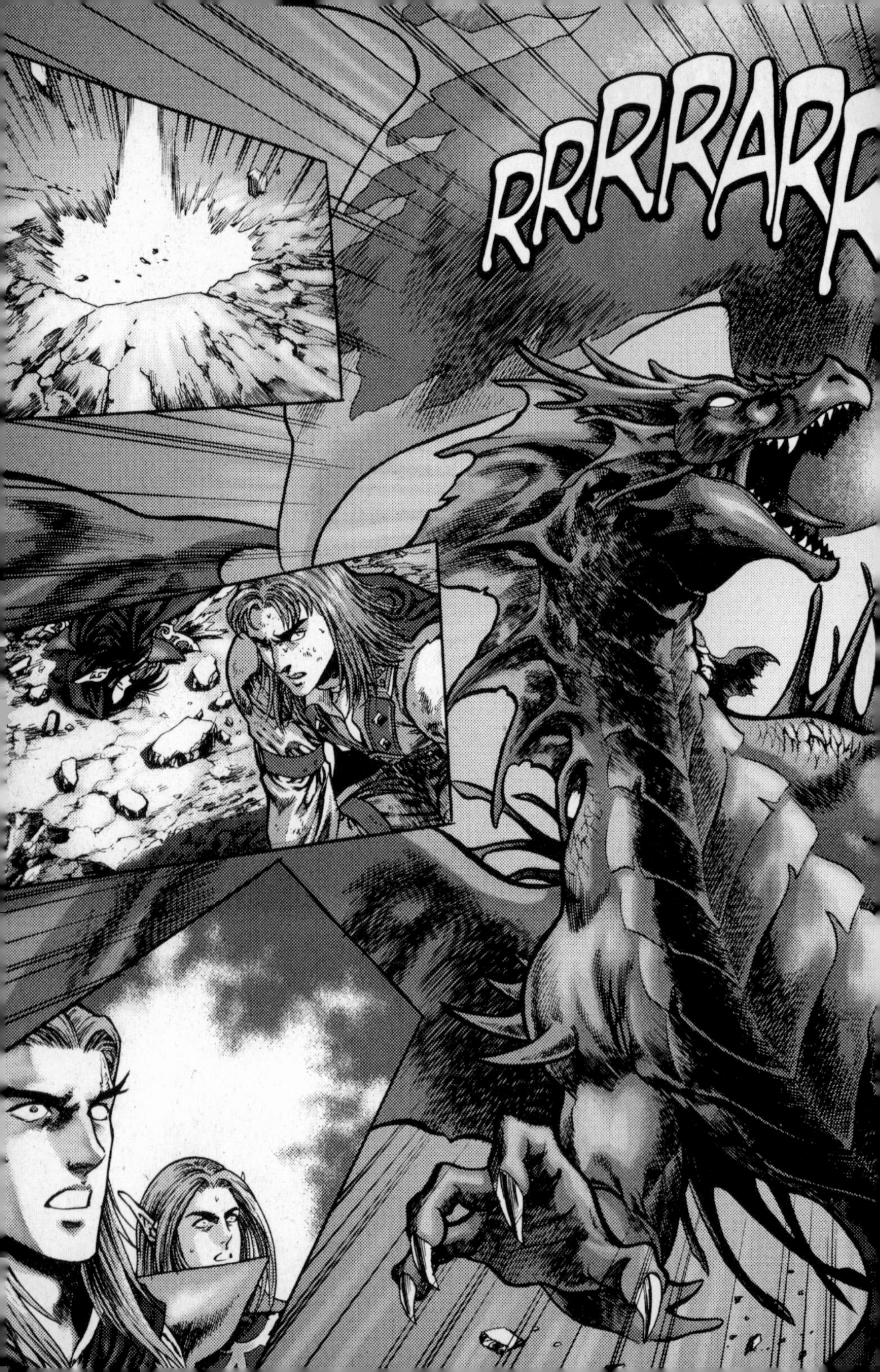
RRRRARR

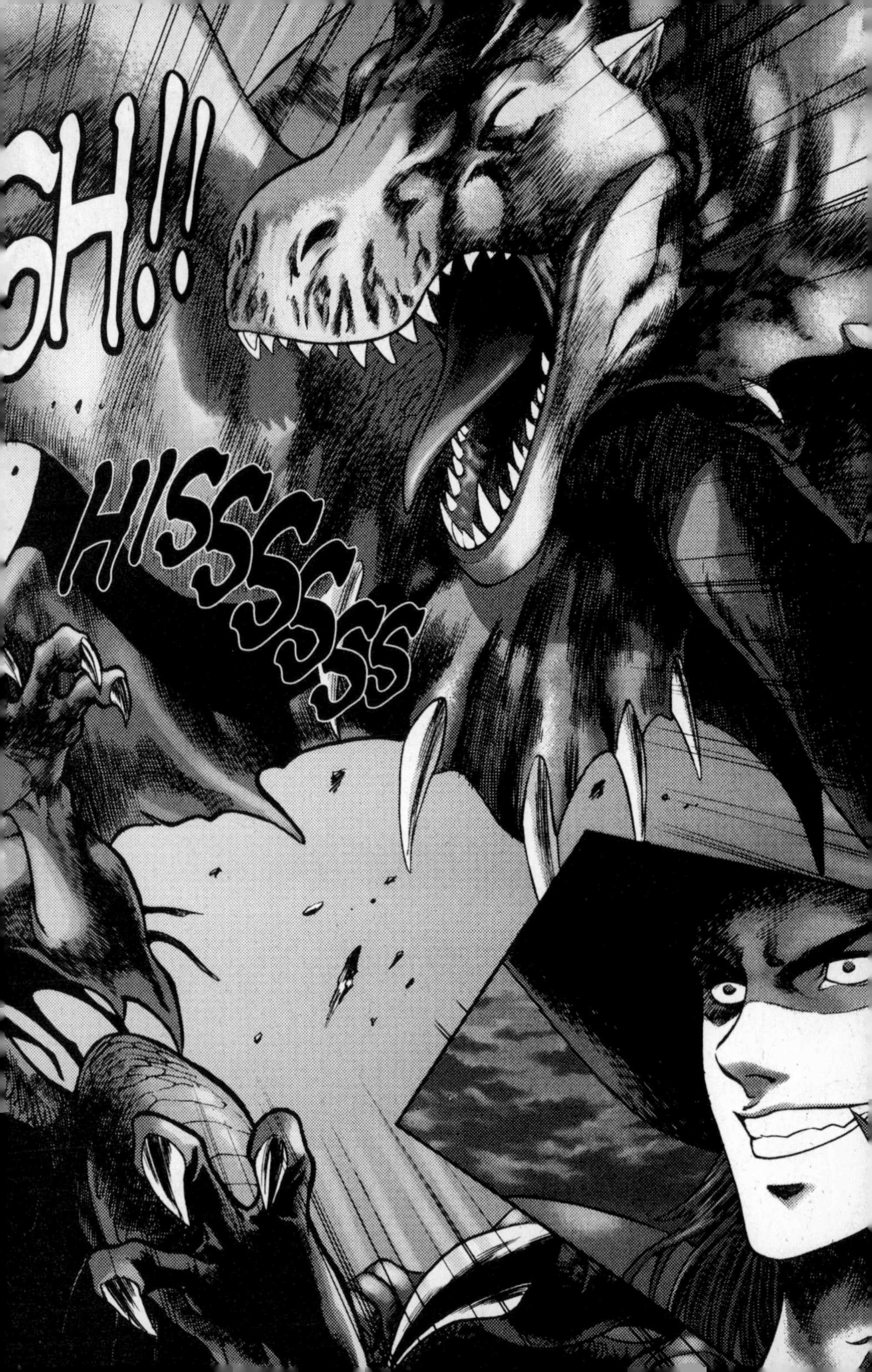
GH!!
HISSSSSSS

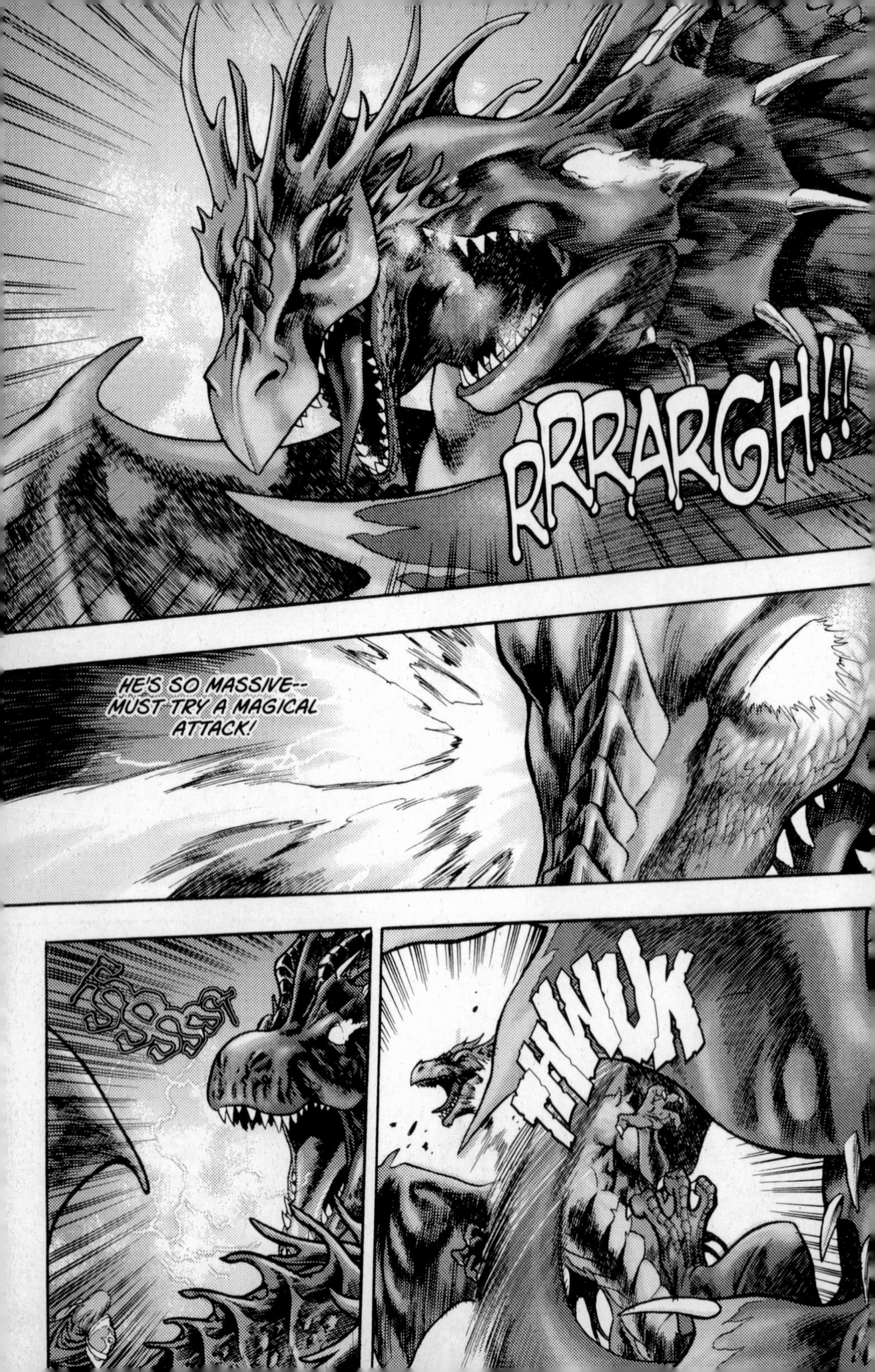
RRRARGH!!
HE'S SO MASSIVE-- MUST TRY A MAGICAL ATTACK!
THWUK
FSSSSST

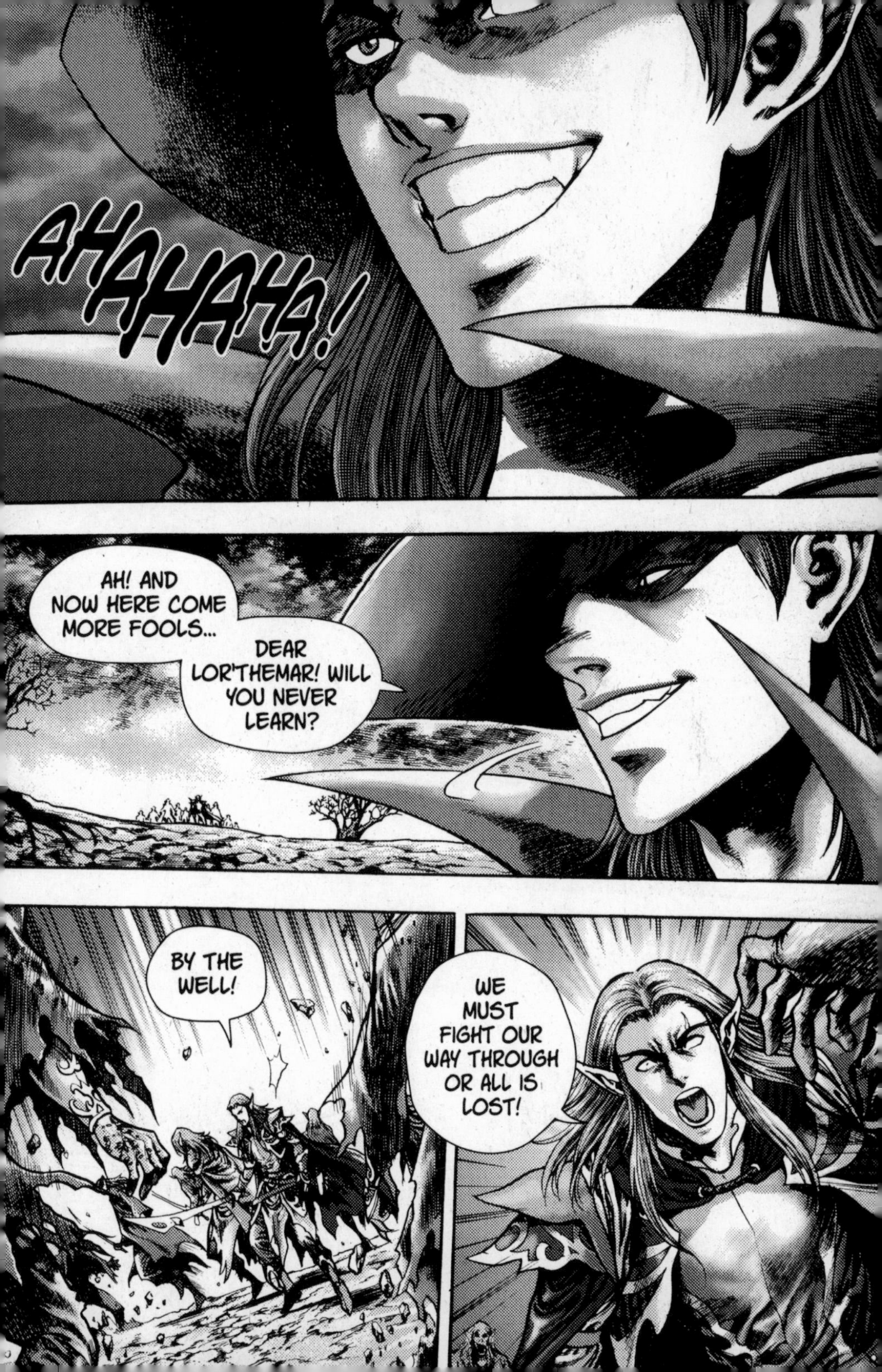
AHAHAHAHA!
AH! AND NOW HERE COME MORE FOOLS...
DEAR LOR'THEMAR! WILL YOU NEVER LEARN?
BY THE WELL!
WE MUST FIGHT OUR WAY THROUGH OR ALL IS LOST!

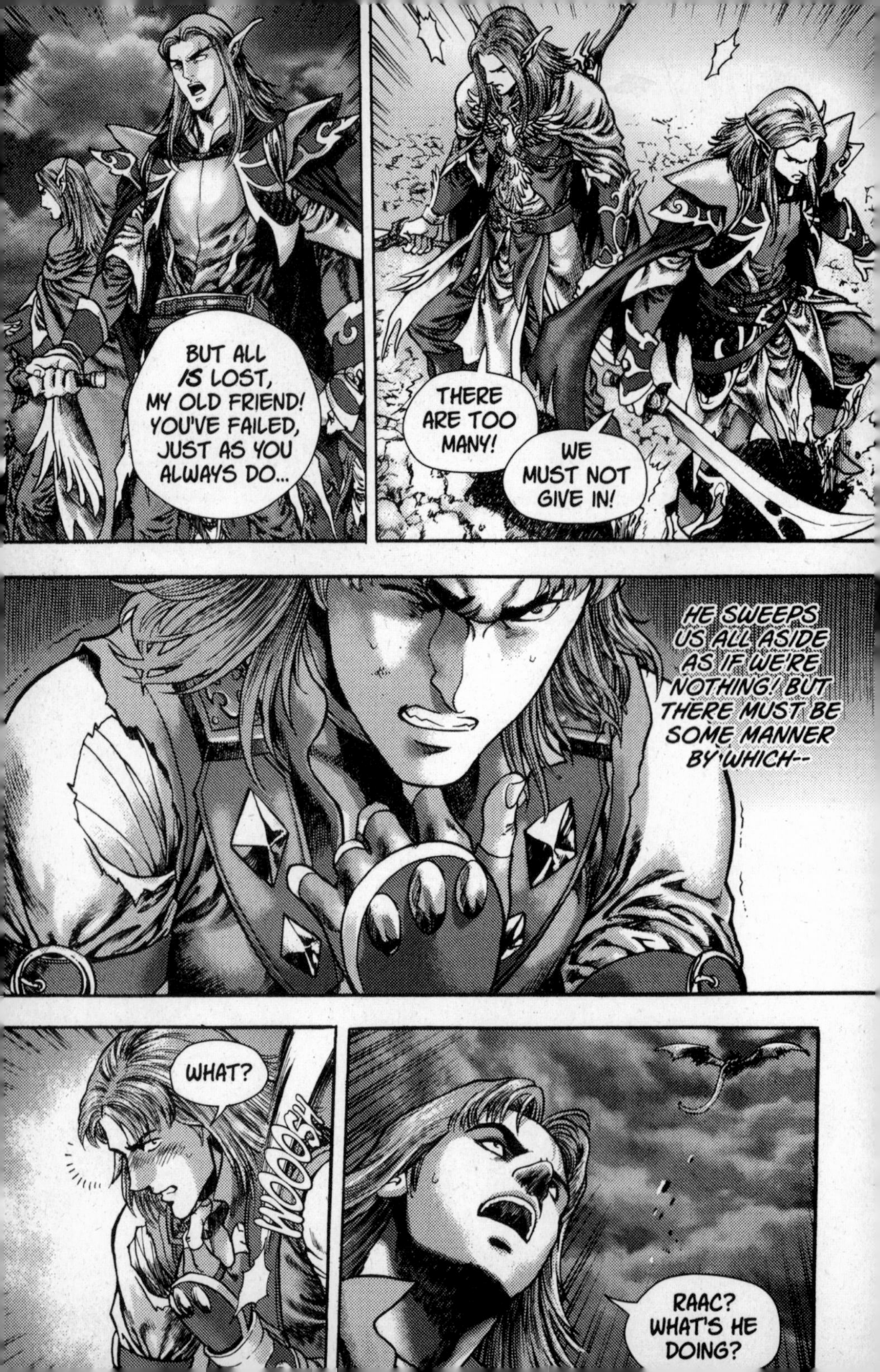
BUT ALL *IS* LOST, MY OLD FRIEND! YOU'VE FAILED, JUST AS YOU ALWAYS DO...
THERE ARE TOO MANY!
WE MUST NOT GIVE IN!
HE SWEEPS US ALL ASIDE AS IF WE'RE NOTHING! BUT THERE MUST BE SOME MANNER BY WHICH--
WHAT?
RAAC? WHAT'S HE DOING?

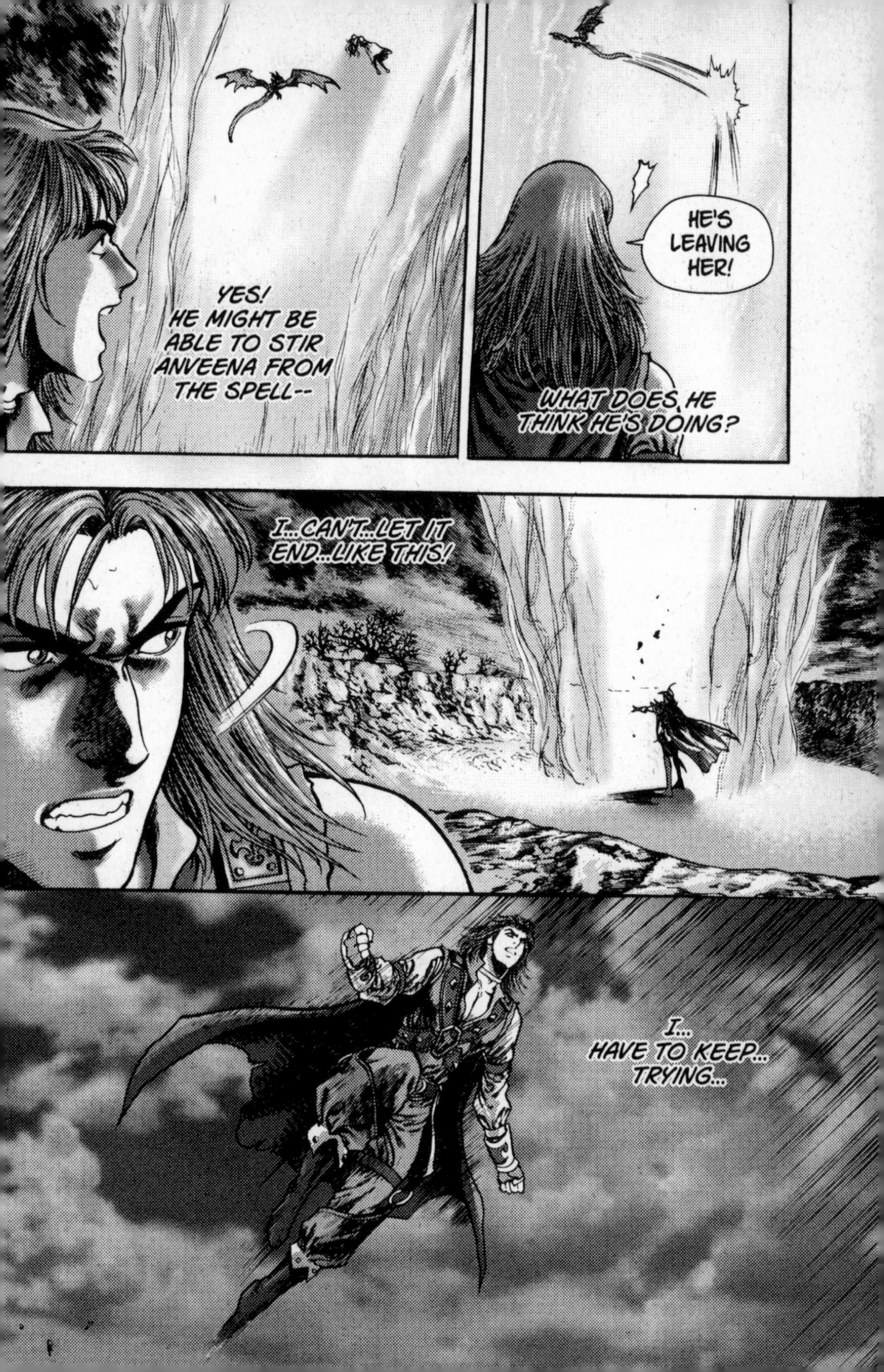
YES! HE MIGHT BE ABLE TO STIR ANVEENA FROM THE SPELL--
HE'S LEAVING HER!
WHAT DOES HE THINK HE'S DOING?
I...CAN'T...LET IT END...LIKE THIS!
I... HAVE TO KEEP... TRYING...

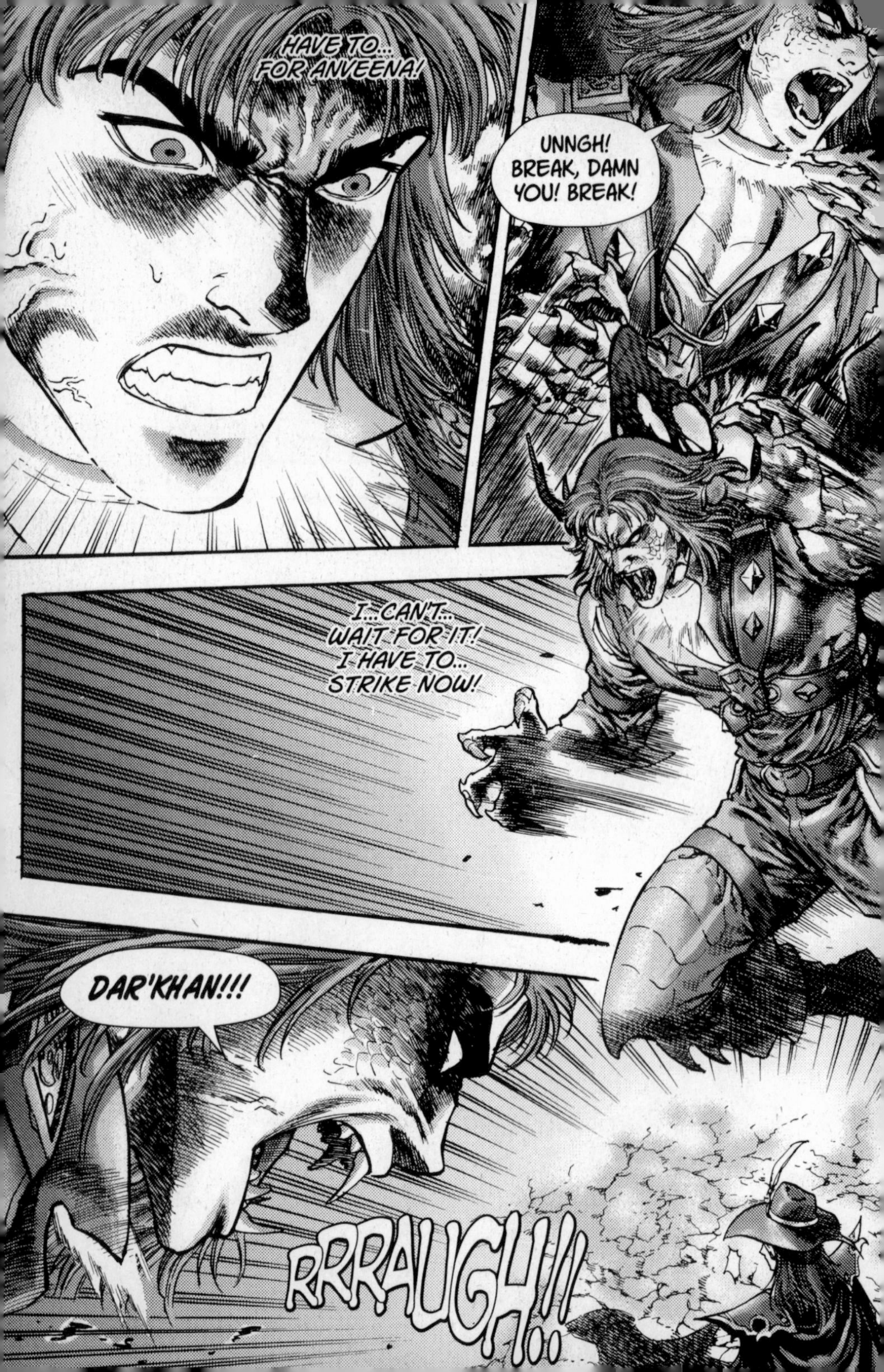
HAVE TO... FOR ANVEENA!
UNNGH! BREAK, DAMN YOU! BREAK!
I...CAN'T... WAIT FOR IT! I HAVE TO... STRIKE NOW!
DAR'KHAN!!!
RRRAUGH!!!

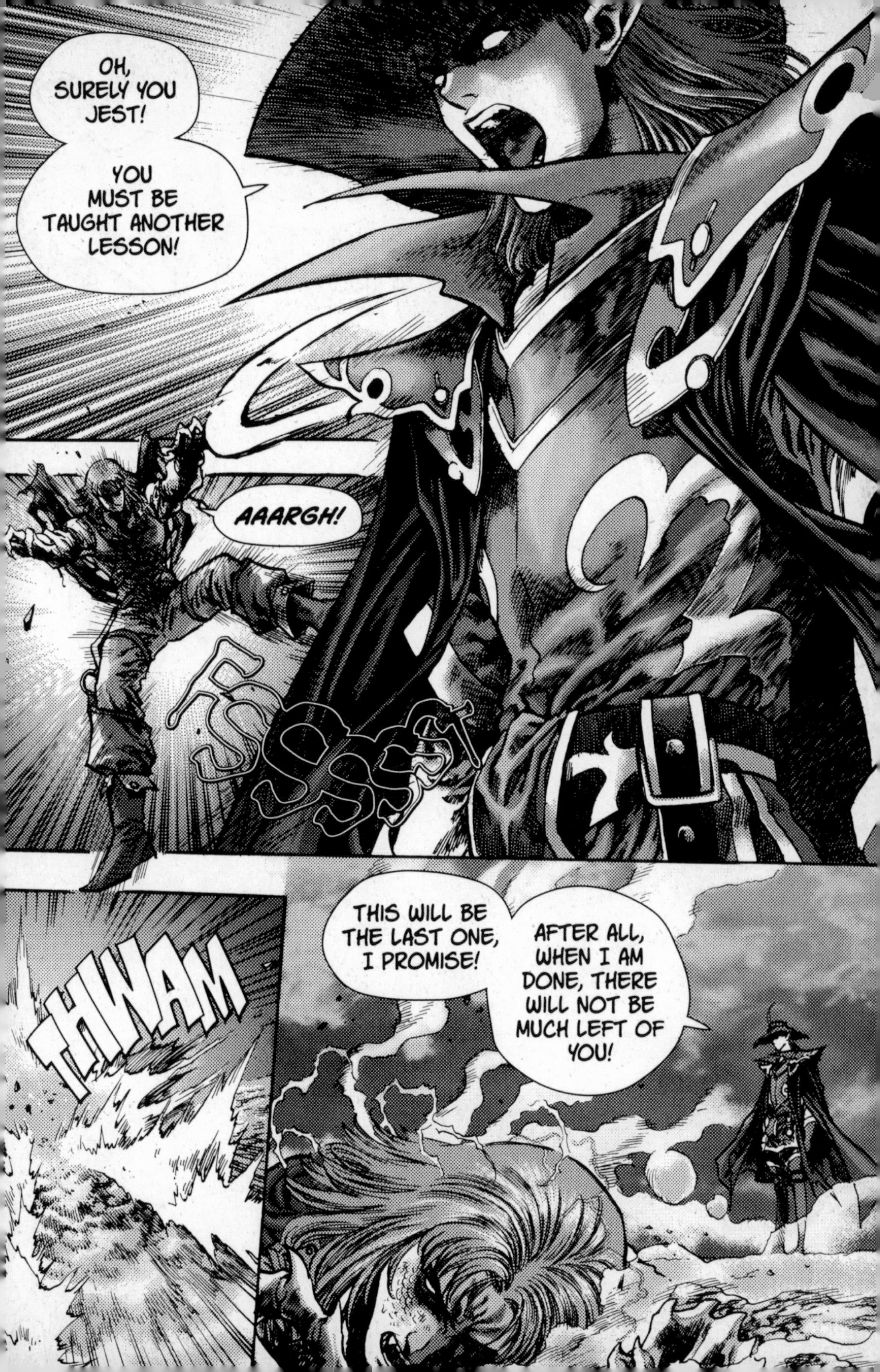
OH, SURELY YOU JEST!
YOU MUST BE TAUGHT ANOTHER LESSON!
AAARGH!
FSSSST
THIS WILL BE THE LAST ONE, I PROMISE!
AFTER ALL, WHEN I AM DONE, THERE WILL NOT BE MUCH LEFT OF YOU!
THWAM

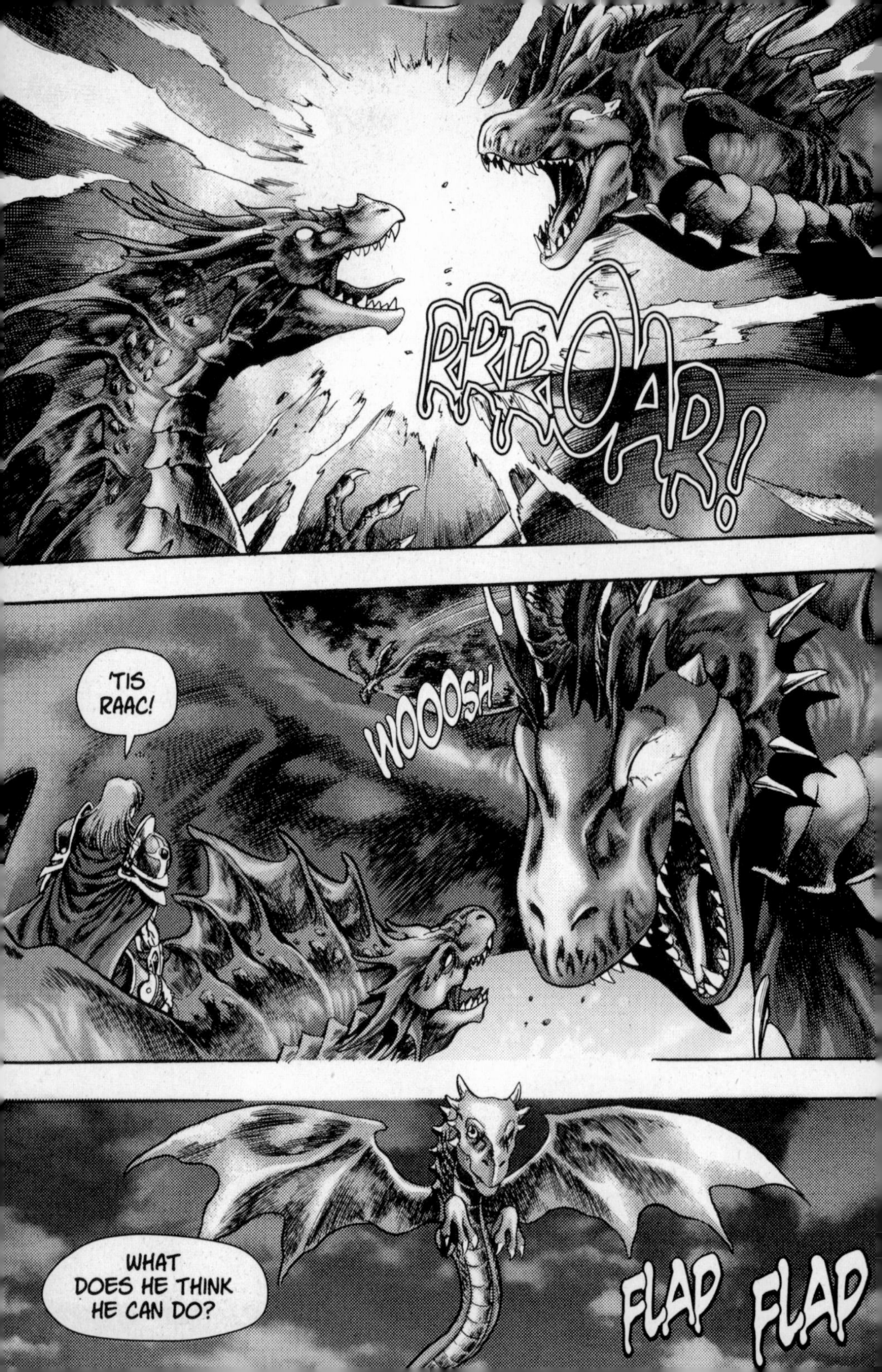
RRRROAR!
WOOOSH
'TIS RAAC!
FLAP FLAP
WHAT DOES HE THINK HE CAN DO?

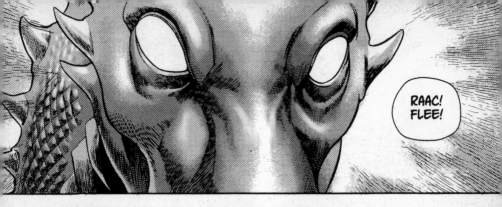

RAAC! FLEE!

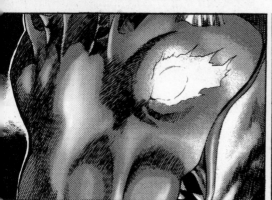
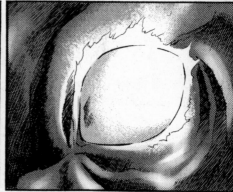

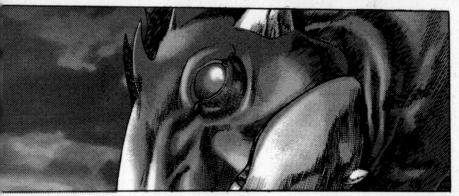

SO, LITTLE ONE...

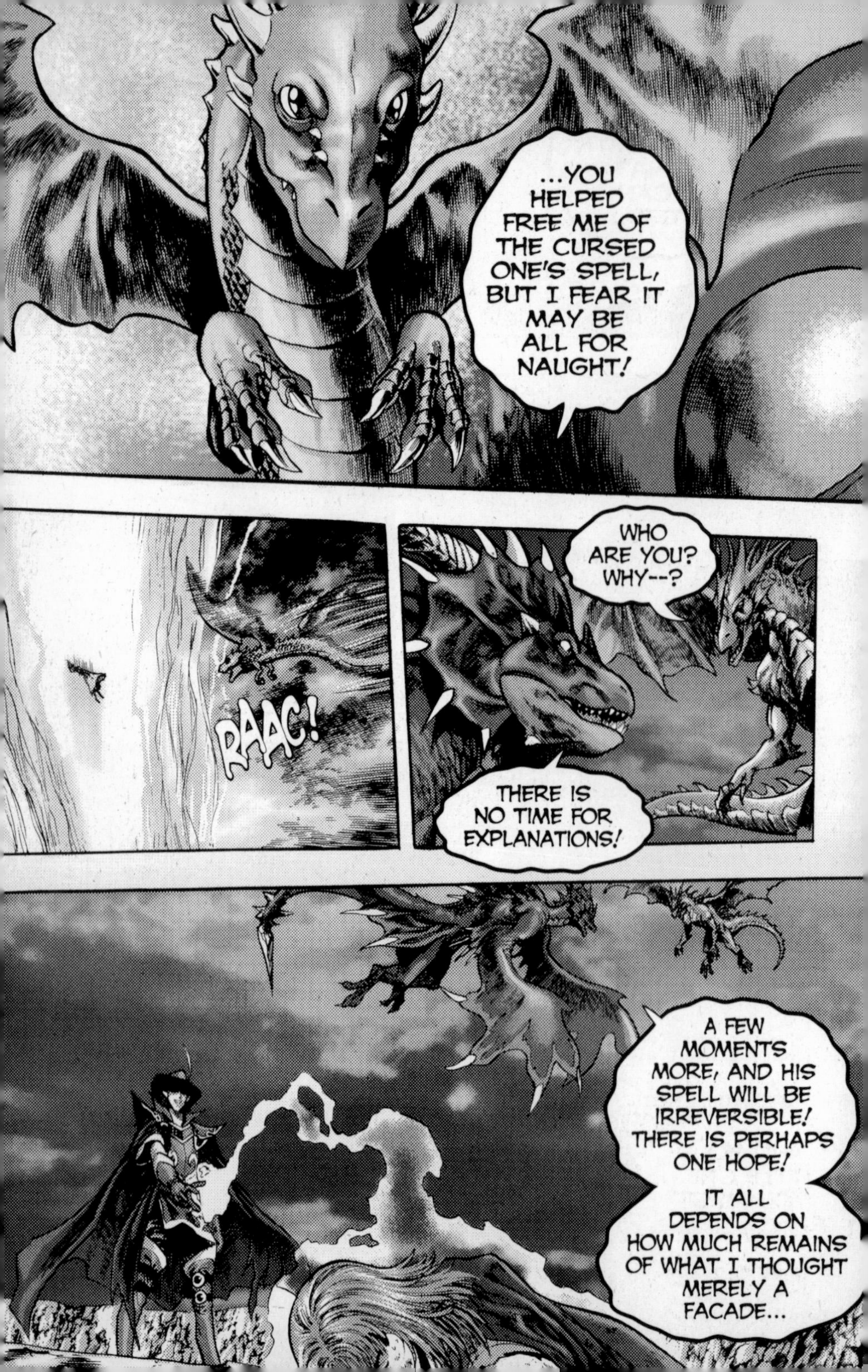
...YOU HELPED FREE ME OF THE CURSED ONE'S SPELL, BUT I FEAR IT MAY BE ALL FOR NAUGHT!
WHO ARE YOU? WHY--?
THERE IS NO TIME FOR EXPLANATIONS!
RAAC!
A FEW MOMENTS MORE, AND HIS SPELL WILL BE IRREVERSIBLE! THERE IS PERHAPS ONE HOPE!
IT ALL DEPENDS ON HOW MUCH REMAINS OF WHAT I THOUGHT MERELY A FACADE...

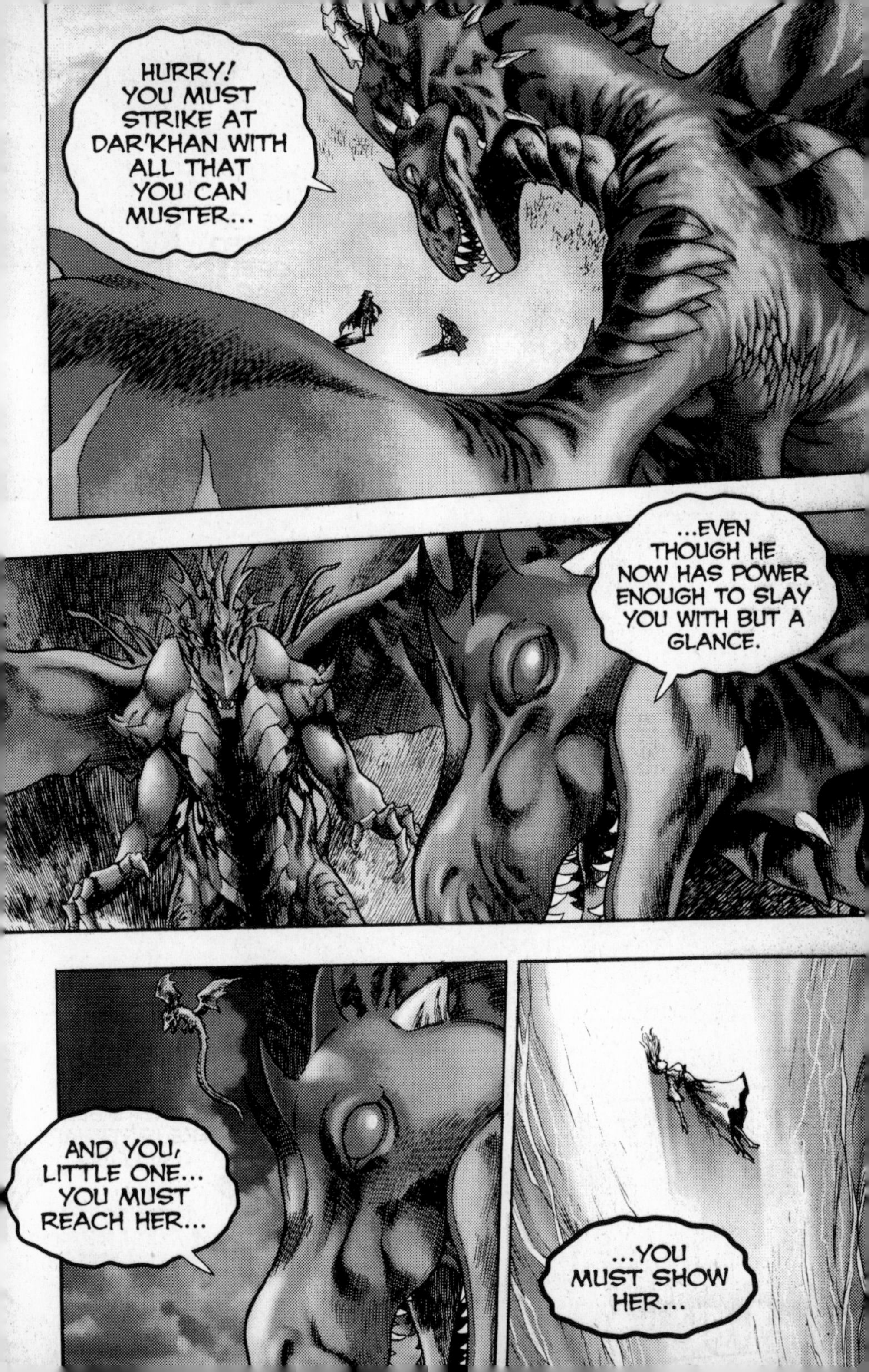
HURRY! YOU MUST STRIKE AT DAR'KHAN WITH ALL THAT YOU CAN MUSTER...
...EVEN THOUGH HE NOW HAS POWER ENOUGH TO SLAY YOU WITH BUT A GLANCE.
AND YOU, LITTLE ONE... YOU MUST REACH HER...
...YOU MUST SHOW HER...

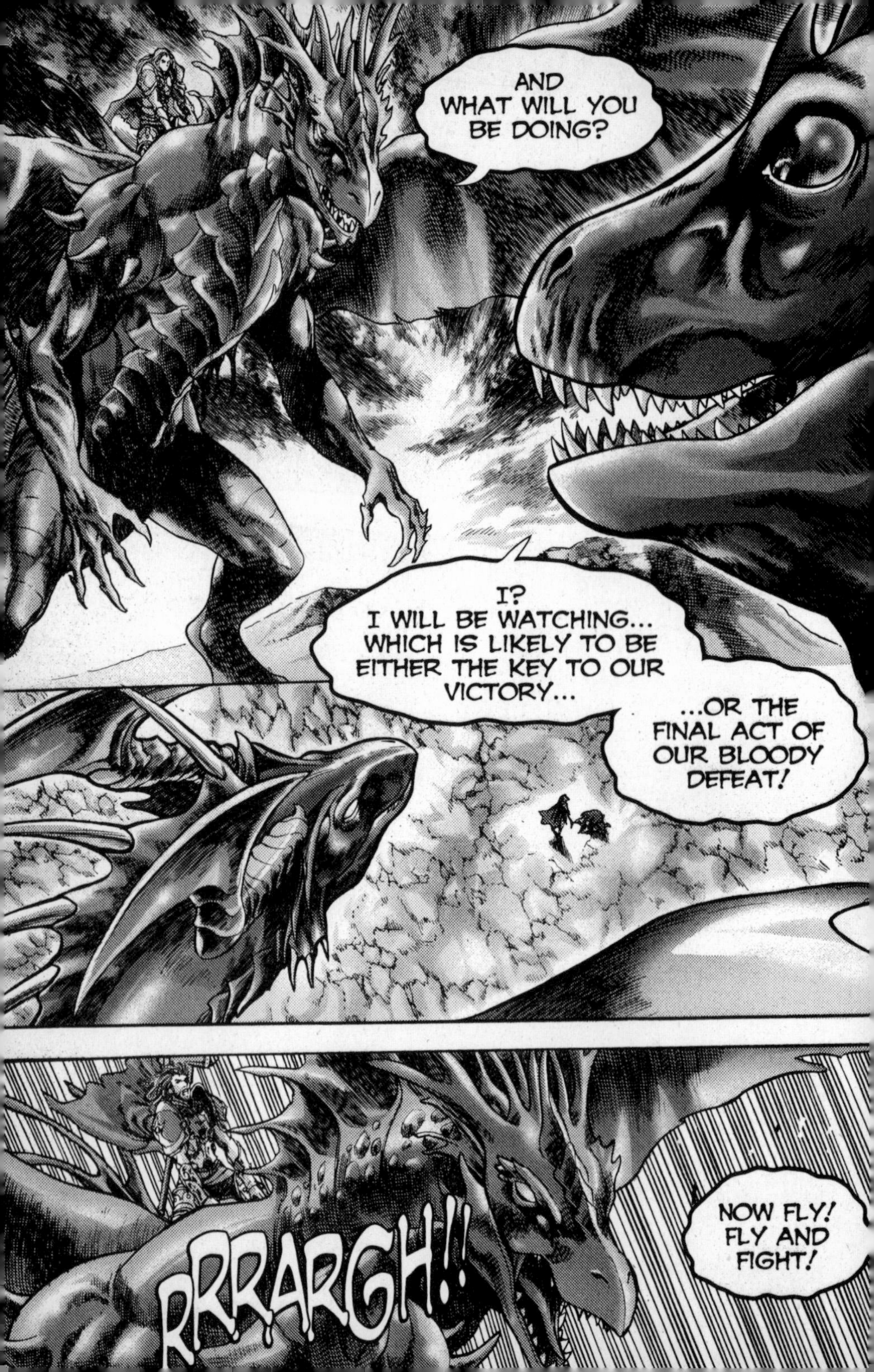
AND WHAT WILL YOU BE DOING?
I? I WILL BE WATCHING... WHICH IS LIKELY TO BE EITHER THE KEY TO OUR VICTORY...
...OR THE FINAL ACT OF OUR BLOODY DEFEAT!
NOW FLY! FLY AND FIGHT!
RRRARGH!!

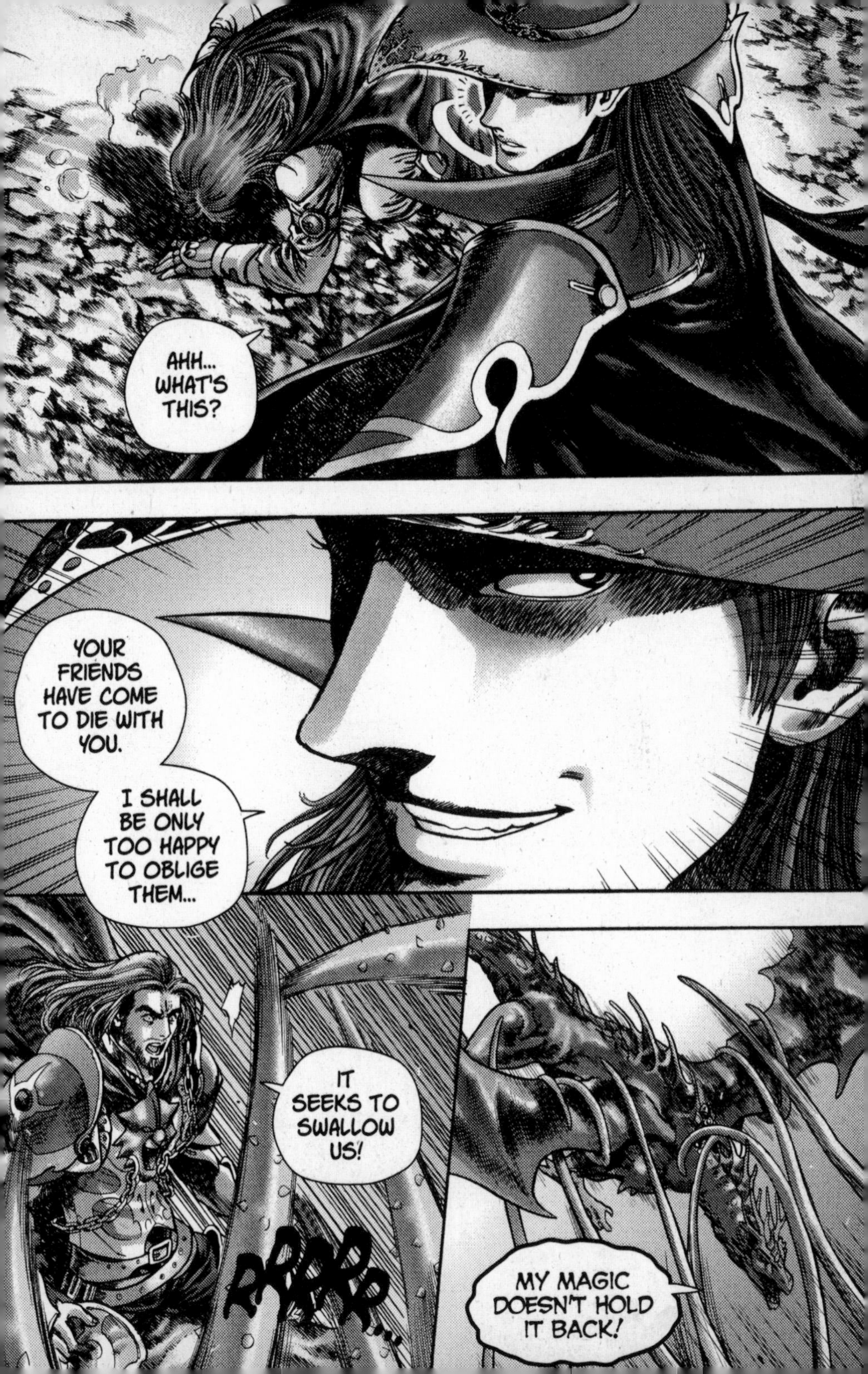
AHH... WHAT'S THIS?
YOUR FRIENDS HAVE COME TO DIE WITH YOU.
I SHALL BE ONLY TOO HAPPY TO OBLIGE THEM...
IT SEEKS TO SWALLOW US!
RRRRR...
MY MAGIC DOESN'T HOLD IT BACK!

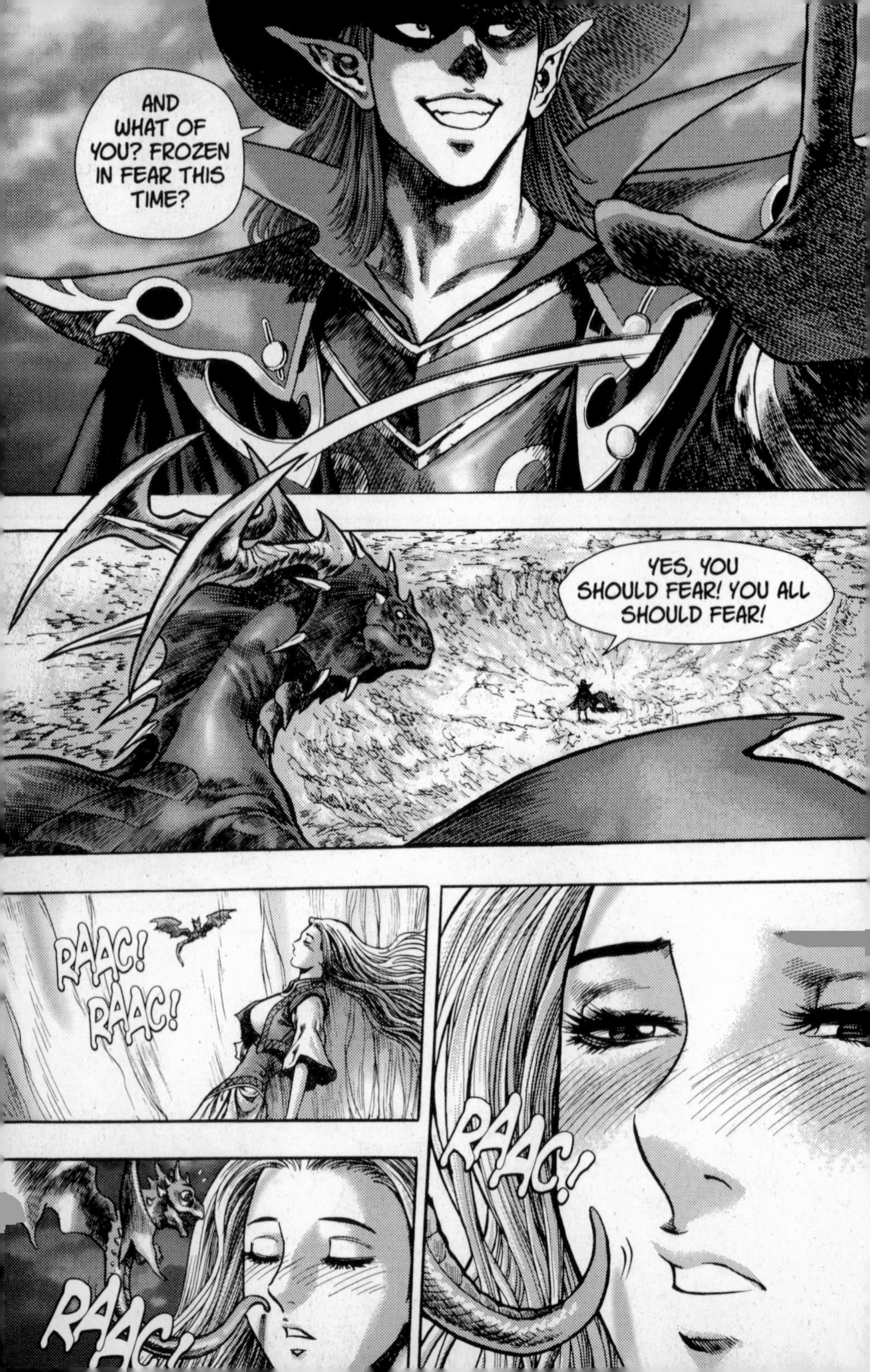
AND WHAT OF YOU? FROZEN IN FEAR THIS TIME?
YES, YOU SHOULD FEAR! YOU ALL SHOULD FEAR!
RAAC!
RAAC! RAAC!
RAAC!

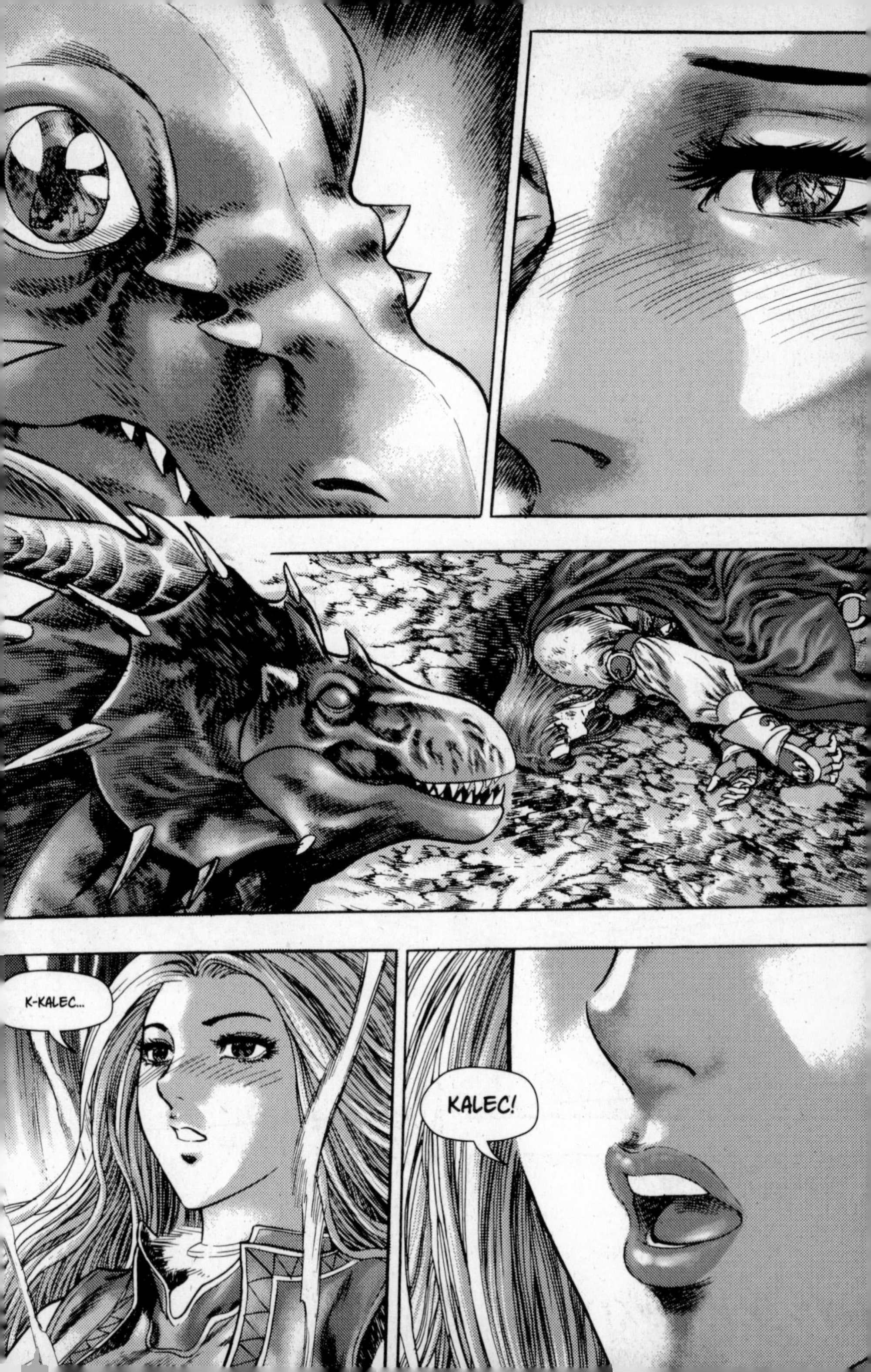
K-KALEC...
KALEC!

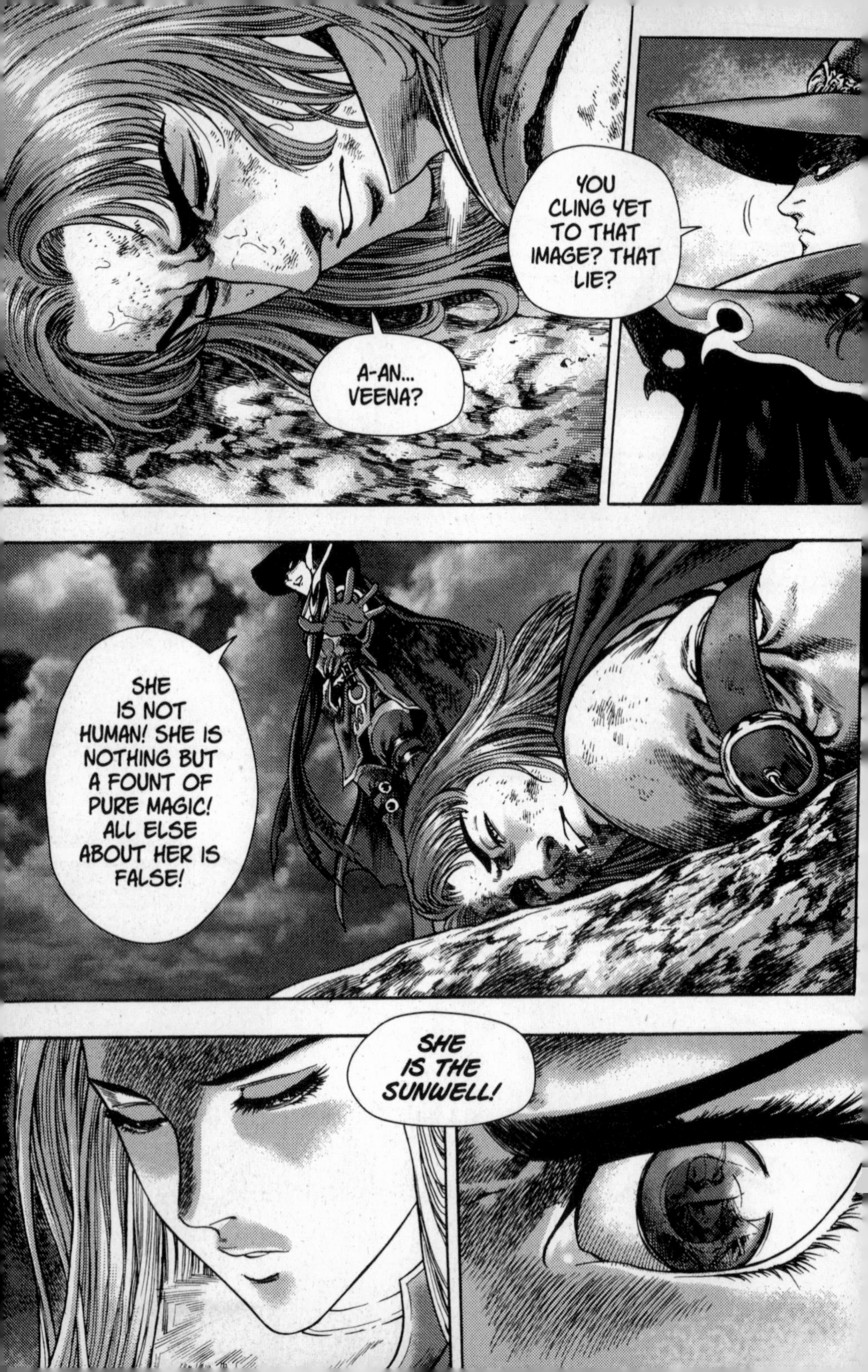
A-AN... VEENA?
YOU CLING YET TO THAT IMAGE? THAT LIE?
SHE IS NOT HUMAN! SHE IS NOTHING BUT A FOUNT OF PURE MAGIC! ALL ELSE ABOUT HER IS FALSE!
SHE IS THE SUNWELL!

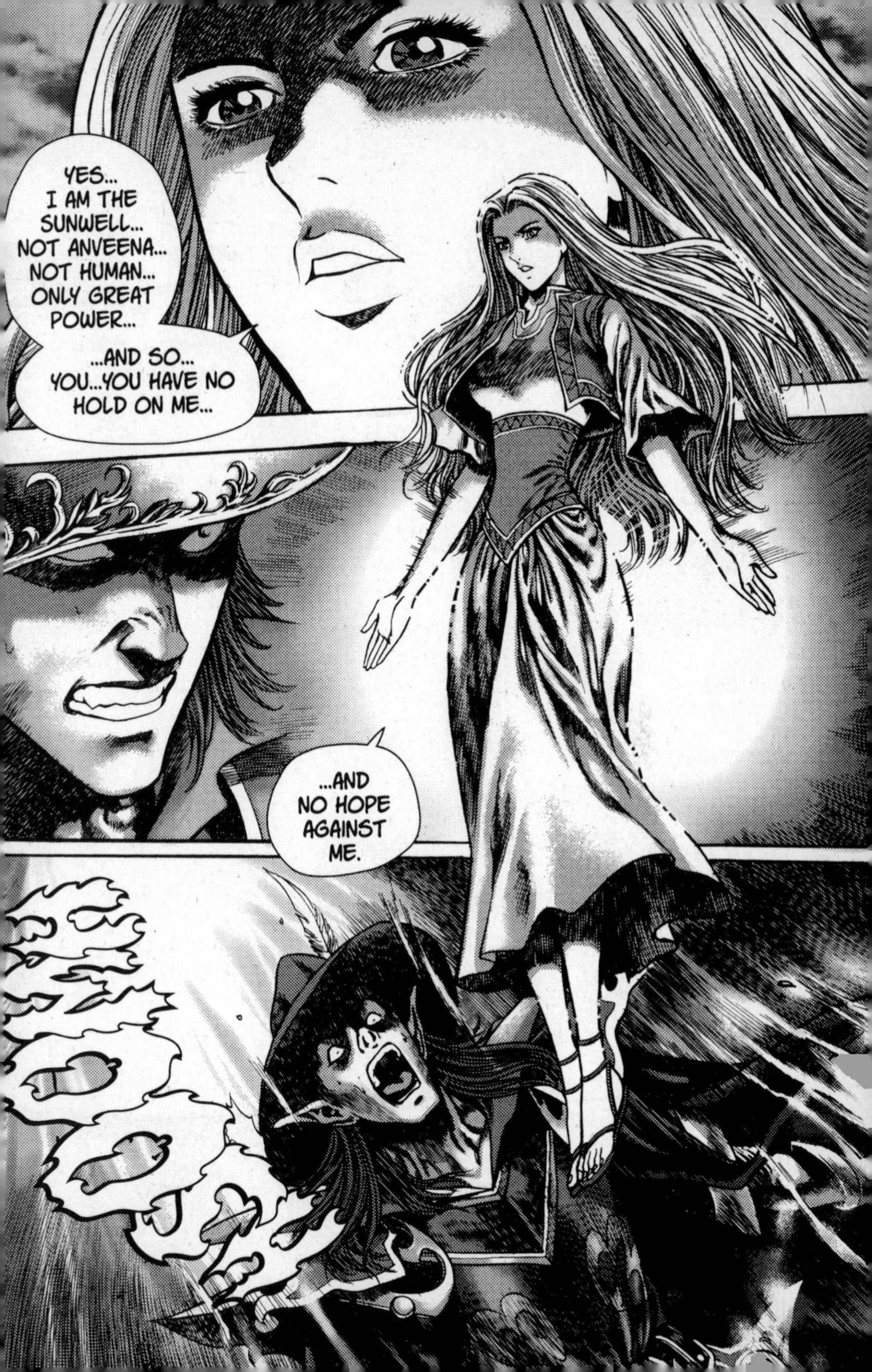
YES... I AM THE SUNWELL... NOT ANVEENA... NOT HUMAN... ONLY GREAT POWER...
...AND SO... YOU...YOU HAVE NO HOLD ON ME...
...AND NO HOPE AGAINST ME.

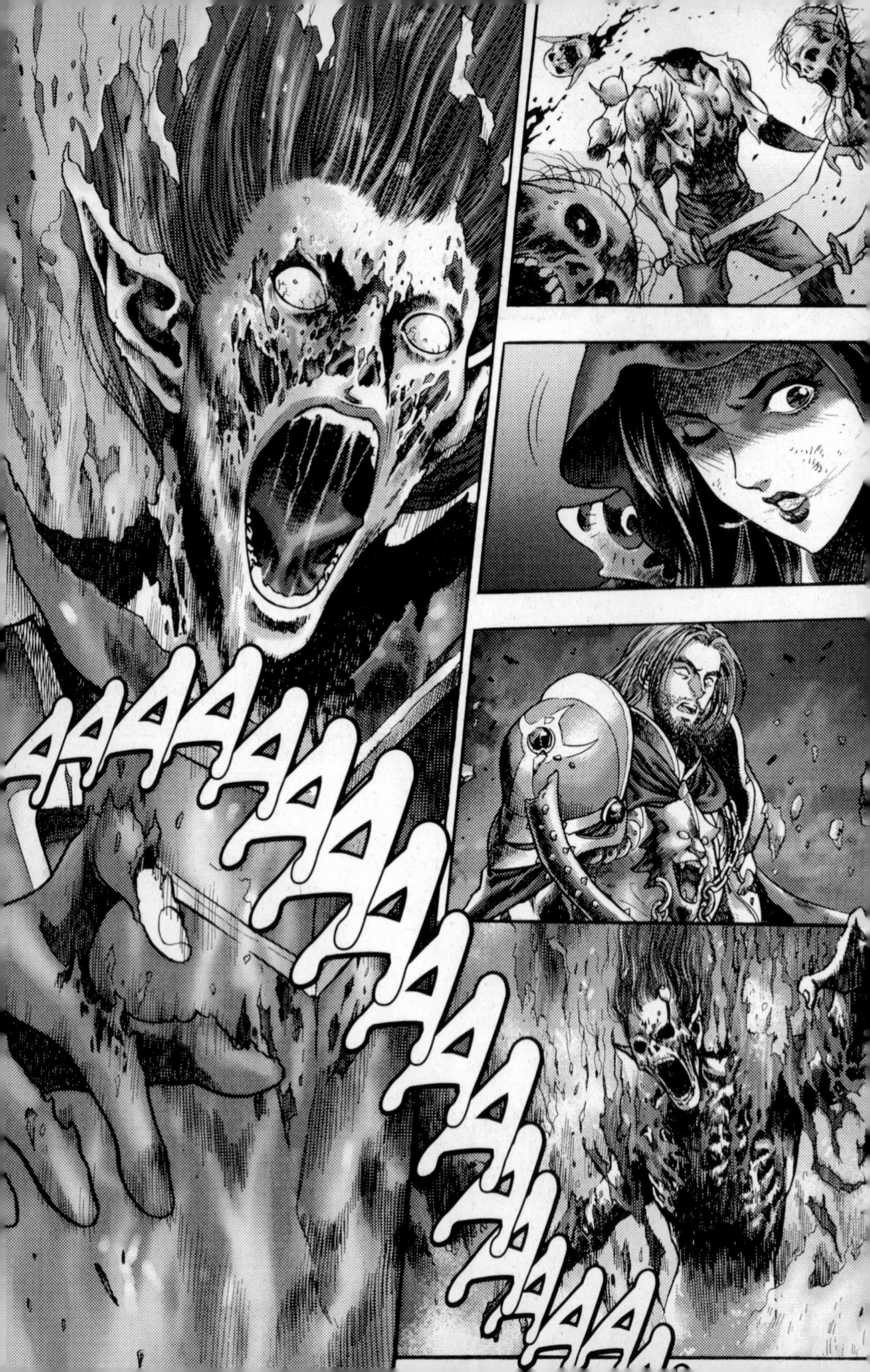
AAAAAAAAAAAAAAAAAAAAAAAA

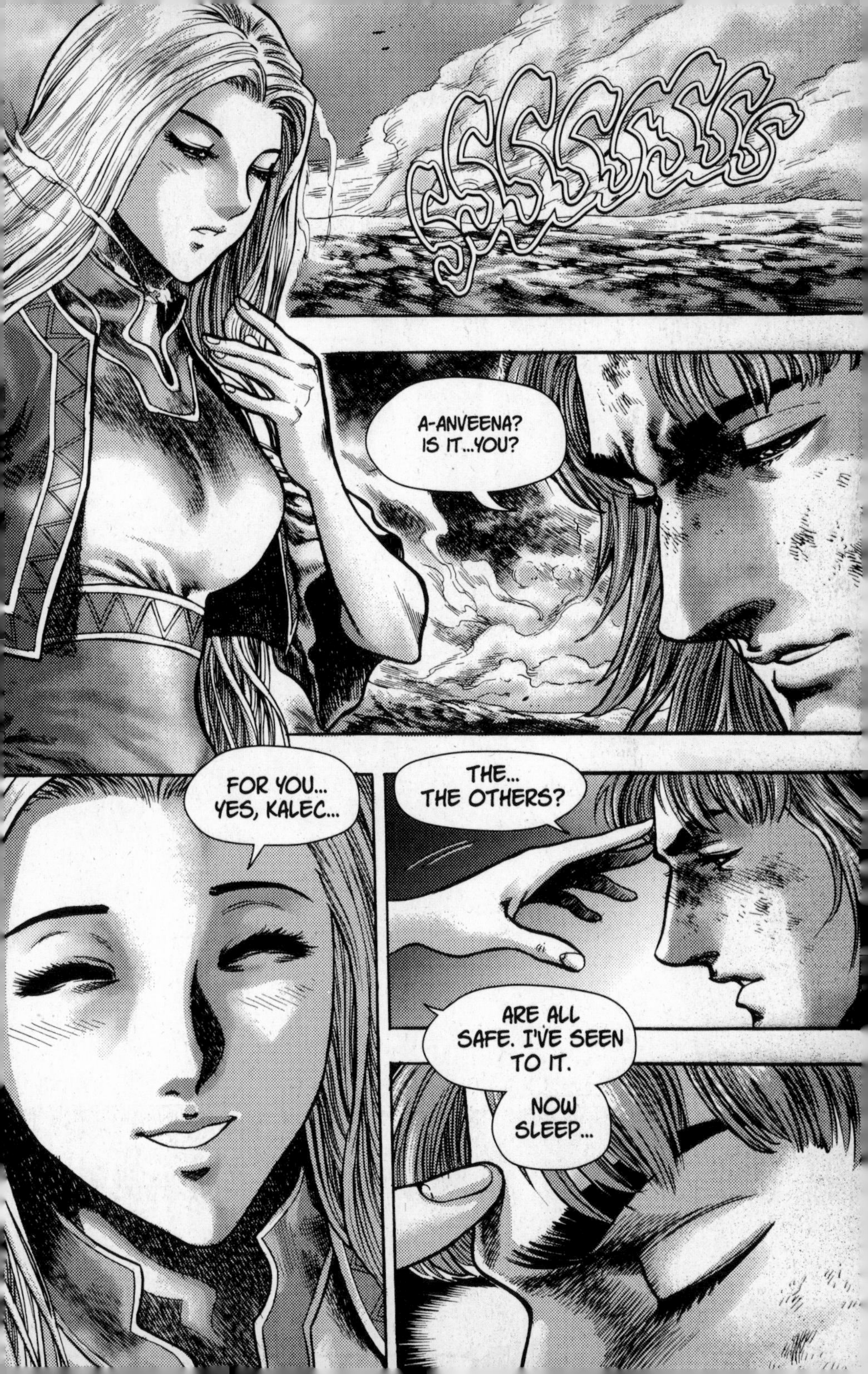
A-ANVEENA? IS IT...YOU?
FOR YOU... YES, KALEC...
THE... THE OTHERS?
ARE ALL SAFE. I'VE SEEN TO IT.
NOW SLEEP...

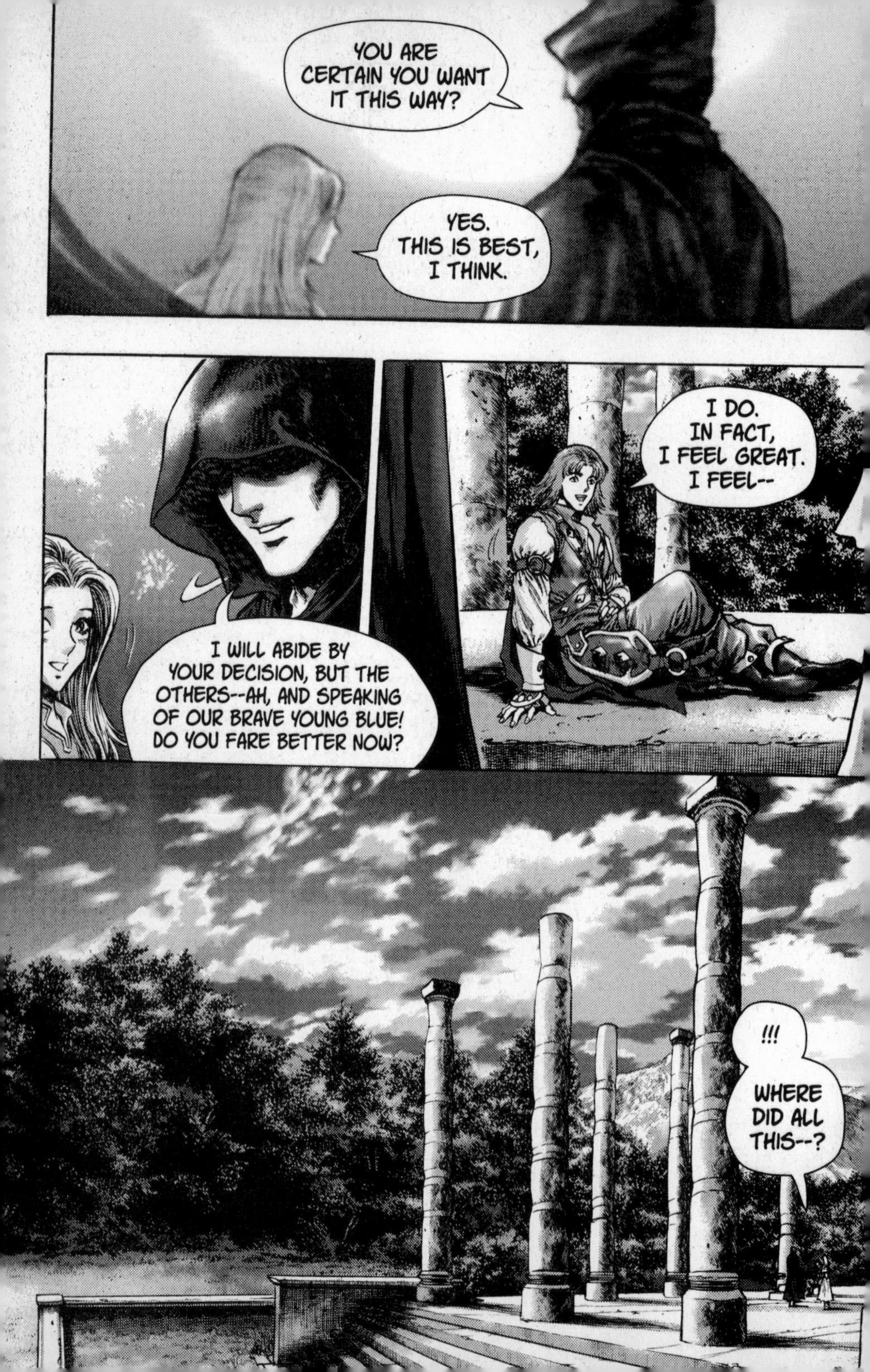
YOU ARE CERTAIN YOU WANT IT THIS WAY?
YES. THIS IS BEST, I THINK.
I WILL ABIDE BY YOUR DECISION, BUT THE OTHERS--AH, AND SPEAKING OF OUR BRAVE YOUNG BLUE! DO YOU FARE BETTER NOW?
I DO. IN FACT, I FEEL GREAT. I FEEL--
!!!
WHERE DID ALL THIS--?

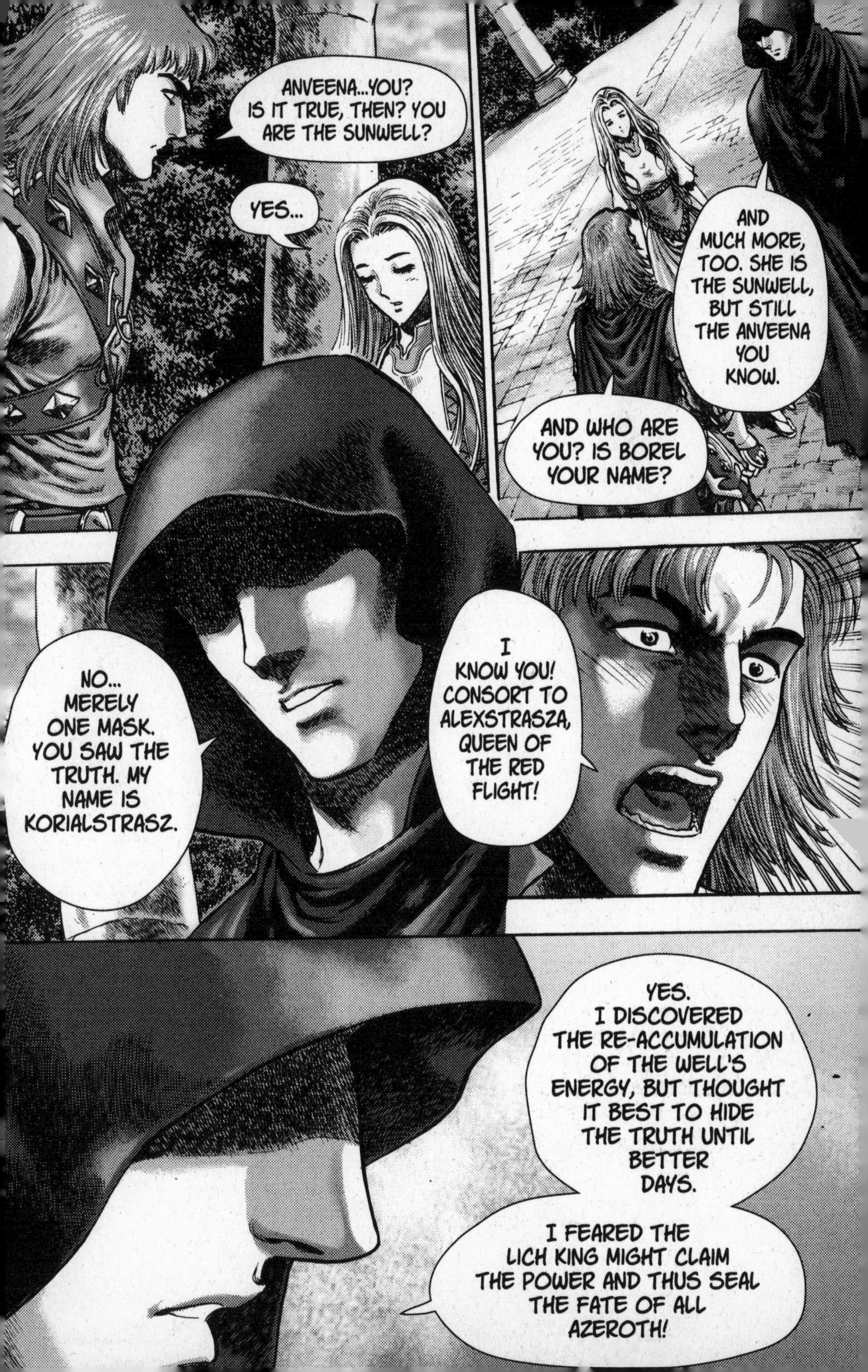
ANVEENA...YOU? IS IT TRUE, THEN? YOU ARE THE SUNWELL?
YES...
AND MUCH MORE, TOO. SHE IS THE SUNWELL, BUT STILL THE ANVEENA YOU KNOW.
AND WHO ARE YOU? IS BOREL YOUR NAME?
NO... MERELY ONE MASK. YOU SAW THE TRUTH. MY NAME IS KORIALSTRASZ.
I KNOW YOU! CONSORT TO ALEXSTRASZA, QUEEN OF THE RED FLIGHT!
YES. I DISCOVERED THE RE-ACCUMULATION OF THE WELL'S ENERGY, BUT THOUGHT IT BEST TO HIDE THE TRUTH UNTIL BETTER DAYS.
I FEARED THE LICH KING MIGHT CLAIM THE POWER AND THUS SEAL THE FATE OF ALL AZEROTH!

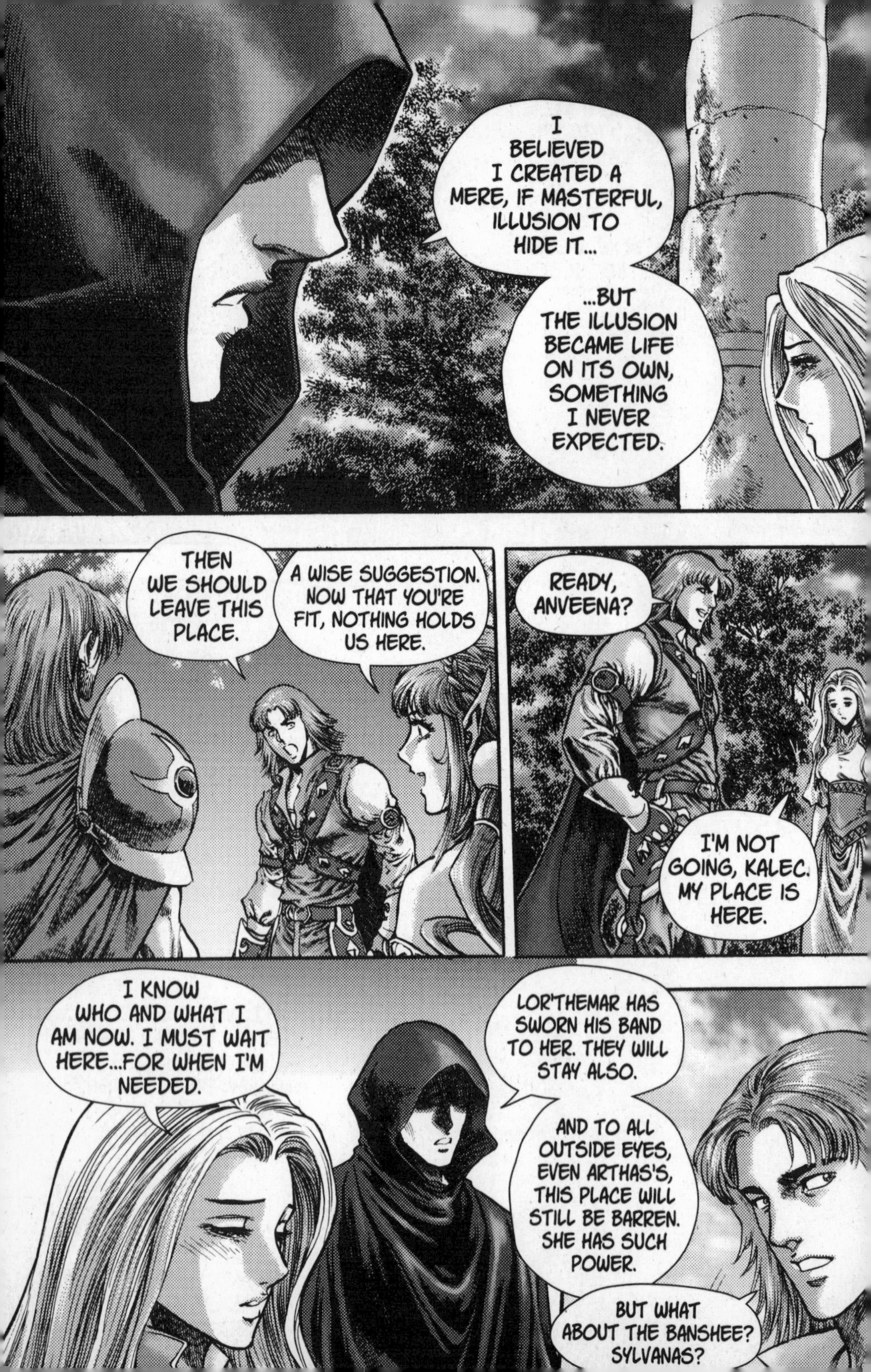
I BELIEVED I CREATED A MERE, IF MASTERFUL, ILLUSION TO HIDE IT...
...BUT THE ILLUSION BECAME LIFE ON ITS OWN, SOMETHING I NEVER EXPECTED.
THEN WE SHOULD LEAVE THIS PLACE.
A WISE SUGGESTION. NOW THAT YOU'RE FIT, NOTHING HOLDS US HERE.
READY, ANVEENA?
I'M NOT GOING, KALEC. MY PLACE IS HERE.
I KNOW WHO AND WHAT I AM NOW. I MUST WAIT HERE...FOR WHEN I'M NEEDED.
BUT WHAT ABOUT THE BANSHEE? SYLVANAS?
LOR'THEMAR HAS SWORN HIS BAND TO HER. THEY WILL STAY ALSO.
AND TO ALL OUTSIDE EYES, EVEN ARTHAS'S, THIS PLACE WILL STILL BE BARREN. SHE HAS SUCH POWER.

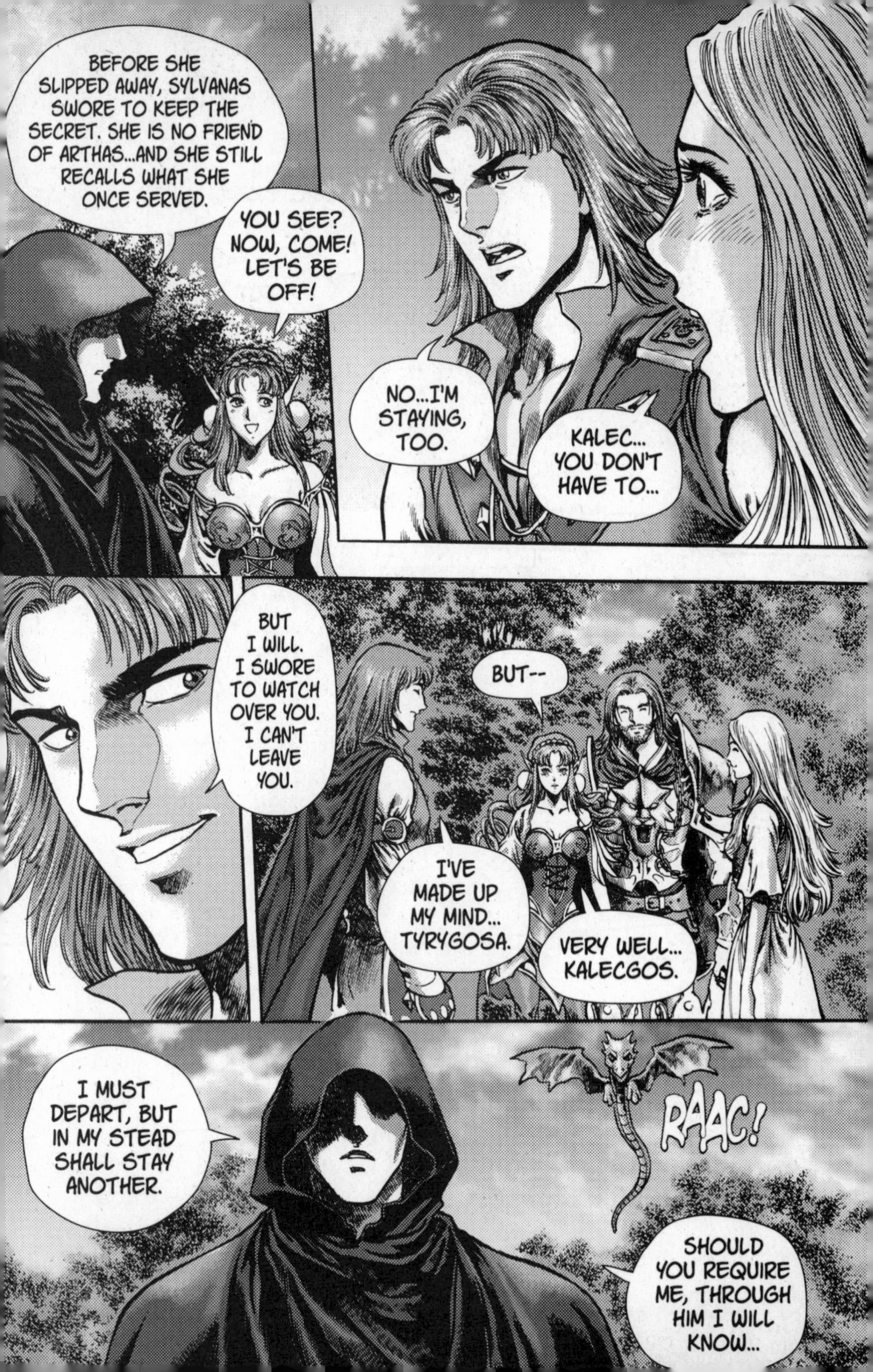
BEFORE SHE SLIPPED AWAY, SYLVANAS SWORE TO KEEP THE SECRET. SHE IS NO FRIEND OF ARTHAS...AND SHE STILL RECALLS WHAT SHE ONCE SERVED.
YOU SEE? NOW, COME! LET'S BE OFF!
NO...I'M STAYING, TOO.
KALEC... YOU DON'T HAVE TO...
BUT I WILL. I SWORE TO WATCH OVER YOU. I CAN'T LEAVE YOU.
BUT--
I'VE MADE UP MY MIND... TYRYGOSA.
VERY WELL... KALECGOS.
I MUST DEPART, BUT IN MY STEAD SHALL STAY ANOTHER.
RAAC!
SHOULD YOU REQUIRE ME, THROUGH HIM I WILL KNOW...

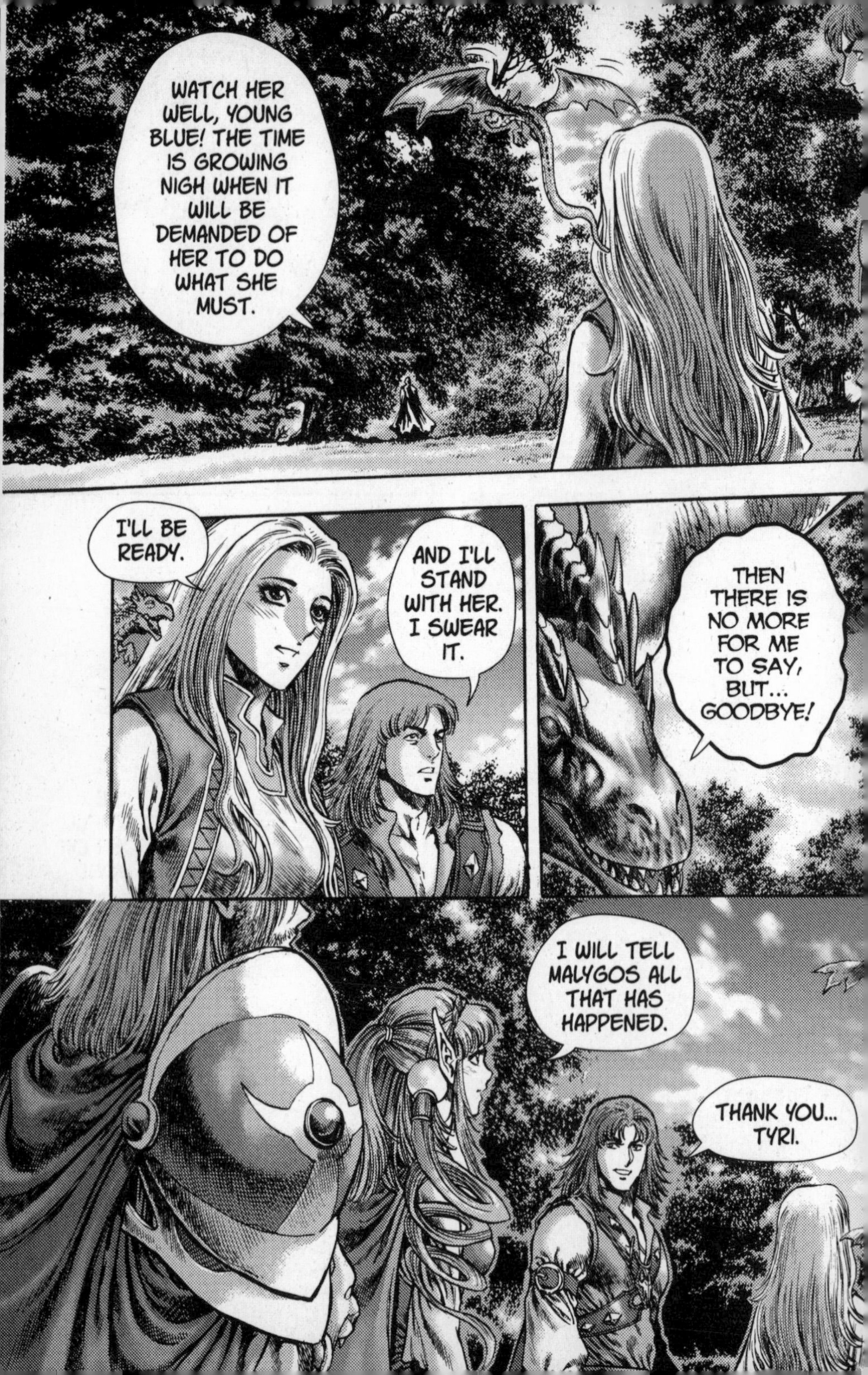
WATCH HER WELL, YOUNG BLUE! THE TIME IS GROWING NIGH WHEN IT WILL BE DEMANDED OF HER TO DO WHAT SHE MUST.
I'LL BE READY.
AND I'LL STAND WITH HER. I SWEAR IT.
THEN THERE IS NO MORE FOR ME TO SAY, BUT... GOODBYE!
I WILL TELL MALYGOS ALL THAT HAS HAPPENED.
THANK YOU... TYRI.

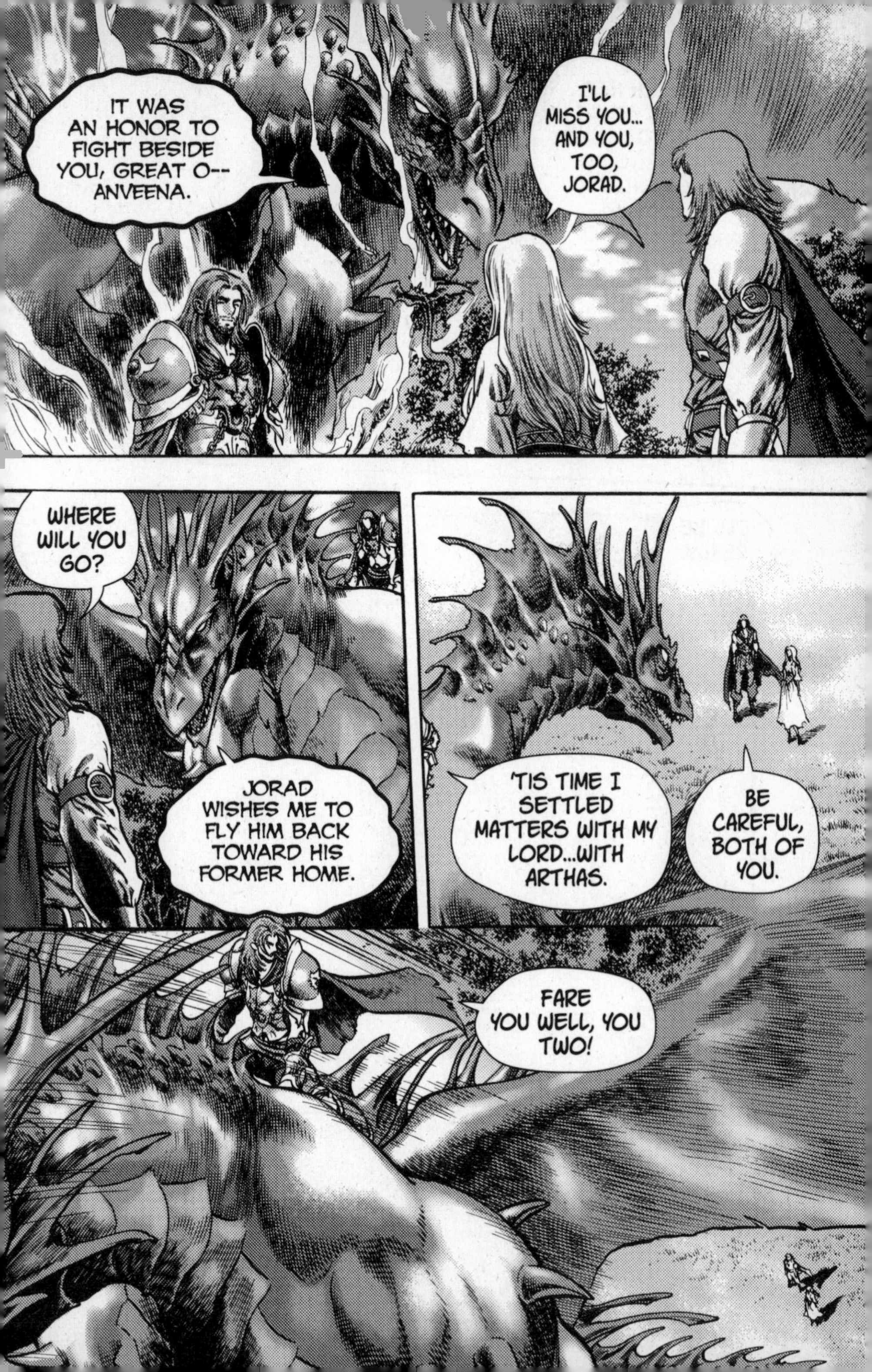
IT WAS AN HONOR TO FIGHT BESIDE YOU, GREAT O-- ANVEENA.
I'LL MISS YOU... AND YOU, TOO, JORAD.
WHERE WILL YOU GO?
JORAD WISHES ME TO FLY HIM BACK TOWARD HIS FORMER HOME.
'TIS TIME I SETTLED MATTERS WITH MY LORD...WITH ARTHAS.
BE CAREFUL, BOTH OF YOU.
FARE YOU WELL, YOU TWO!

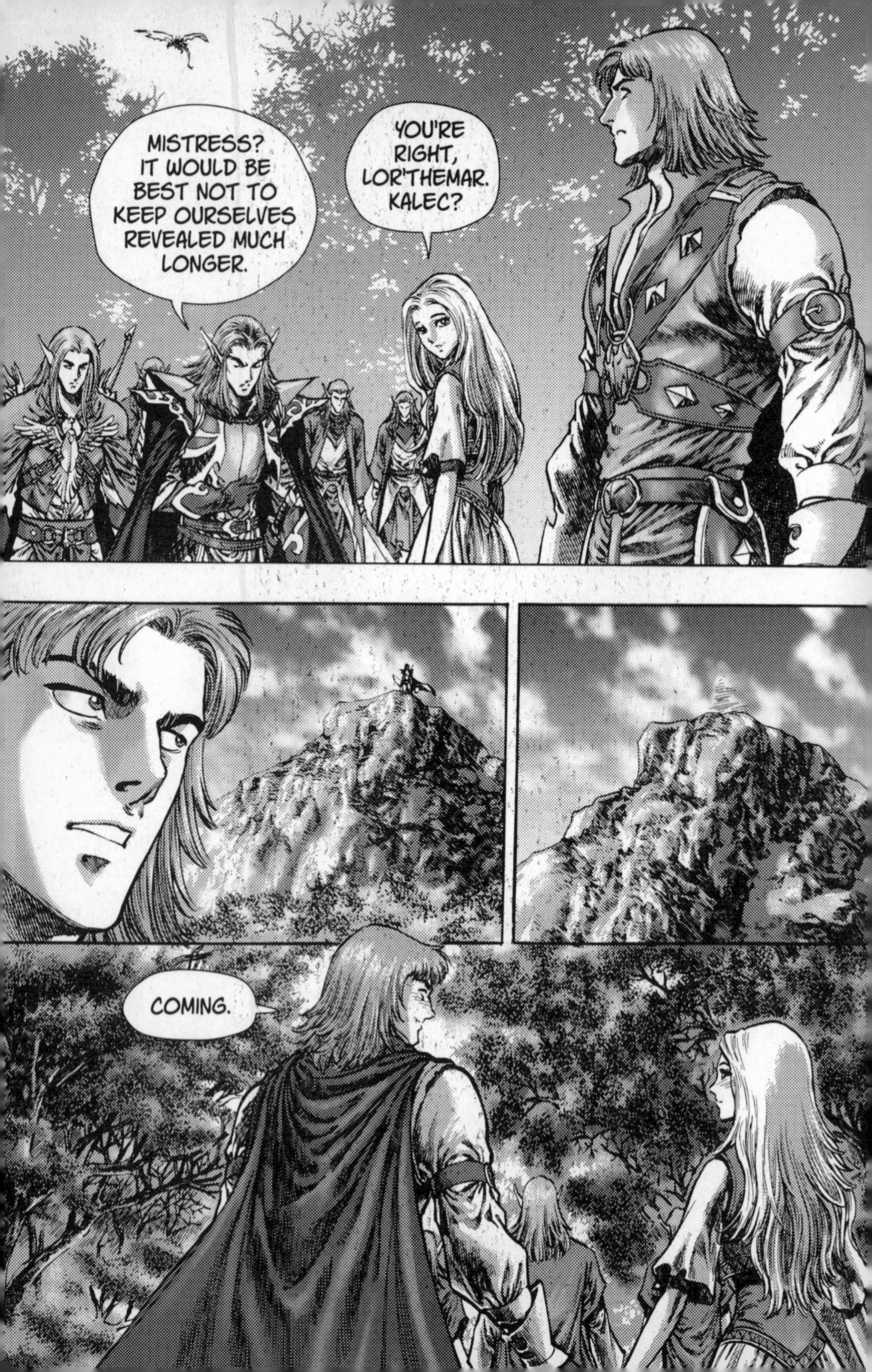
MISTRESS? IT WOULD BE BEST NOT TO KEEP OURSELVES REVEALED MUCH LONGER.
YOU'RE RIGHT, LOR'THEMAR. KALEC?
COMING.

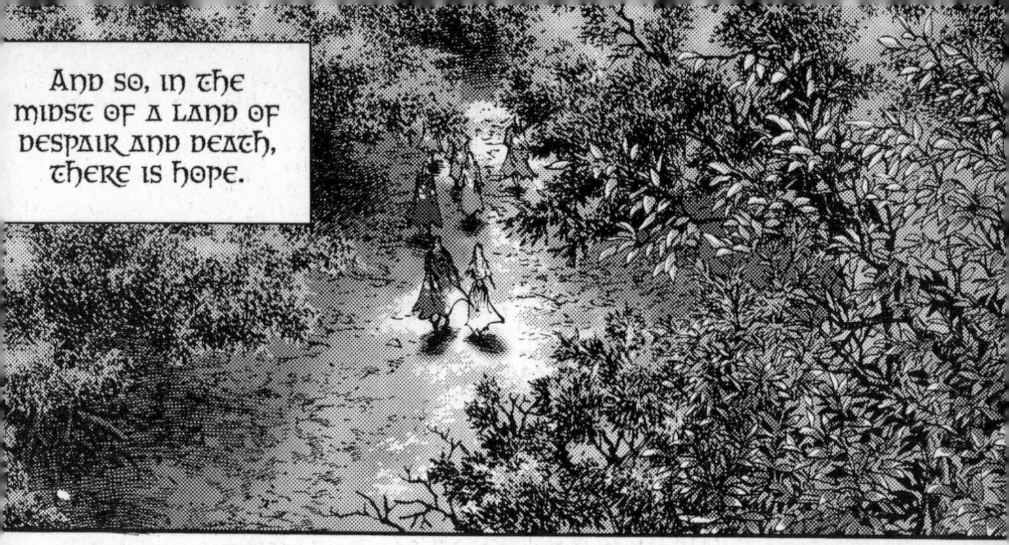
And so, in the midst of a land of despair and death, there is hope.
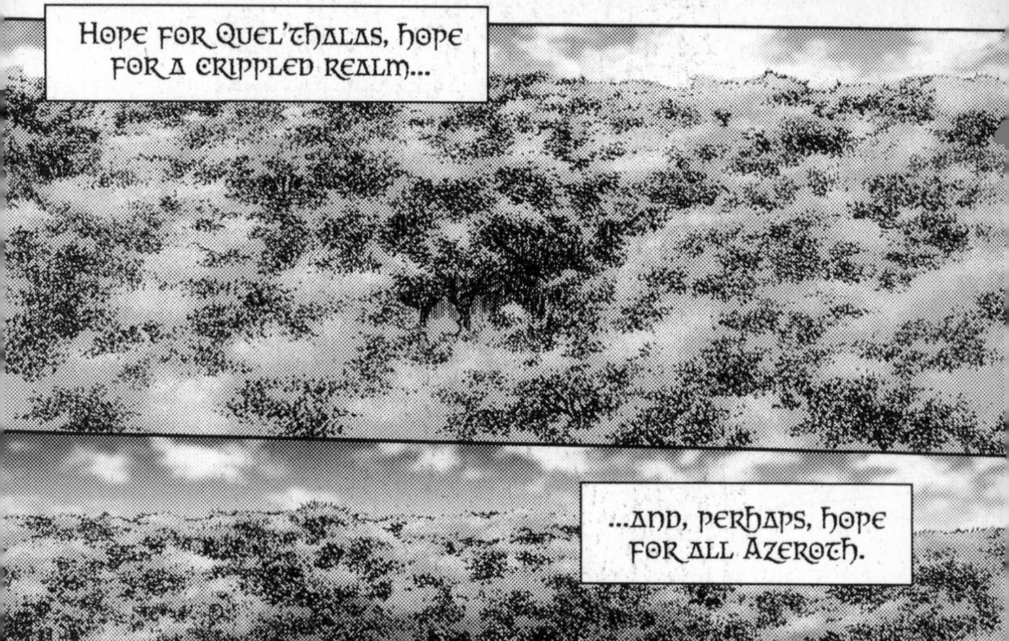
Hope for Quel'thalas, hope for a crippled realm...
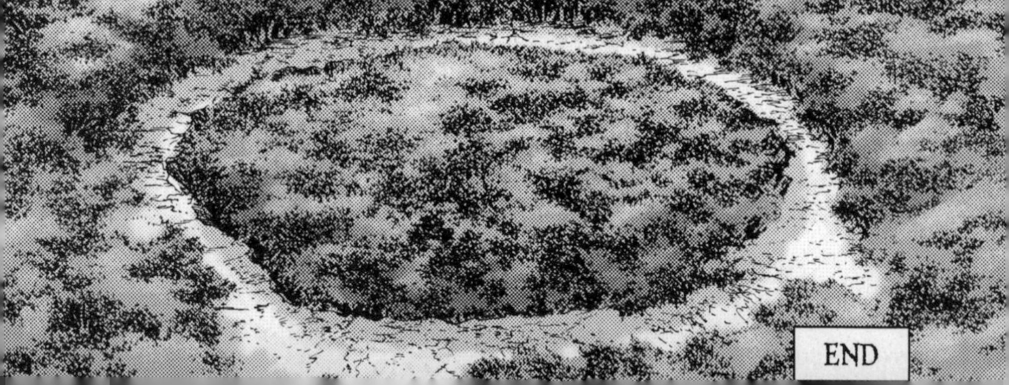
...and, perhaps, hope for all Azeroth.
END

A MESSAGE FROM RICHARD A. KNAAK

I have always been a big fan of minotaurs, be they the ones
Greek myth, the imperial warriors of Ansalon in *Dragonlance*,
of course, the tauren of *World of Warcraft*. I knew that at so
point I wanted to include a tauren in my stories, and that oppor
nity came quickly with *Warcraft: The Sunwell Trilogy*.

Trag Highmountain epitomized the tauren race: a powerful, ho
orable warrior deathly loyal to his friends. However, as you ha
read in the trilogy, in the case of Baron Valimar Mordis this lo
alty proved to be a double-edged sword. When finally coming
the realization that the Baron was no longer the man he knew l
a monster intent on evil, Trag sacrificed himself to stop his form
friend's insidious plans.

But you can't keep a good tauren down--even if he's had a mou
tain dropped on him. There was just something about Trag th
demanded I use him again, so an idea was born that I proposed
Blizzard. The thought of an undead tauren intrigued them, a
so the story of Trag's rise from the grave and the resulting con
quences came to fruition. That tale, serialized in the first four v
umes of the *Warcraft: Legends* anthology series, is now present
together for the first time in this volume.

And so, without further adieu, we enter a forest where a taur
shaman is about to have a most unexpected visitor...

Richard A. Knaak

CHAPTER ONE

FALLEN

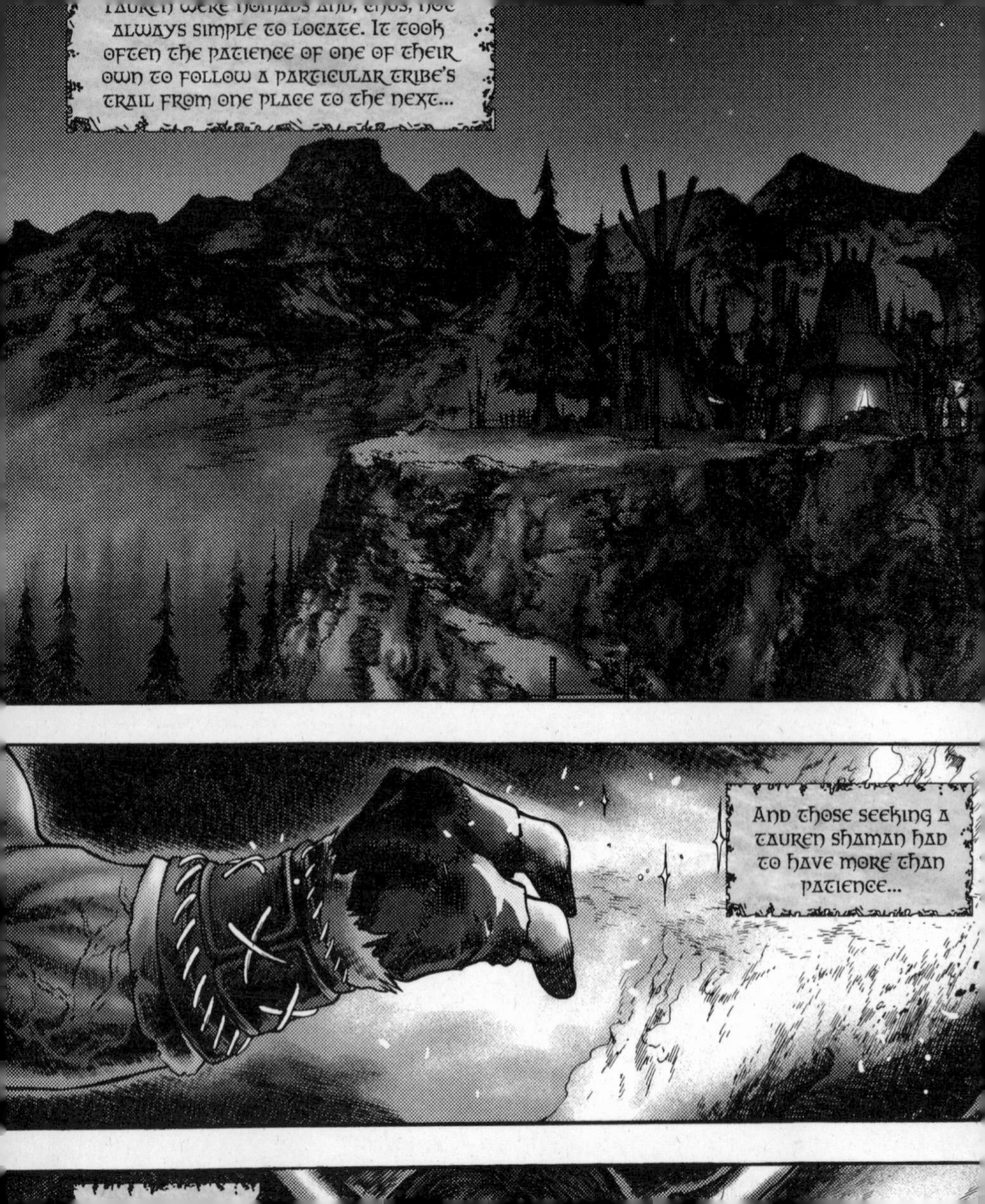
Tauren were nomads and, thus, not always simple to locate. It took often the patience of one of their own to follow a particular tribe's trail from one place to the next...
And those seeking a tauren shaman had to have more than patience...

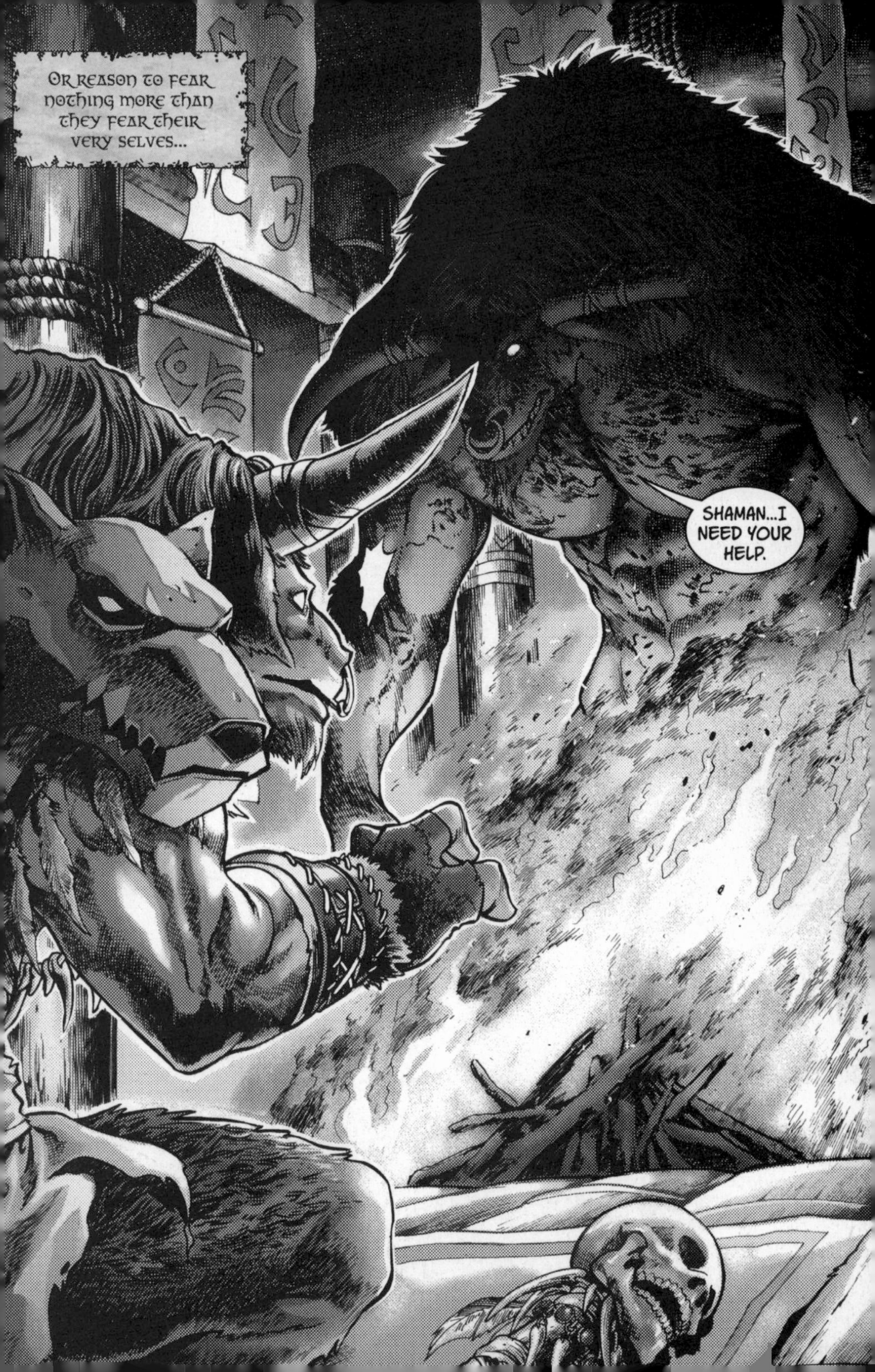
OR REASON TO FEAR NOTHING MORE THAN THEY FEAR THEIR VERY SELVES...
SHAMAN...I NEED YOUR HELP.

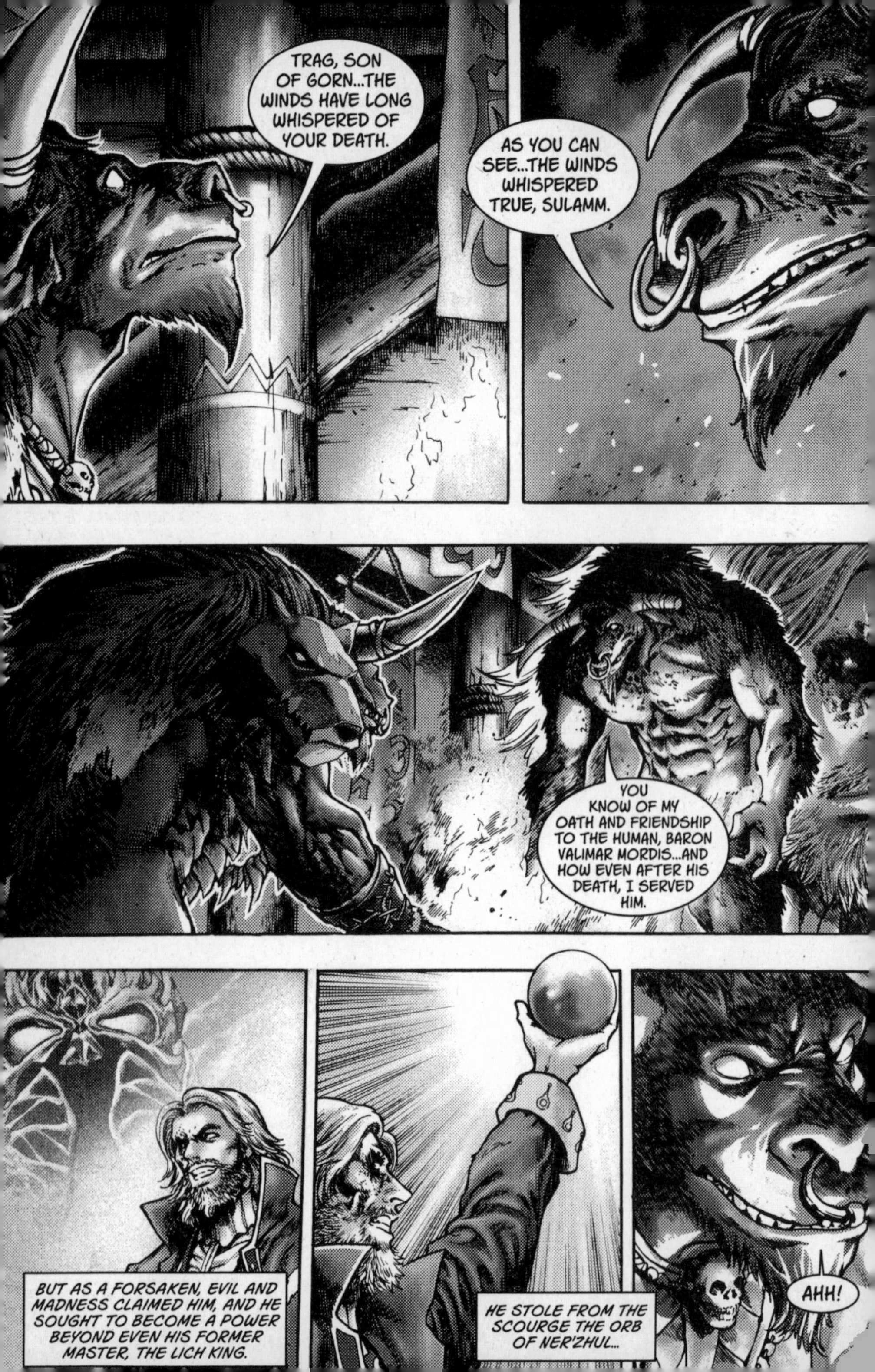
TRAG, SON OF GORN...THE WINDS HAVE LONG WHISPERED OF YOUR DEATH.
AS YOU CAN SEE...THE WINDS WHISPERED TRUE, SULAMM.
YOU KNOW OF MY OATH AND FRIENDSHIP TO THE HUMAN, BARON VALIMAR MORDIS...AND HOW EVEN AFTER HIS DEATH, I SERVED HIM.
BUT AS A FORSAKEN, EVIL AND MADNESS CLAIMED HIM, AND HE SOUGHT TO BECOME A POWER BEYOND EVEN HIS FORMER MASTER, THE LICH KING.
HE STOLE FROM THE SCOURGE THE ORB OF NER'ZHUL...
AHH!

...AND USED IT TO RAISE A TERRIBLE MONSTER!

I DID NOTHING THEN, BUT A YOUNG FEMALE WITH SPECIAL GIFTS CAME INTO HIS GRIP, A FEMALE WHO COULD MAKE THE ORB A THOUSAND TIMES MORE TERRIBLE!

HER FRIENDS SOUGHT TO SAVE HER...

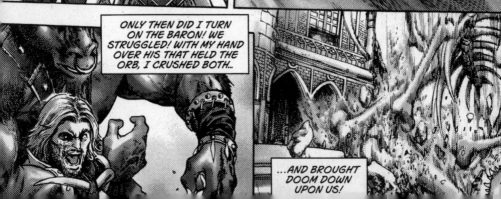

ONLY THEN DID I TURN ON THE BARON! WE STRUGGLED! WITH MY HAND OVER HIS THAT HELD THE ORB, I CRUSHED BOTH...

...AND BROUGHT DOOM DOWN UPON US!

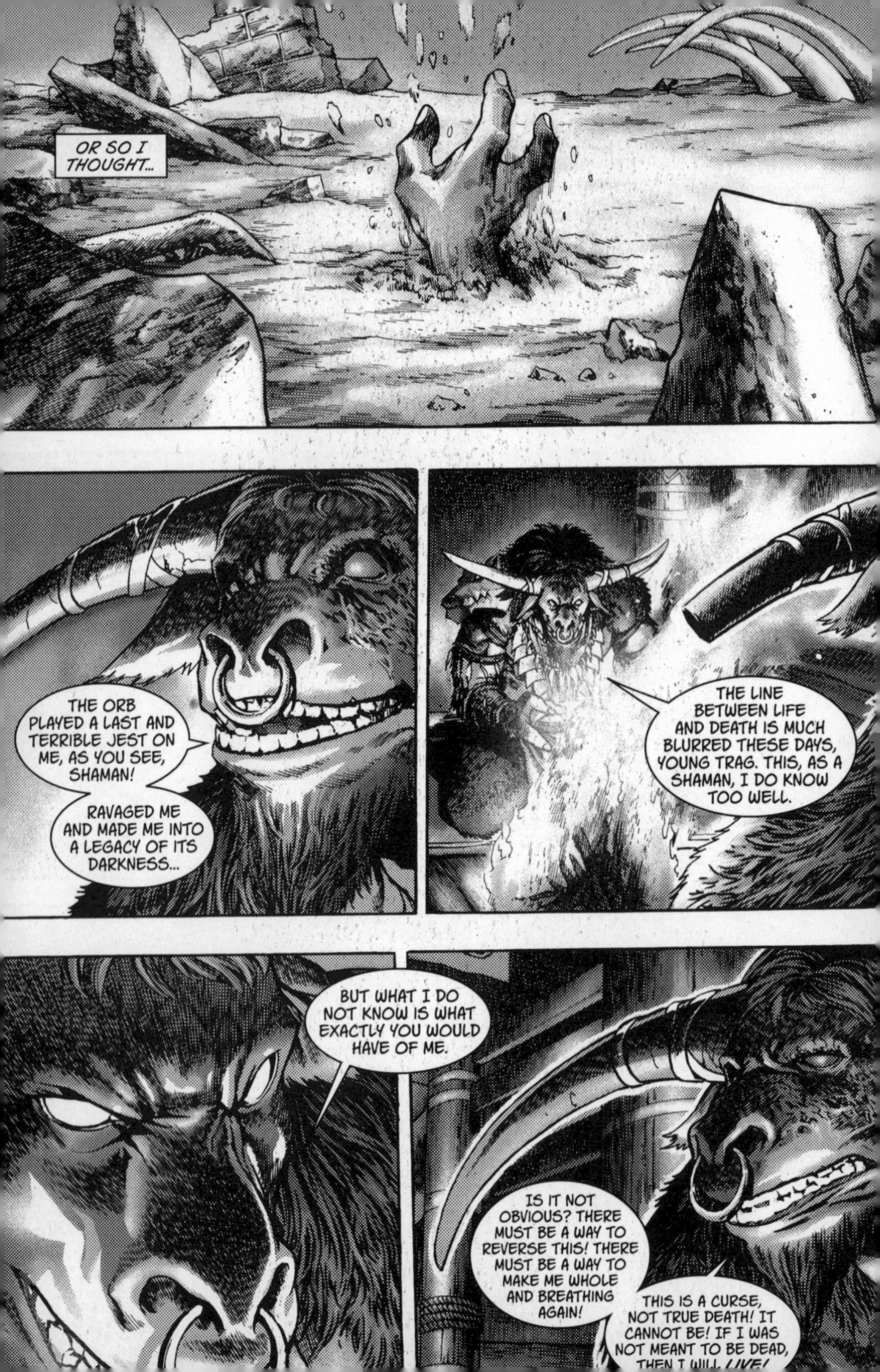
OR SO I THOUGHT...
THE ORB PLAYED A LAST AND TERRIBLE JEST ON ME, AS YOU SEE, SHAMAN!
RAVAGED ME AND MADE ME INTO A LEGACY OF ITS DARKNESS...
THE LINE BETWEEN LIFE AND DEATH IS MUCH BLURRED THESE DAYS, YOUNG TRAG. THIS, AS A SHAMAN, I DO KNOW TOO WELL.
BUT WHAT I DO NOT KNOW IS WHAT EXACTLY YOU WOULD HAVE OF ME.
IS IT NOT OBVIOUS? THERE MUST BE A WAY TO REVERSE THIS! THERE MUST BE A WAY TO MAKE ME WHOLE AND BREATHING AGAIN!
THIS IS A CURSE, NOT TRUE DEATH! IT CANNOT BE! IF I WAS NOT MEANT TO BE DEAD, THEN I WILL *LIVE!*

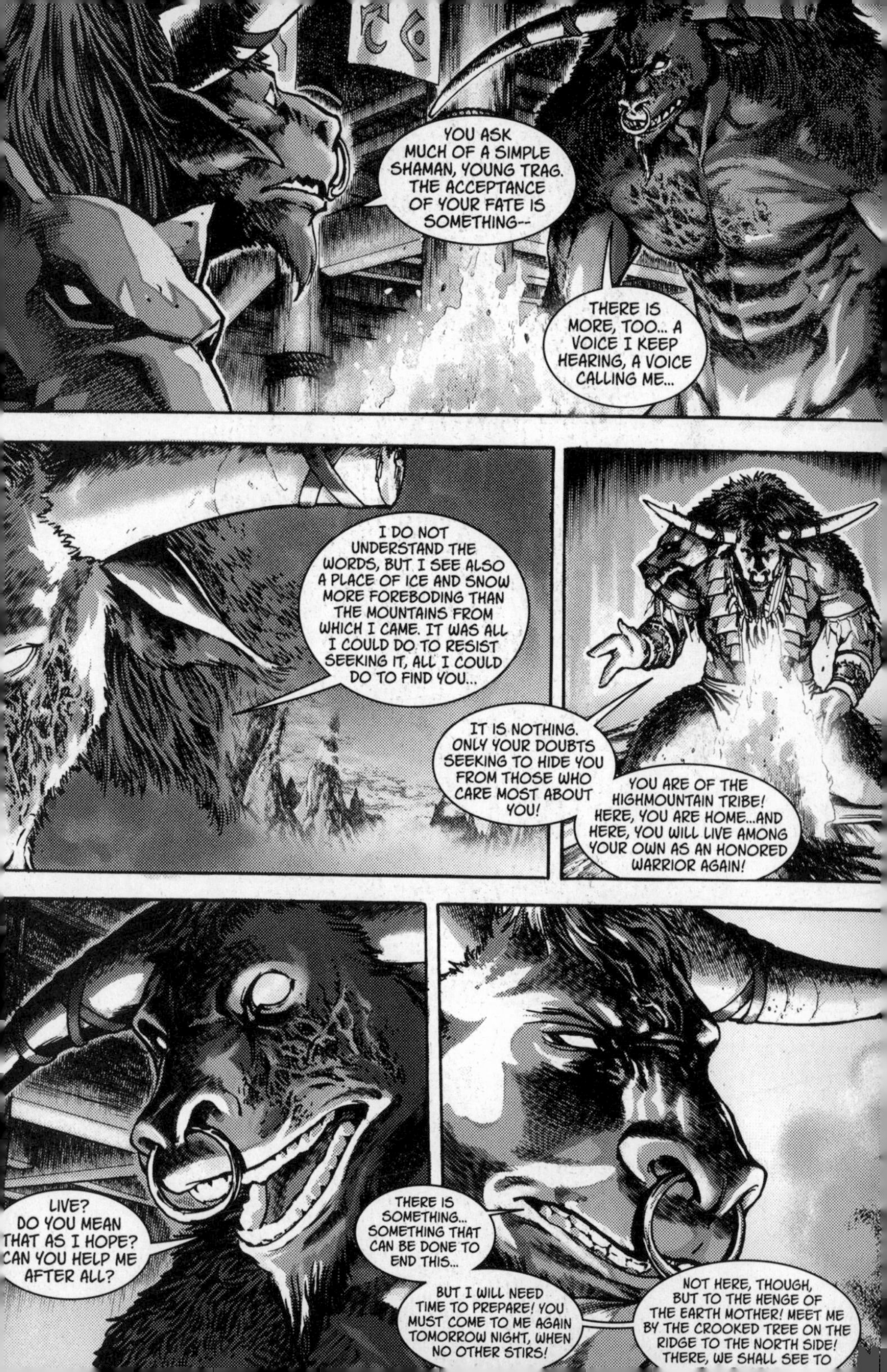
YOU ASK MUCH OF A SIMPLE SHAMAN, YOUNG TRAG. THE ACCEPTANCE OF YOUR FATE IS SOMETHING--
THERE IS MORE, TOO... A VOICE I KEEP HEARING, A VOICE CALLING ME...
I DO NOT UNDERSTAND THE WORDS, BUT I SEE ALSO A PLACE OF ICE AND SNOW MORE FOREBODING THAN THE MOUNTAINS FROM WHICH I CAME. IT WAS ALL I COULD DO TO RESIST SEEKING IT, ALL I COULD DO TO FIND YOU...
IT IS NOTHING. ONLY YOUR DOUBTS SEEKING TO HIDE YOU FROM THOSE WHO CARE MOST ABOUT YOU!
YOU ARE OF THE HIGHMOUNTAIN TRIBE! HERE, YOU ARE HOME...AND HERE, YOU WILL LIVE AMONG YOUR OWN AS AN HONORED WARRIOR AGAIN!
LIVE? DO YOU MEAN THAT AS I HOPE? CAN YOU HELP ME AFTER ALL?
THERE IS SOMETHING... SOMETHING THAT CAN BE DONE TO END THIS...
BUT I WILL NEED TIME TO PREPARE! YOU MUST COME TO ME AGAIN TOMORROW NIGHT, WHEN NO OTHER STIRS!
NOT HERE, THOUGH, BUT TO THE HENGE OF THE EARTH MOTHER! MEET ME BY THE CROOKED TREE ON THE RIDGE TO THE NORTH SIDE! THERE, WE SHALL SEE TO

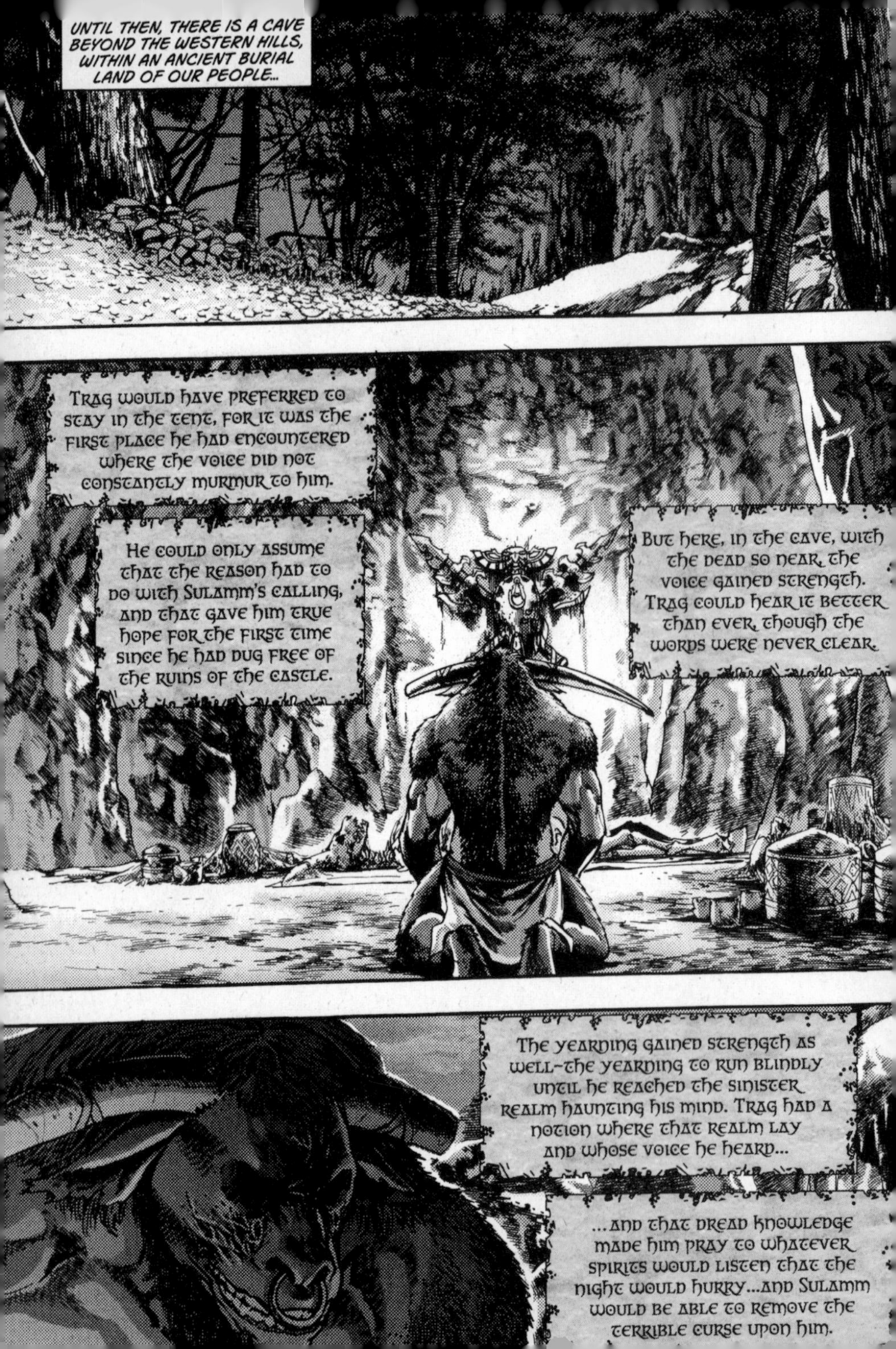
UNTIL THEN, THERE IS A CAVE BEYOND THE WESTERN HILLS, WITHIN AN ANCIENT BURIAL LAND OF OUR PEOPLE...
Trag would have preferred to stay in the tent, for it was the first place he had encountered where the voice did not constantly murmur to him.
He could only assume that the reason had to do with Sulamm's calling, and that gave him true hope for the first time since he had dug free of the ruins of the castle.
But here, in the cave, with the dead so near, the voice gained strength. Trag could hear it better than ever, though the words were never clear.
The yearning gained strength as well—the yearning to run blindly until he reached the sinister realm haunting his mind. Trag had a notion where that realm lay and whose voice he heard...
...and that dread knowledge made him pray to whatever spirits would listen that the night would hurry...and Sulamm would be able to remove the terrible curse upon him.

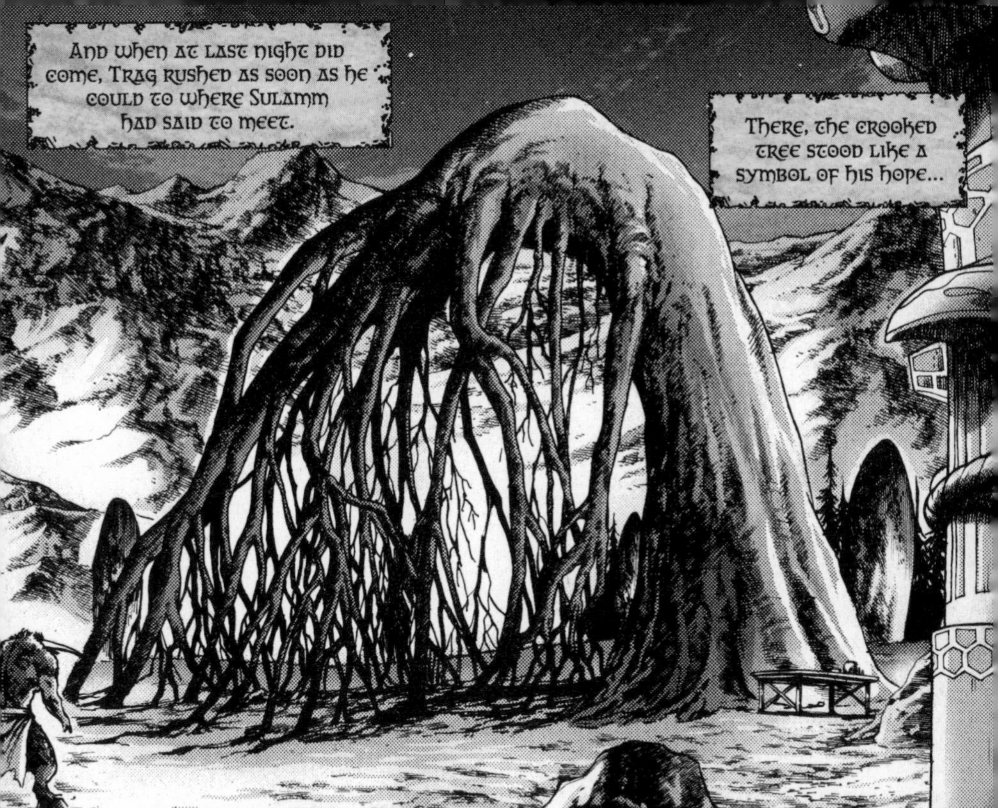
And when at last night did come, Trag rushed as soon as he could to where Sulamm had said to meet.
There, the crooked tree stood like a symbol of his hope...

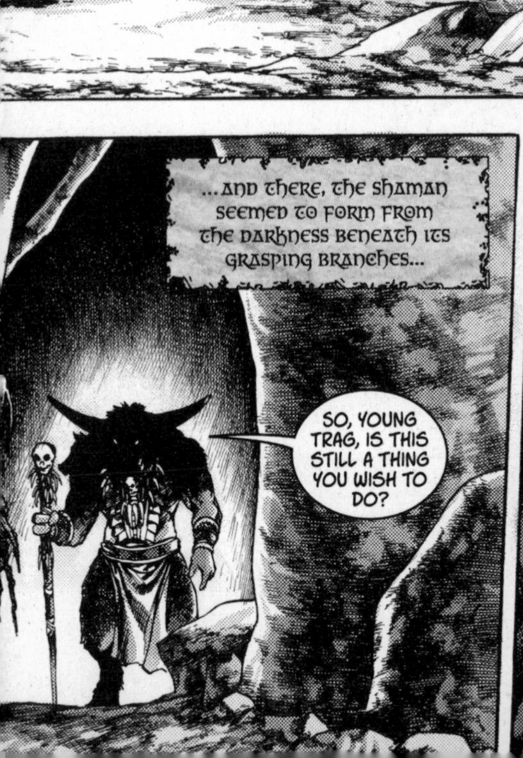
...and there, the shaman seemed to form from the darkness beneath its grasping branches...
SO, YOUNG TRAG, IS THIS STILL A THING YOU WISH TO DO?

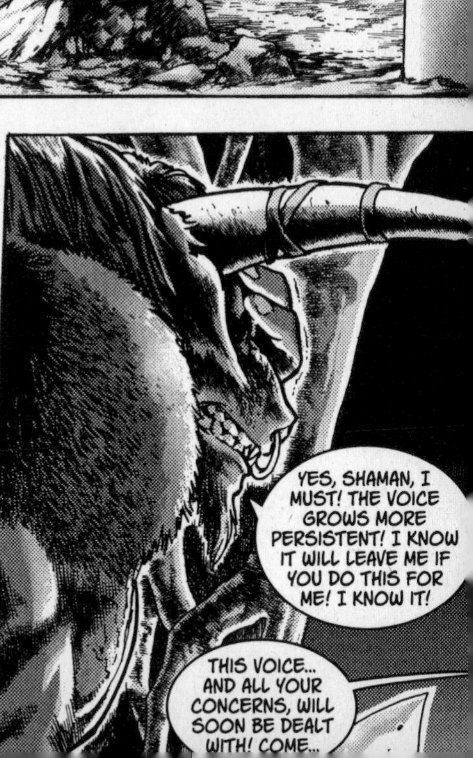
YES, SHAMAN, I MUST! THE VOICE GROWS MORE PERSISTENT! I KNOW IT WILL LEAVE ME IF YOU DO THIS FOR ME! I KNOW IT!
THIS VOICE... AND ALL YOUR CONCERNS, WILL SOON BE DEALT WITH! COME.

WHAT'S THIS?

YOU MUST KNEEL IN THE MIDDLE OF THIS PATTERN WITH YOUR EYES SHUT. I WILL SIT BEYOND YOUR HEAD.

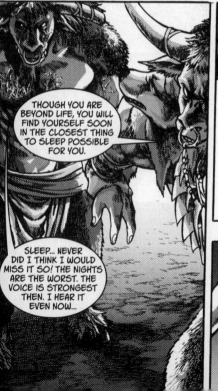

THOUGH YOU ARE BEYOND LIFE, YOU WILL FIND YOURSELF SOON IN THE CLOSEST THING TO SLEEP POSSIBLE FOR YOU.

SLEEP... NEVER DID I THINK I WOULD MISS IT SO! THE NIGHTS ARE THE WORST. THE VOICE IS STRONGEST THEN. I HEAR IT EVEN NOW...

BE AT EASE... I WILL SOON END YOUR SUFFERING...

TO LIVE AGAIN...

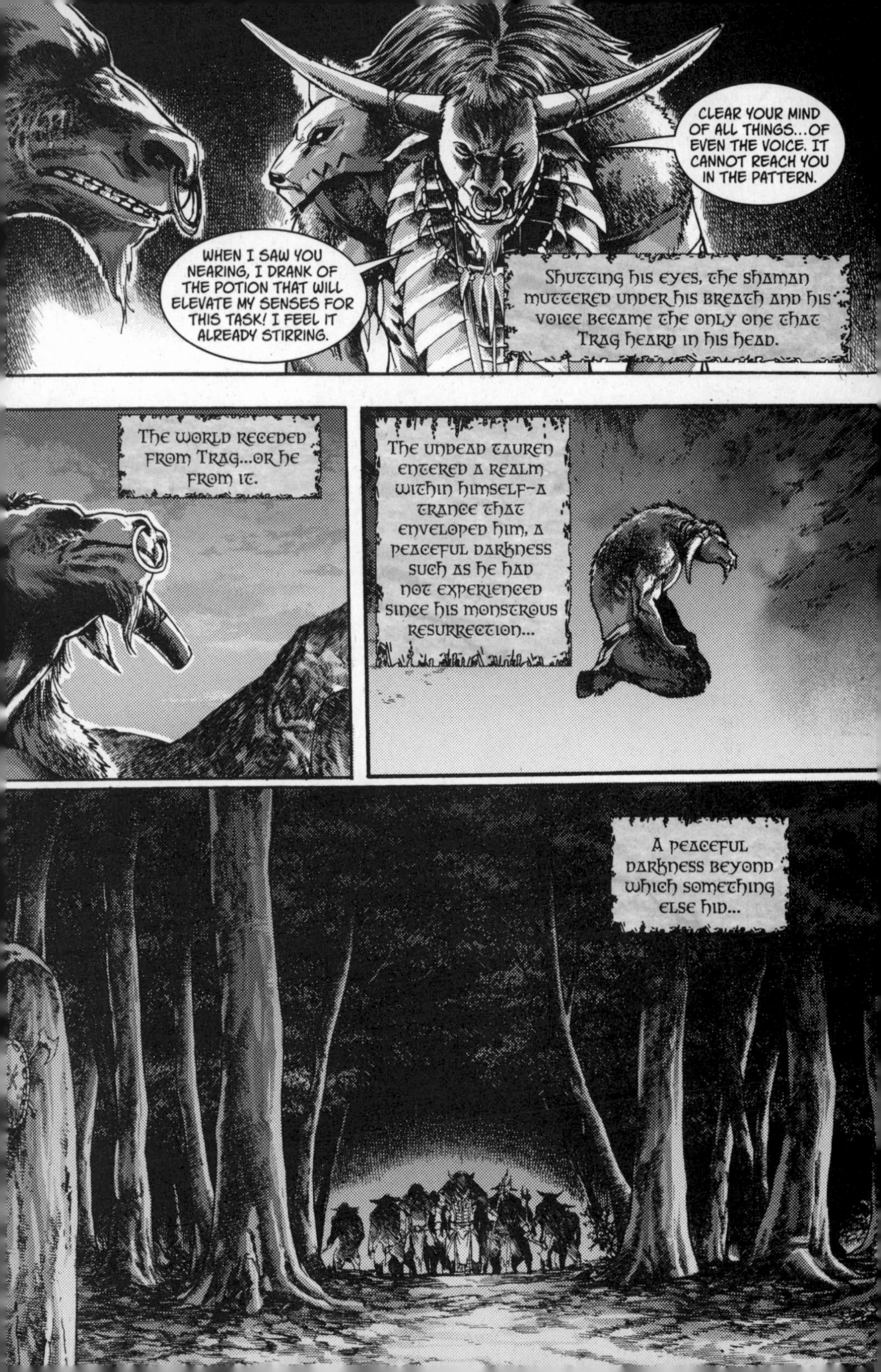

WHEN I SAW YOU NEARING, I DRANK OF THE POTION THAT WILL ELEVATE MY SENSES FOR THIS TASK! I FEEL IT ALREADY STIRRING.
CLEAR YOUR MIND OF ALL THINGS...OF EVEN THE VOICE. IT CANNOT REACH YOU IN THE PATTERN.
Shutting his eyes, the shaman muttered under his breath and his voice became the only one that Trag heard in his head.
The world receded from Trag...or he from it.
The undead tauren entered a realm within himself—a trance that enveloped him, a peaceful darkness such as he had not experienced since his monstrous resurrection...
A peaceful darkness beyond which something else hid...

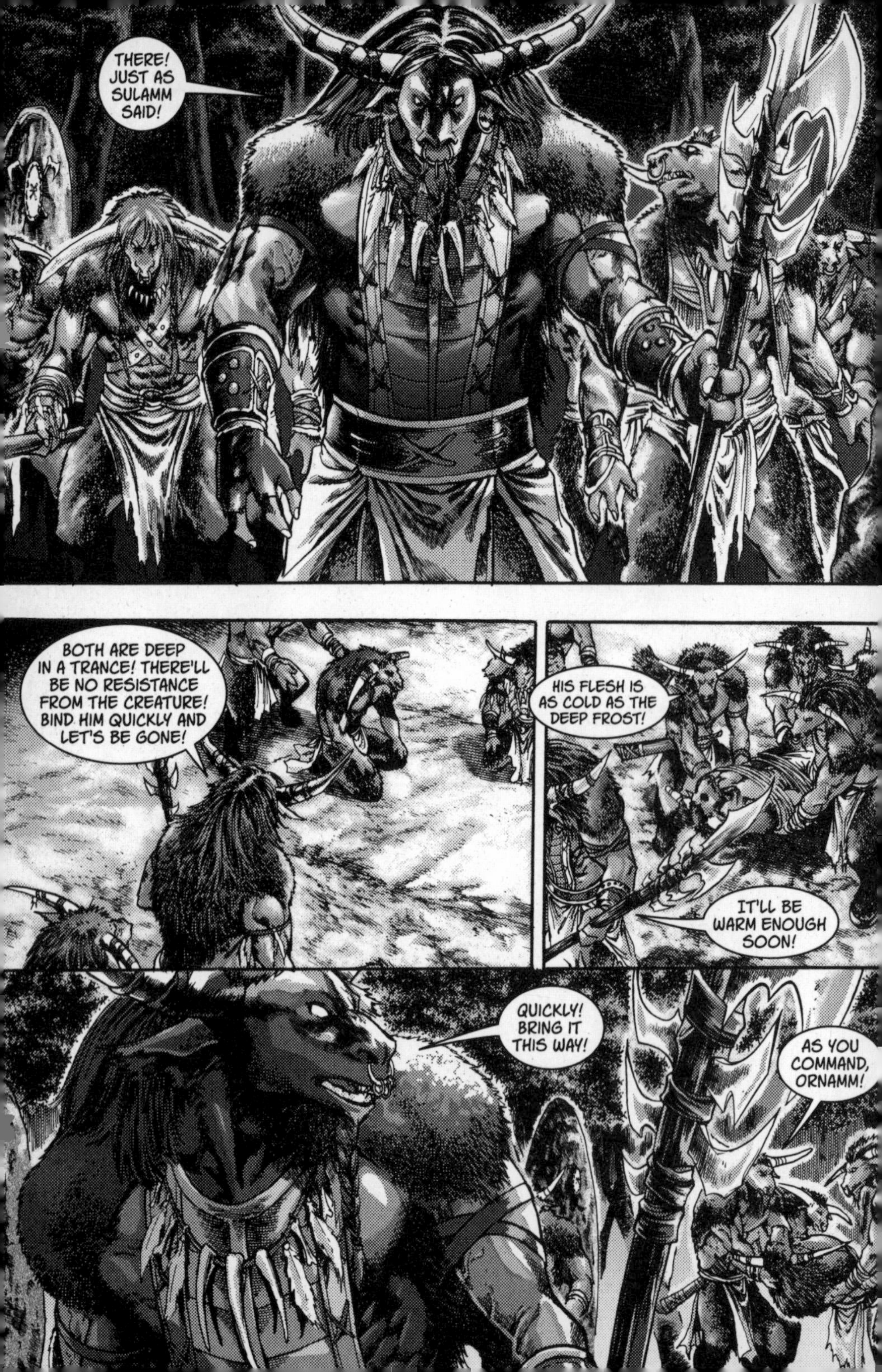
THERE! JUST AS SULAMM SAID!
BOTH ARE DEEP IN A TRANCE! THERE'LL BE NO RESISTANCE FROM THE CREATURE! BIND HIM QUICKLY AND LET'S BE GONE!
HIS FLESH IS AS COLD AS THE DEEP FROST!
IT'LL BE WARM ENOUGH SOON!
QUICKLY! BRING IT THIS WAY!
AS YOU COMMAND, ORNAMM!

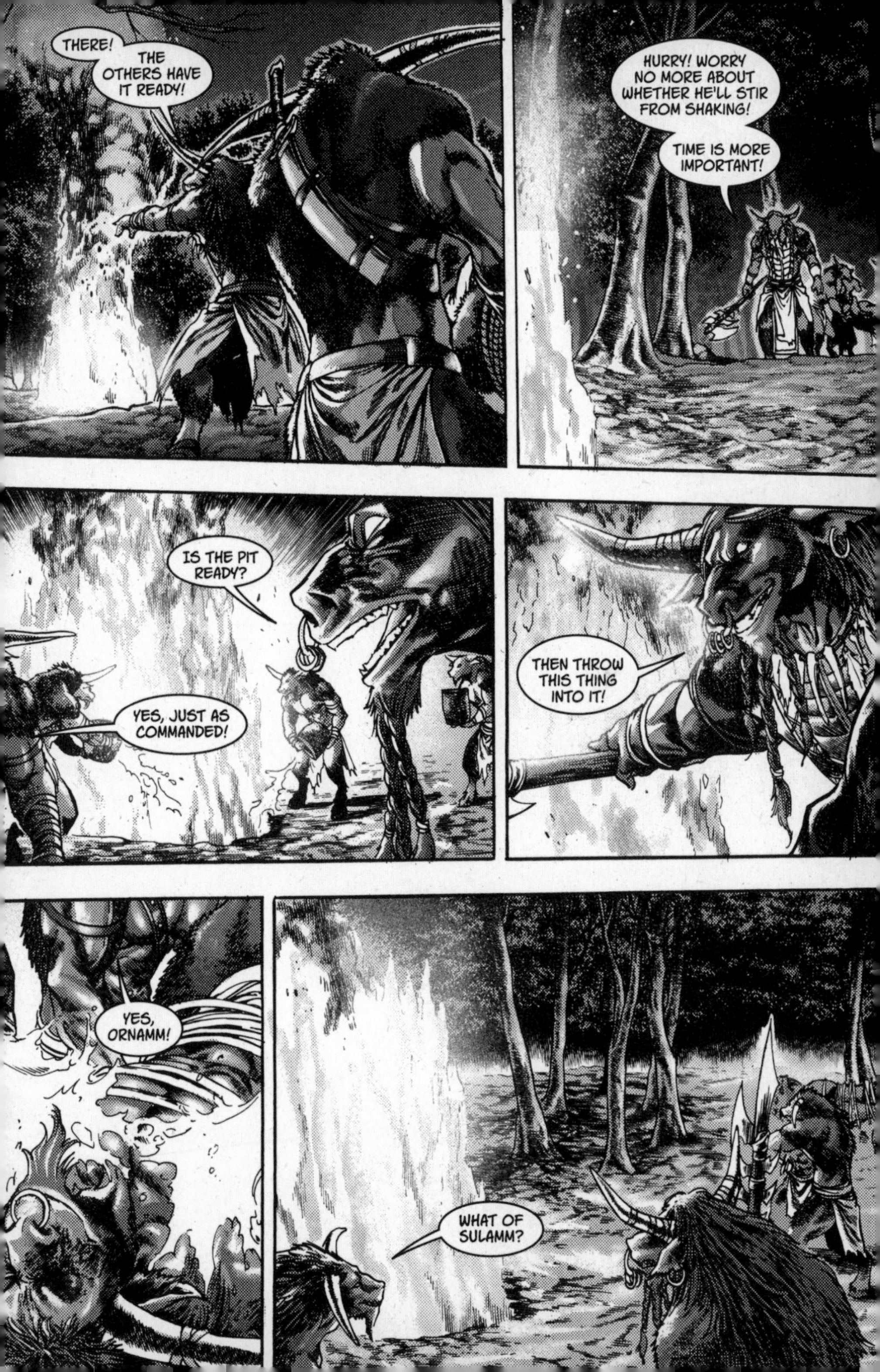
THERE!
THE OTHERS HAVE IT READY!
HURRY! WORRY NO MORE ABOUT WHETHER HE'LL STIR FROM SHAKING!
TIME IS MORE IMPORTANT!
IS THE PIT READY?
YES, JUST AS COMMANDED!
THEN THROW THIS THING INTO IT!
YES, ORNAMM!
WHAT OF SULAMM?

HE WILL
REMAIN IN HIS
TRANCE...

F
W
U
O
M
P

The flames licked
eagerly at dried
flesh and bone.

CRACKLE

CRACKLE

But although on the
outside Trag lay as
one of the dead...

...within, he was at anything
but rest. The shaman's spell
had worked to still his body,
but his consciousness now
stirred uneasily.

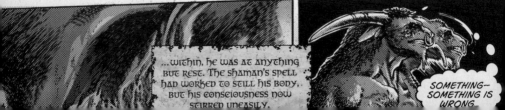

SOMETHING—
SOMETHING IS
WRONG.

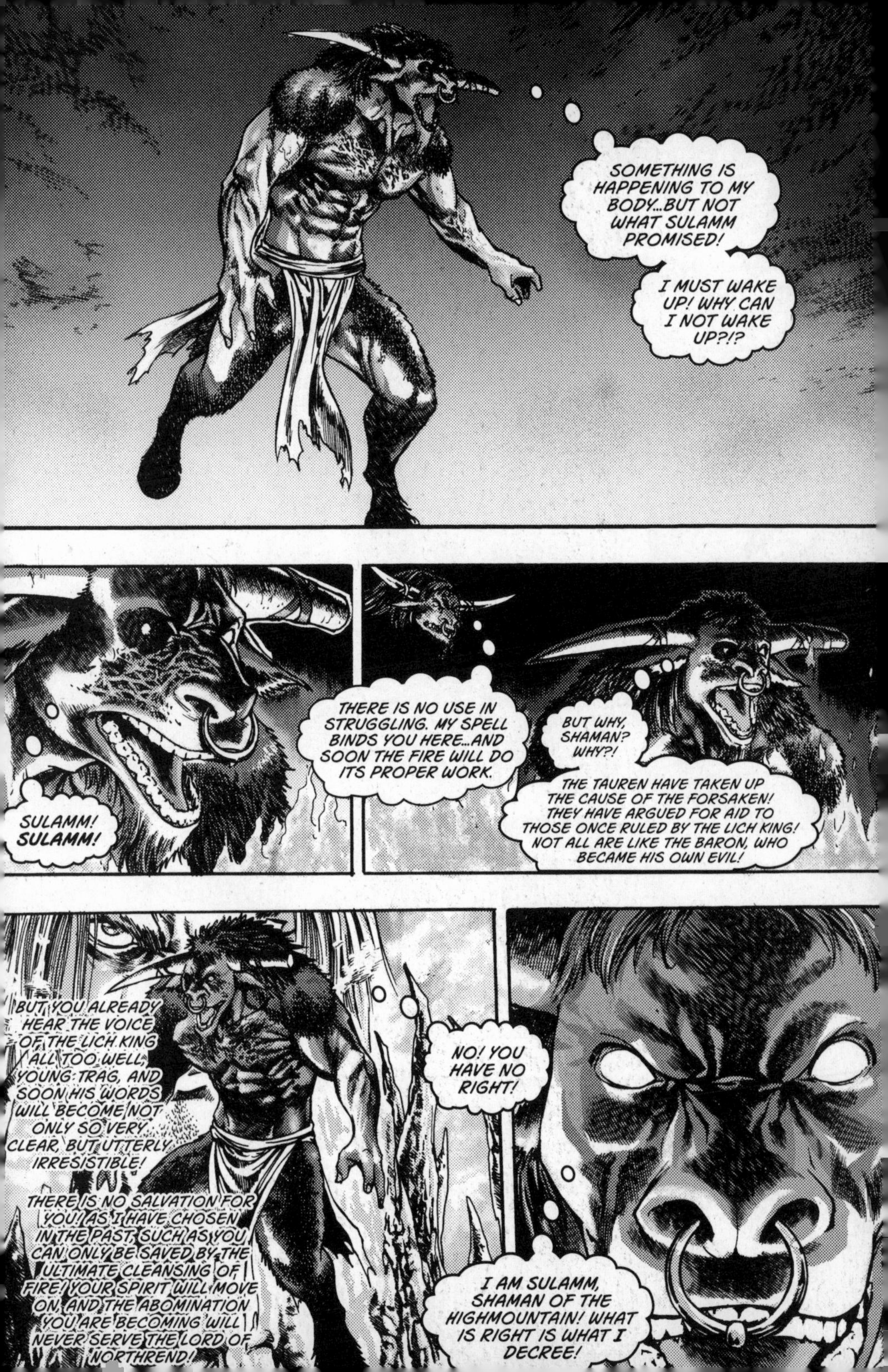
SOMETHING IS HAPPENING TO MY BODY...BUT NOT WHAT SULAMM PROMISED!
I MUST WAKE UP! WHY CAN I NOT WAKE UP?!?
SULAMM! **SULAMM!**
THERE IS NO USE IN STRUGGLING. MY SPELL BINDS YOU HERE...AND SOON THE FIRE WILL DO ITS PROPER WORK.
BUT WHY, SHAMAN? WHY?!
THE TAUREN HAVE TAKEN UP THE CAUSE OF THE FORSAKEN! THEY HAVE ARGUED FOR AID TO THOSE ONCE RULED BY THE LICH KING! NOT ALL ARE LIKE THE BARON, WHO BECAME HIS OWN EVIL!
BUT YOU ALREADY HEAR THE VOICE OF THE LICH KING ALL TOO WELL, YOUNG TRAG, AND SOON HIS WORDS WILL BECOME NOT ONLY SO VERY CLEAR, BUT UTTERLY IRRESISTIBLE!
THERE IS NO SALVATION FOR YOU! AS I HAVE CHOSEN IN THE PAST, SUCH AS YOU CAN ONLY BE SAVED BY THE ULTIMATE CLEANSING OF FIRE! YOUR SPIRIT WILL MOVE ON, AND THE ABOMINATION YOU ARE BECOMING WILL NEVER SERVE THE LORD OF NORTHREND!
NO! YOU HAVE NO RIGHT!
I AM SULAMM, SHAMAN OF THE HIGHMOUNTAIN! WHAT IS RIGHT IS WHAT I DECREE!

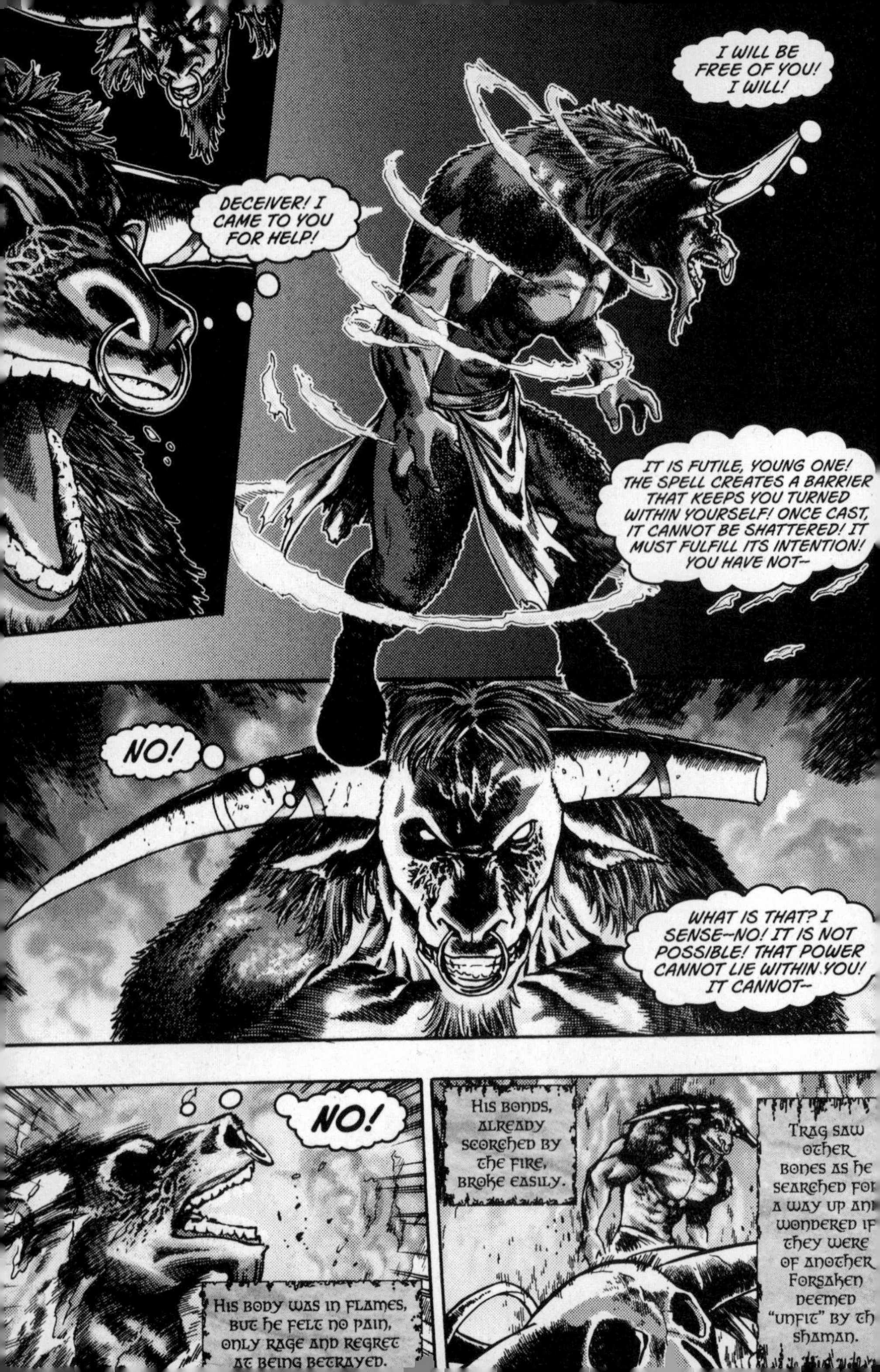
DECEIVER! I CAME TO YOU FOR HELP!
I WILL BE FREE OF YOU! I WILL!
IT IS FUTILE, YOUNG ONE! THE SPELL CREATES A BARRIER THAT KEEPS YOU TURNED WITHIN YOURSELF! ONCE CAST, IT CANNOT BE SHATTERED! IT MUST FULFILL ITS INTENTION! YOU HAVE NOT--
NO!
WHAT IS THAT? I SENSE--NO! IT IS NOT POSSIBLE! THAT POWER CANNOT LIE WITHIN YOU! IT CANNOT--
NO!
His body was in flames, but he felt no pain, only rage and regret at being betrayed.
His bonds, already scorched by the fire, broke easily.
Trag saw other bones as he searched fo a way up an wondered if they were of another Forsaken deemed "unfit" by th shaman.

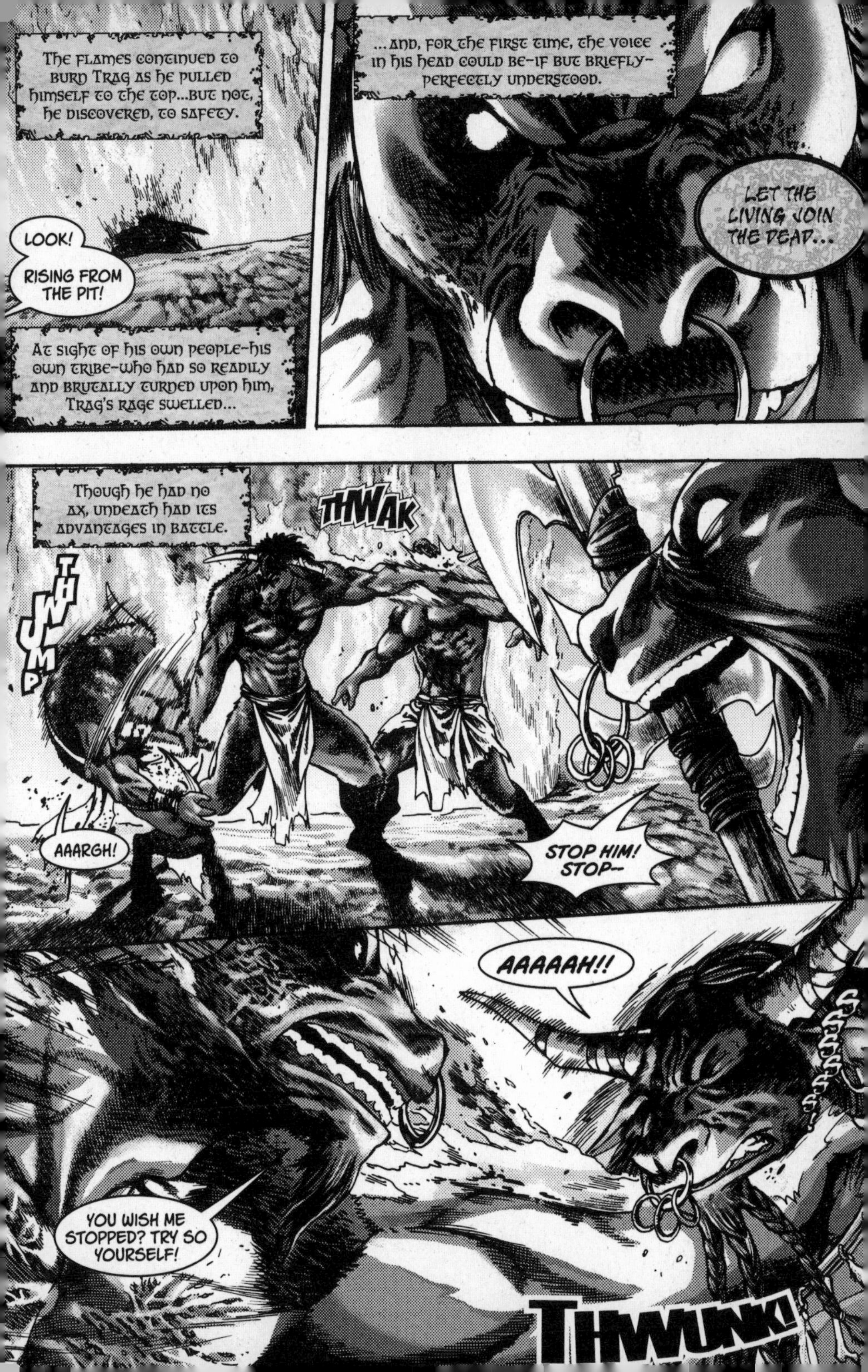

The flames continued to burn Trag as he pulled himself to the top...but not, he discovered, to safety.
LOOK!
RISING FROM THE PIT!
At sight of his own people–his own tribe–who had so readily and brutally turned upon him, Trag's rage swelled...
...and, for the first time, the voice in his head could be–if but briefly–perfectly understood.
LET THE LIVING JOIN THE DEAD...
Though he had no ax, undeath had its advantages in battle.
THWUMP
THWAK
AAARGH!
STOP HIM! STOP--
AAAAAH!!
YOU WISH ME STOPPED? TRY SO YOURSELF!
THWUNK!

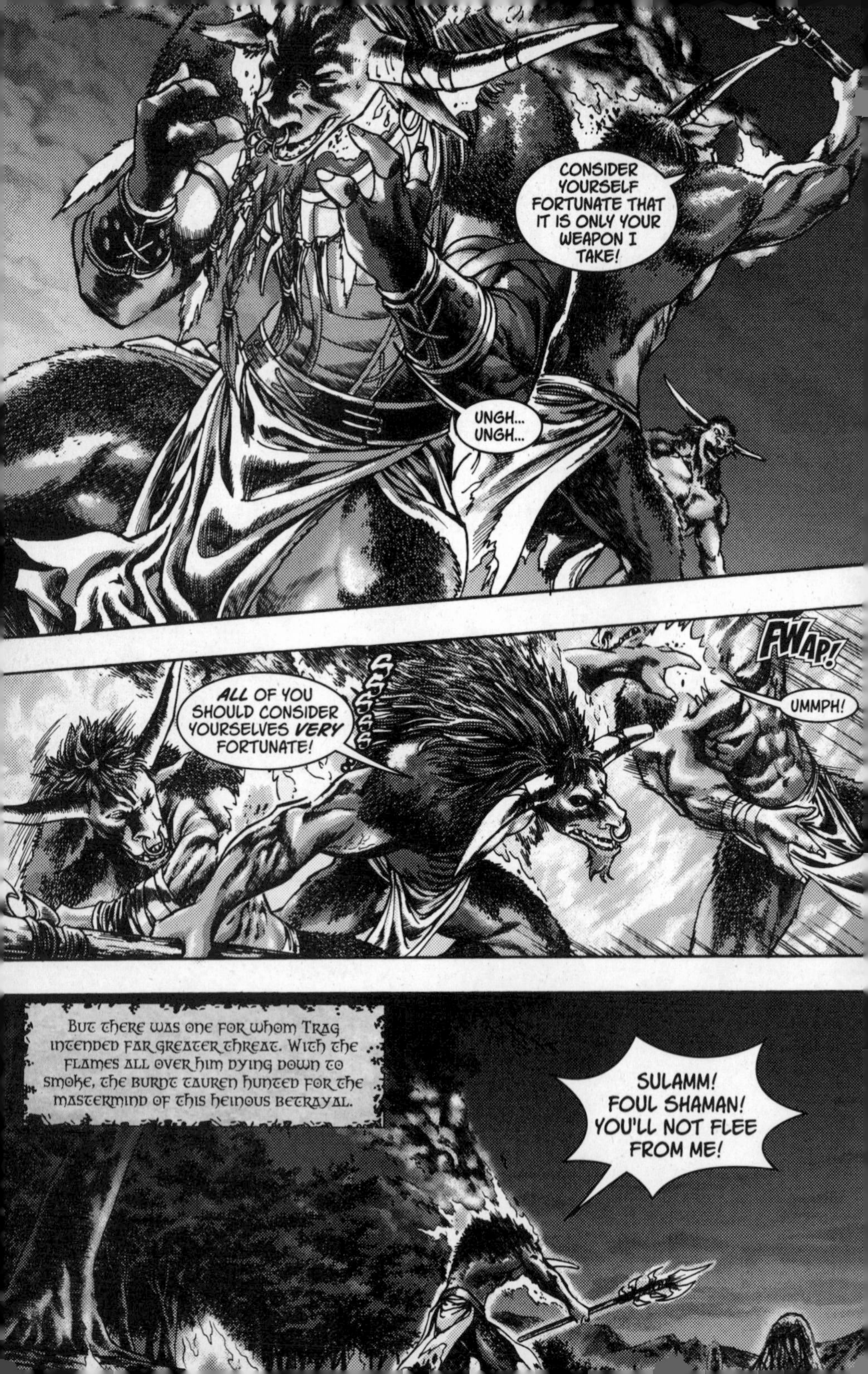
CONSIDER YOURSELF FORTUNATE THAT IT IS ONLY YOUR WEAPON I TAKE!
UNGH... UNGH...
ALL OF YOU SHOULD CONSIDER YOURSELVES VERY FORTUNATE!
FWAP!
UMMPH!
But there was one for whom Trag intended far greater threat. With the flames all over him dying down to smoke, the burnt tauren hunted for the mastermind of this heinous betrayal.
SULAMM! FOUL SHAMAN! YOU'LL NOT FLEE FROM ME!

DO NOT PRETEND TO IGNORE ME! I--

SULAMM?!?

TRAG RECALLED THE SHAMAN'S SPELL AND HOW SULAMM HAD TALKED OF IT AS SOMETHING FROM WHICH HE SHOULD NOT HAVE BEEN ABLE TO ESCAPE...AND YET TRAG HAD.

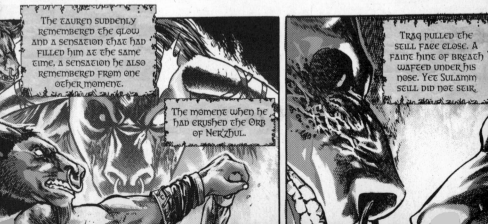

THE TAUREN SUDDENLY REMEMBERED THE GLOW AND A SENSATION THAT HAD FILLED HIM AT THE SAME TIME, A SENSATION HE ALSO REMEMBERED FROM ONE OTHER MOMENT.

THE MOMENT WHEN HE HAD CRUSHED THE ORB OF NER'ZHUL.

TRAG PULLED THE STILL FACE CLOSE. A FAINT HINT OF BREATH WAFTED UNDER HIS NOSE. YET SULAMM STILL DID NOT STIR.

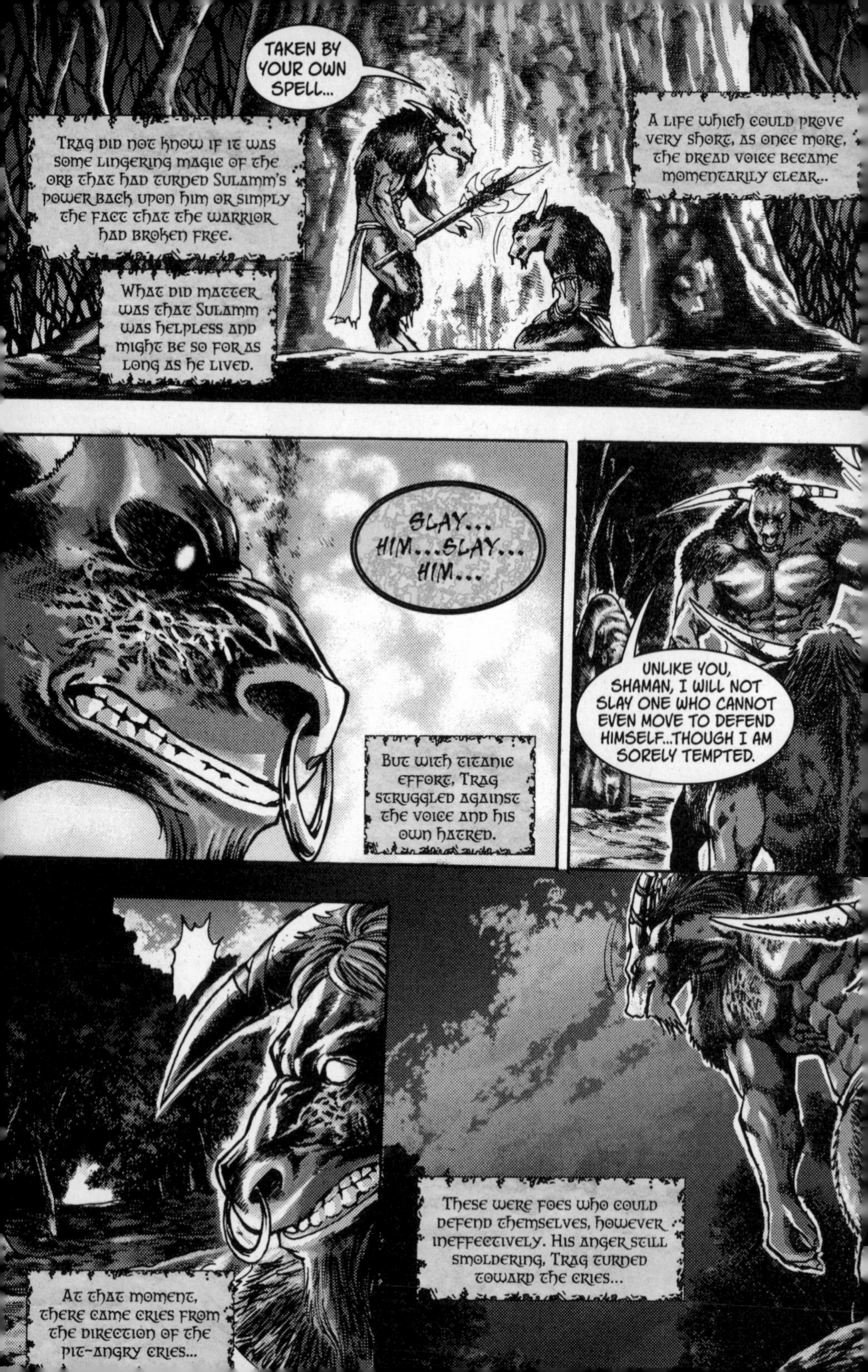
TAKEN BY YOUR OWN SPELL...
Trag did not know if it was some lingering magic of the orb that had turned Sulamm's power back upon him or simply the fact that the warrior had broken free.
What did matter was that Sulamm was helpless and might be so for as long as he lived.
A life which could prove very short, as once more, the dread voice became momentarily clear...
SLAY... HIM...SLAY... HIM...
But with titanic effort, Trag struggled against the voice and his own hatred.
UNLIKE YOU, SHAMAN, I WILL NOT SLAY ONE WHO CANNOT EVEN MOVE TO DEFEND HIMSELF...THOUGH I AM SORELY TEMPTED.
At that moment, there came cries from the direction of the pit-angry cries...
These were foes who could defend themselves, however ineffectively. His anger still smoldering, Trag turned toward the cries...

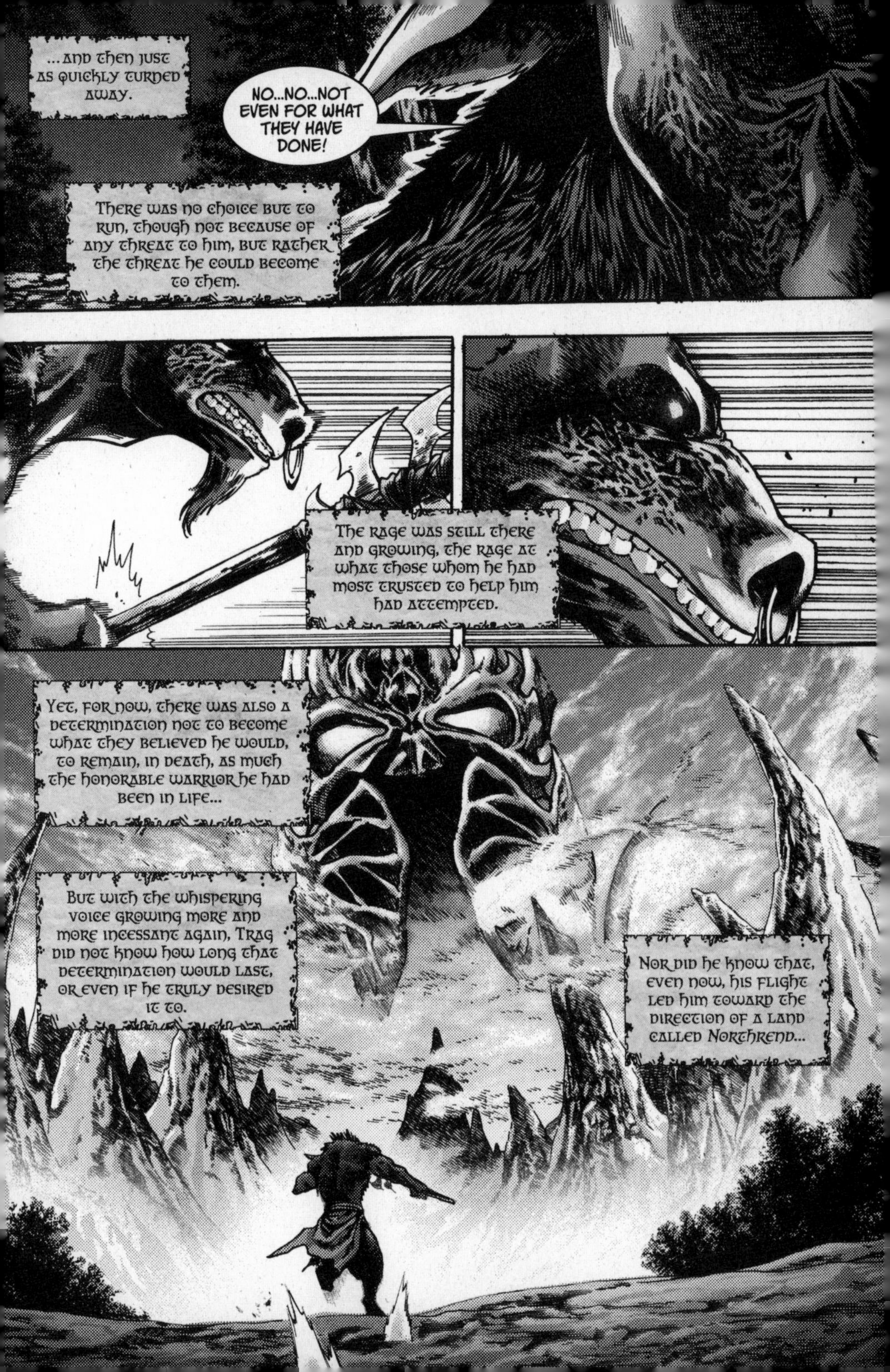

...AND THEN JUST AS QUICKLY TURNED AWAY.
NO...NO...NOT EVEN FOR WHAT THEY HAVE DONE!
THERE WAS NO CHOICE BUT TO RUN, THOUGH NOT BECAUSE OF ANY THREAT TO HIM, BUT RATHER THE THREAT HE COULD BECOME TO THEM.
THE RAGE WAS STILL THERE AND GROWING, THE RAGE AT WHAT THOSE WHOM HE HAD MOST TRUSTED TO HELP HIM HAD ATTEMPTED.
YET, FOR NOW, THERE WAS ALSO A DETERMINATION NOT TO BECOME WHAT THEY BELIEVED HE WOULD, TO REMAIN, IN DEATH, AS MUCH THE HONORABLE WARRIOR HE HAD BEEN IN LIFE...
BUT WITH THE WHISPERING VOICE GROWING MORE AND MORE INCESSANT AGAIN, TRAG DID NOT KNOW HOW LONG THAT DETERMINATION WOULD LAST, OR EVEN IF HE TRULY DESIRED IT TO.
NOR DID HE KNOW THAT, EVEN NOW, HIS FLIGHT LED HIM TOWARD THE DIRECTION OF A LAND CALLED NORTHREND...

FEAR

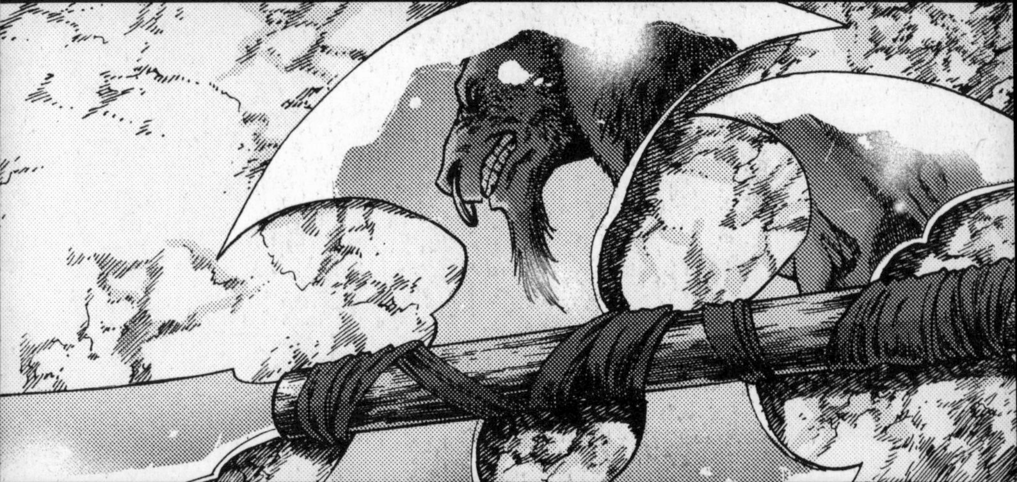

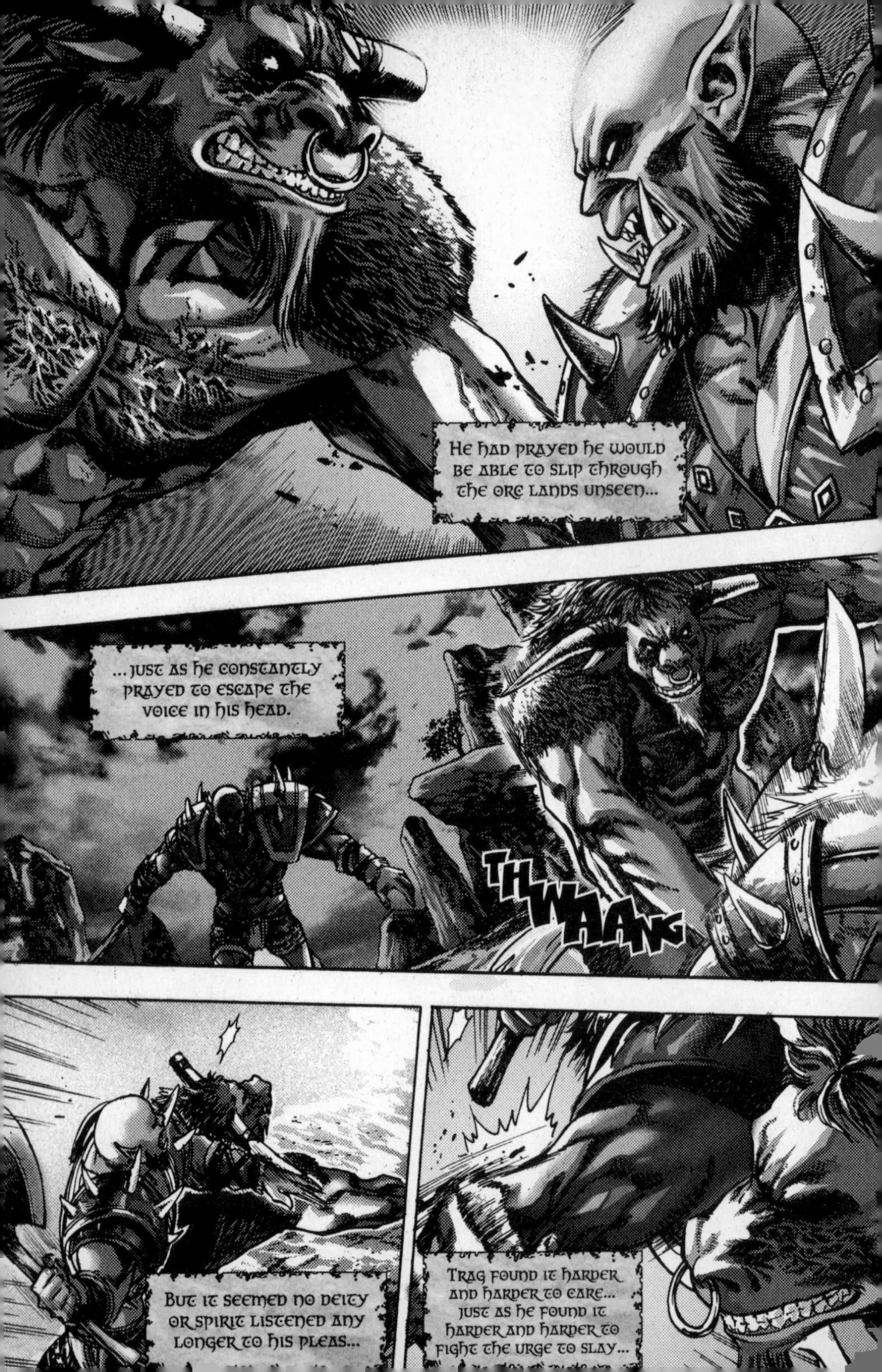
He had prayed he would be able to slip through the orc lands unseen...
...just as he constantly prayed to escape the voice in his head.
THWAANG
But it seemed no deity or spirit listened any longer to his pleas...
Trag found it harder and harder to care... just as he found it harder and harder to fight the urge to slay...

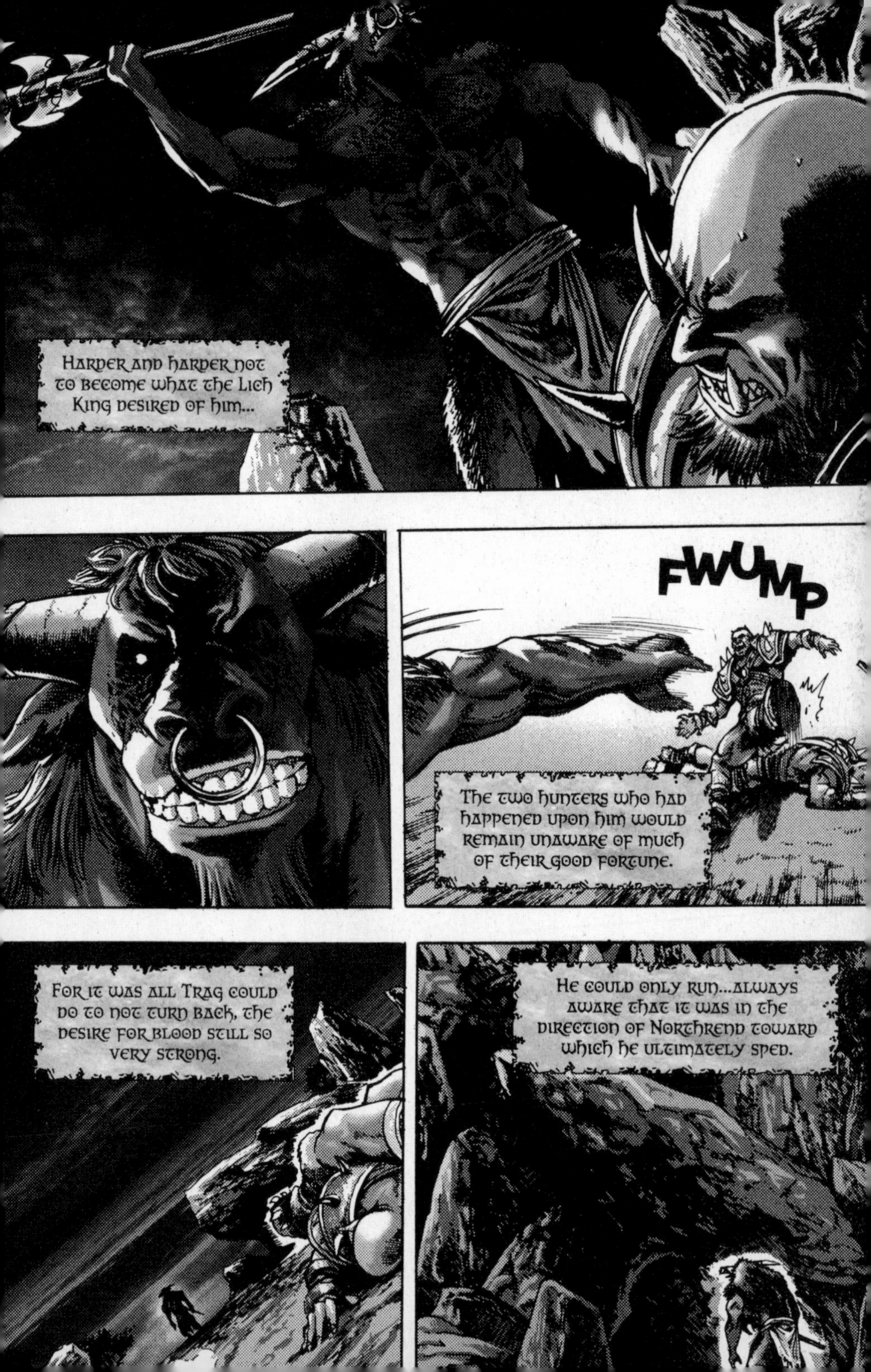
HARDER AND HARDER NOT TO BECOME WHAT THE LICH KING DESIRED OF HIM...
FWUMP
THE TWO HUNTERS WHO HAD HAPPENED UPON HIM WOULD REMAIN UNAWARE OF MUCH OF THEIR GOOD FORTUNE.
FOR IT WAS ALL TRAG COULD DO TO NOT TURN BACK, THE DESIRE FOR BLOOD STILL SO VERY STRONG.
HE COULD ONLY RUN...ALWAYS AWARE THAT IT WAS IN THE DIRECTION OF NORTHREND TOWARD WHICH HE ULTIMATELY SPED.

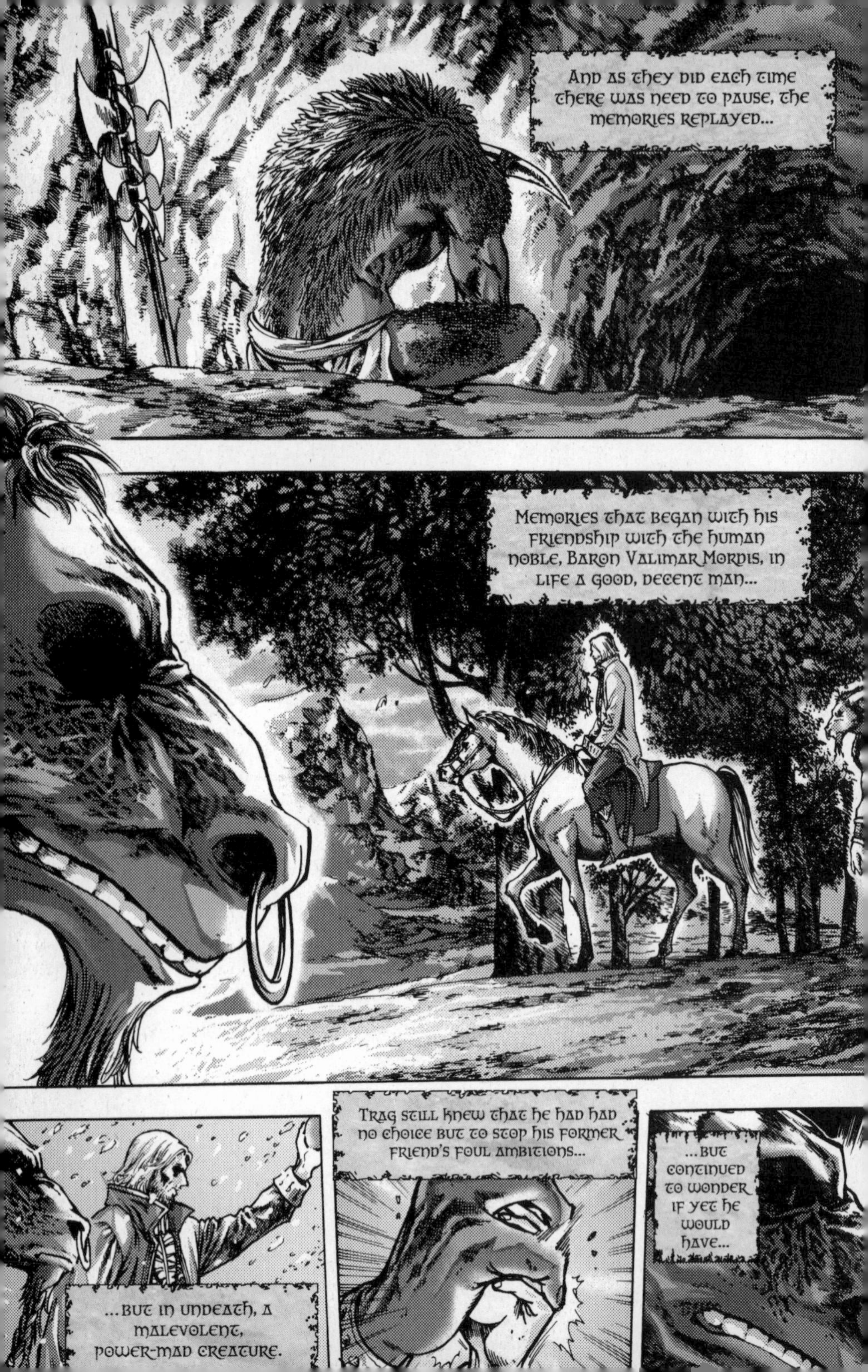
And as they did each time there was need to pause, the memories replayed...
Memories that began with his friendship with the human noble, Baron Valimar Mordis, in life a good, decent man...
...but in undeath, a malevolent, power-mad creature.
Trag still knew that he had had no choice but to stop his former friend's foul ambitions...
...but continued to wonder if yet he would have...

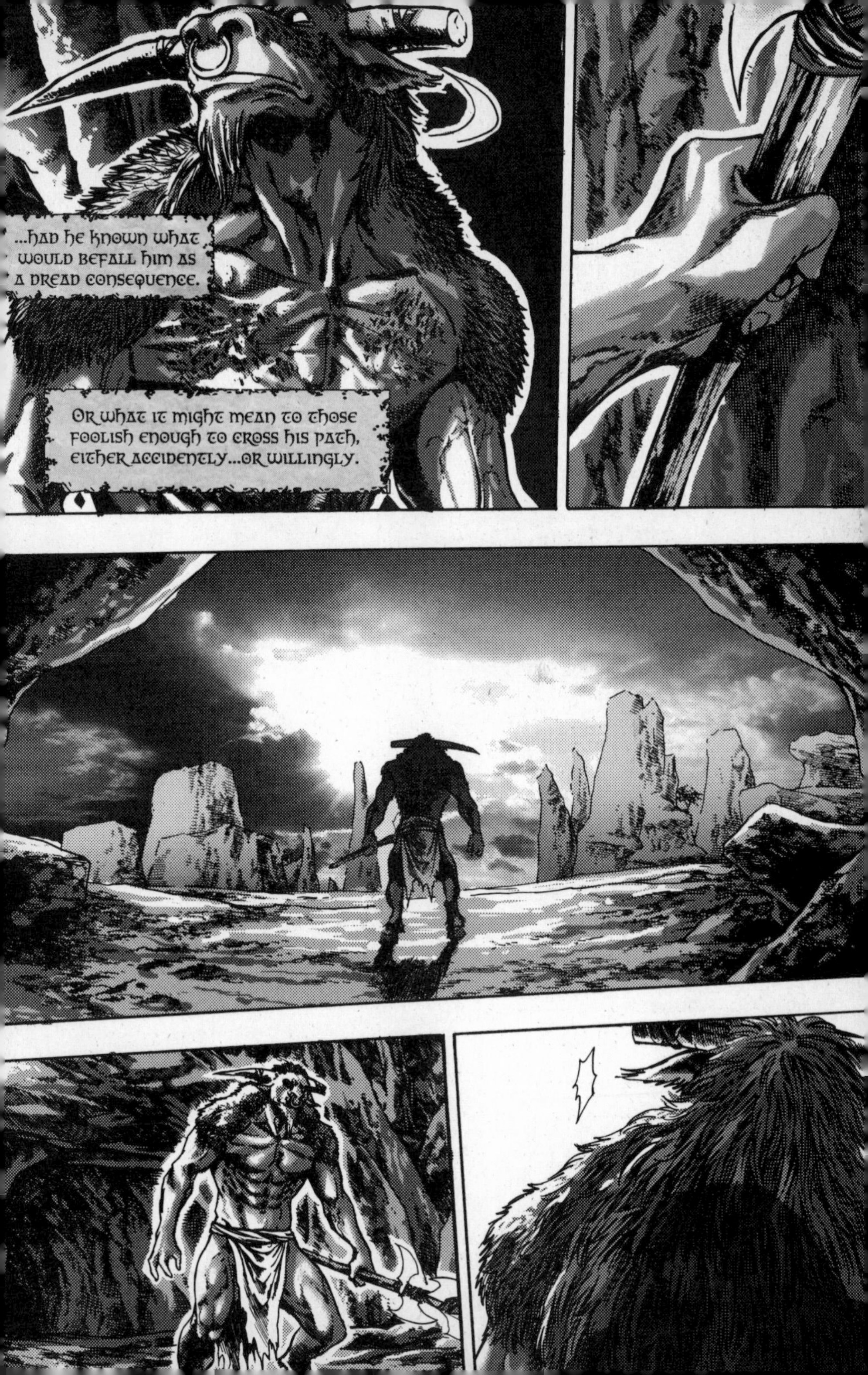
...had he known what would befall him as a dread consequence.
Or what it might mean to those foolish enough to cross his path, either accidently...or willingly.

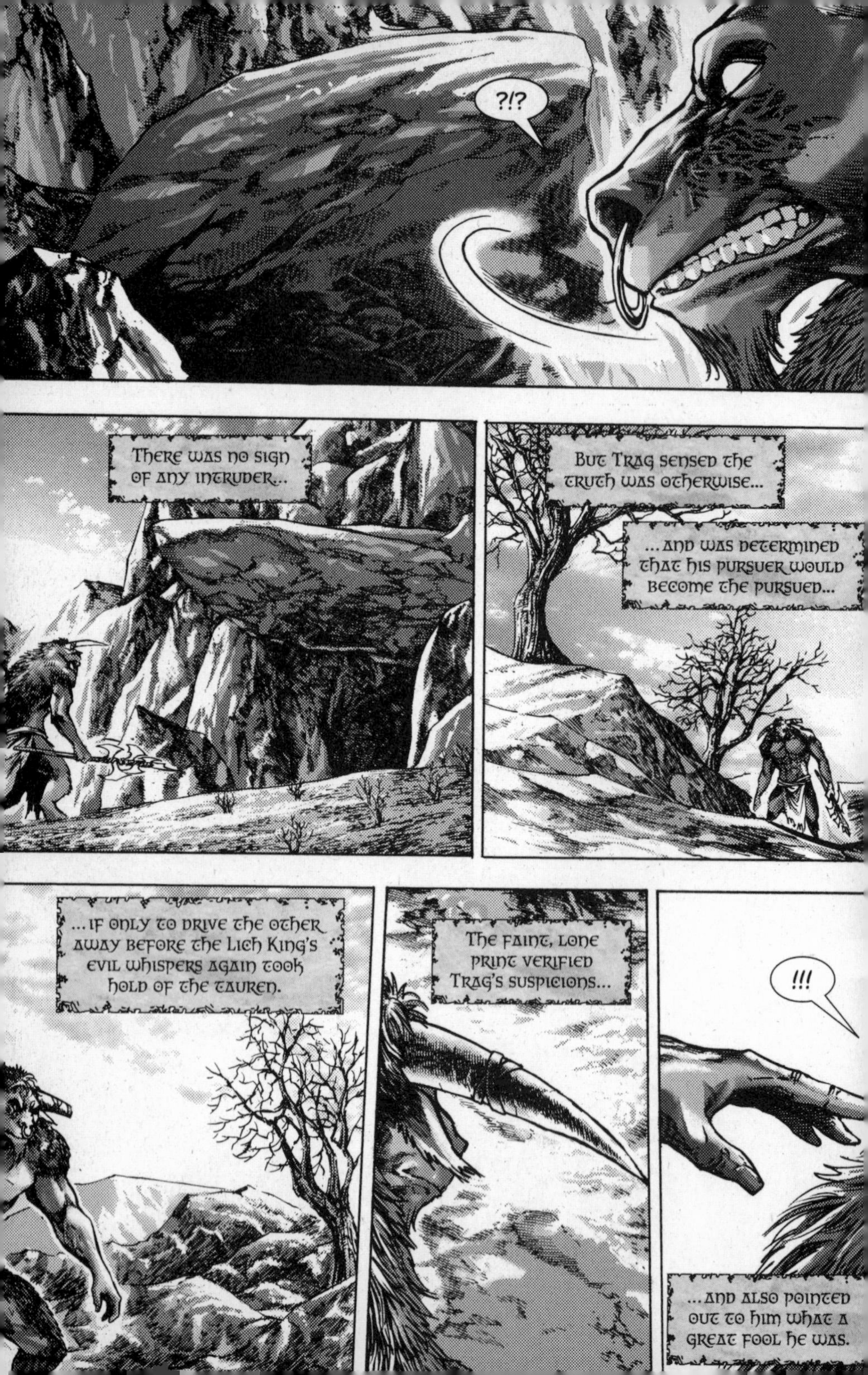
?!?
There was no sign of any intruder...
But Trag sensed the truth was otherwise...
...and was determined that his pursuer would become the pursued...
...if only to drive the other away before the Lich King's evil whispers again took hold of the tauren.
The faint, lone print verified Trag's suspicions...
!!!
...and also pointed out to him what a great fool he was.

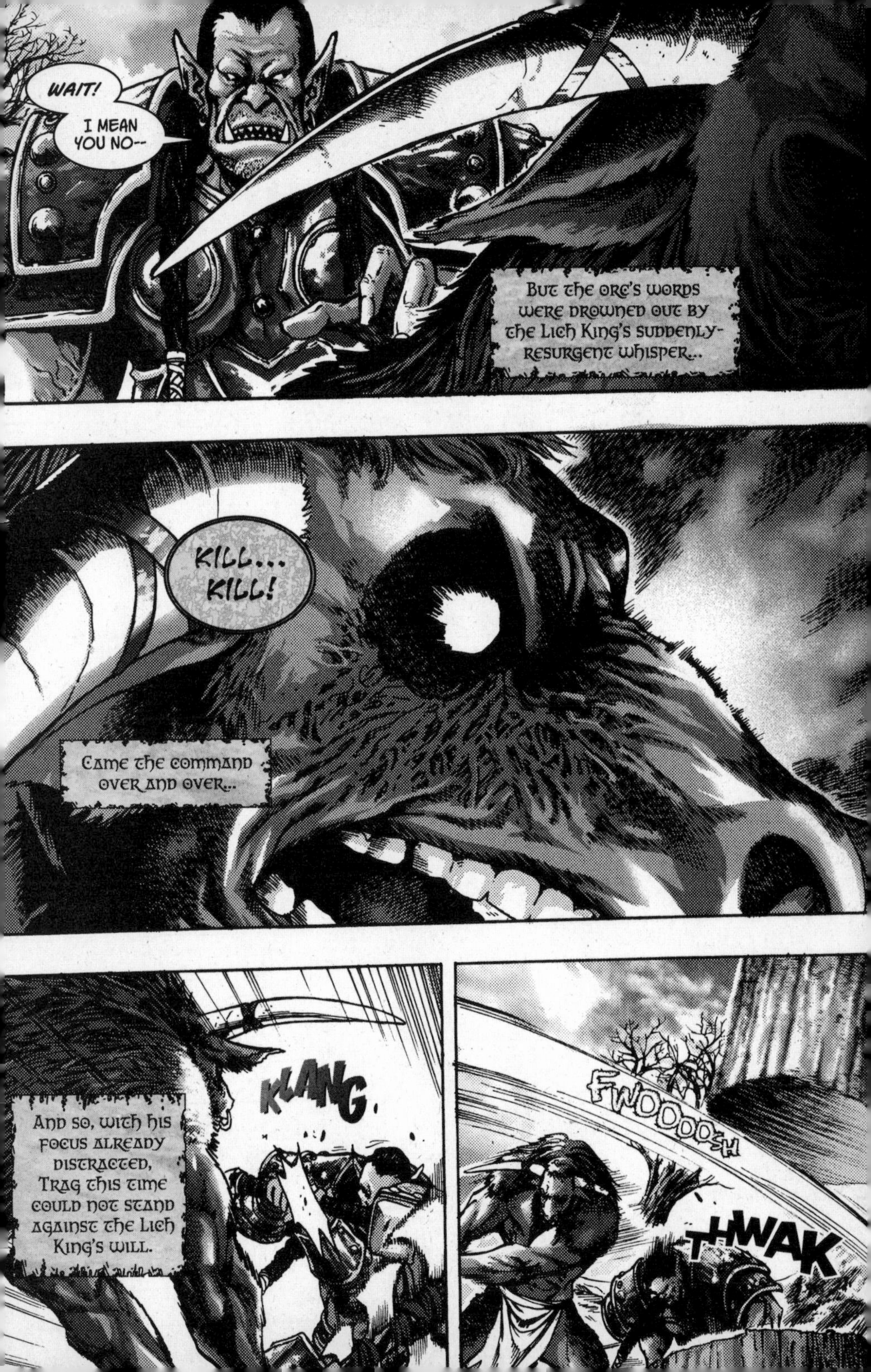
WAIT!
I MEAN YOU NO--
But the orc's words were drowned out by the Lich King's suddenly-resurgent whisper...
KILL... KILL!
Came the command over and over...
And so, with his focus already distracted, Trag this time could not stand against the Lich King's will.
KLANG
FWOOOOOSH
THWAK

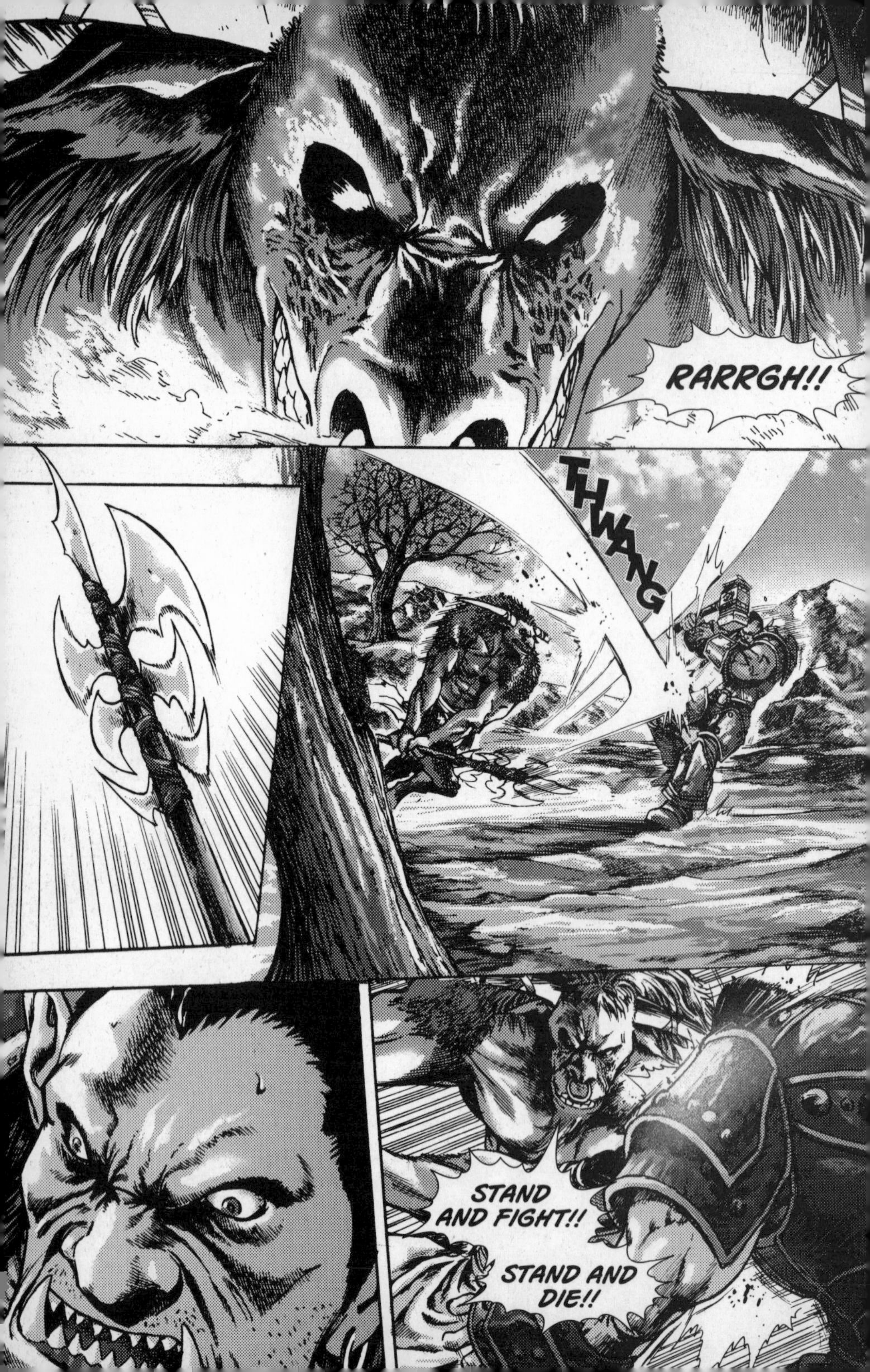
RARRGH!!
THWANG
STAND AND FIGHT!!
STAND AND DIE!!

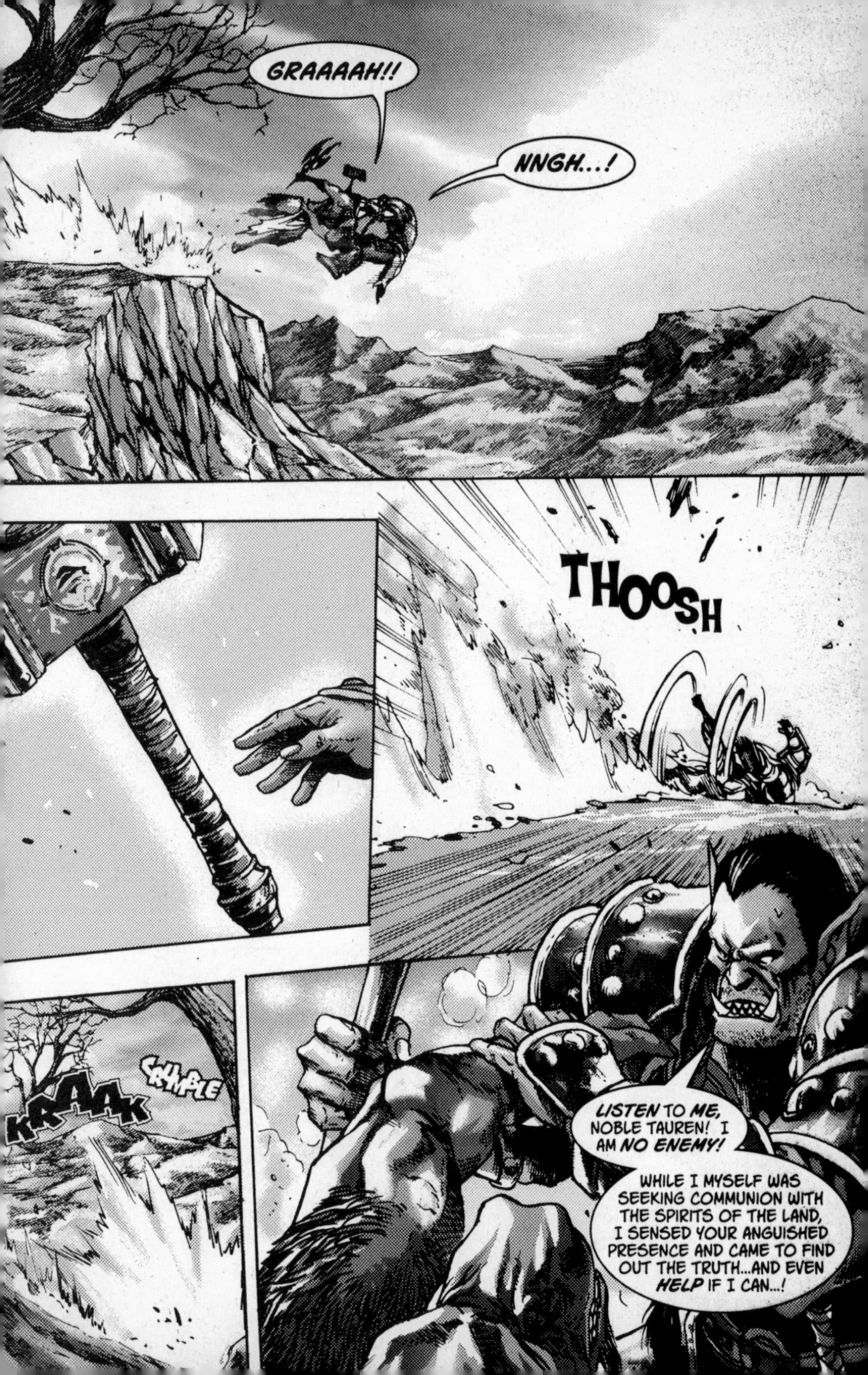
GRAAAAH!!
NNGH...!
THOOSH
KRAAAK
CRUMBLE
LISTEN TO ME, NOBLE TAUREN! I AM NO ENEMY!
WHILE I MYSELF WAS SEEKING COMMUNION WITH THE SPIRITS OF THE LAND, I SENSED YOUR ANGUISHED PRESENCE AND CAME TO FIND OUT THE TRUTH...AND EVEN HELP IF I CAN...!

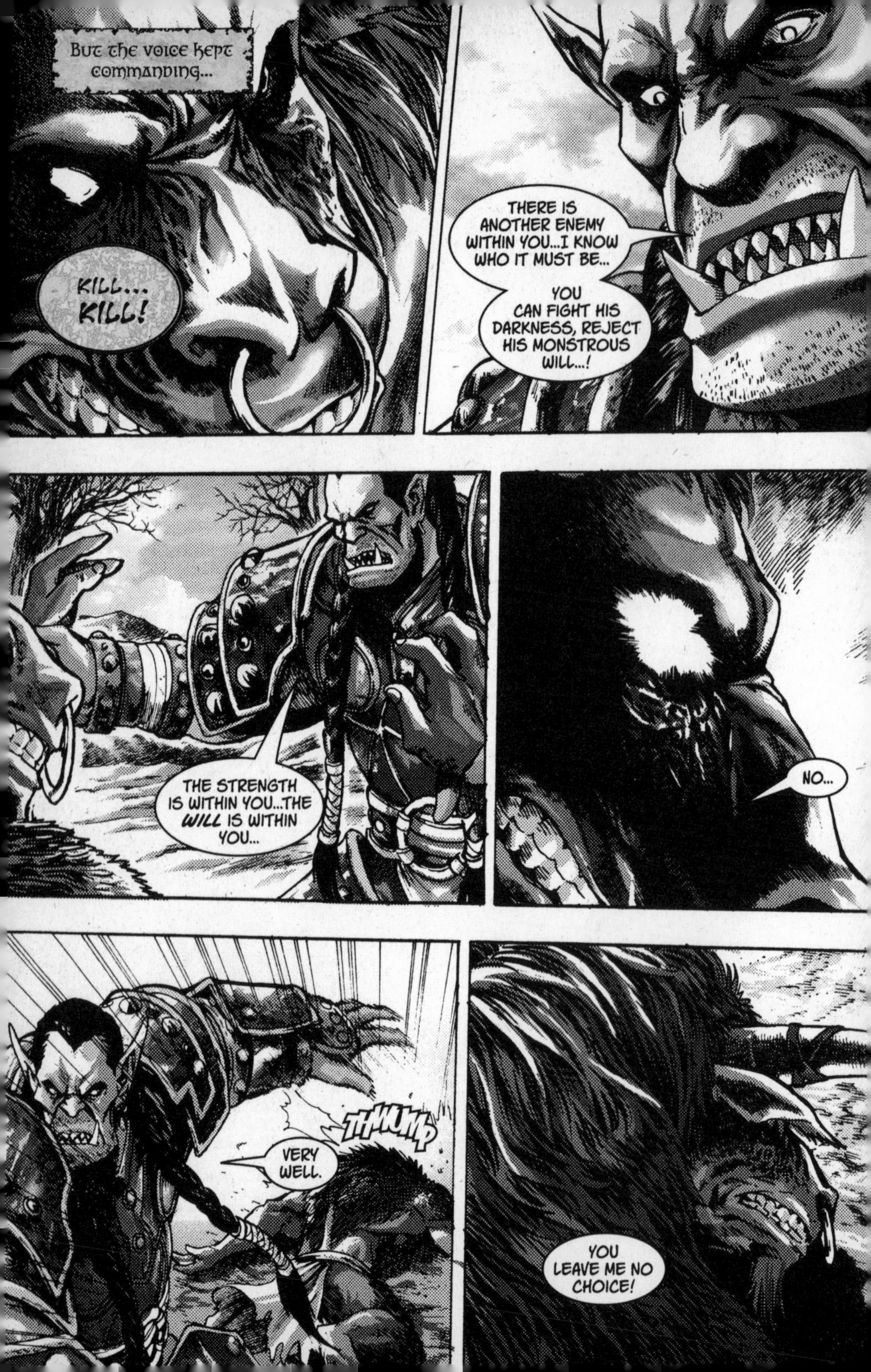
But the voice kept commanding...
KILL... KILL!
THERE IS ANOTHER ENEMY WITHIN YOU...I KNOW WHO IT MUST BE...
YOU CAN FIGHT HIS DARKNESS, REJECT HIS MONSTROUS WILL...!
THE STRENGTH IS WITHIN YOU...THE WILL IS WITHIN YOU...
NO...
THWUMP
VERY WELL.
YOU LEAVE ME NO CHOICE!

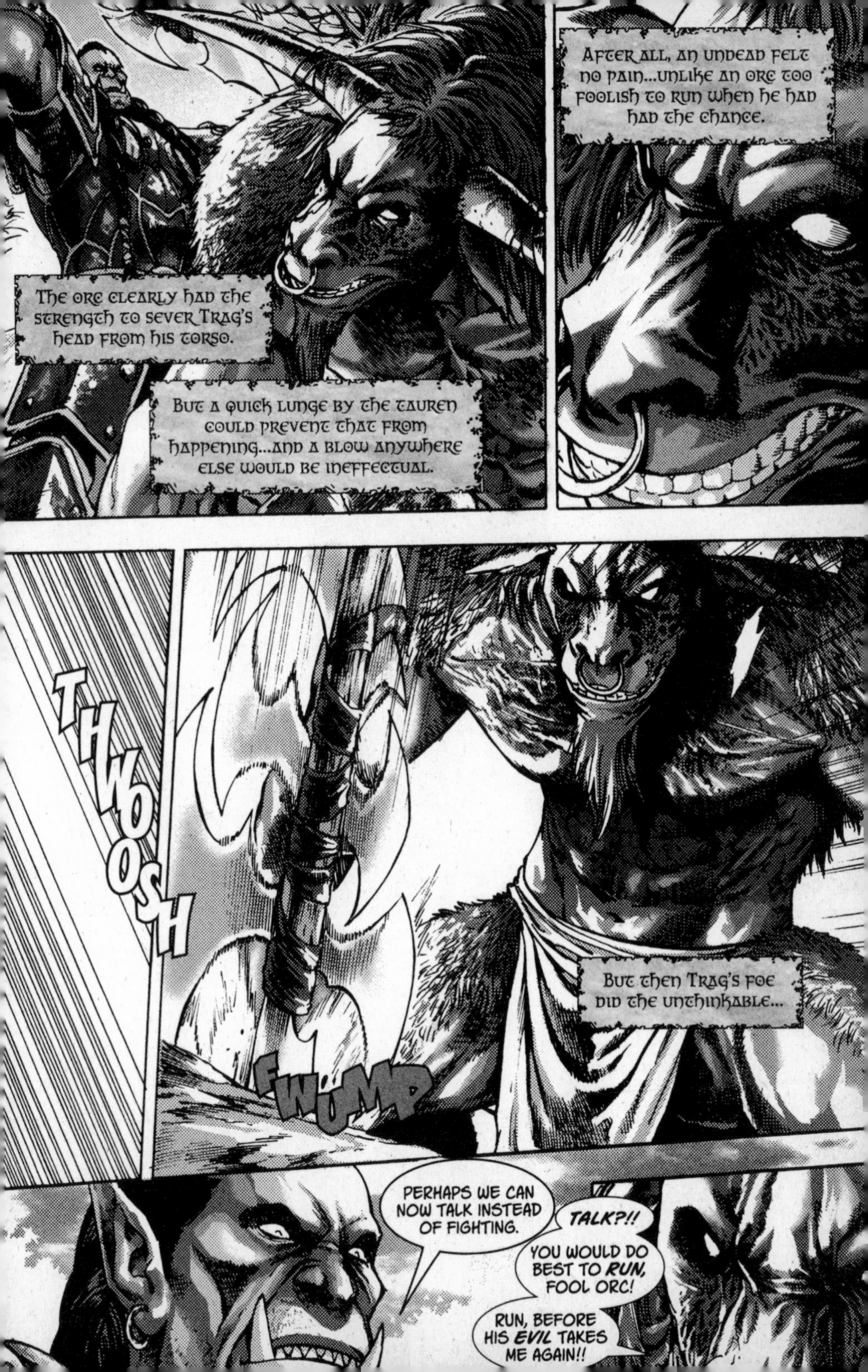
The orc clearly had the strength to sever Trag's head from his torso.
But a quick lunge by the tauren could prevent that from happening...and a blow anywhere else would be ineffectual.
After all, an undead felt no pain...unlike an orc too foolish to run when he had had the chance.
THWOOSH
But then Trag's foe did the unthinkable...
FWUMP
PERHAPS WE CAN NOW TALK INSTEAD OF FIGHTING.
TALK?!!
YOU WOULD DO BEST TO *RUN*, FOOL ORC!
RUN, BEFORE HIS *EVIL* TAKES ME AGAIN!!

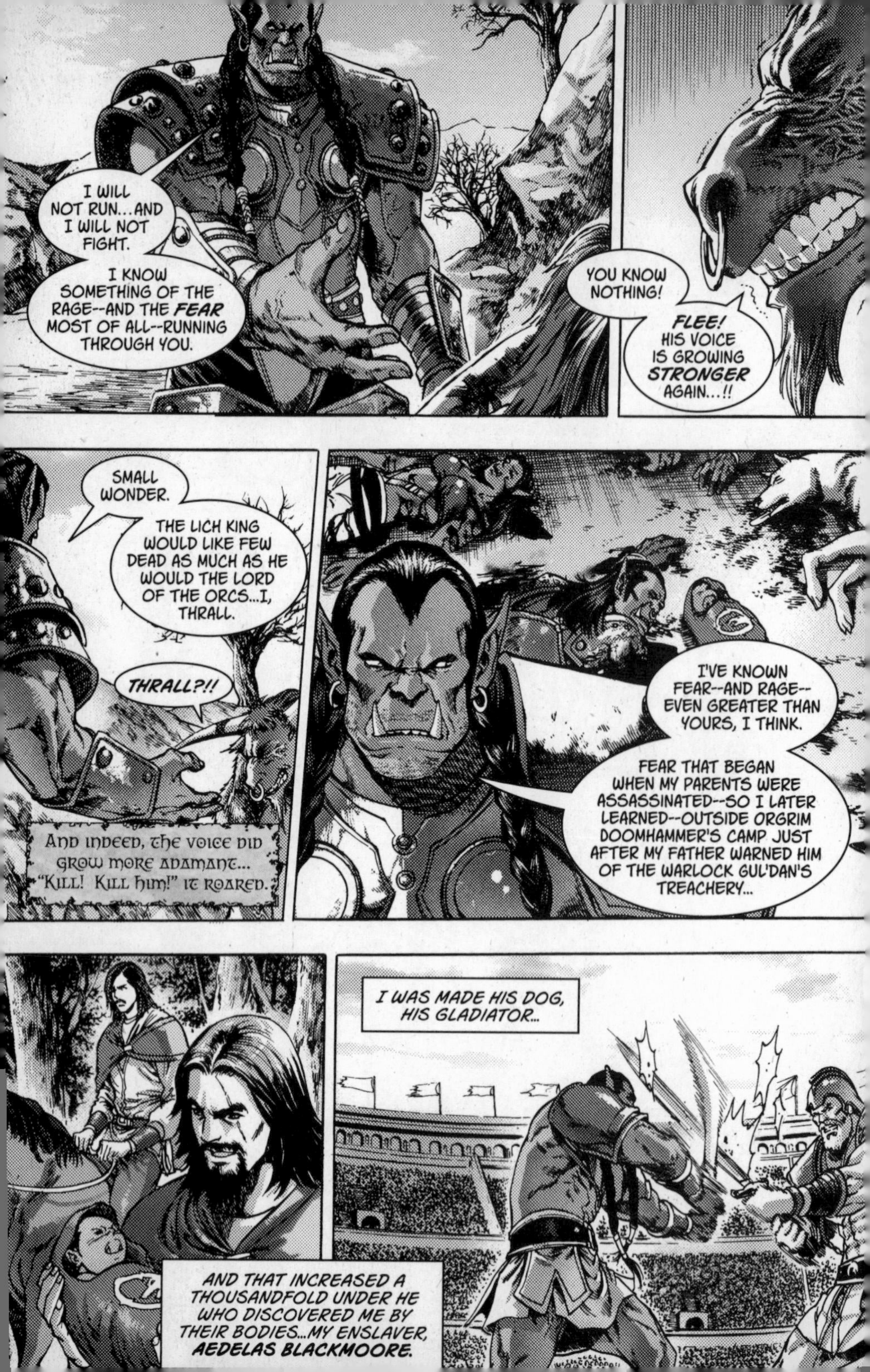
I WILL NOT RUN...AND I WILL NOT FIGHT.
I KNOW SOMETHING OF THE RAGE--AND THE FEAR MOST OF ALL--RUNNING THROUGH YOU.
YOU KNOW NOTHING!
FLEE! HIS VOICE IS GROWING STRONGER AGAIN...!!
SMALL WONDER.
THE LICH KING WOULD LIKE FEW DEAD AS MUCH AS HE WOULD THE LORD OF THE ORCS...I, THRALL.
THRALL?!!
And indeed, the voice did grow more adamant... "Kill! Kill him!" it roared.
I'VE KNOWN FEAR--AND RAGE--EVEN GREATER THAN YOURS, I THINK.
FEAR THAT BEGAN WHEN MY PARENTS WERE ASSASSINATED--SO I LATER LEARNED--OUTSIDE ORGRIM DOOMHAMMER'S CAMP JUST AFTER MY FATHER WARNED HIM OF THE WARLOCK GUL'DAN'S TREACHERY...
AND THAT INCREASED A THOUSANDFOLD UNDER HE WHO DISCOVERED ME BY THEIR BODIES...MY ENSLAVER, AEDELAS BLACKMOORE.
I WAS MADE HIS DOG, HIS GLADIATOR...

AND LIKE SOME MASTERS DO TO THEIR ANIMALS, I WAS BEATEN FOR ALL FAILURES, REAL OR IMAGINED...OR BEATEN FOR NO REASON AT ALL...

THE FEAR CONTINUED TO SWELL WITHIN ME...BUT IT WAS THE FEAR THAT I WOULD BECOME NOTHING MORE THAN THE BEAST HE THOUGHT ME.

I THOUGHT AND EVEN PRAYED THAT I WOULD DIE...BUT THERE CAME ONE CARING HUMAN—TARETHA—WHO FIRST BEFRIENDED ME AS NO OTHER. SHE GAVE ME HOPE...

...AND THEN HELPED ME ESCAPE.

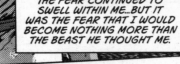

BUT MY FIRST TASTE OF FREEDOM WAS SHORT-LIVED...AND I WAS TOSSED INTO AN INTERNMENT CAMP! FOR THE FIRST TIME I MET MY RACE... ONCE LEGENDARY WARRIORS...

...BUT NOW ALL OF THEM SLAVES SUFFERING A SINISTER LETHARGY DUE—I LEARNED MUCH LATER—TO THEIR FORCED WITHDRAWAL FROM THE DEMONIC FORCES SO LONG A PART OF THEM.

AND IT WAS THERE THAT THE OLD ONE, KELGAR, AWAITED ME...

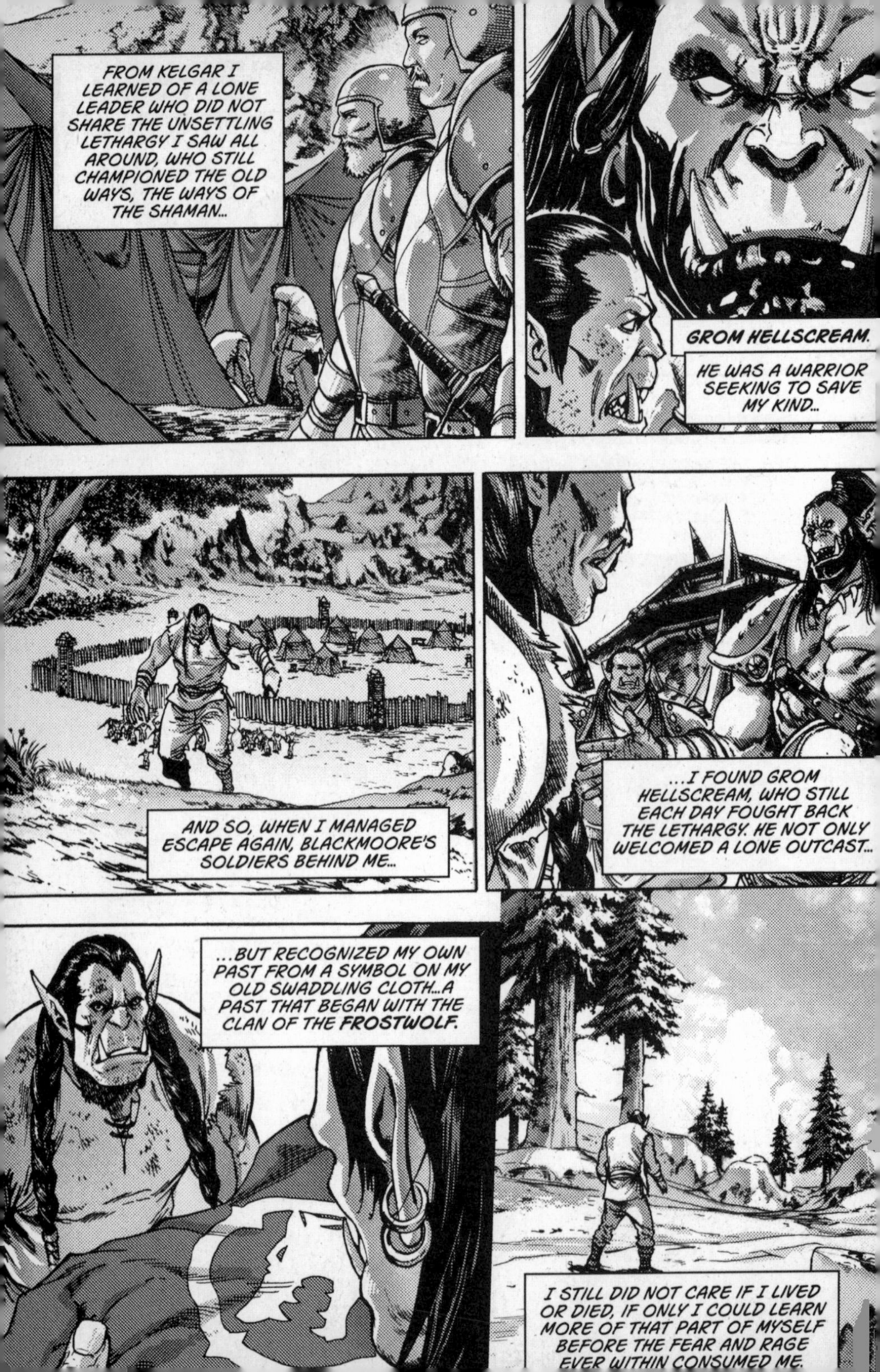
FROM KELGAR I LEARNED OF A LONE LEADER WHO DID NOT SHARE THE UNSETTLING LETHARGY I SAW ALL AROUND, WHO STILL CHAMPIONED THE OLD WAYS, THE WAYS OF THE SHAMAN...
GROM HELLSCREAM.
HE WAS A WARRIOR SEEKING TO SAVE MY KIND...
AND SO, WHEN I MANAGED ESCAPE AGAIN, BLACKMOORE'S SOLDIERS BEHIND ME...
...I FOUND GROM HELLSCREAM, WHO STILL EACH DAY FOUGHT BACK THE LETHARGY. HE NOT ONLY WELCOMED A LONE OUTCAST...
...BUT RECOGNIZED MY OWN PAST FROM A SYMBOL ON MY OLD SWADDLING CLOTH...A PAST THAT BEGAN WITH THE CLAN OF THE FROSTWOLF.
I STILL DID NOT CARE IF I LIVED OR DIED, IF ONLY I COULD LEARN MORE OF THAT PART OF MYSELF BEFORE THE FEAR AND RAGE EVER WITHIN CONSUMED ME.

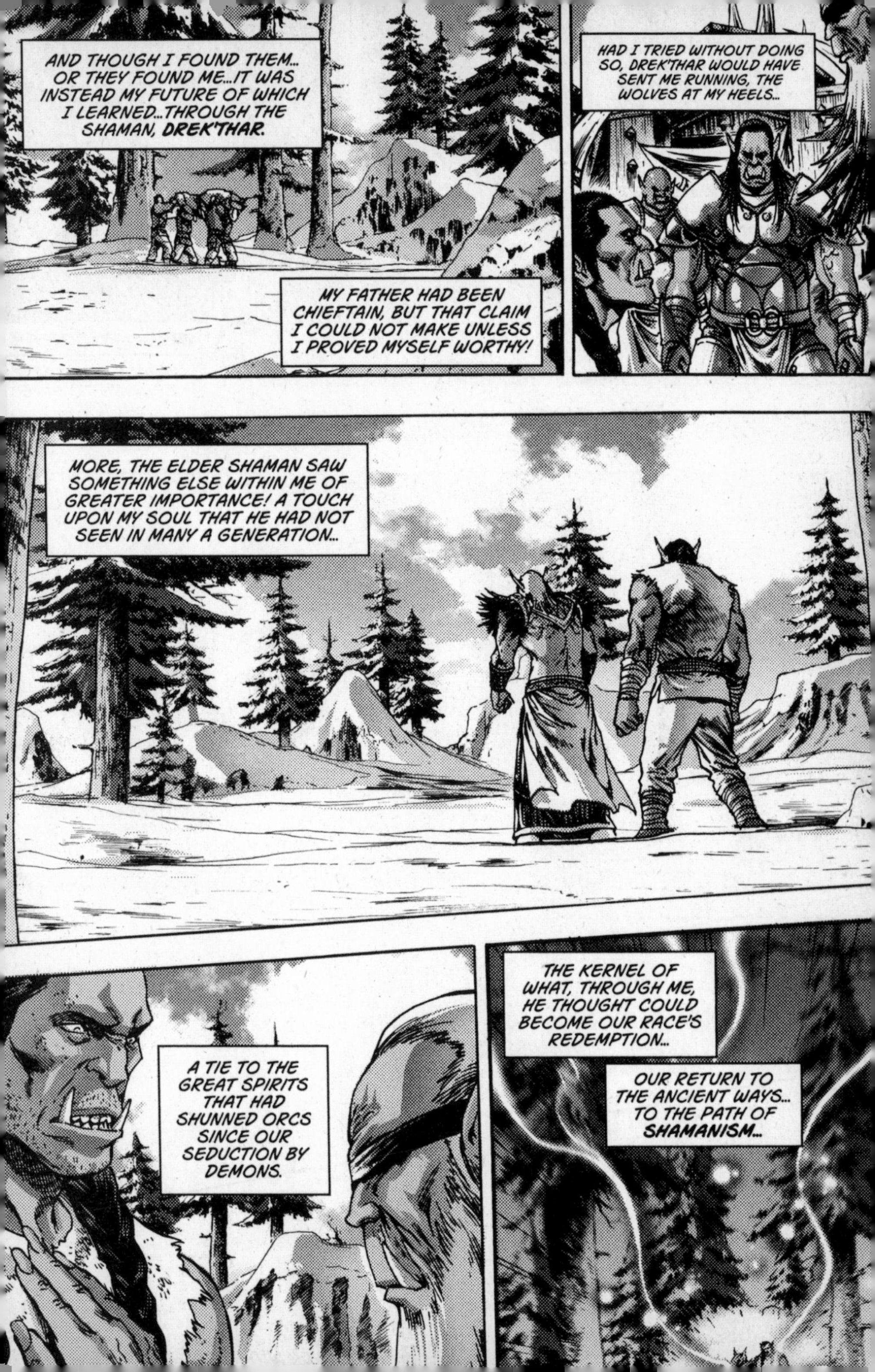
AND THOUGH I FOUND THEM... OR THEY FOUND ME...IT WAS INSTEAD MY FUTURE OF WHICH I LEARNED...THROUGH THE SHAMAN, **DREK'THAR.**
MY FATHER HAD BEEN CHIEFTAIN, BUT THAT CLAIM I COULD NOT MAKE UNLESS I PROVED MYSELF WORTHY!
HAD I TRIED WITHOUT DOING SO, DREK'THAR WOULD HAVE SENT ME RUNNING, THE WOLVES AT MY HEELS...
MORE, THE ELDER SHAMAN SAW SOMETHING ELSE WITHIN ME OF GREATER IMPORTANCE! A TOUCH UPON MY SOUL THAT HE HAD NOT SEEN IN MANY A GENERATION...
A TIE TO THE GREAT SPIRITS THAT HAD SHUNNED ORCS SINCE OUR SEDUCTION BY DEMONS.
THE KERNEL OF WHAT, THROUGH ME, HE THOUGHT COULD BECOME OUR RACE'S REDEMPTION...
OUR RETURN TO THE ANCIENT WAYS... TO THE PATH OF **SHAMANISM...**

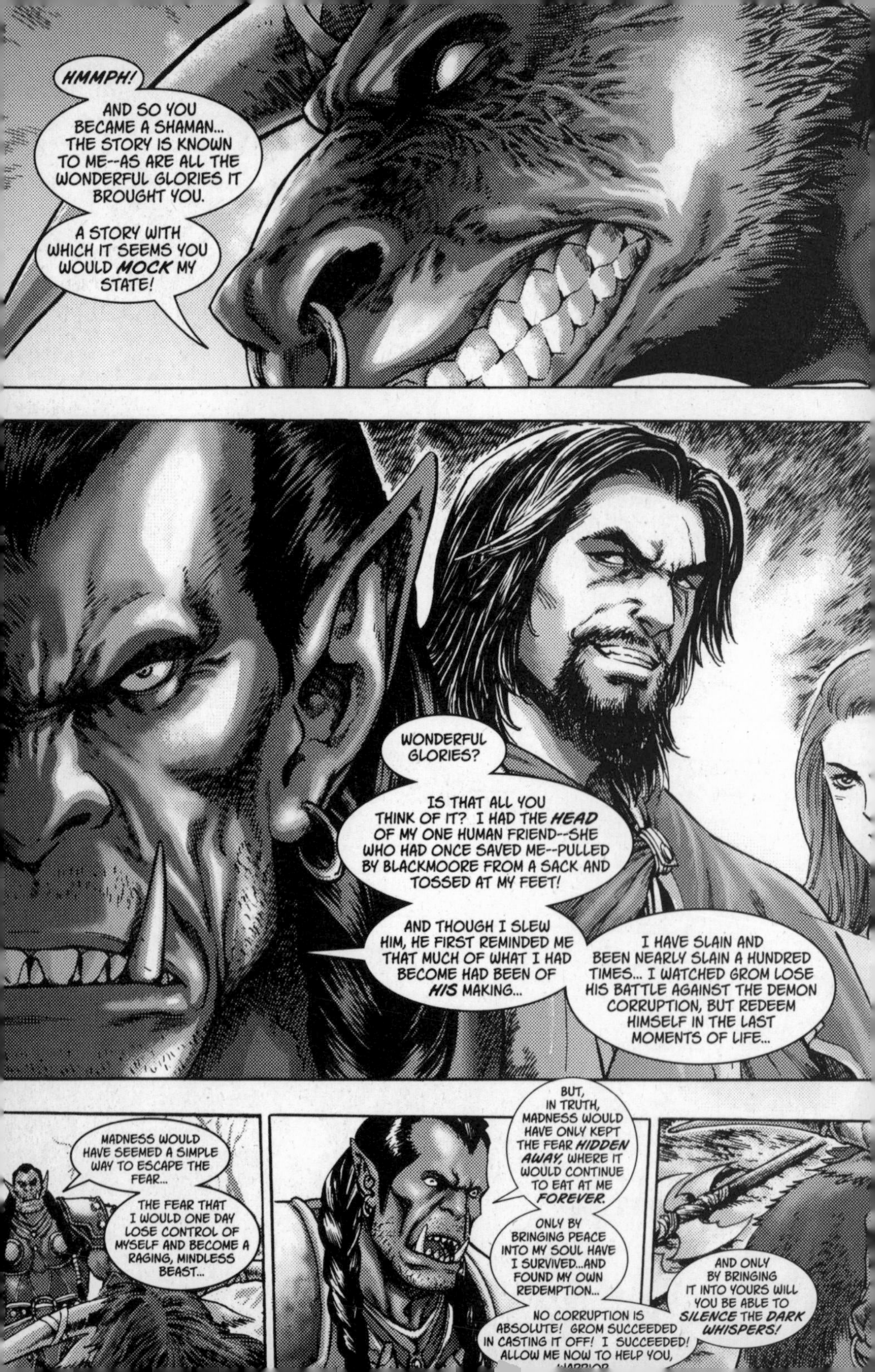
HMMPH!
AND SO YOU BECAME A SHAMAN... THE STORY IS KNOWN TO ME--AS ARE ALL THE WONDERFUL GLORIES IT BROUGHT YOU.
A STORY WITH WHICH IT SEEMS YOU WOULD MOCK MY STATE!
WONDERFUL GLORIES?
IS THAT ALL YOU THINK OF IT? I HAD THE HEAD OF MY ONE HUMAN FRIEND--SHE WHO HAD ONCE SAVED ME--PULLED BY BLACKMOORE FROM A SACK AND TOSSED AT MY FEET!
AND THOUGH I SLEW HIM, HE FIRST REMINDED ME THAT MUCH OF WHAT I HAD BECOME HAD BEEN OF HIS MAKING...
I HAVE SLAIN AND BEEN NEARLY SLAIN A HUNDRED TIMES... I WATCHED GROM LOSE HIS BATTLE AGAINST THE DEMON CORRUPTION, BUT REDEEM HIMSELF IN THE LAST MOMENTS OF LIFE...
MADNESS WOULD HAVE SEEMED A SIMPLE WAY TO ESCAPE THE FEAR...
THE FEAR THAT I WOULD ONE DAY LOSE CONTROL OF MYSELF AND BECOME A RAGING, MINDLESS BEAST...
BUT, IN TRUTH, MADNESS WOULD HAVE ONLY KEPT THE FEAR HIDDEN AWAY, WHERE IT WOULD CONTINUE TO EAT AT ME FOREVER.
ONLY BY BRINGING PEACE INTO MY SOUL HAVE I SURVIVED...AND FOUND MY OWN REDEMPTION...
AND ONLY BY BRINGING IT INTO YOURS WILL YOU BE ABLE TO SILENCE THE DARK WHISPERS!
NO CORRUPTION IS ABSOLUTE! GROM SUCCEEDED IN CASTING IT OFF! I SUCCEEDED! ALLOW ME NOW TO HELP YOU,

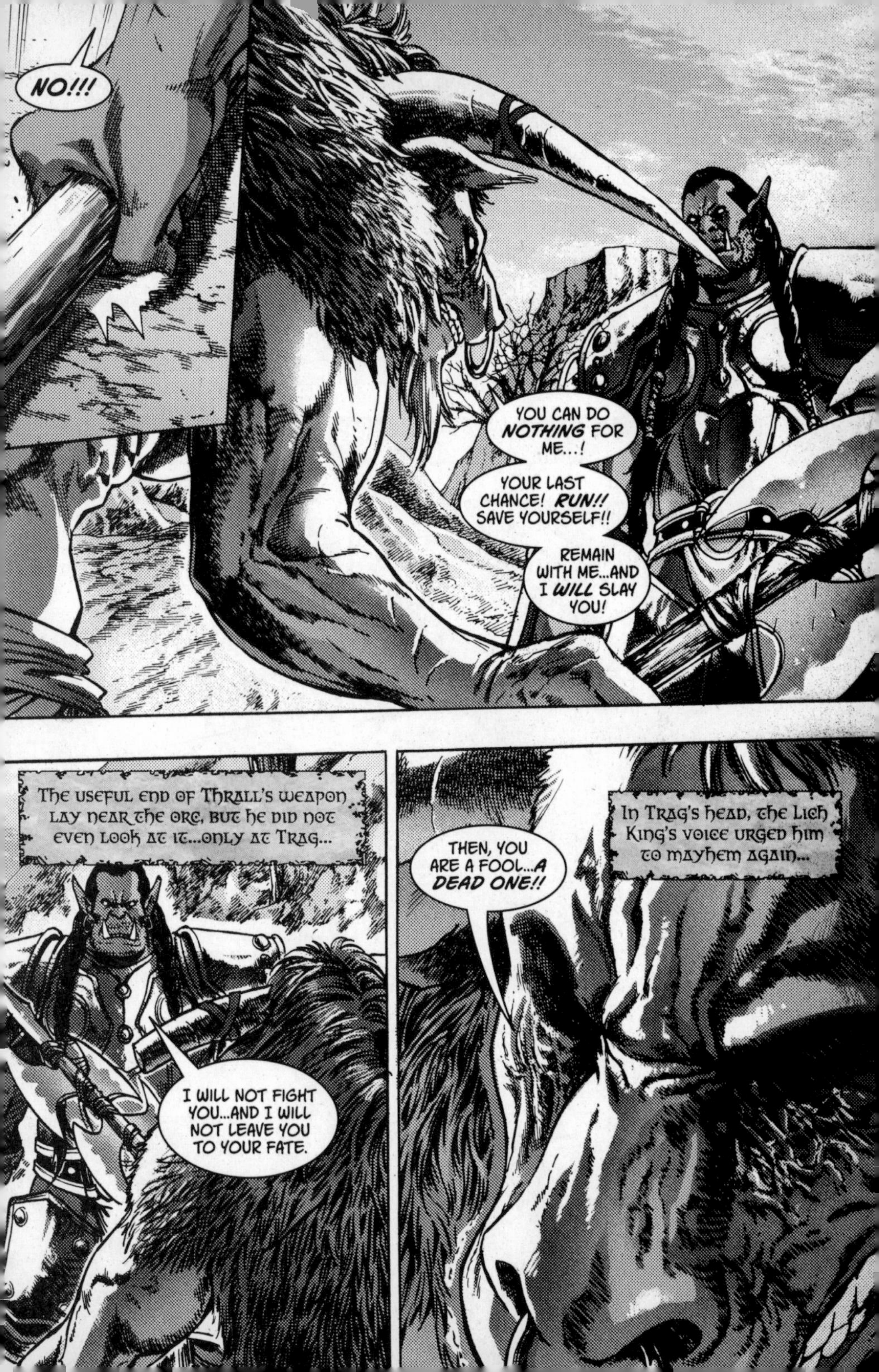
NO!!!
YOU CAN DO NOTHING FOR ME...!
YOUR LAST CHANCE! RUN!! SAVE YOURSELF!!
REMAIN WITH ME...AND I WILL SLAY YOU!
The useful end of Thrall's weapon lay near the orc, but he did not even look at it...only at Trag...
I WILL NOT FIGHT YOU...AND I WILL NOT LEAVE YOU TO YOUR FATE.
THEN, YOU ARE A FOOL...A DEAD ONE!!
In Trag's head, the Lich King's voice urged him to mayhem again...

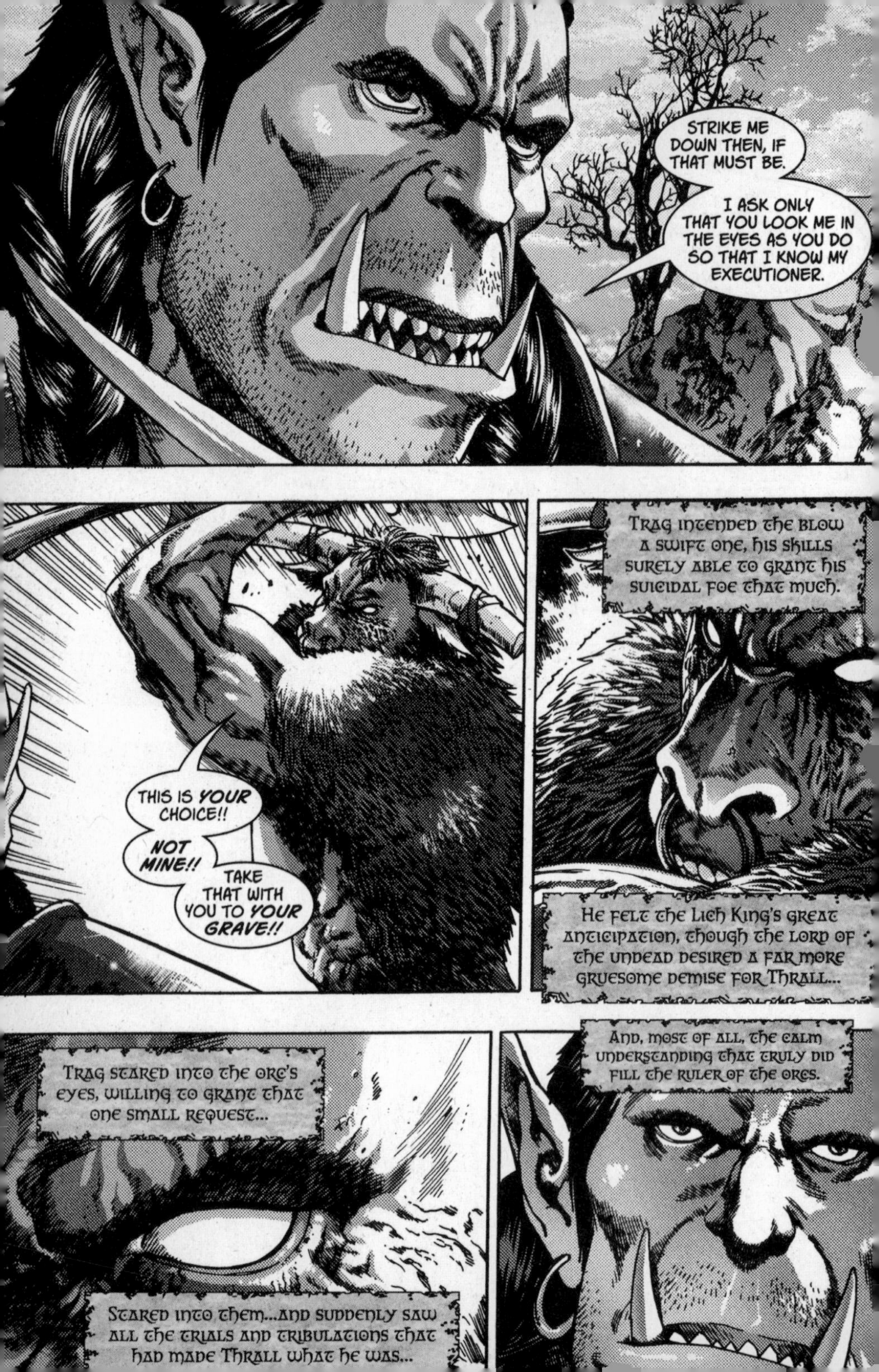
STRIKE ME DOWN THEN, IF THAT MUST BE.
I ASK ONLY THAT YOU LOOK ME IN THE EYES AS YOU DO SO THAT I KNOW MY EXECUTIONER.
THIS IS *YOUR* CHOICE!!
NOT MINE!!
TAKE THAT WITH YOU TO *YOUR GRAVE!!*
Trag intended the blow a swift one, his skills surely able to grant his suicidal foe that much.
He felt the Lich King's great anticipation, though the lord of the undead desired a far more gruesome demise for Thrall...
Trag stared into the orc's eyes, willing to grant that one small request...
Stared into them...and suddenly saw all the trials and tribulations that had made Thrall what he was...
And, most of all, the calm understanding that truly did fill the ruler of the orcs.

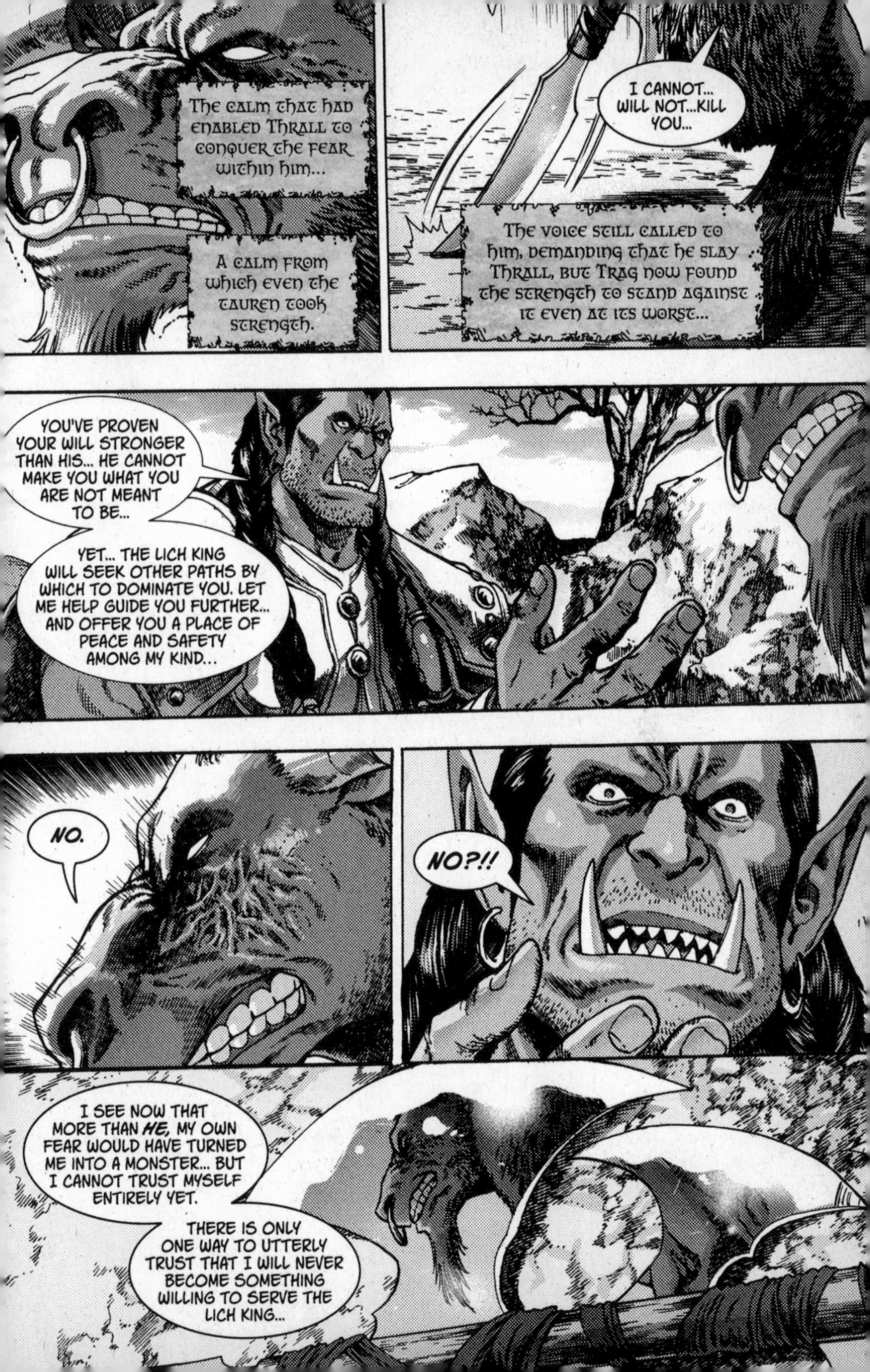

The calm that had enabled Thrall to conquer the fear within him...
A calm from which even the tauren took strength.
I CANNOT... WILL NOT...KILL YOU...
The voice still called to him, demanding that he slay Thrall, but Trag now found the strength to stand against it even at its worst...
YOU'VE PROVEN YOUR WILL STRONGER THAN HIS... HE CANNOT MAKE YOU WHAT YOU ARE NOT MEANT TO BE...
YET... THE LICH KING WILL SEEK OTHER PATHS BY WHICH TO DOMINATE YOU. LET ME HELP GUIDE YOU FURTHER... AND OFFER YOU A PLACE OF PEACE AND SAFETY AMONG MY KIND...
NO.
NO?!!
I SEE NOW THAT MORE THAN *HE*, MY OWN FEAR WOULD HAVE TURNED ME INTO A MONSTER... BUT I CANNOT TRUST MYSELF ENTIRELY YET.
THERE IS ONLY ONE WAY TO UTTERLY TRUST THAT I WILL NEVER BECOME SOMETHING WILLING TO SERVE THE LICH KING...

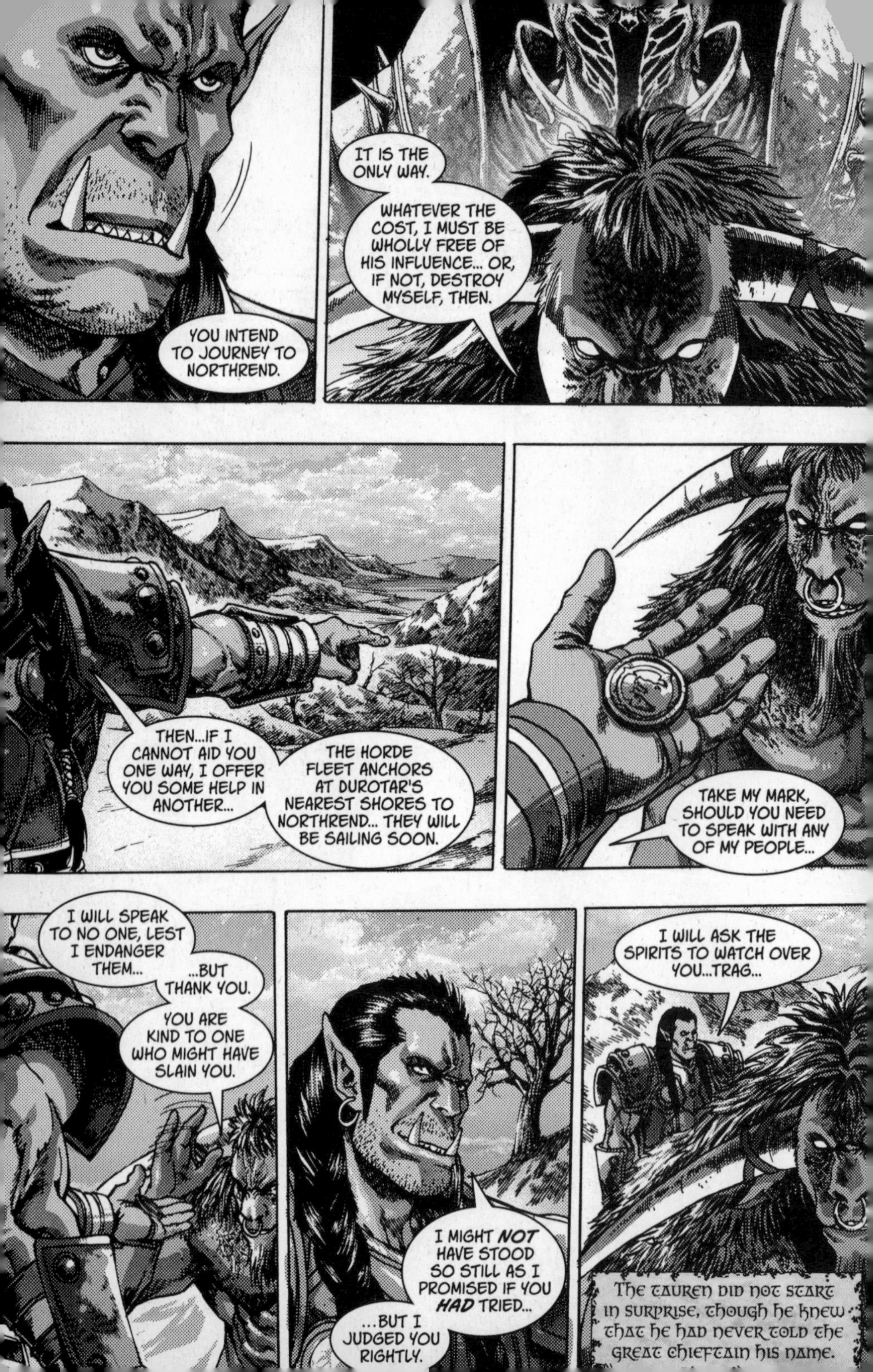
YOU INTEND TO JOURNEY TO NORTHREND.
IT IS THE ONLY WAY.
WHATEVER THE COST, I MUST BE WHOLLY FREE OF HIS INFLUENCE... OR, IF NOT, DESTROY MYSELF, THEN.
THEN...IF I CANNOT AID YOU ONE WAY, I OFFER YOU SOME HELP IN ANOTHER...
THE HORDE FLEET ANCHORS AT DUROTAR'S NEAREST SHORES TO NORTHREND... THEY WILL BE SAILING SOON.
TAKE MY MARK, SHOULD YOU NEED TO SPEAK WITH ANY OF MY PEOPLE...
I WILL SPEAK TO NO ONE, LEST I ENDANGER THEM...
...BUT THANK YOU.
YOU ARE KIND TO ONE WHO MIGHT HAVE SLAIN YOU.
I MIGHT **NOT** HAVE STOOD SO STILL AS I PROMISED IF YOU ***HAD*** TRIED...
...BUT I JUDGED YOU RIGHTLY.
I WILL ASK THE SPIRITS TO WATCH OVER YOU...TRAG...
The tauren did not start in surprise, though he knew that he had never told the great chieftain his name.

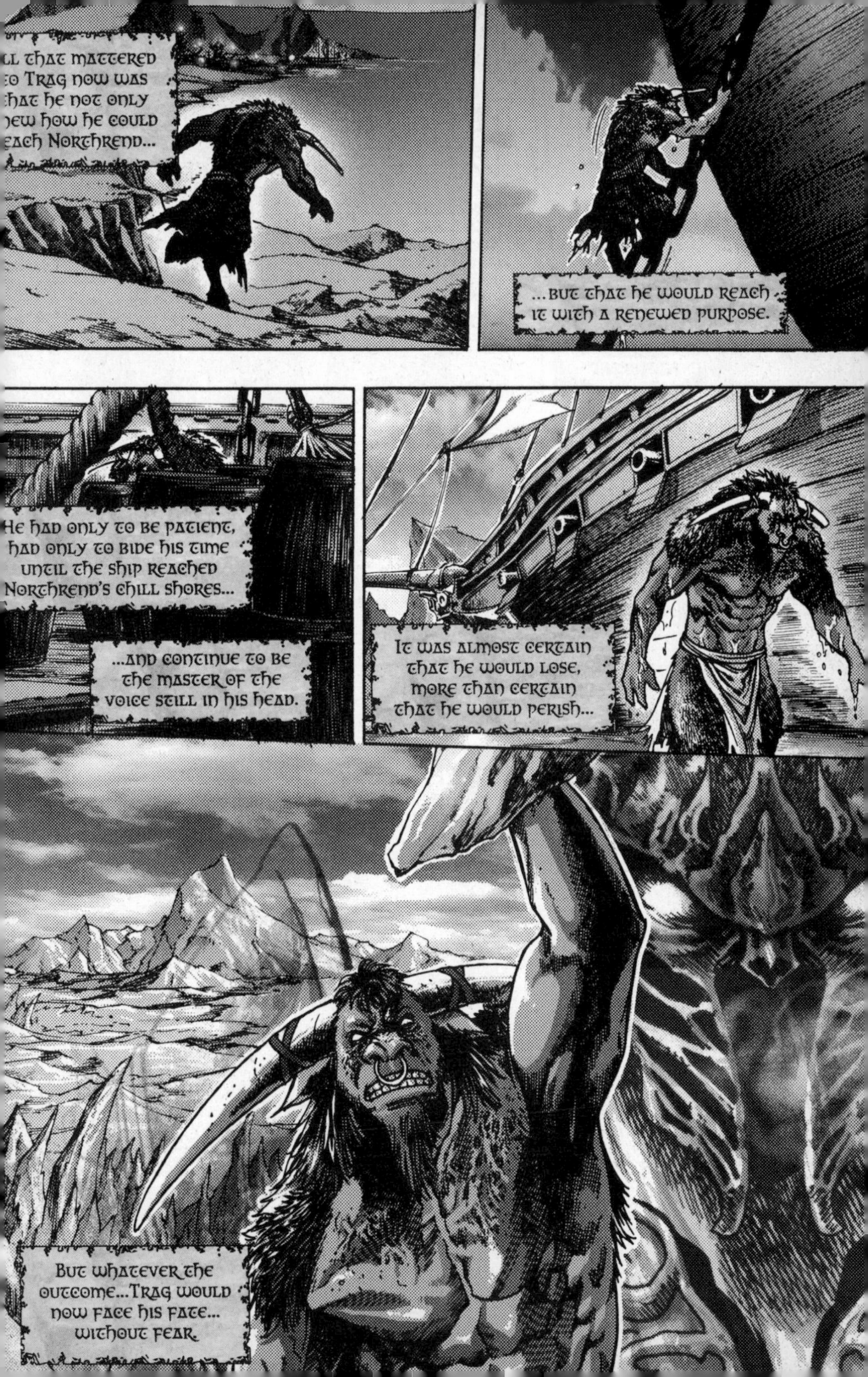

LL THAT MATTERED
TO TRAG NOW WAS
THAT HE NOT ONLY
NEW HOW HE COULD
EACH NORTHREND...
...BUT THAT HE WOULD REACH IT WITH A RENEWED PURPOSE.
HE HAD ONLY TO BE PATIENT, HAD ONLY TO BIDE HIS TIME UNTIL THE SHIP REACHED NORTHREND'S CHILL SHORES...
...AND CONTINUE TO BE THE MASTER OF THE VOICE STILL IN HIS HEAD.
IT WAS ALMOST CERTAIN THAT HE WOULD LOSE, MORE THAN CERTAIN THAT HE WOULD PERISH...
BUT WHATEVER THE OUTCOME...TRAG WOULD NOW FACE HIS FATE... WITHOUT FEAR.

HAPTER THREE

FIEND

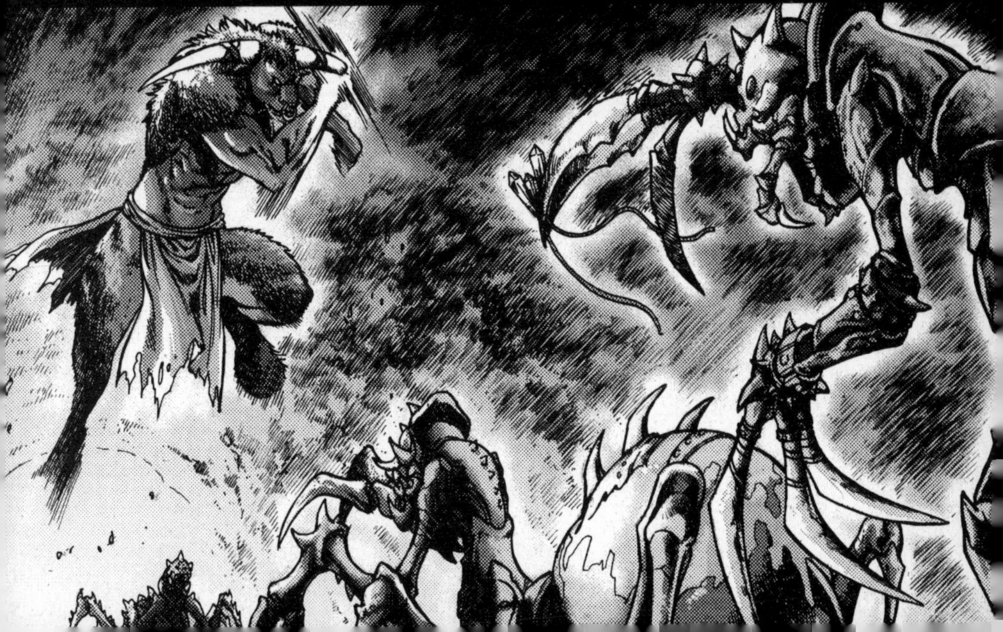

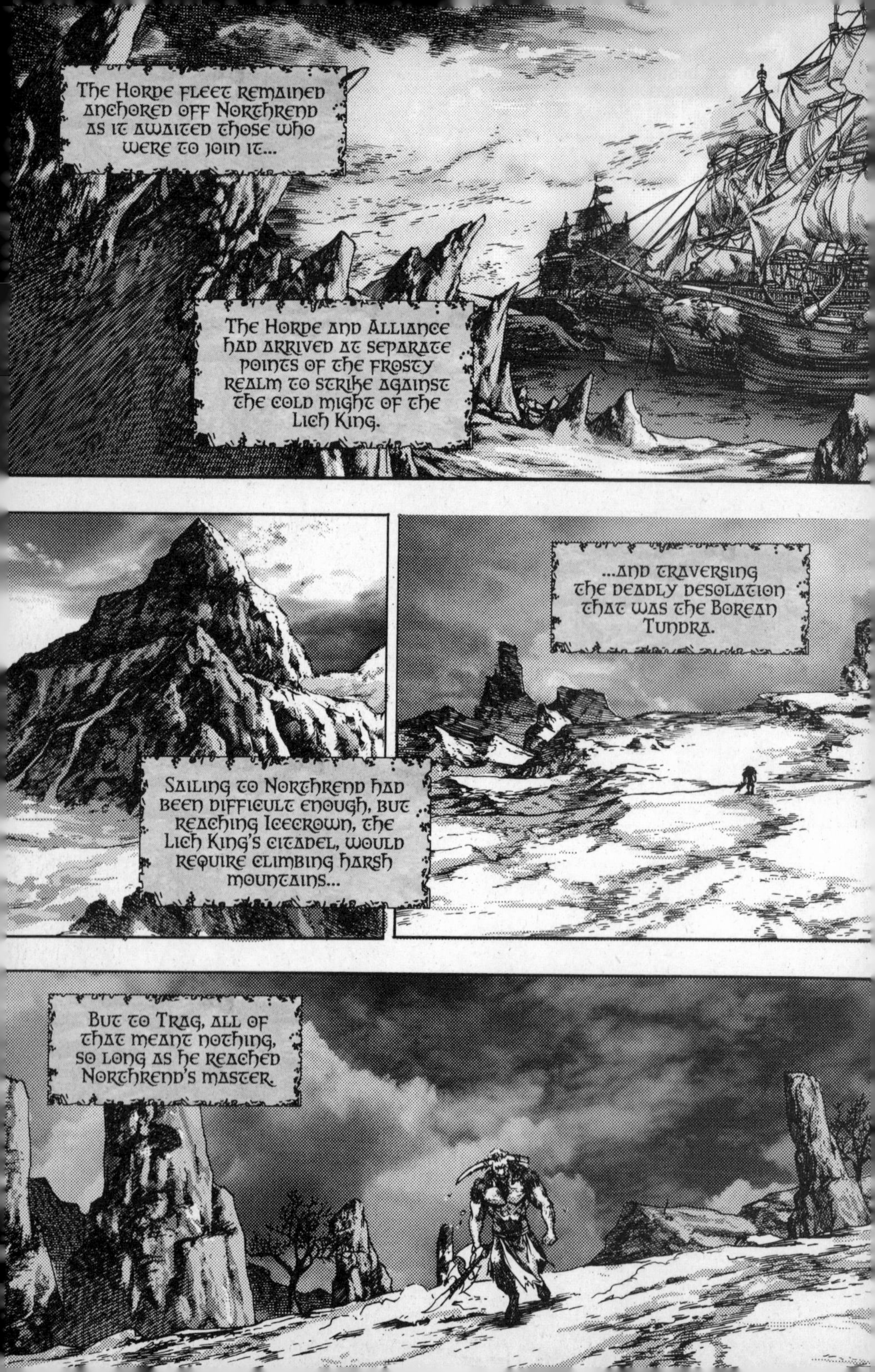
The Horde fleet remained anchored off Northrend as it awaited those who were to join it...
The Horde and Alliance had arrived at separate points of the frosty realm to strike against the cold might of the Lich King.
Sailing to Northrend had been difficult enough, but reaching Icecrown, the Lich King's citadel, would require climbing harsh mountains...
...and traversing the deadly desolation that was the Borean Tundra.
But to Trag, all of that meant nothing, so long as he reached Northrend's master.

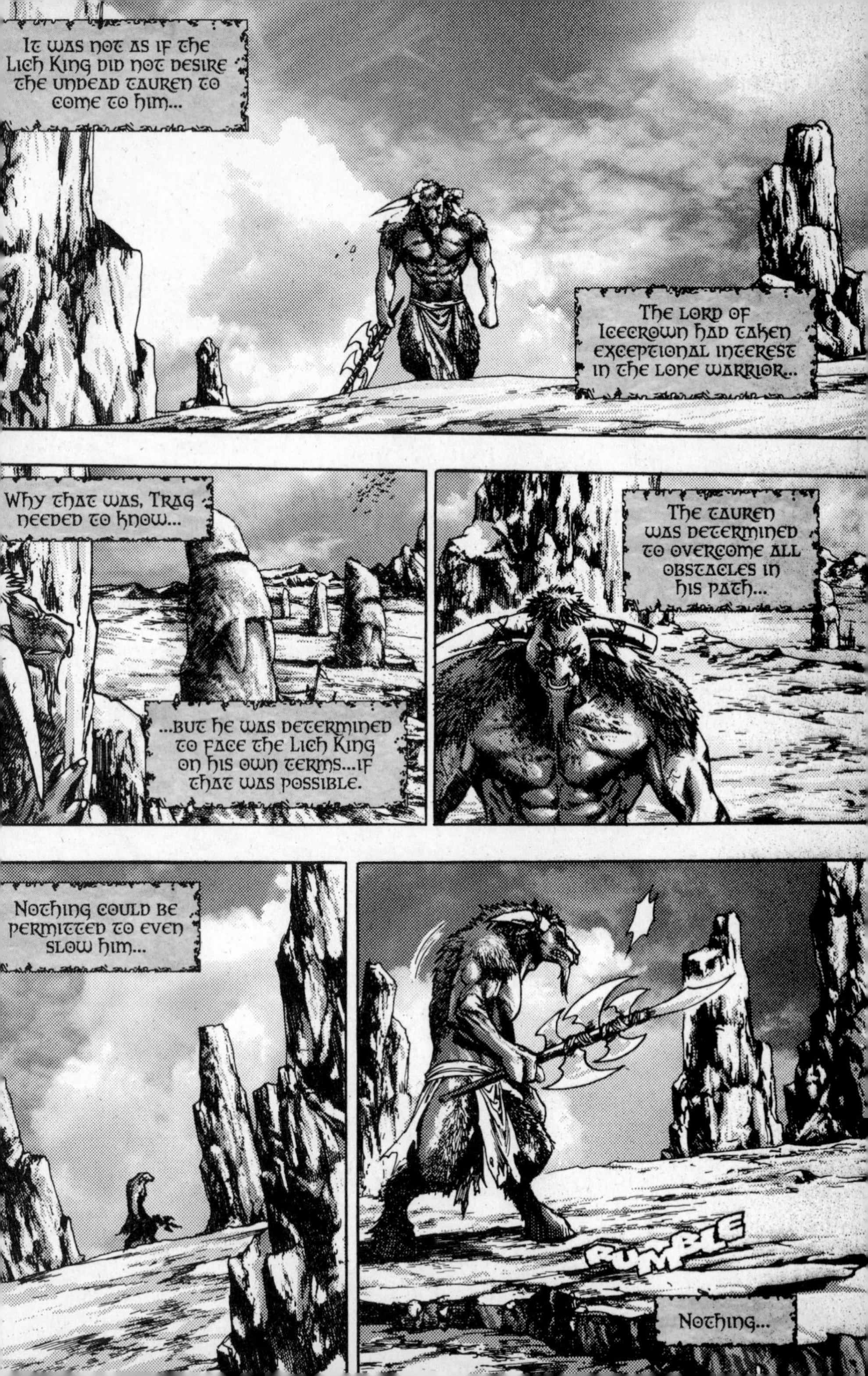
It was not as if the Lich King did not desire the undead tauren to come to him...
The Lord of Icecrown had taken exceptional interest in the lone warrior...
Why that was, Trag needed to know...
...but he was determined to face the Lich King on his own terms...if that was possible.
The tauren was determined to overcome all obstacles in his path...
Nothing could be permitted to even slow him...
RUMBLE
Nothing...

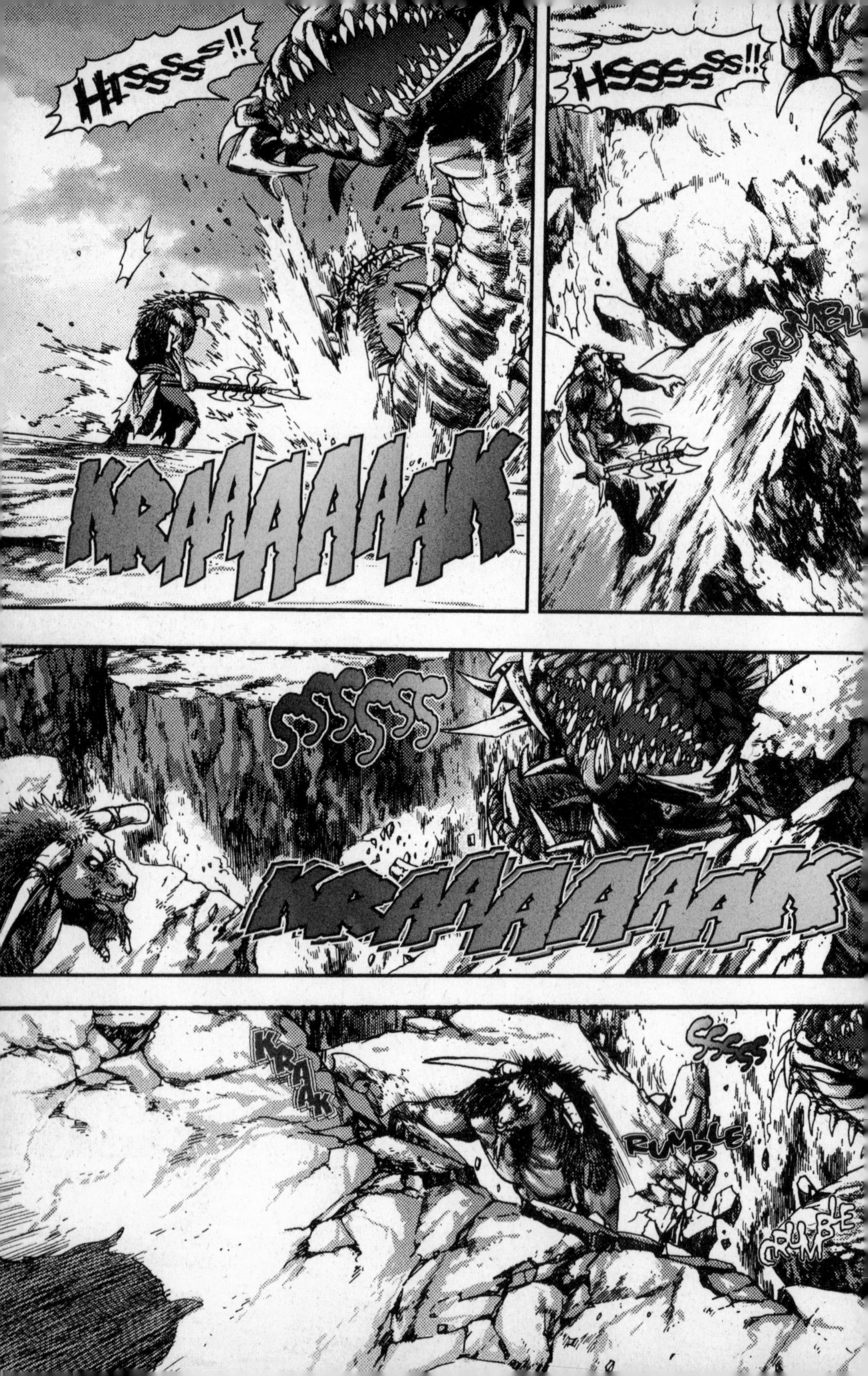
HSSSSSSS!!
CRUMBL
HISSSSS!!
KRAAAAAAK
SSSSSS
KRAAAAAAAK
SSSSS
RUMBLE
CRUMBLE
KRAAK

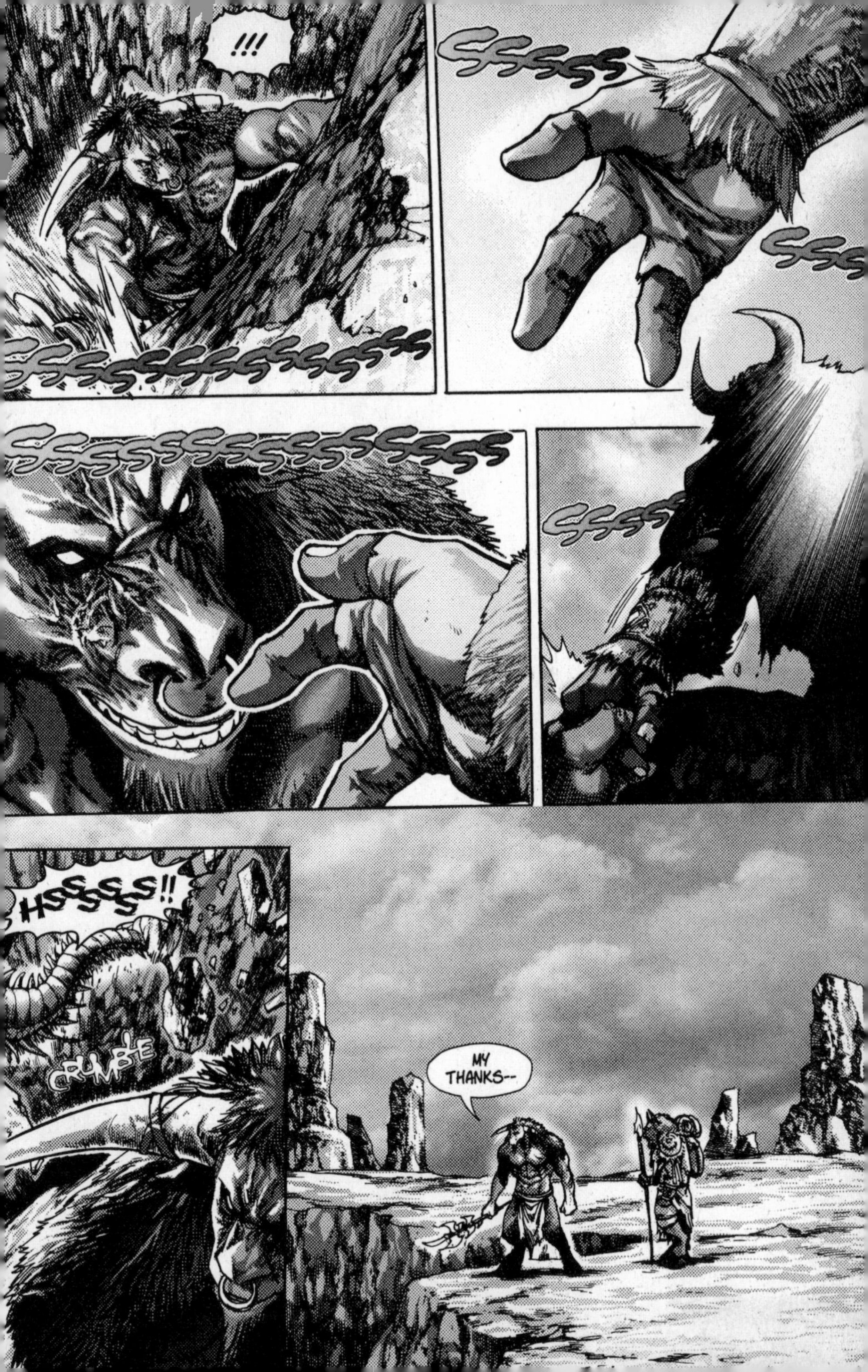
!!!
MY THANKS--
HSSSSSS!!
CRUMBLE

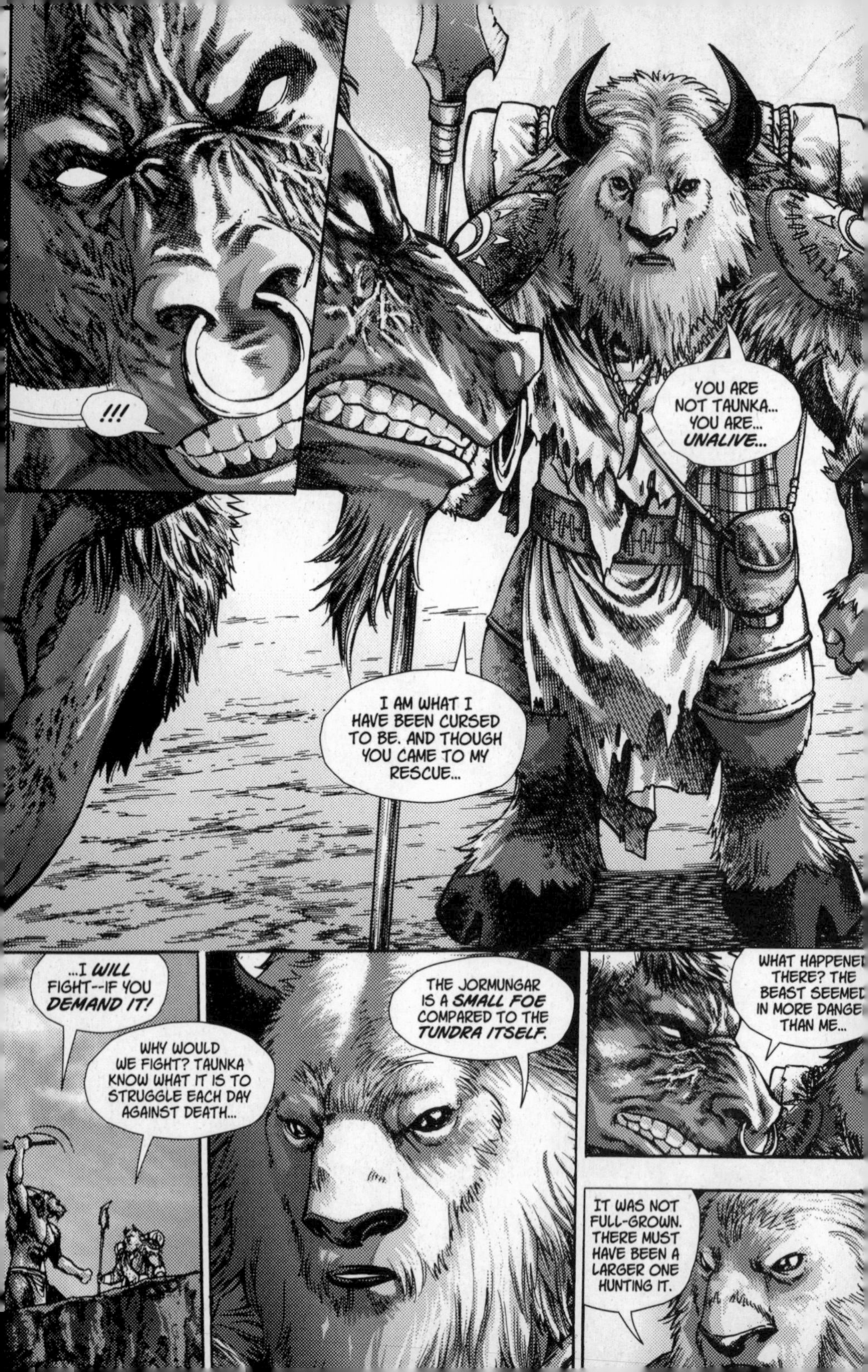

!!!
YOU ARE NOT TAUNKA... YOU ARE... *UNALIVE*...
I AM WHAT I HAVE BEEN CURSED TO BE. AND THOUGH YOU CAME TO MY RESCUE...
...I *WILL* FIGHT--IF YOU *DEMAND IT!*
WHY WOULD WE FIGHT? TAUNKA KNOW WHAT IT IS TO STRUGGLE EACH DAY AGAINST DEATH...
THE JORMUNGAR IS A *SMALL FOE* COMPARED TO THE *TUNDRA ITSELF.*
WHAT HAPPENE THERE? THE BEAST SEEME IN MORE DANGE THAN ME...
IT WAS NOT FULL-GROWN. THERE MUST HAVE BEEN A LARGER ONE HUNTING IT.

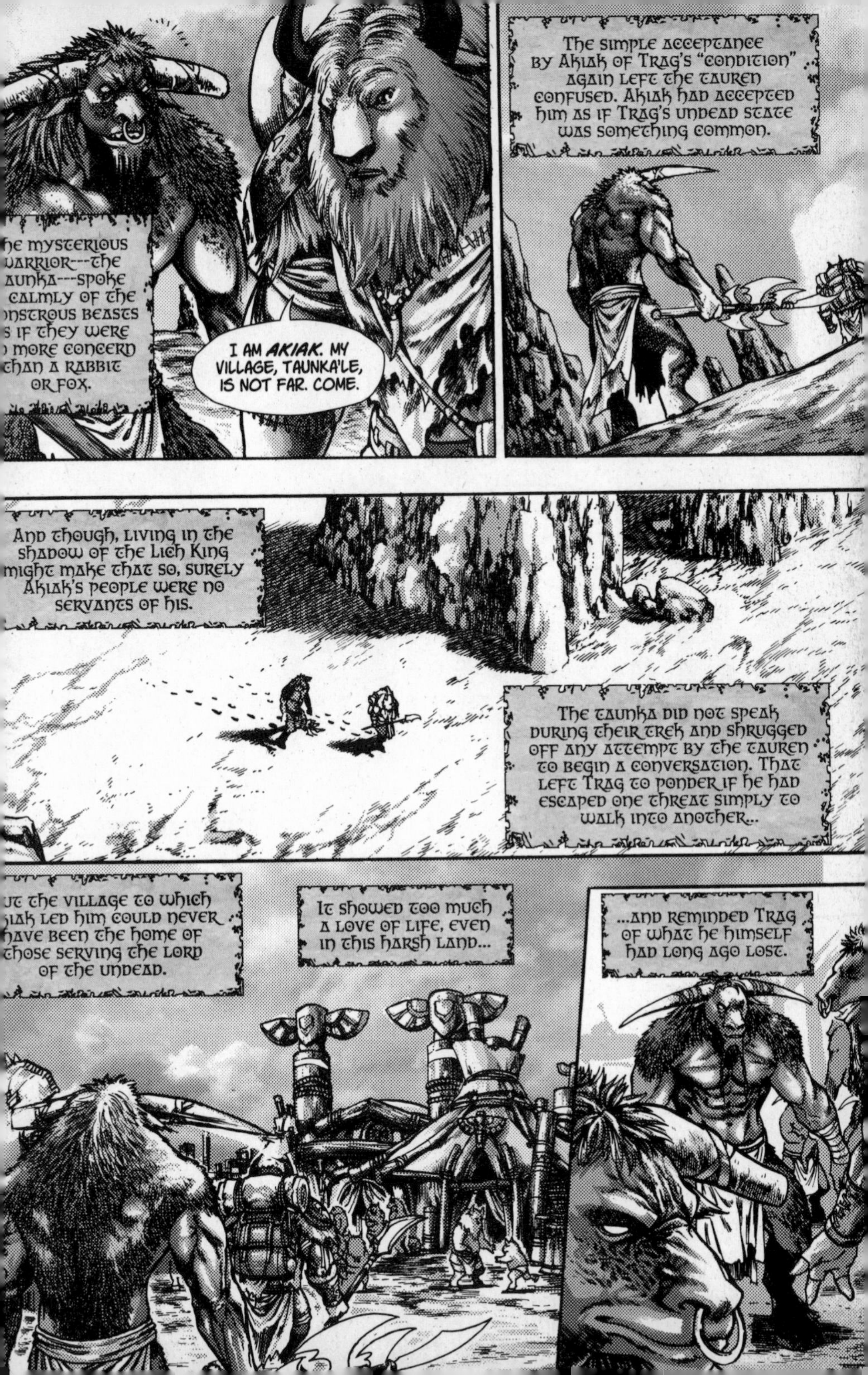
he mysterious warrior---the aunka---spoke calmly of the nstrous beasts s if they were o more concern than a rabbit or fox.
I AM *AKIAK*. MY VILLAGE, TAUNKA'LE, IS NOT FAR. COME.
The simple acceptance by Akiak of Trag's "condition" again left the tauren confused. Akiak had accepted him as if Trag's undead state was something common.
And though, living in the shadow of the Lich King might make that so, surely Akiak's people were no servants of his.
The taunka did not speak during their trek and shrugged off any attempt by the tauren to begin a conversation. That left Trag to ponder if he had escaped one threat simply to walk into another...
ut the village to which kiak led him could never have been the home of those serving the lord of the undead.
It showed too much a love of life, even in this harsh land...
...and reminded Trag of what he himself had long ago lost.

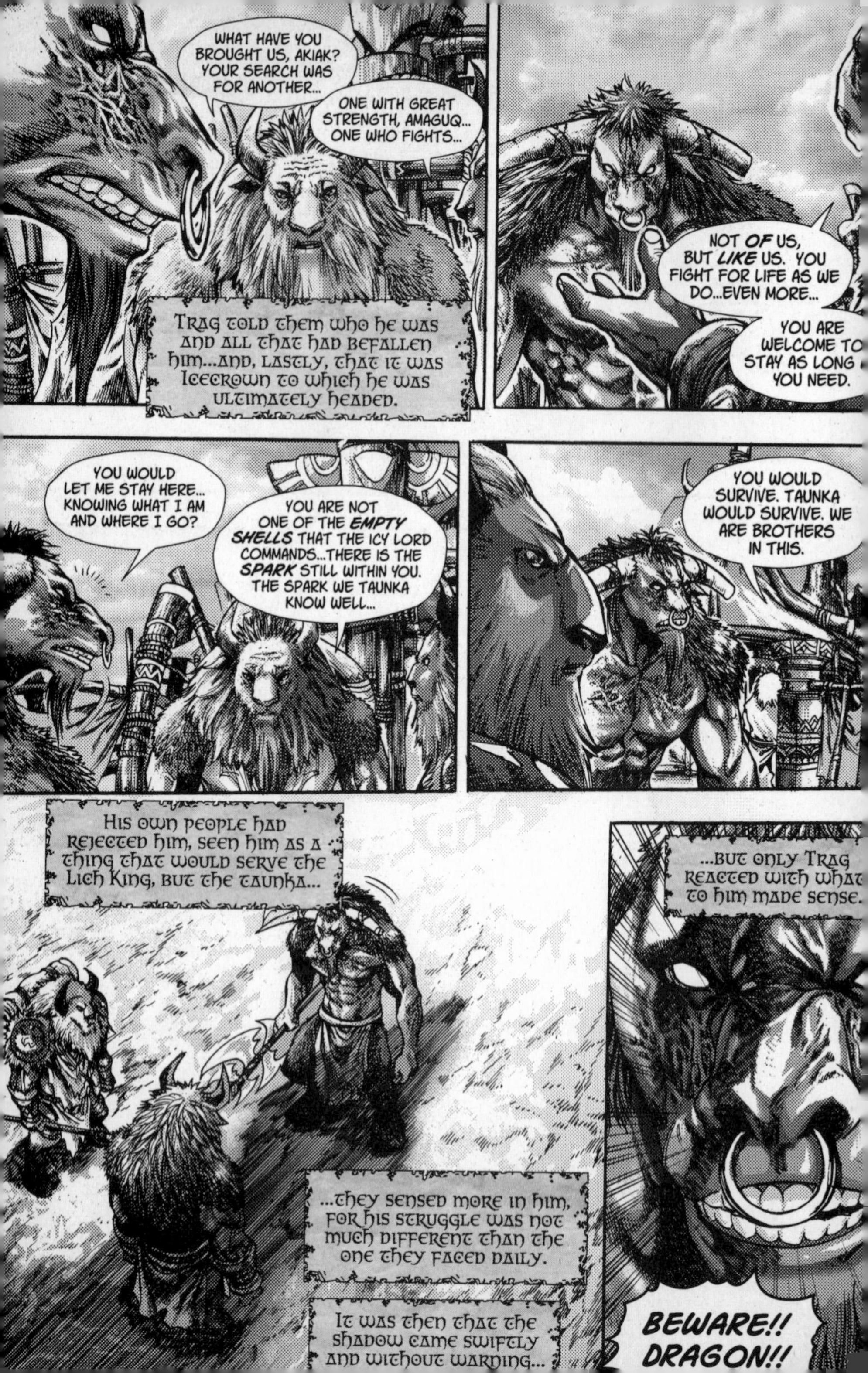
WHAT HAVE YOU BROUGHT US, AKIAK? YOUR SEARCH WAS FOR ANOTHER...
ONE WITH GREAT STRENGTH, AMAGUQ... ONE WHO FIGHTS...
Trag told them who he was and all that had befallen him...and, lastly, that it was Icecrown to which he was ultimately headed.
NOT *OF* US, BUT *LIKE* US. YOU FIGHT FOR LIFE AS WE DO...EVEN MORE...
YOU ARE WELCOME TO STAY AS LONG YOU NEED.
YOU WOULD LET ME STAY HERE... KNOWING WHAT I AM AND WHERE I GO?
YOU ARE NOT ONE OF THE *EMPTY SHELLS* THAT THE ICY LORD COMMANDS...THERE IS THE *SPARK* STILL WITHIN YOU. THE SPARK WE TAUNKA KNOW WELL...
YOU WOULD SURVIVE. TAUNKA WOULD SURVIVE. WE ARE BROTHERS IN THIS.
His own people had rejected him, seen him as a thing that would serve the Lich King, but the taunka...
...they sensed more in him, for his struggle was not much different than the one they faced daily.
It was then that the shadow came swiftly and without warning...
...but only Trag reacted with what to him made sense.
BEWARE!! DRAGON!!

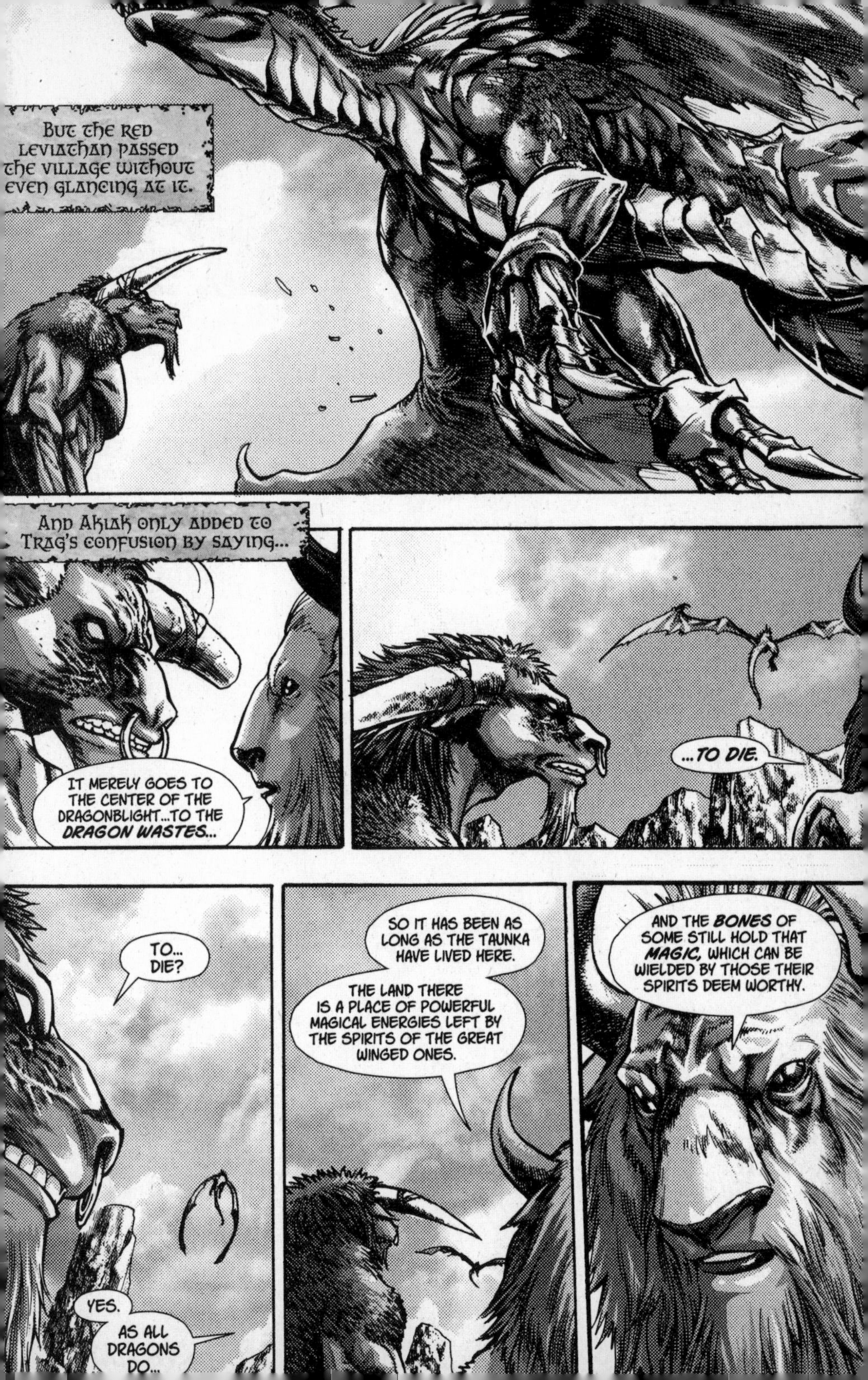
But the red leviathan passed the village without even glancing at it.
And Akiak only added to Trag's confusion by saying...
IT MERELY GOES TO THE CENTER OF THE DRAGONBLIGHT...TO THE *DRAGON WASTES*...
...*TO DIE.*
TO... DIE?
YES.
AS ALL DRAGONS DO...
SO IT HAS BEEN AS LONG AS THE TAUNKA HAVE LIVED HERE.
THE LAND THERE IS A PLACE OF POWERFUL MAGICAL ENERGIES LEFT BY THE SPIRITS OF THE GREAT WINGED ONES.
AND THE *BONES* OF SOME STILL HOLD THAT *MAGIC,* WHICH CAN BE WIELDED BY THOSE THEIR SPIRITS DEEM WORTHY.

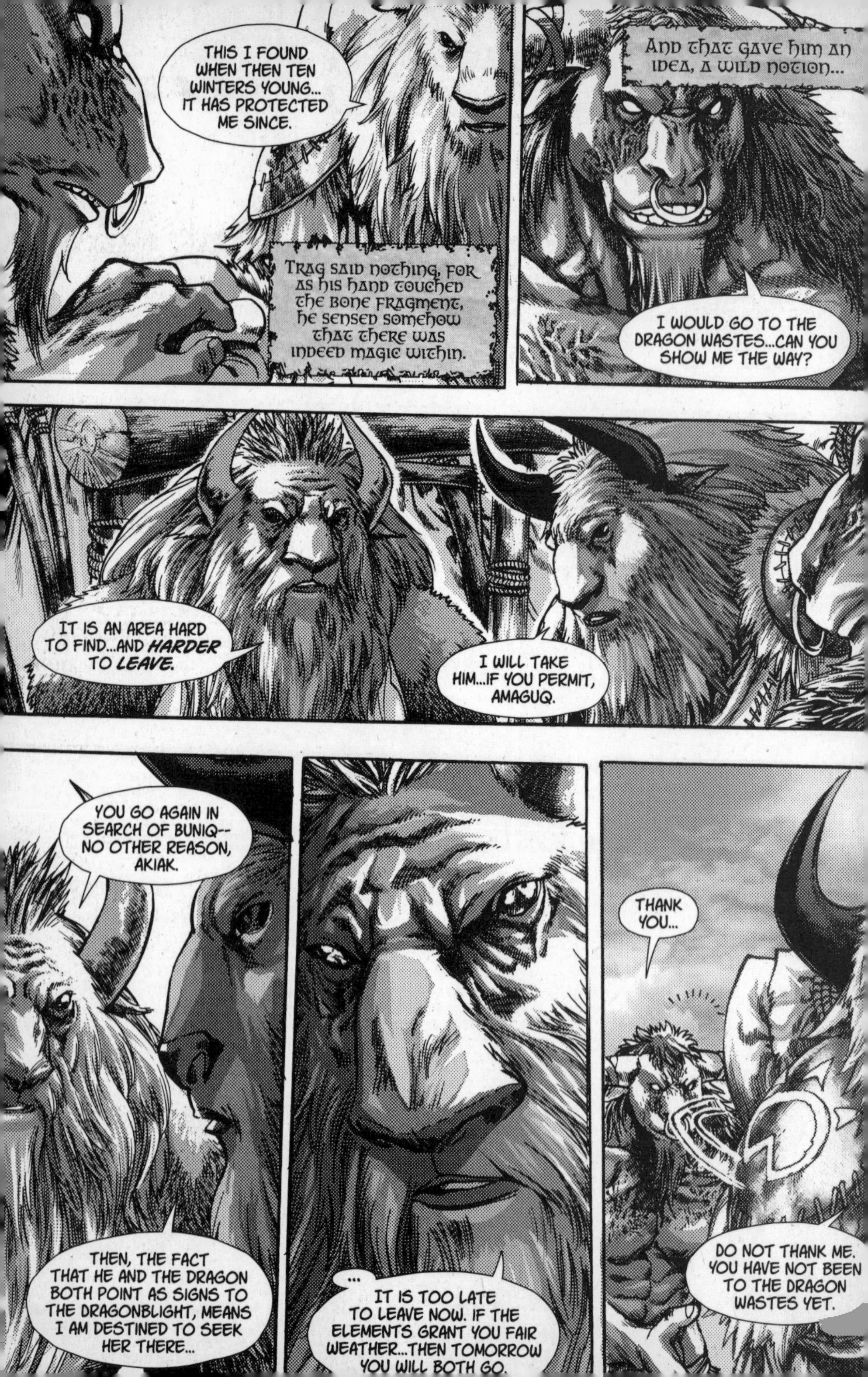
THIS I FOUND WHEN THEN TEN WINTERS YOUNG... IT HAS PROTECTED ME SINCE.
TRAG SAID NOTHING, FOR AS HIS HAND TOUCHED THE BONE FRAGMENT, HE SENSED SOMEHOW THAT THERE WAS INDEED MAGIC WITHIN.
AND THAT GAVE HIM AN IDEA, A WILD NOTION...
I WOULD GO TO THE DRAGON WASTES...CAN YOU SHOW ME THE WAY?
IT IS AN AREA HARD TO FIND...AND *HARDER* TO *LEAVE*.
I WILL TAKE HIM...IF YOU PERMIT, AMAGUQ.
YOU GO AGAIN IN SEARCH OF BUNIQ-- NO OTHER REASON, AKIAK.
THEN, THE FACT THAT HE AND THE DRAGON BOTH POINT AS SIGNS TO THE DRAGONBLIGHT, MEANS I AM DESTINED TO SEEK HER THERE...
...
IT IS TOO LATE TO LEAVE NOW. IF THE ELEMENTS GRANT YOU FAIR WEATHER...THEN TOMORROW YOU WILL BOTH GO.
THANK YOU...
DO NOT THANK ME. YOU HAVE NOT BEEN TO THE DRAGON WASTES YET.

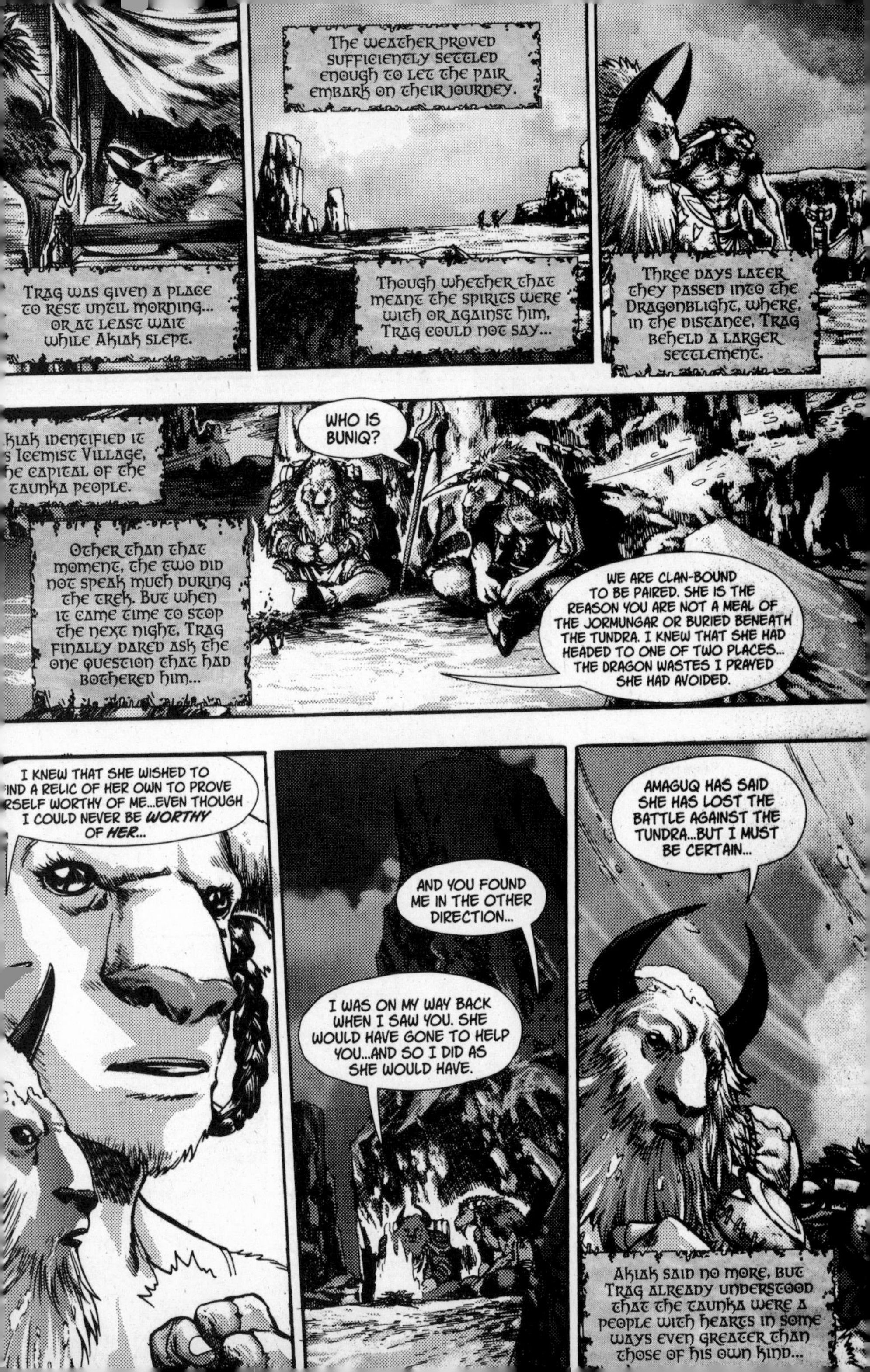
Trag was given a place to rest until morning... or at least wait while Akiak slept.
The weather proved sufficiently settled enough to let the pair embark on their journey.
Though whether that meant the spirits were with or against him, Trag could not say...
Three days later they passed into the Dragonblight, where, in the distance, Trag beheld a larger settlement.
kiak identified it s Icemist Village, he capital of the taunka people.
Other than that moment, the two did not speak much during the trek. But when it came time to stop the next night, Trag finally dared ask the one question that had bothered him...
WHO IS BUNIQ?
WE ARE CLAN-BOUND TO BE PAIRED. SHE IS THE REASON YOU ARE NOT A MEAL OF THE JORMUNGAR OR BURIED BENEATH THE TUNDRA. I KNEW THAT SHE HAD HEADED TO ONE OF TWO PLACES... THE DRAGON WASTES I PRAYED SHE HAD AVOIDED.
I KNEW THAT SHE WISHED TO IND A RELIC OF HER OWN TO PROVE RSELF WORTHY OF ME...EVEN THOUGH I COULD NEVER BE ***WORTHY*** OF ***HER***...
AND YOU FOUND ME IN THE OTHER DIRECTION...
I WAS ON MY WAY BACK WHEN I SAW YOU. SHE WOULD HAVE GONE TO HELP YOU...AND SO I DID AS SHE WOULD HAVE.
AMAGUQ HAS SAID SHE HAS LOST THE BATTLE AGAINST THE TUNDRA...BUT I MUST BE CERTAIN...
Akiak said no more, but Trag already understood that the taunka were a people with hearts in some ways even greater than those of his own kind...

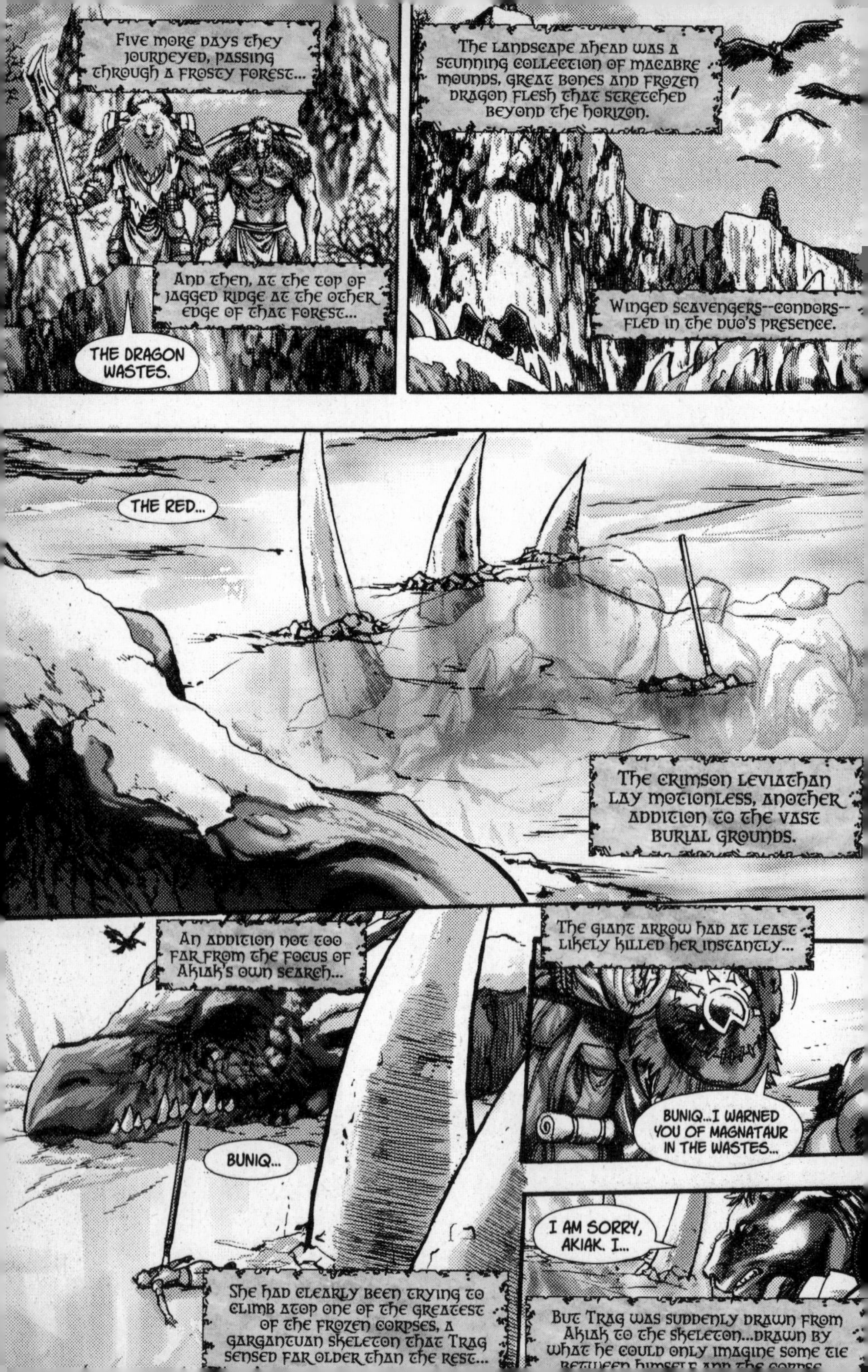
Five more days they journeyed, passing through a frosty forest...
And then, at the top of jagged ridge at the other edge of that forest...
THE DRAGON WASTES.
The landscape ahead was a stunning collection of macabre mounds, great bones and frozen dragon flesh that stretched beyond the horizon.
Winged scavengers--condors--fled in the duo's presence.
THE RED...
The crimson leviathan lay motionless, another addition to the vast burial grounds.
An addition not too far from the focus of Akiak's own search...
BUNIQ...
She had clearly been trying to climb atop one of the greatest of the frozen corpses, a gargantuan skeleton that Trag sensed far older than the rest...
The giant arrow had at least likely killed her instantly...
BUNIQ...I WARNED YOU OF MAGNATAUR IN THE WASTES...
I AM SORRY, AKIAK. I...
But Trag was suddenly drawn from Akiak to the skeleton...drawn by what he could only imagine some tie

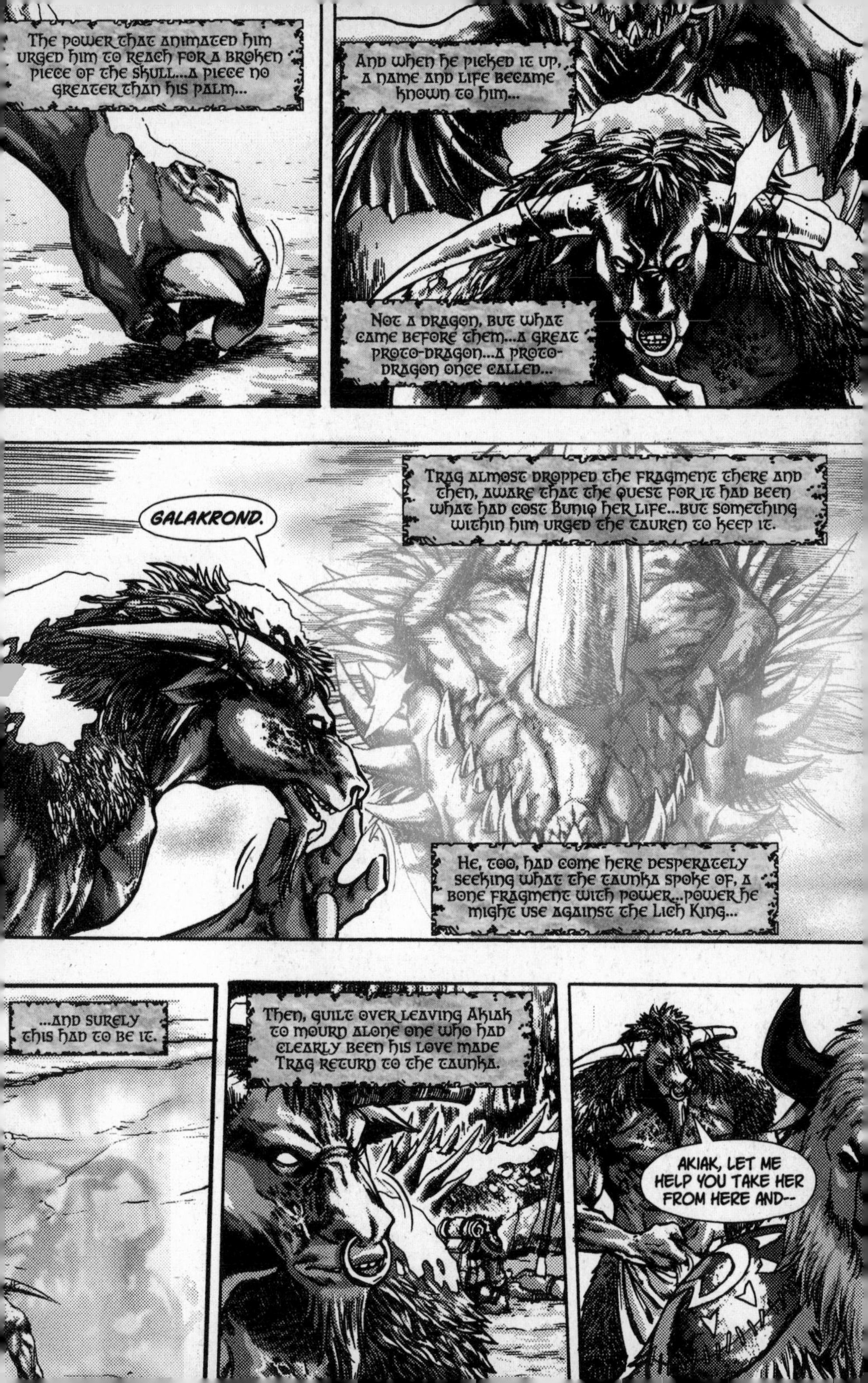
The power that animated him urged him to reach for a broken piece of the skull...a piece no greater than his palm...
And when he picked it up, a name and life became known to him...
Not a dragon, but what came before them...a great proto-dragon...a proto-dragon once called...
GALAKROND.
Trag almost dropped the fragment there and then, aware that the quest for it had been what had cost Buniq her life...but something within him urged the tauren to keep it.
He, too, had come here desperately seeking what the taunka spoke of, a bone fragment with power...power he might use against the Lich King...
...and surely this had to be it.
Then, guilt over leaving Akiak to mourn alone one who had clearly been his love made Trag return to the taunka.
AKIAK, LET ME HELP YOU TAKE HER FROM HERE AND--

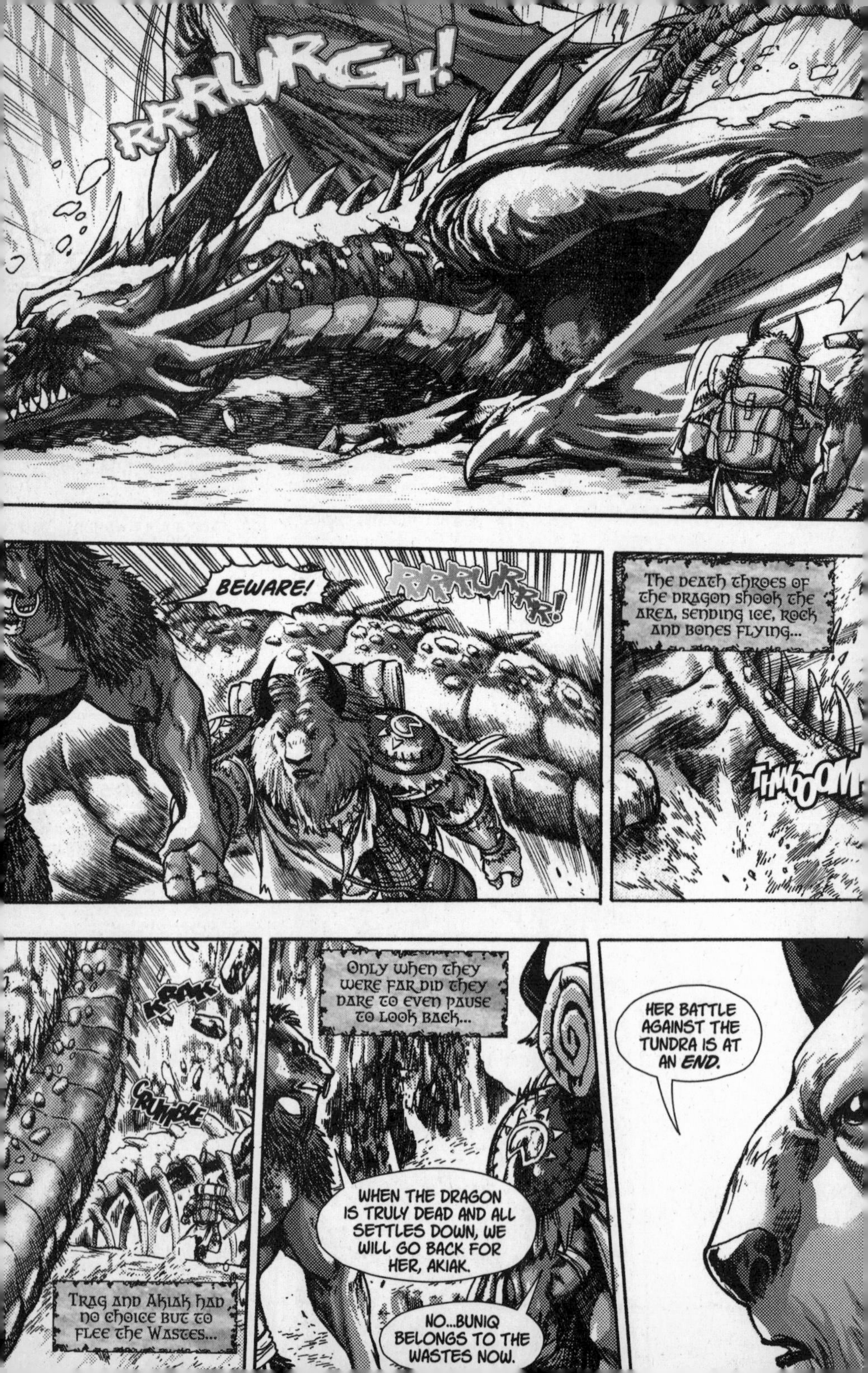
RRRUURGH!
BEWARE!
RRRRURRRR!
The death throes of the dragon shook the area, sending ice, rock and bones flying...
THWOOOM
KRAK
CRUMBLE
Trag and Akiak had no choice but to flee the Wastes...
Only when they were far did they dare to even pause to look back...
WHEN THE DRAGON IS TRULY DEAD AND ALL SETTLES DOWN, WE WILL GO BACK FOR HER, AKIAK.
NO...BUNIQ BELONGS TO THE WASTES NOW.
HER BATTLE AGAINST THE TUNDRA IS AT AN *END*.

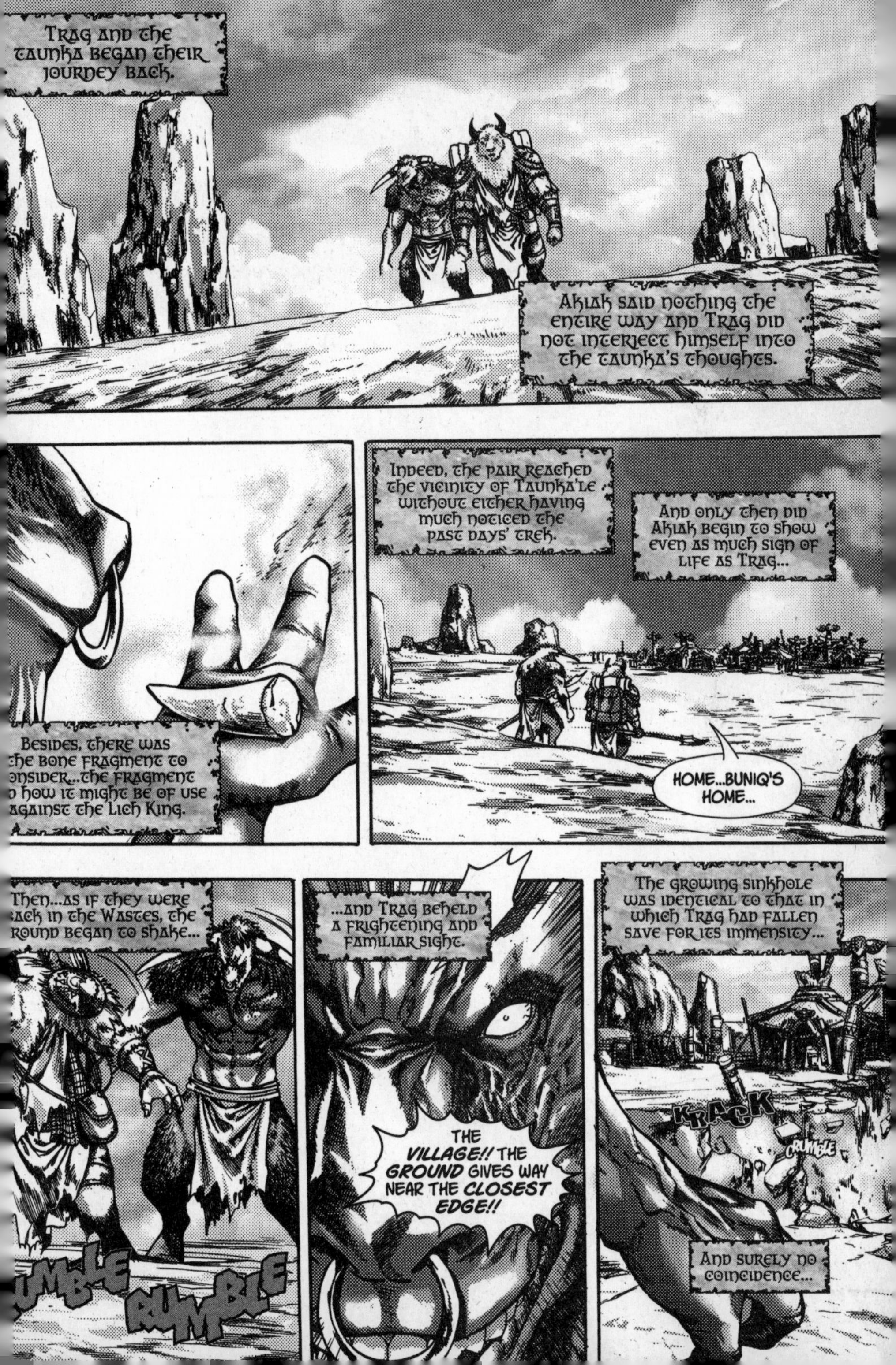
Trag and the taunka began their journey back.
Akiak said nothing the entire way and Trag did not interject himself into the taunka's thoughts.
Besides, there was he bone fragment to onsider...the fragment d how it might be of use against the Lich King.
Indeed, the pair reached the vicinity of Taunka'le without either having much noticed the past days' trek.
And only then did Akiak begin to show even as much sign of life as Trag...
HOME...BUNIQ'S HOME...
Then...as if they were ack in the Wastes, the round began to shake...
UMBLE
RUMBLE
...and Trag beheld a frightening and familiar sight.
THE VILLAGE!! THE GROUND GIVES WAY NEAR THE CLOSEST EDGE!!
The growing sinkhole was identical to that in which Trag had fallen save for its immensity...
KRACK
CRUMBLE
And surely no coincidence...

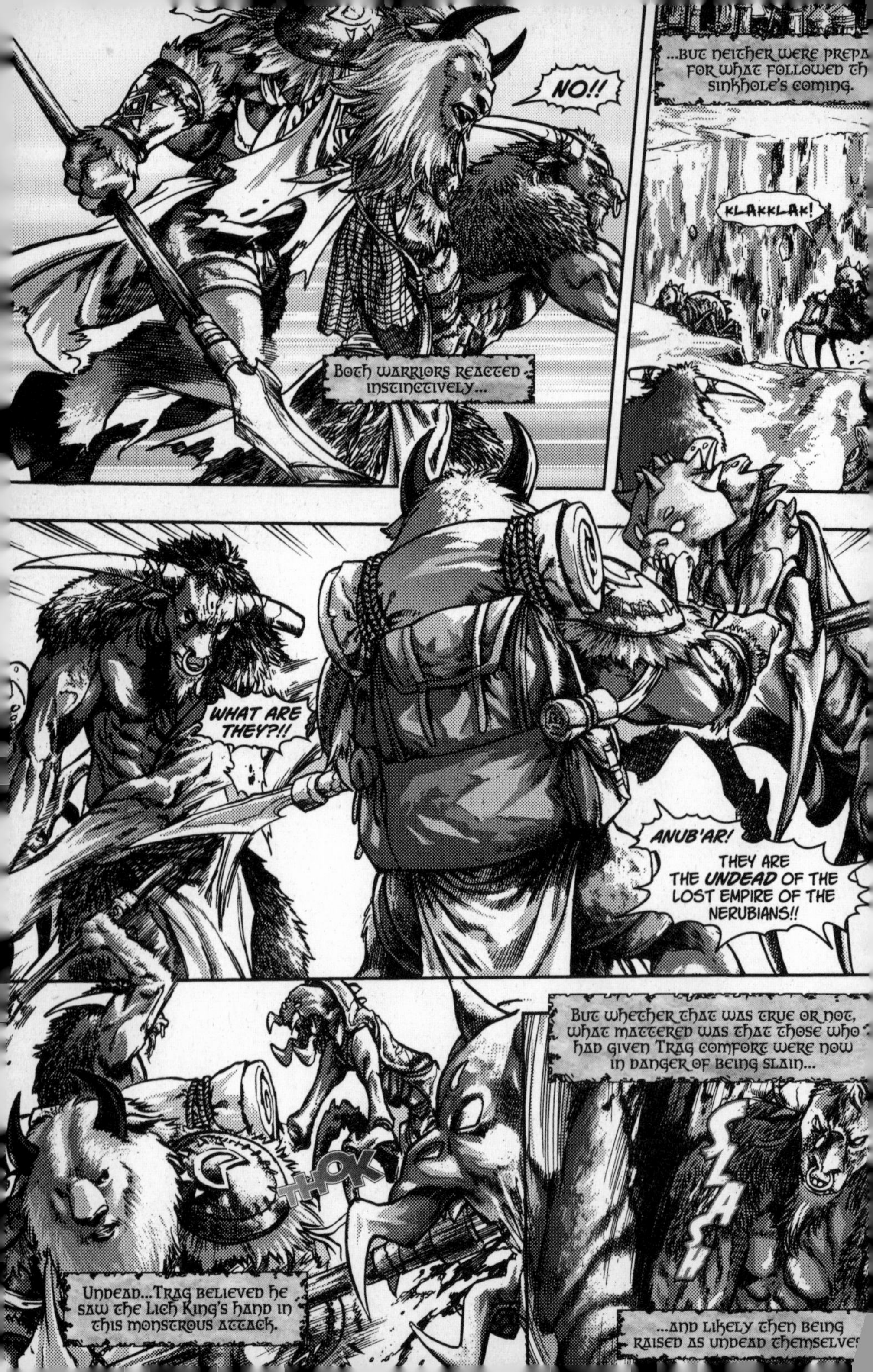
NO!!
Both warriors reacted instinctively...
...But neither were prepa for what followed th sinkhole's coming.
KLAKKLAK!
WHAT ARE THEY?!!
ANUB'AR!
THEY ARE THE UNDEAD OF THE LOST EMPIRE OF THE NERUBIANS!!
Undead...Trag believed he saw the Lich King's hand in this monstrous attack.
THOK
But whether that was true or not, what mattered was that those who had given Trag comfort were now in danger of being slain...
SLASH
...and likely then being raised as undead themselve

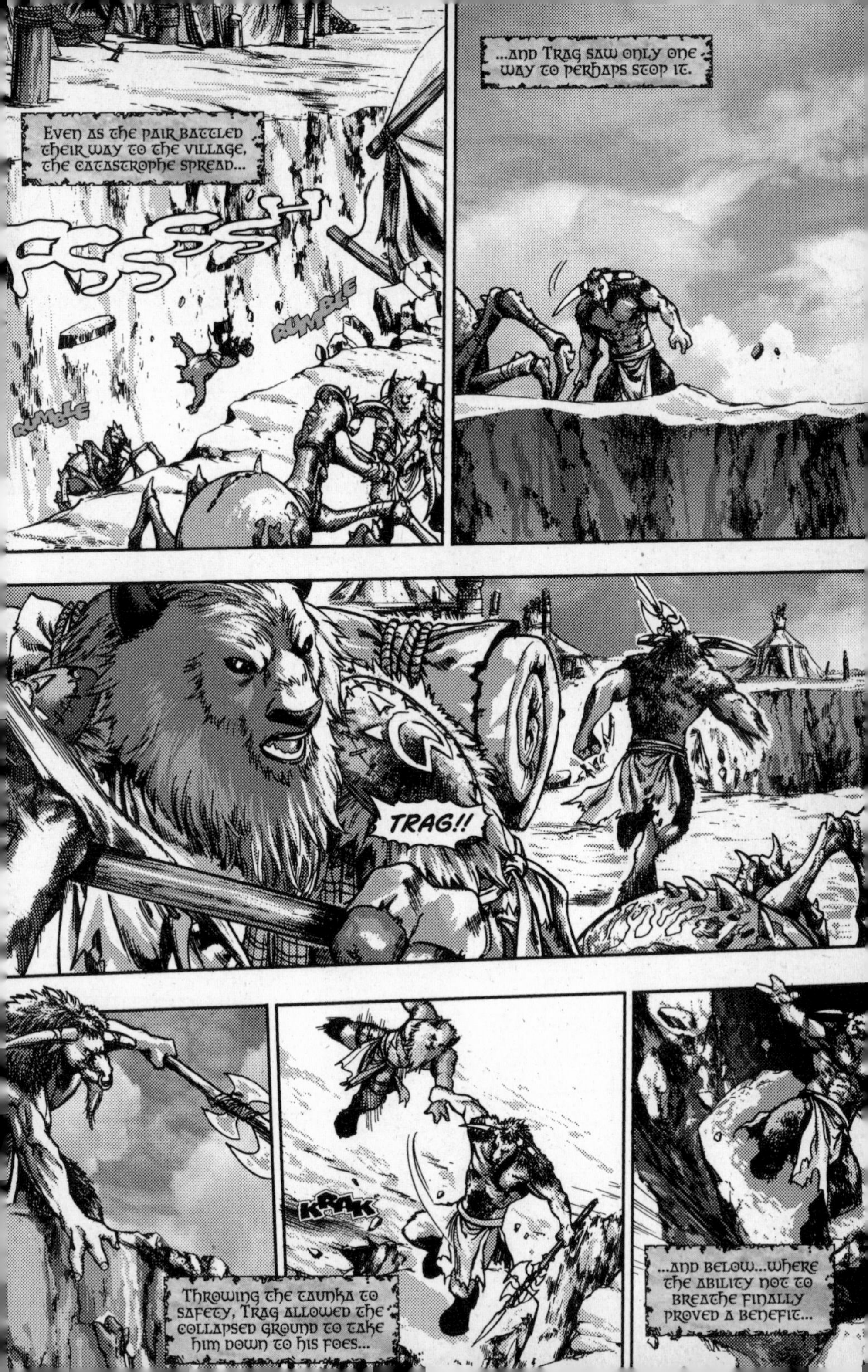

Even as the pair battled their way to the village, the catastrophe spread...
FSSSSHH
RUMBLE
RUMBLE
...and Trag saw only one way to perhaps stop it.
TRAG!!
KRAK
Throwing the taunka to safety, Trag allowed the collapsed ground to take him down to his foes...
...and below...where the ability not to breathe finally proved a benefit...

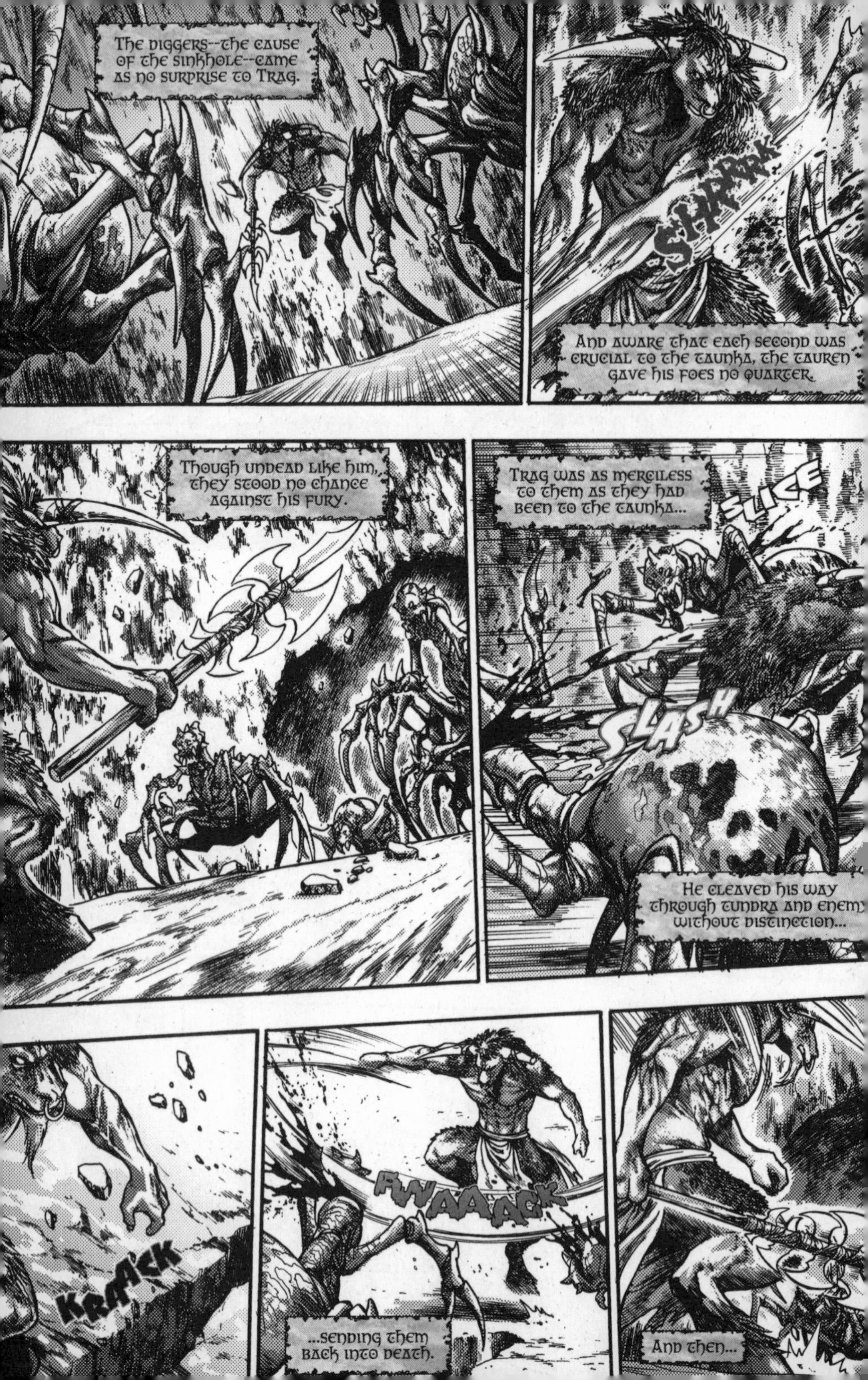
The diggers--the cause of the sinkhole--came as no surprise to Trag.
SHRRRK
And aware that each second was crucial to the taunka, the tauren gave his foes no quarter.
Though undead like him, they stood no chance against his fury.
Trag was as merciless to them as they had been to the taunka...
SLICE
SLASH
He cleaved his way through tundra and enemy without distinction...
KRAACK
FWAAAACK
...sending them back into death.
And then...

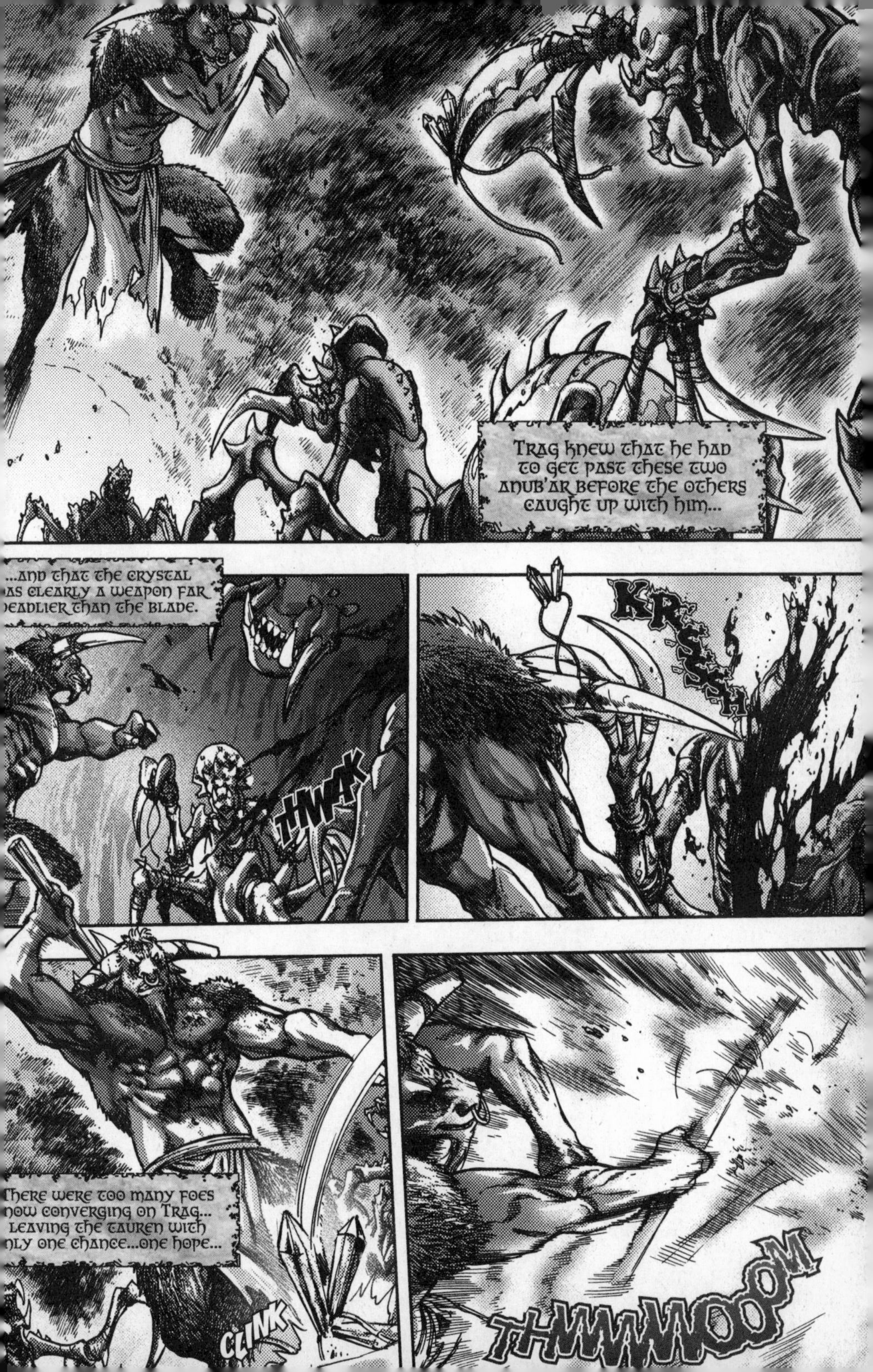
TRAG KNEW THAT HE HAD TO GET PAST THESE TWO ANUB'AR BEFORE THE OTHERS CAUGHT UP WITH HIM...
...AND THAT THE CRYSTAL AS CLEARLY A WEAPON FAR EADLIER THAN THE BLADE.
THWAK
KRSSCH
THERE WERE TOO MANY FOES NOW CONVERGING ON TRAG... LEAVING THE TAUREN WITH NLY ONE CHANCE...ONE HOPE...
CLINK
THMMMOOOM

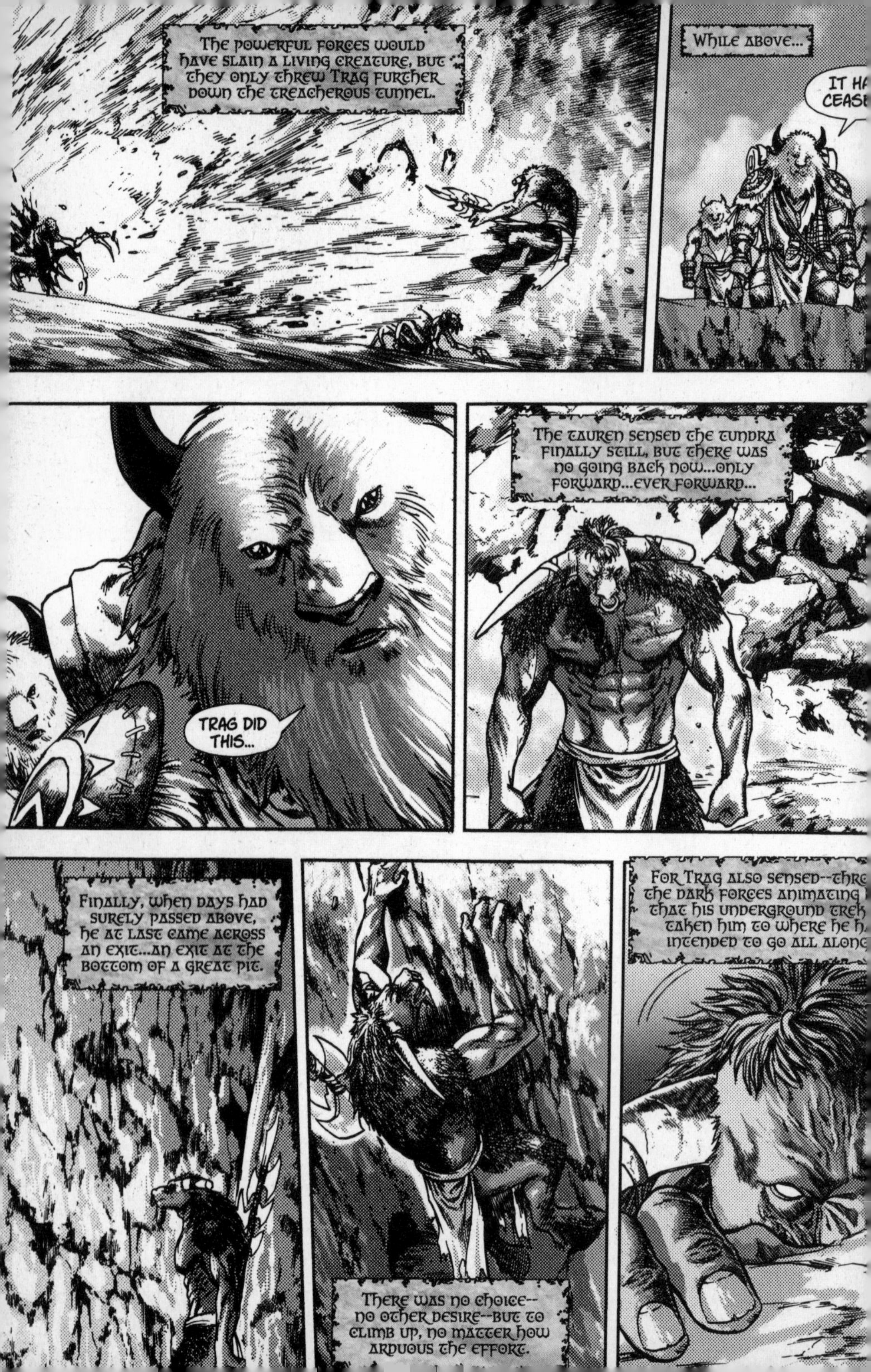
The powerful forces would have slain a living creature, but they only threw Trag further down the treacherous tunnel.
While above...
IT HA
CEAS
TRAG DID THIS...
The tauren sensed the tundra finally still, but there was no going back now...only forward...ever forward...
Finally, when days had surely passed above, he at last came across an exit...an exit at the bottom of a great pit.
There was no choice--no other desire--but to climb up, no matter how arduous the effort.
For Trag also sensed--thro
the dark forces animating
that his underground trek
taken him to where he h
intended to go all along

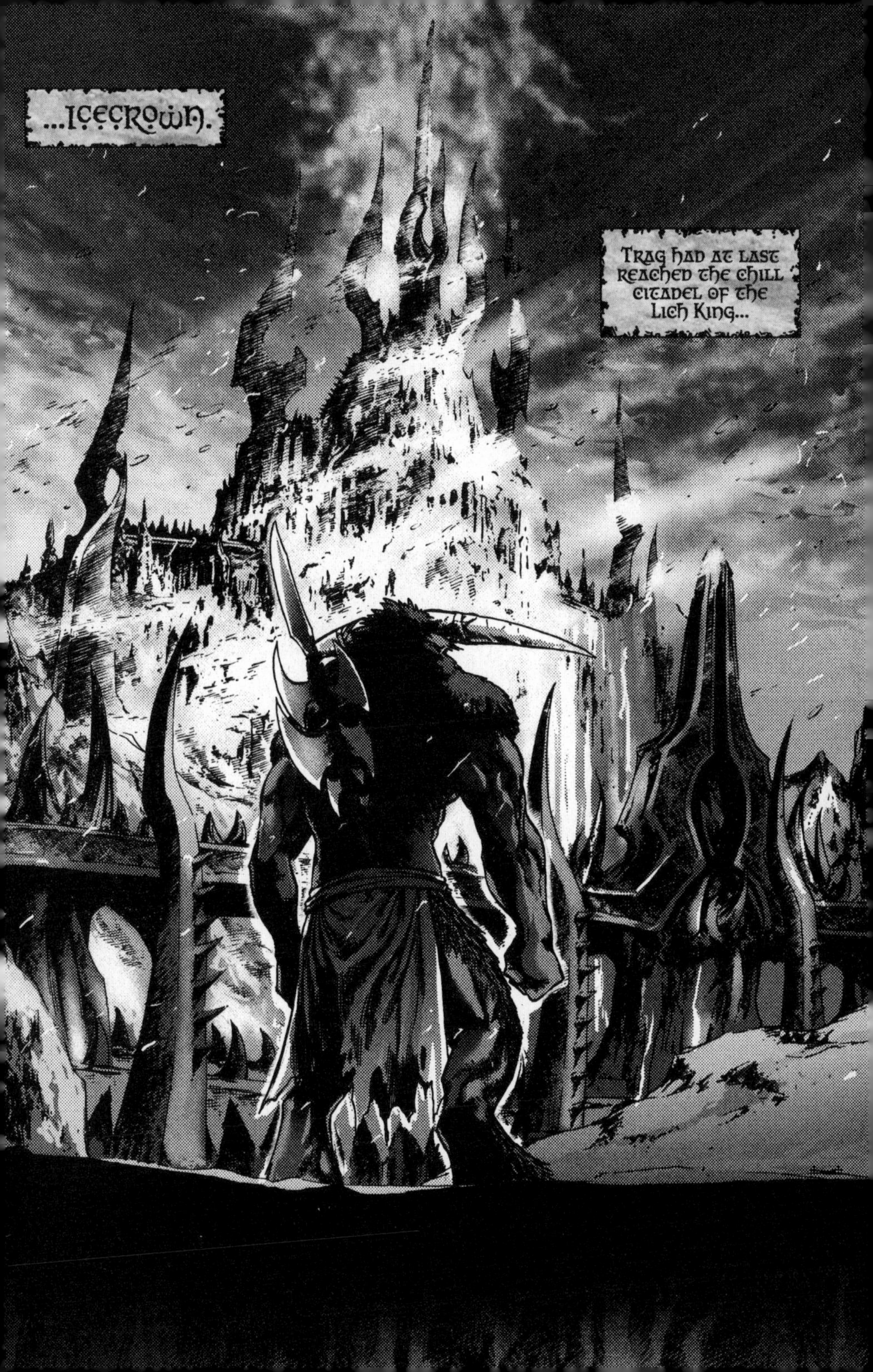
...Icecrown.
Trag had at last reached the chill citadel of the Lich King...

CHAPTER FOUR

FATE

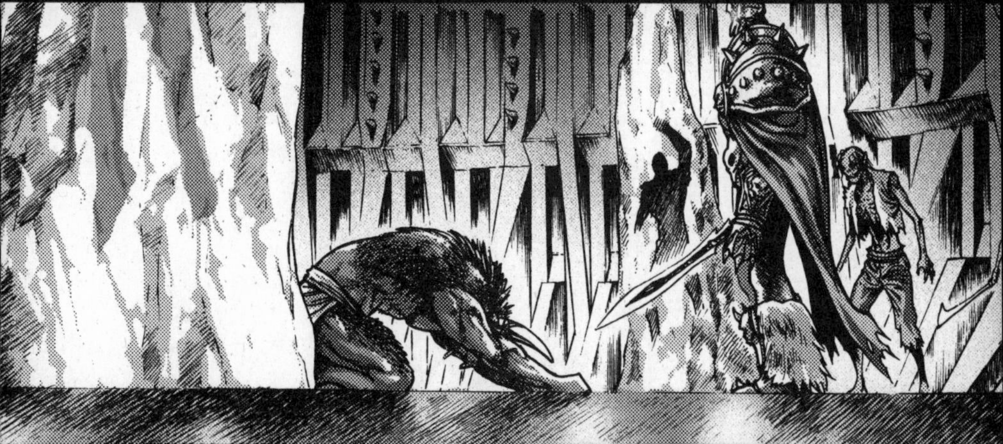

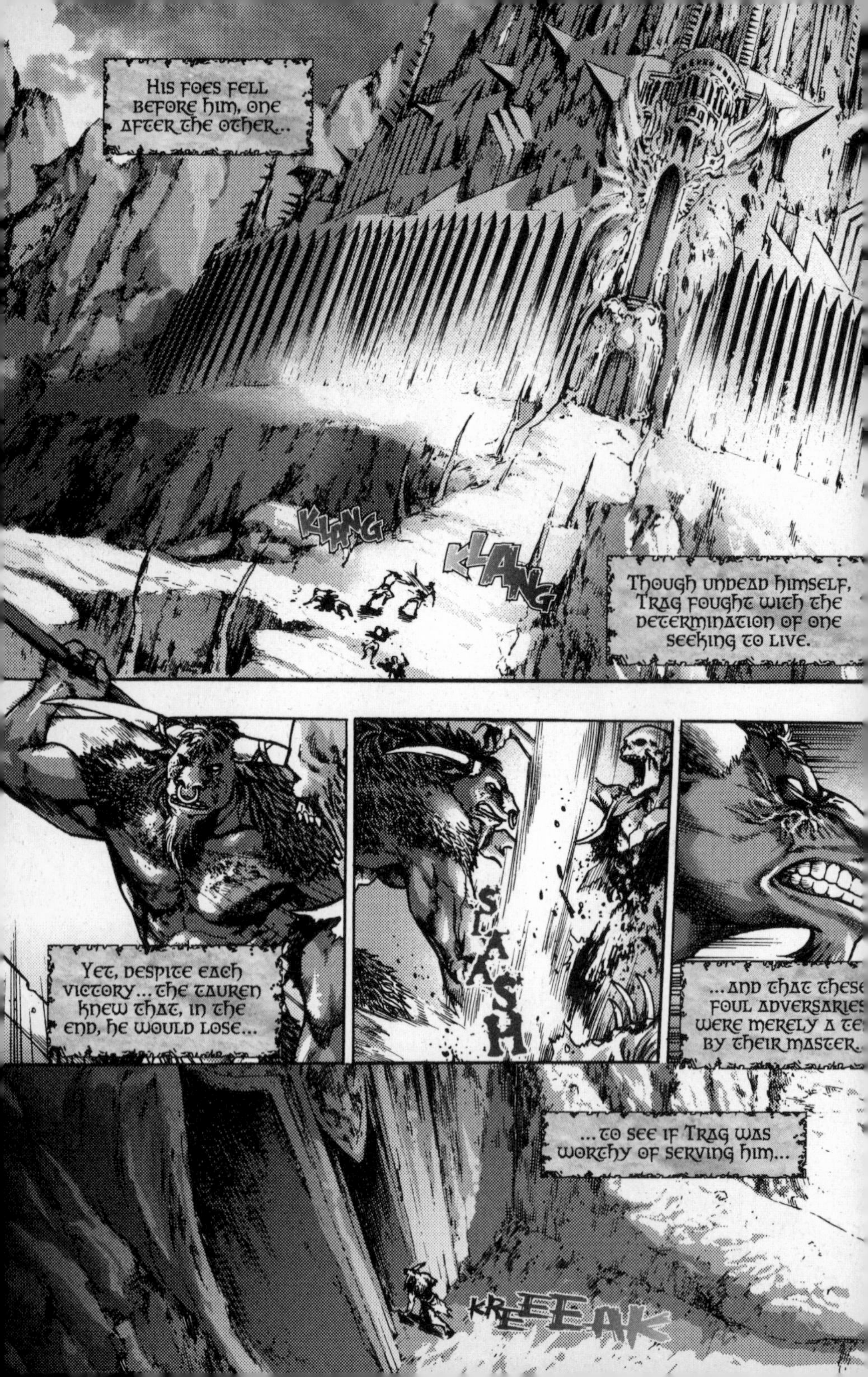
His foes fell before him, one after the other...
KLANG
KLANG
Though undead himself, Trag fought with the determination of one seeking to live.
Yet, despite each victory... the tauren knew that, in the end, he would lose...
SLASH
...and that these foul adversaries were merely a te
by their master.
...to see if Trag was worthy of serving him...
KREEEEAK

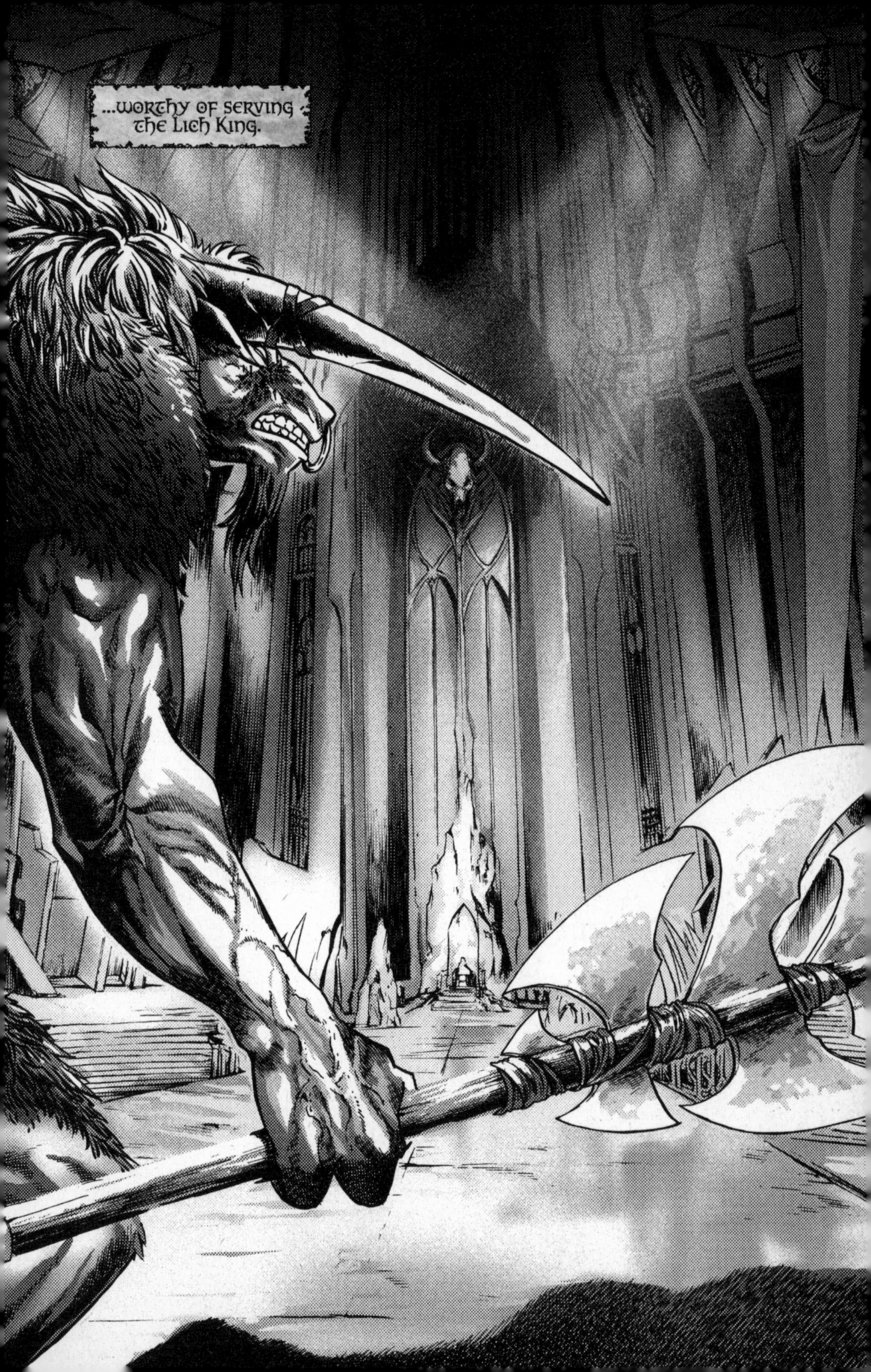
...worthy of serving the Lich King.

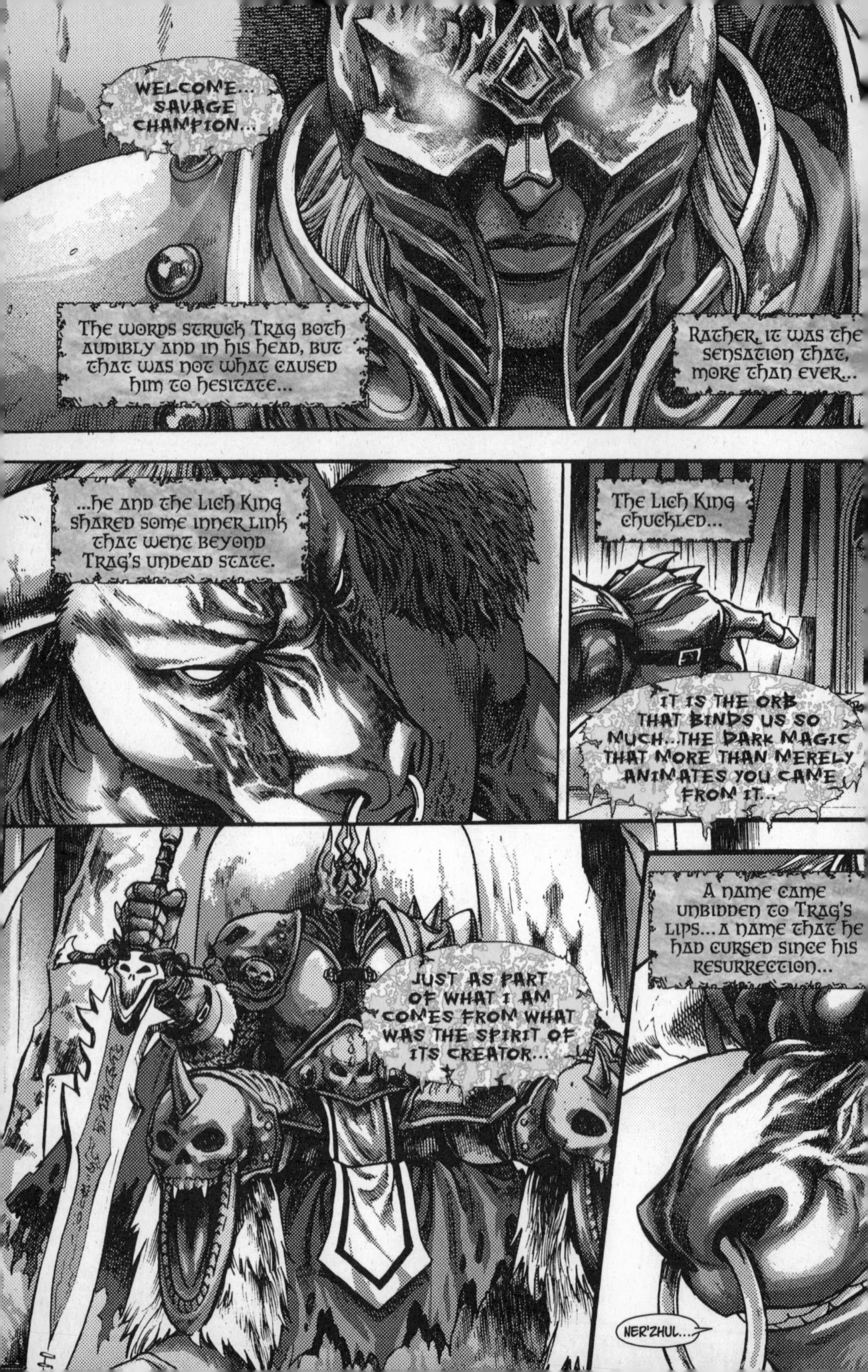
WELCOME... SAVAGE CHAMPION...
The words struck Trag both audibly and in his head, but that was not what caused him to hesitate...
Rather, it was the sensation that, more than ever...
...he and the Lich King shared some inner link that went beyond Trag's undead state.
The Lich King chuckled...
IT IS THE ORB THAT BINDS US SO MUCH...THE DARK MAGIC THAT MORE THAN MERELY ANIMATES YOU CAME FROM IT...
JUST AS PART OF WHAT I AM COMES FROM WHAT WAS THE SPIRIT OF ITS CREATOR...
A name came unbidden to Trag's lips...a name that he had cursed since his resurrection...
NER'ZHUL...

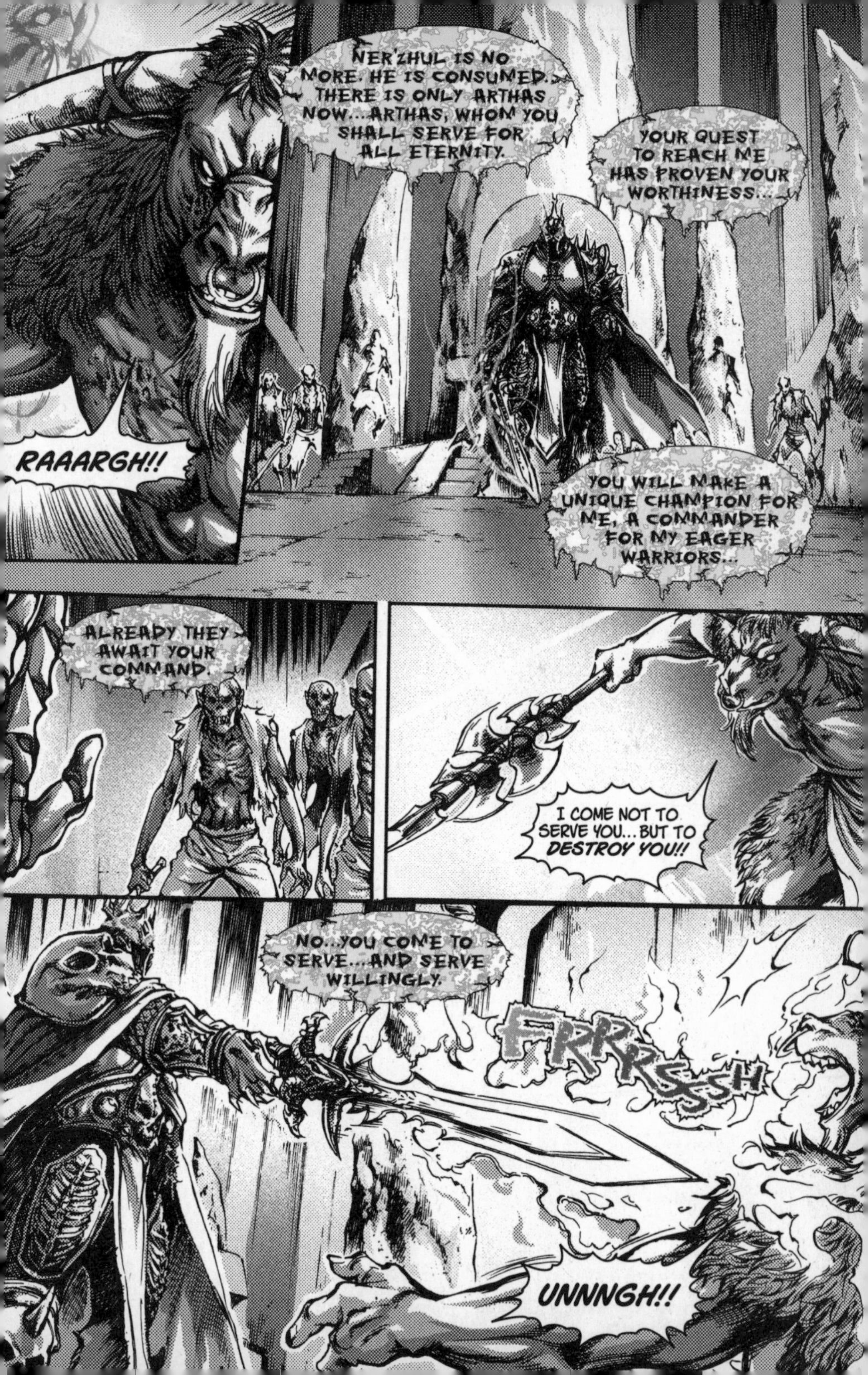
NER'ZHUL IS NO MORE. HE IS CONSUMED. THERE IS ONLY ARTHAS NOW... ARTHAS, WHOM YOU SHALL SERVE FOR ALL ETERNITY.
RAAARGH!!
YOUR QUEST TO REACH ME HAS PROVEN YOUR WORTHINESS...
YOU WILL MAKE A UNIQUE CHAMPION FOR ME, A COMMANDER FOR MY EAGER WARRIORS...
ALREADY THEY AWAIT YOUR COMMAND.
I COME NOT TO SERVE YOU... BUT TO DESTROY YOU!!
NO... YOU COME TO SERVE... AND SERVE WILLINGLY.
FRRRRSSSH
UNNNGH!!

IT WAS OVER. WHAT TRAG HAD KNOWN WOULD HAPPEN HAD, DESPITE HIS FAINT HOPES OTHERWISE, COME TO PASS.

RISE, MY LOYAL WARRIOR.

THE TAUREN RESIGNED HIMSELF TO HIS FATE. HE WAS A CREATION OF THE ORB...AND THE LICH KING WAS THE ORB'S MASTER.

YOU ARE NOW READY FOR YOUR COMMAND.

YOUR WARRIORS AWAIT YOUR LEADERSHIP FOR THIS TASK...

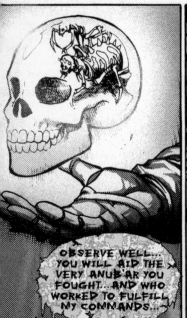

OBSERVE WELL... YOU WILL AID THE VERY ANUB'AR YOU FOUGHT...AND WHO WORKED TO FULFILL MY COMMANDS...

THEY WILL RESUME UNDERMINING THE VILLAGE'S FOUNDATIONS... AND WHEN IT IS NO MORE, MOVE ON TO THE TAUNKA CAPITAL, ICEMIST.

THE GLORIOUS BEGINNING TO SCOURING THE LIVING FROM NOT MERELY NORTHREND...BUT ALL AZEROTH.

AAH! BUT WE HAVE OTHER VISITORS IN OUR MIDST...WOULD YOU CARE TO SEE THEM, TOO?

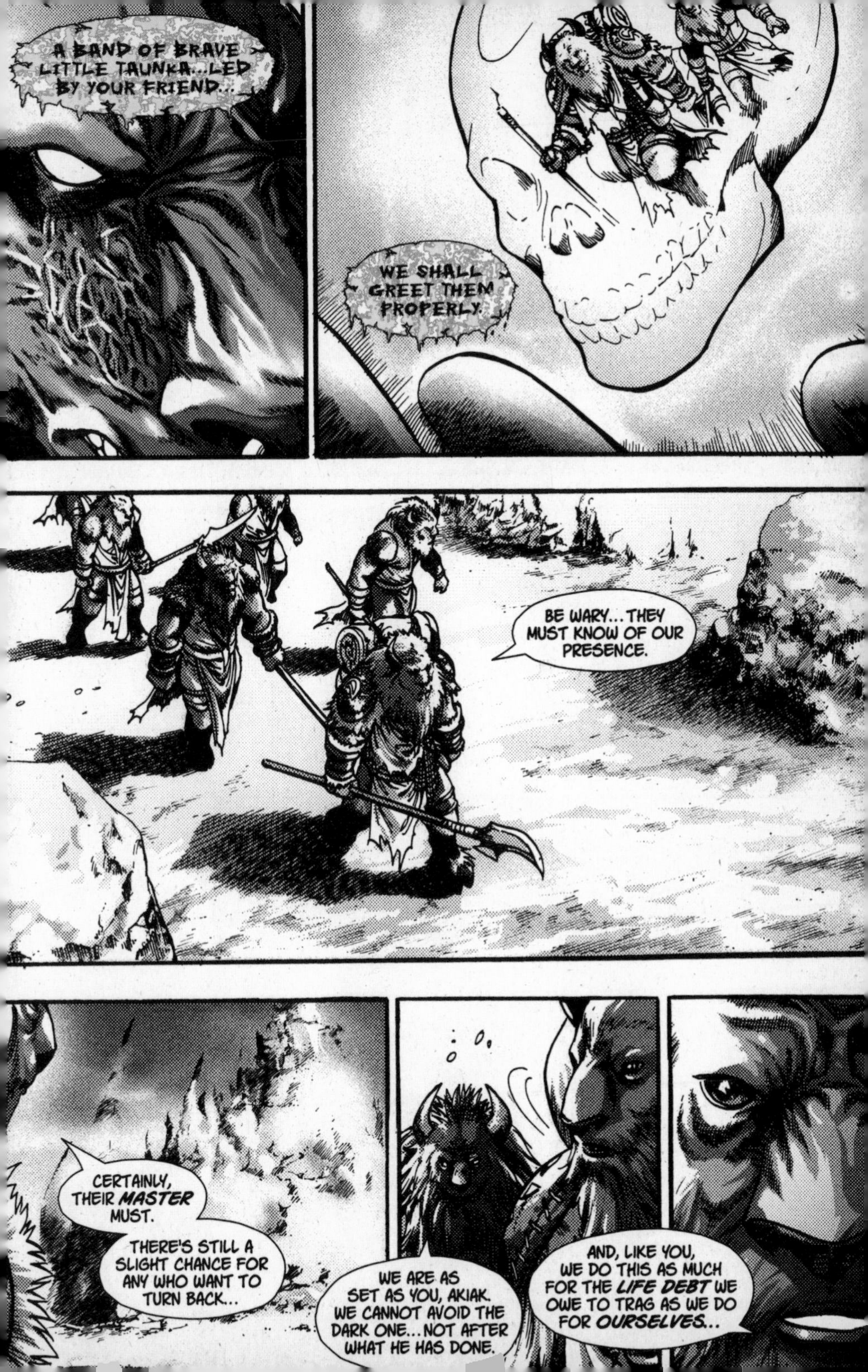
A BAND OF BRAVE LITTLE TAUNKA...LED BY YOUR FRIEND...
WE SHALL GREET THEM PROPERLY.
BE WARY... THEY MUST KNOW OF OUR PRESENCE.
CERTAINLY, THEIR *MASTER* MUST.
THERE'S STILL A SLIGHT CHANCE FOR ANY WHO WANT TO TURN BACK...
WE ARE AS SET AS YOU, AKIAK. WE CANNOT AVOID THE DARK ONE... NOT AFTER WHAT HE HAS DONE.
AND, LIKE YOU, WE DO THIS AS MUCH FOR THE *LIFE DEBT* WE OWE TO TRAG AS WE DO FOR *OURSELVES*...

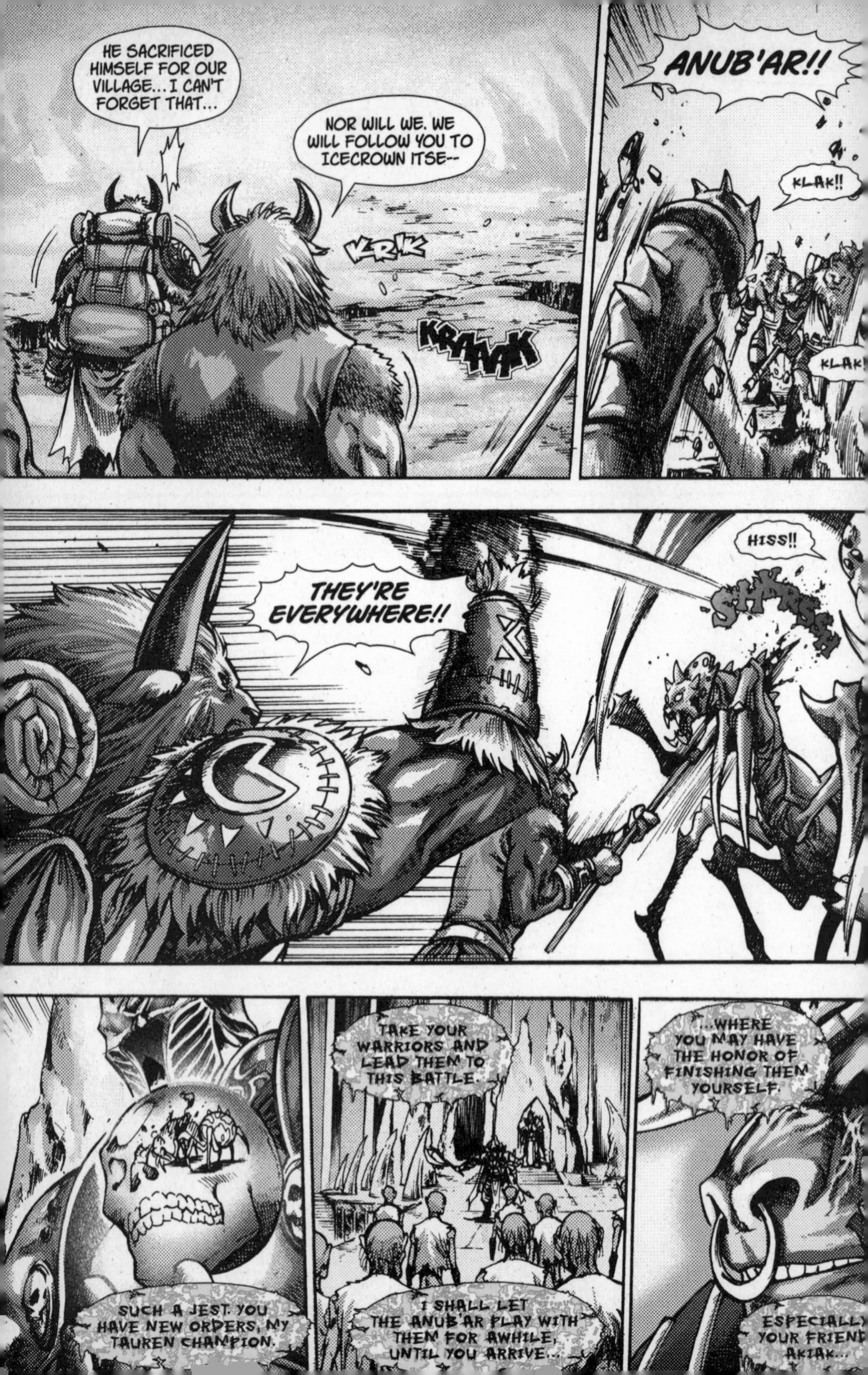
HE SACRIFICED HIMSELF FOR OUR VILLAGE... I CAN'T FORGET THAT...
NOR WILL WE. WE WILL FOLLOW YOU TO ICECROWN ITSE--
KRIK
KRAAAK
ANUB'AR!!
KLAK!!
KLAK
THEY'RE EVERYWHERE!!
HISS!!
SHKRSSH
SUCH A JEST. YOU HAVE NEW ORDERS, MY TAUREN CHAMPION.
TAKE YOUR WARRIORS AND LEAD THEM TO THIS BATTLE.
I SHALL LET THE ANUB'AR PLAY WITH THEM FOR AWHILE, UNTIL YOU ARRIVE...
...WHERE YOU MAY HAVE THE HONOR OF FINISHING THEM YOURSELF.
ESPECIALLY YOUR FRIEND AKIAK...

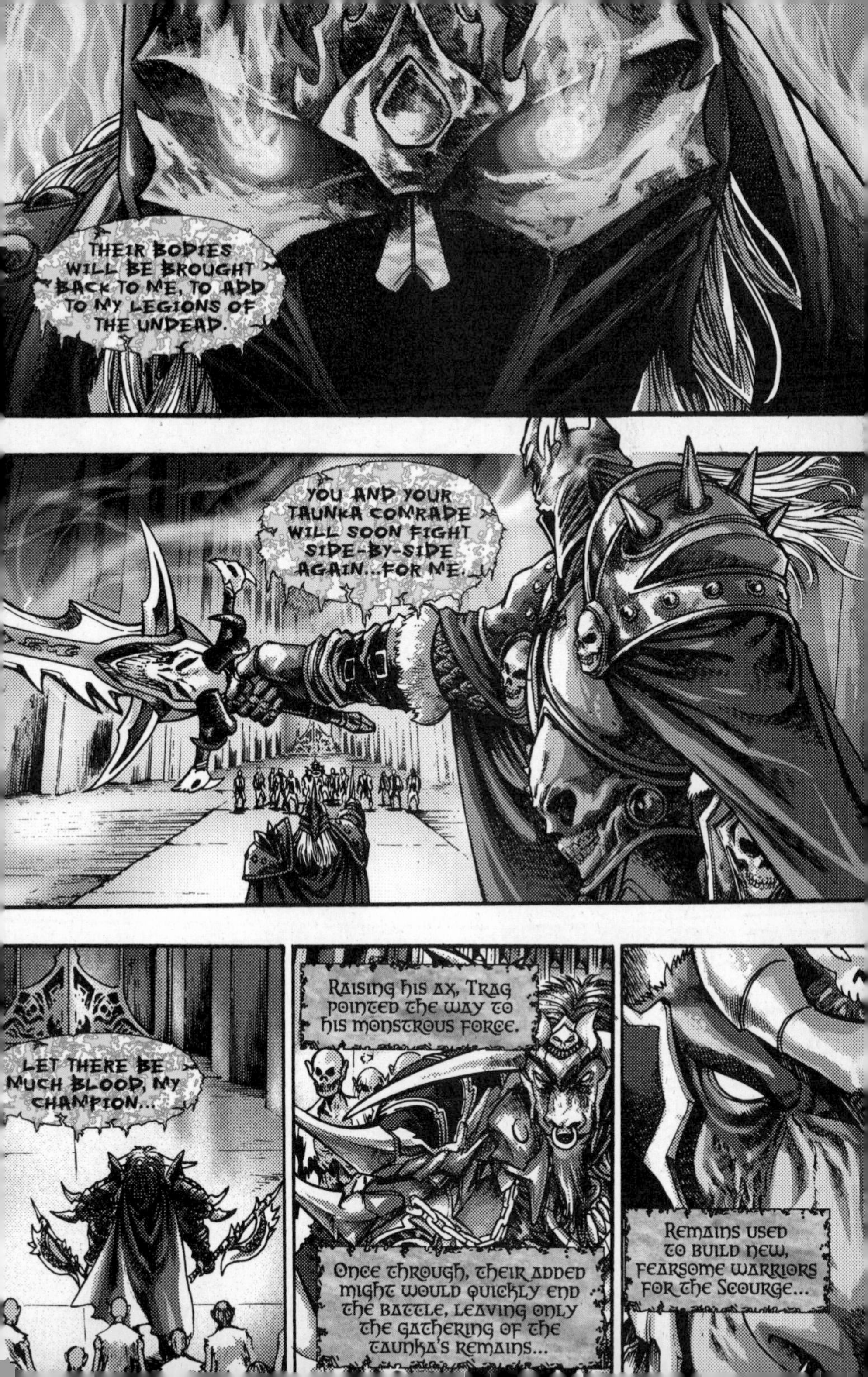
THEIR BODIES WILL BE BROUGHT BACK TO ME, TO ADD TO MY LEGIONS OF THE UNDEAD.
YOU AND YOUR TAUNKA COMRADE WILL SOON FIGHT SIDE-BY-SIDE AGAIN...FOR ME.
LET THERE BE MUCH BLOOD, MY CHAMPION...
Raising his ax, Trag pointed the way to his monstrous force.
Once through, their added might would quickly end the battle, leaving only the gathering of the taunka's remains...
Remains used to build new, fearsome warriors for the Scourge...

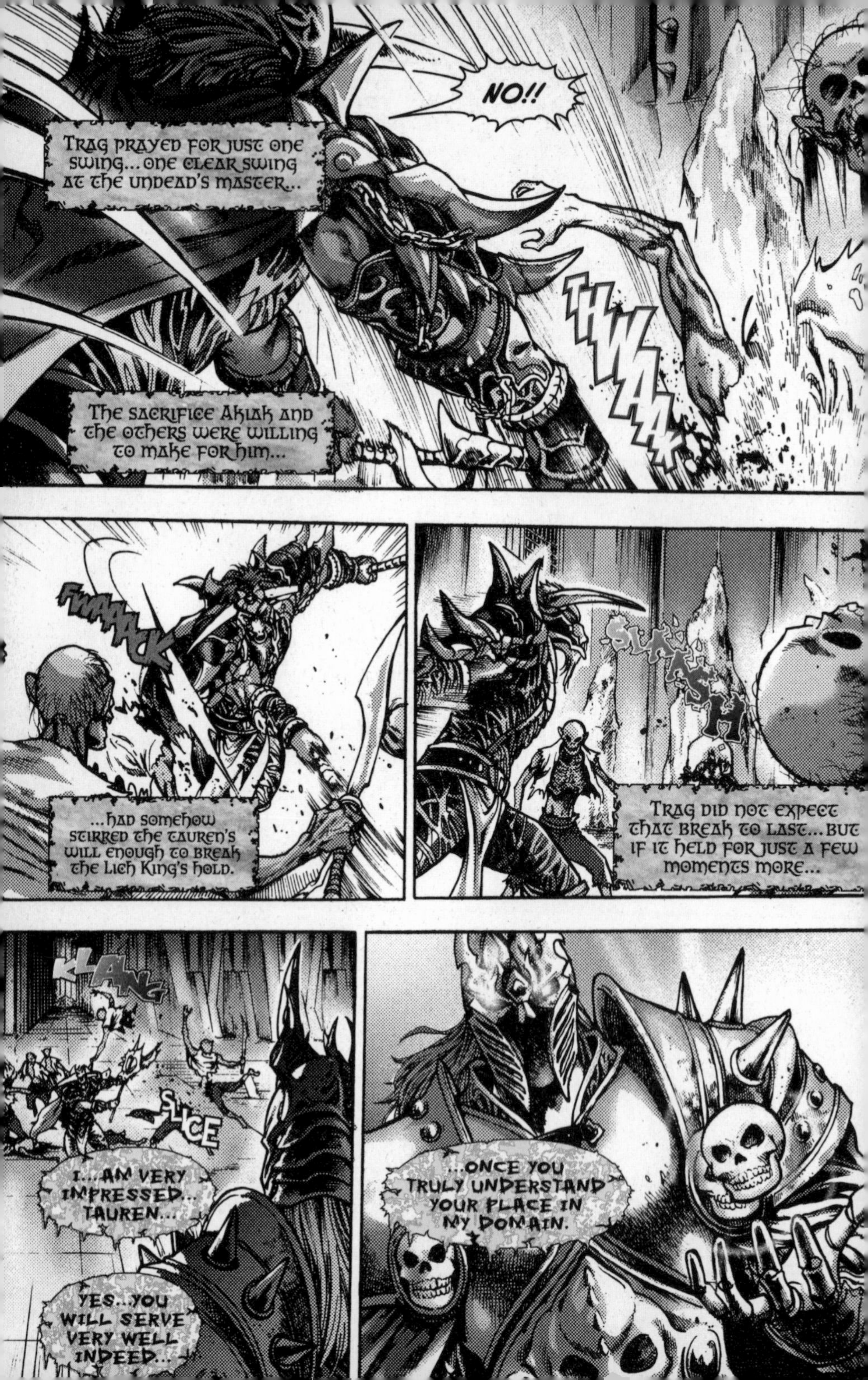
TRAG PRAYED FOR JUST ONE SWING... ONE CLEAR SWING AT THE UNDEAD'S MASTER...
NO!!
THE SACRIFICE AKIAK AND THE OTHERS WERE WILLING TO MAKE FOR HIM...
THWAAK
FWAAACK
...HAD SOMEHOW STIRRED THE TAUREN'S WILL ENOUGH TO BREAK THE LICH KING'S HOLD.
SLASH
TRAG DID NOT EXPECT THAT BREAK TO LAST... BUT IF IT HELD FOR JUST A FEW MOMENTS MORE...
KLANG
SLICE
I...AM VERY IMPRESSED... TAUREN...
YES...YOU WILL SERVE VERY WELL INDEED...
...ONCE YOU TRULY UNDERSTAND YOUR PLACE IN MY DOMAIN.

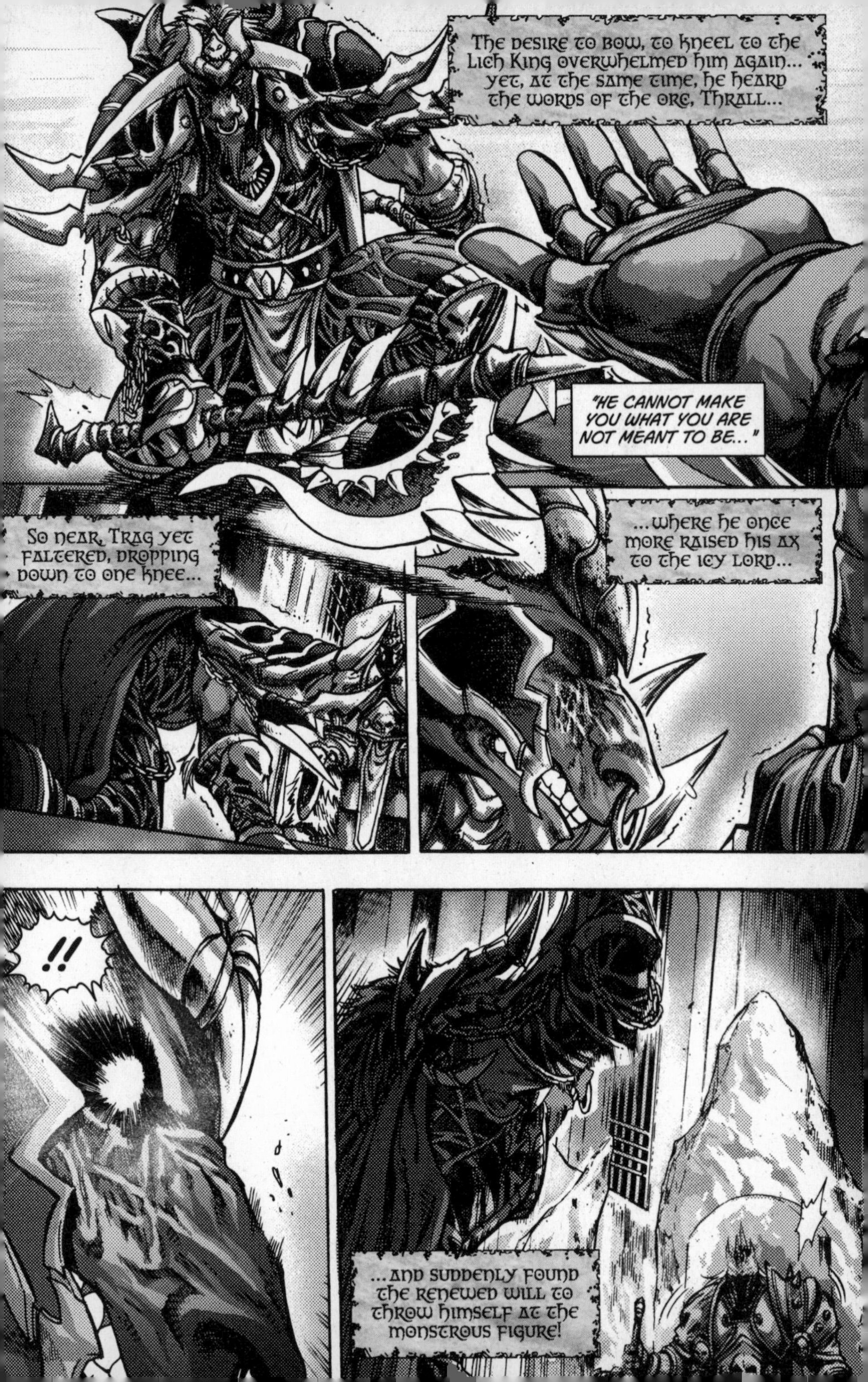
The desire to bow, to kneel to the Lich King overwhelmed him again... yet, at the same time, he heard the words of the orc, Thrall...
"He cannot make you what you are not meant to be..."
So near, Trag yet faltered, dropping down to one knee...
...where he once more raised his ax to the icy lord...
!!
...and suddenly found the renewed will to throw himself at the monstrous figure!

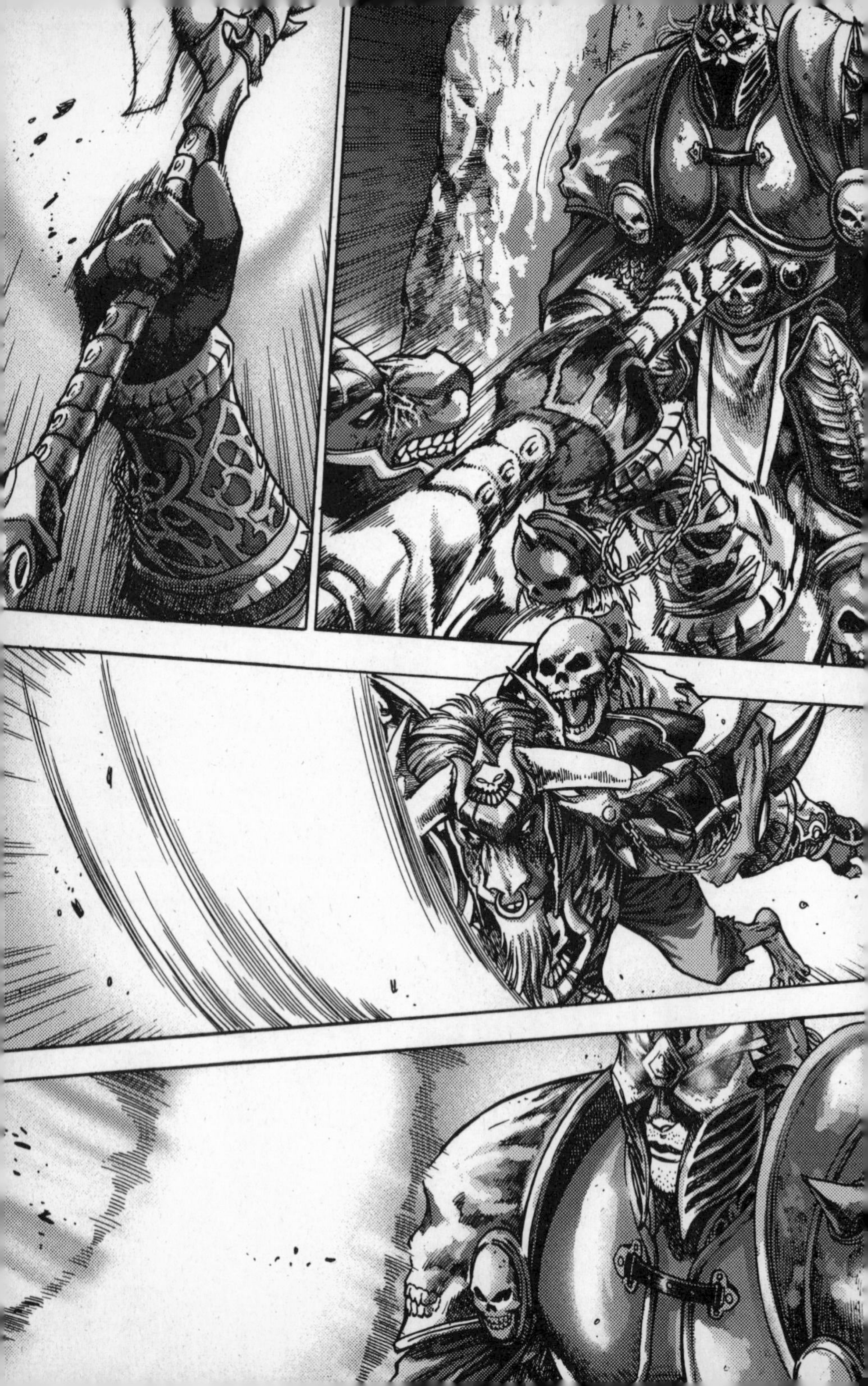

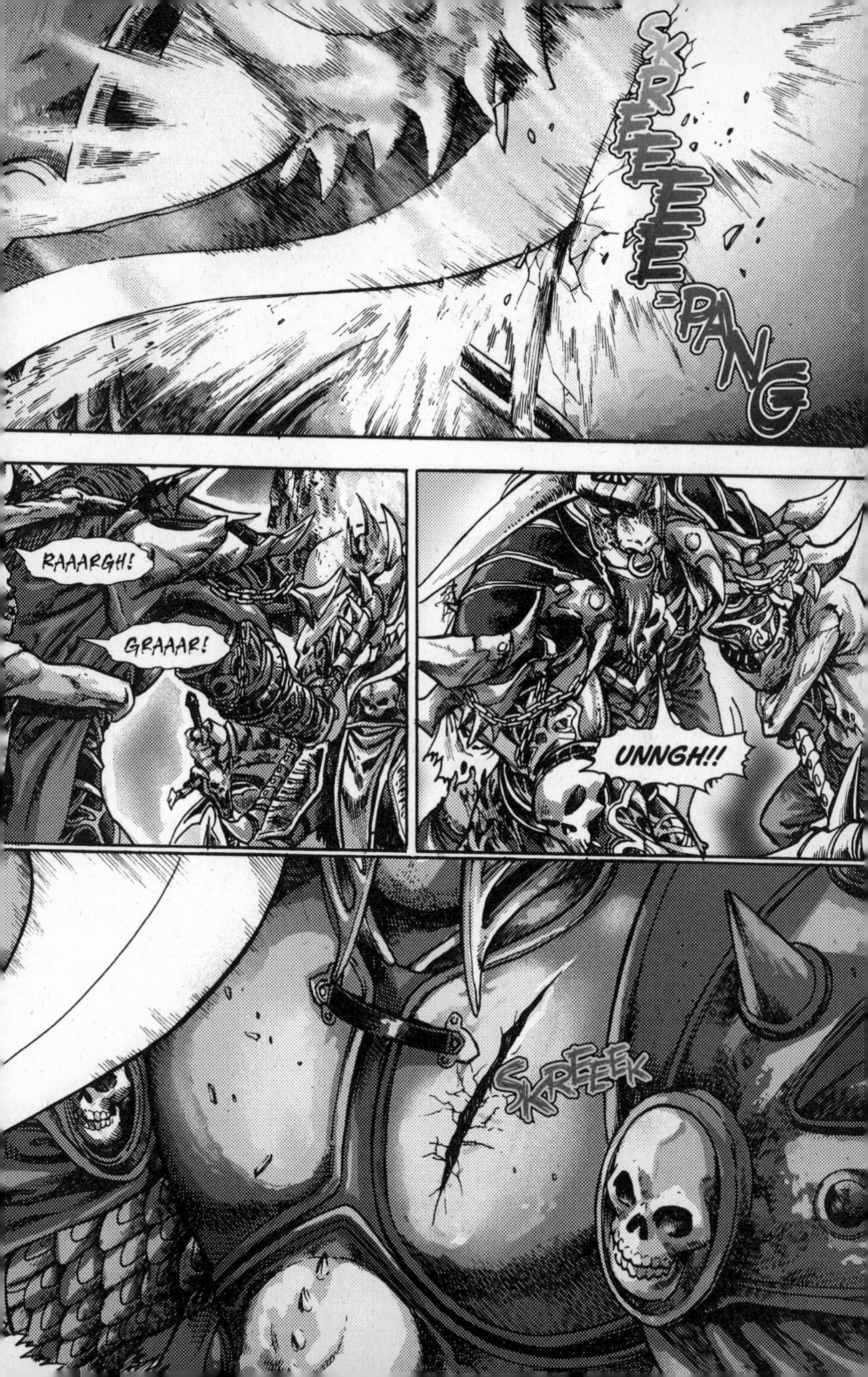
SKREEEEE-PANG
UNNGH!!
RAAARGH!
GRAAAR!
SKREEEK

SCR-EEE

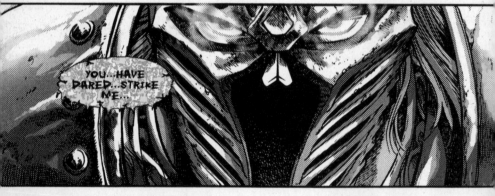

YOU...HAVE DARED...STRIKE ME...

BUT TRAG WAS DISTRACTED FROM THE LICH KING'S IRE AS SOMETHING JABBED AGAINST HIS SIDE...

THE BONE FRAGMENT FROM GALAKROND...

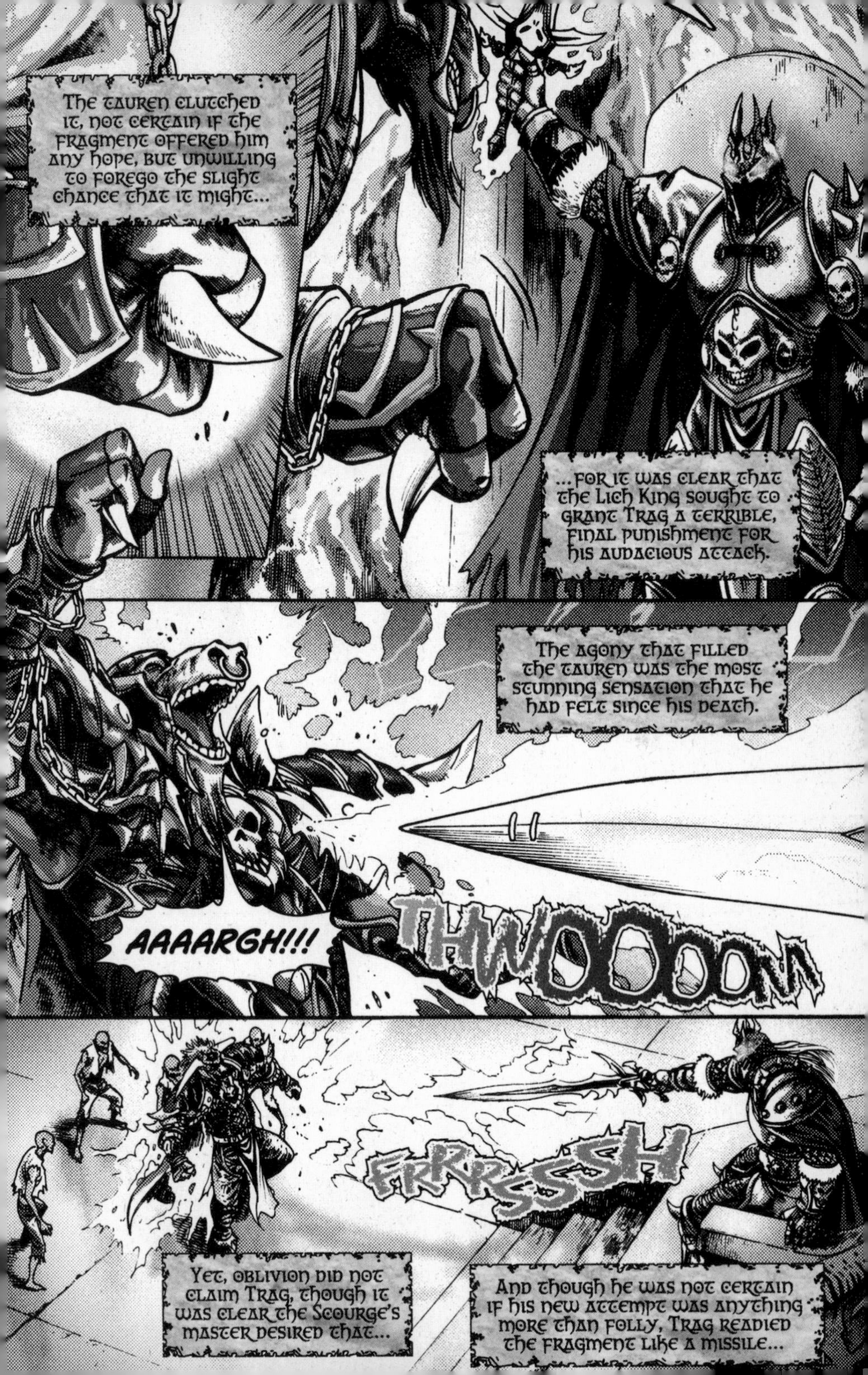
The tauren clutched it, not certain if the fragment offered him any hope, but unwilling to forego the slight chance that it might...
...for it was clear that the Lich King sought to grant Trag a terrible, final punishment for his audacious attack.
The agony that filled the tauren was the most stunning sensation that he had felt since his death.
AAAARGH!!!
THWOOOOM
FRRRSSSH
Yet, oblivion did not claim Trag, though it was clear the Scourge's master desired that...
And though he was not certain if his new attempt was anything more than folly, Trag readied the fragment like a missile...

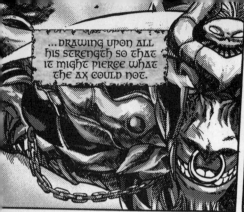

...DRAWING UPON ALL HIS STRENGTH SO THAT IT MIGHT PIERCE WHAT THE AX COULD NOT.

FWOOOSH

BUT THIS TIME, THE CHANCE WAS NOT TO BE HIS...

KRAAK

KA-THOOM

WHAT IS THAT?!

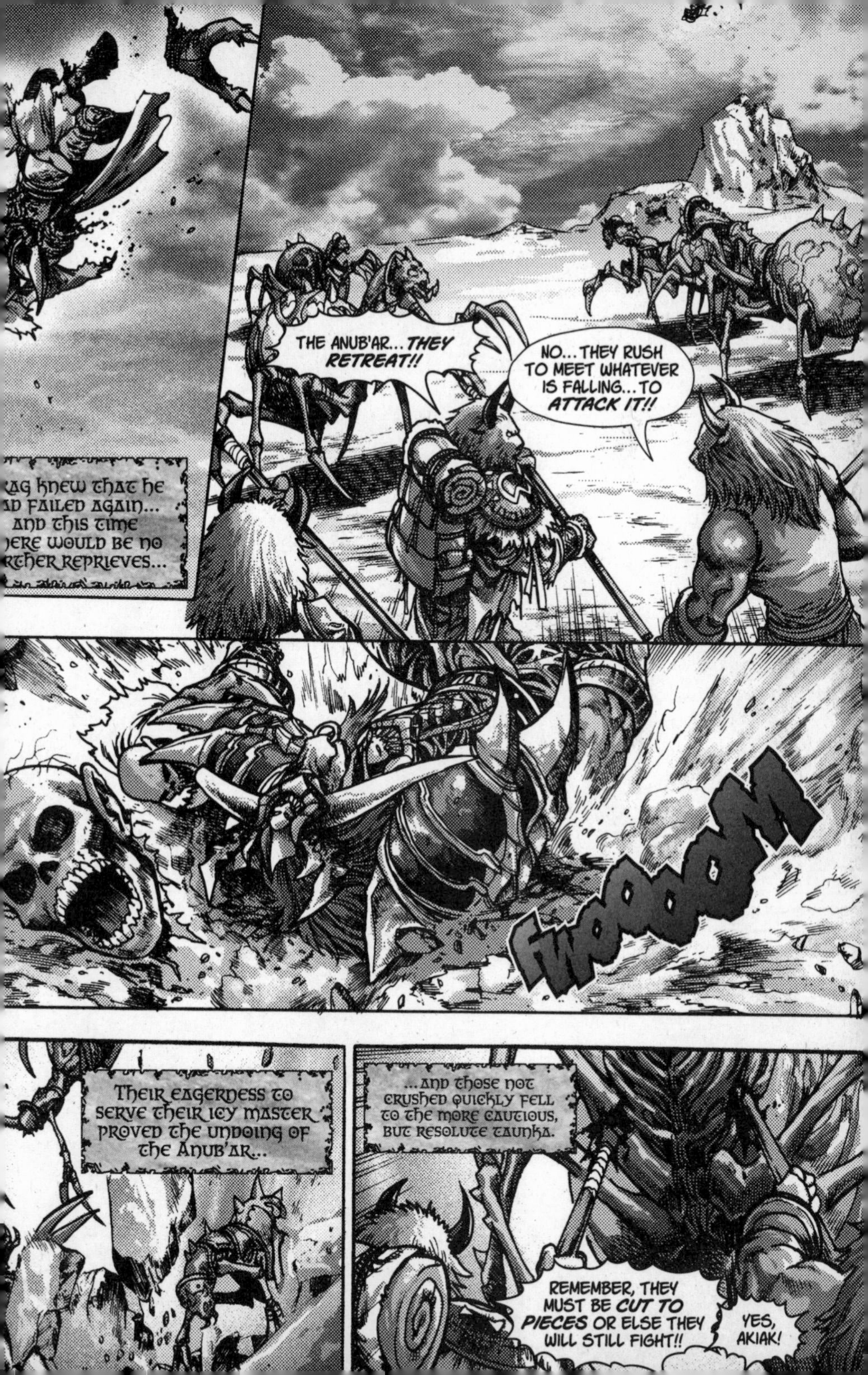

RAG KNEW THAT HE AD FAILED AGAIN... AND THIS TIME HERE WOULD BE NO RTHER REPRIEVES...
THE ANUB'AR... *THEY RETREAT!!*
NO... THEY RUSH TO MEET WHATEVER IS FALLING... TO *ATTACK IT!!*
FWOOOOOM
THEIR EAGERNESS TO SERVE THEIR ICY MASTER PROVED THE UNDOING OF THE ANUB'AR...
...AND THOSE NOT CRUSHED QUICKLY FELL TO THE MORE CAUTIOUS, BUT RESOLUTE TAUNKA.
REMEMBER, THEY MUST BE *CUT TO PIECES* OR ELSE THEY WILL STILL FIGHT!!
YES, AKIAK!

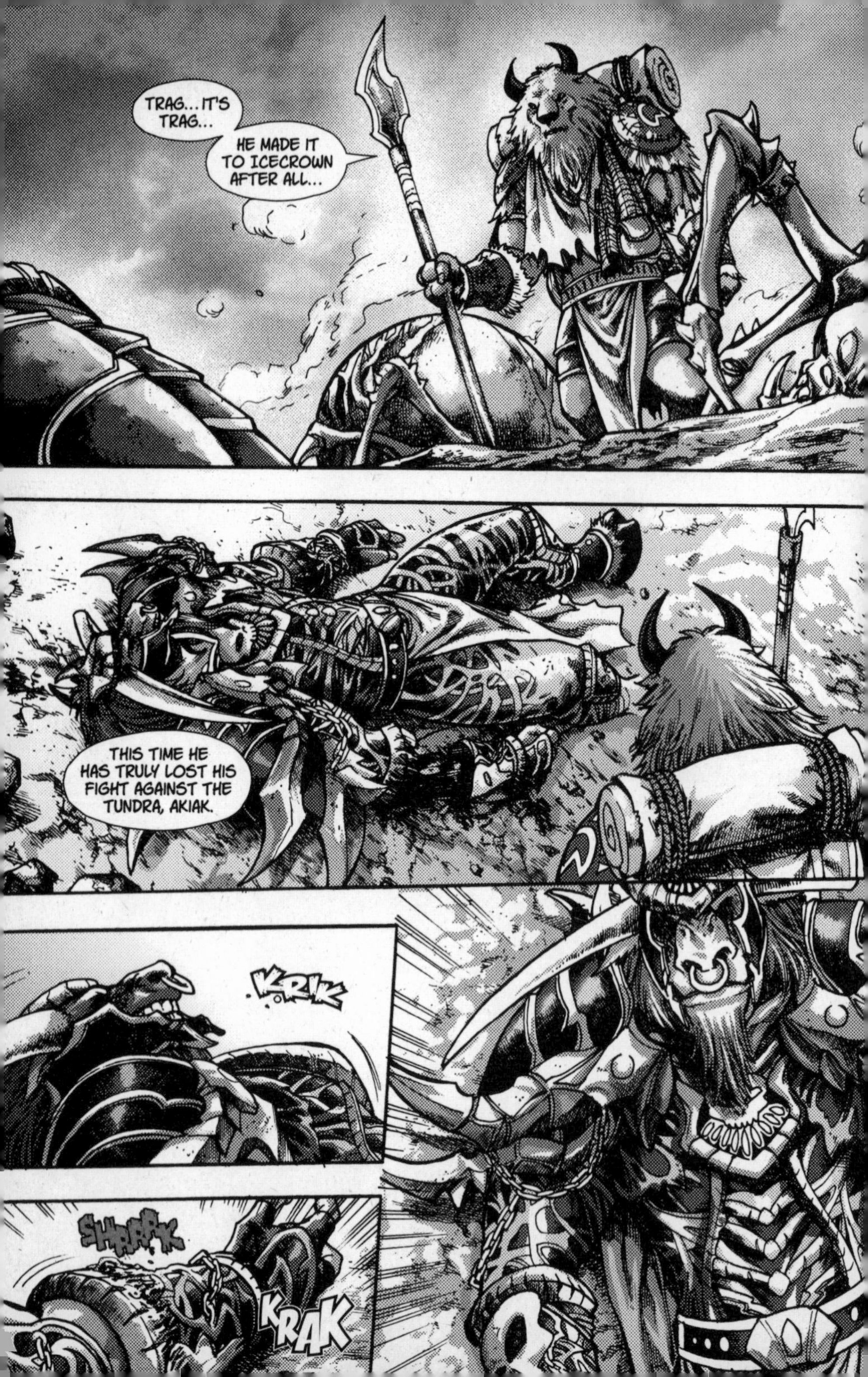
TRAG... IT'S TRAG...
HE MADE IT TO ICECROWN AFTER ALL...
THIS TIME HE HAS TRULY LOST HIS FIGHT AGAINST THE TUNDRA, AKIAK.
KRIK
SHRRPK
KRAK

TRAG SAW THE SHOCK IN THE NORMALLY-STAID TAUNKA'S FACES.

THEY NO DOUBT NOW SAW HIM FOR THE MONSTER THAT HE WAS.

BUT THEN...

LEAN ON ME IF YOU NEED TO...

I-I AM... RECOVERED ENOUGH...

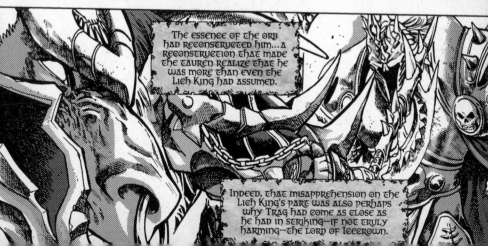

THE ESSENCE OF THE ORB HAD RECONSTRUCTED HIM...A RECONSTRUCTION THAT MADE THE TAUREN REALIZE THAT HE WAS MORE THAN EVEN THE LICH KING HAD ASSUMED.

INDEED, THAT MISAPPREHENSION ON THE LICH KING'S PART WAS ALSO PERHAPS WHY TRAG HAD COME AS CLOSE AS HE HAD IN STRIKING--IF NOT TRULY HARMING--THE LORD OF ICECROWN.

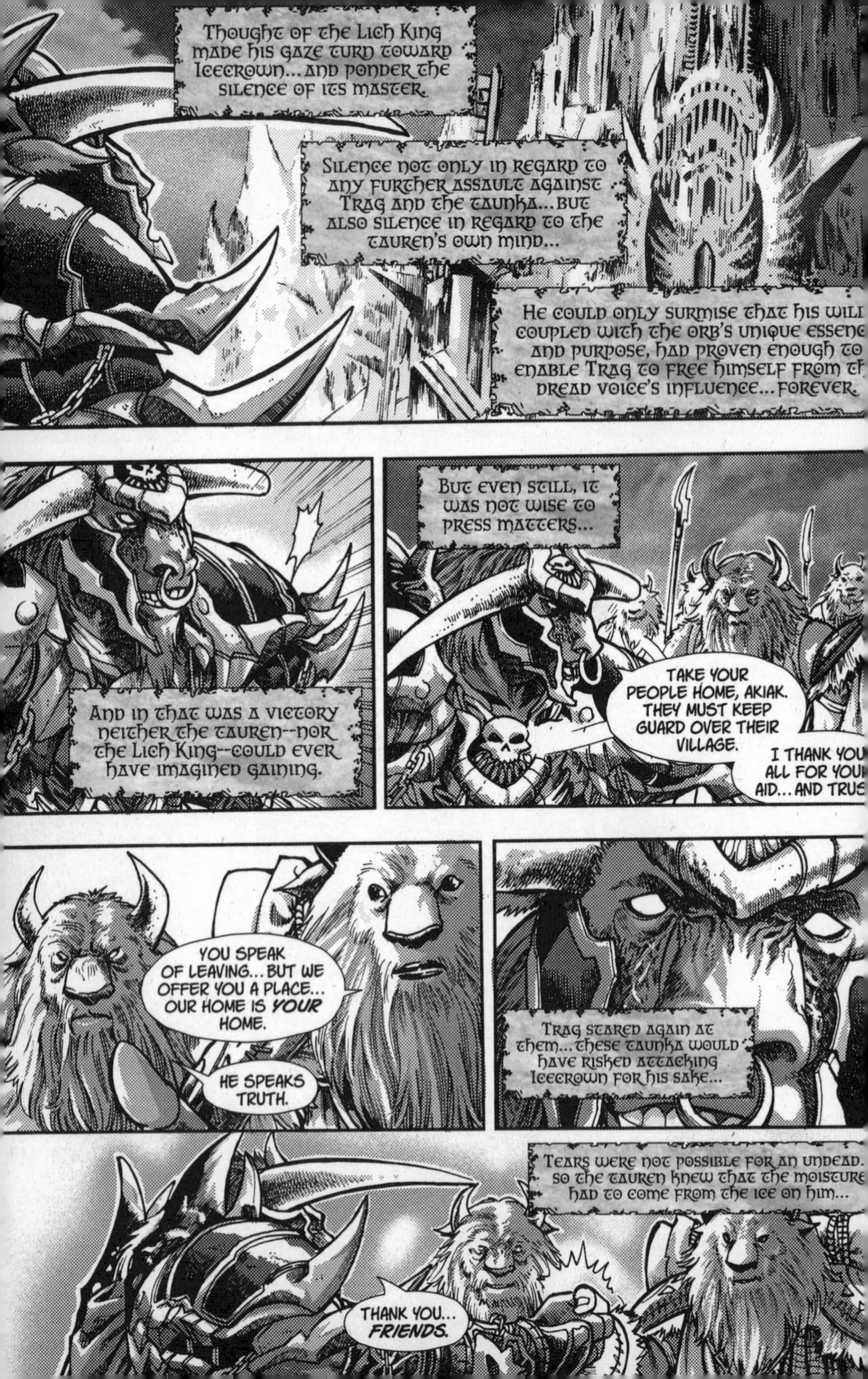
Thought of the Lich King made his gaze turn toward Icecrown... and ponder the silence of its master.
Silence not only in regard to any further assault against Trag and the taunka... but also silence in regard to the tauren's own mind...
He could only surmise that his will coupled with the orb's unique essenc and purpose, had proven enough to enable Trag to free himself from th dread voice's influence... forever.
And in that was a victory neither the tauren--nor the Lich King--could ever have imagined gaining.
But even still, it was not wise to press matters...
TAKE YOUR PEOPLE HOME, AKIAK. THEY MUST KEEP GUARD OVER THEIR VILLAGE.
I THANK YOU ALL FOR YOU AID... AND TRUS
YOU SPEAK OF LEAVING... BUT WE OFFER YOU A PLACE... OUR HOME IS *YOUR* HOME.
HE SPEAKS TRUTH.
Trag stared again at them... these taunka would have risked attacking Icecrown for his sake...
Tears were not possible for an undead. so the tauren knew that the moisture had to come from the ice on him...
THANK YOU... *FRIENDS.*

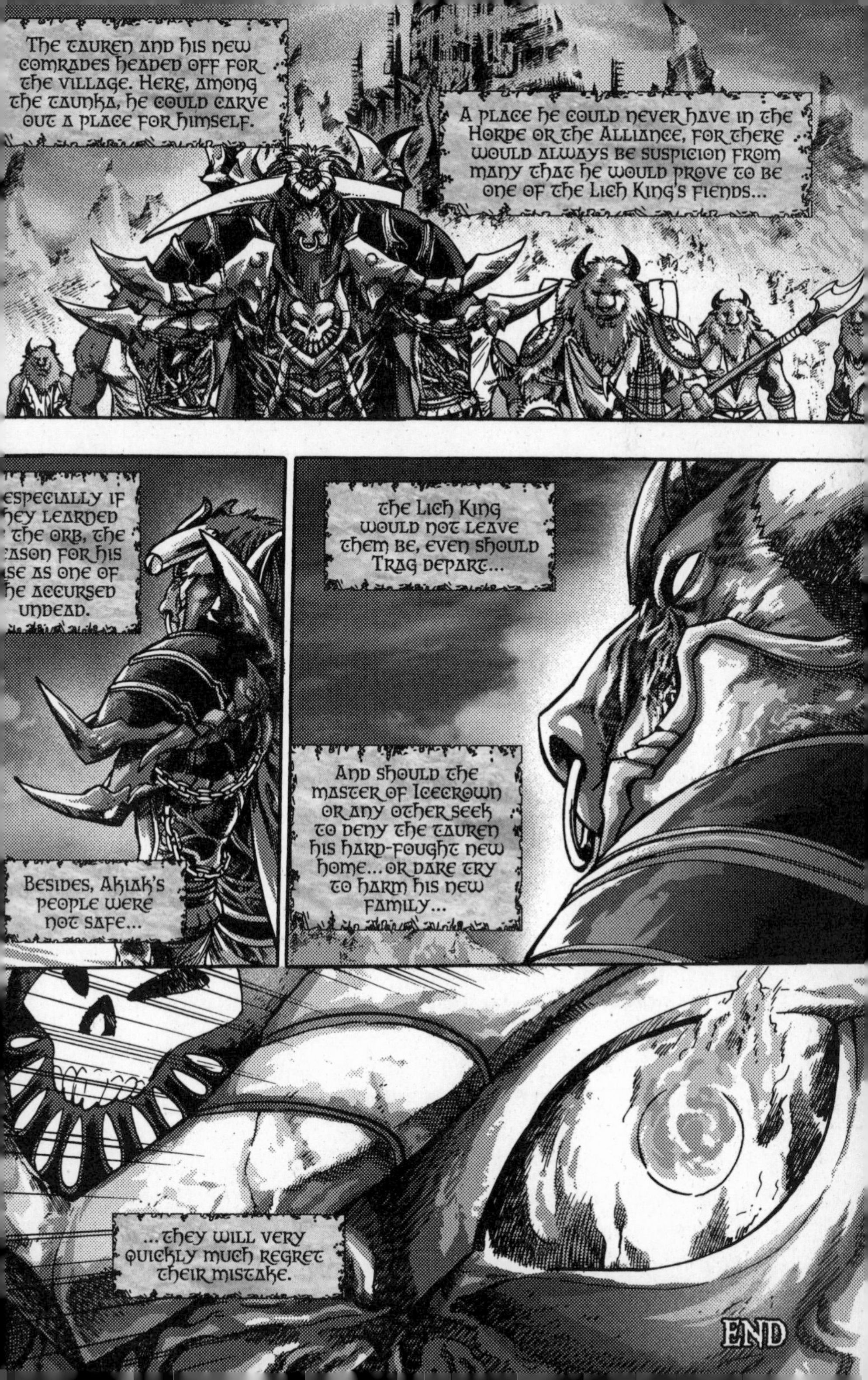
The tauren and his new comrades headed off for the village. Here, among the taunka, he could carve out a place for himself.
A place he could never have in the Horde or the Alliance, for there would always be suspicion from many that he would prove to be one of the Lich King's fiends...
especially if hey learned the orb, the eason for his se as one of he accursed undead.
Besides, Akiak's people were not safe...
The Lich King would not leave them be, even should Trag depart...
And should the master of Icecrown or any other seek to deny the tauren his hard-fought new home...or dare try to harm his new family...
...they will very quickly much regret their mistake.
END

PREVIEW

TOKYOPOP and BLIZZARD ENTERTAINMENT present *World of Warcraft: Shadow Wing,* the thrilling sequel to the international bestseller *Warcraft: The Sunwell Trilogy!*

In *Warcraft: The Sunwell Trilogy,* a good-natured but brash blue dragon, Tyrygosa, and the human Jorad Mace, a paladin struggling to reconnect with the Light, emerged victorious in the Ghostlands after ending the undead Scourge's quest to obtain the Sunwell's potent energies. Yet as arduous as that task was, Tyri and Jorad's journey is far from over. Both are drawn into the Dark Portal and transported to the shattered world of Outland, where they encounter a group of enigmatic creatures unlike any they have ever seen: the incorporeal nether dragons. But watching from the shadows is the ruthless Ragnok Bloodreaver, one of the original death knights. He has evil plans for the nether dragons that can change Outland and Azeroth forever...

Written by bestselling author Richard A. Knaak and drawn by international superstar Jae-Hwan Kim, *World of Warcraft: Shadow Wing* takes readers on an incredible journey through the mysterious regions of Outland. This epic manga also reveals details about the nether dragons' origins and connection to Deathwing, the corrupt Dragon Aspect responsible for the devastating events in the upcoming *World of Warcraft* expansion, *Cataclysm.*

Available now!

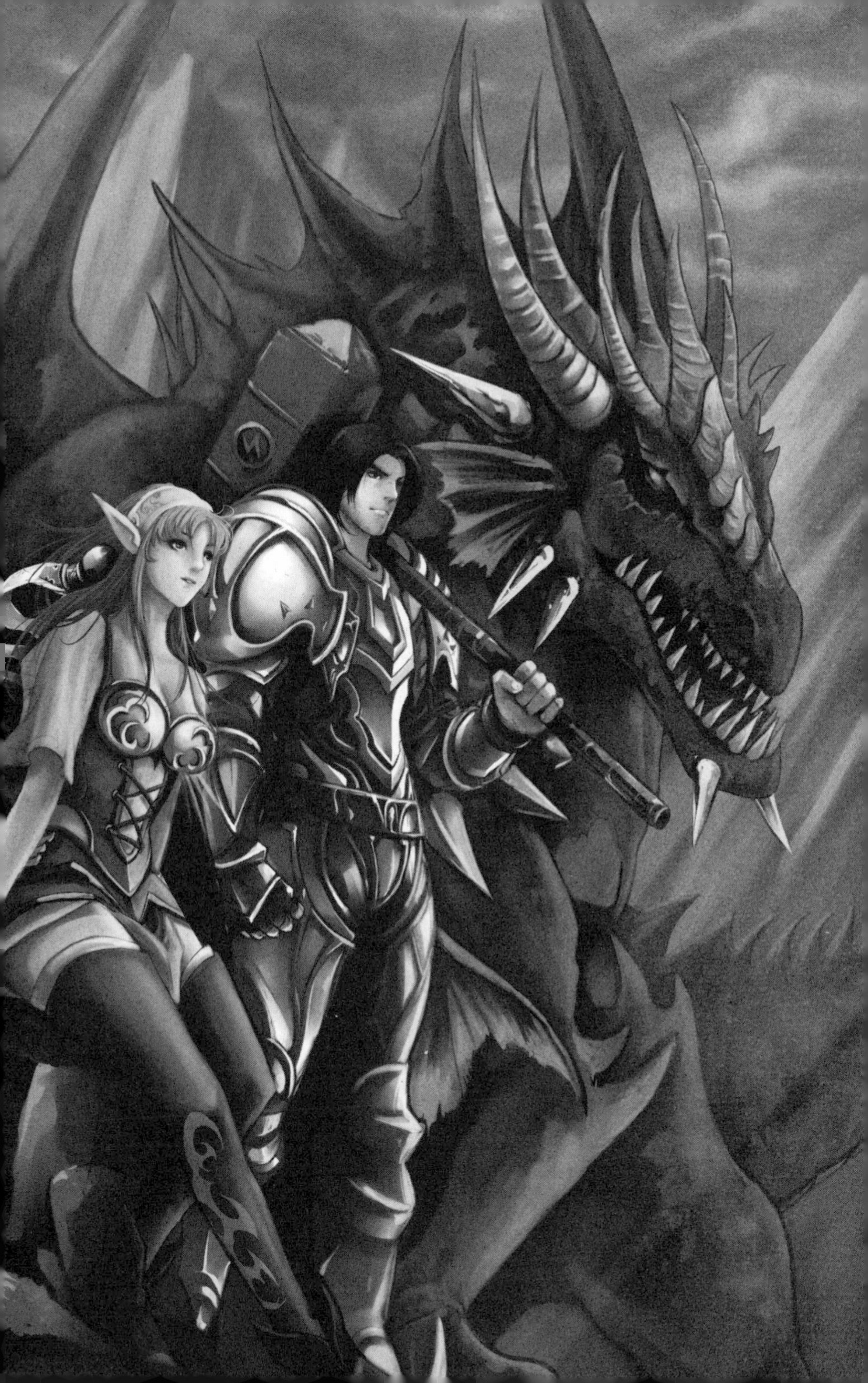

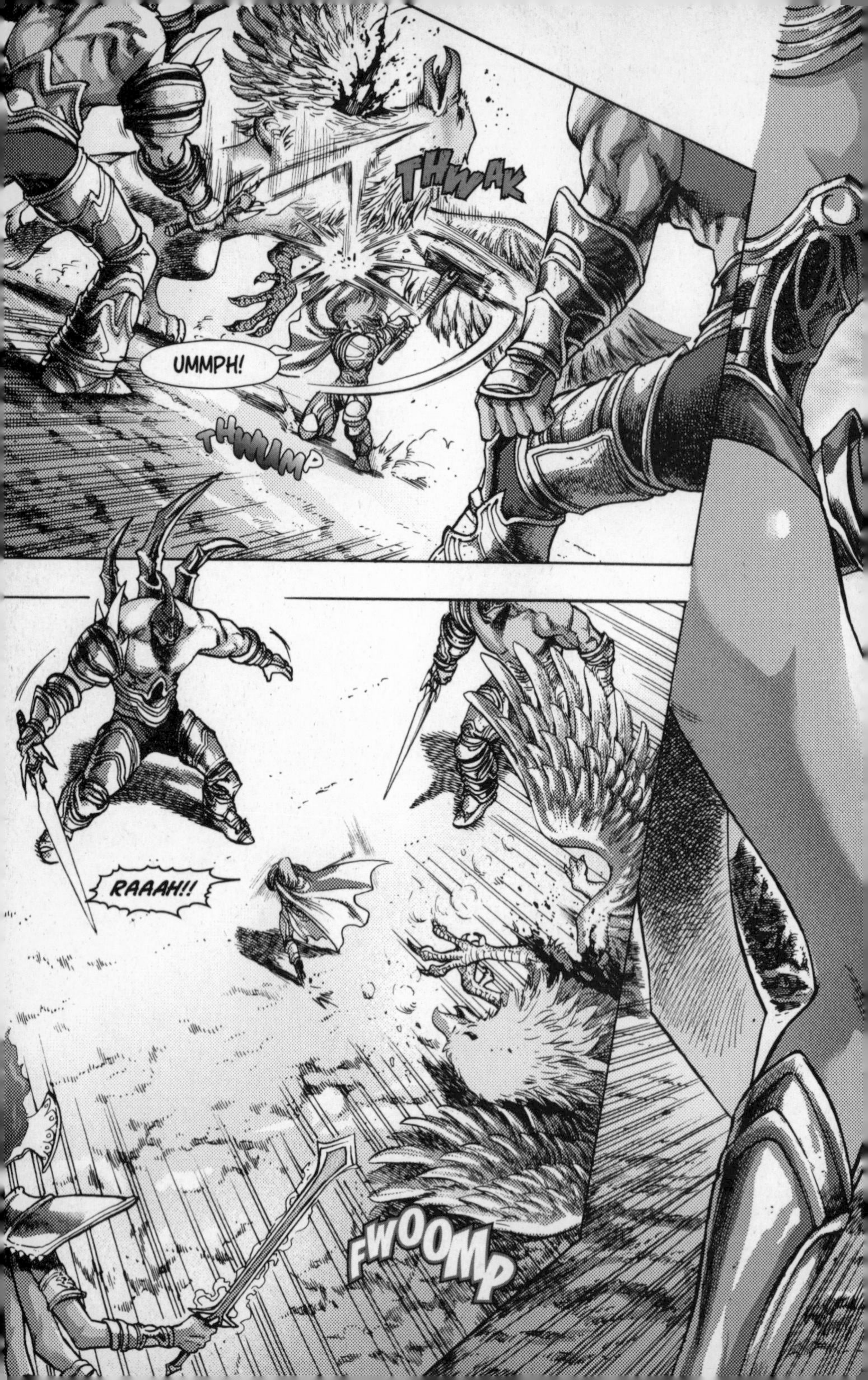
THWAK
UMMPH!
THWUMP
RAAAH!!
FWOOMP

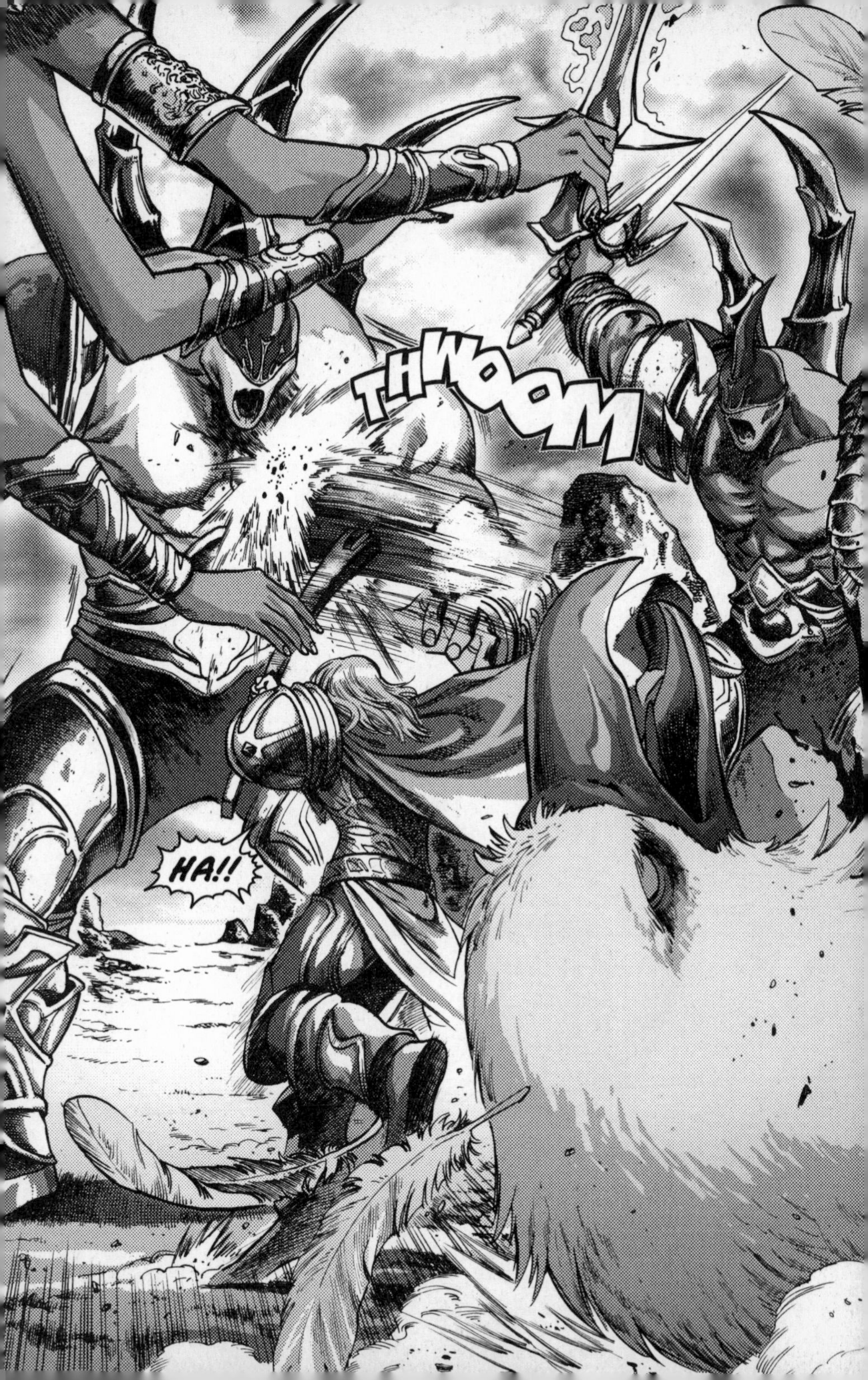
THWOOM
HA!!

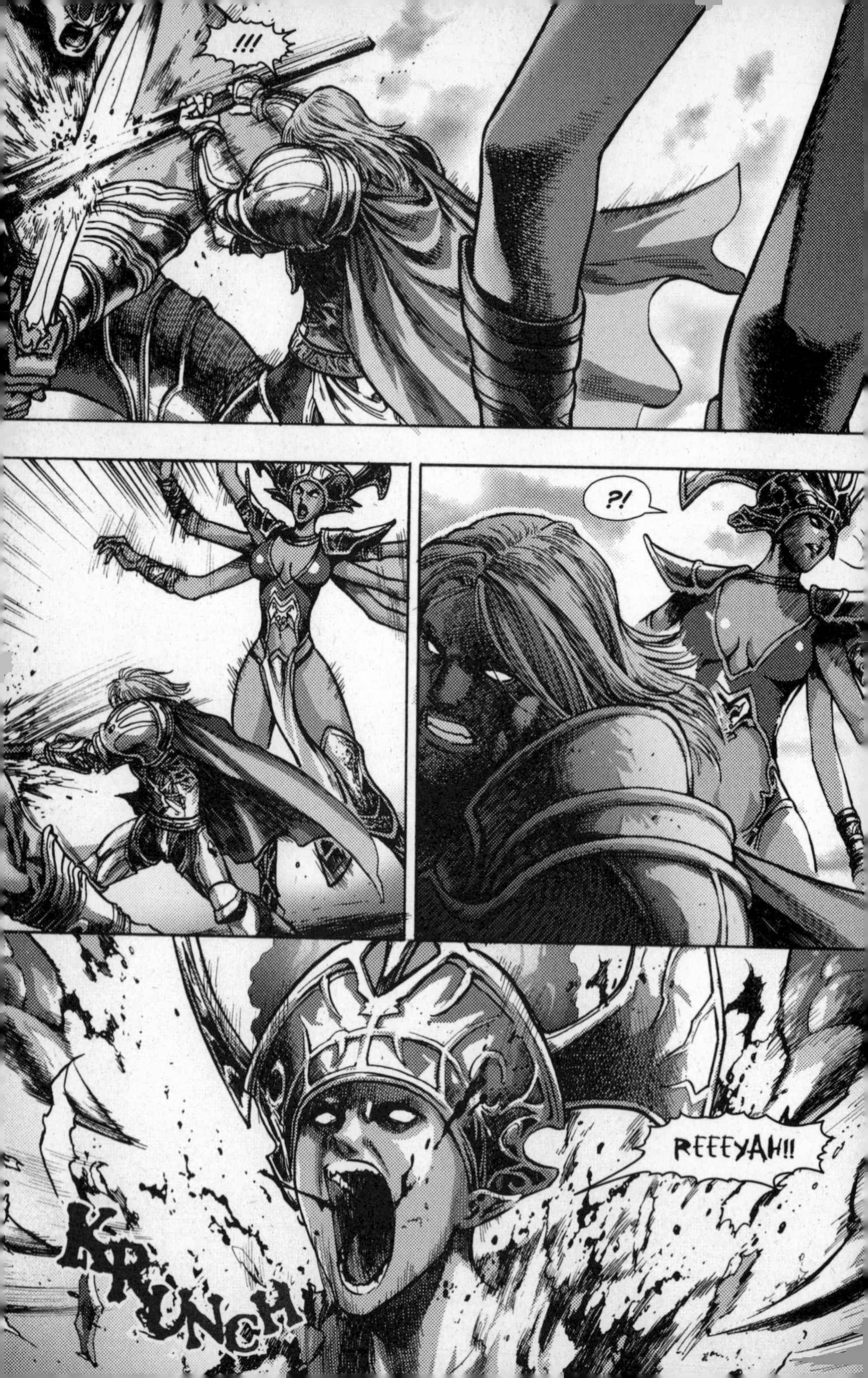
!!!
?!
REEEYAH!!
KRUNCH!!

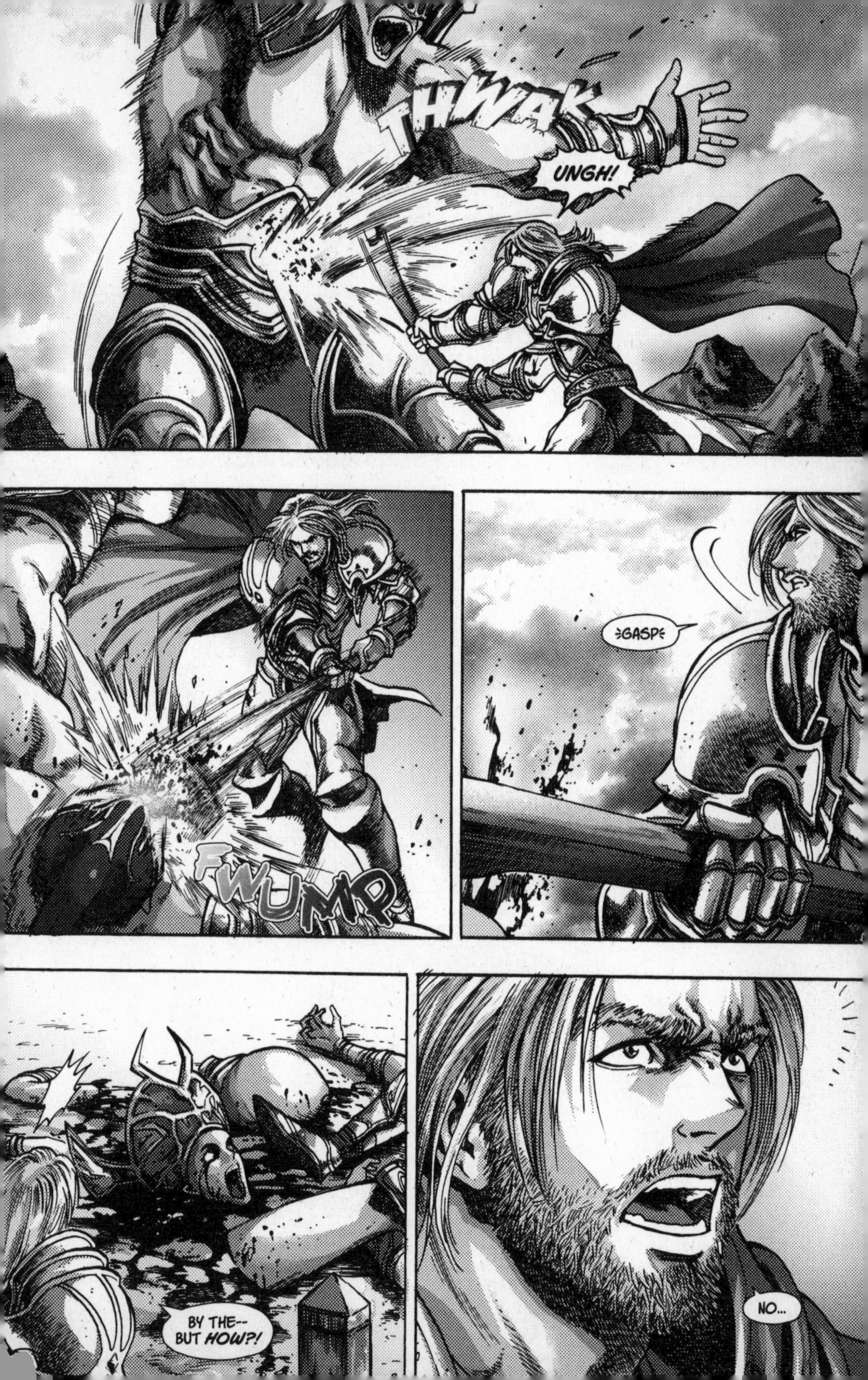
THWAK
UNGH!
FWUMP
GASP
BY THE-- BUT HOW?!
NO...

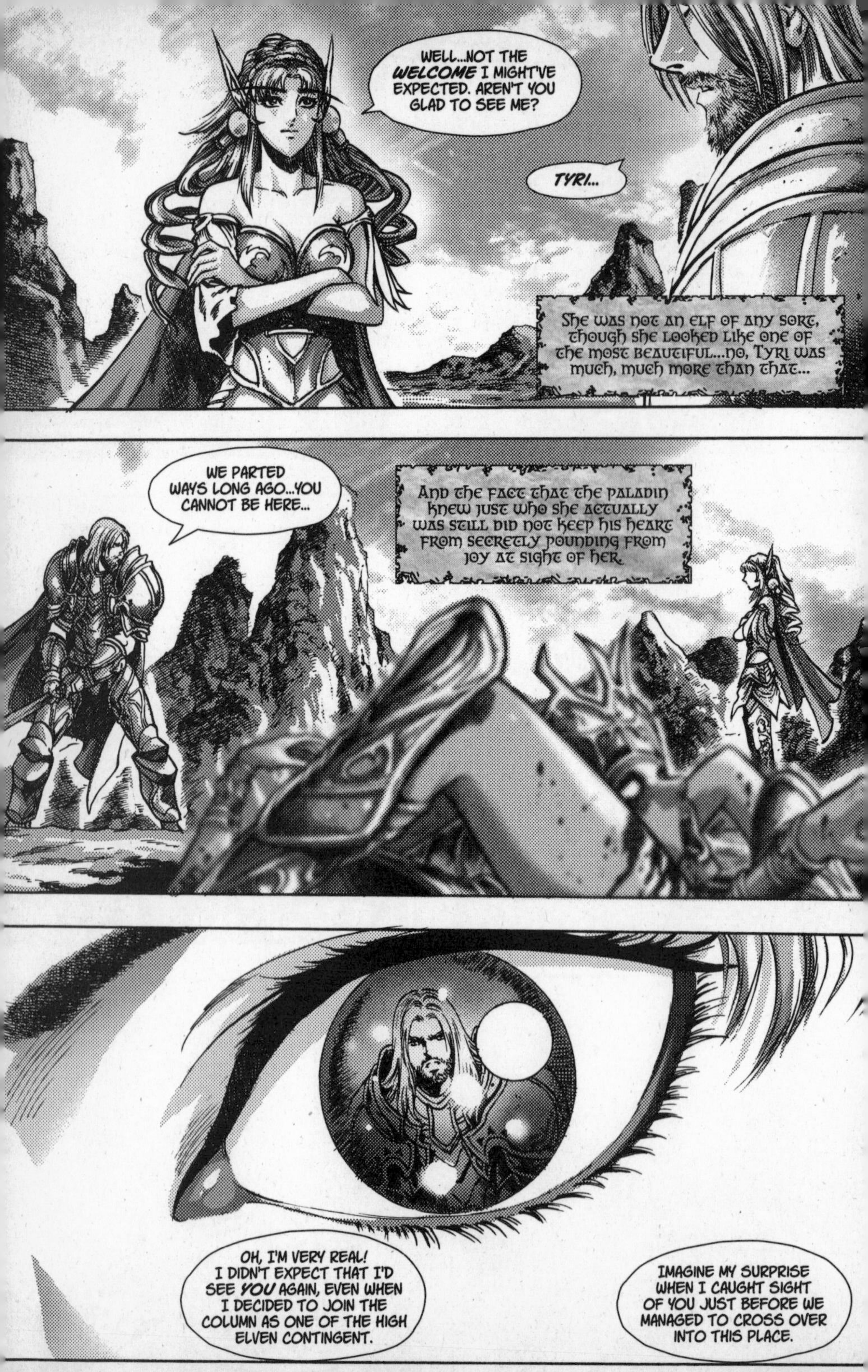
WELL...NOT THE *WELCOME* I MIGHT'VE EXPECTED. AREN'T YOU GLAD TO SEE ME?
TYRI...
She was not an elf of any sort, though she looked like one of the most beautiful...no, Tyri was much, much more than that...
WE PARTED WAYS LONG AGO...YOU CANNOT BE HERE...
And the fact that the paladin knew just who she actually was still did not keep his heart from secretly pounding from joy at sight of her.
OH, I'M VERY REAL! I DIDN'T EXPECT THAT I'D SEE *YOU* AGAIN, EVEN WHEN I DECIDED TO JOIN THE COLUMN AS ONE OF THE HIGH ELVEN CONTINGENT.
IMAGINE MY SURPRISE WHEN I CAUGHT SIGHT OF YOU JUST BEFORE WE MANAGED TO CROSS OVER INTO THIS PLACE.

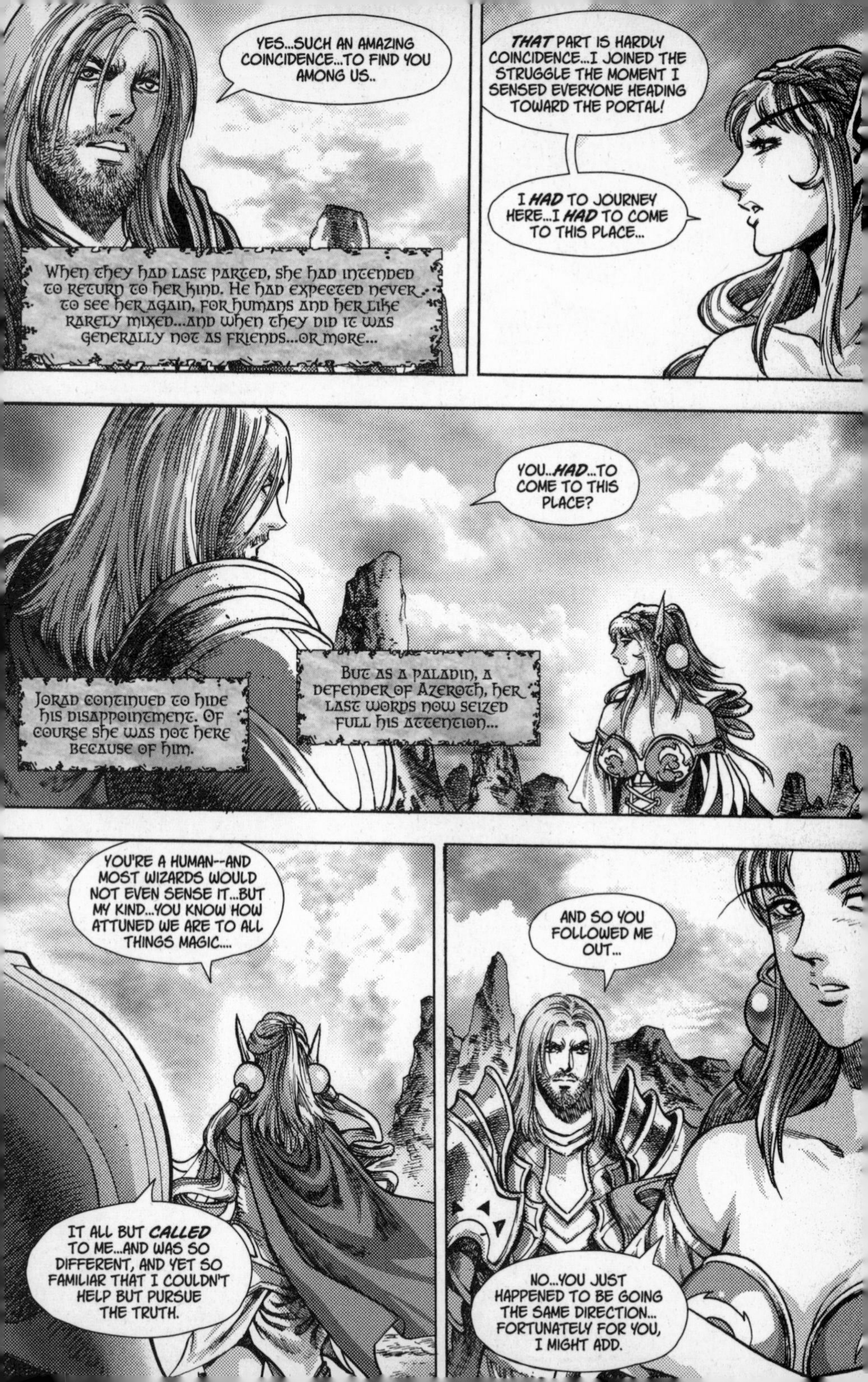
YES...SUCH AN AMAZING COINCIDENCE...TO FIND YOU AMONG US..
When they had last parted, she had intended to return to her kind. He had expected never to see her again, for humans and her like rarely mixed...and when they did it was generally not as friends...or more...
THAT PART IS HARDLY COINCIDENCE...I JOINED THE STRUGGLE THE MOMENT I SENSED EVERYONE HEADING TOWARD THE PORTAL!
I *HAD* TO JOURNEY HERE...I *HAD* TO COME TO THIS PLACE...
YOU...*HAD*...TO COME TO THIS PLACE?
Jorad continued to hide his disappointment. Of course she was not here because of him.
But as a paladin, a defender of Azeroth, her last words now seized full his attention...
YOU'RE A HUMAN--AND MOST WIZARDS WOULD NOT EVEN SENSE IT...BUT MY KIND...YOU KNOW HOW ATTUNED WE ARE TO ALL THINGS MAGIC....
IT ALL BUT *CALLED* TO ME...AND WAS SO DIFFERENT, AND YET SO FAMILIAR THAT I COULDN'T HELP BUT PURSUE THE TRUTH.
AND SO YOU FOLLOWED ME OUT...
NO...YOU JUST HAPPENED TO BE GOING THE SAME DIRECTION... FORTUNATELY FOR YOU, I MIGHT ADD.

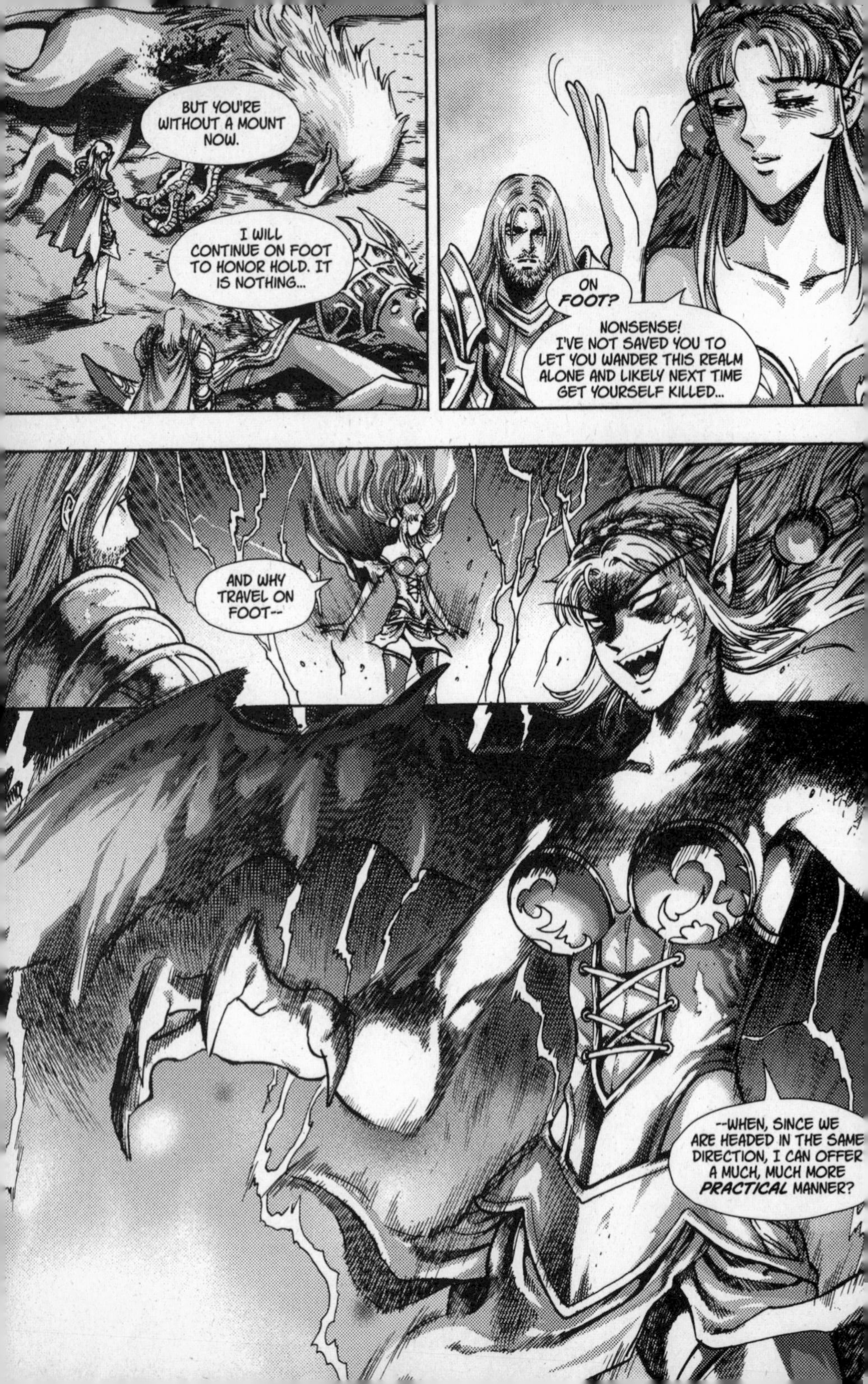
BUT YOU'RE WITHOUT A MOUNT NOW.
I WILL CONTINUE ON FOOT TO HONOR HOLD. IT IS NOTHING...
ON *FOOT?*
NONSENSE! I'VE NOT SAVED YOU TO LET YOU WANDER THIS REALM ALONE AND LIKELY NEXT TIME GET YOURSELF KILLED...
AND WHY TRAVEL ON FOOT--
--WHEN, SINCE WE ARE HEADED IN THE SAME DIRECTION, I CAN OFFER A MUCH, MUCH MORE *PRACTICAL* MANNER?

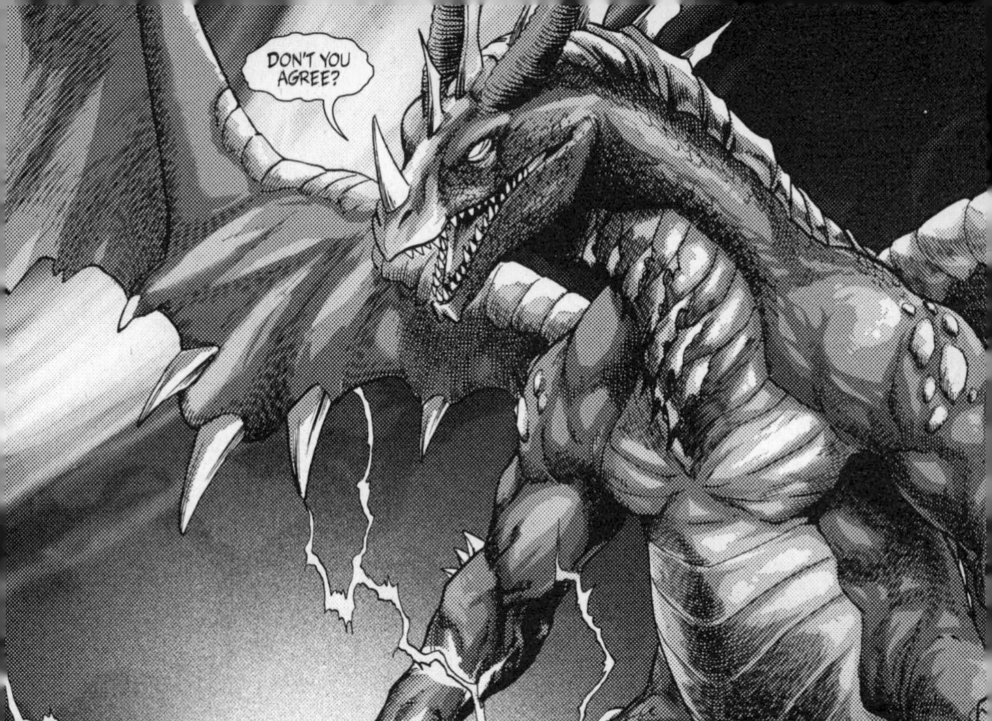
DON'T YOU AGREE?

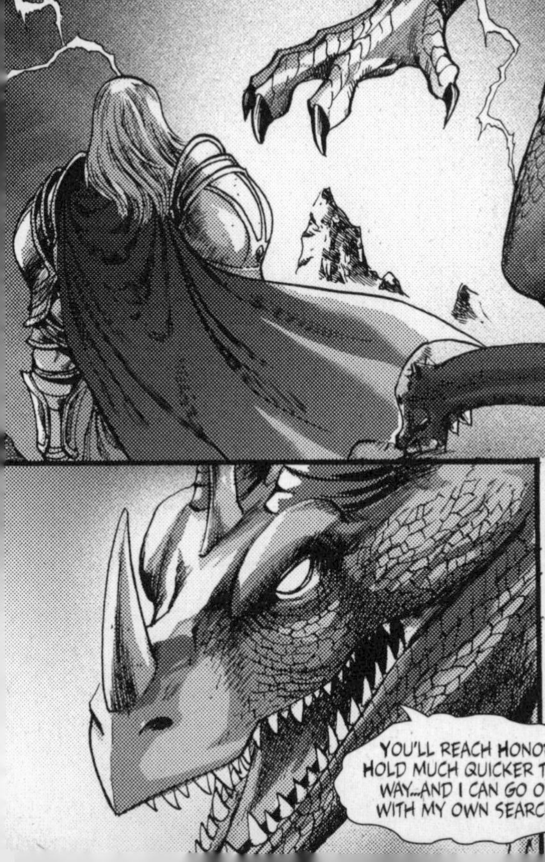
YOU'LL REACH HONOR HOLD MUCH QUICKER THIS WAY...AND I CAN GO ON WITH MY OWN SEARCH.

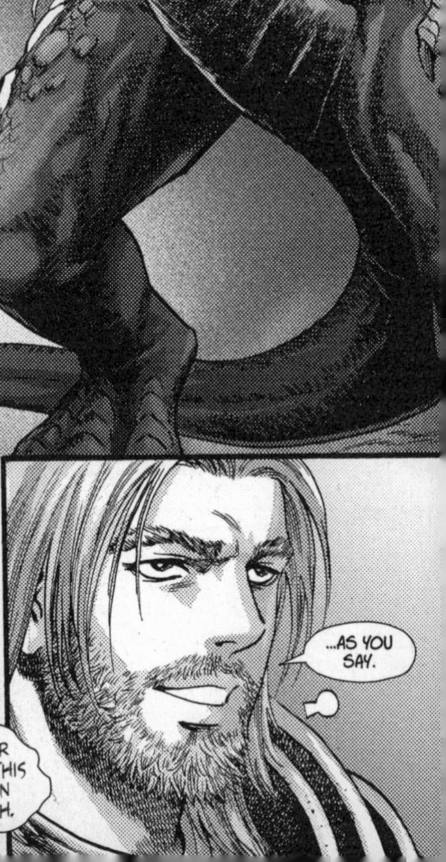
...AS YOU SAY.

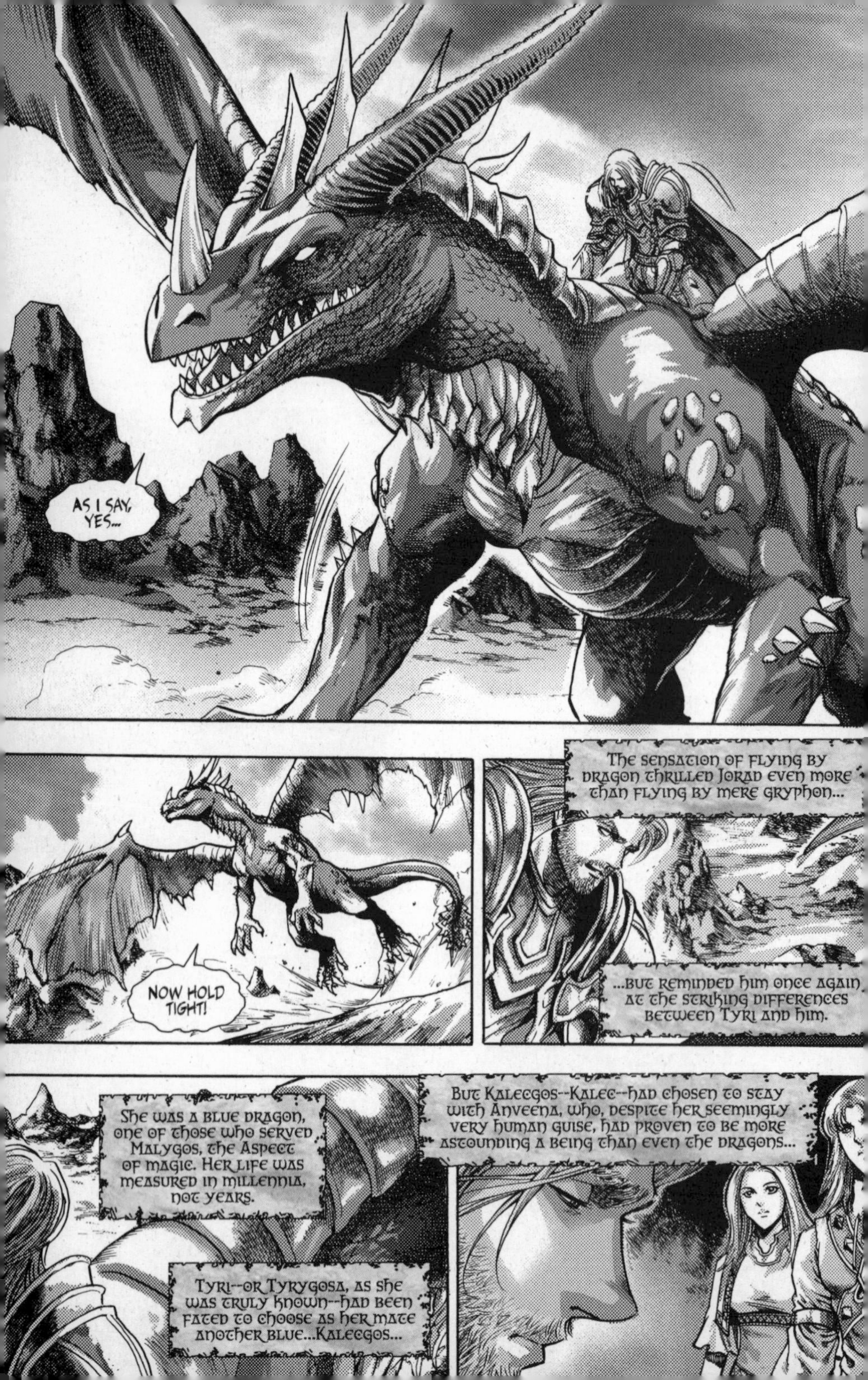

AS I SAY, YES...
NOW HOLD TIGHT!
The sensation of flying by dragon thrilled Jorad even more than flying by mere gryphon...
...but reminded him once again of the striking differences between Tyri and him.
She was a blue dragon, one of those who served Malygos, the Aspect of magic. Her life was measured in millennia, not years.
Tyri--or Tyrygosa, as she was truly known--had been fated to choose as her mate another blue...Kalecgos...
But Kalecgos--Kalec--had chosen to stay with Anveena, who, despite her seemingly very human guise, had proven to be more astounding a being than even the dragons...

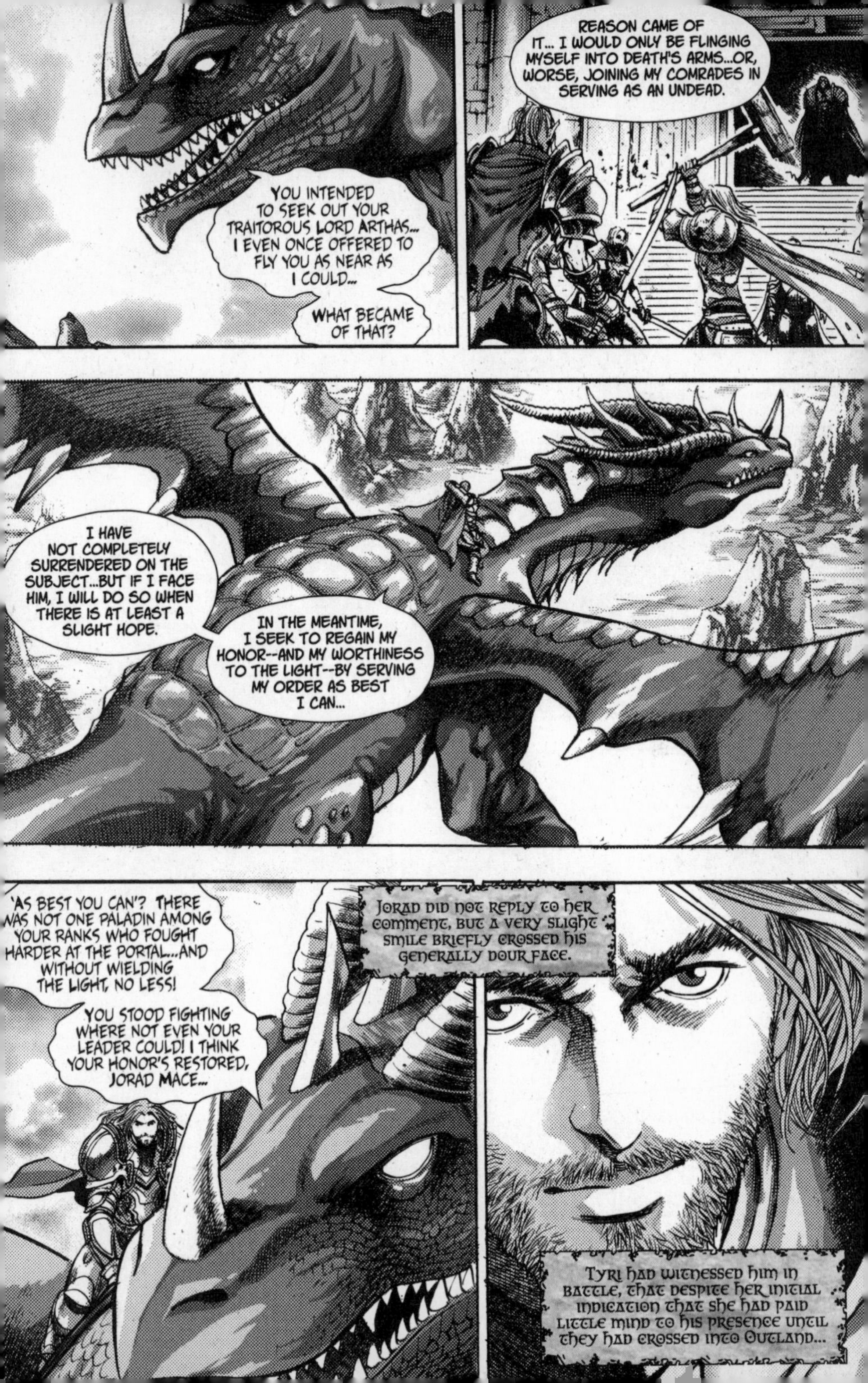
YOU INTENDED TO SEEK OUT YOUR TRAITOROUS LORD ARTHAS... I EVEN ONCE OFFERED TO FLY YOU AS NEAR AS I COULD...
WHAT BECAME OF THAT?
REASON CAME OF IT... I WOULD ONLY BE FLINGING MYSELF INTO DEATH'S ARMS...OR, WORSE, JOINING MY COMRADES IN SERVING AS AN UNDEAD.
I HAVE NOT COMPLETELY SURRENDERED ON THE SUBJECT...BUT IF I FACE HIM, I WILL DO SO WHEN THERE IS AT LEAST A SLIGHT HOPE.
IN THE MEANTIME, I SEEK TO REGAIN MY HONOR--AND MY WORTHINESS TO THE LIGHT--BY SERVING MY ORDER AS BEST I CAN...
'AS BEST YOU CAN'? THERE WAS NOT ONE PALADIN AMONG YOUR RANKS WHO FOUGHT HARDER AT THE PORTAL...AND WITHOUT WIELDING THE LIGHT, NO LESS!
YOU STOOD FIGHTING WHERE NOT EVEN YOUR LEADER COULD! I THINK YOUR HONOR'S RESTORED, JORAD MACE...
Jorad did not reply to her comment, but a very slight smile briefly crossed his generally dour face.
Tyri had witnessed him in battle, that despite her initial indication that she had paid little mind to his presence until they had crossed into Outland...

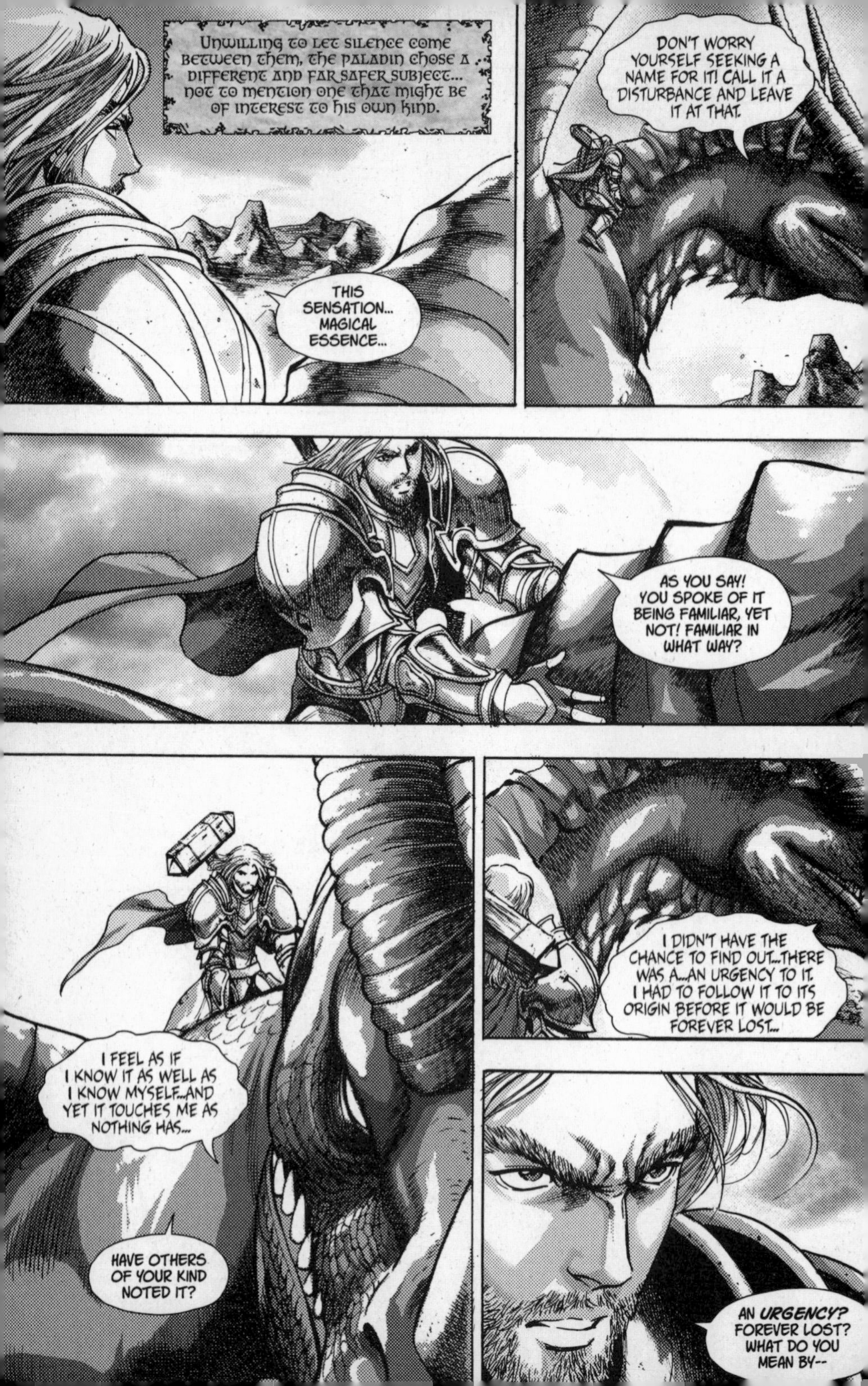
UNWILLING TO LET SILENCE COME BETWEEN THEM, THE PALADIN CHOSE A DIFFERENT AND FAR SAFER SUBJECT... NOT TO MENTION ONE THAT MIGHT BE OF INTEREST TO HIS OWN KIND.
THIS SENSATION... MAGICAL ESSENCE...
DON'T WORRY YOURSELF SEEKING A NAME FOR IT! CALL IT A DISTURBANCE AND LEAVE IT AT THAT.
AS YOU SAY! YOU SPOKE OF IT BEING FAMILIAR, YET NOT! FAMILIAR IN WHAT WAY?
I FEEL AS IF I KNOW IT AS WELL AS I KNOW MYSELF...AND YET IT TOUCHES ME AS NOTHING HAS...
HAVE OTHERS OF YOUR KIND NOTED IT?
I DIDN'T HAVE THE CHANCE TO FIND OUT...THERE WAS A...AN URGENCY TO IT. I HAD TO FOLLOW IT TO ITS ORIGIN BEFORE IT WOULD BE FOREVER LOST...
AN URGENCY? FOREVER LOST? WHAT DO YOU MEAN BY--

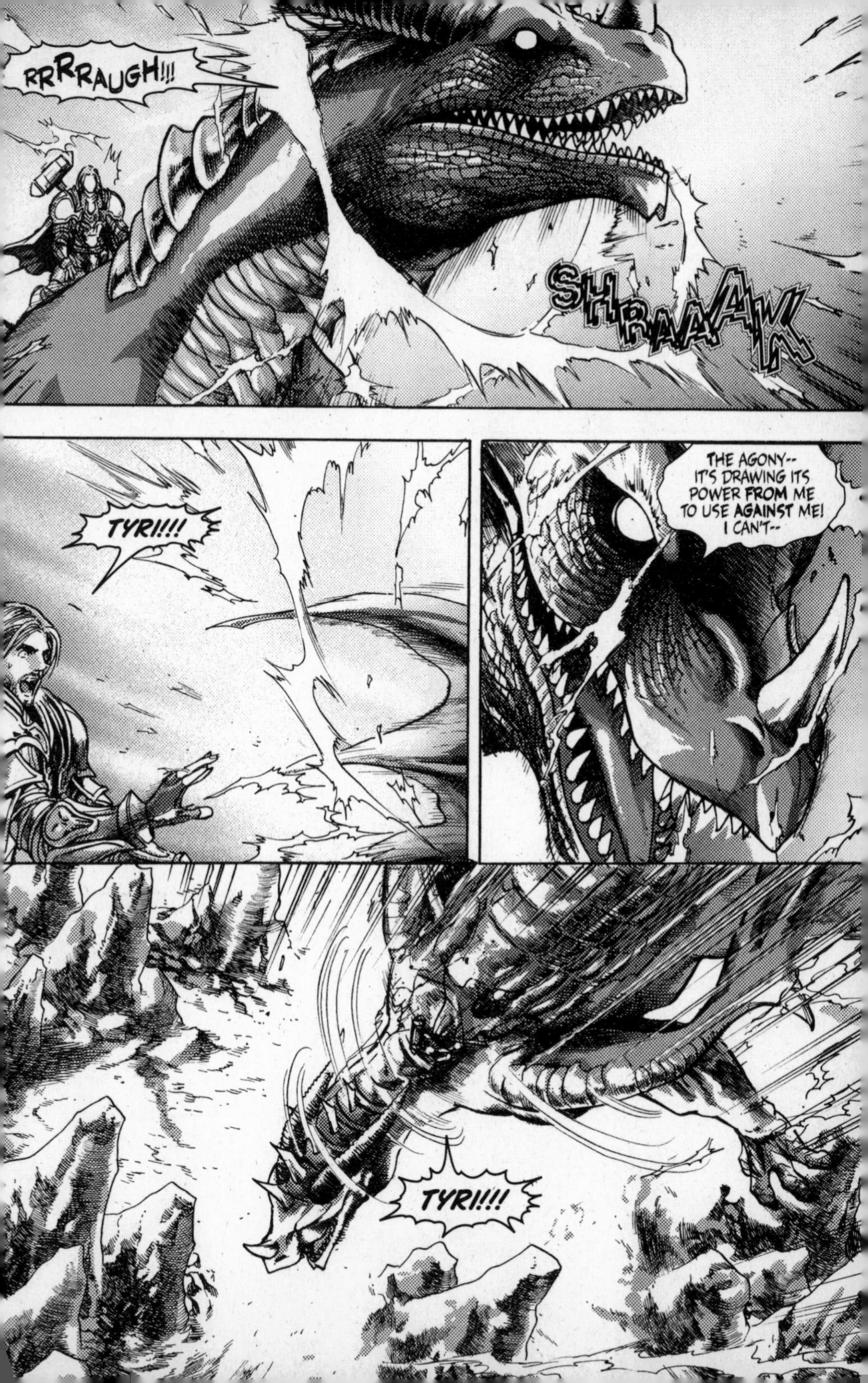
RRRRAUGH!!!
SHRAAAAK
TYRI!!!!
THE AGONY-- IT'S DRAWING ITS POWER FROM ME TO USE AGAINST ME! I CAN'T--
TYRI!!!!

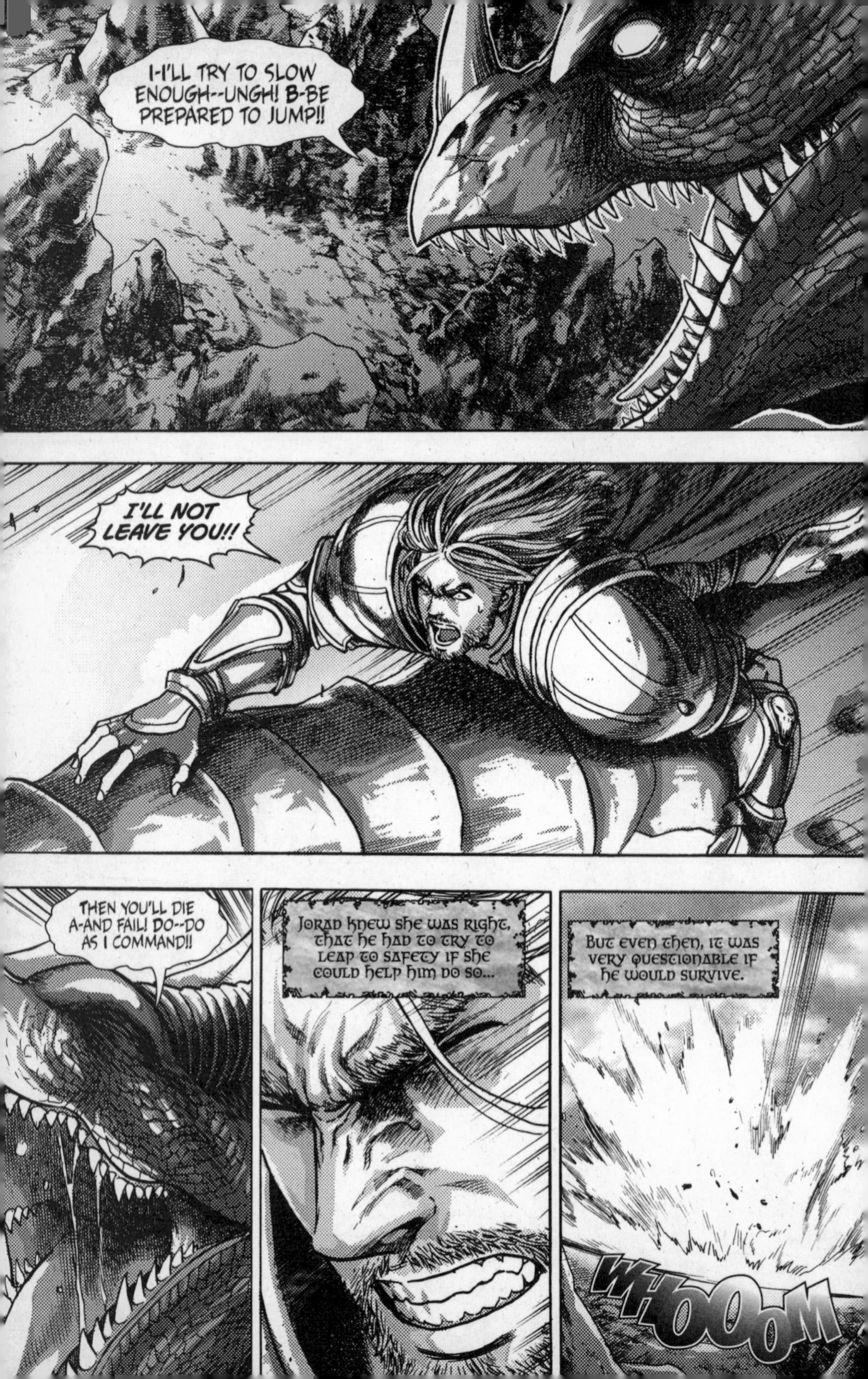
I-I'LL TRY TO SLOW ENOUGH--UNGH! B-BE PREPARED TO JUMP!!
I'LL NOT LEAVE YOU!!
THEN YOU'LL DIE A-AND FAIL! DO--DO AS I COMMAND!!
Jorad knew she was right, that he had to try to leap to safety if she could help him do so...
But even then, it was very questionable if he would survive.
WHOOOM

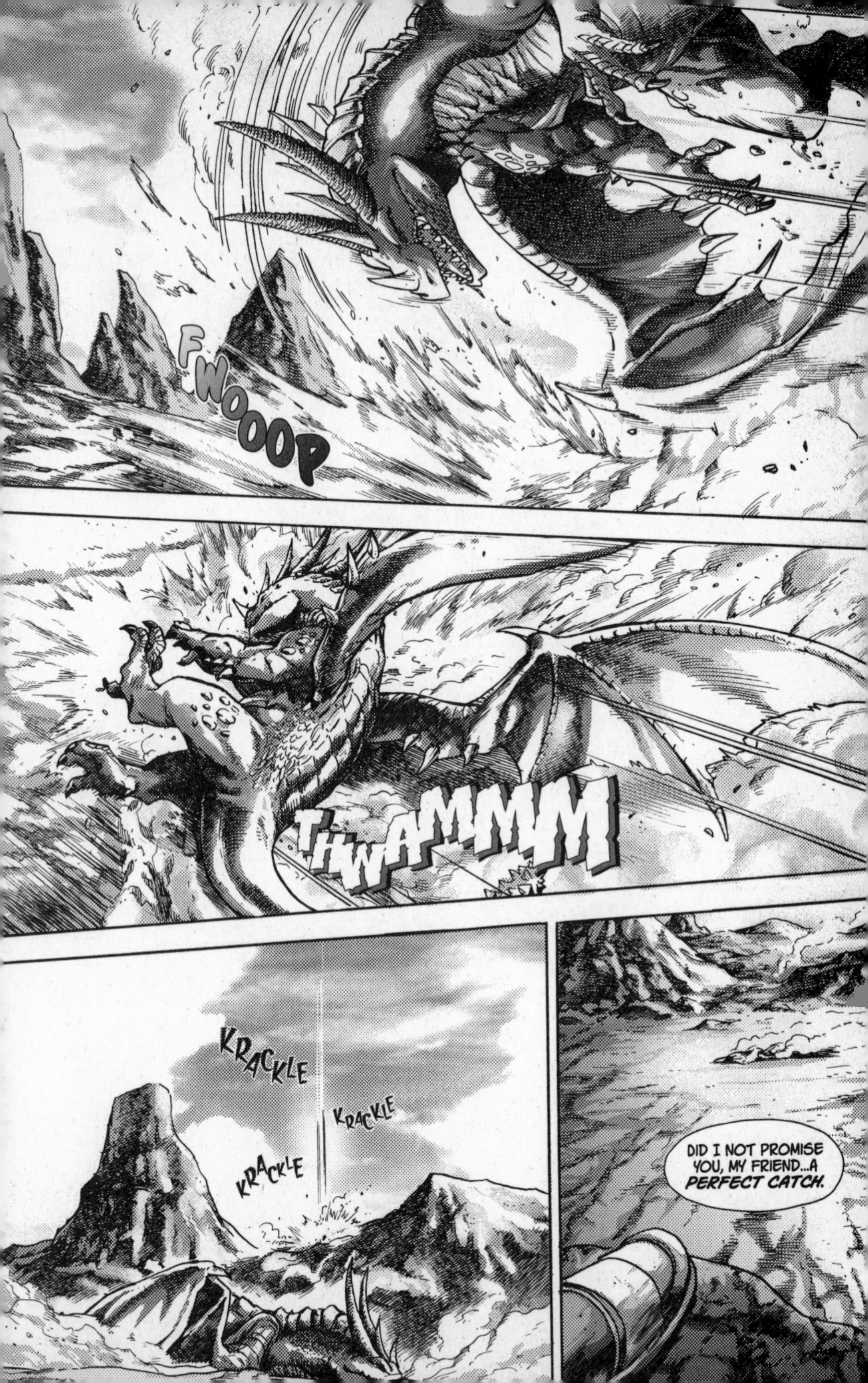
FWOOOOP
THWAMMMM
KRACKLE
KRACKLE
KRACKLE
DID I NOT PROMISE YOU, MY FRIEND...A *PERFECT CATCH.*

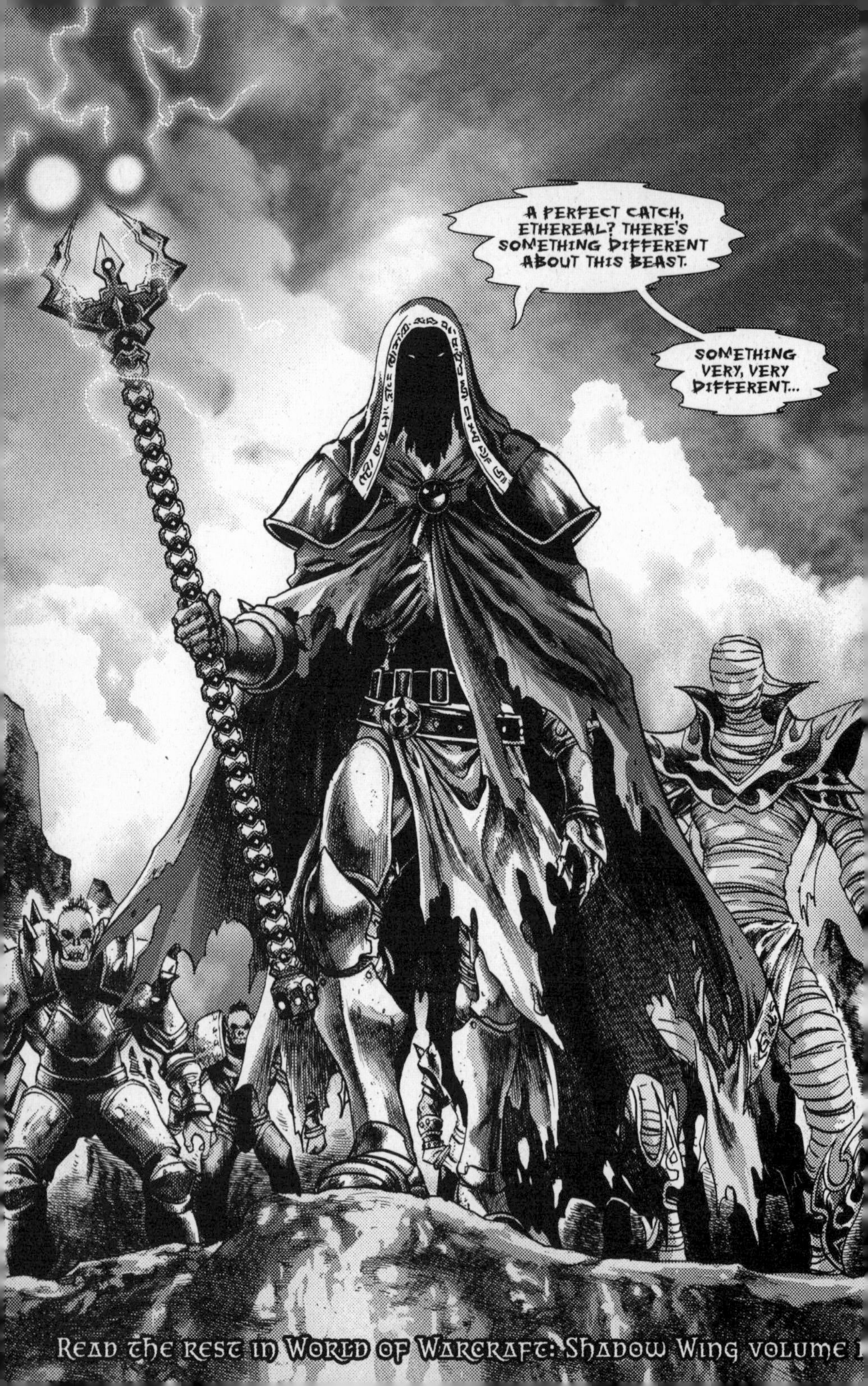
A PERFECT CATCH, ETHEREAL? THERE'S SOMETHING DIFFERENT ABOUT THIS BEAST.
SOMETHING VERY, VERY DIFFERENT...
READ THE REST IN WORLD OF WARCRAFT: SHADOW WING VOLUME 1

CREATOR BIO'S

RICHARD A. KNAAK

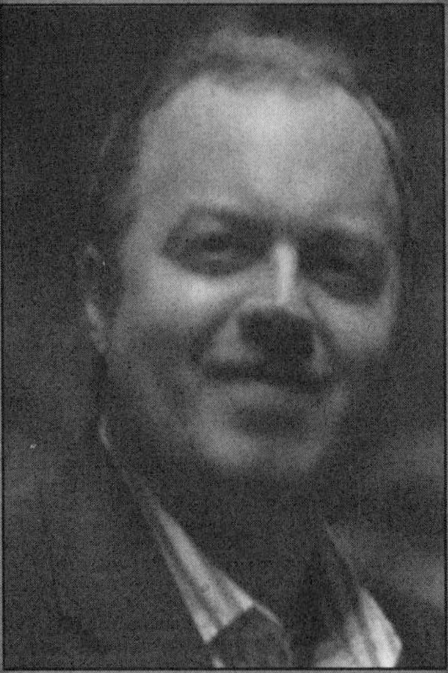

Richard A. Knaak is the New York Times and USA Today bestselling fantasy author of 40 novels and over a dozen short stories, including most recently the national bestseller, *World of Warcraft: Stormrage.* He is also well known for such favorites as *The Legend of Huma* & *The Minotaur Wars* for Dragonlance, the *War of the Ancients* trilogy for *Warcraft,* and his own *Dragonrealm* series. In addition to the TOKYOPOP series *Warcraft: The Sunwell Trilogy,* he is the author of five short stories featured in *Warcraft: Legends* Volumes 1-5 , as well as the sequel series to *Warcraft: The Sunwell Trilogy, World of Warcraft: Shadow Wing.* He also recently released *The Gargoyle King,* the third in his *Ogre Titans* saga for Dragonlance and *Legends of the Dragonrealm,* which combines the first three novels of his world. A second volume was released in October 2010. To find out more about Richard's projects, visit his website at www.richardaknaak.com.

JAE-HWAN KIM

Born in 1971 in Korea, Jae-Hwan Kim's best-known manga works include *Rainbow*, *Combat Metal HeMoSoo* and *King of Hell,* a series published by TOKYOPOP. Along with being the creator of *War Angels* for TOKYOPOP, Jae-Hwan is the artist for TOKYOPOP's *Warcraft: The Sunwell Trilogy,* the Trag Highmountain short stories in *Warcraft: Legends* Volumes 1-4, as well as the sequel series to *Warcraft: The Sunwell Trilogy, World of Warcraft: Shadow Wing.*

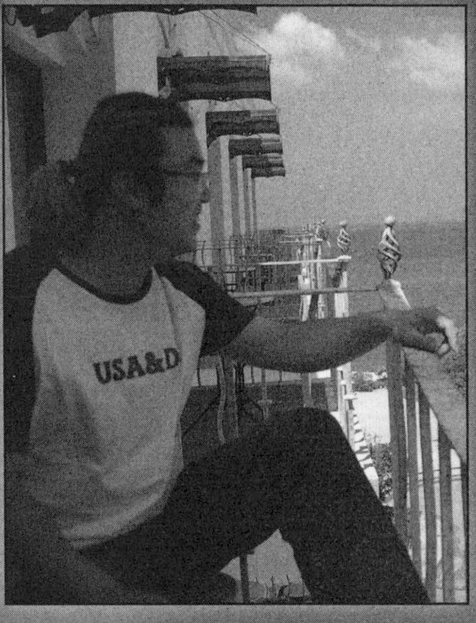
USA&D

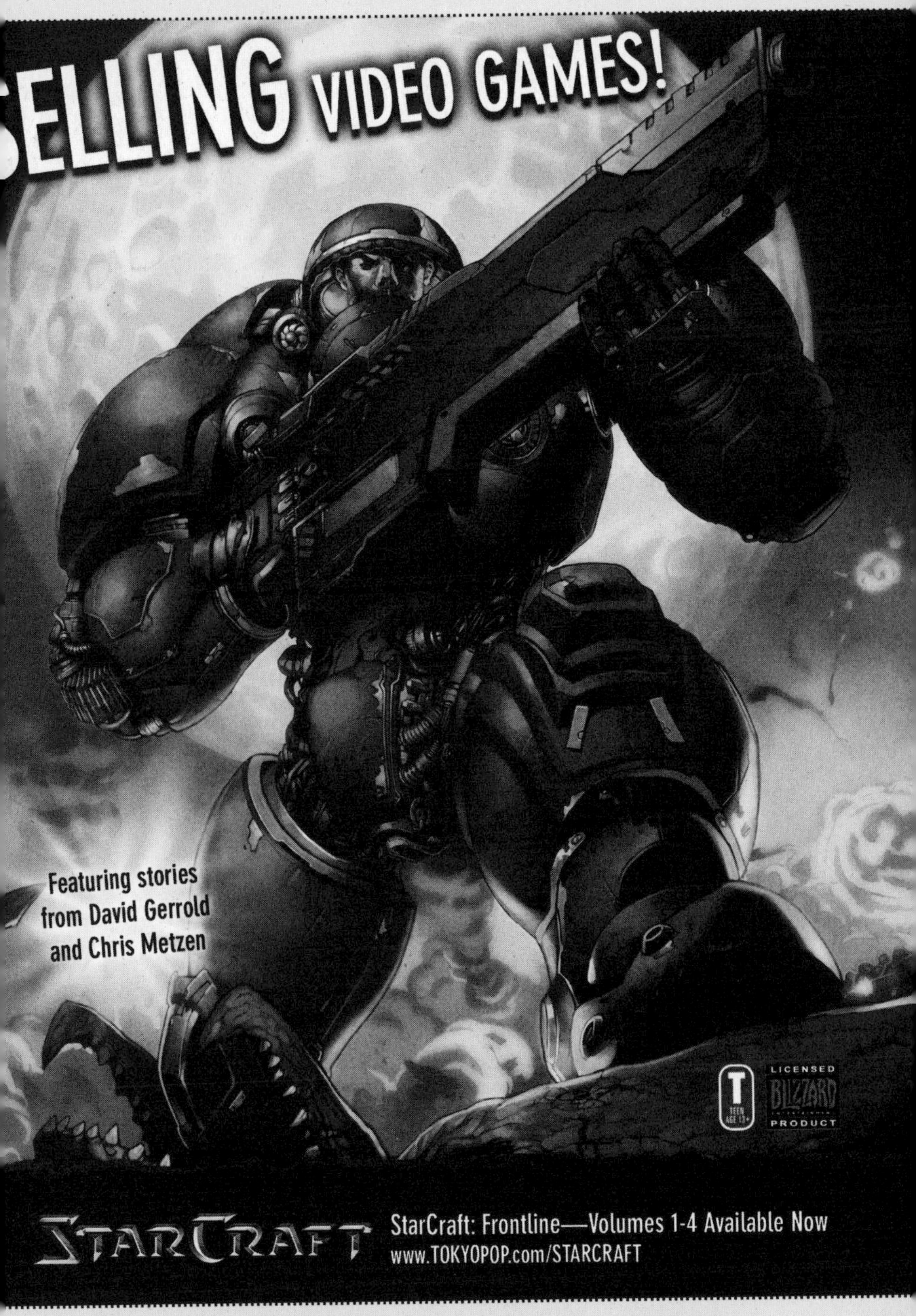
SELLING VIDEO GAMES!
Featuring stories from David Gerrold and Chris Metzen
T TEEN AGE 13+
LICENSED BLIZZARD PRODUCT
STARCRAFT
StarCraft: Frontline—Volumes 1-4 Available Now
www.TOKYOPOP.com/STARCRAFT

Actual Gameplay.

NO. I'D RATHER KILL RATS.

With millions of players online, World of Warcraft has made gaming
history — and now it's never been easier to join the adventure.
Simply visit **www.warcraft.com**, download the FREE TRIAL and join
thousands of mighty heroes for ten days of bold online adventure.

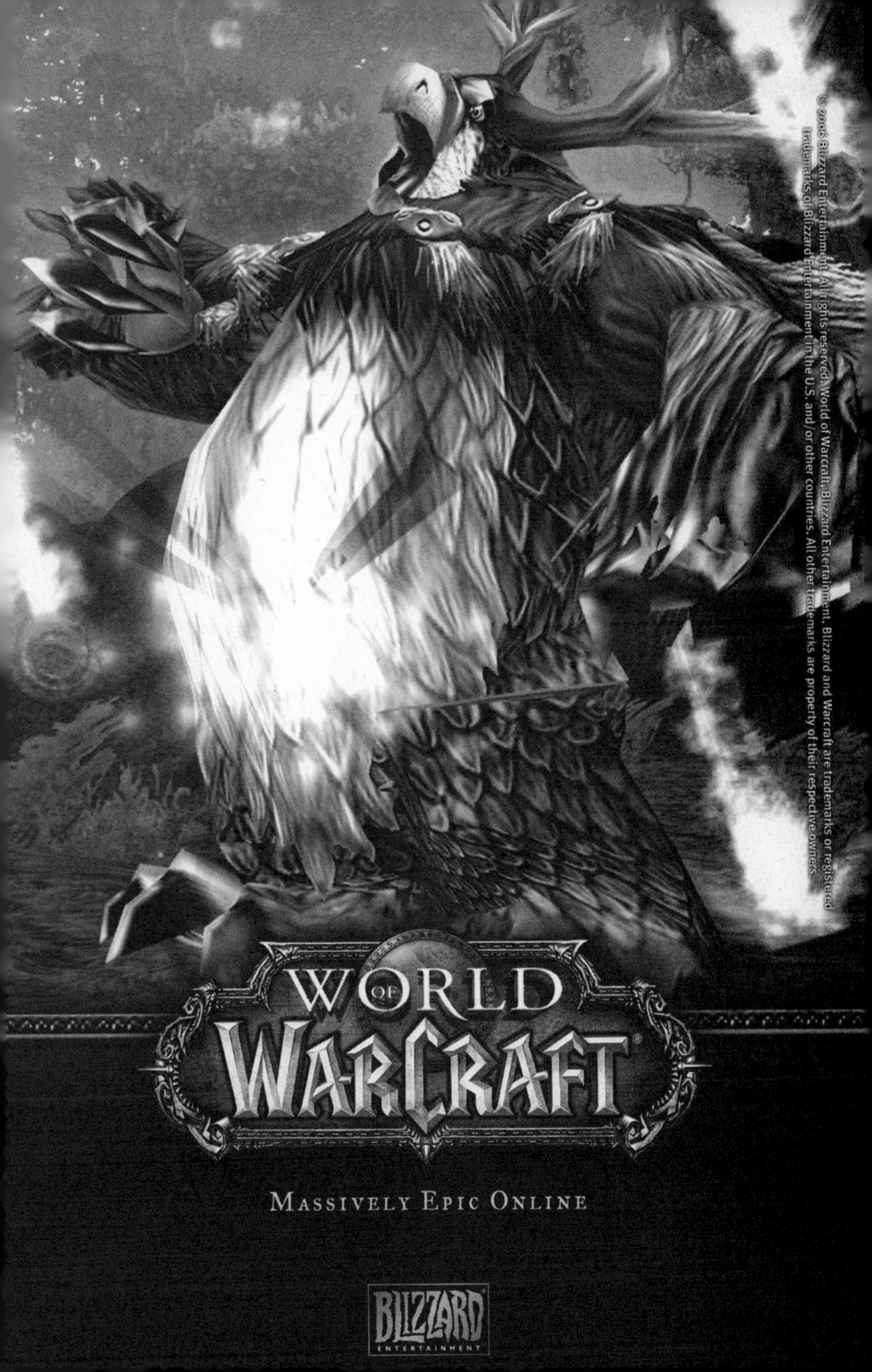
© 2006 Blizzard Entertainment. All rights reserved. World of Warcraft, Blizzard Entertainment, Blizzard and Warcraft are trademarks or registered trademarks of Blizzard Entertainment in the U.S. and/or other countries. All other trademarks are property of their respective owners.
WORLD OF WARCRAFT®
MASSIVELY EPIC ONLINE
BLIZZARD ENTERTAINMENT

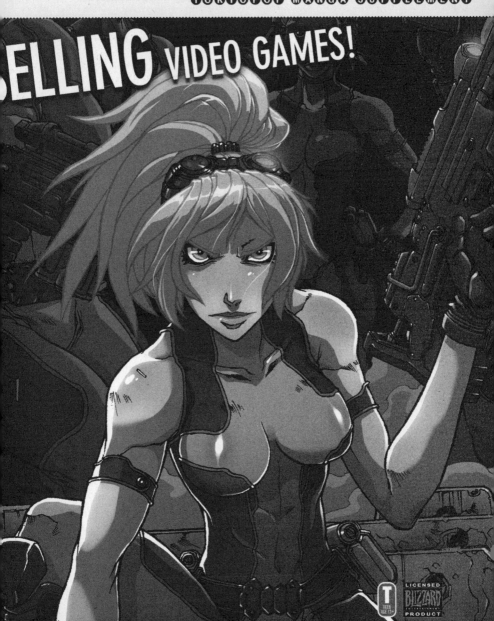

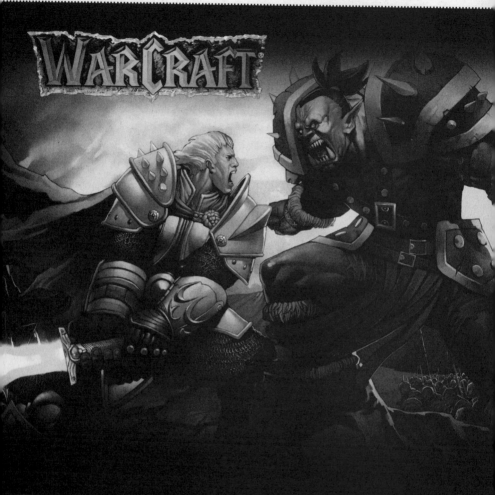

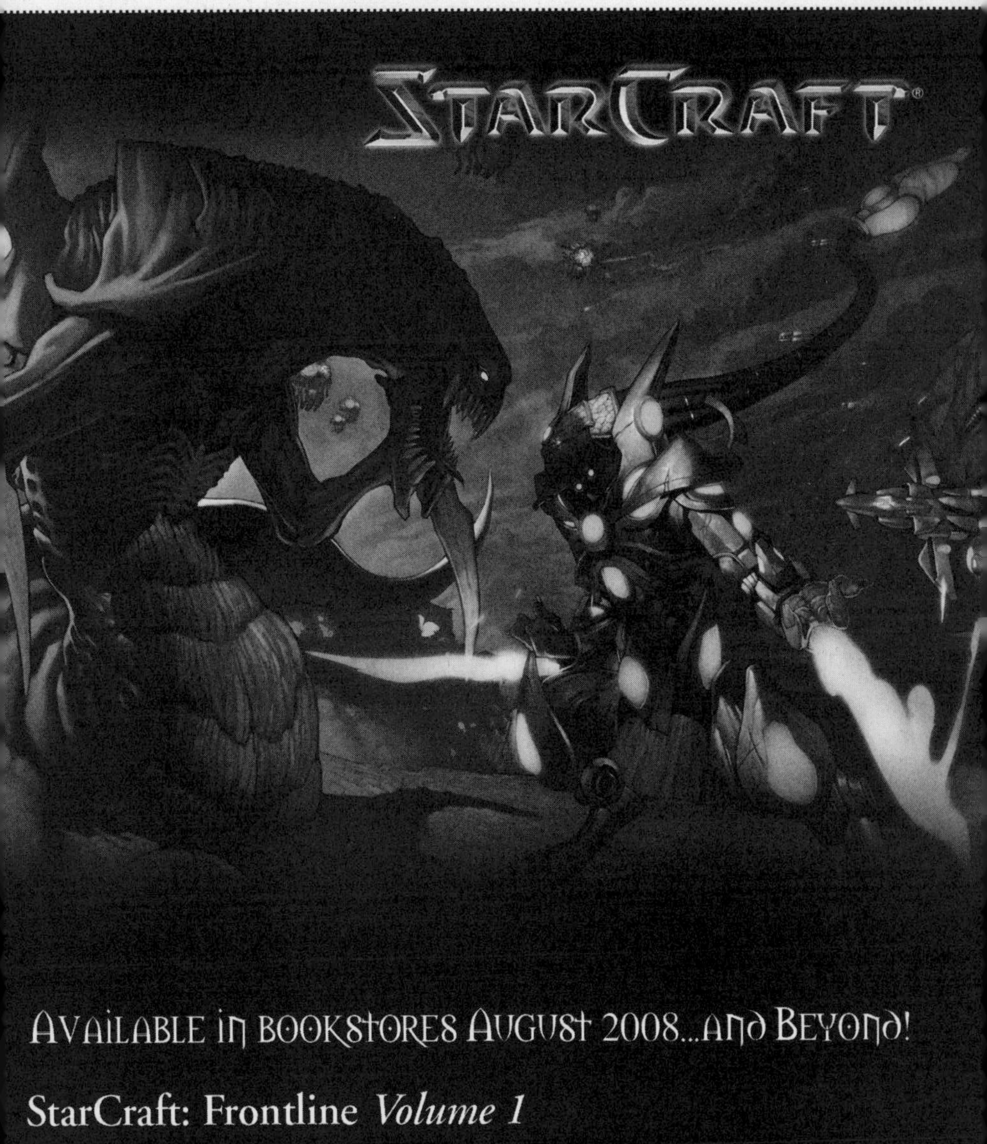
STARCRAFT®
AVAILABLE IN BOOKSTORES AUGUST 2008...AND BEYOND!
StarCraft: Frontline Volume 1
Check out www.TOKYOPOP.com/STARCRAFT
for exclusive news, updates and free downloadable art.
T TEEN AGE 13+
BLIZZARD® ENTERTAINMENT
Art by: UDON with Saejin Oh
Warcraft and StarCraft: © 2008 Blizzard Entertainment, Inc. All rights reserved.

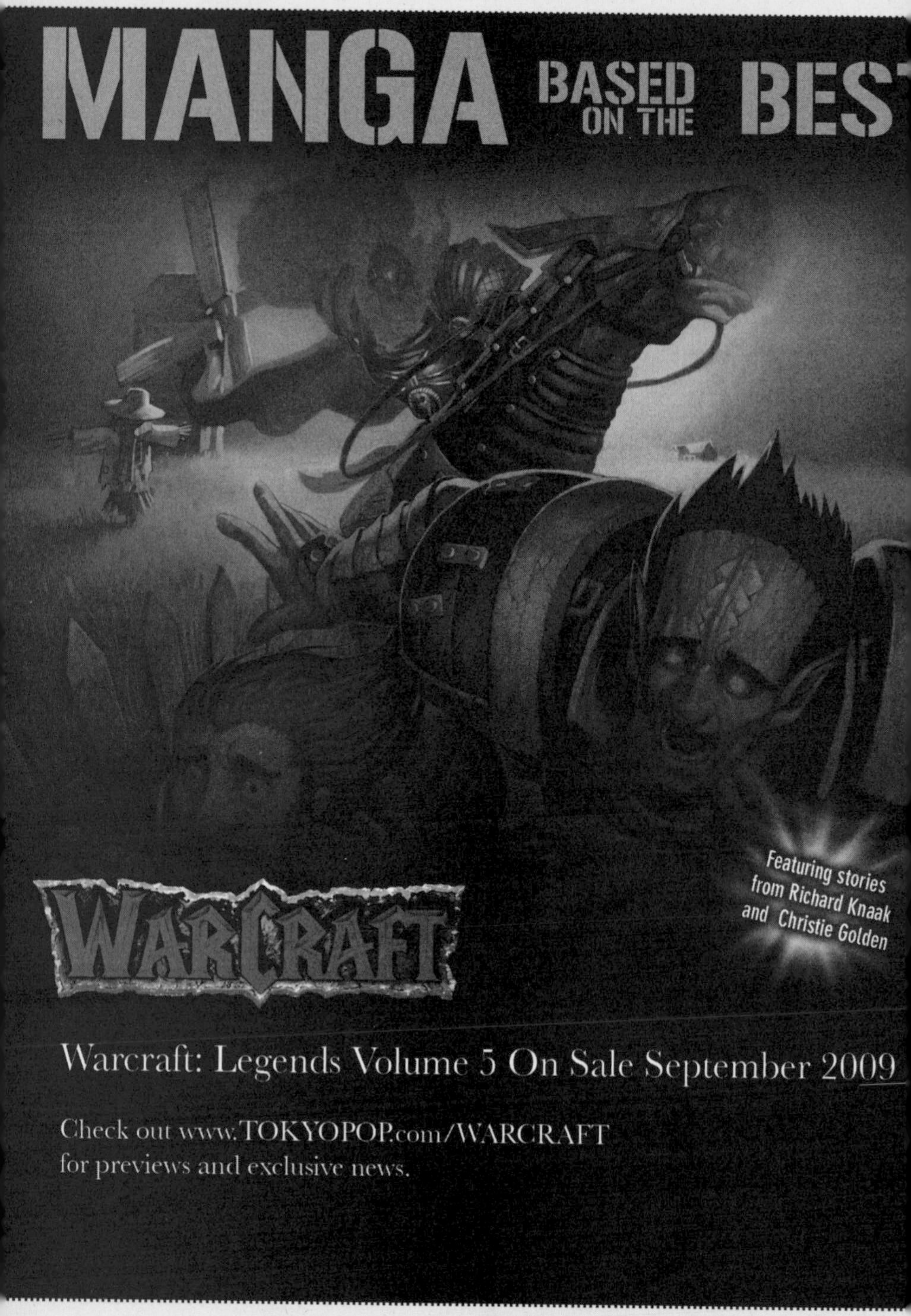
MANGA BASED ON THE BEST
Featuring stories from Richard Knaak and Christie Golden
WARCRAFT
Warcraft: Legends Volume 5 On Sale September 2009
Check out www.TOKYOPOP.com/WARCRAFT for previews and exclusive news.